STP 1219

Exxon Valdez Oil Spill: Fate and Effects in Alaskan Waters

Peter G. Wells, James N. Butler, and Jane Staveley Hughes, Editors

ASTM Publication Code Number (PCN):
04-012190-16

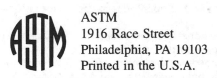

ASTM
1916 Race Street
Philadelphia, PA 19103
Printed in the U.S.A.

Library of Congress Cataloging-in-Publication Data

Exxon Valdez oil spill : fate and effects in Alaskan waters / Peter G.
 Wells, James N. Butler, and Jane Staveley Hughes, editors.
     (STP ; 1219)
     ASTM publication code number (PCN): 04-012190-16.
     Contains papers presented at the Third Symposium on Environmental
 Toxicology and Risk Assessment held in Atlanta, Georgia on 26-28
 April 1993.
     Includes bibliographical references and index.
     ISBN 0-8031-1896-1
     1. Oil spills—Environmental aspects—Alaska—Congresses.   2. Oil
 spills and wildlife—Alaska—Congresses.   3. Exxon Valdez (Ship)—
 Congresses.   I. Wells, P. G.   II. Butler, James Newton.
 III. Hughes, Jane S., 1955–   .   IV. Symposium on Environmental
 Toxicology and Risk Assessment (3rd : 1993 : Atlanta, Ga.)
     V. Series: ASTM special technical publication ; 1219.
 QH545.05E95   1995
 57405'09798'3—dc20   95-25366
                                                             CIP

Photocopy Rights

Peer Review Policy

Each paper published in this volume was evaluated by three peer reviewers. The authors
addressed all of the reviewers' comments to the satisfaction of both the technical editor(s) and
the ASTM Committee on Publications.

To make technical information available as quickly as possible, the peer-reviewed papers in
this publication were prepared "camera-ready" as submitted by the authors.

The quality of the papers in this publication reflects not only the obvious efforts of the authors
and the technical editor(s), but also the work of these peer reviewers. The ASTM Committee
on Publications acknowledges with appreciation their dedication and contribution to time and
effort on behalf of ASTM.

Printed in Ann Arbor, MI

First Printing, October 1995

Second Printing, February 1996

Foreword

This publication, *Exxon Valdez Oil Spill: Fate and Effects in Alaskan Waters,* contains papers presented at the Third Symposium on Environmental Toxicology and Risk Assessment—Exxon Valdez Oil Spill, held in Atlanta, Georgia on 26–28 April 1993. The symposium was sponsored by ASTM Committee E-47 on Biological Effects and Environmental Fate. Dr. Peter G. Wells of Dalhousie University in Nova Scotia, Canada; Dr. James Butler of Harvard University in Cambridge, Massachusetts; and Jane Staveley Hughes of Carolina Ecotox in Durham, North Carolina presided as symposium chairpersons and are editors of the resulting publication.

Contents

IMPACT ASSESSMENT FOR FISH AND FISHERIES

IMPACT ASSESSMENT FOR WILDLIFE

IMPACTS ON ARCHAEOLOGICAL SITES

Introduction, Overview, Issues

Peter G.Wells[1], James N.Butler[2] and Jane S.Hughes[3], Editors

INTRODUCTION, OVERVIEW, ISSUES

REFERENCE: Wells, P.G., Butler, J.N., and Hughes, J. S. "Introduction, Overview, Issues," *Exxon Valdez* Oil Spill: Fate and Effects in Alaskan Waters. ASTM STP 1219. Peter G. Wells, James N. Butler, and Jane S. Hughes, Eds. American Society for Testing and Materials, Philadelphia, 1995

ABSTRACT:

The *Exxon Valdez* oil spill in Prince William Sound, Alaska, in March 1989, was the largest crude spill to date in US waters. It prompted many studies on the fate, transport and effects of the oil on biota in Alaskan waters, as well as on archaeological sites. This book consists of 25 research papers presented at an ASTM Symposium in April 1993. This introductory chapter summarizes topics and highlights of those papers, covering chemistry and fate, shoreline impacts, effects on fish, fisheries and wildlife, and impacts on archaeological sites, and discusses some of the issues arisiing from the study of this spill.

   Some lessons learned from this research included:
- The need for accurate identification of the spilled oil-derived hydrocarbons in all samples,
- The extensive movement of the oil down the Alaskan coast, with its unique fate characteristics,
- The strong chemical basis required for interpreting the biological significance of sedimented hydrocarbons,
- The difficulty of separating oil effects on biological populations from changes due to other variables (biotic and abiotic),
- The need for sensitive hydrocarbon biomarkers, and
- The need to have established definitions and criteria to determine whether biological recovery had occurred.

   To provide a context for the papers in this volume, other published literature and symposia on this spill are discussed. Some of the more important remaining issues include:
- The duration of effects of the residual oil,
- The extent of intertidal impact and recovery,
- The extent and duration of impacts of the spill on fisheries and wildlife populations, including seabirds and sea otters.

Additional issues, of considerable importance, but not concerned primarily with the fate and effects of the spilled oil, include:
- The need for the oil spill community as a whole to agree ahead of time on how to study such accidental spills, and select appropriate monitoring tools.

[1] Environment Canada, Bedford Institute of Oceanography, Dartmouth Nova Scotia B2Y4A2, and School for Resource and Environmental Studies, Dalhousie University, Halifax Nova Scotia B3H3E2, Canada
[2] Division of Applied Sciences, Pierce Hall, Harvard University, 29 Oxford St. Cambridge, MA 02138
[3] Carolina Ecotox, Inc. 710 W. Main St., Durham NC 27701

• The effect of impending litigation on the type and extent of the research conducted,

This volume provides the reader with detailed insights into the ecological impacts of such accidents in cold sub-arctic waters, and some of the outstanding scientific issues on the effects and recovery patterns after such spill events.

KEYWORDS: *Exxon Valdez*, Prince William Sound, petroleum, hydrocarbons, fate and effects of oil spills, oil spill source identification, oil spill shoreline impacts, fisheries, wildlife, birds, sea otters, ecological recovery.

INTRODUCTION

Oil Spills in the Sea

Oil spills from shipping, particularly during the carriage of crude and refined oils, continue to occur each year in the world's oceans, especially in coastal regions (GESAMP 1993). The past three decades have seen a number of very large (100,000 to 200,000 metric tons) spills from tankers – from the *Torrey Canyon* in the English Channel in 1967 to the *Amoco Cadiz* off Brittany, France in 1978, and the grounding of the *Braer* off the southern Shetland Islands in 1993. Each spill raises similar challenges and responsibilities for marine pollution damage control and prevention, as well as impact assessment. Each raises expressions of concern from the public, the media and governments for the protection of fisheries resources, wildlife and marine habitats. Each raises scientific questions about acute and long-term ecological impacts of such spills. Often lengthy legal battles take place to recover costs and compensate for damage.

The occurrence of a large spill in a northern area noted for its wildlife, fishing, and aquatic recreation brings to mind the *Amoco Cadiz* spill of 220,000 tons off the coast of Brittany, France – arguably the largest coastal spill in history and six times the size of the *Exxon Valdez* spill. Public outcry in France in 1978 was certainly as great as in Alaska in 1989, and the acute damage to fisheries and shoreline biotic communities was widespread, dramatic, and well-documented (Hess, 1978; Conan *et al.* 1981; NOAA, 1983). Some effects persisted but were obscured by physical cleanup and by other spills in the area (Gundlach *et al.* 1981). The damage suits that resulted from the *Amoco Cadiz* were settled only after 14 years of litigation (Oil Spill Intelligence Report, Jan 30, 1992 and July 30 1992).

However, each spill has unique features of oil type, location, timing, release pattern and fate that make impact prediction difficult and often inaccurate, and create concerns about the chronic deleterious effects of petroleum hydrocarbons on local marine resources and ecosystems. The highly publicized *Exxon Valdez* spill proved to be no exception.

The Exxon Valdez Oil Spill

The Tank Vessel *Exxon Valdez* grounded on Bligh Reef in Prince William Sound, Alaska, on March 24, 1989, spilling 10.9 million gallons[4] of Alaska North Slope (Prudhoe Bay) Crude. The spill response was described in some detail in NOAA (1992), and in great detail by the US Coast Guard (1993).

[4.] 37,000 of its 180,000 metric ton cargo; this is equivalent to 4.1×10^7 liters.

During the 12 years Port Valdez had operated, there had been over 8500 tanker loadings, with 6.8 billion barrels (10^9 metric tons) of oil transported (American Petroleum Institute, *Response Bulletin R-424*, March 1989). The *Exxon Valdez* accident was only 1 part in 25,000 of that total, and was the first large spill originating from the port. Although the *Exxon Valdez* spill was far from the largest coastal spill recorded, it has certainly been the most expensive – at $3 billion total to date for cleanup, damage assessment, and payment of damages, nearly $12,000 per barrel or $80,000 per metric ton of oil lost.[5]

What made the *Exxon Valdez* oil spill special? It was the largest spill to date in US waters. The acute impact of this spill was certainly severe, in an area valued for its scenery and wildlife, and the public was certainly outraged (See Lethcoe & Nurnberger (1989) and Davidson (1990), as well as thousands of newspaper, magazine and television stories). The extremely heavy attention paid by the media was an important factor. Hundreds of millions of people in the US, Canada and Europe were repeatedly shown the oiled birds and otters, and the thousands of people and machines busy at the cleanup. Vice Admiral Clyde Robbins, Federal On-Scene Coordinator at the spill from April to September 1989, recalled what drove the program: "There was the pervasive view that we had to do something…We couldn't just leave the oil on the shoreline" (Robbins, 1993).

As with many other spills, an immediate priority was to protect commercially valuable resources – fish hatcheries and the habitat of local fisheries. Another overlapping priority was to protect the "most sensitive resources," but there was not good agreement about what those were, or how best to protect them (Robbins, 1993). And as at other large spills, many of the people responding had little experience with spill response nor any historical perspective on the fate and effects of other spills.

Nevertheless, a number of valuable lessons were learned again: Effective containment and cleanup requires well-equipped, well-trained and timely spill response teams. Practical contingency plans are essential. The capacity of nature to recover is greater than it seems at first. But concern about ecological effects drove the cleanup and the biological, chemical and resource (e.g. fisheries) studies initiated after public interest waned.

In this introduction, we describe topics and highlights of the research covered in this book, and discuss some key issues pertaining to the fate and effects of spilled oil in Alaskan waters.

TOPICS COVERED IN THIS BOOK

This book contains papers presented at a symposium of the American Society for Testing and Materials, held in April 1993. Most of this work, conducted in the period 1989-91, was revealed to the public for the first time on that occasion. The emphasis was not on how much acute damage had been done by the spill, but on how the environment had responded and the extent to which it had recovered in the three years post-spill.

The assessment of "recovery" has turned out to be a highly controversial matter. The death of large numbers of visible organisms, such as sea otters, and the potential loss of fisheries created a great deal of alarm. For species with large and robust populations

---

[5] In the past, costs of mechanical spill cleanup have ranged from $10 to $5000 per bbl, with an average of $600. This must be compared with a typical sale price of $15 per bbl. (White & Nichols 1983, Moeller et al 1987, Lasday, 1989).

(e.g. snails and amphipods) such mortality is unlikely to be signifiicant. For other species, those endangered or of low fecundity, the loss of large numbers of individuals could be very serious.

Most of the research reported in this symposium volume was supported by Exxon and might therefore be considered biased by some readers. One of the significant differences between the Exxon-sponsored studies and Government-sponsored studies was that the latter focussed primarily on the impacted areas, whereas the Exxon studies were more synoptic, covering unimpacted as well as impacted areas. Such differences in experimental design may influence the detection and interpretation of damage (Parrish and Boersma, 1995). However, an objective reader or scholar will place these rigorously peer-reviewed ASTM papers in the context of other scientific publications on the same topics over time, and strive to make a fair judgement of oil impact and ecosystem response and recovery for Prince William Sound and adjacent Alaskan waters.

Chemistry and Fate

The first section is on chemistry and fate of the crude oil spilled in Prince William Sound (PWS). This includes identification of hydrocarbon sources in sediments (Paper #1)[6] and biota (Paper #2) of local waters, oil concentrations in the water column (Paper #3), clay-oil flocculation (Paper #4), sheen surveillance (Paper #5), and bioavailability of hydrocarbons (Paper #6).

Page *et al*. (Paper #1) made a clear distinction between the main sources of polycyclic aromatic hydrocarbons (PAH) in each sediment sample from PWS – natural seeps, Alaska North Slope crude oil (such as the *Exxon Valdez* cargo), diesel fuel, pyrogenic and biogenic hydrocarbons. They concluded that there is a natural PAH background due to oil seeps in the eastern Gulf of Alaska, that *Exxon Valdez* cargo residues were sometimes found near shorelines oiled by the spill, and that other oil sources were locally important. Concentrations of total PAH in the sediments, potentially available for uptake by subtidal biota, were much lower than known toxicity threshold concentrations – hence representing low or negligible hazard. Because of the depth (largely over 100 m) of Prince William Sound and the complex movement of the slicks, it is not surprising that most of the sea floor had no detectable PAHs.

Bence and Burns (Paper #2) interpreted a large database of hydrocarbon analyses, distinguishing weathered Alaska North Slope oil (as would result from the *Exxon Valdez* spill) from diesel and other sources. They distinguished the sources of oiling for mussels, herring, sea ducks, and otters in post-spill years.   This work is discussed further below, under "How much residual oil came from the *Exxon Valdez*?"

Total PAHs in the water column over time in PWS were well below levels accepted as Alaskan water quality standards, according to Neff *et al*. (Paper #3). Acute toxicity tests on the water samples, using standard tests with algae, mysid crustaceans, and minnows, showed that the field concentrations of PAHs in PWS, more than a week after the spill, were very much lower than toxicity thresholds from Rice's (1979, 1984) earlier work with Arctic and Subarctic species. Some of the same organisms are found in the Gulf of Alaska (See paper #11).

Bragg and Yang (Paper #4) hypothesized that flocculation of oil with sediment particles accelerated oil removal from shorelines, enhancing oil transport and distribution throughout the water column, and enhancing biodegradation of the oil. This was supported

---

[6] Papers are numbered in the order in which they appear in this book.

by laboratory wave tank studies, as well as tests on some trench samples from Prince William Sound.

Taft *et al.* (Paper #5) reported the results of an aerial sheen surveillance program in Prince William Sound and the Gulf of Alaska during 1989 and 1990. Water samples were also taken and analyzed to identify their source. Sheens from *Exxon Valdez* oil were found to be negligible by the summer of 1990.

Shigenaka *et al.* (Paper #6), in a study sponsored by the Trustee Council[7], tested semipermeable membrane devices as monitoring tools to detect residual PAH, comparing them with mussels. These devices, based on partitioning of organics, have been used previously for monitoring organic pollutants. Shigenaka *et al.* concluded that they also show promise for monitoring oil spills.

Shoreline Impacts

Section Two consists of six papers on shoreline impacts of the oil, covering study design (Papers #7 & 8), condition of the beaches in Prince William Sound after oiling (Papers #9 & 10), and biological and toxicological responses of intertidal biota (Papers #11 &12).

For shoreline communities, Page *et al.* (Paper #7) considered recovery to be demonstrated when measurements on communities at oiled sites were statistically indistinguishable from unoiled reference sites. As mentioned above, such criteria depend on what is measured – these may include chemical concentrations and distribution, attributes of intertidal ecology, or size of bird populations. As well, the longer the study and the more detailed and numerous the observations, the more reliable the testing and conclusion of recovery – thus the statistical bias of small sample size has been minimized. In this study, the level of oiling on shorelines was measured by the width of oil bands on beaches relative to the 1989 oiling. By 1990, a substantial decrease in petroleum residues from the spill was observed, together with a corresponding recovery of plant and animal communities.

McDonald and Erickson (Paper # 8), in a study sponsored by the Trustee Council[7], described formal survey design statistics and statistical inferences for coastal habitat injury assessment. Details for sampling the supralittoral, littoral and sublittoral (shallow) were described. When interpreting changes in habitat that might be attributed to oiling, observed in the 1989 sampling, problems arose because there was too much variation within each stratum, samples were too small, sites were misclassified, stratification was not appropriate for subtidal work, and studies were only conducted on sites >100 meters in length and only on accessible sites. Some of the sites also had been cleaned using undocumented methods. The criteria for choosing the control sites were also discussed. The authors concluded that a much longer study (ten years, by analogy with the *Torrey Canyon* and *Amoco Cadiz* spills), with more carefully monitored sites, would be required to obtain reliable results.

Neff *et al.* (Paper #9) described the rapid reduction in shoreline oiling on many oiled beaches over the period 1989-92. Because of the low sampling frequency, estimating the length of time of oiling at specific sites had high uncertainty. Isolated pockets of

---

[7] The Exxon Valdez Oil Spill Trustee Council was established in 1991 to oversee the allocation of funds from the settlement between Exxon, the US Government and the State of Alaska, to be used for restoration in Prince William Sound and Alaskan waters. It consists of 6 representatives from State and Federal agencies.

subsurface oil were found in decreasing amounts through 1992, most of them being in the upper intertidal and supratidal zones, chiefly in protected areas of coarse cobbles and boulders.

Boehm *et al.* (Paper #10) used the Triad approach (chemical, toxicological, ecological – Long and Chapman, 1985) to assess levels and reduction of oil residues on the shoreline and to estimate biological recovery from 1989 to 1991. There appeared to be minor deposition of oil in the nearshore subtidal sediments. By 1991, much of the shoreline oil had been removed and the remaining oil was heavily degraded. Isolated pockets of oil remained. These might have had adverse effects on the herring spawn, but fortunately they were not in the spawning areas. Later Boehm concluded (SETAC 1993) that there was "almost complete recovery of PWS by 1993"; but only one species of amphipod (*Rhepoxynius abronius*) was used in the sediment assays for this approach, which limits such broad interpretations (Rice *et al.* 1993).

Gilfillan *et al.* (Paper #11) pointed out that the intertidal and subtidal environments are not fragile ecologically, as is sometimes presumed. On the basis of community structure analysis, which is a more sensitive measure than diversity, abundance or richness, they concluded that over 70% of Prince William Sound shorelines that had been exposed to oil had "recovered" by 1990, when their study finished.

Fish and Fisheries

Section Three assesses the spill impact on fish and fisheries, particularly crustaceans and bottomfish (Paper #13), salmon (Papers #14 & 15) and herring (Paper #16).

Armstrong *et al.* (Paper #13) in a study of bottomfish and crustacean species in Prince William Sound, showed that there were few measurable effects on these species. Tanner crabs were not affected by the spill, and any declines noted in shrimp and crab fisheries had been occurring prior to the spill from the 1970s onwards. No effects could be determined on larvae in the field, not surprisingly considering the large spatial and temporal variability in their distribution in the various bays. One statistically significant effect was a lower fecundity of coonstripe shrimp in some oiled bays.

Brannon *et al.* (Paper #14) studied pink salmon spawning in freshwater streams in western PWS. Pink salmon have a two-year life cycle, going to sea and returning to spawn in streams which cross beaches and are potentially vulnerable to stranded or buried oil. Pink salmon were exposed to up to 300 ppb of PAH in oiled streams in 1989, but the hydrocarbon concentration in water in nearshore feeding and rearing areas, and in offshore migratory areas, was 1 to 4 orders of magnitude lower than reported laboratory values for chronic or acute effects. In both oiled and reference streams, 77 to 100% survival of salmon eggs, fry, and juveniles was observed. No substantial effects on critical early life stages and processes of pink salmon were attributed to the spill.

Maki *et al.* (Paper # 15) reported on adult pink salmon studies from 1989 to 1991. Fourteen percent of pink salmon streams in PWS were exposed to *Exxon Valdez* crude oil. In 1990-91, progeny of the year classes most vulnerable to the spill exceeded their parental year returns. In 1989, adult returns were the same in both oiled and reference streams. Effects were studied three ways - qualitatively, by quantitatively comparing oiled and clean streams, and by quantitatively regressing effects against PAH concentrations in the stream beds themselves. No differences were detected amongst the intertidal densities of returning salmon across 4 years of sampling (1989-1992). A number of streams, in 1989 to 1991, were contaminated with *Exxon Valdez* crude oil, but no relationship was obvious between salmon density and PAH concentration in the stream sediments. The effects on salmon are further discussed below under issues.

Pearson *et al.* (Paper # 16) were concerned with Pacific Herring survival and reproduction. Pacific herring spawn intertidally, a particularly vulnerable location, with major risks from stranded oil to spawning fish and their eggs and larvae, particularly the eggs adhering to oiled kelp (Pearson *et al.* 1985) . PAHs were detected in eggs on kelp beds at 2 of 6 oiled sites in PWS in 1989. There was no demonstrated relationship between PAH burdens and biological responses in the eggs and developing embryos.

Many toxic effects have been demonstrated in the laboratory on herring eggs if oil adheres to them (NRC, 1985), but in PWS in 1989 there was little overlap between herring spawning sites and contaminated areas. Pearson *et al.* estimated that 96% of the total 1989 spawn length (158 km) was free of oil and hence only 4% of spawn was exposed in 1989, with no effects in 1990. The expected population decrease was overwhelmed by the 18% additional herring biomass – fish not caught as a result of the commercial fisheries closure – and the 1991 and 1992 harvests of herring were subsequently large. Concern about sublethal effects of oil on herring populations prompted a number of continuing studies (e.g., Hose *et al.* 1993; Funk *et al.* 1993).

Wildlife

Section Four assesses impacts on wildlife, including toxicology (Papers #17 & 18), coastal birds (Papers #19-22), pelagic seabirds (Paper #23) and sea otters (Paper #24).

Stubblefield *et al.* (Paper # 17) studied the toxic properties of naturally weathered *Exxon Valdez* crude oil from shoreline sediments to the mallard duck *Anas platyrhynchos* and the European ferret *Mustela putorius*, as surrogates for the many wildlife species impacted by the spill. No treatment-related mortalities or gross signs of toxicity were noted in ducks at dietary concentrations up to 100 000 mg/kg. Significant reductions in mean eggshell thickness and strength were observed at 20,000 mg/kg. These exposures greatly exceeded those likely in the field.

Hartung, (Paper # 18), presented a conceptual paper on acute and sublethal effects measurement, and dose-duration-effects measurement with seabirds, concluding that long-term sublethal toxic effects from the spill on wildlife are unlikely. This conclusion was based on the comparison of higher laboratory versus much lower field concentrations of hydrocarbons, and presumed shorter exposure times in the field.

Day *et al.* (Paper # 19) evaluated the use and recovery of oiled bird habitats. Oil affects seabirds in a number of ways, such as direct mortality, sublethal effects on reproduction, and effects on habitats on land and at sea. Not all of PWS was oiled, and in the oiled areas, oil distribution was not uniform. It is well known that impact on seabirds is not directly related to the amount of oil spilled. Day *et al.* used an oiling index to describe the amount of oiling at any one location, and three statistical techniques to distinguish effects within and between years. In PWS, 19 out of 42 species of birds showed initial impacts; 14 recovered by late summer of 1991 (perhaps they avoided oiled bays; there is no evidence one way or the other), but 6 did not recover. On the Kenai Peninsula, 12 of 34 species showed negative impacts, and six recovered and six did not. Principal component analysis of habitat attributes showed no difference between impacted and non-impacted sites.

White *et al.* (Paper # 20) reported on density and productivity of bald eagles in PWS. Density of eagle nests with eggs along the coastline is considered a good indicator of marine environmental quality. Eagles were oiled in 1989 by the spill, but effects (fewer eagles, lower nest occupation and fewer young) did not persist to the 1990-91 season. There were no differences in density of nests with eggs between oiled and unoiled areas in 1990 and 1991. This was thought to be due to the large number of replacement eagles for the available nesting sites and less disturbance by people than during the cleanup activity in 1989. There was a decrease in 1991 in success of nesting, which was ascribed to weather rather than to oil. Continued monitoring of eagle distribution, density and reproductive success would be desirable.

Erikson (Paper # 21) reported surveys of murre colony attendance in the Northern Gulf of Alaska. Estimates of mortality of murres at the time of the spill were very high, ranging from 74,000 to 289,000; 22,000 carcasses of murres were collected by August 1, 1989. However, no major devastation of the murre colonies was observed. There were very similar historic and postspill (1989-1991) numbers of murres, and no differences in attendance of murres at the Barren Islands site pre and post-spill. Several reasons may account for the lack of impact, which might have been expected from acute mortality: models used to estimate total mortality from observed counts were too high, losses were being replaced from a non-breeding pool of birds, mortalities included non-breeders or non-local birds, lost birds were rapidly replaced by immigrants, or more birds may have returned to the colonies in post-spill years. The measurable impacts of the spill on murres seem, therefore, to have been short-term.

Boersma *et al.* (Paper # 22) described murre abundance, phenology and productivity of the Barren Islands. This was a detailed study at one major breeding colony. The key question was: What happened to the breeding colony post-spill? Extensive reproductive studies showed that the number of eggs produced in 1989 and 1990 was the same, and that there were no significant differences in population numbers between the 1990-92 period and historical values. As expected, high inter-year variability in population numbers at the site was observed, and there was a reproductive disturbance attributed to weather and low food availability in 1991.

Wiens (Paper #23) gave an overview on the recovery of seabirds. There were impacts on seabirds, but they were highly variable and populations have begun to recover. There are several approaches to determining impacts of oil on seabirds: before and after historical comparisons, treatment-control comparisons, and comparisons on an oiling gradient – and problems are inherent in each approach. There are also multiple dimensions to oil response by seabirds: no response, reduction in population, lowered reproductive success, and less habitat use and value. The seabird colonies also can be grouped into categories of risk, as shown by the murre study (see Erikson, Paper #21) where there was no difference between prespill and postspill numbers, and Boersma's (Paper #22) study of reproductive effects of murres, where there were changes in murre phenology and productivity in 1992 only, but "no dramatic changes between the 1970s and 1990s". Wiens concluded that there was recovery of habitat use by many species, and in colony attendance and reproduction by murres, and that these signs of recovery were well advanced by late 1991.

Johnson and Garshelis (Paper # 24) described sea otter abundance and pup production in PWS. This study, on otter abundance, distribution, pup production, mortality and foraging, concluded that there was no clear relationship between oil amount and population change at each site and that this finding was not due to inter-observer differences, immigration of otters, differences between east and west parts of PWS, or timing of pupping. There were no significant differences between foraging success at oiled and unoiled sites on Green Island. A good prognosis was given for the PWS otters, although some questions arose as to the validity of the foraging data and data on prespill pup patterns (see discussion of issues below).

Impacts on Archaeological sites

The final – and unique – paper by Wooley and Haggarty (#25), on the protection of archaeological sites, concluded that no serious damage to archaeological sites resulted either from oiling or cleanup. This paper is supplemented by two in the Trustee Council Symposium (Reger, 1993; McAllister, 1993).

THE SPILL: ISSUES AND CONTEXT

In preparing this discussion of issues raised by the *Exxon Valdez* oil spill, we considered the 25 papers in this ASTM volume, and in addition, surveyed five data bases for peer-reviewed and government literature, as well as the abstracts of the symposium convened by the *Exxon Valdez* Oil Spill Trustee Council[7] at Anchorage Alaska in February 1993, and papers presented at a symposium of the Society for Environmental Toxicology and Chemistry (SETAC) held at Houston Texas in November 1993. The Trustee Council symposium is still in the process of being published in its full peer-reviewed form. Nevertheless, the more than 100 extended abstracts aleady available from this symposium represent a sizeable fraction of the literature to date on the *Exxon Valdez* spill. Our discussions have utilized these abstracts and other presentations in an attempt to give balance to the discussion of as-yet unresolved issues. A serious reader will consult this volume along with other peer-reviewed literature on this spill as it appears.

We have identified four principal issues: Persistence of residual oil, effects on fisheries, effects on wildlife populations, and how the scientific research on the oil spill was affected by the impending litigation[8]

ISSUES: PERSISTENCE OF RESIDUAL OIL

Effects of residual oil

So much effort went into cleanup at the *Exxon Valdez* spill, that considerable controversy arose over whether the cleanup techniques – particularly high pressure hot water washing of the intertidal zone – did more harm than good, and whether the shorelines would have recovered more effectively if left alone.

---

[8] This volume concerns the fate and effects of the spilled oil, but other issues, omitted from this symposium, are each worthy of a volume of their own.

The immediate response to the spill is detailed in US Coast Guard, 1993 and Davidson, 1990.

Except for the paper (#25 in this Volume) by Wooley and Haggarty on archaeological sites, the social impacts on Alaskan residents, particularly native peoples, were judged to be beyond the scope of this book. See Fall (1993), Palinkas *et al* (1992,1993) for more details.

Although the *Exxon Valdez* Oil spill provided a primary motivation for passaage of the US Oil Pollution Act of 1990, which covered liability and tanker safety as well as contingency plans, this complex topic is also beyond the scope of this book. Canada and Australia also undertook a complete review of their national contingency plans for oil spill response as a result of this spill (Brander-Smith, et al, 1990; Robinson, 1994).

The slogan "how clean is clean?"reflected the frustration of regulators in establishing an acceptable level of hydrocarbon concentrations and ecosystem recovery, given the usual lack of baseline data and poor understanding of contaminant inputs and natural fluctuations in the biota. An obvious criterion of impact is a statistically significant difference between samples exposed to oil and reference samples. Recovery would then be the disappearance through time of such a statistical difference. This concept is limited because it implies a measure of impact with little variability and a well-characterized reference site. In field situations, measurements at sample sites can be highly variable, as are the sites themselves, and reference sites may or may not be the same as the sample site before impact. In addition it is generally acknowledged that the statistical power of wildife population census techniques to detect change is weak. Weins (Paper #23) discusses this issue in the context of the recovery of seabird populations.

Spies (1993) emphasized the difficulty of making accurate damage assessments. Even when there is obvious mortality, as with birds and otters, the effects on the entire population must be estimated using a conceptual or mathematical population model and considerable field data. When there are no baseline data (as is usually the case) the affected area must be compared with a presumably similar but unaffected area. The real differences between the sites, if the spill had not occurred, will never be fully known. The longer the time span since the spill, the greater is the importance of any basic differences between sample and reference sites. In addition, the possibility always remains that subtle longer-term effects from residual oil components are occurring in some organisms or their populations, which are not the focus of study.

Spies (1993) also gave great emphasis to the uncertainty of estimating injury to a number of specific resources of PWS, such as Dolly Varden trout, eagles, herring, various fish, invertebrates and plants. But the heart of the matter was that he considered most recovery estimates for PWS to be unknown.

Although an absolute measure of cleanliness or recovery seems beyond reach, some questions are useful in assessing the studies of this spill which have already been reported: What types of measurements were made? Who made the measurements? Where? How precise and accurate were they? What was their statistical distribution? What statistical tests were employed? How reliable were they?

Intertidal impact and recovery

Three closely interrelated issues pertaining to shoreline recovery have emerged:
1. The impact of oiling on the intertidal biota,
2. The impact of beach cleaning on the oil and intertidal biota,
3. Persistence of the remaining, often pocketed, oil – and effects, especially on mussels and their predators. Remaining bulk oil could also impact birds, marine mammals and terrestrial mammals.
The following discussion supplements the information in Papers #7 through #12, summarized above.

Effects of shoreline treatment
The choice was not obvious between cleanup – aggressive mechanical removal of stranded oil – and permitting natural processes to degrade the oil. Initially, the cleanup option was supported by scientific advisors to the Coast Guard and cleanup proceeded. But by the summer of 1989, the drawbacks in adopting such agressive cleanup were realized, although it took months to change to alternative response strategies (Robinson, 1994).

Houghton *et al.* (1993b, c) and Driskell et al. (1993) reported on studies at three kinds of sites: unoiled reference sites, oiled but untreated sites, and oiled sites which had been washed with high pressure hot water (Table I).

Table 1. Physical and biological observations of shoreline in unoiled reference areas, oiled areas, and oiled areas of PWS which had been washed with high-pressure hot water (Houghton *et al.* 1993)

Physical observations:

Category	Description	PAH conc	Distribution	10-fold decline observed	Beach profile
1	unoiled reference	up to 1000 times less than 2 or 3			
2	oiled		increasing with elevation	3 of 4 elevations	
3	oiled, washed with high pressure hot water		highest at mid- and subtidal elevations.	1 of 4 elevations	unstable, less fine sediment

Biological observations:

Category	Description	Infauna	bivalve *Macoma* spp, copepods, oligochaetes	rockweed, limpets, drills
1	unoiled reference			
2	oiled	similar to Category 1 in 1990-92	high populations	similar to Category 1 by 1991
3	oiled, washed with high pressure hot water	lowest species, numbers, diversity	lowest clam recruitment	partial recovery by July 1991 Rockweed, limpets abundant by July 92

Houghton *et al.* (SETAC 1993) compared the effects of the hot water treatment and oil versus oil alone on intertidal epifauna, hoping to separate out oil effects from treatment effects. He examined epibiota (rockweed, *Littorina* spp., barnacles, and red algae) at oiled, moderate oil and hot water, and heavy oil and hot water sites. He concluded that most of the intertidal dominance survived the original oiling, but that the hot water washing reversed the survivals. As summarized in Table 1 below, beaches not washed have the same distribution of epifauna as unoiled beaches. Beaches that were washed are moving in the direction of recovery and similarity with untreated sites, but with some major fluctuations in species numbers and types.

"Both the NOAA scientists and Exxon scientists studied recovery at some of the same shoreline sites. Houghton had initially selected the sites on a subjective basis in 1989 while he was working for Exxon. He continued studying them for NOAA in 1990, while Gilfillan *et al.* studied a number of them for Exxon as part of the 'fixed-site' portion of their 1990-91 study. Both investigators found that these worst-case sites had not recovered by 1991. NOAA continued studying the sites after 1991 and concluded in 1993 that while few significant differences remained, full recovery appeared to be several years away. Because of the method by which the sites had been selected, the findings reflect conditions only at these sites, but not in the spill zone as a whole." (Maki, 1995)

Driskell *et al.* (SETAC 1993) examined recovery of intertidal infauna from the spill and the shoreline cleanup. They concluded that there was an oil impact on infauna , that washing the beaches further impacted the infauna, and that washing should not have occurred. Recovery is occurring at different rates for different kinds of animals, for example, bivalves and polychaetes are recovering more slowly than crustaceans.

In summary, the effects of oil on intertidal communities were significant, but organisms in areas treated with high pressure hot water recovered more slowly than those in untreated areas. The importance of appropriate reference sites for determining the efficacy of cleanup options cannot be understated. NOAA's scientific advisory group recommended 61 short segments of shoreline to be set aside from cleanup. Unfortunately, political controversies reduced this to only nine sites, a statistically inadequate sample.

Persistence of intertidal oil and effects on mussels

Reports of pockets of weathered oil in the intertidal zone (See paper # 10) raised the question of how persistent hydrocarbon contamination affects sub-Arctic intertidal communities. Long-term trace contamination of the shorelines and their biota in Western PWS is a concern to local residents and fishermen.

On protected shorelines, mussels can form dense beds that prevent oil in underlying sediment from being cleansed by wave action. Mussels in these beds can accumulate oil from the underlying sediment (Maki, 1995). Mussels transplanted in 1991 from reference sites to areas of high residual sediment contamination (Houghton *et al.* 1993b) increased in PAH levels to values as high as those in local mussels. Large reductions in PAH in mussel tissues from Smith Island suggest that leaching rates from subsurface deposits of oil declined from 1990 to 1991.

Mankiewicz et al (1993) found that only 1 to 3 % of the mussel beds available for foraging in PWS were oiled. He estimated oil dosages that wildlife might receive if the mussel portion of their diet came exclusively from these beds, combined these estimates with toxicity data for surrogate species (Stubblefield, Paper # 17, Hartung, Paper # 18, Maki, 1995), and found that the exposure of avian and mammal species was well below the "no-effect" level. The concentration of PAH was also low compared to that producing toxic effects in the mussels themselves. Burns and Bence (1993) also emphasized the importance of fingerprinting the hydrocarbons detected in mussel tissues.

Most surface deposits of oil on the shorelines of PWS decreased by a factor of 10 in one year, the same general time frame as observed in the experimental Baffin Island Oilspill Program (Sergy, 1985, 1987; Koons & Jahns 1992). Sedimented oil in high energy transects decreased even more rapidly, a factor of 8 from Sept. 1989 to March 1990. Oil in low-energy sediment areas and in areas of subsurface burial would be expected to be retained much longer. Jahns (1993) also noted that just because the oil has "gone" from the beach (visually or chemically) does not mean that the impact has necessarily gone. He concluded that most *Exxon Valdez* crude oil was biodegraded, or was present in non-toxic concentrations on shorelines. Pockets of weathered oil might exert local effects. As of 1992, Wolfe *et al.* (1994) estimated that "approximately 2% of the spilled oil remained on intertidal shorelines of PWS and the Gulf of Alaska, much of it highly weathered, biologically inert residues.

How much residual petroleum in Prince William Sound came from the Exxon Valdez?

It was clear that the crude oil observed in the intertidal zone at many locations just after the spill came from the *Exxon Valdez*. However, a controversy exists about the source of petroleum residues detected later in subtidal sediments and biota. Impacts of petroleum, from whatever source, are important to understand, but within the adversarial context of this spill, identifying the source of such oil accurately in each sample is of particular importance.

In part the issue is procedural. Although analytical instruments for volatile hydrocarbons – gas chromatography/mass spectrometry – and trace elements – atomic absorption and plasma emission spectroscopy – are highly sophisticated, their use in source identification is still relatively primitive. A naive assumption would be that all of the hydrocarbons came from the *Exxon Valdez* cargo, as hydrocarbons certainly came from other sources. Boat traffic greatly increased over normal levels during cleanup operations, land-based combustion sources contributed, and there are natural oil seeps in the Gulf of Alaska south-east of PWS.

How much *Exxon Valdez* oil reached and entered the subtidal sediments? Page *et al.* (Paper #1) concluded that only a few percent of the total hydrocarbons found in subtidal sediments in the area originated from Alaska North Slope crude, such as the cargo of the *Exxon Valdez*. This conclusion resulted in part from the wide geographical area of the sampling program, including depths greater than 100 m. In a subsequent paper, Page *et al.*(SETAC, 1993) analyzed for subtidal oil in PWS, using phenanthrene/dibenzothiophene ratios and the presence or absence of oleonane, which is absent in *Exxon Valdez* crude oil. They concluded that the subtidal sediments largely reflect the natural input of Katalia crude oil from the natural oil seeps southeast of PWS. Of course, subtidal sediment samples may have included little of the oil which stranded in the intertidal zone and did the greatest acute damage.

Bence and Burns (Paper #2) interpreted more than 1500 biological tissue hydrocarbon analyses in the Alaska State Oil Spill Health Task Force and the NOAA Prince William Sound Oil (PWSOIL) databases. They found 34% of whole salmon analyzed in 1989 contained *Exxon Valdez* crude, which decreased to 2% in 1990. The corresponding values for salmon fry were 28% and 14 %. Also, 36% of Bald eagle eggshells collected in 1989 showed *Exxon Valdez* crude, compared to only 2% in 1990. In contrast, 1% or less of herring eggs, and no samples of seaduck livers from either 1989 or 1990 contained *Exxon Valdez* crude.

Critics of this work (Stone, 1993) point out that this source-identification approach underestimates the potential impact , as organisms metabolize many crude oil hydrocarbons, and these metabolites would not be identified as *Exxon Valdez* crude. PAH metabolites could produce a potentially toxic impact on individual organisms of the Sound and are being identified in the bile of fish (Krahn *etal*.1992, 1993a, b, c, d). However, tracing these metabolites to a particular oil source appears at present to be beyond the state of the art.

The most surprising conclusion, reached by Bence and Burns (Paper #2) was that 60% of the samples in the databases included a low-level suite of hydrocarbons which matched none of the primary sources. These were called a "procedural artifact" because such data apparently resulted from the minimum reporting requirements set by NOAA – to quantify 25 compounds regardless of their concentrations relative to detection limits.

ISSUES: FISHERIES

Considerable public concern focussed on the potential effects of the spill on the hatcheries and highly valued commercial fisheries of Prince William Sound. Several species (crab, herring and salmon) are sensitive to oil exposures in the laboratory (NRC 1985, 1989), and oil and its constituents may taint fish (Ackman and Heras 1992; GESAMP 1993). However, impacts on field populations of fisheries species has always depended upon the nature and duration of the oiling event, status of the population (including fluctuations) at the time of the perturbing event, the level of fishing impact and the unique biology of each species at risk.

Few fish were found dead after the *Exxon Valdez* spill (this is not atypical at crude oil spill sites), but local rockfish had accumulated hydrocarbons (Meacham and Sullivan, 1993), and intertidal shellfish collected from native subsistence fishing grounds contained oil-derived aromatics (Varanasi *et al.* 1991). It was observed that "Oil was still present in the salmon fishing areas when adult salmon returned in the summer of 1989. Nets could not avoid straining oil and water; oiled nets contaminated the salmon held by them; and oil-tainted salmon could not be sold" (Meacham and Sullivan, 1993; Fall, 1993). Some investigators were concerned about the potential for subtle effects of oil on habitats and life histories of various fish species, particularly during reproduction and development (Meacham and Sullivan, 1993).

Few effects were detected on bottomfish and crustaceans (Armstrong *etal.* Paper #13), even considering the noted sensitivity of larval crustaceans to hydrocarbons. These fisheries remain unimpaired post-spill, as far as was known in 1993.

There was considerable concern for the salmon fisheries and aquaculture facilities after the spill. A number of effects were measured, the full implications of which still are uncertain and the subject of different viewpoints. In the Fall of 1989, eggs and fry suffered higher mortalities in oiled areas than elsewhere. With the fisheries closed, it was thought that too many pink salmon adults in some spawning streams exhausted food resources, and many young salmon starved (Meacham and Sullivan, 1993). The Alaska Department of Fish and Game (Bue *etal.* 1993) reported that salmon egg mortality in oiled streams was greater than in non-oiled streams – this effect apparently had not abated since the spill (1989 to 1992).

In contrast, Brannon *etal.* (Paper #14), through incubation experiments, showed no differences in egg viability between oiled and reference streams. Maki *etal.* (Paper #15) described strong postspill adult returns and spawning. Alaska Department of Fish and Game information for wildstock survival and recruitment showed that the return of natural spawners in the post-spill years (1990-91), fish that were progeny of the year classes most vulnerable to spill effects, were in excess of their parent year classes, in spite of all-time record production and harvest of hatchery returns (Maki, 1995). In addition, any subtle differences Bue et al (1993) measured in egg mortality in the Fall do not show up as differences in fry survival in the spring, illustrating that productivity of these stream environments has not changed (Moulton 1995, Maki and Parker, 1995).

Research continues on the levels of hydrocarbons in juveniles, alterations in migratory routes following the spill, and changes in rates of return by oil-exposed salmon (Nevissi 1991). Bue *et al.* (1993) hypothesized that continuing and increased mortality in pink salmon is the result of genetic damage sustained by eggs and alevins which incubated in oiled gravel during the Fall of 1989 and Spring of 1990. This hypothesis is being tested now by controlled rearing experiments. To date, "...there has been no confirmation of a delayed genetic effect on PWS pink salmon based on actual field experiments" (Maki, 1995).

Potential spill effects on the Pacific Herring were a major concern. Herring are both vulnerable (i.e. likely to be exposed) and sensitive (i.e. affected at low concentrations) to crude oils, based on Pearson's many laboratory studies (See references in Paper # 16). Were predictions of high herring vulnerability and sensitivity to the oil justified? In PWS only a small percentage of the spawning areas was oiled (in 1989, about 4% of the shoreline was oiled, and less than 1% moderately to heavily oiled) (Pearson *et al.* Paper # 16). Where herring spawned on oiled shores, their hatching rate was lower, with fewer viable larvae being produced. One of the largest herring year-classes in 25 years was in 1988; when it dominated the fishery in 1992, the fertility rate of the eggs it produced was lower in the oiled than in the unoiled areas (Meacham and Sullivan, 1993). However it was not possible to ascertain whether their lower fertility rate was due to oil or to some other site-specific effect (Kocan *et al.* 1993). Indeed, a herring egg incubation experiment showed "only a weak relationship between oil exposure in the Sound and effects on the biology of herring embryos" (McGurk *et al.* 1990).

An indirect effect of the spill on herring was the reduction of parasitic nematodes in spawners from oiled sites in PWS, and a change in parasite location in the fish; this phenomenon was used to demonstrate oil exposure of pre-spawn herring at two PWS sites in April 1989 (Moles *et al.* 1993). It has potential of being a novel monitoring tool.

Concerns for the salmon and herring fisheries are justified, if only on economic grounds. However, due to large natural population fluctuations and conflicting impact results, many uncertainties surround predictions of long-term damage from the spill to their populations and spawning areas. To attribute a decrease in a fish population to an oil spill of five years ago is not realistic, as many factors influence population numbers and recruitment. Only continued study of successive year class strength, the health of individual wild fish, and spawning success of the primary fisheries in PWS and adjacent waters will clarify the true causes of changes in fish populations.

ISSUES: WILDLIFE POPULATIONS

Birds

Seabirds and shore dwelling birds are the most conspicuous early victims of marine oil spills. The *Exxon Valdez* spill was no exception. Tens of thousands of birds were oiled by the slicks. "...more than 30,000 dead birds of 90 species were retrieved by Aug. 1, 1989," with early estimates of total mortality as high as 300,000 (Piatt *et al.* 1990). This raised public ire, but the public missed the main concern, whether there would be longer-term impacts of the spill on various coastal and pelagic bird populations. Were there differences in impacts on coastal and pelagic birds? Could subtle sublethal effects be separated from natural fluctuations, habitat loss and food loss? Could impacted seabird populations recover from such losses and if so, through which mechanisms? A number of studies, some reported in this volume, addressed these questions, and indeed, research is still underway to ensure knowledge of the extent of damage and the condition of key species and their breeding colonies.

Bald eagles, living in trees and feeding along the shorelines, were initially disrupted by both the oil and the physical disturbance from boats and people, but they apparently recovered by 1990-91, with nesting success resuming and the young being raised successfully. They have been monitored since then. Trustee studies indicated that the PWS bald eagle population and productivity had recovered by 1993 (Bowman and Schempf, 1993; Trustee Council, 1994. –*Exxon Valdez Oil Spill Restoration plan.*)

Many murres were directly killed by the spill (at least 22,000 carcasses were collected), but subsequent population effects, if they occurred, were obscured by natural variation in their numbers (See Boersma *et al.* paper #22). Boersma *et al.* concluded that there was essentially no longer-term impact on murre numbers at the Barren Islands, based on many summers of careful field observations. It is important to note that inter-year comparisons of murre population sizes at breeding sites are complicated both by unknown numbers of recruits from other locations, as well as by differences in methodology used for the population estimates (see also Parrish and Boersma, 1995).

Wiens (Paper #23) and Hartung (Paper #18) wrote exhaustive reviews of oil effects on birds. They particularly discussed the public perception of massive effects of spilled oil on seabirds and great stability in marine ecosystems, whereas great variability in seabird numbers and breeding success due to natural factors is a common natural event, making detection of the degree of oil effects difficult if not impossible.

The long-term health of other birds such as Harlequin ducks and oystercatchers also was of concern, due to heavily oiled intertidal feeding areas and contaminated mussels and other shellfish. Overall numbers of birds declined and reproductive failures were reported for both species (Patten,1993; Sharp and Cody,1993).

However, the relative roles of oiling *versus* physical disturbance of habitat remain unresolved. For example, Patten (1993) said "…seaducks…were chronically exposed by oil remaining in the intertidal by direct contact to feathers and skin, and internally through preening and ingestion of contaminated food (e.g. in blue mussels). This was especially true of Harlequin Ducks…oil exposure from contaminated intertidal food items ingested by the ducks caused cessation of reproduction." Another potential cause, disturbance from the massive clean-up from 1989 through 1991 seemed less likely because reproductive failure continued in 1992: "…45 blue mussel beds retained significant amounts of *Exxon Valdez* oil…Blue mussels are a key prey species for seaducks…The oil remains trapped beneath byssal thread mats in anoxic conditions and retains toxic components."

In contrast, a number of investigators (Dzinbal and Jarvis, 1984; Vermeer 1983; Gaines and Fitzner, 1987) have shown that mussels are a small portion of the Harlequin diet. Together with the observation by Mankiewicz *et al.* (1993) of relatively low levels of hydrocarbons in spill zone mussels, the long-term effects of oiled food on Harlequins is probably minimal.

Sharp & Cody (1993) reported on the black oystercatchers: "In 1989, daily chick mortality was directly correlated with degree of oiling, with 6% mortality on heavily oiled feeding territories…and no mortality on the control site….In 1990 oiling was still pervasive on "cleaned" shorelines at Green Island".

Some observers saw oil, measured reproductive failure and concluded that the oil caused the reproductive failure. For example, Sharp & Cody (1993) say "…Assuming a complete reproductive failure on bioremediated areas…" – although they gave no direct evidence about effects of bioremediation. It seems likely that disturbance of habitat is far more important than oil-induced toxic reproductive failure, but only long-term monitoring of key attributes of seabird species, both individuals and populations, and their colonies at oiled and unoiled sites, will resolve these issues.

Sea Otters

Between 500 and 4000 sea otters were estimated to have been killed by the spill in PWS and along the Kenai Peninsula (Garrott et al. 1993; Ballachey, et al. 1994), but the central issue remains one of evaluating the long-term hazards of a contaminated food supply, particularly shellfish, to individuals and their populations in PWS. How likely are such hazards? On what evidence is such concern based? Gorbics and Ballachey (1993) noted the extensive work required to determine mortalities caused by the spill, the accuracy of loss estimates, the degree of hydrocarbon contamination of individuals, damage to tissues and organs, population abundance in the years post-spill, and current survival rates in different parts of PWS.

Clearly, otters were killed by floating oil, there were oil-related pathologies , there were lower survival rates in western PWS compared to the eastern section, mortality patterns recurred by 1992 to pre-spill rates, and some physiological injuries may be persisting in individuals in the population. Otter populations seem to be recovering from the event in the western PWS (Johnson and Garshelis, Paper #24) but this requires confirmation by continued monitoring.

Other primary studies on otters reported since the spill have shown that there were toxic effects on individuals during 1989. Duffy et al. (1993) demonstrated differences in blood chemistry (haptoglobin levels) between otters inhabiting oiled and unoiled areas of PWS, and lower body mass in males from oiled areas. They proposed oil-related causes. Oil-exposed otters also suffered a range of histopathologic lesions after the spill; Lipscomb et al. (1993) described interstitial pulmonary emphysema, centrilobular hepatic necrosis, and hepatic and renal lipidosis. In addition, animals exposed to crude oil also suffered hypothermia and hypoglycemia (Williams et al. 1990). Hence there seems little dispute about the occurrence and type of acute toxicological effects on individual sea otters collected in 1989.

The issue with otters is primarily one of extent of chronic population impacts in PWS due to exposed habitats and food supply. On the one hand, Garrott et al. (1993) state that "it is clear that a significant fraction of the otters in the spill zone survived", and that their survival potential is high due to the convoluted coastline of PWS and the likelihood of finding refuge in clean embayments. Alternately, otters feeding on oiled mussel beds where chronic bioaccumulation of hydrocarbons has occurred may be affected directly, or indirectly through transfer of some hydrocarbons to their young. Such possibilities are considered strong by some research groups, less likely by others. In addition, population numbers are considered by some to be lower than before 1989 (Johnson and Garshelis, Paper #24), but within acceptable limits of variation from year to year by other investigators. The different views will only be reconciled through continued research and monitoring of otter numbers and distribution in the Sound. The reader is referred to the recent publication edited by Loughlin (1994) for additional descriptions of marine mammal studies, and sea otters in particular (e.g. Burn, 1994).

ISSUES: HOW WAS SCIENTIFIC RESEARCH ON THE OIL SPILL AFFECTED BY THE IMPENDING LITIGATION?

The final issue of note is the impact of the legal system on the scientific work done during and after the spill. The spirit of the law in a situation like this is to evaluate damage and restoration costs and to compensate for these by monetary payment or actions. There is a related set of research activities to help define the best response techniques, quite independent of research oriented toward damage assessment for litigation. The procedures of the law encourage adversarial roles for those involved. There was an attempt at the beginning of the cleanup to develop a joint research program, but this failed because the US Dept. of Justice imposed confidentiality restrictions on the work of all Government scientists (Robinson, 1994; Maki, 1995).

This meant for the *Exxon Valdez* spill that no joint programs between the parties to the case could easily be developed. It meant that secrecy became a major factor, so that data and papers based on them might be delayed for years pending the outcome of legal action. If the data had entered the public domain as they became available, they might have helped with the understanding of the problem and initiation of other actions to alleviate damage.

Robinson (1994) notes: "To the extent that research conducted during the spill might have offered the potential of changing the course of the cleanup, there were probably several missed opportunities. The adversarial process in which we found ourselves certainly did not work to the benefit of the cleanup. Those of us charged with advising the Coast Guard were effectively blocked from communicating with scientists on either side of the damage assessment issue, much to our unending dismay. People and money to *support cleanup-related* research, as opposed to *damage-related* research, were difficult to come by. Most of the insight that subsequently led to our slowing down the cleanup came from Exxon-supported scientists…who shared some of their observations with us. We were never able to communicate effectively with scientists employed by the State or Federal governments' damage assessment efforts."

Questions are often narrowed to suit the strategy of the case at the moment. Because such studies are hastily organized, they can be fragmentary and incomplete, and the data they produce may be unsuitable for publication in primary scientific journals. For example, a major effort to collect and analyze hundreds of water samples (which had negligible concentrations of hydrocarbons) used resources that might have been spent on studies of situations where the answers were not already known– for example, the actual concentrations and composition of intertidal oil, which was initially estimated visually instead of chemically. However, this extensive water quality study was conducted in response to considerable public concern about the potential risk to herring and salmon fisheries.

Standard toxicity tests were employed on water and sediments, probably because they were thought more likely to be accepted by the courts. From the viewpoint of hazard assessment, experiments with a combination of standard and indigenous species would have been more appropriate.

Long-term studies, particularly, are very important for scientific hazard assessment as well as legal damage assessment. A reliable assessment of fisheries and wildlife impact requires careful work over many years. One of the positive aspects of litigation of this spill is the funding available for such long-term studies. Consequently, new research testing the hypotheses of subtle long-term impacts on marine populations is starting to emerge.

In an attempt to clarify the results of their work for the media and the legal system in the early phases of the adversarial process, many scientists tended to generalize and overstate their conclusions. Both the media and the legal system tend to encourage extreme positions on controversial issues. In contrast, the peer-review system strives toward consensus by criticism from other workers in the field. The ASTM and some other institutions go one step further, and insist on drawing their peer-reviewers from a full range of potential interests. For example, each of the papers in this volume was reviewed by at least one expert each from the academic, government, and industrial arenas. Furthermore, as work continues and more data are obtained, opinions and interpretations based on that data tend to converge. The result of this is that some apparent controversies over the degree and duration of oil impact are indeed resolved.

Finally, political constraints can overwhelm all scientific and legal intentions. One major problem for the authorities on both sides was continued public distrust in their deliberations and outputs. Ideally, public representatives should be involved in study design, through to data dissemination. But even if all of the experts agreed that the best response to the spill was to allow natural processes to take their course, this would have been politically unacceptable because the public was crying "do something!" Political and social factors still overshadow the objective analysis of the impacts or lack of them for this particular oil spill.

CONCLUSIONS – SOME LESSONS LEARNED FROM THE *EXXON VALDEZ* SPILL.

The acute effects, largely lethal, from the *Exxon Valdez* oil spill were severe and obvious in intertidal habitats and on marine wildlife in the spill's path. This was to be expected from such a large spill in semi-enclosed waters in a biologically rich area. That these acute effects occurred is well documented and undisputed. What was of greater concern and largely unpredictable was the potential for chronic effects on important resource and wildlife species, lasting from days to years.

Hence, the possibility of long-term effects of the spilled oil in Prince William Sound and the Gulf of Alaska has been the subject of concern, debate and controversy, largely ahead of the facts. This is not unexpected at major oil spill sites, but there have been only a few well-studied spills in the cold temperate and polar zones as the basis of comparison (Percy and Wells, 1984). The same concern existed at previous spills such as the *Arrow* (Nova Scotia), the *Amoco Cadiz* (France), and the *Nestucca* (Pacific Northwest), and in subsequent spills such as the 1993 *Braer* accident in the Shetland Islands. After the *Braer* spill, a fisheries exclusion zone was established from which seafoods, wild or farmed, could not be sold because some were tainted or contaminated with PAHs. Restrictions on wild fish were lifted in April 1993, but continued until late 1993 for farmed salmon and to late 1994 for shellfish. Oil remained in some seabed sediments a year later, but overall, predicted ecological impacts from the *Braer* spill have not been demonstrated (Ritchie and O'Sullivan, 1994; Spaulding, *et al.* 1994).

Complicating an evaluation of chronic effects from *Exxon Valdez* crude oil are problems such as continuing inputs from other sources, and levels of petroleum residue which are too low to produce acute toxic effects. As discussed above, not all the petroleum residues in Prince William Sound came from the *Exxon Valdez spill.* Although *Exxon*

Valdez oil was found near shorelines oiled by the spill, and most of the seafloor in Prince William Sound has no detectable spill-related PAH, there is interference from natural oil seeps in the eastern Gulf of Alaska, and from local inputs of diesel and pyrogenic hydrocarbons. Most significant, hydrocarbon levels measured in the subtidal sediments are lower than known sediment threshold concentrations for toxic effects to marine organisms.

Investigating potential long-term sublethal effects from such incidents requires careful, long-term research. At this time not all the evidence has been assembled from the pertinent investigations. However, based on papers in this Volume, the Trustee Symposium, the SETAC symposium, and the International Oil Spill Conferences, chronic effects of exposure to *Exxon Valdez* crude oil on wildlife and fisheries appear to be limited, and at the population level, their overall impacts blend with natural factors, causing variability in species abundance and distribution.

Such effects, however short or long in duration, are notoriously difficult to detect and to ascribe to known stresses such as oiling. For example: "Continued elevated egg mortalities of pink salmon in oiled streams is a potential exception. Subtle differences between blood parameters in sea otters and river otters in oiled and unoiled areas are also potential markers of sublethal effects from oil. Another exposure marker (which carries the potential for increasd sublethal effects) is elevated P4501A in some nearshore fishes and perhaps in Harlequin ducks as late as 1993." (Spies, 1994). Because of the importance of the PWS area economically and biologically, selected longer-term studies of the intertidal ecology, fisheries and coastal wildlife should continue. It is in the interest of all parties with concerns about this spill that this be done.

As discussed earlier, there is controversy over whether "the cleanup", which included shoreline washing, oil slick recovery and bioremediation of shorelines, did more good or more harm to the intertidal and adjacent subtidal areas. Studies of the intertidal ecology (e.g. recruitment success of selected species, and diversity of the recovering communities, documented by reliable quantitative techniques such as reported by Houghton *et al.* (1993)) should continue, to establish the rate and processes by which intertidal communities in a high energy subarctic zone will recover from oilings and cleanup interventions. Such knowledge would be a very important contribution to the science of marine ecotoxicology and oil spill impact assessment in cold waters.

What were the surprises, if any, from this spill? What are some of the primary lessons to date? Not all of the oil in PWS came from the *Exxon Valdez* oil spill. Earlier acknowledgement of there being several sources of oils, especially from boat traffic and the natural crude oil from seeps, could have been anticipated. The negative effects of cleaning on intertidal biota might have been anticipated also. "The cleanup approach for each segment of shoreline was subjected to rigorous review by scientists on all sides of the issue, and almost unanimous consent was required before a segment-by-segment go-ahead was authorized by the Coast Guard. Tens of thousands of hours of impartial scientific advice were applied in this process." (Robinson, 1994),

The extensive movement of the spill down the coast of Alaska caused more damage than expected. For the size of the spill, a very large amount of coastline at a very long distance was oiled to varying degrees, an outcome which might have been predicted on the basis of oil type and volume, currents, weather and shoreline topography. Surprisingly little (8 to 16 %) of the *Exxon Valdez* oil found its way to subtidal sediments (Wolfe, *et al..*, 1994). This contrasts with the *Braer* spill, which involved a low viscosity, high volatility crude oil and where 27 to 35% of the oil was found in the subtidal sediments west and east of the Shetland Islands (Ritchie and O'Sullivan, 1994; Spaulding *et al..*, 1994). Each oil spill is unique and its fate is often very difficult to predict accurately in advance!

The difficulties of determining the population impacts of the spill on fish, seabirds and mammals perhaps should have been more openly discussed with all parties, public and media, as such impacts, if they occur, are generally very difficult to detect. This difficulty is due to the high variability in biological processes and population numbers, and the low statistical power of many monitoring techniques to detect significant change. Finally, an unbiased sampling strategy could have been agreed upon by all parties studying the potential effects, if it were not for their immediate adversarial relationship.

Experience from previous spills might have predicted that all of the above responses in marine biota would have occurred to some degree. It is our judgement that very few effects on marine biota will be detectable after a decade. Such effects might be on wildlife (e.g. seabird colonies on oiled shores) and in low energy intertidal areas (e.g. the one 2-acre salt marsh of PWS), and in intertidal mussel beds in localized areas. "There likely were serious multi-year impacts on wildlife species (especially sea otters, marbled murrelets, pigeon guillemots, among others) and the intertidal environment from this spill. There was injury. There was lost use. The environment is recovering; different populations have or ar recovering at different rates. Recovery is apparently not complete for some resources. Those are the issues." (Spies, 1994).

Table 2 is our attempt to summarize observed and anticipated principal effects of the *Exxon Valdez* oil spill in Prince William Sound and adjacent waters exposed to the spill. It is a qualitative assessment of the kinds of exposure and effects and the time scales over which they occur. The longest time scale of most impacts is months to years. A few effects in localized areas might be expected to last for a decade or more. But the Table does not convey important quantitative information. For example, only 4% of the shorelines on which herring spawned in 1989 were oiled. Over 60% of the mussel samples from the spill zone did not contain PAH identifiable as being from the spill. According to the most reliable investigator, there was virtually no detectable change in population at murre colonies one year after the spill. The Table should assist the reader in following the papers of this Volume and understanding the various impacts or lack of them. It should not be taken out of context.

Finally, the studies reported in this Volume suggest that at least some indicators of marine environmental quality at spill sites are worth more thorough investigation. Methods and standards for monitoring in unexposed and oil-exposed parts of the system should be established, and then applied after a particular spill. As a global society, we must stop "reinventing the wheel" each time a catastrophic accident occurs. Rather than broad and unfocussed monitoring of the whole system, we should concentrate on investigating and monitoring the most vulnerable and sensitive components of the ecosystem. Such research should be carried out by impartial teams of researchers trained rigorously in the use of current quantitative chemical, ecotoxicological and ecological methodologies. These researchers should also have extensive background knowledge about the observed responses of marine ecosystems to other large oil spills.

TABLE 2. Anticipated principal effects of the Exxon Valdez oil spill in Prince William Sound, based largely on studies reported in ASTM STP 1219.

Exposure/Effects	Time Scale of Event				
	d	wk	mo	yr	dec
Water column exposures to dispersed oil/WAF's	x	x			
Exposure of shorelines to hydrocarbons	x	x	x	x	x?
Exposure of benthic environments to oil	x	x	x	x?	
Oiling of intertidal organisms	x	x	x	x?	
Bioaccumulation of HC by intertidal shellfish	x	x	x	x	
Oiling of herring spawning areas	x	x	x		
Oiling of salmon spawning streams	x	x	x		
Effects on bald eagles	x	x	x	x?	
Effects on murres	x	x	x	x	
Effects on sea otters	x	x	x	x?	
Effects on other wildlife	x	x	x	x?	x?
Salt marsh	x	x	x	x	x?

ACKNOWLEDGEMENTS

We would like to express our appreciation to all of the people who volunteered to review the papers in this volume and offered their insights and constructive comments. In accordance with ASTM policy, reviewers were selected to provide a balanced cross-section representing industry, academia, and government. In addition, a significant effort was made by the editors to solicit reviewers who, although experts in the various scientific disciplines, did not participate in any research relating to the *Exxon Valdez* oil spill, and who could therefore provide critical, unbiased reviews of the submitted manuscripts. Thanks are also due to the authors of the manuscripts for their patience and cooperation with the revision and publication process.

In particular, we thank Charles H. W. Foster of Harvard University; Peter Howgate, formerly of the U.K. Ministry of Agriculture, Food, and Fisheries; Alan Maki and colleagues at Exxon Company USA; John Robinson, formerly of the NOAA Hazardous Materials Response Team; and Robert B. Spies, Chief Scientist of the *Exxon Valdez* Trustee Council, all of whom read a draft of this chapter. Their critical comments greatly improved the final version. Financial support of this work was provided by the American Society for Testing and Materials, Dalhousie University, Environment Canada, Harvard University, and the Zemurray Foundation.

SELECTED REFERENCES, INCLUDING LITERATURE CITED

This is a complete list of all references we found on the fate and effects of the *Exxon Valdez* oil spill. It includes very little of the literature on spill response or on the legal and economic aspects of the case. These references include abstracts, environmental advocacy reports, government reports, seminar and conference proceedings, as well as peer-reviewed books and journal articles. All are publicly available. Titles of papers have been included for completeness and ease in locating references. Although some of the references in this list are not cited in the text, all are included for the benefit of future scholars.

Ackman, R.G.; Heras, II., 1992, "Tainting by short-term exposure of Atlantic salmon to water soluble petroleum hydrocarbons," *15th Arctic and Marine Oilspill Program Tech. Seminar*, Environment Canada, Ottawa. pp 757-762.

Allen, Alan A., 1990, "Contained Controlled Burning of Spilled Oil During the *Exxon Valdez* Oil Spill," *13th Arctic & Marine Oilspill Program Technical Seminar*, Environment Canada, Ottawa. pp 305-315.

Allen, Alan A., 1990, "Contained controlled burning of spilled oil during the *Exxon Valdez* oil spill," *Spill Technology Newsletter*, Vol. 15, No. 2, pp 1-6.

ASTM (Amerian Society for Testing and Materials), 1993, *Abstracts, Symposium on the Exxon Valdez Oil Spill*, Atlanta GA, April.

Atlas, R.M.; Bartha, R., 1992, "Hydrocarbon biodegradation and oil spill remediation," in K.C. Marshall, ed., *Advances in Microbial Ecology*, Vol. 12, Plenum Press, New York. pp 287-338.

Ballachey, B.E.; Bodkin, J.L., DeGange, A.R., 1994. "An overview of sea otter studies," Chapter 3 in T.R. Loughlin, ed. *Marine Mammals and the Exxon Valdez*, Academic Press, San Diego, pp 47-59

Bayha K; Kormendy J, eds., 1991, *Sea Otter Symposium: Proceedings of a Symposium to Evaluate the Response Effort on Behalf of Sea Otters After the T/V Exxon Valdez Oil Spill into Prince William Sound*, 497 pp. US Fish and Wildlife Service, Anchorage, AK.; National Fish and Wildlife Foundation, Washington, DC. .[Symposium held in Anchorage, Alaska on April 17-19, 1990, NTIS PB91-233791.]

Bence, A.E.; Burns, W.E., 1993, "Fingerprinting hydrocarbons in the biological resources of the *Exxon Valdez* spill area," *16th Arctic & Marine Oilspill Program Tech. Seminar*, Environment Canada, Ottawa. p. 99.

Berkey, Edgar; Cogen, Jessica M.; Kelmeckis, Val J.; McGeehan, Lawrence T.; Merski, A. Thomas, 1991, "Evaluation Process for the Selection of Bioremediation Technologies for the *Exxon Valdez* Oil Spill," *Environ. Science Research - Environ. Biotechnology for Waste Treatment*, Vol. 41, Plenum, NY. pp 95-90.

Bodkin, J. L.; Weltz, F., 1990, "Evaluation of Sea Otter Capture After the T/V *Exxon Valdez* Oil Spill, Prince William Sound, Alaska," in Bayha, K. and Kormendy, J. eds. *Sea Otter Symposium: Proceedings of a Symposium to Evaluate the Response Effort on Behalf of Sea Otters After the T/V Exxon Valdez Oil Spill into Prince William Sound*, US

Fish and Wildlife Service, Anchorage, AK.; National Fish and Wildlife Foundation, Washington, DC., pp 61-69.

Bowman, T.D.; Schempf, P.F., 1993, "Effects of the *Exxon Valdez* oil spill on bald eagles," *Abstracts, Exxon Valdez Oil Spill Symposium,* Feb. 2-5, 1993, Trustee Council, Anchorage, Alaska, pp 142-143.

Bragg, J.R.; Yang, S.H. , 1993, "Effect of clay/oil flocculation on the rate of natural cleansing in Prince William Sound following the *Exxon Valdez* oil spill," *16th Arctic & Marine Oilspill Program Tech. Seminar,* Environment Canada, Ottawa. p 121.

Brander-Smith, D.; Therrien, D.; Tobin, S. , 1990, *Protecting our waters. Public review panel on tanker safety and marine spills response capability,* Final Report, EN21-91/1990E, 263 pp, Minister of Supply and Services Canada, Ottawa. [ISBN 0-662-18089-5]

Brown, D.W.; Wigren, C.A; Burrows, D.G.; Tilbury, K.L.; Pearce, R.W.; Bolton, J.L.; Pierce, S.M.; Field, L.J.; Chan, S.L.;Varanasi, U., 1993, "Petroleum hydrocarbons in Alaskan subsistence seafoods following the 1989 *Exxon Valdez* oil spill," *Abstracts, ASTM Symposium on the Exxon Valdez Oil Spill,* Atlanta, April 1993.

Bue, B.G.; Sharr, S.; Moffitt, S.D.; Craig, A., 1993, "Assessment of injury to pink salmon eggs and fry", *Abstracts, Exxon Valdez Oil Spill Symposium,* Feb. 2-5, 1993, Trustee Council, Anchorage, Alaska. pp 101-103.

Burn, D.M., 1994. "Boat-based population surveys of sea otters on Prince William Sound." Chapter 4 in T.R. Loughlin, ed. *Marine Mammals and the Exxon Valdez,* Academic Press, San Diego, pp 61-80.

Burns, W.A. and Bence, A.E., 1993, "Fingerprinting polycyclic aromatic hydrocarbons (PAH) in subtidal sediments," Abstract #002, in *Ecological Risk Assessment: Lessons Learned.* 14th Annual Meeting, Society of Environmental Toxicology and Chemistry (SETAC) 14-18 November 1993, Houston, TX.

Button, D.K.; Robertson, B.R.; McIntosh, D.; Juttner, F., 1992, "Interactions between marine bacteria and dissolved-phase and beached hydrocarbons after the *Exxon Valdez* oil spill," *Appl. Environ. Microbiol.,* Vol. 58, No. 1, pp 243-251.

Cohen, Maurie J., 1993, "Economic Impact of an Environmental Accident: A Time-Series Analysis of the *Exxon Valdez* Oil Spill in South-Central Alaska." *Sociological Spectrum,* Vol. 13, No. 1, pp 35-63.

Collier, T.K.; Krahn, M.M.; Krone, C.A.; Johnson, L.L.; Myers, M.S.; Chan, S.L.; Varanasi, U., 1993, "Oil exposure and effects in subtidal fish following the *Exxon Valdez* oil spill," *Proc.International Oil Spill Conference*, American Petroleum Institute, Washington DC. pp 301-305

Conan, G.; Laubier, L.; Marchand, M.; d'Ozouville, L., 1981, *Amoco Cadiz: Consequences d'une pollution accidentelle par les hydrocarbures*, 881 pp, Centre National pour l'Exploitation des Oceans (CNEXO), Paris.

Davidson, A. , 1990, *In the Wake of the Exxon Valdez: the Devastating Impact of the Alaska Oil Spill,* Sierra Club Books, San Francisco. 334 pp.

DeGange, A. R.; Lensink, C. J., 1990, "Distribution, Age, and Sex Composition of Sea Otter Carcasses Recovered During the Response to the T/V *Exxon Valdez* Oil Spill," in Bayha, K. and Kormendy, J. eds. *Sea Otter Symposium: Proceedings of a Symposium to Evaluate the Response Effort on Behalf of Sea Otters After the T/V Exxon Valdez Oil Spill into Prince William Sound*, US Fish and Wildlife Service, Anchorage, AK.; National Fish and Wildlife Foundation, Washington, DC., pp 124-129.

DeGange, A. R.; Monson, D. H.; Irons, D. B.; Robbins, C. M.; Douglas, D. C., 1990, "Distribution and Relative Abundance of Sea Otters in South-Central and Southwestern Alaska Before or at the Time of the T/V *Exxon Valdez* Oil Spill , in Bayha, K. and Kormendy, J. eds. *Sea Otter Symposium: Proceedings of a Symposium to Evaluate the Response Effort on Behalf of Sea Otters After the T/V Exxon Valdez Oil Spill into Prince William Sound*, US Fish and Wildlife Service, Anchorage, AK.; National Fish and Wildlife Foundation, Washington, DC., pp 18-25.

DeGange, A. R.; Williams, T. D., 1990, "Procedures and Rationale for Marking Sea Otters Captured and Treated During the T/V *Exxon Valdez* Oil Spill , in Bayha, K. and Kormendy, J. eds. *Sea Otter Symposium: Proceedings of a Symposium to Evaluate the Response Effort on Behalf of Sea Otters After the T/V Exxon Valdez Oil Spill into Prince William Sound*, US Fish and Wildlife Service, Anchorage, AK.; National Fish and Wildlife Foundation, Washington, DC., pp 394-399.

Driskell, W.B., Houghton, J.P., Fukuyama, A.K., 1993, "Long-term effects of *Exxon Valdez* oiling and shoreline treatments on intertidal fauna. Abstract # 091 in *Ecological Risk Assessment: Lessons Learned*. 14th Annual Meeting, Society of Environmental Toxicology and Chemistry (SETAC) 14-18 November 1993, Houston, TX.

Driskell, W.B.; Fukuyama, A.K.; Houghton, J.P.; Lees, D.C.; Shigenaka, G.; Mearns, A.J. , 1993, "Impacts on intertidal infauna: *Exxon Valdez* oil spill and cleanup," *International Oil Spill Conference*, American Petroleum Institute, Washington DC. pp 355-360.

Duffy, L. K.; Bowyer, R. T.; Testa, J. W.; Faro, J. B., 1993, "Differences in blood haptoglobin and length-mass relationships in river otters *Lutra canadensis* from oiled and non-oiled areas of Prince William Sound Alaska," *Journal of Wildlife Diseases*, Vol. 29, No. 2, pp 353-359.

Dyer, Christopher L., 1993, "Tradition Loss as Secondary Disaster: Long-Term Cultural Impacts of the *Exxon Valdez* Oil Spill," *Sociological Spectrum*, Vol. 13, No. 1, 65-88.

Dyer, Christopher L.; Gill, Duane A.; Picou, J. Steven , 1992, "Social Disruption and the Valdez Oil Spill: Alaskan Natives in a Natural Resource Community," *Sociological Spectrum*, Vol. 12, No. 2, pp 105-126.

Dzinbal, A.M; Jarvis, R.L., 1984. "Coastal feeding ecology of Harlequin ducks in Prince William Sound, Alaska during summer," in *Marine Birds, Their Feeding Ecology and Commercial Fishing Relationships*. D.N. Nettleship, et al., eds. Canadian Wildlife Service Ottawa, Canada. pp 6-10.

Estes, J.A., 1991, "Catastrophes and conservation: Lessons from sea otters and the *Exxon Valdez*," *Science*, Vol. 254, No. 5038, p. 1596.

Fall, James A., 1993. "Subsistence", *Abstracts, Exxon Valdez Oil Spill Symposium*, Feb. 2-5, 1993, Trustee Council, Anchorage, Alaska. pp 16-18.

Field, R.; North, M.R.; Wells, J., 1993, "Nesting activity of yellow-billed loons on the Colville River delta, Alaska, after the *Exxon Valdez* oil spill.," *Wilson Bull.*, Vol. 105, No. 2, pp 325-332.

Fraser, J.P.; Tennyson, E.J., 1993, "Oil Spills of opportunity – an appropriate place for response research?", *16th Arctic & Marine Oilspill Program Tech. Seminar*, Environment Canada, Ottawa. pp 255-270.

Gaines, W. L; Fitzner, R.E., 1987. "Winter diet of the Harlequin duck at Sequim Bay, Puget Sound Washington." *Northwest Science* Vol. 61, No.4, pp 213-215.

Galt, J. A.; Payton, D. L., 1990, "Movement of Oil Spilled from the T/V *Exxon Valdez*," in Bayha, K. and Kormendy, J. eds. *Sea Otter Symposium: Proceedings of a Symposium to Evaluate the Response Effort on Behalf of Sea Otters After the T/V Exxon Valdez Oil Spill into Prince William Sound*, US Fish and Wildlife Service, Anchorage, AK.; National Fish and Wildlife Foundation, Washington, DC., pp 4-17.

Galt, J.A.; Lehr, W.J.; Payton, D.L. , 1991, "Fate and transport of the *Exxon Valdez* oil spill," *Environ. Sci. Technol.*, Vol. 25, No. 2, pp 202 209.

Garrott R.A.; Eberhardt, L.L.; Burn, D.M. , 1993, "Mortality of sea otters in Prince William Sound following the *Exxon Valdez* oil spill," *Marine Mammal Science*, Vol. 9, No. 4, pp 343-359.

Glaser J.A.; Venosa, A.D.; Opatken, E.J. , 1991, "Development and Evaluation of Application Techniques for Delivery of Nutrients to Contaminated Shoreline in Prince William Sound," *Proc. International Oil Spill Conference*, American Petroleum Inst. Washington DC. pp 559-562.

Griest, W.H.; Ho, C.; Guerin, M.R.; Tyndall, R.L., 1991, "Chemical comparison of weathered spilled oil and *Exxon Valdez* hold oil from an occupational health standpoint," *Annual Meeting of the Air and Waste Management Association* , Vancouver, B.C. (Canada) [16-21 Jun 1991 - NTIS/DE91009915] p 229.

Gorbics, C, and Ballachery, B., 1993, "The fate of sea otters following the *Exxon Valdez* oil spill." *Abstracts, ASTM Symposium on the Exxon Valdez Oil Spill*, Atlanta, April 1993.

Gundlach, E.R.; Berne, S.; D'Ozouville, L.; Topinka, J.A., 1981, "Shoreline oil two years after *Amoco Cadiz*: New complications from *Tanio*," *Proc. International Oil Spill Conference*, 525-540. American Petroleum Inst. Washington DC.

Gundlach, E.R.; Pavia, E.A.; Robinson, C; Gibeaut, J.C., 1991. "Shoreline surveys at the *Exxon Valdez* Oil Spill: The State of Alaska Response." *Proc. International Oil Spill Conf.*, American Petroleum Inst. Washington DC. pp 519-529.

Hanna, S.R.; Drivas, P.J., 1993, "Modeling VOC emissions and air concentrations from the *Exxon Valdez* oil," *Air & Waste*, Vol. 43, No. 3, pp 298-309.

Harvey, S.; Elashvili, I.; Valdes, J.J.; Kamely, D.; Chakrabarty A. M. , 1990, "Enhanced removal of *Exxon Valdez* spilled oil from Alaskan gravel by a microbial surfactant," *Bio-Technology* (New York), Vol. 8, No. 3, pp 228-230.

Heras, H.; Zhou, S.; Ackman, R.G., 1993, "Uptake and depuration of petroleum hydrocarbons by Atlantic salmon," *16th Arctic and Marine Oilspill Program Technical Seminar*, Environment Canada, Ottawa, pp 343-352.

Hess, W.N., Editor, 1978, "The *Amoco Cadiz* oil spil: A preliminary Scientific Report," NOAA/EPA special report, NOAA and US Environmental Protection Agency, Washington DC. 355 pp. [NTIS PB-285-805]

Holmes, K. , 1990, "The *Exxon Valdez* spill: One year later," *Natl. Fisherman*, Vol. 71, No. 3, pp 14-16,36.

Houghton, J. P., Fukuyama, A.K., Lees, D.C., Driskell, D.B., Chigenaka, G., Mearns, A.J., 1993, "Long-term effects of *Exxon Valdez* oiling and soreline treatments on rocky intertidal epibiota," Abstract # 092 in *Ecological Risk Assessment: Lessons Learned.* 14th Annual Meeting, Society of Environmental Toxicology and Chemistry (SETAC) 14-18 November 1993, Houston, TX.

Houghton, J.P.; Fukuyama, A.K.; Driskell, W.B.; Lees, D.C.; Shigenaka, G.; Mearns, A.J., 1993, "Recovery of Prince William Sound Intertidal infauna from the *Exxon Valdez* spill and treatments 1990-92," *Abstracts, Exxon Valdez Oll Spill Symposium*, Feb. 2-5, 1993, Trustee Council, Anchorage, Alaska. pp 75-78.

Houghton, J.P.; Fukuyama, A.K.; Lees, D.C.; Driskell, W.B.; Mearns, A.J.; Shigenaka, G., 1993, "Recovery of Prince William Sound intertidal epibiota from the *Exxon Valdez* spill and treatments-1990-1992," *Abstracts, Exxon Valdez Oll Spill Symposium*, Feb. 2-5, 1993, Trustee Council, Anchorage, Alaska. pp 79-82.

Houghton, J.P.; Fukuyama, A.K.; Lees, D.C.; Driskell, W.B.; Shigenaka, G.; Mearns, A.J., 1993, "Impacts on intertidal epibiota: *Exxon Valdez* spill and subsequent cleanup," *Proc. International Oil Spill Conference*, American Petroleum Institute, Washington DC. pp 293-300.

Houghton, J.P.; Fukuyama, A.K.; Lees, D.C.; Teas, H.; Cumberland, H.; Harper, P.; Evert, T.; Driskell, W.B., 1992, *1991 Biological Monitoring Survey, Evaluation of the condition of Prince William Sound shorelines following the Exxon Valdez oil spill and subsequent shoreline treatment*. NOAA Tech. Memo. NOS ORCA 67, Vol. 2, National Oceanic and Atmospheric Administration, Seattle Washington. 238 pp

Houghton, J.P.; Lees, D.C.; Driskell, W.B.; Mearns, A.J., 1991, "Impacts of the *Exxon Valdez* spill and subsequent cleanup on intertidal biota - 1 year later," *Proc. International Oil Spill Conference*, American Petroleum Institute, Washington DC. pp 467-475.

Houghton, J.P.; Lees, D.C.; Ebert, T.A., 1991, "Evaluation of the condition of intertidal and shallow subtidal biota in Prince William Sound following the *Exxon Valdez* oil spill and subsequent shoreline treatment, NOAA Report HMRB 91-1, Vol. 1, National Oceanic and Atmospheric Administration, Washington DC.

Houghton, J.P.; Lees, D.C.; Ebert, T.A. , 1991, "Evaluation of the condition of intertidal and shallow subtidal biota in Prince William Sound following the *Exxon Valdez* oil spill and subsequent shoreline treatment." Appendices, NOAA Report No. HMRB 91-1, Vol. 2. National Oceanic and Atmospheric Administration, Washington DC.

Jahns, H.O., 1993, "The fate of the oil from the *Exxon Valdez*: A perspective," *Abstracts, ASTM Symposium on the Exxon Valdez Oil Spill*, Atlanta, April 1993.

Johnson, E., 1991, "Effect on fishermen of the Valdez spill", *Seaways*, 8.

Juday, G.P.; Foster, N.R., 1990, "A preliminary look at effects of the *Exxon Valdez* oil spill on Green Island research natural area," *Agroborealis*, Vol. 22, No. 1, pp 10-17.

Karinen, J.F.; Babcock, M.M.; Brown, D.W.; MacLeod, W.D.; Ramos, L.S., 1993, "Hydrocarbons in Intertidal Sediments and Mussels from Prince William Sound, Alaska, 1977-1980: Characterization and Probable Sources," Report, Contract Number: NOAA-TM-NMFS-AFSC-9, 75 pp. [NTIS/PB93-159093]

Kelso, D. K.; Kendziorek, M., 1991, "Alaska's response to the *Exxon Valdez* oil spill," *Environ. Sci. Technol.*, Vol. 25, pp 18-23.

Khan, R.A., 1990, "Parasitism in marine fish after chronic exposure to petroleum hydrocarbons in the laboratory and to the *Exxon Valdez* oil spill," Bull. Envron. Contam. Toxicol., Vol. 44, No. 5, 759-763.

Kocan, R.M.; Marty, G.D.; Biggs, F.D; Baker, T.T. 1993. "Reproductive success of individual Prince William Sound herring three years after the *Exxon Valdez* oil spill." Alaska Dept. of Fish and Game Report.

Koons, C.B.; Jahns, H.O, 1992, "The fate of oil from the *Exxon Valdez* - a perspective," *Proc. Marine Technology Soc.*, Vol 26, No. 3, pp 61-69. [Also listed as: *MTS '92: Global Ocean Partnership.* Proceedings, Washington, DC (USA) 19-21 Oct '92. pp 105-125.]

Krahn, M.M.; Burrows, D.G.; Ylitalo, G.M.; Brown, D.W.; Wigren, C.A.; Collier, T.K.; Chan, S-L.; Varanasi, U., 1992, "Mass spectrometric analysis for aromatic compounds in bile of fish sampled after the *Exxon Valdez* oil spill," *Environ. Sci. Technol*, Vol. 26, No. 1, pp 116-126.

Krahn, M.M.; Ylitalo, G.M.; Buzitis, J.; Krone, C.A.; Stein, J.E.; Chan, S.L.; Varanasi, U., 1993a, "Screening methods for assessing damage to natural resources following the *Exxon Valdez* oil spill," *Proc. International Oil Spill Conference*, American Petroleum Institute, Washington DC. pp 872-873.

Krahn, Margaret M.; Ylitalo, Gina M.; Buzitis, Jon; Chan, Sin-Lam; Varanasi, Usha; Wade, Terry L.; Jackson, Thomas J., 1993b, "Comparison of High-Performance Liquid Chromatography/Fluorescence Screening and Gas Chromatography/Mass Spectrometry Analysis for Aromatic Compounds in Sediments Sampled After the *Exxon Valdez* Oil Spill," *Environ. Sci. Technol.*, Vol. 27, No. 4, pp 699-708.

Krahn, M.M., Ylitalo, G.M., Burrows, D.G., Buzitis, J., Chan, S.L., and Varanasi, U.. 1993 c, "Methods for determining crude oil contamination in sediments and biota after the *Exxon Valdez* oil spill." *Abstracts, ASTM Symposium on the Exxon Valdez Oil Spill*, Atlanta, April 1993.

Krahn, M.M., Ylitalo, G.M., Burrows, D.G., Buzitis, J., Chan, S.L., and Varanasi, U., 1993d, "Methods for determining crude oil contamination in sediments and biota after the *Exxon Valdez* oil spill." *Abstracts, Exxon Valdez OII Spill Symposium*, Feb. 2-5, 1993, Trustee Council, Anchorage, Alaska. pp 60-62

Kvenvolden, K.A.; Hostettler, F.D.; Rapp, J.B.; Carlson, P.R., 1993, "Hydrocarbons in oil residues on beaches of islands of Prince William Sound, Alaska," *Mar. Pollut. Bull.*, Vol. 26, No. 1, pp 24-29.

Lasday, A.H. , 1989, "Economic evaluation of dispersants to combat oil spills," in Flaherty, L. M. , ed., *Oil Dispersants: New Ecological Approaches*, ASTM STP 1018, Amer. Soc Testing Mater., Philadelphia. pp 41-48.

Lees, D.C.; Houghton, J.P.; Driskell, W.B. , 1993, "Effects of shoreline treatment methods on intertidal biota in Prince William Sound," *Proc. International Oil Spill Conference*, American Petroleum Institute, Washington DC. pp345-354.

Lethcoe, N.R.; Nurnberger, L.; Eds., 1989, *Prince William Sound Environmental Reader 1989 – T/V Exxon Valdez Oil Spill.*, Prince William Sound Conservation Alliance, Valdez Alaska.

Lindstrom, J.E.; Prince, R.C.; Clark, J.C.; Grossman, M.J.; Yeage, T.R.; Braddock, J.F.; Brown, E.J., 1991, "Microbial   populations and hydrocarbon biodegradation potentials in fertilized shoreline sediments affected by the T/V *Exxon Valdez* oil spill," *Appl Environ Microbiol* , Vol. 57, No. 9, pp 2514-2522.

Lipscomb, T.P.; Harris, R.K.; Moeller, R.B.; Pletcher, J.M.; Haebler, R.J.; Ballachey, B.E., 1993, "Histopathologic lesions in sea otters exposed to crude oil," *Vet. Pathol*, Vol. 30, No. 1, pp 1-11.

Long, E. R.; Chapman, P., 1985, "A sediment quality triad: measures of sediment contamination, toxicity and infunal community composition in Puget Sound," *Mar. Pollut. Bull.* , Vol. 16, pp 405-415.

Loughlin, T.R., Ed., 1994. *Marine Mammals and the Exxon Valdez,* San Diego: Academic Press. 395 pp.

Maki, A.W. , 1991, "The *Exxon Valdez* oil spill: Initial environmental impact assessment, *Environ. Sci. Technol.*, Vol. 25, pp 24-29.

Maki, A.W.; Parker, K.R., 1995, "An analysis of post-spill spawning by pink salmon in selected Prince William Sound streams through 1994." Manuscript, presented at 17th Northeast Pacific PInk and Chum Salmon Workshop, March 1-3, 1995. 12 pp.

Maki, A.W., 1995, personal communication to P.G. Wells and J.N. Butler, reviewing a draft of this Introduction.

Mankiewicz, P.J, Boehm, P.E., Neff, J., 1993, "The use of mussel PAH burdens to assess bioavailability and long-term risk to wildlife following the *Exxon Valdez* oil spill." Abstract # 090 in.*Ecological Risk Assessment: Lessons Learned.* 14th Annual Meeting, Society of Environmental Toxicology and Chemistry (SETAC) 14-18 November 1993, Houston, TX.

McAllister, M., 1993, "Generating damage restoration costs for archaeologial injuries of the *Exxon Valdez* oil spill," *Abstracts, Exxon Valdez OIl Spill Symposium,* Feb. 2-5, 1993, Trustee Council, Anchorage, Alaska. pp 219-222.

McGurk, M.; Warburton, D.; Parker, T.; Litke, M., 1990, *Early Life History of Pacific Herring: 1989 Prince William Sound Herring Egg Incubation Experiment,* Ocean

Assessments Div., and Minerals Management Service, Outer Continental Shelf Office, Anchorage, Alaska. 412 pp, [NTIS/PB90-265885]

Meacham, C.P.; Sullivan, J.R., 1993, "Salmon & other fish - eggs & fry," *Abstracts, Exxon Valdez Oil Spill Symposium,* Feb. 2-5, 1993, Trustee Council, Anchorage, Alaska. pp 27-29.

Michel, J.; Hayes, M.O. , 1993, "Persistence and weathering of *Exxon Valdez* oil in the intertidal zone – 3.5 years later," *Proc. International Oil Spill Conference,* American Petroleum Institute, Washington DC. pp 279-286.

Moeller, T.H.; Barber, H.D.; Nichols, J.A., 1987, "Comparative costs of oil spill cleanup techniques., *Proc. International Oil Spill Conf,* Amer. Petrol Inst., Washington DC. pp 123-127.

Moles, A. D.; Rice, S.D.; Okihiro, M.S. , 1993, "Herring parasite and tissue alteration following the *Exxon Valdez* oil spill," *Proc. International Oil Spill Conference,* American Petroleum Institute, Washington DC. pp 325-328.

Moulton, L.L., 1995, "Effects of oil-contaminated sediments on early life stages and egg viability of pink salmon in Prince William Sound, Alaska." Manuscript, presented at the 17th Northeast Pacific Pink and Chum Salmon Workshop, March 1-3, 1995. 13 pp.

Mueller, J.G.; Resnick, S.M.; Shelton, M.E.; Pritchard, P.H., 1992, "Effect of Inoculation on the Biodegradation of Weathered Prudhoe Bay Crude Oil," *Journal of Industrial Microbiology,* Vol. 10, pp 95-102.

National Research Council, 1985. *Oil in the Sea: Inputs, Fates, and Effects.* National Academy Press, Washington DC. 608 pp.

Nauman, S. A. , 1990, "Shoreline cleanup techniques: *Exxon Valdez* operations," *13th Arctic & Marine Oilspill Program Tech. Seminar,* Environment Canada, Ottawa. pp 431-438.

Neff, J.M., 1991, "Long-term trends in the concentrations of polycyclic aromatic hydrocarbons in the water column of Prince William Sound and the western gulf of Alaska Following the *Exxon Valdez* oil spill," *14th Arctic and Marine Oil Spill Program Technical Seminar,* Environment Canada, Ottawa. pp 27-38.

Nevissi, A.E., 1991, *Effects of Exxon Valdez oil spill on pink salmon migration,* US National Science Foundation Grant summary. [FEDRIP-91-01305681]

Nighswander, Thomas, 1993, "Health effects," *Abstracts, ASTM Symposium on the Exxon Valdez Oil Spill,* Atlanta, April 1993.

NOAA, 1983, *Assessing the social costs of oil spills: the Amoco Cadiz case study,* US Dept. of Commerce, National Oceanic and Atmospheric Administration, National Ocean Service, Washington DC. 144 pp.

NOAA , 1992, *Oil Spill Case Histories 1967-1991,* Hazardous Materials Response and Assessment Division, National Oceanic and Atmospheric Administration, Seattle WA., pp 121-133 [NTIS No. PB93-144517].

NOAA , 1992, *Exxon Valdez HindCast (for microcomputers)*, Software,.1 diskette, National Oceanic and Atmospheric Administration, [NTIS : PB92-503176/GAR.]

Norcross, B.L., 1992, "Responding to an oil spill: Reflections of a fisheries scientist," *Fisheries*, Vol. 17, No. 6, p 4.

Ott, Frederica (Riki), 1994, *Sound Truth: Exxon's manipulation of science and the significance of the Exxon Valdez oil spill*,   Greenpeace, PO Box 104432, Anchorage AK 99510. 76 pp

Owens, E.H., 1990, "Suggested improvements to oil spill response planning following the *Nestucca* and *Exxon Valdez* incidents," *13th Arctic & Marine Oilspill Program Tech. Seminar*, Environment Canada, Ottawa, pp 439-450.

Owens, E.H., 1991, "Shoreline conditions following the *Exxon Valdez* spill as of fall 1990", *14th Arctic and Marine Oil Spill Program Technical Seminar*, Environment Canada Ottawa. pp 579-606.

Owens, E.H.; Sergy, G.A.; McGuire, B.E.; Humphrey, B., 1993, "The 1970 *Arrow* oil spill: What remains on the shoreline 22 years later?" *16th Arctic & Marine Oilspill Program Tech. Seminar*, Environment Canada, Ottawa. pp 1149-1168.

Owens, E.H.; Teal, A., 1990, "Shoreline cleanup following the *Exxon Valdez* oil spill – Field data collection and the SCAT program," *13th Arctic & Marine Oilspill Program Tech. Seminar*, Environment Canada, Ottawa. pp 411-422.

Owens, E.H.; Teal, A.R.; Haase, P.C., 1991, Berm relocation during the 1990 shoreline cleanup program following the*Exxon Valdez* spill, *14th Arctic and Marine Oil Spill Program Technical Seminar*, Environment Canada Ottawa. pp 607-630.

Owens, Ed, 1990, "A Brief Overview and Initial Results from the Winter Shoreline Monitoring," *13th Arctic & Marine Oilspill Program Tech. Seminar*, Environment Canada, Ottawa. pp 451-470.

Page, D., Boehm, P.D., Douglas, G.S., Bence, A.E.,1993, "The natural petroleum hydrocarbon background in subtidal sediments of Prince William Sound, Alaska." Abstract # 089 in *Ecological Risk Assessment: Lessons Learned*. 14th Annual Meeting, Society of Environmental Toxicology and Chemistry (SETAC) 14-18 November 1993, Houston, TX.

Page, D.; Boehm, P.D.; Douglas, G.S.; Bence, A.E., 1993, "Identification of hydrocarbon sources in the benthic sediments of Prince William Sound and the Gulf of Alaska following the *Exxon Valdez* oil spill," *16th Arctic & Marine Oilspill Program Tech. Seminar*, Environment Canada, Ottawa, p 45.

Palinkas, L.A.; Downs, M.A.; Petterson, J.S.; Russell, J., 1993, "Social, cultural, and psychological impacts of the *Exxon Valdez* oil spill," *Hum. Organ.*, Vol. 52, No. 1, pp 1-13.

Palinkas, L.A.; Petterson, J.S.; Russell, J.; Downs, M.A., 1993, "Community patterns of psychiatric disorders after the *Exxon Valdez* oil spill," *Am. J. Psychiatry*, Vol. 150, No. 10, pp 1517-1523.

Palinkas, L.A.; Russell, J.; Downs, M.A.; Petterson, J.S., 1992, "Ethnic differences in stress, coping and depressive symptoms after the *Exxon Valdez* oil spill," *Journal of Nervous and Mental Disease*, Vol. 180, No. 5, pp 287-295.

Parrish, J. K.; Boersma, P.D., 1995. "Muddy Waters" *American Scientist*, Vol 83, pp 112-115.

Patten, S.M., 1993, "Acute and sublethal effects of the Exxon Valdez oil spill on Harlequins and other seaducks," *Abstracts, Exxon Valdez Oil Spill Symposium,* Feb. 2-5, 1993, Trustee Council, Anchorage, Alaska. pp 151-154.

Payne, J.R.; Clayton, J.R.; McNabb, G. D.; Kirstein, B.E., 1991, "*Exxon Valdez* oil weathering fate and behavior: Model predictions and field observations," *Proc. International Oil Spill Conference*, American Petroleum Institute, Washington DC. pp 641-654.

Pearson, W.H.; Woodruff, D.L.; Kiesser, S.L.; Fellingham, G.W.; Elston, R.A., *Oil effects on spawning behavior and reproduction in Pacific herring (Clupea harengus pallasi)*, Publication, No. 4412, American Petroleum Institute, Washington DC. 105 pp.

Percy, J.A. and Wells, P.G., 1984 "Effects of petroleum in polar marine environments". *Mar. Technol Soc. Jour.* 18 (3): 51-61.

Peterson, Markus J.; Peterson, Tarla Rai, 1993, "A Rhetorical Critique of 'Nonmarket' Economic Valuations for Natural Resources," *Environmental Values*, Vol. 2, No. 1, pp 47-65.

Piatt, J.F.; Lensink, C.J.; Butler, W.; Kendziorek, M.; Nysewander, D.R., 1990, "Immediate impact of the *Exxon Valdez* oil spill on marine birds," *Auk*, Vol. 107, No. 2, pp 387-397.

Picou, J. Steven; Gill, Duane A.; Dyer, Christopher L.; Curry, Evans W, 1992, "Distribution and Stress in an Alaskan Fishing Community: Initial and Continuing Impacts of the *Exxon Valdez* Oil Spill," *Industrial Crisis Quarterly* , Vol. 6, No. 3, pp 235-257.

Prince, R.C.; Bare, R.E.; George, G.N.; Haith, C.E.; Grossman, M. J.; Lute, J.R.; Elmendorf, D.L.; Bernero, V. M.; Senius, J. D.; Keim, L.G.; Chianelli, R.R.; Hinton, S. M.; Teal, A. R., 1993, "The effect of bioremediation on the microbial populations of oiled beaches in Prince William Sound, Alaska," *Proc. International Oil Spill Conference*, American Petroleum Institute, Washington DC. pp 469-475.

Pritchard, P.H., 1991, "Bioremediation as a Technology: Experiences with the *Exxon Valdez* Oil Spill," *Journal of Hazardous Materials*, Vol. 28, No. 1-2, pp 115-130.

Pritchard, P.H.; Costa, C.F., 1991, "EPA's Alaska oil spill bioremediation project," *Environ. Sci. Technol*, Vol. 25, pp 372-379.

Pritchard, P.H.; Costa, C.F.; Suit, L. , 1991, *Alaska Oil Spill Bioremediation Project.* Science Advisory Board Draft Report. Sections 1 through 6,   250 pp. [EPA/600/9-91/046a]

Pritchard, P.H.; Costa, C.F.; Suit, L. , 1991, *Alaska Oil Spill Bioremediation Project.* Science Advisory Board Draft Report. Sections 7 through 13 and appendices, US

Environmental Protection Agency, Office of Research and Development, Gulf Breeze, Florida. 572 pp. [EPA/600/9-91/046b]

Pritchard, P.H.; Mueller, J. G.; Rogers, J. C.; Kremer, F. V.; Glaser, J. A., 1992, "Oil Spill Bioremediation: Experiences, Lessons and Results from the *Exxon Valdez* Oil Spill in Alaska," *Biodegradation* , Vol. 3, No. 2-3, pp 315-335.

Provant, S.G. , 1992, "Assessment of the Transrec-350 mechanical recovery capacity of the oil spill response equipment in Prince William sound," *15th Arctic & Marine Oilspill Program Tech. Seminar*, Environment Canada, Ottawa. pp 219-238.

Reger, D.R., 1993, "Investigations of crude oil contamination in intertidal archaeological sites around the Gulf of Alaska," *Abstracts, Exxon Valdez Oil Spill Symposium,* Feb. 2-5, 1993, Trustee Council, Anchorage, Alaska. pp 215-218.

Restoration Planning Work Group, 1990, *Restoration following the Exxon Valdez Oil Spill,* State of Alaska, US Depts. of Agriculture, Commerce, Interior, and US Environmental Protection Agency. 178 pp.

Rice, S.D.; Moles, A.; Karinen, J.F.; Korn, S.; Karls, M.G.; Brodersen, C.C.; Gharrett, J.A.; Babcock, M.M., 1984, *Effects of petroleum hydrocarbons on Alaskan aquatic organisms: A comprehensive review of all oil-effects research on Alaskan fish and invertebrates conducted by the Auke Bay Laboratory 1970-1981,* Tech. Memo. NMFS/NWC-67, US Dept. Commerce, National Oceanic and Atmospheric Administration, Auke Bay, Alaska. 128 pp.

Rice, S.D.; Moles, D.A.; Taylor, T.L.; Karinen, J.F., 1979, "Sensitivity of 39 Alaskan marine species to Cook Inlet crude oil and No.2 fuel oil," Proc. International Oil Spill Conf, American Petroleum Institute, Washington DC. pp 549-554.

Rice, S.D.; Wright, B.A. Short, J.W.; O'Clair, C.B., 1993. "Subtidal oil contamination and biological impacts." *Abstracts, Exxon Valdez Oil Spill Symposium,* Feb. 2-5, 1993, Trustee Council, Anchorage, Alaska. pp 23-26

Ritchie, W. and O'Sullivan, M., eds. 1994. *The Environmental Impact of the Wreck of the Braer.* The Scottish Office, Edinburgh. 207 pp. [ISBN 0-7480-0900-0] See also SOED, 1994.

Robbins, C.E. "The Exxon Valdez Cleanup – The first six months," *Abstracts, Exxon Valdez Oil Spill Symposium,* Feb. 2-5, 1993, Trustee Council, Anchorage, Alaska. pp 10-12. [The quotation in the text was taken down by P.G.Wells at the symposium: *Ecological Risk Assessment: Lessons Learned.* 14th Annual Meeting, Society of Environmental Toxicology and Chemistry (SETAC) 14-18 November 1993, Houston, TX.]

Robinson, John, Nov. 5, 1994. Letter to J.N. Butler reviewing a draft of this Introduction.

Rodin, Mari; Downs, Michael; Petterson, John; Russell, John , 1992, "Community Impacts Resulting from the *Exxon Valdez* Oil Spill." *Industrial Crisis Quarterly,* Vol. 6, No. 3, pp 219-234.

Rogers, J.E.; Araujo, R.; Pritchard, P.H.; Tabak, H.H., 1990, *Role of microorganisms in the bioremediation of the oil spill in Prince William Sound, Alaska,* US Environmntal Protection Agency Report [NTIS PB90-263070/GAR]

Sergy, G.A., 1985. "The Baffin Island Oil Spill (BIOS) Project: A Summary." *Proc. International Oil Spill Conf.,* American Petroleum Institute, Washington DC. pp 571-575.

Sergy, G.A., 1987. "The Baffin Island Oil Spill (BIOS) Project," *Arctic* Vol.40, suppl. 1, 279 pp.

SETAC (Society for Environmental Toxicology and Chemistry), 1993, Abstracts, *Ecological Risk Assessment: Lessons Learned.* 14th Annual Meeting, 14-18 November 1993, Houston, TX.

Sharp, B.E.; Cody, M., 1993, "Black oystercatchers in Prince William Sound: Oil spill effects on reproduction and behavior," *Abstracts, Exxon Valdez Oil Spill Symposium,* Feb. 2-5, 1993, Trustee Council, Anchorage, Alaska. pp 155-158.

Shaw, D.G., 1992, "The *Exxon Valdez* oil-spill: Ecological and social consequences," *Environ. Conserv.,* Vol. 19, No. 3, pp 253-258.

Skinner, S. K. and Reilly, W. K., 1989, *The Exxon Valdez Oil Spill – A report to the President of the United States of America* US National Response Team, Washington DC. Reprinted by Cutter Information Corp. Arlington, MA., 68 pp.

SOED (Scottish Office of Environmental Department), 1994. *The environmental impact of the wreck of the Braer.* Ecological Steering Group on the oil spill in Shetland, Edinburgh, Scotland, 207 pp. [See also Ritchie and O'Sullivan, 1994.]

Spaulding, M. L.; Colluru, V.S; Anderson, E; Howlett, E., 1994. "Application of three-dimensional oil spill model (WOSM/OILMAP) to hindcast the Braer Spill," *Spill Science and Technology Bulletin,* Vol.1, No. 1, pp 23-35.

Spies, R. B., 1993. "So why can't science tell us more abou the effects of the *Exxon Valdez* oil spill? *Abstracts, Exxon Valdez Oil Spill Symposium,* Feb. 2-5, 1993, Trustee Council, Anchorage, Alaska. pp 1-5

Spies, R. B.., Dec. 12, 1994 . Letter to J.N. Butler reviewing a draft of this Introduction.

Spraker, T.R., 1990, "Hazards of Releasing Rehabilitated Animals with Emphasis on Sea Otters and the T/V *Exxon Valdez* Oil Spill," in Bayha, K. and Kormendy, J. eds. *Sea Otter Symposium: Proceedings of a Symposium to Evaluate the Response Effort on Behalf of Sea Otters After the T/V Exxon Valdez Oil Spill into Prince William Sound,* US Fish and Wildlife Service, Anchorage, AK.; National Fish and Wildlife Foundation, Washington, DC., pp 385-389.

Stoker, S.W.; Neff, J.M.; Schroeder, T.R.; McCormick, D.M., 1993, "Biological conditions of shorelines following the *Exxon Valdez* spill," *Proc. International Oil Spill Conference,* American Petroleum Institute, Washington DC. pp 287-292.

Stone, R. , 1993, "Dispute over *Exxon Valdez* cleanup data gets messy," *Science,* Vol. 260, p 749 .

Stringer, W.J.; Dean, K.G.; Guritz, R.M.; Garbeil, H.M.; Groves, J.E.; Ahlnaes, K. , 1992, "Detection of petroleum spilled from the MV *Exxon Valdez*," *Int. J. Remote Sens.*, Vol. 13, No. 5, pp 799-824.

Stubblefield, W.A., Pillard, D.A., Boehm, P.D, Page, D.S.,1993, "Evaluation of the toxicity of oil residues in shoreline sediments following the *Exxon Valdez* oil spill." Abstract # 093 in *Ecological Risk Assessment: Lessons Learned*. 14th Annual Meeting, Society of Environmental Toxicology and Chemistry (SETAC) 14-18 November 1993, Houston, TX.

Tabak, H.H.; Haines, J.R.; Venosa, A.D.; Glaser, J.A.; Desai, S., 1991, "Enhancement of Biodegradation of Alaskan Weathered Crude Oil Components by Indigenous Microbiota with the Use of Fertilizers and Nutrients," *Proc. International Oil Spill Conference*, American Petroleum Institute, Washington, DC. pp 583-590.

Teal, A. , 1990, "Shoreline cleanup following the *Exxon Valdez* oil spill – the decision process for shoreline cleanup," *13th Arctic & Marine Oilspill Program Tech. Seminar*, Environment Canada, Ottawa, pp 423-429.

Trustee Council, 1989, *State/Federal Natural Resource Damage Assessment Plan for the Exxion Valdez Oil Spill*. Public Review Draft, Oil Spill Public Information Center, 645 G St., Anchorage AK 99501. 258 pp.

Trustee Council, 1990, *The 1990 State/Federal Natural Resource Damage Assessment and Restoration Plan for the Exxon Valdez Oil Spill*, Appendices A,B.C., Vol. 1, Oil Spill Public Information Center, 645 G St., Anchorage AK 99501. 353+ pp.

Trustee Council, 1990, *The 1990 State/Federal Natural Resource Damage Assessment Plan for the Exxon Valdez Oil Spill*. Appendix D., Vol. 2, Oil Spill Public Information Center, 645 G St., Anchorage AK 99501. 121 pp.

Trustee Council, 1991, *The 1991 State/Federal Natural Resource Damage Assessment and Restoration Plan for the Exxon Valdez Oil Spill*. Appendices A,B.C., Vol. 1, Oil Spill Public Information Center, 645 G St., Anchorage AK 99501. 288pp and Appendices.

Trustee Council, 1991, *The 1991 State/Federal Natural Resource Damage Assessment and Restoration Plan for the Exxon Valdez Oil Spill*. *Response to Public Comment*. Appendix D, Vol. 2, Oil Spill Public Information Center, 645 G St., Anchorage AK 99501. 178 pp.

Trustee Council, 1993, *Exxon Valdez Oil Spill Symposium, Feb. 2-5 1993.*, Abstract book, Oil Spill Public Information Center, 645 G St., Anchorage AK 99501. [Cited as *Abstracts, Exxon Valdez Oll Spill Symposium*, Feb. 2-5, 1993, Trustee Council, Anchorage, Alaska].

Trustee Council, 1994, *Comprehensive Assessment of Coastal Habitat: Final Status Report*, Vol. 1-6. Oil Spill Public Information Center, 645 G St., Anchorage AK 99501.

Trustee Council, 1994. *Exxon Valdez Oil Spill Restoration plan*. Oil Spill Public Information Center, 645 G St., Anchorage AK 99501.

US Coast Guard, 1993, *Federal On-Scene Coordinator's Report: T/V Exxon Valdez Oil Spill*, Vol. 1, US Coast Guard, Washington DC. 581 pp.

US Coast Guard, 1993, *Federal On-Scene Coordinator's Report: T/V Exxon Valdez Oil Spill*, Vol. 2, US Coast Guard, Washington DC. 1012 pp.

Varanasi, U.; Chan, S.L.; MacLeod, W.D.; Stein, J.E.; Brown, D.W., 1991, *Survey of Subsistence Fish and Shellfish for Exposure to Oil Spilled from the Exxon Valdez. First Year: 1989* Report. [NTIS/PB91-152132.]

Venkatesh, S., 1990, "Model simulations of the drift and spread of the *Exxon Valdez* oil spill," *Atmosphere-Ocean*, Vol. 28, No. 1, pp 90-105.

Venosa, A.D.; Haines, J.R.; Allen, D.M., 1992, "Efficacy of commercial inocula in enhancing biodegradaion of weathered crude oil contaminating a Prince William Sound beach," *Journal of Industrial Microbiology*, Vol. 10, No. 1, pp 1-11.

Vermeer, K., 1983, "Diet of the Harlequin duck in the Strait of Georgia, British Columbia," *The Murrelet*, Vol. 64, No.2, pp 54-57.

Westermeyer, W.E., 1991, "Oil spill response capabilities in the United States," *Environ. Sci. Technol*, Vol. 25, 196-202.

White, I.C.; Nichols, J. A. , 1983, "The cost of oil spills," *Proc. International Oil Spill Conf.*, Amer. Petrol. Inst., Washington DC. pp 541-544.

Williams, T. M.; McBain, J.; Wilson, R. K.; Davis, R. W., 1990, "Clinical Evaluation and Cleaning of Sea Otters Affected by the T/V *Exxon Valdez* Oil Spill," Fin Bayha, K. and Kormendy, J. eds. *Sea Otter Symposium: Proceedings of a Symposium to Evaluate the Response Effort on Behalf of Sea Otters After the T/V Exxon Valdez Oil Spill into Prince William Sound*, US Fish and Wildlife Service, Anchorage, AK.; National Fish and Wildlife Foundation, Washington, DC., pp 236-257.

Wolfe, Douglas A; Hamcedi, M.J.; Galt, J.A.; Watabayashi, G; Short, J.; O'Claire, C.; Rice S.; Michel, J.; Payne, J.R.; Braddock, J; Hanna, S; Salel, D., 1994. "The fate of the oil spilled from the *Exxon Valdez*," *Environ. Sci. Technol.* Vol. 28, No.13, pp 561A-568A.

Chemistry and Fate of the Spill

David S. Page,[1] Paul D. Boehm,[2] Gregory S. Douglas,[2] A. Edward Bence[3]

IDENTIFICATION OF HYDROCARBON SOURCES IN THE BENTHIC SEDIMENTS OF PRINCE WILLIAM SOUND AND THE GULF OF ALASKA FOLLOWING THE *EXXON VALDEZ* OIL SPILL

REFERENCE: Page, D. S., Boehm, P. D., Douglas, G. S., and Bence, A. E., "Identification of Hydrocarbon Sources in the Benthic Sediments of Prince William Sound and the Gulf of Alaska Following the Exxon Valdez Oil Spill," *Exxon Valdez Oil Spill: Fate and Effects in Alaskan Waters, ASTM STP 1219*, Peter G. Wells, James N. Butler, and Jane S. Hughes, Eds., American Society for Testing and Materials, Philadelphia, 1995.

ABSTRACT: Advanced hydrocarbon fingerprinting methods and improved analytical methods make possible the quantitative discrimination of the multiple sources of hydrocarbons in the benthic sediments of Prince William Sound (PWS) and the Gulf of Alaska. These methods measure an extensive range of polycyclic aromatic hydrocarbons (PAH) at detection levels that are as much as two orders of magnitude lower than those obtained by standard Environmental Protection Agency methods. Nineteen hundred thirty six (1 936) subtidal sediment samples collected in the sound and the eastern Gulf of Alaska in 1989, 1990, and 1991 were analyzed.

Fingerprint analyses of gas chromatography–mass spectrometry data reveal a natural background of petrogenic and biogenic PAH. The petrogenic background is derived largely from oil seeps in the eastern Gulf of Alaska. Age-dated (^{210}Pb) sediment cores indicate that significant input of seep hydrocarbons into Prince William Sound has been going on for at least 160 years and probably for thousands of years. Superimposed on this natural background are locally elevated concentrations of anthropogenic hydrocarbons from sources such as diesel fuel and pyrogenic PAH that are found primarily adjacent to active or historical sites of human use. *Exxon Valdez* crude, its weathering products, and diesel fuel refined from Alaska North Slope crude are readily distinguished from the natural seep petroleum background and from each other because of their

[1]Bowdoin College, Brunswick, ME 04011
[2]Arthur D. Little, Cambridge, MA 02140
[3]Exxon Production Research Company, Houston, TX 77252-2189

distinctive PAH distributions.

Mixing models were developed to calculate the PAH contributions from each source to each sediment sample. These calculations show that most of the seafloor in PWS contains no detectable hydrocarbons from the *Exxon Valdez* spill, although elevated concentrations of PAH from seep sources are widespread. In those areas where they were detected, spill hydrocarbons were generally a small increment to the natural petroleum hydrocarbon background. Low levels of *Exxon Valdez* crude residue were present in 1989 and again in 1990 in nearshore subtidal sediments off some shorelines that had been heavily oiled. By 1991 these crude residues were heavily degraded and even more sporadically distributed.

KEYWORDS: Polycyclic aromatic hydrocarbons (PAH), oil seeps, oil fingerprinting, *Exxon Valdez*, subtidal sediments, petrogenic hydrocarbons, pyrogenic hydrocarbons.

INTRODUCTION

On March, 24, 1989, the tanker *Exxon Valdez* hit Bligh Reef in Prince William Sound, Alaska, releasing approximately 258 000 barrels of Alaska North Slope (ANS) crude oil into the marine environment. In the aftermath of the spill, many scientific studies were conducted to assess its effects. This paper reports the results of subtidal sediment studies carried out in PWS in 1989, 1990, and 1991, involving 1 936 sediment analyses.

The primary goals of the subtidal sediment studies were to (1) identify and, where present, quantify the contribution of *Exxon Valdez* crude (EVC) to benthic sediments in Prince William Sound (PWS) and the Gulf of Alaska (GOA) in the region of the spill; (2) characterize the prespill hydrocarbon background in the spill zone; and (3) quantify the relative contributions of various polycyclic aromatic hydrocarbon (PAH) sources to seafloor sediments in PWS.

This paper deals primarily with the PAH in the sediments. Some of the PAH, particularly the 3- and 4 ring structures, are relatively resistant to degradation, and their fingerprints can diagnose different sources of hydrocarbon input. In addition, PAH are associated with the toxicity of petroleum. Because of concerns regarding the transport of EVC residues from intertidal areas to the seafloor, an important issue in this study is the degree to which traces of EVC residues in benthic sediments might represent a continuing threat to subtidal biota. Because saturate biomarker data were not available for studies done before 1991, the present study relied on the PAH data for source identification.

Hydrocarbon Sources

Hydrocarbons from both natural and anthropogenic (human) sources are common in the marine environment (Brassell and Eglinton 1980). Even the most isolated regions receive low concentrations of anthropogenic hydrocarbons through atmospheric fallout (see, for example, LaFlamme and Hites 1978), and areas on the continental shelves can receive multiple hydrocarbon inputs from natural sources such as oil seeps and the erosion of organic-rich sedimentary rocks, as well as from localized human activities. For example, Page et al. (1988) documented numerous sources of petroleum in the *Amoco Cadiz* impact zone including diesel fuel from boating activity, fresh crude oil, residual fuel oil, and weathered crude oil. (The use of diesel fuel for vessels and power generation is widespread in PWS.) Other inputs of petroleum were documented at the *Metula* spill site in the Straits of Magellan (Baker et al. 1975) and the *Bahia Paraiso* spill site in the Antarctic (Kennicutt et al. 1991, 1992). Because these ongoing hydrocarbon inputs make up the hydrocarbon background, recognizing the existence of this background and identifying its sources are an essential part of an oil-spill study. Consequently, the spill study design needs to include methods that discriminate spill oil from other hydrocarbons that can be similar in composition to the spill oil.

Types of hydrocarbons--There are three major types of hydrocarbons: (1) *petrogenic*, which are generated in organic-rich source rocks exposed to elevated temperatures for long time periods--a category that includes crude oil and its refined products; (2) *biogenic*, which are generated by biologic processes or in the early stages of diagenesis in marine sediments; and (3) *pyrogenic*, which are generated in combustion processes (Blumer and Youngblood 1975; Brassell and Eglinton 1980). The sources of hydrocarbons contributing to the background in PWS and the GOA are summarized, schematically, in Figure 1. Although PWS is not an industrialized area, it has a history of mining, fishing, and logging. Consequently, there are sites in PWS where human activity has caused localized inputs of hydrocarbons to nearshore marine sediments. In addition, large-scale inputs such as petrogenic hydrocarbons transported from oil-seep areas have contributed to the regional background PAH levels. Due to wide regional and local variations of the contributions from each source to the subtidal, it is not possible to determine their relative inputs to the sound as a whole.

Oil seeps as hydrocarbon sources--Natural oil seeps are found worldwide (see, for example, NRC [National Research Council] 1985; Bayzlinski et al. 1988; Kennicutt et al. 1988). The petroleum hydrocarbons from these seeps serve as carbon sources for heterotrophic bacteria, which, in turn, support biological communities at higher trophic levels (Montagna et al. 1987; Spies et al. 1988; Wade et al. 1989). Oil seeps are potentially important sources of background petrogenic hydrocarbons in Alaskan coastal waters because of the widespread occurrence of oil seeps along the Alaskan coast, including the GOA (Blasko 1976a; McGee 1972; Becker and Manen 1989). Although PWS is not a place where oil seeps would be expected to occur (because of the high metamorphic grade of the underlying sedimentary rocks (Tysdale and Case 1979), Cook Inlet, the Alaska Peninsula, and the east coast of Alaska from the Copper River delta almost to Juneau have numerous active petroleum seeps (Rosenberg 1974): over 75 active petroleum seeps have been identified in the Katalla area alone (Miller 1951). In addition, microseepage of petroleum was detected on the continental shelf seaward of the Hinchinbrook Entrance area by a sediment geochemistry study (J. M. Brooks, Geochemical and Environmental Research Group, Texas A&M University, personal communication, 1990).

The principal sources of subtidal sediments in the sound are associated with active

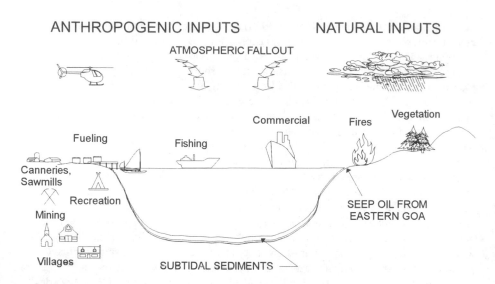

FIGURE 1--Sources of hydrocarbons contributing to the background in Prince William Sound and the Gulf of Alaska.

petroleum seep areas in the eastern GOA. These sediments are transported along the coast and brought into the sound via the Alaskan Coastal Current (Burbank 1974; Feely et al. 1979; Klein 1983; Reimnitz and Carlson 1975; Royer et al. 1990). Organic water from eroding Tertiary source rocks, such as the Katalla and Poul Creek formations (Miller 1951; Miller et al. 1959), is another potential hydrocarbon source.

Studies of previous spills (see, for example, Kolpack et al. 1971; Gundlach et al. 1983; Boehm et al. 1982) as well as experimental studies pertaining to the *Exxon Valdez* spill (Bragg and Yang, this volume) have documented the importance of fine-grained sediments as vehicles for oil transport in the marine environment--oil adheres to the sediment particles to form oil-clay flocculates, which, because of their near-neutral buoyancy, can be transported long distances by ocean currents. Larger and denser oil-mineral aggregates settle to the seafloor.

Payne et al. (1991) reported little EVC contamination in subtidal surface sediments in the first two to three weeks after the spill, even for benthic areas adjacent to heavily oiled shorelines. Jahns et al. (1991) presented evidence that the formation of neutrally buoyant flocculates is an important mechanism for the dispersal of spill residues in the water column. Glacial flour brought in from the Gulf of Alaska by the Alaska Coastal Current is an important source of these fine clay particles in PWS.

It has been estimated that 107 million tons of suspended sediment are discharged from the Copper River annually (Reimnitz 1966). As Figure 2 shows, the Alaska Coastal Current transports this sediment, along with sediments discharged from streams and rivers farther to the east, and associated hydrocarbons, westward along the coastline. Major components of the coastal current enter PWS through Hinchinbrook Entrance and

Hawkins Cutoff, where the decrease in current velocity (from 40 cm/sec at Hinchinbrook Entrance to <10 cm/sec in the body of PWS [Royer et al. 1990]) causes the larger particles of sediment to fall to the seafloor. Although there is some sediment input from the fjords lining Prince William Sound, the major source of sediment in the depositional areas of the sound, as determined by mineralogical criteria, is the eastern Gulf of Alaska (Klein 1983; Sharma 1979).

The suspended sediment in the Alaska Coastal Current can transport sediment-associated petroleum hydrocarbons from active oil seeps in the Katalla and Yakataga areas (Figure 3) along with petroleum residues from eroding source rocks that have been identified along the eastern Alaskan coast (Martin 1908; Blasko 1976b). At Katalla, a small oil field discovered in 1902 produced low-sulfur paraffinic crude until it was destroyed by fire in 1933 (Miller 1951; Rosenberg 1974).

Identifying PAH sources in Prince William Sound--Previous studies in PWS and the adjacent gulf resulted in data indicating that petrogenic hydrocarbons exist in deep subtidal sediments, but their source was not identified (Kaplan and Venkatesan 1981; Kvenvolden et al. 1991). Petroleum from natural sources that contribute to the background in PWS contains the same PAH compounds as EVC, but the relative amounts of individual PAH are different. To separate multiple petrogenic inputs one needs to apply petroleum geochemistry fingerprinting methods (e.g., Mackenzie 1984; Radke, 1987). A variety of oil fingerprinting methods have been used to identify sources in previous spill studies (e.g., Albaiges and Albrecht 1979; Boehm et al. 1981; Overton et al. 1981; Friocourt et al. 1982; Sportstol et al. 1983; Berthou et al. 1984; Butt et al. 1986).

In PWS one needs to separate the contributions from at least three petroleum sources that can be important in a given location: (1) seep oil from the eastern Gulf of Alaska; (2) EVC; and (3) diesel refined from ANS feed stock. This is needed to establish the extent to which EVC is a contributor to the hydrocarbons in these sediments and requires data of higher precision and accuracy than most oil-spill studies have produced to date.

MATERIALS AND METHODS

Study Design

The purposes of the sampling and analytical programs were to detect the EVC contribution to seafloor sediments, to quantify its concentration relative to the pre-existing background, and to characterize the historical input of petrogenic and nonpetrogenic PAH to PWS. The work described here involved field studies carried out from 1989 to 1991.

The study utilizes chemical data from seafloor surface (0-2 cm) sediments and from dated sediment cores that provide samples from depths of up to 32 cm below the seafloor. The sediments were sampled in 1989, 1990, and 1991, but only a small number of nearshore sites were visited in all three years.

Seven separate programs visited 649 subtidal sediment sampling sites in PWS and the eastern GOA and collected 1 936 samples that were subsequently analyzed for PAH (Figure 4). The sites are categorized as (1) nearshore (<100 meters from the nearest shoreline); (2) embayment; (3) offshore (from 100 to 1 000 m from the nearest shoreline);

FIGURE 2 - - September 2, 1973, Landsat MSS image (Band 4; penetration depth about 30m) of eastern PWS one hour after low tide showing sediment plumes (gray) entering PWS via Hinchinbrook Entrance and Hawkins Cutoff. Plumes disappear in the center of the sound as current velocities decrease and larger particles settle to the seafloor. Right inset is an April 22, 1985, Landsat image of the Gulf of Alaska shoreline to the east of PWS. Sediments are carried along the shoreline by the Alaskan Coastal Current from offshore Yakataga, at the eastern edge of the image, around Kayak Island, past Katalla, and westward across the Copper River delta. Key place names are shown on left inset and on Figure 4.

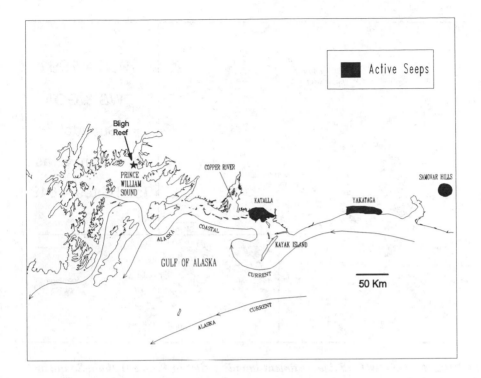

FIGURE 3--General ocean circulation patterns in the Gulf of Alaska and Prince William Sound.

and (4) deep subtidal (> 1 000 m from the nearest shoreline).

Field programs were designed to ensure that sampling sites were properly documented, that rigorous sample collection procedures were followed to minimize the possibility of hydrocarbon contamination (e.g., cross-contamination with oiled samples, diesel soot, hardware lubricants, surface-water oil sheens, or cigarette smoke), and that proper chains of custody were maintained. All samples were frozen at the time of collection and remained frozen until processed for analysis.

Nearshore subtidal stations--Nearshore subtidal stations were located on the extensions of intertidal sampling transects of the shoreline ecology studies. They include nonrandomly chosen fixed sites visited repeatedly in 1989, 1990, and 1991, and 64 randomly chosen sites (stratified random sampling [SRS] design) visited only in 1990 (Page et al., this volume). Four shoreline habitats at four oiling levels (heavy, moderate, light, and none) were sampled in the SRS study.

Stations were established at each site at depths of -1 m; -3 m to -10 m; and -10 m to -30 m. The depths were selected randomly along each transect in the -3-m to -10-m and -10-m to -30-m ranges. Divers sampled each station and recorded the depths relative to mean lower low water.

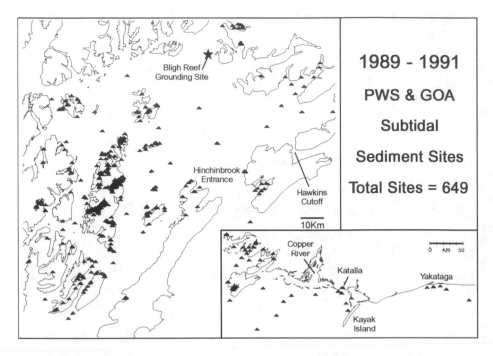

FIGURE 4--1989-1991 subtidal sediment sampling sites in Prince William Sound and the Gulf of Alaska

Embayment subtidal studies--The 1989 and 1990 embayment studies involved sampling stations within oiled and unoiled bays. In 1991, a comprehensive stratified (over depth) random sampling study was conducted to compare an oiled bay (Bay of Isles) and a reference bay (Drier Bay). For each bay, a 100-m grid was computer-projected onto a map for three depth contours. Intersections were randomly chosen and the precise coordinates noted.

Before 1991, embayment stations were located by triangulation from land features by means of nautical charts and ship's radar. In 1991, navigation and station location within embayment systems was achieved to within ±5-m accuracy by using a ranger system, and existing navigational controls were located with maps and other records. Additional control points were established as necessary by using standard land surveying techniques. New controls were installed with recoverable markers and were verified in the field to provide station coordinates. Before and immediately after sample collection, the navigational equipment was calibrated over a known range to verify the accuracy of the systems. Trilateration was used to survey control positions and for all navigational instrument calibrations.

Offshore/deep subtidal studies--A 1989 offshore study sampled locations within and outside the spill zone in Prince William Sound. In 1991 deep subtidal sampling was conducted on a cruise track from Cape Yakataga, 250 km east of Prince William Sound, to locations within the sound.

Station coordinate determinations and navigation for the offshore programs were achieved with nautical and topographical charts, radar, and Loran-C time delays. Because Loran-C chart overlays can be inaccurate in Prince William Sound, all vessels for this program measured a time delay offset at the Bligh Reef buoy to help calibrate the Loran-C. The latitude and longitude of the buoy had been surveyed in April 1989 by the U.S. Coast Guard.

A global positioning satellite (GPS) system was used to locate the deep subtidal stations sampled in 1991. The accuracy of the GPS system used in this study is approximately 50 m. For selected stations in the 1991 deep subtidal program, acoustic sediment profiling was used to identify suitable sites for box-coring. These acoustic sediment profiles were collected with a high-resolution 3.5 Hz ORE model 140.

Sediment Sampling

Several types of sampling equipment were used in the various studies. Smith-MacIntyre and Van Veen grabs were used in water depths of up to 500 m to collect surface samples (nearshore, embayment, offshore, and deep subtidal). In addition, divers collected sediment cores for some embayment and nearshore studies. A Soutar box core was used at some deep subtidal sites in 1991 to collect samples at depths greater than 300 m, or to collect cores in shallower water.

Grab samples were inspected for acceptability (undisturbed sediment surface) upon retrieval. The top (0-2 cm) of the grab was subsampled with a precleaned Kynar-coated or stainless-steel scoop and transferred to a precleaned, labeled, glass container, and frozen.

Core subsamples were collected from the Soutar box cores for hydrocarbon, total organic carbon (TOC), grain size, and ^{210}Pb analysis. After the overlying water was siphoned off, a precleaned acrylic core liner was inserted vertically into the sediments and capped at both ends. A separate surface sample was then collected. Each core was labeled, photographed, and stored frozen in the vertical position.

Field Program Quality-Control Procedures and Sample Documentation

Because vessels release petroleum hydrocarbons during normal operations, extra care was taken to minimize the possibilities for contamination of the field samples. The potential hydrocarbon contaminants were airborne stack gases from ships' engines, diesel-oil slicks, and hand-transferred oils and grease. The precautions taken included (1) positioning the ship's stern into the wind to prevent stack gases from blowing onto the sampling equipment during deployment, recovery, and subsampling; (2) cleaning equipment just prior to arriving on station; (3) ensuring that the sampling equipment was never deployed or recovered through oil slicks or sheens; and (4) closing the top access doors to the sampler when it was not being deployed or cleaned. Field blanks were collected from each piece of equipment at regular intervals during the survey. Potential sources of hydrocarbon contaminants (i.e., stack exhaust, soot, winch lubricant, diesel fuel, lube oil, etc.) were also collected to enable their identification later.

Station logs and chain-of-custody forms served as the primary documentation of station identification, date, time, type of equipment used for sampling, method of subsampling (core, scoop, or both), and type of sample. Additional information on sample collection, including any deviations from specified procedures, was entered on the chain-of-custody forms.

As collected, sediment samples were logged in on the chain-of-custody forms. The original of this form accompanied the samples from the sampling boat to the shipper and subsequently accompanied the samples to the analytical laboratory. Each sample cooler (packed with Blue Ice or dry ice) was sealed with a custody seal or evidence tape, which was initialed and dated by the packer.

Analytical Chemistry Methods

Nearshore, embayment, and offshore subtidal sediment samples were analyzed for alkanes, petroleum hydrocarbons (PHC), PAH, percentage of solids, TOC, and grain size. Additional determinations on embayment and deep subtidal samples collected in 1991 included perylene, benzo[e]pyrene, biphenyl, and dibenzofuran, biomarker compounds (diterpanes, triterpanes, and steranes), post alumina-column residue weights, and ^{210}Pb analysis of selected sediment core samples for age-dating. The general sample processing and analytical approach is outlined in Figure 5.

Sample extraction--A 30- to 50-g (wet) sediment sample was spiked with the appropriate surrogates (ortho-terphenyl, naphthalene-d_8, fluorene-d_{10}, and chrysene-d_{12}), mixed with equal amounts of sodium sulfate to dry the samples, and serially extracted (3 times, 60 mL/extraction) with 1:1 methylene chloride:acetone using an orbital shaker and sonication (EPA Method 3550). The extracts were combined, then dried with sodium sulfate and filtered through glass wool. A 293-mm Gelman-type A/E glass fiber filter was used in the 1991 deep subtidal sediment study to improve the precision of the gravimetric analysis. The extract was then passed through an alumina-column cleanup according to EPA Method 3611, and the saturated (F1) and unsaturated (F2) hydrocarbons were eluted with methylene chloride. The eluant was then concentrated by means of Kuderna Danish evaporation and further concentrated under nitrogen to the internal standards (5-androstane, acenaphthene-d_{10}, phenanthrene-d_{10}, benzo[a]pyrene-d_{12}) and analyzed by gas chromatography with flame ionization detection (GC/FID) and gas chromatography with mass spectrometry detection (GC/MS) operating in the selected ion monitoring (SIM) mode.

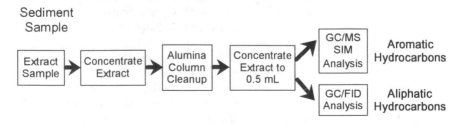

FIGURE 5--Sample processing and analysis.

Polycyclic aromatic hydrocarbon analysis by GC/MS-SIM-modified EPA method 8270--Target PAH and alkylated PAH compounds were analyzed by GC/MS operated in the SIM mode. This method is a modification of EPA Method 8270 "Gas Chromatography/Mass Spectrometry for Semivolatile Organics: Capillary Column Technique." The modifications included: (1) redefining the surrogate, internal standard, and target analyte list to include primarily diagnostic hydrocarbon compounds (see Table 1); (2) the use of selected ion monitoring (SIM) to increase analytical sensitivity; and (3) the quantification of alkylated PAH homologues (e.g., C_3-phenanthrenes, Sauer and Boehm 1991; Douglas et al. 1994).

A 1- to 3-microliter aliquot of the sample extract was injected into a gas chromatograph equipped with a high-resolution capillary column (e.g., J&W fused-silica DB5 column, 30 m, 0.25-mm internal diameter, and 0.25-micron film thickness) operated in the splitless mode. The temperature program and capillary column were selected in order to achieve near-baseline separation of the EPA priority PAH compounds listed in Table 1.

Before sample analysis, a five-point initial calibration composed of the 16 priority pollutant compounds and dibenzothiophene was established, demonstrating the linear range of the analysis. Check standards were analyzed with every ten samples to validate the integrity of the initial calibration. The method of internal standards (EPA Method 8000) using the average relative response factors (RRF) generated from the linear initial calibration was used to quantify the target PAH compounds (Table 1).

PAH alkylated homologues were quantified by using the straight baseline integration of each level of alkylation and the RRF of the respective unsubstituted parent PAH compound. The selection criteria for the integration and reporting of each alkylated homologue were based primarily on retention time, pattern recognition relative to the EVC standard, and on the presence of selected confirmation ions. For all but one (perylene) of the 37 reported PAH analytes and all six of the deuterated surrogate PAH standards, a total of 47 secondary confirming ions were used to verify the assignment of primary quantifying ions. All data were corrected for the recovery of the surrogate compound fluorene-d_{10}. Nonzero results for each PAH analyte below its practical quantification limit (PQL) (see Table 2) were reported with the appropriate qualifier. Total PAH (TPAH) is the sum of all reported PAH analytes. As of 1990, a laboratory standard oil was analyzed with each analytical batch to monitor analytical precision and to provide data for interlaboratory comparisons. Several analytical laboratories were needed to process and analyze the large numbers of samples collected.

The data-quality objectives (DQO) for this method are listed in Table 2. Each laboratory performed sediment method detection limit (MDL) studies according to the procedures described in the EPA protocol titled "Definition and Procedure for the Determination of the Method Detection Limit" (Code of Federal Regulations 40 CFR Part 136). Because of the complex mixtures of resolved and unresolved PAH isomers in each alkylated PAH series, only MDLs for the parent PAH compounds were determined. The MDLs for an alkylated series would generally be higher than for the parent because the instrument response for each series is spread over multiple peaks. To optimize sensitivity for the alkylated PAH compounds, data were collected only when the signal-to-noise ratio of a single isomer in a series was greater than 3:1.

TABLE 1--Target analyte list for subtidal sediment studies.

Polycyclic Aromatic Hydrocarbons (PAH)				Saturated Hydrocarbons (SHC)
Compound	**Code**	**#Rings**	***@Detection Limit**	- Normal (linear) alkanes
+ naphthalene	N0	2	0.27	n-C_{10} - n-C_{33}
C$_1$-naphthalenes	N1	2	0.29	
C$_2$-naphthalenes	N2	2	0.45	- Isoprenoid Hydrocarbons
C$_3$-naphthalenes	N3	2	0.57	pristane
C$_4$-naphthalenes	N4	2	0.42	phytane
biphenyl	Bph	2	0.18	
+ acenaphthylene	ACE	3	-	
dibenzofuran	Dbf	3	0.05	*Biomarkers
+ acenaphthene	ACL	3	-	diterpanes m/e 191
+ fluorene	F0	3	0.07	hopanes m/e 191
C$_1$-fluorenes	F1	3	0.17	steranes m/e 217
C$_2$-fluorenes	F2	3	0.34	
C$_3$-fluorenes	F3	3	0.72	
+ phenanthrene	P0	3	0.11	
+ anthracene	AN	3	0.03	
C$_1$-phenanthrenes/anthracenes	P1	3	0.28	Surrogates and Standards
C$_2$-phenanthrenes/anthracenes	P2	3	0.40	
C$_3$-phenanthrenes/anthracenes	P3	3	0.20	Surrogate compounds added to sample
C$_4$-phenanthrenes/anthracenes	P4	3	0.27	PHC = ortho-terphenyl
dibenzothiophene	DO	3	0.05	PAH = naphthalene-d$_8$
C$_1$-dibenzothiophenes	D1	3	0.10	fluorene-d$_{10}$
C$_2$-dibenzothiophenes	D2	3	0.17	chrysene-d$_{12}$
C$_3$-dibenzothiophenes	D3	3	0.11	* Biomarkers = 5β(H)-cholane
+ fluoranthene	FL	4	0.06	C$_{30}$-17β(H), 21β(H)-hopane
+ pyrene	PY	4	0.05	
C$_1$-fluoranthenes/pyrenes	FP1	4	0.09	Internal standard compounds added to
+ benzo(a)anthracene	BaA	4	0.03	extract
+ chrysene	C0	4	0.04	PHC = 5α androstane
C$_1$-chrysene	C1	4	0.07	PAH = acenaphthene-d$_{10}$
C$_2$-chrysene	C2	4	0.15	phenanthrene-d$_{10}$
C$_3$-chrysene	C3	4	0.13	benzo(a)pyrene-d$_{12}$
C$_4$-chrysene	C4	4	-	*Triterpanes & Steranes =
+ benzo(b)fluoranthene	BbF	5	0.07	fluorene-d$_{10}$, benzo(a)pyrene-d$_{12}$
+ benzo(k)fluoranthene	BkF	5	0.03	
benzo(e)pyrene	BeP	5	0.03	
+ benzo(a)pyrene	BaP	5	0.62	QA/QC Standards
perylene	Per	5	0.05	EV check = cargo oil
+ dibenz(a,h)anthracene	DA	5	0.01	*SRM 1491
+ indeno(1,2,3-c,d)pyrene	1P	6	0.06	EVC521 = topped EVC
+ benzo(g,h,l)perylene	BgP	6	0.06	*Katalla production oil

+ EPA priority pollutant
* 1991 Deep Subtidal Study
@μg/kg dry sediment

TABLE 2--Data-quality objectives for subtidal sediment studies. The exact MDL depends on the compound analyzed. See Table 1 for individual 1991 MDL values.

Parameter	Subtidal Sediment Studies	1991 Deep Subtidal Studies
Units	μg/kg dry weight	μg/kg dry weight
Practical Quantification Limit (PQL)	10 μg/kg	1.0 μg/kg
Estimated Method Detection Limit (MDL)	1.0 μg/kg	0.1 μg/kg (values in Table 1)
Procedural Blank	5 x MDL	5 x MDL
Field Blank	5 x MDL	5 x MDL
Matrix Spike Recovery	40 - 120%[a]	40 - 120%[a]
Surrogate Recovery	40 - 120%[b]	40 - 120%[b]
Duplicate Precision	± 30%	± 30%
EVC Control Oil Standard Precision	± 20%[c]	± 20%
Katalla Control Oil Standard Precision	NA	± 20%
NIST SRM 1941 Precision	NA	± 25%
NIST SRM 1291 Accuracy	NA	± 15%

[a] The average percentage recoveries for all 16 compounds must fall between 40 and 120%. Only one compound can be below its minimum percentage recovery. This allowed a deviation for a single analyte of not less than 10% for chrysene and benzo(a) pyrene and not less than 20% for the others.

[b] Surrogate recoveries must fall between 40 and 120%. The upper control limit may be exceeded by one compound.

[c] The average percentage difference for the target compounds should not exceed 20% of the mean of all previous values, and no single compound/isomer grouping should deviate by more than 30% of its mean value of all previous determinations.

Analytical Methods for the 1991 Deep-Subtidal Sediment Study

Because background hydrocarbon levels for many of the target analytes were at the lower limits of analytical detection (1- to 10-ppb range), a more rigorous set of DQOs was developed and implemented in the 1991 deep subtidal sediment study (see Table 2). The sediment extraction and PAH analytical procedures were refined to achieve lower method detection limits (0.1 to 1.0 ppb) and improved analytical precision and accuracy. The key refinements were as follows:

- Sediment sample size was increased from 30 g to as much as 100 g wet weight.
- Sample extract pre-injection volume was reduced from 0.5 mL to 0.25 mL.
- Sample analysis was optimized for low-level target analytes (as compared with midrange or high-level concentrations) with a signal-to-noise ratio greater than 3:1; target compounds above the highest calibration standard (4 μg/mL) were diluted and reanalyzed.
- A second five-point calibration curve was analyzed midway through the program to improve analytical precision.
- A more rigorous calibration check standard of $\pm$15% was implemented to improve analytical precision.
- One GC/MS instrument and the same analyst were used for the entire program.
- Mass discrimination was minimized to improve the analytical sensitivity of the four- and five-ring PAH compounds (i.e., C_3-chrysenes).
- Alkylated PAH baselines were set manually to improve analytical precision.
- The instrument was carefully maintained and tuned to achieve maximum sensitivity. The lowest analytical PAH calibration standard concentration was 0.05 μg/mL.
- National Institute of Standards and Technology reference materials (SRMs) and Katalla crude oil samples were analyzed with each analytical batch to monitor accuracy and precision.
- The diagnostic compounds perylene, benzo[e]pyrene, biphenyl, and dibenzofuran were measured in addition to the compounds required by the standard operating procedure specified analyte list (see Table 1).
- An alkylated PAH MDL study was performed on sediments, spiked with topped *Exxon Valdez* crude (Prince et al. 1994), following the procedures described in the EPA protocol titled "Definition and Procedure for the Determination of the Method Detection Limit" (Code of Federal Regulations 40 CFR Part 136).

These modifications substantially improved the precision and accuracy of the analytical data in the 0.1- to 10-ppb PAH-concentration range.

Sediment Core Age-Dating

The sedimentation rates in five sediment cores collected in Prince William Sound depositional areas were estimated by using ^{210}Pb dating methods (Koide et al. 1973). ^{210}Pb is a naturally occurring intermediate decay product of the ^{238}U decay series having a half-life of 22 years. It is present in atmospheric and water-column particulates and in crustal minerals. Excess ^{210}Pb enters marine sediments bound to particles derived from atmospheric or terrestrial runoff. As surface sediments are buried, the input of excess ^{210}Pb (^{210}Pb not generated by the *in situ* decay of ^{238}U) stops and its activity in the sediment decreases with depth because of radioactive decay. The activity of "supported" ^{210}Pb, the relatively constant background generated from ^{238}U-containing minerals in the sediment, is estimated from the bottom of the sediment core where excess ^{210}Pb activity approaches zero. This value is subtracted from each core profile to measure the excess ^{210}Pb activity at any point in the core. By combining measurements of excess ^{210}Pb with depth information, the sedimentation rates can be calculated.

The calculation of sedimentation rate assumes the following: (1) the sedimentation rate has been uniform with time between dated points in a core; (2) the sediment composition and ^{210}Pb activity of the surface sediment have been uniform with time; and (3) sediment mixing is restricted to a surface layer. Assumptions (1) and (2) are reasonable for deep subtidal sediments in PWS for the last 200 years. Assumption (3) is confirmed by visual observations of the core and by a linear increase in perylene concentration with depth. Perylene is a naturally produced PAH (Venkatesan 1988) that generally increases in concentration with depth in undisturbed sediments (Radke 1987). It is not found in either EVC or seep petroleum.

Interpretive Methods

The PAH (specifically the 3- and 4-ring PAH) provide diagnostic fingerprints of the hydrocarbon sources in PWS. Because of their resistance to weathering relative to the aliphatic fraction (Friocourt et al. 1982; Sportstol et al. 1983; Berthou et al. 1984) and their occurrence in many sources in proportions diagnostic of those sources, the PAH compounds were used for source discrimination. The criteria used to distinguish various sources of PAH are discussed below.

Distinguishing criteria for petrogenic PAH--Petrogenic hydrocarbons, including residues of EVC, are characterized by their distributions of alkylated homologues of naphthalene, fluorene, phenanthrene, dibenzothiophene, and chrysene, where the parent PAH for each series is least abundant (Figure 6a). In weathered petroleum, the di-, tri-, and tetramethylphenanthrenes and dibenzothiophenes increase relative to the parent compound (NRC 1985). The relative abundances of the alkylated homologues of one PAH family (e.g., phenanthrenes) relative to that of another PAH family (e.g., dibenzothiophenes) can diagnose different petroleum sources (Overton et. al 1981).

Distinguishing criteria for pyrogenic PAH--Pyrogenic hydrocarbon signatures can be diverse but are generally characterized by high concentrations of PAH with molecular weights greater than C_3-dibenzothiophene and/or high concentrations of the unsubstituted parent compound (C_0) (Brassell and Eglinton 1980), as indicated in Figure 6b. Combustion-related (pyrogenic) sources produce a PAH distribution dominated by the parent compounds of the 3-, 4-, and 5-ring PAH and fluoranthene and pyrene (see Figure 6b), which is distinct from that of petroleum (Figure 6a), in which the alkyl-substituted homologues in a given family of PAH compounds are most abundant (NRC 1985). Creosote (Figure 6b) yields PAH with a lower boiling range than combustion sources but is included in the pyrogenic category.

Distinguishing criteria for biogenic PAH--There are a number of individual PAH

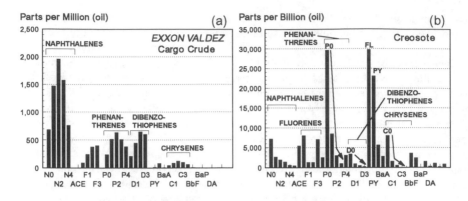

FIGURE 6--PAH fingerprints of petrogenic and pyrogenic hydrocarbon sources in PWS. (a) EVC and (b) creosote from pilings at Chenega Village.

compounds associated with specific recent biological sources (Anderson et al. 1986; Radke, 1987). In subtidal sediments, bacterial modification of recent inputs of organic matter yields perylene (Venkatesan 1988), an unsubstituted PAH produced in subtidal sediments by a process known as early diagenesis. This compound is a widely distributed biogenic PAH in subtidal sediment samples analyzed in this study.

Distinguishing criteria for crude oil versus diesel--Nearly all of the marine diesel sold in the PWS/GOA region from 1989 to 1991 was refined at the Tesoro or Chevron refineries on the east coast of Cook Inlet. The Tesoro refinery used, on average, a feed stock of 83% ANS crude and 17% Cook Inlet crude. The Chevron refinery used 100% ANS. A sample of ANS feed stock and refined diesel was obtained from the Chevron Kenai refinery at Nikiski, Alaska, in the fall of 1990. That refinery, now closed, was designed to maximize the output of diesel (#2 fuel oil) (G. Jackson, Chevron Corp., Nikiski, Alaska, personal communication, September 1990). Furthermore, there were no facilities to remove sulfur during the production of diesel. The cargo oil of the *Exxon Valdez* was an ANS crude.

When crude oil is distilled to manufacture diesel fuel, higher boiling fractions such as the chrysene family and above are almost entirely removed (Figure 7a). Comparison of the PAH profiles for the ANS crude oil (Figure 6a) with that of diesel refined from an ANS feed stock (Figure 7a) shows that the two distributions are nearly identical except for the lack of chrysenes in the diesel.

Distinguishing criteria for crude oils from different sources--Petroleum from different fields can have very different PAH distributions. As shown in the Results section of this paper, an important source of petroleum hydrocarbons in PWS is seep-derived petroleum imported on suspended sediment from the eastern Gulf of Alaska. Coastal seeps in the vicinity of the Katalla oil field and northwest Cape Yakataga are important sources. Katalla oil (Figure 7b) is low in dibenzothiophenes, a sulfur-containing PAH, relative to EVC (Figure 6a), and this difference provides a means of distinguishing the two.

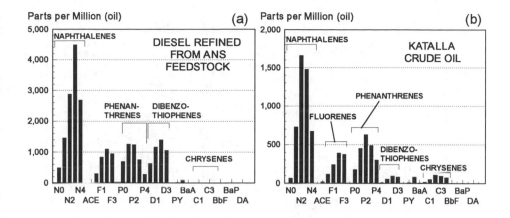

FIGURE 7--PAH fingerprints of diesel (a) refined from ANS feed stock at a Kenai refinery and (b) Katalla crude.

In the Cook Inlet-Kodiak-Alaska Peninsula region, Cook Inlet crude and numerous seeps along the Alaska Peninsula are potentially important contributors to subtidal sediments. Cook Inlet crude is a low-sulfur oil with a PAH distribution that is similar to Katalla oil. Thus, the relative abundances of the alkylated dibenzothiophenes to the alkylated phenanthrenes in its PAH fingerprint serve to distinguish it from EVC. More sophisticated analyses are required to distinguish Cook Inlet crude from Katalla crude.

Oil weathering trends--The combined effects of weathering (dissolution, biodegradation, photo-oxidation) of the spill oil are summarized in Figure 8. Major compositional changes include the following:

- Pronounced decrease in naphthalenes (Np) relative to the other PAH, which occurs rapidly in the first few days of exposure to the atmosphere (Figures 8a, b). By 1991, exposed oil (Figure 8d) had lost most of its naphthalenes.

- Development of a "water-washed" profile for each of the petrogenic groups so that each group has the distribution: Parent $(C_0)<C_1<C_2<C_3$.

- Gradual buildups in the relative abundances of the phenanthrenes, dibenzothiophenes, and chrysenes as the more soluble components are lost (Figures 8a-d). Because of their very low solubilities in water, and resistance to microbial degradation, the chrysenes exhibit the most pronounced relative increase (Figure 8e).

Figure 9 plots C_2-phenanthrene (C_2-Ph) versus C_2-dibenzothiophene (C_2-Db) and C_3-phenanthrene (C_3-Ph) versus C_3-dibenzothiophene (C_3-Db) for several petroleum

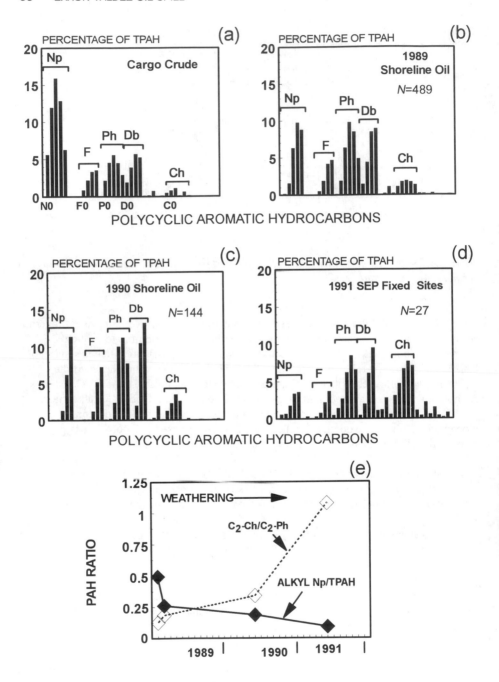

FIGURE 8--EVC PAH weathering trends.

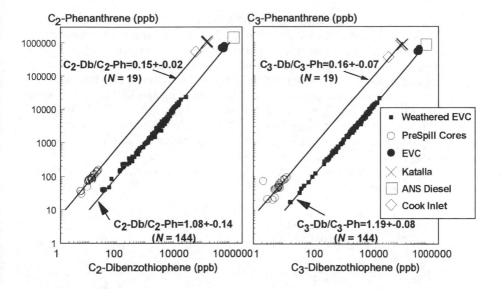

FIGURE 9--C_2-Db/C_2-Ph and C_3-Db/C_3-Ph relationships of weathered EVC, diesel refined from ANS crude feedstock at a Kenai Refinery, PWS regional background hydrocarbons from deep subtidal cores, and Katalla and Cook Inlet crude oils. The weathered EVC data are analyses of 1990 oiled intertidal sediments (surface and subsurface samples) reported by Prince et al. (1991; 1994). Wide ranges of weathering states and concentrations are represented.

sources associated with PWS. As the straight lines in Figure 9 show, an important weathering feature of ANS crude (and diesel refined in Alaskan refineries from ANS crude) is the relative constancy of the ratios C_2-Db/C_2-Ph (1.08 ± 0.14) and C_3-Db/C_3-Ph (1.19 ± 0.08). These data are from the 1990 bioremediation study that measured the decrease of spill residues on treated and untreated shorelines over time (Prince et al. 1991; 1994).

The PWS prespill background measured in the deep subtidal cores has relatively constant ratios of C_2-Db/C_2-Ph = 0.15 ± 0.02 and C_3-Db/C_3-Ph = 0.16 ± 0.07 for a wide range of sediment TPAH concentrations. These ratios are close to those of Katalla crude oil and of subtidal sediments collected off Yakataga and Katalla. This alkylated dibenzothiophene/phenanthrene weathering feature is the single most important fingerprinting criterion used in this study to distinguish ANS crude, its weathering products, and diesel refined from ANS feed stock (Kenai refineries) from other petrogenic hydrocarbons (Katalla crude, Cook Inlet crude, West Coast-refined diesel, and natural PAH background).

Calculation of the EVC Component in a PAH Mixture

The dissimilarity of prespill background and EVC and its weathering products provides a means of calculating the relative proportions of these two hydrocarbon sources in a sediment sample containing both components. A subtidal sediment sample containing both spill and background hydrocarbons will have C_2- and C_3-Db/Ph ratios that fall proportionally between the two end-members. The relative amounts of the two petrogenic PAH sources can then be readily calculated if the analytical data are of sufficiently high quality. This study relied primarily on the C_2-Db/C_2-Ph ratios to calculate petrogenic source composition because the data for these PAH homologues had less scatter at low concentrations (Figure 9). However, either ratio yields similar results.

The approximate amount of ANS-derived PAH in sediment can be calculated using the following equation:

$$TPAH_{ANS} = \frac{C_2 - Ph_{samp}}{0.093} \left[1 - \left[\frac{1.07 - \left(\frac{C_2 - Db}{C_2 - Ph} \right)_{samp}}{0.92} \right] \right]$$

where $TPAH_{ANS}$ is the TPAH derived from ANS and $C_2 - Ph_{samp}$ and $C_2 - Db_{samp}$ are the concentrations of these analytes in the samples. Numbers used in the equation come from the following ratios:

$(C_2 - Db / C_2 - Ph)_{ANS} = 1.07 \pm .17$,

$(C_2 - Db / C_2 - Ph)_{Petro\ Background} = 0.15 \pm .03$, and

$(C_2 - Ph / TPAH)_{ANS} = 0.093 \pm .02$.

The numerical term 0.92 represents the difference between the 1.07 ratio and the 0.15 ratio. The ANS ratios are averages of ratios of the 1990 intertidal sediment samples plotted in Figure 9.

The equation assumes that subtidal ANS for the years 1989-1991 can be approximated by intertidal EVC from 1990. Since intertidal (surface and subsurface) and nearshore subtidal oil residues are in environments that are typically aerobic with much water contact, they probably weather in a similiar fashion though at different rates.

Because this method of separating petrogenic source contributions is based on 3-ring PAH, ANS crude cannot be distingushed from diesel without further data analysis. (See above, *Distinguishing criteria for crude oil versus diesel.*) In the results below, any contribution from diesel containing C_2–dibenzothiophene is included in the EVC component.

The relative constancy of various dibenzothiophene to phenanthrene ratios (i.e., C_0-Db/C_0-Ph, C_1-Db/C_1-Ph, C_2-Db/C_2-Ph, etc) in an oil weathering in the presence of water (Overton et al. 1981) may be the result of similar water solubilities or octanol-water partition coefficients (K_{ow}). For example, Ogata et al. (1984) report a log K_{ow} of 4.42 for C_0-Db and Niimi (1991) reports a log K_{ow} of 4.45 for C_0-Ph. The alkylated dibenzothiophenes and phenanthrenes should be less soluble in water than the parent compounds but their solubilities should be similar for the same level of alkylation.

To quantitatively separate petroleum hydrocarbon sources using the method described, PAH analyses are required that are both precise and accurate. The calculations are highly sensitive to the composition of the background, which can vary--especially at nearshore sites (see below). Small, natural variations in background C_2-Db/C_2-Ph can falsely indicate the presence of EVC. The measured prespill C_2-Db/C_2-Ph ratio in the PWS deep subtidal background varies by approximately ± 0.02. This is $\pm 3\%$ of the difference between the average petrogenic background and average weathered EVC. For a sediment sample containing 500 ppb petrogenic PAH (the rough average for deep subtidal sediments) this is equivalent to ± 15 ppb of the petrogenic component. For a sample containing 100 ppb petrogenic PAH (e.g., a nearshore sample in which petrogenic PAH are usually much lower), this range is equivalent to ± 3 ppb, which approaches the lower limit of detectability in this dataset. Consequently, because an average background ratio is used in the calculations, the practical lower limit for recognition of EVC in an offshore subtidal sediment sample is about 3 to 6% of the measured total petrogenic component. In embayments, the range of background C_2-Db/C_2-Ph values is somewhat higher because of local point-source inputs of petrogenic hydrocarbons. A practical lower limit of $\pm 4\%$ of the petrogenic component is indicated.

RESULTS

The presentation of results begins with a description of the prespill-PAH subtidal background of PWS. Sediment samples corresponding to prespill conditions were obtained by analyzing sediment from core depths greater than 10 cm below the sediment-seawater interface. This corresponds to sediments deposited at least 3 to 10+ years before the spill, as described below. The results of these prespill samples are then compared with results for 1991 deep-subtidal sediment samples taken in PWS and the Gulf of Alaska eastward to Cape Yakataga to establish the regional extent of this PAH background. They can further be compared with the results for offshore subtidal samples taken in April 1989 and March 1990 to determine the extent to which EVC residues were present in PWS seafloor sediments. Results are then presented for subtidal sediment samples taken in oiled and unoiled bays to establish the extent of EVC transport to the seafloor in protected waters nearer to shore. Finally, results are given for nearshore subtidal locations where these locations are on transects covering both intertidal and subtidal stations. The analysis of subtidal sediments from sites adjacent to shorelines that had been heavily oiled provides a conservative estimate of the extent of offshore transport of EVC residues into the nearshore environment.

Regional and Local PAH Fingerprints

Subtidal sediments contain a record of the inputs of hydrocarbons to the seafloor. This record is defined by the distribution of the individual PAH. In PWS, offshore and deep subtidal sediments have a diagnostic regional PAH signature that is almost identical to those of offshore GOA sediments near the seep localities of Katalla and Yakataga and is markedly different from that of weathered EVC (Figure 10). Nearshore locations such as Sawmill Bay (also called Chenega Bay) have variable PAH profiles often dominated by a pyrogenic PAH hydrocarbon signature, as shown by the "Local Sources" component in Figure 10. For nearshore sites such as the Bay of Isles, an EVC PAH pattern can be detected as a small addition to the regional PWS background pattern, as shown by the Bay

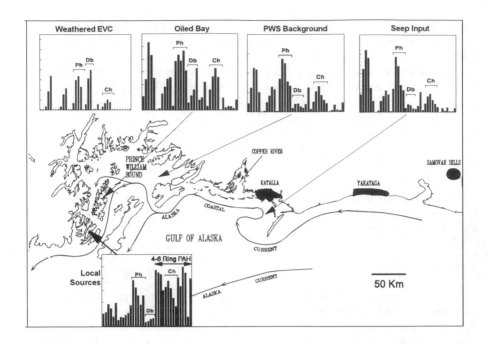

FIGURE 10--Subtidal sediment PAH fingerprints from the PWS-GOA area compared with weathered EVC.

of Isles PAH profile ("Oiled Bay") in Figure 10.

PWS Deep Subtidal Historical PAH Background

Box cores taken at 15 PWS deep subtidal sites in 1991 (Figure 11a) define the historical (prespill) background. Each sediment core was sampled at three levels for hydrocarbon analysis: top (0-2 cm), midpoint, and the bottom (as deep as 32 cm). PAH analyses were obtained on all samples for hydrocarbon analysis. To estimate the prespill age of the sediments, the ^{210}Pb age-dating technique was applied to ten layers in each of five cores.

Depositional environments represented include deep open water basins, embayments, and narrow straits. PAH results for four of the dated cores are reported here. The fifth, Station 44 in Latouche Passage, a shallow strait having strong currents, appears to be disturbed. The PAH distributions for the top, midpoint, and bottom intervals of open-water core #08 (Figure 11b), taken in 212 m of water north of Smith Island, are identical even though TPAH is greater at the bottom than at the top (Figure 11b). The extrapolated ^{210}Pb dating results and sedimentation rates for this core show the bottom has an age of ~130 years. Consequently, the petrogenic hydrocarbons contributing to the natural background from 1989 to 1991 have not changed at this site for ~130 years.

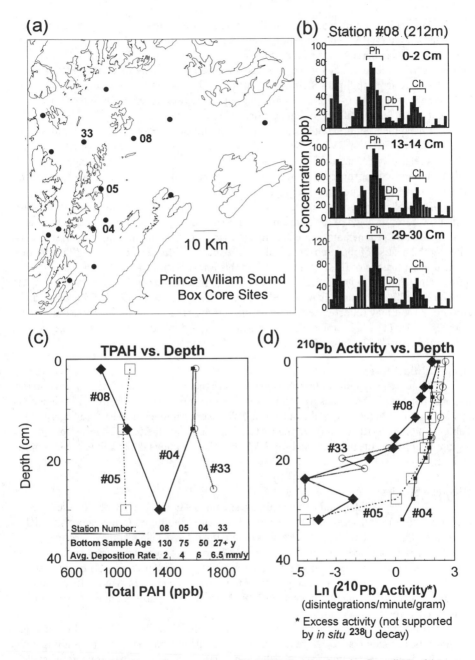

FIGURE 11--(a) PWS box-core stations. (b) PAH fingerprints in Core #08. (c) TPAH-depth profiles in three open-water (08, 04, 33) and one embayment (05). (d) ^{210}Pb decay rates for cores.

The sediment core from Station 33, located at the fringes of the spill area (Figure 11a), has a higher TPAH concentration over its entire length (Figure 11c). This core had one of the highest percentages of clay (78%) of the core samples. The high TPAH is consistent with the tendency for the finer clay particles to carry more adsorbed PAH.

A core from spill-path Station 04 (east of Knight Island), which has no detectable EVC component in the 0- to 2-cm sample, has an average sedimentation rate of ~6 mm/year and 1 300-1 600 ppb of background PAH (Figure 11c).

Embayment Station 05, located near the mouth of the Bay of Isles, has traces (about 6% of TPAH) of EVC in the 0- to 2-cm sample. The concentration of background TPAH is relatively constant at ~1 000 ppb over the cored interval. The average sedimentation rate for this core is ~4 mm/year (Figure 11c), although the upper part of the core may have been deposited at a greater rate.

Plots of the natural logarithm of the excess ^{210}Pb activities as functions of depth within the core, for each of the four cores, are shown in Figure 11d. If the sediments are undisturbed and sedimentation rate is constant these plots should decline in a linear fashion with depth because of the exponential decay of excess ^{210}Pb. The excess ^{210}Pb activities in the upper portions of these cores decline in this linear fashion, although the slopes differ. Only one (#33) has a discontinuity at an age that corresponds to the 1964 earthquake. Discontinuities in excess ^{210}Pb activities for cores #08 and #05 predate the earthquake and may reflect uncertainties in the activity measurements for these older samples. Ages of core bottoms were estimated using sedimentation rate if age exceeded the capability of ^{210}Pb dating (~5 half-lives or ~110 years).

Deep-Subtidal Sites

To test the hypothesis that the seep areas in the eastern Gulf of Alaska provide the regional petrogenic PAH background for PWS, a series of locations from Cape Yakataga 250 km east of PWS to the spill zone within PWS were sampled in 1991 (see Figure 12). Table 3 and Figure 12a summarize the PAH components for the 0- to 2-cm samples by region, spill path, nonspill path, and for PWS prespill sediments taken below a core depth of 10 cm.

Offshore Studies

Offshore subtidal sampling was undertaken in 1989 and early 1990 to assess the extent of offshore transport of EVC residues from oiled shorelines to nearshore subtidal locations. The sampling locations are shown in Figure 13. Table 4 summarizes the analytical results and averages of the various PAH source-components for samples collected on cruises in April 1989 and in March 1990. If offshore transport of oil to the seafloor had taken place as a consequence of the cleansing action of winter storms and the cleanup activities, the samples collected on the March 1990 cruise might be expected to contain EVC residues.

The results, summarized in Figure 13a, show highly variable TPAH values among the stations, reflecting large differences in depositional environment (energy) among locations. Mixing calculations show that, where present, EVC residues are a very small increment superimposed on a natural PAH background dominated by petrogenic hydrocarbons similar to those found near Katalla. Pyrogenic hydrocarbons are important

TABLE 3--Deep subtidal PWS-GOA sediment PAH averages (ppb) plus or minus one standard deviation. The number of individual samples appear in parentheses. The averages of the individual source components are given.

	Total PAH	Pyrogenic PAH	Petrogenic Background PAH	Petrogenic ANS-PAH[**]	Biogenic Perylene
PWS Spill Path (38)	740 ± 460	150 ± 176	565 ± 74	12^a ± 14	14 ± 13
Nonspill Path (12)	619 ± 315	77 ± 35	523 ± 291	10^a ± 22	9 ± 4
PWS Prespill* (20)	1 079 ± 361	137 ± 42	906 ± 334	3^a + 6	34 ± 19
PWS Nonspill Path Embayment (11)	2 051 ± 1 842	1 137 ± 1 216	864 ± 741	5^a ± 5	45 ± 20
Gulf of Alaska (25)	1 481 ± 1 890	144 ± 188	1 329 ± 1 711	0.3^a ± 2	8 ± 9

* Samples from >10-cm core depth.
** ANS-PAH = petrogenic PAH attributable to EVC or some other ANS petroleum source (e.g., diesel or other crude oil discharge).
[a] Calculated EVC concentrations representing ≤3-6% of the petrogenic component are within the scatter caused by the natural variability of the background and are therefore indistinguishable from background.

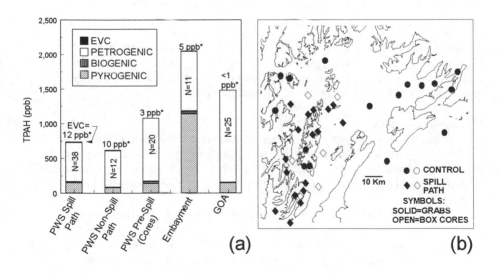

(a)   (b)

FIGURE 12--(a) PAH component averages for 1991 deep-subtidal sediments by categories. (b) Deep- subtidal sediment sampling station locations. Asterisk (*) indicates calculated EVC concentrations <3-6% of petrogenic PAH that are within the scatter caused by the natural variability of the background and are indistinguishable from background.

TABLE 4--PWS offshore subtidal sediment PAH averages (ppb) plus or minus one standard deviation. The number of individual samples appear in parentheses. The averages of the individual source components are given.

	Total PAH	Pyrogenic PAH	Petrogenic Background PAH	Petrogenic ANS-PAH*	Biogenic Perylene
April 1989					
Spill Path(35)	389 ± 269	108 ± 94	252 ± 154	29 ± 33	N.M.
Nonspill Path (26)	517 ± 560	233 ± 379	281 ± 222	$3^a \pm 4$	N.M.
March 1990					
Spill Path(43)	511 ± 293	81 ± 85	333 ± 197	38 ± 48	59 ± 81
Nonspill Path(15)	435 ± 243	100 ± 59	293 ± 199	$2^a \pm 3$	40 ± 32

N.M. = Not measured.
*ANS-PAH = petrogenic PAH attributable to EVC or some other ANS petroleum source.
[a] Calculated EVC concentrations representing ≤3-6% of the petrogenic component are within the scatter caused by the natural variability of the background and are therefore indistinguishable from background.

at some nearshore sites, for example, Sawmill Bay (Johnson Cove, Station SQ09 on Figure 13a). Figure 13c plots C_2-phenanthrene against C_2-dibenzothiophene for these data. This figure clearly shows the grouping of the data (including many spill-path samples) along and near the Katalla background line (Figure 9).

Embayment Studies

Subtidal sediment samples were taken from stations in oiled and unoiled bays in 1989, 1990, and 1991 as shown on the map in Figure 14b. Table 5 summarizes the chemistry results for all embayment and nearshore studies. This table shows the total PAH and the concentrations of the PAH source contributors for spill-path and non-spill-path (control) stations.

Figure 14a presents the total PAH and PAH components for spill-path and non-spill-path embayment sites sampled in February and March 1990, showing that the generalizations indicated in Table 4 also apply to individual locations shown in Figure 14b.

Figure 14c summarizes the results of the mixing calculations applied to hydrocarbon chemistry data for Drier Bay (unoiled) and Bay of Isles (oiled). Averages of the PAH components were calculated for each of three depth zones sampled in each bay. Important features to note include: (1) the overall TPAH increase with depth zone for each bay (parallels decreasing grain size); (2) a relatively small increment of residual EVC to total PAH in Bay of Isles depth zone; (3) similarities between bays in the background petrogenic component; and (4) higher shallow (nearshore) pyrogenic component in Drier Bay.

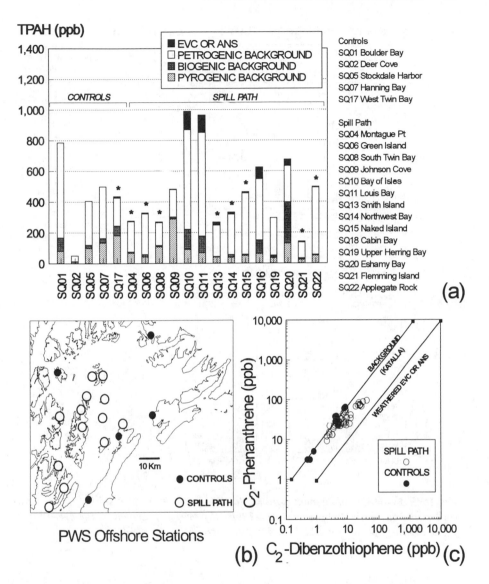

FIGURE 13--(a) Station averages for total PAH, petrogenic, pyrogenic, and biogenic background, and EVC residue, March 1990 cruise. (b) Offshore station locations for March 1990 cruise. (c) C_2-Db versus C_2-Ph for March 1990 offshore sediments showing relationship to natural petrogenic background. Asterisk (*) indicates calculated EVC <3-6% of petrogenic PAH that are within the scatter caused by the natural variability of the background and are indistinguishable from background.

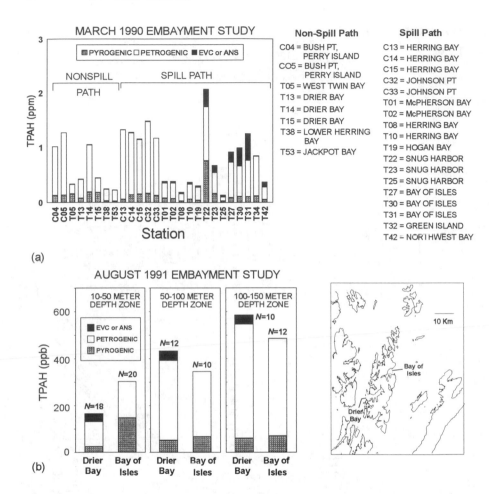

(a)

(b)

FIGURE 14--PWS embayment stations. (a) PAH components in spill-path and non-spill-path stations in February-March 1990. (b) 1991 embayment study averages by water depth zone for Bay of Isles (oiled) and Drier Bay (control).

Nearshore Studies

Nearshore stations are generally located within 100 m of shore. Subtidal sediment samples at these sites can be affected by past or present anthropogenic activities on nearby shorelines. For example, Figure 10 shows that sediment from Sawmill Bay (Chenega Bay) is dominated by pyrogenic hydrocarbons mixed with natural background PAH. Diesel fuel is a key energy source in Prince William Sound, and its presence is indicated in sediments from some nearshore locations by the relative lack of alkylated chrysenes (Figure 7a).

Figure 15 presents time-series data on background PAH and EVC PAH for subtidal sediments in eight nearshore subtidal sites associated with heavily oiled shorelines.

Apparent changes in background levels from year to year reflect the heterogeneity of nearshore subtidal areas where differences in sediment character and exposure regime can have a profound effect on background TPAH levels. At most of the sites, the EVC component is proportionally less important as water depth increases; in general, the EVC component of the PAH decreased from 1989 to 1991. Exceptions occurred in some depth zones of Bay of Isles, Snug Harbor, and Sheltered Bay.

The Mussel Beach (station UPSROIN) subtidal results (Figure 15) show that by 1991 any EVC was indistinguishable from background. This dramatic decrease in sediment PAH parallels the decrease in mussel tissue PAH measured at the same location between 1989 and 1991 (Boehm et al., this volume).

DISCUSSION

The results have been discussed in the context of the overall goals of this program: (1) to identify the subtidal hydrocarbon background in PWS; (2) to quantify the relative contributions of various PAH sources to the PAH measured in a given sample; and (3) to quantify the contribution of *Exxon Valdez* spill oil to benthic sediments in deep and nearshore subtidal locations in the spill zone. The key findings are as follows:

- There is a substantial natural background of petrogenic PAH throughout PWS benthic sediments that originates from seep locations to the east.
- Sediment samples from specific locations can have elevated levels of PAH from pyrogenic and petrogenic sources not associated with the spill.
- Low levels of spill oil PAH were found in 1989-1991 in nearshore subtidal sediments off some shorelines that had been heavily affected by the spill.
- Most of the seafloor in PWS has no detectable PAH from the spill.

The overall average contributions of PAH sources for spill-path and non-spill-path subtidal samples taken in 1990 and 1991 are summarized in Figure 16. The data, arranged by distance from shore, show that the petrogenic background component is greatest in the eastern GOA and is reduced substantially as PWS shorelines are approached. This, plus the similarity of the PAH fingerprints from Katalla and PWS sediments and the GOA-PWS circulation patterns, supports our conclusion that seeps in the eastern Gulf of Alaska are the source of the natural PAH background in PWS. Furthermore, contributions of PAH from the spill are small compared with the ongoing inputs of seep-derived PAH from the GOA.

Regional PAH Background

The regional petrogenic PAH background identified by this study is confirmed by Kinnetic Laboratories (1994) who report it at both spill-path and non-spill-path sites in Prince William Sound and at locations along the Kenai Coast and the Kodiak Archipelago. Its presence is consistent with the fact that petroleum is a naturally occurring material found in marine sediments worldwide. Figure 10 shows the representative PAH profiles for important PAH sources identified by this study. The data summarized in this figure

TABLE 5--Nearshore and embayment subtidal hydrocarbon chemistry. Means and standard deviations (mean ± SD) for total PAH and the sources components of total PAH: pyrogenic PAH; natural background petrogenic PAH; petrogenic Alaska North Slope (ANS); and biogenic PAH (perylene). Data are given as ppb on a dry-sample-weight basis. The concentrations of Total PAH, Pyrogenic PAH and perylene are all measured quantities. The values for Petrogenic Background PAH and Petrogenic ANS-PAH are calculated from the analytical data for each record in a given data set using the mixing model and then averaged.

Study	Depth Range (m)	Oiling Level*	No. of Samples	Total PAH	Pyrogenic PAH	Petrogenic Background PAH	Petrogenic ANS-PAH[o]	Biogenic Perylene
Embayment								
Feb. '90	22-380	NSP	24	518 ± 336	68 ± 41	445 ± 319	6 ± 6	NA
		SP	58	680 ± 497	78 ± 96	494 ± 369	109 ± 235	NA
Sept. '90	NA	NSP	53	294 ± 690	130 ± 323	150 ± 355	8 ± 32	NA
		SP	38	263 ± 583	98 ± 280	148 ± 309	17 ± 28	NA
July '91	10-50	NSP	20	349 ± 404	147 ± 235	198 ± 169	5 ± 8	42 ± 35
		SP	18	225 ± 87	24 ± 20	152 ± 150	49 ± 52	56 ± 109
	50-100	NSP	10	364 ± 149	66 ± 45	293 ± 116	5 ± 5	45 ± 35
		SP	12	488 ± 191	51 ± 20	380 ± 160	57 ± 21	42 ± 27
	100-150	NSP	12	506 ± 224	69 ± 39	427 ± 181	10 ± 8	50 ± 33
		SP	10	622 ± 172	60 ± 19	511 ± 140	52 ± 19	32 ± 15
Nearshore								
1989 SEP	2	NSP	18	79 ± 115	24 ± 51	50 ± 72	5 ± 21	31 ± 71
Fixed Sites		SP	32	446 ± 934	94 ± 421	57 ± 177	317 ± 543	12 ± 37
(Nonrandom)	3-10	NSP	18	206 ± 410	66 ± 136	102 ± 200	38 ± 83	10 ± 13
		SP	37	665 ± 2 717	195 ± 942	305 ± 1 605	175 ± 294	8 ± 22
	10-30	NSP	17	322 ± 321	98 ± 159	205 ± 209	39 ± 61	29 ± 27
		SP	28	534 ± 606	147 ± 325	326 ± 347	86 ± 110	30 ± 29
1990 SEP	3	NSP	57	116 ± 579	58 ± 360	58 ± 219	2 ± 8	6 ± 18
Fixed Sites		SP	33	139 ± 243	16 ± 29	75 + 183	49 ± 10	3 ± 8
(Nonrandom)	3-10	NSP	54	77 ± 272	31 ± 131	46 ± 141	1 ± 4	5 ± 12
		SP	33	91 ± 93	17 ± 25	43 ± 44	33 ± 53	3 ± 6
	10-30	NSP	3	66 ± 34	3 ± 2	64 ± 32	0	6 ± 2
		SP	18	1 159 ± 3 427	462 ± 1 666	647 ± 1 747	50 ± 65	109 ± 261
1991 SEP	3	NSP	27	19 ± 30	4 ± 6	15 ± 24	0	6 ± 13
Fixed Sites		SP	33	998 ± 5014	67 ± 213	78 ± 179	854 ± 4 700[+]	3 ± 8
(Nonrandom)	3-10	NSP	27	18 ± 32	4 ± 8	14 ± 25	0	5 ± 10
		SP	33	184 ± 319	38 + 103	92 ± 169	54 ± 112	9 ± 18
	10-30	NSP	3	13 ± 6	2 ± 1	11 ± 6	0	11 ± 6
		SP	18	179 ± 201	47 ± 70	109 ± 120	23 ± 37	18 ± 27
1990 SEP	3	NSP	54	122 ± 590	61 ± 366	59 ± 225	2 ± 8	7 ± 19
Stratified		SP	134	170 ± 381	54 ± 192	67 ± 145	50 ± 134	2 ± 9
Random	3-10	NSP	54	82 ± 277	33 ± 133	48 ± 144	1 ± 4	5 ± 13
Sites (SRS)		SP	134	155 ± 297	36 ± 111	65 ± 109	54 ± 194	3 ± 5

NA = Not available

* NSP = non-spill-path control (reference stations); SP = spill-path (oiled) stations.

[o] ANS-PAH = PAH attributable to the EVC or other ANS petroleum source.

[+] Values high because of one outlier (TPAH = 29 000 ppb).

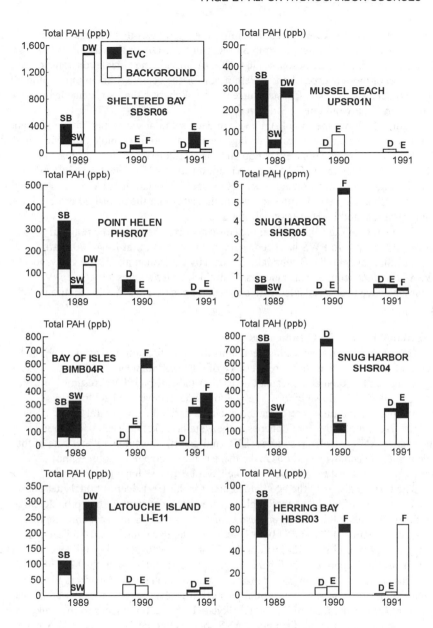

FIGURE 15--PAH components at selected PWS fixed sites by year. SB = -2 m, SW = -10, DW≥ -30m, D = -3m, E = -3 to -10 m, F = -10 to -30 m (all meters below mean lower low water).

and in other parts of the Results section confirm the hypothesis that the background of petrogenic PAH in PWS originates from oil seeps in the GOA to the east of PWS (Figure 2). Suspended sediments from sources in the GOA provide the vehicle for transport and sedimentation of these hydrocarbons. Were it not for the heavy sediment inputs along the eastern GOA and the Alaskan Coastal Current, it is likely that the petrogenic hydrocarbon background in PWS would be very different.

Figure 17 shows the total PAH levels in deep subtidal sediments of the GOA and PWS as a function of distance from Yakataga. There are no discernible differences in the PAH distributions among GOA, PWS non-spill-path, and PWS spill-path sites. Two samples near Yakataga in the GOA had the highest total PAH values found in 1991 and most likely originate from an offshore petroleum seep. The fact that PWS has historically supported a rich and diverse marine ecosystem indicates that the measured prespill levels of sediment-associated PAH are not harmful to biota.

The results of the ^{210}Pb-dating of sediment cores show that the regional petrogenic PAH input to PWS has been an ongoing process for at least 160 years. Seismic profiling of deep PWS subtidal sediments by Carlson et al. (1991) shows locations in PWS with recent sediments as much as 75-m thick. This suggests that seep hydrocarbons have been associated with sediment deposition in PWS for thousands of years.

Dibenzothiophenes as EVC Indicators

One of the major conclusions, related to the identification of the regional PAH background in PWS, is that the mere presence of dibenzothiophenes or other petrogenic marker compounds, taken alone, cannot be used as indicators of EVC residues in PWS subtidal sediments. To do so ignores the well-documented natural background of dibenzothiophenes and other petroleum compounds derived from natural seeps. Even though the fraction of dibenzothiophenes in the Katalla-Yakataga seep background is smaller than in ANS petroleum sources (EVC and diesel), the cumulative effects of the chronic inputs of seep hydrocarbons make these natural petrogenic sources, not EVC residues, the vastly greater contributor to the PWS benthic sediments.

The PAH analyses of the age-dated cores for the 1991 deep subtidal sites show that concentrations of total dibenzothiophenes are nearly constant with depth. Average values for total dibenzothiophenes in these cores are 24 ppb (0- to 2-cm core depth samples; recent deposit), 21 ppb (11- to 16-cm core depth samples; ~20-80 year-old deposits), and 22 ppb (25- to 32-cm core depth samples; ~50-160 year-old deposits). The highest value was 95 ppb for a sediment sample off Cape Yakataga in the Gulf of Alaska.

This underscores the importance of using more sophisticated markers for EVC than just the mere presence of dibenzothiophenes. It is necessary to consider additional information, such as the ratio of individual alkylated dibenzothiophenes to their alkylated phenanthrene counterparts, to distinguish ANS sources like EVC from Katalla-Yakataga sources. It is necessary to consider still other information, such as the amount of chrysenes relative to other PAH, to distinguish ANS crude from ANS diesel.

Nearshore PAH Sources

Villages, sawmills, canneries, camps, etc., can contribute significant amounts of

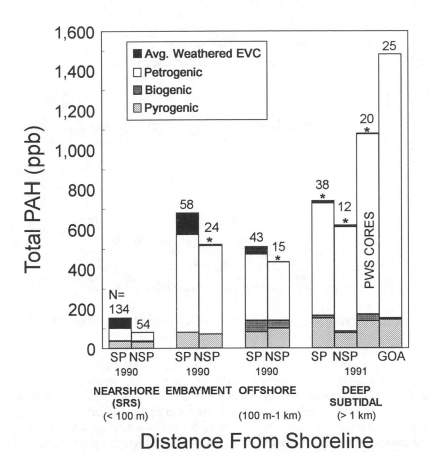

Figure 16--PAH components in PWS and eastern Gulf of Alaska subtidal sediments in 1990 and 1991. Note that the petrogenic PAH component is highest in the eastern GOA (nearest the seeps), is reduced substantially at PWS deep subtidal sites, and is at its lowest levels as the shorelines in PWS are approached. Asterisk (*) indicates calculated EVC concentrations <3-6% of petrogenic PAH that are within the scatter caused by the natural variability of the background and are indistinguishable from background. SP = spill path; NSP = nonspill path; GOA = Gulf of Alaska.

pyrogenic PAH to nearby subtidal sediment. These localized sources of PAH are detectable in the sediment by relatively high concentrations of 4- 6-ring PAH compounds, many of which are not found in EVC at significant levels. High levels of parent 2- 3-ring compounds can also indicate pyrogenic sources.

Pyrogenic PAH form a major part of total PAH in subtidal samples from Chenega Bay, Snug Harbor, Drier Bay, Thumb Bay, Mummy Bay, West Twin Bay, McClure Bay, Stockdale Harbor, McLeod Harbor, the Cordova area, and Boulder Bay. Some of these

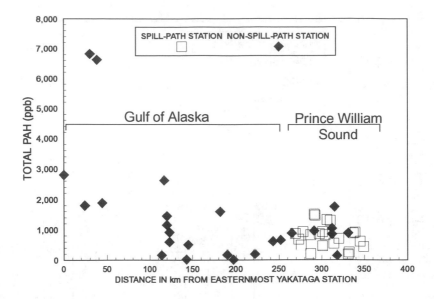

Figure 17--Subtidal (0-2 cm) sediment TPAH (ppm) for 1991 samples as a function of distance from Gulf of Alaska stations off the coast at Yakataga.

locations are associated with current anthropogenic activities (Chenega Bay, Cordova), and others are associated with historic activities such as former fish processing facilities (Drier Bay, Snug Harbor, McClure Bay, Thumb Bay, and Stockdale Harbor). Occurrences of pyrogenic hydrocarbons in nearshore subtidal sediments at Sleepy Bay and at the Alyeska Marine Terminal are reported by Kinnetic Laboratories (1994).

These pyrogenic compounds are sometimes present at very high levels, high enough to exceed ER-L (Effects Range-Low) sediment toxicity threshold values for specific PAH (Long and Morgan 1990). For parent and 4- 6-ring PAH, the ER-L threshold values in sediment are (all in ppb) as follows: C_0-naphthalene = 340; C_1-naphthalene = 65; C_0-fluorene = 35; C_0-phenanthrene = 225; fluoranthene = 600; pyrene = 350; benzo[a] anthracene = 230; C_0-chrysene = 400; and benzo[a]pyrene = 400.

Figure 18 shows concentrations of these compounds (expressed as a percentage of the ER-L value) for subtidal sediment samples from Snug Harbor and Sawmill Bay. PAH distributions for these samples clearly indicate a pyrogenic source, so these compounds are shown in the figure as being of pyrogenic origin.

Biogenic localized sources--Some nearshore subtidal depositional areas act as traps for organic matter. Where this occurs, anaerobic decay and early diagenesis can lead to elevated concentrations of perylene. An example is the West Arm of the Bay of Isles, where subtidal sediment concentrations of perylene exceed 400 ppb.

Diesel sources--Diesel is a potentially important localized petroleum source in Prince William Sound, given the amount of boating activity there. In addition, fresh and weathered diesel fuel and diesel soot are ubiquitous parts of the shipboard environment of

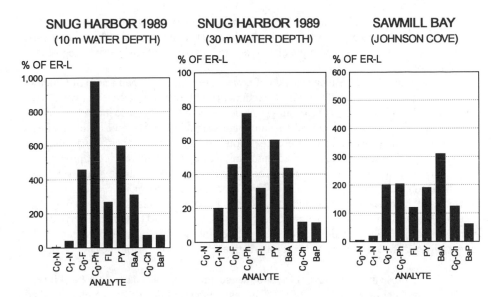

Figure 18--PAH analytes as percentages of Effects Range-Low (ER-L) values (Long and Morgan 1990) for subtidal sediments in two PWS bays in the Spring of 1989. Snug Harbor was heavily oiled; Johnson Cove in Sawmill Bay was lightly oiled.

sampling vessels and may contaminate sediment samples during collection and handling. Diesel contamination of sediment can be confused with *Exxon Valdez* crude residue. Most of the diesel sold in Prince William Sound in 1989 and 1990, was refined from an ANS feed stock, making it difficult to distinguish from EVC residues by the mixing calculation described here, and impossible to distinguish by using single compound petroleum markers alone. However, identification of diesel is possible by comparing the relative amounts of chrysenes (see above, Interpretive Methods). There is little evidence of diesel in the spill-path subtidal samples reported in this paper.

Distribution of EVC residues in subtidal sediments--Our studies show that some nearshore subtidal sediment samples (32 of 84) collected from sites that had been heavily oiled in 1989 had detectable EVC residues in 1991. All but 2 of the 32 had less than 1 000 ppb EVC PAH and 19 had less than 100 ppb. Furthermore, as discussed earlier, our August 1991 stratified random sampling study of one of the most heavily oiled bays (Bay of Isles) demonstrates that high concentrations are not a general phenomenon. The vast majority of the 4 500-km^2 seafloor area of PWS has no detectable traces of EVC residues even though PAH are present from historic seep sources. Where present nearer to shore, EVC residues are generally a small addition to the natural petrogenic background.

Significance of total PAH levels in subtidal sediments--A question that naturally arises is whether the total PAH levels in the subtidal sediments are high enough to have an affect on the ecosystem. Nearshore subtidal sediments from the spill path were not toxic to amphipods or to oyster larvae (Boehm et al., this volume). Furthermore, those toxicity data and similiar intertidal data reported by Boehm et al. support the 4 000 ppb total PAH ER-L proposed by Long and Morgan (1990) as the lower limit of toxic effects reported in the literature.

Obviously, TPAH, which is a sum of concentrations rather than a sum of toxicities, is only an approximate guide for toxicity. Sediments with the same TPAH but widely differing PAH composition probably differ considerably in toxicity since individual PAH analytes vary in toxicity. Additionally, spill oil and seep oil probably have different effects on toxicity, possibly arising from differences in physical state and biological availability of the oil. Seep oil appears to be absorbed onto clay particles; spill oil may exist primarily as droplets or films of bulk oil. Bulk oil may be more bioavailable. In any event, PWS nearshore subtidal sediment was found to have little toxicity. However, the tests of Boehm et al. mentioned above suggest that in the case of sediments contaminated by natural seeps and an oil spill, Long and Morgan's 4 000 ppb TPAH ER-L can serve as a general guideline. Seep oil and spill oil may not be biologically available to the same extent, given differences in droplet size and degree of association with fine clay particles (silt).

In the present study, most of the subtidal sediment samples have total PAH from all sources well below 4 000 ppb. In 1989, a small number of nearshore samples (17) had total PAH levels that exceeded 4 000 ppb. After 1989, only four subtidal sediment samples were found to have TPAH values that exceeded 4 000 ppb. Those that did included two samples collected offshore from Yakataga in the eastern GOA (Figure 17), which are believed to be from an area of submarine seepage, a 1990 sample from Snug Harbor (Figure 15) which contains more than 5 000 ppb of pyrogenic PAH, and a single shallow subtidal sample from the Bay of Isles, collected in 1991, which contains 28 000 ppb petrogenic PAH (24 000 ppb of EVC believed to be from a small tarball).

Studies supported by the *Exxon Valdez* Oil Spill Trustees give similar results. More than 1 500 subtidal sediment samples were collected from Prince William Sound during 1989-91, and their chemical analyses are reported in the Trustees' database PWSOIL (Manen et al. 1993). These data, when adjusted for the presence of outliers (Short and Heintz 1992), show that in 1989, nine samples from Prince William Sound (of 503 reported) had TPAH greater than 4 000 ppb. Two of these, both from Snug Harbor, contained primarily pyrogenic hydrocarbons. After 1989, only five samples (of 869 reported) had TPAH that exceeded 4 000 ppb.

Interested scientists should consult with the authors for information on specific datasets. Because a number of additional technical papers based on these data are in progress, the entire dataset for all parts of the program are not yet available.

CONCLUSIONS

The major conclusions arising from this study are summarized as follows:

1. Most of the seafloor in PWS contains no detectable hydrocarbons from the spill. The subtidal sediment studies show that there has been no significant transport of EVC residues to the seafloor.

2. In those areas where EVC was detected, spill hydrocarbons were generally a small increment to the natural petroleum hydrocarbon background. Fingerprinting methods utilizing the results of high-quality PAH analyses are required to discriminate the spill oil from the background. This natural background is derived largely from oil seeps in the eastern Gulf of Alaska.

3. ^{210}Pb-dated cores indicate the input of seep hydrocarbons has been ongoing for at least the past 160 years and probably for many thousands of years.

4. Anthropogenic hydrocarbon sources including diesel and pyrogenic hydrocarbons are locally important--primarily at subtidal stations adjacent to sites of current or historical human activity.

5. Low levels of EVC residue were present in 1989 and again in 1990 in nearshore subtidal sediments off some shorelines that had been heavily affected by the spill. These remaining traces of EVC are now heavily degraded and are sporadically distributed.

ACKNOWLEDGMENTS

This study was supported by Exxon Company, U.S.A. We appreciate the participation of Ted Sauer, Sandra Tate, Tony Parkin, Larry LeBlanc, John Brown, and others of Arthur D. Little; Dierdre Dahlen and Eric Butler of Batelle Ocean Sciences; Eric Crecelius of Battelle Marine Sciences; and Lisa Haas, Mike Bronson and others at America North (Emcon).

REFERENCES

Albaiges, J. and P. Albrecht. "Fingerprinting Marine Pollutant Hydrocarbons by Computerized Gas Chromatography-Mass Spectrometry." *International Journal of Environmental Analytical Chemistry*. 6: 171-190; 1979.

Anderson, J. W., J. M. Neff, and P. D. Boehm. "Sources, Fates, and Effects of Aromatic Hydrocarbons in the Alaskan Marine Environment with Recommendations for Monitoring Strategies." Contract Report: U. S. Environmental Protection Agency #EPA/600/3-86/018. Corvallis, OR. 123 pp; 1986.

Baker, J. M., I. Campodonico, L. Guzman, J. J. Texera, B. Texera, C. Venegas, and A. Sabhueza. "An Oil Spill in the Straits of Magellan." In *Marine Ecology and Oil Pollution*, J. M. Baker (editor) New York: J. Wiley and Sons; 441-471; 1975.

Bayzlinski, D. A., J. W. Farrington, and H. W. Jannasch. "Hydrocarbons in Surface Sediments from a Guaymas Basin Hydrotherma Vent Site." *Organic Geochemistry.* 12: 547-558; 1988.

Becker, P. R. and C.A. Manen. "Natural Oil Seeps in the Alaskan Marine Environment." Outer Continental Shelf Environmental Assessment Program. Final Report, Volume 62. OCS Study, MMS 89-0065. 126 pp; 1989.

Berthou, F., Y. Dreano, and P. Sandra. "Liquid and Gas Chromatographic Separation of Isomeric Methylated Dibenzothiophenes." *Journal of High Resolution Chromatography and Chromatography Communications.* 7: 675-686; 1984.

Blasko, D. P. "Oil and Gas Seeps in Alaska: Alaskan Peninsula, Western Gulf of Alaska." U.S. Bureau of Mines, Report of Investigations 8122, Washington, DC. 78 pp; 1976a.

Blasko, D. P. "Occurrences of Oil and Gas Seeps Along the Gulf Coast of Alaska." *Offshore Technology Conference Abstracts.* Society of Petroleum Engineers—American Institute of Mechanical Engineers. Houston, TX; 211-220; 1976b.

Blumer M. and W. W. Youngblood. "Polycyclic Aromatic Hydrocarbons in Soils and Recent Sediments." *Science.* 188: 53-55; 1975.

Boehm, P. D. "The *AMOCO CADIZ* Analytical Chemistry Program." In: NOAA-CNEXO Joint Scientific Commission Report: Ecological Study of the *AMOCO CADIZ* Oil Spill. National Oceanic and Atmospheric Administration, Washington, DC, 35-100; 1982.

Boehm, P. D., D. L. Fiest, and A. Elskus. "Comparative Weathering Patterns of Hydrocarbons from the *Amoco Cadiz* Oil Spill Observed at a Variety of Coastal Environments." In *Proceedings of the International Symposium on the* Amoco Cadiz: *Fate and Effects of the Oil Spill. Brest (France), November 19-22, 1979.* Le Centre National pour L'Exploitation des Oceans, Paris. 159-173; 1981.

Brassell, S. C. and G. Eglinton. "Environmental Chemistry—An Interdisciplinary Subject. Natural and Pollutant Organic Compounds in Contemporary Aquatic Sediments." In *Analytical Techniques in Environmental Chemistry.* J. Albaiges (editor) Oxford: Pergamon Press; 1-22; 1980.

Burbank, D. C. "Suspended Sediment Transport and Deposition in Alaskan Coastal Waters: With Special emphasis on Remote Sensing By the ERTS-1 Satellite." M.S. Thesis. University of Alaska, Fairbanks. 222 pp; 1974

Butt, J. A., D. F. Duckworth, and S. G. Perry. *Characterization of Spilled Oil Samples.* Institute of Petroleum. New York: John Wiley and Sons; 95 pp; 1986.

Carlson, P.R., P.W. Barnes, E. Hayden, and B.A. Carbin. "Morphology of Bottom Sediment of Prince William Sound Along the Oil Spill Trajectory." In *Sediment of Prince William Sound, Beach to Deep Fjord Floor, a Year After the* Exxon Valdez *Oil Spill.* P.R. Carlson (editor) U. S. Geological Survey Open File Report; 91-631. P; 69-98; 1991.

Douglas, G.S., R.C. Prince, E.L. Butler, and W.G. Steinhauer. "The use of internal chemical indicators in petroleum and refined products to evaluate the extent of biodegradation." In: *Hydrocarbon Biomediation.* R.E. Hinchee, B.C. Alleman, R.E. Hoeppel, R.N. Miller (editors); Ann Arbor, Michigan: Lewis Publishers; 219-236; 1994.

Feely, R. A., E. T. Baker, J. D. Schumacher, G. J. Massoth, and W. M. Landing. "Processes Affecting the Distribution and Transport of Suspended Matter in the Northeast Gulf of Alaska." *Deep Sea Research*, Part A, 26, 4A, 445-464; 1979.
Friocourt, M. P., F. Berthou, and D. Picart. "Dibenzothiophene Derivatives as Organic Markers of Oil Pollution." *Toxicological and Environmental Chemistry.* 5: 205-215; 1982.

Gundlach, E. R., P. D. Boehm, M. Marchand, D. M. Atlas, D. M. Ward, and D. A. Wolfe. "The Fate of the *Amoco Cadiz* Oil." *Science.* 221: 122-129; 1983.

Jahns, H. O., J. R. Bragg, L. C. Dash, and E. H. Owens. "Natural Cleansing of Shorelines Following the *Exxon Valdez* Spill." *Proceedings of the 1991 Oil Spill Conference.* American Petroleum Institute Publication No. 4529. 167-176; 1991.

Kaplan, I. R. and M. I. Venkatesan. "Characterization of Organic Matter in Sediments from Gulf of Alaska, Bering and Beaufort Seas." Final Report to Outer Continental Shelf Environmental Assessment Program. DOC/DOI, 88 pp, Boulder, CO; 1981.

Kennicutt, M. C., J. M. Brooks, R. B. Bidgare, and G. J Denoux. "Gulf of Mexico Hydrocarbon Seep Communities: Part II: Regional Distribution of Hydrocarbon Seepage and Associated Fauna." *Deep Sea Research.* 35: 1639-1651; 1988.

Kennicutt, M. C. III, S. T. Sweet, W. R. Fraser, M. Culver, and W. L. Stockton . "The Fate of Diesel Fuel Spilled by the *Bahia Paraiso* in Arthur Harbor, Antarctica." In *1991 Oil Spill Conference Proceedings. San Diego.* 493-500; 1991.

Kennicutt, M. C., III, T. J. McDonald, G. J. Denoux, and S. J. McDonald. "Hydrocarbon Contamination the Antarctic Peninsula I. Arthur Harbor—Subtidal sediments." *Marine Pollution Bulletin.* 24: 499-506; 1992.

Kinnetic Laboratories. Prince William Sound RCAC: Long-term environmetal monitoring program. Annual monitoring report-1993. Anchorage: Prince William Sound Regional Citizens Advisory Council. 1994

Klein, L. H. "Provenances, Depositional Rates and Heavy Metal Chemistry of Sediments, Prince William Sound, Alaska." M.S. Thesis, University. Alaska, Fairbanks, 96 pp; 1983.

Koide, M., K. E. Bruland, and E. D. Goldberg. "$^{228}Th/^{232}Th$ and ^{210}Pb Geochronologies in Marine and Lake Sediments." *Geochimica et Cosmochimica Acta.* 37: 1171-1183; 1973.

Kolpack, R. L. and T. J. Meyers. "(Gas Chromatographic) Characterization of Some Crude Oil and Natural Seep Oil from Santa Barbara Channel, California." 161st American Chemical Society National Meeting, Los Angeles; Division of Water Air and Waste Chemistry, Abstract No. WATER017; 1971.

Kvenvolden, K. A., Rapp, J. B., and Hostettler, F. A. "Tracking Hydrocarbons from the *Exxon Valdez O*il Spill in Beach, Shallow-Water, and Deep-Water Sediments of Prince William Sound, Alaska." In *Sediment of Prince William Sound, Beach to Deep Fjord Floor, a Year After the* Exxon Valdez *Oil Spill.* P.R. Carlson (editor) U. S. Geological Survey Open File Report; 91-631. P; 69-98; 1991.

LaFlamme, R. E. and R. A. Hites. "The Global Distribution of Polycyclic Aromatic Hydrocarbons in Recent Sediments." *Geochimica et Cosmochimica Acta.* 42: 289-303; 1978.

Long, E. R. and L. G. Morgan. "The Potential for Biological Effects of Sediment-sorbed Contaminants Tested in the National Status and Trends Program." NOAA Technical Memorandum NOS OMA 52, National Oceanic and Atmospheric Administration, U.S. Department of Commerce, Rockville, MD; 175 pp + appendices; 1990.

Mackenzie, A. S. "Application of Biological Markers in Petroleum Geochemistry." In *Advances in Petroleum Geochemistry. Volume 1.* J. Brooks and D. Welte (editors) New York: Academic Press. 115-214; 1984.

Manen, C. A., J. R. Price, S. Korn, and M. G. Carls. "Natural Resource Damage Assessment: Database Design and Structure." National Oceanic and Atmospheric Administration Technical Memorandum NOS/ORCA; 1993, in press.

Martin, G. C. "Geology and Mineral Resources of the Controller Bay Region, Alaska." *U. S. Geological Survey Bulletin.* 335: 3-141; 1908.

McGee, D. L. "Gulf of Alaska Petroleum Seeps." State of Alaska Department Natural Resources, Open File Report. 32, 7 pp; 1972.

Miller, D. J. "Preliminary Report on the Geology and Oil Possibilities at the Katalla District, Alaska." U.S. Geological Survey Open File Report 50, 66 pp; 1951.

Miller, D. J., R. Payne, and G. Gryc. "Geology of Possible Petroleum provinces in Alaska." *U. S. Geological Survey Bulletin.* 1094. 9-131; 1959.

Montagna, P. A., P. A. Bauer, J. E. Toal, J. Hardin, D. Hardin, and R. B. Spies. "Temporal Variability and the Relationship between Benthic Meiofaunal and Microbial Populations of a Natural Coastal Petroleum Seep." *Journal of Marine Research.* 45: 761-769; 1987.

Niimi, A. J. "Solubility of Organic Chemicals in Octanol, Triolein and Cod Liver Oil and Relationships Between Solubility and Partition Coefficients." *Water Research.*; 25: 1515-1521; 1991.

(NRC) National Research Council. "Oil in the Sea: Inputs, Fates, and Effects." Washington, DC: National Academy Press; 601 pp; 1985.

Ogata, M., F. Kuniyasu, Y. Ogino and E. Mano. "Partition Coefficients as a Measure of Bioconcentration Potential of Crude Oil Compounds in Fish and Shellfish." *Bulletin of Environmental Contamination and Toxicology,* 33: 561-567; 1984.

Overton, E. B., J. A. McFall, S. W. Mascarella, C. F. Steele, S. A. Antoine, I. R. Politzer, and J. L. Laseter. "Identification of Petroleum Residue Sources After a Fire and Oil Spill." *Proceedings of the 1981 Oil Spill Conference.* American Petroleum Institute Publication # 720. 541-546; 1981.

Page, D. S., J. C. Foster, P. M. Fickett, and E. S. Gilfillan. "Identification of Petroleum Sources in an Area Impacted by the *Amoco Cadiz* Oil Spill." *Marine Pollution Bulletin.* 19: 107-115; 1988.

Payne, J. R., J. R. Clayton, G. D. McNabb, and B. E. Kirstein. "*Exxon Valdez* Oil Weathering Fate and Behavior: Model Predictions and Field Observations." *Proceedings of the 1991 Oil Spill Conference.* 641-654; 1991.

Prince, R. C., J. R. Clark, and J. E. Lindstrom. "Bioremediation Monitoring Program." Joint Exxon, U.S.E.P.A., and Alaska Department of Environmental Conservation Report. Anchorage, AK, 99503. 85 pp; 1991.

Prince, R. C., J. R. Clark, and J. E. Lindstrom, E. L. Butler, E. J. Brown, G. Winter, M. J. Grossman, P. R. Parrish, R. E. Bare, J. F. Braddock, W. G. Steinhauer, G. S. Douglas, J. M. Kennedy, P. J. Barter, J. R. Bragg, E. J. Harner, and R. M. Atlas. "Bioremediation of the *Exxon Valdez* Oil Spill: Monitoring Safety and Efficacy." In: *Hydrocarbon Bioremediation.* R. E. Hinchee, B. C. Alleman, R. R. Hoeppel, R. N. Miller (editors); Ann Arbor, Michigan: Lewis Publishers; 107-124; 1994.

Radke, M. "Organic Geochemistry of Aromatic Hydrocarbons." In *Advances in Petroleum Geochemistry Volume 2.* J. Brooks and D. Welte (editors) Orlando: Academic Press; 141-205; 1987.

Reimnitz, E. "Late Quaternary History and Sedimentation of the Copper River Delta and Vicinity, Alaska." Ph. D. Dissertation; University of California, San Diego. 160 pp; 1966.

Reimnitz, E. and P. R. Carlson. "Circulation of Nearshore Surface Water in the Gulf of Alaska." In: Carlson, P. R., Conomos, T. J., Janda, R. J., and Peterson, D. H. (editors) *Principal Sources and Dispersal Patterns of Suspended Particulate Matter in Nearshore Waters of the Northeast Pacific Ocean.* National Technical Information Service, E75-102666, Springfield VA, 10-25; 1975.

Rosenberg, D. H. "Oil and Gas Seeps of the Northern Gulf of Alaska." In *A Review of the Oceanography and Renewable Resources of the Northern Gulf of Alaska.* Rosenberg, D. H. (editor) University of Alaska Institute of Marine Science Report R72-23. 143-148; 1974

Royer, T. C., J. A. Vermersch, T. J. Weingartner, H. J. Niebauer, and R. D. Muench. "Ocean Circulation Influencing the *Exxon Valdez* Oil Spill." *Oceanography.* 3:2; p. 3-10; 1990.

Sauer, T. and P. D. Boehm. "The Use of Defensible Analytical Chemical Measurements for Oil Spill Natural Resource Damage Assessment." *Proceedings of the 1991 Oil Spill Conference,* 363-369; 1991.

Sharma, G. D. *The Alaskan Shelf. Hydrographic, Sedimentary, and Geochemical Environment.* New York: Springer-Verlag; 498 pp; 1979.

Short, J. and R. Heintz. "Descriptive Documentation for Identification of Biased Sediment and Mussel Tissue Samples in the NRDA Hydrocarbon Database." Draft Report for Exxon Valdez Natural Resource Damage Assessment Project, Subtidal 8. October 30, 1992. (Available through Oil Spill Public Information Center, 645 G Street, Anchorage, Alaska.)

Spies, R. B., D. D. Hardin, and J. P. Teal. "Organic enrichment or toxicity? A Comparison of the Effects of Kelp and Crude Oil in Sediments on the Colonization and Growth of Benthic Infauna." *Journal of Experimental Marine Biology and Ecology.* 124: 261-282; 1988.

Sporstol, S., N. Gjos, R. G. Lichtenthaler, K. O. Gustavson, K. Urdall, and F. Oreld. "Source Identification of Aromatic Hydrocarbons in Sediments Using GC/MS." *Environmental Science & Technology.* 17: 282-286; 1983.

Tysdale, R. G. and J. E. Case. "Geology Map of the Seward and Blying Sound Quadrangles, Alaska." U. S. Geological Survey Miscellaneous Investigation Series Map I-1150; 1979.

Venkatesan, M. I. "Occurrence and Possible Sources of Perylene in Marine Sediments—A Review." *Marine Chemistry.* 25: 1-27; 1988.

Wade, T. L., M. C. Kennicutt, and J. M. Brooks. "Gulf of Mexico Hydrocarbon Seep Communities: Part III. Aromatic Hydrocarbon Concentrations in Organisms, Sediments and Water." *Marine Environmental Research.* 27: 19-30; 1989.

A. E. Bence,[1] W. A. Burns[1]

FINGERPRINTING HYDROCARBONS IN THE BIOLOGICAL RESOURCES OF THE *EXXON VALDEZ* SPILL AREA

REFERENCE: Bence, A. E. and Burns, W. A., "Fingerprinting Hydrocarbons in the Biological Resources of the Exxon Valdez Spill Area," Exxon Valdez Oil Spill: Fate and Effects in Alaskan Waters, ASTM STP 1219, Peter G. Wells, James N. Butler, and Jane S. Hughes, Eds., American Society for Testing and Materials, Philadelphia, 1995.

ABSTRACT: A procedure has been developed that discriminates *Exxon Valdez* crude from other sources of hydrocarbons found in Prince William Sound and the Gulf of Alaska. The procedure uses polycyclic aromatic hydrocarbon (PAH) distributions, measured by gas chromatography/mass spectrometry (GC/MS), to fingerprint sample extracts. The relative abundances of alkylated phenanthrenes, dibenzothiophenes, and chrysenes are used to differentiate *Exxon Valdez* crude and its weathering products from other hydrocarbons. Saturate fraction distributions are used to confirm the PAH identification whenever possible.

The procedure has been applied to the more than 1 500 PAH analyses of tissues reported by the Oil Spill Health Task Force, formed after the spill to assess subsistence food safety, and nearly 4 700 PAH analyses of biological samples in PWSOIL, the government's damage-assessment chemistry database. These two datasets constitute the largest collection of hydrocarbon analyses of biological samples from the spill-impact zone.

Excluding shellfish, only a small fraction of the samples contain recognizable *Exxon Valdez* crude residues, and most of those are samples that were collected in 1989. Only rarely is *Exxon Valdez* crude identified in samples collected in 1990, and never in 1991 samples. The majority of samples containing *Exxon Valdez* crude residues are associated either with external surfaces (e.g., eggshells, skin, hair, carcasses) or with the gastrointestinal tract (e.g., stomach contents, intestines). Many of these samples contain diesel in various stages of weathering, as do sediment samples also archived in the database. For example, diesel is observed on approximately one-half of the bald eagle and common murre eggshells collected in both 1989 and 1990. Rarely is *Exxon Valdez* crude seen in internal tissues (e.g., liver) and never in body fluids (e.g., blood, milk), because of

[1]Exxon Production Research Company, Houston, TX 77252-2189

lack of exposure, lack of uptake, or metabolic effects. Low concentrations of low-molecular-weight PAH compounds, the source(s) of which cannot be identified, are present in some internal tissues and fluids at comparable levels in samples collected from both within the spill path and without. This suggests a source other than the spill. Additionally, more than 60% of the fish and wildlife samples in PWSOIL contain a distinct nonpetrogenic fingerprint, an artifact of laboratory analytical and reporting procedures. This fingerprint consists of 25 specific PAH compounds that were required to be reported, without corrections for baseline or detection limit, regardless of their concentration.

Mussels and clams from some heavily oiled shorelines contained high levels of *Exxon Valdez* crude in 1989. Subsequently, these levels dropped by approximately an order of magnitude annually, and many had reached or were approaching background by 1991. This is consistent with the sharply decreasing oiling levels detected during shoreline surveys in 1989 through 1992.

This empirical analysis shows that PAH fingerprinting is highly diagnostic for samples of external surfaces where selective uptake and metabolism are not issues. It also appears applicable to samples from the gastrointestinal tract. For external surfaces and gastrointestinal tract samples, it has a major advantage over other techniques in that it can quantitatively differentiate among multiple sources of hydrocarbons having generally similar compositions. Although the method is less diagnostic for internal tissues and fluids, it does offer a way to compare spill-path and non-spill-path sites, and it clearly identifies fingerprints that are artifacts of the analytical procedure.

Results show that the exposure of biota to spill oil in 1989 was restricted to the spill path where it was sporadically distributed. Very little evidence of *Exxon Valdez* crude was seen in 1990. Consequently, these data do not indicate widespread or persistent biologic exposure to *Exxon Valdez* crude.

KEYWORDS: Oil spill, *Exxon Valdez*, polycyclic aromatic hydrocarbons, fingerprinting, tissue hydrocarbons, biological exposure, Oil Spill Health Task Force, PWSOIL, hydrocarbon uptake, diesel

---

INTRODUCTION

The Prince William Sound-Gulf of Alaska region affected by the *Exxon Valdez* oil spill has important commercial and subsistence fisheries. Local reliance on natural resources is particularly high, and the majority of natural foods are taken from the sea. Consequently, there was concern immediately following the spill about the contamination of the subsistence food supply as well as about potential longer-term effects on the abundant wildlife in the spill zone.

An ad hoc Oil Spill Health Task Force (OSHTF) was established to study subsistence foods from the traditional harvest areas, determine their safety for human consumption, and communicate its findings to the users. Members of the task force were drawn from local, state, and federal agencies and from Exxon. Public health organizations were also represented. The results and conclusions of their investigations were published in a series of newsletters, which were distributed to the subsistence users (e.g., OSHTF 1990). Scientific results (primarily chemistry) were published by the National Oceanic and Atmospheric Administration (NOAA) (Varanasi et al. 1990) or released in a series of memoranda from NOAA to the task force. The chemistry dataset represented by the subsistence food safety study is hereafter referred to as OSHTF.

In addition, the Trustees (State of Alaska Departments of Law, Fish and Game, and Environmental Conservation; U.S. Departments of the Interior and Agriculture; and NOAA) carried out Natural Resource Damage Assessment (NRDA) studies--parts of which were designed to determine the potential for longer-term impacts on the fish, shellfish, and wildlife. The hydrocarbon chemistry of tissue, sediment, and water samples analyzed during their investigations is reported in the database PWSOIL. This database is managed by NOAA (Manen et al. 1993) which has the lead responsibility for data interpretation and analysis. It is the official chemistry database for all of the Trustees' NRDA studies including Air/Water, Coastal Habitat, Fish/Shellfish, Marine Mammals, Terrestrial Mammals, and Birds.

The November 1993 version of PWSOIL contains nearly 4 700 hydrocarbon analyses of tissues (excluding replicate, quality control, and matrix spike samples). Each analysis reports wet weight concentrations of the polycyclic aromatic hydrocarbons (PAH) measured by gas chromatography-mass spectrometry and the C_{10}-C_{34} alkanes plus the unresolved complex mixture (UCM) measured by gas chromatography. In addition, more than 2550 FAC (fluorescent aromatic contaminants) analyses of bile (excluding replicates and quality control samples) are reported. An interpretation as to the presence or absence of "oil" is provided for more than 1 250 of the biological sample PAH analyses reported in PWSOIL.

To ensure that the hydrocarbon chemistry results were interpreted consistently, the Trustees' Technical Services Group established a set of criteria for determining oil contamination in NRDA samples (Manen 1991). These criteria, which include saturated fraction (presence of phytane, carbon preference index ~1, and unresolved complex mixture) and aromatic fraction (alkylated naphthalenes, phenanthrenes, and dibenzothiophenes) parameters, are all valid indicators of petrogenic hydrocarbons. However, they fail to distinguish among multiple petrogenic sources characteristic of the Prince William Sound environment (i.e., background component related to seeps, Cook Inlet and ANS crudes, and diesel). The task of discriminating *Exxon Valdez* crude is complicated by the presence of these other petroleum hydrocarbons in the area, particularly diesel.

For example, the Trustees frequently relied upon the presence of fluorescent aromatic contaminants in bile (the bile FAC method) as an indicator of exposure to crude. This method can identify exposure to the polycyclic aromatic hydrocarbons (PAH) found in petroleum, refined petroleum products, and combustion products, but it is not source-specific, i.e., it cannot identify the source of the hydrocarbons (Varanasi et al. 1990; Krahn et al. 1992), and it must be used on freshly killed animals (Krahn et al. 1986). NOAA is developing a new method based on the analysis of bile metabolites by GC/MS (Krahn et al. 1992) with the potential to be source-specific. This method shows promise but requires additional field testing.

A principal component analysis approach to identify *Exxon Valdez* crude and its weathering products in sediments is described by Short and Heintz (1993). This method relies primarily on the PAH. Its major shortcoming is that it does not include the alkylated chrysenes and, consequently, cannot distinguish diesel from crude.

Krahn et al. (1993) describe an HPLC (high-pressure liquid chromatography) method of analysis to rapidly and inexpensively screen sediment samples for possible oil contamination. Using this technique, which is based upon pattern recognition, they were able to distinguish weathered *Exxon Valdez* crude in oiled bay sediments from diesel in sediments from unoiled locations. This distinction was confirmed by GC/MS analysis. However, only the alkylated naphthalenes, phenanthrenes, and dibenzothiophenes were used to distinguish *Exxon Valdez* crude. Their diesel control was a west coast product (M. M. Krahn, National Marine Fisheries, NOAA, personal communication, February, 1993) that lacked alkylated dibenzothiophenes. Alkylated dibenzothiophenes are important PAH components of diesel refined from ANS crude feed stock.

Assessments of the extent of exposure of biological communities to *Exxon Valdez* crude required the development of techniques that are capable of differentiating spill residue from other hydrocarbon sources in different types of biologic samples. This paper describes a hydrocarbon fingerprinting technique and its application to the OSHTF and PWSOIL datasets. It examines fingerprints (primarily the PAH) of biological sample extracts in a way that permits low concentrations of spill oil and its weathering products to be distinguished from other crudes, refined products including diesel, the water-soluble fractions of crude and diesel, combustion products, natural biological sources, and artifacts of the analytical methods. Results of this fingerprint analysis can be used to determine whether or not hydrocarbons have passed into the tissues (addressing food-chain issues). Many sample types may be analyzed, including sediments and tissues from animals found dead. The method works well with samples of external surfaces and the gastrointestinal tract. Because selective uptake and differential metabolism change the relative distributions of PAH in internal tissues and body fluids, the results of the method, when applied to such samples, are subject to some uncertainty. The method has been applied to more than 5 200 PAH analyses, measured by gas chromatography/mass spectrometry (GC/MS), from PWSOIL and OSHTF. Fish tissues, shellfish, eggshells and egg contents, blubber, fat, muscle tissue, brain tissue, hair, liver, kidney, blood, milk, stomach contents, etc., have been fingerprinted with the technique.

HYDROCARBON FINGERPRINTING

This section explains why the PAH analytes are useful in determining the source of hydrocarbons in biological samples. It describes the characteristic PAH fingerprints of various sources of hydrocarbons found in the area, weathering patterns for *Exxon Valdez* crude, and the importance of laboratory reporting limits and detection limits. A flow chart is included that describes application of the step-by-step fingerprinting procedure to the PWSOIL and OSHTF datasets.

Methods of Fingerprinting Hydrocarbon Sources

The hydrocarbon analyses commonly used to identify spill oil include total hydrocarbon measurements (extractable hydrocarbons) and analyses of aliphatic and aromatic components. Aliphatic indicators include the normal alkane carbon preference index (CPI), the ratio of the isoprenoids (branched alkanes) pristane and phytane (Rasmussen 1975), and the magnitude of the unresolved complex mixture (UCM) (i.e., the "hump" under the normal alkanes on a gas chromatographic trace). Excluding the pristane/phytane ratio, none of these are source-specific, i.e., none discriminate among different sources of petroleum. Furthermore, depending upon climate, the alkanes in exposed oil degrade fairly quickly and may be unrecognizable only months after a spill. Traces of cyclic alkane (hopane) and C_{27}-C_{29} sterane and diasterane "biomarkers" (Mackenzie 1984) found in oils are useful oil indicators because of their resistance to degradation and their differences among oils (e.g., Connan 1983; Kvenvolden et al. 1991), but their quantitative analysis in environmental samples is not yet done routinely. No biomarker analyses of biological samples are reported in either the PWSOIL or OSHTF datasets.

We note that diesel can be distinguished from *Exxon Valdez* crude by differences in the distribution of C_{18}-C_{30} alkanes, but the distribution is sometimes obscured by the odd-even ratios of plant waxes, rapid weathering, and other factors. Where possible, we use reported alkane analyses (measured by gas chromatography) to confirm or augment PAH fingerprinting of PWSOIL samples.

Polycyclic Aromatic Hydrocarbons--The aromatic fraction includes the PAH (Table 1), some of which are relatively stable and diagnostic constituents of petroleum. They have been used as environmental indicators of oil in sediments (e.g., Overton et al. 1979; Overton et al. 1981; Boehm et al. 1981; Gundelach et al. 1983) and tissues (e.g., Friocourt et al. 1983; Sinkkonen 1983). Overton et al. (1981), who were the first to use the ratios of specific alkylated PAH (alkylated phenanthrenes/alkylated dibenzothiophenes) to identify spill oil in sediments, noted that two different oils (Louisiana sweet crude and Arabian light crude) were readily distinguished by these ratios. Furthermore, they noted that these ratios appeared to be unaffected by weathering one year after a spill. Many recent assessments of both chronic inputs of hydrocarbons (Anderson et al. 1986) and oil spill impacts on the marine environment have focused on PAH because of their resistance to degradation and their source specificity. Page et al. (Identification of Hydrocarbon Sources in the Benthic Sediments of Prince William Sound and the Gulf of Alaska Following the *Exxon Valdez* Oil Spill, this volume) use PAH analyte ratios (alkylated dibenzothiophenes/alkylated phenanthrenes) to quantitatively distinguish natural seep background hydrocarbons from spill oil residues in Prince William Sound subtidal sediments.

PAH Uptake by Organisms--Organisms can ingest the PAH or incorporate them through the skin or membranes. In fish and higher vertebrates, only a small fraction of the PAH ingested in oil-contaminated food is absorbed through the gut wall (Van Veld et al. 1988; Varanasi et al. 1989; Lemaire et al. 1992). The majority of the PAH are

TABLE 1--*Polycyclic aromatic hydrocarbons*

ANALYTE	SYMBOL	# RINGS
*Naphthalene	N0	2
C$_1$-Naphthalenes (*2-Methylnaphthalene, *1-Methylnaphthalene)	N1	2
C$_2$-Naphthalenes (*2,6-Dimethylnaphthalene)	N2	2
C$_3$-Naphthalenes (*2,3,5-Trimethylnaphthalene)	N3	2
C$_4$-Naphthalenes	N4	2
*[Biphenyl]	Bph	2
*Acenaphthylene	Acl	3
*Acenaphthene	Ace	3
*Fluorene	F0	3
C$_1$-Fluorenes	F1	3
C$_2$-Fluorenes	F2	3
C$_3$-Fluorenes	F3	3
*Anthracene	AN	3
*Phenanthrene/anthracene	P0	3
C$_1$-Phenanthrenes/anthracenes(*1-Methylphenanthrene)	P1	3
C$_2$-Phenanthrenes/anthracenes	P2	3
C$_3$-Phenanthrenes/anthracenes	P3	3
C$_4$-Phenanthrenes/anthracenes	P4	3
*Dibenzothiophene	D0	3
C$_1$-Dibenzothiophenes	D1	3
C$_2$-Dibenzothiophenes	D2	3
C$_3$-Dibenzothiophenes	D3	3
*Fluoranthene	FL	4
*Pyrene	PY	4
C$_1$-Fluoranthenes/pyrenes	FP1	4
*Benz(a)anthracene	BaA	4
*Chrysene	C0	4
C$_1$-Chrysenes	C1	4
C$_2$-Chrysenes	C2	4
C$_3$-Chrysenes	C3	4
C$_4$-Chrysenes	C4	4
*Benzo(b)fluoranthene	BbF	5
*Benzo(k)fluoranthene	BkF	5
*[Benzo(e)pyrene]	BeP	5
*Benzo(a)pyrene	BaP	5
*[Perylene]	Per	5
*Indeno(1,2,3-c,d)pyrene	ID	6
*Dibenz(a,h)anthracene	DA	5
*Benzo(g,h,i)perylene	BgP	6

    *   Required reporting analyte
    [ ] Analyte not present in all datasets
    (*) Individual isomers of analytes that are required reporting analytes

excreted in feces, and some are converted to metabolites by a mixed-function oxygenase (MFO) system in the intestines. Unmetabolized PAH and PAH metabolites may be absorbed through the gut wall where they enter the portal-vein system, which drains the gastrointestinal tract, and transported directly to the liver. In the liver, they are converted to more polar metabolites and excreted (e.g., Neff 1979; Lee 1981). This process occurs relatively rapidly (Neff et al. 1976; Varanasi et al. 1989; Stegeman 1981; Pritchard and Bend 1991). Because of the portal-vein system, very little of the PAH absorbed through the gut are passed on through the general circulatory system to other tissues. Consequently, the liver of fish and wildlife is the tissue of choice for the detection of PAH if ongoing exposure to petroleum hydrocarbons via the food chain is suspected. However, the mechanisms by which petroleum PAH are incorporated into tissues may fractionate them according to ring size or water solubility (Eastcott et al. 1988), and the resulting fingerprint can have little resemblance to that of the oil.

Fatty tissues, which are stored for later nutritional use, can be sites of longer-term PAH retention (Neff 1979). The blubber of pinnipeds and cetaceans is included in this category (e.g., Engelhardt 1978). In situations where exposure is high, the PAH may build up in lipid-rich tissues such as brain, muscles, and kidney (e.g., Neff et al. 1985; Broman et al. 1990). Even then, individual analyte levels rarely exceed a few tens of ppb (Heras et al. 1992; Law and Whinnett 1992). More commonly, individual PAH analyte levels in tissue samples are at or below the limits of detection of current analytical methods. Internal tissues are difficult to analyze, and because of these low concentrations of PAH, sample handling, preparation, analysis, and interpretation of the data must be conducted with extreme care and appropriate concerns for contamination.

Hydrocarbon Sources in Prince William Sound Biological Samples

Three generic types of hydrocarbons are recognized by their PAH constituents in Prince William Sound and Gulf of Alaska biological analyses: petrogenic (related to oil, oil source rocks, and refined products of oil), pyrogenic (products of incomplete combustion), and biogenic (produced during biologic and diagenetic processes). Some represent natural or anthropogenic environmental exposure of the living organism, some could be contaminants introduced at the time of sampling, some could be contaminants introduced during sample preparation and analysis, and others could be artifacts of the analytical procedure.

The petrogenic PAH component (represented by weathered *Exxon Valdez* crude in Figure 1A) contains the alkylated homologues of naphthalene, fluorene, phenanthrene, and chrysene. The sulfur-containing heteroatom, dibenzothiophene, and its alkylated homologues, are usually included in PAH analyses. Each group consists of a parent compound made up of multiple benzene rings (e.g., parent phenanthrene {P0} contains 3 rings) and an homologous series of alkylated compounds, which consists of the parent structure to which methyl, ethyl, and other alkyl groups have been added. For example, C_1-phenanthrene (P1) contains one methyl substitution with 4 observed configurations (isomers), C_2-phenanthrene (P2) contains two methyl or one ethyl substitution with 12 observed configurations (Radke et al. 1990).

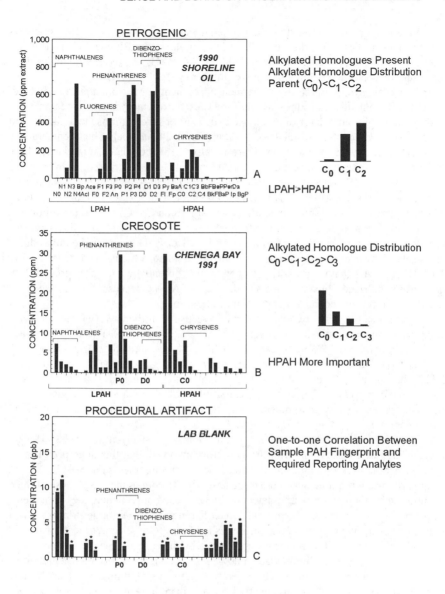

FIGURE 1--Criteria used to distinguish the PAH fingerprints of petrogenic hydrocarbons, creosote, and procedural artifacts in analyses of biological samples from Prince William Sound and the Gulf of Alaska. Note the difference in concentration scales. (* indicates required reporting analyte)

In crudes and their refined products, the alkylated homologues are almost always in higher concentrations than the parent PAH (Youngblood and Blumer 1975). They are further characterized by the dominance of light PAH (LPAH, i.e., those with molecular weights less than C_3-dibenzothiophene) over the heavy PAH (HPAH).

Pyrogenic hydrocarbons in the marine environment come from atmospheric fallout, surface runoff from villages and towns, old forest fire burns, campfire sites, and peat (which is a natural accumulator of pyrogenic hydrocarbons from atmospheric fallout and surface runoff). Creosote, a distillate of coal tar (distilled from coal at high temperatures in the absence of oxygen) and a common preservative of wood pilings at marine facilities, is included in this category. The pyrogenic PAH component is characterized by increased HPAH (relative to LPAH) and high concentrations of parent (C0) fluorene, phenanthrene, dibenzothiophene, and chrysene relative to the alkylated homologues (Figure 1B). The alkylated homologues may show a rapidly decreasing trend $C_0 > C_1 > C_2 > C_3$, as shown in Figure 1B, or they may be absent. Specific analytes, including anthracene, fluoranthene, pyrene, benzo(a)anthracene, benzo(a)pyrene, and heavier PAH, may also be important constituents. However, diesel soot, which is the incomplete combustion product of diesel, has a PAH signature that is primarily petrogenic. It is potentially a major source of PAH contaminants in Prince William Sound and the Gulf of Alaska because diesel is used extensively in electrical power generation and as boat fuel.

In our analysis of the two datasets, we have also identified a very large number of samples having a diagnostic, nonpetrogenic fingerprint (Figure 1C). This fingerprint is pervasive throughout the PWSOIL database, where it is restricted to analyses reported by one of the two laboratories involved in PAH analysis, and is occasionally found in OSHTF. It consists of 25 compounds (Table 1), all but 5 of which are parent or unsubstituted compounds. Forty samples classified as oiled in PWSOIL and many of the tissue samples reported by government scientists to be contaminated with oil contain only these compounds.

The diagnostic fingerprint appears in the lab blanks usually at low levels. It is our understanding, after discussions with the laboratory involved, that this fingerprint is a procedural artifact of the sample analysis and reporting requirements imposed by NOAA. Minimum reporting requirements were to quantify the 25 compounds regardless of their concentration levels with respect to detection limits. As a consequence, they consistently appear and, in many cases, they represent "quantified noise." Their fingerprint is so unusual, however, that they are easily distinguished from petrogenic hydrocarbons.

The biogenic PAH component, represented by the early diagenetic compound perylene, is rarely significant in the PAH analyses of biological samples; consequently, a biogenic classification is not made. However, the alkane distributions, which are used to confirm the PAH classifications, frequently have dominant biogenic characteristics (odd-over-even preference in the C_{26}-C_{34} region; Wakeham and Farrington 1980).

Exxon Valdez *crude fingerprints--Exxon Valdez* crude is a mixture of Alaska North Slope (ANS) produced crudes transported via the trans-Alaska pipeline (in the approximate percentages of 76% Prudhoe Bay, 17% Kuparuk, 5% Endicott, and 2% Lisburne). The PAH fingerprint of fresh *Exxon Valdez* crude is dominated by alkylated naphthalenes, followed by approximately equal abundances of alkylated fluorenes,

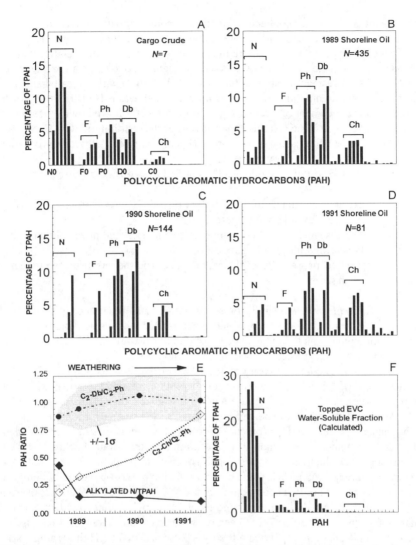

FIGURE 2--PAH fingerprints illustrating recognition criteria and weathering trends for **Exxon Valdez** *crude* **(EVC)**. *(A) Cargo crude is a sample of the* **Exxon Valdez** *cargo. Aliquots are used for interlaboratory calibration. The analysis reported is an average of values obtained by Battelle Ocean Sciences for the fall of 1991. (B) 1989 shoreline oil is the average of all Shoreline Ecology Program (SEP) intertidal fixed-site samples having total PAH (TPAH)>100 ppb(Boehm et al. this volume). (C) 1990 shoreline oil is the average of 144 intertidal samples from the bioremediation study (Prince et al. 1991; 1994). (D) 1991 shoreline oil is the average of SEP intertidal fixed-site samples having TPAH >100 ppb. (E) EVC weathering trends for selected PAH ratios. Data points are for the averages shown in figures A, B, C, and D. (F) Calculated PAH distribution for the WSF of topped EVC (see text).*

phenanthrenes, and dibenzothiophenes, and minor amounts of chrysenes (Figure 2A). As it weathers, *Exxon Valdez* crude is depleted in the most water-soluble constituents (naphthalenes more than fluorenes, more than phenanthrenes, etc.) and relatively enriched in the least water-soluble constituents (chrysenes) (Figures 2B-D). As a consequence, the light PAH (LPAH) decrease relative to the total PAH (TPAH) with increased aging (weathering). With weathering, the PAH acquire a "water-washed" distribution in which the most-soluble component of a series, C_0, disappears first followed by the next most-soluble (C_1), and so on. The result is enhancement of the distribution: $C_0 < C_1 < C_2 < C_3$ for each of the series naphthalene (N), fluorene (F), phenanthrene (Ph), dibenzothiophene (Db), and, to a lesser degree, chrysene (Ch).

Important *Exxon Valdez* crude weathering features considered here are the following:

- Relative constancy of C_2-Db/C_2-Ph (and C_3-Db/C_3-Ph) regardless of the degree of weathering (Figure 2E)
- Increase in alkylated chrysenes relative to alkylated phenanthrenes (and dibenzothiophenes) (Figure 2E)
- Preferential removal of the naphthalenes and the unsubstituted parent of each series

Water Soluble Fraction (WSF) Fingerprints--A small fraction of fresh crude oil is soluble in water. Its PAH fingerprint, which is determined by the solubilities of the individual compounds, can look like and be mistaken for that of fresh diesel. However, the two are readily distinguished by their alkane composition.

The WSF is a complex mixture of low-molecular-weight alkanes (C_1-C_{10}) and aromatics (C_6-C_{16}). Solubilities decrease rapidly with increasing molecular weight, and, for a given carbon number, aromatics are much more soluble than alkanes (McAuliffe 1987). Alkanes with carbon numbers greater than C_{10} (decane) and aromatics with carbon numbers greater than C_{16} (pyrene) have very low solubilities in water. Under spill conditions the low-molecular-weight ($< C_{10}$) compounds evaporate quickly, and the light PAH, although individually in low- or sub-ppb concentrations, dominate the WSF. These concentrations are commonly below the detection limits for most biological samples.

The distribution of PAH compounds in the WSF of topped *Exxon Valdez* crude (heated until 20% by weight has evaporated to simulate spill oil that stranded on Prince William Sound shorelines in 1989) has been determined experimentally and has also been calculated from equilibrium partitioning theory. The calculated PAH fingerprint (plotted as a percentage of TPAH) is shown in Figure 2F. Important features are: (a) dominance of the naphthalenes (83% of TPAH), (b) absence of or very low levels of chrysenes, and (c) $C_0 > C_1 > C_2 > C_3$ for each parent-alkylated homologous series. As the oil weathers the more soluble constituents are removed and the composition of the WSF fraction in equilibrium with the residual oil changes concomitantly. The calculated WSF for the 1990 shoreline oil (shown in Figure 3C) has lower TPAH (64 ppb) than the WSF of the topped oil, continuing dominance of alkylated naphthalenes, and a PAH fingerprint similar to that of relatively fresh diesel. We distinguish the two by their alkanes. Diesel typically has an alkane distribution of from about C_{10} to about C_{25} with a maximum at about C_{15}-C_{17}. C_{10}-C_{25} alkanes are

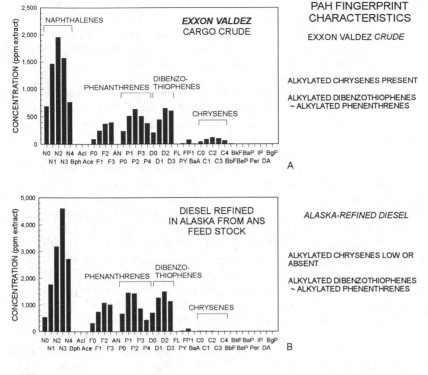

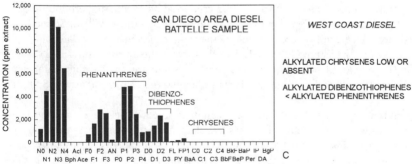

FIGURE 3--PAH fingerprints for petroleum hydrocarbon sources in Prince William Sound and the Gulf of Alaska. (A) **Exxon Valdez** *cargo crude. (B) diesel refined from ANS crude at a Kenai (Alaska) refinery. C_0, C_1, C_2, C_3, and C_4 Chrysene concentrations are 7.4, 7.1, 4.5, 0, and 0 ppm, respectively (C) West coast-refined diesel (San Diego area). C_0, C_1, C_2, C_3, and C_4 Chrysene concentrations are 11.8, 13.4, 0, 0, and 0 ppm, respectively. All analyses conducted by Battelle Ocean Sciences Laboratory on individual samples.*

usually not detected in the WSF. In fact, their presence in a water analysis is commonly used to confirm that a liquid hydrocarbon phase is present. Our interpretations of diesel made in the succeeding sections have been confirmed, whenever possible, by a diesel alkane fingerprint. We have identified no unequivocal WSF fingerprints in any of the biological samples reported in the OSHTF and PWSOIL datasets.

Other Petrogenic Sources--Multiple petrogenic sources (both natural and anthropogenic) of PAH are recognized in the Prince William Sound-Gulf of Alaska area. These include: ANS crude from tanker operations as well as the *Exxon Valdez* cargo crude; refined products (including diesel, kerosene, jet A, gasoline) from ANS and other crudes; Cook Inlet crude (CIC); Monterey, California, tars (Kvenvolden et al. 1993); and Katalla-Yakataga area seep oil (primarily a subtidal component in Prince William Sound; Page et al. Identification of Hydrocarbons Sources in the Benthic Sediments of Prince William Sound and the Gulf of Alaska Following the *Exxon Valdez* Oil Spill, this volume).

Diesel refined largely from ANS crude at Kenai refineries was the dominant diesel sold in the Prince William Sound-Gulf of Alaska region through 1991. The PAH distributions of diesel refined from 100% ANS feed stock at Chevron's Nikiska refinery (shut down in 1991) and fresh *Exxon Valdez* crude are shown in Figures 3A and 3B. Both have similar distributions of the LPAH. In particular, the relative abundances of the alkylated phenanthrenes and dibenzothiophenes are similar and approximately 1. This is because the Kenai refineries were not required to produce low-sulfur diesel. The primary difference between the diesel and *Exxon Valdez* crude PAH fingerprints is the absence or low concentrations of the chrysenes in the diesel. We also differentiate *Exxon Valdez* crude from diesel by the fact that the crude has a wider range of alkanes, typically from the lower end of our analysis technique, C_8-C_{10} (for fresh crudes), to $C_{34}+$. We have used these two features to discriminate *Exxon Valdez* crude and its weathering products from diesel in biological samples. Applying the chrysene feature to Prince William Sound subtidal sediment fingerprints is complicated by the significant levels of alkylated chrysenes derived from eastern Gulf of Alaska seeps that make up the natural PAH background (Page et al. Identification of Hydrocarbon Sources in the Benthic Sediments of Prince William Sound and the Gulf of Alaska Following the *Exxon Valdez* Oil Spill, this volume).

Diesel refined on the U. S. west coast is another potential petrogenic marine contaminant because of the number of vessels traveling along the west coast to and from Alaska. West coast refineries meet lower sulfur emission requirements. Consequently, they commonly have sulfur-removal facilities to handle high sulfur feed stocks, or they blend in low-sulfur crude. A diesel sample collected in San Diego has lower C_2- and C_3-Db/Ph ratios (Figure 3C) than *Exxon Valdez* crude.

The other petroleum sources (Cook Inlet crude, Alaska Peninsula and Katalla-Yakataga seep oils, and Monterey, California, tars) are distinguished from *Exxon Valdez* crude by their lower alkylated dibenzothiophene/alkylated phenanthrene ratios (reflecting lower sulfur contents), and by their higher relative abundances of alkylated chrysenes to alkylated dibenzothiophenes (Page et al. Identification of Hydrocarbon Sources in the Benthic Sediments of Prince William Sound and the Gulf of Alaska Following the *Exxon*

Valdez Oil Spill, this volume). They can be further distinguished by differences in their saturate biomarkers (steranes and hopanes) and carbon isotopes (Kvenvolden et al. 1993).

Chemical parameters diagnostic of the hydrocarbon sources found in Prince William Sound and the Gulf of Alaska are available from the authors.

REPORTING LIMITS

Detection of the alkylated homologues of phenanthrene, dibenzothiophene, and chrysene is crucial to the identification of the source of petrogenic hydrocarbons found in biological tissues from the spill area. Thus, the ability of GC/MS to detect an analyte (called the instrument detection limit), the 99% confidence that a measured and reported value is greater than zero (method detection limit), and the guidelines a laboratory uses for reporting the data (called the reporting limit) are important.

Method detection limits (MDL) are usually determined by statistical analysis of a prescribed series of analytical runs. These limits not only vary among analytes but also can vary significantly among laboratories and among individual instrument and technician combinations in a single laboratory. They are sensitive to sample size. Reporting limits are normally a factor of three to five greater than the method detection limit. It is common practice to report analyte concentrations that are below the reporting limit with an attached qualifier code indicating lower confidence in that analysis. Some laboratories also report analyte concentrations that are below the method detection limit but above the instrument detection limit. Confidence that these values are greater than zero is less than 99%, and they are usually qualified accordingly. Qualifier codes and MDLs are not provided for any of the OSHTF data or for many analyses reported in PWSOIL. Accordingly, we have fingerprinted all reported analyses in both datasets.

Estimates of analyte reporting limits in a dataset (e.g. eggshells, livers, etc.) can be obtained by plotting the reported concentrations of analyte pairs (e.g., C_2-Ph vs C_2-Ch) against each other for the entire range of concentrations. The estimated reporting limit for an analyte is, essentially, the lowest reported value for that analyte. In 1989 the estimated reporting limits for these analytes in PWSOIL mussels appear to be 4 to 10 ppb. In 1990 and 1991 they are somewhat lower. OSHTF (1989-1991) shellfish reporting limits for these analytes ranged from 0.3 to 1 ppb depending upon the analyte.

Some 1989 analyses of fish samples are reported in PWSOIL with individual PAH analyte values below the lab reporting limit of 1 ppb. However, in 1990 and 1991 the 1 ppb reporting limit was adhered to by that lab (T. J. McDonald, Geochemical and Environmental Research Group, Texas A&M University, personal communication, March 1993). To make the data compatible for the purpose of fingerprinting, 1989 values of alkylated PAH < 1 ppb (after rounding to the nearest 0.1 ppb), reported by that laboratory, are assigned concentrations of zero.

FINGERPRINTING PROCEDURES

The procedure described below specifically applies to the PAH analyses of biological samples reported in PWSOIL and OSHTF. The principles, however, have general application to other spill situations where the criteria needed to discriminate among the various hydrocarbon components may differ. It is important to note that distinguishing criteria, such as PAH analyte ratios, are laboratory-dependent, and direct comparisons of analyses from two laboratories may not be possible without interlaboratory calibrations. This does not diminish the effectiveness of the method but serves as a note of caution regarding how the method is applied.

Classification of Components

Nomenclature--Our procedures recognize the specific patterns of PROCEDURAL ARTIFACTS alone; EVC (*Exxon Valdez* crude) (or ANS crude); DIESEL; WSF (the water-soluble fraction) of crude or diesel; and NON-ANS petrogenic hydrocarbons. In addition it recognizes a component (PETRO) that is related to ANS sources (*Exxon Valdez* crude, diesel, or WSF) but cannot be further defined. PETRO has a diesel fingerprint (alkylated dibenzothiophenes present and alkylated chrysenes absent). This may be explained in one of four ways: (1) it is *Exxon Valdez* crude, but the levels of the alkylated phenanthrenes (e.g., C_2-Ph) are low, indicating that the chrysenes, which are usually in much lower concentrations than the phenanthrenes, might be below their detection limits for the sample; (2) it is EVC, but the chrysenes have been excluded by selective uptake; (3) it is a WSF of crude or diesel; or (4) it is diesel.

Selective uptake of the PAH in internal tissues can preferentially exclude the alkylated chrysenes. Consequently, the C_2-Ph levels at which *Exxon Valdez* crude chrysenes can be detected differ with tissue types. For example, the C_2-Ph level required for the detection of C_2-Ch from *Exxon Valdez* crude is 10 ppb for samples containing external surfaces collected in 1990-1991 and 35 ppb for liver (based on limited data). The amount of C_2-Ph required for *Exxon Valdez* crude alkylated chrysenes detection in fats and other lipid-rich internal tissues and fluids is unknown and may depend on the type and duration of exposure. In PWSOIL, alkylated chrysenes were not detected in the fat of heavily oiled sea otters, even with C_2-Ph as high as 190 ppb.

Two other categories, alkylated naphthalenes (ALKYL NAPH) and UNRESOLVED, are used to classify low levels of petrogenic PAH, the sources of which cannot be identified. ALKYL NAPH contains only alkylated napthalenes plus the analytes in PROCEDURAL ARTIFACTS. It is commonly observed in internal tissues from samples collected from both within the spill path and without. The classification UNRESOLVED is used when alkylated fluorenes or phenanthrenes (plus the alkylated napthalenes and required reporting analytes) are present but alkylated dibenzothiophenes are not. The PAH levels are too low for the source to be identified.

The sources of ALKYL NAPH and UNRESOLVED could be light refined products such as kerosene (Jet A), laboratory contaminants such as cleaning solvents, low levels of unweathered ANS crude, low-sulfur Cook Inlet crude, diesel, or the WSF of any of these. Additional information such as location and year of collection can limit the

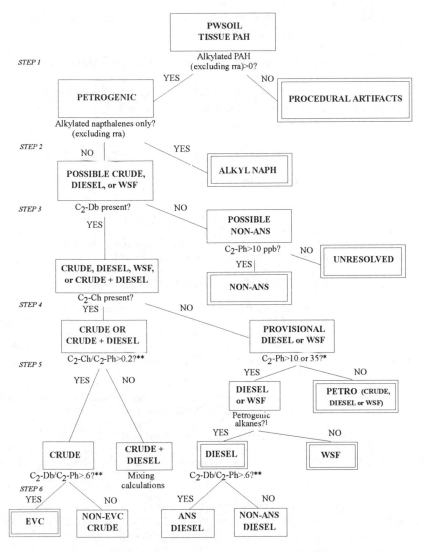

*   Depends on tissue type and weathering state of oil. No limit was established for fat, blubber, brain, blood, or other internal tissue other than liver) and C_2-Ch/C_2-Ph ratio (see text).
[1]   See text for discussion of criteria.
** These ratios vary among labs and are procedure-dependent. Ratios involving Db varied so widely in PWSOIL that we did not do Step 6. High-quality data can resolve ANS crude and ANS-refined diesel from low-S crudes and diesel.

Figure 4--Fingerprint flow chart for PWS-GOA tissue PAH reported in PWSOIL.

number of possibilities. For example, if the sample represents a control collected in eastern Prince William Sound, well outside of the spill path, there is little likelihood it contains *Exxon Valdez* crude.

Creosote and pyrogenic components are recognized only in OSHTF shellfish samples.

Figure 4 summarizes the steps followed in fingerprinting biological samples. Distinguishing criteria are summarized in Table 2.

TABLE 2--*Distinguishing criteria for PAH components in biological samples*

PROCEDURAL ARTIFACTS	Only the required reporting analytes (rra) are reported.
ALKYL NAPH	Only alkylated naphthalenes are present (in addition to rra).
UNRESOLVED	Alkylated PAH other than naphthalenes present in addition to rra; concentrations are too low to assign a more specific classification.
NON-ANS	Alkylated PAH present in addition to rra; no C_2- Db; C_2-Ph > 10 ppb.
DIESEL	Alkylated PAH present in addition to rra; C_2-Db present; C_2- and Ch not present; C_2-Ph > 10 ppb (weathered external surfaces); C_2-Ph > 35 (unweathered external surfaces, liver, gastrointestinal tract). A diesel designation was not made for other internal tissues/fluids except for one sea-otter-blood sample from the Juneau area collected in 1991, which as a consequence of its location, could not be EVC.
PETRO	Diesel signature but chrysenes are below reporting limits for the tissue involved (defined by C_2-Ph levels; see DIESEL above).
EVC	EVC signature including presence of C_2-Db and C_2-Ch.
WSF (ANS, Diesel)	WSF can have a diesel PAH signature but lacks >C_{10} petrogenic alkanes

Step 1: Identification of Procedural Artifacts and Petrogenic Signatures--The first step in fingerprinting assigns either a petrogenic or a PROCEDURAL ARTIFACTS classification. A petrogenic classification is made if *any* of the alkylated compounds (excluding those among the required reporting analytes) are present.

This first step eliminates more than 60% of the PWSOIL fish and wildlife sample analyses from further consideration because they contain no petrogenic hydrocarbons. The next step ordinarily would be to look at the heavy molecular weight PAH relative to the light molecular weight PAH and the relative distributions of C_1, C_2, and C_3 homologues to identify pyrogenic (and creosote) components (see Figure 1B). However, because many of the biological samples in PWSOIL contain the unsubstituted PAH of the procedural artifacts, we have found it impossible to make reliable pyrogenic distinctions. We have identified pyrogenic hydrocarbons in shellfish reported in OSHTF.

Step 2: Alkylated Naphthalenes--A nongeneric classification, ALKYL NAPH, is given to an analysis that contains only the alkylated naphthalenes (all isomers of C_2-N and C_3-N, excluding those included among the required reporting analytes and C_4-N) in addition to procedural artifacts.

Step 3: Non-ANS and Unresolved--If C_2-Db is present, the fingerprint is crude, diesel, or a crude-diesel mixture. If C_2-Db is not present, and C_2-Ph > 10 ppb, the fingerprint is definitive NON-ANS. However, if C_2-Ph < 10 ppb, further resolution is not possible, and an UNRESOLVED classification is assigned.

Step 4: Classification into Crudes, Provisional Diesels, WSF, or Crude-Diesel Mixtures--Crudes or crude-diesel mixtures (alkylated chrysenes present) and diesels or WSF (alkylated chrysenes absent) are then separated. If C_2-Ch is reported, a crude or crude-plus-diesel mixture assignment is made.

Step 5: Crudes, Diesels, and WSF--The provisional diesel or WSF category on the right side of Figure 4 can be resolved in the following way. If the dataset contains evidence that the contaminating oil is substantially weathered (i.e., C_2-Ch/C_2-Ph $\geq$ 0.5) or if it contains reliable C_2-Ch values down to 2-4 ppb, C_2-Ph has to be >10 ppb (and C_2-Ch = 0) before a classification of DIESEL or WSF is assigned. Samples in this category commonly contain external surfaces. If the contaminating oil is not weathered, or if the dataset contains no reliable C_2-Ch values below 4 ppb, C_2-Ph has to be greater than 35 ppb (and C_2-Ch = 0) before a DIESEL or WSF classification is assigned. With the possible exception of livers, *Exxon Valdez* crude and diesel cannot be distinguished from one another in the internal tissue PAH analyses reported in PWSOIL, even when C_2-Ph = 190 ppb. The concentration levels of the other alkylated phenanthrenes and alkylated chrysenes should be examined at this time to ensure that the reported values for C_2-Ph and C_2-Ch are not aberrant.

In cases where there is no C_2-Ch, and C_2-Ph concentrations are less than the values previously stated, diesel, crude, and WSF cannot be distinguished using the PAH analysis alone. A nongeneric PETRO (crude, diesel, crude-diesel mixtures, or WSF) classification is assigned. If these cannot be resolved by their alkane distributions, additional information such as visual evidence of oiling, year of collection, or the fact that the sample is from a control area should be considered.

The crude or crude-diesel mixture category, on the left side of Figure 4, is handled as follows. All crude-diesel mixtures identified in PWSOIL are classified as *Exxon Valdez* crude in this paper. However, the relative proportions of fresh crude and diesel in the mixture can be estimated by simple mass balance. Fresh ANS in PWSOIL had C_2-Ch/C_2-Ph ~ 0.2 (some 1989 shoreline sediments with high concentrations of oil had C_2-Ch/C_2-Ph ~ 0.1). With weathering this ratio increased, and by July 1990, weathered shoreline oil residues (as determined from the mussel analyses) had C_2-Ch/C_2-Ph ~ 0.6-0.7. Diesel has a C_2-Ch/C_2-Ph = 0. Samples having 0 < C_2-Ch/C_2-Ph < 0.2 are assumed to be mixtures of diesel and crude. The relative proportions of each are calculated assuming two-component mixing. Results are approximate, given the observed variability of the ratio. In this calculation scheme, all C_2-Ch is treated as though it came from crude. In fact, some diesels contain low concentrations of C_2-Ch. Samples having C_2-Ch/C_2-Ph > 0.2 are assumed to be 100% crude, although they could be mixtures of highly weathered crude and diesel. For the reasons discussed above, this calculation should be applied only to external surface or gastrointestinal tract samples.

Fresh diesel and the water-soluble fraction of ANS crude can have very similar PAH fingerprints. When the hydrocarbon concentrations are sufficiently high, diesel is identified by its characteristic petrogenic alkane distribution in the C_{10} to C_{25} range. Alkanes in this range in the WSF are normally too low to be detected.

Step 6: Classification of Crudes and Diesels by Sulfur Content--The crudes and diesels found in the spill area may be subdivided into high-sulfur (e.g., ANS-related) and low-sulfur (e.g., Cook Inlet) categories on the basis of the C_2- and C_3-Db/Ph ratios. These ratios vary among and within laboratories because of procedural differences. For example, when only the parent compound response factors are used in the GC/MS quantification procedure, *Exxon Valdez* crude has C_2-Db/C_2-Ph ~ 1 (Figures 2 and 3) In some laboratories the response factors of the alkylated homologues of phenanthrene are used to quantify the alkylated phenanthrenes. When this procedure is followed, the alkylated phenanthrenes are enhanced relative to the alkylated dibenzothiophenes and the respective C_2- and C_3- ratios are lowered. Consequently, it is important that each laboratory independently determine these values using well-calibrated interlaboratory standards. Inconsistencies in the ratios of alkylated dibenzothiophenes to alkylated phenanthrenes in PWSOIL samples containing obvious *Exxon Valdez* crude may relate to procedural changes in the laboratory. Consequently, all crudes and crude-diesel mixtures identified in Step 5 are classified as *Exxon Valdez* crude, and we have not attempted to separate low-sulfur crudes (Cook Inlet) and diesels (refined on the west coast).

For numerous reasons--e.g., mixed components, high method detection limits, matrix interferences, operator error, transcription errors--some analyses fall into gray areas between classifications. Resolution of these is a judgment call that requires, at a minimum, looking at the overall fingerprint to see if it makes sense (e.g., no single analyte widely out of range) and may even require examination of the individual isomer distributions. The distribution of alkanes can also be used to confirm a PAH fingerprint classification.

DATASETS

Our PAH fingerprinting procedure has been applied to analyses of biological samples in two chemistry datasets: OSHTF and PWSOIL. Together they form the most comprehensive set of hydrocarbon analyses of biological samples collected to study the effects of the *Exxon Valdez* spill. OSHTF contains more than 1 500 tissue sample hydrocarbon analyses (PAH and saturate fraction) and some bile FAC analyses of subsistence foods collected from traditional harvesting sites in the spill area. Results are reported by Varanasi et al. (1990) and in later memos from NOAA, National Marine Fisheries Service (NMFS), to the OSHTF. Analyses are reported for the edible tissues of fish (salmon, halibut, bottom fish, rockfish), pinnipeds (harbor seal, sea lion), intertidal and subtidal shellfish, sea ducks, and deer. The species and tissues selected and the harvesting sites chosen for study were identified by the subsistence users from native villages in Prince William Sound, the Kenai, and Kodiak. Two of the sites, Chenega Bay-Sawmill Bay-Crab Bay area (hereafter referred to as Chenega Bay) and Windy Bay, were in the general spill path. Windy Bay was heavily oiled in 1989; however, Chenega Bay was protected with multiple booms (up to five) and received minimal oil.

Our version of PWSOIL (November 1993) was obtained from Dr. Carol-Ann Manen, National Ocean Service, National Oceanic and Atmospheric Administration, Silver Springs, MD 20910. It contains information on nearly 42 000 samples (tissues, sediments, water, and QA/QC samples). There are nearly 4 700 PAH (plus alkane) analyses (excluding replicates and standards) of biological samples collected in 1989, 1990, and 1991.

RESULTS

The results of our fingerprint analysis that follow are organized by species (fish, birds, mammals, shellfish) and sample type (external surfaces, gastrointestinal tract, and internal tissues/fluids). This distinction enables us to establish that for external surfaces, where tissue uptake, selective metabolism, and depuration are not issues, the procedure works quite well. Hydrocarbons from sources other than *Exxon Valdez* crude (including diesel and procedural artifacts) are clearly recognizable.

Gastrointestinal tract samples are important because they establish an unequivocal link to exposure. For these samples, some modification of the PAH fingerprints by digestive processes might be anticipated. However, we find that, for the majority of gastrointestinal tract analyses, this is not the case. Clear fingerprints of the recognized hydrocarbon sources are found.

Internal tissue/fluid samples are, for two reasons, much more difficult to fingerprint. As noted previously, selective uptake, metabolism, and depuration can alter the fingerprint and, more importantly, PAH levels are usually around the limits of detection for individual analytes. Very few of the internal tissue/fluid samples in PWSOIL and OSHTF have the diagnostic PAH analytes above detection limits. However, several, including liver and blood, have clearly recognizable fingerprints of *Exxon Valdez* crude or diesel. Fat and blubber, on the other hand, appear to fractionate the PAH and make it impossible to differentiate *Exxon Valdez* crude from diesel at the reported concentration levels.

Fish

Contamination of fish by *Exxon Valdez* crude in 1989 was a primary concern because of the important commercial and sport fisheries in Prince William Sound and the Gulf of Alaska and because fish is a major subsistence food harvested in the spill area. Consequently, in 1989, 427 fish samples and sample composites (OSHTF = 200; PWSOIL = 227) of various species were tested and the analyses reported. The OSHTF numbers do not include the more than 900 halibut caught and inspected (81 tested for bile FAC) by

NOAA/NMFS and the International Pacific Halibut Commission (Varanasi 1990). Those results indicated no exposure for halibut caught in the spill-impact zone. In 1990, an additional 251 fish tissues were analyzed (OSHTF = 70; PWSOIL = 181). In addition, more than 2 500 bile samples were collected and analyzed for FAC. Their analyses are reported in PWSOIL.

Salmon--Our fingerprint analysis detected *Exxon Valdez* crude residues in 11.5% (48 of 415) salmon tissue samples (all types) collected in 1989 and 1990 and reported in OSHTF and PWSOIL (Table 3). All of the samples with recognizable *Exxon Valdez* crude contain external surfaces or are from the gastrointestinal tract.

One hundred ninety-nine edible tissue samples pink, red, silver, and chum salmon were analyzed in 1989 and 1990 and the results reported in OSHTF. More than one-half (102) of the analyzed tissues contain less than 1 ppb TPAH (wet weight). Because of these very low TPAH levels (Figure 5A), the Oil Spill Health Task Force pronounced the salmon tissues safe to eat (OSHTF 1990). About one-third (69) of the edible tissue samples contain low levels of nonpetrogenic procedural artifacts. The TPAH levels obtained for smoked salmon from Tatitlek and Kodiak are shown in Figure 5A for the sake of comparison.

A few Kodiak Harbor samples exceed the FDA guideline of 50 ppb TPAH. However, all samples exceeding that guideline contain diesel (Figure 5B) and/or procedural artifacts (and not *Exxon Valdez* crude). Independent of field observations, the fingerprint in Figure 5B could also be classified as a mixture of procedural artifacts and possible traces of *Exxon Valdez* crude, but this is precluded by the time and place the salmon was caught. It is an August 1990 sample from Kodiak Harbor, which was not oiled by *Exxon Valdez* crude. The signature is too fresh for an 18-month-old sample of *Exxon Valdez* crude, and these salmon were caught during clean-up activities following a diesel spill the previous day in Kodiak Harbor (D. S. Page, Bowdoin College, personal communication, April, 1993).

No *Exxon Valdez* crude fingerprints were found in our analysis of the OSHTF data for salmon. Results for all reported tissue analyses are summarized in Figure 5C.

PWSOIL contains PAH analyses of 133 pink salmon samples collected in 1989 (Table 3). Forty-four of these contain detectable *Exxon Valdez* crude PAH (Figure 5D) in concentrations ranging from less than 50 ppb to about 2 000 ppb. By 1990, 4 of 83 samples analyzed had EVC fingerprints (TPAH range 150-450 ppb). In both years, approximately 6-7% of samples analyzed contain diesel (up to 425 ppb TPAH). Procedural artifacts (Figure 5E) and low levels of light alkylated PAH dominate PWSOIL salmon analyses (Table 3, Figure 5F).

Exxon Valdez crude residues (and diesel) are observed in reported analyses of viscera, whole salmon, and salmon fry. All of these samples contain external surfaces or are associated with the gastrointestinal tract. In view of the OSHTF results (no detectable *Exxon Valdez* crude in internal tissues), it is unlikely that the *Exxon Valdez* crude residues detected are in the edible tissues. More likely, they are associated with the external surfaces and the linings and contents of the gastrointestinal tract.

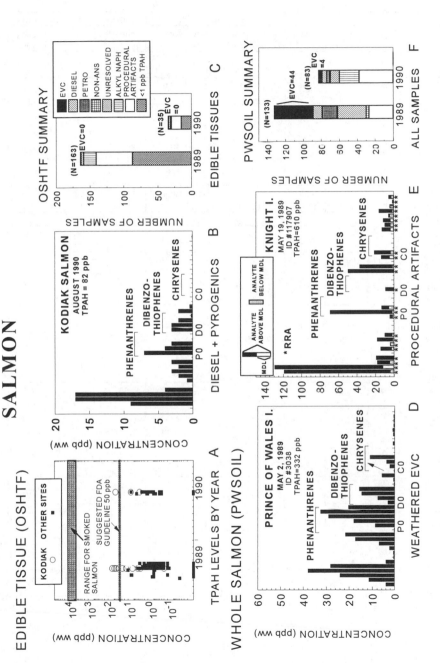

FIGURE 5--Salmon tissue PAH fingerprints and component summaries. RRA = Required Reporting Analyte (see text). Analyses from PWSOIL and OSHTF. MDL = Method detection limit reported in PWSOIL.

TABLE 3--*Salmon and Herring*

SAMPLE TYPE	YEAR	NO. OF SAMPLES	EVC	DEFINITIVE NON-EVC			OTHER NON-EVC FINGERPRINTS		
				PROCEDURAL ARTIFACTS	DIESEL	NON-ANS	PETRO	UNRESOLVED	ALKYL NAPH

PWSOIL — SALMON

SAMPLE TYPE	YEAR	NO. OF SAMPLES	EVC	PROCEDURAL ARTIFACTS	DIESEL	NON-ANS	PETRO	UNRESOLVED	ALKYL NAPH
Whole Salmon	1989	41	14	13	2	1	2	7	2
" "	1990	61	1	38				5	17
Alevin	1989	10		9					1
Viscera	1989	16	12		1		1	2	
Carcass	1989	17	5		1		8	3	
Muscle	1989	1						1	
Fry	1989	47	13	5	6		5	19	
"	1990	22	3		5	1	3	5	5
TPAH	1989	133	40-2000	10-610	100-425	30<100	10-90	5-85	<10-150
RANGE (ppb)	1990	83	150-450	10-135	50-425	20-60	20-30	5-25	<10-35

OSHTF

SAMPLE TYPE	YEAR	NO. OF SAMPLES	EVC	PROCEDURAL ARTIFACTS	DIESEL	NON-ANS	PETRO	UNRESOLVED	ALKYL NAPH
Edible tissue	1989	164*		54	1			4	18
" "	1990	35*		15	1			3	1
TPAH	1989	164		1-117	5			<1-3	<1-5
RANGE (ppb)	1990	35		1-62	20			1-3	1

	SALMON TOTALS	415*	48	134	17	2	19	49	44

* Includes 87 analyses reporting < 1 ppb TPAH in 1989 and 15 in 1990

PWSOIL — HERRING

SAMPLE TYPE	YEAR	NO. OF SAMPLES	EVC	PROCEDURAL ARTIFACTS	DIESEL	NON-ANS	PETRO	UNRESOLVED	ALKYL NAPH
Roe	1989	78	1	52			3	2	20
"	1990	26		23					3
Gonad	1989	9		5					4
Gut	1989	12						1	11
"	1990	9		9					
Viscera	1990	10		8					2
Testes	1990	10		10					
Ovary	1990	10		10					
Muscle	1990	10		10					
Stomach Contents	1990	1		1					

	HERRING TOTALS	175	1	128			3	3	40

TPAH	1989	99	300	<10-200		50-90		10-40	5-140
RANGE (ppb)	1990	76		<10-90					6-17

Bottom fish (Halibut, Sole)--All TPAH analyses of bottom fish tissues reported in OSHTF are at background levels (TPAH ranges from non detect to 2 ppb). Results for fish from spill-path and control sites are indistinguishable. The OSHTF reports hydrocarbon analyses of internal tissues (edible flesh) for 32 halibut caught in 1989 and 1990. No spill-oil fingerprints were detected in our analysis of the data. The PAH reported for 7 sole (5 rock sole and 1 yellowfin sole caught in 1990 and 1 undesignated sole caught in 1989) are low concentrations of procedural artifacts.

PAH fingerprints of the stomach contents of 3 Dover sole and 8 flathead sole caught in 1990 and reported in PWSOIL contain no *Exxon Valdez* crude. Five of the flathead sole have petrogenic PAH fingerprints from non-ANS sources or are unresolved (concentration range 2 to 250 ppb alkylated PAH). The remaining 3 are procedural artifacts with TPAH concentrations ranging from 10 to 110 ppb.

Herring--One of 78 herring roe samples collected in 1989 contains *Exxon Valdez* crude (~300 ppb TPAH attributable to *Exxon Valdez* crude) (Table 3). This sample is from Cabin Bay on Naked Island. Three additional samples from the same location have lower TPAH concentrations, and it is not possible to unequivocally assign their fingerprints *Exxon Valdez* crude classifications. Accordingly, they are classified as PETRO; however, it is likely that they represent low levels of *Exxon Valdez* crude. This finding is consistent with Exxon study results in which *Exxon Valdez* crude residues were found on herring roe in Cabin Bay in April 1989 (Pearson et al. this volume). Other PWSOIL herring samples (74 in 1989 and 97 in 1990) are dominated by procedural artifacts alone (20 to 120 ppb) or procedural artifacts plus up to ~150 ppb of alkylated naphthalenes. While alkylated naphthalenes by themselves do not indicate source, other fingerprints, such as the distributions of C_{18}-C_{24} normal alkanes, indicate that 1989 herring gut samples contain diesel, not *Exxon Valdez* crude.

No herring tissue PAH are reported in OSHTF.

Other Fish--PAH fingerprints of other fish, including several species of cod, rockfish, greenling, Dolly Varden, and Irish lord (22 in 1989 and 15 in 1990), reported in OSHTF, are due to very low levels (<10 ppb) of procedural artifacts.

PWSOIL reports tissue analyses for rockfish (3) and greenling (2) caught in 1989 and prickleback (6), sculpin (1) and unidentified fish (1) caught in 1990. In addition, it reports analyses for the stomach contents of 3 Pacific cod caught in Orca Bay in 1990. For 1989, 3 of the 5 tissue analyses report procedural artifacts, 1 greenling has alkylated naphthalenes, and 1 rockfish has either diesel or EVC (PETRO). In 1990, 1 of the 8 tissue analyses contains either diesel or EVC. The remainder are procedural artifacts. Two of the Pacific cod stomach contents analyses report procedural artifacts. The other is unresolved.

Birds

Sea Ducks--*Exxon Valdez* crude residues ranging from about 60 to 1 000 ppb are identified in the stomach contents of 7 sea ducks (6 in 1989 and 1 in 1990) from all species reported in PWSOIL (Table 4; Figures 6A, C). None of the 40 sea-duck liver

SEA DUCKS

A. Main Bay, September 15, 1989

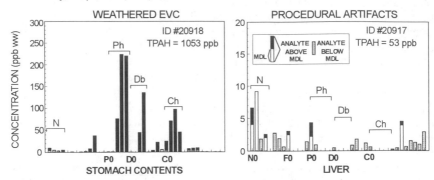

B. Foul Bay, January 15, 1990

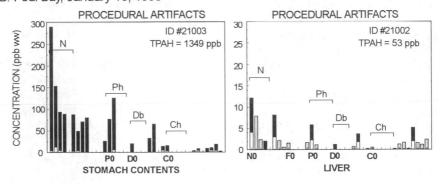

C. Sea-Duck Fingerprint Summary Results

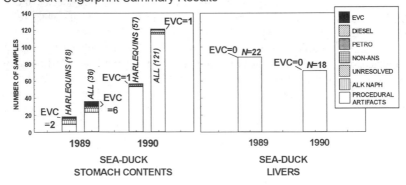

FIGURE 6--PAH fingerprints for the stomach contents and liver of two Harlequin Ducks collected at Main Bay (A) and Foul Bay (B) in western Prince William Sound. Summary of PAH fingerprint results for all sea duck analyses reported in PWSOIL. MDL = Method detection limit reported in PWSOIL.

TABLE 4--*Sea ducks*

SPECIES	YEAR	NO. OF SAMPLES	EVC	DEFINITIVE NON-EVC			OTHER NON-EVC FINGERPRINTS		
				PROCEDURAL ARTIFACTS	DIESEL	NON-ANS	PETRO	UNRESLVD	ALKYL NAPH
LIVER									
Barrows	1989	2		2					
Goldeneye	1990	6		6					
Common	1989	3		3					
Goldeneye	1990	2		2					
Harlequin	1989	10		10					
	1990	8		8					
White Wing	1989	5		5					
Scoter	1990	1		1					
Surf Scoter	1989	2		2					
	1990	1		1					
LIVER TOTALS		40		40					
STOMACH CONTENTS									
Barrows	1989	12	3	9					
Goldeneye	1990	37		35				1	1
Common	1989	1	1						
Goldeneye	1990	10		10					
Harlequin	1989	18	2	9				2	5
	1990	56	1	52				2	1
	-	1		1					
White Wing	1989								
Scoter	1990	13		13					
Surf Scoter	1989	5		5					
	1990	3		3					
Black Scoter	1989								
	1990	1		1					
STOMACH CONTENT TOTALS		157	7	138				5	7
WHOLE DUCK									
Harlequin	1989	1		1					
GRAND TOTALS		198	7	179				5	7
TPAH RANGE (ppb)	1989	59	60-1 000	33-2064				40-50	20-40
	1990	138	1 100	23-3 708				15-100	8-15
	-	1		49					

analyses reported in PWSOIL, including those from birds having recognizable crude residues in their stomach contents, contain detectable levels of petrogenic PAH (Table 4). Only procedural artifacts (Figures 6A, B), at TPAH levels ranging from 35 to 269 ppb, are identified (Figure 6C). This suggests that the majority of the PAH are passed through the duck's digestive system and excreted rather than entering the blood stream and passing on to the liver. This conclusion is supported by bile FAC analyses reported in PWSOIL for 3 of the 7 sea ducks that have detectable *Exxon Valdez* crude residue in their stomachs. Only 1 of the 3 have bile FAC elevated above values for controls collected in eastern Prince William Sound and in the Juneau area.

The large majority of reported stomach-contents analyses (~90%) contain only the required reporting analytes (Table 4, Figure 6B) and are classified as procedural artifacts. Their TPAH concentrations range from <25 ppb to as high as 3 700 ppb for a very small sample (0.029 grams wet weight)(Table 4).

OSHTF reported summary results for 20 livers of sea ducks shot by Alaska Department of Fish and Game personnel in Prince William Sound and on Kodiak in the winters of 1989 and 1990. Because dates and locations of collection as well as the investigator sample numbers are similar, some of these may be the same birds reported in PWSOIL. Consequently, the OSHTF results are not included in Table 4. None of the OSHTF livers contain any detectable petrogenic hydrocarbons. Unsubstituted PAH, alkylated naphthalenes and methyl phenanthrene, are present at levels ranging from a few ppb to 120 ppb. They are attributed to procedural artifacts.

Eagles--Twenty-four of 66 bald eagle eggshells collected in 1989 and reported in PWSOIL have extensively weathered *Exxon Valdez* crude PAH (Table 5 and Figure 7A) in concentrations ranging from less than 100 ppb to ~5 000 ppb. By 1990, only 1 of 54 eggshells analyzed contained traces of *Exxon Valdez* crude (450-800 ppb *Exxon Valdez* crude TPAH), and those traces are mixed with diesel.

Thirty-two of the 66 eggshells from 1989 and 36 of the 54 eggshells from 1990 contain high concentrations of diesel (<100-30 000 ppb TPAH) (Figure 7B). Unexpectedly high concentrations of relatively fresh diesel (ppm levels of individual analytes and up to 27 000 ppb TPAH) are found on eggshells collected in eastern Prince William Sound in 1990 at sites far removed from the spill path. Of the 68 samples having diesel PAH, 59 have alkanes from petroleum sources. The remainder (9) have alkane concentrations that are too low to be recognizable. The alkanes confirm a diesel classification for 55 of the 59 (93%) samples. Plant wax alkanes (C_{25}-C_{33}) are also evident in the eggshell data (Figure 7B). Egg and egg-contents analyses also indicate diesel contamination at levels ranging from 225 to 500 ppb TPAH (Table 5). The remainder contain low levels of alkylated PAH that cannot be further resolved or procedural artifacts. Figure 7C summarizes the eggshell PAH fingerprint analyses by year.

Twenty-eight of 68 prey remnant analyses reported in PWSOIL for samples collected in 1989 contain *Exxon Valdez* crude residues (up to 260 ppm TPAH *Exxon Valdez* crude), and 17 contain diesel (up to 2 100 ppb) (Table 5). The remainder contain low levels of alkylated PAH that cannot be further resolved or procedural artifacts. By 1990, 2 of 20 analyses of prey remnants contain *Exxon Valdez* crude residues (150 and 2

BALD EAGLE EGGSHELLS

A. Spill Path: Heavily Weathered EVC

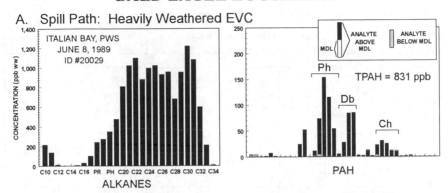

B. Eastern Prince William Sound Control: Water-washed Diesel

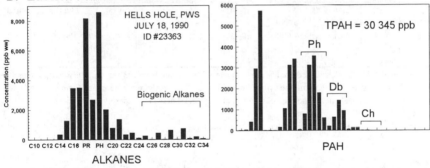

C. Eggshell Summary Results

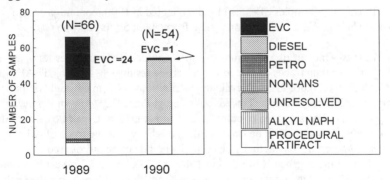

FIGURE 7--Alkane and PAH fingerprints of weathered EVC (A) and water-washed diesel (B) on two bald eagle eggshells collected in Prince William Sound from a spill-path and a control site, respectively. The alkane fingerprints confirm the PAH identifications. (C) Summary results for bald eagle eggshell analyses reported in PWSOIL.

TABLE 5--*Bald eagles*

SAMPLE TYPE	YEAR	NO. OF SAMPLES	EVC	DEFINITIVE NON-EVC			OTHER NON-EVC FINGERPRINTS		
				PROCEDURAL ARTIFACTS	DIESEL	NON-ANS	PETRO	UNRESOLVED	ALKYL NAPH
Egg	1989	3				3			
Egg	1989	20	1	15					4
contents	1990	27		25	1				1
Eggshells	1989	66	24	7	33		1	1	
"	1990	54	1	17	36				
Prey	1989	68	28	7	17		5	5	6
remnants[1]	1990	20	2	7				3	8
"	undated	1		1					
Feather	1989	1				1			
Eagle blood	1989	22		22					
TOTALS		**282**	**56**	**101**	**91**		**6**	**9**	**19**
TPAH RANGE (ppb)	1989	180	50-260 000*	10-277	55 30 000		50-150	25-235	<10-55
	1990	101	150-1000	10-130	235-27 000			<10-115	<10-50
	undated	1		150					

[1]Early version of PWSOIL classified these as "prey remnants;" the November 1993 version of PWSOIL reclassified them as "stomach contents." We retain the original classification because these are samples of animal carcasses found in the vicinity of eagle nests and are not residues of prey found in the stomachs of eagles (Schempf and Bowman 1990).
*EVC concentration >4 800 ppb are restricted to prey remnants.

700 ppb TPAH). The remainder contain procedural artifacts or low levels of alkylated PAH.

Twenty-two samples of eagle blood, collected in 1990, contain procedural artifacts (Table 5). Their TPAH concentrations range from about 50 to 225 ppb.

Murres--One out of 103 common-murre eggshell PAH analyses reported in PWSOIL may contain traces of *Exxon Valdez* crude residues (~400 ppb TPAH) (Table 6) mixed with diesel (Figure 8A). The alkane distributions confirm a diesel component on this sample. All of these eggshells were collected at Puale Bay (Alaska Peninsula) in 1989 and 1990. Puale Bay is an area of active petroleum seeps (Oil Creek flows into Shelikof Strait immediately south of Puale Bay), so the possibility that the trace of what appears to be *Exxon Valdez* crude may actually be seep oil should not be discounted.

Many of the eggshells (34 of 64 in 1989 and 17 of 39 in 1990) are contaminated with weathered diesel in concentrations ranging from about 100 ppb to 5 100 ppb TPAH (Table 6 and Figure 8A). Ninety percent of these PAH classifications are confirmed by their alkane distributions. The remainder cannot be confirmed because the alkane concentrations are too low. Twelve eggshells most likely contain diesel, but these are classified PETRO (diesel or *Exxon Valdez* crude) because of low levels of phenanthrenes and no detectable chrysenes. However, alkane distributions confirm that 9 of the 12 contain diesel. Nearly one-third of the samples analyzed in 1989 contain only low levels

COMMON MURRE EGGSHELLS

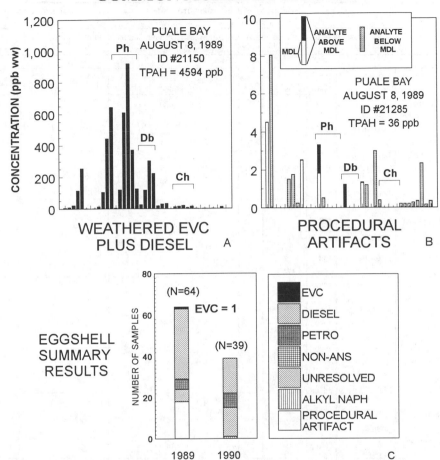

FIGURE 8--Selected PAH fingerprints and summary of results for murre eggshells.
Analyses from PWSOIL. MDL = Method detection limit reported in PWSOIL.

of procedural artifacts (Figure 8B). Table 6 and Figure 8C summarize the fingerprinting
results by year.

Other Birds--Table 6 summarizes our fingerprint analysis of other bird results
reported in PWSOIL. Of 342 analyses (all tissue types), 16 samples (13 collected in 1989
and 3 in 1990) have Exxon Valdez crude PAH fingerprints. Weathered Exxon Valdez
crude occurs in the stomach oils of 10 of 39 fork-tailed storm petrels (400 - 6 400 ppb
TPAH Exxon Valdez crude) from Elizabeth Island on the southwest Kenai and on 2 petrel
eggs (~3 250 ppb TPAH Exxon Valdez crude). In addition, feathers from 3 tufted

TABLE 6--*Murres and other birds*

SPECIES	SAMPLE TYPE	YEAR	NO. OF SAMPLES	EVC	DEFINITIVE NON-EVC PROCEDURAL ARTIFACTS	DIESEL	NON-ANS	OTHER NON-EVC FINGERPRINTS PETRO	UNRESLVD	ALKYL NAPH
Murres	Eggshells	1989	64	1	18	33		5	7	
	"	1990	39			17		7	14	1
Black Oystercatcher	Egg	1989	8		2	5				1
	Eggshells	1989	4		1			1		2
	Egg Contents	1989	1		1					
Pigeon Guillemots	Liver	1989	5		5					
	Egg Contents	-	5		4	1				
	Eggshells	1989	3		1	2				
	"	-	5			5				
	Whole	-	1		1					
Fork-Tailed Storm Petrel	Stomach Oil	1989	39	10	16	4	2	7		
	Egg	1989	3	2	1					
	Egg Contents	1989	2		1					1
	" "	1990	17		14					3
	Eggshells	1989	2			2				
	"	1990	17*		1					15
Black-Legged Kittiwake	Eggshells	1989	1			1				
	"	1990	4		4					
	Egg Contents	1989	1		1					
	" "	1990	4		4					
	Liver	1989	10		10					
	"	1990	14		14					
	Stomach Contents	1990	14		1			12		
		1991	1					1		
	Feather	1990	1			1				
Marbled Murrelets	Liver	1989	9		6				2	1
	"	1990	18		18					
Black Turnstones	Liver	1989	7		7					
	"	1990	4		4					
	Eggshell	-	1			1				
Rock Sandpipers	Liver	1989	2		2					
	Kidney	1989	1		1					
Surfbirds	Liver	1989	1		1					
	"	1990	4		4					
Tufted Puffin	Feather	1990	3	3						
	Gut	1989	1		1					
	Liver	1989	1		1					
Horned Puffin	Feather	1989	1			1				
	Gut	1989	1		1					
Peregrine Falcons	Egg Contents	1990	12		12					
	Eggshells	1990	13							13
	TOTALS		**342***	**16**	**155**	**73**	**2**	**33**	**24**	**37**

*Includes one non-detect

TABLE 6 (Continued)--*Murres and other birds*

SPECIES	SAMPLE TYPE	YEAR	NO. OF SAMPLES	EVC	DEFINITIVE NON-EVC			OTHER NON-EVC FINGERPRINTS		
					PROCEDURAL ARTIFACTS	DIESEL	NON-ANS	PETRO	UNRESLVD	ALKYL NAPH
TPAH RANGE (ppb)		1989	169	63-6 400	12-400	100-5 100	75-200	30-720	13-90	20-82
		1990	162	1 100-	8-700	100-750		10-216	15-140	5-35
		1991	1	10 000				30		
		-	12	000	40-340	200-20 000				

puffins collected in 1990 also contain *Exxon Valdez* crude residues (1 400 -10 000 ppb TPAH *Exxon Valdez* crude).

In addition to the eagle and murre analyses summarized above, diesel is also found in the analyses of eggs and eggshells collected in 1989 by other bird studies. These include the eggs of black oystercatchers (5 eggs containing up to 470 ppb TPAH diesel) and pigeon guillemots (7 eggs with up to 20 000 ppb TPAH diesel). The stomach oils of 4 fork-tailed storm petrels, collected in 1989, also contain up to 700 ppb TPAH diesel.

Of the 342 analyses from bird studies reported in PWSOIL, 155 contain only procedural artifacts in concentrations ranging from 8 to over 700 ppb (Table 6).

MAMMALS

Marine Mammals

Sea Otters--Overall, 17 of the 574 PAH analyses of otter samples reported in PWSOIL have recognizable *Exxon Valdez* crude. An additional 25 assigned to the PETRO category are probably *Exxon Valdez* crude because they came from visibly oiled animals and have most, but not all, of the characteristics of *Exxon Valdez* crude (i.e., alkylated chrysenes were absent).

To assess oil exposure in different tissues, we have subdivided sea-otter samples into three categories: those containing external surfaces (e.g., skin, hair); those associated with the gastrointestinal tract (e.g., intestines, viscera, stomach contents); and samples of internal tissues and body fluids (e.g., liver, fat, brain, blood, milk). Results are reported in Table 7.

Most of the samples having recognizable *Exxon Valdez* crude (Figure 9A) have external surfaces (Table 7; Figure 9C). Two samples (both hair) contain diesel PAH (Figure 9B). These are confirmed by their alkane distributions. Two intestine samples have identifiable *Exxon Valdez* crude (Table 7). One intestine sample appears to contain diesel, but it is near the reporting limit for alkylated chrysene and may not be definitive.

More than half of the gastrointestinal tract samples contain only procedural artifacts (Figure 9F).

Two of the internal tissue/fluid samples (livers) showed *Exxon Valdez* crude (Figure 9D), suggesting that the technique may work, at least for liver. A complete *Exxon Valdez* crude fingerprint was not seen in fat even at 7 000 ppb petrogenic PAH. At these PAH levels, fat from heavily oiled animals has a fingerprint resembling that of ANS diesel (Figure 9E). Reported analyses of body fluids, such as blood and milk, have considerably less petrogenic PAH than fat, and none have *Exxon Valdez* crude fingerprints. Diesel PAH are identified in the blood of a reference-area sea otter sampled in 1991 from southeast Alaska (Figure 9G), and procedural artifacts are identified in a sea otter-milk sample (Figure 9H). The only PAH found in the majority of internal tissue/fluid samples are procedural artifacts (Figure 9I). The petrogenic PAH (i.e., PAH other than procedural artifacts) reported for internal tissues/fluids are generally too low for source identification by this fingerprinting technique. Taking the visibly oiled otters as a basis, the highest levels of petrogenic PAH in internal tissue/fluids are found in fat, followed by the brain, kidney, liver, and muscle, in roughly that order.

Petrogenic PAH in Table 7 and Figure 9 reflect the year the sea otters were collected from the field, not the sample collection year reported in PWSOIL, which was often the date tissue was taken from frozen carcasses (B. E. Ballachey, U. S. Fish and Wildlife Service, personal communication, February 1993; Mulcahy and Ballachey 1992, 1993). The reported analyses of many of these samples contained only alkylated naphthalenes. As petrogenic PAH increased, alkylated compounds other than naphthalenes were detected, but generally only at the highest PAH levels.

In 1990, sea otter pups from unoiled eastern Prince William Sound and western Prince William Sound control bays generally have the same levels of alkylated napthalenes and other alkylated PAH in their fat as otters from western Prince William Sound spill-path locations (Figure 10). Procedural artifacts form the dominant PAH component in each sample group. The alkylated PAH levels are 5 to 10 times lower than levels in the fat of heavily oiled animals collected in 1989. There appears to be little correlation between petrogenic naphthalenes and phytane, the branched alkane often used to identify oil. Reference sea otters from southeast Alaska sampled in 1991 have no petrogenic napthalenes in their fat. There are no otter fat data in PWSOIL for Prince William Sound otters in 1991.

Pinnipeds--Edible tissues (liver, blubber, kidney, and skeletal muscle) from 6 harbor seals and 9 sea lions collected for the OSHTF in 1989 from locations along the spill path in Prince William Sound and the Gulf of Alaska contain no recognizable *Exxon Valdez* crude. Low levels (up to ~7 ppb) of procedural artifacts are reported. These animals were, at most, only moderately oiled.

PWSOIL contains 72 harbor seal tissue analyses for samples collected in 1989 and 25 from 1990. Analyses of 23 sea lion tissues from 1989 and one from 1990 are also reported. As with sea otters, the only PAH in most of these samples are procedural artifacts. A number of internal tissue and fluid samples contain low levels of alkylated naphthalenes other than procedural artifacts.

SEA OTTERS

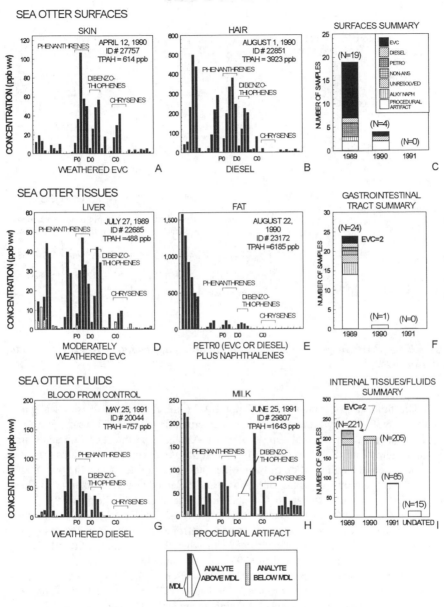

FIGURE 9--PAH fingerprints and summary of components in sea otter tissue, fluids, and surfaces. Analyses from PWSOIL. MDL = Method detection limit reported in PWSOIL.

SEA OTTER PUPS

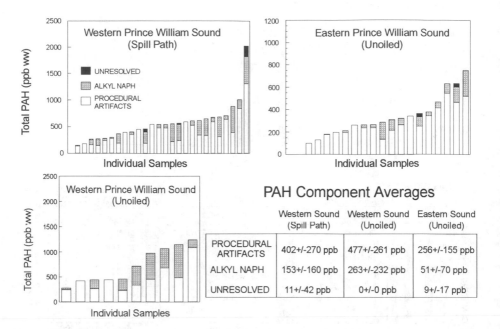

FIGURE 10--PAH components in fat from sea otter pups captured in Prince William Sound in 1990.

One fluid sample containing 1 200 ppb PAH (milk from a Bay of Isles seal pup collected in 1989) has a weathered *Exxon Valdez* crude fingerprint. This sample was taken from the stomach of a seal pup (K. J. Frost, Alaska Department of Fish and Game, personal communication, February 1993). The *Exxon Valdez* crude it contains probably came from external contamination of the mother, and was ingested when the pup nursed.

Two surface samples (skin) of harbor seals, collected near Ketchikan in southeast Alaska in 1990, contain 1 150 and 3 400 ppb diesel (Figure 11A). The diesel PAH classification is confirmed by the alkane distribution (Figure 11B). None of the internal tissues from these two animals contain detectable petrogenic hydrocarbons. This suggests that exposure to diesel occurred shortly before or when the seals were collected. No *Exxon Valdez* crude was detected in any 1990 or 1991 samples.

Figures 11C and 11D summarize the PAH fingerprint analysis by year for harbor seals and sea lions, respectively, as reported by the OSHTF and PWSOIL. The single sample having an *Exxon Valdez* crude PAH fingerprint is the 1989 harbor seal milk sample. Alkanes confirm that identification. One blubber sample taken from a Bay of Isles seal collected in 1989 contains what is probably *Exxon Valdez* crude, but at concentrations too low to be certain. It is classified as PETRO. No samples collected in 1990 contain recognizable *Exxon Valdez* crude.

TABLE 7--*Sea otters*

SAMPLE TYPE	YEAR	NO. OF SAMPLES	EVC	DEFINITIVE NON-EVC PROCEDURAL ARTIFACTS	DIESEL	NON-ANS	OTHER NON-EVC FINGERPRINTS PETRO	UNRESLVD	ALKYL NAPH
INTERNAL TISSUES/FLUIDS									
Blood	1989	18		15					3
"	1990	95		66				1	28
"	1991	39		38	1				
Brain	1989	17		3			6	4	4
Fat	1989	46		23			6	1	16
	1990	91		21				8	62
	1991	2		2					
	undated	15		15					
Kidney	1989	16		6			2	3	5
"	1991	10		10					
Liver	1989	102	2	59			3	5	33
"	1990	18		18					
"	1991	11		11					
Milk	1990	1						1	
"	1991	11		11					
Muscle	1989	15		8			2	2	3
"	1991	12		12					
Placenta	1989	3		3					
Testes	1989	4		2			2		
EXTERNAL SURFACES									
Hair	1989	16	10	1	1		3		1
"	1990	4	1	2	1				
Skin	1989	3	2	1					
GASTROINTESTINAL TRACT									
Stomach Con	1990	1		1					
Intestines	1989	24	2	14	1	1	1	2	3
TOTALS		575[+]	17	343[+]	4	1	25	27	158

	YEAR	NO. OF SAMPLES	EVC	PROCEDURAL ARTIFACTS	DIESEL	NON-ANS	PETRO	UNRESLVD	ALKYL NAPH
	1989	265	155-30 000	<10-725	100-700	155	25-7 000	22-490	<10-180
TPAH RANGE (ppb)	1990	210[+]		10-610	100-3 400		730	10-350	<10-680
	1991	85		11-1 640	620				
	undated	15		50-145					

[+]Includes 1 sample with an 8/30/90 date but no sample-type designation

MARINE MAMMALS

HARBOR SEAL SKIN

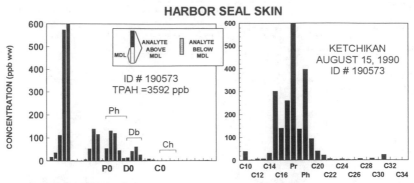

A. Polycyclic Aromatic Hydrocarbons B. Alkanes

PINNIPED SUMMARY

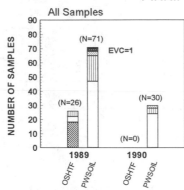 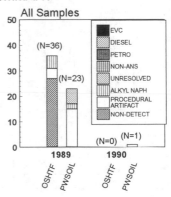

C. Harbor Seals   D. Sea Lions

FIGURE 11--Pinniped diesel PAH fingerprints (A, B) and summary of results for Harbor Seals (C) and Sea Lions (D). Analyses from PWSOIL and OSHTF. MDL = Method detection limit reported in PWSOIL.

Cetaceans--PWSOIL reports PAH analyses for 10 internal tissue samples of cetaceans (whales) collected in 1989 and 4 collected in 1990. The Oil Spill Health Task Force did not arrange to have any cetacean tissues tested. No *Exxon Valdez* crude signature is present in the PWSOIL analyses of any tissues from cetaceans found dead. With one exception, the analyses consist of procedural artifacts (40 to 400 ppb TPAH) plus non-ANS petrogenic PAH. Blubber from one gray whale contains 400 ppb TPAH from an unspecified source (PETRO). Liver tissue from what may be the same animal contains less than 150 ppb unresolved petrogenic hydrocarbons plus an estimated 160 ppb procedural artifacts. The PAH analysis of liver tissue from a killer whale found dead in Port Gravina (eastern Prince William Sound) in April 1990 contains ~100 ppb alkylated naphthalenes and about 400 ppb procedural artifacts.

Terrestrial Mammals

Brown Bear--Forty-five hydrocarbon analyses are reported in PWSOIL for brown bear feces collected on the Alaska Peninsula in 1989. An additional 10 feces samples are undated, and the collection sites are not indicated.

Our analysis of the PAH data indicates that one sample contains low levels (~150 ppb) of weathered *Exxon Valdez* crude, 4 contain up to 650 ppb diesel plus 100 to 200 ppb procedural artifacts (Figure 12A), and 5 may be either highly weathered *Exxon Valdez* crude or diesel but are assigned PETRO on the basis of detection limit criteria. The remainder report only procedural artifacts (19), procedural artifacts plus alkylated naphthalenes (23), or such low concentrations of petrogenic hydrocarbons that they cannot be further resolved (3). The normal alkane distributions of all feces samples are dominated by biogenic (structured terrestrial) compounds in the C_{21}-C_{31} region (Figure 12B). No analyses are reported for samples collected in 1990. These results, summarized in Figure 12C, indicate that the Alaskan brown bear was only minimally exposed to spill oil in 1989.

Two internal tissue (liver and brain) and 2 stomach contents analyses for bears shot in 1989 report only procedural artifacts (<10 to 100 ppb TPAH).

Sitka Black-Tailed Deer--OSHTF reports tissue analyses (liver and muscle) for 23 animals collected along the spill path in Prince William Sound and the Gulf of Alaska. One liver sample from Whale Bay, an unoiled or possible slightly oiled site, contains low levels of petrogenic hydrocarbons from a non-ANS source. All other liver and muscle tissue PAH show low levels of procedural artifacts or alkylated naphthalenes plus procedural artifacts (Figure 12D). The saturated fraction of one liver sample from Bligh Island has a waxy alkane distribution. In the absence of any petrogenic PAH, we conclude that it is a wax contaminant probably introduced from the wax septa used to seal extract vials in the laboratory.

PWSOIL contains hydrocarbon analyses for 7 livers and 3 rumen contents from animals collected on the Kenai during late spring 1989. The livers all have low levels (20-70 ppb) of procedural artifacts. Two of the rumen contents contain weathered *Exxon Valdez* crude. One of these reports nearly 12 ppm *Exxon Valdez* crude TPAH. The liver analysis from the same animal contains only procedural artifacts.

Mink--Fingerprint analysis finds no detectable EVC in 116 internal tissue analyses (livers, fat, mammary) collected in 1990 and reported in PWSOIL. The PAH fingerprints consist of procedural artifacts at concentrations ranging from 80 to more than 500 ppb.

TERRESTRIAL MAMMALS

BROWN BEAR FECES

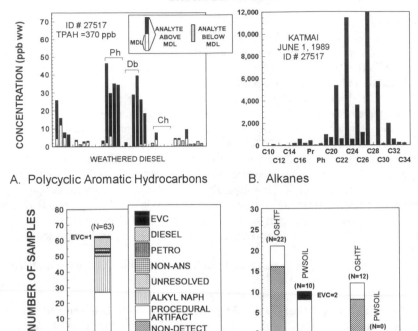

A. Polycyclic Aromatic Hydrocarbons

B. Alkanes

C. Brown Bear Summary (All Samples)

D. Sitka Black-tailed Deer
   Summary (All Samples)

FIGURE 12--Terrestrial mammal PAH fingerprint results. Analyses from PWSOIL and OSHTF.

Shellfish

Shellfish, in particular those from the intertidal zone in the spill path, were heavily impacted initially by the spill. The Oil Spill Health Task Force, because of its concerns for human safety, concentrated its shellfish studies on the traditional harvest regions of Prince William Sound and the Gulf of Alaska. All of these were sites of regular human activity before the spill. Only two, Windy Bay and some locations in the Chenega Bay area, received significant oiling at the time of the *Exxon Valdez* spill. Shellfish sites in the areas sampled by governmental scientists and reported in PWSOIL encompassed a much broader category of sites and only occasionally included subsistence food sites.

Mussels and some species of clams that are filter feeders bioconcentrate hydrocarbons. They filter large volumes of water to obtain suspended food particles.

Any dispersed particles and dissolved constituents of oil present in the water column are ingested at the same time. These hydrocarbons are depurated (on a time scale of several days to weeks) to background levels when the source is removed (Farrington et al. 1982; Clements et al. 1980). However, if the initial oiling is heavy, or if there is a chronic source of bioavailable hydrocarbons, the depuration process can be extended. Hydrocarbons are ubiquitous in the marine environment, and Prince William Sound and the Gulf of Alaska are no exceptions (see, for example, Page et al. Identification of Hydrocarbon Sources in the Benthic Sediments of Prince William Sound and the Gulf of Alaska Following the *Exxon Valdez* Oil Spill, this volume). Consequently, hydrocarbon concentrations can be substantial locally because of anthropogenic activities.

Mussels--Figure 13A shows plots of TPAH versus time for the OSHTF and PWSOIL mussel data. Spill-path and non-spill-path sites are identified for PWSOIL. Windy Bay and Chenega Bay are the only spill-path sites in the OSHTF dataset. Both figures show high levels of TPAH in some spill-path samples immediately after the spill. However, the TPAH concentrations are highly variable and many spill-path samples are indistinguishable from background. This reflects the discontinuous manner in which an oil spill affects a shoreline. Both datasets also show that the most heavily oiled samples have depurated at a rate of about one order of magnitude per year each year since the spill. This is consistent with the finding of sharply decreasing oiling levels reported by shoreline surveys conducted in 1989 through 1992 (Neff et al. Condition of Shorelines in Prince William Sound Following the *Exxon Valdez* Oil Spill, this volume) and with the fixed-site studies described by Boehm et al. (this volume).

The natural background TPAH levels for mussels from the Prince William Sound-Gulf of Alaska area, as determined from non-spill-path sites, generally range from <1 ppb to ~100 ppb; however, outliers as high as 800 to 1 000 ppb are observed. Reference-site TPAH from PWSOIL are in general an order of magnitude greater than that for the OSHTF reference sites (Figure 13A) This is due to the higher levels of procedural artifacts in the PWSOIL analyses.

Other sources of hydrocarbons recognized in the mussel-tissue datasets include creosote at Windy Bay and Kodiak and weathered diesel at Kodiak, Tatitlek, Chenega Bay, and Old Harbor.

Clams--Clams are a major food source for sea otters (Garshelis and Johnson, this volume). Because they are largely subtidal organisms, clams from spill-path sites have markedly lower TPAH concentrations than mussels from the same sites. Some contain low levels of weathered *Exxon Valdez* crude, while others contain weathered diesel as well as the unsubstituted PAH. The OSHTF and PWSOIL TPAH data for affected sites (Figure 13B) show that depuration has occurred at a rate of approximately an order of magnitude per year since the spill and that TPAH levels in clams from many spill-path sites were at or approaching reference values by 1991.

PWSOIL reference site TPAH levels are about a factor of 3 to 4 higher than the non-spill-path sites in OSHTF. The difference appears to be a consistently higher level of lab procedural artifacts in the PWSOIL data.

SHELLFISH AND CRUSTACEANS

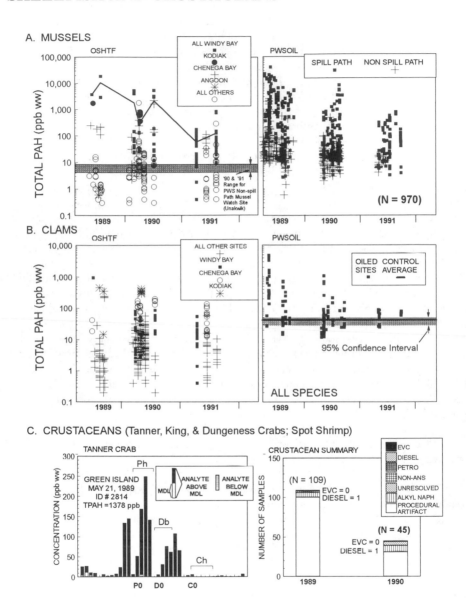

FIGURE 13--TPAH distributions in mussels, clams, and crustaceans. Analyses from the OSHTF and PWSOIL.

TABLE 8--*Other shellfish and crustaceans*

SAMPLE TYPE	YEAR	NO. OF SAMPLES	EVC	DEFINITIVE NON-EVC			OTHER NON-EVC FINGERPRINTS		
				PROCEDURAL ARTIFACTS	DIESEL	NON-ANS	PETRO	UNRESOLVED	ALKYL NAPH
Tanner	1989	35		32	1			1	1
Crab	1990	24		17	1			5	1
King Crab	1989	10		8				1	1
Dungeness	1989	47		47					
"	1990	11		11					
Spot	1989	17		13					4
Shrimp	1990	10		3					7
Oysters	1989	29	7	11	6		1	4	
"	1990	9		7				2	
Sea Urchin	1989	17		7		1		5	4
Scallops	1989	21	4	6	8			3	
Cockles	1989	4	3					1	
TOTALS		234	14	162	16	1	1	22	18

Other Shellfish and Crustaceans--PWSOIL contains analyses from 1989 and 1990 for dungeness, king, and tanner crabs, spot shrimp, oysters, scallops, sea urchins, and cockles. The majority (162 of 234) contain only procedural artifacts. *Exxon Valdez* crude residue is present in a small number of oyster, scallop, and cockle samples collected in 1989 and a few (6 oysters, 8 scallops, and 2 tanner crabs) contain diesel (Figure 13C). *Exxon Valdez* crude was not detected in any 1990 samples. Our interpretation of the PAH fingerprints is summarized in Figure 13C and in Table 8.

DISCUSSION

The PAH fingerprinting procedure we have described, when applied to the PAH analyses reported in OSHTF and PWSOIL, can, in most cases, discriminate *Exxon Valdez* crude residues from other PAH sources. Identification of hydrocarbon sources permits us to address the issues of both short-term and long-term exposure of the fish and wildlife in Prince William Sound and the Gulf of Alaska to *Exxon Valdez* crude.

Exposure of Fish and Wildlife to Hydrocarbons

PAH fingerprint analysis of external surfaces (e.g., hair, feathers, skin, eggshells), where selective uptake, metabolism, and depuration are not issues, shows evidence of exposure to *Exxon Valdez* crude for a number of fish and wildlife samples collected in 1989. For samples collected in 1990, the number containing *Exxon Valdez* crude diminished significantly. An even larger number of samples, collected in 1989 and 1990, contain high concentrations of diesel, probably originating from boat traffic.

Gastrointestinal tract samples (e.g., intestines, viscera, stomach contents, feces) are important because they may be used to establish exposure to petroleum hydrocarbons via the food chain. Our fingerprint analysis of gastrointestinal tract samples reported in PWSOIL indicates that digestion has had little effect on the PAH fingerprints. Clear examples of *Exxon Valdez* crude fingerprints are found, as are fingerprints of diesel and procedural artifacts.

For internal tissues and fluids (e.g., liver, kidney, brain, fat, blubber, lungs, reproductive organs, blood, and milk), the analysis of PAH fingerprints is less certain because of possible selective tissue uptake, metabolism, and depuration. In higher life forms, the fraction of PAH that is assimilated is rapidly metabolized (primarily in the liver) and eliminated (e.g., Brown and Neff 1993). This is the natural process by which animals and fish eliminate the PAH. The results of this study provide limited empirical evidence that the fingerprinting method works for some internal tissues/fluids when analyte concentration levels are above their method detection limits. Generally, however, the levels of PAH reaching the internal tissues of exposed animals are very low. This is probably due to a combination of low initial exposure, low assimilation, and effective metabolism. The majority of the PAH reported for internal tissues/fluids in PWSOIL can be definitively classified as procedural artifacts. As noted above, this component may represent "noise" calculated as PAH through an artifact of the data collection and reporting procedures, or it may represent physical contaminants unrelated to environmental exposure of the living animal.

It seems possible that, in some animal species, upon exposure to petroleum hydrocarbons the alkylated chrysenes may not be absorbed into internal tissues and body fluids while the lighter PAH are. This is based upon the observation that, in fish, the heavier PAH (including the chrysenes) have lower efficiencies of absorption from food than the lighter PAH (Niimi and Doochran 1989). The alkylated chrysenes are important because our method of fingerprinting uses them to discriminate *Exxon Valdez* crude from diesel (in which alkylated chrysenes are absent or very low). However, we have evidence that it is possible to distinguish *Exxon Valdez* crude from diesel in some sea-otter tissues and fluids. The PAH analysis of the livers of sea otters exposed to *Exxon Valdez* crude in 1989 show clearly recognizable *Exxon Valdez* crude fingerprints containing alkylated chrysenes. On the other hand, blood from a control specimen collected near Juneau in 1991, far beyond any possible impact from *Exxon Valdez* crude, has a distinct diesel fingerprint. (Of course, one would not expect to see the crude fingerprint containing alkylated chrysenes there.)

Laboratory studies show that, if exposure levels for mammals and birds are high enough over a sufficient time period and the PAH are not fully metabolized and eliminated, they will be passed to some internal tissues (e.g., liver) and body fluids (Tarshis and Rattner 1982; McEwan and Whitehead 1980; Englehardt 1978). It is possible that the PAH fingerprints in those tissues/fluids will be recognizable if the exposure has been chronic and if the tissues were collected very soon (hours) after the source of exposure was removed.

Some internal tissues (i.e., fat and blubber) deserve additional comment. In addition to questions about selective tissue uptake and metabolism, these tissues are also difficult to analyze because care must be taken to separate hydrocarbon contaminants from the lipids. Consequently, we are cautious with our interpretation of their petrogenic PAH fingerprints. Many of the fat and blubber analyses in PWSOIL report only procedural artifacts or alkylated naphthalenes. For example, sea otters from eastern Prince William Sound contain alkylated naphthalenes in their fat, suggesting that sources other than spill oil were involved.

Very few (2 of more than 500 samples) of the internal tissue/body fluid samples reported in PWSOIL contain recognizable *Exxon Valdez* crude PAH. This would indicate that no exposure occurred, the PAH were not taken up by internal tissues in concentrations sufficiently high to be detected, or they were eliminated before sampling. If petrogenic PAH are present in the tissues but at levels below the method detection limit, the data cannot be used to distinguish *Exxon Valdez* crude from diesel or other refined products.

Potential For Long-Term Exposure

The results indicate that although there was initial exposure in 1989, there is little evidence that fish, birds, and mammals continued to be exposed to *Exxon Valdez* crude residues after 1989. These results are consistent with observational evidence of substantial reductions in shoreline hydrocarbons after 1989.

Our analysis of more than 5 200 PAH analyses of biological samples reported in OSHTF and PWSOIL shows that, while *Exxon Valdez* crude PAHs were recognized in a number of fish, bird, and mammal samples collected in 1989 (138 of more than 1 175 samples in PWSOIL and none of more than 300 samples in OSHTF; Figures 14A, B), only rarely were they identified in samples collected in 1990 (11 of nearly 1 000 samples in PWSOIL and none of more than 50 in OSHTF). None was found in 97, 1991 samples, but few 1991 spill-path samples were reported in PWSOIL. In the majority of cases where *Exxon Valdez* crude was recognized, it appears to correlate with external surfaces or gastrointestinal tract samples and does not appear to be in the tissues at detectable levels. Specifically, when *Exxon Valdez* crude PAH residue was found in stomach contents, only rarely was it also detected in the animal's liver. The majority of the individual PAH must pass through the animal without being retained in the fluids or tissues at levels we can detect. Consequently, claims of continuing harmful exposure of the fish, birds, and mammals in Prince William Sound and the Gulf of Alaska to *Exxon Valdez* oil via the food chain are not supported by available chemical data reported in OSHTF and PWSOIL.

Some shellfish from spill-path sites contained high levels of *Exxon Valdez* crude in 1989. In 1990 and again in 1991, spill hydrocarbon levels in mussels dropped by approximately an order of magnitude each year, and, by 1991, many samples had returned to background. Recent reports of mussel PAH levels from "oiled mussel beds," i.e., those beds overlying oiled sediment (Babcock et al. 1993), are generally consistent with the mussel depuration trends shown on Figures 11A and 11B. The maximum range of TPAH concentrations by GC/MS recently reported for one of these beds is 0.1 to 6 ppm dry weight (~15 to 850 ppb wet weight) (Rounds et al. 1993).

Petrogenic and pyrogenic hydrocarbons from sources unrelated to the spill (primarily diesel and pyrogenic hydrocarbons near sites of human activity) are present in

SAMPLE SUMMARY

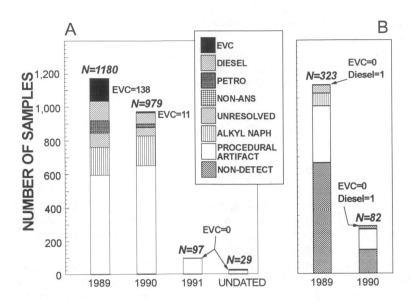

FIGURE 14--Summaries of fingerprint results for bird, mammal, crustacean, and fish PAH analyses reported in PWSOIL (A) and OSHTF (B).

some shellfish samples collected for all three years in Prince William Sound and the Gulf of Alaska. Any assessments of hydrocarbon exposure must include an evaluation of these other sources, some of which are more toxic than weathered *Exxon Valdez* crude.

Specific Claims of Injury

Sea Otters--Claims that continuing long-term exposure may be resulting in a chronic effect on the sea otter (Ballachey et al. 1990; Monson and Ballachey 1993) are not substantiated by the 1990 tissue analyses reported in PWSOIL. One basis for these claims includes higher total aromatics and naphthalenes in fat and blood samples from living adult female sea otters captured within the spill zone compared with otters from outside the spill zone (DeGange et al. 1990). Subsequent reports (e.g., Mulcahy and Ballachey 1992), however, made no attempt to interpret these chemistry results. Our fingerprint analysis of the PAH distributions for samples collected in 1990, as noted above, detects slight differences in total PAH levels but no differences in the PAH analytes reported for fat samples from sea otters collected in the spill path when compared to those from eastern Prince William Sound. The same PAH compounds, primarily the alkylated naphthalenes plus procedural artifacts, are reported for fat tissues from both areas.

Herring--Biggs and Baker (1993) note that the total PAH, total naphthalenes, and phytane contents of adult herring guts for fish taken in 1989 from spill-path locations are elevated relative to controls. Those differences continued through 1990, although hydrocarbon levels were lower. Fingerprint analysis of the herring PAH data reported in PWSOIL does not support their conclusion that the differences are due to *Exxon Valdez* crude.

Gut contents from Naked Island (oiled site) samples collected in 1989 have slightly elevated alkylated PAH (75 to 142 ppb) compared with controls from Galena Bay (38 to 104 ppb) and Cedar Bay (29 to 33 ppb). However, the same analytes (primarily alkylated naphthalenes) are observed in the controls as at spill-path sites. Procedural artifacts constitute 60 to 75% of the total PAH in these samples. Alkane distributions in gut samples show diesel exposure, not exposure to *Exxon Valdez* crude.

In 1990 samples of adult-herring-gut contents, spill-path sites have slightly elevated total PAH relative to controls. Fingerprint analysis indicates that all gut-content samples, both from spill-path and control sites, contain only procedural artifacts. Roe, ovary, viscera, and gonad samples were also tested in 1990. Alkylated PAH occur only in roe and viscera samples from two sites: Sitka, a control in southeast Alaska, and Wells Bay, a control in northwest Prince William Sound. All of the other samples, including those from along the spill path, contain only low levels of procedural artifacts.

The PAH data in PWSOIL show that, although there was some exposure of herring roe to *Exxon Valdez* crude in 1989, exposure was quite limited and at low concentration. There is no chemical evidence for continuing exposure in 1990.

Harlequin Ducks--Claims have been made for sea ducks in general, and Harlequin Ducks in particular, of continuing exposure to spill-oil residues via the consumption of mussels from contaminated mussel beds (Patten 1990; Patten et al. 1991; Patten 1993). Apparent reproductive failures for harlequins in western Prince William Sound in 1991 and 1992 are blamed primarily on continuing chemical exposure to oil and secondarily on disturbance (Patten 1993). The chemical basis for these claims is that, in 1989 and 1990, about 40% of the harlequins had tissues (livers) contaminated with hydrocarbons (Patten et al. 1991). This study shows, however, that the only PAH reported in PWSOIL for harlequin tissues are procedural artifacts.

A few sea ducks (7, including 3 harlequins, of 151 analyzed) contained *Exxon Valdez* crude residue in their stomach contents in 1989 and 1990, and the concentrations were low ($\leq$ 1 100 ppb TPAH). Furthermore, even when *Exxon Valdez* crude residues were detected in the stomach contents of a duck, they could not be detected in the livers, suggesting that tissue uptake was negligible and that most of the *Exxon Valdez* crude ingested was excreted.

Stubblefield et al. (this volume) found no reproductive failures of ducks fed substantial quantities of partially weathered *Exxon Valdez* crude, which was considerably fresher than the *Exxon Valdez* crude content of 1991 mussels. Bile FAC results reported in PWSOIL show no difference in the range of hydrocarbon exposure levels between sea ducks from western Prince William Sound and controls collected in eastern Prince William Sound, Kodiak, and the Juneau area. No analyses are reported for 1991 or 1992.

Therefore, claims that the Harlequin Duck population has suffered complete reproductive failure as a consequence of continuing exposure to *Exxon Valdez* crude (via the oiled mussel beds) are not consistent with evidence of exposure in the chemistry data.

The alternative explanation for the reported poor reproductive success of harlequins in western Prince William Sound is disturbance (Patten 1993). Dzinbal (1982), in a study of Harlequin Ducks in Prince William Sound, observed a major reduction in reproductive success for birds that had been tagged as part of his study (7% successful) compared with that of untagged birds (55% successful). He further noted that those effects carried beyond the tagging year. Patten (1993) characterized the impacts of disturbance as temporary and discounted the effects of disturbance associated with spill cleanup as the cause for reproductive failure in 1992. If disturbance had been a contributor to reduced reproduction, then the very limited effort in 1991 and 1992 would not have been a significant factor and the environment for reproduction would logically have been restored.

Eagles--Some investigators have claimed exposure on the basis of observed egg and prey contamination by hydrocarbons (Schempf et al. 1990; Bowman 1992). Our analysis of the PWSOIL data shows *Exxon Valdez* crude residues on about one-third of the eggshells collected in 1989 and on 1 of 54 collected in 1990. Nearly one-half of the 1989 eggshells and two-thirds of those collected in 1990 were contaminated with diesel. Some were at TPAH levels significantly higher than the highest measured EVC concentrations. The low number of samples (1) containing *Exxon Valdez* crude in 1990 indicated that there had been almost no continuing exposure. In addition, because so many of the eggshell samples were contaminated with diesel, it would be impossible to separate any chemical effects of the spill on reproductivity from effects caused by the diesel.

Pigeon Guillemots--Claims have been made that unhatched eggs showed internal and external contamination in 1989 and 1990 (Kuletz 1992a; Oakley and Kuletz 1993). They claim that the presence of oil on these eggs one year after the spill indicates continuing exposure of the pigeon guillemot to *Exxon Valdez* crude even though most of the area beaches had been cleaned (Oakley and Kuletz 1993). Our analysis of the PWSOIL data, summarized in Table 6, indicates that what was inferred to be spill oil is diesel. No *Exxon Valdez* crude was detected in any of the samples.

Common Murres--Hydrocarbon contamination from spill oil is one possible explanation given for delays and failures to lay eggs at the murre colony in Puale Bay in 1989 (Nysewander et al. 1993). Delays in egg-laying were also noted for 1990 but were not attributed to the spill because there was no apparent oil remaining near the breeding sites and clean-up activity had diminished. Continued delays in egg-laying and reproductive success, which were reported at some locations in 1992 (Nyswander and Byrd 1993), were attributed to the initial mortalities in 1989 and the effect they had on community structure. Our fingerprint analysis of eggshell chemistry in PWSOIL for samples collected in 1989 and 1990 suggests that another factor, diesel contamination, may play a role. More than 60% of the samples from both years were contaminated with diesel. The Puale Bay region is an active commercial fishing area, and the probable source of diesel is the fishing fleet.

Marbled Murrelets--Kuletz (1992b; 1993a, b) reported that petroleum hydrocarbons were found in 5 of 18 bird livers from oiled areas and in none of 10 from unoiled areas in 1989. PWSOIL contains the analyses of 9 marbled murrelet livers collected in 1989 and 18 from 1990. No site locations are given. Examination of the PAH distributions indicates that 6 of 9 contain only procedural artifacts (37 to 60 ppb TPAH). The remaining 3 report low concentrations (20 to 30 ppb) of alkylated PAH (primarily naphthalenes) plus 70 to 80 ppb procedural artifacts. No petrogenic hydrocarbons from any source were found in the 18 liver tissues analyzed in 1990. Consequently, although there may have been low levels of exposure to *Exxon Valdez* crude in 1989, there is no chemical evidence of continuing exposure in the data reported in PWSOIL.

Black-legged Kittiwakes--Declines in the reproductive successes for black-legged kittiwakes in 1989, 1990, 1991, and 1992 are associated with observations of 1 oil-contaminated liver and 1 contaminated eggshell in 1989, and two contaminated stomach contents in 1990 (Irons 1993a, b). Fingerprint analysis indicates that the 10 livers collected in 1989 (and the 14 livers collected in 1990) report only procedural artifacts (30 to 80 ppb TPAH). The single eggshell analysis from 1989 contains 950 ppb of high-sulfur diesel. Low concentrations of petrogenic PAH (8 to 90 ppb) occur in the stomach contents of 13 out of 14 samples from 1990. However, the concentrations of the diagnostic analytes are too low to provide a definitive PAH fingerprint. Liver tissues from the same birds report only procedural artifacts, indicating that any PAH uptake by internal tissues are too low to be detected by the methods used.

Bears--Claims that brown bears have been exposed to hydrocarbons have been made because 4 of 27 fecal samples contained elevated levels of petroleum hydrocarbons (Lewis and Sellers 1991). Of 57 fecal sample analyses reported in PWSOIL, 1 contains low levels of *Exxon Valdez* crude (150 ppb PAH), indicating only limited exposure to spill oil. However, 4 samples contain up to 650 ppb weathered diesel. An additional 5 contain probable highly weathered diesel but have been assigned to the PETRO category (crude or diesel).

Diesel and Procedural Artifacts

Many of the analyses of biological samples reported in PWSOIL, including those for eagle, pigeon guillemot, and murre eggshells and eagle prey, show contamination with diesel. Some of this contamination may have been introduced at the time of collection or subsequent handling, but most appears to be environmental. Dekin (1993) found evidence of widespread contamination by low levels of refined petroleum hydrocarbons at a number of upland archaeological sites.

Few if any of the OSHTF samples are contaminated with diesel. However, eggshells and eagle prey are not included in that dataset. Diesel PAH detected in some samples (e.g., Kodiak salmon and shellfish) is a consequence of its presence in the environment.

PWSOIL field blanks indicate that at least some of the diesel contamination was introduced during sampling. A number of the field blanks for coastal habitat and air and water studies (mainly mussel and sediment analyses) for all years reported in PWSOIL contain weathered diesel to TPAH levels exceeding 1 000 ppb. Large numbers of subtidal sediments collected from 1989 to 1991 contain fresh and weathered diesel. Fresh diesel has not yet been found in the field-blank data analyzed to date, although it does show up clearly in subtidal sediment samples collected in 1989 and 1990.

Inputs of ANS diesel can be differentiated from *Exxon Valdez* crude in sediments that naturally contain alkylated chrysenes by the relative amounts of alkylated chrysenes present for the state of weathering of the *Exxon Valdez* crude. Double ratio plots of C_3-N/C_2-Ph versus C_2-Ch/C_2-Ph are particularly useful in that regard (Burns and Bence, in preparation).

The procedural artifacts component, which at 60% is the largest single category recognized in PWSOIL fish, bird, and mammal samples, is present at levels ranging from ~10 ppb to nearly 4 000 ppb. The highest values appear to correlate with very small sample sizes, and in most cases individual analyte levels are at or near the method detection limit. This component also occurs with other components in all but a very few of the remaining 40% of the samples. Its fingerprint is highly diagnostic and should not readily be confused with any petrogenic fingerprint.

CONCLUSIONS

PAH fingerprinting, applied to the OSHTF and PWSOIL datasets, differentiates among spill oil residues and other sources of hydrocarbons found in Prince William Sound and the Gulf of Alaska as well as procedural artifacts of the laboratory methods.

Fingerprinting works well for biological samples having external surfaces. It also appears to work on gastrointestinal tract samples. It appears less diagnostic for internal tissues and fluids, but it offers a way to compare exposure at spill-path and non-spill-path sites and can clearly identify procedural artifacts in these tissues and fluids. In those cases where *Exxon Valdez* crude was recognized, it appears to be primarily on external surfaces and in samples associated with the gastrointestinal tract rather than with internal tissue or fluids.

Excluding shellfish, only a fraction of the tissues collected, analyzed, and reported in OSHTF and PWSOIL contain identifiable *Exxon Valdez* crude. Most were from samples collected in 1989 (138 out of more than 1 175 analyses in PWSOIL). Only rarely was *Exxon Valdez* crude detected in samples collected in 1990 (11 of nearly 1 000 analyses). None was found in more than 100 samples collected in 1991 and reported in the two datasets. However, most of these were from nonspill sites.

Criteria used by others to identify oil contamination recognize petrogenic hydrocarbons but are unable to separate the multiple sources of petrogenic hydrocarbons found in the Prince William Sound-Gulf of Alaska environment, including diesel.

Consequently, an interpretation of oil contamination in studies using these criteria should not be interpreted as implying the presence of *Exxon Valdez* crude.

Tissue PAH has been used by some as evidence of exposure to *Exxon Valdez* crude. Claims that fish, birds, and mammals continue to be exposed to spill oil are not supported by the OSHTF and PWSOIL datasets.

Some mussels and clams from heavily affected shorelines had high levels of *Exxon Valdez* crude PAH in 1989. In 1990 and again in 1991, PAH levels at the same sites sampled in 1989 dropped by approximately an order of magnitude each year and, in 1991, many were at or approaching background. Many shellfish, especially those in the vicinities of subsistence villages, contain both petrogenic and pyrogenic hydrocarbons from nonspill sources.

ACKNOWLEDGMENTS

This research was supported by Exxon Company, U.S.A. We acknowledge helpful and stimulating discussions on the issues of uptake, metabolism, and depuration of the PAH with J. Neff, A. Maki, R. Lee, P. Boehm, and R. Huggett. Carol-Ann Manen, NOAA, provided us with PWSOIL. B. Ballachey, USFWS, clarified questions of sampling date and identification codes pertaining to the sea otters. D. Erickson and T. Schroeder provided information on commercial fishing activities in Cook Inlet, the Kenai coast, and the Alaska Peninsula. Unpublished interim and final reports of the various investigations conducted by Trustee scientists are available from the Oil Spill Public Information Council, 645 G Street Anchorage, AK 99501 (tel. 1-800-283-7745). These reports are labeled (OSPIC) in the References.

REFERENCES

Anderson, J. A., J. M. Neff, and P. D. Boehm. "Sources, Fates, and Effects of Aromatic Hydrocarbons in the Alaskan Marine Environment with Recommendations for Monitoring Strategies." Environmental Protection Agency Project Report EPA/600/3-86/018; 1986.

Babcock, M., G. Irvine, S. Rice, P. Rounds, J. Cusick, and C. Brodersen. "Oiled Mussel Beds Two and Three Years After the *Exxon Valdez* Oil Spill. In: Exxon Valdez *Oil Spill Symposium Abstracts; Feb 2-5, 1993; Anchorage, AK*. 184-185; 1993.

Ballachey, B. E., J. L. Bodkin, and D. Burn. "Assessment of the Magnitude, Extent and Duration of Oil Spill Impact on Sea Otter Populations in Alaska." United States Fish and Wildlife Service Interim Report, November 19, 1990. (OSPIC)

Biggs, E. D. and T. T. Baker. "Summary of Known Effects of the *Exxon Valdez* Oil Spill on Herring in Prince William Sound, and Recommendations for Future Inquiries." In: Exxon Valdez *Oil Spill Symposium Abstracts; Feb 2-5, 1993; Anchorage, AK*. 264-267; 1993.

Boehm, P. D., D. L. Fiest, and A. Eiskus. "Comparative Weathering Patterns of Hydrocarbons from the *Amoco Cadiz* Oil Spill Observed at a Variety of Coastal Environments. *In: Proceedings of the International Symposium on the* Amoco Cadiz: *Fates and Effects of the Oil Spill. Brest, France, November 19-22, 1979.* Publie' Par Le Centre National pour L'Exploitation des Oceans, Paris; 1981.

Bowman, T. D. "Effects of the *Exxon Valdez* Oil Spill on Bald Eagles." In: *Proceedings of the Annual Meeting of the Raptor Research Foundation; Bellvue, WA. Nov 11-15, 1992.* 46; 1992.

Broman, D, C. Naf, I. Lundbergh, and Y. Zebuhr. "An *in situ* Study on the Distribution, Biotransformation and Flux of Polycyclic Aromatic Hydrocarbons (PAHs) in an Aquatic Food Chain (seston -*Mytilus edulis* L.-*Somateria mollissima*) From the Baltic: An Ecotoxicological Perspective." *Environmental, Toxicology and Chemistry.* 9: 429-442; 1990.

Brown, B. and J. M. Neff, "Bioavailability of Sediment-Bound Contaminants to Marine Organisms." Preprint prepared for National Ocean Pollution Program Office. National Oceanic and Atmospheric Administration, Washington, DC; 1993.

Clements, L. E., M. S. Stekoll, and D. G. Shaw. "Accumulation, Fractionation and Release of Oil by the Intertidal Clam *Macoma Balthica*." *Marine Biology.* 57: 41-50; 1980.

Connan, J. "Biodegradation of Crude Oils in Reservoirs." In: *Advances in Petroleum Geochemistry.* Vol. 1. J. M. Brooks and D. Welte (editors). New York: Academic Press; 299-355; 1983.

Dekin, A. A., Jr. "The Impact of the *Exxon Valdez* Oil Spill on Cultural Resources." Exxon Valdez *Oil Spill Symposium.* Preprint; Anchorage, AK; 1993. (OSPIC)

DeGange, A. R., B. E. Ballachey, M. S. Udevitz, and A. M. Dorott. "Hydrocarbon Contamination of Sea Otter Tissue Samples." In: *Assessment of the Magnitude, Extent, and Duration of Oil Spill Impact on Sea Otter Populations.* United States Fish and Wildlife Service Interim Report. Section 6. November 19, 1990. (OSPIC)

Dzinbal, K. A. "Ecology of Harlequin Ducks in Prince William Sound, Alaska, During Summer." Oregon State University, Corvallis. MS. thesis; 1982.

Eastcott, L., W. Y. Shiu, and D. Mackay. "Environmentally Relevant Physical-Chemical Properties of Hydrocarbons: A Review of Data and Development of Simple Correlations." *Oil Chemical Pollution* 4: 191-216; 1988.

Englehardt, F. R. "Petroleum Hydrocarbons in Ringed Seals, *Phoca hispida*, Following Experimental Oil Exposure." In: *Proceedings of the Conference on Assessment of Ecological Impacts of Oil Spills*. Washington, DC: American Institute of Biological Sciences; 614-628; 1978.

Farrington, J. W., A. C. Davis, N. M. Frew, and S. K. Rabin. "No. 2 Fuel Oil Compounds in *Mytilus Edulis*." *Marine Biology*. 66: 15-26; 1982.

Friocourt, M. P., F. Berthou, and D. Picart.   "Dibenzothiophene Derivatives as Organic Markers of Pollution". In: *Chemistry and Analysis of Hydrocarbons in The Environment*. J. Albaiges, R. W. Frei, and E. Merian (editors); New York: Gordon and Breach, Science Publishers; 125-135; 1983.

Gundelach, E. R., P. D. Boehm, M. Marchand, R. M. Atlas, D. M. Ward, and D. A. Wolfe. "The Fate of the *Amoco Cadiz* Oil." *Science*. 221: 122-129; 1983.

Heras, H., R. G. Ackman, and E. J. MacPherson. "Tainting of Atlantic Salmon (*Salmo salar*) by Petroleum Hydrocarbons During Short-Term Exposure." *Marine Pollution Bulletin*. 24: 310-315; 1992.

Irons, D. B. "Effects of the *Exxon Valdez* Oil Spill on Black-legged Kittiwakes in Prince William Sound." *Pacific Seabird Group Twentieth Annual Meeting Abstracts*; *Seattle; Feb 9-13, 1993*. 29; 1993a.

Irons, D. B. "Effects of the *Exxon Valdez* Oil Spill on Black-legged Kittiwakes in Prince William Sound." In: Exxon Valdez *Oil Spill Symposium Abstracts. Feb 2-5; Anchorage, AK*. 159; 1993b.

Krahn, M. M., L. K. Moore, and W. D. MacLeod, Jr. "Standard Analytical Procedures of the National Oceanic and Atmospheric Administration, National Analytical Facility, 1986: Metabolites of Aromatic Compounds in Fish Bile." U. S. Department of Commerce Technical Memorandum NMFS F/NWC-102; 1986.

Krahn, M. M., D. G. Burrows, G. M. Ylitalo, D. W. Brown, C. A. Wigren, T. K. Collier, S.-L. Chan, and U. Varanasi.   "Mass Spectrometric Analysis for Aromatic Hydrocarbons in Bile of Fish Sampled After the *Exxon Valdez* Spill." *Environmental Science Technology*. 26: 116-126; 1992.

Krahn, M. M., G. M. Ylitalo, D. G. Burrows, J. Buzitis, S.-L. Chan, and U. Varanasi. "Methods for Determining Crude Oil Contamination in Sediments and Biota After the *Exxon Valdez* Oil Spill." In: Exxon Valdez *Oil Spill Symposium Abstracts. Feb 2-5, 1993; Anchorage, AK*. 60-62; 1993.

Kuletz, K. J. "A Preliminary Summary of the *Exxon Valdez* Damage Assessment Studies on the Pigeon Guillemot." United States Fish and Wildlife Service Preliminary Report, May 12, 1992a. (OSPIC)

Kuletz, K. J. "Assessment of Injury to Marbled Murrelets from the *Exxon Valdez* Oil Spill." United States Fish and Wildlife Service Draft Report. February 5, 1992b. (OSPIC)

Kuletz, K. J. "Effects of the *Exxon Valdez* Oil Spill on Marbled Murrelets at Naked Island in Prince William Sound and Kachemak Bay." *Pacific Seabird Group Twentieth Annual Meeting Abstracts*; Seattle; Feb 9-13, 1993. 28; 1993a.

Kuletz, K. J. "Effects of the *Exxon Valdez* Oil Spill on Marbled Murrelets." In: Exxon Valdez *Oil Spill Symposium Abstracts. Feb 2-5, 1993; Anchorage, AK.* 148-149; 1993b.

Kvenvolden, K. A., F. D. Hostettler, and J. B. Rapp. "Short-Term Effects of Oil Spills on the Molecular Record in Sediments of San Francisco Bay, California, and Prince William Sound, Alaska." In: *Organic Geochemistry: Advances and Applications in Energy and the Natural Environment.* D. A. C. Manning (editors); Manchester: Manchester University Press; 527-730; 1991.

Kvenvolden, K. A., P. R. Carlson, C. N. Threlkeld, and A. Warden. "Possible Connection Between Two Alaskan Catastrophes Occurring 25 Years Apart (1964 and 1989)." *Geology.* 21: 813-816; 1993

Law, R. J. and J. A. Whinnett. "Polycyclic Aromatic Hydrocarbons in Muscle Tissue of Harbour Porpoises (*Phocoena phocoena*) from U.K. Waters." *Marine Pollution Bulletin.* 24: 550-553; 1992.

Lee, R. F. "Mixed Function Oxygenases (MFO) in Marine Invertebrates." *Marine Biology Letter.* 2: 87-105; 1981.

Lemaire, P., S. Lemaire-Gony, J. Berhaut, and M. Lafaurie.   "The Uptake, Metabolism, and Biological Half-life of Benzo(a)pyrene Administered by Force-feeding in Sea Bass (*Dicentrarchus labrax*)." *Ecotoxicology and Environmental Safety.* 23: 244-251; 1992.

Lewis, J. P. and R. Sellers. "Assessment of the *Exxon Valdez* Oil Spill on Brown Bears on the Alaskan Peninsula." Alaska Department of Fish and Game. Final Report. November 28, 1991. (OSPIC)

Mackenzie, A. S. "Applications of Biomarkers in Petroleum Geochemistry." In: *Advances in Petroleum Geochemistry. Vol. 1.* J. M. Brooks and D. H. Welte (editors). London: Academic Press; 115-214; 1984.

Manen, C. A. "Hydrocarbon Analytical Support Services and Analysis of Distribution and Weathering of Spilled Oil." NRDA Technical Services #1 Preliminary Draft Report, Appendix C. 1991. (OSPIC)

Manen, C. A., J. R. Price, S. Korn, and M. G. Carls. "Natural Resource Damage Assessment: Database Design and Structure." National Oceanic and Atmospheric Administration Technical Memorandum NOS/ORCA; 1993, in press.

McAuliffe, C. D. "Organism Exposure to Volatile/Soluble Hydrocarbons From Crude Oil Spills - A Field and Laboratory Comparison". In: *Proceedings 1987 Oil Spill Conference; April 6-9, 1987; Baltimore, MD*. 275-288; American Petroleum Institute; 1987

McEwan, E. H. and P. M. Whitehead. "Uptake and Clearance of Petroleum Hydrocarbons by the Glaucous-winged Gull (*Laras glaucescens*) and the Mallard Duck (*Anas platyrhynchos*)." *Canadian Journal of Zoology*. 58: 723-726; 1980.
Monson, D. H. and B. E. Ballachey. "Age Distribution of Sea Otters Dying in Prince William Sound, Alaska, After the *Exxon Valdez* Oil Spill." In: Exxon Valdez *Oil Spill Symposium Abstracts; Feb 2-5, 1993; Anchorage, AK*. 282-284; 1993.

Mulcahy, D. and B. E. Ballachey. "Hydrocarbon Contamination of Sea Otter Tissue Samples." In: *Assessment of the Magnitude, Extent, and Duration of Oil Spill Impacts on Sea Otter Populations in Alaska*. B. E. Ballachey, J. L. Bodkin, and D. Burn. (Project Leaders). U. S. Fish and Wildlife Service and Alaska Fish and Wildlife Research Center. Natural Resource Damage Assessment Draft Preliminary Status Report, Section 6. Revised May 12, 1992. (OSPIC)

Mulcahy, D. and B. E. Ballachey. "Hydrocarbon Concentrations in Tissues of Sea Otters Collected Following the *Exxon Valdez* Oil Spill." In: Exxon Valdez *Oil Symposium Abstracts*; *Feb 2-5, 1993; Anchorage, AK*. 293-295; 1993.

Neff, J. M. *Polycyclic Aromatic Hydrocarbons in the Aquatic Environment: Sources, Fates and Biological Effects*. London: Applied Science Publishers; 262; 1979.

Neff, J. M., B. A. Cox, D. Dixit, and J. A. Anderson. "Accumulation and Release of Petroleum-derived Aromatic Hydrocarbons by Four Species of Marine Animals." *Marine Biology*. 38: 279-289; 1976.

Neff, J. M., P. D. Boehm, and W. E. Haensley. "Petroleum Contamination and Biochemical Alterations in Oysters (*Crassostrea virginica*) and Plaice (*Pleuronectes platessa*) From Bays Impacted by the *Amoco Cadiz* Crude Oil Spill." *Marine Environmental Research*. 17: 281-283; 1985.

Niimi, A. J. and G. P. Doochran. "Dietary Absorption Efficiencies and Elimination Rates of Polycyclic Aromatic Hydrocarbons (PAHs) in Rainbow Trout (*Salmo gairdneri*)." *Environmental Toxicology and Chemistry*. 8: 719-722; 1989.

Nysewander, D. R., and G. V. Byrd. "Effects of the *Exxon Valdez* Oil Spill on Murres: A Perspective From Observations at Breeding Colonies." *Pacific Seabird Group Twentieth Annual Meeting Abstracts; Feb 9-13, 1993. Seattle.* 29; 1993.

Nysewander, D. R. C. Dipple, G. V. Byrd, and E. P. Knudtson. "Effects of the *T/V Exxon Valdez* Oil Spill on Murres: A Perspective From Observations at Breeding Colonies." In: Exxon Valdez *Oil Spill Symposium Abstracts, Feb 2-5, 1993; Anchorage, AK.* 135-138; 1993.

Oakley, K. L. and K. J. Kuletz. "Effects of the *Exxon Valdez* Oil Spill on Pigeon Guillemots (*Cepphus columba*) in Prince William Sound, AK." In: Exxon Valdez *Oil Spill Symposium Program and Abstracts. Feb 2-5, 1993. Anchorage, AK.* 144-146; 1993

OSHTF (The Oil Spill Health Task Force) Report, March 1990. (OSPIC)

Overton, E. B., J. R. Patel, and J. L. Laseter. "Chemical Characterization of Mousse and Selected Environmental Samples From the *Amoco Cadiz* Oil Spill." In: *Proceedings of the 1979 Oil Spill Conference; March 19-22, 1979; Los Angeles, CA.* 169-174; American Petroleum Institute; 1979.

Overton, E. B., J. A. McFall, S. W. Mascarella, C. F. Steele, S. A. Antoine, I. R. Politzer, and J. L. Laseter. "Identification of Petroleum Residue Sources After a Fire and Oil Spill." In: *Proceedings of the 1981 Oil Spill Conference; March 2-5, 1981; Atlanta, GA.* 541-546; American Petroleum Institute; 1981.

Patten, S. M. "Injury Assessment of Hydrocarbon Uptake by Sea Ducks in Prince William Sound and Kodiak Archipelago, Alaska." Alaska Department of Fish & Game Draft Report; November 28, 1990. (OSPIC)

Patten, S. M. "Acute and Sublethal Effects of the *Exxon Valdez* Oil Spill on Harlequins and Other Sea Ducks." In: Exxon Valdez *Oil Spill Symposium Program and Abstracts. Feb 2-5, 1993; Anchorage, AK.* 151-154; 1993.

Patten, S. M., Jr., R. Gustin, and T. Crowe. "Injury Assessment of Hydrocarbon Uptake by Sea Ducks in Prince William Sound and Kodiak Archipelago, Alaska." Alaska Department of Fish & Game Draft Report; November 20, 1991. (OSPIC)

Prince, R. C., J. R. Clark, and J. E. Lindstrom. "Bioremediation Monitoring Program." Joint Exxon, U.S. Environmental Protection Agency, and Alaska Department of Environmental Conservation Report, Anchorage, AK; 85; 1991. (Available from Alaska

Department of Environmental Conservation, P. O. Box 0 Juneau, AK 99811-1800, tel. (907) 465-2606.)

Prince, R. C., J. R. Clark, J. E. Lindstrom, E. L. Butler, E. J. Brown, G. Winter, M. J. Grossman, P. R. Parrish, R. E. Bare, J. F. Braddock, W. G. Steinhauer, G. S. Douglas, J. M. Kennedy, P. J. Barter, J. R. Bragg, E. J. Harner, and R. M. Atlas. "Bioremediation of the Exxon Valdez Oil Spill: Monitoring Safety and Efficacy." In: *Hydrocarbon Bioremediation*. R. E. Hinchee, B. C. Alleman, R. E. Hoeppel, and R. N. Miller (editors); Ann Arbor, Michigan: Lewis Publishers; 107-124; 1994.

Pritchard, J. B. and J. R. Bend. "Relative Roles of Metabolism and Renal Excretory Mechanisms in Xenobiotic Elimination in Fish." *Environmental Health Perspective.* 90: 85-92; 1991.

Radke, M., P. Garrigues, and H. Willsch. "Methylated Dicycylic and Tricyclic Aromatic Hydrocarbons in Crude Oils From the Handil Field, Indonesia." *Organic Geochemistry.* 15: 17-34; 1990.

Rasmussen, W. V. "Characterization of Oil Spills by Capillary Column Gas Chromatography." *Analytical Chemistry.* 48: 1562-1566; 1975.

Rounds, P., S. Rice, M. M. Babcock, C. C. Brodersen. "Availability of *Exxon Valdez* Hydrocarbon Concentrations in Mussel Bed Sediments." In: Exxon Valdez *Oil Spill Symposium Program and Abstracts. Feb 2-5, 1993; Anchorage, AK.* 182-183; 1993.

Schempf, P. F., T. D. Bowman, J. Bernatowicz, and T. Schumacher. "Assessing the Effects of the *Exxon Valdez* Oil Spill on Bald Eagles. Bird Study Number 4". United States Fish and Wildlife Service Preliminary Report, November 19, 1990. (OSPIC)

Short, J. W. and R. A. Heintz. "Qualitative and Quantitative Determination of *Exxon Valdez* Crude Oil in Sediment Samples Using Principal Component Analysis of Hydrocarbon Data." In: Exxon Valdez *Oil Spill Symposium Abstracts; Feb 2-5, 1993; Anchorage, AK.* 63; 1993.

Sinkkonen, S. "Appearance and Structure Analysis of Aromatic Oil Residues in Baltic Mussels and Fish." *In Chemistry and Analysis of Hydrocarbons in The Environment.* J. Albaiges, R. W. Frei, and E. Merian (editors). New York: Gordon and Breach Science Publishers; 207-215; 1983.

Stegeman, J. J. "Polynuclear Aromatic Hydrocarbons and their Metabolism in the Marine Environment." In: *Polycyclic Hydrocarbons and Cancer, Vol. 3.* H. V. Gelboin and P. O. P. Ts'o (editors). New York: Academic Press; 1-60; 1981.

Tarshis, I. B. and B. A. Rattner. "Accumulation of ^{14}C-Naphthalene in the Tissues of Redhead Ducks Fed Oil-contaminated Crayfish." *Archives of Environmental Contamination and Toxicology.* 11: 155-159; 1982.

Van Veld, P. A., J. S. Patton, and R. F. Lee. "Effect of Exposure to Dietary Benzo(a)pyrene (BP) on the First-pass Metabolism of BP by the Intestine of Toadfish (*Opsanus tau*): *in vivo* Studies Using Portal Vein-catheterized Fish." *Toxicology and Applied Pharmacology.* 92: 255-256; 1988.

Varanasi, U., J. E. Stein, and M. Nishimoto. "Biotransformation and Disposition of Polycyclic Aromatic Hydrocarbons (PAH) in Fish. In: *Metabolism of Polycyclic Aromatic Hydrocarbons in the Aquatic Environment.* U. Varanasi (editors). Boca Raton, FL: CRC Press, 93-149; 1989.

Varanasi, U., S.-L. Chan, W. D. MacLeod, J. E. Stein, D. W Brown, D. G. Burrows, K. L. Tilbury, J. T. Landahl, C. A. Wigren, T. Hom, and S. M. Pierce, "Survey of Subsistence Fish and Shellfish for Exposure to Oil Spilled from the *Exxon Valdez*. First Year: 1989." National Oceanic and Atmospheric Administration Technical Memorandum NMFS F/NWC-191; December 1990.

Wakeham, S. G. and J. W. Farrington. "Hydrocarbons in Contemporary Aquatic Sediments." *In Contaminants and Sediments, Volume 1*, R. A. Baker (editors). Ann Arbor, MI: Science Publishers, 3-32; 1980.

Youngblood, W. W. and M. Blumer. "Polycyclic Aromatic Hydrocarbons in the Environment: Homologous Series in Soils and Recent Marine Sediments." *Geochemica Cosmochimica Acta.* 39: 1303-1314; 1975.

Jerry M. Neff[1] and William A. Stubblefield[2]

CHEMICAL AND TOXICOLOGICAL EVALUATION OF WATER QUALITY FOLLOWING THE *EXXON VALDEZ* OIL SPILL

REFERENCE: Neff, J.M. and Stubblefield, W.A. "**Chemical and Toxicological Evaluation of Water Quality Following the *Exxon Valdez* Oil Spill,** "*Exxon Valdez Oil Spill: Fate and Effects in Alaskan Waters, ASTM STP 1219,* Peter G. Wells, James N. Butler, and J.S. Hughes, Eds. American Society for Testing and Materials, Philadelphia, 1995.

ABSTRACT: As part of a comprehensive water-quality assessment program performed in Prince William Sound and the western Gulf of Alaska following the *Exxon Valdez* oil spill of March 24, 1989, water samples were collected from 417 locations, most of them in areas through which the oil drifted, to assess the distribution and concentrations of petroleum hydrocarbons in the water column. Over 5 000 water samples were analyzed for individual and total petroleum alkanes and for aromatic hydrocarbons by very sensitive gas chromatographic techniques. A total of 2 461 of these samples were analyzed for polycyclic aromatic hydrocarbons (PAHs). Concurrent with some of these samples, an additional 123 water samples were collected in April 1989 (a week to a month after the spill) at 32 offshore locations and in June 1989 at 7 nearshore sites in Prince William Sound to determine the toxicity of the water to representative species of marine organisms. The toxicity of Prince William Sound water was assessed with standard Environmental Protection Agency (EPA) and American Society for Testing and Materials (ASTM) marine toxicity tests with representative species of three taxonomic groups: (1) *Skeletonema costatum* (a marine diatom), (2) *Mysidopsis bahia* (a crustacean), and (3) larval/juvenile *Cyprinodon variegatus* (a fish, the sheepshead minnow).

Highest concentrations of total PAHs, the best indicator of the potential toxicity of the spilled oil to water-column organisms, were observed in the water column of Prince William Sound in the first two months after the spill. Measured PAH levels were below the state of Alaska's water quality standard of 10 ppb total aromatic hydrocarbons. This finding is consistent with National Oceanic and Atmospheric Administration (NOAA) water samples collected during the same time period. PAH concentrations in the water

---

[1]Senior Research Leader, Battelle Ocean Sciences, 397 Washington, St., Duxbury, MA 02332. Formerly with Arthur D. Little, Inc., Cambridge, MA.

[2]Senior Aquatic Toxicologist, ENSR Consulting and Engineering, 1716 Heath Parkway, Fort Collins, CO 80524

column of the sound declined rapidly with time after the spill to essentially background concentrations of 0.01 to 0.1 ppb by mid to late summer of 1989. No water samples from spill path areas of the western Gulf of Alaska contained more than 1.0 ppb total PAHs. These concentrations are well below concentrations reported in the scientific literature to be toxic to marine plants and animals. Eight of 329 samples (2.4%) of the water surface contained between 10 and 29.3 ppb total PAHs; these samples probably contained oil sheen material.

Toxicity tests with full strength Prince William Sound water showed no acute or chronic toxicity to three representative species of marine organisms. There was no dose-response relationship for any species or seawater sample, and there was no relationship between the concentration of total PAHs in the undiluted seawater samples and percentage of survival or relative growth rates in the test organisms.

These studies show that the traces of petroleum hydrocarbons present in the water column of Prince William Sound and the western Gulf of Alaska shortly after the spill were well below concentrations capable of producing harmful effects in populations of sensitive species and life stages of marine organisms.

KEY WORDS: Prince William Sound, *Exxon Valdez*, oil spill, water column, crude oil, toxicity, marine organisms, polycyclic aromatic hydrocarbons, PAH.

INTRODUCTION

Following the grounding of *T/V Exxon Valdez* on Bligh Reef in northeastern Prince William Sound on March 24, 1989, approximately 11 million gallons (41.6 million liters) of the tanker's cargo of Alaskan North Slope crude oil was spilled. The spilled oil was driven by the prevailing winds and water currents toward the island system in the western sound and eventually, after about March 30, into the northwestern Gulf of Alaska. The drifting oil slick formed a water-in-oil emulsion (mousse) and broke up into bands and stringers. The oil that reached the Gulf of Alaska was swept to the west along the coast by the Alaska Coastal Current.

Shortly after the spill, there was concern that petroleum hydrocarbons from the surface slicks might enter the water column (the area between the water surface and the bottom) of Prince William Sound and threaten important fisheries species and food-chain organisms. In order to address these concerns, a massive water-quality monitoring program was begun in Prince William Sound and the western Gulf of Alaska within a few days after the spill. The objectives of the water-quality monitoring program were to document the distribution and composition of petroleum hydrocarbons in the water column over time after the spill and to determine whether the small amounts of oil in the water column in the weeks immediately after the spill were toxic to water-column organisms.

The water quality program included two components: (1) determination of the concentrations and distribution over space and time after the spill of petroleum hydrocarbons in the water column of Prince William Sound and the western Gulf of Alaska and (2) assessment of the toxicity of Prince William Sound water collected shortly after the spill to sensitive species of marine plants and animals. Sixteen hundred seventy water-quality samples analyzed for PAH were reported earlier (Neff 1991a). In the present paper, 791 additional water samples collected in association with special biological studies, 1990 shoreline studies, sample duplicates, and samples collected inside and outside containment booms during cleanup operations are now included, bringing the total to 2 461. In addition, NOAA collected 243 water samples that were analyzed for PAH (Short and Rounds 1993). As part of several of the Exxon-supported studies, many water samples also were analyzed for benzene, toluene, ethylbenzene, and xylenes (VOAs), individual saturated hydrocarbons and total resolved and unresolved petroleum hydrocarbons (PHCs) by gas chromatography-flame ionization detection, and total petroleum hydrocarbons (TPHs) by infrared analysis. The PAH analyses provided the best indication of the distribution of North Slope crude oil from the spill in the marine environment and the potential toxicity of the spilled oil to water-column organisms. Therefore, this paper focuses on the PAH data.

In the second component of the water quality program, water-column samples collected at the same times and locations as some samples for PAH analysis from spill path and nonspill path areas of Prince William Sound in the month after the spill and from nearshore waters adjacent to heavily oiled shores in June and July were evaluated for acute and chronic toxicity to sensitive marine plants and animals.

This paper provides a summary of the results of the toxicity tests performed in 1989 and the water-quality investigations performed in 1989 and 1990. Results of some of the water quality studies have been reported in elsewhere (Neff 1991a,b; Neff et al. 1990). The results of these PAH analyses and results from other studies supported by Exxon are summarized here. In addition, results of the water quality program performed by NOAA (Short and Rounds 1993) are included for completeness. The results of these studies provide a context for interpreting the results of the toxicity tests.

MATERIALS AND METHODS

Field Surveys

Sampling Locations--There were eleven damage assessment studies in Prince William Sound and three studies in the western Gulf of Alaska, supported by Exxon, that included sampling and analysis of water samples for polycyclic aromatic hydrocarbons (PAHs). NOAA also performed a water quality study in western Prince William Sound in April and May 1989. The results of all of these studies will be summarized below.

As part of the Exxon-sponsored water-quality program, water samples were collected at least once for hydrocarbon analysis from 327 stations in Prince William Sound between March 31, 1989 and August 9, 1990 (Figure 1) and from 90 stations in the western Gulf of Alaska between April 13 and August 30, 1989 (Figure 2). Water samples from biology studies (e.g., salmon, herring, etc.) are included. NOAA collected water samples for hydrocarbon analysis at least once from an additional 32 sampling stations in

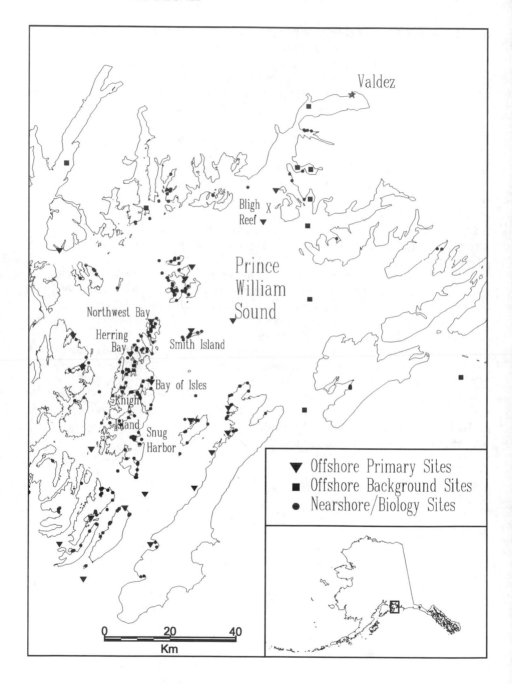

Figure 1--Station locations in Prince William Sound where hydrocarbon concentrations were measured.

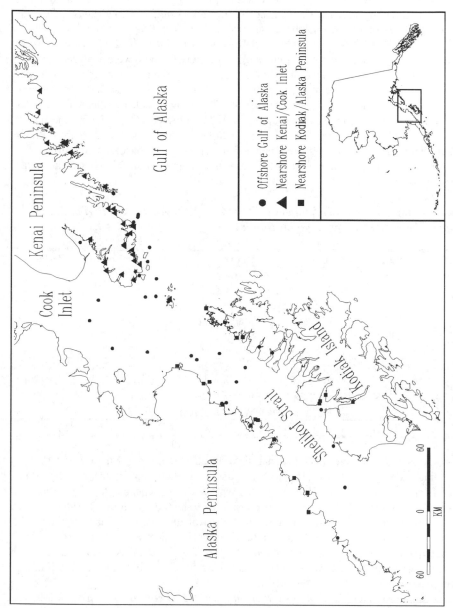

Figure 2--Station locations in western Gulf of Alaska where hydrocarbon concentrations were measured.

the Prince William Sound between March 31 and May 8, 1989 (Short and Rounds 1993).

Most sampling locations were in nearshore waters (<100 m from shore) adjacent to shores that had been oiled. An offshore water-quality study in Prince William Sound included 35 sampling stations 100 m or more from shore (Neff 1991a). The NOAA study also included several offshore sampling stations.

A total of 2 704 water samples from these stations, including 2 461 samples from Exxon-sponsored studies and 243 samples from the NOAA study, were analyzed for individual and total PAHs (Table 1). Most samples were from the water column in areas known or suspected of being within the spill path. Additional reference water samples were collected from locations known or suspected of being outside the spill path, in order to document the background concentrations of PAHs in Prince William Sound and the western Gulf of Alaska. A total of 601 water samples, including 418 samples from Prince William Sound and 183 samples from the Gulf of Alaska, were collected from surface waters. These "surface" samples included water from below the surface, as well as surface sheens, if present.

Table 1--Summary of Water Samples Collected for PAH Analysis as Part of Exxon-Supported and NOAA Water Quality Studies.

Study	Location	Area	Depth	Number	Total
Exxon	PWS	Spill Path	Surface	329	
			Water Column	1 238	1 567
		Reference	Surface	89	
			Water Column	295	384
	GOA	Spill Path	Surface	183	
			Water Column	327	510
	Subtotal				2 461
NOAA	PWS	Spill Path	Water Column	207	
		Reference	Water Column	36	243
	Total				2 704

Most water samples for PAH analysis were collected from (1) the water surface (including water from below the surface), (2) just below the water surface, and (3) from several depths between 1 and 30 m below the water surface, depending on the particular study. The 0 to 30-m depth interval was considered to be the region of the water column most likely to contain elevated concentrations of petroleum hydrocarbons from the spill. It also encompasses the euphotic zone and is the most biologically productive region of the water column of Prince William Sound. As part of a biological assessment of demersal fisheries, water samples also were collected from just above the bottom in 20 to 55 m of water in several bays in the western sound.

Collection and Handling of Water Samples for Chemical Analysis--Various water sampling devices were used in the different studies. During the first two offshore water-quality surveys, most surface-water samples were collected with samplers that collected water from the upper 50 cm of the water column. After the second survey, surface samples were collected in wide-mouth jars and were intended to include any surface sheen material that might be present. Most subsurface water-column samples were collected with water samplers that could be lowered and retrieved through the water surface in a closed position, avoiding possible contamination of the sample with surface sheen material. Some samples were collected directly into sample bottles by divers.

All water samples for PAH analysis were stored and shipped in precleaned amber glass bottles or jars with Teflon®-lined caps (I-CHEM or equivalent). All samples were shipped and stored chilled to 3-4°C. Water samples were collected from survey boats in the field on a daily basis by small float plane or fast boat and returned to Valdez for shipment by air freight to the analytical laboratory. Most water samples were received at the analytical laboratory within two days of collection.

Standard EPA methods for collection of water samples for analysis of organic priority pollutants, including PAHs, recommend that the samples be chilled on ice but not preserved during shipment and storage before analysis. Therefore, water samples collected for PAH analysis during the first two offshore water quality surveys were not preserved. However, there was concern that, since ambient water temperatures in Prince William Sound were only slightly higher than the recommended storage temperature, indigenous microbiota might degrade some of the hydrocarbons during transport and storage. Therefore, after the second offshore field survey, all water samples for PAH analysis were preserved immediately in the field with 5 mL of a 50% aqueous solution of HCl per liter of sample.

Collection and Handling of Water Samples for Toxicity Tests--During the second and third field surveys of the Prince William Sound offshore water-quality program, performed between April 3 and 14 and April 20 and 30, 1989, a total of 123 water samples were collected concurrently with samples for hydrocarbon analyses at 1 and 3 m below the water surface at 30 and 32 stations, respectively, to evaluate the toxicity of the water to representative species of marine organisms. These sampling depths were chosen to be consistent with the offshore water-quality program and to represent the region of the water column most likely to contain the highest concentrations of petroleum hydrocarbons and the largest numbers of marine organisms. Samples were collected from 10 reference and 22 spill-path stations.

Water samples for toxicity tests were collected with a Teflon®-lined piston pump and Teflon® tubing. A few samples were collected with discrete water samplers (e.g., GoFlo samplers). Water samples were placed in 5-gallon (18.9-liter) polyethylene containers. The sample containers were filled completely, leaving no head space, and sealed with Teflon®-lined caps. They were stored in the dark at 4°C and were shipped by air freight to Springborn Laboratories, Wareham, MA, where the toxicity tests were performed.

Between June 21 and July 6, 1989, water samples also were collected in nearshore waters of seven bays in western Prince William Sound. These samples were taken a short distance off oiled shores by submerging 5-gallon polyethylene containers approximately 20 cm below the water surface and allowing them to fill. These samples were collected to determine whether toxic amounts of petroleum were washing off heavily oiled shorelines into the nearshore water column. These water samples were handled in the same fashion as the samples collected for toxicity tests in April.

Quality Assurance and Quality Control--Duplicate water samples were collected periodically (1 pair of duplicates for every 20 or so samples) to determine reproducibility of the sampling and analysis scheme. Field blank samples (high-purity distilled water poured into a sample bottle in the field) and matrix spike/spike duplicates were also collected with every batch of 20 samples for quality control. These quality control samples were used to identify extraneous sources of hydrocarbon contamination in the samples, as from chemical reagents, sampling gear, or exhaust fumes from the sampling vessel.

Rigorous quality assurance procedures were used in all phases of the field and analysis programs. They included strict chain-of-custody procedures to ensure sample integrity from the time of collection through analysis in the laboratory and reporting of the final data. Each water sample was given a unique sample identification code, which allowed matching and comparison of results for samples collected concurrently for chemical and toxicological analysis.

Laboratory Methods (Toxicology)

Three standard marine toxicity tests were performed with water samples from Prince William Sound: (1) the mysid (*Mysidopsis bahia*) static acute toxicity test; (2) the sheepshead minnow (*Cyprinodon variegatus*) 7-day larval survival and growth test; and (3) the marine diatom (*Skeletonema costatum*) 96-hour growth test. These species have been shown to be among the most sensitive test organisms to toxic chemicals in sea water (Suter and Rosen 1988), and are considered suitable surrogates for indigenous species. Mysids and sheepshead minnows were as sensitive as two indigenous species, coonstripe shrimp and pink salmon, to treated ballast water effluents discharged from the Alyeska terminal (Stubblefield unpublished results).

All toxicity tests were performed in accordance with standard procedures described by the U.S. Environmental Protection Agency (U.S. EPA 1985, 1988) and the American Society for Testing and Materials (ASTM 1992a,b). Nearly all tests were initiated within 48 hours of sample receipt; however, recommended sample-holding times were exceeded in a few cases because test organisms were not readily available.

Seawater for dilution, control tests, and diatom cultures was collected from the Cape Cod Canal, Bourne, MA, and filtered through a 5-μm filter and an activated carbon filter. The quality of the dilution water was monitored biologically in the laboratory by maintaining continuous cultures of mysids; satisfactory survival, growth, and reproduction of these sensitive organisms were used to substantiate the quality and acceptability of the natural sea water used as dilution water in laboratory toxicity tests (ASTM 1992a,b). Representative samples of dilution water were analyzed periodically for several pesticides, polychlorinated biphenyls, and metals in accordance with EPA Good Laboratory Practices and ASTM guidelines (ASTM 1992a,b; U.S. EPA 1989). Concentrations of all target chemicals in dilution water samples were below limits set by EPA (i.e., ambient water quality criteria). Toxicity tests were performed periodically with reference toxicants (dodecyl sodium sulfate and potassium dichromate) and test organisms to confirm that the health of the test organisms was within an acceptable range at the initiation of all toxicity tests.

Mysid Acute Toxicity Test--The mysids used in these tests were obtained from in-house laboratory cultures. Mysids in culture were fed live brine shrimp (*Artemia* sp.) nauplii twice daily and Hatchfry Encaplulon®, a high-protein food, three times weekly. Culture water temperature was maintained at 25±1°C. Mysids less than 24 hours posthatch were collected from the cultures and acclimated at the test temperature (20±1°C) for about 24 hours before initiation of the tests.

Mysids were exposed for 96 hours to five dilutions of water samples collected between April 3 and 14, 1989 (6.4, 13, 25, 50, and 100% Prince William Sound water) and to a dilution water control. The salinity of all exposure media was adjusted to that of the full-strength Prince William Sound water sample being investigated (10 to 36 parts per thousand). Test media were aerated and mysids were fed *Artemia* nauplii during the tests. Duplicate test solutions, with ten animals per duplicate, were used at each treatment level in all tests. A minimum of two, but usually four, dilution water controls were run with each test.

Because no acute toxicity was observed in these tests, the test procedure was modified for subsequent tests; mysids were exposed to only the full-strength (100%) Prince William Sound water samples and a dilution water control. All other aspects of the tests were not changed.

The relationship between nominal concentrations in the test media (percentage Prince William Sound water) and mortality data for each observation period was evaluated by probit analysis with a computer program (Stephan 1977a,b) to estimate the median lethal concentration at 96 hours (96h LC_{50}) and its 95% confidence interval.

Sheepshead Minnow Larva 7-Day Survival and Growth Test--The larval sheepshead minnow 7-day test is a rapid-chronic toxicity test developed by EPA for estimating the chronic toxicity of effluents and receiving waters (U.S. EPA 1988). It is used as a surrogate for a full life cycle test and, because it focuses on the most sensitive life stages and biological responses, is considered by EPA to be a good predictor of possible chronic effects.

Most of the larvae used in toxicity tests were obtained from in-house cultures of reproducing sheepshead minnows; however, at times, the number of toxicity tests being performed concurrently exceeded the local supply, and additional embryos were obtained from a commercial supplier, Aquatic Biosystems, Inc., Fort Collins, CO. All developing embryos were incubated and hatched in the testing laboratory in egg cups suspended in an aquarium containing aerated natural dilution water.

Sheepshead minnow larvae were exposed for seven days to five dilutions of Prince William Sound water samples collected between April 3 and 14, 1989 (6.4, 13, 25, 50, and 100% Prince William Sound water) and a dilution water control. The salinity of all exposure media was adjusted to that of the undiluted Prince William Sound water being tested. Duplicate test solutions, each containing 15 fish larvae, were used at each treatment level in all tests. A minimum of two dilution water controls were run with each test. The fish larvae, about 24 hours posthatch at the start of the test, were fed *Artemia* nauplii daily.

Test media were not aerated during the tests but were replaced with freshly prepared exposure media on days three and five of the tests. The stock exposure medium

(100% Prince William Sound water) was kept refrigerated in the dark during the tests and was warmed to the test temperature before preparation of replacement exposure media.

Because no mortality or growth retardation were observed in these tests, the test procedure was modified for subsequent tests; fish larvae were exposed to only the full-strength (100%) Prince William Sound water samples from subsequent field surveys and a dilution water control. All other aspects of the rapid chronic tests were not changed.

Fish survival and growth (increase in dry weight) data were analyzed statistically with a computer program (TOXSTAT, Version 3.2: Gulley et al. 1990) to identify significant ($P<0.05$) treatment-level effects. Statistical analyses were performed on the mean response of fish in each replicate vessel rather than on individual response values. Percentage survival data were transformed to the arcsine square root for analysis, as is appropriate for normalizing proportional data (Sokol and Rohlf 1981). A one-tailed Student's t-test (Sokol and Rohlf 1981) was used to identify significant differences in survival and growth of fish exposed to 100% Prince William Sound water and the control. If a significant difference was observed at the highest treatment level, a one-tailed Dunnett's test (Dunnett 1955, 1964) was used to analyze data for all treatment groups.

The theoretical threshold concentrations expected to produce no deleterious effects at the 95% level of certainty were estimated as the chronic value (ChV), which is equal to the geometric mean of the limits set by the lowest concentration that showed a statistically significant effect (Lowest Observed Effect Concentration, LOEC) and the highest test concentrations that showed no statistically significant difference from the control (No Observed Effect Concentration, NOEC) (U.S. EPA 1988).

Marine Phytoplankton 96-Hour Growth Test--Cultures of the marine diatom *Skeletonema costatum* were obtained from Bigelow Laboratory, Boothbay Harbor, ME, and maintained in stock cultures at the test facility. The diatoms were cultured in a standard culture medium (U.S. EPA 1978) except that natural seawater from Cape Cod Canal, Bourne, MA, rather than synthetic seawater, was used. The cultures were maintained under conditions similar to those used for the toxicity tests (shaking rate of 60 rpm, temperature of $20\pm2°C$, photoperiod of 16 hours of light to 8 hours of dark at a light intensity of approximately 4 000 lm/m^2) for a period of 3 to 7 days before testing. The salinity of test and control media was adjusted to that of the full strength Prince William Sound water sample being evaluated.

The first series of tests included two concentrations (50 and 100%) Prince William Sound water and a control; only 100% Prince William Sound water and a control were tested for samples collected between April 20 and 30. No algal growth tests were performed with samples collected in June and July. There were three replicates in each treatment group.

Tests were initiated by adding 10^4 algal cells to each flask containing 50 mL of the appropriate test or control medium. Mean growth rate of algae was estimated as the increase in the number of cells in each flask (number of cells at the end of the test minus the average number at the start of the test). The growth response of cells to each exposure concentration and control was calculated as the arithmetic mean response for the 3 replicates in each treatment group. Mean responses were evaluated statistically to identify differences among treatments at $P<0.05$. For tests performed with only a control and 100% Prince William Sound water, a Student's t-test (Sokol and Rohlf 1981) was used to identify significant differences in cell numbers between the treatment and control. For tests consisting of a control and 2 treatment levels, significant differences between treatments and control were identified with Dunnett's test (Dunnett 1955, 1964).

Laboratory Methods (Analytical Chemistry)

Water samples for chemical analysis were stored in the laboratory at 4°C in the dark until they were extracted. Most water samples were extracted for analysis within five days of delivery. Samples were not filtered before analysis; therefore, analytical results are for the sum of dissolved and dispersed/particulate hydrocarbons in water.

Methods used in the analysis of water samples for individual and total PAHs have been described in detail elsewhere (Sauer and Boehm 1991; Boehm et al. this volume; Page et al., Benthic Sediments, this volume). Water samples for hydrocarbon analysis were extracted by a modification of EPA SW-846 Method 3510B involving ambient temperature, separatory-funnel liquid-liquid extraction with dichloromethane. The bottles in which water samples were shipped from the field and stored before extraction were rinsed with the extracting solvent to ensure recovery of any hydrocarbons that may have adsorbed to the inner walls of the bottles.

The dichloromethane extracts were concentrated and analyzed by capillary gas chromatography with quantification of target PAH analytes by mass spectrometry in the selected ion monitoring mode. This is a modification of EPA Method 8270. Modifications include changing the surrogate, internal standard, and target analytes to include PAHs commonly encountered in crude oil, using selected ion monitoring to increase analytical sensitivity, and quantification of alkylated PAHs.

The target analytes included naphthalene, phenanthrene, and chrysene and their C_1 through C_4 alkylated homologues, fluorene and dibenzothiophene and their C_1 through C_3 alkylated homologues, acenaphthylene, acenaphthene, anthracene, fluoranthene, pyrene, methyl fluoranthenes and pyrenes, benz(a)anthracene, benzo(b)fluoranthene, benzo(k)fluoranthene, benzo(a)pyrene, dibenz(a,h)anthracene, benzo(g,h,i)perylene, and indeno(1,2,3-cd)pyrene. Surrogate standards added to water samples included d_8-naphthalene, d_{10}-fluorene, and d_{12}-chrysene. Internal standards added to the final extracts included d_{10}-acenaphthene, d_{10}-phenanthrene, and d_{12}-benzo(a)pyrene. The method of internal standards (EPA Method 8000) using the average relative response factors (RRF) generated from the linear initial calibration was used to quantify the target PAHs. PAH alkylated homologues were quantified by a straight line integration of each level of alkylation and the RRF of the respective unsubstituted, parent PAH compound.

Detection limits for many individual PAHs were better than 0.005 µg/L (parts per billion: ppb). This represented more than a hundred-fold improvement over available EPA methods.

Quality control procedures for chemical analyses included the analysis of field and laboratory blanks with every batch of samples, analysis of spiked and standard reference samples, and regular calibration of all analytical instruments (Page et al., Benthic Sediments, this volume).

RESULTS

Toxicity of Prince William Sound Water to Marine Organisms

Toxicity to Mysids and Larval Fish--In tests performed with water samples collected during the April 3-14 survey, juvenile mysids and larval sheepshead minnows were exposed to a series of test media containing 6.3 to 100% Prince William Sound seawater. In no case was there a dose-response relationship between exposure concentration or duration and mortality of either species. Mortality never exceeded 50% in combined replicates at any exposure concentration (highest mortality in any treatment group of minnow larvae was 36.7%; highest mortality in a mysid treatment group was 25%). Because there was no dose-response relationship and mortalities in all treatment groups were never significantly different from those of the concurrent controls and were always less than 50%, median lethal concentrations (LC_{50}) and chronic values (ChV) could not be estimated (ASTM 1992a,b). (These toxicity endpoints could not be estimated because they are in excess of actual concentrations of petroleum hydrocarbons in the water samples tested, i.e., greater than 100% Prince William Sound water).

Because there was no dose-response relationship for any water samples collected in early April, tests performed with samples collected in late April and June-July were performed at only the highest possible exposure concentration, 100% Prince William Sound water. In a few cases where the full-strength seawater sample produced a response significantly different from that of the concurrent controls (four tests with sheepshead minnow larvae), the test was repeated at a series of exposure concentrations. As for the early April samples, all values for LC_{50} and ChV in the mysid acute tests and the sheepshead minnow larvae rapid chronic tests for samples collected in late April and June-July were greater than 100% Prince William Sound water.

In all cases for mysids and nearly all cases for minnow larvae, survival among animals exposed to full-strength Prince William Sound was greater than 80% of control survival. When water samples that produced less than 80% survival among minnow larvae were retested, survival among the larvae exposed to 100% Prince William Sound water was always greater than 93%.

Full-strength water samples collected between June 21 and July 6, 1989 from about 20 cm below the water surface a short distance off seven oiled shorelines also were nontoxic to mysids and sheepshead minnows. These samples contained 0.05 to 1.95 ppb total PAHs. Thus, oil was not washing off these seven shores in toxic amounts.

Because water samples for chemical analysis were collected concurrently with most water samples for toxicity testing (214 water samples, including many duplicate and triplicate samples, were collected concurrently with 115 of 130 water samples collected for toxicity tests and were analyzed for PAH), it is possible to evaluate the relationships between the responses of test organisms to exposure to full-strength Prince William Sound water and concentrations of PAHs in the water. The endpoint used in this evaluation was mean survival (among replicates) of animals exposed to full-strength Prince William Sound water expressed as a percentage of the survival among concurrent controls (Figures 3 and 4). No correlation was found between relative survival and PAH concentration in either case ($R^2 < 0.001$ and $R^2 < 0.0037$, respectively).

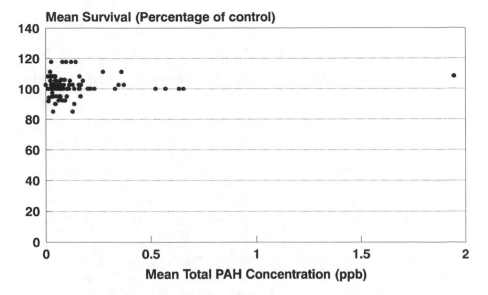

*Figure 3--Mean survival (as percentage of controls) versus mean
total PAH concentration for mysid shrimp acute toxicity tests.*

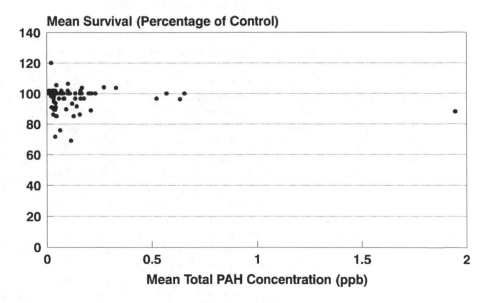

*Figure 4--Mean survival (as percentage of controls) versus mean total
PAH concentration for sheepshead minnow 7-day survival test.*

There was little difference in survival between exposed and control animals at the highest concentrations of PAHs (greater than about 0.4 ppb) in the water samples. At low concentrations of total PAHs (less than about 0.2 ppb) in the water samples, there was more variability in the relative survival of mysids and minnow larvae. This may reflect the greater statistical variability associated with the larger number of Prince William water samples in the very low PAH concentration range and to effects of variation in salinity of the Prince William Sound water samples.

Effects on Growth of Diatoms and Fish Larvae--Exposure for four days (diatoms) or seven days (minnows) to Prince William Sound water had highly variable effects on growth. There was no relationship between the exposure concentration of Prince William Sound water and the change in cell numbers of diatoms and weight of fish. As an example of the extreme variability of results for the algal growth test, the maximum range of responses to exposure to full strength Prince William Sound water, as a percentage of control growth, from -98% (inhibition) to +219% (stimulation), was for two water samples taken from the same unoiled reference station in early and late April.

In most *Skeletonema* growth tests (68%), exposure to test water resulted in a slight inhibition of growth (relative to control). Full-strength samples of 41 of the 123 water samples collected in April for toxicity tests produced a statistically significant inhibition of growth rate in *Skeletonema*. However, there was no dose-response relationship in any test, and a ChV could not be estimated. No algal growth tests were performed with nearshore water samples collected in June and July.

Considering the high variability in the responses of the algae and the fact that the greatest responses were produced with Prince William Sound water from unoiled reference stations, it is probable that the algae were responding primarily to differences in the natural chemical composition and salinity of Prince William Sound water and control culture water (from the Cape Cod Canal, MA) and not to petroleum hydrocarbons in Prince William Sound water.

Growth (measured as increase in body weight) of sheepshead minnow larvae exposed to Prince William Sound water for seven days usually was within 20% of the growth of concurrent controls and ranged from about 45 to 170% of control growth. Most differences between treatment and control fish were not statistically significant. Two water samples collected on April 20 and 22, 1989, produced a significant inhibition of growth in sheepshead minnow larvae, relative to controls. One sample was from an unoiled reference station; the other was from Herring Bay, a heavily oiled site. These samples contained 0.035 ppb and 0.16 ppb, respectively, total PAH; concentrations of total resolved and unresolved petroleum hydrocarbons were below the detection limit. Because there was no dose-response relationship for mortality or growth in sheepshead minnow larvae, ChVs could not be estimated for any water samples.

The relative growth of sheepshead minnow larvae exposed for seven days to seven water samples collected just below the water surface off heavily oiled shores in June-July ranged from 86.8 to 119% of control growth, well within acceptable limits for this test. Thus, none of these water samples collected near oiled shorelines in Prince William Sound can be considered toxic to the test animals in a rapid chronic test.

There was no relationship between relative growth rates of algae ($R^2 < 0.001$) and sheepshead minnow larvae ($R^2 < 0.029$) during exposure to full-strength Prince William

Sound water and concentrations of total PAHs in the water samples (Figures 5 and 6). As expected, the relative growth rates of algae and minnows were more variable than relative survival of mysids and minnows. However, the greatest variability was at the lowest PAH concentrations, indicating that the traces of petroleum hydrocarbons in the water samples did not contribute to the variability in growth responses.

Petroleum Hydrocarbons in the Water Column

Data Quality--There was good agreement in concentrations of total PAHs in the duplicate samples collected periodically during the Exxon studies. There were 176 sets of replicates involving 375 samples and duplicates. The average coefficient of variation between these replicate samples and their replicate means was 0.084, and $R^2 = 0.95$. Recoveries of analytes were good in matrix spike samples and standard reference materials. Field blank samples typically contained only trace concentrations of PAHs.

About 50 water samples from the summer of 1990 contained elevated levels (i.e., above 0.1 ppb) of either naphthalene or methylnaphthalene. The source of these compounds was traced to the solvent used for extraction. Short and Rice (1993) report that some of the NOAA samples contained elevated levels of naphthalene, also from a solvent. These elevated spikes of individual analytes are not spill related and are easily differentiable from the rest of the PAH fingerprint.

Water samples collected for chemical analysis during the first two offshore water-quality field-surveys supported by Exxon (124 samples collected between March 31 and April 14, 1989), as well as samples for toxicity tests, were not preserved in the field. The samples were kept chilled on ice or in a refrigerator (0-4°C) until extraction for analysis or initiation of toxicity tests. However, ambient seawater temperatures in Prince William Sound during March and April 1989 were generally near 4°C; therefore, hydrocarbons in the samples could have been subject to degradation by cold-adapted hydrocarbon-degrading bacteria between the time of collection and analysis or testing. Stewart et al. (1993) reviewed the published literature on the rates of crude oil biodegradation in seawater and concluded that rates vary widely, depending on the concentration of hydrocarbons present, mixing energy of the system, and ambient temperature.

Temperature-normalized (to 20°C) microbial degradation is first order with respect to oil concentration in the water, with a mean rate constant of 0.011 d^{-1}. The degradation rate constant would have been lower for temperature-acclimated microbes at 4-5°C. Thus, the concentration of total petroleum hydrocarbons in water might be expected to decrease by up to 1% per day under ambient conditions. All but three of the water samples collected during these two field surveys were processed for chemical analysis or toxicity testing within ten days of collection. Therefore, total biodegradation probably did not exceed about 10%. PAHs are degraded by water-column microorganisms more slowly than saturated hydrocarbons (Oudot 1984; Heitkamp and Cerniglia 1987). Therefore, degradation rate of the petroleum PAH assemblage in the water samples that were not preserved in the field probably was less than 10%. Subsequent to the second offshore water-quality field-survey in Prince William Sound, all water samples for chemical analysis were preserved by acidification.

Toxicity Test Samples-- A total of 214 water samples were collected for PAH analysis concurrently (same time, location, and water depth) with 115 of the water

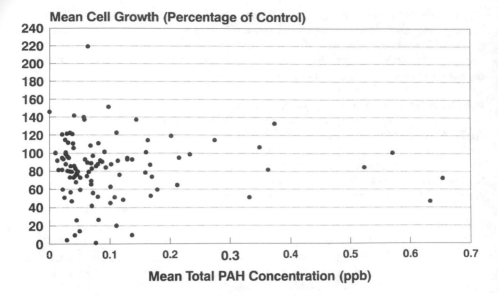

Figure 5--Mean cell growth (as percentage of controls) versus mean total PAH concentration for marine phytoplankton 96-hour growth test.

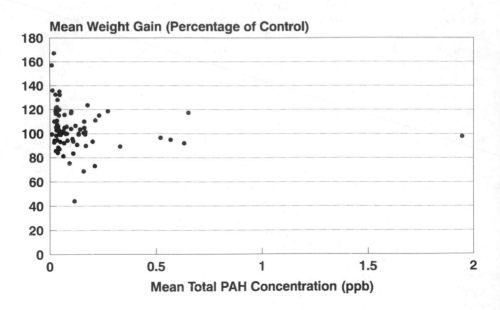

Figure 6--Mean weight gain (as percentage of controls) versus mean total PAH concentration for sheepshead minnow 7-day growth test.

samples for toxicity tests. The mean concentration of total PAHs in water-column samples collected concurrently with samples from offshore stations in Prince William Sound for toxicity tests in April 1989 was about 0.1 ppb (range <0.01 to 0.73 ppb). The mean PAH and standard deviation concentration in water samples collected from 1 and 3 m between April 4 and 14, 1989 was 0.09±0.09 ppb; the concentration of PAH in water samples from the same depths and locations collected between April 20 and 30, 1989 was 0.10±0.14 ppb. Near-surface (0.2 m), shallow water samples collected for toxicity testing between June 21 and July 6, 1989 contained 0.046 to 1.95 ppb total PAHs (average and standard deviation, 0.40±0.69). The highest concentrations of total PAHs were in the water column of heavily oiled bays, such as the Bay of Isles and Snug Harbor, both on Knight Island. This range of concentrations is within the range of about 85% of the concentrations of total PAHs in water column samples collected throughout spill path areas of Prince William Sound during March, April and May of 1989 (Figure 7). Therefore, the results of the toxicity tests provide a reasonable approximation of the toxicity of the spill-path water column in the few months after the spill.

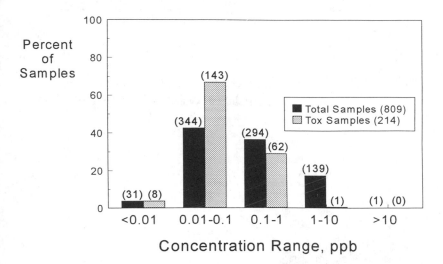

Figure 7--Comparison of distribution of PAH concentrations for toxicology water samples with all water-quality samples (including NOAA's) during March - May, 1989.

Distribution of PAHs in the Water Column--A total of 2 461 water samples from Prince William Sound and the western Gulf of Alaska were analyzed for total and individual PAHs as part of several environmental assessment programs sponsored by Exxon (Table 1). Of these samples, 384 were from nonspill path areas of the Sound (reference sites); the remainder were from areas documented or suspected of having been in the path of the spreading oil slick. Short and Rounds (1993) collected an additional 243 water samples for PAH analysis from Prince William Sound in April and May 1989. Thirty-six of these samples were from reference sites; the remainder were from the spill

.th, particularly in nearshore waters of heavily oiled bays in the western sound. The
results of these analyses are summarized here.

Concentrations of total PAHs in the "open" water-column of spill path areas of
western Prince William Sound were highly variable in time and space during the spring and
summer of 1989. (The phrase "open" water-column refers to the nearshore and offshore
water column not within a containment boom. Water column samples do not include
samples taken at the surface.) Concentrations greater than 1 ppb total PAHs were
encountered most frequently in April 1989 and concentrations throughout the sound
generally decreased with time after the spill (Figure 8). (Figure 8 includes all samples
other than those collected inside containment booms, which are discussed separately.) A
total of 17.3% (140 samples) of open water column samples collected in April and May
1989 contained more than 1 ppb total PAHs (Figure 7). Only one sample contained more
than 10 ppb total PAHs, the state of Alaska standard for total aromatic hydrocarbons in
sea water.

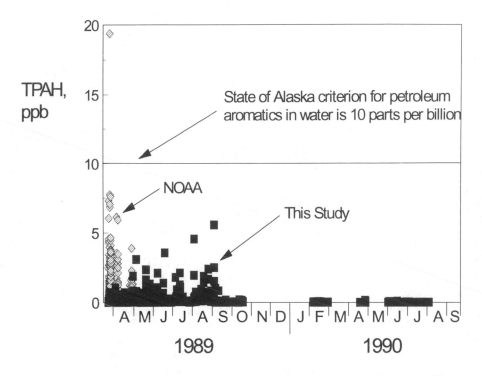

*Figure 8--Total PAH concentrations in the open-water-column of spill
path areas of Prince William Sound.*

The highest PAH concentration in an open-water-column sample was 19.38 ppb in
a sample collected by Short and Rounds (1993) at 5 m off the north shore of Green Island
(a heavily oiled site) on April 3, 1989. Two replicate water samples collected at the same

time and location contained 1.66 and 2.96 ppb total PAHs, and the sample containing 19.38 ppb total PAHs contained anomalously high concentrations (compared to the sp oil) of naphthalene, C2-naphthalene and other individual analytes. Short and Rounds (1993) do not discuss this high sample specifically; it apparently failed their statistical tes for correlation with *Exxon Valdez* oil composition. Most other water samples collected b. Short and Rounds (1993) and in Exxon-sponsored studies and containing elevated concentrations of PAHs did have a PAH composition similar to that of weathered North Slope crude oil.

Other than the one high NOAA sample, none of the open-water-column samples contained more than 10 ppb total PAHs, the state of Alaska's water quality standard for total dissolved aromatic hydrocarbons in seawater. Therefore, concentrations of PAHs in the samples were well below concentrations known or suspected of causing harmful effects in Alaskan marine organisms.

Highest concentrations of total PAHs were found in open-water-column samples from heavily oiled bays in the western sound and adjacent to heavily oiled shorelines. The most heavily oiled bays were Northwest Bay, Herring Bay, Snug Harbor, and Bay of Isles. In early April, but not later, water-column samples collected offshore in Montague Strait (the main route of exit of oil slicks from the sound: Galt et al. 1991) also contained elevated concentrations (about 0.9 ppb) of PAHs (Short and Rounds 1993). After mid-May, the highest concentrations of total PAHs in the open water column of Prince William Sound were in samples collected during shoreline cleanup just outside booms deployed off shorelines being treated to remove oil (Figure 8).

Water-column samples were also collected from within the primary containment boom during shoreline treatment. Oil droplets from cleanup operations were for the most part retained inside the containment booms, where they were allowed to coalesce at the surface for removal by skimmers and absorbants. The results of those analyses are not included in Figure 8.

Seventeen water samples collected inside the primary booms during shoreline cleanup contained 0.42 to 77.65 ppb total PAHs (average and standard deviation 16.03 ±26.65 ppb). Three water samples collected from inside the primary booms on the day after completion of shoreline cleanup contained 0.31 to 0.91 ppb total PAHs (average 0.54 ppb). Water samples collected just outside the booms during shoreline cleanup contained an average of 0.75±0.93 ppb total PAHs (range 0.05-5.59 ppb). Shortly after shoreline cleanup had been completed, water-column samples collected just outside the booms contained an average of 0.21±0.23 ppb total PAHs (range 0.02-1.02 ppb). Thus, although shoreline cleanup did flush petroleum hydrocarbons into the nearshore water column, relatively little of the oil escaped the booms deployed to prevent escape of oil sheens, and PAH concentrations in the water column returned rapidly to low levels after cessation of cleanup at the site.

PAH concentrations in the offshore water-column of Prince William Sound decreased to background levels within a couple of months. Surface samples generally had higher arithmetic average concentrations than subsurface samples, the result of a few samples containing surface sheens. Surface samples collected during the first two cruises were collected with sampling devices that sampled the upper half meter of water. Later

e samples contained water only from the top 3 cm. This difference in sampling
ique contributes to the apparent peak in surface samples during late April (Figure 9).

PAH concentrations in the open nearshore water column of heavily oiled bays
ually decreased rapidly after the spill (Figure 10). For example, in Snug Harbor, highest
concentrations (mean 6.24 ppb) were observed in early April and had decreased by nearly
two thirds by mid-April (2.41 ppb at 1 m). By May, all concentrations were at or below 1
ppb; by late June and early July, concentrations had dropped below about 0.1 ppb. Similar
trends were observed in most other heavily oiled bays.

The exception was Northwest Bay. Northwest Bay, was very heavily oiled; it was
boomed shortly after the spill to prevent oil from escaping and oiling other shores. The
bay remained boomed from the rest of the sound for most of the summer. During the
summer of 1989, the shorelines of Northwest Bay were intensively and repeatedly cleaned.
Elevated concentrations of PAHs were observed on the water surface (in sheens) and in
the water column of the bay throughout most of the summer of 1989.

PAHs in the Water Column of Reference Areas in Prince William Sound--Of
295 water samples collected during Exxon-sponsored studies in nonspill path (reference)
areas of Prince William Sound, four samples contained more than 0.2 ppb total PAHs.
Most of the remaining samples contained less than 0.1 ppb total PAHs. A duplicate to the
sample containing the highest PAH concentration (0.78 ppb) contained 0.018 ppb. These
duplicate samples were from 1 m below the water surface in Hinchinbrook Entrance and
the high sample probably contained a micro-tar ball. These results indicate that
background concentrations of total PAHs in the water column of Prince William Sound
are generally less than 0.1 ppb.

PAHs in Surface Water Samples in Prince William Sound--A total of 329
samples from spill-path areas in Prince William Sound and 89 samples from reference
areas were taken at the water surface for analysis of petroleum hydrocarbons as part of
two Exxon-sponsored studies. These samples were intended to include any oil-sheen
material that may have been present on the water surface at the time of sampling. Most
surface water samples included water from the top few centimeters of the ocean and so do
not represent a quantitative estimate of the concentrations of PAHs in sheens themselves.
Eight of the surface samples from spill-path areas (2.4%) contained more than 10 ppb
total PAHs; the highest concentration measured in a surface-water sample was 29.27 ppb
total PAHs. Most surface samples contained less than 1 ppb total PAHs. Highest PAH
concentrations were consistently observed throughout the summer of 1989 in surface
samples from Northwest Bay. Several surface samples collected in February and March of
1990 contained trace or undetectable concentrations of total PAHs. Only two surface
water samples from reference locations in Prince William Sound (2.2%) contained more
than 0.4 ppb total PAHs. The two samples containing more than 0.4 ppb total PAHs were
from Lower Herring Bay (1.3 ppb) and College Fjord (1.0 ppb), both well outside the spill
path. Most samples from reference locations contained less than 0.1 ppb total PAHs.
These results, though not quantitative for sheen material, indicate that sheens were rare
and unevenly distributed in Prince William Sound during the summer of 1989.

PAHs in the Water Column of the Gulf of Alaska--Concentrations of PAHs in
the offshore water-column of spill-path areas of the western Gulf of Alaska (Figure 2) in

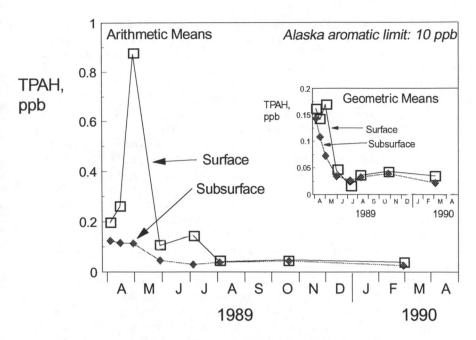

Figure 9--Average PAH concentrations for surface and subsurface water at primary offshore stations in Prince William Sound.

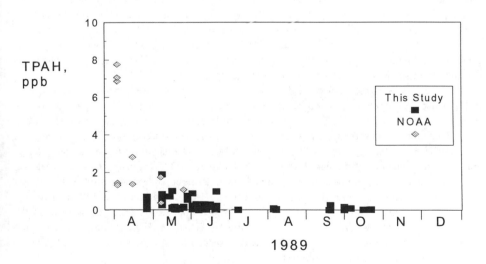

Figure 10--Concentrations of Total Polycyclic Aromatic Hydrocarbons (TPAH) in water samples from Snug Harbor

April and May 1989, when slicks of weathered oil and mousse were drifting through the area, generally were very low. The average concentration of total PAHs in 140 water samples collected between April 13 and May 21 was 0.11±0.14 ppb. PAH concentrations ranged from nondetectable to 0.99 ppb.

An additional 370 water samples were collected in shallow nearshore waters off oiled shores along the Kenai Peninsula, Kodiak Island, and the Alaska peninsula (Figure 2) in July and August. They contained an average of 0.03±0.05 ppb total PAHs. The highest concentration of total PAHs in the water column was 0.42 ppb.

One hundred and eighty-three surface-water samples, collected in the Gulf of Alaska between April 21 and August 30, 1989, contained an average of 0.03±0.05 ppb total PAHs (range <0.005 to 0.31 ppb). A surface water sample, not included in the above average and containing mousse material, collected in Morning Cove during a storm in early August 1993, contained 4 320 ppb total PAHs; a water sample collected from the water column 1 m below the mousse contained 0.32 ppb total PAHs. The water sample from 9 m below the surface mousse contained 0.008 ppb total PAHs (Neff 1991b). These results indicate that very little oil from floating mousse penetrated down into the water column to depths of 1 or more meters.

Composition of the PAH Assemblage in the Water Column--Initially, the composition of the PAH assemblage in the water column appeared to be enriched in the low molecular weight, more water soluble analytes (i.e., parents and lightly alkylated PAH) compared to the high-molecular-weight, less-water-soluble analytes (Figure 11A). Later, the composition of the PAH assemblage in most water-column samples resembled that of weathered North Slope crude oil, with reduced naphthalenes. Water column samples were still generally enriched in the more-water-soluble PAH compared to sheens on the surface (Figure 11B). The relative concentrations of different PAHs in the water samples was variable, depending on the degree of weathering and relative proportions of dissolved and dispersed oil present. Early water samples had a PAH assemblage roughly resembling that of the water-accommodated fraction of crude oil used in most laboratory toxicity tests (Anderson et al. 1974). Dispersed and particulate oil is less toxic to water column organisms than dissolved hydrocarbons (Anderson et al. 1974).

Many water samples also are depleted in lower molecular weight n-alkanes (C_{10} to C_{18}) and slightly enriched in higher molecular weight n-alkanes ($>C_{24}$) compared to the unweathered oil (Neff 1991b). The presence of high molecular weight n-alkanes with more than about 20 carbon atoms, which have extremely low aqueous solubilities (Coates et al. 1985), indicated that some of the petroleum hydrocarbons were present in the water column in dispersed or particulate forms. Short and Rounds (1993) also concluded that many of their water-column samples contained both dissolved and particulate PAHs.

Several water samples from throughout the spill-path and non-spill-path areas of Prince William Sound and the western Gulf of Alaska contained PAH assemblages that did not resemble that of weathered North Slope crude oil. These PAH assemblages may have been derived from diesel fuel or seep oil, as was observed for several sediment and tissue samples (Bence and Burns this volume).

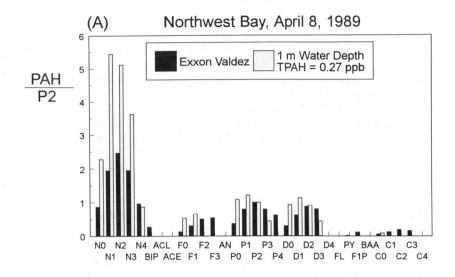

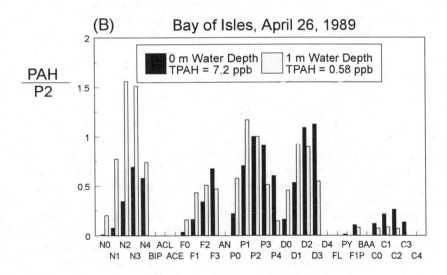

Figure 11--Fingerprint profiles of PAH analytes relative to C_2-phenanthrene (P2). (A) Northwest Bay, April 8, 1989, (B) Bay of Isles, April 26, 1989.

DISCUSSION

The combination of water quality and toxicology test results provides a broad perspective for assessing possible adverse biological effects of the oil spill on marine plants and animals living in the water column of Prince William Sound and the western Gulf of Alaska. The most compelling data for estimating potential effects are direct toxicological studies using water sampled from the water column of spill-path areas of Prince William Sound shortly after the spill. These data, coupled with the results of the most extensive water-quality monitoring program ever conducted following an oil spill, provide a strong basis for extrapolating the aquatic toxicology results to the larger expanse of Prince William Sound and the western Gulf of Alaska.

Petroleum Hydrocarbons in the Water Column

Hydrocarbons Responsible for Toxicity of Oil to Water Column Organisms--Volatile aromatic hydrocarbons (benzene, toluene, ethylbenzene, and xylenes), sometimes called VOAs, and low-molecular-weight polycyclic aromatic hydrocarbons (PAHs) are the constituents of crude oil that are responsible for most of its toxicity to water-column organisms (Rice et al. 1977; Neff and Anderson 1981). The State of Alaska has a water quality standard for total dissolved aromatic hydrocarbons (VOAs plus PAHs) of 10 μg/L (parts per billion: ppb). The VOAs, although slightly soluble in seawater, are so volatile that they evaporate rapidly from an oil slick on the water surface or from solution in the upper water column (Stiver and Mackay 1984). Therefore, they may contribute to the toxicity of spilled oil for only a few days after a spill. Two- and three-ring PAHs and their alkylated homologues are abundant in many crude oils, slightly soluble in seawater, and are persistent enough to contribute to the toxicity of oil in the water column for a longer period of time. VOAs were analyzed in many of the water samples analyzed for PAHs. VOA concentrations in water samples were highly variable and did not correlate with concentrations of PAHs and total petroleum hydrocarbons in the samples (Neff 1991a).

Therefore, PAH analyses provided the most useful information about the temporal and spacial distribution and concentrations of potentially toxic fractions of the spilled oil in the water column. North Slope crude oil contains about 14 000 mg/kg (parts per million) total two- and three-ring PAHs and their alkylated homologues (Page et al., Benthic Sediments, this volume).

Hydrocarbons in the Water Column During the Week After the Spill--The first water samples gathered in either NOAA or Exxon-sponsored studies were collected on March 30, 1989, six days after the spill. Therefore, no empirical data are available on concentrations of petroleum hydrocarbons and PAHs in the water column of Prince William Sound during the first week after the spill. However, Wolfe et al. (1994) used the NOAA oil weathering model to predict the concentration of dissolved and dispersed oil in the upper water column under the spreading oil slick between March 27 and March 30, the time period of the gale in the sound. They estimated that the average concentration of total petroleum hydrocarbons was 800 ppb in the top 10 meters under the slick during the storm, which corresponded to a volume less than 0.1 % of the water in the sound. This concentration of total petroleum hydrocarbons corresponds to an average PAH concentration of about 12 ppb, based on a total petroleum hydrocarbon to PAH ratio of

67. The larger dispersed droplets doubtless resurfaced after the storm. The model predicted subsequent rapid dilution of hydrocarbons as the slick spread into the western part of the sound and as tidal mixing and turnover of the surface waters occurred. This prediction was confirmed by the empirical water quality studies described above.

Temporal and Spatial Trends in PAH Concentrations in the Water Column-- More than 90% of the 2 268 water samples collected for PAH analysis from spill-path areas in Prince William Sound in 1989 and 1990 contained less than 1 ppb total PAHs. Nine samples, all but one from the water surface, contained more than 10 ppb total PAH (the state of Alaska standard for total dissolved aromatics in sea water). Most of the surface samples containing elevated concentrations of PAHs were collected off heavily oiled shores, particularly in Northwest Bay, during shoreline cleanup activities during the summer of 1989 and probably contained surface sheen material. Within a month after the spill, concentrations of PAHs in the water column of all but a few protected spill path locations had dropped below 1 ppb. Most water samples contained less than 0.1 ppb total PAHs.

Other Spills--This range of PAH concentrations in the water column of the spill path generally was similar to concentrations reported in the water column after other major crude oil spills in the marine environment. PAH concentrations in the water column may be somewhat higher after spills of light and medium distilled products, such as jet fuel and diesel fuel.

Grahl-Nielsen (1978) reported that concentrations of total low-molecular-weight PAHs in the water column near the Ekofisk Bravo oil platform shortly after a blowout in April 1977 ranged from 8 ppb near the well to about 0.1 ppb at the edge of the area of floating oil emulsion. At 6.4 km downcurrent from the well, the PAH concentration was 4.1 ppb; 17.7 km from the well, the concentration was 0.38 ppb. Two weeks after the well was capped, PAH concentrations had dropped to 0.40 ppb near the well to 0.05 ppb at the edge of the spill-affected zone. Boehm et al. (1979) reported that concentrations of individual petroleum PAHs in the water column down-current from the *Argo Merchant* spill of heavy fuel oil were in the range of 0.01 to 0.066 ppb shortly after the spill. Water from a depth of 2 m near the well head of the Ixtoc I blowout in Campeche Bay, Mexico, contained 2 860 ppb total particulate PAHs and 81 ppb dissolved PAHs (Boehm and Fiest 1982). Kennicutt et al. (1991) reported 50 to 100 ppb total PAHs in the water column near the *Bahia Paradiso* diesel oil spill in the Antarctic. PAH concentrations returned to nondetectable levels within a month after the spill. One year after the Iraq-Kuwait war, concentrations of total low-molecular-weight PAHs in the nearshore water-column off heavily oiled shores were in the range of 0.005 to 0.105 ppb (Ehrhardt and Burns 1993).

Natural Background--Most water samples from non-spill-path areas of Prince William Sound collected during the Exxon offshore water-quality study contained less than 0.1 ppb total dissolved and particulate PAHs. It is probable that the natural background concentration of total PAHs in the water column of Prince William Sound is in the range of 0.01 to 0.1 ppb. These PAHs probably are derived in large part from natural oil seeps to the southeast (up-current) from the sound (Page et al. Benthic Sediments, this volume). These PAHs are carried into Prince William Sound associated with suspended clay-sized particles and are deposited in sediments throughout the sound and the western Gulf of Alaska.

Natural background concentrations of PAHs in the marine water column vary widely depending on the proximity to natural and anthropogenic sources. Wade et al. (1989) reported an average concentration of 0.028 ppb total PAH in water samples collected near a hydrocarbon seep in 570 m of water in the Gulf of Mexico. Concentrations of total semivolatile PAH in the water near a shallow-water seep off southern California are in the range of 0.15 to 0.52 ppb (Stuermer et al. 1982).

The total concentration of phenanthrene, dibenzothiophene, fluoranthene, pyrene, and their alkylated homologues in the water column of the northern Arabian Gulf in 1986 was 0.019 ppb (Ehrhardt and Douabul 1989). Phenanthrene and monomethylphenanthrenes were the most abundant PAH present. The total concentrations of naphthalene, fluorene, phenanthrene, dibenzothiophene, fluoranthene, pyrene, and their alkylated homologues in water samples from three nearshore locations around Bermuda ranged from 0.003 to 0.062 ppb (Ehrhardt and Burns 1990). A water sample from an offshore reference station contained only 0.01 ng/L (parts per trillion) fluoranthene. Surface waters from the open Mediterranean Sea contained 0.049 to 0.051 ppb total PAHs (Ehrhardt and Petrick 1993). The dominant PAHs were phenanthrene and alkylphenanthrenes. Water samples collected from 1 m below the water surface in Faringehavn, Greenland contained 0.005 to 0.22 ppb total light PAHs (Futsaeter 1991). By comparison, the concentration of light PAHs in offshore water was 0.005 ppb.

Water from the Mackenzie River and estuary, Canada, contained 0.054 to 1.824 ppb total PAH in solution (Carey et al. 1990). Suspended particulate matter in Mackenzie River water contained 0.052 to 0.418 µg/g total PAH. Fluorene was the most abundant PAH in solution and naphthalene was the most abundant PAH associated with the suspended particulate phase. These PAHs were derived primarily from weathering of peat and coal along the Mackenzie River drainage. Water from the Rhône River, France, contained 0.004 to 0.120 ppb dissolved PAH and 0.4 to 9.2 µg/g particulate PAH (Bouloubassi and Saliot 1993). Thus, background concentrations of total PAHs in marine and estuarine waters usually is in the range of 0.01 to 0.1 ppb.

Toxicity of Prince William Sound Water

Water samples collected from 1 and 3 m below the water surface of Prince William Sound in the month after the spill were not toxic to three widely-used marine bioassay organisms, representing three major taxonomic groups (marine plants, invertebrates, and vertebrates) in acute and rapid chronic toxicity tests. The sensitivity of representatives of these three taxa to chemicals in the water varies widely and covers the range of sensitivity expected in organisms from most marine and aquatic ecosystems (Kimerle et al. 1983). The sheepshead minnow is a representative toxicity-test organism, and the mysid is among the most sensitive test organisms to toxic chemicals in seawater (Suter and Rosen 1988). Marine microalgae, such as *Skeletonema*, are sensitive to many chemical contaminants, but also are sensitive to small differences in seawater composition. Thus, they are less useful than most marine animals for assessing toxic chemicals in bulk water samples. However, the lack of a dose-response relationship in the algae during exposure to Prince William Sound water indicates that concentrations of petroleum hydrocarbons in the water column of the sound were below effects concentrations.

No relationship was found between either the exposure concentration of Prince

William Sound water or total PAH concentration in water samples and toxicity endpoints (acute [survival] or sublethal [growth rate] responses) for any of the test organisms. Therefore, concentrations of petroleum hydrocarbons in seawater collected from the spill area, not toxic to these sensitive test species, would not likely be toxic to marine organisms indigenous to Prince William Sound.

The initial concentrations of total PAHs (the most toxic fraction of slightly weathered crude oil) in the water samples used in toxicity tests (<0.05 to 1.95 ppb total PAHs) were comparable to the range of concentrations measured in a much larger number of water samples from throughout the spill-path area of Prince William Sound and the Gulf of Alaska (Figure 7). A small number of water-column samples contained slightly higher concentrations of PAHs than those in toxicity test samples. During static and static-renewal toxicity tests, such as those performed as part of this study, slightly volatile chemicals, such as low molecular weight PAHs, may evaporate from the exposure media. As a result, test organisms were exposed to lower mean concentrations of PAHs than reported. However, natural populations of marine water-column organisms in Prince William Sound also were being exposed to rapidly fluctuating concentrations of spill-derived PAHs. Therefore, the laboratory toxicity tests represent a reasonable approximation of exposure in the environment. However, the decreasing concentrations in exposure media should be considered in extrapolating from test results to estimates of adverse effects in water column organisms in the field. This can be done by comparing PAH concentrations shown to be nontoxic in the tests with Prince William Sound water to results of acute and chronic toxicity tests with crude oil and specific PAHs from the scientific literature.

Relation to Published Values for Oil Toxicity--The oil-water preparation used most frequently to evaluate the toxicity of crude and refined oils to marine organisms is the water-soluble or water-accommodated fraction prepared by gently mixing oil and water for a set period of time (Anderson et al. 1974). The dominant hydrocarbons in the water-soluble fraction include benzene, C_1 to C_3 alkylbenzenes, and low-molecular-weight PAHs. Benzene and alkylbenzenes leave the water soluble fraction rapidly (Riley et al. 1981), leaving low molecular weight 2- and 3-ring PAHs, which are responsible for most of the toxicity of crude oil (Rice et al. 1977; Neff and Anderson 1981). Thus, the water soluble fraction roughly resembles the composition of the hydrocarbon fraction accommodated in the water column of Prince William Sound after the spill.

Concentrations of crude oil, and particularly petroleum-derived PAHs in the water column of Prince William Sound and the western Gulf of Alaska after the *Exxon Valdez* oil spill, were well below the range of concentrations that have been shown in previous laboratory studies to be toxic to or produce sublethal biological effects in marine organisms from southern Alaska. The acute toxicity of water-soluble fractions of Alaskan crude oils to Alaksan crustaceans, echinoderms, and fish (measured as the median lethal concentration, LC_{50}, after 24 to 96 hours of exposure) ranges from about 0.8 to 32 mg/L (parts per million: ppm), equivalent to 800 to 32 000 ppb total aromatic hydrocarbons (Table 2). Weathering substantially decreases the toxicity of crude oil to marine organisms. Water-soluble fractions of weathered Prudhoe Bay crude oil were practic[?] nontoxic to several species of marine animals, including species indigenous to south[?] Alaska (Anderson 1985).

Table 2--Acute toxicity (96 hr LC$_{50}$) of crude oils to Alaskan marine animals. Median lethal concentrations in seawater recorded as concentration of aromatic hydrocarbons (mg/L: ppm) derived from the water-soluble fraction of the oil.

Species	Oil	LC$_{50}$ (ppm)	Reference
Crustaceans			
Amphipod *Anonyx nugax*	Prudhoe Bay	32.00	Foy, 1982.
Amphipod *Orchomene pinguis*	Cook Inlet	>7.98	Rice et al., 1979.
Mysid *Acanthomysis pseudomacropsis*	Cook Inlet	>9.02	Rice et al., 1979.
Grass shrimp *Crangon alaskensis*	Cook Inlet	0.87	Rice et al., 1979.
Kelp shrimp larvae *Eualus sucklevi*	Crude oil	1-3*	Rice et al., 1984.
Adults	Cook Inlet	1.86	Rice et al., 1979.
	Cook Inlet	1.40	Rice et al., 1984.
Shrimp *Eualus* sp. (4 °C)	Cook Inlet	1.68	Korn et al., 1979.
Pink shrimp *Pandalus borealis*	Cook Inlet	4.94	Rice et al., 1979.
	Cook Inlet	1.20**	Stickle et al., 1987.
Humpy shrimp *Pandalus goniurus*	Cook Inlet	1.79	Rice et al., 1979.
	Cook Inlet	1.94	Korn et al., 1979.
Coonstripe shrimp *Pandalus hypsinotus*	Cook Inlet	1.40	Rice et al., 1984.
Red king crab *Paralithodes camtschatica*	Cook Inlet	1.50	Rice et al., 1983.
Purple shore crab *Hemigrapsus nudus*	Cook Inlet	8.45	Rice et al., 1979.
Echinoderms			
Tarspot *Cucumaria vega*	Cook Inlet	>6.84	Rice et al., 1979.
Six-armed starfish *Leptasterias hexactis*	Cook Inlet	>10.58	Rice et al., 1979.
White cucumber *Eupentacta quinquesimita*	Cook Inlet	>12.29	Rice et al., 1979.
Green sea urchin *Stongylocentrotus drobachiensis*	Cook Inlet	>10.58	Rice et al., 1979.
Mottled sea star *Evasterias troschelii*	Cook Inlet	0.82	Rice et al., 1984.
Fish			
Crescent gunnel *Pholis laeta*	Cook Inlet	>11.72	Rice et al., 1979.
Cockscomb prickleback *Anoplarchus purpurescens*	Cook Inlet	>11.72	Rice et al., 1979.
Tubesnout *Aulorhynchus flavidus*	Cook Inlet	2.55	Rice et al., 1979.
Starry flounder *Platichthys stellatus*	Cook Inlet	>5.34	Rice et al., 1979.
Dolly varden *Salvelinus malma*	Cook Inlet	1.55	Rice et al., 1979.
Pacific herring *Clupea harengus pallasi*	Cook Inlet	1.22	Rice et al., 1979.
	Cook Inlet	2.20	Rice et al., 1987.
Great skulpin *Myoxocephalus polyacanthocephalus*	Cook Inlet	3.96	Rice et al., 1979.
Walleye pollock *Therugra chalcogrammus*	Cook Inlet	1.73	Rice et al., 1979.
Pink salmon fry *Onchorhynchus gorbuscha*	Cook Inlet	1.45	Korn et al., 1979.
fingerlings	Cook Inlet	1.69	Rice et al., 1979.
juveniles	Cook Inlet	1.20	Moles and Rice, 1983.

4 hr LC$_{50}$

hr LC$_{50}$

Sublethal and chronic responses to chemicals often are elicited at concentrations well below those that are acutely toxic (Table 3). Water-soluble fractions of crude oils produce a variety of sublethal responses in Alaskan marine animals at minimum concentrations ranging from 0.2 to 1.89 ppm (200 to 1 890 ppb) total aromatic hydrocarbons. Most of these concentrations are two or three orders of magnitude higher than the highest concentrations of PAHs measured in the water column of Prince William Sound in the months immediately after the spill.

Table 3--Sublethal responses to crude oil exposure in Alaskan marine animals. Effective concentrations recorded as concentration (mg/L: ppm) of total aromatic hydrocarbons in seawater.

Species	Effective Concentration (ppm)	Response	Reference
Mottled sea star *Evasterias troschelli*	≥0.20	decreased feeding/growth @ 28 d	Rice et al. 1984.
Kelp shrimp *Eualus suckleyi*	1.00	cessation of swimming @ 20 m	Rice et al. 1979.
King crab larvae *Paralithodes camtschatica*	0.50	cessation of swimming @ 20 m	Rice et al. 1984.
	1.87	reduced molting success @ 6 h	Mecklenburg et al. 1977.
	0.50	stopped feeding @ 35 d	Rice et al. 1983.
Pacific herring larvae *Clupea barengus pallasi*	0.70	decreased feeding @ 12 d	Rice et al. 1986.
Coho salmon *Onchorhynchus kisutch*	1.89	50% avoidance @ 1 h	Maynard and Weber 1981.
Pink salmon *Onchorhynchus gorbuscha*	1.50	decreased growth @ 30 d	Moles et al. 1986.
	0.40	increased respiration & decreased growth	Rice 1985.
	0.40	decreased growth	Moles and Rice 1983.

Following an oil spill, organisms in the water column are exposed to continuously changing concentrations of petroleum hydrocarbons, an exposure regime that is not easily simulated in the laboratory. Two factors must be considered when evaluating the exposure of marine organisms to a chemical: (1) the concentration of the chemical and (2) the duration of exposure at that concentration. Even considering exposure in these terms, it is likely that the safety factor (ratio of effects concentration to environmental concentration) for marine organisms in Prince William Sound following the spill was in excess of 100 and possibly as high as 10 000 during April and May 1989 (Neff 1991a).

No empirical data are available for concentrations of PAHs in the water column of the sound during the first week after the spill. Although modeled concentrations of PAH in the water column averaged no more than 12 ppb during this time, it is possible that concentrations in the upper water column under the thick oil slick near Bligh Reef may have been somewhat higher for a short period of time during the storm of March 27 to 30.

In early spring, relatively few animals are present in the upper water column of the sound. Adult salmon do not return to the sound until summer; salmon fry do not emerge from anadromous streams until April and May. Small numbers of adult, prespawning Pacific herring (*Clupea harengus palassi*) could have been present in the northeastern sound at that time of year. However, prespawning herring do not feed actively in the month or so before spawning and tend to remain in deep water until they collect in large numbers at the surface to spawn. Prespawning adult herring are not very sensitive to oil (Rice et al. 1984). Thus, it is unlikely that many adult herring came in contact with harmful concentrations of petroleum in the upper water column shortly after the spill. Very little spawning occurred in the spill path area in 1989. Spawning density and survival of herring eggs and larvae was good in the northeastern sound in the spring of 1989 (McGurk 1992; Pearson et al. this volume). Therefore, possibly elevated concentrations of petroleum in the upper water column of northeastern Prince William Sound in the week after the spill did not produce measurable population-level effects in Pacific herring.

Although oil sheens have never been documented in previous spills to pose a hazard to water-column organisms or even to animals that use the water surface, such as marine birds and mammals, there was considerable concern expressed by state and federal scientists that sheens from the spilled oil might harm fish and wildlife. Oil sheens are extremely thin (an iridescent sheen is approximately 0.3 µm thick) and contain very little oil per unit area of the water surface. A typical iridescent sheen of moderately weathered North Slope crude oil would contain about 0.3 µg of oil per cm^2 of sea surface. Pink salmon and herring do jump during feeding and other activities. A jumping pink salmon might come in contact with approximately 10 cm^2 of sheen material containing 0.05 µg of total PAHs (assuming an oil/PAH ratio of 60), particularly during reentry into the water. Most contact would be with the relatively impermeable, scale-covered general body surface. There would be little or no exposure of the permeable gill and gut epithelia to sheen material. Therefore, sheen PAHs are not likely to have contributed significantly to body burdens of PAHs in fish tissues.

CONCLUSIONS

Seawater samples collected from the upper water column of spill-path areas of Prince William Sound in April 1989 (less than one month after the *Exxon Valdez* oil spill) and June-July 1989 were not toxic to representative sensitive species of marine plants, invertebrates, and fish. Water column samples collected between one week and more than a year after the spill from throughout the spill-path and non-spill-path area of Prince William Sound and the northwestern Gulf of Alaska contained low concentrations of petroleum-derived PAHs, ranging from less than 0.005 ppb to slightly more than 10 ppb. Only one water column sample contained more then 10 ppb total PAHs, the state of Alaska water quality standard for total aromatic hydrocarbons in seawater. More than 90% of samples collected in the two months after the spill contained less than 1 ppb total PAHs. By midsummer, PAH concentrations in the water column declined to background concentrations, 0.01 to 0.10 ppb. Surface water samples, some containing oil sheen material, contained up to 30 ppb total PAHs; highest concentrations were adjacent to oiled shorelines undergoing shoreline cleanup. Oil sheens posed minimal risk to water column organisms.

ACKNOWLEDGEMENTS

The aquatic toxicology and water quality studies reported here were performed by a large number of independent scientists under contract with Exxon Company, USA. Field surveys were performed by America North, Inc., Kinnetic Laboratories, Inc., Battelle Ocean Sciences Laboratory, Arthur D. Little, Inc., and Dames & Moore, Inc. Toxicity tests were managed by ENCK Consulting and Engineering and performed by Springborn Life Sciences, Inc. Analyses of water samples for PAHs were performed by Battelle Ocean Sciences Laboratory, ENSECO, Inc. Authur D. Little, Inc., Geological and Environmental Research Group, ATI, and Alden Laboratories, Inc. Most survey vessels were leased from local fishermen.

REFERENCES

American Society for Testing and Materials (ASTM), 1992a, "Standard Guide for Conducting Life-Cycle Toxicity Tests with Saltwater Mysids. ASTM E1191.90," American Society for Testing and Materials, Philadelphia, PA.

American Society for Testing and Materials (ASTM), 1992b, "Standard Guide for Conducting Acute Toxicity Tests with Fishes, Macroinvertebrates, and Amphibians. ASTM E729-88a," American Society for Testing and Materials, Philadelphia, PA.

Anderson, J.W., 1985, "Toxicity of Dispersed and Undispersed Prudhoe Bay Crude for Shrimp, Fish, and their Larvae," Publ. 4441 American Petroleum Institute, Washington, DC. 49 pp.

Anderson, J.W., Neff, J.M., Cox, B.A., Tatem, H.E., and Hightower, G.M., 1974, "Characteristics of Dispersions and Water-Soluble Extracts of Crude and Refined Oils and Their Toxicity to Estuarine Crustaceans and Fish," *Marine Biology*, Vol. 27, pp.75-88.

Boehm, P.D. and D.L. Fiest, D.L., 1982, "Subsurface Distribution of Petroleum From an Offshore Well Blowout - The Ixtoc I Blowout, the Bay of Campeche,"*Environmental Science and Technology*, Vol.16, pp. 67-74.

Boehm, P.D., Steinhauer, W.G., Fiest, D.L., Mosesman, N., Barak, J.E., and Perry, G.H. 1979, "A Chemical Assessment of the Present Levels and Sources of Hydrocarbon Pollutants in the Georges Bank Region " *Proceedings of the 1979 International Oil S*

Conference, Prevention, Behavior, Control, Cleanup. American Petroleum Institute, Washington, DC, pp. 333-341.

Bouloubassi, I. and Saliot, A., 1993, "Dissolved, Particulate and Sedimentary Naturally Derived Polycyclic Aromatic Hydrocarbons in a Coastal Environment: Geochemical Significance," *Marine Chemistry*, Vol. 42, pp.127-143.

Carey, J.H., Ongley, E.D., and Nagy, E. 1990, "Hydrocarbon Transport in the Mackenzie River, Canada," *Science of the Total Environment*, Vol. 97/98, pp. 69-88.

Coates, M., Connell, D. W. and Banon, D. N., 1985, "Aqueous Solubility in Octan-1-ol to Water Partition Coefficients of Aliphatic Hydrocarbons." *Environmental Science and Technology*, Vol. 19, pp. 828-832.

Dunnett, C.W., 1955, "A Multiple Comparison Procedure for Comparing Several Treatments With a Control," *Journal of the American Statistical Association*, Vol. 50, pp. 1096-1121.

Dunnett, C.W., 1964, "New Tables for Multiple Comparisons with a Control," *Biometrics*, Vol. 20, pp. 482-491.

Ehrhardt, M.G. and Burns, K.A., 1990, "Petroleum-Derived Dissolved Organic Compounds Concentrated from Inshore Waters in Bermuda", *Journal of Experimental Marine Biology and Ecology*, Vol. 138, pp. 35-47.

Ehrhardt, M.G. and Burns, K.A., 1993, "Hydrocarbons and Related Photo-Oxidation Products in Saudi Arabian Gulf Coastal Waters and Hydrocarbons in Underlying Sediments and Bioindicator Bivalves," *Marine Pollution Bulletin*, Vol. 27, pp. 187-197.

Ehrhardt, M.G. and Douabul, A., 1989, "Dissolved Petroleum Residues and Alkylbenzene Photo-Oxidation Products in the Upper Arabian Gulf," *Marine Chemistry*, Vol. 26, pp. 363-370.

Ehrhardt, M.G. and Petrick, G., 1993, "On the Composition of Dissolved and Particle-Associated Fossil Fuel Residues in Mediterranean Surface Water," *Marine Chemistry*, Vol. 42, pp. 57-70.

Foy, M.G., 1982, "Acute Lethal Toxicity of Prudhoe Bay Crude Oil and Corexit 9527 to Arctic Marine Invertebrates and Fish from Frobisher Bay, N.W.T.," EPS-4-Environment Canada-82-3. Environmental Protection Service, Environment Canada, Ottawa, Canada.

Futsaeter, G. 1991, "Oil Pollution in the Arctic Marine Environment," *Proceedings of the 4th Arctic and Marine Oil Spill Technical Seminar*, Environment Canada, Ottawa, Canada, pp. 307-324.

Galt, J.A., Lehr, W.J., and Payton, D.L., 1991, "Fate and Transport of the *Exxon Valdez* Oil Spill," *Environmental Science and Technology*, Vol. 25, pp. 202-209.

Grahl-Nielsen, O., 1978, "The Ekofisk Bravo Blowout. Petroleum Hydrocarbons in the Sea," *Proceedings of the Conference on Assessment of Ecological Impacts of Oil Spills*, American Institute of Biological Sciences, Washington, DC, pp 477-487.

Gulley, D.D., Boelter, A.M., and Bergman, H.L., 1990, "TOXSTAT Version 3.2," Fish Physiology and Toxicology Laboratory, Dept. of Zoology and Physiology, University of Wyoming, Laramie, WY.

Heitkamp, M.A. and Cerniglia, C.E., 1987, "Effects of Chemical Structure and Exposure on the Microbial Degradation of Polycyclic Aromatic Hydrocarbons in Freshwater and Estuarine Ecosystems," *Environmental Toxicology and Chemistry*, Vol. 6, pp. 535-546.

Kennicutt, M.C. II, Sweet, S.T., Fraser, W.R., Culver, M., and Stockton, W.L., 1991, "The Fate of Diesel Fuel Spilled by the *Bahia Paraiso* in Arthur Harbor, Antarctica," *Proceedings of the 1991 International Oil Spill Conference. Prevention, Behavior, Control, Cleanup*, American Petroleum Institute, Washington, DC, pp. 493-500.

Kimerle, R.A., Werner, A.F., and Adams, W.J., 1983, "Aquatic Hazard Evaluation Principals Applied to the Development of Water Quality Criteria," *Aquatic Toxicology and Hazard Assessment: Seventh Symposium. ASTM STP 854*, R.D. Cardwell, R. Purdy, and R.C. Bahner, Eds., American Society for Testing and Materials, Philadelphia, PA.

Korn, S., Moles, D.A., and Rice, S.D., 1979, "Effects of Temperature on the Median Tolerance Limit of Pink Salmon and Shrimp Exposed to Toluene, Naphthalene, and Cook Inlet Crude Oil," *Bulletin of Environmental Contamination and Toxicology*, Vol. 21, pp. 521-525.

Maynard, D.J. and Weber, D.D., 1981, "Avoidance Reactions of Juvenile Coho Salmon (*Oncorhunchus kisutch*). to Monocyclic Aromatics," *Canadian Journal of Aquatic Science*, Vol. 38, pp. 772-778.

McGurk, M.D., 1992, "Petroleum Effects on Herring Eggs and Larvae in Prince William Sound, Alaska, 1989," *Alaska OCS Region Fourth Information Transfer Meeting. Conference Proceedings*, OCS Study MMS 92-0046, U.S. Dept. of the Interior, Minerals Management Service, Alaska OCS Region, Anchorage, AK, pp. 119-124.

Mecklenberg, T.A., Rice, S.D., and Karinen, J.F., 1977, "Molting and Survival of King Crab (*Paralithoides camtschatica*) and Coonstripe Shrimp (*Pandalus hypsinotus*) Larvae Exposed to Cook Inlet Crude Oil Water-Soluble Fraction," *Fate and Effects of Petroleum Hydrocarbons in Marine Organisms and Ecosystems*, D.A. Wolfe, Ed., Pergamon Press, New York, pp. 221-228.

Moles, A., Babcock, M.M., and Rice, S.D., 1986, "Effects of Oil Exposure on Pink Salmon (*Oncorhynchus kisutch*) Alevins in a Simulated Intertidal Environment," *Marine Environmental Research*, Vol. 21, pp. 49-58.

Moles, A. and Rice, S.D., 1983, "Effects of Crude Oil and Naphthalene on Growth, Caloric Content, and Fat Content of Pink Salmon Juveniles in Seawater," *Transactions of the American Fisheries Society*, Vol.112, pp. 205-211.

Neff, J.M., 1991a, "Water Quality in Prince William Sound and the Gulf of Alaska," Report to Exxon Co. USA, Houston, TX. 37 pp. Available from J.M. Neff, Battelle Ocean Sciences Laboratory, 397 Washington St., Duxbury, MA.

Neff, J.M., 1991b, "Long-Term Trends in the Concentrations of Polycyclic Aromatic Hydrocarbons in the Water Column of Prince William Sound and the Western Gulf of Alaska Following the *Exxon Valdez* Oil Spill," *Proceedings of the 14th Annual Arctic and Marine Oilspill Program Technical Seminar*, Environment Canada, Ottawa, Canada, pp. 27-38.

Neff, J.M., and Anderson, J.W., 1981, *Responses of Marine Animals to Petroleum and Specific Petroleum Hydrocarbons*, Halsted Press, New York, 177 pp.

Neff, J.M., Boehm, P.D., Haas, L., and Kinney, P.J., 1990, "Petroleum Hydrocarbons in the Water Column of Prince William Sound, Alaska," *Oil Spills. Management and Legislative Implications*, M.L. Spaulding and M. Reed, Eds., American Society of Civil Engineers, New York, pp. 426-443.

Oudot, J., 1984, "Rates of Microbial Degradation of Petroleum Components as Determined by Computerized Capillary Gas Chromatography and Computerized Mass Spectrometry." *Marine Environmental Research*, Vol.13, pp. 277-302.

Rice, S.D. 1985, "Effects of Oil on Fish," *Petroleum Effects in the Arctic Environment*, F.R. Englehardt, Ed., Elsevier Applied Science Publishers, New York, pp.157-182.

Rice, S.D., Babcock, M.M., Brodersen, C.C., Carls, M.G., Gharrett, J.A., Korn, S., Moles, A., and Short, J.W., 1986, "Lethal and Sublethal Effects of the Water-Soluble Fraction of Cook Inlet Crude Oil on Pacific Herring (*Clupea harengus pallasi*) Reproduction," *Report: Outer Continental Shelf Environmental Assessment Program. Research Unit 66*, National Oceanic and Atmospheric Administration, Anchorage, AK, pp. 323-489.

Rice, S.D., Babcock, M.M., Brodersen, C.C., Gharrett, J.A., and Korn, S., 1987, "Uptake and Depuration of Aromatic Hydrocarbons by Reproductively Ripe Pacific Herring and the Subsequent Effect of Residues on Egg Hatching and Survival," *Pollution Physiology f Estuarine Organisms*, W.B. Vernberg, A. Calabrese, F.P. Thurberg, and F.J. Vernberg, s., U. of South Carolina Press, Columbia, SC, pp.139-154.

Rice, S.D., Karinen, J.F., and Brodersen, C.C., 1983, "Effects of Oiled Sediment on Juvenile King Crab," *Report: Outer Continental Shelf Environmental Assessment Program. Research Unit 62*, National Oceanic and Atmospheric Administration, Anchorage, AK, pp. 287-310.

Rice, S.D., Moles, A., Karinen, J.F., Korn, S., Carls, M.G., Brodersen, C.C., Gharrett, J.A., and Babcock, M.M., 1984, "Effects of Petroleum Hydrocarbons on Alaskan Aquatic Organisms: a Comprehensive Review of All Oil-Effects Research on Alaskan Fish and Invertebrates Conducted by the Auke Bay Laboratory, 1970-81" *NOAA Technical Memorandum NMFS F/NWC-67. Outer Continental Shelf Environmental Assessment Program Final Report 29*, National Oceanic and Atmospheric Adminsitration, Anchorage, AK, pp. 311-427.

Rice, S.D., Moles, D.A., Taylor, T.L., and Karinen, J.F., 1979, "Sensitivity of 39 Alaskan Marine Species to Cook Inlet Crude Oil and No. 2 Fuel Oil, *Proceedings of the 1979 International Oil Spill Conference. Prevention, Behavior, Control, Cleanup*, American Petroleum Institute, Washington, DC, pp. 549-554.

Rice, S.D., Short, J.W., and Karinen, J.F., 1977, "Comparative oil toxicity and comparative animal sensitivity," *Fate and Effects of Petroleum Hydrocarbons in Marine Organisms and Ecosystems*, D.A. Wolfe, Ed., Pergamon Press, New York, pp. 78-94.

Riley, R.G., Thomas, B.L., Anderson, J.W., and Bean, R.M., 1981, "Changes in the Volatile Hydrocarbon Content of Prudhoe Bay Crude Oil Treated under Different Simulated Weathering Conditions," *Marine Environmental Research*, Vol.4, pp.109-119.

Sauer, T.C. and Boehm, P., 1991, "Use of Defensible Analytical Chemical Measurements for Oil Spill Natural Resource Damage Assessment," *1991 International Oil Spill Conference. Prevention, Behavior, Control, Cleanup*, American Petroleum Institute, Washington, DC, pp. 363-369.

Short, J.W. and Rounds, P.,1993, "Petroleum Hydrocarbons in the Near-Surface Seawater of Prince William Sound, Alaska, Following the *Exxon Valdez* Oil Spill I: Chemical Sampling and Analysis," Report from the Auke Bay Laboratory, Alaska Fisheries Science Center, National Marine Fisheries Service, National Oceanic and Atmospheric Administration, Juneau, AK.32 pp. + Appendices.

Sokol, R.R. and F.J. Rohlf, 1981, *Biometry*, Second Edition. Chapter 14, W.H. Feeman and Co., New York, pp. 496-498.

Stephan, C., 1977a, U.S. Environmental Protection Agency, Environmental Research Laboratory, Duluth, MN. Personal communication.

Stephan, C.E., 1977b," Methods for Calculating an LC_{50}," *Aquatic Toxicology and Hazard Evaluation. ASTM STP 634*, F.L. Mayer and J.L. Hamelink, Eds., American Society for Testing and Materials, Philadelphia, PA, pp. 65-84

Stewart, P.S., Tedaldi, D.J., Lewis, A.R., and Goldman, E., 1993. "Biodegradation Rates of Crude Oil in Seawater," *Water Environment Research*, Vol. 65, pp. 845-848.

Stickle, W.B., Kapper, M..A., Shirley, T.C., Carls, M.g., and Rice, S.D., 1987, "Bioenergetics and Tolerance of the Pink Shrimp (*Pandalus borealis*) During Long-Term Exposure to the Water-Soluble Fraction and Oiled Sediment from Cook Inlet Crude Oil," *Pollution Physiology of Estuarine Organisms*, W.B. Vernberg, A. Calabrese, F.P. Thurberg, and F.J. Vernberg, Eds., U. of South Carolina Press, Columbia, SC, pp. 87-106.

Stiver, W. and Mackay, D., 1984, "Evaporation Rate of Spills of Hydrocarbons and Petroleum Mixtures," *Environmental Science and Technology*, Vol. 18, pp. 834-840.

Stuermer, D.H., Spies, RB, Davis, P.H., Ng, D.J., Morris, C.J., and Neal, A., 1982, "The Hydrocarbons in the Isla Vista Marine Seep Environment," *Marine Chemistry*, Vol.11, pp. 413-426.

Suter, G.W., II and Rosen, A.E., 1988 "Comparative Toxicology for Risk Assessment of Marine Fishes and Crustaceans," *Environmental Science and Technology*, Vol. 22, pp. 548-556.

U.S. Environmental Protection Agency (U.S. EPA), 1978, *Bioassay Procedures for the Ocean Disposal Permit Program*, EPA 600/9-78/010. U.S. Environmental Protection Agency, Washington, DC.

U.S. Environmental Protection Agency (U.S. EPA), 1985, *Methods for Measuring the Acute Toxicity of Effluents to Freshwater and Marine Organisms*, EPA-600/4-84-013. U.S. Environmental Protection Agency, Washington, DC. 216 pp.

U.S. Environmental Protection Agency (U.S. EPA), 1988, *Short-Term Methods for Estimating the Chronic Toxicity of Effluents and Receiving Waters to Freshwater and Marine Organisms*, EPA-600/4-86/028. U.S. Environmental Protection Agency, Washington, DC. 416 pp.

U.S. Environmental Protection Agency (EPA), 1989, *Fish Toxicity Screening Data. Part 2. Lethal Effects of 2014 Chemicals Upon Sockeye Salmon. Steelhead Trout, and Threespine Stickleback*,. U.S. Environmental Protection Agency, Washington, DC.

de, T.L., Kennicutt, M.C., and Brooks, J.M., 1989, "Gulf of Mexico Hydrocarbon Communities: Part III. Aromatic Hydrocarbon Concentrations in Organisms, nts and Water," *Marine Environmental Research*, Vol. 27, pp. 19-30.

Wolfe, D.A., Hameedi, M.J., Galt, J.A., Watabayashi, G., Short, J., O'Clair, C., Rice, S., Michel, J., Payne, J.R, Braddock, J., Hanna, S., and Sale, D., 1994, "Fate of the oil spilled from the T/V *Exxon Valdez* in Prince William Sound, Alaska," *Environmental Science and Technology* (in press).

James R. Bragg[1] and Shan H. Yang[1]

CLAY-OIL FLOCCULATION AND ITS ROLE IN NATURAL CLEANSING IN PRINCE WILLIAM SOUND FOLLOWING THE *EXXON VALDEZ* OIL SPILL

REFERENCE: Bragg, J. R. and Yang, S. H., "Clay-Oil Flocculation and Its Role in Natural Cleansing in Prince William Sound Following the Exxon Valdez Oil Spill," Exxon Valdez Oil Spill: Fate and Effects in Alaskan Waters, ASTM STP 1219, Peter G. Wells, James N. Butler, and Jane S. Hughes, Eds., American Society for Testing and Materials, Philadelphia, 1995.

ABSTRACT: Natural interactions of fine mineral particles with residue oil and seawater, in a process called clay-oil flocculation, were found to create solids-stabilized oil-in-water emulsions on shoreline sediments at numerous locations in Prince William Sound following the *Exxon Valdez* spill. In laboratory tests using oiled sediment samples from Prince William Sound, these emulsions were shown to facilitate natural cleansing and dispersion of oil from sediments by moving water.

Microscopic examination showed that the emulsions consisted of complex and varied floc aggregates of about 1-100 microns in diameter. Fluorescence under ultraviolet light revealed that the interior of these particles consisted of numerous spheres of oil surrounded by mineral fines and seawater. X-ray diffraction and scanning electron microscope studies showed the minerals to consist of clays, quartz, and feldspar--typical components of glacial flour. Chemical analyses of the oil revealed a correlation between the fraction of polar hydrocarbons present and the amount of mineral fines bound with the oil. These factors were also related to the ease by which the oil could be removed from substrate sediments by hydrodynamic forces.

To investigate the effect of flocculation on natural cleansing, studies were conducted to determine the hydrodynamic energy needed for seawater to remove flocculated oil residues from sediments sampled from shorelines. Water was pumped at different velocities through a column packed with oiled sediment, and the amount and composition of oil removed from the sediment were measured as functions of water velocity and sediment movement. In separate tests, oil removal was observed in a wave tank that generated wave heights less than and greater than needed to move sediments. These tests

---

[1] Exxon Production Research Company, Houston, TX 77252

demonstrated that, with clay-oil flocculation, substantial amounts of the oil could be removed at wave energies less than those needed to cause sediment movement and abrasion, which helps to explain observed removal of oil from the subsurface and from low energy shorelines where waves were not large enough to move sediments. Further, the large hydraulic cross section and nearly neutral buoyancy of floc particles removed from the sediment help to explain their efficient dispersal. The flocculation process also significantly increases the oil-water interfacial area, enhancing access to the oil by bacteria for biodegradation.

Clay-oil flocculation was found to be a beneficial process that we believe accelerated the removal of oil from shoreline sediments following the *Exxon Valdez* spill. The physical properties of the floc should have facilitated dispersion of the oil over large distances, thus helping to reduce buildup of hydrocarbons in subtidal sediments. Clay-oil flocculation, therefore, is another natural cleansing process that must be considered when studying the fate of oil spilled on shorelines.

KEYWORDS: oil, flocculation, natural cleansing, shoreline, *Exxon Valdez*, clay-oil interactions, oil-mineral interactions.

INTRODUCTION

Following the *Exxon Valdez* oil spill on March 24, 1989, extensive scientific studies were conducted in Prince William Sound and the Gulf of Alaska to measure the impacts of the spill and determine where and how long the oil persisted in the environment. From summer 1989 to summer 1992, numerous surveys of shoreline oiling conditions were conducted jointly by Exxon and federal and state agencies (Owens 1991; Neff, Owens, Stoker, and McCormick this volume). These studies measured shoreline oiling over time, in terms of length of shoreline oiled, surface area oiled, area containing subsurface oil, and sediment oil concentrations.

The length of shoreline initially oiled in 1989 in Prince William Sound was approximately 780 km (486 miles), or about 16% of the total Prince William Sound shoreline. By 1992, however, shoreline treatments by Exxon and natural cleansing had reduced the length of shoreline containing significant surface oil to 10.3 km (6.4 miles) -- or about 1.3% of the initial length oiled. For the same locations surveyed in 1991 and 1992, the area containing subsurface oil decreased by 69% in a single year (Neff, Owens, Stoker, and McCormick this volume).

As expected, rapid natural oil removal was observed on high-energy, exposed shorelines where wave action, combined with sediment abrasion, was especially effective during storms (Michel et al. 1991; Jahns et al. 1991). However, the cleansing of low-energy, sheltered shorelines, and reduction of deep subsurface oil were also relatively rapid. For example, between September 1989 and March 1990, National Oceanic and Atmospheric

Administration (NOAA) measured a 40% reduction in subsurface oil content (by weight) for 338 shoreline samples, most of which were collected at depths of 25 to 45 cm (Michel et al. 1991). NOAA considered those depths to be generally below the depth of sediment reworking by wave action, and we therefore surmise that abrasion should not have been a significant cleansing mechanism for that deep subsurface oil.

Absence of Subtidal Oil
While the rapid reduction of shoreline oil was evident, no substantial amounts of *Valdez* oil were measured in subtidal sediments (Page, Boehm, Douglas, and Bence this volume), even near oiled shorelines. During cleanup operations in 1989, oil removed from exposed rock surfaces or from buried sediments floated on the water surface, where it was picked up by various skimming devices (Harrison 1991). Natural cleansing processes that followed also appear to have effectively removed and widely dispersed the oil. On high-energy shorelines, where sediments were reworked extensively during storms, sediments were either transported seaward to the near subtidal under erosional wave conditions, or moved landward toward the storm berm under depositional energy conditions (Hayes et al. 1991). Under such high-energy conditions, oil could be expected to be removed and dispersed widely as very fine droplets, such as has been observed in prior spills (e.g., following the *Arrow* spill in Nova Scotia (Forrester 1971). However, for low-energy, sheltered shorelines, such mechanisms could not account for the observed efficient removal and dispersion of *Exxon Valdez* oil, nor for the lack of significant accumulation in subtidal sediments.

Laboratory Observations of Clay-Oil Flocculation
In late 1989, laboratory experiments were being conducted to measure natural rates of oil biodegradation on shoreline sediments from Prince William Sound (Bragg et al. 1990; Bragg et al. 1992). Oiled sediments had been collected on Smith Island in November 1989 and preserved in refrigerated containers during transit from the shoreline to the laboratory. In these tests, seawater was pumped through large Plexiglas columns filled with the oiled sediments at velocities, times, and directions to simulate tidal flow and ebb. No fertilizers or chemicals were introduced. Although oil on the sediment before its submersion in seawater appeared black, thick, and sticky, once submerged, much of the oil took on the fluffy appearance of a flocculated emulsion. Some of the flocculated oil tended to float upward with the rising tide until it became trapped at points of contact between sediment particles, while other oil appeared to be flocculated in thin sheets remaining on the sediment surfaces. Under a microscope, the emulsion appeared to consist of aggregates of micron-sized droplets of oil surrounded by micron-sized mineral fines. For simplicity, we call the emulsion clay-oil floc. The flocculated oil did not appear to adhere strongly to the sediment, suggesting that, on shorelines, such a state of the oil might affect how easily it is removed by waves and tides.

Prior Studies of Interactions Between Oil and Mineral Fines
Several investigators have previously studied interactions between hydrocarbons and fine minerals such as clay with respect to adsorption of dissolved hydrocarbons from seawater onto the minerals as a pathway for removing contaminants from the water column

(Meyers and Quinn 1973; Meyers and Oas 1978). Malinky and Shaw (1979) specifically investigated adsorption of petroleum hydrocarbons onto suspended marine sediments from south-central Alaska, and concluded that removing hydrocarbons solely by adsorption from solution in water would not be a significant hydrocarbon transport mechanism. More pertinent to this study, Bassin and Ichiye (1977) first showed that clays spontaneously interact with crude oil in seawater to produce flocculated emulsions. Delvigne et al. (1987) studied flocculation of Prudhoe Bay and Ekofisk crude oils and mineral fines in seawater as functions of water turbulence and concentrations of oil and fines.

Prior to the *Exxon Valdez* spill, NOAA (Payne et al. 1989) conducted studies to investigate the potential for interactions between oil and suspended particulate matter (SPM) in case North Slope oil were spilled on Arctic waters containing SPM such as clays and quartz of glacial origin. As defined by Payne et al., oil-SPM interactions could be of two types. The first, adsorption of dissolved hydrocarbons from water onto surfaces of mineral fines, was not believed to be a significant hydrocarbon transport process following a spill. The second type is the interaction of droplets of bulk oil with SPM to form stable emulsions--i.e., clay-oil flocculation. Payne et al. considered this a possible process for dispersing oil floating in the water column, with the potential for transporting significant amounts of that oil to offshore benthic environments by sedimentation.

Concerned that such spontaneous interactions between SPM and the floating oil slick from the *Exxon Valdez* spill might lead to the sinking of very fresh and potentially toxic oil, NOAA conducted surveys in Prince William Sound following the spill (April 12-15, 1989) in an attempt to detect the presence of SPM and oil-SPM interactions in the water column (Payne et al. 1989). Three types of samples were collected and analyzed for oil and particulate loadings: (1) bulk oil samples, (2) water-column samples, and (3) samples of the surficial flocculant layer of sediment in shallow, nearshore areas. Sampling locations were concentrated in the western portion of Prince William Sound around Knight Island and Eleanor Island, and near glacial sources.

Levels of SPM were very low in most water-column samples (0-2.2 mg dry weight/L), and even the "milky" water near the face of the Columbia Glacier contained only about 4.3-4.6 mg/L of suspended solids. However, the surficial flocculant layer samples, from locations such as Northwest Bay, contained about 63-110 mg solids/L. No significant levels of oil-SPM interactions were detected, however, and NOAA concluded that, at the time of the spill, SPM concentrations were too low and the waters too calm to lead to significant oil-SPM interactions before the oil reached the shorelines.

In summary, prior studies investigating the formation of oil-in-water emulsions stabilized by micron-sized mineral fines have concentrated on the offshore environment because of the concern that sudden, large-scale interactions of oil with SPM would lead to oil sinking to the subsurface sediments. This paper is the first to consider the significance of clay-oil floc formation on oiled shorelines and its beneficial role in removing oil in a way that mitigates its redeposition in nearshore subtidal sediments.

Objectives of this Study

Our observation of clay-oil flocculation led to laboratory tests and analyses of sediment samples from Prince William Sound that were designed to investigate the following questions:

- To what extent could the mechanism of clay-oil flocculation affect the rate of oil removal from shorelines in Prince William Sound, and how would this process interact with the major natural cleansing processes of wave action, sediment abrasion, and biodegradation?

- How would clay-oil flocculation affect the ultimate fate of oil removed from shorelines? Where would the oil likely be transported, and how would the physical properties of the floc affect its dispersal and further biodegradation?

METHODS

We conducted four types of laboratory studies:

- The structure and chemical composition of emulsions found on sediments from Smith Island and Perry Island in Prince William Sound were investigated.
  - Visible macrostructures of emulsions on shoreline sediments were studied by normal and ultraviolet (UV) light microscopy.
  - The composition, including polars content, of the flocculated oil was measured by gas chromatography and high-performance liquid chromatography (HPLC).
  - Composition of incorporated mineral fines was determined by x-ray diffraction and scanning electron microscopy. Size distribution of mineral fines was also measured.

- Small-scale studies of interactions of mineral fines with different oils, seawater, and freshwater were conducted in test tubes to gain understanding of the factors responsible for formation of flocculated emulsions in Prince William Sound.

- Using oiled sediments collected from Prince William Sound, hydrodynamic flow-experiments were conducted in a packed column and in a wave tank to determine the amount of oil floc removed from the sediments at various water velocities or wave heights, including flow regimes with and without sediment movement.

- Oiled sediment samples obtained in January 1990 from seven locations in Prince William Sound were screened to determine if, and to what extent, they contained flocculated oil.

Oiled Sediments and Seawater Used in Laboratory Studies

Oiled sediments used in the initial laboratory flow experiments were sampled from Smith Island (at survey site AP-1; see Jahns et al. 1991 for AP-1 site description) on November 11, 1989, and Perry Island (survey site Meares Point, N-17) on December 7, 1990. Additional samples were collected in January 1990 from subsurface trenches at seven other locations in Prince William Sound. Sediments were placed in plastic bags inside ice chests and kept moist and cold during the two-to-three day transit to Exxon laboratories in Houston.

Sediments from Smith Island were sampled from depths of from 0 to 15 cm below the base of the cobble armor and consisted of particle sizes ranging from sand and pebbles to cobble of 12 cm in diameter, mixed with smaller amounts of fines and silt. Sediments from Perry Island were collected from depths of from 15 to 76 cm but were similar to those from Smith Island. Sediments arrived in four batches (two from each location). Each batch was individually homogenized by gentle hand mixing to obtain a uniform size distribution and was tested for oil loading. Oil loadings for individual batches ranged from 0.46-1.85 g oil/kg dry sediment; at least three samples of each batch were measured, with standard deviations of about 6% of mean oil loading. These loadings were typical for sediment on exposed, high-energy shorelines in late 1989 (Jahns et al. 1991).

Two sources of seawater were used: preserved seawater taken from Prince William Sound and synthetic seawater made to a salinity of 2.5% total dissolved solids by weight (same as the preserved seawater, and typical for shallow shoreline waters in Prince William Sound [Lung et al. 1993]) using tap water and sea salts (Sigma Chemical No. S-9883). The source of water was not found to affect the formation or properties of the oil-water emulsions.

Analytical Procedures
   Emulsion structure studies--Particles of oil-water emulsion were observed suspended in drops of seawater under two optical microscopes. One microscope was a Nikon Biophot (V series), using transmitted light and phase contrast, a Plan 40X objective, and a high-resolution color video camera and monitor connected, providing an effective magnification of about 475X-950X. The structure of floc particles under transmitted and UV light was observed with a Leitz Orthoplan model with either transmitted light or epi-illuminated UV (wavelengths of about 350-400 nm) produced by a XENOPHOT HLX xenon bulb. With a Plan 20X objective the effective magnification of the Leitz was about 270X. A glass slide with an etched micrometer grid scale was used with both microscopes as a scale reference to determine the actual size of observed particles, and attached 35-mm cameras were used to obtain still photographs.

   Oil concentrations--Oil was extracted from sediment samples to measure the concentration of oil (oil loading) and to obtain oil for compositional analyses by the following gravimetric technique. First, 2-kg samples of sediment were batchwise extracted with toluene (about 1.0 L volume). Extracts were decanted from nonsuspended sediment (sand, pebbles, etc.) and then filtered through a Whatman Reeve pleated filter paper (Fisher Cat. No. 09-790-14E) of known tare weight to remove suspended mineral fines. Mineral residue was washed with distilled water and methanol to remove salt and dried to constant weight. Large sediment was washed in distilled water and dried to constant weight. The extract was partly distilled at 110°C to remove the bulk of toluene. When the distillation temperature began rising above 110°C, distillation was stopped, and the remaining toluene was evaporated from the distillation flask in a vacuum oven at a constant temperature of 25°C until constant weight of oil residue was obtained. Oil loading (oil concentration) was reported as g oil/kg dry sediment.

Oil and mineral fines from floc aggregates collected from water during oil-removal tests in columns and wave tanks were concentrated, extracted, and weighed using the following techniques. For column-flow tests, water exiting the column flowed into a 150-L plastic drum where floc particles floated to the surface and were collected by skimming with a stainless steel mesh and a stainless steel spatula. The floc was centrifuged, and the free water was decanted. For wave-tank tests, water in the tank containing floc particles was removed by pipet while waves were still in motion, and floc was then concentrated by centrifugation, and free water was decanted. Liberated floc adhering to tank walls was collected on cotton swabs that were subsequently extracted with toluene, and oil in that floc was also included in the mass balance.

The concentrated emulsion floc was extracted with toluene to solubilize oil and separate it from remaining water and mineral fines. For emulsions from column-flow tests, toluene extracts were filtered, distilled, and the oil residues dried to constant weight using the same procedures as described above for determining oil loadings on sediments. The mass of mineral fines in the emulsion was determined by washing the filter cake with distilled water and then methanol to remove salt and polars, and then by drying and weighing the filter paper. The specific water content of the flocculated emulsion could not be measured accurately, but, on the basis of floc volumes in centrifuge tubes and masses before and after water removal, we estimated that floc particles typically contained about 80% water by volume.

To determine the oil content of small amounts of floc liberated in intermediate tests in the wave tank, a colorimetric method was used by which the light absorbance (at a wavelength of 650 nm) of the toluene extract was measured by spectrophotometer (Sequoia-Turner Model 340). The absorbance was calibrated versus oil concentration in toluene using oil extracted from Smith Island sediment. This method measured oil contents within ±5% of the true values, and it was more accurate than gravimetric analysis for small masses of floc.

Oil compositional analyses--The oils recovered by toluene extraction of either the original oiled sediments or the floc samples recovered from water were chemically analyzed by an HPLC (high performance liquid chromatography) system that coupled two columns and two detectors. This system was operated by two different methods to provide a different measures of composition. In the first, identified here as **HPLC Method 1**, samples were fractionated with a flow of 1.5 mL/min through a combination of a charge transfer column and a modified silica column as described in U.S. Patent 4,988,446 (Haberman et al.). The solvent gradient of hexane, methylene chloride, and isopropyl alcohol was patterned after that reported by Grizzle and Thomson (1982). This aromatics-type separation provided fractions consisting of saturates, 1- to 4-ring aromatics, and polars (mainly consisting of 5+ -ring aromatics and N-heterocyclics). The fractionated components were passed through a Hewlett Packard 8451 diode array detector (DAD) and an Applied Chromatography Systems 750/14 evaporative mass detector (EMD), allowing quantification of each type of ring, the percentage of aromatic carbon (from the DAD) and the percentage of total mass (from EMD).

The polar hydrocarbons are of particular interest in flocculation studies because their heteroatoms usually impart an electrostatic charge on the oil, thus affecting the attraction of oil to charged mineral particles in seawater. To further investigate subtle changes in polars composition of oil in floc aggregates sequentially removed from sediments during the column-flow experiments, expanded separations of polar components were conducted with the same detection system. With this modified technique, identified as **HPLC Method 2**, the separation was performed on a cyano-modified silica gel system using a gradient of hexane, methylene chloride, and methanol containing 200 ppm diethylamine. The hexane eluted the hydrocarbons (at least through 4-ring aromatics), and methylene chloride yielded intermediate polars (ketones, esters, alcohols, pyrroles, etc.). The gradient to 25% methanol displaced the most polar multifunctional components that were designated as strong polars. In this separation, most of the compound types found in the intermediate polars were believed to be the initial oxidation products of hydrocarbons, while most of the strong polars were believed to be the more severely oxidized and degraded compounds. Because of differences in methods, total polars measured by Method 2 are different from those by Method 1.

Mineral fines analyses--Mineral fines separated from the emulsion were analyzed for composition by scanning electron microscopy (SEM) and x-ray diffraction (MINDIF). The size distribution of fine particles was measured using laser diffraction (System 3601 Particle Size Analyzer from Malvern). The particles were dispersed in 25 mL water containing 0.5% hexametaphosphate and agitated for 10 min in an ultrasonic mixer to ensure complete dispersion. Particle diameters of less than 1 μm were reported as 1 μm or smaller.

Small-Scale Flocculation Screening Tests
Screening tests to determine the effect of mineral type and size, oil composition, and water salinity on the formation of flocculated emulsions were conducted in 48 test tube experiments at a temperature of 22°C. The tests used mineral fines consisting of feldspar, chlorite, illite, and quartz obtained from a geological supply firm (Wards Geological Supply, Rochester, NY). None of these materials had ever been oiled prior to testing. Two ranges of particle sizes were used: <1μm and 1-5 μm. Particles were sized by standard centrifuge techniques (Jackson 1979).

Three different oils were used: a degassed Alaska North Slope (ANS) crude oil with low polars content, weathered oil from the *Exxon Valdez* spill collected by skimmer on May 10, 1989 (referred to hereafter as weathered EVOS oil), and 600 °F topped ANS oil [distilled at 600 °F (316 °C) to remove light ends]. Properties of the three oils are compared in Table 1 with typical properties of oil extracted from intertidal sediments collected on Smith Island on November 11, 1989. Finally, two water salinities were included in the matrix of test parameters--a low salinity water (0.1% total dissolved solids by weight) and synthetic seawater with a salinity of 2.5% total dissolved solids (by weight) made with sea salt (Sigma No. S-9883).

To observe flocculation behavior, 0.05 g of mineral fines were first mixed with 20 mL of water in a test tube, mixed with an ultrasonic vibrator, and left to settle in the test tube overnight. Then five drops of oil were introduced, and the tube was shaken by hand. The appearance of any floc formed was recorded by still and video cameras. Visual and microscopic examinations were used to assess the size, shape, and approximate number density of floc particles formed, as well as the visual appearance of other oil-mineral interactions not leading to flocculation.

TABLE 1--Typical properties of oils used in flocculation screening tests compared to oil extracted from sediments from Smith Island, Prince William Sound. (Oil compositions measured by HPLC Method 1)

Oil Source	Low-Polars ANS Crude Oil	Weathered EVOS (Collected by Skimmer 5-10-89)	600 °F Topped ANS	Oil Extracted from Smith Island Subsurface Sediments (Collected 11-11-89)
Density, g/cc	0.91	0.90	0.96	0.96
Viscosity, cp	16	27.8	3000	3900
Saturates, wt %	46.8	46.4	48.6	34.7
Aromatics, wt %	43.4	18.1	32.8	44.8
Total Polars, wt %	9.8	26.5	18.6	20.5

Column-Flow Tests of Oil Mobilization
A series of column-flow tests were conducted in the apparatus shown in Figure 1. This apparatus was initially constructed to measure rates of biodegradation (Bragg et al. 1992). Water was pumped into the bottom of the 30.5-cm (1-ft) diameter Plexiglas column packed with a 91.5-cm (3-ft) deep bed of oiled sediment, and the amount of oil liberated from the sediment was measured as a function of time and water velocity. Flow from the top of the column entered a 150-L tank (see Figure 1) where oil liberated from the column floated to the water surface and was collected. (Under these conditions, no significant amount of floc was ever observed to sink in the tank.)

The column contained about 87.7 kg of sediment from Smith Island (batch 1) with an average oil loading of about 0.90 ± 0.09 g oil/kg dry sediment. Porosity of the packed sediment ranged from about 31.5% to 33.0%, and permeability was measured at 200 000 darcies. Prior to initiation of flow tests of oil removal, we cycled seawater for three weeks upward and downward through the column at flowrates and time intervals to simulate typical ebb and flow of tides in Prince William Sound (Bragg, Yang, and Roffall 1990). No significant amount of oil was removed from sediment at these rates, which produced a vertical velocity of 61 cm/hr (2.0 ft/hr). Then higher water velocities up to 579 cm/min were established for six-hour periods (referred to as a flow trials), and the amount of floc liberated from the sediment during each trial was measured. At an intermediate point in the test, 2 kg of sediment was removed to analyze for oil composition, and at the end of the test three 2-kg samples of sediment were analyzed to determine the amount and composition of oil remaining on the sediment for comparison with mobilized floc.

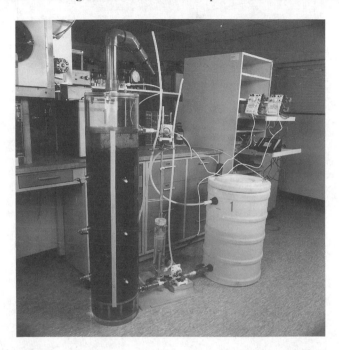

FIGURE 1--Column-flow apparatus containing oiled sediment.

Wave-Tank Experiments

A wave-tank apparatus was constructed to study oil removal from sediments by oscillatory water movement, which simulated swash and wave action on a shoreline. The apparatus, shown in Figure 2, consisted of a counterbalanced tank of optical glass (24.1 cm high, 24.1 cm long, and 7.1 cm wide), mounted on a rocking table whose period of motion could be controlled electronically. Approximately 1.0 kg of oiled sediment was placed in the tank for observation, and video and 35-mm still cameras were mounted at a fixed position relative to the tank to record wave heights and the dynamics of clay-oil floc removal. (The second, dummy, tank was filled with ballast as needed for balance.) As shown in Figure 2, oiled sediment (from Smith Island or Perry Island) was placed in the test tank, which contained a measured depth, h, of seawater above the sediment. By rocking the table at a controlled and constant frequency, waves of height d could be generated and measured from video images. Under such shallow wave conditions, the water velocity generally would be proportional to the wave height, but would vary with location and depth. The main objective was to observe visually how the oil floc was removed from the rock at various levels of wave energy less than or greater than needed to move the sediment. However, we did not attempt to correlate wave heights in the tank with actual wave heights or wave energies on shorelines in Prince William Sound.

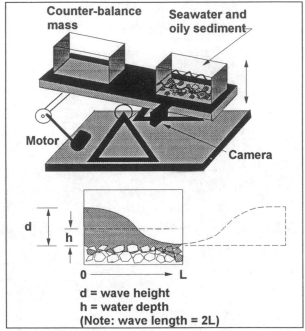

**FIGURE 2--Schematic of wave tank and rocking
mechanism. (Note: dimension L = 24.1 cm.)**

Wave height could be varied from a gentle swash, with no movement of sediment, to waves causing sediment movement. In all wave tank experiments, video images and still photography recorded the macro structure of the flocculated emulsion removed from the sediment. After a trial wave motion, the amount of oil removed from sediment was measured by quickly withdrawing the seawater by pipet while the table was still rocking to capture any floc particles that might sink in quiescent water, concentrating the floc by centrifuging, and then extracting the floc as described earlier. A typical oil-removal test in the wave tank involved a sequential series of trial runs utilizing different wave heights and rocking times with the same batch of oiled sediment. Clean seawater was recharged to the tank after each floc removal step. At the end of the series the sediment was removed and extracted to determine remaining oil. A mass balance on oil removed at various steps was used to compute the original sediment oil loading.

Verification of Flocculated Oil in Field Samples
Field sediment samples were obtained from trenches dug at seven locations in January 1990 (Teal 1991). At low tide, field personnel observed that, unlike previously at the

same locations, subsurface oil did not adhere to sediment, and a substantial amount of the oil could easily be washed off rocks and their hands by cold water. These samples were analyzed in a semiquantitative manner to determine the amount of flocculated oil that would spontaneously be released by simply submerging a weighed amount (about 20 g) of oiled sediment under quiescent seawater in a beaker. Oil released from the sediment was examined to determine its tendency to coalesce or disperse in seawater, and particles suspected of being floc were examined under a microscope. The mobilized floc was collected, extracted, and weighed to determine the mass of oil and mineral fines within the floc. Oil remaining on the sediment was also extracted and measured. Oil that was spontaneously released was reported as a fraction of the total oil in the sample. This relative measure of the oil liberated from sediment is only useful to demonstrate the presence of clay-oil floc on field samples when collected.

RESULTS
Results are first presented for studies that investigated the basic structure and composition of the clay-oil floc aggregates through microscopic and chemical analyses. The results of small-scale screening tests are then presented to show that flocculation in the laboratory is spontaneous when oil and mineral fines similar to those on shoreline sediments were brought together in the presence of seawater and to demonstrate the factors that caused clay-oil flocculation on shoreline sediments. Finally, results of oil-removal tests in column-flow experiments and wave tanks are provided to establish the relative ease of removal of flocculated oil from shoreline sediments under conditions where sediments do or do not move. For brevity, results are shown only for tests using Smith Island sediment, but results of additional tests conducted using Perry Island sediment were similar.

Structure of Clay-Oil Floc Emulsion Particles
Figure 3 illustrates the appearance of sediment from Smith Island just prior to being loaded into the column-flow apparatus. So long as it was not submerged under seawater, the oil appeared black and sticky, as it did on shorelines exposed at low tide, with no visual suggestion of having undergone interactions with mineral fines. Figure 4 shows some of the same sediment while it was under seawater in a simulated rising tide in the column-flow apparatus shown in Figure 1. Note that the oil had taken on the appearance of a fluffy colloidal emulsion and did not appear to adhere strongly to the sediment. The oil had flocculated with mineral fines to form an emulsion that was stable so long as it was submerged under seawater. When the seawater was drained during the low-tide cycle, the floc collapsed but reformed during the next rising tide.

Aggregates (or "particles") of clay-oil floc were easily visible to the unaided eye once flowing water liberated them from the sediment. For example, Figure 5(a) shows a photograph of aggregates of floc in seawater 1 minute after rocking motion was stopped in a wave tank containing Smith Island sediment; prior rocking for 10 minutes had generated wave heights of about 9 cm. Immediately upon removal from sediment, some floc particles appeared as thin, translucent sheets. These then coiled into more compact aggregates of smaller diameter. The photograph in Figure 5(b), taken 25 minutes later without further motion, shows that most of the floc had floated to the water surface, but

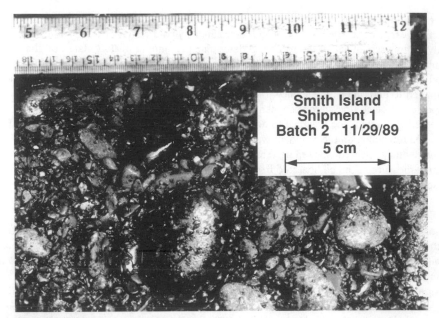

FIGURE 3--Oiled sediment from intertidal zone of Smith Island prior to being loaded into the column-flow apparatus.

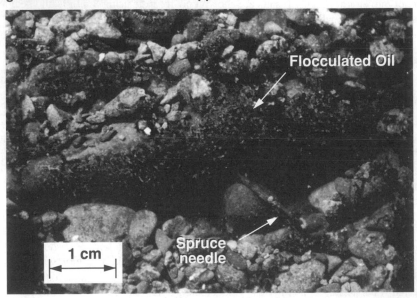

FIGURE 4--Oil flocculated with mineral fines on sediments from Smith Island while submerged under seawater in column-flow apparatus. Note that fluffy colloidal structure of the floc does not allow it to adhere strongly to sediment.

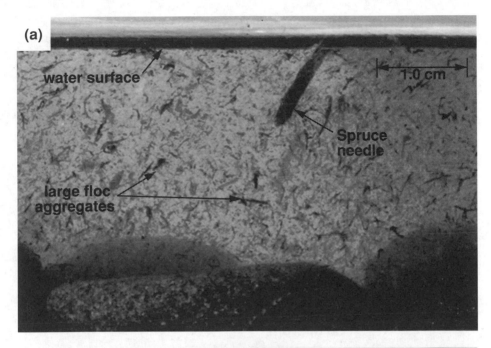

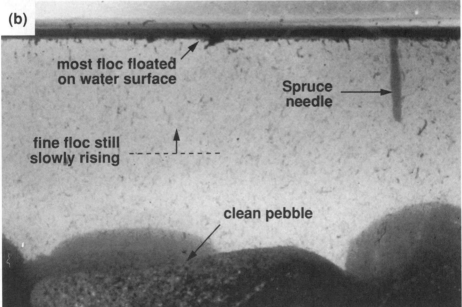

FIGURE 5--Photograph of wave tank containing oiled pebbles from Smith Island submerged in quiescent seawater: (a) 1 minute after wave action was stopped and (b) 25 minutes later. Floc aggregates mostly floated on surface or remained suspended in water.

smaller diameter floc particles were still slowly rising. Few floc particles sank. Floc aggregates liberated in the column tests appeared similar, but smaller, with diameters averaging about 100 μm. In quiescent water, most particles from the column floated, with a minor portion sinking at rates of a few centimeters per hour.

Under a light microscope, structures of individual floc aggregates appeared varied and complex (Figure 6). The outer surfaces of all aggregates were covered with mineral fines. Floc aggregates contained active zooplankton and appeared to contain motile bacteria on and within the floc; however, because the bacteria are only about 1 μm long, it was difficult to confirm their presence visually. Microbial cultures of oil from the sediments used in these tests showed high concentrations of viable hydrocarbon degrading bacteria, and not all were motile (Bragg et al. 1990).

Figure 7 shows photomicrographs of the same aggregates under normal light and ultraviolet (UV) light. UV light, which causes the oil to fluoresce, reveals that the interior consisted of numerous micron-sized spheres of oil surrounded by mineral fines and seawater. Thus, the dimensions of oil droplets were much smaller than the width of the total clay-oil floc aggregate, with actual oil droplet dimensions in the range of approximately 1 to 10 μm.

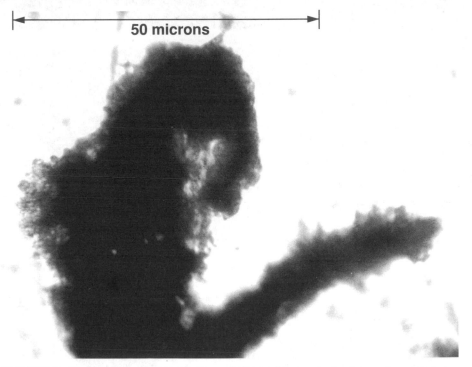

FIGURE 6--Photomicrograph of clay-oil floc aggregate in drop of seawater. Note mineral fines coating all surfaces. (Magnification is approximately 1360X.)

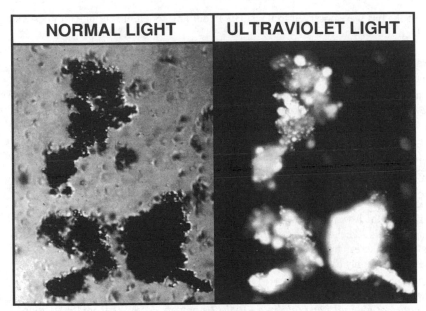

| NORMAL LIGHT | ULTRAVIOLET LIGHT |

Scale: 100 microns ⊢————————⊣

FIGURE 7--Photomicrographs of the same clay-oil floc aggregates viewed in normal and ultraviolet (UV) light. The UV light causes oil droplets to fluoresce, revealing smaller oil spheres inside floc aggregates. (Magnification is approximately 270X.)

Composition and Size Distribution of Mineral Fines

Scanning electron micrography and x-ray diffraction analyses of mineral solids separated from the floc particles revealed minerals typical of glacial flour. On average, they consisted of approximately 50% clay, 25% quartz, and 25% feldspar; however, the clay content in some samples ran as high as 77%. The clay fraction was mainly chlorite with minor amounts of illite and traces of kaolinite.

Small-Scale Flocculation Screening Studies

We conducted a total of 48 screening tests in test tubes to determine flocculation behavior for various combinations of mineral fines type, particle size range, oil type, and water salinity. In all cases, spontaneous interactions among mineral fines, oil, and seawater occurred upon mixing, however relatively little interaction was observed with low salinity (0.1% total dissolved solids) water. Lack of strong flocculation in the low salinity water is consistent with prior flocculation theory for other colloid systems where lack of electrolytes allows repulsive charges on particles (the "double layer") to prevent flocculation (Lyklema 1978). (In seawater, ions suppress the repulsive double layer and allow mineral particles to move sufficiently close to flocculate by attraction of van der Waals forces.) Small, finely-divided floc particles were formed most extensively with the more polar, weathered EVOS oil, mineral sizes less than 1μm, and seawater.

None of the oils were observed to flocculate under any conditions if mineral fines were not added to the water.

Figure 8 illustrates flocculation behavior observed for key combinations in seawater: (1) low-polars ANS crude with fines < 1 μm in size, (2) weathered EVOS oil with fines <1 μm in size, and (3) weathered EVOS oil with fines 1 to 5 μm in size. Low-polars ANS crude oil and <1 μm solids flocculated to form some finely dispersed structures. (The most were formed with chlorite--the major clay constituent found in mineral fines from Prince William Sound). However, weathered EVOS oil and all types of mineral solids of <1 μm size flocculated extensively to form very finely dispersed spheres of oil coated with mineral fines. The larger mineral particles (1 to 5 μm) interacted with weathered EVOS oil, but the oil was not dispersed as effectively and formed larger droplets. The 600°F topped ANS oil did not flocculate under these conditions, probably because its high viscosity and the low mixing energy used in the test tubes prevented adequate contact of oil and minerals. The same combination might flocculate in the presence of higher fluid shear. (These screening tests were not designed to investigate all conditions leading to flocculation but only to identify key parameters.)

Column-Flow Tests

Amount of clay-oil floc mobilized--Table 2 summarizes results from the various flow tests conducted sequentially in the packed column, including flow times, vertical interstitial water velocities, and the amounts of oil and mineral solids removed as clay-oil floc at the end of each flow trial. Table 3 and Table 4 show the compositions of oil floc recovered in water that flowed out of the column as well as compositions of oil remaining on the oiled sediment sampled at the times indicated. Figure 9 shows the data in Table 2 plotted to show cumulative oil removal versus water velocity and sediment movement.

Tidal cycling of seawater at a velocity of 1.02 cm/min (2 ft/hr) for three weeks removed only an insignificant amount of oil floc. At a water velocity of 338 cm/min (11.0 ft/min) which produced no rock movement, 13.6% of the total oil in the column was mobilized and removed as finely divided floc particles over a six-hour period (most of this was removed in the first 30 minutes). Thus, sediment movement and abrasion were not needed for oil removal in the presence of the clay-oil floc, but water velocities considerable higher than normal tides are needed to remove significant amounts of oil *in a short time span* (episodic events such as storms are likely needed).

In tests at higher velocity, where sediment did move gently, oil was removed faster. Further, restarting flow and establishing different flow paths through the sediment likely removed additional material not contacted at the same velocity in prior runs. This suggested that sediment movement facilitated oil removal not so much by abrasion as by simply exposing more surface area of sediment to effective water velocities. A material balance summary in Table 5 shows that 70% of the total oil on sediment at test start was removed within 24 hours by water flowing at velocities that would exceed tidal velocities.

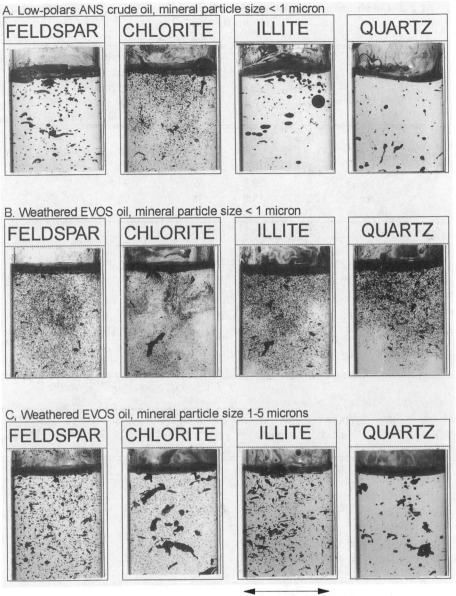

A. Low-polars ANS crude oil, mineral particle size < 1 micron

FELDSPAR   CHLORITE   ILLITE   QUARTZ

B. Weathered EVOS oil, mineral particle size < 1 micron

FELDSPAR   CHLORITE   ILLITE   QUARTZ

C, Weathered EVOS oil, mineral particle size 1-5 microns

FELDSPAR   CHLORITE   ILLITE   QUARTZ

Scale: 1.0 inch (2.54 cm)

FIGURE 8--Interactions among oils, mineral fines, and seawater observed in test tube screening tests. Particle sizes <1 μm and weathered EVOS (with increased polars) formed most finely dispersed floc.

TABLE 2--Oil and mineral fines in clay-oil floc emulsions washed from sediments in column-flow tests .

Flow Trial No.	Flow Time	Interstitial Water Velocity (cm/min)	Oil Removed (g)	Instan- taneous Rate of Oil Removal (%/hr) *	Mineral Solids Removed (g)	Fraction of Solids on Water-Free Basis (wt %)
0	none	0	0	0	0	0
1	3 weeks	0.085	sheen	$\cong 0$	$\cong 0$	NA**
2	6 hours	338	10.7	3.2	0.79	6.9
3	6 hours	579	20.3	6.1	1.94	8.7
4	6 hours	579	15.9	4.8	3.06	16.1
5	6 hours	579	8.2	2.5	3.13	27.6
		Totals	55.1		8.92	

* Instantaneous rate of removal expressed as % of initial oil on sediment.
** Not measured because of insufficient sample size.

TABLE 3--Composition of oil in clay-oil floc emulsions washed from sediments in column-flow tests compared to composition of oil on sediments at start of test.

				Oil Composition by HPLC Method 2			
Flow Trial No.	Flow Time	Water Velocity (cm/min)	Oil Sampled	Hydrocarbons (%)	Intermediate Polars (%)	Strong Polars (%)	Total Polars (%)
0	none	0	bulk oil on sediment	84.3	7.8	7.9	15.7
2	6 hours	338	mobilized floc	84.7	7.6	7.7	15.3
2	6 hours	338	oil left on sediment	84.3	7.6	8.1	15.7
4	6 hours	579	mobilized floc	83.5	8.1	8.4	16.5
5	6 hours	579	mobilized floc	82.5	8.3	9.2	17.5
5	6 hours	579	oil left on sediment	83.0	8.0	9.0	17.0

TABLE 4--Composition of oil in clay-oil floc washed from sediments in column-flow tests compared to composition of oil on sediments at start of test.

Flow Trial No.	Flow Time	Interstitial Water Velocity (cm/min)	Oil Sampled	Oil Composition by HPLC Method 1					
				Sats (%)	1-Ring Arom. (%)	2-Ring Arom. (%)	3-Ring Arom. (%)	4+ - Ring Arom. (%)	Polars (%)
0	none	0	bulk oil on sediment	34.7	14.2	12.4	8.1	10.1	20.5
2	6 hours	338	mobilized floc	34.7	14.6	12.9	7.7	11.4	18.7

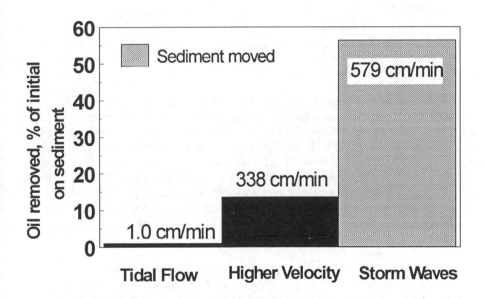

FIGURE 9--Cumulative oil removed from Smith Island sediment versus vertical water velocity in column-flow experiment (Table 2). Note that sediment moved only at highest water velocity (likely equivalent to storm waves on field scale).

TABLE 5--Material balance for oil initially on sediments, removed as floc,
or left on sediments during column-flow test.

Sample Identification	Oil Mass, (g)
Total oil in column at start of flow test:	78.9
(87.7 kg sediment with 0.90 ± 0.09 g oil/kg sediment)	
Less: oil removed with each flow trial:*	
Oil removed in flow trial 1	(0.0)
Oil removed in flow trial 2	(10.7)
Oil removed in flow trial 3	(20.3)
Oil removed in flow trial 4	(15.9)
Oil removed in flow trial 5	(8.2)
Less: oil remaining on sediment at end of test determined by extracting sediment	(18.0)
(85.8 kg sediment with 0.21 ± 0.029 g oil/kg sediment)	
Less: oil removed on 2.0 kg of sediment sampled between flow trials	(1.6)
Net oil unaccounted for:	4.2 g (5.3% of initial)

* Total oil removed as flowing floc was 55.1 g, or 70% of oil in
column at start of test.

Composition of mobilized clay-oil floc--Figure 10 shows how the composition of the oil floc removed from the column changed during the course of the test (points represent data for flow trials shown in Tables 2-3). The fraction of mineral fines in the mobilized floc and the polars content of oil in that floc increased as higher water velocities and flow times increased cumulative oil removal. This suggests that, as polars increase, interactions with the rock substrate become stronger even though more mineral fines are also attracted to the oil, thus requiring more hydraulic energy for removal from the substrate. Our column-flow experiments therefore demonstrated a subtle chromatographic separation of polar components in the clay-oil floc being removed from the sediment.

Wave-Tank Experiments

Clay-oil floc buoyancy--By stopping the wave-tank motion and observing particle movement with time-lapse video, we were able to observe floc buoyancy. (Normal procedure, however, was to remove water and suspended floc before stopping the tank motion to capture any floc that might sink.) Figure 5 shows clay-oil floc particles one and 26 minutes after the water motion had stopped. By 26 minutes, most of the floc particles had floated to the water surface, a few had sunk (at a maximum rate of about 6 cm/hr), and many smaller flocs still remained suspended with almost neutral buoyancy. As shown in Figure 5(b), the water cleared faster near the bottom of the tank, *indicating that most of the floc particles were rising, not sinking.*

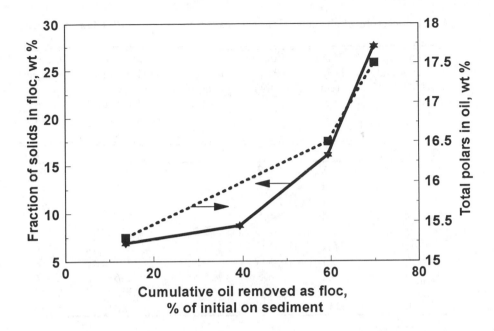

FIGURE 10--The weight fraction of mineral solids in the floc (on a water-free basis) and the concentration of polar hydrocarbons in the oil increased with cumulative oil removed in column-flow test. (Data points are for flow trials in Tables 2-3.)

Floc removal at various wave heights--Table 6 shows amounts and instantaneous rates of oil removal estimated for a series of wave-tank tests conducted at 2°C and a series at 15 °C. At any given wave height, most of the incremental oil was removed during the first few minutes. Nevertheless, some wave heights were run for several hours just to confirm that steady-state removal had been attained. Figure 11 shows the wave height achieved, and incremental oil removed, for each trial run. General trends are similar for the two series, suggesting that temperature was not a major factor in the floc removal mechanism over a range typical of water temperatures from summer to winter in Prince William Sound. Results show two significant trends. First, significant amounts of oil were removed at lower wave heights without sediment movement. Second, the highest rate of oil removal occurred at the first instance where sediment moved, with lesser amounts of oil removed in later trials even though later test durations were extended as long as 17 to 23 hours. This shows that abrasion was not needed for effective oil removal, but sediment movement did increase the rate of oil removal by several-fold, most likely by exposing more of the sediment surfaces to effective shear by water.

TABLE 6--Results of oil-removal tests in wave tank using Smith Island sediments.

Test Series and Wave Trial	Wave Height (cm)	Rocking Period (hr)	Oil Removed (% of initial mass)	Instantaneous Oil-Removal Rate (% /hr of initial oil mass)	Distance Sediment Was Moved (cm)
Test 1 (2°C)					
1	4.8	0.7	0.62	1.6	0
2	5.1	17	0.22	0.02	0
3	6.1	1	0.27	0.49	0
4	6.4	0.5	3.1	11.1	0
5	6.4	0.25	2.2	15.8	0
6	9.1	0.17	17	179	2 - 7
7	9.1	0.17	12	126	2 - 7
8	9.1	4.5	6.5	2.6	2 - 7
9	11.7	0.3	5.9	35.2	5 - 13
10	11.7	17	8.0	0.8	5 - 13
total			55.8		
Test 2 (15°C)					
1	5.1	0.83	0.11	0.23	0
2	5.3	0.5	0.97	3.3	0
3	6.6	1	0.91	1.54	0
4	6.6	0.5	5.2	17.7	0
5	6.6	0.17	4.0	39.9	0
6	9.1	0.17	13	130	2 - 6
7	9.1	0.17	8.8	87.9	0 - 6
8	9.1	4.5	11.0	4.2	0 -6
9	11.4	0.5	8.6	29.2	5 - 13
10	11.4	23	6.3	0.5	5 - 13
total			58.9		

Just as with the column-flow tests, oil removal had reached an apparent plateau at the end of each run, but, after stopping and restarting water movement, more floc was removed within moments of achieving a wave height of at least equal to that in the previous run. This suggests that the process of stopping and restarting, even with great care taken, may have allowed some additional sediment movement so that new surfaces were exposed to water motion. However, whether sediment moved or not, the basic structure and composition of mobilized floc particles appeared similar for all wave heights (data not

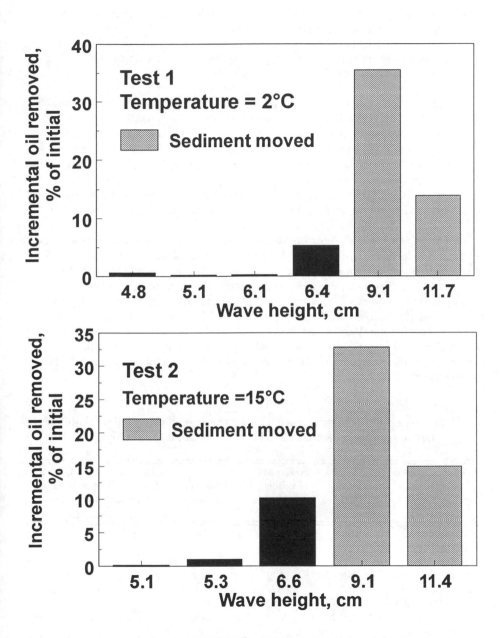

FIGURE 11--Amount of oil removed in wave-tank tests (Table 6)
versus wave height and presence or absence of sediment movement.

shown), suggesting that the mechanism for removal of floc from the sediment was not fundamentally different for the two regimes. With rock movement, however, the size of floc aggregates appeared to be smaller than sometimes observed for removal at lower wave heights, suggesting that the larger aggregates may have been broken into smaller units by the increased water velocity and sediment abrasion.

Size distribution of mineral fines--Figure 12 shows the particle-size distributions by weight of all mineral fines in floc particles liberated from the wave-tank test 2 (top) and those in clay-oil floc particles remaining on the sediment at the end of the test (bottom), with the latter being shifted to larger particle sizes. This shows that smaller particles flocculate the oil more efficiently, facilitating its removal from the sediment. There may also have been an increase in the size of mineral fines as cumulative floc removal increased, but individual floc samples did not contain sufficient fines for accurate analysis of size distribution, and all fines were combined for the analysis shown in Figure 12.

Additional verification of clay-oil floc in January 1990 trench samples--The seven sediment samples from trenches dug in January 1990 were subjected to submergence tests to determine if they contained clay-oil floc. Table 7 shows the estimated fraction of the total oil on the sediment that spontaneously separated from the rock (most floated) when it was placed under quiescent seawater. Also shown are the sediment oil loading and the ratio of mass of fines/mass of oil in the liberated floc. Only one sample--a sample of asphalt pavement from West Herring Bay--did not exhibit the easy oil removal typical of clay-oil floc. However, this oil contained virtually no mineral fines. Microscopic examination of oil released from all other six samples confirmed that in all cases the oil was extensively flocculated.

TABLE 7--Results of submergence tests for presence of clay-oil flocculation in trench samples collected in Prince William Sound in January 1990

Location Sampled	Sample Depth (cm)	Sediment Oil Loading (g oil/kg sed.)	Mass Fines Mass Oil	Fraction of Total Oil that Spontaneously Floated off Sediment in Quiescent Seawater, (%)
NW Ingot Island	80	0.36	2.8	64
NW Bay, BP-5	30	2.57	0.3	58
NW Bay, BP-5	30	0.46	2.2	28
NW Bay, East Cove	NR	1.29	0.8	12
W. Herring Bay*	0-3	32	0.1	0
Point Helen, AP-10	40	1.59	0.6	33
NW Ingot Island (Injection test site)	NR	0.37	2.8	36

* Sample consisted of asphalt pavement.   NR= not reported

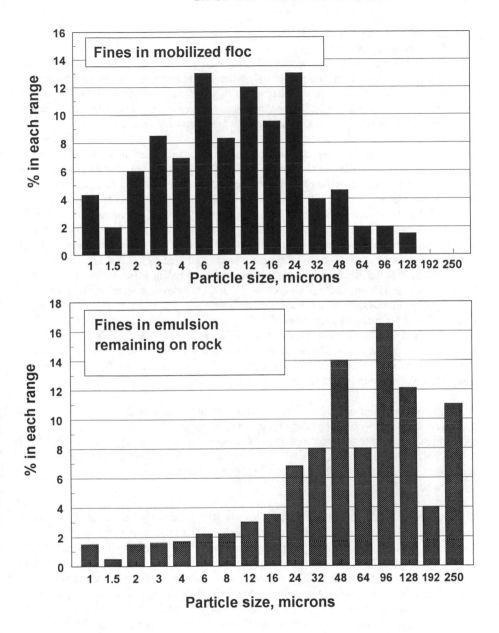

FIGURE 12--Particle-size distributions of mineral fines in combined floc removed from sediment and in floc remaining on sediment at end of wave-tank test 1 (Table 6).

INTERPRETATION OF RESULTS
Floc Formation and Structure
Results of extensive visual observations of sediments containing flocculated oil show that the emulsion structures form and persist only when the oil and minerals are submerged under seawater--the floc structures collapse out of water. The presence of the clay-oil emulsion therefore would not be noticed by casual observation on shorelines at low tide, but could be identified by careful inspection of submerged sediment.

Figure 13 illustrates our conceptual view of the floc structures seen under the microscope. We estimate that about 80% of the gross volume of a typical clay-oil floc particle is water. Flocculated emulsions form because of attractions among electrostatic charges on polar hydrocarbon molecules in the oil, on surfaces of mineral fines, and ions in seawater (Ives 1978). The polar molecules in the oil near the oil-water interface are attracted to the positive charges on cations such as calcium and magnesium in the seawater. Charges on surfaces of the mineral fines are likewise attracted to cations in the seawater, and the result is a stable emulsion in which small oil droplets are surrounded by mineral fines in water. A "cation bridge" in the film of seawater therefore serves to balance the electrostatic forces between the minerals and the oil. Uptake of H^+ or OH^- by oxides on minerals, such as silanol groups on the surface of a silica particle, can render the surface positive or negative (Ives 1978). Clay platelets gain much of their charge from isomorphic substitution (Ives 1978) in which Si^{4+} ions in the crystal lattice are exchanged by Al^{3+} or Ca^{2+}, rendering the surfaces negative, but with their edges still carrying a positive charge. Thus, the clay, quartz, and feldspar in the glacial flour generate varied surface charges that, in seawater, cause flocculation among themselves and the oil.

Polar charges in the oil result from heteroatoms such as nitrogen, sulfur, and oxygen. Biodegradation and weathering of the oil increase its polars content primary by oxidization, likely generating carboxy groups (Bragg et al. 1992; Bragg et al. 1993; Bragg et al. 1994). Thus, it is not surprising that in our small-scale screening experiments we found that weathered oil flocculates more readily than oil containing fewer polar hydrocarbons (Figure 8).

The finer the minerals, the more effective they are at dispersing the oil into small, micron-sized droplets because their surface area and electrical charge density per unit of mass increase as particle size decreases. If the oil contains sufficient polar hydrocarbons and the minerals are sufficiently fine, such as glacial flour, the interaction is spontaneous even with weak fluid shear (Payne et al. 1989). Although the resulting small floc particles are stable, aggregates of these can take on an almost infinite number of shapes and sizes depending on water turbulence (Lick 1987). We noted, for instance, that in wave-tank tests the size of floc aggregates removed from the sediment was somewhat dependent on the wave energy at the time of removal (data not shown). Further, some aggregates removed as thin films (identified as large aggregates in Figure 5(a)) appeared to later coil up into more compact particles after floating in the water for a few minutes. These coiled particles, now smaller in size, appeared similar to the floc particles removed from the column flow tests. Thus, the exact structure and size of aggregates is dependent on numerous factors, but the basic structural unit of individual floccules (small spheres of oil surrounded by mineral solids) appears common to most aggregates.

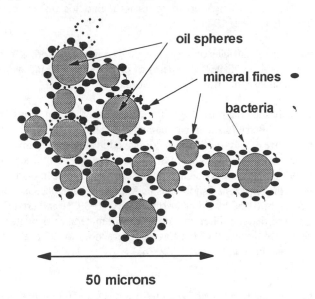

50 microns

FIGURE 13--Conceptual structure of clay-oil floc aggregates. Individual oil spheres surrounded by fine mineral particles and seawater (floccules) are loosely bound by weak interactions with neighbor floccules. Bacteria (scale exaggerated) gain increased access to oil via expanded oil-water interfacial area.

Prior literature and our screening studies suggest that most of the particles larger than clay (> 2μm) found in floc removed from sediment in Prince William Sound (see Figure 12) likely were incorporated into the emulsion floc by circumstance--by their close proximity to the flocculated oil and abundance in the sediment. However, they probably are not important contributors to the flocculation process because their masses are too large for the amount of surface areas they contribute. Kitchener (1978) concluded from prior studies of the effect of particle size that mineral particles up to at least 10 μm can exhibit colloidal phenomena such as flocculation, but activity diminishes rapidly as the mineral particle size increases.

Implications for Oil Removal and Ultimate Fate of Oil
   Timing of formation of clay-oil flocculation on Prince William Sound shorelines-- We believe that the following conditions led to formation of the clay-oil floc found on shorelines in Prince William Sound:

- Clay-oil emulsions formed on shorelines primarily after the oil had started to weather and generate increased concentrations of polar hydrocarbons. Screening tests showed that low-polars ANS crude oil did not readily form the finely dispersed clay-oil floc. However, weathered EVOS oil collected on May 10, 1989, already had sufficient polars to form the fine flocculates observed on sediment in November 1989.

- Very fine mineral particles of < 1μm in size were much more effective in generating the finely dispersed spheres of oil commonly found within the clay-oil floc from sediments in Prince William Sound.

This study first established the presence of flocculated clay-oil emulsions on samples taken from Smith Island and Perry Island in November and December of 1989. More widespread occurrence of clay-oil floc was confirmed in samples obtained from trenches dug at various locations in Prince William Sound in January 1990. Because NOAA (Payne et al. 1989) did not observe significant interactions between oil and suspended particulates before the oil reached shorelines in April 1989, and because our analysis of the oil collected off Knight Island by skimmer on May 10, 1989, (weathered EVOS in Table 1 and Figure 8) showed that it did not contain sufficient mineral fines by itself to flocculate in seawater, we believe that most of the clay-oil interactions must have occurred on the shorelines over the summer and fall of 1989.

One source of mineral fines in Prince William Sound is glacial flour that is transported by a portion of the Alaska Coastal Current that enters the sound and carries suspended glacial flour from the Copper River plume and numerous glaciers located east of Prince William Sound. This source is vividly illustrated by satellite images such as those produced by the Coastal Zone Color Scanner (Royer et al. 1990; Page, Boehm, Douglas, and Bence this volume) that show suspended fines entering Prince William Sound. Other sources of fine mineral particles within Prince William Sound are runoff--primarily from Columbia Glacier and Nellie Juan Glacier located within Prince William Sound (Payne et al. 1989). Runoff is seasonal, with highest transport of fines occurring during summer and early fall.

Once they enter the sound, only the smallest of these mineral fines remain suspended in the water column because of the water depth and relative quiescent conditions offshore. However, fines do remain along the subtidal and lower intertidal zones along shorelines, particularly in the surficial flocculant layer in shallow, nearshore areas (Payne et al. 1989). It is most likely that formation of clay-oil emulsions was initiated on shorelines shortly after oil arrived, but we can only guess at the rate or extent of flocculation during the summer of 1989.

The flocculation process was likely accelerated in the fall and winter of 1989 as storm activity caused resuspension of nearshore sediments and onshore transport of mineral fines (Feely et al. 1979) that then contacted the stranded oil. Further, clay-oil flocculation was probably enhanced with time as the oil became increasingly more polar as it continued to biodegrade and weather.

Natural oil removal was assisted following floc formation--Compositional analyses of oil removed from sediment as clay-oil floc (Tables 3-4) show that, except for subtle differences in the content of polar hydrocarbons, the oil removed as floc had the same composition as the bulk oil originally on the sediment. Thus, clay-oil flocculation is a bulk oil removal process.

Results of the column and wave-tank experiments may imply that small, but steady reductions of oil on sediment occurred with each tidal ebb and flow. Certainly, these results show that significant oil removal occurred when the oiled sediments were subjected to wave action even without sediment movement.

On the basis of our lab results, we would expect that oil removal would be very rapid where wave energy is sufficiently high to cause sediment movement. High rates of oil removal were observed on shorelines during storms, and sediment reworking with abrasion is considered the primary natural cleansing process on high-energy shorelines in Prince William Sound and the Gulf of Alaska (Owens 1991; Jahns et al. 1991; Neff, Owens, Stoker, and McCormick this volume). Results from this laboratory study confirm that sediment movement increases the rate of oil removal several-fold (Figures 9,11), but in the presence of clay-oil flocculation, physical abrasion of the sediment is not necessary to achieve rapid cleansing. Even gentle movement of sediment, with insignificant abrasion, exposes more of the floc on sediments to high water velocities, facilitating more thorough oil removal. Still, we view the flocculation process as merely augmenting abrasion for cleanup of high-energy shorelines, where extreme wave heights and abrasion would have efficiently removed the oil even in the absence of flocculation. These studies, however, show that the flocculation process was likely a very important contributor to oil removal for low-energy shorelines and deep subsurface oil where sediment movement and abrasion either did not occur or was negligible.

In our laboratory flow tests, complete oil removal was not achieved even though the bulk of the oil was readily removed from sediments. This is likely because floc with finely dispersed oil droplets, which is easiest to remove, requires mineral fines of about 1 μm or less in size for formation (as shown in the small-scale flocculation screening studies in Figure 8 and the work of Payne et al. [1989]), and these small (1 μm or less) mineral fines are differentially depleted as clay-oil floc is removed. Figure 12 shows that oil remaining on the sediment after floc removal contained very few of the small fines beneficial for flocculation. However, in the shoreline environment, the finer minerals would be replenished over time, leading to additional clay-oil flocculation, hence more complete oil removal. Thus, laboratory tests conducted in this study do not correctly simulate the ultimate end point of oil removal that should be expected in the dynamic shoreline environment where additional flocculation is likely a continuous process.

The abundance of mineral fines at most locations in Prince William Sound relative to the minimum amount needed to form floc is illustrated in Table 7 by the ratio of mineral fines to oil contained in flocculated emulsions on field sediment samples. These locations represented a wide range of shoreline energy levels. Except for the sample of asphalt pavement from West Herring Bay, the oil in all samples was flocculated, and a significant fraction of that floc was spontaneously removed from the sediment when the sample was placed in a beaker of seawater. There is a statistically significant linear correlation between the ratio of mass fines to mass oil in the floc and the oil loading on the sediment:

$$(\text{mass fines/mass oil in floc}) = 2.91 - 0.925(\text{oil loading, g oil/kg rock}).$$
$$[\text{for the fit, } R^2 = 0.82, p = 0.008.]$$

For the tests in Table 7 we did not measure oil composition, so we cannot determine whether oils with higher ratios of mass fines to mass of oil contained more polar hydrocarbons. There was no apparent correlation in Table 7 between the amount of oil spontaneously released and the ratio of fines to oil in the floc for the various samples. The main test result was simple confirmation that the oil was flocculated. Table 2 and Figure 10 show that the first floc removed from sediments in the column-flow test had a ratio of mass fines to mass oil as small as 0.074, so all samples in Table 7 contained far more minerals than needed to flocculate the amount of oil present. There simply was insufficient data on the prior histories for these samples (amount of oil originally present, local water energy level, shoreline geomorphology, etc.) to attempt to determine if there should be a general correlation between the ratio of fines to oil in the floc and its ease of removal from the various sediment samples.

Removal of oil as clay-oil floc particles helps explain absence of subtidal oil--The presence of clay-oil flocculation helps explain the lack of subtidal oil (Page, Boehm, Douglas, and Bence this volume) because the flocculated oil is removed as light aggregates that should either float or settle at very low velocities and thus become dispersed over wide areas to insignificant concentrations by waves and currents. Column-flow tests and wave-tank tests show that, although the rate of removal of flocculated oil is increased by sediment movement, the floc is removed in generally the same structural and chemical form regardless of whether the water velocity is high enough to move sediment.

Waves and currents can easily disperse the floc over wide areas. The large hydrodynamic cross-sections of the floc particles both enhance the ability of water to remove oil from the rock and to allow the water to transport the floc long distances, even in slow currents.

Effect of Clay-Oil Flocculation on Biodegradation and Weathering.
In clay-oil floc, oil exists as aggregates of small micron-sized spheres of oil surrounded by seawater. In the absence of flocculation, the oil exists as larger globules trapped within sediment or as a relatively thick film of residue on sediment particles. Calculations of oil-water interfacial areas for these two scenarios for typical sediment oil loadings (1 to 20 g oil/kg dry sediment) suggest that flocculation can increase oil-water interfacial area by up to three orders of magnitude. This should increase the rate of leaching of water-soluble hydrocarbons such as lower molecular weight aromatics and PAHs (polynuclear aromatic hydrocarbons), thus speeding up natural weathering.

Microscopic examination and microbial culturing of numerous floc particles from sediments in Prince William Sound showed that the floc contained substantial numbers of bacteria. Many of these bacteria are likely to remain with the floc particle as it is removed from the beach and, together with additional microbes from the water column, further biodegrade the remaining hydrocarbons.

Environmental Conditions where Clay-Oil Floc is Beneficial
Given the ease of the spontaneous interactions between crude oil and micron-sized mineral particles shown in this and other studies (Bassin and Ichiye 1977; Payne et al. 1989), flocculation should likely occur on a variety of marine shorelines that contain clays or other mineral fines. However, other factors, including competing interactions between oil and other sediments, may dominate in some environments. The major factors apparently required for clay-oil flocculation to be beneficial for cleansing oil from shoreline sediments are: (1) shoreline sediments that are primarily rocky (pebble, cobble) and not easily transported by waves and tides; (2) a supply of mineral fines of about 1 μm or less in size; (3) an oil containing a substantial fraction of polars--these form rapidly as the oil weathers, and many crudes contain sufficient polars to form clay-oil floc even when fresh; and (4) saline water. The first factor is primarily related to the differences in density and mass of the oiled substrate and the oil floc. If the sediment substrate is not greatly larger and heavier than the oil droplets (e.g., fine sand or silt), oil will be mobilized by water motion but it will also mobilize sediments that get incorporated into the oil, preventing effective removal of floc.

Many northern arctic and subarctic marine shorelines are rocky, but not all may contain the necessary micron-sized mineral fines if inputs from rivers or glaciers do not provide a source. Sandy beaches and marshes such as those prevalent on shorelines along the Gulf of Mexico are rich in clays of micron sizes that could cause flocculation. Unfortunately, major shoreline substrates for many of these beaches are sand, silt, and mud, which, like the mineral fines, are relatively light and mobile. These substrates have particle sizes that are too large to form flocculated emulsions, yet they are small enough to be incorporated into the oil droplets without emulsification. While a number of factors such as degree of weathering of the oil also must be considered (Payne and Phillips 1985), we can speculate that shorelines with fine sandy or silty sediments would more likely promote the formation of tarballs rather than clay-oil flocculation. While flocculation would occur, its effect likely would be overwhelmed by the incorporation of larger-grain sediments.

Implications for Future Clean-up Response
While this study has addressed the role of clay-oil flocculation as a natural cleansing process only in Prince William Sound, the findings suggest that the clay-oil flocculation process could perhaps be used to clean up future marine oil spills. Additional site-specific studies would need to be done, but adding clay-size mineral fines on affected beaches as part of the cleanup process during water washing or bioremediation treatments may help remove oil residues under certain conditions--especially on rocky shorelines or in coarse sediments where mineral fines are not naturally present.

CONCLUSIONS

On the basis of our laboratory studies of the structure and physical properties of oil residues remaining on sediment in Prince William Sound several months after the *Exxon Valdez* spill, we conclude that much of the oil had formed solids-stabilized oil-in-water emulsions through a process called clay-oil flocculation. These emulsions, which began forming in 1989 after the oil reached the shorelines, were generated from interactions among micron-sized mineral fines, seawater, and weathered oil. It is probable that the flocculation significantly affected the rate of natural cleansing, including physical removal of residues from shorelines, biodegradation, and leaching of soluble hydrocarbons. Clay-oil flocculation likely accelerated with time as the oil became more weathered, biodegraded, and polar (Bragg et al. 1993; Bragg et al. 1994). The structure and hydrodynamic properties of these emulsions provide new insight into how oil was removed from shorelines without causing substantial concentrations of oil residues in subtidal sediments.

Our specific conclusions are the following:

1. Flocculated clay-oil emulsions formed after oil from the *Exxon Valdez* reached the shorelines. These emulsions formed through interactions of oil and seawater with micron-sized mineral fines consisting of clay, quartz, and feldspar. The resulting structures are complex and varied but stable. The oil is distributed within the emulsion as micron-sized spheres surrounded by seawater and mineral fines. The entire structure is probably stabilized by electrical charges from polar components in oil, cations in seawater, and charges on mineral surfaces.

2. Flocculation of oil residues with fine mineral particles reduces the ability of the oil to adhere to sediment substrates such as sand, pebbles, and cobbles. Laboratory tests in column-flow and wave-tank experiments show that flocculated oil can be removed from subsurface and surface sediments by water energy levels less than those needed to move sediments. This provides an explanation as to how oil on subsurface sediments and low-energy shorelines can be cleaned in the absence of sediment movement by waves. However, tests also confirm that the rate of oil removal is much higher when sediments are moved, which is consistent with observed high rates of oil cleansing during storms.

3. The extensive flocculation of oil observed on sediment samples at different locations in Prince William Sound beginning in late 1989 (representing both high-energy and low-energy shorelines) suggests that a significant portion of the oil removed from shorelines, at least from that time forward, was likely removed as fine particles of flocculated clay-oil emulsion.

4. Chemical analyses show that, except for minor differences in the concentrations of polar hydrocarbons, the oil removed from sediments as flocculated emulsions is the same as oil on sediments prior to removal. Thus, flocculation is a bulk oil removal process.

5. The observed large hydrodynamic cross section and buoyancy of the clay-oil floc particles removed from field sediment samples suggest that, when washed from the shoreline, such floc particles should easily be transported by waves, tides and offshore currents and be widely dispersed. Laboratory tests show that most of these particles either float or are nearly neutral in buoyancy. Some heavier particles sink at very low velocities of centimeters to meters per day. Thus, we believe that floc particles swept by offshore currents moving at kilometers per hour were likely transported long distances before they settled to the seafloor. Such dispersion over wide areas helps to explain why *Exxon Valdez* oil residue, where it was identified in subtidal sediments, generally occurred only as a small increment over and above the natural hydrocarbon background in the region (Page, Boehm, Douglas, and Bence this volume).

6. Clay-oil flocculation significantly increases the oil-water interfacial area by reducing the oil to micron-sized droplets. We believe this makes the oil more accessible to microbes for biodegradation and enhances leaching of soluble hydrocarbons, which are the most toxic components of the oil. Thus, floc formation likely works in concert with other natural processes to hasten degradation of the oil to a biologically inert residue.

Overall, clay-oil flocculation was found to be a beneficial process that interacts synergistically with other natural (and active clean-up) processes to remove oil from shorelines. The process is initiated naturally in rocky shoreline environments such as Prince William Sound where the required micron-sized mineral fines are readily available. However, it may be possible to actively promote this process in other environments by prudent use of mineral fines as a supplement to other clean-up methods.

REFERENCES
Bassin, N. J. and T. Ichiye. "Flocculation Behavior in Suspended Sediments and Oil Emulsions." *Journal of Sedimentary Petrology.* 47: 671-677; 1977.

Bragg, J. R., J. C. Roffall, and S. J. McMillen. "Column Flow Studies of Bioremediation in Prince William Sound." Houston, TX: Exxon Production Research Company; 50 pp; 1990a.

Bragg, J. R., S. H. Yang, and J. C. Roffall. "Experimental Studies of Natural Cleansing of Oil Residue From Rocks in Prince William Sound by Wave/Tidal Action." Houston, TX; Exxon Production Research Company; 31 pp; 1990b.

Bragg, J. R., R. C. Prince, J. B. Wilkinson, and R. M. Atlas. "Bioremediation for Shoreline Cleanup Following the 1989 Alaskan Oil Spill." Houston, TX; Exxon Company, USA; 94 pp; 1992.

Bragg, J. R., R. C. Prince, E. J. Harner, and R. M. Atlas. "Bioremediation Effectiveness Following the *Exxon Valdez* Spill." *Proceedings of the 1993 Oil Spill Conference.*

Prevention, Behavior, Control, Cleanup, March 29-April 1, 1993, Tampa, FL.
Washington, DC: American Petroleum Institute; 435-447; 1993.

Bragg, J.R., R.C. Prince, E.J. Harner, and R.M. Atlas. "Effectiveness of Bioremediation
for the Exxon Valdez Oil Spill." *Nature.* 386; (No. 6470): 413-418; 1994.

Delvigne, G. A. L., J. A. van der Stel, and C. E. Sweeney. "Measurement of Vertical
Turbulent Dispersion and Diffusion of Oil Droplets and Oiled Particles, Final Report." U.
S. Department of the Interior, Minerals Management Service, OCS Study MMS 87-111;
Anchorage, AK; 501 pp; 1987.

Feely, R. A., E. T. Baker, J. D. Schumacher, G. J. Massoth, and W. M. Landing.
"Processes Affecting the Distribution and Transport of Suspended Matter in the Northeast
Gulf of Alaska." *Deep Sea Research.* 26A: 445-464; 1979.

Forrester, W. D. "Distribution of Suspended Oil Particles Following the Grounding of the
Tanker *Arrow.*" *Journal of Marine Research.* 29: 151-170; 1971.

Grizzle, P.L. and J.S. Thomson. "Liquid Chromatographic Separaton of Aromatic
Hydrocarbons with Chemically-bonded (2,4-Dinitroanilinopropyl) Silica." *Analytical
Chemistry,* 54: 1071, 1982.

Haberman, R.E., R.E. Overfield, and W.K. Robbins. "Method for Spectroscopic Analysis
of Hydrocarbons." U.S. Patent 4,988,446; January 29, 1992.

Harrison, O. R. "An Overview of the *Exxon Valdez* Oil Spill." *Proceedings of the 1991
International Oil Spill Conference. Prevention, Behavior, Control, Cleanup.*
Washington, DC: American Petroleum Institute; 313-319; 1991.

Hayes, M. O., J. Michel, and D. C. Noe. "Factors Controlling Initial Deposition and
Long-Term Fate of Spilled Oil on Gravel Beaches." *Proceedings of the 1991
International Oil Spill Conference. Prevention, Behavior, Control, Cleanup.*
Washington, DC: American Petroleum Institute; 453-460; 1991.

Jackson, M.L. *Soil Chemical Analysis -- Advanced Course,* 2nd Edition, 11th Printing.
Published by the author, Madison, WI: 127; 1979.

Jahns, H. O., J. R. Bragg, L. C. Dash, and E. H. Owens. "Natural Cleaning of Shorelines
Following the *Exxon Valdez* Spill." *Proceedings of the 1991 International Oil Spill
Conference. Prevention, Behavior, Control, Cleanup. March 4-7, 1991, San Diego, CA.*
Washington, DC: American Petroleum Institute; 167-176; 1991.

Kitchener, J. A. "Flocculation in Mineral Processing," in *The Scientific Basis of
Flocculation,* Kenneth J. Ives (Editor); NATO Advanced Study Institute Series E, No.

27; Alphen aan den Rijn, The Netherlands: Sijthoff & Noordhoff International Publishers; 283-328; 1978.

Lick, W. "The Transport of Sediments in Aquatic Systems." in *Fate and Effects of Sediment-Bound Chemicals in Aquatic Systems*, K. L. Dickson, A. W. Maki, and W. A. Brunges (Editors); New York: Pergamon Press; 61-74; 1987.

Lyklema, J. "Surface Chemistry of Colloids in Connection with Stability," in *The Scientific Basis of Flocculation*, Kenneth J. Ives (Editor); NATO Advanced Study Institute Series E, No. 27; Alphen aan den Rijn, The Netherlands: Sijthoff & Noordhoff International Publishers; 3-61; 1978.

Lung, W. S., J. L. Martin, and S. C. McCutcheon. "Eutrophication Analysis of Embayments in Prince William Sound, Alaska." *Journal of Environmental Engineering.* 119 (No. 5): 814-815; 1993.

Malinky, G. and D. G. Shaw. "Modeling the Association of Petroleum Hydrocarbons and Sub-Arctic Sediments." *Proceedings of the 1979 Oil Spill Conference. Spill Behavior and Effects. March 19-22, 1979, Los Angeles, CA.* Washington, DC: American Petroleum Institute; 621-623; 1979.

Meyers, P. A. and J. G. Quinn. "Association of Hydrocarbons and Mineral Particles in Saline Solution." *Nature.* 244: 23-24; 1973.

Meyers, P. A. and T. G. Oas. "Comparison of Associations of Different Hydrocarbons with Clay Particles in Simulated Seawater." *Environmental Science & Technology.* 12(8): 934-937; 1978.

Michel, J., M. O. Hayes, W. J. Sexton, J. C. Gibeaut, and C. Henry. "Trends in Natural Removal of the *Exxon Valdez* Oil Spill in Prince William Sound from September 1989 to May 1990." *Proceedings of the 1991 International Oil Spill Conference. Prevention, Behavior, Control, Cleanup. March 4-7, 1991, San Diego, CA.* Washington, DC: American Petroleum Institute; 181-187; 1991.

Owens, E. H. "Shoreline Conditions Following the *Exxon Valdez* Spill as of Fall 1990." *Proceedings of the Fourteenth Arctic and Marine Oilspill Program (AMOP) Technical Seminar. June 12-14, 1991, Vancouver, BC.* Ottawa, Canada: Environment Canada; 579-606; 1991.

Payne, J. R., J. R. Clayton, Jr., G. D. McNabb, Jr., B. E. Kirstein, C. L. Clary, R. T. Redding, J. S. Evans, E. Reimnitz, and E. W. Kempema. "Oil-Ice-Sediment Interactions During Freezup and Breakup." U.S. Department of Commerce, National Oceanic and Atmospheric Administration (NOAA), *OCSEAP Final Report.* 64: 1-382; 1989.

Payne, J. R. and C. R. Phillips. *Petroleum Spills in the Marine Environment*. Chelsea, MI: Lewis Publishers, Inc.; 1-148; 1985.

Royer, T. C., J. A. Vermersch, T. J. Weingartner, H. J. Neiibaure, and R. D. Muench. "Ocean Circulation Influencing the *Exxon Valdez* Oil Spill." *Oceanography*. 3(2): 3-10; 1990.

Teal, A. R. "Shoreline Cleanup--Reconnaissance, Evaluation, and Planning Following the Valdez Oil Spill." *Proceedings of the 1991 International Oil Spill Conference. Prevention, Behavior, Control, Cleanup. March 4-7, 1991, San Diego, CA*. Washington, DC: American Petroleum Institute; 149-152; 1991.

D. G. Taft[1], D. E. Egging[1], and H. A. Kuhn[2]

SHEEN SURVEILLANCE: AN ENVIRONMENTAL MONITORING PROGRAM
SUBSEQUENT TO THE 1989 *EXXON VALDEZ* SHORELINE CLEANUP

REFERENCE: Taft, D. G., Egging, D. E., and Kuhn, H. A., "Sheen
Surveillance: An Environmental Monitoring Program Subsequent to the 1989
Exxon Valdez Shoreline Cleanup," Exxon Valdez Oil Spill: Fate and Effects in
Alaskan Waters, ASTM STP 1219, Peter G. Wells, James N. Butler, and Jane
S. Hughes, Eds., American Society for Testing and Materials, Philadelphia,
1995.

ABSTRACT: In the fall of 1989, an aerial surveillance program was implemented to
locate oil sheens (or slicks) originating from shorelines affected by the *Exxon Valdez* spill.
The objectives of the program were to identify any oil on the water that warranted
response and to identify those sections of shoreline that would be priority candidates for
further cleanup in 1990. The program initially surveyed the entire affected area, but,
because proportionally fewer sheens were spotted in the Gulf of Alaska, the program was
refocused on Prince William Sound in early 1990.

The surveillance program consisted of frequent low-altitude flights with trained
observers in a deHavilland Twin Otter outfitted with observation ports and communication
equipment. The primary surveillance technique used was direct visual observation. Other
techniques, including photography, were tested but proved less effective. The flights
targeted all shorelines of concern, particularly those near fishing, subsistence, and
recreational areas. The observers attempted to locate all sheens, estimate their size and
color, and identify the source of the oil found in the sheen. Size and color were used to
estimate the volume of oil in each sheen. Samples were collected whenever possible
during the summer of 1990 using a floating Teflon™ sampling device that was developed
for easy deployment from a boat or the pontoon of a float plane. Forty four samples were
analyzed by UV-fluorescence spectroscopy. Eleven of these samples were also analyzed
by GC/MS. In general, the analyses confirmed the observers' judgement of source.

The flights from late September 1989 through early September 1990 identified 827
petroleum hydrocarbon sheens. About two-thirds of the sheens were related to the *Exxon
Valdez* or were of indeterminate source. For the purposes of analyses these were
combined and treated as if their origins were all from the *Exxon Valdez*. The numbers and
volumes of these sheens decreased dramatically with time after the onset of winter storms.

[1]Exxon Production Research Co., Houston Tx
[2]Shoreline Resources, Rathdrum, ID

The *Exxon Valdez* related sheens sighted during the spring and summer of 1990 contained volumes averaging less than two litres of oil each. By the summer of 1990, the number and size of *Exxon Valdez* sheens were smaller than those associated with normal vessel activity in Prince William Sound. There was no disruption of commercial fishing activities because of *Exxon Valdez* related sheens in 1990. The program was discontinued in September 1990 because the number and volume of spill-related sheens had declined to low levels.

KEYWORDS: Oil sheen, oil slick, monitoring, oil spill, *Exxon Valdez*, aerial surveillance

---

INTRODUCTION

Exxon Valdez oil-spill (EVOS) cleanup operations were suspended in September 1989 because of weather-related safety considerations. In spite of the cleanup effort, oil residue remained on some shorelines. This residue could potentially be removed by winter storms and tidal action. This paper describes an environmental monitoring program, called the Sheen Surveillance program, which was established to monitor releases of oil from shorelines.

Sheens are very thin films of organic materials typically less than 1 mm thick. Sheens containing small volumes of oil were not expected to pose a hazard to water-column organisms or to wildlife on the sea surface (Neff 1991; Baker et al. 1990). This surveillance program was designed to identify sheens and their likely source.

The sheen surveillance program involved frequent overflights using a specially equipped aircraft and trained observers. Its objectives were to document the releases of oil from shorelines affected by the EVOS so that response vessels could be directed to locations of large sheens in the event a response was warranted, and to identify locations of persistent sheening to assist in planning the 1990 shoreline assessment and cleanup. Particular emphasis was placed on areas near shorelines that were known to have residual oil and on areas of environmental concern, such as fishing grounds. Although the principal focus of the surveillance program was to locate and quantify sheens related to the EVOS, other sheens not related to the spill were frequently observed and documented.

The sheen surveillance program operated from late September 1989 through early September 1990. The program assessed the locations and associated volumes of hydrocarbon sheens using visual techniques. A sheen sampling technique was developed and used during the program to collect samples for lab analyses and source confirmation by fingerprinting.

Over 80 000 km were safely flown on 121 days during the 12-month duration of the aerial surveillance program. The program was discontinued in September 1990 because the number and volume of EVOS-related sheens had declined to levels less than those associated with normal activities.

METHODS

Extent of Surveys

The aerial sheen surveillance program consisted of two phases. Phase 1, which included both the Gulf of Alaska (GOA) and Prince William Sound (PWS), began in late September 1989 and lasted into March 1990. There were proportionally fewer sheens in the GOA during this period compared with PWS. In addition, greater weather downtime and safety risks were associated with operations in the GOA. Therefore, the program that became Phase 2 was refocused to concentrate on only PWS from early March until its termination in September 1990.

Flights during Phase 1 were conducted weekly over areas affected by the spill (weather and daylight permitting) as shown in Figure 1. Short daylight periods during the winter (e.g., about 10 h in October and February, less than 6 h in December) and long distances meant monitoring the Kodiak Archipelago and Alaska Peninsula in two separate flights. These flights, as shown in Figure 1, were conducted on alternate weeks. Flights over PWS were performed each week along the flight line shown in the inset on Figure 1. Each week's flight was about 3 000 km.

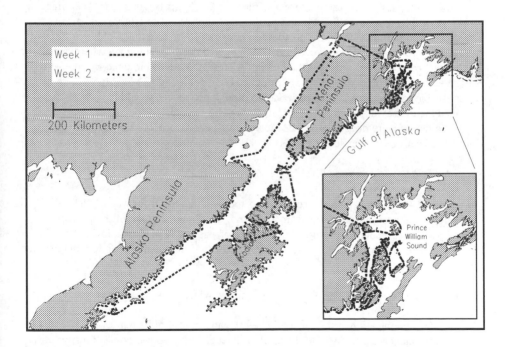

Figure 1--Flight lines for the sheen surveillance program over the spill-affected area during the winter (PWS and the GOA) and summer (PWS).

During Phase 2, flights were conducted daily (weather permitting). Monitoring concentrated on EVOS-affected areas of PWS. Emphasis was placed on shorelines that produced sheens during Phase 1 and on areas that were important to fishing, subsistence, or recreational use.

Flight schedules were planned around weather and tidal cycles, because EVOS-related sheens generally resulted from high waves and tides exposing oil residue to the sea. Therefore, the optimal observation times for sheen surveillance usually corresponded to times near high tide. Flight schedules during winter did not always coincide with the high-tide cycle because of short daylight periods. However, the data from fall and winter flights do not show a bias due to tide level. Daylight was usually not a consideration for planning flights at high tide during Phase 2 of the program, because longer daylight periods during spring and summer (e.g., about 15 h in April and August; 19 h in June) allowed more flexible flight scheduling. Weather conditions, including low visibility and high winds, did cause flight cancellations or alterations throughout the program, but there were progressively fewer changes to flight plans as the year advanced from winter to summer.

Flights over PWS encompassed essentially the same areas during the two phases of the program. A typical day's flight over PWS in Phase 2 was over 400 km.

Sheen observations were also recorded in areas outside the affected area along the aircraft's flight path. For example, because most of the flights originated in Anchorage, areas along the most direct flight path to PWS, including Whittier Harbor and areas east, were surveyed during each flight. In addition, areas en route to either Valdez or Seward on refueling runs were also surveyed. All nonbiogenic sheens sighted anywhere during the flight were recorded and are reported herein. A large number of biogenic sheens were observed, particularly in the spring and summer when some flights could have documented over 100 biogenic sheens. Since observation of all these sheens would have severely reduced the time available to locate and document EVOS-related sheens, only large biogenic sheens were documented. Because a complete record was not maintained, biogenic sheens are not included in this paper.

Standard Observation Procedures

Aircraft -- Sheens can be very difficult to spot and identify from water level. Therefore, overhead observations from an aircraft are essential. One of the principal features of the surveillance program was the use of a specially modified deHavilland Twin Otter aircraft. Features added to the Twin Otter for the surveillance program included the following:

- A large, optically clear observation window, which replaced one rear door.

- A communication system that allowed the observers (in the rear of the aircraft) to communicate directly with the pilot or independently with Exxon's transportation center in Anchorage.

- A global positioning system (GPS) for real-time recording of the aircraft's position and, hence, the locations of sheens or other significant observations.

- A portable computer with menu-driven software and linkage to the GPS to facilitate the recording and reporting of observations and their locations.

- Video and still cameras for photo documentation.

- Floats, installed in the spring of 1990, to allow the aircraft to land near sheens of interest to take samples for source verification.

Flights were planned to obtain the best possible observations given weather, tide, and daylight conditions and subject to fuel and safety considerations. Survey altitudes typically ranged from 100 m to 300 m above sea level. Airspeeds ranged from 80 knots to 120 knots. When a possible sheen was sighted, the observer communicated with the pilot to obtain the best viewing position. This often required circling the sheen to record the size and color and, if possible, to identify the source.

All the surveillance flights were conducted within the environmental constraints placed on cleanup activities by regulatory authorities. These constraints included zones of exclusion that varied in size from 400 m to 800 m around all eagle nests, seabird colonies, and pinniped haulouts during specific time periods. Within these zones, the flight altitude was maintained above 300 m. The locations of these zones sometimes prevented sampling of sheens near shorelines. However, the exclusion zones did not unduly constrain the observations of sheens.

Identification and Measurement of Sheens -- Standardized procedures for visual observations and data recording developed by Kuhn and MacDonald (1990) were followed. The procedures included safety practices and constraints, flight patterns, protocol for determining sheen size and identifying color, standardized reporting definitions, and U. S. Coast Guard reporting requirements. The initial observer, H. A. Kuhn, was trained as a pilot and in aerial surveillance by the U. S. Navy. He gained oil spill experience during the summer of 1989. Training typically included study of photographs and video of various sheens, and a review of the survey area for fresh water outflows and other features that affect observations. Other observers were trained by Kuhn to ensure consistency in their ability to detect and report sheens. The airborne program was supplemented with sampling for source confirmation in the late spring and summer after weather conditions allowed floats to be used on the aircraft.

Many organic materials, including crude oil and refined products, form sheens on water that refract light in a variety of colors. Refraction of light through a sheen results in certain colors that characterize its thickness. For example, a rainbow-colored sheen, typical of a refined petroleum product such as diesel, has a thickness usually between 0.00015 mm and 0.00030 mm. Thinner sheens are silvery or gray; thicker sheens tend to have dull colors. Sheens thicker than a few thousandths of a millimeter take on the color of the material forming the sheen. Because sheens are so thin, they contain very little petroleum per unit area of water surface. For example, 15 mL of oil could form a rainbow sheen of about 50 m^2 in surface area.

The volume of material in a sheen can be estimated from the area covered by the sheen and from its thickness (determined from its color). The color standards used in the sheen surveillance program and their corresponding maximum thicknesses are shown in Table 1

(Koops 1985; ITOPF 1981; Fingas, Duval, and Stevenson 1979). Because maximum thicknesses were used in estimating sheen volumes, volume estimates were generally at the upper limits, and the actual volume of oil contained in each sheen was probably less than noted in this paper.

TABLE 1--CORRELATION BETWEEN SHEEN COLOR AND UPPER BOUND THICKNESS

Sheen Color	Maximum Thickness (mm)	Description
Very light	0.00005	Like fresh water but faint pearly blue-gray hue. Difficult to locate at water level for sampling. Possibly from seaweed. Dissipates easily.
Silver	0.0001	Reflects color of sky. Mirror-like. Possibly from seaweed.
First color	0.00015	A few light colors begin to appear. Mirror-like.
Rainbow	0.0003	Vivid luminescent rainbow of colors. Broken by aircraft prop-wash. Very conspicuous.
Dull colors	0.001	Dull, greasy rainbow hues. May calm surface ripples on water. Not significantly affected by aircraft prop-wash.
Yellow-Brown	0.01	Dull yellow-brown hue. May calm surface of water. Not affected by aircraft prop-wash.
Light brown	0.1	Appears thick on the water surface. Light brown hue ringed by yellow-brown and rainbow colors.
Brown-black	1.0	Appearance of thick black motor oil. Calms seas. Readily adheres to any surface.

Note: All hydrocarbon films with these colors are referred to as sheens in the text. In some of the oil spill literature, the thicker ones would be called slicks.

Sheen dimensions near the coast were often estimated by comparison with coastline features or objects with identifiable sizes, or by using a map for scale if the sheen was large. Away from the coast, objects on or near the water were often used to estimate size: seagulls have a wingspan of about 1 m; sea lions are about 2.5 m long; and boat lengths could be approximated with experience, especially if crew members were visible. Observers learned from experience to estimate field-of-view dimensions at the normal survey altitudes. The speed over ground and time of flight also allowed the observer to calculate the size of large sheens. The percentage of the area covered by the sheen was also estimated. Photographs of sheens showing various percentages of coverage were used to calibrate the observers.

Sheens were classified into five categories on the basis of their potential originating source. These sources and their respective classification criteria are as follows:

1. *Exxon Valdez* crude oil
   - Sheens bleeding, or down current, from EVOS-oiled shorelines that had an appearance consistent with weathered Alaska North Slope (ANS) crude. (ANS crude was carried by the *Exxon Valdez*.) The appearance of sheens produced by EVOS ANS crude changed over the course of the surveillance program. Repeated observations of sheens emanating from EVOS-oiled shorelines allowed the observers to "recalibrate" as the amount of ANS crude available to produce sheens was reduced and the oil continued to weather.
   - Sheens located near cleanup crews.

2. Indeterminate (potentially EVOS)
   - Sheens located near, or down current from, oiled shorelines that did not appear to be similar to weathered ANS crude due to color or character.
   - Sheens that could not be classified into one of the other four categories.

3. Vessel-related
   - Sheens typical of those produced by refined products (fuel oil, diesel, lubricating fluids, bilge liquids) in the immediate vicinity of vessels.
   - Sheens typical of refined products in high traffic areas and not near EVOS-oiled shorelines.

4. Other man-made sources
   - Sheens bleeding from visible man-made sources such as creosoted logs or leaking drums not associated with cleanup activities.

5. Biogenic
   - Sheens from plant matter usually visible within or very close to the sheen. Biogenic sheens were so common during the spring and summer that a decision was made to document only the largest. Biogenic sheen data are not included in this paper.

Experienced observers could usually distinguish the source material of a sheen from the sheen's color, luster, shape and location. The identifying characteristics of sheens from different types of hydrocarbons are shown in Table 2. The observers used the visual characteristics noted in Table 2 with the classification criteria cited above to determine the originating source of a sheen.

TABLE 2--VISUAL IDENTIFICATION OF SHEENS

Source of Sheen	Characteristic Appearance
Light refined hydrocarbons	Dull to rainbow colors when fresh, becoming silver with time (volatile liquids like aviation gasoline go from bright rainbow to silver in minutes, as they evaporate). Often noticeably rounded and localized.
Diesel fuel	Rainbow to dull colors; very conspicuous
Hydraulic fluid	Commonly rainbow; fairly persistent.
Bilge fluid (oil, water)	Sheens from bilge oil are usually rounded in shape, with conspicuous, dull to rainbow colors. Bilge-water sheens may show brown froth or streaks from the fuel and lubricants they contain.
Crude oil	Distribution (shape) and thickness (color) of crude-oil sheens are influenced by the amount of weathering. Color varies with thickness, as shown in Table 1; with time they become pale, and the shape tends to elongate. Fresh crude oil forms rounded or wide sheens that in time form ribbons, streaks, and wisps.
Natural (biogenic)	Off Alaska, a common source of plant sheen is rockweed or popweed (genus *Fucus*) that produces a silver to very light blue sheen. The shape tends to be in ribbons and streaks, forming wisps in light winds.

To the untrained observer, numerous phenomena can appear to be hydrocarbon sheens. These false indications include outflows of fresh water at stream mouths, wind sheens, turbid water, debris in riptides, and rafts of pollen or pine needles. Identifying these non-hydrocarbon sheen-like phenomena often required knowledge of the local waters and wind patterns. Observers frequently needed multiple very low altitude passes from different directions over suspicious material to determine whether it was really a hydrocarbon sheen or one of these phenomena. In general, non-hydrocarbon sheen-like phenomena are easily distinguished if the observer's relative angle with the sun is significantly changed. The ability of trained observers to successfully identify the source of oil in sheens was confirmed by sampling and fingerprinting of numerous sheens as discussed below.

Data Reporting and Information Sharing -- Observations were recorded in a consistent manner. General data recorded about each flight included aircraft ID, pilot, observer, flight line, weather (including wind, visibility, cloud cover, sea state, and air temperature), and tidal range.

A computer-based system was used to enhance the observers' ability to map a flight path, map the positions of sheens, and consistently document sheen characteristics. The observers recorded the location, size, and dominant color of each sheen. They also identified its most likely source (if possible) and its general description. Since sheens tended to be discontinuous and patchy over the water surface, observers also recorded the fraction of the area covered by the sheen. All documentation became part of the daily flight report. Large sheens and other unusual or significant features were photographed and/or videotaped.

Reports were generated for each flight. The date, flight line, sheen locations, and sheen attributes were loaded on to a geographic information system (GIS), or mapping system. The data in the GIS were used to determine sheen trends near shorelines of persistent sheening, fisheries, and other areas of interest.

The volume of each sheen was estimated following the flight by multiplying the surface area (length x width x percent of coverage) of the sheen by its thickness, using the maximum thickness-color relationship shown in Table 1.

Weekly summaries of the surveillance flights were provided to federal and state agencies. In addition, federal and state agency personnel were invited to participate in the daily observation flights. A U.S. Coast Guard (USCG) observer was present on about one-half of the flights.

Identification and Fingerprinting of Sheens -- Observers identified the sources of sheens with a reasonable degree of certainty. Confirming these sources required the collection and analyses, or fingerprinting, of sheen samples. Samples were collected by means of a sheen lure based on USCG technology (United States Coast Guard 1974). The sheen lure is a weighted fishing float with several strips of Teflon™ attached, as shown in Figure 2. Hydrocarbons would adhere to the surface of the Teflon™ strips, thereby permitting trace amounts to be captured from the water. The captured hydrocarbons were extracted from the strips for subsequent laboratory analysis.

Sheens were selected for sampling on the basis of their size and location. Because sheens are often very difficult to see at water level, the only sheens sampled were those large enough and of a sufficiently contrasting color that they could be located after landing on the water. These requirements generally precluded sampling small sheens or those that were silver or very lightly colored. Sheens that were clearly bleeding from shorelines containing remains of EVOS oil or originating from other clearly identifiable sources were not routinely sampled. In addition, the observers tried to minimize the impact of the sampling on wildlife or commercial and recreational activities by not sampling sheens near sensitive environmental resources or vessels.

To obtain samples, the aircraft would land on the water near the sheen and taxi downwind from it. The aircraft would then use reverse thrust to back within casting range (about 10 m) so the lure could be cast into the sheen with a fishing rod to obtain an uncontaminated sample. Three or four casts would generally capture an adequate sample on the Teflon™ strips for fingerprinting. The Teflon™ strips were immediately placed in a chemically sterilized bottle with an extraction solvent, hexane, added prior to sealing and transport to the laboratory. These field procedures reduced the chance of inadvertent contamination of the sample. Great care was needed in the sampling and extraction procedures because of the sensitivity of the sheen lure to airborne hydrocarbons. Laboratory analyses would normally identify aviation fuel in the sample if the sheen lure was exposed to aircraft exhaust.

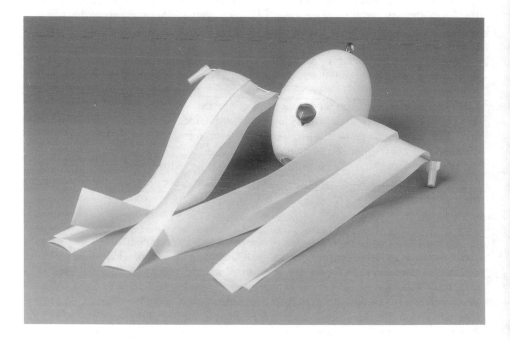

Figure 2.--Photograph of sheen lure used for collecting sheen samples from the water surface. The sheen lure consists of Teflon™ strips suspended from a weighted fishing net float.

Although several analytical techniques are useful for source-oil fingerprinting, USCG and National Oceanic and Atmospheric Administration (NOAA) oil-spill-response experience since the early 1970's has led to standard methodology and general use of two techniques for identification and classification of oil from oil spills (United States Coast

Guard 1977). These techniques are ultraviolet fluorescence (UV-F) spectroscopy and gas chromatography/mass spectrometry (GC/MS). Both techniques were used in Exxon's laboratory in Anchorage. The UV-F methods used in this laboratory were qualitative and quite different from the quantitative methods used to identify the origins of low concentrations of hydrocarbons in biological tissues and sediment studies (Bence and Burns, this volume).

UV-F spectroscopy measures the emission of radiation from a sample excited by ultraviolet light. The resulting emission spectrum, grouped according to emissions from multi-ring hydrocarbons, was used to identify the source. Spectra from both constant excitation and synchronous scanning were used. Identification was accomplished by comparing the spectra from the unknown sample with known reference spectra. Regular monitoring of weathered EVOS oil samples provided observable trends in the spectra.

Analysis by UV-F spectroscopy was conducted on all samples as a preliminary screening tool to distinguish EVOS-related oil from oil from other sources. The Alaska North Slope crude oil carried on the *Exxon Valdez* has a distinctive fingerprint that differentiates it from refined products (e.g., diesel). The graphs in Figure 3 are examples of fluorescence emission spectra, from a synchronous emission scan, for (a) crude oil from the *Exxon Valdez* and (b) #2 diesel fuel from Alaska. Both samples were diluted/concentrated to test just below the saturation limit of the UV-F spectrograph. The horizontal axis is the wavelength of the emission, and the vertical axis is the relative intensity. The difference between the crude oil and the diesel fuel are obvious. A strong two-ring component peak, occurring at or below an excitation wavelength of 310 nm, is the principal feature of most light, refined products such as diesel fuel. The peaks from the other components, especially the 4+ ring compounds, in refined products are very weak in comparison to those of the ANS crude. The refining process for diesel and other light fuels removes the 4+ ring compounds.

In a few cases (4 out of 44), the analysis by UV-F spectroscopy did not produce conclusive results. These four samples were analyzed with GC/MS. GC/MS analysis characterizes a complex mixture by separating the sample into its individual molecular components on the basis of their relative retention times on a chromatographic column (GC) and mass/charge ratios (MS). The GC/MS analysis of these four samples concluded that one was definitely not ANS crude and that the other three sheens were of indeterminate origin. Additional GC/MS analysis was conducted on 11 sheen samples to either quantify the characteristics of weathered ANS crude or to determine the origin of non-ANS crude sheens.

The USCG and NOAA techniques adopted in Exxon's oil identification laboratory in Anchorage could differentiate, or fingerprint, the sources of hydrocarbons taken from sheens. However, the extraction methods used for the sheen surveillance program were different from the more time-consuming extraction methods required to quantify the concentrations and relative contributions of hydrocarbons from multiple sources. Therefore, the techniques for fingerprinting outlined here were not applicable to a quantitative analysis of low concentrations of weathered hydrocarbons from mixed sources, such as the techniques employed in the shoreline-sediment-monitoring programs (Gilfillan, Suchanek et al., this volume; Page et al., this volume; Boehm et al., this volume)

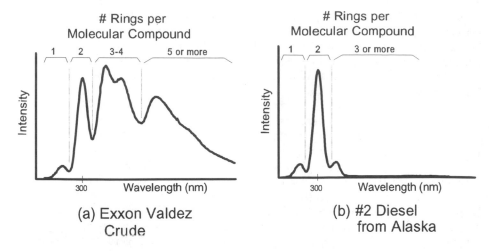

(a) Exxon Valdez Crude

(b) #2 Diesel from Alaska

Figure 3.--Example emission spectra from ultraviolet fluorescence for (a) *Exxon Valdez* crude and (b) #2 diesel from Alaska. These spectra are one type of "fingerprint" that can be used to identify the sources of crude oils or oil products.

and the tissue sampling programs (Gilfillan, Page et al., this volume; Bence and Burns, this volume) reported elsewhere in this volume. However, the UV-F procedures that identified the presence of 4+ ring compounds in EVOS-related ANS crude are based on the same principles used in the fingerprinting techniques employed in the above referenced studies. A review of the results using the GC/MS data where available showed the analysis procedure used in this study produced qualitative results consistent with those used by the other referenced studies.

Other Sheen-Detection Procedures

Other techniques for locating and identifying sheens were tested. An ultraviolet (UV) and an infrared (IR) video camera were mounted in the aircraft. The UV camera could detect the presence of petroleum hydrocarbons on the water due to their fluorescence properties. The IR camera could approximate the thickness of the hydrocarbon layer by sensing the temperature difference between the hydrocarbon layer and the surrounding water. These cameras, which were designed for initial spill response, were tested for about one month with poor results. Their main deficiency was the small field of view resulting from the low altitude of flights which was necessary to see the average sheen. These cameras did not identify a single sheen that had not been seen visually by the observer. Therefore, their use was discontinued. A wide angle version of this equipment may be useful for any future sheen surveillance programs. However, the small sheen sizes may still require low altitude flights and make detection using this equipment less effective and quite tedious.

High-altitude and low-altitude still photography was also tested during the winter of 1989. In the high altitude photography, the scale of the photographs taken from an altitude of 12 500 m was too small to allow reliable identification of most of the sheens that were identified visually from low-flying aircraft. Therefore, the high-altitude photography program was abandoned. The low altitude (600 m) photographs did identify several sheens that were about the same size as those reported in this paper. However, the time and effort that would have been required to photograph the entire southwest portion of Prince William Sound and interpret those photographs on a daily basis eliminated this option. Visual observations became the standard procedure because these other techniques had limited success, did not identify any additional sheens, or were impractical.

RESULTS

The surveillance program was successful in identifying and documenting sheen locations, sizes, and trends. This program provided important information for response planning, for defining priority areas for shoreline cleanup in 1990, for facilitating normal operations of the fisheries in 1990, and for understanding natural cleansing processes.

Sheen Observations

A total of 827 sheens were observed on 121 days during the 12-month program. Of this figure, 799 were sighted in PWS, and 28 were observed in the GOA. About 69% of the total number (or 567 sheens) were from the EVOS or from indeterminate sources. About 31% of the total number (or 260 sheens) were caused by non-spill-related vessels or from other man-made sources. Combining the sheens from the EVOS and indeterminate sources should result in an upper limit for spill-related sheens observed during the program. The number of sheens observed during a single day varied from 0 to 30. A high number of sheens were sighted in October 1989 with the onset of fall and winter storms, in mid-March 1990 during a period of exceptionally high tides and warm days, and during periods of intense fishing vessel activity in the summer of 1990. Undoubtedly other sheens occurred that were not observed, but they would be unlikely to change the overall observed trends

The surface areas of sheens ranged from less than 1 m^2 to greater than 2.3 km^2 with a median size of 525 m^2. The sheen with the largest surface area covered 45% of the water surface over an area about 900 m by 5 600 m and was sighted in the Valdez Narrows on December 7, 1989. This sheen was estimated from its rainbow color to contain 695 L of refined product (e.g., diesel) and because of the color and location was clearly not associated with the EVOS.

Individual sheen volumes ranged from negligible amounts (< 0.01 L) to over 50 000 L. The sheen with the greatest volume of oil was observed on October 24, 1989, after the first significant fall storms following a week of high autumn tides. This sheen covered 90% of the water surface over an area about 20 m by 3 000 m. It was located in southern PWS, southwest of Green Island, and was estimated from its brown color to contain 54 000 L of oil. Although logistical constraints precluded response to this sheen, the stormy weather that caused the oil in this sheen to be released also caused it to dissipate over a large area (NOAA, 1991). Although flight lines were similar, sheens of this order of magnitude were not observed during the remainder of the program.

A total of 19 sheens, all located in PWS, had oil volumes equal to or greater than 1 000 L: eighteen occurred during the fall and winter of 1989 and 1990 and were attributed to the EVOS or indeterminate sources. One was observed during the summer of 1990 and was attributed to a non-spill-related vessel. Thirteen of these large EVOS-related or indeterminate sheens were observed on October 24, 1989, and included the eight largest sheens seen during the program. The locations and volumes of all sheens observed on October 24, 1989, are illustrated by vertical bars in Figure 4. The bases of the vertical bars give the geographic locations of the sheens, and the heights represent the estimated volumes of oil within the sheens. The height scale increases linearly with volume to a maximum at 54 000 L of oil. The three bars in the legend illustrate relative scale and represent the maximum observed volume (54 000 L), a volume one order of magnitude lower (5 400 L), and a volume two orders of magnitude lower (540 L). The 13 large sheens were from 600 m to 17 km long and from 5 m to 20 m wide. They contained estimated volumes of oil that ranged from 1 350 L to 54 000 L. Many appeared to be moving in a southerly direction out of southwestern PWS and into the GOA. The other five EVOS-related sheens with estimated volumes greater than 1 000 L occurred on separate days during September, October, and November 1989, and March 1990.

The next largest accumulation of oil in sheens during the winter occurred on March 15-16, 1990. Forty-nine sheens were observed in PWS on these dates, when warm days occurred in conjunction with high tides. The locations and volumes of sheens observed during these two days are illustrated in Figure 5. Of these 49 sheens, 45 were classified as EVOS or indeterminate in source, and 19 contained 10 or more litres of oil. The total volume of oil in all 49 sheens was estimated to be 4 460 L; the estimated volume of individual sheens ranged from 0.02 L to 1 000 L. The volumes of oil within these sheens were small in comparison with the volumes observed on October 24. The difference in numbers and volumes can be visualized by comparing March 15-16 observations in Figure 5 with October 24 observations in Figure 4.

After the beginning of spring on March 21, no sheens with oil volumes greater than 65 L were observed that could be attributed to the EVOS or indeterminate sources. In fact, non-spill-related vessels contributed the greatest sheen volume during the spring and summer. The largest vessel-related sheen sighted during the program occurred on June 17, 1990, in Whittier Harbor. A diesel-like spill by a tour ship produced a rainbow-colored sheen estimated to contain 6 000 L. Numerous other fuel oil spills were also seen near Whittier in Passage Canal during the program. Vessel-related sheens during the spring and summer of 1990 accounted for a total oil volume in excess of 6 800 L. The total volume of oil in sheens observed during the fall and winter was greater than the total volume during the spring and summer. The source confirmation procedures involving the analytical lab were not employed until the spring of 1990. Even so, most of the fall and winter sheens were attributed to the EVOS or indeterminate sources. By contrast, most of the oil volume in sheens observed during the spring and summer were attributed to non-spill-related vessels and other man-caused sources.

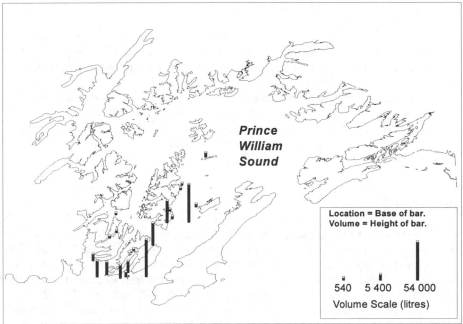

Figure 4.--Location and volume of sheens observed on October 24, 1989, in PWS.

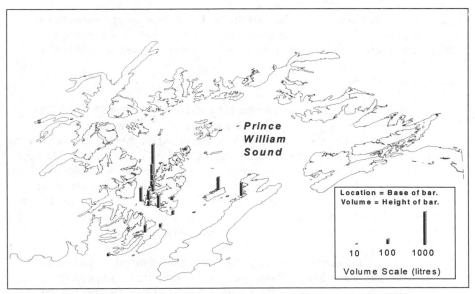

Figure 5.--Location and volume of sheens observed on March 15-16, 1990, in PWS. Note the significant change in volume bar scale between Figure 4 and Figure 5.

Laboratory Confirmation of Source

Forty-four sheens were sampled and analyzed between May 1990 and September 1990 with the methods discussed earlier. Six were attributed to the EVOS, 3 were indeterminate, and 35 were attributed to non-spill-related vessels, biogenic, and other sources.

Cross-checking of visually determined sources with the laboratory analyses showed that no EVOS-related sheens had been mistakenly attributed to other sources. Conversely, several sheens that had been visually attributed to the EVOS or indeterminate sources were found by the analyses to actually be refined product (from a vessel or other source).

DISCUSSION

Sheens were infrequently sighted in the GOA during the fall of 1989, consistent with the generally low initial shoreline impact in those areas compared with PWS. In addition, the sheens that were sighted indicated that no single area was generating large sheens on a regular basis. Because of the small number of sheens and the increased weather downtime and safety risks, the surveillance program focused on only PWS early in 1990. All observations from that time forward relate only to PWS. Field observations confirmed the expected trends of declining number and volume of EVOS-related sheens with time. These observations are consistent with the findings of studies that natural cleansing processes would continue the removal of oil residue from shorelines. Among the processes contributing to natural cleansing are the breaking of waves, tidal pumping, weathering, and biodegradation (Jahns et al. 1991; Owens 1991a,b; Koons and Jahns 1992). Natural cleansing is accelerated by storms, as was observed in October 1989.

Trends in Observations

For analyses, the source categories were collapsed into two groups: (1) EVOS or indeterminate sources and (2) non-spill-related vessels or other man-made sources.

The number of sheens observed during the program and the average volume of oil per sheen are summarized on the time series bar charts shown in Figures 6 and 7. The height of the bars in Figure 6, plotted as a function of time, represents the total number of sheens observed during each flight that could be attributed to (1) the EVOS or indeterminate sources (top chart) or (2) non-spill-related vessels or other sources (bottom chart). The height of the bars in Figure 7, in logarithmic scale, represent the average volume of oil for sheens observed during each flight, grouped the same way as in Figure 6.

Sheens from EVOS or Indeterminate Sources -- During the fall and winter of 1989-1990, most of the sheens observed during the program were attributed to EVOS or indeterminate sources. Sheens from these sources, observed from October through December, after the onset of fall and winter storms, were high in number (Figure 6) and had relatively large average volumes of oil per sheen (Figure 7). A number of large sheens

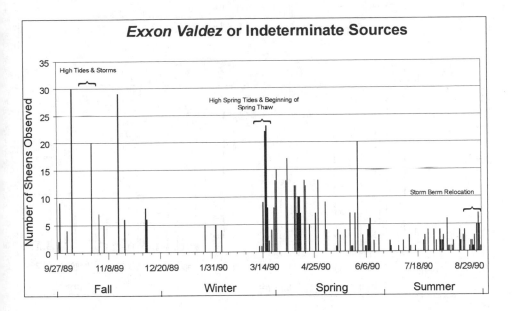

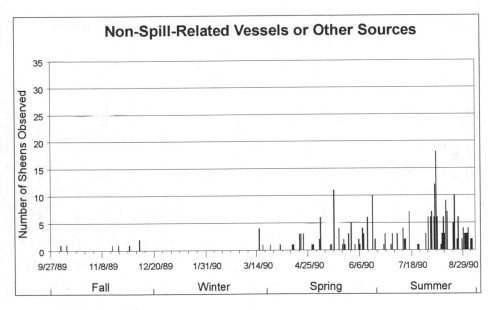

Figure 6.--Cumulative number of sheens observed during each flight that were attributed to non-biogenic sources. These bar charts illustrate the differences between the number of sheens from the *Exxon Valdez* or indeterminate sources and those from non-spill-related vessels or other sources.

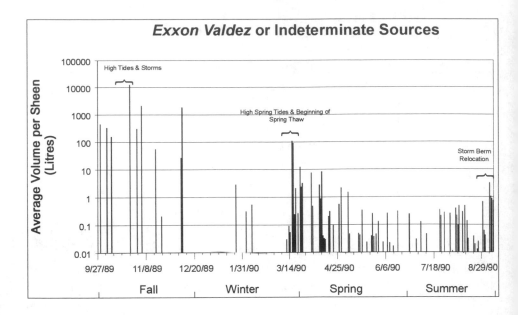

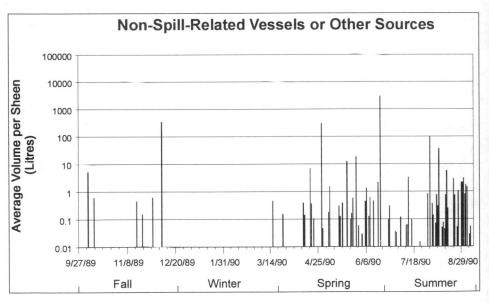

Figure 7.--Average volume of oil per sheen for each flight for sheens attributed to nonbiogenic sources. These bar charts illustrate the difference between the volumes of sheens from the *Exxon Valdez* or indeterminate sources and those from non-spill-related vessels or other sources.

were sighted on October 24, 1989, after an early winter storm that followed a week of high autumn tides. Average volumes of these sheens from EVOS or indeterminate sources exceeded 12 500 L of oil, as shown in Figure 7. As the winter progressed (January and February), the number of sheens diminished, and the corresponding volume of oil within these sheens declined to an average of less than 2 L per sheen. This was likely due to a combination of (a) much less stranded oil being available to produce sheens after the fall and winter storms in October through December and (b) colder weather, which reduced the mobility of the remaining oil residue.

Sheen numbers and volumes increased during a period of high tides and warm weather in mid-March. Warmer temperatures increased the mobility of stranded oil by reducing its viscosity. Sheens were more prevalent because the remaining oil was more easily washed off shorelines by spring tides, storms, and snow-melt (Jahns et al. 1991; Koons and Jahns 1992). From March 1 to March 21, the average volume of oil in sheens from the EVOS or indeterminate sources was 64 L per sheen; the average volume on March 15 and 16, during the highest spring tides, was about 100 L per sheen.

The average volume of oil in sheens attributed to the EVOS or indeterminate sources decreased again in spring and summer 1990 (Figure 7) to an average of less than 2 L of oil per sheen. Average volumes were several orders of magnitude lower than those recorded in the fall of 1989. In September 1990, a slight increase in the volumes of EVOS-related sheens was noted. This increase was attributed to the storm berm relocation activities that occurred near the end of the 1990 cleanup program. These activities moved oiled debris and sediments from the storm berms into the middle intertidal zones to provide more effective natural cleansing.

These trends suggest that most of the mobile oil remaining on shorelines following the 1989 cleanup was dissipated by storms during the 1989-1990 winter. The decrease in oil volumes in sheens from October 1989 through March 1990 emphasizes the efficiency of the natural process of winter storms in cleansing oiled shorelines. The EVOS-related sheens observed during the summer of 1990 were generally located near EVOS-affected shorelines and not in open water or in the large numbers or volumes observed during the preceding winter.

Sheens from Non-Spill-Related Vessels or Other Sources -- Because major fishing and tourist activities in Alaska cease toward the end of summer, vessel activity during the fall and winter 1989-1990 was at a minimum. The average volume of oil in sheens caused by non-spill-related vessel activity during that time was less than 6 L in all but one case. This exception occurred on December 7, 1989, as already discussed in this paper, when a rainbow-colored sheen estimated to contain 695 L of diesel or other refined product was observed in Valdez Narrows.

The number of sheens from non-spill-related vessels in open-water areas of PWS increased during the spring and summer of 1990 apparently in proportion to the increase in commercial-vessel activities (mainly fishing). Sheens from non-spill-related vessels were typically a bright rainbow of colors, indicating that their source, confirmed by fingerprinting or location alongside vessels, was diesel fuel or another refined product. Sheens from these sources, observed during the spring and summer, contained an average of 6 L of oil per sheen if the large 6 000 L sheen observed on June 17, 1990, in Whittier

Harbor is excluded. The average volume per sheen would be significantly distorted by including this large sheen, since the figure would increase to 30 L of oil per sheen. After May 1990, sheens from non-EVOS sources were greater in number (Figure 6) and generally contained more oil (Figure 7) than EVOS-related sheens.

Frequency Distribution and Geographic Locations of Sheens -- The frequency distributions of oil volumes within all sheens observed during (1) the fall and winter of 1989 and 1990 and (2) the spring and summer of 1990 are shown in Figure 8. Oil volumes in sheens were combined into volume bins that vary by one order of magnitude, as shown on the abscissa. The heights of the bars represent the percentage of the total number of sheens containing the given volume range of oil for each phase of the program. Each bar also shows the proportions in the total number of sheens having an EVOS or indeterminate source and those from non-spill-related vessels or other man-made sources. This distribution illustrates that most of the sheens during Phase 2, including the EVOS-related ones, contained very small volumes of oil. More than 85% of all sheens during Phase 2 (and 75% of all sheens observed) had a volume less than 1 L of oil. The chart also shows the dramatic reduction of large sheens in the spring and summer of 1990 compared with the fall and winter 1989-1990.

There were some locations in PWS where sheens caused by EVOS-impacted shorelines were persistent during the surveillance program. These included areas containing subsurface oil or locations with oil in the high intertidal zones. Mobile oil in these intertidal zones would sheen only when reached by large waves and/or high tides. These locations were regularly monitored during surveillance flights. As a first step in the 1990 cleanup program, containment booms were deployed at areas of persistent sheening to prevent the sheens from migrating offshore. Observers in the surveillance aircraft would notify work crews of the status and effectiveness of the booms in those locations. All areas that persistently produced sheens were included in the summer 1990 cleanup program. By the end of that program, any sheens emanating from these areas contained little oil (at most a few litres).

The distribution of cumulative number and geographic locations of sheens observed within PWS during the entire program are shown on the maps in Figure 9 for EVOS and indeterminate sources (top map) and non-spill-related vessels and other man-made sources (bottom map). The height of each bar represents the total number of sheens within 7.5 km^2 grids; the location of the base of the bar is the approximate center of the grid. This grid size was chosen for illustrative purposes to allow specific geographic areas to be represented by a single bar. For example, all the EVOS or indeterminate sheens within Northwest Bay on Eleanor Island (an area heavily affected by the EVOS) are shown on the top map by the tallest single bar. Similar to Figures 4 and 5, the height scale in Figure 9 increases linearly with the number of sheens to the maximum of 84 sheens falling within a single grid. After reviewing all sheen volumes, it was concluded that illustrating the number of sheens in a geographic area was better than illustrating corresponding sheen volumes since most sheens contained very small volumes of oil. The median sheen volume for the program was 0.1 L.

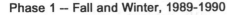

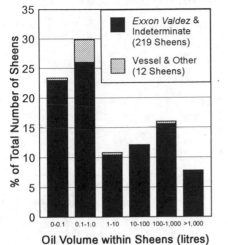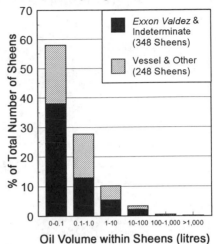

Figure 8.--Frequency distribution of oil volumes within the nonbiogenic sheens observed during the aerial sheen surveillance program.

As expected, the greatest number of sheens caused by EVOS-affected shorelines were near areas where there was the greatest amount of stranded oil in 1989. The locations of non-EVOS-related sheens were mainly in areas of high fishing or commercial-vessel activity.

The number and volume of all sheens declined through the summer of 1990. Oiled shorelines were not producing sheens in large numbers, and the sheens from oiled shorelines that were occurring contained small volumes of oil. Sheens from commercial-vessel activity decreased as the major fishery openings ended and fewer vessels were present in PWS. Because the number and volume of EVOS-related sheens had declined by late summer 1990 to numbers and volumes smaller than those associated with non-EVOS-related activity (at most a few litres of oil), the sheen surveillance program was discontinued in September 1990.

The sheen surveillance program provided an extensive amount of information that was used to define response and cleanup priorities. The program also showed that the volumes of EVOS-related oil on the water were of the same order of magnitude or smaller than those from non-EVOS-spill-related activities. Throughout 1990 the fisheries operated normally in PWS and the GOA (Royce et al. 1991). There were no closures of fisheries due to sheens on the water, and only two small shoreline areas were placed off-limits because oil residue on the shore could have affected set-net operations (Brady 1990a,b).

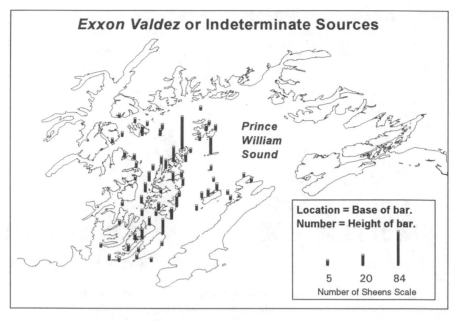

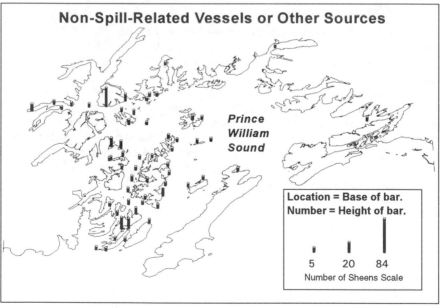

Figure 9.--Geographic distribution in the cumulative number of sheens observed in PWS during the aerial sheen surveillance program that were attributed to EVOS or indeterminate sources (top map) or non-spill-related vessels or other man-made sources (bottom map).

CONCLUSIONS

The aerial surveillance program was conducted successfully over a one-year period. Results showed that the combination of the 1989 cleanup and the 1989-1990 winter storms was effective in removing essentially all mobile oil from spill-affected shorelines. Sheens caused by mobile oil remaining from the EVOS diminished to very low levels by the summer of 1990. The observations from the sheen surveillance program helped to prioritize 1990 cleanup operations and to ensure inclusion of all shorelines producing sheens. The program also confirmed that there was no need to maintain a capability to respond to sizable sheens or continue sheen surveillance beyond the summer of 1990, because the volumes of free oil on the water were too small for response.

Significant sheening from EVOS-impacted shorelines was not expected in 1991. The 1991 and 1992 shoreline surveys and scientific programs confirmed the absence of significant quantities of mobile oil in shoreline sediments.

One year after the spill, no fisheries were affected or closed because of the presence of EVOS oil on the water. In fact, by the end of summer 1990, EVOS-related sheens were generally lower in number and volume than those associated with normal commercial-vessel activity in Prince William Sound.

REFERENCES

Baker, J. M., R. B. Clark, P. F. Kingston, and R. H. Jenkins. 1990. "Natural Recovery of Cold Water Marine Environments After an Oil Spill." *in: Proceedings of the Thirteenth Arctic and Marine Oilspill Program Technical Seminar, June 6-8, 1990, Chateau Lacombe, Edmonton, Alberta, Canada.* Ottawa, Ontario, Canada: Environment Canada. 173 - 177.

Brady, J. A. 1990a. "1990 PWS Salmon Season Summary." November 11, 1990. Alaska Department of Fish and Game, Commercial Fisheries Division. Cordova, AK. Unpublished memorandum; 11 pp.

Brady, J. A.. 1990b. "PWS Herring Season Summary, 1990." May 23, 1990. Alaska Department of Fish and Game, Commercial Fisheries Division. Cordova, AK. Unpublished memorandum; 7 pp.

Fingas, M. F., W. S. Duval, and G. B. Stevenson. 1979. *The Basics of Oil Spill Cleanup with Particular Reference to Southern Canada.* Environmental Emergency Branch, Environmental Protection Service, Environment Canada.

International Tanker Owners Pollution Federation Ltd.(ITOPF). 1981. "Aerial Observation of Oil at Sea." London: International Tanker Owners Pollution Federation, Ltd., Technical Information Paper No. 1.

Jahns, H. O., J. R. Bragg, L. C. Dash, and E. H. Owens. 1991. "Natural Cleaning of Shorelines Following the *Exxon Valdez* Spill." *in: Proceedings of the 1991 International Oil Spill Conference (Prevention, Behavior, Control, Cleanup), March 4 - 7, 1991, San Diego, CA.* Washington, DC: American Petroleum Institute; Publication 4529. 167 - 176.

Koons, C. B. and H. O. Jahns. 1992. "The Fate of Oil from the Exxon Valdez — A Perspective" in: Marine Technology Society Journal, Vol. 26, No. 3, 61-69.

Koops, W. 1985. "The Oil Spill Slide Rule to Predict the Fate of an Oil Spill." *in: Proceedings of the 1985 International Oil Spill Conference (Prevention, Behavior, Control, Cleanup), February 25-28, 1985, Los Angeles, CA.* Washington, DC: American Petroleum Institute; Publication 4385. 647.

Kuhn, H. A. and G. M. MacDonald. 1990. *Aerial Surveillance Standard Operating Procedures.* Exxon Company, U.S.A. — Alaska Operations. Anchorage, AK. (Contact Exxon Company, U.S.A., Public Affairs, P.O. Box 2180, Houston, TX 77001).

National Oceanic and Atmospheric Administration (NOAA). 1991. "Summary of NOAA's review of the status of Prince William Sound shorelines following two years of treatment by Exxon." Seattle, WA: NOAA Hazardous Materials Response Branch, Spill Response Program. Unpublished report sent to Admiral David E. Ciancaglini (U.S. Coast Guard), Juneau, AK, by David M. Kennedy (NOAA), Seattle, WA; March 15, 1991.

Neff, J. M. 1991. "Water Quality in Prince William Sound and the Gulf of Alaska." Arthur D. Little, 20 Alcorn Park, Cambridge, MA 02140; 37 pp.

Owens, E. H.. 1991a. *Changes in Shoreline Oiling Conditions 1 1/2 Years After the 1989 Prince William Sound Spill.* Woodward-Clyde Consultants, 3440 Bank of California Center, 900 Fourth Ave., Seattle, WA 98164.

Owens, E. H.. 1991b. "Shoreline Conditions Following the *Exxon Valdez* Spill as of Fall 1990." *in: Proceedings of the Fourteenth Annual Arctic and Marine Oil Spill Program Technical Seminar, June 12 - 14, 1991, Hotel Georgia, Vancouver, British Columbia, Canada.* Ottawa, Ontario, Canada: Environment Canada. 579 - 606.

Royce, W. F., T. R. Schroeder, A. A. Olsen, and W. J. Allender. 1991. *Alaskan Fisheries — Two Years After the Spill.* Cook Inlet Fisheries Consultants, P.O. Box 636, Homer, AK 99603.

United States Coast Guard. 1974. *Oil Spill Identification System (Interim report).* Coast Guard Research and Development Center, Groton, CT. NTIS Report No.: AD-A003 803/4.

United States Coast Guard. 1977. *Oil Spill Identification System.* Coast Guard Research and Development Center, Groton, CT. NTIS Report No.: AD-A044 750/8.

Gary Shigenaka[1] and Charles B. Henry, Jr.[2]

USE OF MUSSELS AND SEMIPERMEABLE MEMBRANE DEVICES TO ASSESS
BIOAVAILABILITY OF RESIDUAL POLYNUCLEAR AROMATIC HYDROCARBONS THREE
YEARS AFTER THE *EXXON VALDEZ* OIL SPILL

REFERENCE: Shigenaka, G. and Henry, C. B., Jr., "Use of Mussels and
Semipermeable Membrane Devices to Assess Bioavailability of Residual
Polynuclear Aromatic Hydrocarbons Three Years After the Exxon Valdez Oil
Spill," Exxon Valdez Oil Spill: Fate and Effects in Alaskan Waters,
ASTM STP 1219, Peter G. Wells, James N. Butler, and Jane S. Hughes,
Eds., American Society for Testing and Materials, Philadelphia, 1995.

ABSTRACT: Mussels (*Mytilus* cf. *trossulus*) were transplanted to a
heavily oiled and extensively treated site on Smith Island, Prince
William Sound, Alaska, in 1992. A new monitoring and assessment tool,
the semipermeable membrane device, was also deployed to compare
hydrocarbon uptake with mussels and to evaluate the route of exposure to
mussels. Both mussels and semipermeable membrane devices accumulated
polynuclear aromatic hydrocarbons during 14- and 52-day deployments,
particularly at the oiled site. Accumulation levels were similar
between mussels and the semipermeable membrane devices, but the
distribution of individual hydrocarbons differed. The results permit
some inference about route of exposure to mussels. Sheens leaching from
subsurface deposits of residual oil, and particulate material with
adsorbed hydrocarbons were apparently more important exposure pathways
than dissolved hydrocarbons in water. Semipermeable membrane devices
show promise as monitoring tools and to provide insights into exposure
pathways for biota.

KEYWORDS: bioaccumulation, *Exxon Valdez* oil spill, mussels, *Mytilus*,
polynuclear aromatic hydrocarbons, semipermeable membrane devices

---

[1]Marine biologist, Hazardous Materials Response and Assessment Division,
National Oceanic and Atmospheric Administration, 7600 Sand Point Way
N.E., Seattle, WA 98115.
[2]Research chemist, Institute for Environmental Studies, Louisiana State
University, 42 Atkinson Hall, Baton Rouge, LA 70803.

INTRODUCTION

Smith Island, in north-central Prince William Sound, Alaska, was heavily impacted by Prudhoe Bay crude oil which spilled from the tanker *Exxon Valdez* when it grounded on March 24, 1989. Located approximately 37 kilometers from the grounding site at Bligh Reef (Figure 1), Smith Island, in particular, its northern shore, was directly in the path of the oil slick as it moved to the southwest. The coastline was heavily oiled by relatively fresh crude oil on March 26, 1989 (Michel and Hayes 1991). The large grain size characteristic of many beaches on the island permitted the crude oil to penetrate deeply, where it proved to be difficult to remove.

During 1989 and 1990, many heavily oiled beaches along the northern shoreline of Smith Island were aggressively cleaned, using high-pressure hot water, chemical cleaners, mechanical tilling and movement of portions of the beaches with heavy equipment, and bioremediation. The remedial efforts required many personnel and substantial logistical support. Despite these efforts, subsurface oil pockets have persisted at the site sampled for this study.

BACKGROUND: PREVIOUS RESULTS FROM SMITH ISLAND

In 1990, a team of biologists from the Hazardous Materials Response and Assessment Division (HAZMAT) of the National Oceanic and Atmospheric Administration (NOAA) visited a site on the northwest shore of Smith Island as part of a monitoring program in Prince William Sound to assess the effects of both oiling and cleanup activities on intertidal biological communities (Houghton et al. 1991). An integral part of the monitoring effort was the analysis of tissue samples from important representatives of the intertidal communities by gas chromatography/mass spectrometry (GC/MS) for levels of polynuclear aromatic hydrocarbons (PAHs). Mussels (*Mytilus* cf. *trossulus*) were a key part of these collections, as bivalve molluscs of this genus have been extensively used as "sentinel", or biomonitoring organisms in many programs around the world (Goldberg et al. 1978; Widdows and Donkin 1992).

In 1990, mussels from the Smith Island site contained the highest levels of total target PAHs, 84,000 ng/g dry weight, among 23 sites sampled for the monitoring program. In contrast, 21 samples had PAH levels ≤ 8,000 ng/g (Houghton et al. 1991).

In 1991 a transplant experiment was established in which mussels from a reference site in Prince William Sound (Eshamy Bay, Figure 1) were placed at two stations on the east and west sides of the Smith Island pocket beach site. The mussels were deployed for a two month period, after which they were analyzed by GC/MS for tissue PAH levels. Comparison of PAH levels in the reference mussels and transplants showed a significant uptake over the two month period: the Eshamy Bay transplant stock contained 760 ng/g summed PAH, while samples of this stock transplanted to the east and west ends of the Smith Island beach site contained 20,000 and 4,800 ng/g, respectively.

In 1992, the mussel transplant experiment at Smith Island was expanded to further investigate and define conditions there. The present manuscript describes this experiment and its results.

FIG. 1--Central Prince William Sound, Alaska, showing relative locations of the *Exxon Valdez* grounding site, Smith Island, Barnes Cove, and Eshamy Bay.

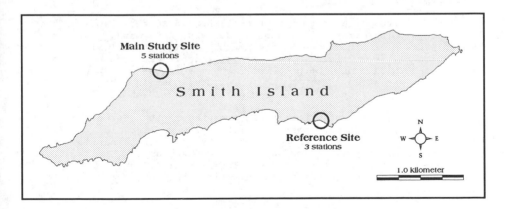

FIG. 2--Location of study sites on Smith Island.

EXPERIMENTAL METHODS

Mussel Collections

Mussels (*Mytilus* cf. *trossulus*) used as transplant stock for the experiment were collected on June 24, 1992, in Barnes Cove, Knight Island, in the central part of Prince William Sound (Figure 1). Shoreline surveys indicated that this area had been only lightly oiled from the spill, and GC/MS analyses of mussels collected at this site had confirmed a low level of hydrocarbon contamination (Babcock et al. 1993). Collection was restricted to mussels with shells greater than 30 mm in length in order to minimize variability due to size and age (Salazar and Salazar 1990).

Three samples of the Barnes Cove mussels were collected for GC/MS analysis to quantify "baseline" levels of PAH contamination in the transplant stock. Each of these samples was comprised of 25 individual mussels.

Semipermeable Membrane Devices

Semipermeable membrane devices (SPMDs) are a recently developed tool for assessing availability of nonpolar organic compounds to aquatic organisms and for estimating concentrations of such materials in the environment (Huckins et al. 1990). SPMDs are simple in design, consisting of a heat-sealed low-density polyethylene bag containing triolein. Transient holes in the polyethylene ranging from five to ten Å are believed to permit dissolved low molecular weight lipophilic compounds to diffuse into the enclosed triolein, where they are retained until the SPMDs are recovered, extracted, and analyzed. The devices potentially offer several advantages over traditional biological monitoring tools such as bivalves, primarily consistency, comparability, and utility in situations where living sentinel organisms are not available or practical.

Semipermeable membrane devices (SPMDs) for this study were prepared by the Battelle Marine Sciences Laboratory in Sequim, WA, using the methods of Huckins et al. (1990), and Lebo et al. (1992). Two SPMDs were held in sealed containers in the laboratory as method blanks.

Site Sampling

Two 60 m study transects were established on Smith Island for the 1992 study. The first was located on June 25, 1992, at a previously established NOAA study site on the northwest side of the island (Figure 2), which had been heavily oiled. This transect was located in the middle intertidal zone, between two recognizable beach features (bedrock outcrops), and at an elevation where resident mussels were found. The tidal elevation of the transect ranged between 2.23 and 2.32 m above mean lower low water (MLLW).

Samples collected near the transect on the north side of the island for PAH analysis included nearshore water from two locations; visible oil sheen leaching from the beach substrate on the falling tide; and beach sediment samples collected from 30 cm deep pits. The sheen sample was opportunistically collected by dragging a pre-cleaned, porous Teflon filter across a visible oil sheen in a tide pool formed during a falling tide.

Five stations were located along the north transect, with the first station located at the 3 m mark, and the remaining four located at equally spaced intervals of 14.25 m (17.25, 31.50, 45.75, and 60 m marks on the transect).

The second transect was established at a boulder/cobble beach on the southeast side of the island (Figure 2) on June 25, 1992. Shoreline assessment and cleanup records had indicated that beaches on this side of Smith Island were either unoiled or only lightly oiled. In order to minimize differences attributable to beach elevations and submergence time, the tidal elevation of the north transect was used as a reference for the location of the south transect. The south transect range was 2.23 to 2.28 m above MLLW. Three stations were located on the south transect, with the first established at 8 m, and the other two at equally spaced 26 m intervals (34 and 60 m marks on the transect).

At each station on both transects, the large boulders and cobbles overlying, or "armoring", smaller-grained substrate underneath were removed. Once the armoring layer had been moved, samples of the gravel layer were collected in pre-cleaned 500 mL jars for chemical analysis.

Three 10 cm x 10 cm x 15 cm vinyl-coated wire cages were placed in a row on the gravel substrate. The two end cages contained a single SPMD each, and the middle cage contained 55 mussels collected from Barnes Cove (Figure 3). Cages were anchored in place with beach boulders and cobbles.

FIG. 3--Transect station consisting of cages for transplanted mussels (center) and semipermeable membrane devices (left and right).

The sites were revisited on July 9, 1992 (14-day exposure), and one of the SPMDs and approximately 25 mussels were recovered at each station. Final sample collection took place on August 16, 1992 (52-day exposure).

Field sampling handling and processing procedures were adapted from those of environmental monitoring programs such as the National Status and Trends Program (Wade et al. 1993). All samples were frozen in the field, packed in "blue ice", and shipped by overnight carrier to the appropriate analytical facility after the vessel returned to port.

Chemical Methods

Sediment and mussel tissue samples were analyzed at the Institute for Environmental Studies at Louisiana State University in Baton Rouge, LA. Semipermeable membrane devices were analyzed at Battelle Marine Sciences Laboratory in Sequim, WA. As a laboratory calibration standard, both facilities analyzed a mussel tissue standard reference material (SRM 1974) prepared and certified by the National Institute of Standards and Technology (Schantz et al. 1993).

Sediment samples--Methods for analysis of sediment PAHs were adapted from those of Krahn et al. (1988a, 1988b). Sediment samples were weighed into 600 mL beakers for extraction. Approximately 100 cc of material was extracted for each sample. Samples were dried before extraction by the addition of anhydrous sodium sulfate (Na_2SO_4). Sodium sulfate not only removed any water as an extraction interference, but also enhanced the extraction of weathered oil residue from the pebbles and gravel by acting as an abrasive. Surrogate standards acenaphthene-d_{10}, phenanthrene-d_{10}, and terphenyl-d_{14} were added. Samples were extracted three times using nanograde hexane solvent and a bath sonication technique. Hexane was used as the extraction solvent because of the relatively large concentrations of PAHs and coarser grain size of samples collected. An advantage of using hexane to extract samples contaminated with crude oils is that centrifugation prior to analysis by GC/MS removes such hexane-insoluble compounds as asphaltenes as potential interferences. The extracts were combined and then reduced in volume by a combination of rotary-evaporation and solvent reduction under a stream of high purity nitrogen. The final concentration varied between 1 mL and 150 mL depending on the degree of contamination. The extracts were analyzed by gas chromatography/mass spectrometry GC/MS using a Hewlett Packard™ 5890 gas chromatograph (GC) equipped with a DB-5 high-resolution capillary column directly interfaced to a Hewlett Packard™ 5970B mass spectrometer (MS). The GC was optimized to provide the required degree of separation (i.e., baseline resolution between nC-17 and pristane). The GC was operated in the temperature program mode with an initial column temperature of 55°C for 3 minutes, then increased to 290°C at a rate of 6°C/minute, and held at the upper temperature for 17 minutes. The MS was operated in the selective ion mode to enhance quantitative analyses. The injection temperature was held constant at 250°C, and only high-temperature, low-thermal bleed septa were used. The interface to the MS was maintained at 280°C.

At the beginning of each analysis period, the MS was tuned to perfluorotributylamine. Quantitative analysis was accomplished by using authentic standards for the non-alkylated PAHs, with the exception of naphthobenzothiophene, which was estimated using the response of dibenzothiophene. Because standards are not widely available for the alkylated homologues, non-alkylated parent compounds were used to estimate values for the alkylated compounds. The following internal standards were co-injected: naphthalene-d_8, anthracene-d_{10}, chrysene-d_{12}, and perylene-d_{12}.   Blanks and duplicates were extracted with each set of samples.

The detection limit for each target compound differed by approximately an order of magnitude between the lowest molecular weight compound quantified, naphthalene (128 amu), and the highest, dibenz(a,h)anthracene (278 amu).   For example, in trace analyses, the estimated detection limit for naphthalene was 1 ng/g wet weight, while that for dibenz(a,h)anthracene was 10 ng/g.   This range was due to the differences in response of the GC/MS for analytes spanning a wide boiling point and molecular weight range.   For this study, the reported detection limits were calculated from the lowest value of the five-point standard curve.   Minimum peak detection required a greater than three-to-one signal-to-noise ratio.

Mussel tissues--Analytical methods for tissues were adapted from the procedures of MacLeod et al. (1985).   Mussels were rinsed, shelled, and thoroughly rinsed again with deionized water before extraction.   The tissue sample was homogenized to composite the sample into a uniform consistency.   A subsample of the homogenate, 8 g, was treated with potassium hydroxide pellets to digest the lipids and cellular materials in the samples for 24 hours.   Known amounts of surrogate standards (acenaphthene-d_{10}, phenanthrene-d_{10}, and terphenyl-d_{14}) were added to the digested homogenate.   The homogenate was then extracted three times using dichloromethane.   The extracts were combined and filtered through anhydrous sodium sulfate to eliminate traces of water.   The resulting filtrate was concentrated to 4 mL using a combination of rotary evaporation and reduced in volume under a nitrogen stream.   The extract was fractionated using an alumina and silica gel column to isolate PAHs from interfering compounds present in the extract.   Fractionated extracts were analyzed qualitatively and quantitatively using GC/MS.

A Hewlett Packard 5890 GC equipped with a J&W Scientific DB-5 capillary column (0.25 mm ID and 0.25 μm film thickness) directly interfaced to a Hewlett Packard™ 5971 MS and operated in the selected ion detection mode was used.   The analysis method provided source-fingerprinting information as well as compound-specific quantities of selected petrogenic and pyrogenic PAH and sulfur heterocyclic compounds. Internal standards (naphthalene-d_8, anthracene-d_{10}, chrysene-d_{12}, and perylene-d_{12}) were co-injected at the time of analysis.   Blanks and duplicates were extracted with each set of samples.   Detection limits were calculated as described for sediment samples.

Semipermeable membrane devices--SPMDs were constructed following the methods of Lebo et al. (1992).   Each SPMD contained 1.0 g of triolein. The triolein (1,2,3-tri-[(cis)-9-octadecenoyl]glycerol) was obtained from Sigma Chemical Co., St. Louis, MO.   It was sold as 99 percent pure and did not receive further processing before being used for the SPMDs. Polyethylene tubing used for the SPMDs was custom-produced by Brentwood Plastics Inc., St. Louis, MO to specifications of Lebo et al.   To accommodate ease of transport and handling, the polyethylene envelope was not loop-configured as described by Lebo et al., but was simply heat-sealed at each end.

Analytical methods for SPMDs were adapted from the procedures of Krahn et al. (1988a and 1988b) and are essentially standard analytical methods used in the NOAA/National Status and Trends Program (Battelle Memorial Institute, 1990).   Individual SPMDs were cleaned of algae and sediment by wiping with laboratory tissues, and then solvent-extracted in 100 mL of hexane, containing stable isotopically-labeled surrogate compounds, and 10 g of anhydrous sodium sulfate, for 24 hours. The extract was evaporated to a volume of 1.0 mL, processed by high performance liquid chromatography to remove possible interfering compounds, and then analyzed by GC/MS.

A total of 30 PAHs were common to both mussel tissue results and SPMD results. When comparisons were made within a matrix group (for example, among mussel tissue results), the full suite of PAH results available was used. When comparisons were made across matrices, only the PAHs measured in common were used.

Water samples--Water samples were analyzed following procedures outlined in Baker (1991). Samples were collected directly into pre-cleaned containers, then extracted aboard the support vessel using Empore™ extraction disks with bonded C-18 octadecyl. Extracts were transported to Louisiana State University for analysis by GC/MS. Target analytes were the same as those for mussels and sediments.

Sheen sample--A pre-cleaned Zitex™ 47 mm/20-30 μm Teflon™ filter was used as a sampling device by placing it in direct contact with a visible sheen on the surface of a tide pool, the filter was placed in a 40 mL vial with 5 mL nanograde hexane and transported back to the analytical facility. In the laboratory, anhydrous sodium sulfate was added to remove water, and the sample volume was reduced to 100 μL. The extract was then analyzed by GC/MS. Target analytes were the same as those for mussels, sediments, and water.

RESULTS

Two of the SPMDs were missing from their cages at the first collection. At these stations, the remaining SPMD was collected, leaving none for collection at the subsequent visit. However, as a result, a full set of eight SPMDs (five on the north side, three on the south side) was collected in July. A complete set of mussels was also sampled. During the second visit, four of eight mussel cages had shifted, and one was missing entirely. Of the six SPMD cages left on the beaches, two had shifted and three were missing. Table 1 summarizes disposition of samples. Only station N-5 had intact mussel and SPMD cages for both sampling periods. Table 2 summarizes results of GC/MS analyses, in ng/g, of sediments, mussels and SPMDs.

Sediment Results

Sediment result are reported as ng/g wet weight due to the large grain size found on Prince William Sound beaches: moisture content of gravel samples is not an interpretable parameter.

The mean surrogate recovery values for sediment samples were 78 percent for acenaphthene-d_{10} (range 44-110 percent), 75 percent for phenanthrene-d_{10} (range 48-90 percent), and 92 percent for terphenyl-d_{14} (range 29-160 percent). Reported sediment values were not corrected for surrogate recovery.

Results for summed PAH concentrations in sediments are shown in Table 2. They ranged over two orders of magnitude, with all concentrations along the unoiled/lightly oiled south transect < 0.5 ng/g, and all concentrations on the heavily oiled north transect > 11 ng/g. Differences between the two transects were significant (Mann-Whitney U test, p = 0.025).

TABLE 1--Disposition of samples at Smith Island.

SAMPLE-DATE	STATION							
	N-1	N-2	N-3	N-4	N-5	S-1	S-2	S-3
Mussel-July	✓	✓	✓	✓	✓	✓	✓	✓
Mussel-Aug	✳	✓	✳	✓	✓	✳	●	✳
SPMD-July	✓	●	✓	✓	✓	✓	✓	●
SPMD-Aug	✳	✗	●	●	✓	✳	●	✗

✓ = sample collected as scheduled
✳ = cage displaced, sample collected
● = sample missing, not collected
✗ = collected early, in place of missing sample

TABLE 2--Summed PAH results from Smith Island deployments. Results for sediments (ng/g wet), mussels (ng/g dry), and SPMDs, (ng/SPMD).

SAMPLE-DATE	STATION							
	N-1	N-2	N-3	N-4	N-5	S-1	S-2	S-3
Sediments								
Sed-June			26	160	34	12	88	0.5	0.3	0.4
Mussels								
Xplant stock	11	27	---	---	---	---	---	---	---	---
Mussel-July	---	---	1200	1600	1300	1800	1900	46	17	37
Mussel-Aug	---	---	3100*	4200	4700*	5000	5500	57*	---	n/a*
SPMDs								
SPMD blank	300	400	---	---	---	---	---	---	---	---
SPMD-July	---	---	1000	–	1100	1200	2300	380	640	---
SPMD-Aug	---	---	460*	1900[a]	---	---	2200	330*	---	280[a]

*   = cage moved from original deployment location on transect
[a] = SPMD originally scheduled for collection in August but collected in July in place of missing device
n/a = not analyzed

Mussel Results

The mean surrogate recovery values for the mussel samples were 76 percent for acenaphthene-d_{10} (range 54-140 percent), 82 percent for phenanthrene-d_{10} (range 56-120 percent) and 78 percent for terphenyl-d_{14} (range 55-120 percent). The tissue values reported were corrected for surrogate recoveries. This permitted the use of a greater number of internal standards to counter matrix effects inherent in biological material. Variance of results for laboratory replicates (samples split after homogenization) was ≤ 12 percent for all mussel samples.

Summed PAH results were compared for three groups of mussels (Barnes Cove transplant stock, reference Smith-south transplants, and Smith-north transplants). Results from the July collection were used, because that data set is complete across all stations. Using the nonparametric Mann-Whitney U test, significant difference was found between the PAH concentrations in tissues of the Barnes Cove stock mussels and the mussels deployed on the unoiled south side of Smith Island. Mussel tissue levels measured on the heavily oiled north side of the island, however, differed significantly from those on the south side (p = 0.034).

On the north side of the island, three mussel cages (N-2, N-4, and N-5) on the transect remained at the designated stations and were not laterally displaced by wave and tidal action over the entire 52-day deployment. This permitted an assessment of temporal changes in levels of accumulated PAHs between 14 and 52 days. In all three cases, summed levels of PAHs increased between the 14-day collection and the 52-day collection (Table 2). At station N-2, the PAH level increased from 1,600 ng/g to 4,200 ng/g; at N-4, from 1,800 ng/g to 5,000 ng/g; and at N-5, from 1,900 ng/g to 5,500 ng/g. The difference between the 14-day PAH levels and the 52-day levels was significant (p = 0.05) in the Mann-Whitney U test.

SPMD Results

Analytical results for PAH levels in the SPMDs were subjected to the same nonparametric tests as the mussel results, and similar patterns were obtained. July SPMD results were used in these tests because collections were complete across both transects. Application of the Mann-Whitney U test showed that there was no significant difference between summed PAH levels in laboratory blank SPMDs and the SPMDs deployed to the south side of Smith Island. Concentrations of PAHs in SPMDs deployed on the north side of the island differed significantly (p = 0.025) from those in SPMDs from the south side.

Only one SPMD station from either side of the island remained intact over the entire 52-day deployment. This station was N-5, along the northern transect. While other SPMDs were recovered on both sides of Smith Island in August, these had shifted in location between the 14- and 52-day collections and could not be directly compared. The single intact pair of SPMDs contained essentially the same levels of PAHs at both 14 and 52 days, 2,300 and 2,200 ng/g, respectively.

Comparison of Sediment, Mussel and SPMD Results

The summed concentrations of PAHs in sediments, mussels, and SPMDs at stations on the north and south sides of Smith Island were compared using the Spearman rank correlation coefficient. Application of the test showed that results in all three matrices were significantly correlated in the levels of hydrocarbon uptake on the two sides of the island. Results from the Spearman rank procedure are summarized below in Table 3.

Although the uptake patterns of total target PAHs in both mussels and SPMDs were similar at the north and south transects (i.e., significantly higher concentrations at the oiled site relative to the unoiled/lightly oiled site; and no significant differences between the unoiled/lightly oiled site and blank or reference materials), the distribution of specific PAH compounds was different in mussels and SPMDs. Figure 4 shows a typical example of these differences from the 14-day collections at station N-5 on the north side of Smith Island. Concentrations of individual PAHs are portrayed as percent of total target PAHs in order to focus on distributional patterns and minimize absolute concentration effects. The most readily apparent differences between the mussel and SPMD results are the compounds occurring in highest proportion. In the mussel sample, the alkylated phenanthrenes, and especially C-3 phenanthrene, are most prevalent. In the SPMD sample, the lighter PAHs, naphthalenes and fluorenes, dominate.

Table 3--<u>Results of Spearman rank correlation tests on summed hydrocarbon results from Smith Island</u>

Test	N	D^2	r_s	z	p
Sed vs. Mussel	8	16	0.810	2.142	0.032
Sed. vs. SPMD	8	11.5	0.862	2.281	0.022
Mussel vs. SPMD	8	9.5	0.886	2.345	0.019

N   = number of cases (5 north stations, 3 south stations)
D^2 = sum of squares of differences of ranks
r_s = Spearman rho value
z   = distribution transformation of r_s for significance testing
p   = probability/significance

    Cluster analysis is a descriptive multivariate technique used to group cases by the degree of "similarity" to each other. It is considered descriptive in that significance of relationships is not tested. However, cluster analysis can elicit structure in the data that might not otherwise be apparent (Everitt 1993).

    In this study, the procedure involved a complete linkage hierarchical clustering based on a Euclidean distance metric. It was used to evaluate the 14-day mussel and SPMD results and to determine whether the differences in distribution of individual PAH compounds observed at station N-5 were consistent; and furthermore, whether the differences in PAH distribution were sufficiently great to result in distinct grouping of the samples by matrix and location.

    Figure 5 shows the resultant tree diagram from the cluster analysis. As can be seen in the figure, the clusters correspond well to combinations of matrix and deployment location. Branch "A", for example, includes all ten SPMD results, including the method blanks. Branch "B" encompasses all of the mussels, including the transplant stock collected at Barnes Cove. Branch "C" represents all of the SPMDs deployed on the oiled north side of the island and one from the south side. The remaining SPMDs from the south side of Smith Island, and the method blanks, are grouped at the next level into this branch, at "D". Branch "E" contains all five of the mussels transplanted to the north side transect; and finally, "F" clusters the south side mussels and the Barnes Cove stock mussels.

<u>Ancillary Sample Results</u>

    Several samples in other matrices were used to further characterize residual oil occurring at the Smith Island north site. These were collected within 10 m of the established transect. The ancillary samples resulted in summed PAHs ranging from below detection in two bulk water samples, to 78,000 ng/g in a sample of heavily oiled sediment taken from a 30 cm pit dug in the upper intertidal zone of the beach. Although a sample of oil sheen was collected and analyzed, it resulted in a "unitless" measurement, in that the analytical matrix was the sheen itself; therefore, no summed PAH concentration was possible, although relative abundance of individual PAHs could be calculated.

    The pit sample was included in this collection because previous geomorphological surveys at the site (Michel and Hayes 1991) had documented the presence of a large reservoir of buried residual oil. Although surface sediment samples (e.g., Houghton et al. 1993) had

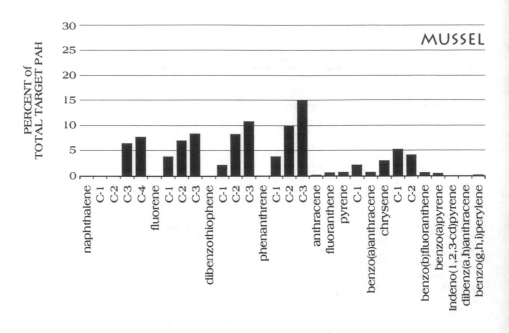

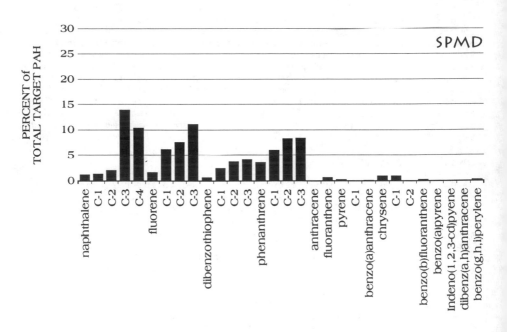

FIG. 4--PAH profiles for transplanted mussel (top) and SPMD (bottom)
samples collected at station N-5 on Smith Island in July 1992.

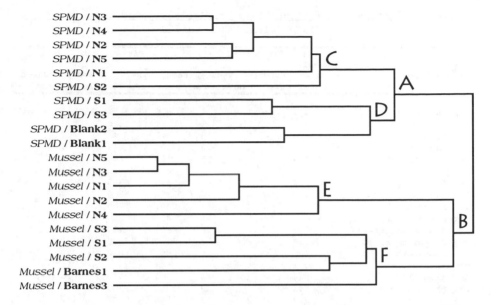

FIG. 5--Tree diagram for cluster analysis of PAH distributions in Smith Island mussel transplants and SPMDs collected in July 1992.

reflected little measurable oiling, trenching, particularly in upper intertidal berms, revealed heavy sediment oiling at depth. The pit sample was collected to evaluate this oil as a potential source of exposure to mussels at the site.

Results for ancillary samples collected on the north side of Smith Island are shown in Table 4 (two samples of nearshore water with all results below detection limits are omitted).

Differences between water samples were observed during collection. The two bulk samples were collected at the water's edge, at the interface between beach and ocean, while the other sample was collected in a tide pool above the actual tidal level. There was little particulate material noted in the nearshore water samples, while the tide pool sample was visibly clouded by fine particulates.

Figures 6A and 6B show the distribution of individual PAHs in selected ancillary samples, a surface sediment sample collected at station N-5, and *Exxon Valdez* cargo oil (included for reference). The use of normalized concentration data permits these distribution profiles to be compared to those in Figure 4. Relative to the original product spilled (*Exxon Valdez* cargo), all samples are noticeably deficient in lighter aromatic hydrocarbons, particularly the naphthalenes.

Cluster analysis was performed on PAH distribution results in the selected ancillary sample matrices, mussel tissue (station N-5), SPMD (N-5), surface sediment (N-5), and the sample of *Exxon Valdez* cargo oil. The resultant tree diagram (Figure 7) shows a hierarchy of similarities based on the PAH profiles. At grouping level "A" on the figure, the cargo oil and the SPMD samples group together, likely because of the proportionally higher levels of the lighter aromatic hydrocarbons found in both. Branch "B" includes the other sample matrix types, including mussel, both sediments, tide pool water, and oil sheen. The grouping of

Table 4--<u>GC/MS results for ancillary samples collected on north side of Smith Island, June, 1992.</u>

Sample name:	Tide Pool	Pit 1	Pit 2	Pit 3	Pit 4	Pit 9	-
Sample Type:	Water	Sed.	Sed.	Sed.	Sed.	Sed.	Sheen
COMPOUND	ng/ml	ng/g wet	ng/g wet	ng/g wet	ng/g wet	ng/g wet	unitless
naphthalene	<0.1	<0.1	1.5	<10	<10	5.0	<10
C-1 naphthalene	<0.1	<0.1	3.1	<10	<10	<10	<10
C-2 naphthalene	0.6	<0.1	5.5	<10	93	<10	<10
C-3 naphthalene	0.8	<0.1	5.3	190	440	86	<10
C-4 naphthalene	0.9	2.7	15	1400	7600	1400	200
fluorene	<0.1	<0.1	<0.1	<10	<10	<10	<10
C-1 fluorene	0.2	<0.1	2.2	200	1300	110	<10
C-2 fluorene	0.8	<0.1	4.8	1100	5500	810	240
C-3 fluorene	2.8	<0.1	32	3400	7700	3700	2200
dibenzothiophene	<0.1	<0.1	0.5	<10	<10	<10	<10
C-1 dibenzothiophene	0.3	0.2	3.3	64	2100	<10	90
C-2 dibenzothiophene	1.8	4.3	12	1600	7900	2100	920
C-3 dibenzothiophene	4.1	11	76	3900	9500	5400	3400
phenanthrene	0.1	0.4	1.0	24	<10	<10	13
C-1 phenanthrene	0.4	<0.1	3.0	62	1900	<10	89
C-2 phenanthrene	2.3	5.3	29	1300	9200	9800	1700
C-3 phenanthrene	3.7	9.2	72	3200	9700	4100	4100
anthracene	<0.1	0.2	0.1	<10	<10	<10	<10
naphthobenzothiophene	0.4	0.2	4.4	130	1000	100	430
C-1 naphthobenzothiophene	1.7	1.6	19	610	2900	1500	2200
C-2 naphthobenzothiophene	2.7	3.3	28	790	2400	2100	3200
C-3 naphthobenzothiophene	2.5	7.1	22	560	1500	1800	2200
fluoranthene	<0.1	1.6	<0.1	60	<10	<10	<10
pyrene	0.1	2.5	2.3	200	160	12	27
C-1 pyrene	0.3	10	13	980	780	530	190
C-2 pyrene	1.1	18	32	2000	2500	1500	780
benzo(a)anthracene	<0.5	<0.5	<0.5	<50	<50	<50	<10
chrysene	0.5	4.6	11	520	840	500	310
C-1 chrysene	0.7	4.2	14	500	900	530	610
C-2 chrysene	0.7	5.7	14	460	690	540	650
benzo(b)fluoranthene*	<0.5	1.0	<0.5	94	130	94	<50
benzo(e)pyrene	<0.5	2.6	<0.5	110	130	160	<50
benzo(a)pyrene	<0.5	<0.5	<0.5	<50	<50	<50	<50
perylene	<0.5	<0.5	<0.5	<50	<50	<50	<50
indeno(1,2,3-cd)pyrene	<1.0	<1.0	<1.0	<100	<100	<100	<100
dibenz(a,h)anthracene	<1.0	<1.0	<1.0	<100	<100	<100	<100
benzo(g,h,i)perylene	<1.0	6.0	<1.0	<100	900	140	<100
Total Target PAH†	29	102	430	23000	78000	37000	24000

*Sum of benzo(b)fluoranthene and benzo(k)fluoranthene.
†Below detection values not included in Total PAH summation.

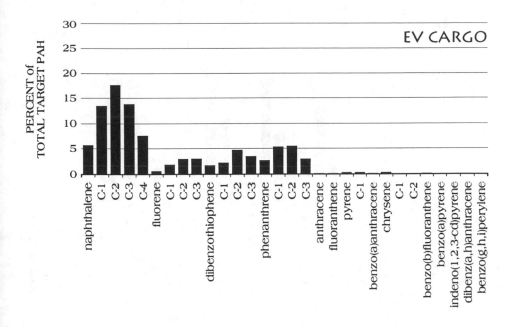

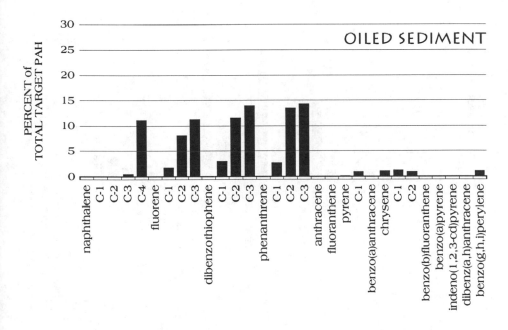

FIG. 6A--PAH profiles for reference *Exxon Valdez* cargo oil, and oiled subsurface sediment collected near the north sample transect on Smith Island in July 1992.

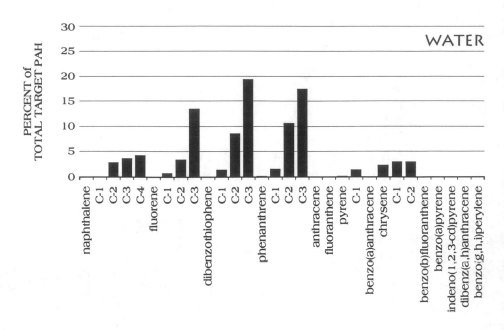

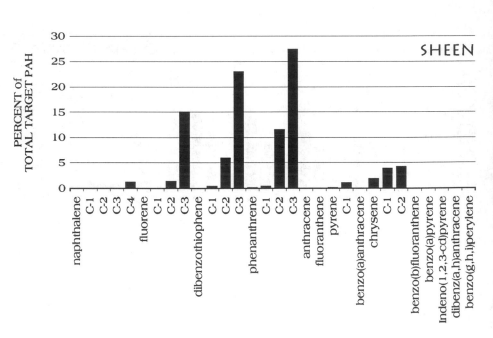

FIG. 6B--PAH profiles for tide pool water, and oil sheen samples collected near the north sample transect on Smith Island in July 1992.

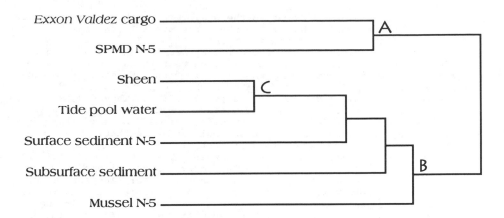

FIG. 7--Tree diagram for cluster analysis of PAH distributions for seven
matrices from the north Smith Island site.

sheen and tide pool water at branch "C", and the relatively short length
of the branch, suggests that these two samples are most similar in their
PAH profiles.

DISCUSSION

The large grain size of sediments characterizing Prince William Sound
beaches complicated interpretation of PAH results. Concentrations of
organic compounds like PAHs are known to negatively correlate with
sediment grain size (see, for example, Burton 1992). As a result,
sediment hydrocarbon results from Prince William Sound may not compare
well with results from other spill-affected shorelines with typically
smaller grain size characteristics. The results from this study suggest
that surface or shallow subsurface sediment concentrations of PAHs at
the Smith Island site do not adequately reflect the biological
availability of residual oil.

Because semipermeable membrane devices, by design, passively sample
the dissolved fraction of PAHs in the aquatic environment, their
deployment in the environment in association with mussels can offer some
insight into the mechanism of PAH exposure to the mussels.
Specifically, comparison of results in SPMDs and mussels may highlight
the relative roles of dissolved PAHs vs. PAHs associated with food or
particulate material ingested during filter-feeding activities, in
determining accumulation in mussel body tissues. For the intertidal
deployments in this study, oil sheens may also be an important source of
PAHs to mussels, but it is not clear how the organisms would be exposed:
sheens are water surface phenomena, and mussels are not likely to be
filtering unless they are completely covered by water. SPMDs, on the
other hand, may come directly into contact with sheens as the water
level on the beaches rises or falls.

Comparison of PAH results in mussels and SPMDs was complicated by the
interferences encountered in the laboratory at GC elution times for the
alkylated phenanthrenes. As these compounds are important constituents
of the source and original oil, inability to quantitate them affected
results of PAH profile comparisons. It is not clear whether the

interferences were attributable to the deployment method, e.g., the use of plastic-coated wire cages, or whether they are inherent for PAH compounds of this type that partition into SPMDs. In future deployments, modified cleanup procedures may address these problems.

Regardless of their origin, the differences between the PAH uptake characteristics in mussels and SPMDs in this study are similar to those reported elsewhere for polychlorinated biphenyl uptake in paired deployments of clams and SPMDs (Prest et al. 1992). They suggest that passive uptake processes (equilibrium partitioning) do not completely account for levels of PAHs found in mussels exposed to residual petroleum hydrocarbons. This in turn would indicate that: the route of exposure to SPMDs and mussels is different, i.e., PAHs in solution vs. PAHs adsorbed to particulate material or incorporated in food items; the mussels selectively metabolize some PAHs over others, perhaps eliminating lighter fractions such as naphthalenes or fluorenes more readily than other PAHs; or some combination of exposure and metabolism. However, the relative similarity of PAH profiles found in water/sheens/ oiled sediments, and in mussels, coupled with the relative dissimilarity of the exposure source profiles and profiles in SPMDs, suggests that mussels do not substantially alter target PAHs by metabolism.

The fact that levels of PAHs were significantly accumulated in SPMDs on the north side of Smith Island indicates that PAHs are available in the water flooding over the SPMDs and mussels. This would suggest that the route of exposure is associated either with dissolved PAHs, or with PAHs in the sheens regularly observed to leach from the substrate on the north side. The analysis of bulk water samples collected at the beach-water interface yielded no detectable concentrations of any of the targeted PAHs, which would implicate sheens as a more important route of exposure over PAHs partitioned into the water column. However, these observations are based on a limited sample size, and a more targeted study would be necessary to definitively investigate exposure mechanisms.

The cluster analysis across the six different matrices in Figure 7 suggests that mussels reflect the PAH composition of sources (as represented by oiled sediment, water, and sheen) to a relatively greater degree than SPMDs. Moreover, the relative dissimilarity between the sheen/water/sediment/mussel results and the original *Exxon Valdez* cargo analysis indicates that a substantial degree of weathering has occurred in the environment over the past three years. This is not unexpected, given the degree of physical exposure typical of sites in Prince William Sound, the large grain size of the beaches, and the length of time that has passed since the spill occurred.

SUMMARY AND CONCLUSIONS

Summarizing the findings of this study:

• Sediments collected from stations on the north (heavily oiled) side of Smith Island contained significantly higher concentrations of target PAHs than did sediments collected from stations on the south (unoiled/lightly oiled) side.
• Both mussels and SPMDs deployed at the north side transect accumulated PAHs to concentrations significantly greater than those deployed at the south side transect.
• Total target PAH results in sediments, mussels, and SPMDs collected at the same stations were significantly correlated.

- Hydrocarbon uptake kinetics in mussels and SPMDs appear to be different. There was little difference in PAH levels in SPMDs collected after 14 and 52 days, while mussels showed significantly higher levels after 52 days.
- Although target PAH concentrations were similar in mussels and SPMDs, the distribution of individual PAHs was different, particularly along the oiled transect.
- PAH profiles in north side samples of tide pool water, oil sheen, and surface and subsurface sediments were similar to that in mussel tissue; the profile in a comparable SPMD was relatively dissimilar.
- The results suggest that particulate material with adsorbed PAHs and sheens leaching from subsurface deposits of residual oil may be important routes of exposure to intertidal mussels, but further investigation would be necessary for confirmation and determination of the relative importance of the two potential pathways.

Despite the fact that SPMDs showed clear differences in the nature of PAH uptake at oiled stations relative to that in mussels, they demonstrated their potential utility as monitoring tools. The devices effectively sequester lipophilic contaminants that occur at trace levels, and with further research into equilibrium partitioning coefficients, eventually could offer a means for estimating concentrations of contaminants in the environment. Furthermore, because of the selectivity in the mechanism of hydrocarbon uptake, SPMDs deployed in conjunction with traditional monitoring organisms can facilitate insights into ecological routes of exposure. However, the analytical difficulties encountered in this study with respect to interferences in quantitation of the alkylated phenanthrenes remain an area of concern, as these compounds are important constituents of crude oil.

Although it is clear that PAHs remain biologically available to mussels on the oiled side of Smith Island, comparison of mussel PAH results from 1990 and those from the 1992 transplant experiment indicates that the degree of bioavailability of residual hydrocarbons has declined substantially. Nevertheless, the biological and ecological significance of the levels accumulated in intertidal organisms remains undetermined. The pathological consequences of a continued, relatively low-level chronic exposure to the mussels are not known. It is also not known whether the tissue levels in the mussels pose any risk to predators that feed on them. While a NOAA study in 1990 (Houghton et al. 1991) found no evidence of biomagnification of PAHs from mussels further up the food web into intertidal predators such as starfish and drills, recently some wildlife biologists (e.g., Patten 1993) have asserted that reproductive failure in harlequin ducks in oiled regions of Prince William Sound is attributable to ingestion of contaminated mussels by the ducks. However, at this time, this link remains speculative, and clearly remains a subject for further research before disruptive mussel removal projects are implemented.

DISCLAIMER

The views expressed in this manuscript do not necessarily represent those of the U.S. Government or the National Oceanic and Atmospheric Administration. Mention of trade names or commercial products does not constitute endorsement or recommendation for their use.

ACKNOWLEDGMENTS

    The authors would like to acknowledge and thank the many people who participated in the funding, collection and analytical phases of this study. The work was supported by NOAA, the U.S. Environmental Protection Agency, the American Petroleum Institute, and the Minerals Management Service (U.S. Department of Interior). Rebecca Hoff of NOAA (Seattle, WA), Cristina Rumbaitis-del Rio of Montgomery Blair High School (Silver Spring, MD), and Paulene Roberts of Louisiana State University (Baton Rouge, LA) assisted in field collections and deployment. Crewmembers from the vessels *Renown*, *Arctic Dream*, and *Good Times* provided safe passage to and from the collection sites, often in less than optimal weather conditions. Paulene Roberts was responsible for the chemical analyses of mussel tissues. Dr. Eric Crecelius of Battelle Marine Sciences Laboratory supervised the preparation and analysis of semipermeable membrane devices, and Dr. Jim Huckins of the National Fisheries Contaminant Research Center (U.S. Fish and Wildlife Service) provided valuable advice on the deployment and use of SPMDs. Malin Babcock and Patricia Rounds of the National Marine Fisheries Service Auke Bay Laboratory shared their considerable experience in mussel research in Prince William Sound and identified a suitable source stock for mussel transplants. Gini Curl of NOAA produced graphics for the manuscript and offered critical guidance for the aesthetically impaired. There are many others who assisted in this effort, and omission from this necessarily wordy listing should not minimize the importance of their contributions.

REFERENCES

Babcock, M., G. Irvine, S. Rice, P. Rounds, J. Cusick and C. Brodersen, 1993, "Oiled mussel beds two and three years after the *Exxon Valdez* oil spill," <u>Program and Abstracts</u>, *Exxon Valdez* Oil Spill Symposium Anchorage, Alaska, *Exxon Valdez* Oil Spill Trustee Council, University of Alaska Sea Grant College Program, and American Fisheries Society, Alaska Chapter, Anchorage, pp. 184-185.

Baker, J.T., "Extraction of PAHs from water," Application Note EMP-002, J.T. Baker, Inc., Phillipsburg, NJ, 1991.

Battelle Memorial Institute, "Phase 4 draft final report on National Status and Trends Mussel Watch Program: Collection of bivalves and surficial sediments from coastal U.S. Atlantic and Pacific locations and analyses for organic chemicals and trace elements," Battelle Memorial Institute, Duxbury Operations, Duxbury, MA, 1990.

Burton, G.A., Jr., 1992, "Sediment collection and processing: Factors affecting realism," <u>Sediment Toxicity Assessment</u>, Lewis Publishers, Inc., Chelsea, MI, pp. 37-66.

Everitt, B., 1993, <u>Cluster Analysis</u>, New York: Halsted Press, New York.

Goldberg, E.D., V.T. Bowen, J.W. Farrington, G. Harvey, J.H. Martin, P.L. Parker, R.W. Risebrough, W. Robertson IV, E. Schneider and E. Gamble, 1978, "The Mussel Watch," <u>Environmental Conservation</u>, Vol. 5, pp. 101-125.

Houghton, J.P., D.C. Lees, H. Teas, H. Cumberland, S. Landino, and W.B. Driskell, "Evaluation of the condition of intertidal and shallow subtidal biota in Prince William Sound following the Exxon Valdez oil spill and subsequent shoreline treatment: Volume 1," Pentec Environmental, Inc., and ERC Environmental and Energy Services, 1991.

Houghton, J.P., A.K. Fukuyama, D.C. Lees, H. Teas, III, H.L. Cumberland, P.M. Harper, T.A. Ebert, and W.B. Driskell, "Evaluation of the 1991 condition of Prince William Sound shorelines following the Exxon Valdez oil spill and subsequent treatment: Volume II, 1991 biological monitoring survey," NOAA Technical Memorandum NOS ORCA 67, NOAA, Hazardous Materials Response and Assessment Division, Seattle, WA, 1993.

Huckins, J.N., M.W. Tubergen and G.K. Manuweera, 1990, "Semipermeable membrane devices containing model lipid: A new approach to monitoring the bioavailability of lipophilic contaminants and estimating their bioconcentration potential," Chemosphere, Vol. 20, No. 5, pp. 533-552.

Krahn, M.M., C.A. Wigren, R.W. Pearce, L.K. Moore, R.G. Bogar, W.D. MacLeod, Jr., S.L. Chan, and D.W. Brown, 1988a, "Standard analytical procedures of the NOAA National Analytical Facility, 1988: New HPLC cleanup and revised extraction procedures for organic contaminants," NOAA Technical Memorandum NMFS F/NWC-153, Northwest and Alaska Fisheries Center, National Marine Fisheries Service, Seattle, WA.

Krahn, M.M., C.A. Wigren, R.W. Pearce, L.K. Moore, R.G. Bogar, W.D. MacLeod, Jr., S.L. Chan, and D.W. Brown, 1988b, "A rapid high-performance liquid chromatographic method for isolating organic contaminants from tissue and sediment extracts," Journal of Chromatography, Vol. 437, pp. 161-175.

Lebo, J.A., J.L. Zajicek, J.N. Huckins, J.D. Petty, P.H. Peterman, and R.W. Gale, 1992, "A demonstrated method for the application of semipermeable membrane devices to in situ monitoring of environmental waters for polycyclic aromatic hydrocarbons," Chemosphere, Vol. 25, No. 5, pp. 697-718.

MacLeod, Jr., W.D., D.W. Brown, A.J. Friedman, D.G. Burrows, O. Maynes, R.W. Pearce, C.A. Wigren, and R.G. Bogar, 1985, "Standard analytical procedures of the NOAA National Analytical Facility, 1985-1986: Extractable toxic organic compounds, second edition," NOAA Technical Memorandum NMFS F/NWC-92, Northwest and Alaska Fisheries Center, National Marine Fisheries Service, Seattle, WA..

Michel, J. and M.O. Hayes, "Geomorphological controls on the persistence of shoreline contamination from the Exxon Valdez oil spill," NOAA Hazardous Materials Response Branch, Seattle, WA, 1991.

Patten, S., 1993, "Reproductive failure of harlequin ducks," Alaska's Wildlife, Vol. 25, No. 1, p. 15.

Prest, H.F., W.M. Jarman, S.A. Burns, T. Weismüller, M. Martin and J.N. Huckins, 1992, "Passive water sampling via semipermeable membrane devices (SPMDs) in concert with bivalves in the Sacramento/San Joaquin River delta," Chemosphere, Vol. 25, No. 12, pp. 1811-1823.

Salazar, M.H. and S.M. Salazar, 1990, "Mussels as bioindicators: A case study of tributyltin effects in San Diego Bay," Proceedings, 17th Annual Aquatic Toxicity Workshop, Vancouver, Canada, pp. 47-75.

Schantz, M.M., B.A. Benner, Jr., S.N. Chesler. R.G. Christensen, B.J. Koster, J. Kurz, R.M. Parris, and S.A. Wise, 1993, "NIST methods for certification of SRM 1941 and SRM 1974," In Sampling and Analytical Methods of the National Status and Trends Program National Benthic Surveillance and Mussel Watch Projects 1984-1992, Vol. IV, Comprehensive Descriptions of Trace Organic Analytical Methods, NOAA Technical Memorandum NOS ORCA 71, pp. 165-182.

Wade, T.L., J.M. Brooks, M.C. Kennicutt II, T.J. McDonald, J.L. Sericano, and T.J. Jackson, 1993, "GERG trace organics contaminant analytical techniques," In Sampling and Analytical Methods of the National Status and Trends Program National Benthic Surveillance and Mussel Watch Projects 1984-1992, Vol. IV, Comprehensive Descriptions of Trace Organic Analytical Methods, NOAA Technical Memorandum NOS ORCA 71, pp. 121-139.

Widdows, J. and P. Donkin, 1992, "Mussels and environmental contaminants: Bioaccumulation and physiological aspects," In The Mussel Mytilus: Ecology, Physiology, Genetics and Culture, Elsevier Science Publishers B.V., Amsterdam, pp. 383-424.

Shoreline Impacts of the Spill

David S. Page [1], Edward S. Gilfillan [1], Paul D. Boehm [2], and E. James Harner [3]

SHORELINE ECOLOGY PROGRAM FOR PRINCE WILLIAM SOUND, ALASKA, FOLLOWING THE *EXXON VALDEZ* OIL SPILL: PART 1—STUDY DESIGN AND METHODS

REFERENCE: Page, D. S., Gilfillan, E. S., Boehm, P. D., and Harner, E. J., "Shoreline Ecology Program for Prince William Sound, Alaska, Following the Exxon Valdez Oil Spill: Part I--Study Design and Methods," *Exxon Valdez Oil Spill: Fate and Effects in Alaskan Waters, ASTM STP 1219,* Peter G. Wells, James N. Butler, and Jane S. Hughes, Eds., American Society for Testing and Materials, Philadelphia, 1995.

ABSTRACT: Part 1 of a three-part series, this paper describes the design and analysis of a large field and laboratory program to assess shoreline recovery in Prince William Sound following the *Exxon Valdez* oil spill. The study was designed so that results could be generalized area-wide (biology, chemistry) or habitat-wide (toxicology) and projected forward in time (chemistry). It made use of the "sediment quality triad" approach, combining biological, chemical, and toxicological measurements to assess shoreline recovery. Key aspects of the study include the following:

- Coordinated field sampling for chemical, toxicological, and biological studies
- Stratified random sampling (SRS) as a basis for spatial generalization
- Periodic sampling to assess trends, including sites with worst-case conditions
- Analysis of oil-spill effects on hundreds of species
- Statistical methods based on normal and non-normal theory, consistent with the structure of the data, including generalized linear models and multivariate correspondence analysis

[1] Bowdoin College, Brunswick, ME
[2] Arthur D. Little, Inc., Cambridge, MA
[3] West Virginia University, Morgantown, WV

Prince William Sound shorelines were stratified into four types of habitat (exposed bedrock/rubble, sheltered bedrock/rubble, boulder/cobble, and pebble/gravel) and four different levels of oiling (unoiled, light, moderate, and heavy). Sixty-four SRS sites were randomly selected with an average of four replicates in each combination of habitat type and oiling level. The SRS sites were sampled in 1990 to assess the state of recovery in the sound. Twelve additional non-random sites, including some of the most heavily oiled locations in the sound, were monitored annually to assess trends from 1989 to 1991.

At sedimentary sites, sediment samples were taken for hydrocarbon analysis, sediment toxicology, and biological (infaunal) analysis. At bedrock/rubble sites, filter wipes and surface scrape samples were taken to assess chemistry and epibiota. Where present, mussel samples were taken to determine the bioavailability of any petroleum residues.

Spill-affected shorelines are judged to have recovered when the biological communities are statistically indistinguishable from those at unoiled reference sites. Given the large natural variability observed among sites, this study provides a more accurate and comprehensive picture of shoreline recovery than approaches that focus on only a few species at subjectively chosen locations.

KEYWORDS: *Exxon Valdez*; oil spill; shoreline ecology; shoreline recovery; stratified random sampling; generalized linear models; correspondence analysis.

INTRODUCTION

The March 24, 1989, grounding of the *Exxon Valdez* on Bligh Reef in Prince William Sound resulted in the release of about 258 000 barrels of Alaska North Slope crude oil into the marine environment. Nearly 500 miles of shorelines in the sound were oiled to some degree (Maki 1991; Neff et al., Shoreline Conditions, this volume). In the aftermath of the spill, many scientific studies were undertaken to assess spill effects as part of the Natural Resource Damage Assessment (NRDA) process under the Comprehensive Environmental Response, Compensation, and Liability Act (CERCLA). This shoreline ecology program (SEP) had the objectives of providing an unbiased independent assessment of shoreline injury, shoreline recovery, and oil loss.

The shoreline ecology program was designed to assess the recovery of hundreds of miles of oiled shorelines in Prince William Sound by using a limited number of sampling stations. The number of sampling stations had to be small enough for a survey to be accomplished in the summer weather window, but large enough to detect important spill effects. The stratified random selection of 64 sample sites permitted results to be generalized to the affected area of the sound. Periodic sampling of 12 sites of special interest allowed sediment chemistry to be projected forward in time and recovery at worst-case sites to be assessed. The design of this program was strongly influenced by the "sediment quality triad" approach to impact assessments, a combined strategy of chemical, toxicological, and biological measurements (Long and Chapman 1985; Chapman et al. 1991).

In order to form a statistically valid link between exposure and effect, all samples taken in 1990 and 1991 for chemistry, biology, and sediment toxicology at any given site were taken at one time by the same personnel. Sediment samples were obtained wherever possible for hydrocarbon analysis, sediment toxicology, and biological (infaunal) analysis. In bedrock/rubble habitats, filter wipes and surface scrape samples were collected for chemical and biological (epibiota) analyses, respectively. Samples of mussels were taken to assess the bioavailability of any petroleum residues. Surface conditions (epibiota) were also documented photographically.

This paper describes the study design and analysis of data. The two companion papers (Boehm et al., Part 2: Chemistry, this volume; Gilfillan et al., Part 3: Biology, this volume) present chemistry and biology results respectively. The results of a complementary shoreline ecology program in the Gulf of Alaska are presented separately (Gilfillan et al., Shoreline Impacts, this volume).

Definition of Recovery

The design of an oil-spill injury/recovery assessment study depends on the criteria used to define recovery. The Federal NRDA regulations under CERCLA (U. S. Code of Federal Regulations, 1987: 11.60–11.73) define "recovery period" as the "length of time required to return the services of the injured resource to their baseline condition." Baseline services "should reflect conditions that would have been expected at the assessment area had the discharge of oil not occurred, taking into account both natural processes and those that are the result of human activities." Thus, determining the recovery of affected plant and animal communities requires that measurements be made in oiled and unoiled (reference) areas.

Recovery of a biological resource can be defined in terms of specific derived parameters (statistical variables) related to community structure. These parameters include the number of individuals present, the number of species present, and the community's diversity. When such classical community parameters are used, both negative (fewer species and reduced diversity) and positive (more species and increased diversity) effects are possible. In keeping with CERCLA, recovery can be considered complete when negative effects (injuries) are no longer present. More conservatively, we consider recovery to be incomplete as long as any differences (positive or negative) can be detected in these community parameters.

Recovery can also be defined more broadly in terms of the overall structure of the biological community: when the community structure in oiled locations is indistinguishable from unoiled reference locations, recovery has occurred. For this second, more inclusive definition of recovery, we used multivariate correspondence analysis to assess any differences from reference.

Past Oil-Spill Studies

Because fine-grained sediments tend to sustain effects from oil spills the longest (National Research Council [NRC] 1985), most shoreline studies of prior oil spills have dealt with environments such as salt marshes, mud flats, and sand beaches (Mielke 1990; NRC 1985). Even though there is a good ecological database for exposed and sheltered rocky environments (Grant 1977; Markham and Munda 1980; McGuiness 1987a, 1987b; Murray and Horn 1989), relatively little work has been reported on the recovery of epifaunal communities from oil spills (Southward and Southward 1978; Chasse 1978; Chan 1975). Information on infaunal communities in boulder and gravel beaches is very limited because these locations are difficult to sample quantitatively.

Most shoreline studies in areas with fine-grained sediments have compared subjectively chosen oiled sites and subjectively chosen reference sites. The classic example is the work of Sanders et al. (1980) on the effects of the West Falmouth oil spill of 1969. This was the first comprehensive oil-spill study to link biological and chemical data and to define recovery in terms of the succession from a perturbed infaunal biological community structure back to a reference community structure. In addition to combining biological and chemical measurements, a key feature of this work was that it involved repeated sampling over several years. Another reason for the success of the West Falmouth study was the nature and extent of the oil spill. The spill occurred near shore and was of moderate size (4 600 barrels). The affected zone was limited in extent and consisted primarily of an intertidal salt marsh and a soft-sediment subtidal environment. Oiling within the spill zone varied from heavy to none. It was therefore possible to represent the ranges of oiling and habitat types and to monitor recovery with a limited number of subjectively chosen sites.

A number of studies of subsequent oil spills were modeled on the West Falmouth spill study (Gilfillan et al. 1986; Glemarec and Hussenot 1982; Thomas 1978). A problem with many such studies was that assessing overall recovery was difficult because only a few sites were sampled. Successful systematic oil-spill studies based on the West Falmouth model have been reported for small affected zones, i.e., when it was possible to sample with sufficient density over the affected area to provide a valid basis for estimating recovery. This can involve sampling grids covering the entire spill zone (Gilfillan et al. 1977).

Strategy for Prince William Sound

This study differed from past shoreline studies by combining the traditional "fixed-site" approach with a stratified random sampling (SRS) component. The 1990 SRS component was designed to assess shoreline recovery in area-wide terms. The 1989-1991 fixed site program assessed changes in the amount and character of petroleum residues at certain locations of environmental concern.

SRS component—A SRS design allows findings to be generalized to the spill zone as defined by the sampling plan. This approach has been used by ecologists to sample deep-sea marine organisms (Grassle et al. 1975) and to estimate the population densities of clams (Russell 1972), fish (Jolly and Hampton 1990), fur seal pups (York and Kozloff 1987), forest community types (St. Jaques and Gagnon 1988), and black rhinoceros (Goddard 1969).

The SRS component of the study was designed to assess spill effects in each of four major habitats. This was accomplished by (1) selecting sampling locations randomly from a set of candidate sites stratified by habitat and oiling level and (2) quantifying site-specific natural factors, i.e., wave exposure, percentage sand, percentage silt/clay, and total organic carbon (TOC), all of which can affect biological communities. Area-wide natural factors that affect biota (such as temperature) should have approximately the same effect on all sites in a given habitat. With an SRS design and removal of major site-specific variables, statistically significant differences in biota between oiled and unoiled categories can be attributed to the effects of the spill. In accordance with the study plan, significant tests were done to establish whether or not differences existed ($\alpha = 0.05$) between biological communities for oiled and unoiled sites for each tide zone in each habitat.

This approach was facilitated by the fact that extensive shoreline surveys of habitat and oiling level were available in a computerized geographical information system (GIS). This GIS system was used to subdivide the shoreline into many segments of equal length, categorized by habitat and oiling level, and to select sampling sites at random from each category.

Fixed-site component—The fixed-site component of the shoreline ecology program assessed conditions at 12 non-randomly chosen sites. These were sites of special interest or concern, representing mainly sedimentary habitats and some of the worst oiling conditions in the sound. Included were two soft-sediment sites, habitats not common enough in Prince William Sound to be included in the SRS design. Eight of these 12 sites had been sampled previously in 1989. Four of those sites were "set-aside" sites, i.e., they received no cleanup treatment. In contrast to the SRS sites, which were sampled only once (in 1990), the fixed sites were sampled during two or three successive summers (ending in 1991).

An important role of the fixed sites was to conservatively estimate the rate of shoreline recovery and oil loss. This could be done either by periodically resampling the complete set of SRS sites or by complementing a single set of 1990 SRS data with periodic sampling of a smaller number of fixed sites. We chose the latter approach. While the fixed site biological data were not used to quantitatively project recovery beyond 1990 as was done for oil loss, the fixed site biological data did give an estimate of recovery trends for heavily oiled locations.

No prespill baseline data existed; but, in any case, it is often not meaningful to use prespill data as a benchmark for recovery because of interannual variation. This is particularly true in Prince William Sound, where plant and animal communities change over time because of the stresses of severe winters, storms, shoreline battering by ice and logs, and beach movement. It is, therefore, more appropriate to compare spill sites with reference sites that have been exposed to similar area-wide environmental factors, except oiling. Unoiled reference sites suitable for this purpose were sampled in both the SRS and the fixed-site programs.

SHORELINE HABITATS IN PRINCE WILLIAM SOUND

Prince William Sound is a large, partially enclosed body of water with many islands and a mainland having a complex coastline formed by passages, fjord-like indentations, and irregular bays. Much of the present shoreline topography where oiling occurred is a result of uplifting (1-3 m) during the 1964 earthquake (Plafker 1965; Haven 1971), which means that much of the present shoreline of the sound is geologically young. The tides range from 3 m (neaps) to 6 m (springs). Wind velocities are greatest between October and March, and storms can be severe. The environment of Prince William Sound is far from fragile: the continuing stress of physical factors relating to harsh winters and severe storms has resulted in plant and animal communities that are very resilient.

Four shoreline habitats dominate in the area of the sound affected by the spill: exposed bedrock/rubble; sheltered bedrock/rubble; boulder/cobble beaches; and pebble/gravel beaches (Figure 1). Sheltered and exposed bedrock/rubble habitats comprise over 70% of the spill-affected zone, and boulder/cobble and pebble/gravel beaches make up almost all of the remainder. Soft-sediment intertidal habitats and salt-marsh environments are very rare in Prince William Sound (<1%). The four principal habitats are described briefly in the following paragraphs.

Sheltered and exposed bedrock habitats are characterized by bedrock outcrops, often with rock rubble or rocky ledges comprising a narrow low-tide platform. Although these are not sedimentary intertidal habitats, it is often possible to find isolated shallow pockets of sedimentary material, particularly in the lower intertidal zone of sheltered bedrock sites. Many of the intertidal biota in sheltered and exposed bedrock habitats live on the rock surfaces.

Boulder/cobble shorelines are commonly found on exposed shorelines, where a lower layer of mixed sand, gravel, boulders, and cobbles is overlain by wave-washed and rounded boulders and cobbles. In some cases, boulder/cobble beaches form a veneer over a bedrock platform. These are generally high-energy beaches where breaking waves can cause cobbles and small boulders to move. Because these beaches are relatively porous, water percolates readily with tide and wave action. The intertidal biota in these habitats are commonly associated with finer-grained sediments in interstices and under the boulder/cobble armor.

Pebble/gravel beaches range in character from gravel/sand in more protected locations to pebble/gravel in more exposed areas. Such habitats are often found between outcrops of bedrock shorelines and at the heads of bays and inlets. These are sedimentary habitats where the intertidal biota are primarily infaunal species.

STUDY DESIGN

Sampling Sites

At each site, sampling stations were established to provide synoptic data on chemistry, toxicology, and biology. Systematic sampling was done at intertidal elevations or subtidal depths that were comparable from site to site. Three intertidal zones and one subtidal zone were sampled for biology. For chemistry, one additional subtidal zone was

FIGURE 1 - Examples of four habitat types in Stratified Random Sampling Program. Percentages are in terms of oiled PWS Shoreline.

sampled in the SRS program and one or two additional subtidal zones in the fixed-site program. The tide zones were defined as follows:

Tide Zone	Designation	Definition
Upper intertidal	UI	Mean high tide
Middle intertidal	MI	Mean tide level
Lower intertidal	LI	Mean lower low water (MLLW)
Subtidal	SB	3-m depth*
Shallow water	SW	3- to 10-m depth*, randomly selected
Deep water	DW	10- to 30-m depth*, randomly selected

(*relative to MLLW)

The upper intertidal zone was the area most affected by the spill, with its communities of plants and animals receiving the greatest exposure to oil. The middle intertidal zone included the upper part of the *Fucus gardneri* (rockweed) zone and reflects the effects of the spill on members of the rockweed plant and animal community. The lower intertidal and the subtidal zones were sampled to assess the extent and effects of downward transport of oil residues from higher tide zones. At each site, three sampling transects were established across these tide zones. In order to form a statistically valid link between exposure and effect, all samples taken in 1990 and 1991 for chemistry, toxicology, and biology at any given site were taken at one time by the same personnel.

Each habitat presented different sampling problems. Sediment samples for biology (infauna), hydrocarbon chemistry, and sediment toxicology were obtained where possible. Sediment samples were taken with a hand coring tool or a metal scoop, but only core samples were used for biological analyses. Sediment cores were taken at all subtidal sampling stations, including those at bedrock sites. The rationale for obtaining sediment core samples whenever possible was that animals living in a sedimentary environment are generally those at greatest risk from the effects of oil. At bedrock/rubble habitats, we took filter wipes for chemistry and surface scrape samples of plants and animals.

Mussels were also sampled, where present, for chemical analysis to assess the bioavailability of petroleum residues in the nearshore water column. Photographs were taken to document surface coverage by epibiota (mussels, barnacles, algae, etc.).

Stratified Random Sampling Program

Goals—The goals of the SRS component of the shoreline ecology program were (1) to establish and sample randomly chosen study sites stratified by habitat type and degree of initial oiling; (2) to measure hydrocarbon concentrations in intertidal and nearshore subtidal filter-wipe, sediment, and mussel samples; (3) to measure the toxicity of any petroleum residues in the sediments; (4) to measure the concentrations of key hydrocarbon compounds; (5) to measure the abundance of epibiota or infaunal species; and (6) to statistically compare the results of measurements made at oiled and unoiled sites to estimate the extent of recovery by the summer of 1990. Because bias was rigorously eliminated by the random site selection process, the conclusions drawn from comparisons of oiled and unoiled sites could be generalized to the spill zone as a whole.

Statistical design considerations—Statistical design consists of three interrelated components: treatment design, experimental design, and sampling design. Together, these determine the statistical power of the design, i.e., the ability to separate effects caused by oiling from effects caused by other factors, including natural variability (see the Discussion section). *Treatment design* (not to be confused with shoreline cleanup treatment) consists of the definition of initial oiling levels and the determination of physical variables that are taken into account prior to testing for an oiling effect. The use of initial oiling levels reported from shoreline surveys (Neff et al., Shoreline Conditions, this volume) reduced or eliminated bias in oiling comparisons. Cleanup effects are considered to be part of an overall spill effect (see the Discussion in Gilfillan et al., Part 3: Biology). Habitat type and tide zone are not "treatments" because data analyses are done within the levels of each of these factors. *Experimental design* consists of defining experimental units to which "treatments" are applied (sites), and the sampling units (transects). The objective is to minimize the "within treatment" variability in order to sharpen oiling comparisons. The error terms for the models are described in the Statistical Data Analysis section. *Sampling design* consists of determining the required number of sites and transects for making the oiling comparisons with acceptable power.

Stratification—To provide an unbiased basis for assessing recovery, sampling sites were stratified by habitat type and by initial oiling level. Figure 1 shows examples of the four major habitats found in the oiled area of Prince William Sound, and Table 1 gives the distribution of initial oiling levels among the four habitat types. These four habitats constitute more than 99% of the impact zone (Neff et al., Shoreline Conditions, this volume). Although soft-sediment environments were too rare in the oiled area to be included in the SRS, representative soft-sediment sites were included in the fixed-site program.

Shoreline data on initial oiling levels, physical characteristics, and environmental conditions are based on extensive shoreline surveys conducted in 1989 (Teal 1990; Neff e: al., Shoreline Conditions, this volume). These surveys were done by teams of biologists and geomorphologists in 1989 as part of the spill cleanup/response effort. The survey teams used the following classifications according to the width of shoreline oiling:

Unoiled	No oil observed
Very Light	< 1-m–wide band of oil
Light	1- to 3-m–wide band
Moderate	3- to 6-m–wide band
Heavy	>6-m–wide band

At the time when the shoreline ecology program was designed, the Light and Very Light oiling categories had not been separated; therefore, the Light oiling category in this paper includes both lightly and very lightly oiled sites.

The wave energy at a given site can have major ecological consequences. For this reason, in the SRS study, bedrock/rubble sites were stratified into "exposed" or "sheltered" on the basis of wave-exposure estimates (Neff et al., Shoreline Conditions, this volume). Although the broad range of actual wave exposures made it impractical to include more detailed categories, calculated wave energies for all SRS sites were included as a concomitant variable to remove the effect of wave energy on biological variables before testing for the effect of oiling.

TABLE 1—Percentages of oil-affected shorelines in Prince William Sound by habitat type and oiling level, based on shoreline survey data. The numbers of candidate segments available for random selection of study sites are shown in parentheses.

| Habitat Type | Percentage | | | Totals (%) |
	Heavy Oiling	Moderate Oiling	Light Oiling	
Exposed Bedrock	2.8 (159)	1.8 (49)	12.2 (493)	16.8
Sheltered Bedrock	7.5 (429)	7.3 (348)	41.8 (1352)	56.6
Boulder/Cobble	6.4 (362)	2.7 (100)	13.8 (1076)	22.9
Pebble/Gravel	1.1 (40)	0.4 (22)	2.2 (104)	3.7
Totals (%)	17.8	12.2	70.0	100% = 486 Miles

Study site selection—Information on oiling level, substrate type, and estimated wave-energy categories was stored in GIS map files (ARC/INFO®), which were merged into a single file containing each of these attributes. These GIS data were then used to break up the entire surveyed shoreline up into 100 m shoreline segments for each habitat/oiling level combination. Because pebble/gravel beaches tend to occur as smaller pocket beaches, the shoreline corresponding to this habitat was broken up into 60 meter segments to ensure a large number of candidate sites. A random number was assigned to each segment, and 16 lists of randomly ordered candidate sites were developed, corresponding to the 16 combinations of habitat types and oiling levels. The first four sites in each list were selected as replicates (subject to verification), making a total of 64 randomly selected sites. The numbers of candidate segments available in various habitat/oiling level categories are shown in Table 1. A certain number of sites given in Table 1 were not available for sampling due to the presence of human activity or eagle nests. Other sites were not available because they were too short in length or because of habitat misclassifications in the GIS database.

Each candidate site was visited in the field in the spring of 1990 to verify that the habitat type and segment length were correctly identified, and to make sure that there was no active eagle nest or human activity near the site. If a site failed to meet any one criterion, the next candidate site in the random list was visited. Using these objective criteria to remove sites from the list of candidate sites was the only practical way to eliminate bias in final site selection. Since relatively few sites would be reallocated to other SRS cells due to habitat classification, the effect of habitat misidentification on data analysis and conclusions would be minimal. At each site that met the criteria, a headstake with an identification tag was placed above the high-tide line at the approximate center of the segment. This headstake later served as the reference point for selecting three

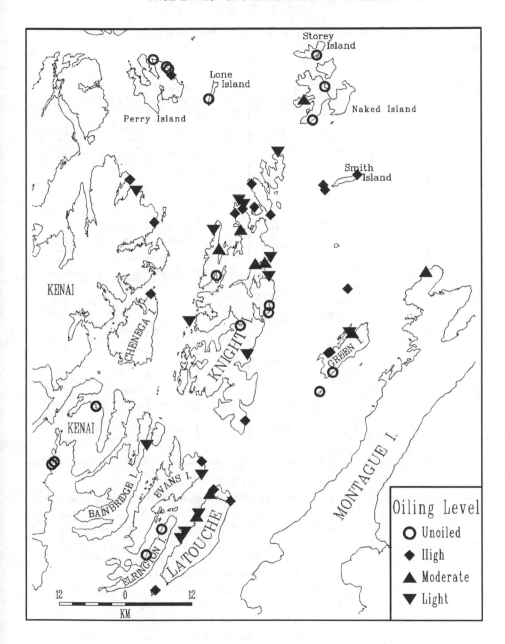

FIGURE 2—1990 SRS sites in Prince William Sound.

TABLE 2—SRS study site locations showing habitat, initial oiling level, site name, and shoreline segment code.

HABITAT TYPE	OILING LEVEL	SITE LOCATION	CODE	HABITAT TYPE	OILING LEVEL	SITE LOCATION	CODE
Exposed Bedrock/ Rubble	None	Marsha Bay	KN-214	Boulder/ Cobble	None	Green Island	GR-301
		Bass Harbor	NA-27			Knight Island	KN-551
		Perry Island	PR-11			Rua Cove	KN-213
		Perry Island	PR-09			Little Green I.	LG-50
		Perry Island	PR-09			Storey Island	ST-1
	Light	Evans Island	EV-36		Light	Green Island	GR-104
		Bay of Isles	KN-20			Latouche I.	LA-38
		Snug Harbor	KN-705			Latouche I.	LA-35
	Moderate	Montague Island	MN-4		Moderate	Bay of Isles	KN-18
		Montague Island	MN-4			Herring I.	KN-121
						Cabin Bay	NA-25
	Heavy	Applegate Rock	AP-38		Heavy	Green Island	GR-09`
		Ingot Island	IN-33			Green Island	GR-1A
		Latouche I. (NE)	LA-15			Knight Island	KN-103
		Little Smith I.	LS-49			Knight I. (SE)	KN-405
		Little Smith I.	LS-48			Latouche I. (NW)	LA-21
		Smith Island	SM-05				
Sheltered Bedrock/ Rubble	None	Elrington Island	ER-04	Pebble/ Gravel	None	Bainbridge Island	None
		Elrington Island	ER-01			Drier Bay.	KN-575
		Lone Island	LN-11			Port Bainbridge	None
		McPherson Bay.	NA-6			Whale Bay	WH-3
	Light	Knight Island	KN-102		Light		
		Knight Island	KN-501			Panhat Pt.	BA-1
		Bay of Isles	KN-207			Latouche Island	LA-38
		Passage Pt.	KN-108-9			Main Bay	MA-9
		Point Eleanor	EL-104				
		Squirrel Island	SL-1				
	Moderate	Bay of Isles	KN-19		Moderate	Green Island	GR-103
		Herring Bay	KN-132			Wilson Bay	LA-36
						Latouche Island	LA-21
	Heavy	Chenega Island	CH-10		Heavy	Disk Island	DI-67
		Danger Island	DA-1			Eshamy Bay	EB-1
		Herring Bay	KN-112			Evans Island	EV-12
		Perry Island	PR-07			Ingot Island	IN-24
						Latouche I. (W)	LA-21
						Main Bay	MA-4

sampling transects. Each verified site was fully documented so that field sampling crews could locate the site and the headstake. The locations of the 64 SRS sites are shown in Figure 2. Table 2 provides the habitat type, degree of initial oiling, and the shoreline segment code for each of these sites.

SRS matrix—The matrix of four habitats by four oiling levels, with each cell containing four replicates, constituted a reasonable compromise between project cost, the need to complete sampling within the short Alaskan summer, and the need for statistical power. Because the principal objective was to compare means within strata (habitat/oiling level) and not to obtain overall estimates, it was not statistically efficient or appropriate to use proportional sampling in this study. The final assignment of sites to the design matrix was not balanced, however. The SRS program was designed according to the best shoreline survey data available in early 1990. The original ARC/INFO® (GIS) data files used for this study underwent QA/QC in late 1990. The result was the reassignment of some shoreline segments from one oiling level to another oiling level within the same habitat classification. Although this resulted in a less-balanced design, there were still at least two sites per SRS matrix cell and, in some cases, as many as six sites. This resulted in either no change or an increase in the number of heavily oiled and reference sites and thus, the power to test for differences between heavily oiled and unoiled categories was unchanged for the sheltered-bedrock/rubble habitat and increased for the other three.

Table 3 shows the modified SRS design matrix, as well as the number of biological samples available for statistical analysis (by tide zone) in each habitat/oiling level combination. The goal of three samples per site (one from each transect) was not always attained, i.e., when sampling stations at bedrock sites contained sediment, or vice versa. Although samples appropriate to the local substrate were usually taken, each dataset used for statistical analysis could only include one type of sample: surface or sediment. As seen in Table 3, reduced replication occurred more often at bedrock sites than at sedimentary sites. In most cases, the number of samples used for chemical analyses was equal to the number of biological samples. Slight differences arose on some rocky sites, for example, when it was possible to collect sediment samples with a scoop but not with the coring tool.

TABLE 3—SRS design matrix with the number of replicate sites and biological samples within each category. Sample numbers (in parentheses) are given by tide zone in the following order (UI; MI; LI; SB); italicized numbers indicate biological samples from rock surfaces.

Habitat	Degree of Initial Oiling				Totals
	Heavy	Moderate	Light	None	
Exposed Bedrock					
Sites	6	2	3	5	16
Samples	*(18;17;17;18)*	*(6;6;6;6)*	*(6;5;4;8)*	*(15;15;15;15)*	*(45;43;42;47)*
Sheltered Bedrock					
Sites	4	2	6	4	16
Samples	*(12;12;11;12)*	*(6;6;5;6)*	*(18;17;12;18)*	*(9;9;5;12)*	*(45;44;33;48)*
Boulder/Cobble					
Sites	5	3	3	5	16
Samples	(15;15;15;10)	(9;9;9;9)	(9;9;9;9)	(14;15;15;13)	(47;48;48;41)
Pebble/Gravel					
Sites	6	3	3	4	16
Samples	(18;18;18;18)	(9;9;9;9)	(9;9;9;9)	(12;12;12;12)	(48;48;48;48)

Fixed-Site Sampling Program

Goals—The goals of the fixed-site study component of the shoreline ecology program were (1) to establish and sample study sites in areas of special interest that were not reflected in the SRS design; (2) to measure temporal trends in hydrocarbon concentrations in intertidal and nearshore subtidal samples; (3) to measure hydrocarbon-related toxicity in the sediments; (4) to measure the concentrations of key hydrocarbon compounds to assess weathering trends; (5) to measure the condition of infaunal species; and (6) to measure hydrocarbon concentrations in mussel samples as an estimate of the bioavailability of petroleum residues present at these sites. The sites were chosen to represent worst-case oiling conditions, as well as special habitats. Some of them had been designated as set-aside sites for scientific monitoring of oil impacts, natural cleaning, and recovery in the absence of cleanup operations. Measurements at the fixed sites were to be compared with conditions at appropriate reference sites. The fixed site data were not used to estimate shoreline recovery, as in the case of the SRS data. The fixed site program carried out over the period 1989-1991 was used to assess oil loss, oil weathering, and changes in exposure to mussels for a group of non-randomly chosen worst case locations and sites of environmental concerns.

Site selection—This study began in 1990 but adopted eight of a larger number of oiled locations sampled in 1989 by other investigators (Maki 1991). The 1989 sites had been selected in the field as shoreline oiling occurred, and reflected the desire to sample heavily oiled locations, areas of particular biological sensitivity (e.g., near salmon streams), and to achieve some replication of habitat types. Four fixed sites were added in 1990. They included two sites (one oiled, one reference) in soft-sediment habitats. The other ten fixed sites belonged to sedimentary (boulder/cobble and pebble/gravel) habitats represented in the SRS design. Therefore, we used unoiled SRS sites as a reference for these fixed sites. Table 4 lists the twelve fixed study sites and the times when they were sampled. Figure 3 shows their map locations.

The twelve fixed sites were sampled in 1990 and 1991 along with corresponding reference sites from the SRS program. The rest of the SRS sites were not sampled in 1991. All the fixed-site biological data taken in 1990 and 1991 were from sediment samples. Because the 1989 studies tended to focus on epibiota, the biological data available for comparisons with 1990 and 1991 were very limited. Samples of infauna

TABLE 4—SEP fixed-site program.

Habitat	Location	Site/Segment	Oiling	1989*	1990	1991
					Sampling	
Boulder/Cobble						
	Latouche	E11/LA15	Heavy		X	X
	Latouche (SA)	E11SA/LA15	Heavy	X	X	X
	Point Helen	SR07/KN405	Heavy	X	X	X
	Sleepy Bay	SL01/LA19	Heavy		X	X
	Reference	(5 SRS sites)	None		X	X**
Pebble/Gravel						
	Bay of Isles West	SRMB4/KN07	Light	X	X	X
	Herring Bay (SA)	SR03/KN5000	Moderate	X	X	X
	Mussel Beach	SR01N/EL13	Moderate	X	X	X
	Shelter Bay	SR06/EV21	Heavy	X	X	X
	Snug Harbor W (SA)	SR05/KN401	Heavy	X	X	X
	Snug Harbor E (SA) _	SR04/KN401	Heavy	X	X	X
	Reference	(4 SRS sites)	None		X	X
Soft Sediment						
	Bay of Isles Marsh	BI01/KN136	Heavy		X	X
	McClure Bay	MB01/ -	None		X	X
SA	Designates set-aside sites.					
_	Snug Harbor E (SA) is partially a sheltered bedrock site; however, only sediment samples were included in the analysis.					
*	Only chemistry samples from 1989 were included in the analyses for this program.					
**	Only 4 of the 5 boulder/cobble reference sites were sampled in 1991.					

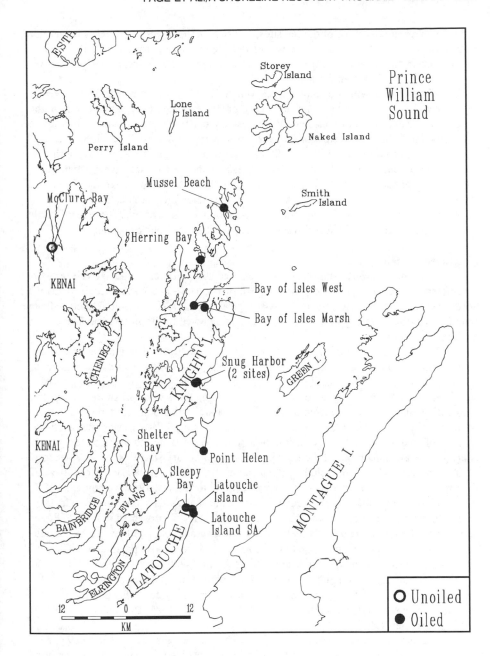

FIGURE 3—SEP fixed sites in Prince William Sound.

had been taken at only three of the ten sites, and only in the lower intertidal. Furthermore, no grain-size and TOC measurements were available for these cores and there was no synoptic chemistry or sediment toxicology sampling done. Therefore, no 1989 biology data were included in the analysis.

The soft-sediment site (Bay of Isles Marsh; KN136), which was added in 1990, together with its reference site (McClure Bay), presented a habitat type that is rare in the sound. It was a location of considerable interest and concern because similar sites studied in previous spills have been slow to recover (see Introduction: Past Oil-Spill Studies).

The other two sites added in 1990 are Latouche (E11) and Sleepy Bay, both heavily oiled boulder/cobble beaches. Both sites had undergone extensive mechanical cleanup to expose and remove subsurface oil in 1990, and to a lesser degree in 1991. Point Helen, another boulder/cobble site, underwent major "berm relocation" in 1991, when oiled sediments from the supratidal storm berm were spread over the upper intertidal zone. This occurred in July, a few weeks before the 1991 sampling program.

Measured Variables

Physical Variables—Physical variables used as covariates included two grain-size parameters (percentage sand and percentage silt/clay), TOC, and wave-energy. They were needed to help interpret the chemical, toxicological, and biological results. Each sediment sample taken for chemistry and toxicology was subsampled for grain size and TOC analyses.

Wave-energy is a key physical stress factor for plant and animal communities in Prince William Sound. A numerical wave model (e.g., Allen 1985) was used to estimate the relative wave exposure for all sites in the shoreline ecology program. Hindcasts of significant wave height and peak period were calculated for a point off shore each of the sites with wind-field data collected by three automatic weather stations deployed in the sound from September 1, 1989, to May 25, 1990. A history of wave-energy at each site was established by using the wave height and period to calculate the wave-crest unit energy at the breaking point of the shoaling waves. Summary statistics for wave-energy at each beach were calculated, including the mean and the value that was exceeded 10% of the time. The latter was used as a concomitant variable in the statistical analyses.

Chemical variables—A detailed list of chemical analytes determined in this program (mainly polycyclic aromatic hydrocarbons [PAH]) is presented in Part 2 (Boehm et al., this volume). PAH are relatively resistant to degradation, and they are associated with the toxicity of petroleum. The overall strategy was to choose parameters that would allow determination of the quantities and composition of petroleum residues, determination of background levels of petrogenic compounds, differentiation of background petrogenic compounds from *Exxon Valdez* oil residues, and quantification of biogenic and pyrogenic hydrocarbon residues (Boehm et al. 1981; Boehm et al. 1989; Sauer and Boehm 1991).

Sediment toxicology variables—Bioassay measurements were made to evaluate the acute toxicity of sediment samples to the petroleum-sensitive infaunal marine amphipod *Rhepoxynius abronius*. Five replicates of 20 healthy animals each were exposed for 10 days to 2 cm of test sediment in containers with clean sea water (see Boehm et al., Part 2:

Chemistry, this volume). Live and dead (or missing) animals were counted after the 10-day exposure period and the results expressed as percentage mortality.

Biological variables—The basic biological variables measured were abundances of animal species and the biomass of algal species in a sample. Details are given in Part 3 (Gilfillan, et al., this volume). Because both core and scrape samples had standard dimensions (10 cm diameter and 12.5 x 25 cm, respectively), these measurements reflect the density (per unit-area) of plants and animals on the shoreline. The following three widely used community parameters were calculated for the fauna at both sedimentary and bedrock/rubble sites:

- Total abundance: the total number of individuals present regardless of species
- Species richness: the number of individual species present
- Shannon diversity index: Shannon diversity is a community parameter defined by the expression: $\Sigma_i \log_2 p_i$, where p_i is the relative abundance of species i, expressed as a fraction of total abundance (Shannon 1948; Shannon and Weaver 1949). Diversity increases as the number of species increases and as the total number of individuals is more evenly distributed among species. High diversity is considered a positive attribute of a community.

At bedrock/rubble sites, the total biomass of each of the algae species present was determined in addition to the abundance of animal species. This was done because, for many species of algae, it is difficult to determine the number of individuals at a site. Biomass measurements also provide estimates of the amount of food available for herbivores and detritivores. Total algal biomass (all species combined) was used as a fourth community parameter on bedrock sites. Photographs were taken at each sampling station to estimate percentage cover for major epibiota.

FIELD METHODS

Layout of Study Sites

The sampling of shorelines included a three-step process: transect selection, sampling station selection, and acquisition of samples. Figure 4 is a schematic of the sampling layout at each site. The intertidal samples were of two basic types: sediment samples or surface samples. The former were taken when possible. Surface samples included filter wipes for chemistry and scrape samples for biology. All aspects of the field program were guided by written standard operating procedures that were tested in the field, modified, and finalized before sampling. In June 1990, before actual sampling began, the sampling teams conducted two full field rehearsals of all station selection and sampling methods. The three-year program involved the collection of thousands of samples, by more than 100 professional personnel, using both ships and helicopters for a total of over 2 500 person-days in the field.

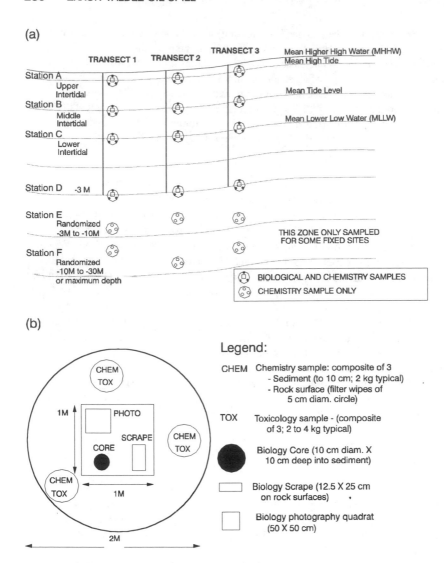

FIGURE 4—Typical layout for SEP sampling sites (a) and sampling stations (b).
Sampling points at each station were not rigidly fixed, but the search for suitable
substrate within the 2 m circle was guided by written standard operating
procedures. Either surface or sediment samples were taken at a given station.
(Drawings not to scale.)

Transect selection and location—The field procedures ensured that transects were well separated (20 to 30 m) and their locations selected in an unbiased manner. At each site, a headstake was placed near the center, where it remained through 1991. Three sampling transects were established perpendicular to the water line at each site. The center transect was randomly selected within ±15 m offset from the headstake, and two others were located 30 m on either side of the center transect (as little as 20 m for some pebble/gravel SRS sites and some fixed sites that were less than 100 m wide). Sites resampled in 1991 used the same transects as in 1990. Beach elevation profiles were surveyed along each center transect.

Station selection—As shown in Figure 4a, stations were sampled along each transect at three intertidal zones and two subtidal zones. Synoptic sampling for chemistry, toxicology, and biology was done in 1990 and 1991 in accordance with a consistent station layout (Figure 4b). During the 1989 fixed-site surveys, intertidal chemistry sampling stations were established along each transect on the basis of beach characteristics. Upper intertidal stations were just below the spring-tide debris line; middle intertidal stations were in the rockweed zone (if present) or mid-beach area; lower intertidal stations were at the low-tide line. In 1990, intertidal station locations were surveyed into position relative to MLLW. To avoid resampling at exactly the same spot, the stations were positioned to the right of the transects by 1 m during 1990, and to the left of the transects by 1 m in 1991.

Field Sampling

Sampling was conducted at each site in accordance with preplanned and written standard operating procedures by using a variety of well-tested techniques. For the SRS program, all sites for each habitat type were sampled within a 2-3 week period to minimize variability. The sampling plan was implemented by field managers who used written work plans and standard operating procedures as approved by the principal investigators. In addition, the principal investigators or their representatives supervised the actual field sampling and conducted the subsequent data analysis. Samples for chemistry were obtained at each station, biological samples at each intertidal station and the shallowest subtidal station; toxicology samples were obtained at selected tide zones along the center transect in 1989 and at all three transects in 1990 and 1991 (Figure 4).

Sediment samples for chemical analysis and toxicology were composited from sediments collected at three locations within a 2 m circle that defined the sampling station (Figure 4b). These samples were representative of surface sediments (0-10 cm). In addition, subsurface sediments (for chemical analysis only) were collected from the 10- to 60 cm depth interval when feasible. Filter-wipe samples were collected by wiping the rock surface with filter paper and solvent.

Sediment cores for biology were taken with a hand-held coring tube. Epibiota from rock surfaces were sampled in two stages: first, the macro-algae attached within the sampling quadrant were collected, then the remaining biota were scraped off the surface with hand tools.

Mussel samples (from 30 to 50 individuals) for tissue hydrocarbon analysis were obtained along each of the three transects when possible, preferably from within one of the three intertidal tide zones. If mussels were present only outside the area of the transects, samples were taken and the sampling areas noted on the site diagram. Photographs were taken of a 50-x-50 cm square at each intertidal station.

Sample Handling

Samples were labeled and immediately preserved or processed in the field as necessary. All sample labeling incorporated a bar-code system. Bar-code scanning provided an immediate database of samples collected, established a tracking system that followed the samples through all phases of custody transfer and analysis, and provided the basis for the tracking of data submissions. Custodial integrity of the samples was maintained by controlled-access storage and tamper-evidence seals on containers during shipment and custody transfers. All aspects of sample collection, tracking, and data logging were linked to the program's database, creating complete records of all steps in the process. All sample handling and chain-of-custody procedures were also explicitly documented in written standard operating procedures contained in the field manual.

Field Quality Assurance/Quality Control

The field quality-assurance program included written manuals and standard operating procedures for each step of the operation, training of field personnel, written procedures for establishing the need for, and making changes to, standard operating procedures in the field. Field quality-assurance/quality-control procedures included the collection of predetermined types of quality control samples, which included field blanks corresponding to each type of sample and procedure.

ANALYTICAL METHODS

To avoid repetition, the laboratory procedures for chemical and biological analyses and for measuring sediment toxicity are detailed elsewhere in their appropriate context. Chemical analytical methods and sediment bioassay procedures are described in other papers in this volume (Boehm et al., Part 2: Chemistry; Page et al., Hydrocarbon Sources). The biological analytical methods are described in Part 3: Biology (Gilfillan et al., this volume).

STATISTICAL DATA ANALYSIS

The goal of the statistical data analysis for this study was to detect oiling effects and quantify differences between reference sites and oiled SRS and fixed sites. SRS data were to be used to extrapolate findings to the sound as a whole for 1990, whereas fixed-site time-series data were to provide a basis for projecting observed trends into the future.

Overview of Approach

Traditionally, a limited number of dominant species and a few community-level indices, are investigated by using normal-theory models. In contrast, this study took a broad view of the shoreline biota by including many different species, and by using generalized linear models to analyze species count data. Important concomitant variables, such as wave exposure, grain size, and TOC, were quantified and included in the data analysis. These physical variables explained approximately as much of the biological variability measured at the SRS sites as did the oiling effect (Gilfillan et al., Part 3: Biology, this volume). Prior to selecting these concomitant variables, we ascertained that they were not strongly correlated with oiling.

Chemical data—Oil residues present in the spill zone were analyzed to test whether the geometric means of the analyte concentrations in a given oiled SRS cell were significantly different from unoiled reference. The analytes tested were the following sums of alkyl PAH that are generally associated with petroleum sources: $C_2+C_3+C_4$ naphthalenes, C_2+C_3 phenanthrenes, C_2+C_3 dibenzothiophenes, and C_2+C_3 chrysenes. For the fixed sites, the rate at which oil residues were disappearing through natural processes was estimated from fixed-site data assuming exponential decay. Sediment bioassay data were analyzed to determine whether petroleum residues had a toxic effect.

Biological data—Because many biological species are not distributed according to normal theory, a strategy was developed to accommodate other population distributions (Poisson, binomial, or negative binomial) before applying univariate statistical tests.

Examining each species separately does not provide an adequate analysis of the biological community as a whole. Therefore, we conducted two types of community level analyses: (1) univariate analysis of traditional community parameters: total abundance, species richness and diversity and (2) multivariate correspondence analysis of community structure, based on combinations of many species present in a sample. (Gilfillan et al., Part 3: Biology, this volume.)

Site and transect models—In conducting univariate tests to detect an oiling effect on a given chemical or biological variable, two different models were run. The object was to use the model with the greater power to detect differences. First a "site model" was run in which "among-site" variability was used to test for oiling effects. In addition, among-site variability was compared with "within-site" variability. If among-site variability was not statistically different, at a 0.05 significance level, from within-site variability, a "transect model" was used in which within-site variability and among-site variability were pooled and used to test for oiling effects. Because the study design separated transects by 20 to 30 m, it was often valid to treat observations from different transects as statistically independent.

The stringent requirement of an 0.05 significance level for rejection of the transect model in the tests described above was intentional, as was the wide separation of the transects. Conventional statistical practice in this instance would use significance levels of 0.1 or larger (Winer, 1971) for accepting the site model to avoid concluding that oiling effects exist when in fact they don't (Type I Error). By using more stringent significance levels (and consequently pooling variances more frequently), we nearly always reduced the Type II Error, i.e., we reduced the probability that oiling effects might go undetected. The practical consequence of this was that the transect model was used 80 percent of the time for the SRS study. Because there were three transects per site, the transect model effectively tripled the sample size compared to the site model, which combined with generally smaller estimates of error variability, increased the probability of detecting an oiling effect (power).

As a check of the method, these same criteria were applied to data from another study, one involving transects only a few meters apart. In that case, the site model was accepted every time because observations from the transects were not statistically independent, i.e., there was little transect to transect variability relative to site to site variability.

The rationale and implications of pooling are treated further in the Discussion section.

Detailed Statistical Procedures

Because the goals of the SRS and fixed site components of this study were different, details of the data analyses for each differed. This paper presents an overview of the methods used with details presented in papers 2 and 3 (Boehm et al., Part 2: Chemistry, this volume; Gilfillan et al., Part 3: Biology, this volume).

The strategies for analyzing the chemistry and biology datasets were similar. In both datasets, the data were first transformed as $\log_{10}(x+1)$, where x represents a species count or analyte concentration (usually expressed as parts per billion), or other data. Log-transformation is often applied to positively-skewed data that are inherently non-negative, to better approximate a normal distribution.

One-way analysis of covariance (ANCOVA) was carried out with initial oiling level as the factor related to the spill. Concomitant variables (i.e., natural site-specific factors) were fit before testing for oiling effect. Removing the effect of these variables eliminated some of the natural differences between oiled and reference sites. For core data, concomitant variables included percentage sand, percentage silt/clay, TOC, and wave-energy. For scrape and filter-wipe data from bedrock/rubble sites, the only appropriate concomitant variable used was wave-energy. In addition to testing for an overall oiling effect, Dunnett's test was performed in SuperANOVA (Abacus Software, Inc.) to compare individual oiling level means with the reference.

The residuals from each ANCOVA analysis were tested for normality by using a standard Shapiro-Wilks test. If the residuals were normally distributed (Shapiro-Wilks $P > 0.05$), the ANCOVA results were accepted. If the residuals were not normally distributed, tests for significant differences were carried out with GLIM (Generalized Linear Interactive Model: Numerical Algorithm Group, Inc.) by using either a Poisson, binomial, or a negative binomial distribution, as appropriate, for the residual variation of the response variable. In each of these distributions, the appropriate model (site model or transect model) was used to test for an overall oiling effect and individual comparisons of oiling level means to the reference.

Chemistry data analysis—The data analysis for the SRS chemistry followed the approach described above. If GLIM failed to converge for a given variable, site averages for this analyte were calculated over each tide zone to make the data more normal. The averages were then log-transformed and the ANCOVA/normality test/GLIM process was repeated. In some cases, site-averaged variables could not be analyzed, i.e., when there were too many zero values in the dataset. In these cases, tests for significant differences between means of affected and reference cells were performed by using nonparametric statistics (Wilcoxon/Kruskal-Wallace tests: JMP – SAS Institute, Inc.). This overall procedure ensured that the chemistry data were analyzed by the most powerful statistical method appropriate to the structure of the data.

Sediment toxicity data analysis—The results of the sediment toxicity bioassays were reported in terms of percentage survival of a standard population of test animals. Tests for significant differences in sediment toxicity values were done with the GLIM binomial model. Because the test animal, *Rhepoxynius abronius,* a petroleum-sensitive infaunal marine amphipod, is very sensitive to sediment grain size (DeWitt et al. 1988; Spies 1989), percentage sand and percentage silt/clay were used as concomitant variables in the data analysis.

Biology data analysis—Biological data analyses included univariate analysis of species counts, algal biomass, and community parameters, as well as multivariate analysis of community structure. The univariate analysis of the biological data followed an ANCOVA/GLIM procedure similar to that described above for the chemical data. GLIM models will fail to converge if too many zeros are present in a dataset. In particular, the models were unstable and failed frequently for species that occurred in less than 20% of the samples. Therefore, the analysis was limited to species that were present in at least 20% of the samples in a given dataset. If GLIM still failed to converge, that species was not analyzed further. Additional details are described in Part 3: Biology (Gilfillan et al., this volume).

Multivariate analyses were conducted to identify linear combinations of species abundances that showed the strongest correlation with oiling level. One of the best ways to show associations within datasets is to use ordination methods (Gilfillan et al. 1991). Ordination arranges samples along statistical axes that are defined in terms of species composition. Samples that are similar in composition will lie close together in the statistical space defined by these axes.

De-trended partial canonical correspondence analysis (Ter Braak 1986; 1987) was the ordination method used to analyze the biology data. This procedure can be applied to non-normally distributed data and was used to maximally differentiate between oiled and unoiled sites, and to assess the degree of similarity or dissimilarity in species composition between oiled and reference sites. Whereas analysis of covariance makes comparisons for one response variable at a time, correspondence analysis makes use of many variables simultaneously. Because correspondence analysis is sensitive to the random occurrence of rare species, it was necessary to remove from the datasets all those species that occurred in less than 20% of the samples (consistent with the ANCOVA/GLIM models). This and other aspects of the method are discussed in detail in Part 3: Biology (Gilfillan et al., this volume).

DISCUSSION

The following discussion focuses on topics that are germane to the design and methodology used in the shoreline ecology program. Specifically, it addresses (1) the two-pronged study design, combining SRS and fixed-site components; (2) the question of statistical power to detect an oiling effect; and (3) the statistical models that were used in a synergistic manner to interpret the data. For discussions of results, refer to Part 2: Chemistry and Toxicology (Boehm et al., this volume) and Part 3: Biology (Gilfillan et al., this volume).

Study Design

The study design described here involved a combined strategy of chemical, ecological, and toxicological measurements on samples taken in the field. The sampling plan was designed to meet the requirements of the information goals and the data analysis plan described in the preceding section. The two key elements of the sampling plan were the 1990 SRS program and the 1989-1991 fixed-site program. The SRS program provided data that enabled a generalized estimate of ecological recovery (Gilfillan et al., Part 3: Biology, this volume) and the state of petroleum residues from the spill (Boehm et al., Part 2: Chemistry, this volume) to be made for 1990. Because factors other than oiling can affect biological community structure, sediment PAH profiles, and sediment bioassay results, the study design included the measurement of covariates, such as wave exposure, sediment grain size, and sediment organic carbon content.

In the data analysis plan, the null hypothesis of no significant difference among mean population densities of individual species or of community structure parameters for oiling levels was tested for oiled *vs.* unoiled SRS cells within each habitat and tide zone. These results were used to estimate recovery within each habitat/tide zone/oiling level stratum. Overall recovery of the spill area was estimated by combining the estimates for recovery of individual strata weighted by the length of the shoreline belonging to each particular SRS habitat/oiling level cell. This plan was successfully used to quantify positive and negative differences in the chemical and biological parameters measured for oiled and unoiled sites to estimate recovery in 1990 using the SRS results. Recovery trends for the chemical parameters were projected into the future by using the results from the non randomly chosen time-series sites.

An important part of the overall study plan was sediment bioassay measurements made on sediment toxicology samples taken concurrently with the chemical and biological samples in order to give an exposure/effect link and to aid in the interpretation of the chemistry and biology data. Because it is possible to measure PAH at levels far below those associated with toxic effects (e.g., see Long and Morgan 1990), sediment bioassay measurements, coupled with biological species counts, are useful in determining whether petroleum residues are acting as a toxicant or as a carbon source for microorganisms (e.g., Spies et al. 1988). Statistical comparisons of bioassay results for sediments from oiled versus unoiled SRS sites permit generalizations to be made concerning any remaining toxic effects of spill residues (see Boehm et al., this volume).

Statistical Power

This section discusses statistical power and the strategies used to increase the power to detect oiling effects within the constraints of the sampling effort.

Strategies to increase power—Within the context of this study, power is the probability of detecting an oiling effect. Power depends on the significance level ($\mathcal{D}$), the natural variability (noise), the magnitude of effects (signal), and the sample size (n). The sampling effort (the number of sites and transects) should ensure sufficient power to detect an effect of ecological importance. A reasonable strategy is to ensure that the effect of interest, φ, will be detected if it is comparable to, or greater than, the (unexplained) natural variation, $\bullet$ (Skalski 1994).

Figure 5 is a plot of the power as a function of the signal-to-noise ratio ($\varphi/\bullet$) for various sample sizes using univariate normal theory. For any given sample size, the power increases from $\mathscr{O}$ (the significance level) to 1, when $\varphi/\bullet$ increases from 0 to sufficiently large values. In the absence of an oiling effect, the probability that an effect will be "detected" by random chance is equal to $\mathscr{O}$, in this case 0.05. The power can be increased if the sample size is increased or if the unexplained variability is reduced. Both methods were used in the SRS analysis.

To increase the ability to detect an oiling effect, equal weight was given to sites in all oiling levels even though lightly oiled sites were most common (Table 1). Proportional sampling would have reduced the probability of finding oiling effects since 70% of the impacted sites were lightly oiled. Sampling only heavily oiled sites would have optimized the ability to detect an oiling effect but would have prevented the ability to draw inferences for the 82.2% of the impacted sites that were not heavily oiled (Table 1). Equal allocation of sites among oiling levels was a design strategy to balance the ability to detect an oiling effect with the ability to draw broader inferences (see Skalski 1994). Moreover, the fixed site component of the present study ensured that heavily oiled sites would be studied more intensively even though they were a minority of the total body of oiled sites.

A balance was also sought in determining the number of sites (replicates) versus the number of transects per site (pseudo-replicates). Although it would have been desirable to have additional sites for each habitat, the required sampling effort precluded that possibility given the short Alaskan summer. Three widely separated transects were selected for each site in the hope that transect-to-transect variability, pooled with site-to-site variability, could be used to represent error variability. The advantage of pooling is two-fold: not only is the sample size (n) increased from 16 to 48, but also the estimate of residual variability ($\bullet$) is usually reduced. Both of these effects of pooling increase the power. We favored the transect model by using a stringent criterion for rejecting it, even though more liberal criteria are often recommended (Winer 1971). This strategy leads to liberal use of the transect model and increases the probability of finding an oiling effect, whether or not an oiling effect exists.

The power was also increased by removing the effects of concomitant variables (wave-energy, grain size, and TOC) prior to testing the oiling effect. Again, the effect is to reduce the estimate of unexplained variation and, thus, to increase the power. Although partial confounding between the physical variables and oiling could mask an oiling effect, this was not a serious problem here; the physical variables were not strongly correlated with oiling level.

The power may not be high, even after making these adjustments to the analysis. The result could be an overly optimistic picture of recovery because recovery is operationally defined in terms of establishing no difference from reference. This can be addressed in two ways: the significance ($\mathscr{O}$) can be increased or the estimate of recovery can be viewed as an upper limit. The first approach was used in a major wildlife study (Day et al., this volume), in which testing was done sequentially at significance levels of

0.05, 0.10, and 0.20. In this study, we used the commonly accepted significance level of 0.05 in hypothesis testing of community parameters. Therefore, the recovery estimate based on community parameter analyses is viewed as an upper limit. A related lower-limit estimate of recovery was obtained via correspondence analysis of community structure (Gilfillan et al., Part 3: Biology, this volume).

Reallocation of study sites—The next issue concerns the statistical effect on power of reallocating sites among oiling levels. The overall effect of site reallocation on the data analyses and conclusions was minimal. Site reallocation was the only practical way to minimize bias in site selection based on the use of GIS data.

The reallocation of sites was uneven, with the number of rocky sites in the various oiling levels becoming the most unequal (Table 3). Certain comparisons, specifically those for exposed and sheltered bedrock shores with moderate oiling, had reduced power. On the other hand, the most important comparisons for detecting an oiling effect, those between reference and heavily oiled sites, generally had increased numbers of sites and increased power.

Generally, reallocating sites to different oiling levels had little effect on power for either the site or the transect models. The degrees of freedom for testing the overall oiling effect remained unchanged for both models. Power increased slightly for Dunnett's comparisons because the number of reference sites increased by one for two of the four substrate types, which moved the site allocation toward the optimum for this test (Dunnett 1955; Hochberg and Tamhane 1987).

Assessment of power—Finally, we used JMP (SAS Institute, Inc.) for *a posteriori* estimates of power for detecting oiling effects in the biological data presented in Part 3: Biology (Gilfillan et al., Part 3: Biology, this volume). A limitation is that many of the tests used non-normal models and little is known about power calculations for these generalized models. However, power calculations can be made for normal models, and approximations can be obtained for non-normal models by using approximate F-test statistics.

The oiling signal was weak relative to the natural background variability, even after we adjusted for the concomitant variables. Estimates of the signal-to-noise ratio based on the community parameter analyses for normal-theory models ranged from near 0 to 0.8 for the various substrates and tide zones. If we compare this with Figure 5, the power to detect an oiling effect would range from 0.05 to near 1 for the transect models ($n = 48$). (Only one community-level analysis used the site model.) The average power was low: 0.34 for species richness, 0.37 for abundance, and 0.49 for Shannon diversity (Gilfillan et al., Part 3: Biology, this volume). However, had the oiling effect been close to the natural variability, the power would have been near 1.

Statistical Models

The modeling strategy used in this program provided a comprehensive analysis of the chemistry, toxicology, and biology data by using advanced statistical methodologies. Weighting based on sampling fraction was not part of the statistical model because the sampled sites in each SRS cell were a small fraction of a large number of possible candidate sites (see Table 3), i.e., the analysis was not based on a finite sampling model.

Furthermore, weighting would have emphasized lightly oiled sites (70% of the total) thus reducing the power to detect oiling effects for heavy and moderately oiled sites.

The chemistry data consisted of relatively few variables (mainly PAH components). The major problem in analyzing these variables was the spike of values at zero, mixed with positively skewed values. An adequate distribution was seldom found, often resulting in the use of nonparametric techniques.

Species abundance data were difficult to model because of the sporadic species counts. Therefore, classical statistical methods like normal-theory linear models and ordination techniques were generally inappropriate. In similar situations, many researchers have restricted their analyses to the most abundant species. The goal of this study was to assess recovery broadly by analyzing as many species as possible.

Abundances can often be modeled approximately by the log-normal, Poisson, binomial, or negative binomial probability distributions (Elliott 1971). Therefore, a decision tree was developed that sought the most appropriate model. If log-normality of the residuals was not supported, a Poisson model was fit, assuming tentatively that species abundances are "random." This model was then tested for lack of fit. If the Poisson assumption was rejected, either a binomial or negative binomial model was fit, depending on whether the abundances were under- or over-dispersed. The combination of linear (log) normal-theory models and generalized linear non-normal models allowed a large number of species to be analyzed. Most species present in 20% or more of the samples were analyzed. The models usually did not work on rare species, i.e., those present in less than 20% of the samples. Otherwise, these models performed very well and extended the range of analyzable species considerably.

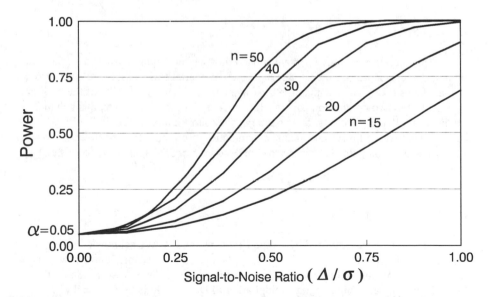

FIGURE 5—Plot of power for testing the oiling effect as a function of signal-to-noise ratio (Δ/σ) and sample size (n).

The univariate models of individual species did not give a complete picture because species assemblages were not assessed. Therefore, additional approaches were used in Part 3: Biology (Gilfillan et al., this volume): univariate analyses of community parameter variables and correspondence analysis. Both methods allowed an overall community assessment. The community parameter analysis followed the same strategy as the individual species abundances, but included all species present.

Correspondence analysis gave a quantitative and visual assessment of the state of recovery. The first two ordination axes were constrained to maximally separate samples on the basis of oiling level, after adjusting for concomitant variables. This approach allowed a conservative estimate of recovery to be developed. The method was unstable for rare species, as discussed in Part 3: Biology (Gilfillan et al., this volume), and thus a 20% cut was used, as for the univariate species analyses.

The statistical methodologies used here allowed a relatively complete assessment of shoreline recovery. Overall, the analytical strategy was successful by using both normal and non-normal models, as well as correspondence analysis. This methodology approached the limits of what is feasible with currently available techniques. In fact, results of the analyses tended to become unstable when the rare-species cutoff was reduced below 20%. Pushing the analysis further would probably require complex nonlinear models based on mixtures of distributions, e.g., the log-normal with the binomial, or the Poisson with the binomial.

Interested scientists should consult with the authors for information on specific datasets. Because a number of additional technical papers based on these data are in progress, the entire dataset for all parts of the program are not yet available.

CONCLUSION

This shoreline ecology program applied the "sediment quality triad" approach, combining chemical, toxicological, and biological measurements to assess recovery from oil-spill effects (Long and Chapman 1985; Chapman et al. 1991). Results of the program are described in two companion papers (Boehm et al., Part 2: Chemistry, this volume; Gilfillan et al., Part 3: Biology, this volume). They show evidence, in 1990, of a substantial recovery of plant and animal communities throughout the affected zone, as well as a rapid and ongoing decrease in petroleum residues from the spill at the fixed study sites.

ACKNOWLEDGMENTS

This study was supported by Exxon Company, U.S.A. We acknowledge the participation of Ted Sauer, Sandra Tate, Tony Parkin, Larry LeBlanc, John Brown, and many others of Arthur D. Little; Cecile Kresja of Bowdoin College; David Pillard of ENSR Consulting and Engineering; Keith Parker of Data Analysis Group; Cathy McPherson of EVS Consulting and Lane Cameron, Bob Cimberg and others from Dames & Moore.

REFERENCES

Allen, J.R.L. *Physical Sedimentology*. London: George, Allen and Unwin Publishers; 272 pages; 1985.

Boehm, P. D., D. L. Fiest, and A. Elskus. "Comparative Weathering Patterns of Hydrocarbons From the *Amoco Cadiz* Oil Spill Observed at a Variety of Coastal Environments." *in:* Amoco Cadiz, *Consequences d'une Pollution Accidentelle par les Hydrocarbures; Fates and Effects of the Oil Spill.* Paris: Centre National Pour l'Exploitation des Oceans; 159-173; 1981.

Boehm, P. D., J. S. Brown, and T. C. Sauer. "Physical and Chemical Characterization of San Joaquin Valley Crude Oil." Final Report prepared for ENTRIX, Inc., Walnut Creek, CA; 1989.

Chan, G.L. "A Study of The Effects of the San Francisco Oil Spill on Marine Life. Part II. Recruitment." *in: Proceedings of the 1975 Oil Spill Conference.* Environmental Protection Agency/American Petroleum Institute/United States Coast Guard; 457-461; 1975.

Chapman, P. M., E. A. Power, R. N. Dexter, and H. B. Andersen. "Evaluation of Effects Associated With an Oil Platform, Using the Sediment Quality Triad." *Environmental Toxicology and Chemistry.* 10:407-424; 1991.

Chasse, C. "The Ecological Impact on and Near Shores by the *Amoco Cadiz* Oil Spill." *Marine Pollution Bulletin.* 9:298-301; 1978.

DeWitt, T. H., G. R. Ditsworth, and R. C. Swartz. "Effects of Natural Sediment Features on Survival of the Phoxocephalid Amphipod, *Rhepoxynius abronius*." *Marine Environmental Research.* 25:99-124; 1988.

Dunnett, C.W. "Multiple Comparison Procedures for Comparing Several Treatments and a Control." *Journal of the American Statistical Association.* 50:1096-1121; 1955.

Elliott, J.M. Some Methods for the Statistical Analysis of Samples of Benthic Invertebrates. Freshwater Biological Association, Scientific Publication No. 25; 1971.

Gilfillan, E.S., S.A. Hanson, D.S. Page, D.W. Mayo, J. Cooley, J. Chalfant, T. Archambeault, A. West, and J.C. Harshbarger. Final Report: Comprehensive Study of Petroleum Hydrocarbons in the Marine Environment at Long Cove, Searsport Maine--An Ecological, Physiological, Chemical and Histopathological Survey. Maine Department of Environmental Protection Contract #906439. 196 pages; 1977.

Gilfillan, E.S., D.S. Page, and J.C. Foster. "Tidal Area Dispersant Project: Fate and Effects of Chemically Dispersed Oil in the Nearshore Benthic Environment." *American Petroleum Institute Publication No. 4440.* Washington, DC; 215 pages; 1986.

Gilfillan, E.S., D.S. Page, C.M. Krejsa, S.A. Hanson, J.C. Foster, G.C. Trussell, and B.S. Whalon. "Use of Ordination Techniques to Follow Community Succession from Oil Impact to Recovery in the Field." *Chemistry and Ecology.* 5: 85-97; 1991.

Glemarec, M. and E. Hussenot. "Reponses des Peuplements Subtidaux a la Perturbation Cree par l' *Amoco Cadiz* dans les Abers Benoit et Wrac'h." *in: Ecological Study of the* Amoco Cadiz *Oil Spill, Report of the NOAA-CNEXO Joint Sea Commission, Part II, Biological Studies of the* Amoco Cadiz *Oil Spill.* M. Marchand (ed.) National Oceanic and Atmospheric Administration; Washington, DC; 191-204; 1982.

Goddard, J. "Aerial Census of Black Rhinoceros Using Stratified Random Sampling." *East African Wildlife Journal.* 7:105-114; 1969.

Grant, W.S. "High Intertidal Community Organization on a Rocky Headland in Maine, USA." *Marine Biology.* 44(1):15-26; 1977.

Grassle, J. F., H. L. Sanders, R. R. Hessler, G. T. Rowe, and T. McLellan. "Pattern and Zonation: A Study of the Bathyl Megafauna Using the Research Submersible Alvin." *Deep-Sea Research.* 22:457-481; 1975.

Haven, S. B. "Effects of Land Level Changes on Intertidal Invertebrates with Discussion of Postearthquake Ecological Succession." *in: The Great Alaska Earthquake of 1964: Biology.* Publication No. 160. National Academy of Science; Washington, DC; 82-106; 1971.

Hochberg, Y. and A.C. Tamhane. *Multiple Comparison Procedures.* New York: Wiley; 450 pages; 1987.

Jolly, G. M. and I. Hampton. "A Stratified Random Transect Design for Acoustic Surveys of Fish Stocks." *Canadian Journal of Fisheries and Aquatic Science.* 47:1282-1291; 1990.

Long, E. R. and P. M. Chapman. "A Sediment Quality Triad: Measures of Sediment Contamination, Toxicity, and Infaunal Community Composition in Puget Sound." *Marine Pollution Bulletin.* 16:405-415; 1985.

Long, E. R. and L. G. Morgan. "The Potential for Biological Effects of Sediment-sorbed Contaminants Tested in the National Status and Trends Program." *NOAA Technical Memorandum NOS OMA 52.* National Oceanic and Atmospheric Administration, U.S. Department of Commerce, Rockville, MD; 175 pages + appendices; 1990.

Maki, A. "The *Exxon Valdez* Oil Spill: Initial Environmental Impact Assessment." *Environmental Science and Technology.* 25:24-29; 1991.

Markham, J.W. and I. M. Munda. "Algal Recolonization in the Rocky Eulittoral at Helgoland, Germany." *Aquatic Botany.* 9(1):33-72; 1980.

McGuiness, K.A. "Disturbance and Organisms on Boulders I. Patterns in the Environment and the Community." *Oecologica.* 71(3):409-419; 1987a.

McGuiness, K.A. "Disturbance and Organisms on Boulders II. Causes of Patterns in Diversity and Abundance." *Oecologica* . 71(3):420-430; 1987b.

Mielke, J. E. "Oil in the Ocean: The Short- and Long-Term Impacts of a Spill." *90-356 SPR.* Congressional Research Service, The Library of Congress, Washington, DC; 34 pages; 1990.

Murray, S.N. and M. H. Horn. "Seasonal Dynamics of Macrophyte Populations from an Eastern North Pacific Rocky Intertidal Habitat." *Botanica Marina.* 32:457-473; 1989.

National Research Council. *Oil in the Sea: Inputs, Fates, and Effects.* Washington, DC: National Academy Press; 601 pages; 1985.

Plafker, G. "Tectonic Deformation Associated with the 1964 Alaska Earthquake." *Science.* 148:1675-1687; 1965.

Russell, H. J. "Use of a Commercial Dredge to Estimate a Hardshell Clam Population by Stratified Random Sampling." *Journal of the Fisheries Research Board of Canada.* 29:1731-1735; 1972.

Sauer, T.C. and P. D. Boehm. "The Use of Defensible Analytical Chemical Measurements for Oil Spill Natural Resource Damage Assessment." *in: Proceedings of the 1991 Oil Spill Conference.* American Petroleum Institute, Washington, DC. 363-369; 1991.

Sanders, H. L., J. F. Grassle, G. R. Hampson, L. S. Morse, S. Garner-Price, and C. C. Jones. "Anatomy of an Oil Spill: Long Term Effects from the Grounding of the Barge *Florida* off West Falmouth, Massachusetts." *Journal of Marine Research.* 38:265-380; 1980.

Shannon, C.E. "The Mathematical Theory of Communication." *Bell System Technical Journal.* 27: 379-623; 1948.

Shannon, C.E. and W. Weaver. *The Mathematical Theory of Communication.* Urbana, IL: University of Illinois Press; 1949.

Skalski, J. R. "Statistical Considerations in the Design and Analysis of Oil Spill Assessment Studies." *Journal of Environmental Management.*. Submitted for publication 1994.

Southward, A.J. and E. C. Southward. "Recolonization of Rocky Shores in Cornwall After Use of Toxic Dispersants to Clean up the *Torrey Canyon* Spill." *Journal of the Fisheries Research Board of Canada.* 35:682-706; 1978.

Spies, R.B. "Sediment Bioassays, Chemical Contaminants and Benthic Ecology: New Insights or just Muddy Water?" *Marine Environmental Research.* 27:73-75; 1989.

Spies, R. B., D. D. Hardin, and J. P. Toal. "Organic Enrichment or Toxicity? A Comparison of the Effects of Kelp and Crude Oil in Sediments on the Colonization and Growth of Benthic Infauna." *Journal of Experimental Marine Biology and Ecology.* 124:261-282; 1988.

St. Jaques, P. and D. Gagnon. "The Forest Vegetation of the Northwest Section of the St. Lawrence River Valley, Quebec, Canada." *Canadian Journal of Botany.* 66: 793-804; 1988.

Teal, A. R. "Shoreline Cleanup Following the *Exxon Valdez* Spill—The Decision Process for Cleanup Operations." *Proceedings of the 13th Arctic and Marine Oilspill Program (AMOP) Technical Seminar, June 6-8, Edmonton.* 422-429; 1990.

Ter Braak, C. J. F. "Canonical Correspondence Analysis: A New Eigenvector Technique for Multivariate Direct Gradient Analysis." *Ecology.* 67:1167-1179; 1986.

Ter Braak, C. J. F. "The Analysis of Vegetation-Environment Relationships by Canonical Correspondence Analysis." *Vegetatio.* 69:69-77; 1987.

Thomas, M. L. H. "Comparison of Oiled and Unoiled Intertidal Communities in Chedabucto Bay, Nova Scotia." *Journal of the Fisheries Research Board of Canada.* 35:707-716; 1978.

U. S. Code of Federal Regulations. 43 C.F.R. part 11, as amended by 53 Federal Register 5166 (February 22, 1988) and 53 Federal Register 9769 (March 25, 1988): §11.60-11.73; 1987.

Winer, B.J. *Statistical Principles in Experimental Design.* New York: McGraw Hill; 1971.

York, A. E. and P. Kozloff. "On the Estimation of Northern Fur Seal *Callorhinus ursinus* Pups Born on St. Paul Island, Alaska, USA." *US National Marine Fisheries Service Bulletin.* 85:367-376; 1987.

Lyman L. McDonald[1], Wallace P. Erickson[1], and M. Dale Strickland[1]

SURVEY DESIGN, STATISTICAL ANALYSIS, AND BASIS FOR STATISTICAL INFERENCES IN COASTAL HABITAT INJURY ASSESSMENT: EXXON VALDEZ OIL SPILL

REFERENCE: McDonald, L. L., Erickson, W. P., and Strickland, M. D., "Survey Design, Statistical Analysis, and Basis for Statistical Inferences in Coastal Habitat Injury Assessment: Exxon Valdez Oil Spill," Exxon Valdez Oil Spill: Fate and Effects in Alaskan Waters, ASTM STP 1219, Peter G. Wells, James N. Butler, and Jane S. Hughes, Eds., American Society for Testing and Materials, Philadelphia, 1995.

ABSTRACT: The objective of the Coastal Habitat Injury Assessment study was to document and quantify injury to biota of the shallow subtidal, intertidal, and supratidal zones throughout the shoreline affected by oil or cleanup activity associated with the *Exxon Valdez* oil spill. The results of these studies were to be used to support the Trustee's Type B Natural Resource Damage Assessment under the Comprehensive Environmental Response, Compensation, and Liability Act of 1980 (CERCLA). A probability based stratified random sample of shoreline segments was selected with probability proportional to size from each of 15 strata (5 habitat types crossed with 3 levels of potential oil impact) based on those data available in July, 1989. Three study regions were used: Prince William Sound, Cook Inlet/Kenai Peninsula, and Kodiak/Alaska Peninsula. A Geographic Information System was utilized to combine oiling and habitat data and to select the probability sample of study sites. Quasi-experiments were conducted where randomly selected oiled sites were compared to matched reference sites. Two levels of statistical inferences, philosophical bases, and limitations are discussed and illustrated with example data from the resulting studies.

KEYWORDS: damage assessment, injury assessment, meta-analysis, Fisher's procedure, Stouffer's procedure, oil spill, subtidal, intertidal, supratidal, Prince William Sound, natural resource damage assessment, CERCLA, NRDA

The Coastal Habitat Injury Assessment (CHIA) was designed to document and quantify injury to biological resources within the supratidal, intertidal, and shallow subtidal zones affected by the *Exxon Valdez* oil spill/cleanup (EVOS). The results of these studies were to be used to support the Trustee's Type B Natural Resource Damage Assessment (NRDA) under the Comprehensive Environmental Response, Compensation, and Liability Act of 1980 (CERCLA). To quantify injury for the entire shoreline habitat affected by the spill/cleanup, a probability based sample of shoreline segments within the universe of

---

[1]Senior Biometrician, Biometrician, and Senior Ecologist respectively, WEST, Inc., 1402 South Greeley Highway, Cheyenne, WY 82007.

potentially oiled shoreline was needed.   Based on data available in
July, 1989, a Geographic Information System (GIS) was utilized to
combine oiling and shoreline habitat classification data to define the
universe of potential affected segments (sites).   Because of the great
extent of the oil spill, three study regions were identified: Prince
William Sound (PWS), Cook Inlet-Kenai Peninsula (CIK), and Kodiak-Alaska
Peninsula (KAP) (Figure 1).   The GIS was employed to select a stratified
random sample of study sites for study beginning in the fall of 1989.

      To counter problems with high intra-strata variation in the
original 1989 study design, accessible moderate to heavily oiled sites
selected in the stratified random sample were retained for the
supratidal-intertidal study (Sundberg et al. 1993).   Each oiled site was
matched with a reference site on the basis of physical characteristics
of the oiled sites.   Biota of the oiled and reference pairs were
subsampled by the supratidal-intertidal survey crews using standard
protocols.   The shallow subtidal study was completely redesigned using a
stratification independent of the supratidal-intertidal surveys.

      Two levels of statistical inferences and their philosophical bases
are discussed and illustrated with example data from the resulting
studies.   Both levels use techniques from the emerging field of "meta-
analysis".   The first level relies on subsampling of sites and restricts
statistical inferences to the observed differences (or mean difference)
between specific pairs of matched oiled and reference sites.   In this
level, no statistical inferences were made to the broader set of oiled
sites.   Fisher's procedure for combining results of independent
experiments (Steel and Torrie 1980; Folks 1984) was used for this level
of analysis.

      For the second and more important level, another technique from
meta-analysis was used to draw inferences to the universe of oiled (and
accessible) sites.   A generalization of Stouffer's meta-analysis
procedure by Liptak (Folks 1984) which utilized the initial unequal
inclusion probabilities was used to make inductive statistical
inferences to the universe of moderate-heavily oiled (accessible) sites.

FIELD METHODS

Site Selection Procedures

      The GIS data layers used for definition of the sampling universe
included: 1) the mean high high water shoreline digitized from U.S.
Geological Survey 1:63,360 quadrangles in the spill-affected area, 2)
digitized Environmental Sensitivity Index maps (Hayes and Ruby 1979; RPI
1983A, 1983B, 1985, 1986) which classified the shoreline into nineteen
geomorphologic types, and 3) digitized Oil Spill Impact maps (ADEC 1989)
which classified the shoreline by degrees of oiling as of July 1989.
The shoreline was divided into sites (arcs) ranging in length from 100
to 600 meters.   Arcs less than 100 meters were eliminated from the GIS
before sample sites were selected because they were judged to be too
small to allow for the required number of transects and study plots for
multiple years of destructive data collection.   Arc lengths were limited
to 600 meters to ensure that the study site could be subsampled
efficiently during a low tide event.   Each arc was then given a unique
identification number (site number) in the GIS.   The three degrees of
oiling originally utilized for site selection included moderate to
heavily oiled, very light to lightly oiled, and non-oiled.

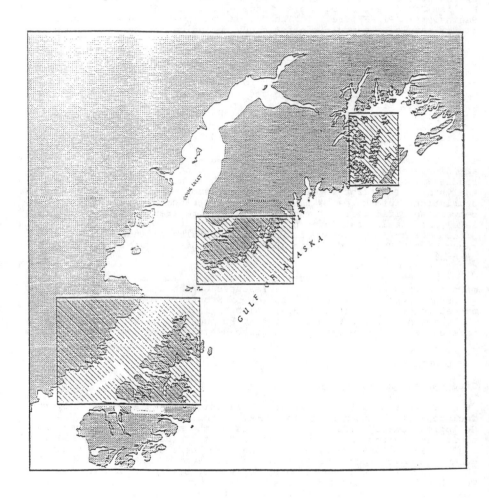

Figure 1--Map showing the locations of the three regions sampled during this study. The upper right shaded region represents the Prince William Sound (PWS) region, the middle shaded region represents the Cook Inlet-Kenai Peninsula (CIK) region, and the lower left shaded region represents the Kodiak Island-Alaska Peninsula (KAP) region. Map produced by ADNR, Land Records Information Section, Technical Services 3.

The various geomorphologic types were combined into five habitat types: exposed rocky, fine textured, coarse textured, sheltered rocky and sheltered estuarine. All arcs were placed in one of these 15 categories.

    Potential study sites were selected by personnel of the Alaska Department of Natural Resources and the Alaska Department of Fish and Game using a stratified random sampling procedure with probability proportional to arc length for each of the 15 habitat-oiling categories using commercial software for the GIS (ESRI 1989). Sites were then visited during a reconnaissance survey (Sundberg et al. 1993) to determine accessibility by field crews for collection of samples of biological and substrate material. All sites were retained in the order selected except those with slope greater than 30 degrees which were judged to be unsafe and not accessible by field crews. Other objectives of the reconnaissance survey were to describe the sites, verify habitat and oiling classifications, reclassify sites when necessary, collect oil and sediment samples, and mark the study sites (Sundberg et al. 1993).

    Biological data collected on study sites were further stratified by one meter elevation zones below mean high high tide. Regardless of the stratification by shoreline type and tidal height, there was unacceptable variation within the strata in 1989. With the original design and feasible sample sizes, it would not have been possible to detect important effects between oiled and reference strata with acceptable statistical precision. For example, in PWS the reference strata had unacceptable variation in many variables because they included sites on the islands with high salinity and sites on the mainland with lower salinity. Most oiled sites were on the islands of the central and western Sound where salinity was high. Extreme variation in habitat was noted within all strata. Also, a large proportion of sites were misclassified by oil classification, habitat type, or both in the original stratification of sites in the GIS (Sundberg et al. 1993). For these reasons the survey design and planned statistical analyses were modified during the winter of 1989-1990.

    The shallow subtidal study was completely redesigned using a stratification independent of the supratidal-intertidal surveys (Jewett et al. 1993). Oiled sites within a given stratum were visited in a random order and checked to determine if required characteristics contained in a written protocol were satisfied. The first site found to satisfy the protocol was accepted for the study. Each oiled site was then matched to a "reference" site. Potential reference sites were identified, randomly ordered, visited and the first one to satisfy the protocol was selected. This process generated a quasi-experiment with statistical inferences limited to the matched pairs of sites and the protocols for site selection. The shallow subtidal study will not be considered further because the statistical analysis procedures follow standard methods (Jewett et al. 1993).

    The original stratified random sample remained a valid probability sample of the universe of oiled shoreline sites (> 100 m) in a given region, admittedly with inappropriate labels for the stratum. For the supratidal and intertidal studies, each of the accessible, moderate-heavily oiled sites selected in the original stratified random sample was post-classified into the correct habitat strata based on results of the reconnaissance survey (Sundberg et al. 1993). Following a written protocol, each accessible, moderate-heavily oiled site was deductively matched with a reference site (Manly and Wright 1982). Matching was based on those physical characteristics of the unique oiled site which would influence the biological community present if there was absence of an oil/cleanup effect. Biological variables could not be directly used to select matching reference sites because variables on oiled sites were potentially affected by the oil/cleanup.

Physical characteristics considered for selection of matching reference sites, included substrate composition, wave exposure regime, slope, proximity of freshwater, nearshore bathymetry, and absence of oil based on 1989 oil distribution maps or the site visit (Sundberg et al. 1993). Initial unequal probability sampling and post-classification of oiled sites combined to yield sites pooled into "new strata" with unequal probabilities of inclusion for a given site. Some additional oiled sites were subjectively selected for habitat strata which did not meet the minimum objective for sample sizes. These sites have 100% probability of inclusion and relatively less weight in the resulting meta-analyses. Figures 2, 3, and 4 identify the locations of oiled and reference sites selected for study in the PWS, CIK, and KAP regions.

Subsampling Procedures

The site visits were made by field crews once in 1989, twice in 1990, and twice in 1991 (Highsmith et al. 1993). The invertebrates, algae, and sediment were collected from 20 X 50 cm rectangular quadrats systematically placed within the intertidal zone stratified by vertical relief following procedures reported in Highsmith et al. (1993). Percent cover of algae and invertebrates were measured at the quadrats using a point contact method and macro invertebrates were counted in larger strip transects (Highsmith et al. 1993). The samples of biological material collected at the sites were returned to the laboratory for sorting, counting and weighing of plants, algae, and invertebrates. This paper will illustrate statistical methods using example intertidal data collected from the 20 X 50 cm quadrats for the abundance of the family of barnacles, *Balanomorpha*. Supratidal zones and intertidal fish were subsampled by similar methods.

STATISTICAL METHODS

There were two levels of statistical inferences used in the analyses. The first, known commonly as "fixed effects analysis" used Fisher's procedure for combining results of independent tests (Folks 1984) to make inferences to the unique set of oiled and reference pairs in the sample. No statistical inferences were drawn beyond the specific set of sites in the quasi-experiments and pairs of sites were given equal weight (importance) in the analyses regardless of the final probability of inclusion associated with the sites. In the second level, another meta-analysis procedure, the Stouffer-Liptak method (Folks 1984), was used to provide inferences to the universe of oiled sites subject to the protocols for selection of matching reference sites and subsampling of sites.

Initially, the null hypothesis of no significant difference between variables for a specific pair of matched oiled and reference sites was tested. For a given variable, Levene's test (Milliken and Johnson 1984) was used to test for homogeneity of variances within sites of the same habitat type, time period, and elevational zone. If variances were not significantly different at the $P = 0.01$ level, then ordinary one-way analysis of variance was conducted to obtain the pooled estimate of variance. Pairs of oiled and reference sites were then compared by a two-sample t-test (Milliken and Johnson 1984) using the pooled estimate of variance. If variances were significantly different, data were transformed to logarithms and the above tests were repeated. If Levene's test remained significant on the transformed values, then regular two-sample t-tests were conducted to compare matched pairs (with Satterthwaite's correction on the degrees of freedom for unequal variances). Proportional data were transformed using the arcsine square root transformation (Steel and Torrie 1980) before comparisons were made between each matched pair of sites.

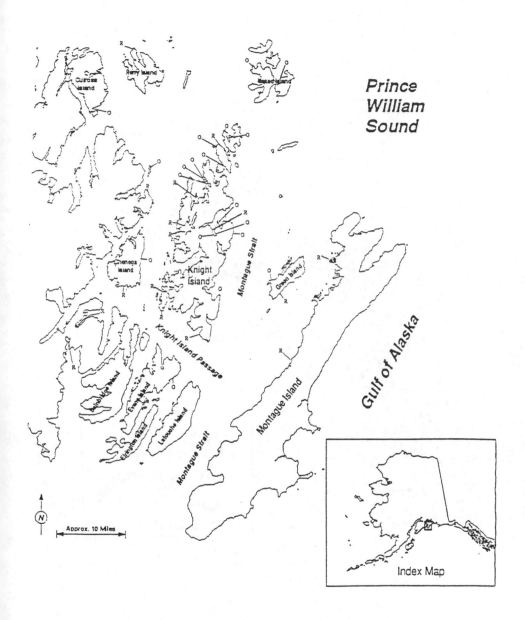

Figure 2--Prince William Sound (PWS) study area showing site locations. The symbol "R" refers to reference sites and the symbol "o" refers to oiled sites. Map produced by ADNR, Land Records Information Section, Technical Services 3.

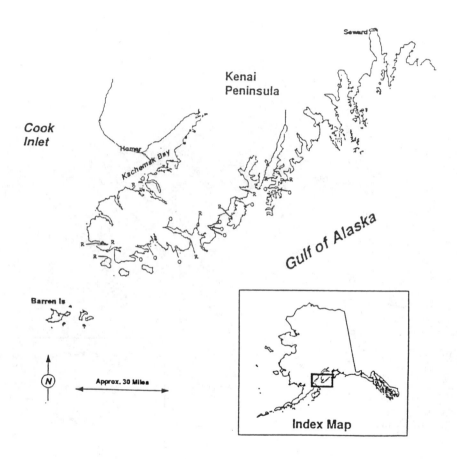

Figure 3--Cook Inlet-Kenai Peninsula (CIK) study area showing site locations. The symbol "R" refers to reference sites and the symbol "o" refers to oiled sites. Map produced by ADNR, Land Records Information Section, Technical Services 3.

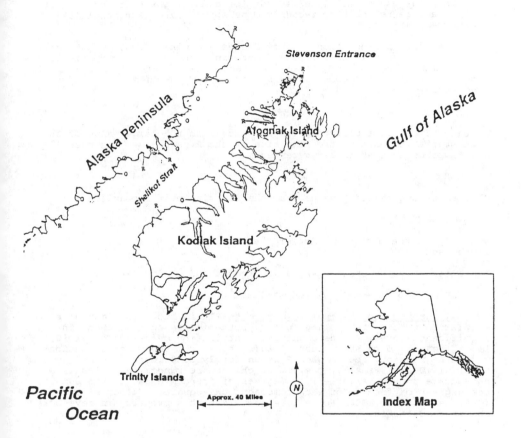

Figure 4--Kodiak Island-Alaska Peninsula (KAP) study area showing site
locations. The symbol "R" refers to reference sites and the symbol "o"
refers to oiled sites. Map produced by ADNR, Land Records Information
Section, Technical Services 3.

Meta-Analysis

     The term meta-analysis was coined by Glass (1976) and defined as the use of quantitative methods for research synthesis. One quantitative method for combining results of independent studies is to calculate an "overall significance level" for a group of independent studies. Based on a literature review of methods for combining results of independent studies we selected the Fisher and Stouffer-Liptak methods and applied them in combination to test for oil/cleaning effects. The use of multiple methods for combining results of independent tests has been recognized as appropriate (Rosenthal 1978, Wachter and Straf 1990).

     We adopt the notation used by Hedges and Olkin (1985). Consider k independent site pair comparisons, where in each of these comparisons the parameters θ_1, θ_2,...θ_k (mean differences, etc.) are of interest. In each of the site pair comparisons a statistic T_i is used to test the hypothesis

$$H_{oi} :\quad \theta_i = 0, \quad i = 1,2,...,k. \tag{1}$$

In each of the site pair comparisons, assume that a large value of the test statistic leads to the rejection of the hypothesis. The overall null hypothesis that is being tested is

$$H_o:\quad \theta_1 = \theta_2 = ... = \theta_k = 0. \tag{2}$$

Define the one-tailed P-value from the ith site pair comparison as:

$$P_i = Pr\{T_i \geq t_{io}\}$$

where t_{io} is the observed value of the t statistic in the ith comparison.

The alternative hypothesis stated by Hedges and Olkin (1985) is

$$H_1:\quad \theta_i \geq 0 \quad i = 1,...,k \text{ and at least one } \theta_i > 0. \tag{3}$$

     Inferences to the quasi-experiments--It is known from mathematical statistics theory that if the "null hypothesis" is correct then, the significance level, P, has a uniform distribution on the interval [0, 1]. It can also be shown that -2*ln(P) has a chi-square distribution with 2 degrees of freedom when P is uniformly distributed on the interval [0,1]. Finally, the sum of chi-square random variables is a chi-square random variable with degrees of freedom equal to the sum of the degrees of freedom of each component chi-square. Fisher's method (Steel and Torrie 1980, Folks 1984) utilizes this property in developing the test statistic:

$$X = \sum_{i=1}^{n} -2*\ln(P_i) \tag{4}$$

where P_i is the P-value from the comparisons between the ith pair of oiled and reference sites, i = 1,2,...,n. The test of no overall effect is rejected if

$$X > \chi^2_{2n,\alpha}$$

where $\chi^2_{2n,\alpha}$ is the upper $(1-\alpha)100$ percentile of the chi-square distribution with 2n degrees of freedom. This method treats sites with equal weight. This test can yield a significant result when one or more components yields a highly significant effect, or when most components yield results with moderately low P-values. Fisher's procedure was used to synthesize the results of fixed effects tests on the same variable. Inferences were to the specific set of site pairs in the quasi-experiment following the logic that each site pair was a separate independent quasi-experiment with equal weight.

Inference to the universe of oiled sites--The basic philosophy behind Stouffer's test (Folks 1984) is that if there is no effect of the oil/cleanup and the protocols for selection of reference sites are unbiased then the mean of the P-values in comparison of statistics on each pair of sites will be 0.5. Stouffer's method tests whether the mean P-value is significantly lower than 0.5. Therefore, Stouffer's method rejects the hypothesis of no overall effect when all component tests yield "significant" results in the same direction. Stouffer's method has been extended by Liptak (Folks 1984) to the case of unequal weights. The method is sometimes referred to as the inverse normal method (Hedges and Olkin 1985) and Rice (1990) referred to it as a "consensus test" in that it yields significant results when all component tests tend to refute the same common null hypothesis. We refer to the method as the Stouffer-Liptak procedure.

The significance levels are transformed to standard normal z scores. The standard normal z-score, Z_i, corresponding to the ith significance level is defined by:

$P_i = \Phi(Z_i)$ where $\Phi(x)$ is the standard normal cumulative distribution function. The overall test statistic Z is then defined by:

$$ Z = \frac{Z_1 + Z_2 + \ldots + Z_k}{\sqrt{k}} = \frac{\phi^{-1}(P_1) + \ldots + \phi^{-1}(P_k)}{\sqrt{k}} \qquad (5) $$

where k is the number of component tests (site pairs). Under the null hypothesis, the statistic Z has the standard normal distribution. The null hypothesis of no oil/cleanup effect is rejected when Z is greater than the critical value Z_α.

This inverse normal method is easily used when unequal weights (w_i, i = 1,...,k) are assigned to individual studies (Liptak, in Folks 1984). In this case, the method is based on the test statistic

$$ Z_w = \frac{w_1 Z_1 + w_2 Z_2 + \ldots + w_k Z_k}{\sqrt{w_1^2 + \ldots + w_k^2}} = \frac{w_1 \phi^{-1}(P_1) + \ldots + w_k \phi^{-1}(P_k)}{\sqrt{w_1^2 + \ldots + w_k^2}}, \qquad (6) $$

where w_i is the reciprocal of the probability of inclusion of the ith site. When the null hypothesis is true, Z_w follows a standard normal distribution.

The Stouffer-Liptak meta-analysis procedure was used to test for oil/cleanup effects in the universe of oiled sites within a given habitat type and time period. This method utilized the unequal inclusion probabilities inherent for each site pair in the original site selection process. Inferences are to the universe of oiled-reference site pairs which could have been obtained by the sampling and site selection protocol in the sense that if the whole process could be repeated using sites selected by the same protocols, then similar statistical inferences would be expected.

RESULTS AND DISCUSSION

We illustrate results of the statistical methodology for design, sampling, and analysis of coastal habitat injury assessment due to the EVOS with a simple example. Results of the coastal habitat injury assessment are contained in Highsmith et al. (1993) and Jewett et al. (1993), and numerous papers presented at national meetings and submitted for publication.

Example: Biomass (g/m^2) of *Balanomorpha* on intertidal sites in PWS-- Table 1 contains results for biomass of the family of barnacles *Balanomorpha* for Prince William Sound sheltered rocky sites in the second meter of vertical drop during May 1990. The conjecture is that mean biomass per m^2 is less on the oiled sites. The column labeled I_i is the probability of inclusion of the particular site pair in the study. The column labeled, P-value, contains the significance level of the one-tailed t-tests comparing the mean biomass (g/m^2) on each oiled site with mean biomass on the matched reference site. First, values of biomass measured on members of a given site pair are compared. One site pair, 453C/453, had significantly more biomass on the reference site at the P = 0.015 level. The site pair, 598C/598, had significantly more biomass on the reference site at the P = 0.052 level, a value which is slightly larger than the target size 0.05. The other 3 pairs have more biomass on the reference sites, but the differences in biomass are not large when compared to the standard errors. These results point toward an overall oil/cleanup effect on biomass of *Balanomorpha* on sheltered rocky intertidal sites in PWS, but the results are hardly convincing. We use meta-analysis to formalize the combination of these individual comparisons.

Simultaneous inference to the fixed set of 5 site pairs in this quasi-experiment is made using Fisher's test and assigning equal weight (importance) to each pair. For this example, the critical value calculated from equation 4 for Fisher's test is:

$$X = -2*(\ln(.3740)+\ln(.0146)+\ln(.1673)+\ln(.0515)+\ln(0.1479))$$
$$= 23.751$$

The significance level of the test is calculated as:

$$P = \Pr(X \geq 23.751 | df = 10) = 0.0083,$$

where X is a chi-square random variable with 10 degrees of freedom. The statistical result is that there is an overall significant effect of the oil/cleanup on biomass of *Balanomorpha* in the second meter of vertical drop in this fixed set of 5 pairs of sites (P = 0.0083).

Simultaneous inference to the effect of oil/cleanup in the universe of oiled sheltered rocky sites in Prince William Sound is made

TABLE 1--Statistical results for biomass of _Balanomorpha_ on PWS sheltered rocky sites in the second meter of vertical drop during May 1990.

Site pair	C^a	SE^b	O^c	SE^d	$I_i{}^e$	weight^f	P-value^g
4825C/1424	22.767	13.175	8.363	6.207	1.000	1.000	0.374
453C/453	62.814	32.024	2.185	1.022	0.262	3.820	0.015
601C/601	428.387	232.679	267.108	86.242	0.600	1.667	0.167
598C/598	385.859	132.767	124.783	23.992	0.179	5.591	0.052
1522C/1522	213.705	112.880	66.702	39.725	0.668	1.496	0.148

[a] reference site mean abundance (No./0.1 m²)
[b] Standard error of reference site mean
[c] Oiled site mean abundance (No./0.1 m²)
[d] Standard error of oiled site mean
[e] probability of inclusion of the site pair
[f] importance value
[g] one-tailed t-test P-value

using the Stouffer-Liptak test. For this example, the critical value calculated from equation 6 for the Stouffer-Liptak test is:

$$Z_w = \frac{1.0*0.321+3.82*2.181+1.667*0.965+5.591*1.63+1.496*1.045}{\sqrt{1.0^2+3.820^2+1.667^2+5.591^2+1.496^2}}$$

$$=2.907$$

The significance level of the test is calculated as:

$$P = Pr(Z_w \geq 2.907) < 0.0018$$

where Z_w is a standard normal random variable. The statistical result is that there is an overall significant effect of the oil/cleanup on biomass of _Balanomorpha_ in the second meter of vertical drop in the universe of oiled protected rocky sites in Prince William Sound ($P < 0.0018$).

Assessing Injury and/or Recovery Over Time

Two questions of interest in the CHIA studies were:

1.   Was there injury to the intertidal community because of the EVOS?

2.   If injury occurred, has recovery taken place by the end of the study?

Our approach to answer Question 1 for a specific point in time is described above. The second question can best be addressed by checking for interaction of the biological variable with time (Skalski and Robson 1992). We plotted the means of the variables across time periods and considered the interpretation of results of the Fisher and Stouffer-Liptak tests. If a significant adverse effect was detected in 1990, but not in 1991 then interaction with time was detected. This is statistical inference of an initial oil/cleanup effect followed by indication of at least some recovery for that variable. Significant adverse oil effect in both 1990 and 1991 was considered to be grounds for the statistical inference that there was an oil/cleanup effect and recovery had not taken place by the end of the field season in 1991.

The purpose of this paper is to provide a overview of the design, sampling, and data analysis procedures of the Trustee's CHIA studies and to relate all three to our philosophical ideas for making proper statistical inferences. The overall objective of the CHIA studies (Highsmith et al. 1993, Jewett et al. 1993) was to document and quantify injury to the biota due to the EVOS. This objective differs from many other EVOS studies where the objectives were to understand the mechanisms, processes and pathways for injury due to oil in the environment. When interest is in the amount of injury to a resource, a probability based sample of the universe of oiled habitat must be studied. This was the heart of the statistical philosophy behind the Trustee's CHIA studies.

When quantifying injury, the most important component is to precisely define the universe to which the inductive inferences apply. In our study, the universe was defined by the information in the GIS system used for site selection. Sites were classified into oil class and habitat class by written protocols during the reconnaissance survey (Sundberg et al. 1993). These protocols are an integral part of the definition of the universe. Also, several factors existed to reduce the size of the sampled universe in this study. These limitations were: 1) sites which were not safe for subsampling by a large field crew were not included, 2) segments less than 100 m were excluded because small sites would not accommodate repeated visits with multiple destructive subsamples over three years, and 3) only sites in the moderate-heavily oiled class were included.

Difficulties exist in developing cause and effect relationships in injury assessment studies when no pre-accident data exist (Green 1979; Hurlbert 1984; Stewart-Oaten et al. 1986). In most cases a single undisturbed site is chosen as a reference site for comparative purposes. This approach has been criticized by the above authors and others because of the variability among sites and lack of replication. We addressed this potential shortcoming by utilizing randomly selected oiled sites matched with reference sites where the reference sites were selected by an unbiased protocol. Reference sites were also spatially interspersed with the oiled sites in the study areas. With this study design, statistically significant differences in variables, (e.g., abundance and biomass of an organism) between reference and oiled sites can serve as inductive proof of oil and/or cleanup impact on the sampled universe. In the absence of impact due to oil or cleanup and with an unbiased protocol for selection of reference sites, one would expect approximately half the oiled sites to have greater abundance and biomass than the matching reference sites and the other half to have lower abundance and biomass than their matched reference sites. Therefore, if consistent differences are noted between oiled and reference sites, one can be confident in the inductive statistical inference that these differences are due to impact of oil and/or cleanup.

The clean up activities were confounding factors in this study. We were unable to determine specific cleaning methods used on many of the randomly selected sites. Consequently, injuries detected are attributed to the combination of oil and/or cleaning activities associated with the spill. Potentially, the use of Fisher's method can aid in understanding treatment effects, because it can yield a significant effect when one or more components of the test are significant. If information concerning treatments applied to those sites can be determined, then perhaps the effect can be attributed to oil or oil/cleanup as the cause. However, without replication of the specific oil/cleanup treatments such inferences could be due to habitat differences and should be viewed only as interesting conjectures.

If the environment is subjected to a single pollution event, such as the EVOS, a convergence of experimental and reference data over an extended period following the spill/cleanup would provide strong evidence that differences observed immediately after the spill/cleanup are oil-related (Skalski and Robson 1992). With only two years of data, it is difficult to assess recovery with statistical confidence and one must rely more on professional judgement. A longer study would also aid in validating the precision of the protocols used to match oiled and reference sites. Recovery of rocky intertidal communities on the coast of Cornwall following the Torrey Canyon spill was judged to have required up to ten years (Southward and Southward 1978). Subtidal ampeliscid amphipod communities also were judged to have required approximately ten years to recover following the *Amoco Cadiz* spill of France (Dauvin 1987). Thus, given estimates of recovery times for previous spills in temperate-boreal marine habitats and the short duration of the EVOS intertidal study, statements concerning recovery should be considered preliminary.

ACKNOWLEDGEMENTS

Many people participated and assisted in the actual design, data collection, and data analysis for the CHIA studies and should be acknowledged. In particular, Kim Sundberg and Earl Becker with the Alaska Department of Fish and Game and Richard McMahon with the Alaska Department of Natural Resources (and other personnel) were responsible for implementing the initial definition and selection of sites. Kim Sundberg and Lawrence Deysher were the principal scientists responsible for the reconnaissance survey and selection of reference sites. Kim Sundberg, Raymond Highsmith, Mike Stekoll, Steve Jewett, Tom Dean, Lawrence Deysher, and Will Barber were not only the principal investigators on the CHIA studies but their input during our discussions was invaluable in development of the final philosophy for statistical design, sampling, and analysis. Roger Green and Douglas Robson provided excellent peer review of the statistical issues.

REFERENCES

Alaska Department of Environmental Conservation (ADEC), 1989, Impact maps and summary reports of shoreline surveys of the *Exxon Valdez* spill site, Seward area; 3 September - 19 October 1989. Alaska Department of Environmental Conservation, Anchorage, Alaska. approx. 350 pp.

Dauvin, J. C., 1987, "Evolution a long term (1978-1986) des populations d'ampipodes des sables fins de la Pierre Noire (Baie de Morlaix, Manche occidentale) apres la catastrophe de l'Amaco Cadiz," Marine Environmental Research, Vol. 21, No.4, pp. 247-273.

Environmental Systems Research Institute (ESRI), 1989, "Arc/Info geographic information system software," Version 5.0, Redland, California.

Folks, J. L., 1984, "Combination of Independent Tests", In P. R. Krishnaiah and P. K. Sen (eds.), Handbook of Statistics 4. Nonparametric Methods, North-Holland, New York.

Glass, G. V., 1976, "Primary, Secondary, and Meta-analysis of Research," Educational Researcher, Vol 5, pp. 3-8.

Green, R. H., 1979, Sampling Design and Statistical Methods for Environmental Biologists, Wiley Press, New York.

Hayes, M. O. and Ruby C. H., 1979, Oil spill vulnerability index maps, Kodiak Archipelago, Unpublished maps, 47 leaves.

Hedges, L. V. and Olkin I., 1985, Statistical Methods for Meta-Analysis, Academic Press, Inc., New York.

Highsmith, R. C., Stekoll, M. S., Barber, W. E., McDonald, L., Strickland, D., and Erickson, W. P., 1993, "Comprehensive Assessment of Coastal Habitat: Final Status Report," Volumes I-VI, Coastal Habitat Study No. 1A, Exxon Valdez Oil Spill Trustee Council, Simpson Building, 645 G Street, Anchorage, AK 99503.

Hurlbert, S. H., 1984, "Pseudoreplication and the Design of Ecological Field Experiments," Ecological Monographs, Vol. 54, pp. 187-211.

Jewett, S. C., Dean, T. A., Haldorson, L. J., Laur, D., Stekoll, M., and McDonald, L., 1993, "The effects of the Exxon Valdez oil spill on shallow subtidal communities in Prince William Sound, Alaska," Final Report, Study No. ST2A, Exxon Valdez Oil Spill Trustee Council, Simpson Building, 645 G Street, Anchorage, AK 99503.

Manly, B. F. J. and Wright, V. L., 1982, "Report of workshop on design of environmental impact statements," Special Report 82-01, Department of Experimental Statistics, Louisiana State University, Baton Rouge, LA 70803.

Milliken, G. A. and Johnson, D. E., 1984, Analysis of Messy Data: Volume I, Designed Experiments, Van Nostrand Reinhold Company, New York.

RPI (Research Planning Institute, Inc.), 1983a, "Sensitivity of coastal environments and wildlife to spilled oil, Prince William Sound, Alaska, an atlas of coastal resources," Prepared for National Oceanic and Atmospheric Administration, Office of Oceanography and Marine Services, Seattle, Washington, 48 leaves.

RPI (Research Planning Institute, Inc.), 1983b, "Sensitivity of coastal environments and wildlife to spilled oil, Shelikof Strait Region, Alaska, an atlas of coastal resources," Prepared for National Oceanic and Atmospheric Administration, Office of Oceanography and Marine Services, Seattle, Washington, 43 leaves.

RPI (Research Planning Institute, Inc.), 1985, "Sensitivity of coastal environments and wildlife to spilled oil, Cook Inlet/Kenai Peninsula, Alaska, an atlas of coastal resources", Prepared for National Oceanic and Atmospheric Administration, Office of Oceanography and Marine Assessment Services, Seattle, Washington, 64 leaves.

RPI (Research Planning Institute, Inc.), 1986, "Sensitivity of coastal environments and wildlife to spilled oil, Southern Alaska Peninsula, Alaska, an atlas of coastal resources," Prepared for National Oceanic and Atmospheric Administration, Office of Oceanography and Marine Assessment Services, Seattle, Washington, 64 leaves.

Rice, W. R., 1990, "A Consensus Combined P-value Test and the Family-wide Significance of Component Tests," Biometrics, Vol 46, pp. 303-308.

Rosenthal, R., 1978, "Combining Results of Independent Studies", Psychological Bulletin, Vol. 85, pp. 185-193.

Skalski, J. R. and Robson D. S., 1992, Techniques for Wildlife Investigations, Design and Analysis of Capture Data, Academic Press, Inc., New York.

Southward, A. J. and Southward E. C., 1978, "Recolonization of Rocky Shores in Cornwall After Use of Toxic Dispersants to Clean Up the Torrey Canyon Spill," Journal of the Fisheries Research Board Canada, Vol. 35, pp. 682-703.

Steel, R. G. D. and Torrie, J. H. 1980, Principles and Procedures of Statistics, a Biometrical Approach, McGraw-Hill, New York.

Stewart-Oaten, A., Murdoch, W. W., and Parker, K. R., 1986, "Environmental Impact Assessment: Pseudoreplication" in Time?," Ecology, Vol. 67, No. 4, pp. 929-940.

Sundberg, K. A., Deysher, L., and McDonald, L. L., 1993, "Intertidal-Supratidal Site Selection Utilizing a Geographic Information System", presented at the Exxon Valdez Oilspill Symposium, Anchorage, AK, February 1993, and to be published in the Proceedings of the Exxon Valdez Oilspill Symposium, American Fisheries Journal.

Wachter, K. W. and Straf, M. L., eds., 1990, The Future of Meta-Analysis, Russel Sage Foundation, New York.

Jerry M. Neff[1], Edward H. Owens[2], Sam W. Stoker[3], and Deborah M. McCormick[4]

SHORELINE OILING CONDITIONS IN PRINCE WILLIAM SOUND FOLLOWING THE *EXXON VALDEZ* OIL SPILL

REFERENCE: Neff, J. M., Owens, E. H., Stoker, S. W., and McCormick, D. M., "Shoreline Oiling Conditions in Prince William Sound Following the Exxon Valdez Oil Spill," Exxon Valdez Oil Spill: Fate and Effects in Alaskan Waters, ASTM STP 1219, Peter G. Wells, James N. Butler, and Jane S. Hughes, Eds., American Society for Testing and Materials, Philadelphia, 1995.

ABSTRACT: Following the *Exxon Valdez* oil spill of March 24, 1989, in Prince William Sound, Alaska, Exxon conducted comprehensive, systematic shoreline surveys in cooperation with federal and state authorities to obtain information on the distribution and magnitude of shoreline oiling and to identify natural and cultural resources requiring special protection. Similar joint surveys were performed during the springs of 1990, 1991, and 1992 on all Prince William Sound and Gulf of Alaska shorelines that were suspected of having remnants of weathered oil and that would benefit from further cleanup.

The extent of oiling declined substantially between 1989 and 1992: in 1989, survey teams found oil on about 16% (783 km) of the approximately 5 000 km of shoreline in Prince William Sound; in the spring of 1991, they found oil on about 96 km; and, in May 1992, on only about 10 km of shoreline in the sound. During this period, most of the oil was located in the biologically least productive upper intertidal and supratidal zones.

In the springs of 1990, 1991, and 1992, isolated pockets of subsurface oil were found, chiefly in small scattered zones in coarse cobble/boulder sediments in the upper intertidal or supratidal zones. In 1991, about one-third of the subdivisions in Prince William Sound with surface oil also contained some subsurface oil. The areal extent of this subsurface oil declined by nearly 70% between 1991 and 1992, from about 37 000m^2 to about 12 000m^2. Moreover, where subsurface oil remained in 1992, it was present in lesser amounts.

Rates of oil removal were greatest on coastal sections treated early in the spring and summer of 1989. Where shoreline treatment was

[1]Battelle Ocean Sciences Laboratory, 397 Washington St., Duxbury, MA 02332
[2]Owens Coastal Consultants, Bainbridge Island, WA 98110
[3]Beringian Resources, Inc., Fairbanks, AK 99709
[4]U.S. Army Corps of Engineers, Anchorage, AK 99524

delayed, the subsequent rate of removal of oil from the shore by natural processes was slower.

Key Words: oil, Prince William Sound, shoreline, intertidal zone, subsurface oil

---

INTRODUCTION

Spill History

On March 24, 1989, the tanker *Exxon Valdez* ran aground on Bligh Reef in northeastern Prince William Sound, spilling approximately 41 million liters of North Slope crude oil. It was the largest marine oil spill ever in United States territorial waters and prompted the largest containment and cleanup operation ever mobilized.

At the time of the spill, there was little or no wind or wave activity to move the oil. During the first few days after the spill, the slick was spread to the southwest by a combination of water currents, gravity, and surface tension. However, on March 26, two and a half days after the spill, a violent windstorm, moving from the east to northeast, drove the oil slick toward the extensive island system in the western sound and eventually, after March 30, into the northwestern Gulf of Alaska (Figure 1). The storm caused some of the oil to form a water-in-oil emulsion (mousse), and broke up the original slick into bands and streaks that drifted to the southwest at a rate of about 21 km/day (Koons and Jahns 1992). The oil that reached the Gulf of Alaska was swept to the west along the shore by the Alaska Coastal Current. Approximately 30% of the oil evaporated within a few days of the spill and was diluted, dispersed, and photooxidized in the atmosphere. Additional oil dissolved or dispersed in the water column where much of it was biodegraded by microorganisms. Most of the remaining oil that did not strand on the shoreline was eventually swept out into the open north Pacific Ocean. Some of the weathered oil washing off the shore was deposited in near-shore subtidal sediments.

Oil came ashore in both western Prince William Sound and the northwestern Gulf of Alaska. A total of 783 km of the roughly 5 000 km of shoreline in Prince William Sound, and another 1 300 km of the approximately 10 000 km of shoreline of the western Gulf of Alaska, was eventually oiled to some degree (Owens 1991b). The most heavily oiled shores were on islands of western Prince William Sound, along the Kenai Peninsula, in the northern and northwestern Kodiak Island group, and along the Alaska Peninsula. Some oil in the form of tarballs was observed as far south as Chignik Bay, more than 970 km in a straight line from the spill site.

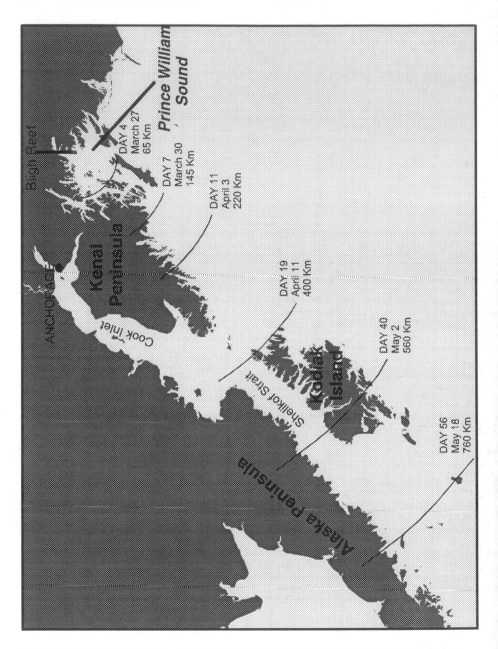

Figure 1--The path of the spilled oil through Prince William Sound and the western Gulf of Alaska

The Physical Environment

Prince William Sound is a large (39 000 km^2) subarctic embayment of the northern Gulf of Alaska with numerous fjords and active glaciers. It is bordered by the mountains of the Kenai-Chugach ranges rising steeply out of the ocean. The extremely convoluted coastline of islands, bays, and rocky shores is roughly 5 000 km long. An extensive archipelago of islands fills the western part of the sound. Most shores in the western sound where oil came ashore are steep bedrock cliffs, interspersed with deep bays and pocket beaches with boulder, cobble, and, occasionally, sandy sediments (Owens 1991a).

Oceanic water from the Alaska Coastal Current enters Prince William Sound primarily through Hinchinbrook Entrance, moves in a counterclockwise direction throughout the sound, and exits primarily through Montague Strait (Royer et al. 1990). Semidiurnal tides average about 3 m, with a maximum tidal range of about 5 m. Tidal currents provide substantial daily exchange of water in coastal inlets and bays. The turnover rate (exchange period) of seawater in Prince William Sound is once every three to four weeks (Royer et al. 1990).

Prevailing winds are primarily from the east and northeast during most of the year, with highest velocities in December and January (Royer et al. 1990). Severe storms, with wind speeds of 80 to 97 km/hour and moderately high seas, are frequent in the sound, particularly in the fall and winter. Precipitation is quite high throughout the year, averaging about 150 cm/year in Valdez and 635 cm/year on Montague Island (Lethcoe and Lethcoe 1989). Because of the high annual precipitation, surface runoff of freshwater from hundreds of small streams and from the many glaciers that line the northern and western mainland is very high, particularly in the spring. Although extensive sea ice does not develop in the sound, ice and deep snow are common on the shores during much of the winter, particularly in sheltered areas protected from winter storms.

Shoreline Cleanup

Under the direction of the Federal On-Scene Coordinator (FOSC), and with the concurrence of state authorities, Exxon conducted cleanup operations in the sound and the Gulf of Alaska during the summers of 1989-1991 and the spring of 1992. During 1989, cleanup efforts focused on removing bulk oil from the shorelines as quickly as possible. By September, 15, 1989, when cleanup operations were halted for the winter, crews had treated all designated oiled shores as directed by the FOSC (Harrison 1991). Some heavily oiled shores, particularly those in areas important to marine mammals and seabirds, were treated several times during the first summer after the spill.

Cleanup operations in 1989 included manual pick-up of oil with sorbent pads; low- and moderate-pressure washing with cold and warm water (up to 60°C); mechanical tilling and removal of oiled sediments; and bioremediation (Harrison 1991). Most cleanup efforts focused on the more heavily oiled upper and middle intertidal zones, with appropriate measures taken to minimize injury and disturbance to the biologically more productive (and usually unoiled) lower intertidal areas.

The removal of bulk oil in 1989 and natural cleaning of oiled shores during winter storms allowed more selective, and less intrusive, cleanup techniques to be used in subsequent years. In order to minimize impact on intertidal biological communities and wildlife, cleanup operations after 1989 were conducted on the basis of "Net Environmental Benefit" (NOAA 1990). Under this guideline, oil remaining on a particular shore was removed or treated if the FOSC determined that further cleaning would provide a net benefit to the environment. Consequently, some isolated areas containing oil residues were not cleaned in 1990 and later years because further action was not seen to be beneficial. In 1990, cleanup operations included manual and mechanical removal of tarmats (thick deposits of weathered oil and sediment), oiled debris, mousse, and significant subsurface oil deposits; storm berm relocation; surface tilling; and bioremediation (Owens et al. 1991).

In 1991, cleanup consisted primarily of manual pickup and bioremediation. At a few sites, oiled sediments in the storm berm were relocated to the middle intertidal zone, where natural cleansing processes removed the oil. In May and June 1992, treatments included manual removal of scattered and weathered asphalt patches or oiled sediments, local manual tilling, and bioremediation. On June 12, 1992, both the federal and state governments declared that no additional cleanup of shoreline was needed, and the cleanup was concluded.

Shoreline Assessment Program

Soon after the spill, Exxon started survey programs to determine the location and extent of shoreline oiling and to plan and set priorities for natural resource protection and cleanup programs. One survey program, a systematic aerial reconnaissance videotape survey, was initiated in Prince William Sound in April 1989. By August, about 8 300 km of shoreline in the sound and the Gulf of Alaska had been videotaped, catalogued, and mapped (Teal 1991). All shorelines within the spill trajectory where oil might have stranded were surveyed.

Data on shore-zone characteristics and shoreline oiling conditions were obtained through subsequent detailed ground-based surveys carried out between mid April and early September 1989 by Shoreline Cleanup Assessment Teams (SCAT). These data were used as the basis for recommendations on environmentally sound and effective cleanup techniques for individual shoreline segments and to identify natural and/or cultural resources requiring special protection (Teal 1991). Similar surveys were conducted in the springs of 1990, 1991, and 1992 and were designated SSAT, MAYSAP and FINSAP, respectively.

These surveys were designed to accomplish the following:
- Assess the presence, distribution, and amount of surface and subsurface oil on the shorelines
- Provide information needed to make environmentally sound decisions regarding the need for additional cleanup
- Identify areas in which special actions were needed to minimize disturbance of sensitive ecological or cultural resources

The process and methods developed for conducting shoreline surveys have been incorporated into protocols adopted by the Canadian government (Environment Canada 1992).

Each survey team consisted of an oil spill geomorphologist, a marine ecologist, an archaeologist (in 1989), and often other members that varied from year to year. In some situations in 1989 and in all surveys in 1990, 1991, and 1992, representatives of government agencies, landowners, and Exxon joined the teams to facilitate cleanup recommendations and decisions.

Cleanup Decision Process

In 1989, the data from shoreline surveys were evaluated by an Interagency Shoreline Cleanup Committee (ISCC) composed of representatives from the National Oceanic and Atmospheric Administration (NOAA), the Alaska Department of Environmental Conservation (ADEC), federal and state land and resource management agencies, Alaska Natives, commercial fishermen, environmental groups, and Exxon (Knorr et al. 1991). The ISCC made joint recommendations to help the FOSC and Exxon set priorities and methods for cleanup and to protect sensitive natural and cultural resources.

The survey and review processes were changed slightly in 1990 to further strengthen the joint nature of the survey process and to allow decisions to be made in a more timely manner. That spring, representatives of the Coast Guard, NOAA, state and federal regulatory agencies, and landowners joined the survey teams. Their shoreline observations were reviewed, and cleanup recommendations were developed by the Technical Advisory Group (TAG), a successor of the ISCC. This group contained representatives of all appropriate state and federal regulatory agencies and Exxon. TAG was able to process survey reports and make recommendations on surveyed shorelines within two weeks of the survey. All cleanup recommendations were reviewed by the State Historic Preservation Office (SHPO) to ensure protection of cultural resources and were then submitted to the FOSC for approval. This timely review process enabled the cleanup to proceed quickly and efficiently in 1990, 1991, and 1992.

Supplemental Shoreline Monitoring Data

A separate study program, focusing on time-series observations of shoreline oiling and biological conditions at 18 moderately oiled to heavily oiled shoreline locations in Prince William Sound, was initiated in the summer of 1989 and continued through September 1990 (Owens 1991a). This program of detailed, site-specific monitoring studies was called the Fate and Persistence (FAP) program. To ensure consistency between the shoreline surveys and FAP, all of the field scientists involved in the FAP program also participated in the shoreline assessment program.

This report summarizes the observations of shoreline oiling made from 1989 through 1992 during the surveillance programs described above. An earlier paper summarizes the condition of intertidal biological communities on formerly oiled shores (Stoker et al. 1993). Together, these two papers describe the distribution of oil and biological impacts of the spill in 1989, and the recovery of the intertidal habitats and communities in succeeding years.

METHODS

1989 Surveys

The first ground-based shoreline survey was initiated on April 13, 1989, and the last segment was surveyed on September 3 that year (Teal 1991). A total of 5 500 km of shoreline was surveyed during 1989, including nearly 1 500 km in Prince William Sound and 4 000 km in the northwestern Gulf of Alaska.

Shoreline survey methods varied slightly from year to year, reflecting the evolving objectives of the surveys. In 1989, shoreline assessment teams, composed of an oil spill geomorphologist, a biologist, an archaeologist and, in some cases, state and federal agency personnel, visited and surveyed all shores identified by the aerial video surveys as possibly containing stranded oil. As many as seven shoreline assessment teams worked at a time, with first priority given to biologically sensitive areas and the most heavily oiled shores. To provide a georeference system, the geomorphologists divided the shorelines into segments, each up to about 2.5 km long, on the basis of geographic features that could be related back to detailed maps of the shoreline (Owens 1991b). The survey team either walked the full length of each segment or inspected it from a boat if access was impossible.

The geomorphologists recorded observations and drew maps showing the physical features of the shore; substrate types; degree of exposure of the shore to storms; and the distribution, relative abundance, and physical characteristics of the oil. The biologists and archaeologists recorded and mapped the characteristics, condition, and distribution of biological and archaeological resources in each segment. Because of the sensitivity of archaeological resources, information concerning locations and characteristics of such resources was kept confidential, in accordance with state and federal regulations(Wooley and Haggarty this symposium 1994). These detailed data on oiling distribution, biological resources, and cultural/social sensitivities provided the basic information needed by ISCC to formulate cleanup priorities and plans.

1990-1992 Surveys

In April 1990, the FOSC asked government authorities, landowners, and Exxon to identify shoreline segments from among those surveyed in 1989 that might still contain oil and require further cleanup. The 725 shoreline segments subsequently identified for surveys were then subdivided into 1 033 shorter subdivisions to provide a higher level of resolution in terms of site descriptions. Most of the 711 subdivisions in Prince William Sound were 0.8 km or less in length. Each subdivision was surveyed by one of 20 six-member teams made up of an oil spill geomorphologist, a biologist, and representatives of state and federal governments, landowners, and Exxon.

In April and May, the teams surveyed a total of nearly 2 000 km of shoreline in four weeks, including about 1 109 km in Prince William Sound and about 855 km in the Gulf of Alaska. In addition to recording observations of the distribution of surface oil deposits, the geomorphologist dug pits to document and map the presence, distribution, and character of subsurface oil deposits. In 1990, subsurface oil was defined as any oil deposit that had penetrated or was buried more than 10 cm below the general surface of the sediment.

In 1991, shoreline areas to be surveyed were identified by government authorities or landowners as possibly containing remnant oil requiring cleanup. Between April 26 and May 30, 1991, six 10- or 11-member survey teams visited 582 subdivisions and surveyed about 385 km of shoreline in Prince William Sound, and about 120 km in the Gulf of Alaska. Team members walked the full length of each subdivision and recorded their observations as described above for previous surveys.

As in 1990, pits were dug to determine the presence, type and depth of subsurface oil deposits. Where subsurface oil was found, additional pits were dug to delineate its approximate areal extent. The geomorphologist recorded the depth of the oiled zone in each pit, physical characteristics of the oil, type of subsurface sediments, and pit locations within the intertidal zone. In 1991, subsurface oil was redefined as oil found at a depth greater than 5 cm below the surface of sediments located beneath the armor layer (Mastracchio 1991). The modified definition facilitated measurements on shorelines with irregular armor or boulders resting on finer-grained sediments. Subsurface oil deposits were categorized as Oil-Filled Pores, Heavy, Medium, or Light Oil Residue, Traces of Oil, or No Oil (Table 2).

Between May 14 and June 5, 1992, two vessel-based, 11-person survey teams surveyed 76 subdivisions in Prince William Sound and 6 subdivisions along the Kenai Peninsula that government agencies, landowners, or Exxon had nominated as being likely cleanup candidates. In addition, because the 1991 cleanup focused on subsurface oil, those subdivisions where work to remove subsurface oil was done in 1991 were priority candidates for survey in 1992. Teams surveyed about 32 km of shoreline in Prince William Sound and 2 km of shoreline along the Kenai Peninsula. Surveyors again recorded and mapped the distribution of oil present by type (asphalt, tarballs, mousse, surface oil residues, cover, coat, stain, film, oiled debris, or no oil). Following procedures developed in the 1991 survey, the geomorphologists also dug pits and recorded the amount, type, and distribution in the intertidal zone of any deposits of subsurface oil.

In 1992, shorelines did not generally require cleanup beyond the work that could be done while the survey teams were on site. Consequently, most decisions about cleanup were delegated to appropriate members of the survey teams.

Survey Protocols

Very early in the program (April 1989), it was evident that a systematic survey program and more than one field team would be required to provide an adequate database for response decisions. A standard form, incorporating mutually agreed-upon definitions and terminology, was developed for use by the field teams to describe the character of the shoreline and the shoreline oiling conditions in a consistent manner on a segment-by-segment basis (Owens 1991b). This approach ensured that each team was recording a set of objective parameters (oil band width, surface-oil cover, etc.) in the same format. From the start of the shoreline survey program in 1989, teams worked together to develop appropriate procedures and, as the program progressed, a system of cross-training was established for crew change-overs and the introduction of new participants to the system. Before each of the 1990, 1991, and 1992 field surveys, training sessions ensured that all team members were fully briefed on and familiar with the field data collection procedures and terminology.

TABLE 1--Categories of surface oiling used by shoreline survey teams in 1989 and in 1990-1992

Year	Degree of Oiling	Shore Width Affected		Percent Oil Cover
1989	Heavy	>6 m		. . .
	Moderate	3 to 6 m		. . .
	Light	<3 m		. . .
	Very Light	. . .		<10
1990-92	Wide	≥6 m	and	≥50%
	Medium	≥6 m	and	<50% & ≥10%
			or	
		3 to 6 m	and	≥10%
	Narrow	<3 m	and	≥10%
	Very Light	any amount		<10%

TABLE 2--Categories for subsurface oil description in 1991 and 1992

Type	Description
OP	Oil-filled Pore Spaces
HOR	Heavy Oil Residue
MOR	Medium Oil Residue
LOR	Light Oil Residue
OF	Oil Film
TR	Trace
NO	No Oil Observed

Shoreline Oiling Definitions

    The protocols used in the surveys were also checked each year to ensure they met the data demands imposed by the cleanup program. A reconnaissance survey in February 1990 indicated that shoreline oiling conditions had declined substantially since the 1989 survey and that modifications to the survey forms were needed to document and record the character of the shoreline oiling more accurately . The 1990, 1991, and 1992 surveys used a definition of oiling conditions based on a more detailed description than had been used in 1989, involving both width and surface distribution, whereas only width was considered in 1989 (Table 1). The new definition enabled a more quantitative description of oil distribution on the shore after much of the bulk oil had been removed by the 1989 cleanup effort and winter storms.

Likewise, standardized definitions were adopted to characterize subsurface oil. Table 2 shows the categories assigned to various degrees of subsurface oil observed in 1991 and 1992.

An example of the survey form prepared by the shoreline geomorphologist in 1991 to describe each subdivision is provided in Appendix A. The actual format of the survey forms changed from year to year, reflecting both changes in the amounts and modes of occurrences of the remaining oil and changing information needs for the cleanup decision process. Data from each survey form (Appendix A) were entered into computer databases to facilitate record keeping and analysis.

The surface and subsurface oiling data for each subdivision were reviewed, proof-read for consistency of data entries, and entered into the geographic information and mapping system (GIS), which produced maps showing distribution of oiled shores, amounts and types of oil present within each subdivision, and changes in amounts and distributions of oil from year to year.

RESULTS

The shoreline assessment program (SCAT) provides data on changes in the distribution of stranded oil on an annual basis from April 1989 through May 1992. The 1989-1990 Fate and Persistence (FAP) monitoring data identify local monthly time-series changes in shoreline oiling conditions. Both the regional and local data sets of surface and subsurface oiling are discussed here.

Surface Oiling

Initial Oil Distribution--As the oil slick moved among the islands of western Prince William Sound, some of the oil was carried into the intertidal zone by incoming tides and became stranded, primarily in the biologically less-productive upper intertidal and supratidal zones (Owens 1991a,b). Subsequent high tides refloated some of this oil and, in some instances, transported it to other shores. Cleanup methods, such as warm- or cold-water washing, and probably storms, at times transported oil or oil-coated sandy sediments into the middle and lower intertidal zones (Lees et al. 1991). However, in most cases, oiling was heaviest and most persistent in coarse sediments of the upper intertidal zone.

Not all shorelines in western Prince William Sound were oiled. The most heavily oiled shores faced eastward or northward. Some of the westward-facing shores of islands in the spill path were also oiled, particularly by oil that was refloated in the weeks immediately after the spill. Results of the 1989 shoreline assessment program indicated that approximately 783 km of the shoreline in western Prince William Sound (54% of the shores surveyed and 16% of the total shoreline of the sound) was oiled to some degree (Table 3). However, only 10% of the shoreline in the spill path (18% of the oiled shoreline) was classified as heavily oiled and, on a majority of oiled shorelines, there were areas adjacent to the oiled zone with little or no oil cover. The 1 450 km of surveyed shoreline in Prince William Sound (Table 3) represents those sections of coast in the spill path that were identified by the aerial videotape reconnaissance survey as being oiled or possibly oiled.

This does not include many sections of coast in the spill path, such as Southern Herring Bay, Drier Bay, Mummy Bay, and Northern Montague Island, where the aerial survey showed no oil.

TABLE 3--Linear kilometers of surface oiling of shores in Prince William Sound 1989-92 (Distances were converted to metric units)

Year	Surveyed Seg-ments	Subdiv-isions	Km	Very Light	Narrow /Light	Medium/ Moderate	Wide/ Heavy	Total Oiled
1989	550	...	1450	223	326	94	141	783
1990	493	711	1109	323	80	46	21	420
1991	305	432	386	68	15	12	0.1	96
1992	59	76	32	8.7	0.8	0.6	0.2	10

* Oiling coverage definitions changed in 1990; see Table 1.

Reduction of Surface Oil Cover--Table 3 shows oiling distribution in various categories from 1989 to 1992. Figures 2 through 5 illustrate the changes over time in the distribution of surface oiling indicated by the surveys. Between 1989 (Figure 2) and 1990 (Figure 3), total shoreline oiling decreased by approximately 46%, from 783 km to 420 km, due to the intensive 1989 shoreline cleanup effort and several large winter storms (Table 3). The heaviest deposits of oil remaining in 1990 were in sheltered bays in the Knight Island group and on some exposed boulder/cobble shores, such as Point Helen and Sleepy Bay (shown in Figure 2), where oil had penetrated below the surface boulder/cobble layer.

By the spring of 1991, surface deposits of oil were still present on about 96 km of shoreline in the sound. Most of the deposits were classified as either Very Light or Narrow, with only about 0.1 km (100 m) of shore still classified as Wide (Table 3). Most shores still containing surface oil deposits were in sheltered low-energy bays (Figure 4). By the spring of 1992, only isolated pockets of surface oil remained in a few protected bays such as Shelter Bay and Bay of Isles, and a few exposed boulder/cobble beaches such as Point Helen and Sleepy Bay. Surface oiling in the Wide category persisted only in two locations, in Bay of Isles on Knight Island and on northwestern Disk Island (Figure 5). The linear kilometers of oiled shorelines in Prince William Sound declined by an average of about 75% per year between 1989 and 1992, from approximately 16% of the shoreline of Prince William Sound in 1989 to about 0.2% of the shoreline (10 km) in 1992 (Figure 6).

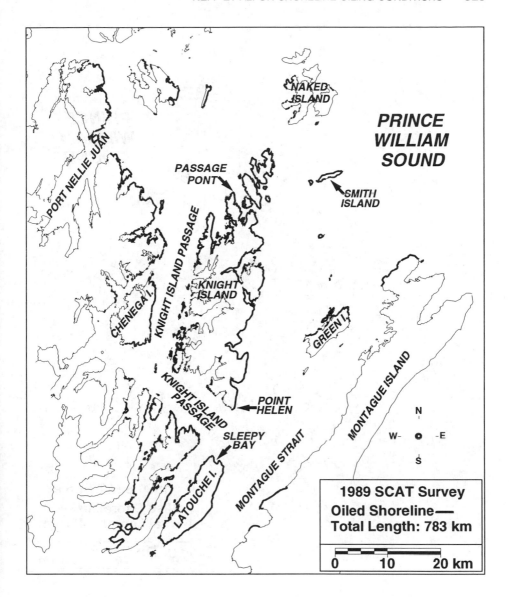

Figure 2--Distribution of oil on shorelines of Prince William Sound in 1989.

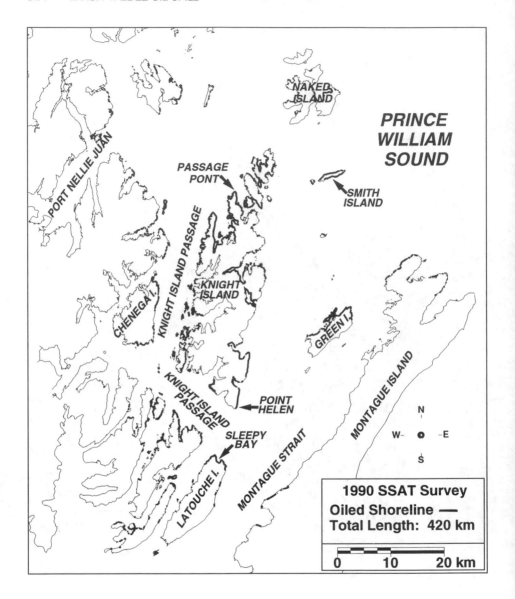

Figure 3--Distribution of oil on shorelines of Prince William Sound in 1990.

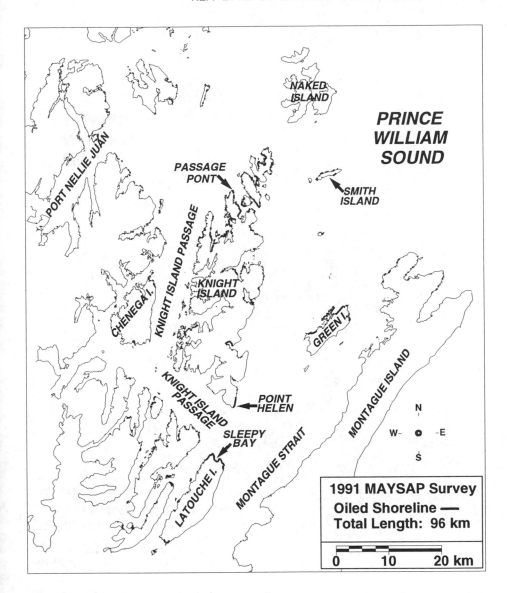

Figure 4--Distribution of oil on shorelines of Prince William Sound in 1991.

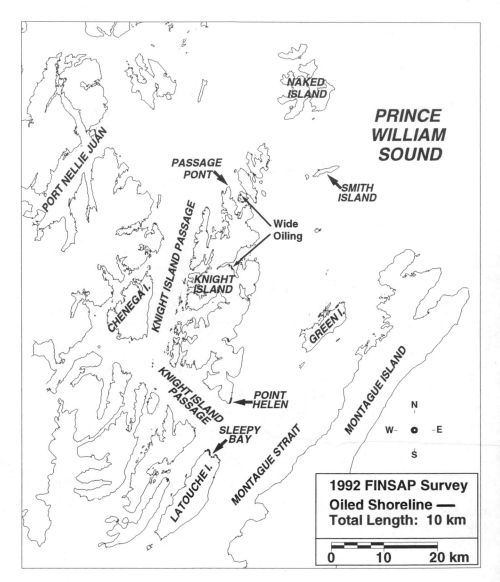

Figure 5--Distribution of oil on shorelines of Prince William Sound in 1992.

Oil Removal on Individual Shores: Effects of Cleanup--Rates of
oil reduction varied among shoreline segments because of differences in
both wave exposure and intensity of cleanup effort. Surface oiling
tended to decrease most rapidly on lightly oiled shores, exposed
shorelines, and shores that received intensive cleanup shortly after the
spill (Owens 1991a). When heavy deposits of oil were allowed to remain
on the shore through the summer of 1989, some surface and subsurface oil
tended to persist into 1991 and, occasionally, 1992.

This trend can be seen schematically in Figures 7a and 7b, which
shows the amount and distribution of surface oil over time on a small
section of the northeast shore of Smith Island (shown in Figure 2) that
was in the direct path of the drifting oil slick (Owens 1991a,b). This
site is indicated by the arrow within segment SM-05 in Figure 8, and was
one of the shorelines monitored in the FAP program.

Observations in April 1989 show that surface oil cover was 100% in
the middle and upper intertidal zones of segment SM-05. In this area
all the surface and near-surface pore spaces were completely filled with
oil. Because the site was near a harbor seal haulout area, intensive
effort was made shortly after the spill to wash off and recover as much
oil as possible from the shore. By late June, the surface oil cover at
the site had been reduced to about 79% by a combination of cleanup
activities and wave action. Additional shoreline washing was performed
during the summer, and the surface oil cover declined to about 28% by
mid-September. Winter storms in October 1989 and January and February
1990 removed most of the residual oil, so that only about 1% oil cover
could be detected on the partially snow-covered shore during a survey in
early March 1990 (Owens, 1991a). A resurvey of the site in early June
1990 revealed 2% oil cover, with most of the oil located in the storm
berms in the supratidal zone. In July, the berms were relocated into the
upper intertidal zone to allow wave action to more effectively remove
the remaining oil. Because berm relocation exposed some buried oil,
total surface oil coverage increased to about 9% in early September.
Estimates of oil cover from September 1989 on were derived from
quantitative transect surveys performed as part of the Fate and
Persistence (FAP) program. The survey methods for FAP were described by
Owens (1991a).

Less-intensive cleanup allowed oil to persist longer on other
shores. For example, shoreline cleanup was not uniform along the
northern coast of Smith Island, with most effort focused on segment SM-
05. Shorelines to the west, such as segment SM-06, were not cleaned as
intensively and, by the spring of 1990, still contained a predominantly
Wide oil cover. Conversely, the intensively cleaned portion of segment
SM-05 described above was classified as having No Oil, Very Light, or
Narrow Oil by that time (Figure 8a).

Rates of natural cleaning also varied among shores. For example,
the removal of oil on the northern shore of Smith Island by shoreline
cleanup and by wave action during the first winter (1989-1990) was more
rapid than that recorded on northern Latouche Island. Both sections of
coast are similar in their physical character (coarse sediments and
bedrock outcrops), exposure to wave action, and initial oiling
conditions (Heavy oil loadings).

Part of this difference may be related to the degree of cleanup in
1989. Except for a small effort in late June and early July, which was
curtailed because of fisheries openings, cleanup on northern Latouche

did not begin until late in the summer (August). Even then, the level of effort was considerably less than that on Smith Island (SM-05). Less oil was removed from the northern Latouche coast in 1989, so that winter wave action there was less effective in removing the remaining surface oil than it was on northern Smith Island (Figures 8a and 8b). The spring 1990 oil-cover map (Figure 8b) shows that the oil cover on most (55%) of this section of the Latouche coast was still categorized as Wide. By spring 1991, after treatment during the previous summer and a further season of winter wave action, the oil cover on approximately half of the shore in this area was still categorized as either Medium or Wide, whereas on northern Smith Island the 1991 data indicate the cover on less than 6% of the shore could be classified as either Medium or Wide. By 1992, the oil cover on northern Latouche was substantially reduced, although traces (Narrow or Very Light cover) were still evident on over a quarter of this coast.

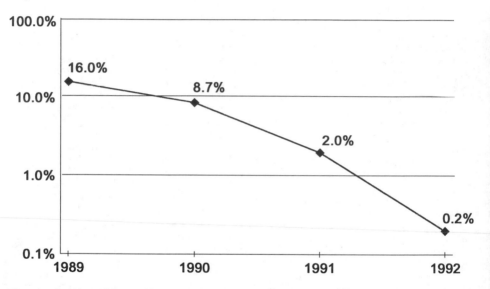

Figure 6--Shoreline oil coverage in Prince William Sound as a percent of the total shoreline length (4840 km) in the sound.

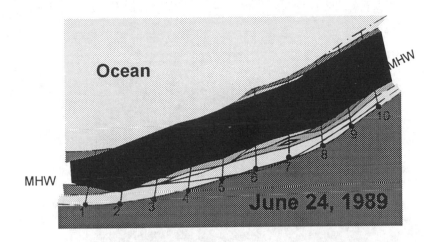

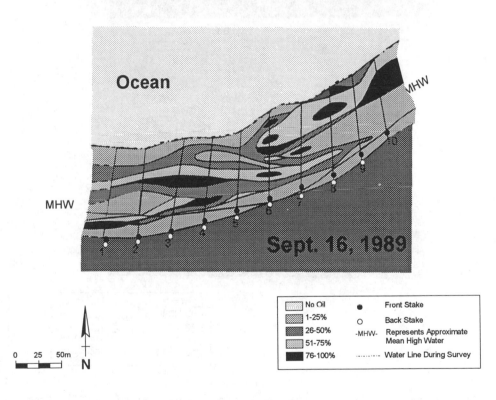

Figure 7a--1989 Surface oiling on northeast Smith Island (SM-05) (from FAP Survey data)

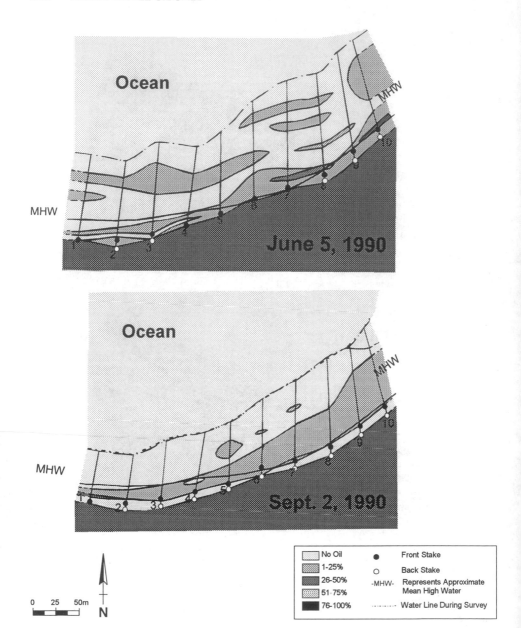

Figure 7b--1990 Surface oiling on northeast Smith Island (SM-05) (from FAP Survey data)

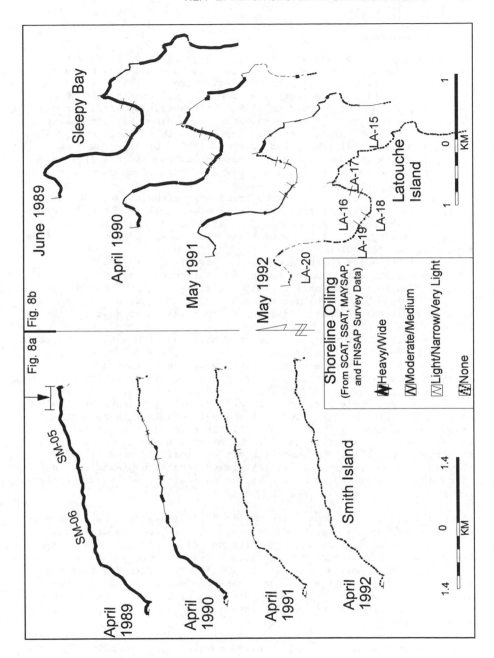

Figure 8--Maps of surface oil distribution for N. Smith segments SM 5 and 6 and N. Latouche segments LA 15 through 20. (The arrow indicates the location of the study site shown in Figures 7a and 7b.). Data were derived from the annual shoreline surveys.

Subsurface Oiling

Distribution of Subsurface Oil in 1990--In 1989, oil was seen to penetrate coarse sediment shorelines to a depth of as much as several decimeters. However, where fine sediments were present, oil was restricted to the surface layer. Although no systematic data on subsurface oil were collected in 1989, a concentrated effort was made in 1990 to document the degree and extent of such deposits. In the spring and summer of 1990, 3 534 pits were dug in the intertidal zone of 493 segments in Prince William Sound (Voskamp 1990). Oil was found at a depth greater than 10 cm below the sediment surface in 624 pits on 218 shoreline segments. Most of the oil was less than 60 cm deep, although some isolated deposits were as deep as 100 cm.

Subsurface oil deposits were found most frequently in the upper intertidal or supratidal zones of high-energy shores composed of coarse-grained cobble/boulder sediments. Four areas in Prince William Sound contained 35% by area of the subsurface oil. These locations were (see Figure 2) the following:

- Point Helen on the southeast shore of Knight Island
- Passage Point on the north shore of Knight Island
- The northwest shore of Smith Island
- Sleepy Bay on the north shore of Latouche Island

At some locations in these segments, oil penetrated to depths of 15 to 100 cm.

Several techniques were used to remove subsurface oil deposits in 1990 (Voskamp 1990). When subsurface oil deposits were covered by a surface coating of mousse or tarmat, cleanup crews removed surface deposits manually or exposed them to natural or bioremediated weathering by raking, tilling, and adding fertilizer. Most subsurface oil deposits were in coarse cobble/boulder sediments frequently flushed by tidal action and having well-aerated pore spaces. Usually, these shores were treated with granular or soluble fertilizers to enhance bioremediation rates. Heavy oil deposits in storm berms were moved into the middle intertidal zone where they were subject to tidal and wave action and treated with bioremediation fertilizers to enhance degradation. Warm- or cold-water washing and manual pickup were also used in some isolated cases.

Distribution of Subsurface Oil in 1991--The shoreline surveys in 1991 also included a comprehensive search for subsurface oil. Seven survey teams dug a total of 2 990 pits on 368 of 432 Prince William Sound subdivisions surveyed to determine the presence and magnitude of subsurface oil deposits (Mastracchio 1991). Pits were dug to explore for the presence of oil and to determine the degree of oiling, the aerial extent, and the depth of penetration or burial. The extent of subsurface oiling was obtained by integrating data from multiple pits at each site where subsurface oil was encountered.

About one-third of the subdivisions with surface oil in 1991 also had subsurface oil. Surveyors observed several types of subsurface oil deposits, including:

- Soft mousse/tar under consolidated surface asphalt patches
- Oil lenses buried under coarse pebble/cobble/boulder sediments and/or resting on a layer of peat or clay

- Oily sediments beneath clean, coarse sediments in storm berms in the upper intertidal and supratidal zones
- Oil trapped in finer sediments under mussel beds

Survey crews found significant subsurface oil deposits, defined as Oil-Filled Pores, Heavy Oil Residue, or Medium Oil Residue (Table 2), on about 1.2% of shoreline areas surveyed--an estimated 50 000 m^2 of shoreline. Individual subsurface oil deposits ranged in size from about 4 000 m^2 to less than 1 m^2. The largest deposits of subsurface oil were in a boulder/cobble beach in Sleepy Bay on the north shore of Latouche Island.

Seventy percent of the total shoreline area with subsurface oil, was treated using berm relocation, tilling, bioremediation, or manual pickup during the 1991 cleanup (Mastracchio 1991).

Distribution of Subsurface Oil in 1992--Identifying remaining subsurface oil was a priority in the 1992 survey; survey teams found scattered deposits on 69 of the 81 subdivisions surveyed in Prince William Sound and along the Kenai Peninsula. Most of the 712 pits dug were on shores that had subsurface oil in 1991 and were suspected of still having subsurface oil in 1992. The survey participants did not dig pits on the other 12 subdivisions because of the type of substrate encountered (bedrock/boulder) or because evidence from prior surveys indicated that no subsurface oil was present. These subdivisions were designated as having no subsurface oil.

In 1992, survey teams resurveyed sixty of the subdivisions surveyed in 1991. Figure 9 shows how the nature of oiling changed on these shores: the pits containing oil categorized as Light Oil Residue or less increased from 39% in 1991 to 69% in 1992. Correspondingly, the heaviest oiling category (OP) fell from 12% to 2%.

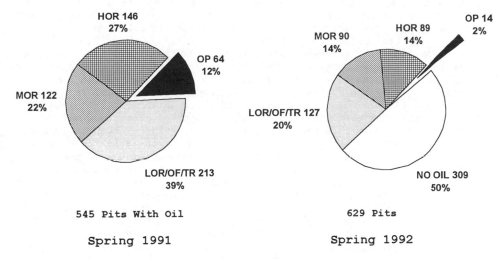

Figure 9--Subsurface oiling in 60 subdivisions surveyed in both 1991 and 1992 (abbreviations are defined in Table 2)

Reductions were even more substantial on an areal basis. On
shorelines common to both surveys, the total area of shoreline
containing subsurface oil deposits decreased by nearly 70% between 1991
and 1992, from about 33 000 m^2 in 1991 to 11 500 m^2 in 1992.
Subdivisions still containing subsurface oil in 1992 also exhibited
substantial improvement in the degree of oiling compared with 1991.
Subsurface oil deposits containing OP decreased by nearly 98% overall,
from 14 500 m^2 in 1991 to 345 m^2 in 1992.

Manual pickup and some tilling, followed in many cases by
application of granular fertilizer, were performed immediately by the
survey crews on most shores requiring treatment. Three subdivisions
required more intensive manual work.

Effects of Cleanup on Subsurface Oil Deposits--Most subsurface oil
was confined to small, isolated deposits in the upper intertidal and
supratidal zones on cobble and boulder shorelines. In 1991, the three
areas in Prince William Sound with the largest estimated areas of
subsurface oil were northwest Smith Island, Point Helen on Knight
Island, and sections of northern Latouche Island. Comparison of data
from these three locations with that from northeast Smith Island
illustrates the effects of the cleanup efforts on rates of change in
subsurface oiling in similar environments. All four sites had a similar
heavy oil loading in 1989 and are predominantly coarse-sediment beaches
into which the stranded oil could penetrate.

The effect of early cleanup is illustrated by considering
Subdivision SM-05 on northeast Smith Island. The cobble beach on
northeast Smith Island was studied as part of the FAP monitoring program
and was one of the most heavily oiled locations anywhere in the sound in
1989 (Owens 1991a). As noted above, this beach was cleaned intensively
in both May and August 1989 because of the proximity to a harbor seal
haulout. A trench dug across the upper intertidal zone in November 1989
revealed that the sediments were virtually free of oil down to the
underlying bedrock (Owens 1991a).

By contrast, northwest Smith Island (Subdivision SM-06B) was not
treated to the same degree as SM-05 in 1989. Similarly, the Point Helen
and northern Latouche Island segments were not treated to the same
degree in 1989, and most work was done later in the summer, in August.
On three of the nine subdivisions on northern Latouche (LA-15B, LA-15E,
and LA-20C) that contained significant amounts of subsurface oil in
1991, 75 to 100% was in the OP category, indicating substantially higher
subsurface oil content than on northwest Smith Island. In the case of
LA-15E, all of the 4 200 m^2 subsurface oil documented was in the OP
category. In the nine subdivisions combined, 62% of the subsurface oil
was in the OP category in 1991. By contrast, subsurface oil residue on
northeastern Smith Island (SM-05) in 1991 was present predominantly as a
coat or cover (LOR) on the subsurface sediments, with no OP. As shown
in Figure 10, 1991 cleanup activities, along with natural removal of oil
during the 1991-92 winter, were also very successful in reducing
subsurface oiling on northern Latouche. The heaviest oiling category,
OP, declined from 62% to 3% between 1991 and 1992.

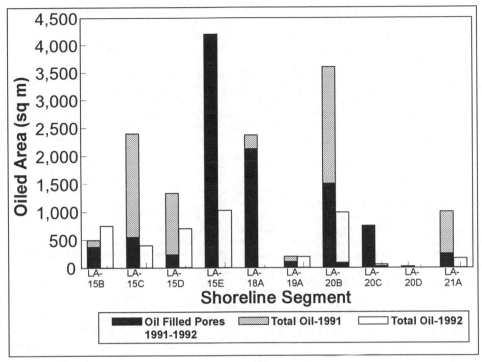

FIGURE 10--Bar graphs of 1991-1992 subsurface oil in northern Latouche subdivisions.

DISCUSSION

In the three years since the *Exxon Valdez* oil spill, the amount of surface and subsurface oil on the shoreline of Prince William Sound has decreased dramatically, by nearly 75% each year between 1989 and 1992. By the spring of 1992, only about 0.2% of the shoreline in Prince William Sound still had any surface oil. The areal extent of subsurface oil on the shores of the sound, most of it in the biologically least productive upper intertidal zone, decreased at a similar rate.

A large amount of oil was removed from the shore by the massive cleanup effort mounted during the summer of 1989 (Carpenter, Dragnich, and Smith 1991; Harrison 1991). Many shores were treated several times by different cleanup methods during the summers of 1989, 1990, and in a few cases 1991 and 1992. Additional oil was removed from oiled shores by natural weathering processes such as evaporation, dissolution, photooxidation, biodegradation, and wave action (Jahns et al. 1991; Koons and Jahns 1992; Bragg and Yang this symposium 1994).

The total amount of oil on the shoreline of Prince William Sound decreased by an estimated order of magnitude during the winter of 1989/90 (Owens, 1991a,b). Michel et al. (1991) reported that winter storms removed up to 90% of the surface oil from exposed, high-energy shorelines and as much as 50% of the surface oil from sheltered shores.

Their survey showed that reworking of cobble sediments by wave action removed subsurface oil from the top 20 cm of the shore and from even greater depths in storm berms on the upper shore. Approximately 40% of oil buried at greater depths was removed by the storm waves of 1989-90 (Michel et al. 1991).

Substantial amounts of oil also disappeared from intertidal sediments on protected shorelines. Oil residues tended to form flocculated aggregates with fine clay-sized particles (glacial flour) present in shoreline sediments. The aggregates, composed of small oil droplets coated with micron-sized mineral particles, do not adhere to surfaces and are readily washed off the shore by tidal flushing and wave action (Bragg and Yang this symposium).

Koons and Jahns (1992) estimated that after two cleanup seasons and two winters, less than about 1% of the oil that originally stranded on the shoreline of the sound remained on shorelines. They also estimated that the total amount of oil remaining on the shoreline in the fall of 1991 was less than about 40 882 L or one-tenth of one percent of the amount of oil originally spilled. Additional oil was removed from the shoreline during the winter of 1991-92, and only a few isolated patches of shore in Prince William Sound contained any oil by May 1992.

Comparison with Previous Spills

The rates of loss of oil from the shorelines of Prince William Sound in the three years after the spill generally were greater than rates of oil loss from shorelines with similar morphology following other large oil spills (Humphrey, Sergy, and Owens 1990; Koons and Jahns 1992).

It is widely accepted that oil is more persistent on protected shores than on exposed areas. For example, during the Baffin Island Oil Spill (BIOS) project, an experimental spill of Lago Medio crude oil was monitored for eight years (Humphrey, Sergy, and Owens 1990; Humphrey, Owens, and Sergy 1991). The rate of natural removal of oil from a sheltered pebble/cobble beach was rapid initially, but slowed as the easily weathered components of the oil were removed. Conversely, experimentally applied heavy No. 5 fuel oil was eroded rapidly between mean water level and 5 m above mean water level from exposed rocky shores of nontidal portions of the Baltic Sea (Jonsson and Broman 1989). Like BIOS, however, the oil was quite persistent on protected rocky shores. Similar patterns have been observed following the *Arrow* and *Esso Bernicia* spills (Owens 1978; Rolan and Gallagher 1991).

These studies all show that natural wave action on exposed rocky shores is effective in removing heavy deposits of crude, refined, and residual oils. However, in sheltered environments that are not cleaned, oil can persist for long periods. For example, field observations at Black Duck Cove in Nova Scotia during 1992, fully 22 years after the 1970 *Arrow* spill of bunker C residual fuel oil, documented the presence of oil on coarse-sediment beaches in sheltered environments where no cleanup was done. At several sheltered locations the oil remains in large quantities, filling the surface and near-surface pore spaces between pebble and cobble sediments in the upper half of the intertidal zone (Owens,et al. 1993).

Even allowing for differences in the environmental fate of different types of oil, the experience in these previous spills

contrasts with the results reported here. The extent of shoreline
surface oiling of Prince William Sound decreased dramatically between
1989 and 1992, from approximately 16% in 1989 to about 0.2% in the
spring of 1992. The extent of heavy oiling decreased even more
dramatically, from 2.9% of the shoreline of Prince William Sound in 1989
to 0.003% in 1992.

Prince William Sound Cleanup Program

     Rates of change were not uniform in time or space. The spatial
variability in the reduction of oil cover over the first year (1989 to
1990) can be explained by an evaluation of the dominant variables
(initial oiling, cleanup effort and timing, and natural removal). The
result of this first phase of recovery, in terms of the amount of oil
remaining after the winter of 1989-90, is reflected in data collected
during the following spring and summer. By the spring of 1990, most of
the coastal segments in Prince William Sound that were initially heavily
oiled were reduced to the Narrow, Very Light, or No Oil categories.
Segments that retained Wide or Medium oil cover in 1990 were those
treated later in the summer of 1989 or were segments that either did not
receive as much cleanup effort or were less exposed to tidal and wave
action. With a few exceptions, all heavily oiled shores in Prince
William Sound were treated at least once in 1989.
     On the basis of these comparisons, it is evident that the
intensive shoreline cleanup efforts, particularly during the summer of
1989, undoubtedly contributed substantially to the rapid decline in the
amounts of oil on the shores of Prince William Sound. By removing most
of the heavy deposits of bulk oil and weathered mousse from the shore,
the cleanup effort allowed natural shoreline cleaning to proceed more
effectively during the winter and decreased the likelihood that bulk oil
washed off one shore by storm waves would wash up on another nearby
shore.
     It is quite conceivable that many sheltered areas in Prince
William Sound, such as Upper and Lower Passage, Northwest Bay, and
Herring Bay, as well as more open coasts such as Sleepy Bay, could have
resembled the situation in Black Duck Cove, Nova Scotia, following the
Arrow spill, had bulk oil cleanup not occurred in 1989.
     One of the primary objectives of spill response operations is to
prevent or minimize the biological injuries and habitat contamination
that might result from the spilled oil. Injury to some of the animals or
plants is inevitable if the oil reaches a shoreline; the objective of a
cleanup program then is to ensure that the system recovers as quickly as
possible.
     In some instances the system can recover quickly without
intervention. In other situations, recovery can be accelerated by
treatment, as opposed to allowing the oil residue to weather naturally.
Development of an appropriate response program involves assessing the
potential effects of the different cleanup options and selecting the
approach, or combination of techniques, that will efficiently remove the
maximum amount of oil and, at the same time, cause minimal injuries to
plants and animals on the shore.
     In evaluating cleanup effectiveness, the surface and subsurface
oiling data from Prince William Sound indicate that it is prudent to

remove oil in the early stages following a spill, before weathering occurs.

SUMMARY

1. Oil was removed rapidly from the shorelines of western Prince William Sound by a combination of the shoreline cleanup effort, weathering of oil residues on the shore, and natural cleansing by wave action from winter storms. The linear kilometers of shoreline in Prince William Sound containing surface oil decreased by an average of 75% each year. The amounts of subsurface oil on the shores of Prince William Sound showed a similar rapid decline from 1991 to 1992.

2. As shown by comparisons of the heavily oiled north shores of Smith and Latouche Islands, reduction rates of surface and subsurface oil were accelerated where 1989 treatment was conducted early (May and June) or where intensive and repeated cleanup was used. Reduction rates were slower in areas treated later that summer and/or less intensively.

3. The systematic collection of data on shoreline oiling conditions using standardized definitions and observation protocols facilitated direct comparison among sites, segments, and coastal sections over time.

4. The shoreline survey and committee review and approval process which evolved following the *Exxon Valdez* spill effectively identified and developed priorities for shoreline segments requiring treatment and protection. The information gathered allowed selection of effective and environmentally acceptable shoreline treatment methods for different oiling conditions while protecting vulnerable natural and cultural resources.

ADDENDUM

During the summer of 1993, an additional shoreline survey was conducted in the spill-impacted areas of Prince William Sound, the Kenai Peninsula, and the Kodiak Archipelago – Alaska Peninsula region. This survey was conducted by personnel familiar with prior shoreline surveys. The primary objectives of the 1993 survey were to assess residual surface and subsurface oiling and shoreline biological conditions. Because shoreline cleanup had terminated in 1992 under the order of federal and state authorities, the surveys teams were not asked to consider the advisability of additional cleanup activities.   In 1993, the team focused on finding subsurface oil. Consequently, more shorelines were visited and more pits were dug than in prior years.

Ninety-seven subdivisions were surveyed in Prince William Sound during June. Sixty one of these were the sites that had been surveyed in 1992. The 36 sites added to the 1993 survey were areas of high interest because of their previous oiling or cleanup history. An additional 34 subdivisions not inspected in 1992 were surveyed in the

Kenai Peninsula - Kodiak Archipelago - Alaska Peninsula region during the first half of July.

A single team was employed for this survey, which included two, and in some cases three, oil spill geomorphologists, a biologist, an Exxon logistics coordinator, and, during the Prince William Sound phase, a data manager. Each of these individuals had been involved in prior joint agency surveys and was very familiar with the spill area and survey methodologies.

The results of the 1993 survey demonstrated a continuing decline of residual surface oiling, with only scattered and weathered remnants remaining at some locations. Of the approximately 80 km of shoreline surveyed, only 119 m at a single location (Bay of Isles, Knight Island) retained Wide surface oiling. An additional 558 m was categorized as Moderate. Surface oiling in the Moderate to Wide category was found only in Prince William Sound, and in total lengths greater than 10 m at only 12 locations (Harrelson, 1994).

Overall, a somewhat larger area of subsurface oil was located in 1993 than in 1992 because more effort was expended in searching for subsurface oil. In 1993, approximately 1 500 pits were dug on 96 subdivisions, as opposed to fewer than 700 pits on 76 subdivisions in 1992. However, when specific locations are compared on a location to location and pit to pit basis, a continuing decline in subsurface oiling from year to year was observed. In all such comparisons, both the category of residual subsurface oil and the thickness of the oiled layer declined between 1992 and 1993.

The 1993 survey also demonstrated that the techniques and procedures described above can be adapted to serve a variety of purposes. In 1989 through 1992, the procedures were used to prioritize and select the shorelines that were to be worked on by cleanup crews. In 1993, they provided a disciplined methodology to continue to monitor and document the reduction in shoreline oiling on shores affected by the spill (Harrelson, 1994).

ACKNOWLEDGMENTS

The studies that are reported here constitute one of the largest, most detailed coastal survey programs ever undertaken. The success of the program is due to the considerable effort of the several dozen geomorphologists and support staff who conducted the field surveys or reduced the large volume of data that was generated. A.R. Teal was the program manager for Exxon throughout the 4-year study. The authors wish to acknowledge two unknown reviewers for their attention to detail and constructive input to the manuscript.

REFERENCES

Bragg, J.R. and Yang, S.R. "Clay-Oil Flocculation and Its Effects on the Rate of Natural Cleansing in Prince William Sound Following the *Exxon Valdez* Oil Spill." *Third Symposium on Environmental Toxicology and Risk Assessment: Aquatic, Plant, and Terrestrial.* American Society for Testing and Materials, Philadelphia; 1993.

Carpenter, A.D., R.G. Dragnich, and M.T. Smith. "Marine Operations and Logistics During the *Exxon Valdez* Spill Cleanup." *Proceedings of the 1991 International Oil Spill Conference. Prevention, Behavior, Control, Cleanup.* Washington, DC: American Petroleum Institute. 205-211; 1991.

Environment Canada. *"Oilspill SCAT Manual for the Coastlines of British Columbia."* Prepared by Woodward-Clyde Consultants for: Environment Canada, Technology Development Branch, Conservation and Protection; Edmonton, Alberta; 245 pp.; 1992.

Harrelson, R.C. "POSTSAP Survey Summary Report (Final)" Exxon Company, U.S.A., Houston, TX., 22 pp;1994.

Harrison, O.R. "An Overview of the *Exxon Valdez* Oil Spill." *Proceedings of the 1991 International Oil Spill Conference. Prevention, Behavior, Control, Cleanup.* Washington, DC: American Petroleum Institute. 313-319; 1991.

Humphrey, B., E.H. Owens, and G. Sergy. "Long-term Results from the BIOS Shoreline Experiment-Surface Oil Cover." *Proceedings of the 1991 International Oil Spill Conference. Prevention, Behavior, Control, Cleanup.* Washington, DC: American Petroleum Institute. 447-452; 1991.

Humphrey, B., G. Sergy, and E.H. Owens. "Stranded Oil Persistence in Cold Climates." *Proceedings of the Thirteenth Arctic and Marine Oilspill Program Technical Seminar.* Ottawa, Canada: Environment Canada; 401-410; 1990.

Jahns, H.O., J.R. Bragg, L.C. Dash, and E.H. Owens. "Natural Cleaning of Shorelines Following the *Exxon Valdez* Spill." *Proceedings of the 1991 International Oil Spill Conference. Prevention, Behavior, Control, Cleanup.* Washington, DC: American Petroleum Institute. 167-176; 1991.

Jonsson, A. and D. Broman. "Natural Erosion on Oil of Rocky Shores in Non-Tidal Areas." *Oil & Gas Journal* 5: 273-284; 1989.

Knorr, J.R., A. Teal, N. Lethcoe, S. Christopherson, and J. Whitney. "The Interagency Shoreline Cleanup Committee: A Cooperative Approach to Shoreline Cleanup-The *Exxon Valdez* Spill." *Proceedings of the 1991 International Oil Spill Conference. Prevention, Behavior, Control, Cleanup.* Washington, DC: American Petroleum Institute. 189-191; 1991.

Koons, C.B. and H.O. Jahns. "The Fate of Oil from the *Exxon Valdez*—A Perspective." *Journal Marine Technology Society.* 61-69; Fall 1992.

Lees, D.C., J.P. Houghton, H. Teas, Jr., H. Cumberland, S. Landino, W.B. Driskell, and T.A. Ebert. "Evaluation of the Condition of Intertidal and Shallow Subtidal Biota in Prince William Sound Following the *Exxon Valdez* Oil Spill and Subsequent Shoreline Treatment." Report to NOAA, Hazardous Materials Section, Seattle, WA; 1991.

Lethcoe, J. and N. Lethcoe. 1989. "*Cruising Guide to Prince William Sound.*" Volume 1. Western Part. Valdez, AK: Prince William Sound Books; 152 pp.

Mastracchio, R.L. "Subsurface Oil Evaluation July 12, 1991." Anchorage, AK: Exxon Company, U.S.A., Box 2180, Houston, TX 77252; 1991.

Michel, J., M.O. Hayes, W.J. Sexton, J.C. Gibeaut, and C. Henry. "Trends in Natural Removal of the *Exxon Valdez* Oil Spill in Prince William Sound from September 1989 to May 1990." *Proceedings of the 1991 International Oil Spill Conference. Prevention, Behavior, Control, Cleanup.* Washington, DC: American Petroleum Institute. 181-187; 1991.

NOAA (National Oceanic and Atmospheric Administration). "Excavation and Rock Washing Treatment Technology. Net Environmental Benefit Analysis." Seattle, WA: NOAA; 178 pp.; 1990.

Owens, E.H., "Mechanical Dispersal of Oil Stranded in the Littoral Zone." *Journal Fisheries Research Board of Canada.* 35(3): 563-572; 1978.

Owens, E.H. "Changes in Shoreline Oiling Conditions 1-1/2 Years after the 1989 Prince William Sound Spill." Seattle, WA: Woodward-Clyde; 55 pages; 1991a.

Owens, E.H. "Shoreline Conditions Following the *Exxon Valdez* Spill as of Fall 1990." *Proceedings of the Fourteenth Arctic and Marine Oilspill Program (AMOP) Technical Seminar, Vancouver, Canada, June 12-14.* Environment Canada; 579-606; 1991. Or Seattle, WA: Woodward-Clyde; 49 pages. 1991b.

Owens, E.H., G.A. Sergy, B. E. McGuire, and B. Humphrey "The 1970 *Arrow* Oil Spill—What Remains On the Shoreline 22 Years Later?" *Proceedings of the Sixteenth Arctic and Marine Oilspill Program (AMOP) Technical Seminar.* Ottawa, Canada, Environment Canada; 1149-1167; 1993.

Owens, E.H., A.R. Teal, and P.C. Haase. "Berm Relocation During the 1990 Shoreline Cleanup Program Following the *Exxon Valdez* Spill." *Proceedings of the Fourteenth Arctic and Marine Oilspill Program (AMOP) Technical Seminar.* Ottawa, Canada; Environment Canada; 607-630; 1991.

Rolan, R.G. and R. Gallagher. "Recovery of Intertidal Biotic Communities at Sullom Voe Following the *Esso Bernicia* Oil Spill of 1978." *Proceedings of the 1991 International Oil Spill Conference. Prevention, Behavior, Control, Cleanup.* Washington, DC: American Petroleum Institute. 461-465; 1991.

Royer, T.C., J.A. Vermersch, T.J. Weingartner, H.J. Neibauer, and R.D. Muench. "Ocean circulation Influencing the *Exxon Valdez* Oil Spill." *Oceanography* 3(2): 3-10; 1990.

Stoker, S.W., J.M. Neff, T.R. Schroeder, and D.M. McCormick. "Biological Conditions of Shorelines Following the *Exxon Valdez* Spill." *1993 International Oil Spill Conference.* Washington, DC.: American Petroleum Institute. 287-292; 1993.

Teal, A.R. "Shoreline Cleanup-Reconnaissance, Evaluation, and Planning Following the Valdez Oil Spill." *Proceedings of the 1991 International Oil Spill Conference. Prevention, Behavior, Control, Cleanup.* Washington, DC: American Petroleum Institute. 149-152; 1991.

Voskamp, W.E. "Spring 1990 Joint Shoreline Assessment Subsurface Oil Report." June 27, 1990. Exxon Co. U.S.A., Box 2180, Houston, TX 77252; 1990.

Wooley C.B. and J.C. Haggarty. "Archaeological Site Protection: An integral Component of the Exxon Valdez Shoreline Cleanup." This Symposium.

APPENDIX A

Surface Oil Type Definitions	
Code	Description
AP	Asphalt
MS	Mousse Patches/Pooled Oil
TB	Tarballs/Patties
SOR	Surface Oil Residue
CV	Cover (>1 mm - <1 cm)
CT	Coat (<1 mm)
ST	Stain (<0.1 mm)
FL	Film or Sheen
DB	Oiled/Cleanup Debris
NO	No Visible Oil

Surface Oiling Description Definitions	
Code	Distribution
C	Continuous: 91-00
B	Broken: 51-90%
P	Patchy: 11-50%
S	Sporadic: 1-10%
T	Trace: <1%
...	None: 0%
TR	Trash
VG	Vegetation
LG	Logs
?	Questionable

Subsurface Oil Character Definitions	
Code	Description
OP	Oil-Filled Pores
HOR	Heavy Oil Residue
MOR	Medium Oil Residue
LOR	Light Oil Residue
OF	Oil Film
TR	Trace
NO	No Oil

Pit Zone Definitions	
Code	Tidal Zone
S	Supratidal
U	Upper Intertidal
M	Middle Intertidal
L	Lower Intertidal
SU	Supra-Upper
SUM	Supra-Upper-Mid
SUML	Supra-Upper-Mid-Lower
UM	Upper-Mid
UML	Upper-Mid-Lower
ML	Mid-Lower

Table A-1--Abbreviations used in Figures A-1 and A-2

MAYSAP SHORELINE OILING SUMMARY

PAGE 1 OF 2

TEAM NO. 3

OG HARPER   BIO STOKER

SEGMENT KN-211

ADEC GHORMLEY   LANDMANAGER BLANCHET for USFS

SUBDIVISION B

EXXON CZARNECKI   USCG/NOAA GLEASON / DAHLIN

DATE 17 / MAY / 91

TIME 11 : 00 to 12 : 05   TIDE LEVEL -1.55 ft. to 1.61 ft.   ENERGY LEVEL: [X] H [ ] M [ ] L

SURVEYED FROM: [X] FOOT [X] BOAT [ ] HELO   WEATHER: [X] SUN [ ] CLOUDS [ ] FOG [ ] RAIN [ ] SNOW

TOTAL LENGTH SHORELINE SURVEYED: 431 m   NEAR SHORE SHEEN: [ ] BR [ ] RB [ ] SL [X] NONE

EST. OIL CATEGORY LENGTH: W 19 m M 75 m N 75 m VL 112 m NO 150 m US 0 m

LOC	SURFACE OIL CHARACTER											SURFACE SEDIMENT TYPE	SHORE SLOPE V H M L	AREA		ZONE				NOTES
	AP	MS	TB	SOR	CV	CT	ST	FL	DB	NO			WIDTH m	LENGTH m	S	UI	MI	LI	
A				S							BC	HM	2	30		X			SOR/H/I*
B				P							CPB	M	10	10		X			SOR/H/I
C	T										PCG	M	2	3		X			MOSTLY COLLECTED
D				T							PCB	M	10	20		X			SOR/H/I - MOSTLY LEE SIDE BOULDERS, BETWEEN CRACKS
E1				S							BR	M	5	40		X			
E2					P						BR	M	2	40		X			
F				S							BCP	M	10	10		X	X		SOR/H MOUSSE PATTIES ON LEE
G				S		P					BCP	M	10	20		X			SOR/H
H						P					RB	M	2	20		X			
																			* INTERSTITIAL

DISTRIBUTION: C = 91-100%; B = 51-90%; P = 11-50%; S = 1-10%; T = <1%
SLOPE: V = VERTICAL; H = HIGH ANGLE; M = MEDIUM ANGLE; L = LOW ANGLE   PHOTO ROLL # MAYSAP- 3 - 17 FRAMES # 11-18

PIT NO.	PIT DEPTH (cm)	SUBSURFACE OIL CHARACTER							OILED ZONE cm-cm	CLEAN BELOW Y/N	H2O LEVEL (cm)	SHEEN COLOR B R S N	PIT ZONE				SURFACE-SUBSURFACE SEDIMENTS	NOTES
		OP	HOR	MOR	LOR	OF	TR	NO					S	UI	MI	LI		
1	50							X	-					X			P-P-P-ORG	
2	20							X	-					X			P-P	
3	20						X		-?	Y					X		P-SGP	
4	20						X		-?	Y						X	P-P	
5	35							X	-						X		P-SG	
6	35							X	-							X	P-SGP	
7	20							X	-						X		P-R	
8	20							X	-							X	P-SGP	
9	30							X	25-30	Y					X		P-GPS	CLUMPS OIL ON CLASTS

SHEEN COLOR: B = BROWN; R = RAINBOW; S = SILVER; N = NONE

OG COMMENTS:

THIS IS A RELATIVELY HIGH EXPOSURE PEBBLE-COBBLE-BOULDER POCKET BEACH WITH WAVE FETCH DISTANCES TO THE EAST IN EXCESS OF 30 KM.

THE SURFACE OILING DISTRIBUTION IS COMPLEX, WITH A WIDE VARIETY OF OILING TYPES EVIDENT. THE "FLANKS" OF THE BEACH HAVE RESIDUAL 'COATS' ON BOULDER-RUBBLE AND SPORADIC SOR/H IN INTERSTITIAL CRACKS BETWEEN BOULDER RUBBLE. REMNANTS OF HEAVIER OILING ARE STILL APPARENT ON THE UPPER BEACH, PARTICULARLY AT LOCATIONS 'B' AND 'F' WHERE AN ESTIMATED 60 m² OF SOR/H OR AP REMAINS; MOST OF THE REMAINING PAVEMENT AND/OR MOUSSE PATTIES ARE LOCATED BETWEEN CRACKS IN BOULDERS OR ON THE LANDWARD SIDE

Figure A-1--Geomorphologist report on shoreline oiling at KN-211B on May 17, 1991

MAYSAP SHORELINE OILING SUMMARY (cont.)   PAGE _2_ OF _2_

TEAM NO. _3_

SEGMENT _KN-211_   SUBDIVISION _B_   DATE _17_ /_MAY_/ 91

PIT NO.	PIT DEPTH (cm)	SUBSURFACE OIL CHARACTER							OILED ZONE cm-cm	CLEAN BELOW Y/N	H2O LEVEL (cm)	SHEEN COLOR B R S N	PIT ZONE				SURFACE-SUBSURFACE SEDIMENTS	NOTES
		OP	HOR	MOR	LOR	OF	TR	NO					S	UI	MI	LI		
10	2∅							X	-					X			P-G	
11	2∅						X		-					X			P-P	
12	2∅							X	-					X			P-SG-LOG	
13	~2∅							X	-							X	P-GS	
14	16	X	X						5-15	Y				X			PC-SG	PHOTO 18
									-									ESTIMATE <1m²
									-									
									-									
									-									
									-									
									-									
									-									
									-									
									-									
									-									
									-									
									-									
									-									
									-									
									-									

SHEEN COLOR: B = BROWN; R = RAINBOW; S = SILVER; N = NONE

OG COMMENTS:

OF BOULDERS. THE TARMAT AT LOCATION 'C' WAS COLLECTED.

SUBSURFACE OILING APPEARS TO BE LIMITED TO THE AREAS WHERE SOR/H IS PRESENT. AT THE SOUTH END OF THE BEACH, LOCATION 'B', THE SOR IS GREATER THAN 5-7CM THICK AND PROBABLY GRADES INTO AN HOR CONDITION AT LESS THAN 20% OF LOCATION 'B'. HOR SUBSURFACE OILING CONDITION WAS ALSO IDENTIFIED IN PIT #14; HOWEVER, NUMEROUS NEARBY UNDOCUMENTED PITS INDICATE A VERY LIMITED EXTENT (<1m²).

A LARGE LOG-LIKE, ORANGE OBJECT WAS NOTED AT THE NORTH END (NOT COLLECTED).

Figure A-2--Geomorphologist report on subsurface oiling at KN-211B on May 17, 1991

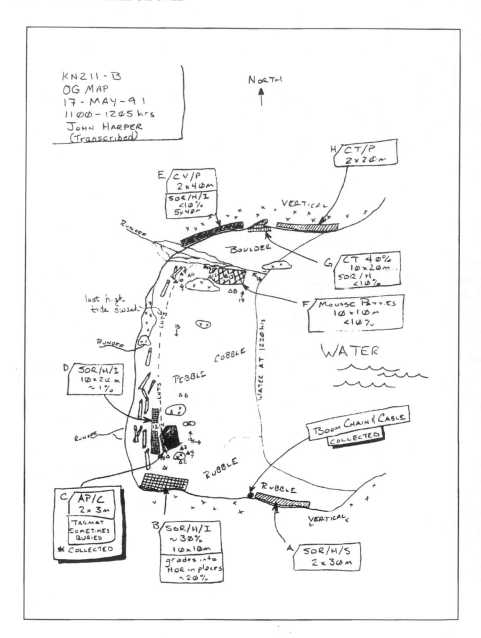

Figure A-3--Geomorphologist sketch of shoreline oiling at KN-211B on May 17, 1991

Paul D. Boehm[1], David S. Page[2], Edward S. Gilfillan[2], William A. Stubblefield[3], E. James Harner[4]

SHORELINE ECOLOGY PROGRAM FOR PRINCE WILLIAM SOUND, ALASKA, FOLLOWING THE *EXXON VALDEZ* OIL SPILL: PART 2—CHEMISTRY AND TOXICOLOGY

REFERENCE: Boehm, P. D., Page, D. S., Gilfillan, E. S., Stubblefield, W. A., and Harner, E. J., "Shoreline Ecology Program for Prince William Sound, Alaska, Following the Exxon Valdez Oil Spill: Part 2--Chemistry and Toxicology," Exxon Valdez Oil Spill: Fate and Effects in Alaskan Waters, ASTM STP 1219, Peter G. Wells, James N. Butler, and Jane S. Hughes, Eds., American Society for Testing and Materials, Philadelphia, 1995.

ABSTRACT: Part two of a three-part series, this paper describes chemical and toxicological results of a comprehensive shoreline ecology program that was designed to assess recovery in Prince William Sound following the *Exxon Valdez* oil spill of March 24, 1989. The program is an application of the "sediment quality triad" approach, combining chemical, toxicological, and biological measurements. Other parts of the program are described in Part 1: Study Design and Methods (Page et al., this volume) and Part 3: Biology (Gilfillan et al., this volume). The study was designed so that results could be extrapolated to the entire spill zone in the sound and projected forward in time. It combined one-time sampling of 64 randomly chosen study sites representing four major habitats and four oiling levels (including unoiled reference sites), with periodic sampling at 12 subjectively chosen "fixed" sites. Sediment samples—or when conditions required, filter-wipes from rock surfaces—were collected in each of three intertidal zones and from subtidal stations up to 30-m deep.

Oil removal was generally quite rapid: by 1991 the concentration of oil spilled from the *Exxon Valdez* had been dramatically reduced on the majority of shorelines by both natural processes and cleanup efforts. Moderate concentrations of petroleum residues remain only in limited, localized areas; however, most of these residues are highly asphaltic, not readily bioavailable, and not toxic to marine life.

[1]Arthur D. Little, Inc., Cambridge, MA
[2]Bowdoin College, Brunswick, ME
[3]ENSR Consulting and Engineering, Ft. Collins, CO
[4]West Virginia University, Morgantown, WV

Acute sediment toxicity from oil (as measured by standard toxicity tests) was virtually absent by 1990-'91, except at a small number of isolated locations. The petroleum residues had degraded below the threshold of acute toxic effects. Measurable polycyclic aromatic hydrocarbon (PAH) levels are, in general, well below those conservatively associated with adverse effects, and biological recovery has been considerably more rapid than the removal of the last chemical remnants. The remaining residues continue to degrade and are, in general, predicted to become indistinguishable from background hydrocarbon levels by 1993 or 1994. Localized residues of weathered oil will no doubt exist beyond 1994 at certain locations, but their environmental significance will be negligible compared with other stresses ongoing in the sound.

Samples of nearshore subtidal sediments showed surprisingly low concentrations of oil residue, as an increment to the natural petrogenic hydrocarbon background. Sediment toxicity tests showed that they were essentially non toxic. It appears that most of the oil leaving the shoreline was swept away and dissipated at sea. It is concluded that long-term ecological effects resulting from shoreline oiling or subtidal contamination are highly unlikely.

KEYWORDS: *Exxon Valdez*, polycyclic aromatic hydrocarbons, sediment chemistry, bioavailability, sediment toxicity, mussels, oil-spill recovery

---

INTRODUCTION

The *Exxon Valdez* oil spill released about 11 million gallons of Alaska North Slope (ANS) crude on March 24, 1989, into Prince William Sound. Approximately 486 miles of shoreline in western and southwestern Prince William Sound were affected (Neff et al., Conditions of Shorelines, this volume). Shorelines along the Kodiak archipelago and the Kenai and Alaska peninsulas were also oiled, but less than those in the sound (Gilfillan et al., Shoreline Impacts, this volume). Additional accounts of the spill history may be found in Maki (1991).

Other studies (e.g., Maki 1991; Michel et al. 1991; Jahns et al. 1991; Owens 1991) have shown that, over the first year following the spill, dramatic reductions in shoreline oiling and improvement in shoreline conditions occurred. Such reductions in oiling levels were the result of natural processes and cleanup activities (Neff et al., Conditions of Shorelines, this volume).

The shoreline ecology program was designed to assess biological recovery and the level and rate of reduction of chemical residues through 1991. The program consisted of biological (Gilfillan et al., Part 3: Biology, this volume) as well as chemical and toxicological components (this study). Details of the program design are described in a separate paper (Page et al., Part 1: Study Design and Methods, this volume).

BACKGROUND

The Prince William Sound Environment

Prince William Sound is a high-energy subarctic environment characterized by rocky and boulder/cobble shorelines and, to a much lesser extent, those having pebble/gravel and fine-grained substrates. It is not a fragile environment; plant and animal communities populating the shorelines are subjected to severe storms and harsh winters on an annual basis. Consequently, they are very resilient and capable of rapid recolonization (Gilfillan et al., Part 3: Biology, this volume).

The spill affected area in the sound is dominated by four shoreline types: exposed bedrock/rubble, sheltered bedrock/rubble, boulder/cobble beaches, and pebble/gravel beaches. Bedrock shoreline habitats, the least likely to exhibit long-term oil retention (Gundlach and Hayes 1978), comprise over 70% of the total impact zone; soft-sediment depositional habitats and salt-marsh environments, the most likely to show long-term effects, are extremely rare in Prince William Sound (Gilfillan et al., Part 3: Biology, this volume).

Previous Spill Histories

Most previous studies on the persistence of oil on shorelines have focused on fine-grained sediments in low-energy environments (e.g., the Baffin Island Oil Spill [BIOS] experiment, the *Florida* spill at West Falmouth, Massachusetts). The same is true for the *Amoco Cadiz* spill, even though much of the shoreline affected by the *Amoco Cadiz* spill consisted of moderate-to high-energy environments.

On the basis of previous spills in high-energy environments, such as the rocky coast of Brittany exposed to the *Amoco Cadiz* spill, the expectation was that the oil spilled into Prince William Sound would be physically removed from the great majority of the shoreline by wave action and other mechanisms. In general, the longest duration of oil-spill impact occurs when oil is mixed with fine-grained sediments (NRC 1985). In the aftermath of the *Amoco Cadiz* oil spill, shoreline surveys showed that oil had largely disappeared from exposed bedrock, exposed boulder, and exposed sand and gravel beaches within 12 to 18 months after the spill. However, oil persisted longer in more sheltered, low-energy locations (d'Ozouville et al. 1980; Gundlach et al. 1983).

Similarly, in the BIOS experiment, oil persisted on the shoreline for several years because of low wave-energy and predominantly fine sediments (Boehm et al. 1987; Owens et al. 1987). The fact that the site is ice-bound for much of the year further slowed natural cleaning processes. Two years after the release, 50% of the oil originally on the beach remained in the form of an asphaltic pavement in the upper intertidal zone.

The long-term persistence of fuel oil in West Falmouth (Teal et al. 1992) is also not readily extrapolatable to Prince William Sound. The West Falmouth spill affected low-energy peat marshes typical of New England, but not of the sound, which has very few soft, fine-grained shoreline sites. It is in fine-grained sediments that previous oil-spill studies (e.g., Gundlach et al. 1983; Boehm et al. 1987; Owens et al. 1987; Teal et al. 1992) have documented that oil residues persist in for a long time.

Oil-Spill Chemistry

Oil-spill chemical studies have evolved from the pioneering work of Blumer and colleagues (e.g., Blumer and Sass 1972; Teal et al. 1978) on the characterization of oil residues in samples taken at West Falmouth and other spill sites. Improved oil-spill chemistry characterized the scientific studies of the Ixtoc-1 blowout, the *Amoco Cadiz* tanker spill, and the BIOS experimental oil release. Through the application of gas chromatography/mass spectrometry, spilled oil is being increasingly characterized in terms of the concentrations of individual hydrocarbon components rather than in terms of broader semiquantitative hydrocarbon profiles. These analyses are targeted at a wide range of compounds, which are used to measure the concentration and weathering state of the spilled oil in order to help assess its biological impact and to discriminate among different hydrocarbon sources (Boehm et al. 1981; Boehm and Fiest 1982; Boehm et al. 1987; Page et al. 1988; Sauer and Boehm 1991).

Prince William Sound, with its predominantly rocky and boulder/cobble shorelines and its relative isolation, presented unique opportunities and challenges for study. The sampling methods for this study adhered to the norms of best current practice (API 1984; NRC 1985). However, the features of the shoreline habitats in the sound required the development of new methods for sampling hydrocarbon residues adhering to rocky faces (i.e., filter wipes) as well as new sampling strategies for boulder/cobble beaches, where fine sediments are rare (i.e., sampling matrix in boulder/cobble).

Linkage of Chemistry and Sediment Toxicity

The presence of hydrocarbons alone is not a reliable indicator of the state of recovery from an oil spill. Spilled oil rapidly loses the more acutely toxic hydrocarbon fractions upon exposure to the environment and a threshold level is passed below which petroleum hydrocarbons serve more as a carbon source for bacteria, and thus, indirectly, for higher organisms, than as a toxicant (Montagna et al. 1987; Spies et al. 1988). Data are presented elsewhere (Page et al., Identification of Hydrocarbon Sources, this volume) that show the presence of a petroleum-hydrocarbon background in the subtidal sediments in Prince William Sound. These hydrocarbons originate from natural seeps in the Gulf of Alaska and are brought into the sound by prevailing currents. Studies at other natural oil-seep areas (e.g., Spies et al. 1980, 1988) have shown that chronic inputs of weathered petroleum from seeps cause changes in biological community structures similar to those observed for inputs of other sources of organic enrichment. These findings mean that the detection of weathered petroleum traces at a site alone is not sufficient to indicate (1) whether *Exxon Valdez* Crude (EVC) is present or (2) if EVC is present, that environmental injury is occurring, i.e., without concurrent biological and/or toxicological measurements.

Polycyclic aromatic hydrocarbons (PAH) and other components of petroleum are found in sediments throughout the world (Neff 1979) and are important contaminants in many coastal marine sediments. A sediment toxicity threshold value for PAH in subtidal sediments has been discussed by Long and Morgan (1990) and Long (1992). On the basis of field data taken from a number of contaminated harbors, this "Effects Range-Low" (ER-L) value conservatively estimates the level of PAH at which there is a potential for adverse biological effects. It also provides a framework to compare the chemistry and toxicity data from this study and to evaluate (along with the results from Gilfillan et al. Part 3: Biology, this volume) the effects of shoreline oiling in terms of potential toxic effects on marine animals.

GOALS AND APPROACH

The overall goal of the chemistry part of the shoreline ecology program was to assess the exposure of the shoreline environment to petroleum hydrocarbons and to document changes in the quantities and composition of petroleum residues over time. The exposure was evaluated through a combination of sediment chemistry (focusing mainly on PAH), sediment toxicology, and mussel body-burden measurements. The chemical assessments were designed to be selective, sensitive, and precise analytical measurements.

The overall program was an application of the "sediment quality triad" approach to contaminant assessment, which combines measurements of chemistry and toxicity with biological/ecological measurements. This approach has been applied to studies of harbor pollution, but not to oil spills (Long and Chapman 1985; Chapman et al. 1991). In addition, the bioavailability of oil residues in intertidal sediments was assessed through the sampling and analysis of mussels, an application of the Status and Trends/Mussel Watch approach (NRC 1980).

The program was guided by the desire to acquire data for chemistry, toxicology, and biology in a synoptic manner (API 1984; NRC 1985) so that relationships between oil exposure and biological response could be developed. This close pairing of biological and chemical observations represents a marked improvement over many previous studies in which sampling locations and/or replication strategies differed between the chemical exposure and biological response components. For example, weathering studies previously undertaken in spill assessments have seldom dealt with the biological implications of the concentration and composition of the remaining oil residues (e.g., Gilfillan et al. 1986).

METHODS AND MATERIALS

The study design consisted of two field components: fixed sites and stratified random sampling (SRS) sites (see Page et al., Part 1: Study Design and Methods, this volume). The 12 fixed sites provided information on the changes in amount and composition of petroleum residues over the period 1989-1991 (Table 1). Unoiled reference sites for the fixed-site program were sampled in 1990 and 1991. Although several "set-aside" (untreated) sites were among the fixed sites, most of the fixed sites were chosen from very heavily oiled shorelines. This paper does not compare set-aside and treated sites. As discussed by Page et al. (Part 1: Study Design and Methods, this volume), the study design did not separate cleanup effects from oiling effects in comparing oiled and reference sites.

The 64 SRS sites of the program provided data that could be extrapolated to the entire spill zone in Prince William Sound. These sites were chosen by stratified random sampling from a large number of candidate sites representing four habitat types (exposed bedrock, sheltered bedrock, boulder/cobble, and pebble/gravel) and four initial oiling levels (heavy, moderate, light, and none = reference). The general locations of study sites are shown in Figure 1.

To assess chemical exposure, three types of samples were obtained from each site:

- Intertidal and nearshore subtidal sediment samples, or bedrock filter wipes, for chemical analysis of hydrocarbon residue;

- Mussel (*Mytilus sp.*) samples from intertidal locations for tissue analysis as indicators of bioavailability of oil residues to nearshore animal communities; and

- Sediment samples for toxicity tests to determine acute toxic effects of petroleum residues remaining in shoreline sediments.

Sampling

Sediment, filter-wipe, and mussel samples were obtained from the 76 study sites. Table 1 summarizes the extent of the sampling program conducted at the 12 fixed sites, and their reference sites, between 1989 and 1991. The 64 SRS sites were surveyed once in 1990. The site selection, site survey, and sampling methods are described in detail in Page et al. (Part 1: Study Design and Methods, this volume).

Synoptic chemical, toxicological, and biological samples were obtained from three generally parallel transects at each site; for chemical analysis, intertidal sediment samples (from 0 to 10-cm depths) were obtained at three tide zones, and nearshore subtidal samples (from 0 to 2-cm depths) were obtained at two or three subtidal depths. Sediment samples for toxicity tests were obtained at two intertidal zones and two or three subtidal depths on all three transects in 1990-'91 (only on the center transect but from three intertidal zones in 1989). Samples were obtained by scooping or coring (with a sampling tube) to the prescribed depth in the sediment. Subsurface samples (from 10 to 60 cm) were collected for chemical analysis in the upper intertidal zone at fixed sites in 1990-'91 and at moderately and heavily oiled boulder/cobble and pebble/gravel SRS sites in 1990. All samples were collected as composites of three subsamples taken from the perimeter of the biological sampling station (see Figure 4b in Page et al., Part 1: Study Design and Methods, this volume).

Mussel samples were collected from the middle intertidal zone of soft sediment and pebble/gravel sites and from rock outcrops or large boulders at bedrock and boulder/cobble sites. At pebble/gravel sites, mussels occurred throughout the intertidal zone and were collected in proximity to sediments. At the Mussel Beach site (SR01N), the middle intertidal zone represented the upper part of a large mussel bed.

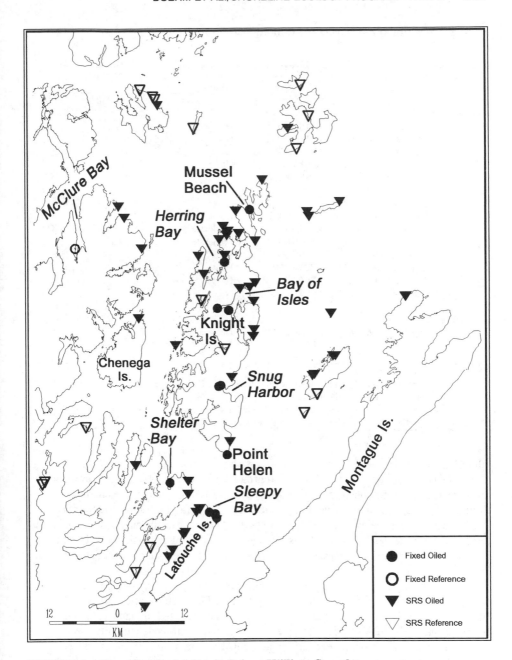

FIGURE 1—Shoreline study sites in Prince William Sound.

TABLE 1—Summary of fixed-site sampling program.

Habitat	Location	Site/Segment	Initial Oiling	Sampling		
				1989*	1990	1991
Boulder/Cobble						
	Latouche	E11/LA15	Heavy		X	X
	Latouche (SA)	E11SA/LA15	Heavy	X	X	X
	Point Helen	SR07/KN405	Heavy	X	X	X
	Sleepy Bay	SL01/LA19	Heavy		X	X
	Reference	(5 SRS sites)	None		X	X**
Pebble/Gravel						
	Bay of Isles West	SRMB4/KN07	Light	X	X	X
	Herring Bay (SA)	SR03/KN5000	Moderate	X	X	X
	Mussel Beach	SR01N/EL13	Moderate	X	X	X
	Shelter Bay	SR06/EV21	Heavy	X	X	X
	Snug Harbor W (SA)	SR05/KN401	Heavy	X	X	X
	Snug Harbor E (SA)†	SR04/KN401	Heavy	X	X	X
	Reference	(4 SRS sites)	None		X	X
Soft Sediment						
	Bay of Isles Marsh	BI01/KN136	Heavy		X	X
	McClure Bay	MB01	None		X	X

SA	Designates set-aside sites.
†	Snug Harbor E (SA) is partially a sheltered bedrock site; however, only sediment samples were included in the analysis.
*	Only chemistry samples from 1989 were included in the analyses for this program.
**	Only 4 of the 5 boulder/cobble reference sites were sampled in 1991.

Chemical Analysis

General approach--The analytical approach included the use of compound-specific measurements for saturated hydrocarbons (SHC) and PAH to quantify the chemical exposure regime, to examine weathering processes, and to facilitate source identification. Table 2 summarizes the overall analytical strategy. The focus of the chemistry covered in this paper is on the PAH concentrations. In addition, sediment-grain-size distribution and organic carbon content were measured and used as concomitant variables in the statistical analysis.

The quality-assurance program for analytical chemistry used a number of safeguards, including written standard operating procedures, laboratory work plans, and internal data auditing. The quality-control program consisted of blanks, standard reference materials (SRMs), check samples, spiking, and rigorous data quality objectives including surrogate recovery ranges, SRM accuracy limitations, etc. Also included in the sampling effort (see Page et al., Part 1: Study Design and Methods, this volume) were complete field verifications of all sampling methods and a training program.

TABLE 2—Description of analytical strategy.

Target Group	Analytes	Sample Matrix	Assessment Use	Method Summary
Polycyclic Aromatic Hydrocarbons (PAH)	2-6 ringed PAH and selected alkylated homologues	Sediments, mussel tissue, filter wipes	1. Determine the presence of *Exxon Valdez* crude oil in samples. 2. Differentiate among sources (e.g., various petrogenic sources vs. pyrogenic sources). 3. Determine oil weathering rates.	Sonication extraction with acetone-methylene chloride, HPLC silica gel fractionation-cleanup, alumina column pre-cleanup for tissue samples, GC/MS SIM analysis.
Saturated Hydrocarbons (SHC)	nC_{10}-nC_{32} alkanes and isoprenoids (pristane and phytane)	Sediments, mussel tissue, filter wipes	1. Measure the petroleum content of samples. 2. Determine stage of oil weathering. 3. Assess the rate of oil biodegradation.	Sonication extraction with acetone-methylene chloride, HPLC silica gel fractionation-cleanup, alumina column pre-cleanup for tissue samples, GC/FID analysis.
Grain Size	Percentage gravel, sand, silt, clay, and phi class size distribution	Sediments	1. Provides information on the particle-size distribution of sediments and the nature of the sedimentary environment. 2. Used as a normalization factor for organic chemical parameters.	Wet and dry sieving to separate gravel, sand, and silt/clay. Wet pipette analysis to further fractionate the silt/clay fraction.
Total Organic Carbon (TOC)	Organic Carbon	Sediments	1. A measure of organic carbon load in sediments. 2. Used to normalize organic chemical parameters.	Solvent extraction to remove petroleum from "heavily oiled" samples, acid treatment to remove inorganic carbon, combustion at 900°C in a C,H,N analyzer.

HPLC = High performance liquid chromatography; GC/MS = Gas chromatography/mass spectrometry; GC/FID = Gas chromatography/flame ionization detector; SIM = Selected ion monitoring

Details of procedures--All analytical procedures were documented as detailed standard operating procedures. The flowchart in Figure 2 summarizes the analytical methodology, which included two important features. First, we used automated high-performance liquid chromatography (HPLC) for extract fractionation. The procedure was geared to the reproducible fractionation of large numbers of samples. Second, we used two sets of standards: surrogate recovery standards added to the sample prior to processing and internal standards added to the extract prior to analysis. This allowed the values, quantified by the internal standards, to be corrected on the basis of surrogate standard recoveries. Additional analytical details and data quality objectives are presented in Page et al. (Identification of Hydrocarbon Sources, this volume).

A list of the individual target analytes is presented in Table 3. It is a relatively extensive, but not exhaustive, list of petrogenic, pyrogenic, and biogenic/diagenetic PAH compounds. The petrogenic compounds on the target list represent between 1% (unweathered oil) and 5% (weathered oil) of the total petroleum present in a typical sample with *Exxon Valdez* crude oil. However, neither the presence of petrogenic PAH nor the presence of any particular PAH homologous series (e.g., the dibenzothiophenes) is sufficient to indicate the presence of spill-related oil (Bence and Burns, this volume; Page et al., Identification of Hydrocarbon Sources, this volume). The PAH values shown in the figures and listed in the appendix do not include biogenic aromatic compounds (perylene) or C_0-and C_1-naphthalenes. The latter compounds were excluded because they were often present in procedural blanks.

Sediment Toxicology

Measurements were taken to evaluate the toxicity of sediment samples to the petroleum-sensitive infaunal marine amphipod *Rhepoxynius abronius*. The bioassays followed the methods of Swartz et al. (1985) and Chapman and Becker (1986). Sediment samples received from the field were refrigerated until testing. Sediment bioassays were normally conducted within two weeks of receipt of the samples. A portion of each sediment sample was taken for grain-size analysis. Five replicates with 20 animals each were exposed for 10 days in containers with clean seawater containing 2 cm of test sediment. Live animals were counted after the 10-day exposure period, and the results expressed as percentage mortality.

Data Analysis

Details of the data analysis procedures are presented in Page et al. (Part 1: Study Design and Methods, this volume). Data were analyzed to determine if the means of the chemical variables measured at oiled study sites were significantly different from those at unoiled reference sites. The methods were chosen to permit hypothesis testing with maximum power. The tests for significant differences in the means between oiled and reference sites were conducted in a manner appropriate to the structure of each dataset. Initially, analysis of covariance (ANCOVA) was applied to log-transformed data with measures of grain size (% sand, % silt/clay), total organic carbon (TOC), and wave exposure as concomitant variables, using either sites or transects (as appropriate) as replicates. The residuals of these models were tested to determine whether normal error

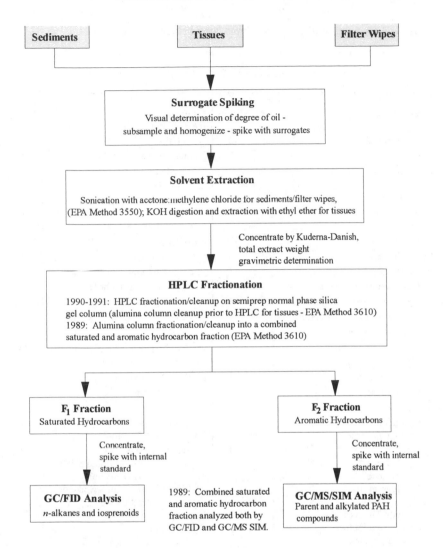

FIGURE 2—Summary flowchart of analytical methods. EPA Methods are derived from U.S. EPA (1986).

theory was applicable, using a standard Shapiro-Wilks test. Those datasets that failed the test were analyzed with a generalized linear model (GLIM), using a Poisson, binomial, or negative binomial distribution, as appropriate. Finally, those datasets with structures that did not permit hypothesis testing by ANCOVA or GLIM were tested by nonparametric comparisons (Wilcoxon's and Kruskal-Wallace ranked-sum tests). Analysis of the amphipod toxicity was conducted with GLIM using a binomial distribution. Data were adjusted using the same concomitant variables as in the statistical analysis of the chemistry data.

TABLE 3—Listing of target analytes, surrogates and standards.

Polycyclic Aromatic Hydrocarbons (PAH)			Aliphatic Hydrocarbons (SHC)	
Compound	Surrogate Reference	#Rings	Compound	Surrogate Reference
naphthalene	1	2	(Normal linear) alkanes•	
C_1-naphthalenes	1	2	nC_{10}-nC_{32}	3
C_2-naphthalenes	1	2	Isoprenoid hydrocarbons	
C_3-naphthalenes	1	2	pristane	3
C_4-naphthalenes	1	2	phytane	3
acenaphthylene	1	3		
acenaphthene	1	3		**Surrogate**
fluorene	1	3	**Surrogates and Standards**	**Reference**
C_1-fluorene	1	3	Surrogates	
C_2-fluorene	1	3	SHC = d$_{24}$-tetracosane	3
anthracene	2	3	PAH = d$_8$-naphthalene	
C_1-phenanthrenes/anthracenes	2	3	d$_{10}$-acenaphthene	1
C_2-phenanthrenes/anthracenes	2	3	d$_{10}$-phenanthrene	2
C_3-phenanthrenes/anthracenes	2	3	d$_{12}$-benzo(a)pyrene	
dibenzothiophene	2	3		
C_1-dibenzothiophenes	2	3	Internal Standards (added to the final extract)	
C_2-dibenzothiophenes	2	3	SHC = d$_{60}$-triacontane	
C_3-dibenzothiophenes	2	3	PAH = d$_{10}$-fluorene	
fluoranthene	2	4	d$_{12}$-chrysene	
pyrene	2	4		
C_1-fluoranthenes/pyrenes	2	4	Quality-Assurance/Quality-Control Standards	
benzo(a)anthracene	2	4	(each batch of 20 samples)	
chrysene	2	4	EV check - *Exxon Valdez* cargo oil solution	
C_1-chrysene	2	4	NIST SRM 1491 (PAH and SHC)	
C_2-chrysene	2	4	NIST SRM 1941 (PAH only)	
C_3-chrysene	2	4	Matrix Spike and Matrix Spike duplicate	
C_4-chrysene	2	4	Procedural Blank	
benzo(b)fluoranthene	2	5		
benzo(k)fluoranthene	2	5		
benzo(a)pyrene	2	5		
dibenzo(a,h)anthracene	2	5		
perylene	2	5		
benzo(g,h,l)perylene	2	6		
indeno(1,2,3-cd)pyrene	2	6		

RESULTS

The results presented in this section include data on the petroleum hydrocarbon content and hydrocarbon chemical composition of sediment samples, surface wipes, and mussel tissues, as well as data on the toxicity of intertidal and nearshore subtidal sediments. Most PAH found in intertidal samples from oiled sites were derived from weathered oil from the spill. However, at some sites, PAH were detected from other sources (peat, diesel, or other refined products). PAH found in subtidal sediment comes from a number of sources, and spill oil is often only a minor constituent (Page et al., Identification of Hydrocarbon Sources, this volume). For purposes of statistical analysis, we did not differentiate sources of PAH other than perylene, which was subtracted from all analyses.

The results from the fixed sites (1989-1991), which are presented first, show the levels of oil residue in terms of total PAH (TPAH) concentrations and their decreases over time. Trends in mussel-body burden and sediment toxicity are also shown.

Data are then presented for the SRS sites sampled in 1990. These data reflect the status in 1990 of chemical and toxicological conditions in the spill-affected portion of Prince William Sound. Results are presented as geometric means to better reflect the large variability in the data and to minimize the effect of outliers. Large variability is typical for oil-spill datasets (e.g., Boehm et al. 1987) because of the patchy distribution of shoreline oiling.

Time Trends at Fixed Sites

The results from the eight sites that were sampled in 1989, 1990, and 1991 are presented in this section. These sites include six pebble/gravel sites (Bay of Isles, Mussel Beach, Herring Bay, Snug Harbor W, Snug Harbor E, and Shelter Bay) and two boulder/cobble sites (NE Latouche Island, Point Helen). (See Figure 1.)

As indicated in Table 1, these sites include lightly, moderately, and heavily oiled sites; some were treated to remove oil and others were not. Results for three additional sites, which were added in 1990 (Latouche Island-E1, Sleepy Bay-SL1, Bay of Isles Marsh-BI1), are presented separately. The fixed-site results represent temporal trends at some of the locations of heaviest initial oiling. Therefore, they cannot be extrapolated to the entire spill zone in Prince William Sound.

Sediment chemistry: PAH--The analytical results for TPAH in intertidal sediments of the eight fixed sites sampled in 1989, 1990, and 1991, as well as reference data from sedimentary SRS sites sampled in 1990 and 1991, are summarized in Figure 3a. TPAH data listings are presented in the Appendix (Table A-1), which include data for fixed sites added in 1990, as well as nearshore subtidal sampling locations. Figure 3a shows that the TPAH decreased steadily over the first two years after the spill. Initial mean TPAH levels (ca. 200 ppm, upper intertidal; 50 ppm, middle intertidal; 2 ppm, lower intertidal) had decreased by two orders of magnitude by 1991 (ca. 2, 0.8, and 0.08 ppm, respectively). Nevertheless, according to nonparametric Wilcoxon statistical tests, mean TPAH levels at the fixed sites in 1991 were still significantly higher than at reference sites in all intertidal zones.

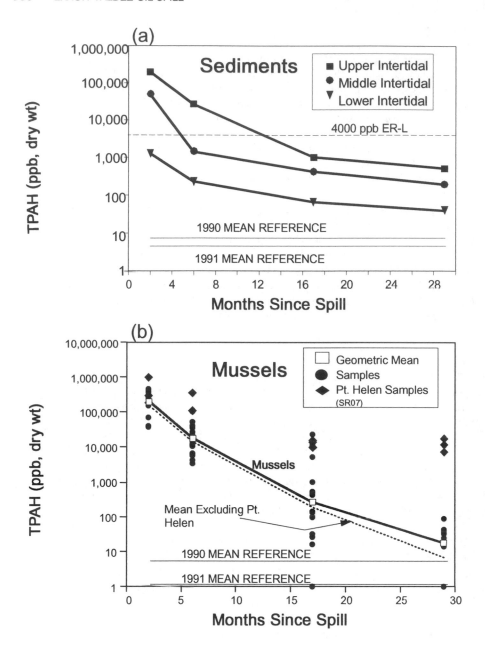

FIGURE 3—Summary of sediment (a) and mussel (b) PAH data for fixed sites sampled in 1989, 1990, and 1991. Values are geometric means in parts per billion (ppb) on a dry-weight basis. PAH totals include all analytes listed in Table 3 except perylene, naphthalene, and C_1-naphthalenes.

The highest TPAH levels were typically found at the upper intertidal zone. The nearshore subtidal zones show evidence of oil from the spill, but the TPAH values are several orders of magnitude lower than those for intertidal levels (see Table A-1). The mean nearshore subtidal TPAH levels ranged from 0.2 to 0.3 ppm in May 1989, and decreased to become statistically indistinguishable from reference in 1990 (-3-m subtidal) and 1991 (-3-to -10-m subtidal).

Weathering indicators--Two weathering indicator ratios were computed from the PAH and saturated hydrocarbon (SHC) data: C_2-C_4-naphthalenes/TPAH and C_{18}/phytane (Table A-2). The first ratio illustrates the weathering of the aromatic hydrocarbons, starting with a value of 0.4 in the spilled oil, and decreasing to values close to zero as the naphthalene homologues are lost because of weathering. The ratio is analogous to an "aromatic weathering ratio" (Boehm et al. 1982b), which decreases as the more easily weathered naphthalene homologous series decreases in concentration relative to the TPAH in the sample. The data in Table A-2 show that a substantial amount of aromatic-hydrocarbon weathering took place the first six months after the spill, when the ratio decreased to, or below, 0.1 at most sites. Sporadic values above 0.1 were observed in 1990. By 1991, values at all sites other than the heavily oiled Bay of Isles site (BI01) were close to zero in all tide zones. The value of 0.2 to 0.3 at BI01 in 1991 is consistent with the finding of substantial quantities of oil remaining at this unique, soft-substrate site that covers roughly two acres. It should be noted that the more volatile aromatic compounds (i.e, the alkylated benzenes and the C_0-C_1-naphthalenes) weathered even faster. Most of the volatile aromatic hydrocarbons were completely removed from the oil residues in three to six months.

The second ratio, C_{18}/phytane, indicates the relative loss of the straight-chain alkanes compared with the isoprenoid alkanes, a progression that is associated with biodegradative loss (Atlas et al. 1981). The C_{18}/phytane ratio is 1.8 in the spilled oil and decreases to a value close to zero (Table A-2). This decrease in the C_{18}/phytane ratio indicates active biodegradation, beginning as early as May 1989.

Mussel chemistry--The TPAH data from indigenous, intertidal mussels from the eight fixed sites sampled in 1989, 1990, and 1991 are plotted in Figure 3b below the corresponding sediment data. The figure shows two average trends, one including Point Helen (SR07), the site of large berm relocation efforts in 1990 and in 1991, and the second excluding this site. When Figures 3a and 3b are compared, a relationship emerges between TPAH levels in the sediments and in the mussel tissues—both decreased steadily. By 1991, while elevated TPAH levels could still be found in the sediments, the body burdens in the mussels were in many cases below the detection limit of the analytical method. The 1991 mean was approaching reference levels.

The mussel PAH data are presented in Table A-3, together with ratios of alkylated naphthalenes to TPAH. These two-ringed aromatics decreased rapidly with time as oil residues weathered on the shoreline.

Subsurface sediment chemistry data--In general, the subsurface PAH levels and the relation of surface to subsurface concentrations tended to be highly variable, indicating a very patchy distribution of subsurface oil. In 1990, samples from depths of 10 to 60 cm were taken at all three transects in the upper intertidal zone of heavily and moderately oiled sedimentary sites (fixed and SRS) to examine the occurrence and chemical state of oil residues in subsurface sediments. These measurements were repeated at the fixed sites in 1991.

The PAH results in Figure 4 indicate that subsurface oil concentrations were dependent on the degree of oiling and the habitat. For the fixed sites (Figure 4a), both surface and subsurface PAH concentrations are highest at the boulder/cobble sites, which represent worst-case oiling conditions in the sound. Subsurface oil concentrations at the fixed pebble/gravel sites were much lower. PAH in the subsurface was generally lower in 1991 than in 1990. Two of the fixed boulder/cobble sites (Point Helen and LaTouche Island) had been subjected to berm relocation activities about two weeks before they were sampled in 1991; in 1990, the Point Helen site was sampled four weeks following berm relocation. Thus, the comparison of surface oiling data may reflect the fact that these berm relocation activities were effective in exposing oiled subsurface layers as intended.

As shown in Figure 4b, the PAH concentrations at the SRS sites were lower than those at the fixed sites and decreased with decreasing oiling level. Like the fixed sites, the extent of oil penetration into the subsurface layers was greater in the boulder/cobble habitat than in the pebble/gravel substrates.

Sediment toxicology--Results of the fixed-site sediment toxicity measurements are summarized in Figure 5 as means (over sites) of percentage amphipod mortality for the boulder/cobble (Figure 5a) and pebble/gravel (Figure 5b) shoreline habitats. Each plot shows true means, by tide zone, for 1990 and 1991, together with the data for the appropriate SRS reference sites. Different symbols (open or solid) are used to indicate whether a statistically significant difference from reference sites was found. Such differences occurred in upper intertidal locations at boulder/cobble beaches in 1990 and 1991 and at pebble/gravel beaches in 1990. No significant differences were found for subtidal sediments.

Sites of Special Interest

Sites that were of special interest because of the possibility of oil persistence included the soft-sediment Bay of Isles marsh site, the mussel bed on Eleanor Island (Mussel Beach), the boulder/cobble site at Point Helen that received berm relocation treatment prior to sampling in 1990 and 1991, and the set-aside site in Herring Bay.

Sediments--TPAH concentrations at the Bay of Isles marsh did not decrease between 1990 and 1991, and relatively high levels (e.g., 800 ppm in the upper intertidal) remained when this site was last sampled in 1991 (see Table A-1). The nearshore subtidal samples show TPAH levels from 0.8 to 2 ppm. This is not unexpected; the site contains a thick layer of peat and is similar to certain marsh environments studied at other spills—it is "the West Falmouth of Prince William Sound."

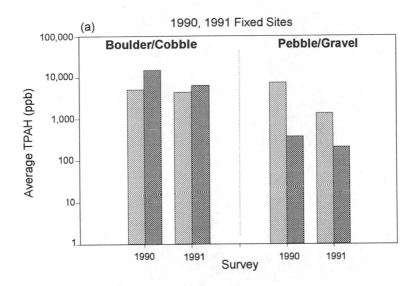

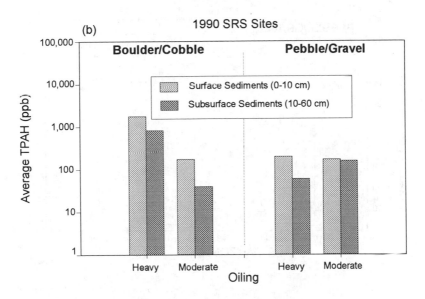

FIGURE 4—Subsurface-sediment chemistry TPAH results for the fixed sites from 1990 and 1991 (a) and the boulder/cobble and pebble/gravel SRS sites in 1990 (b). Data for the boulder/cobble sites in (a) are from three sites: Pt. Helen, Sleepy Bay, and Latouche Island (E11); the set-aside site on Latouche Island was not included. Results are shown as geometric means and include all analytes listed in Table 3 except perylene, naphthalene, and C_1-naphthalenes.

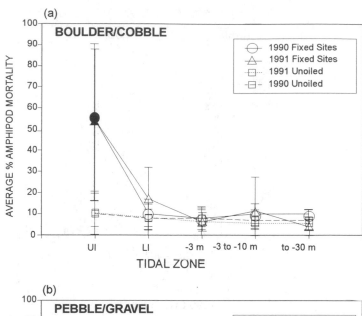

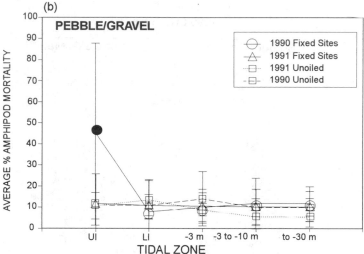

FIGURE 5—Summary of 1990 and 1991 sediment-toxicity data for fixed sites, showing percentage amphipod mortality for boulder/cobble (a) and pebble/gravel (b) sites. Solid symbols are used where the estimated means are statistically different from reference. Data are true means and not adjusted for concomitant variables. Error bars are ± 1 SD.

The sediment data from Mussel Beach (Table A-1) indicate a rapid decrease in TPAH over the period from 1989 to 1991, with concentrations in the lower intertidal statistically similar (at the 95% confidence level) to reference in 1990, whereas levels in the middle intertidal remained statistically different from reference (TPAH = 0.5 ppm). The TPAH results from Point Helen indicated heavy initial oiling followed by a decrease of two to three orders of magnitude at all tide levels; however, the 1991 value in the upper intertidal shows an increase over the previous survey, likely the result of berm relocation only two weeks prior to sampling. The data from the set-aside site in Herring Bay showed TPAH levels decreasing markedly over time. Visual examination indicated that the small amounts of oil residues remaining at this site in 1991 existed as asphaltic residues mixed into the sediments.

Mussel chemistry--The results of the mussel-tissue analyses from several individual sites, shown in Figure 6, demonstrate three important aspects regarding the availability of sediment hydrocarbons to marine animals: (1) the decreasing bioavailability of oil residues trapped in intertidal mussel beds (Mussel Beach), (2) the decreasing bioavailability of oil residues at set-aside sites (Herring Bay), and (3) the effect on bioavailability of berm relocation (Point Helen).

The TPAH values at Mussel Beach (Figure 6a) are particularly interesting because this site contains one of the largest mussel beds in the sound. The mussels at this site were initially covered with oil in May 1989 (Boehm 1989, personal observation). Figure 6a shows the trend in mussels from the upper part of the mussel bed, corresponding to the middle intertidal zone. PAH concentrations in mussels had returned to background by 1991 despite the significant levels of PAH in the underlying sediment (ca. 1 ppm; Table A-1). Note that indigenous mussels of a range of 2-3 cm were sampled. Therefore samples did not include new spat.

The set-aside site in Herring Bay (Figure 6b) also illustrates the rapid decline of mussel-tissue PAH, which reached background levels 17 months after the spill, even though sediment PAH values were still elevated in August 1990 (43 ppm in the upper intertidal zone, Table A-1).

At Point Helen, where sampling occurred four weeks and two weeks after berm relocation in 1990 and 1991, respectively, the effect of sediment redistribution seems to be reflected in the mussel tissue PAH data (Figure 6c). Instead of exhibiting a steady decrease as at other sites, PAH levels in mussels from this site leveled off, probably reflecting the increased bioavailability of buried oil that had been brought to the surface.

Sediment toxicology--Site-specific sediment-toxicity data for three heavily oiled sites (Bay of Isles, Snug Harbor E, Point Helen) are presented in Figure 7. Because of limited replication (i.e., only the center transects were sampled at each site), statistical testing of the results was not performed, but error bars (±1 SD) are presented to illustrate the variance of the data.

Although sediment toxicity is demonstrated by results from the September 1989 samples from most of the tide zones for these three heavily oiled locations, by 1991, only the upper intertidal samples from the Bay of Isles site and Snug Harbor sites showed any

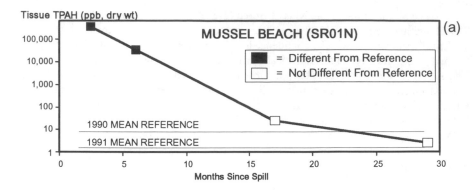

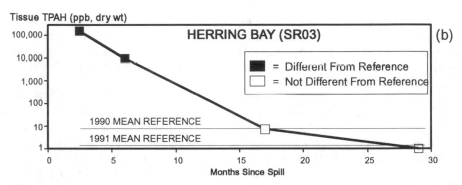

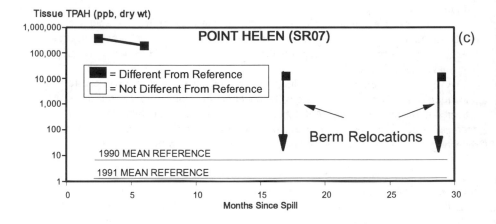

FIGURE 6—Summary of TPAH data for mussels at selected fixed sites. Temporal trends of the geometric means of replicate samples are plotted for Mussel Beach (a), Herring Bay (b), and Point Helen (c). All values are expressed in ppb dry weight.

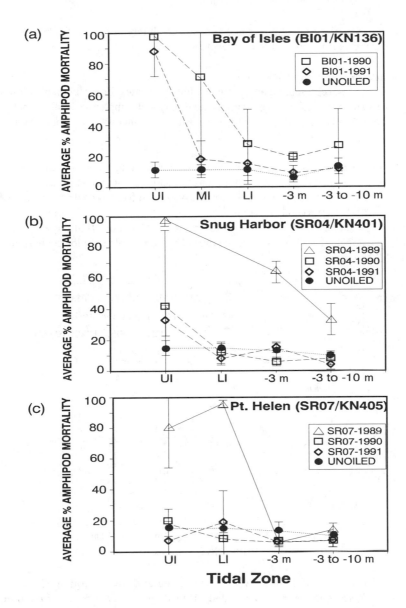

FIGURE 7—Sediment toxicity at selected sites by year. Percent mortality averaged over triplicate samples from each tide zone are shown for Bay of Isles marsh (a), Snug Harbor (b), and Point Helen (c). Also given are unoiled mean reference data (solid circles) for comparison. UI = Upper Intertidal; MI = Middle Intertidal; LI = Lower Intertidal. Error bars are ± 1 SD.

residual toxicity. Samples from all other tide zones from all three sites are similar in
toxicity to the samples from unoiled reference sites.

Stratified Random Sampling (SRS) Sites
　　Sixty-four sites, representing an average of four replicates for each combination of
four oiling levels and four habitats, were chosen randomly and sampled in 1990 so that
results could be extrapolated to the spill-affected portion of Prince William Sound as a
whole.

　　Sediment chemistry--The differences in oiling levels among fixed sites and heavily
oiled SRS sites, as revealed through the PAH measurements, are shown in Figure 8. The
mean (geometric) TPAH levels of the three most heavily oiled fixed sites that were added
to the program in 1990 are roughly an order of magnitude higher than those of the eight
sites that were first sampled in 1989. In turn, the intertidal TPAH levels at these eight
sites are higher (roughly five-fold) than the averages for heavily oiled boulder/cobble and
pebble/gravel SRS sites.

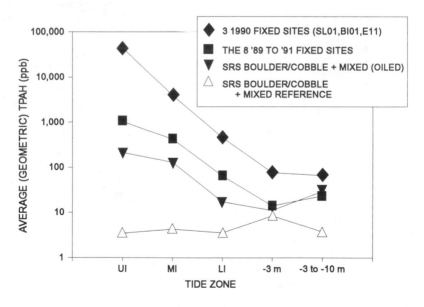

**FIGURE 8—Comparison of 1990 TPAH levels in fixed and SRS sampling sites.
Data points are geometric means. SRS (oiled) data show averages for all three oiling
levels (heavy, moderate, light) combined.**

　　Figure 9 presents a summary of the SRS sediment chemistry data for 1990 as the
geometric mean of TPAH over the tide zones for the boulder/cobble (Figure 9a) and
pebble/gravel sites (Figure 9b). The boulder/cobble beaches (Figure 9a) exhibit again the
highest TPAH levels, especially in the upper and mid-intertidal zones of heavily oiled sites.

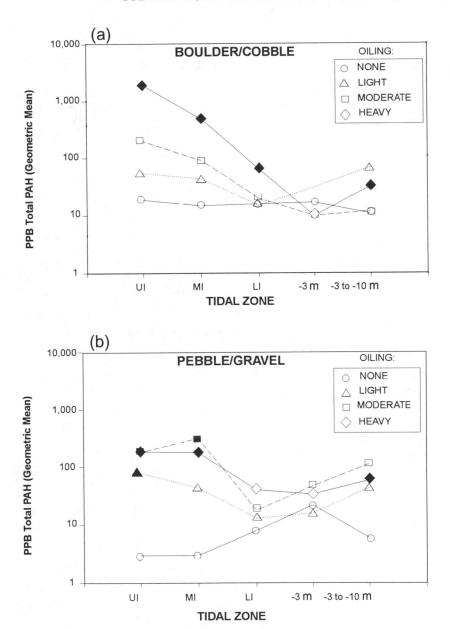

FIGURE 9—SRS sediment TPAH results at boulder/cobble (a) and pebble/gravel
(b) sites. Data points are geometric means of the TPAH values for the sites. Solid
symbols are significantly different ($p < .05$) from unoiled reference based on
C_2-and C_3-dibenzothiophenes. Data are from 1990.

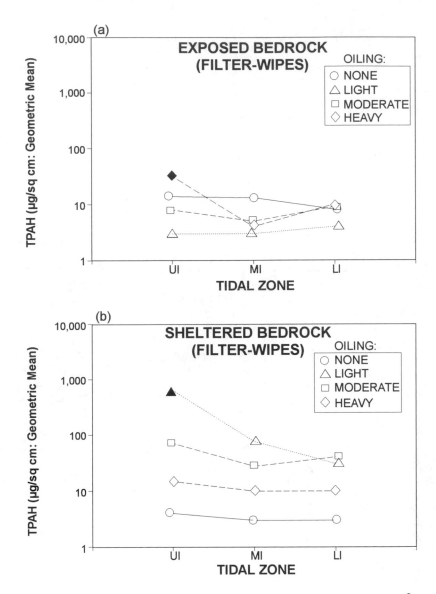

FIGURE 10—SRS filter-wipe TPAH results at bedrock sites. TPAH ($\mu g/cm^2$) on bedrock surfaces as determined from filter-wipe samples; data points are geometric means averaged over sites. Solid symbols are significantly different ($p < .05$) from unoiled reference based on C_2- and C_3-dibenzothiophene. Data are from 1990.

On the basis of statistical testing, significant differences (solid symbols) are noted for heavily oiled boulder/cobble sites and for heavily and moderately oiled pebble/gravel sites (Figure 9). Note that significant differences occur in the subtidal depth of -3 to -10 m at heavily oiled sites, even though these groups of sites (e.g., heavily-oiled, boulder/cobble sites represent a group or "cell") do not show the highest TPAH in Figure 9. Statistical tests were based on the sum of C_2- and C_3-dibenzothiophenes, which were highest on the heavily oiled sites.

The filter-wipe results for the intertidal zones of bedrock sites are summarized in Figure 10. TPAH levels significantly different from those of the unoiled reference sites were found only at the upper intertidal zone, and these were not systematically linked to the initial degree of oiling. The highest values were observed at lightly oiled sheltered bedrock sites. Lightly oiled sites received considerably less cleanup activity than did heavily oiled shorelines (Teal, 1990). Because these sites received less cleanup than the more heavily oiled sites, it appears that cleanup activities before sampling were effective in reducing the chemical exposure.

Mussel chemistry--TPAH levels for the mussels sampled from the SRS sites are presented in Figure 11. This figure shows the geometric mean for each of the 16 habitat and oiling level combinations. As indicators of integrated petroleum exposure, the mussels show that PAH were available to filter-feeders in 1990, consistent with the data from the sediment and filter-wipe samples. Mean TPAH levels ranged from 100 to over 1 000 ppb (dry weight basis) at the heavily oiled sites. Lower ranges of mean values are found in the other SRS site groups. The TPAH values for individual SRS unoiled sites ranged from about 5 to 200 ppb (not shown).

Sediment toxicity results--The results of the SRS sediment toxicity measurements for heavily oiled and reference sites in boulder/cobble, pebble/gravel, and sheltered bedrock (subtidal) habitats are summarized in Figure 12. Toxicity tests were not run on subtidal sediments from exposed bedrock sites. The figure presents the averages of the percentage amphipod mortality in each tide zone where sediment samples were taken. Only the upper intertidal zone of the boulder/cobble habitat showed a significant increase in sediment toxicity compared to the reference. The difference in the shallow subtidal (-3 m) at pebble/gravel sites (Figure 12b) was shown by the statistical tests, which treated grain size as a covariate, to indicate that the difference was due to grain size differences rather than oiling (TPAH) level.

DISCUSSION

Overall Objectives

This component of the shoreline ecology program included chemical, toxicological, and mussel body-burden measurements to assess the extent of exposure of the shoreline environment to petroleum hydrocarbons from the *Exxon Valdez* oil spill. The study had two main components: (1) measuring temporal trends at nonrandomly selected fixed sites that were tracked from 1989 through 1991 and (2)

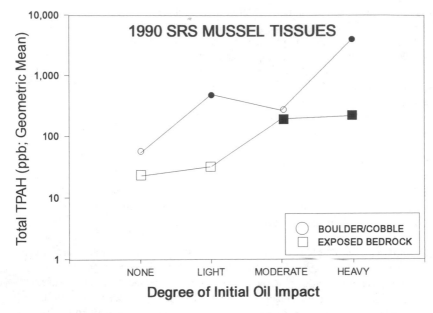

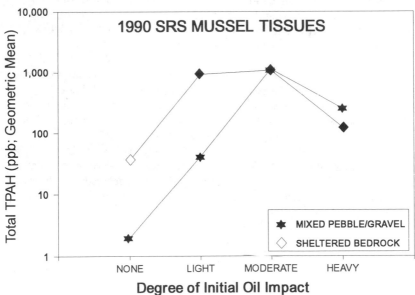

FIGURE 11—SRS mussel tissue TPAH concentrations. Data points are geometric means (ppb dry weight) averaged over sites. Solid symbols are significantly different ($p < .05$) from unoiled reference.

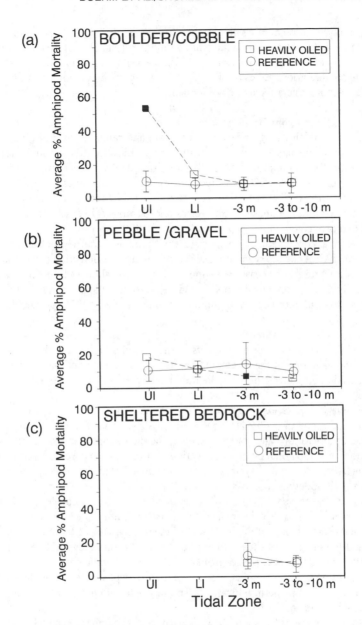

FIGURE 12—SRS sediment toxicity results for (a) boulder/cobble sites; (b) mixed pebble/gravel sites; (c) sheltered bedrock sites. Solid symbols are significantly different ($p < .05$) from unoiled reference.

assessing conditions at randomly selected sites so that results could be extrapolated to the sound as a whole. There is little information in the oil-spill literature dealing with high-energy, subarctic environments similar to Prince William Sound (NRC 1985). We are not aware of any prior studies of oiled shorelines that included both stratified random site selection and a fixed-site component.

Visual Observations From Other Studies
        The results of this study indicate a significant and rapid removal of oil and, hence, reduction in chemical exposure over the first 17 months after the spill and beyond. The continuous improvement in the condition of Prince William Sound shorelines between 1989 and 1991 has been reported by several investigators (Maki 1991; Jahns et al. 1991; Owens 1991; Baker et al. 1991; Neff et al., Condition of Shorelines, this volume). Published time-series photographs (Owens 1991) illustrated the dramatic improvement in the shorelines between 1989 and 1990.
        These visual observations are consistent with the quantitative data reported in this study. Analytical chemistry methods are very effective at detecting petroleum hydrocarbons long after they cease to be apparent from visual inspection, and long after they cease to be an environmental problem and begin to become a carbon food source for marine micro- and, indirectly, macrobiota (Montagna et al. 1987; Spies et al. 1988).

Chemical Exposure Assessment
        A detailed assessment of the impacts of the spilled oil along the shorelines begins with an evaluation of the extent and nature of the exposure of marine organisms to the more toxic components of the spilled oil, namely the PAH compounds.

        Sediment TPAH levels (fixed sites)--By reconstructing the weathering of petroleum residues and the removal of petroleum hydrocarbons from the shoreline through cleanup operations and natural cleaning, the data support several important themes. Soon after the initial oiling in the spring of 1989, physical removal processes became effective; the removal of bulk oil from heavily affected shorelines gave way to increased natural biodegradation of residues as the surface-area-to-volume ratio of the remaining oil increased. By 1991, many of the oiled shorelines contained very low levels of petroleum, just barely distinguishable from those at unoiled reference sites. By 1991, only a small subset of the fixed sites (Sleepy Bay, Bay of Isles, Point Helen) lagged behind the majority of sites in their return to background levels. However, when sampled in 1991, mussel tissues from these same sites indicated very low bioavailability of these remaining petroleum residues, except where the sediments had been recently disturbed by berm relocation. Toxicity tests suggest that the residues were nontoxic to intertidal organisms.
        The initial oiling of the shoreline was greatest at the upper intertidal zone. Fortunately, for boulder/cobble and pebble/gravel substrate shorelines, the zone of maximum oiling and the zone of maximum biological activity did not coincide. The latter occurs in the lower intertidal zone, which received very little, if any, oil on most shorelines. It is also important to note that the residual oil, still present in 1991 at some pebble/gravel sites (e.g., Herring Bay, Snug Harbor E), was generally confined to the

upper intertidal zone where it persisted in asphalt-like bands of largely inert material mixed into the sediments.

The initial oiling of shorelines was very patchy. Total extractable hydrocarbon values along horizontal sections of one shoreline (Point Helen) varied by factors of from 10 to 100 along all intertidal zones on the beach (Boehm 1989, unpublished data). Thus, exposure to oil is not uniform at any given site. This patchiness is characteristic of oil spills (NRC 1985) and is confirmed by the variability in responses observed in the amphipod toxicity tests.

Sediment TPAH levels (SRS sites)--Although it is possible to find persistent spill residues in isolated locations with unusual features, using an SRS design allowed us to estimate oil loss from the impact zone as a whole in an unbiased manner. According to the results of our present study, 30 out of 48 SRS cells were not distinguishable, by hydrocarbon chemistry, from unoiled reference sites from 15 to 17 months after the spill. Because of the high energy of much of the shoreline in the sound, this is not surprising.

Given the abundance of bedrock/rubble and boulder/cobble habitats in Prince William Sound, the results presented here are consistent with prior experience. Low-energy depositional environments, where prior studies have found spilled oil to be most persistent (Gundlach and Hayes 1978; API 1984; NRC 1985), are rare in the spill-affected zone of Prince William Sound. From long-term studies following the *Amoco Cadiz* spill, Baca et al. (1987) found that heavily oiled salt marshes, a habitat in which oil tends to persist, recovered biologically within five to eight years, depending on the extent of cleanup activities. Low-energy depositional mudflat environments showed oil persistence as long as eight years in the *Amoco Cadiz* spill (Page et al. 1989), but the analysis of the effects was complicated by the role such areas play as short-term traps for sediment-bound hydrocarbons from higher-energy areas. The overall loss rate from the *Amoco Cadiz* spill, summarized by Gundlach et al. (1983), shows that within three to four years much of the oil was removed from the affected shorelines by cleanup and natural processes. Higher-energy shores, such as exposed bedrock and boulder/cobble, lost oil residues within one to two years (d'Ozouville et al. 1980).

Implications of mussel data--Mussels bioconcentrate PAH from water from 10^2 to 10^6 times, depending on the solubility of the PAH (McElroy et al. 1989). As filter-feeders, mussels can accumulate hydrocarbons via uptake of hydrocarbons dissolved in seawater or by ingesting hydrocarbons adsorbed on suspended sediment. Where the petroleum residues are present in sediments, but are not available in either dissolved or particulate form, the mussels will have low PAH levels.

Mussels occur in Prince William Sound in four patterns: (1) widely distributed on the intertidal substrate at the pebble/gravel sites, (2) in clusters attached to boulders, (3) attached to bedrock, and (4) in mussel beds. The last consist of high concentrations of mussels that cover the surface in patches at certain low-to-moderate energy locations (typically pebble/gravel habitats).

The results presented in this paper define mussel hydrocarbon levels for the first three patterns described above, both sound-wide (i.e., SRS results) and at sites of special interest (i.e., fixed sites). However, the results from Mussel Beach provide limited time-series data for a large mussel bed.

These results indicate that, in 1990, TPAH levels in mussels from initially oiled locations in the sound were still substantially higher than reference levels. However, the fixed-site time series and results from most individual fixed sites indicated that these levels were decreasing by at least one order of magnitude per year, consistent with decreasing bioavailability of PAH from shorelines. By 1991, TPAH levels were at or near reference levels.

Exceptions were noted at some places, for example, at Bay of Isles Marsh and Point Helen, where TPAH levels decreased more slowly because of unique circumstances—soft sediments and berm relocation, respectively. There are also locations within mussel beds where high concentrations of residual oil and elevated TPAH levels in mussels have been found (Babcock et al. 1993; Rounds et al. 1993). Our own data showed TPAH levels near background even at Mussel Beach.

Thus, bioavailability in the mussel beds appears to have been localized and may be related to local disturbance of the oiled sediments. Where subsurface oil existed at significant levels, but where the beach was not disturbed, the mussels showed low TPAH levels (e.g., 1991 values for Sleepy Bay); thus, bioavailability of the remaining oil residues is minimal as long as they remain undisturbed. National Oceanic and Atmospheric Administration (NOAA), in its 1990 net environmental benefits assessment of subsurface oil removal, came to essentially the same conclusion (NOAA 1990).

The mussel tissue results presented in Figure 3 show a geometric mean value of 20 ppb in 1991 for the eight sites monitored since 1989. This increases to 70 ppb if the three sites monitored since 1990 are included (Bay of Isles Marsh, Sleepy Bay, Latouche). These values are lower than the geometric mean calculated from data reported by NOAA (Manen 1993) for spill-affected sites (350 ppb) but are similar to those reported by the Oil Spill Health Task Force (OSHTF) (45 ppb for Prince William Sound; 110 ppb when sites in the Gulf of Alaska [Windy Bay] are included). (Note: the wet-weight values reported by NOAA and OSHTF were converted to a dry-weight basis, assuming 85% water content.) However, substantially higher values were measured at some of our fixed sites (Sleepy Bay, Latouche Island, Point Helen, and Bay of Isles Marsh; see Table A-3). Although PAH concentrations in mussels were elevated at these sites, the residual oil in the mussels was highly weathered, with less than 3% of the total PAH consisting of naphthalenes.

The differences between the values reported here and those in the NOAA database and OSHTF reports reflect different sampling strategies. The OSHTF focused on subsistence areas and the NOAA data results from a number of National Resource Damage Assessment (NRDA) studies conducted by government scientists. This shoreline ecology study endeavored to assess both site-specific and area-wide trends in hydrocarbon removal and bioavailability. The results reported here show that, except for a few unique sites, the remaining petroleum residues are for the most part highly asphaltic and not bioavailable to any significant degree.

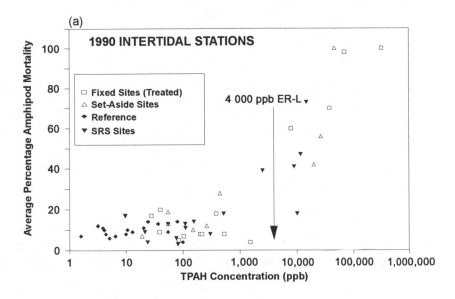

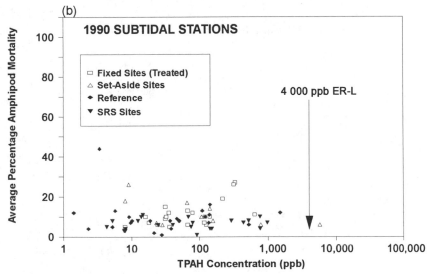

FIGURE 13—Summary of 1990 and 1991 sediment toxicity test results. The results are compared with the proposed ER-L sediment toxicity threshold value of 4 000 ppb TPAH (Long and Morgan 1990); plotted data are actual means, not adjusted for covariates. (a) Intertidal sediments from 1990 surveys; (b) subtidal sediments from 1990 surveys. Arithmetic means of percentage mortality for each site versus geometric means TPAH from the same sediment composite are plotted.

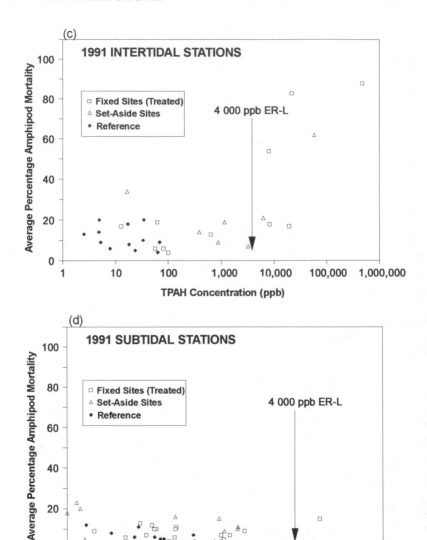

Figure 13 (continued)—Summary of 1990 and 1991 sediment toxicity test results. The results are compared with the proposed ER-L sediment toxicity threshold value of 4 000 ppb TPAH (Long and Morgan 1990); plotted data are actual means, not adjusted for covariates. (c) Intertidal sediments from 1991 surveys; (d) Subtidal sediments from 1991 surveys. Arithmetic means of percentage mortality for each site versus geometric means TPAH from the same sediment composite are plotted.

Sediment Toxicology

Sediment quality criteria--Results of the analysis of specific PAH analytes and the sums of PAH analytes (TPAH) in sediments can be compared with the Effects Range-Low (ER-L) sediment toxicity threshold values proposed by Long and Morgan (1990). The ER-L value of 4 000 ppb TPAH is a conservative indicator of the potential for toxic effects in subtidal sediments. It should be noted that the TPAH values in this study and those used by Long and Morgan differ with respect to the specific analytes being summed. Because this study includes the alkylated PAH and the work of Long and Morgan does not, it would be justified to increase the ER-L criterion three- to five-fold before comparing it with the TPAH values presented in this study.

The four plots in Figure 13 summarize the relationships between TPAH and average percentage amphipod mortality for intertidal and subtidal stations sampled in 1990 and 1991. In each plot, different symbols differentiate oiled and reference sites, as well as treated and set-aside fixed sites.

The results are compared with the ER-L sediment quality value of 4 000 ppb (Long and Morgan 1990). Figure 13 shows that the threshold of amphipod toxicity for the intertidal and subtidal sediments, as determined in this study, is in reasonable agreement with that proposed by Long and Morgan (1990). The elevated subtidal sediment toxicity at an unoiled reference site (Port Bainbridge) in Figure 13b illustrates the importance of grain size (high gravel content) in determining the results of the sediment toxicity test.

In view of the above, comparing the ER-L threshold and our TPAH data gives a very conservative interpretation. The comparison shows that, by the summer of 1990, most intertidal samples, and all but one subtidal sample, had TPAH values below the 4 000 ppb level (Figure 13a). Some "problem" sites still exceeded this value even in 1991 (Figure 13c) in the upper intertidal zone and again in one subtidal sample. All of the exceptions in 1991 were at fixed sites that were either disturbed (Point Helen, Latouche Island) or had soft sediments (Bay of Isles Marsh). These sites are not representative of the broad range of spill-affected shorelines in the sound as a whole.

The average TPAH values at the SRS sites (Figure 13a) exceeded the 4 000 ppb ER-L value only in the heavily oiled boulder/cobble habitat, and only in the upper and mid-intertidal zones. The fixed-site sediment toxicology data (Figure 5) show that from 1990 to 1991 sediment toxicity was rapidly lost, consistent with concurrent PAH loss to concentrations below the 4 000 ppb ER-L threshold.

Statistical analysis--Statistical analyses by ANCOVA/GLIM (Page et al., Part 1: Study Design and Methods, this volume) of the sediment toxicity results show that by 1990-'91 sediment-grain size was as important in determining the observed bioassay results as the presence of oil. The amphipod test organisms have a strong preference for fine, well-sorted sandy sediment (Oakeden et al. 1984). Sediments with either high percentages of gravel or high percentages of silt/clay generally had higher mortality values, consistent with the environmental preferences of the test organism, regardless of oil exposure (Oakeden et al. 1984; DeWitt et al. 1988). This illustrates the importance of including in the study design, in addition to the factor of interest, those variables that can influence a measured response (Gilfillan et al. 1987; DeWitt et al.1988; Gilfillan et al., Part 3: Biology, this volume).

Elevated sediment toxicity (i.e., statistically distinguishable from reference) was observed in two of the ten SRS habitat/tide zone combinations for which toxicity tests were conducted (Figure 12). Only one of these differences was related to oiling, and the other one was attributable to the effect of sediment-grain size. The 1990-'91 fixed-site bioassay results for treated sites and reference sites (Figure 5a, b) showed significant effects attributable to oiling only in the upper intertidal zone at boulder/cobble beaches in 1990-'91, and at pebble/gravel sites in 1990. At the SRS sites, sediment grain size was again more important than oiling in determining amphipod mortality. These results showed that by 1990, oil had degraded to the point that there was little sediment toxicity resulting from the spill.

Findings of the biological studies (Gilfillan et al., Part 3: Biology, this volume) indicate that petroleum residues that are no longer toxic can provide a carbon (food) source for hydrocarbon-degrading microbes, and, hence, indirectly for marine biota, which is consistent with other studies (Spies et al. 1980; Montagna et al. 1987; Spies et al. 1988).

Other Processes

Offshore transport and deposition--Although petroleum residues from the *Exxon Valdez* spill have been largely removed from the shorelines by physical processes and biodegradation, there is little evidence of deposition of such residues in the nearshore subtidal sediments. Concern about the possible transport of a fine-grained fraction of oiled sediment to the nearshore subtidal environment caused NOAA to undertake a subtidal diving and sampling survey. Results indicated that "deposition of oiled sediments, derived from either surface or subsurface sources, may be minimal" (NOAA 1990: p. 188). The mechanisms of oil removal from the shorelines are further discussed in Owens (1991), Jahns et al. (1991), and Bragg and Yang (this volume).

In general, the contribution of *Exxon Valdez* crude to the preexisting petroleum hydrocarbon background as revealed by fingerprinting was found to be a relatively minor addition. Subtidal studies by Page et al. (this volume) found that the increment of *Exxon Valdez* PAH added to the subtidal sediments averaged about 200 ppb at the shallow subtidal (less than 30-m deep) off the fixed sites in 1989, and 50 ppb in the nearshore subtidal (less than 10-m deep) off the SRS sites in 1990. Concentrations of spill-related hydrocarbons decreased further with depth and distance from shore. Moreover, the observed levels of oil in the subtidal sediments are orders of magnitude lower than those observed at previous spills (Kolpack et al. 1970, Santa Barbara Blowout; Gundlach et al. 1983, *Amoco Cadiz*; Boehm et al. 1982a, BIOS). The probable origin of the background hydrocarbons in Prince William Sound are discussed by Page et al. (this volume) and include hydrocarbons from eastern Gulf of Alaska seeps and from human activities in the sound.

Biodegradation--The classical biodegradation pattern indicated by the relative loss of normal alkanes compared with the branched-chain (isoprenoid) hydrocarbons was evident in the shoreline sediment samples as early as 30 days after the spill (see

Table A-2). Biodegradation was further enhanced through the bioremediation component of the shoreline cleanup (Bragg et al. 1993).

Our findings indicate that the physical, chemical, and biodegradative weathering of PAH from crude oil is much more rapid than previously expected for this environment, compared with predictions made by Payne et al. (1984).

Degradation rates and half-lives--The temporal trends of PAH in surface sediments from 1989 to 1991 at the fixed sites can be used to estimate degradation rates and environmental half-lives for TPAH or individual PAH constituents. Apparent first-order rate constants and environmental half-lives were obtained from the fixed-site chemistry data for groups of sites sampled in all three years. (1989-1991). Rate constants for the PAH loss were calculated by fitting the data to the following exponential decay equation:

$$[\text{ppb}_{\text{analyte}} \text{ at any given time}] = [\text{ppb}_{\text{analyte}} \text{ at time zero}]e^{-kt}$$

where t = months from the spill and k = the apparent PAH decay-rate constant.

The environmental half-life is the time required for a given initial concentration of PAH to decay to half of that concentration and is computed as $t_{1/2} = 0.693/k$. Two sets of half-life estimates were calculated from the fixed-site chemistry data: (1) half-lives based on oil removal observed during the first 17 months postspill and (2) half-lives based on oil removal from 1990 to 1991. The latter were used for projecting oil removal beyond 1991 (Table 4). The half-life estimates range from 2 to 3.8 months within the first 17 months and 7.4 to 16 months for the 1990-'91 data. The calculation of two sets of half-lives was justified because of the rapid weathering of the oil and the dominance of physical removal processes (both natural and cleanup) during the first year (see Table A-2; Koons and Jahns 1992). After the first year or so, remaining oil residues are removed more slowly by natural processes because they tend to be highly weathered and residual higher-molecular-weight compounds or are sequestered in wave shadows or below the depth of sediment reworking by winter storms.

TABLE 4—Environmental half-lives ($t_{1/2}$) of TPAH in intertidal surface sediments of Prince William Sound.

ENVIRONMENTAL HALF-LIFE (MONTHS) FOR TOTAL PAH

Tide Zone	May '89 to Aug '90	Aug '90 to Aug '91
Upper Intertidal	2.0	7.4
Middle Intertidal	2.5	10.6
Lower Intertidal	3.8	16.0

The half-life values reported here are generally consistent with data reported from other studies. Miller (1989) presented data yielding a half-life of 1.4 months for a coarse intertidal beach oiled with Alaska North Slope crude by the *ARCO Anchorage* spill in Puget Sound. Data reported by Berne et al. (1980) for the hydrocarbon loss from sandy intertidal environments affected by the *Amoco Cadiz* spill yield an environmental half-life of approximately 2.4 months. The half-life values reported by

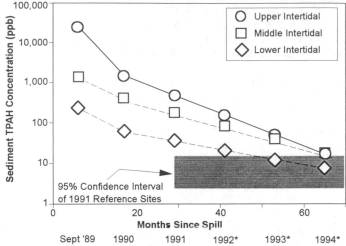

Decreasing TPAH in Prince William Sound Fixed-Site Intertidal Sediments

* Projected concentrations using half-life values calculated from geometric
means from seven sites in 1990 and 1991

FIGURE 14—Projections of TPAH levels for fixed sites, with decay rates based on geometric means of seven fixed sites. Because of extensive berm relocation in 1990 and 1991, data from Point Helen were excluded from the calculation of decay rates.

Miller (1989) and Berne et al. (1980) are similar to our estimates for the first 17 months after the spill and to that reported by Koons and Jahns (1992) for total oil removal during the winter of 1989-90 following the *Exxon Valdez* spill. The half-lives we used to project TPAH losses into the future are longer than those based on Anderson et al. (1981), who presented data for the loss of PAH from a 5- to 10-cm stratum of intertidal sediments that had Alaska North Slope crude oil mixed into it. Their data yield an environmental half-life for TPAH loss of 5.3 months. However, their experiment started with fresher oil than the weathered petroleum residues observed on the shores of Prince William Sound in 1990-'91 and the ambient temperatures were somewhat warmer in Puget Sound than in Prince William Sound.

By using the slower PAH degradation rates and assuming that the exponential decay equation describes the system beyond 1991, we can estimate the TPAH levels in intertidal sediments after 1991. Figure 14 presents projected average TPAH sediment concentrations for 1992, 1993, and 1994 for the fixed sites and the 95% confidence interval for 1991 SRS boulder/cobble and pebble/gravel unoiled reference sites. Although not a formal statistical test, the projections suggest that the lower intertidal TPAH concentrations will be similar to unoiled reference by 1993, and that the upper and middle intertidal zones will be near the reference in 1994.

Using the 1990 SRS data as a basis and applying the loss rates obtained from the fixed sites in an exponential decay model, we can project concentration of TPAH and individual PAH analytes into the future for the sound as a whole. Results of applying the fixed-site degradation rates to the SRS sites are shown in Figure 15. The generalizations made possible by the SRS design indicate that heavily oiled pebble/gravel beaches, on average, will be similar to reference by 1993, and the heavily oiled boulder/cobble beaches will be at or near reference concentrations by 1994. As indicated in this and other oil-spill studies, isolated pockets of more persistent oil residues can be found (see also Babcock et al. 1993; Rounds et al. 1993); however, such isolated locations are insignificant when the impact zone in the sound is viewed in its entirety.

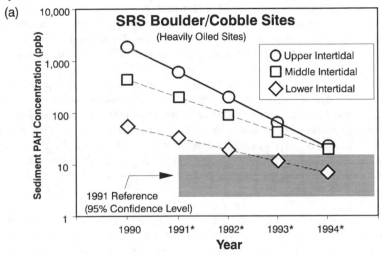

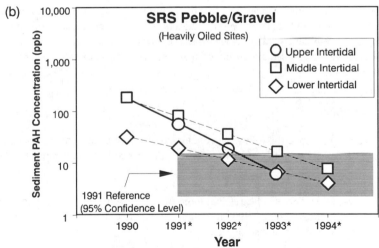

FIGURE 15—Projections of PAH levels for heavily oiled SRS sites: (a) boulder/cobble sites and (b) pebble/gravel sites. Decay rates are based on results of fixed sites. *Projected concentrations using half-life values calculated from geometric means from seven fixed sites in 1990 and 1991.

Subsurface Oil

The persistence and nature of subsurface oil is highly location-specific. Data presented by Jahns et al. (1991) on a group of high-energy sites in Prince William Sound indicate a much greater decrease in subsurface oil over a six-month period during the winter of 1989-1990 than that reported here for the 1990-1991 period. These observations are consistent with the expectation that the rate of oil removal would be highest during the first winter following the spill and subsequently decrease with time.

At typical oiling conditions on boulder/cobble beaches represented by the SRS sites (Figure 4b), the subsurface oil penetration and resulting TPAH concentrations are less than those found at the very heavily oiled fixed sites (Figure 4a). Hence, the fixed-site time-series results (Figure 4a) are not representative of boulder/cobble sites in Prince William Sound.

The important question is, what degree of environmental risk is posed by the subsurface oil? Although present at some locations, this residue continues to degrade and remains sequestered unless it is physically brought to the surface and released to the water and, hence, made bioavailable. The rate at which subsurface oil is released to the surface dictates the exposure that organisms will see and, given the low solubility of the residual oil, the exposure concentration should be quite low. The lack of effect is demonstrated by the results of the three measurement types in the SEP studies: mussel tissue burdens (bioavailability), sediment toxicology, and abundance of shoreline biota (Gilfillan et al., Part 3: Biology, this volume).

Other studies have evaluated the implications of the existence of subsurface residual oil on shorelines in Prince William Sound (e.g., Stoker et al. 1992; NOAA 1990) with similar results. Stoker et al. (1992) found that, although isolated pockets of subsurface oil were found at scattered locations, the remnants posed no biological threat. A study by NOAA (1990: p. 187) addressed the net environmental benefit of removing oiled sediments and concluded that the subsurface oil was, at that time (1990), "relatively stabilized and insulated from exposure to vulnerable resources through sheening."

CONCLUSIONS

We have reached the following conclusions from this study of the chemical and toxicological aspects of petroleum hydrocarbons on Prince William Sound shorelines that:

- Visual evidence indicates that most of the shorelines were cleaned of bulk oil by the spring of 1990, although chemically detectable hydrocarbons remained on many study sites.

- By 1991, much of the oil spilled from the Exxon Valdez had been removed from the shoreline by natural processes or by cleanup. Remaining traces of oil residues were generally very degraded. These residues will continue to degrade and disappear over time.

- The remaining residues of *Exxon Valdez* crude on oiled shorelines are generally at such low concentrations that they pose little risk of adverse biological effects. Except for a few sediment samples, acute sediment toxicity owing to oil, as measured by standard toxicity tests, was absent in 1990-91. For the most part, the petroleum residues had degraded below the threshold of acute toxic effects. Measurable PAH levels were, in general, well below those conservatively associated with adverse effects.

- Isolated patches of subsurface oil exist on certain beaches. These patches may continue to persist for some time, but they are being removed gradually by winter storms and biodegradation. These patches must have been effectively isolated from the rest of the environment to have persisted so long after the spill. Consequently, they should have little effect on shoreline biota unless the shoreline is disturbed by intrusive intervention.

- Projections made by combining area-wide results with fixed-site time trends indicate that PAH residues should be indistinguishable from reference by 1994, with few exceptions.

- Fixed-site studies indicate that only a few sites (e.g., Bay of Isles, Sleepy Bay) had substantial concentrations of oil residue still present in 1991 and that some of them may remain elevated for several more years. The findings from such "worst-case" sites have comprised the conventional wisdom of oil-spill exposure assessments for many years. This study has shown that in the Prince William Sound environment the removal and degradation processes are operating much faster than at other well-studied spills that had a higher proportion of low-energy habitats.

- Well-publicized concerns about long-term persistence of *Exxon Valdez* crude in shoreline and subtidal sediments, which are based on comparisons with other spills in environments different from Prince William Sound, have generally proven to be unfounded. While oil was being eroded from, or was degrading on, the shorelines of Prince William Sound, most of the residue was swept away and dissipated at sea.

ACKNOWLEDGMENTS

This study was supported by Exxon Company, U.S.A. We acknowledge the participation of Ted Sauer, Sandra Tate, Tony Parkin, Larry LeBlanc, John Brown, and many others of Arthur D. Little; Cecile Kresja of Bowdoin College; Dave Pillard of ENSR Consulting and Engineering; Keith Parker of Data Analysis Group, and Cathy McPherson of EVS Consulting, Ltd.

REFERENCES

Anderson, J.W., R.G. Riley, S.L. Messer, B.L. Thomas, and G.W. Feuingham. "Natural weathering of oil in marine sediments: Tissue contamination and growth of the littleneck clam, *Protohaca staminea.*" *Canadian Journal of Fisheries and Aquatic Science.* 40(supplement 2): 70-77; 1981.

API (American Petroleum Institute). *Oil Spill Studies: Measurement of Environmental Effects and Recovery. Guidelines based on workshops sponsored by the American Petroleum Institute.* J.R. Gould (ed.). American Petroleum Institute, Washington, DC; 128 pp.; 1984.

Atlas, R.M., P.D. Boehm, and J.A. Calder. "Chemical and biological weathering of oil from the *Amoco Cadiz* oil spillage within the littoral zone." *Estuarine and Coastal Marine Science.* 12: 589-608; 1981.

Babcock, M., G. Irvine, S. Rice, P. Rounds, J. Cusick, and C.C. Brodersen. "Oiled mussel beds in Prince William Sound two and three years after the *Exxon Valdez* oil spill." Exxon Valdez *Oil Spill Symposium-February 2-5, 1993: Program and Abstracts.* The Oil Spill Public Information Center, Anchorage, Alaska; 184-186; 1993.

Baca, B.J., T.E. Lankford, and E.R. Gundlach. "Recovery of Brittany coastal marshes in the eight years following the *Amoco Cadiz* incident." *Proceedings of the 1987 Oil Spill Conference, American Petroleum Institute, Washington, DC.* 459-464; 1987.

Baker, J.M., R.B. Clark, and P.F. Kingston. *Two Years After the Spill: Environmental Recovery in Prince William Sound and the Gulf of Alaska.* Houston: Exxon Company, U.S.A.; 1991.

Berne, S., M. Marchand, and L. d'Ozouville. "Pollution of sea water and marine sediments in coastal areas." *Ambio.* 9: 287-293; 1980.

Blumer, M. and J. Sass. "Oil pollution: Persistence and degradation of spilled fuel oil." *Science.* 176: 1120-1122; 1972.

Boehm, P.D. and D.L. Fiest. "Subsurface distributions of petroleum from an offshore well blowout: The IXTOC I Blowout, Bay of Campeche." *Environmental Science and Technology.* 16: 67-74; 1982.

Boehm, P.D., D.L. Fiest, and A. Elskus. "Comparative weathering patterns of hydrocarbons from the *Amoco Cadiz* oil spill observed at a variety of coastal environments." *Proceedings of the International Symposium* on the Amoco Cadiz: *Fate and Effects of the Oil Spill. Brest, France, November 19-22, 1979.* Centre National pour l'Exploration des Oceans, Brest; 1981.

Boehm, P.D., D.L. Fiest, P. Hirtzer, L. Scott, R. Nordstrom, and R. Engelhardt. "A biogeochemical assessment of the BIOS experimental spills: Transport pathways and fates of petroleum in benthic animals." *Proceedings of the Fifth Arctic Marine Oil Spill Program Technical Seminar.* Ottawa, Ontario: Environment Canada; 581-618; 1982a.

Boehm, P.D., D.L. Fiest, D. Mackay, and S. Paterson. "Physical chemical weathering of petroleum hydrocarbons from the IXTOC blowout: Chemical measurements and a weathering model." *Environmental Science and Technology.* 16: 498-505; 1982b.

Boehm, P.D., M.S. Steinhauer, D.R. Green, B. Fowler, B. Humphrey, D.L. Fiest, and W.S. Cretney. "Comparative fate of chemically dispersed and beached oil in subtidal sediments of the arctic nearshore." *Arctic* 40 (suppl. 1): 133-148; 1987.

Bragg, J.R., R.C. Prince, E.J. Harner, and R.M. Atlas. "Bioremediation effectiveness following the *Exxon Valdez* oil spill." *Proceedings of the 1993 Oil Spill Conference, March 29-April 1, 1993, Tampa, Florida.* Washington, DC: American Petroleum Institute; 435-447; 1993.

Chapman, P.M. and S. Becker. "Recommended protocols for conducting laboratory bioassays for marine sediment toxicity." Puget Sound Estuary Program; U.S. Environmental Protection Agency, Seattle, WA; 55 pp.; 1986.

Chapman, P.M., E.A. Power, R.N. Dexter, and H.B. Andersen. "Evaluation of effects associated with an oil platform, using the sediment quality triad." *Environmental Toxicology and Chemistry.* 10: 407-424; 1991.

DeWitt, T.H., G.R. Ditsworth, and R.C. Swartz. "Effects of natural sediment features on survival of the Phoxocephalid amphipod, *Rhepoxynius abronius.*" *Marine Environmental Research.* 25: 99-124; 1988.

d'Ozouville, L., S. Beme, E.R. Gundlach, and M.O. Hayes. "Coastal morphology and oil spill pollution: The *Amoco Cadiz* experience." *Petroleum and the Marine Environment. Proceedings of PETROMAR 80.* 657-571; 1980.

Gilfillan, E.S., D.S. Page, and J.C. Poster. *Tidal Area Dispersant Project. Fate and Effects of Chemically Dispersed Oil in the Nearshore Benthic Environment.* American Petroleum Institute Publication No. 4440; 215 pp; July (1986).

Gilfillan, E.S., D.S. Page, B. Griffin, S.A. Hanson, and J.C. Foster. "The importance of using appropriate experimental designs in oil spill impact studies: An example from the *Amoco Cadiz* oil spill impact zone." *Proceedings of the 1987 Oil Spill Conference,* American Petroleum Institute; Washington, DC: 503-507; 1987.

Gundlach, E.R. and M.O. Hayes. "Classification of coastal environments in terms of potential vulnerability to oil spill damage." *Marine Technology Journal.* 12: 18-17; 1978.

Gundlach, E.R., P.D. Boehm, M. Marchand, R.M. Atlas, D.M. Ward, and D.A. Wolfe. "The fate of the *Amoco Cadiz* oil spill." *Science.* 221: 122-131; 1983.

Jahns, H.O., J.R. Bragg, L.C. Dash, and E.H. Owens. Natural cleaning of shorelines following the *Exxon Valdez* oil spill. *Proceedings of the 1991 International Oil Spill Conferenc.* Washington, DC: American Petroleum Institute. 167-176; 1991.

Kolpack, R.L., J.S. Mattson, J.B. Mark, Jr., and T.C. Tu. "Hydrocarbon content of Santa Barbara Channel sediments." *In:* R.L. Kolpack (ed.) *Biological and Oceanographic Survey of the Santa Barbara Channel Oil Spill 1969-1970. Vol II, Physical, Chemical, and Geological Studies.* Allan Hancock Foundation, University of Southern California, Los Angeles; 1970.

Koons, C.B. and H.O. Jahns. "The fate of oil from the *Exxon Valdez*—A perspective." *Marine Technology Society Journal.* 26: 61-69; 1992.

Long, E.R. "Ranges in chemical concentrations in sediments associated with adverse biological effects." *Marine Pollution Bulletin.* 24: 38-45; 1992.

Long, E.R. and P.M. Chapman. "A sediment quality triad: Measures of sediment contamination, toxicity, and community composition in Puget Sound." *Marine Pollution Bulletin.* 16: 405-415; 1985.

Long, E.R. and L.G. Morgan. "The potential for biological effects of sediment-sorbed contaminants tested in the National Status and Trends Program." NOAA Technical Memorandum NOS OMA 52. National Atmospheric and Oceanic Administration, U.S. Department of Commerce, Rockville, MD; 175pp + appendices; 1990.

Maki, A. "The *Exxon Valdez* oil spill: initial environmental impact assessment." *Environmental Science and Technology.* 25: 24-29; 1991.

Manen, C. A., J. R. Price, S. Koan, and M. G. Carls. "Natural resource damage assessment: Database design and structure." National Oceanic and Atmospheric Administration Technical Memorandum (in revision) 1993.

McElroy, A.E., J.W. Farrington, and J.M. Teal. "Bioavailability of polycyclic aromatic hydrocarbons in the aquatic environment." *In:* U. Varanasi (ed.) *Metabolism of Polycyclic Aromatic Hydrocarbons in the Aquatic Environment.* Boca Raton, FL: CRC Press; 1-39; 1989.

Michel, J., M.O. Hayes, W.J. Sexton, J.C. Gibeaut, and C. Henry. Trends in natural removal of the *Exxon Valdez* oil spill in Prince William Sound from September 1989 to May 1990. *Proceedings of the 1991 Oil Spill Conference;* Washington, DC: American Petroleum Institute; 181-188; 1991.

Mielke, J.E. Oil in the ocean: "The short- and long-term impacts of a spill." 90356 SPR. Congressional Research Service, The Library of Congress, Washington, DC; 34 pp.; 1990.

Miller, J.A. "Physical and chemical recovery of intertidal and shallow subtidal sediments impacted by the *Arco Anchorage* oil spill, Ediz Hook, Washington." *Proceedings of the 1989 Oil Spill Conference,* Washington, DC: American Petroleum Institute; 487-491; 1989.

Montagna, P. A., P. A. Bauer, J. P. Toal, J. Hardin, D. Hardin, and R. B. Spies. "Temporal variability and the relationship between benthic meiofaunal and microbial populations of a natural coastal petroleum seep." *Journal of Marine Research.* 45: 761-769; 1987.

NOAA (National Oceanic and Atmospheric Administration). Excavation and rock washing treatment technology. Net environmental benefit analysis. NOAA, Seattle, WA; 199 pp. + appendices. 1990.

NRC (National Research Council). *The international mussel watch.* Washington, DC: National Academy Press; 243pp; 1980.

NRC (National Research Council). *Oil in the Sea–Inputs, Fates, and Effects.* Washington, DC: National Academy Press; 601 pp; 1985.

Neff, J.M. *Polycyclic Aromatic Hydrocarbons in the Aquatic Environment: Sources, Fates, and Biological Effects.* Barking Essex, England: Applied Science Publishers; 262pp. 1979.

Oakeden, J.M. "Feeding and substrate preference in five species of Phoxocephalid amphipods from central California." *Journal of Crustacean Biology.* 4: 233-47; 1984.

Owens, E. "Shoreline conditions following the *Exxon Valdez* spill as of fall 1990." *Proceedings of the Fourteenth Arctic and Marine Oil Spill Program Technical Seminar.* Ottawa, Ontario: Environment Canada; 579-606; 1991.

Owens, E.H., J.R. Harper, W. Robson, and P.D. Boehm. "Fate and persistence of crude oil stranded on a sheltered beach." *Arctic* (suppl. 1): 198-123; 1987.

Page, D.S., J.C. Foster, P.M. Fickett, and E.S. Gilfillan. "Identification of petroleum sources in an area impacted by the *Amoco Cadiz* oil spill." *Marine Pollution Bulletin.* 19: 107-115; 1988.

Page, D.S., J.C. Foster, P.M. Fickett, and E.S. Gilfillan. "Long-term weathering of *Amoco Cadiz* oil in soft intertidal sediments." *Proceedings of the 1989 Oil Spill Conference.* Washington, DC: American Petroleum Institute; 401-406; 1989.

Payne, J.R., B.E. Kirstein, G.D. McNab, J.L. Lambach, R. Redding, R.E. Jordon, W. Hom, C. de Oliveira, G.S. Smith, D.M. Baxter, and R. Gaegel. "Multivariate analysis of petroleum weathering in the marine environment—Sub Arctic." Final Report, Vol. I—Technical Results, 686 pp; Vol.II, 209 pp. NOAA, National Ocean Service, Rockville, MD; 1984.

Sauer, T. C. and P. D. Boehm. "The use of defensible analytical chemical measurements for oil spill natural resource damage assessment." *Proceedings of the 1991 Oil Spill Conference.* Washington, DC: American Petroleum Institute; 363-369; 1991.

Rounds, P., S. Rice, M.M. Babcock, and C.C. Brodersen. "Variability of *Exxon Valdez* hydrocarbon concentrations in mussel bed sediments." Exxon Valdez *Oil Spill Symposium-February 2-5, 1993: Program and Abstracts,* The Oil Spill Public Information Center, Anchorage, Alaska; 182-184; 1993.

Spies, R. B., P. H. Davis, and D.H. Stuermer. "Ecology of a submarine petroleum seep off the California coast." *In:* R.A. Geyer (ed.) *Marine Environmental Pollution. Vol. 1, Hydrocarbons.* New York: Elsevier; 229-263; 1980.

Spies, R. B., D. D. Hardin, and J. P. Toal. "Organic enrichment or toxicity? A comparison of the effects of kelp and crude oil in sediments on the colonization and growth of benthic infauna." *Journal of Experimental Marine Biology and Ecology.* 124: 261-282; 1988.

Stoker, S.W., J.M. Neff, T.R. Schroeder, and D.M. McCormick. *Biological Conditions in Prince William Sound, Alaska, Following the Exxon Valdez Oil Spill: 1989-1992.* Woodward-Clyde Consultants, Anchorage Alaska, 116 pp; 1992.

Swartz, R.C., W.A. DeBen, J.K. Phillips, J.O. Lambertson, and F.A. Cole. "Phoxocephalid amphipod bioassay for marine sediment toxicity." *In:* R.D. Cardwell, R. Purdy, and R.C. Banner (eds.) *Aquatic Toxicology and Hazard Assessment: 7th Symposium.* American Society for Testing and Materials; STP 854; 284-307; 1985.

Teal, A.R., "Shoreline cleanup following the *Exxon Valdez* oil spill-the decision process for cleanup operations". *Proceedings of the 13th Arctic and Marine Oil Spill Program (AMOP) Technical Seminar.* Ottawa, Ontario: Environment Canada; 422-429, 1990.

Teal, J.M., K. Burns, and J.W. Farrington. "Analyses of aromatic hydrocarbons in intertidal sediments resulting from two spills of No. 2 fuel oil in Buzzards Bay, Massachusetts." *Journal of the Fisheries Research Board of Canada.* 35: 510-520; 1978.

Teal, J.M., J. W. Farrington, K.A. Burns, J.J. Stegeman, B.W. Tripp, B. Woodin, and C. Phinney. "The West Falmouth oil spill after 20 years: Fate of fuel oil compounds and effects on animals." *Marine Pollution Bulletin.* 24: 607-614; 1992.

U.S. EPA (U.S. Environmental Protection Agency.) *Test Methods for Evaluating Solid Waste (SW-846).* Vol 1B, Office of Solid Waste and Emergency Response, Washington, D.C. 1986.

APPENDIX

TABLE A-1—Summary of PAH data for sediments. **This table presents geometric means of PAH levels for the May 1989, September 1989, August 1990, and August 1991 samples.** **TPAH totals include all analytes listed in Table 3, except perylene, naphthalene, and C_1-naphthalenes.**

Substrate/Site	Date Sampled	Mean TPAH Concentrations (ppb x 10^3)					
		UI	MI	LI	-3 m	-3 To -10 m	to -30 m
Boulder/Cobble							
Sleepy Bay (SL01)							
	Aug '90	5.04	0.45	0.09	0.07	0.10	0.09
	Aug '91	31.96	1.39	0.05	0.03	0.05	0.22
Point Helen (SR07)							
	May '89	644.58	104.43	9.69	0.51	0.13	
	Sept '89	7.72	3.68	0.72	0.33	0.02	0.06
	Aug '90	0.10	0.51	0.11	0.02	0.01	
	Aug '91	0.63	0.21	0.06	0.01	<0.01	
Latouche Is. (E11SA)							
	Sept '89	1.28	3.16	ND	0.02	<0.01	0.33
	Aug '90	0.42	0.35	0.02	<0.01	0.01	
	Aug '91	1.50	1.31	0.01	<0.01	<0.01	
Latouche Is.(E11)							
	Aug '90	305.87	0.95	0.07	0.02	0.02	
	Aug '91	4.80	0.83	0.07	0.01	0.01	
SRS Reference Sites							
	Aug '90	0.01	0.01	0.01	0.01	0.01	
	Aug '91	0.02	0.02	0.01	0.01	0.01	
Pebble/Gravel							
Herring Bay(SR03)							
	May '89	333.37	0.38	0.68	0.24	0.11	
	Sept '89	16.87	0.03	0.04	0.01		
	Aug '90	43.05	0.13	0.01	<0.01	<0.01	0.04
	Aug '91	5.46	0.05	0.01	ND	<0.01	0.01
Snug Harbor W (SR05)							
	Sept '89	19.93	1.12	0.19	0.20	0.06	
	Aug '90	20.43	2.24	0.14	0.08	0.09	2.56
	Aug '91	2.09	0.48	0.62	0.08	0.16	0.21
Shelter Bay (SR06)							
	May '89	501.59	212.33	0.61	0.12	0.23	
	Sept '89	96.62	10.22	0.73	0.36	0.12	0.97
	Aug '90	1.49	1.39	0.44	<0.01	0.03	0.06
	Aug '91	0.36	1.31	0.02	0.01	0.09	0.04
Mussel Beach (SR01N)							
	May '89	25.94	811.23	9.53	0.14	0.07	
	Sept '89	603.35	123.80	2.92	0.18	0.06	0.46
	Aug '90		0.46	0.01	0.01	0.01	
	Aug '91		0.67	0.01	0.01	<0.01	

TABLE A-1 (con't):—Summary of TPAH data for sediments.

Substrate/Site	Date Sampled	Mean PAH Concentrations (ppb x 10^3)					
		UI	MI	LI	-3 m	-3 To -10 m	to -30 m
Bay of Isles West (SRMB4)							
	Sept '89	13.41	0.23	0.91	0.14	0.03	0.41
	Aug '90	0.01	0.03	0.07	0.01	0.07	0.33
	Aug '91	0.01	0.01	0.01	0.01	0.13	0.28
Snug Harbor E (SR04)							
	May '89	174.27	17.47	0.50	1.07	0.32	
	Sept '89	48.66	0.14	0.31	0.87	0.24	
	Aug '90	1.41	1.08	0.19	0.58	0.11	
	Aug '91	0.35	0.15	0.55	0.21	0.15	
SRS Reference Sites							
	Aug '90	<0.01	ND	<0.01	<0.01	<0.01	
	Aug '91	<0.01	<0.01	<0.01	<0.01	<0.01	
<u>Soft</u>							
Bay of Isles Marsh (BI01)							
	Aug '90	58.81	142.23	14.58	0.26	0.19	0.06
	Aug '91	368.47	146.24	3.32	2.12	0.60	0.01
McClure Bay Reference (MB01)							
	Aug '90	ND	ND	<0.01	<0.01	ND	<0.01
	Aug '91	ND	ND	ND	<0.01	<0.01	<0.01

ND = None detected

TABLE A-2—Summary of key diagnostic ratios for sediment samples, including C_2-C_4-naphthalenes/TPAH and C_{18}/phytane ratios, which indicate the effects of physical/chemical weathering and biodegration, respectively.

Substrate/Site	Date Sampled	RATIO: C_2-C_4 NAPH/TPAH				RATIO: C_{18}/PHYTANE			
		UI	MI	LI	-3 m	UI	MI	LI	-3 m
Boulder/Cobble									
Sleepy Bay (SL01)									
	Aug '90	0.14	0.11	0.07	0.04	0.72	0.67	0.93	0.29
	Aug '91	0.27	0.18	0.11	0.00	0.97	1.05	1.09	0.32
Point Helen (SR07)									
	May '89	0.30	0.26	0.15	0.04	1.57	1.35	1.01	0.71
	Sept '89	0.09	0.15	0.16	0.03	0.76	0.88	1.07	0.31
	Aug '90	0.05	0.04	0.04	0.01	0.41	1.06	0.69	0.23
	Aug '91	0.09	0.06	0.00	0.00	0.61	0.79	0.88	0.36
Latouche Is. (E11SA)									
	May '89								
	Sept '89	0.06	0.04	No PAH	0.03	0.63	0.26	0.00	0.00
	Aug '90	0.13	0.13	0.34	0.19	0.78	0.71	0.39	0.00
	Aug '91	0.11	0.12	0.34	0.00	0.68	0.78	0.39	0.00
Latouche Is.(E11)									
	Aug '90	0.32	0.18	0.20	0.39	1.57	0.72	0.92	0.00
	Aug '91	0.08	0.04	0.01	0.00	0.68	0.85	1.22	1.09
SRS Reference Sites									
	Aug '90	0.03	0.02	0.03	0.06	0.31	0.46	0.00	0.43
	Aug '91	0.03	0.04	0.07	0.06	0.35	1.41	0.72	0.30
Pebble/Gravel									
Herring Bay (SR03)									
	May '89	0.33	0.11	0.08	0.26	1.44	0.56	0.87	1.09
	Sept '89	0.12	0.02	0.05	0.06	0.63	1.12	0.75	1.15
	Aug '90	0.13	0.08	0.30	0.59	0.53	0.69	0.37	0.00
	Aug '91	0.07	0.01	0.00	No PAH	0.39	0.36	1.12	0.85
Snug Harbor W (SR05)									
	May '89					1.60	1.33	0.51	0.93
	Sept '89	0.17	0.20	0.09	0.03	0.90	1.20	0.54	0.22
	Aug '90	0.10	0.09	0.06	0.10	0.34	0.38	0.37	0.60
	Aug '91	0.06	0.01	0.01	0.03	0.55	0.69	0.64	0.15
Shelter Bay (SR06)									
	May '89	0.24	0.26	0.09	0.09	1.82	1.61	0.25	0.00
	Sept '89	0.19	0.07	0.07	0.14	0.88	0.31	0.29	0.99
	Aug '90	0.03	0.03	0.01	0.00	0.54	0.68	0.84	0.40
	Aug '91	0.02	0.06	0.00	0.00	0.66	0.60	1.16	1.03
Mussel Beach (SR01N)									
	May '89	0.14	0.33	0.12	0.10	0.76	1.44	0.64	0.18
	Sept '89	0.29	0.16	0.10	0.00	1.40	0.58	0.45	0.16
	Aug '90		0.06	0.00	0.27		0.38	0.18	0.00
	Aug '91		0.03	0.00	0.00		0.07	1.05	0.49

TABLE A-2 (con't)—Summary of key diagnostic ratios for sediment samples.

Substrate/Site Date Sampled	RATIO: C_2-C_4NAPH/TPAH				RATIO: C_{18}/PHYTANE			
	UI	MI	LI	-3 m	UI	MI	LI	-3 m
Bay of Isles West (SRMB4)								
May '89								
Sept '89	0.12	0.14	0.08	0.03	0.84	0.95	0.50	0.26
Aug '90	0.00	0.04	0.09	0.03	0.69	0.95	0.64	1.00
Aug '91	0.03	0.00	0.04	0.00	0.08	0.19	0.09	0.00
Snug Harbor E (SR04)								
May '89	0.27	0.13	0.07	0.09				0.72
Sept '89	0.11	0.02	0.05	0.22	0.17	0.17	0.39	0.86
Aug '90	0.09	0.05	0.05	0.34	0.85	0.55	0.78	0.00
Aug '91	0.01	0.02	0.01	0.07	0.99	1.35	0.52	1.21
SRS Reference Sites								
Aug '90	0.00	No PAH	0.00	0.03	0.09	0.00	0.11	0.25
Aug '91	0.00	0.06	0.06	0.01	0.24	0.36	0.41	0.56
<u>Soft Sediment</u>								
Bay of Isles Marsh (BI01)								
Aug '90	0.29	0.25	0.18	0.03	0.98	0.53	0.74	7.05
Aug '91	0.24	0.25	0.13	0.02	0.77	0.40	0.42	0.24
McClure Bay Reference (MB01)								
Aug '90	No PAH	No PAH	0.00	0.00	0.00	0.00	0.00	0.00
Aug '91	No PAH	No PAH	No PAH	0.00	0.00	0.00	0.00	0.24

TABLE A-3—Summary of TPAH results for indigenous mussels (*Mytilus sp.*).
Geometric means of TPAH and C_2-C_4 naphthalenes/TPAH ratio for mussels at each
fixed site are presented. TPAH totals include all analytes listed in Table 3, except
perylene, naphthalene, and C_1-naphthalenes.

Substrate/Site	Date Sampled	TPAH (ppb x 10^3) dry weight, (geometric mean)	Ratio: C_2-C_4 Naphthalene/TPAH
Boulder/Cobble			
Sleepy Bay (SL01)			
	Aug '90	24.70	0.047
	Aug '91	0.12	0.000
Point Helen (SR07)			
	May '89	375.86	0.175
	Sept '89	194.84	0.176
	Aug '90	12.66	0.074
	Aug '91	11.37	0.020
Latouche Is. (E11SA)			
	Aug '90	<0.01	0.000
	Aug '91	0.01	0.000
Latouche Is.(E11)			
	May '89		
	Sept '89		
	Aug '90	ND	ND
	Aug '91	9.70	0.030
SRS Reference Sites			
	May '89		
	Sept '89		
	Aug '90	0.02	0.065
	Aug '91	<0.01	0.000
Pebble/Gravel			
Herring Bay(SR03)			
	May '89	154.11	0.072
	Sept '89	9.49	0.058
	Aug '90	0.01	0.000
	Aug '91	ND	ND
Snug Harbor W (SR05)			
	Sept '89	7.54	0.019
	Aug '90	0.44	0.000
	Aug '91	0.01	0.000
Shelter Bay (SR06)			
	May '89	82.9	0.069
	Sept '89	24.8	0.055
	Aug '90	10.93	0.061
	Aug '91	0.03	0.000
Mussel Beach (SR01N)			
	May '89	336.2	0.162
	Sept '89	30.95	0.119
	Aug '90	0.02	0.000
	Aug '91	<0.01	0.000

TABLE A-3(con't)—Summary of TPAH results for indigenous mussels (*Mytilus sp.*).

Substrate/Site	Date Sampled	TPAH (ppb x 10^3) dry weight, (geometric mean)	Ratio: C_2-C_4 Naphthalene/TPAH
Bay of Isles West SRMB4)			
	Aug '90	0.07	0.000
	Aug '91	0.01	0.000
Snug Harbor E (SR04)			
	May '89	73.56	0.138
	Sept '89	21.78	0.032
	Aug '90	0.63	0.000
	Aug '91	0.01	0.000
SRS Reference Sites			
	Aug '90	<0.01	0.000
	Aug '91	ND	ND
Soft Sediment			
Bay of Isles Marsh (BI01)			
	Aug '90	1.26	0.075
	Aug '91	18.22	0.011
McClure Bay Reference (MB01)			
	Aug '90	0.08	0.000
	Aug '91	ND	ND

ND = None detected

Edward S. Gilfillan[1], Dave S. Page[2], E. James Harner[3] ,Paul D. Boehm[4]

SHORELINE ECOLOGY PROGRAM FOR PRINCE WILLIAM SOUND, ALASKA, FOLLOWING THE *EXXON VALDEZ* OIL SPILL: PART 3—BIOLOGY.

REFERENCE: Gilfillan, E. S., Page, D. S., Harner, E. J., Boehm, P. D., "Shoreline Ecology Program For Prince William Sound, Alaska, Following the *Exxon Valdez* Oil Spill: Part 3—Biology," Exxon Valdez *Oil Spill: Fate and Effects in Alaskan Waters, ASTM STP 1219,* Peter G. Wells, James N. Butler, and Jane S. Hughes, Eds., American Society for Testing and Materials, Philadelphia, PA, 1995.

ABSTRACT

This study describes the biological results of a comprehensive shoreline ecology program designed to assess ecological recovery in Prince William Sound following the *Exxon Valdez* oil spill on March 24, 1989. The program is an application of the "Sediment Quality Triad" approach, combining chemical, toxicological, and biological measurements. The study was designed so that results could be extrapolated to the entire spill zone in Prince William Sound.

The spill affected four major shoreline habitat types in Prince William Sound: pebble/gravel, boulder/cobble, sheltered bedrock, and exposed bedrock. The study design had two components: (1) one-time stratified random sampling at 64 sites representing four habitats and four oiling levels (including unoiled reference sites) and (2) periodic sampling at 12 nonrandomly chosen sites that included some of the most heavily oiled locations in the sound. Biological communities on rock surfaces and in intertidal and shallow subtidal sediments were analyzed for differences resulting from to oiling in each of 16 habitat/tide zone combinations. Statistical methods included univariate analyses of individual species abundances and community parameter variables (total abundance, species richness, and Shannon diversity), and multivariate correspondence analysis of community structure.

The communities of animals and plants inhabiting the bedrock and coarse sediments on Prince William Sound's shorelines responded much differently to oiling than communities in soft-sediment environments that were the subject of a majority of shoreline studies conducted after other oil spills.

Sedimentary environments in Prince William Sound did not become anacrobic but showed evidence of increased biological activity as the oil residue became a source of

---

[1]Bowdoin College, Brunswick, ME
[2]Bowdoin College, Brunswick, ME
[3]West Virginia University, Morgantown, WV
[4]Arthur D. Little, Inc.,Cambridge, MA

organic carbon—without the usual succession of opportunistic invaders. Similarly, some bedrock sites showed increases in abundance, species richness, and diversity, as the spaces created by oiling were recolonized. This was to be expected in a high-energy environment dominated by "patch dynamics"; the rock surfaces and sediments support a mosaic of species that are adapted to rapidly colonize new spaces created by wave action and other physical factors.

Two measures of ecological shoreline recovery are reported: an upper-limit estimate based on univariate analysis of community parameters and a lower-limit estimate based on multivariate correspondence analysis of community structure. Overall, the results indicate that between 73% and 91% of the oiled shoreline in Prince William Sound was ecologically recovered (i.e., it was indistinguishable from reference) in the summer of 1990. These results reflect rapid recovery of the biological communities and are consistent with chemical and toxicological studies (this volume), which found that hydrocarbon-related toxicity was virtually absent in the shoreline sediments by 1990-1991.

KEYWORDS: *Exxon Valdez,* oil-spill effects, oil-spill recovery, shoreline ecology, stratified random sampling, generalized linear models, correspondence analysis, patch dynamics, rocky shores, boulder/cobble beaches, pebble/gravel beaches.

INTRODUCTION

On March 24, 1989, the *Exxon Valdez* ran aground on Bligh Reef in Prince William Sound, releasing approximately 258,000 barrels of Alaska North Slope crude into the marine environment and oiling 500 miles of shoreline (Maki 1991; Neff et al., this volume). Following the spill a shoreline ecology program was initiated to provide an unbiased assessment of shoreline recovery in Prince William Sound. This paper represents the biology portion of a comprehensive shoreline ecology program that spanned three field seasons from 1989 to 1991, with the most extensive effort undertaken in 1990. Its objective was to provide an unbiased assessment of shoreline recovery following the spill. The design of the study is described in Part 1: Study Design and Methods (Page et al., this volume), and results of the chemistry and toxicology studies are presented in Part 2: Chemistry and Toxicology (Boehm et al., this volume). This paper describes the shoreline biology studies and summarizes the entire program.

Most previous studies of spill-affected shorelines have been carried out in soft-sediment areas, because it is in these areas that oil persists and has the greatest ecological impacts (National Research Council [NRC] 1985; Mielke 1990). Typically, such studies have involved a relatively small number of sampling locations that have been heavily affected by oil. They were designed to study the ecological processes involved in recovery from oil spills, not to provide quantitative assessments of recovery of the spill zone as a whole.

The general patterns of community response to, and recovery from, oil spills are now understood (NRC 1985; Mielke 1990). For any given habitat, the degree of initial impact from an oil spill is a function of the amount of oil reaching a location, and its toxicity. When toxic oil is incorporated into sediments, the infauna may be killed and sediments may become anaerobic as a result of reduced oxygen transport in animal burrows and the added biochemical oxygen demand (BOD) of the oil (Sanders et al., 1980). If more weathered (i.e., less toxic) oil is incorporated, the added BOD of the oil may drive the sediments anaerobic and kill the infauna even if they survive the initial exposure to oil (Glemarec and Hussenot 1981). The finer the sediments, the more easily they will become anaerobic. This effect of oil spills is similar to that observed with other types of organic enrichment (Pearson and Rosenberg 1978).

Anaerobic sediments undergo a succession to a recovered state as the excess inventory of organic carbon is metabolized by bacteria. At the beginning of the succession, the community is dominated by opportunistic polychaete worms (Grassle and Grassle 1974; Sanders et al. 1980; Glemarec and Hussenot 1981; Gilfillan et al., 1986). Over time, the opportunists are replaced by normally occurring species. At the end of the succession, a normally diverse community again occupies the environment.

This was not the expected process in Prince William Sound. The kinds of shoreline oiled by the spill are very different from those studied most intensely in previous oil spills. Virtually all of the shoreline in the sound falls into one of the following three categories: bedrock/rubble, boulder/cobble, or pebble/gravel. Most shorelines in Prince William Sound are eroding, not accumulating; as a result, sediments tend to be coarse, and total organic carbon (TOC) levels are generally low. These sediments do not easily become anaerobic, and weathered oil can become a food source for micro-organisms, and indirectly, stimulate normal infaunal activity.

The ecology of rocky shores in Prince William Sound depends strongly on the degree of wave exposure. Where wave exposure is low, the observed distribution of animals and plants is largely a result of competition for space, predator-prey interactions, and resistance to physical stress. However, where wave exposure is high, space is constantly recycled, and the activity of predators or other means of competition for space become less important; thus, more species can coexist. In many locations, loose sediment particles become missiles when waves are high (Shanks and Wright 1986). Logs and ice cakes add to the effects of wave exposure. This process of space creation is called patch dynamics (Dayton 1971; Paine and Levin 1981; Nakahara and Ueno 1985; McGuinness 1987a,b; Sousa 1985; Osman 1977; Sousa 1979 a,b). Similar sorts of processes involving smothering by drift algae, wave action, etc., can occur in sedimentary environments (Thistle 1981). The resulting communities are a mosaic of species whose existence in a given location is less a function of their competitive ability than their colonizing ability and the timing of their breeding cycle (Grant 1977). The ecology of many plant and animal communities affected by the *Exxon Valdez* oil spill is strongly influenced by patch dynamics.

Open space for recolonization is created where animals and plants are killed by the oil or subsequent cleanup. However, it is rare for all individuals of a species to be eliminated from an area, even where rocky shorelines are heavily oiled (Chan 1975; Clark et al. 1978; Southward and Southward, 1978; Chasse 1978; Bonsdorf and Nelson 1981; Nelson 1982). Ecological effects of oiling on rocky shores can also result from disruptions in competitive or predator-prey relationships.

There are two general patterns of competitive interaction between two species, A and B, when A normally displaces B. If a disturbance kills A, B becomes more common.

On the other hand, if the oil makes open space available for A and B, the competition is temporarily reduced, and both species can coexist (Denslow 1985). This is similar to the situation where open space is made by waves or other agents of disturbance, e.g., foot traffic, clearing, or predation (Paine 1974; Lubchenco 1978; Ghazanshahi et al. 1983; Sousa 1985; Povey and Keogh 1991). Another possible disruption on rocky shores occurs when a predator is reduced in number, leading to increases in the population of its prey (Robles 1982). When large amounts of space are created, the invading opportunists are usually filamentous green algae (Southward and Southward 1978; Markham and Munda 1980).

The goal of this study was to understand and assess recovery from the impacts of the *Exxon Valdez* oil spill in the intertidal and shallow subtidal communities in Prince William Sound in the context of natural ecological processes in those environments. In the context of this study, impact is defined as the sum of oil and cleanup effects that occurred in 1989. There is no universally accepted definition of recovery of an ecosystem, whether damage occurs from natural episodic environmental factors or from anthropogenic events like an oil spill.

Definition of Recovery

Recovery of a spill-affected biological community could be considered complete when negative spill impacts ("injuries") are no longer detectable. This definition would exclude the increases in abundance resulting from effects of space creation (as discussed above) or those from low-level oil residues serving as a food source for hydrocarbon-degrading bacteria. In this paper, we have adopted a conservative approach: recovery is not considered complete as long as an oiling effect on the biological community, either increases or decreases, can be detected.

Despite the relatively simple definition of recovery we have proposed in this paper, there is still no generally accepted way to measure it. The described process of patch dynamics makes measuring recovery especially difficult, because it introduces great variation in species distributions, both in space and over time. Such variability is difficult to reconcile with the concept that recovery involves a gradual return to equilibrium. Thus, we believe that no single species, or even a small group of "key" species, will suffice as an indicator of recovery when patch dynamics play such an important role. Some broader measure of the structure and composition of the shoreline community is required.

Two approaches were used to assess recovery of intertidal biota. The first uses classical community parameters—total abundance, algal biomass, species richness, and Shannon diversity (Shannon 1948; Shannon and Weaver 1949). A significant difference in the means for any of these variables at oiled sites, relative to reference means, was taken as an indication that recovery had not yet occurred. The second approach was correspondence analysis. This multivariate statistical technique was used to detect differences in species composition between oiled and unoiled sites in a given habitat. As discussed later in this paper, the estimates obtained by these two approaches can be viewed as upper and lower limits, respectively, on the extent to which biological recovery was evident in Prince William Sound by the summer of 1990.

Approach

The approach taken in this study (Part 1: Study Design and Methods, Page et al., this volume) was to combine a one-time effort of stratified random sampling (SRS) in 1990 with studies carried out over time at 12 subjectively chosen "fixed" sites of special interest. The SRS component focused on the four major habitats (exposed and sheltered bedrock/rubble, boulder/cobble, pebble/gravel), and a range of oiling levels (none = reference, light, moderate, and heavy). Thus, oiling effects within each habitat could be determined by statistical comparison with randomly chosen reference sites and the results generalized to conditions in the spill-affected zone as a whole.

The fixed-site component provided information about recovery at some of the most heavily oiled sites in Prince William Sound, including special habitats too rare to be sampled in the SRS study. The fixed-site program extended over three years (1989-1991) for chemistry and two years (1990-1991) for biology. SRS reference sites for boulder/cobble and pebble/gravel substrates were also resampled in 1991.

At each SRS or fixed site, four tide zones (upper, middle and lower intertidal, and shallow subtidal) were sampled along three transects. Sediment cores for analysis of infaunal communities were taken whenever sufficient sediment could be found at the sampling stations. Otherwise, scrape samples of epibiota were collected from bedrock/rubble surfaces. The basic variables measured on these samples were abundances of animal species and the biomass of plant species (algae) attached to rock surfaces. Our objective was to obtain as complete a description of the macrobiota (> than 1 mm) as possible. Hence, the resulting datasets were very large, containing more than 1 055 species in about 1 200 samples. However, most species occurred in only a few samples, consistent with the patch dynamics characteristic of Prince William Sound shorelines.

Three common measures of community structure were derived for each sample from the abundance data of animal species: the total number of organisms (total abundance); the total number of species (species richness); and the Shannon diversity index. A fourth parameter, total algal biomass, was determined for samples from rock surfaces. In addition, we used canonical correspondence analysis to assess overall differences in the structure and composition of biological communities at oiled and reference sites.

METHODS

All methods were codified as written standard operating procedures, and frequent quality-assurance and quality-control exercises in field and laboratory procedures ensured that they were being followed. Site selection, as well as field and analytical procedures, are described in detail in Part 1: Study Design and Methods (Page et al., this volume). The following sections focus on those procedures that apply specifically to the biological portion of the program.

Field Sampling

Depending on the substrate, two types of samples were obtained in the field: on *rocky substrates,* all epibiota within a 12.5- x 25-cm sampling "quadrat" were collected. These samples were taken in two stages: first, all macro-algae attached within the sampling quadrat were removed; then the remaining biota were scraped off the surface. The algae samples were sorted and weighed (by species). Any animals found associated with the algae were removed from the biomass sample and combined with the corresponding scrape sample. In addition, photographs of a 0.5- x 0.5-m quadrat were taken to document surface conditions, including coverage by epibiota (mussels, barnacles, rockweed, etc.). For colonial organisms and encrusting algae their presence or absence within a quadrat was recorded.

On *sedimentary substrates,* core samples were taken whenever possible to assess the infauna. If necessary, surficial layers of coarse sediment (boulders, cobble, etc.) were removed to reach the underlying finer sediments so that a core sample could be taken. Core samples were 10 cm in diameter and (usually) 10- cm deep. Any macro-algae that were attached to the surface of the core sample were collected separately. Only data on the infauna at sedimentary sites are reported here.

The scrape and core samples were sieved in the field to yield those organisms and other material that would not pass through a 1.0-mm mesh. All samples were preserved in 10% buffered formalin. We expected ecological communities to change over the summer growing season. All samples collected from a given habitat, e.g., sheltered bedrock, were collected in the same ~ 2-week low tide period.

Laboratory Methods

As described above, samples arriving at the laboratory were of two types: (1) algal biomass samples and (2) sieved samples from cores or scrapes. Whereas the algal biomass samples had been sorted and weighed in the field, the sieved samples were sorted in the laboratory. Upon arrival, samples were inventoried to ensure that the sample code numbers and number of samples matched the chain-of-custody documentation. Then the >1.0-mm sieved samples were drained of formaldehyde, washed with water, transferred into 75-80% ethanol, and stained with Rose Bengal. Following the transfer, samples were labeled externally with the field label; an additional label was placed inside the container. The >0.5-mm (and <1.0-mm) sieved samples were archived.

Prior to sorting, the samples were washed to remove the ethanol and placed in water in small glass jars. Each sample was placed, a portion at a time, in glass petri dishes and sorted under a dissecting microscope. Organisms found in the sample were sorted into eight taxonomic groups and placed in labeled vials:

- Annelids (polychaetes and oligochaetes)
- Mollusks
- Crustaceans (except copepods)
- Copepods
- Insects and mites
- Nematodes
- Fish

- Miscellaneous taxa (echinoderms, nemerteans, bryozoa, siphuncula, anthozoa, echiura, and urochordata)

The accuracy of the sorting was assessed by re-sorting 10% of the residue (the material left after organisms were removed) from each sample. If fewer than 1% of the total number of organisms found in the sample were found on the re-sort, the sample passed. If more organisms were found, all the residue was re-sorted.

Following sorting, the individual vials were sent to appropriate primary taxonomists for identification, maintaining chain of custody. Organisms were identified to the lowest practical taxonomic level (called "species" for simplicity) and enumerated. The samples and data sheets with species counts were returned to the laboratory. In order to check identifications made by the primary taxonomists, 10% of the samples were verified by secondary taxonomists. Differences were reconciled between the primary and secondary taxonomists; any changes in classification resulting from this reconciliation were applied consistently throughout the dataset.

Data Management

Raw data for species counts were entered into Microsoft EXCEL (Microsoft, Inc., Redmond, WA 98073-9717) data tables. Data in these files were checked completely (100%) against the original data sheets by personnel other than those who had entered the data into the database. Once the files passed the 100% check, they were subjected to a Continuous Sampling Procedure (CSP-1) at the Mean Quality Level (AQL) of 1% (Hanson 1963). If more than five errors were detected during CSP-1 sampling, the 100% check was repeated, followed by a second CSP-1 check.

Statistical Analysis

Two types of statistical analysis were carried out: univariate modeling of individual species abundances and community parameters, and multivariate correspondence analysis of community structure. In both cases, the objective was to compare samples from oiled and unoiled (reference) areas. The null hypothesis was that there was no oiling effect. The comparisons were conducted separately for each of the 16 combinations of four habitats and four tide zones because species abundances and composition depend strongly on these factors. Model residuals were tested to determine whether normality was an appropriate assumption: for most datasets of species abundances, it was not; thus non-normal modeling techniques were used extensively. A significance level of $\alpha = 0.05$ was used for hypothesis testing.

Univariate analysis—For univariate analyses, the null hypothesis of no oiling effect was tested using a model that adjusted the means for important environmental parameters (concomitant variables). The oiling effects for any biological variable in question (species abundance or community parameter) were estimated on the basis of differences among the model means for the different oiling levels. All means mentioned in the text or in graphs are actually model means adjusted for concomitant variables, but they will be referred to as means for simplicity. When the null hypothesis was rejected, the direction (positive or negative) of the difference from reference was noted.

The occurrence of animals and plants in a given habitat is influenced by environmental factors other than the spill. To remove potential bias from our analysis, and to decrease variability, we measured several environmental variables for each site or sample. For core data, these variables included percentage sand, percentage silt/clay, TOC, and wave exposure. For scrape data, the only environmental variable included was wave exposure. These variables were included as concomitant variables in the statistical models.

Two different models were used in the univariate analyses. The goal was to use a model that satisfied the appropriate statistical assumptions and had high power to detect differences. First a "site model" that used among-site variability as an error term was run to test oiling effects. By using this model, among site variability was also compared to within-site (transect) variability. If the among-site variability was not significantly greater than the within-site variability, a "transect model" was run in which the within-site and among-site variabilities were pooled into a single error term. Oiling effects were then tested against this pooled error term. The transect model almost always had greater power to detect differences resulting from oiling and was used when appropriate (Part 1: Study Design and Methods, Page et al., this volume). Based on the statistical test described above, the transect model was found to be appropriate for about 78% of the species.

Testing of oiling effects for individual species abundances (number of individuals or algal biomass) was first done with normal-theory methods on log-transformed data. If the residuals from this analysis were not distributed normally (based on a Shapiro-Wilks test; $P \leq 0.05$), we switched to non-normal theory methods.

Normal-theory testing was carried out by using one-way analysis of covariance (ANCOVA) with oiling level as a factor (Super ANOVA: Abacus Softwares, Inc.). The significance test for overall oiling effects was conducted after adjusting for the concomitant variables. Dunnett's two-tailed test was used to test for significant differences among each of the three oiling levels (light, moderate, and heavy) and reference.

Non-normal theory analyses were conducted with the General Linear Interactive Model (GLIM: Numerical Algorithms Group, Inc.). This allowed us to analyze many species whose abundances were not lognormally distributed. This method is analogous to the ANCOVA, but abundances were tested by using Poisson, binomial, or negative binomial distributions. The approach was to first run GLIM assuming a Poisson error distribution. If the fit to the Poisson model was unacceptable ($P \leq 0.05$) and the data were over-dispersed (finding one of a species in a sample makes it more likely to find another), a negative binomial model was used. If the data were under-dispersed (finding one of a species in a sample makes it less likely to find another), a binomial model was used. The significance test for overall oiling effects was conducted after adjusting for the concomitant variables. Post-hoc tests were conducted to compare oiling level means to the reference. Those species for which the GLIM algorithm did not converge were not analyzed further.

The community parameters were analyzed with the same ANCOVA/GLIM procedure used for the individual species, except that the data were not transformed for the ANCOVA runs. GLIM was invoked in some of these runs, particularly for the abundance data.

Multivariate analysis—When species abundances are analyzed one at a time, they may show inconsistent or contradictory trends with respect to the effect being investigated (e.g., oiling). This is to be expected when the effect is small relative to the natural variability and, hence, the power to detect this effect is low (Part 1: Study Design and Methods, Page et al., this volume). As an alternative to univariate modeling, multivariate techniques have been developed for simultaneous modeling of multiple dependent variables such as individual species abundances.

We used detrended partial canonical correspondence analysis (DCCA) (Ter Braak 1986a,b) to assess effects of oiling on community structure. Correspondence analysis is an ordination technique that arranges samples along axes defined in terms of weighting factors for each species in the dataset. Canonical correspondence analysis constrains one or more of the ordination axes to reflect some effect of interest, such as oiling, i.e., the weighting factors are subject to the condition (constraint) that they must separate, as much as possible, the plotting positions of samples corresponding to different levels of the variable of interest. Partial canonical correlation analysis performs the ordination after removing the effects of other physical or environmental variables. Detrending removes an artifact (arching) that tends to distort the scores for the second ordination axis (Ter Braak 1986b). Correspondence analysis was chosen for these data because it does not require species abundances to be normally distributed, as do other multivariate ordination techniques such as discriminant analysis.

In the correspondence analyses performed for the SRS, the first two ordination axes were constrained to maximally differentiate among samples on the basis of initial oiling level. In addition, the same physical variables that were used in the ANCOVA and GLIM models were also included in the DCCA model to remove their effects prior to assessing oiling effects. Individual transects were treated as independent sampling units because current theory does not allow for multiple random effects. This approximation is justified by the wide separation of the transects within sites and is reasonable because nearly four out of five of the univariate models used the transect model. The DCCA analysis was carried out using CANOCO for the Macintosh (Microcomputer Power).

In the correspondence analysis performed for the fixed sites, the data from 1990 and 1991 were treated differently. The fixed-site data from 1990 were analyzed along with the data from the SRS sites. The fixed sites were carried as "passive sites"— i.e., they were not used to define the axes but sample scores were calculated for each of them. The fixed sites were compared with the appropriate SRS reference sites. In 1991, only the fixed sites and the appropriate SRS reference sites were sampled. For the pebble/gravel habitat, all oiling levels were represented, and two axes were constrained by initial oiling as in the analysis for 1990. For the boulder/cobble habitat, only heavily oiled and unoiled shorelines were represented; therefore, with only one degree of freedom, only one axis could be constrained by initial oiling.

Datasets for Statistical Analysis

The basic biological dataset contained species abundance data for about 936 samples (723 samples from the SRS program and 213 samples from the fixed-site program, including SRS reference sites revisited in 1991). The SRS samples consisted of 252 scrape samples from bedrock locations and 471 core samples from sediment locations, including subtidal core samples from bedrock sites. In addition, each scrape sample had an associated sample of attached macro-algae. With one exception (upper intertidal zone at Mussel Beach), only core samples were obtained in the fixed-site program.

Subsets for habitat/tide level combinations—The basic dataset was divided into subsets for statistical analysis (one subset for each habitat/tide zone combination). A typical subset from the SRS program consisted of species abundance data and any associated biomass data (at bedrock sites) for 48 sampling locations (16 sites sampled at three transects each). Some datasets had fewer than 48 samples (a minimum of 33 samples for lower intertidal sheltered bedrock), because the desired type of sample (scrape or core) was not always available at each sampling station. (Some stations on bedrock sites would fall on sediment, and vice versa.)

Table 3 in Page et al. (Part 1: Study Design and Methods, this volume) gives the number of sites and samples for each combination of habitat, tide zone, and oiling level. These range from 2 sites and 5 samples for lower-intertidal sheltered bedrock reference to 6 sites and 18 samples for several oiled (principally heavily oiled) locations. The relatively small number of samples from sheltered-bedrock intertidal reference sites (a minimum of 5 at the lower intertidal) reduces the statistical power for individual comparisons with reference in this habitat.

Rare species—The properties of the datasets reflected the importance of patch dynamics in the ecology of Prince William Sound: the distribution of animals and plants was extremely patchy. Hence, the most common data value was 0; no species occurred in all samples of any dataset. Figure 1 shows the mean distribution of species in core samples from the SRS sites. Nearly 23% of the species found occurred in only one sample; 68% of the species were found in 10 or fewer samples.

Because the most frequently occurring value for species abundance was 0, the raw datasets were not well suited to classical statistical analysis. Although there is broad agreement that rare species distort results of statistical analysis, there is no general agreement as to what proportion of rare species should be eliminated prior to statistical analysis. Some investigators have dealt with the rare-species problem by selecting a group of the most common species and working with them (Sanders et al. 1980; Stephenson et al. 1970). Others eliminated various percentages of the rare species (Burd et al. 1990; Field et al. 1982; Smith et al. 1988). In this paper, we followed an approach that allowed us to include a large number of species in the analysis while ensuring that the statistical tests were valid. Specifically, we included all those species that occurred in at least 20% of the samples for a given habitat/tide zone combination. Even so, a number of these species could not be analyzed— i.e., GLIM failed to converge. On the other hand, *all* species were included in the calculation of community parameter values and, hence, in the statistical analysis of these variables.

For correspondence analysis, those species that occurred in fewer than 20% of the samples were eliminated (as was done for univariate species analyses). Correspondence analysis is very sensitive to rare species, especially those that have a good chance of occurring in only one cell of an experimental design. By retaining only those species that

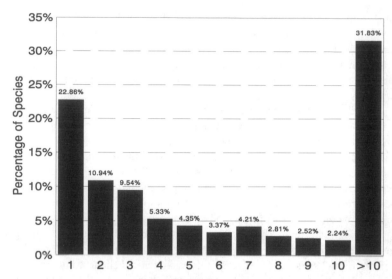

Number of Samples in Which a Species Occurred
FIGURE 1—Mean distribution of species in core samples from SRS sites.

occur in more than 20% of the samples, there was only a small probability (less than 3%) that any of the remaining species would occur in only one cell of our SRS design (assuming no oiling effect). Thus, the effects of random occurrences of a species were greatly reduced. In fact, the 20% cutoff was selected after we explored the sensitivity of the analysis over a range of cutoff values; results tended to stabilize at about 20%.

Numbers of species analyzed—Table 1 lists the numbers of species present in the raw datasets of the SRS program, the numbers of those successfully analyzed by univariate models, and the numbers of those retained for the correspondence analysis. The same data files were used for both univariate modeling and correspondence analysis (containing those species that occurred in at least 20% of the samples for a given habitat/tide zone combination. Univariate modeling required that a species fit a recognized normal or non-normal distribution of abundances. Some species did not fit any of the available distributions, and thus could not be modeled with this technique. Correspondence analysis was not as sensitive to the underlying distribution. As a result, the number of species successfully modeled for univariate analysis is frequently less than the number of species used in correspondence analysis.

Distributions used for hypothesis testing—Table 2 provides a breakdown by the type of distribution used for hypothesis testing of individual species in the ANCOVA/GLIM procedures. The fractions of successful analyses conducted with lognormal, Poisson, binomial, and negative binominal distributions are shown separately for intertidal and subtidal samples in each of the four habitats.

The table demonstrates the importance of using generalized linear models for hypothesis testing; lognormal distributions were found in only about one-third of the species we were able to analyze. For intertidal species, the lognormal distribution was

TABLE 1—Numbers of species* in various habitat/tide zone combinations used for statistical analyses. All species present were used in the community parameter analyses.

Habitat/ Tide Level	Total Numbers of Species Present	Number of Species Successfully Modeled	Number of Species Used for Correspondence Analysis
Exposed Bedrock			
Upper Intertidal	102	12	17
Middle Intertidal	200	36	42
Lower Intertidal	318	50	67
Subtidal (-3 m)	433	62	78
Sheltered Bedrock			
Upper Intertidal	51	6	9
Middle Intertidal	63	32	35
Lower Intertidal	237	48	56
Subtidal (-3 m)	419	55	61
Boulder/Cobble			
Upper Intertidal	93	7	7
Middle Intertidal	161	9	13
Lower Intertidal	283	32	39
Subtidal (-3 m)	324	46	54
Pebble/Gravel			
Upper Intertidal	57	4	4
Middle Intertidal	73	6	8
Lower Intertidal	222	10	25
Subtidal (-3 m)	308	28	33

*Organisms that had been identified to the lowest practicable taxonomic level.

most frequent in the core data (sediment sites), whereas the negative binomial distribution was most common in the scrape data (bedrock sites). This latter distribution reflects patch dynamics, which produces a patchwork of communities with individual patches that are often large compared with the sampling area.

Datasets for community parameter analyses—The community parameter variables used for univariate analysis included the total abundance or biomass of organisms in a sample, the total number of species present (species richness), and the Shannon diversity index. These variables were calculated from the complete set of raw species data for each sample. In contrast to the individual species counts, these data were not log-transformed for the statistical analysis.

The Shannon diversity index (Shannon 1948; Shannon and Weaver 1949) is defined by the expression $-\sum p_i \log_2 p_i$, where p_i is the relative abundance of species i, expressed as a fraction of the total abundance. The diversity index increases with increasing species richness; it also increases as the total number of individuals is more

TABLE 2—Statistical distributions used for hypothesis testing of individual species abundances. Italics and underlining identify data from surface scrape samples; all others are from sediment cores.

Habitat	Percentage of Species Tested							
	Lognormal		Poisson		Binomial		Negative Binomial	
	Inter-tidal	Sub-tidal	Inter-tidal	Sub-tidal	Inter-tidal	Sub-tidal	Inter-tidal	Sub-tidal
Exposed Bedrock	_33_	27	_4_	9	_7_	17	_56_	27
Sheltered Bedrock	_34_	31	_2_	18	_2_	7	_62_	34
Boulder/Cobble	44	24	6	13	8	11	42	37
Pebble/Gravel	55	33	30	12	0	3	15	36

evenly distributed among the species in a community. The more diverse the community, the larger the value of the index.

RESULTS

Results of the statistical analyses are presented first for the SRS program and then for the fixed sites. For the SRS sites, summary results and specific examples of individual species analyses will be presented, followed by results of community parameter and correspondence analyses. For the fixed sites, comparisons of community parameters with those at corresponding SRS reference sites (without statistical testing) will be presented, followed by the results of correspondence analysis.

SRS Program Results

For site locations and methodological aspects of the SRS program, refer to Part 1: Study Design and Methods (Page et al., this volume). However, for perspective, Table 3 includes relevant information on the numbers of sites, and length of oiled shoreline represented, for each of the 16 habitat/oiling level combinations in the SRS matrix. This information is used for extrapolating SRS results to the spill-affected portion of Prince William Sound.

Summary of species tests—We tested whether the mean abundance of a species at oiled sites is greater than, less than, or the same as the mean at corresponding reference sites. Results are summarized in Table 4 by habitat and tide zone. The proportion of species showing an oiling effect ranged from less than 10% to 70%. The highest percentages occurred in the lower intertidal and shallow subtidal zones of pebble/gravel

TABLE 3—Stratified Random Sampling (SRS) sites. The number of sites and the percentages of total oiled shoreline in Prince William Sound are shown for each habitat/oiling level category.

Habitat	Heavy	Oiled Sites Moderate	Light	Reference Sites	Totals
Exposed Bedrock					
Sites	6	2	3	5	16
% Oiled Shoreline	2.8	1.8	12.2	-	16.8
Sheltered Bedrock					
Sites	4	2	6	4	16
% Oiled Shoreline	7.5	7.3	41.8	-	56.6
Boulder/Cobble					
Sites	5	3	3	5	16
% Oiled Shoreline	6.4	2.7	13.8	-	22.9
Pebble/Gravel					
Sites	6	3	3	4	16
% Oiled Shoreline	1.1	.4	2.2	-	3.7
Totals					
Sites	21	10	15	18	64
% Oiled Shoreline	17.8	12.2	70.0		100*

* 100% = 486 miles

sites. However, the post-hoc comparisons with reference sites showed only increases of mean abundances for this habitat (Table 4).

Overall, 83 (18.7%) of the total of 443 species tests showed an oiling effect, and most of the significant changes were increases rather than decreases in species abundance. Thus, if recovery estimates were based on the fraction of species tests showing no difference from reference, one could conclude that about 81% of the biota in the spill-affected area of Prince William Sound had recovered by the summer of 1990. However, as previously discussed, it is preferable to base our assessment of recovery on statistical analyses of the biological community as a whole, rather than on results for individual species.

Dunnett's test for normal-theory models and post-hoc t-tests for non-normal models were run to determine which of the oiling levels (light, moderate, and heavy) were different from reference. Since the follow-up t-test requires significance of an overall oiling effect, but Dunnett's does not, these test results are summarized in Table 4 both conditionally and unconditionally on the significance of the overall oiling effect. The number of decreases and increases observed for each oiling level are reported and compared with reference.

These results show that in summer 1990, the majority of the differences were increases rather than decreases in species abundances at oiled sites relative to reference sites for both the conditional tests (16 decreases versus 52 increases) and the unconditional tests (40 decreases versus 72 increases). In some cases, no differences

TABLE 4—Summary of significant oiling effects overall and by individual comparisons classified by increasing (Incr.) or decreasing (Decr.) abundances for individual species.

Habitat/Tide Zone*	Total Number of Species	Species Showing Significant Overall Oiling Effect		Species different from reference at one or more oiling levels**	
		Number	Percent	Conditional (Decr./Incr.)	Unconditional (Decr./Incr.)
Exposed Bedrock					
UI	12	2	17	0/0	1/0
MI	36	6	17	1/4	4/6
LI	50	4	8	1/2	3/9
-3 m	62	15	24	4/7	7/8
Totals (# of Tests)	**160**	**27**	**16.9**	**6/13**	**15/23**
Sheltered Bedrock					
UI	6	1	17	0/1	0/1
MI	32	3	9	2/1	7/1
LI	48	9	19	1/5	2/8
-3 m	55	6	11	1/2	6/5
Totals (# of Tests)	**141**	**19**	**13.5**	**4/9**	**15/15**
Boulder/Cobble					
UI	7	1	14	1/0	2/0
MI	9	1	11	1/0	2/0
LI	32	5	16	2/3	3/3
-3 m	46	10	22	2/7	3/7
Totals (# of Tests)	**94**	**17**	**18.1**	**6/10**	**10/10**
Pebble/Gravel					
UI	4	1	25	0/1	0/2
MI	6	1	17	0/1	0/1
LI	10	7	70	0/7	0/9
-3 m	28	11	39	0/11	0/12
Totals (# of Tests)	**48**	**20**	**41.7**	**0/20**	**0/24**
Grand Totals (# of Tests)	**443**	**83**	**18.7**	**16/52**	**40/72**

*Tidal Zones: UI - Upper Intertidal, MI - Middle Intertidal, LI - Lower Intertidal, -3 m - Subtidal from three meters below zero tidal datum.

**Test results are given for both conditional tests (given that an overall oiling effect was detected) and unconditional tests (whether or not overall oiling effect was significant).

between individual oiling levels and reference were detected in the post-hoc test, even when the overall oiling effect was significant.

Selected species—Detailed results are presented here for certain species that are especially important to the shoreline ecology of Prince William Sound. They include an alga (*Fucus gardneri*) that provides food and shelter, two types of herbivores (limpets and littorine snails), and mussels (*Mytilus edulis*), an important prey for certain birds and mammals. All of these taxa are epibiota that are clearly visible even to the casual observer. However, estimates of recovery will be based on broad measures of the biological communities. The individual species data exhibit very large natural variability, which would tend to mask any oiling effects.

Figure 2 shows mean biomass estimates of *Fucus gardneri* as a function of intertidal height and oiling level for sheltered and exposed bedrock sites. The symbols UI, MI, and LI designate the upper, middle, and lower intertidal zones, respectively. Exposed bedrock sites had significantly more *Fucus gardneri* biomass in the heavily oiled middle intertidal zone than at the reference sites; on the other hand, there was significantly less *Fucus gardneri* biomass in the lightly oiled upper intertidal zone than at the corresponding reference sites. At sheltered bedrock sites, a significant difference from reference was found in the lightly oiled lower intertidal zone, where the biomass was less than that at the corresponding reference sites. At the upper intertidal, all three oiling levels show less biomass than reference; however, GLIM failed to converge for this dataset, so hypothesis testing was not possible.

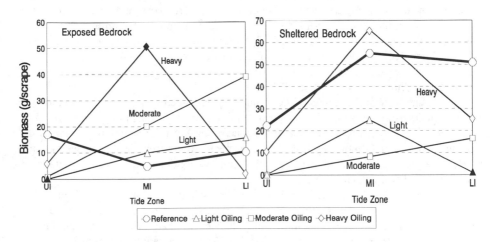

FIGURE 2—**Mean biomass estimates of *Fucus gardneri* (g/scrape) as a function of oiling level and intertidal height for exposed (left) and sheltered (right) bedrock sites. Solid symbols indicate significant differences from reference, UI - Upper Intertidal, MI - Middle Intertidal, LI - Lower Intertidal.**

Two species of littorine snails were tested: *Littorina scutulata* and *L. sitkana*. The abundance of *L. scutulata* at light, moderate, and heavily oiled shorelines was not different from reference sites (*P*<0.05) in 15 tests for the intertidal zone of bedrock shorelines. The abundance of *L. sitkana* was statistically different from reference sites (*P*<0.05) in 2 of 15 tests in the intertidal zone of bedrock shorelines. *L. sitkana* was less abundant in the middle intertidal zone of heavily oiled exposed bedrock shorelines and more abundant in the lower intertidal zone of moderately oiled exposed bedrock shores.

Figure 3 shows the mean abundance estimates of limpets by tide zone and oiling level for exposed and sheltered bedrock habitats. Significant differences from reference (fewer limpets) were found in the upper intertidal, but only at lightly oiled sites (both bedrock habitats) and moderately oiled sites (sheltered bedrock only). In addition, Figure 3 (left) shows much higher mean abundance at the reference sites in the lower intertidal compared with all three oiling levels. Inspection of the individual samples showed a large degree of overlap in the ranges of limpet abundance; therefore, the differences among oiling levels were not statistically significant.

Figure 4 shows the mean abundance of mussels as a function of tide zone and oiling level for exposed and sheltered bedrock sites. No significant differences from reference were found. It is clear from Figures 2 to 4 that there is no consistent pattern of response to oiling in these taxa of epibiota, regarding either the direction of change (increase or decrease) or the tide zone or oiling level where differences from reference were observed.

Community parameter analyses—Results of the community parameter analyses are shown in Figures 5, 6, and 7 as a function of tide zone and oiling level. Data for bedrock habitats represent epifauna. Data for boulder/cobble and pebble/gravel represent infauna. In general, sample means of abundance, species richness, and diversity are seen to increase from the upper intertidal to the lower intertidal zone. This reflects the fact that stress from heat, light, and desiccation decreases with decreasing intertidal elevation. There are relatively few instances of significant differences between oiled sites and reference sites. Most of the differences that were detected are positive, i.e., increased abundance, richness, or diversity at oiled sites.

A summary of the results of the community parameter analyses is provided in Table 5. The parameters that showed positive or negative significant differences from reference are identified for each habitat/tide zone/oiling-level combination. Eleven of the 48 "bins" show one or more significant positive mean differences; the only negative mean difference (reduced diversity) occurred in the shallow subtidal zone of the moderately oiled sheltered bedrock category.

In exposed bedrock and pebble/gravel habitats, significant differences from reference correlate somewhat with oiling level: more significant differences are seen at moderate and heavy oiling than at light oiling. However, all significant differences are increases relative to reference. In the boulder/cobble and sheltered bedrock habitats, only one significant difference was found in each, and no trends are apparent. Overall only 1 of 20 significant differences was negative; i.e., at oiled sites 19 out of 20 species were significantly more numerous.

The data in Table 5 were used to develop estimates of recovery for each habitat and oiling level. Each bin was given a value of either 0% (not recovered) or 100% (recovered), depending on whether or not any significant differences in community parameter means were found. These values were then averaged across oiling levels and

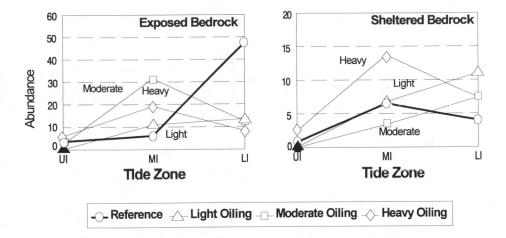

FIGURE 3—Mean abundance (#/scrape) estimates of limpets (sum of *Lottidae* and *Lottia pelta*) as a function of oiling level and intertidal height for exposed (left) and sheltered (right) bedrock sites. Solid symbols indicate significant differences from reference, UI - Upper Intertidal, MI - Middle Intertidal, LI - Lower Intertidal.

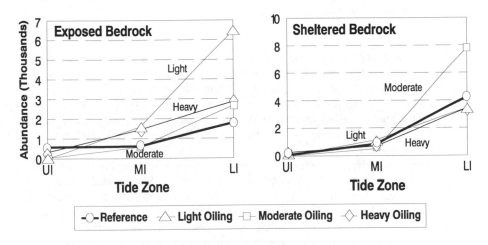

FIGURE 4—Mean abundance (#/scrape) estimates of mussels (*Mytilus edulis*) as a function of oiling level and intertidal height for exposed (left) and sheltered (right) bedrock sites. Note that there are no significant differences from reference. UI - Upper Intertidal, MI - Middle Intertidal, LI - Lower Intertidal

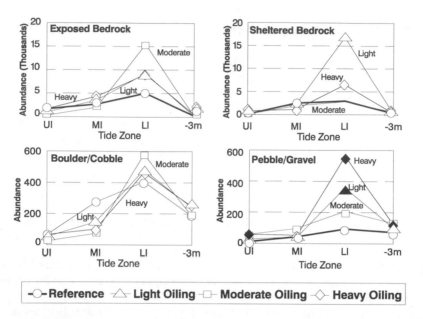

FIGURE 5—Mean total abundance (#/sample) of animals as a function of tide zone and oiling level in the four habitats sampled in the SRS program. Solid symbols indicate significant differences from reference, UI - Upper Intertidal, MI - Middle Intertidal, LI - Lower Intertidal.

habitats, using appropriate weighting factors to reflect the length of oiled shoreline represented by each bin (Table 3). The resulting estimates are shown in Table 5, both individually by tide level, and averaged over all four tide levels, for each habitat (right-most column) and oiling level (bottom row). The means range from about 40% (pebble/gravel) to 97 % (sheltered bedrock). The overall mean is approximately 91%; i.e., weighted by shoreline length the originally oiled shoreline was estimated to be 91% recovered by summer 1990.

Correspondence analysis—Correspondence analysis was used to compare the structure of animal communities at oiled and reference sites. As discussed above, only those species occurring in at least 20% of the samples of a given dataset were included in the analysis. The first two ordination axes were constrained to maximize differences among sample scores from different oiling levels. These scores were used to construct scatter plots as shown in Figure 8, an ordination diagram showing the scores for all middle intertidal samples from pebble/gravel sites. A 95% probability ellipse was drawn on the basis of the scores for the reference samples, assuming a bivariate normal distribution. Scores for all except one of the samples from oiled sites fall within the reference ellipse. The exception is 1 of 18 samples from heavily oiled sites (3 samples per tide level at each of 6 sites in this category). Assuming that samples taken on

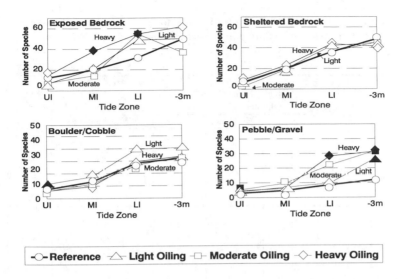

FIGURE 6—Mean species richness as a function of tide zone and oiling level in the four habitats sampled in the SRS program. Solid symbols indicate significant differences from reference, UI - Upper Intertidal, MI - Middle Intertidal, LI - Lower Intertidal.

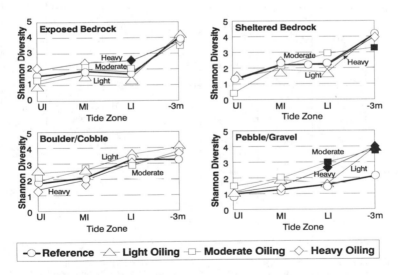

FIGURE 7—Mean Shannon diversity as a function of tide zone and oiling level in the four habitats sampled in the SRS program. Solid symbols indicate significant differences from reference, UI - Upper Intertidal, MI - Middle Intertidal, LI - Lower Intertidal.

TABLE 5—Summary of statistical analyses of community parameters. Recovery estimates are weighted means based on oiled Prince William Sound (PWS) shoreline length.

| Habitat Type | Tide Zone | Degree of Initial Oiling in Summer 1989 | | | Estimated Recovery by Habitat (% Initially Oiled PWS Shoreline) | Mean |
		Light	Moderate	Heavy		
Exposed Bedrock	UI	0	0	0	100	89.0
	MI	0	0	+S	83.3	
	LI	0	+S	+S,H	72.6	
	-3 m	0	0	0	100	
Sheltered Bedrock	UI	0	0	0	100	96.8
	MI	0	0	0	100	
	LI	0	0	0	100	
	-3 m	0	-H	0	87.1	
Boulder/Cobble	UI	+S	0	0	39.7	84.9
	MI	0	0	0	100	
	LI	0	0	0	100	
	-3 m	0	0	0	100	
Pebble/Gravel	UI	0	+S	+A	59.5	39.9
	MI	0	0	0	100	
	LI	+A	+H	+A,S,H	0	
	-3 m	+S,H	+S,H	+A,S,H	0	
					Weighted Overall Mean	
Estimated Recovery by Oiling Level (% Initially Oiled PWS Shoreline)	UI	80.3	96.7	93.8	**84.7**	
	MI	100.0	100.0	84.3	**97.2**	
	LI	96.9	82.0	78.1	**91.7**	
	-3 m	96.9	36.9	93.8	**89.0**	
Mean	All	93.5	78.9	87.5		90.7

Legend:
  0 Not different from reference ($P > 0.05$)   UI - Upper Intertidal
  + Positive difference from reference   MI - Middle Intertidal
  − Negative difference from reference   LI - Lower Intertidal
  A Total abundance of individuals per sample   -3 m - Subtidal from three
  B Algal biomass (Intertidal bedrock sites only)   meters below zero tidal
  S Species richness   datum
  H Shannon diversity

TABLE 6—Summary results from correspondence analyses showing the percentage of Prince William Sound (PWS) shoreline indistinguishable from reference for all habitat/tide zone/oiling-level combinations (UI - Upper Intertidal, MI - Middle Intertidal, LI - Lower Intertidal, -3 m - Subtidal from three meters below zero tidal datum).

Habitat Type	Tide Zone	Degree of Initial Oiling in Summer 1989			Estimated Recovery by Habitat (% Initially Oiled PWS Shoreline)	Mean
		Light	Moderate	Heavy		
Exposed Bedrock	UI	100	100	89	98.2	54.8
	MI	40	83	94	53.6	
	LI	0	17	82	15.5	
	-3 m	50	17	83	52.0	
Sheltered Bedrock	UI	75	75	83	76.1	72.8
	MI	94	83	75	90.1	
	LI	83	60	27	72.6	
	-3 m	61	50	8	52.6	
Boulder/Cobble	UI	78	44	100	80.1	85.3
	MI	100	56	80	89.2	
	LI	100	67	93	94.2	
	-3 m	67	78	100	77.5	
Pebble/Gravel	UI	86	100	94	89.9	91.1
	MI	100	100	94	98.2	
	LI	63	100	100	78.0	
	-3 m	100	100	94	98.2	
					Weighted Overall Means	
Estimated Recovery by Oiling Level (% Initially Oiled PWS Shoreline)	UI	80.3	72.6	90.7	**81.2**	
	MI	86.0	77.6	81.0	**84.0**	
	LI	71.3	56.5	63.9	**68.1**	
	-3 m	61.5	53.0	58.2	**59.9**	
Mean	All	**74.8**	**64.9**	**73.4**		**73.3**

different transects at the same site are statistically independent, 94.4% (17/18) of middle intertidal heavily oiled shorelines in the pebble/gravel habitat were indistinguishable from reference in 1990.

Similar estimates of the "percentage of shoreline indistinguishable from reference" were derived for all categories in the SRS matrix (Table 6). These estimates are used as a second (lower-limit) estimate of recovery.

Table 6 includes weighted mean values for estimates of recovery by habitat (right) and oiling level (bottom), and for all impacted shorelines in Prince William Sound (lower right corner). The weighting factors reflect the length of oiled shoreline represented by each habitat/oiling-level combination (Table 3). The overall means shown in the lower right corner of Table 6 indicate the following estimates of recovery on oiled shorelines in Prince William Sound: upper intertidal, 81%; middle intertidal, 84%; lower intertidal, 68%; shallow subtidal, 60%. The arithmetic mean of these estimates for the four tide zones provides an overall lower-limit estimate of 73.3% recovery. Limitations of this approach to estimating recovery are described in the Discussion section.

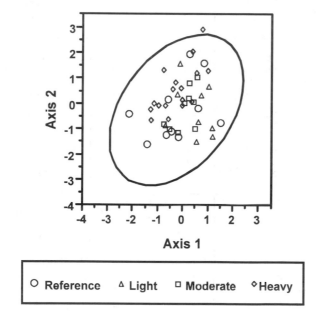

FIGURE 8—Ordination diagram for middle intertidal pebble/gravel samples from the 1990 SRS program. The 95% probability ellipse is estimated from the subset of samples from unoiled reference sites, assuming a bivariate normal distribution of sample scores.

Signal-to-noise ratio—The univariate and correspondence analysis models both assess the magnitude of the oiling effect (signal) relative to the unexplained variability (noise). For both models, the signal-to-noise ratio can be estimated. Estimates of this ratio lead to retrospective (a posteriori) power analyses for the univariate models and to informal assessments for the correspondence models. Power is the probability of detecting an oiling effect. For normal-theory models, it depends on the significance level (α), the sample size (n), and the signal-to-noise ratio (Δ/σ). Figure 5 in Part 1 shows the power as a function of the signal-to-noise ratio for various sample sizes at a significance level of $\alpha = 0.05$.

The a posteriori estimates of the signal-to-noise ratio and power for detecting an overall oiling effect in the abundance, species richness, and diversity data are shown in Figure 9. These estimates are based on normal-theory models. This is reasonable for species richness and Shannon diversity (which were usually fit with normal error terms), but less so for abundance since it was always fit with negative binomial error terms. The mean signal-to-noise ratios (weighted by oiled shoreline length) ranged from 0.28 for species richness, to 0.32 for abundance, to 0.38 for Shannon diversity, and the corresponding mean power estimates are 0.34, 0.37, and 0.49, respectively. The overall mean of these signal-to-noise ratios is 0.33, and the overall mean for power is 0.40.

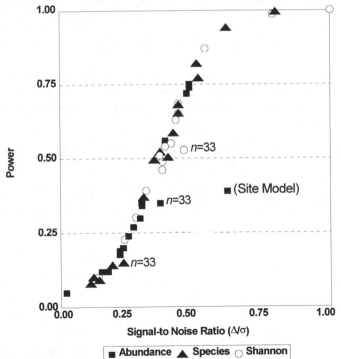

FIGURE 9—Plot of the estimated power for detecting an oiling effect as a function of the computed signal-to-noise ratio for community parameters.

The plot in Figure 9 would exactly follow the theoretical power curve for $n = 48$ (see Part 1, Figure 5) if the transect model were always selected and if all data were present. Only one analysis (out of 48) used the site model for these community variables. However, 36 of the 47 transect models had fewer samples with the minimum (sheltered bedrock) being $n = 33$.

The overall mean for power, 0.40, is not high. This reflects the overall low signal-to-noise ratio estimate of 0.33 of these community variables. The variation explained by the oiling effect relative to the unexplained variability, the square of the signal-to-noise ratio, is only 10.9%. Without the removal of the physical variables from the natural variability, the percentage of variation explained by oiling would even be lower.

The output of the DCCA analysis separates the total variability in the dataset into three parts: (1) the portion associated with the physical factors included as concomitant variables; (2) the portion associated with the constrained ordination axes (i.e., oiling levels); and (3) the unexplained remainder. Table 7 shows a summary of this breakdown for each habitat, averaged over all tide zones. The oiling effect and concomitant variables, together, explain at most a third of the total variability. In bedrock habitats, the unexplained variability is greater than 80%. This is an expected consequence of the patch dynamics in Prince William Sound. The variability associated with oiling (from 10 to 13%) is about the same in all habitats; the variability associated with the concomitant variables is considerably higher at sedimentary sites than at bedrock sites, perhaps because more concomitant variables were included in the sediment habitats.

TABLE 7—Proportions of total variance explained by concomitant variables and oiling. Table entries are means (over tide zones) for each habitat. A high percentage of unexplained variance is to be expected in an environment dominated by patch dynamics.

Shoreline Habitat Type	Percentage of Total Variance			Multivariate Signal-to-Noise
	Physical Covariates*	Oiling (Δ^2)	Unexplained (σ^2)	$[(\Delta/\sigma)^2 \times 100]$**
Exposed Bedrock	7	12	81	14.8
Sheltered Bedrock	5	11	84	13.1
Boulder/Cobble	16	10	74	13.5
Pebble/Gravel	22	13	65	20.0

*   Covariates include percentage sand, percentage silt, and TOC at boulder/cobble and pebble/gravel sites, as well as wave energy at all sites.

** The ratio (Δ/σ) can be interpreted as a signal-to-noise ratio, but should not be used to estimate power since it is not based upon univariate normal theory (as is Figure 10).

The last column in Table 7 shows the variability resulting from oiling as a percentage of the unexplained variability. This ratio is equivalent to the square of a signal-to-noise ratio. It ranges from 13 to 20%; its overall mean, weighted by shoreline length (Table 3), is 13.7%. This value is similar to the weighted mean (10.9%) obtained from the community parameter variables.

Fixed-Site Program Results

The purpose of collecting ecological data at fixed sites was to sample severely oiled shorelines and special habitats that were not represented in the SRS design. All fixed-site biology data reported here are for infaunal communities found in sediment cores at boulder/cobble, pebble/gravel, or soft-sediment sites (Table 8). The fixed-site program was initiated in 1990 and includes seven sites at which biological samples were collected in 1989 (eight sites for chemistry). However, most biology samples taken at these seven sites in 1989 were for epibiota and therefore are not comparable to the infaunal cores collected in 1990 and 1991. All fixed sites, as well as appropriate SRS reference sites, were sampled in 1990 and 1991.

TABLE 8—SEP Fixed-Site Program

Habitat	Location	Site/Segment	Oiling	1989*	1990	1991
Boulder/Cobble						
	Latouche	E11/LA15	Heavy		X	X
	Latouche (SA)	E11SA/LA15	Heavy	X	X	X
	Point Helen	SR07/KN405	Heavy	X	X	X
	Sleepy Bay	SL01/LA19	Heavy		X	X
	Reference	(5 SRS sites)	None		X	
						X**
Pebble/Gravel						
	Bay of Isles West	SRMB4/KN07	Light	X	X	X
	Herring Bay (SA)	SR03/KN5000	Moderate	X	X	X
	Mussel Beach	SR01N/EL13	Moderate	X	X	X
	Shelter Bay	SR06/EV21	Heavy	X	X	X
	Snug Harbor W (SA) †	SR05/KN401	Heavy	X	X	X
	Snug Harbor E (SA) ††	SR04/KN401	Heavy	X	X	X
	Reference	(4 SRS sites)	None		X	X
Soft Sediment						
	Bay of Isles Marsh	BI01/KN136	Heavy		X	X
	McClure Bay	MB01/ –	None		X	X

SA	Designates set-aside sites.
†	No biological samples were collected at this location in 1989.
††	Snug Harbor E (SA) is partially a sheltered bedrock site; however, only sediment samples were included in the analysis.
*	Only chemistry samples from 1989 were included in the analyses for this program.
**	Only the four original boulder/cobble reference sites were resampled in 1991.

The results of the fixed-site program can be presented only in summary form in this paper. Community parameters measured for heavily oiled fixed sites and results of multivariate correspondence analyses for all fixed sites are presented and compared to the appropriate reference sites.

Community parameter analyses—Figures 10 through 13 use a common format to present community parameter variables (abundance, richness, and diversity) for selected fixed sites as follows:

- Means for the three heavily oiled pebble/gravel sites (Figure 10)
- Means for three heavily oiled boulder/cobble sites—excluding Point Helen (Figure 11)
- The heavily oiled boulder/cobble site at Point Helen (Figure 12)
- The soft-sediment site in Bay of Isles (Figure 13)

Each plot shows the means for the oiled sites by year (1990, 1991), and a reference band representing the 95% confidence interval for the applicable reference sites, based on data from both years.

Figure 10 shows the means of abundance, richness, and diversity at the three heavily oiled pebble/gravel sites for 1990 and 1991. Most of the data fall near the top or above the 95% confidence band for the corresponding SRS reference sites. Year-to-year changes show no consistent trend.

Figure 11 shows the means for the three boulder/cobble sites generally in the lower portion of the reference bands in the upper and middle intertidal zones. These sites, all on Latouche Island, were among the most heavily oiled in the sound. The lower intertidal and subtidal means are generally in the upper range of the reference bands. Again, there is no consistent trend with time.

Figure 12 shows that Point Helen followed the same pattern as the other boulder/cobble sites, except that abundance was lower in 1991 than in 1990 across all tide zones. This could be a consequence of the extensive berm relocation program undertaken at this site prior to sampling in 1991. Shannon diversity in 1991 remained within the reference band even in those tide zones most affected by berm relocation (upper and middle intertidal), and was above the reference band in the lower intertidal and shallow subtidal.

Figure 13 compares the soft-sediment site in Bay of Isles with its single reference site in McClure Bay. Although the two habitats may not be strictly comparable, the Bay of Isles site showed mean increases from 1990 to 1991 in most tide zones for all three community parameters, which may be a sign of ongoing recovery at this heavily oiled site.

Correspondence analysis—Results of the correspondence analysis for fixed-site core samples are summarized in Table 9. The 1990 fixed-site data were run as "passive" samples in connection with the correspondence analysis of the 1990 SRS data, and their sample scores were based on the same weighting factors as those from the SRS sites in the same habitat. Table 9 lists the number of samples that fell outside the appropriate

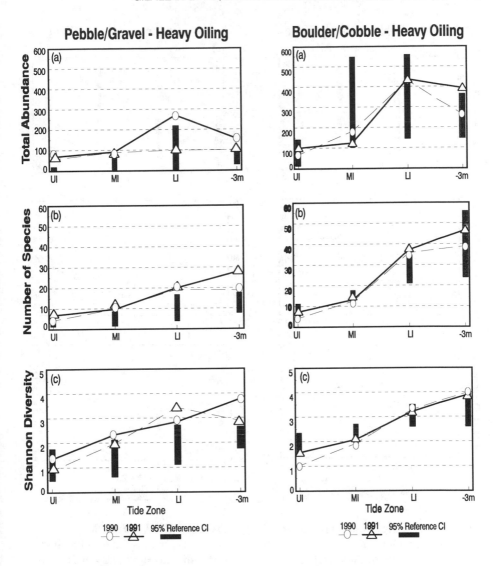

FIGURE 10—Community parameter means for three heavily oiled pebble/gravel sites: Shelter Bay, Snug Harbor W(SA), and Snug Harbor E(SA) by tide zone: (a) Total abundance, (b) Species richness, and (c) Shannon diversity.

FIGURE 11—Community parameter means for three heavily oiled boulder/cobble sites, excluding Point Helen (Sleepy Bay, Latouche, and Latouche [SA]): (a) Total abundance, (b) Species richness, and (c) Shannon diversity.

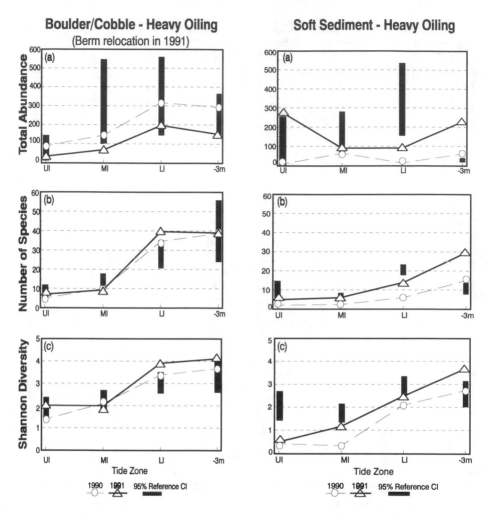

FIGURE 12—Community parameter means for heavily oiled boulder/cobble site at Point Helen: (a) Total abundance, (b) Number of species, and (c) Shannon diversity.

FIGURE 13—Community parameter means for heavily oiled soft-sediment site in Bay of Isles: (a) Total abundance, (b) Number of species, and (c) Shannon diversity.

TABLE 9—Results of correspondence analyses for 1990 and 1991 fixed-site core samples. The 1990 fixed-site data were run as "passive" samples in the correspondence analysis for the 1990 SRS data.

Habitat	Site	Degree of Oiling in 1989	Tide Zone*	Number of Cores Outside 95% Reference Ellipse** 1990 $n = 117$***	Number of Cores Outside 95% Reference Ellipse** 1991 $n = 117$***	
B/C	Sleepy Bay (00SL01)	High	UI	0	0	
			MI	0	0	
			LI	0	0	(1)
			-3m	0	0	
	Pt. Helen (00SR07)	High	UI	0	1	
			MI	1	1	
			LI	0	0	(1)
			-3m	0	0	
	Latouche† (OLIE11)	High	UI	0	0	
			MI	0	1	
			LI	0	0	(1)
			-3m	0	0	
	Latouche (SA) (0E11SA)	High	UI	0	1	
			MI	2	2	
			LI	0	1	(1)
			-3m	0	3	
P/G	Bay of Isles West (0SRMB4)	Low	UI	0	1	
			MI	0	0	
			LI	1	2	
			-3m	0	0	
	Herring Bay (SA) (00SR03)	Moderate	UI	1	0	
			MI	0	0	
			LI	0	1	
			-3m	0	0	
	Mussel Beach (0SR01N)	Moderate	UI	-	-	
			MI	0	0	
			LI	0	0	
			-3m	1	0	
	Shelter Bay (00SR06)	High	UI	0	0	
			MI	0	0	
			LI	0	0	
			-3m	1	0	
	Snug Harbor E (SA) (00SR04)	High	UI	1	0	
			MI	0	0	
			LI	0	0	
			-3m	1	0	
	Snug Harbor W (SA) (00SR05)	High	UI	0	0	
			MI	0	0	
			LI	0	0	
			-3m	2	1	
Totals	All	All	All	11	15	

*   UI - Upper Intertidal, MI - Middle Intertidal, LI - Lower Intertidal,
     -3 m - Subtidal from three meters below zero tidal datum.

**   Reference ellipse based on data from unoiled SRS sites for the appropriate year, habitat, and tide zone.

** n = Total number of fixed site samples.

(1)   1991 results for boulder/cobble habitat based on one-dimensional comparison with 95% reference range.

†   SA designates set-aside sites.

95% reference ellipse, by tide zone, for each of the 10 pebble/gravel and boulder/cobble sites. The soft-sediment site in Bay of Isles is not included.

The 1991 fixed-site data were analyzed in a separate correspondence analysis together with their appropriate SRS reference sites. For pebble/gravel sites, all three levels of oiling were represented, and two axes were constrained for oiling. A 95% reference ellipse was used to assess recovery, as was done in the 1990 SRS analysis. In contrast, all of the boulder/cobble sites were heavily oiled; thus, with only one degree of freedom in oiling level, only one axis could be constrained to reflect the oiling effect, and the test for recovery had to be based on a one-dimensional comparison with the reference sites (i.e., the 95% probability reference range).

Because the fixed sites were subjectively chosen to represent worst-case or unique sites, the data in Table 9 cannot be extrapolated to derive estimates of recovery. Nevertheless, it is interesting to note that relatively few samples from these sites were distinguishable from unoiled sites in similar habitats. Overall, only 11 (9.4%) of the 117 fixed-site samples taken in 1990 were found to be distinguishable from reference. Of these, three were from boulder/cobble and eight from pebble/gravel sites; six were from set-aside sites and one from Point Helen, where berm relocation had occurred prior to sampling.

In 1991, a total of 15 of 117 fixed-site samples (12.8%) were distinguishable from reference. However, as explained above, the 1990 and 1991 results are not strictly comparable since the data were not analyzed in the same way.

DISCUSSION

The goal of this study was to provide an assessment of shoreline recovery following the *Exxon Valdez* oil spill. Recovery was evaluated within the context of natural ecological processes occurring in the major habitats in Prince William Sound.

Recovery occurred much more quickly than would be predicted on the basis of previous studies. Many previous oil-spill studies dealt only with environments where spill effects tended to be severe and long-lasting (soft-sediment environments). Many studies have also been carried out in very heavily oiled areas that are analogous to our fixed-site program. Data from these studies can predict recovery of the most severely oiled areas, but not recovery of the impact zone as a whole, although these data have often been used to do so.

Although the major habitat types found in Prince William Sound exist in other spill sites, for example, the *Amoco Cadiz* spill site, oil-spill effects have rarely been studied in these environments. Most sedimentary habitats in the sound are not soft-sediment, accumulating habitats, but coarse-sediment, eroding habitats. Because the rock-surface habitats differ from those studied previously, in that disturbance (patch dynamics) is very important in the ecology of Prince William Sound, the effects of oiling have been different from those described in past oil-spill studies.

This study was designed to assess the recovery of the impact zone as a whole by using randomly chosen sampling sites. Its results show that, although spill effects were still evident in the summer of 1990, based on biological community criteria (i.e., total abundance, algal biomass, species richness, Shannon diversity, and correspondence analysis), most of the shorelines in the sound had already recovered by that time.

Sedimentary Habitats

Typically, when oil is incorporated into fine-grained sediments, they become anaerobic and the infaunal community is killed (Sanders et al. 1980; Glemarec and Hussenot 1981). As the oil weathers, the sediment is invaded by a population of one or a few species of opportunistic polychaete worms. This community is characterized by low diversity and species richness and by high total abundance. Over time, as the oil is metabolized by bacteria, this opportunistic community is replaced by a normal, more diverse community (Grassle and Grassle 1974; Sanders et al. 1980; Glemarec and Hussenot 1981; Gilfillan et al. 1986).

However, in those sedimentary areas that were affected by the *Exxon Valdez* oil spill, the sediments are relatively coarse. As a result, oxygen was readily transported into sediments by percolation to prevent development of sediment anoxia. At the same time, large numbers of bacteria were able to metabolize the oil and became available as food for animals living in the sediments. Because of their eroding nature, intertidal sediments in Prince William Sound are generally very low in TOC (i.e., less than 1%, compared with typical levels of from 1 to 5% in nearshore sediments and from 10 to 15% in marshes) (Parsons et al. 1977). Bacteria that metabolize oil appear to have been an important source of food, especially in the pebble/gravel habitat: infaunal communities found in oiled areas tended to have more individuals, more species, and higher diversity than those found in reference areas. It is very likely that the increased availability of food (resulting from increased biomass of bacteria metabolizing the weathered oil residue) reduced competition for food and allowed more species to coexist in oil-affected areas than in reference areas (Robles 1982).

Bedrock/Rubble Habitats

Rocky sites have not been studied as much as soft-sediment areas because long-lasting effects are not expected on rocky shores. Typically, few species are completely eliminated on oiled rocky shores, although many species may be reduced in abundance. Competitive interactions and predator-prey relationships may be disrupted.

Recovery of rocky sites from oiling effects is more rapid than at sedimentary sites (Chan 1975; Clark et al. 1978; Southward and Southward 1978; Chasse 1978; Bonsdorf and Nelson 1981; Nelson 1982). Prince William Sound is an area with high wave-energy. The ecology of its rocky shores is driven by the random creation of space by waves, logs, and moving sediment particles (Shanks and Wright 1986); effects of the resulting patch dynamics are apparent everywhere in the sound. Numerous experiments and observations have shown that the artificial creation of space (by scientists) or the natural creation of space (by predators or wave action) reduces competition for space and allows more species to coexist (Paine 1974; Osman 1977; Lubchenco 1978; Sousa 1979 a,b; Paine and Levin 1981; Ghazanshahi et al. 1983; Nakahara and Ueno 1985; Sousa 1985; McGuinness 1987a,b; Povey and Keogh 1991). Thus, one of the ecological consequences of the spill and the attendant cleanup was the creation of open space, which enabled the epifaunal communities living in oiled areas to respond to the relaxation of competition for space, resulting, in many cases, in more individuals, more species, and greater diversity in oiled than in reference areas.

SRS Sites—Estimation of Shoreline Recovery

Definition of recovery—The results of this study illustrate the difficulties involved in arriving at a reasonable definition of recovery from oil spills. Because oil from the spill was detected in many locations where there are no apparent ecological effects (Part 2: Chemistry, Boehm et al., this volume), it would be unreasonable to characterize all these areas as still impacted. Modern chemical methods allow detection and identification of petroleum in concentrations far below those required to produce negative ecological effects, as shown by sediment toxicology. Thus, it is not reasonable to call these areas affected when oil is present at *de minimis* levels and, moreover, is only detectable by sophisticated analytical methods.

It makes sense to define recovery in ecological terms. An area is recovered when there are no statistically significant ecological differences between communities at reference and oiled locations. Ecological differences could include reduced species richness, reduced diversity, dominance by opportunistic species, or the existence of a community composed of species not present in the reference community. In many oiled areas in Prince William Sound, animal communities are richer and more varied than in reference areas.

Recovery estimates based on community parameters—Recovery was estimated with respect to total abundance of individuals, algal biomass, species richness, and Shannon diversity. An overall recovery estimate, made in terms of any difference from reference in these community parameters, is 91%. There are three important aspects to the above analysis: (1) community structure variables may not be particularly sensitive measures of response to environmental change (Camargo 1992; Chadwick and Canton 1984; Hughes 1978; Samways 1984); (2) the statistical analyses of the community structure variables generally do not have high power to detect differences from reference resulting from a low oiling signal (see below and Part 1: Study Design and Methods, Page et al., this volume); and (3) four community structure variables were tested, any one of which could lead to a statement of nonrecovery.

These last two points need additional explanation. An oiling effect almost certainly exists, but at what point is it ecologically relevant? If the oiling effect (signal) exceeds the natural variability (noise), it is reasonable to posit ecological significance. On the other hand, oiling signals that are small compared with the noise will have minimal impact, compared with disruptions resulting from natural processes. (A detailed discussion of statistical power is presented in Part 1: Study Design and Methods, Page et al., this volume.)

The estimates of the oiling effect for the community parameter variables ranged from nearly 0 to 80% of the unexplained variability with a mean signal-to-noise-ratio of about 33% after effects of the concomitant variables had been removed (Figure 10). Thus, the oiling effect generally had a relatively small signal-to-noise ratio, and the power to detect it was low. However, these studies had good power (>85%) to detect meaningful oiling effects (e.g., 50% of natural variability) had they occurred (Part 1: Study Design and Methods, Page et al., this volume).

The power to detect even these marginal oiling effects was enhanced by using four community parameter variables. At the 0.05 significance level, assuming independence of the variables, the probability of rejecting the null hypothesis of no oiling effect when none is present is 0.185, whereas it is 0.05 assuming complete dependence. Therefore, the estimate of recovery should be somewhere between 81.5% (100 - 18.5) and 95% (100 - 5) even when no oiling effect is present. The estimate of 91% recovery could only come about if the community variables are highly correlated (which they are) and if the oiling signal is small (which it is).

The estimate of recovery based on the community parameter analyses is near the upper bound of expected recovery when no oiling effect is present. We view 91% as an upper limit on recovery since the power to detect the observed oiling effects generally is low (a consequence of low signal-to-noise ratio, not experimental design) and the estimate depends on discrete rejections of the null hypothesis.

Recovery estimates based on correspondence analysis—Correspondence analysis is a more sensitive and comprehensive method of detecting changes in community structure. Results of correspondence analysis of the SRS data showed that, averaged over all tide zones, 73% of the shoreline originally affected by the spill was similar to reference in the summer of 1990, seventeen months after the spill. The limitations of this method, discussed now, lead us to view 73% as a lower limit on recovery.

First, DCCA is a very sensitive way to detect differences among communities. A small signal will generally result in some shift of the ellipses representing the oiling levels so that a certain percentage of the samples from oiled sites will fall outside the reference ellipse, even though the effect would not be detected by traditional hypothesis testing.

Second, a certain proportion of the observations from the oiled sites will lie outside the reference ellipse, even if no oiling effect exists. The probability that a random observation lies outside an estimated (random) 95% reference ellipse exceeds 0.05. This probability increases as the sample size with which the reference ellipse is estimated decreases. This applies to all cases, but particularly to the bedrock sites.

Third, rare species and outliers may distort the estimated ellipse, which will cause unpredictable results, sometimes increasing and sometimes decreasing the estimated percentage of recovery.

Last, there are groups of species (guilds) living in Prince William Sound, any member of which could provide the same ecological services. The members of a guild that are present at any given location are a matter of chance. DCCA will find differences between communities that contain different guild members, even though these differences are ecologically irrelevant. Unfortunately, current knowledge concerning the ecology of the sound does not allow identification of the various guilds present and their membership.

Both of these shoreline recovery estimates (based on community parameters or correspondence analysis) are reasonable for a study designed to examine the entire spill zone. In 1989, government scientists initiated a similar study to examine all of the shorelines in the oiled area of Prince William Sound. These scientists were unable to detect significant injuries on light and very lightly oiled shorelines based on their 1989 data and chose not to study them in subsequent years. Furthermore, very lightly oiled shorelines were even made available for selection as reference sites in 1990. By such actions, these two categories could be considered recovered as of 1990. Together, these two oiling categories account for 70% of the oiled portion of Prince William Sound (Table 3 - light and very light oiling levels were lumped as light in the table). Thus, even the government scientists considered about 70% of the oiled portion of Prince William Sound "recovered" in 1990, not counting portions of the remaining oiled shorelines which may also have recovered.

Fixed Sites

The fixed sites were chosen because they were representative of the most heavily oiled areas in Prince William Sound or because they represented habitats too rare to be adequately sampled by the SRS. Results obtained at the fixed sites cannot be used to predict recovery for Prince William Sound as a whole, but they can be used to follow recovery of sites that were particularly heavily oiled or were particularly vulnerable to the effects of oiling (such as the Bay of Isles marsh).

Community parameters—Results of the analysis of community parameters at the boulder/cobble fixed sites showed a tendency for lower total abundance at a site where berm relocation had occurred prior to sampling in 1991 (Point Helen; Figure 12). At other boulder/cobble sites, observed 1991 values of total abundance, species richness, and Shannon diversity were either within or above the 95% reference confidence interval. Although there was a tendency for the means of the community parameters to be higher in 1991 than in 1990, the differences between years were not large.

In the pebble/gravel fixed sites, values for community parameters fell within or exceeded the 95% reference confidence interval. As in the boulder/cobble habitat, there was a tendency for 1991 values to exceed 1990 values, but the observed differences between years were small.

Results of analysis of community parameter data for the boulder/cobble and pebble/gravel fixed sites yielded a similar picture to that seen in the SRS results: The differences from reference that occurred were small and frequently in a positive direction.

Results of analysis of community parameters (Figure 13) for samples from the Bay of Isles marsh and its reference showed that values for 1991 were consistently higher than values for 1990. However, diversity and species richness in the intertidal zone were still below the 95% reference confidence interval in the intertidal zone. This location, which is the only oiled site of its kind in Prince William Sound, with a total area of less than two acres, had not recovered by 1991. This is consistent with chemical and toxicological results obtained at the same site. These results are also consistent with results of other oil-spill studies carried out at heavily oiled soft-sediment areas (Part 1: Study Design and Methods, Page et al., this volume).

Correspondence analysis—Although recovery estimates for both 1990 and 1991 are discussed for the fixed sites, they are not strictly comparable. For 1990, estimates of recovery were obtained by treating the fixed sites as passive samples relative to the entire set of SRS samples. This approach was not possible for 1991, since only reference sites from the SRS were sampled. Therefore, the correspondence analysis for 1991 was based on the fixed sites (along with their SRS reference sites). Furthermore, only one constrained axis could be determined for the boulder/cobble sites since all of these sites were heavily oiled. Thus, a one-dimensional 95% probability reference range was used to assess recovery of the boulder/cobble sites in 1991, rather than a 95% probability reference ellipse. For these reasons, caution must be exercised in interpreting the following comparisons.

Results from pebble/gravel fixed sites show that fewer samples (five) were distinguishable from reference in 1991 than in 1990 (eight). This is consistent with chemical and toxicological data that show that remaining oil at these sites was becoming more weathered and was virtually nontoxic by 1991.

Results of correspondence analysis for the boulder/cobble fixed sites show more samples distinguishable from reference in 1991 (ten) than in 1990 (three). Some of this increase is explained by the berm relocation activities prior to sampling in 1991 at Point Helen and Latouche Island. However, most of the increase occurred at the Latouche Island set-aside site where two samples were distinguishable from reference in 1990 and seven in 1991. The major differences from reference in the composition of infauna at the Latouche island set-aside site were an under-representation of amphipod species and an absence of nematodes.

The Latouche set-aside site was never cleaned. The remaining oil is distributed very patchily (unpublished observations). The locations sampled in 1990 were displaced 4 m laterally from those locations sampled in 1991. For 1991, both the total PAH and sediment toxicities were generally higher than values observed in 1990 (Boehm et al., Part 2: Chemistry, this volume). The increased number of differences in community structure in 1991 is consistent with chemical and toxicological data showing that a portion of the site in 1991 had sediments that contained more oil and were more toxic in 1991 than in 1990. Thus, these differences most likely represent an artifact of sampling resulting from the patchy distribution of the oil remaining at this untreated site.

Except for those sites where berm relocation was carried out prior to sampling in 1991 and the Latouche Island set-aside site, the trends in the boulder/cobble and pebble/gravel fixed sites are for continued biological recovery of those locations that are still distinguishable from reference. Complete biological recovery of these severely affected sites will likely occur within the time frame forecast for chemical recovery (See Part 2: Chemistry, Boehm et al., this volume). The soft-sediment site will probably recover more slowly, but there is no reason to expect that it will not recover completely.

Natural Variation and Cleanup Effects

Species abundances, and measures derived from them, are highly variable in Prince William Sound even when measured within habitat/tide zone combinations. The sources of variation are those resulting from oiling level, the cleanup effort, physical variables, as well as site-to-site, transect-to-transect, and year-to-year variability.

Cleanup effects, as expected, were highly correlated with oiling. Therefore, and because the cleanup effort would be difficult to quantify for each study site, our models contained no explicit terms for cleanup. Thus, the oiling effects discussed in this study reflect the combined effects of direct oiling and cleanup. Quantitative evidence that most of the cleanup effect is confounded with oiling is presented below.

Our results focus on the significance of a signal and the power to detect this signal, both of which are assessed relative to the *unexplained* variation. We removed important physical variables from the error terms in order to increase the probability of detecting an oiling effect. Overall, we concluded that oiling was 10.9% of the unexplained variation in the univariate models and 13.7% of the unexplained variation in the correspondence analysis models. These percentages would be less if expressed in terms of the total variation (without removing the variation resulting from the measured physical variables). While the unexplained variation is viewed here as a measure of natural variability, we recognize that it may contain a portion of the cleanup effect, namely to the extent that cleanup is separable from the oiling effects. As discussed in the following paragraphs, this contribution to the unexplained variability is small (approximately 2.4%).

We defined a working measure of cleanup as the total person hours of water-wash treatment per shoreline segment in order to assess the effect of cleanup on power and percentage recovery. The community parameter models (based only on normal theory) were updated by adding this "cleanup" variable. Cleanup effects adjusted for oiling (and the physical variables) were significant in only three out of the 48 tests performed, compared with seven out of 48 unadjusted for oiling. In addition, cleanup affected the variation accounted for by oiling with a median percentage change of only 13.7% for the three community parameter variables. Taken together, these illustrate the extent of confounding between cleanup and oiling. Since the relationship between cleanup and oiling is always positive, whether the variation explained by oiling adjusted for cleanup is increased or decreased depends on whether the community parameter variable is negatively or positively related to oiling and cleanup. On the basis of the change in variation explained by oiling adjusted for cleanup, the power was slightly reduced in 25 models and increased in 23 models.

The effect of the cleanup on the recovery estimates is small. If cleanup is included in the models as a concomitant variable (which can only be done crudely because of the difficulty of "measuring" cleanup), the unexplained variability (σ^2) would be reduced by a small amount (2.4%). The resulting small increase in power might result in a few more rejections of the null hypothesis and a corresponding decrease in the estimate of recovery using the univariate models. On the other hand, the signal (Δ) is sometimes increased and sometimes decreased, but with slightly more decreases. Overall, the number of rejections resulting from oiling effect would change little. Therefore, the effects on the upper-limit recovery estimate of 91% would be minimal. The effect on the lower-limit recovery estimate of 73% for correspondence analysis would also be small. The canonical axes defined by oiling would change only to the extent that the site variability associated with cleanup is correlated with oiling level and the abundance data. However, once the axes are determined, the reference ellipse is based only on the natural variability among the reference sites.

Comparisons With Results of Other Studies

Our shoreline chemistry findings (Boehm et al., this volume) are consistent with the rapidly declining amounts of oiled sediment found by the joint shoreline surveys (Neff et al., this volume). The fact that spill-related hydrocarbons in samples of finfish and wildlife were rare after 1989 (Bence and Burns, this volume) agrees with this picture of the sound. Similarly, National Oceanic and Atmospheric Administration (NOAA) mussel data (Manen et al. 1992) confirm our findings of substantial reductions in PAH over time.

Our toxicity results (Boehm et. al., this volume) are consistent with the effects-range threshold suggested by Long and Morgan (1990) and with observations of Rice et al. (1993) that subtidal oil contamination levels in Prince William Sound were not acutely toxic. The toxicity of oiled intertidal sediments has declined to background levels at most sites, confirming observations about the weathered state of spill residues. In fact, hydrocarbons remaining on pebble/gravel beaches are generally nontoxic, serving as a food source for biota, similar to what has been suggested for oil at seeps (Spies et al. 1988). Houghton et al., 1993 reported that on a heavily oiled beach on Block Island there were elevated populations of nematodes, oligochaetes, harpactacoid copepods and *Macoma spp* in 1991, which were lower in 1992. They suggest that the elevated populations in 1991 were feeding on hydrocarbon degrading bacteria. Fleeger et al. (1993) report that differences in oil-related effects in meiofauna disappeared after 29 days of exposure to Prudhoe Bay crude oil. Our findings of substantial biological recovery are consistent with the oil-spill literature (Mielke 1990) but differ from some conclusions of other *Exxon Valdez* studies described below.

Houghton et al. (1991a) report that the effects of the 1989 cleanup on biota in 1990 were significant and widespread. By the summer of 1991, on the other hand, Houghton et al. (1993) found that "few statistically significant differences remained between the biota of unoiled rocky shores and those of hot-water-washed shores." The latter conclusion is generally consistent with our 1990 and 1991 results.

Disagreement about the state of recovery in 1990 probably stems from differences in site selection and statistical analysis. For example, our study used a stratified random site-selection process. Together, the sites in our different categories (habitat, oiling level, tidezone) were representative of all possible sites in that category. Houghton et al. selected sites in a nonrandom manner (Lees, personal communication). These sites were the most impacted and cleaned sites in the sound. One of them, the rocky islet in Northwest Bay, Eleanor Island, was hot water washed for 72 hours from 18–20 June 1989. In many other locations in the sound, ecological constraints allowed hot water washing only when the midintertidal zone was covered with water, reducing the impacts of the hot water. Sites that were washed as much as the rocky islet site were rare in the oiled portion of Prince William Sound. The impact of washing at this site was still visible in 1990, but was not apparent at more than 150 other shoreline segments visited in 1990 (unpublished observations). The Houghton et al. studies accurately depict conditions at this location over time, but this site is certainly not representative of all shorelines in the oiled region of Prince William Sound. Their results, therefore, cannot be extrapolated to the spill zone as a whole. Although Houghton et al. did sample in a stratified random manner within each subjectively chosen site, that is not the same as randomly choosing sites representative of the sound.

Oiling levels and cleanup treatment are confounded in the Houghton et al. studies, where statistical comparisons are based on treatment alone. Most heavily oiled sites received hot-water treatment, while many lightly oiled ones did not. Thus, when effects are found, it is not clear which are due to oil and which to treatment. Additionally, treatment histories for specific locations within shoreline segments are not generally well documented, casting further doubt on study conclusions.

Houghton et al. did not account for concomitant variables such as wave energy, which can significantly affect plant and animal community structure. Since a number of their oiled sites appear more exposed to winter storms than their unoiled sites, study results could be affected, depending on the severity of recent storms.

Many of the same comments can be made about the work of Highsmith et al. (1993) and Stekoll et al. (1993), who report continuing impact on intertidal invertebrates and algae in 1990 and 1991 at sites in Prince William Sound, Cook Inlet/Kenai, and Kodiak Island/Alaska Peninsula. Initially, sites in these studies were chosen randomly. Then, unsatisfied with the findings from randomly chosen control sites, investigators subjectively picked different control sites in 1990 and filled out the matrix with fixed sites from 1989. At this point, the ability to project results to the sound as a whole was lost.

Again, these investigators did not correct for the variability introduced by concomitant variables. As we have shown in this paper, part of shoreline variability is explained by these factors.

Stekoll et al. (1993) note significantly less *Fucus gardneri* cover at all habitats in 1991. Our study showed significantly less *Fucus* in the upper intertidal zone of oiled bedrock sites, but significantly more in the middle intertidal zone of exposed bedrock sites. In general, for *Fucus* and other dominant species such as littorines, mussels, and limpets, we found no consistent pattern of significant differences, suggesting that natural variability plays a dominant role in determining the biota at specific sample locations.

CONCLUSION

The overall design of the shoreline ecology program relied on the "sediment quality triad" approach to pollutant impact assessment (Long and Chapman 1985). The "triad" approach combines measurements of chemistry and toxicology of sediments (Part 2: Chemistry, Bochm et al., this volume) with ecological measurements (this study). To assess recovery and remaining impact, it is important to measure all three. Hydrocarbon chemistry alone is not a measure of oil-spill recovery because spilled oil rapidly loses the more acutely toxic hydrocarbon fractions. A toxic threshold level is passed below which petroleum hydrocarbons serve more as a carbon source for bacteria, and thus, indirectly, for higher organisms, than as a toxicant (Spics ct al. 1988).

The chemistry results of this study (Part 2: Chemistry, Boehm et al., this volume) show that oil removal was generally quite rapid. By 1991 the oil spilled from the *Exxon Valdez* was dramatically reduced in concentration from the majority of the Prince William Sound shorelines by both natural processes and the cleanup effort. Toxicological results indicate that the toxic effects were generally limited to a period ranging from the first few months to one year after the spill. Toxic effects of the oil were no longer observed well before all petroleum residues were removed (i.e., no longer detectable by chemical methods). Although localized deposits of weathered oil may exist in isolated areas beyond this time, their environmental significance is negligible compared with other ongoing stress factors in the sound.

These findings mean that the detection of traces of weathered petroleum at a site is not an indicator of actual or potential environmental injury without concurrent biological and/or toxicological measurements. The biological results presented here are entirely consistent with the sediment bioassay results. Both indicate a low level of adverse effects in 1990. We used sensitive ecological measurements to assess ecological recovery of the spill area. Over 440 univariate tests were carried out on abundances of individual species and community structure parameters. A sensitive multivariate technique, DCCA, was used to analyze community structure. Results presented here show that, 15 to 18 months after the spill, approximately 73-91% of the initially affected shorelines in Prince William Sound were statistically indistinguishable from unoiled reference shorelines. In the shoreline areas that were still different from reference, with few exceptions, the communities present were more diverse, and had more species and more individuals than the corresponding reference sites. This result is not surprising given the effects of physical factors in the environment of the sound discussed in this paper, as well as the rapid loss of toxicity of the oil before the summer of 1990 when the sampling was done.

In conclusion, the following points about biological recovery of previously oiled shorelines in Prince William Sound can be made:

- The recovery of Prince William Sound shorelines from the impacts of the spill was effectively determined through a one-time stratified random sampling program combined with periodic monitoring of fixed sites representing unique habitats or worst-case oil exposures. This approach permits one to generalize to the spill-affected zone as a whole, and to project observed trends to the future.

- The best way to define recovery is in ecological, not chemical, terms. Recovery has occurred when no statistical differences exist between biological communities at oiled and reference sites.

- The shoreline of Prince William Sound affected by the *Exxon Valdez* oil spill had largely recovered from the effects of the spill by the summer of 1990, 15 to 18 months after the spill.

- Estimates of recovery in 1990 ranged from 73% based on correspondence analysis to 91% based on univariate community parameters analyses; 82% of the individual species abundances analyzed were indistinguishable from reference.

- The oiling effect in 1990 was small in comparison with the natural variability; thus, the remaining impact was small compared with disruptions resulting from natural stress factors. Estimates of the overall variability associated with the oiling signal were 10.9% of the unexplained variation using univariate community parameter analysis, and 13.7% using correspondence analysis.

- Ecological conditions at the fixed sites, with a few explainable exceptions, are also improving with time. This is consistent with the observation that the remaining oil at these locations is being removed from the environment and has been rendered virtually nontoxic by weathering processes.

- There is no reason that complete shoreline biological recovery will not have taken place within a few years following the 1991 survey.

ACKNOWLEDGMENTS

This study was supported by Exxon Company, U.S.A. We acknowledge the participation of Cecile Krejsa and Nicole Maher of Bowdoin College; Bob Cimberg; Lane Cameron and others of Dames and Moore, Inc; Tony Parkin, Sandra Tate and others of Authur D. Little, Inc; Keith Parker of Data Analysis Group.

REFERENCES

Bonsdorf, E. and W. G. Nelson. "Fate and Effects of Ekofisk Crude Oil in the Littoral of a Norwegian Fjord." *Sarsia*. 66: 231-240; 1981.

Burd, B. J., A. Nemec, and R. O. Brinkhurst. "The Development amd Application of Analytical Methods in Benthic Marine Infaunal Studies." *Advances in Marine Biology*. 26: 169-247; 1990.

Camargo, J. A. "Temporal and Spatial Variations in Dominance Diversity and Biotic Indices along a Limestone Stream Receiving a Trout Farm Effluent." *Water Air Soil Pollution*. 63: 343-359; 1992.

Chadwick, J. W. and S. P. Canton. "Inadequacy of Diversity Indices in Discerning Metal Mine Drainage Effects on a Stream Invertebrate Community." *Water Air Soil Pollution*. 22(2): 217-223; 1984.

Chan, G. L. "A Study of the Effects of the San Francisco Oil Spill on Marine Life. Part II. Recruitment." *In Proceedings 1975 Oil Spill Conference*. Washington, DC: American Petroleum Institute; 457-461; 1975.

Chasse, C. "The Ecological Impact on and Near Shores by the *AMOCO CADIZ* Oil Spill." *Marine Pollution Bulletin*. 9(11): 298-301; 1978.

Clark, R. C., B. G. Patten, and E. E. Denike. "Persistent Spill from the GENERAL E.C. MEIGS." *Journal Fisheries Research Board Canada*. 35: 754-765; 1978.

Dayton, P. K. "Competition, Disturbance and Community Organization: The Provision and Subsequent Utilization of Space in a Rocky Intertidal Community." *Ecological Monographs.* 41: 351-389; 1971.

Denslow, J. S. "Disturbance Mediated Coexistence of Species." *In The Ecology of Natural Disturbance and Patch Dynamics.* New York: Academic Press; 307-323; 1985.

Field, J. G., K. R. Clarke, and R. M. Warwick. "A Practical Strategy for Analysing Multispecies Distribution Patterns." *Marine Ecology Progress Series* 8: 37-52; 1982.

Fleeger, J. W., M. A. Todaro, T. C. Shirley, and M. G. Carls. "Meiofaunal Recolonization Experiment with Oiled Sediments: The Harpacticoid Copepod Assemblage." *In* Exxon Valdez *Oil Spill Symposium Abstracts*; Anchorage, AK; 169-172; 1993.

Ghazanshahi, J., T. Huchel, and J. S. Devinny. "Alteration of Southern California, USA, Rocky Shore Ecosystems by Public Recreational Use." *Journal of Environmental Management.* 16(4): 379-394; 1983.

Gilfillan, E. S., D. S. Page, and J. C. Foster. "Tidal Area Dispersant Project: Fate and Effects of Chemically Dispersed Oil in the Nearshore Benthic Environment." Washington, DC: *American Petroleum Institute Publication No. 4440*; 215 pp; 1986.

Glemarec, M. and E. Hussenot. "Definition d'une Secession Ecologique en Milieu Meuble Abnormallement Enrichi en Matieres Organique a la Suitre de la Catastrophe de l'*Amoco Cadiz*." *In* Amoco Cadiz*: Conseuquences d'une Pollution Accidentelle par les Hydrocarbures; Fates and Effects of the Oil Spill.* Paris: Centre pour l'Exploitation des Oceans; 499-525; 1981.

Grant, W. S. "High Intertidal Community Organization on a Rocky Headland in Maine, USA." *Marine Biology.* 44(1): 15-26; 1977.

Grassle, J. F. and J. R. Grassle. "Opportunistic Life Histories and Genetic Systems in Benthic Polychaetes." *Journal Marine Research.* 32: 253-284; 1974.

Hanson, B. L. *Quality Control: Theory and Applications.* Englewood Cliffs, NJ: Prentice Hall; 1963.

Highsmith, R. C., S. M. Saupe, K. O. Coyle, T. Rucker, and W. Erickson. "Impact of the Exxon Valdez Oil Spill on Intertidal Invertebrates Throughout the Oil Spill Region." *In* Exxon Valdez *Oil Spill Symposium Abstracts*; Anchorage, AK; 166-168; 1993.

Houghton, J. P., D. C. Lees, W. B. Driskell, and A. J. Mearns. "Impacts of the *EXXON VALDEZ* Spill and Subsequent Cleanup on Intertidal Biota—One Year Later." *In Proceedings 1991 Oil Spill Conference.* Washington, DC: American Petroleum Institute; 467-475; 1991a.

Houghton, J. P., D. C. Lees, H. Teas, III, H. L. Cumberland, S. Landino, W. B. Driskell, and T. A. Ebert. "Evaluation of the Condition of Intertidal and Shallow Subtidal Biota in Prince William Sound following the *Exxon Valdez* Oil Spill and Subsequent Shoreline Treatment." Report No. HMRB 91-1; Submitted to National Oceanic and Atmospheric Administration, National Ocean Service, Hazardous Materials Response Branch; NOAA WASC Contract No. 50ABNC-0-00121 and 50ABNC-0-00122; 1991b.

Houghton, J. P., A. K. Fukuyama, Lees, D. C., W. B. Driskell, G. Shigenaka, and A. J. Mearns. "Impacts on Intertidal Epibiota: *Exxon Valdez* Spill and Subsequent Cleanup." *In Proceedings, 1993 International Oil Spill Conference.* Washington, DC: American Petroleum Institute; 293-300; 1993.

Hughes, B. D. "The Influence of Factors Other than Pollution on the Value of Shannon's Diversity Index for Benthic Macro Invertebrates in Streams." *Water Research.* 12(5): 359-364; 1978.

Lees, D. C. Ogden Environmental and Energy Services Co., Inc., San Diego, CA.

Long, E. R. and P. M. Chapman. "A Sediment Quality Triad: Measures of Sediment Contamination, Toxicity, and Infaunal Community Composition in Puget Sound." *Marine Pollution Bulletin.* 16: 405-415; 1985.

Long, E. R. and L. G. Morgan. "The Potential for Biological Effects of Sediment-sorbed Contaminants Teseted in the National Status and Trends Program." NOAA Technical Memorandum NOS OMA 52, 175pp + appendices; 1990.

Lubchenco, J. "Plant Species Diversity in a Marine Intertidal Community: Importance of Herbivore Food Preference and Algal Competitive Abilities." *American Naturalist.* 112: 23-39; 1978.

Maki, A. W. "The *Exxon Valdez* Oil Spill: Initial Environmental Impact Assessment." *Environmental Science and Technology.* 25: 24-29; 1991.

Manen, C. A., J. R. Price, S. Korn, and M. G. Carls. "Natural Resource Damage Assessment: Database Design and Structure." NOAA Technical Memorandum NOS/ORCA (in review); National Oceanic and Atmospheric Administration, U. S. Department of Commerce, Rockville, MD; 1992.

Markham, J. W. and I. M. Munda, "Algal Recolonization in the Rocky Eulittoral at Helgoland, Germany." *Aquatic Botany.* 9(1): 33-72; 1980.

McGuinness, K. A. "Disturbance and Organisms on Boulders I. Patterns in the Environment and the Community." *Oecologica.* 71(3): 409-419; 1987a.

McGuinness, K. A. "Disturbance and Organisms on Boulders II. Causes of Patterns in Diversity and Abundance." *Oecologica*. 71(3): 420-430; 1987b.

Mielke, J. E. "Oil in the Ocean: The Short- and Long-Term Impacts of a Spill." 90-356 SPR. Congressional Research Service, The Library of Congress, Washington, DC; 34 pp; 1990.

Nakahara, H. and M. Ueno. "A Mechanism of Succession in Seaweed Communities." *Bulletin Japanese Society Fisheries*. 51(9): 1437-1440; 1985.

Nelson, W. G. "Experimental Studies of Oil Pollution on the Rocky Intertidal Community of a Norwegian Fjord." *Ecology*. 65(2): 121-138; 1982.

NRC (National Research Council). *Oil in the Sea: Inputs, Fates, and Effects*. Washington, DC: National Academy Press; 601 pp; 1985.

Osman, R. W. "The Establishment and Development of a Marine Epifaunal Community." *Ecological Monographs*. 47(1): 37-63; 1977.

Paine, R. T. "Intertidal Community Structure: Experimental Studies on the Relationship Between a Dominant Competitor and its Principal Predator." *Oecologia*. 15: 93-120; 1974.

Paine, R. T. and S. A. Levin. "Intertidal Landscapes Disturbance and the Dynamics of Pattern." *Ecological Monographs*. 51(2): 145-178; 1981.

Parsons, T. R., M. Takahashi, and B. Hargrave. *Biological Oceanographic Processes*. Oxford: Pergamon Press, 2nd Edition; 332 pages; 1977.

Pearson, T. H. and R. Rosenberg. "Macrobenthic Succession in Relation to Organic Enrichment and Pollution of the Marine Environment." *Oceanography and Marine Biology Annual Review*. 16: 229-311; 1978.

Povey, A. and M. J. Keogh. "Effects of Trampling on Plant and Animal Populations on Rocky Shores." *Oikos*. 61(3): 355-368; 1991.

Rice, S. D., B. A. Wright, J. W. Short, and C. E. O'Clair. "Subtidal Oil Contamination and Biological Impacts." *In* Exxon Valdez *Oil Spill Symposium Abstracts*; Anchorage, AK; 23-26; 1993.

Robles, C. "Disturbance and Predation in an Assemblage of Herbivorous Diptera and Algae on Rocky Shores." *Oecologica*. 54(1): 23-31; 1982.

Samways, M. J. "A Practical Comparison of Diversity Indices Based on a Series of Small Agricultural Art Communities." *Phytophylactica.* 16 (4): 275-278; 1984.

Sanders, H. L., J. F. Grassle, G. R. Hampson, L. S. Morse, S. Garner-Price, and C. C. Jones. "Anatomy of an Oil Spill: Long-Term Effects from the Grounding of the Barge *Florida* off West Falmouth, Massachussetts." *Journal Marine Research.* 38: 265-380; 1980.

Shanks, A. L. and W. G. Wright. "Adding Teeth to Wave Action: The Destructive Effects of Wave Born Rocks on Intertidal Organisms." *Oecologica.* 69: 420-428; 1986.

Shannon, C. E. "The Mathematical Theory of Communication." *Bell System Technology Journal.* 27: 379-623; 1948.

Shannon, C. E. and W. Weaver. *The Mathematical Theory of Communication.* Urbana, Il.: University of Illinois Press, 1949.

Smith, R.W., B. B. Bernstein, and R. L. Cimberg. "Community-Environmental Relationships in the Benthos: Applications of Multivariate Analytical Techniques." *In Marine Organisms as Indicators.* D. F. Soule and G. S. Kleppel (eds.); New York: Springer-Verlag; 247-326; 1988.

Sousa, W. P. "Disturbance in Marine Intertidal Boulder Fields: The Nonequilibrium Maintenance of Species Diversity." *Ecology.* 60(6): 1225-1239; 1979a.

Sousa, W. P. "Experimental Investigations of Disturbance and Ecological Succession in a Rocky Intertidal Algal Community." *Ecological Monographs.* 49(3): 227-254; 1979b.

Sousa, W. P. "Disturbance and Patch Dynamics on Rocky Intertidal Shores." *In The Ecology of Natural Disturbance and Patch Dynamics.* New York: Academic Press; 101-124; 1985.

Southward, A .J. and E. C. Southward. "Recolonization of Rocky Shores in Cornwall After Use of Toxic Dispersants to Clean Up the TORREY CANYON Spill." *Journal Fisheries Research Board of Canada.* 35: 682-706; 1978.

Spies, R. B., D. D. Hardin, and J. P. Toal. "Organic Enrichment or Toxicity? A Comparison of the Effects of Kelp and Crude Oil in Sediments on the Colonization and Growth of Benthic Infauna." *Journal of Experimental Marine Biology and Ecology.* 124: 261-282; 1988.

Stekoll, M. S., L. Deysher, and Z. Guo. "Coastal Habitat Injury Assessment: Intertidal Algal Communities." *In Exxon Valdez Oil Spill Symposium Abstracts*; Anchorage, AK; 169-172; 1993.

Stephenson, W., W. T. Williams, and G. N. Lance. "The Macrobenthos of Moreton Bay." *Ecological Monographs.* 40(4): 459-494; 1970.

Ter Braak, C. J. F. "Canonical Correspondence Analysis: A New Eigenvector Technique for Multivariate Direct Gradient Analysis." *Ecology.* 67: 1167-1179; 1986a.

Ter Braak, C. J. F. "The Analysis of Vegetation-Environment Relationships by Canonical Correspondence Analysis." *Vegetatio.* 69: 69-77; 1986b.
Thistle, D. "Natural Physical Distubances and Communities of Marine Soft Bottoms." *Marine Ecological Progress Series.* 6: 223-228; 1981.

Edward S. Gilfillan[1], Thomas H. Suchanek[2], Paul D. Boehm[3], E. James Harner[4], David S. Page[5], Norman A. Sloan[6]*

SHORELINE IMPACTS IN THE GULF OF ALASKA REGION FOLLOWING THE *EXXON VALDEZ* OIL SPILL

REFERENCE: Gilfillan, E. S., Suchanek, T. H., Boehm, P. D., Harner, E. J., Page, D. S., and Sloan, N. A., "Shoreline Impacts in the Gulf of Alaska Region Following the Exxon Valdez Oil Spill," *Exxon Valdez Oil Spill: Fate and Effects in Alaskan Waters, ASTM STP 1219*, Peter G. Wells, James N. Butler, and Jane S. Hughes, Eds., American Society for Testing and Materials, Philadelphia, 1995.

ABSTRACT: Forty-eight sites in the Gulf of Alaska region (GOA–Kodiak Island, Kenai Peninsula, and Alaska Peninsula) were sampled in July/August 1989 to assess the impact of the March 24, 1989, *Exxon Valdez* oil spill on shoreline chemistry and biological communities hundreds of miles from the spill origin. In a 1990 companion study, 5 of the Kenai sites and 13 of the Kodiak and Alaska Peninsula sites were sampled 16 months after the spill.

Oiling levels at each site were estimated visually and/or quantified by chemical analysis. The chemical analyses were performed on sediment and/or rock wipe samples collected with the biological samples. Additional sediment samples were collected for laboratory amphipod toxicity tests. Mussels were also collected and analyzed for hydrocarbon content to assess hydrocarbon bioavailability.

Biological investigations at these GOA sites focused on intertidal infauna, epifauna, and macroalgae by means of a variety of common ecological techniques. For rocky sites the percentage of hard substratum covered by biota was quantified. At each site, up to 5 biological samples (scrapes of rock surfaces or sediment cores) were collected intertidally along each of 3 transects, spanning tide levels from the high intertidal to mean-lowest-low-water (zero tidal datum). Organisms (down to 1.0 mm in size) from these samples were sorted and identified. Community parameters including organism abundance, species richness, and Shannon diversity were calculated for each sample.

[1] Bowdoin College, Brunswick, ME 04011
[2] University of California, Davis, CA 95616
[3] Arthur D. Little, Inc., Cambridge, MA 02140-2390
[4] West Virginia University, Morgantown, WV 26506
[5] Bowdoin College, Brunswick, ME 04011
[6] Dames and Moore, Seattle, WA 98121
* Current address: EVS Consultants, North Vancouver, B. C., Canada

As expected for shores so far from the spill origin, oiling levels were substantially lower, and beached oil was more highly weathered than in Prince William Sound (PWS). Samples of oiled GOA shoreline sediment were not statistically more toxic in bioassay tests than sediment from unoiled reference sites.

As a consequence of the lower oil impact, the biological communities were not as affected as those in the sound. Biological impacts, although present in 1989 in the GOA, were localized, which is consistent with the patchy and discontinuous nature of much of the oiling in GOA. Some organisms were locally reduced or eliminated in oiled patches but survived in unoiled patches nearby. In areas where oiling occurred, impacts were generally limited to middle and upper intertidal zones.

Analyses of mussel samples indicate that by 1990 little of the shoreline oil remained bioavailable to epifauna. Quantifiable measures of the overall health and vitality of shoreline biological communities, such as organism abundance, species richness, and Shannon diversity for sediment infauna, show few significant differences between oiled and reference sites in 1990.

KEYWORDS: *Exxon Valdez* oil spill, far-field spill impacts, shoreline ecology, shoreline recovery

INTRODUCTION

This paper describes the impact of the March 24, 1989, *Exxon Valdez* oil spill (EVOS) on Gulf of Alaska (GOA) shoreline sediments and biological communities that were hundreds of miles from the origin of the spill in Prince William Sound (PWS). The GOA region included in this study contains the Kenai Peninsula, the Alaska Peninsula, and the Kodiak Island complex (Shuyak Island, Afognak Island, and Kodiak Island).

In general, the types of shoreline habitats oiled by the EVOS in the GOA region are similar to those found in PWS. However, in total, GOA shores are characterized by generally higher wave energy because they are exposed to the long fetch of the GOA and the Shelikof Strait. As a result, the GOA shorelines are fairly rugged, consisting of mostly bedrock, rock rubble, and boulder/cobble habitats with some pebble/gravel shores.

The major impacts of the EVOS occurred within PWS. However, after 7 days some of the EVOS oil was transported out of PWS into the GOA (Neff et al. this volume). Figure 1 shows the progression of EVOS oil into the GOA region. Roughly 800 shoreline miles of this region were oiled, compared with roughly 500 shoreline miles in PWS.

Oil typically traveled 1 to 8 weeks before reaching GOA sites. Therefore, this oil was more weathered and less toxic than the oil that impacted sites in PWS. Winds and waves also dispersed the oil into separate wind rows or isolated pancakes of oil or mousse, resulting in very patchy distributions of oil along GOA shorelines.

The ecology of GOA shoreline communities is very strongly influenced by the effects of wave exposure, which, in other studies, has been shown to create disturbance patches of open space, typically during storm events (Dayton 1971; Osman 1977; Sousa 1979a,b, 1985; Paine and Levin 1981; Nakahara and Ueno 1985; McGuinness 1987a,b). In many

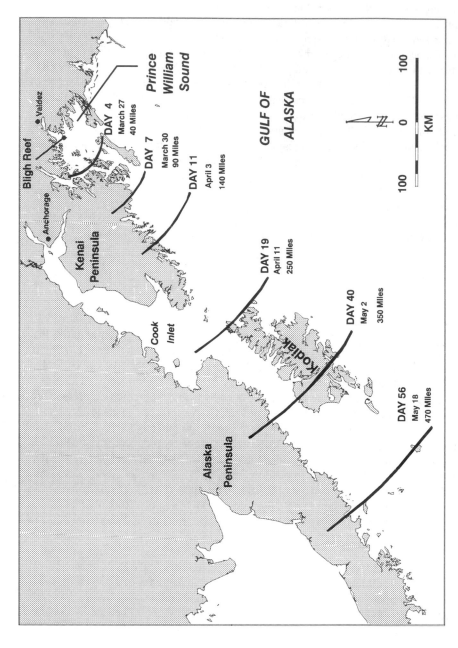

FIGURE 1—Progression of the leading edge of oil from the *Exxon Valdez* oil spill into the Gulf of Alaska Region (Neff et al. this volume).

locations in the GOA, loose sediment particles, logs, and ice chunks become projectiles when waves are high (Shanks and Wright 1986), dislodging sessile organisms and contributing to the formation of some level of natural disturbance patches formed each year. When the availability of space is constantly renewed by intense wave action in concert with natural projectiles, predator activity, oil spills, or scientific experimentation, competition for space is reduced and usually more species can coexist (Grant 1977).

The response of rock surface communities to oil spills is dictated by their ecology as well as oil toxicity (Suchanek 1993). On rock surfaces space is a limiting resource, and competition for this space plays a significant role in determining community structure (Connell 1961; Paine 1974; Suchanek 1985). Following an oil spill, shoreline biota may be killed by the oil, subsequent cleanup, a disruption in competitive interactions, or predator-prey relationships, creating open space for future colonization. It is rare for all individuals of a species to be eliminated on shorelines affected by an oil spill (Chan 1975; Clarke et al. 1978; Southward and Southward 1978; Chasse 1978; Bonsdorf and Nelson 1981; Nelson 1982) and open patches are rapidly recolonized by juveniles from surrounding areas.

In general, very little historical information is available on the ecology of the affected shorelines in the GOA (Druehl 1970; Lindstrom and Calvin 1975). Furthermore, no specific prespill data existed for the sites in this study.

Patterns of community response to, and recovery from, oil spills in soft substrata (i.e., sediments) are generally understood (National Research Council 1985; Mielke 1990). In these types of substrata, the degree of initial impact from an oil spill is a function of the amount of oil reaching a location and its toxicity. When toxic oil is incorporated into sediments, the infauna may be killed and sediments may become anaerobic as a result of reduced oxygen transport in animal burrows (Sanders et al. 1980) and the added biological oxygen demand (BOD) of the oil. If more weathered (i.e., less toxic) oil is incorporated, the added BOD of the oil may drive the sediments anaerobic and kill the infauna even if it survived the initial exposure to oil (Glemarec and Hussenot 1982). The area will then undergo a succession during recovery as the excess inventory of organic carbon is metabolized by bacteria. At the beginning of the succession, the community will be dominated by one or a small number of opportunistic polychaete worms (Grassle and Grassle 1974; Sanders et al. 1980; Glemarec and Hussenot 1982; Gilfillan et al. 1986). At the end of the succession a normally diverse community occupies the environment. Effects of oil spills are usually similar to those of other types of organic enrichment (Pearson and Rosenberg 1978; Spies et al. 1988; Suchanek 1993).

PURPOSE

This study was a reconnaissance exercise to determine whether stranded oil was having similar ecological effects on shorelines in the GOA region as in the PWS region. Data are provided on chemical, toxicological, and biological studies that were begun in July 1989 and from a subset of companion studies that were conducted during the summer of 1990. The purpose of this paper is two-fold: (1) to provide a preliminary description of the impact of the EVOS on shoreline communities in the GOA region in

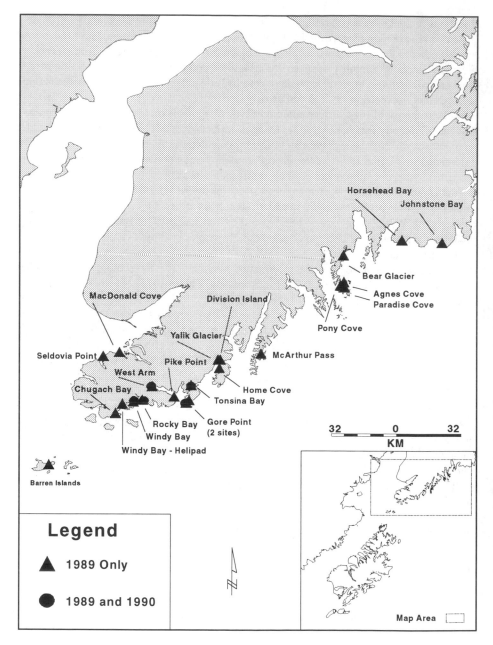

Figure 2—Location of sites (22) sampled in the Kenai Peninsula region in 1989 and 1990.

1989 and (2) to compare trends of chemical change in the GOA with those observed in PWS. There is no direct comparability between the community studies that were conducted in the Kodiak/Alaska Peninsula region in 1989 with those infaunal community studies conducted in that same region in 1990. Therefore, this paper does not imply any measured change in these communities from one year to another; it only presents two separate measurements of community status in relation to original oiling levels during two different years, using different methodologies. For the 1989 data, this paper only gives a preliminary overview of the results in the Kodiak/Alaska Peninsula region. Much more detailed publications in preparation will incorporate more site-specific and quadrat-specific oiling information; species information, species specific impacts and algal biomass data for this region not included here (Suchanek, in prep).

APPROACH

In the summer of 1989, biological and chemical field collections were made at 48 sites in the GOA region; 22 from the Kenai Peninsula, 11 from the Alaska Peninsula, and 15 from the Kodiak Island Complex (Figures 2 and 3; Table 1). Site selection was based on oiling assessments from the shoreline survey oiling designations (Neff et al., this volume) and a preliminary reconnaissance by an advance team. These sites were not chosen randomly, but were chosen specifically to represent a wide range of both habitat types and oiling conditions within the GOA region; therefore, conditions at the sites may not be representative of the GOA as a whole. The following numbers of GOA sites were sampled and analyzed for oil impacts: bedrock (14), boulder/cobble (18), and pebble/gravel (11). Five sand/mud habitats were sampled but not analyzed statistically because all sand sites visited were oiled to some degree and all mud habitats visited were unoiled; therefore, no comparisons could be made that could discriminate between both oiling levels and grain size. Each of the aforementioned habitat types was, in turn, represented by from 2 to 6 sites for each of three subjective levels of oiling: unoiled, light, moderate-heavy. These oiling designations were derived from the results of shoreline surveys conducted in 1989 (Teal 1990; Neff et al. this volume) by combining the moderately and heavily oiled categories.

In 1990 additional samples were collected at 18 of the same sites sampled in 1989 (Figures 2 and 3; Table 1), using chemistry sampling protocols identical to those employed in 1989. However, in most cases the sample types collected for biological sampling differed between the two years, i.e., in 1989 most samples collected were species removal samples, whereas in 1990 most were core samples.

METHODS

Study Design

The shoreline surveys conducted in 1989 were initiated to assess the potential effects of oiling on the biological community and the weathering of stranded oil. Study sites

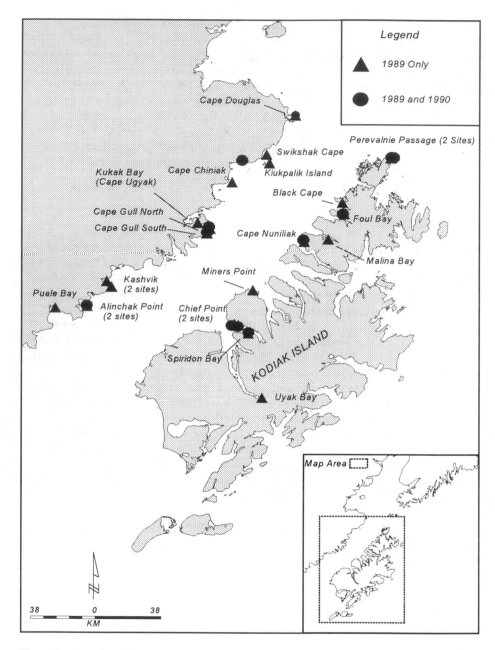

Figure 3—Location of sites (26) sampled in the Kodiak Island complex and Alaska Peninsula region in 1989 and 1990.

were subjectively chosen to encompass the variety of habitats occurring in the region and the degrees of shoreline oiling. Data were acquired at 22 sites along the Kenai Peninsula (Figure 2) and 26 sites in the Kodiak/Alaska Peninsula region (Figure 3). Samples of shoreline biota (infauna and epibiota) were collected along with samples for hydrocarbon analysis, sediment grain size, and amphipod toxicity. In the 1990 survey, 18 of these 48 sites were resampled to measure physical (grain size), chemical, and biological parameters (primarily infauna).

Several types of data were collected directly in the field or derived from collected samples. In 1989 the following types of data were obtained at each site:
- Sediment or rock wipe samples for hydrocarbon analysis.
- Percent cover observations of macroscopic fauna and flora by using the lowest reasonable taxonomic unit (usually to species).
- Removals of macrofauna/macroflora for community parameter analysis (e.g., organism abundance, species richness, diversity). These samples consisted of both species removals from hard surfaces and sediment core samples.

At selected sites the following additional samples were collected:
- Sediment samples for laboratory amphipod toxicity analyses.
- Mussel (*Mytilus* cf. *"edulis"*) samples for tissue hydrocarbon analyses.

In 1990 the following types of data were obtained at each site:
- Sediment or rock wipe samples for hydrocarbon analysis.
- Biological cores for community parameter analysis (organism abundance, species richness, Shannon diversity).
- Epibiota scraped from rock surfaces at some locations.

At selected sites the following additional samples were collected:
- Mussel (*Mytilus* cf. *"edulis"*) samples for tissue hydrocarbon analyses.

Table 1 provides reference information on site identity, location, tide zones, dominant site substratum, oiling levels, and types of samples collected at each site.

Field Methods—Chemistry

Sediment and rock wipe samples for hydrocarbon analysis—For the 1989 survey, chemistry samples were collected alongside the biology samples and consisted of the top 2 cm of sediment. When appropriate, separate samples were collected for grain size and organic carbon analysis. On boulder/cobble beaches, the surface armor of boulders was removed and the loose finer-grained matrix collected for analysis. On rock surfaces an area of about 100 cm^2 was wiped with solvent-impregnated (hexane) glass-fiber filter paper. The splash zone sample was established at the line of flotsam on the beach.

The field methods for chemical sampling during the 1990 survey are summarized in Page et al. (Shoreline Ecology Program: Part 1–Study Design and Methods, this volume). Sediment samples for chemistry consisted of a composite of three subsamples collected around the perimeter of the biology sample. Samples were frozen and shipped to the laboratory. The samples for grain size and organic carbon analysis were subsampled from the chemistry sample at the laboratory. In 1990 boulder/cobble beaches were sampled as described for the 1989 survey. In contrast to the 1989 survey, which took the chemistry samples from one location, the 1990 samples consisted of a composite of three subsamples collected around the perimeter of the biology sample. A 5-cm diameter template was used to scrape the rock surface, then the surface was wiped with a solvent-impregnated (methylene chloride) glass-fiber filter. The rock wipe sample consisted of the scrape material and the filter-wipe from three samples collected around the perimeter of the biology sample (total area of 60 cm^2). Sediment samples for chemistry represented the top 10 cm of intertidal sediment and the top 2 cm of subtidal sediment. Splash zone chemistry samples were not collected in 1990.

Quantification of oiling levels—Hydrocarbon analyses were used to document (1) levels of Total Polycyclic Aromatic Hydrocarbons (TPAH) in GOA sediments and their change over time (i.e., 1989-1990), (2) chemical changes in the composition of oil over time (i.e., 1989-1990), (3) hydrocarbon concentrations in GOA mussel tissues, and (4) hydrocarbon levels in amphipod toxicity tests.

In 1989, TPAH concentrations were compared with visual estimates of oiling levels on a quadrat by quadrat basis for some, but not all, quadrats in the Kodiak/Alaska peninsula region, but not the Kenai region. Because of the patchy nature of oiling in the GOA region, this approach was better at describing localized oiling conditions than the use of a single "oil band width" approach used in most other EVOS studies. However, even this method was not perfect. While both the visual and chemical oiling estimates were obtained from the same square meter area of intertidal shoreline, there was even finer scale variability within these quadrats that affected these comparisons. Visual estimates were obtained from within 25-x-25 cm or 50-x-50 cm quadrats taken from the "biological side" of the transect line, but chemically measured estimates were obtained from only a very small wipe region on the "chemistry side" of the transect line (see Figure 4). With a high degree of patchiness, this led to considerable variability between these two estimates (see Figure 6).

While direct chemical measurement of TPAH or direct visual estimates of oil cover are preferable to the assignment of a single oiling level for an entire site using an oil band width, neither visual nor chemical methods were utilized for all quadrats in all regions. Therefore, for purposes of cross-comparisons between Kodiak, Alaska Peninsula and Kenai sites in 1989, and for the reporting of the subsequent studies in 1990, oiling designations of "moderate to heavy", "light" and "reference" were used. These were originally derived from oil band width surveys reported by Teal (1990) and Neff et al. (this volume).

Mussel collections for tissue hydrocarbon analyses—Mussels, commonly used as indicator organisms, were collected from several locations for tissue hydrocarbon analysis estimating bioavailable hydrocarbon concentrations of epifaunal species. Usually 20 to 30 individuals of *Mytilus cf. "edulis"* were collected from mid or low intertidal regions at 13 of the 35 sites (Table 1), placed in chemically cleaned containers, frozen, shipped to the laboratory, and maintained in a frozen condition (-17 °C) until analyzed for their hydrocarbon content.

Table 1–Sites sampled in 1989 and 1990 in the GOA region with information on habitat type, 1989 shoreline oiling classifications, and numbers of various sample types collected at sites in 1989 and 1990.*

Site	Site Name	Location	Latitude (° N)	Longitude (° W)	Substrate	Oiling	1989 Hydrocarbon (Sed./Wipe/Mussel)	# Cores ('89/'90)	Species Removals ('89/'90)	Percent Cover ('89/'90)	Sediment Toxicity** ('89/'90)
Bedrock/Rock Rubble											
PXR01	Paradise Cove	KEN	59.8	149.6	SB	N	N/N/N	0/0	6/0	6/0	0/0
SPR01	Seldovia Point	KEN	59.5	151.7	EB	N	Y/N/N	0/0	6/0	9/0	0/0
OFOR01	Foul Bay	KOD	58.3	152.9	SB	N	N/N/N	0/8	9/1	9/1	0/0
ORBR01	Rocky Bay	KEN	59.3	151.4	SB	L	Y/N/Y	0/4	9/5	9/5	1/0
PCR01	Pony Cove	KEN	59.8	149.6	SB	L	N/N/N	0/0	8/0	9/0	0/0
OCFR01	Chief Point	KOD	57.7	153.9	SB	L	Y/Y/Y	0/3	0/4	9/6	1/0
ONUR01	Cape Numiliak	KOD	58.2	153.2	SB	L	N/N/N	0/0	0/9	6/9	0/0
0ALM01	Alinchak Bay	AP	57.8	155.3	SB	L	N/N/Y	0/9	0/0	8/0	1/0
KPRO01B	Kiukpalik Island B	AP	58.6	153.6	EB	L	N/Y/N	0/0	0/0	6/0	0/0
WBR01	Windy Bay (WB1)	KEN	59.2	151.5	SB	M-H	Y/Y/Y	0/0	9/0	7/0	0/0
0PPR01	Perevalnie Passage	KOD	58.6	152.4	SB	M-H	Y/Y/Y	0/9	9/0	9/0	1/0
KPRO01A	Kiukpalik Island A	AP	58.6	153.6	EB	M-H	N/N/N	0/0	0/0	6/0	0/0
Boulder/Cobble											
BBC01	Horsehead Bay	KEN	60.0	149.0	B/C	N	Y/N/N	0/0	0/0	0/0	0/0
HHC01	Home Cove	KEN	59.4	150.7	B/C	N	Y/N/N	6/0	0/0	9/0	4/0
JBC01	Johnstone Bay	KEN	59.9	148.7	B/C	N	Y/N/N	0/0	0/0	0/0	0/0
0FOS01	Foul Bay	KOD	58.3	152.8	B/C	N	Y/N/N	6/9	3/0	9/0	1/0
FBBO01	Foul Bay	KOD	58.3	152.8	B/C	N	N/N/N	0/0	9/0	9/0	1/0
0CGM01	Cape Gull South	AP	58.2	154.2	B/C	N	Y/Y/Y	0/9	9/0	9/0	1/0
DIC01	Division Island	KEN	59.4	150.7	B/C	L	Y/N/Y	7/0	0/0	9/0	4/0
GPS01	Gore Point	KEN	59.2	151.0	B/C	L	Y/N/N	6/0	0/0	0/0	4/0
MBCO01	Malina Bay	KOD	58.2	153.0	B/C	L	N/N/N	0/0	0/0	4/0	1/0
MPBO01	Miner's Point	KOD	57.9	153.7	B/C	L	N/N/N	0/0	0/0	6/0	1/0
PMBO01	Perevalnie Mouth	KOD	58.6	152.4	B/C	L	Y/Y/Y	0/0	9/0	9/0	0/0
0GUM01	Cape Gull North	AP	58.2	154.2	B/C	L	Y/N/N	0/9	9/0	9/0	1/0
CBC01	Chugach Bay (2)	KEN	59.2	151.6	B/C	M-H	Y/N/N	0/0	0/0	0/0	1/0
0CFR02	Chief Point(Egg Island)	KOD	57.7	153.9	B/C	M-H	Y/N/Y	0/9	9/0	9/0	1/0
0CDR01	Cape Douglas	AP	58.9	153.3	B/C	M-H	Y/N/N	0/8	9/1	9/1	3/0
KBCO01	Kashvik	AP	57.9	155.1	B/C	M-H	Y/N/Y	6/0	3/0	9/0	5/0

Table 1—Sites sampled in 1989 and 1990 in the GOA region with information on habitat type, 1989 shoreline oiling classifications, and numbers of various sample types collected at sites in 1989 and 1990. *, cont'd.

Site	Site Name	Location	Latitude (°N)	Longitude (°W)	Substrate	Oiling	1989 Hydrocarbon (Sed./Wipe/Mussel)	# Cores (89'/90)	Species Removals (89'/90)	Percent Cover (89'/90)	Sediment Toxicity** (89'/90)
Pebble/Gravel											
MSC01	MacDonald Spit	KEN	59.5	151.6	P/G	N	Y/N/N	9/0	0/0	0/0	1/0
PIC01	Pike Point	KEN	59.3	151.1	P/G	N	Y/N/N	0/0	0/0	0/0	0/0
OSPR01	Spiridon Bay	KOD	57.7	153.8	P/G	N	N/N/N	0/9	0/0	9/0	4/0
0WAC01	West Arm	KEN	59.3	151.3	P/G	L	Y/N/N	0/9	0/0	0/0	1/0
BIC01	Barren Islands	KEN	58.9	152.2	P/G	L	Y/N/N	0/0	0/0	0/0	1/0
PMGR01	Perevalnie Mouth	KOD	58.6	152.4	P/G	L	Y/N/Y	8/0	0/0	0/0	1/0
OCHS01	Cape Chiniak	AP	58.5	153.9	P/G	L	Y/N/N	0/9	0/0	0/0	0/0
OGCM01	Gore Point Control	KEN	59.2	151.0	P/G	M-H	Y/N/Y	6/9	0/0	0/0	4/0
OTBC01	Tonsina Bay	KEN	59.3	151.0	P/G	M-H	Y/N/N	0/9	0/0	0/0	1/0
0WBC01	Windy Bay (2)	KEN	59.2	151.5	P/G	M-H	Y/N/Y	8/9	0/0	0/0	4/0
OPPS01	Perevalnie Passage	KOD	58.6	152.4	P/G	M-H	Y/N/N	9/9	0/0	9/0	1/0
Sand											
BCSA01	Black Cape	KOD	58.4	152.9	SAND	L	Y/N:Y	0/0	0/0	0/0	1/0
PBSA01	Puale Bay	AP	57.8	155.6	SAND	L	Y/N/N	9/0	0/0	0/0	1/0
SCSA01	Swikshak Cape	AP	58.7	153.6	SAND	L	Y/N/N	9/0	0/0	0/0	3/0
Mud											
UBMU01	Uyak Bay	KOD	57.3	153.6	MUD	N	Y/N/N	0/0	0/0	0/0	1/0
KKMU01	Kukak Bay	AP	58.3	154.3	MUD	N	N/N/N	9/0	0/0	0/0	1/0

Key:

EB = Exposed Bedrock; SB = Sheltered Bedrock; B/C = Boulder/Cobble; P/G = Pebble/Gravel
N = Unoiled; L = 1 to 3 meter wide band of oil or less; M-H = >3 meter wide band of oil
KEN = Kenai Peninsula region, KOD = Kodiak Island complex, AP = Alaska Peninsula region
Samples: Sed. = Sediment; Wipe = Rock wipe; Mussel = Mussel tissue; Tox. = Sediment toxicity
Species Removals = Scrapings of Epibiota from Hard Substrata and removal of any sediment to depth of 15 cm within 25-x-25 cm quadrat (see Methods section for more detail).

*Further information on substrate types can be found in Page et al., Part 1, this volume.
**Amphipod toxicity test (Swartz et al. 1985 and Chapman and Becker 1986).

Sediment collections for amphipod toxicity tests—Sediments were collected for acute toxicity testing on the petroleum-sensitive infaunal marine amphipod *Rhepoxynius abronius*. Sediment samples were collected from 25 sites (Table 1) at various intertidal levels and stored refrigerated until tested. A portion of each sediment sample was also retained for an independent determination of grain size. No samples for sediment toxicity determinations were collected in the Gulf of Alaska region during the 1990 survey.

Field Methods–Biology

1989 surveys—A "headstake" marker was established in the approximate center of the shoreline to be sampled (Figure 4) at each site in 1989. The headstake marked the upper end of the center transect (B) of three transects (A, B, C) that were established at each site. The distance along a line from the headstake normal to the water line from the highest sessile biological assemblage (typically the barnacles *Balanus glandula* or *Semibalanus balanoides*) to the mean lower low water (MLLW) level was measured. The height of MLLW was determined from the Commercial Fishermen's Guide (1989), and corrected to the closest locality listed and the time of observation.

The linear distance from the highest biological assemblage (level B1) to MLLW was divided into four equal segments (B1-B2, B2-B3, B3-B4, B4-B5). Two additional transects (A and C) were established from 2 to10 m on either side of and parallel to the 'B' transect; the intertransect distance was determined randomly. On each of the replicate A and C transects, sampling levels 1 through 5 were established at the same intertidal height as sampling levels B1 through B5 by means of a transit or sighting level.

Percent cover observations. At each sampling level along each transect a 50-x-50 cm quadrat was established to determine percent cover of macrofauna, macroalgae, and oil. Percent cover of all macroscopic sessile organisms occupying ~1% of the substratum was estimated visually. Those organisms that were present, but that occupied <1% of the substratum, were assigned a value of 0.5%. A field check of precision among various observers estimating known areas yielded values in the range of ±10%.

Species which form a three-dimensional canopy above the substratum, such as the rockweed *Fucus*, may obscure species occurring beneath their canopy. Therefore, two different measures of percent cover ("primary" versus "tertiary" - sensu Suchanek 1979) were used in this study. "Primary" percent cover represents the area of direct attachment of an organism to the substratum. "Tertiary" percent cover is the surface area covered by the organism as viewed from above. Because various species of algae or different fronds of the same alga may lie on top of each other, tertiary percent cover may exceed 100%. In addition, although an alga may not have its holdfast within the quadrat, some of its fronds may fall within the quadrat; therefore, in some cases there may be tertiary percent cover by a species, but no primary percent cover.

Community removal samples (scrapes or cores). At sites consisting primarily of rock substrata, samples of organisms for the analysis of community parameters were removed by scraping. A 25-x-25 cm quadrat (effective internal area = 0.0625 m²) was placed within the upper (upslope) left-hand corner of the larger 50-x-50 cm quadrat (described above). All fauna, flora, and sediments were removed by scraping the rock surfaces (top and bottom if applicable) and/or by removing all sediment down to a 15-cm depth. At sites consisting primarily of fine-grained sediments, community samples were collected with a 10-cm diameter aluminum core (effective internal area = 0.0078 m^2) that was inserted into the sediment to a depth of 15-cm if possible, capturing both epibiota on the sediment surface and infauna within the sediments. Fragile animals such as juvenile barnacles or encrusting species were identified and recorded before scraping and later added to the dataset for final analysis. Since it was nearly impossible to evaluate numerical abundance of individual algae from scraped samples, statistical analyses of removal samples presented in this paper include only faunal results. Algal biomass analyses will be presented in future publications (Suchanek, in prep.).

In the Shelikof Strait region (Alaska Peninsula and Kodiak Island complex), samples were collected into plastic bags, frozen immediately, shipped, thawed within 1 year, fixed with 4% formalin for ~48 hours, and transferred to 70% ethanol. Organisms >1mm were sorted and identified to the lowest reasonable taxonomic level, usually to species. Samples heavily contaminated with oil were first washed with De-Solv-It™, a citrus-based solvent that very effectively removed oil from the samples without harming the fauna or flora.

In the Kenai region, samples from quadrat removals were bagged and fixed with 10% buffered formalin in seawater. Core samples were sieved on board ship and material >1mm was retained and fixed in a 10% buffered formalin in seawater solution. Samples were transferred to 70% ethanol for long-term storage and sorting. The different field preservation techniques used for infauna in the Kodiak/Alaska Peninsula region (freezing) and the Kenai region (formalin) did not produce any systematic errors for those fauna under consideration (down to 1 mm in size). Suchanek (1979) utilized both types of techniques and found no substantive differences in identifiability of fauna and flora.

1990 surveys—In 1990 core samples were collected at 17 of the original 35 sites, although in most cases core samples had not been taken at these sites in 1989. Field methods for this portion of the study followed those used in the Shoreline Ecology Program (see Page et al., Part 1—Study Design and Methods, this volume). Briefly, samples were collected at the upper, middle, and lower intertidal zones and at one subtidal zone (-3 meters depth). The upper intertidal station represented mean high tide, the middle intertidal represented mean tide, and the lower intertidal represented mean lower low water (MLLW). At any given tide zone, tidal elevations were identical for all three transects. For sediments in the intertidal zones, the 1-m^2 quadrat was divided into one hundred 10 cm-x-10 cm subsections. One of the subsections was selected by means of a random number table and a 10-cm diameter core was taken to a depth of 10 cm. In the subtidal, cores were taken by divers. Each core sample was sieved onboard ship into 1.0-mm and 0.5-mm fractions and preserved in formalin.

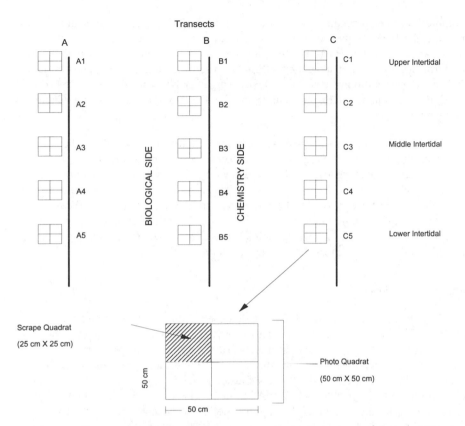

FIGURE 4—Schematic diagram of an intertidal site with transects A, B, and C in place with their associated quadrat positions.

Laboratory Methods/Analyses

Once the samples requiring chemical analysis and toxicity tests reached the laboratory they were handled in the same way as the 1990 PWS stratified-random-sampling and fixed-site samples. Sediment toxicity tests were conducted at EVS Consultants, Ltd, Vancouver, BC, using the amphipod *Rhepoxynius abronius.* Chemical analysis for polycyclic aromatic hydrocarbons (PAH) and saturate hydrocarbons were run at Arthur D. Little, Cambridge, MA.

Hydrocarbon analyses—The sediment, filter wipe, and tissue samples collected as part of this study were solvent-extracted and analyzed for saturated hydrocarbons (SHC) by gas chromatography/flame ionization detection (GC/FID), and PAH by gas chromatography/mass spectrometry (GC/MS) utilizing the same techniques established for the PWS Shoreline Ecology Program (Page et al., Shoreline Ecology Program: Part 1—Study Design and Methods, this volume; Page et al. Identificaiton of Hydrocarbon Sources, this volume; Boehm et al., Shoreline Ecology Program: Part 2—Chemistry, this volume). The one procedural difference between the 1989 and 1990 chemical analyses was that the 1989 samples were analyzed as a combined saturated and aromatic hydrocarbon extract, whereas the 1990 samples were fractionated by normal phase high performance liquid chromatography (HPLC) into separate saturated (F1) and aromatic (F2) fractions prior to instrumental analysis. Target analytes included the 2- to 6-ringed PAH analytes reported in Boehm et al. (Shoreline Ecology Program: Part 2—Chemistry, this volume).

Sediment toxicity to amphipods—Amphipod toxicity bioassays followed the methods of Swartz et al. (1985) and Chapman and Becker (1986). Sediment samples received from the field were refrigerated and bioassays were normally conducted within 2 weeks of receipt of the samples. Five replicates of 20 healthy amphipods each (obtained offshore of West Beach, Whidbey Island, Washington) were exposed for 10 days to a 2-cm bed (175 mL) of test sediment in containers with 800 mL of clean seawater. The number of live and dead (or missing) animals was determined after the 10-day exposure period and the results expressed as percentage survival.

Statistical Methods

Data management—Raw data from field observations of percent cover and laboratory counts were entered into Microsoft EXCEL (Microsoft, Inc.) spreadsheet tables. These data were checked completely (100%) against those from original field data sheets by personnel other than those who had entered the data into the database. Once the files passed the 100% check, they were subjected to a Continuous Sampling Procedure (CSP-1) at the Average Quality Level (AQL) of 1% (Hanson 1963). If more than five errors were detected during CSP-1 sampling, the 100% check was repeated, then followed by a second CSP-1 check.

Using the individual species counts from the scrape and core removal samples we calculated (1) organism abundance (total number of individuals per sample), (2) species richness (total number of species per sample), and (3) Shannon diversity using log to base 2 (Shannon 1948; Shannon and Weaver 1949).

Statistical analyses for 1989 data—Two types of statistical analyses were carried out: (1) one-way statistical modeling of community parameter variables and percent cover and (2) regression modeling of these same variables. In both models, the objective was to assess the impact of oil on the biological variables of interest.

These two analytical approaches are different because of the methods of "measuring" oiling levels. In the first approach, oiling is categorized according to the shoreline survey team's oiling designations— none, light, and moderate-heavy—which means the biological variables are modeled in terms of a single oiling factor. In the second approach, percentage oiling is determined by visual inspection. The resulting "numeric" variable leads to the modeling of the biological variables in terms of a single oiling predictor variable.

The biological variables of interest are percent cover (primary and tertiary), species abundance, species richness, and Shannon diversity as overall community parameter variables. None of these variables were transformed except primary biological cover. This variable was truncated at 100% (because values greater than 100% represent measurement error), converted to a proportion, and transformed by the arcsine of the square root of the proportions. Abundances and percent covers of individual species were not analyzed.

One-way analysis. Both parametric (ANOVA) and nonparametric (Kruskal-Wallis) one-way models were run to test the oiling effect on percent cover and community parameter variables. However, the results presented in Figures 10-12 are based on the Kruskal-Wallis one-way tests because the distributional properties of the response variables were not extensively checked. In essence, the biological variables were subjected to a rank transform prior to analysis. As described below, the transect was always used as the "replication" unit for the Kruskal-Wallis models. On the other hand, both site and transect were used as replication units for the ANOVA models. Table 2 gives the number of replicate sites and transect samples for each tide zone within each habitat type and type of sample (core, scrape, or % cover).

Follow-up tests were conducted to determine whether light and/or moderate-heavy oiling differed significantly from the unoiled category. Dunnett's test for comparing treatments to a control was run subsequent to the ANOVA, whether or not the overall test was significant. As a follow-up to the Kruskal-Wallis test, individual Mann-Whitney tests compared light oiling to none and moderate-heavy oiling to unoiled. These tests were not modified to control the overall probability of incorrectly rejecting the null hypothesis (i.e., they do not represent multiple comparisons). As a consequence, the resulting Mann-Whitney tests are more likely to find significant evidence of oiling when no effect is present than the nominal significance level of 0.05. In fact, 13 Mann-Whitney differences were found in comparison with only 4 Dunnett differences. The results in Figures 10-12 are given in terms of the Mann-Whitney tests.

Regression analysis. Linear regression models were run to test the effect of "visible oil" cover on the biological variables. These response variables were untransformed except for primary biology percent cover as described above. The null hypothesis, that the slope parameter is zero, was tested by the standard t-test.

Detection of Oiling Effects. The Gulf of Alaska studies used transects that were typically only a few meters apart. As a consequence, transect-to-transect variability tested significantly less than site-to-site variability 67% of the time. In such cases, the more appropriate source of variability to use as an error term in statistical models is site-to-site variability. This model is termed the "site" model.

In contrast, the Prince William Sound Shoreline Ecology Program: Part 3—Biology (Gilfillan et al., this volume) found that a "transect" model, which used transect-to-transect variability, was usually more appropriate for Prince William Sound data. In that study, the site model was statistically indistinguishable from the transect model 80 percent of the time. The difference between the Gulf of Alaska and Prince William Sound models arises because the transects in the Prince William Sound program were purposefully set further apart than in the Gulf of Alaska study.

Table 2—The number of replicate sites and transect samples collected in 1989 for each type of sample within each habitat and oiling level. Replicate sites and biological samples are given in the following order: (UI-Upper Intertidal; MI-Middle Intertidal; LI-Lower Intertidal).

| | 1989 Oiling Level | | | |
	None	Low	Med-High	Totals
Cores: Pebble/Gravel				
Sites	(1;2;2)	(1;1;1)	(2;3;3)	(4;6;6)
Samples	(3;6;6)	(3;3;2)	(5;9;9)	(11;18;17)
Cores: Boulder/Cobble				
Sites	(0;1;1)	(0;2;2)	(0;1;1)	(0;4;4)
Samples	(0;3;3)	(0;6;6)	(0;3;3)	(0;12;12)
Scrapes: Boulder/Cobble				
Sites	(3;2;2)	(2;2;2)	(3;2;2)	(8;6;6)
Samples	(9;6;6)	(6;6;6)	(9;6;6)	(24;18;18)
Scrapes: Rock				
Sites	(3;3;2)	(2;2;2)	(2;2;2)	(7;7;6)
Samples	(9;7;5)	(6;5;6)	(6;6;6)	(21;18;17)
% Cover: Boulder/Cobble				
Sites	(3;3;3)	(5;5;4)	(3;2;2)	(11;10;9)
Samples	(12;9;9)	(13;13;11)	(9;6;6)	(34;28;26)
% Cover: Rock				
Sites	(3;3;2)	(6;6;5)	(3;3;2)	(12;12;9)
Samples	(9;9;6)	(17;16;14)	(9;9;6)	(35;34;26)

The use of the site model for the Gulf of Alaska studies means that the chance of detecting an oiling effect was small (unless the effect was large) because relatively few sites were sampled, particularly for certain substrates (Table 2). There are several ways of increasing the probability of detecting oiling impacts: increasing the sample size; reducing error variability by matching sites; removing variability by accounting for concomitant variables; increasing the significance level; and pooling error terms.

Each of these will now be discussed. Increasing the number of study sites is not possible since each site required a full day for collecting biological and chemical data and only a limited number of days were available due to the extensive monitoring program conducted in Prince William Sound. Matching oiled to reference sites cannot be done accurately unless data are available from extensive surveys prior to the specification of the sampling design (which was not the case for these shorelines). Concomitant variables —e.g., grain size and TOC—were not included in the models for 1989 data since they were not collected at all sites in 1989. Therefore, variability associated with the concomitant variables will be part of the unexplained variability for the 1989 data. Only the latter two options, increasing the significance level and pooling (i.e., using the pooled site-to-site and transect-to-transect variability as an error term), were available to us in analyzing the 1989 data. We chose the latter.

Thus, our analysis strategy for the Gulf of Alaska data was two pronged. First, we took a rigorous approach which utilized the site model. Second, we increased the chances of detecting oiling impacts in this limited set of data by using the transect model—even at the risk of attributing to oiling apparent effects that did not result from oiling. Results of both models are presented.

The practical consequence of using the transect model was to increase the probability of detecting apparent oiling effects (power) since the sample size was effectively tripled (Table 2) and the error variability generally was reduced. Technically, the transects are not true replicates—Hurlbert (1984) calls them pseudo-replicates. However, using transects has the same effect on power as using the site model with a higher significance level. A disadvantage of using the transect model is the increased likelihood that an effect attributed to oiling is actually related to other factors. The rationale and implications of pooling are discussed further in Shoreline Ecology Program: Part 3— Biology (Gilfillan et al., this volume). Both the site and transect models were run using normal theory approaches for community parameters such as total abundance; only the transect model was used for the non-parametric approach. The site model has two error terms (i.e., site error and transect error) and hence is not amendable to non-parametric analyses.

Statistical analyses of 1990 core data—Community structure parameters, organism abundance, species richness, and Shannon diversity (Shannon 1948; Shannon and Weaver 1949) derived from the 1990 core data were analyzed using ANCOVA and the same analysis protocols for the 1990 and 1991 Shoreline Ecology Program (SEP) data from Prince William Sound. The null hypothesis of no oiling effect was tested using models that adjusted the means for important environmental parameters (concomitant variables: percent sand, percent silt/clay, and TOC). The oiling effect of any biological variable (organism abundance, species richness, or Shannon diversity) was tested using differences between adjusted means.

Two different models were used, the goal being to use a model that satisfied the appropriate statistical assumptions and had high power to detect differences. First a "site" model that used among-site variability as an error term was run to test oiling effects. Using the same model, among-site variability was compared to within-site (transect) variability. If among-site variability was not significantly greater than within-site variability, a "transect" model was run in which the two error terms were pooled into a single term. Oiling effects were then tested against this new error term. The transect model almost always had greater power to detect differences due to oiling and was used when appropriate.

Testing for oiling effects was first done with normal theory methods. If the residuals from this model were not distributed normally (based on Shapiro-Wilks test; $P < 0.05$), non-normal theory methods were employed.

Normal theory testing was carried out using one-way analysis of covariance (ANCOVA) with oiling level as a factor (SuperANOVA, Abacus Concepts). The significance test for oiling differences was carried out using Dunnett's two-tailed test to test for differences between each of the two oiling levels (light and moderate-to-heavy) and unoiled sites.

Non-normal theory analyses were carried out with the General Linear Interactive Model (GLIM: Numerical Algorithms Group, Inc.). This method is analogous to ANCOVA, but data were tested using Poisson, binomial, or negative binomial distributions. The approach was to first run GLIM to fit a model assuming a Poisson error distribution. If the fit to the Poisson model was unacceptable ($P < 0.05$) and the data were under-dispersed (finding one of a species in a sample makes it less likely to find another), a binomial model was used. If the data were over-dispersed (finding one of a species in a sample makes it more likely to find another), a negative binomial model was used.

RESULTS

Chemistry

Oiling levels—Hydrocarbon concentrations in GOA intertidal sediments were substantially lower than those in Prince William Sound. Figure 5A shows the geometric mean concentrations of polycyclic aromatic hydrocarbons (PAH), the hydrocarbons of most concern, in 1989 by tide zone for Prince William Sound, Kenai, and Kodiak Island/Alaska Peninsula. The highest mean concentrations were found at the splash and upper intertidal zones—zones that naturally contain the fewest biota. Consequently, the maximum degree of oiling did not coincide with the most biologically abundant and productive tide zone, the lower intertidal zone.

In at least two instances (upper and middle intertidal of Tonsina Bay), the levels of oil reported at a site in 1989 was less than that measured at the same site in 1990. In both cases the 1989 data represents one sample in each tide zone. It is possible that due to the patchiness of the oil at many sites in 1989, that little oil was collected in these two samples. It is also possible that there was some movement of the oil on the shoreline subsequent to sampling in 1989.

Oil patchiness—Oiling levels were very uneven (i.e., patchy) along the GOA shorelines. This variability can be observed in the PAH data provided in Table 3 . The typical variability of total PAH (TPAH), as measured by the coefficient of variation of geometric means (defined as the standard deviation times 100 divided by the mean), is shown in Figure 5B for various tide zones. Higher values of this coefficient indicate greater variability or patchiness. On this basis, oiling on GOA shorelines exhibited substantially greater patchiness than on PWS shorelines.

Visible oil—In some cases, the only individual oiling estimates that were obtained on a quadrat-by-quadrat basis were visually estimated oiling levels, termed "visible oil." For some of these quadrats, coincident rock wipe samples were also collected from that half of the sample quadrat used for chemistry, and total PAH was measured for these

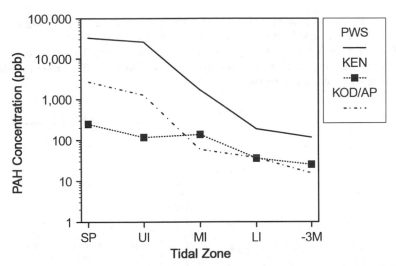

FIGURE 5A—Average 1989 TPAH concentrations (geometric means) for oiled sites in PWS and the GOA region. (Tidal zonation definitions: SP-Splash Zone, UI-Upper Intertidal, MI-Middle Intertidal, LI-Lower Intertidal, -3m shallow subtidal three meters below zero tidal datum; Location: PWS-Prince William Sound, KEN-Kenai Peninsula, KOD/AP-Kodiak Island complex/Alaska Peninsula)

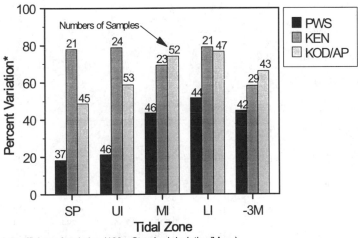

* Coefficient of variation (100 x Standard deviation/Mean)
  for Geometric Means of Total PAH

FIGURE 5B—The percent variation in the 1989 TPAH concentrations for Prince William Sound and the Gulf of Alaska region.

TABLE 3—Chemically measured TPAH by site, tide zone, and 1989 oiling levels (from shoreline surveys) in the GOA region. UI = Upper Intertidal, MI = Middle Intertidal, LI = Lower Intertidal, -3m = subtidal samples from 3 meters below zero tidal datum. Reported values are geometric means. The overall average coefficient of variation was 70% (ranging from 44 to 115%).

Site	Habitat	1989 Oiling Level	Year	UI	MI	LI	-3m
Kenai							
Gore Point (GCM01)	P/G	Moderate	1989	25	112	2	14
			1990	4	4	0	12
Rocky Bay (RBR01)	SB	Light	1989	3	22	- -	35
			1990	2	0	- -	0
Tonsina Bay (TBC01)	P/G	Moderate	1989	2	11	100	76
			1990	72 138	54 026	231	42
West Arm (WAC01)	P/G	Light	1989	1 849	18 520	268	3
			1990	50	1 934	67	1
Windy Bay (WBC01)	P/G	Heavy	1989	10 667	2 428	96	23
			1990	703	243	43	13
Kodiak/Alaska Peninsula							
Alinchak Bay (ALM01)	SB	Light	1989	- -	- -	- -	- -
			1990	2 463	1 178	479	37
Cape Douglas (CDR01)	B/C	Moderate	1989	301 231	14	0	3
			1990	9 818	149	35	11
Chief Point (CFR01)	SB	Light	1989	169	16	332	203
			1990	- -	33	8	21
Chief Point, Egg Island (CFR	B/C	Heavy	1989	650 286	364	8	7
			1990	21	208	3	6
Cape Gull South (CGM01)	B/C	None	1989	1	4	1	4
			1990	7	9	18	24
Cape Chiniak (CHS01)	P/G	Light	1989	193	6	8	- -
			1990	34	29	2	4
Foul Bay (FOR01)	SB	None	1989	- -	- -	- -	1
			1990	1	2	1	2
Foul Bay (FOS01)	P/G	None	1989	2	2	2	- -
			1990	0	0	1	1
Cape Gull North (GUM01)	B/C	Light	1989	4 537	497	109	196
			1990	192	171	92	227
Cape Nuniliak (NUR01)	SB	Light	1989	- -	- -	- -	- -
			1990	- -	- -	- -	0
Perevalnie Passage (PPR01)	SB	Heavy	1989	36 566	953	280	19
			1990	25 564	294	214	65
Perevalnie Passage (PPS01)	P/G	Heavy	1989	74	23	122	32
			1990	119	19	402	178
Spiridon Bay (SPR01)	P/G	None	1989	- -	- -	- -	- -
			1990	8	2	2	2

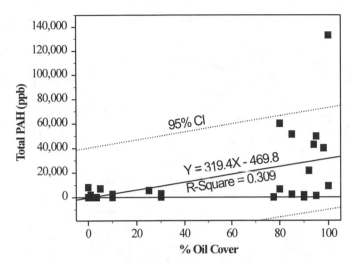

FIGURE 6—Percent cover of "visible oil" estimated in the field (from 0.5 x 0.5 m quadrats) versus chemically analyzed wipe TPAH samples from bedrock sites in 1989. Dashed lines represent the 95% confidence interval for individual predictions.

samples. The relationship between these two measures of oiling is presented in Figure 6 for 48 wipe samples from rocky substrata in the Kodiak/Alaska Peninsula region.

The highest TPAH corresponds to the highest percent oil cover, but there is considerable variability. This variability is perhaps not surprising, given the patchiness and variability of the oiling itself. The relationship is significant ($P = 0.00001$; $R^2 = 0.31$). Figure 6 gives the mean prediction line of best fit and the corresponding 95% individual prediction bands. If the single outlier at about 135 000 ppb is removed, a better fit is realized ($R^2 = 0.35$). Although these tests are highly significant, the correlations are not high. However, the graphs do suggest that stronger relationships could be found if chemical measurements were made on the same quadrats as visible oil.

Oil weathering—With time, oil exposed to the environment loses some of its more toxic constituents by dissolution, vaporization, and biodegradation. This process is called weathering. Generally speaking, the more weathered oil is, the less impact it will have on biota.

The degree of weathering of oil or oiled sediment can be ascertained from the amount of naphthalenes it contains relative to other PAH compounds. Naphthalenes are the lightest, most-soluble portion of the PAH. Consequently, the naphthalenes disappear from oil more quickly than other PAH compounds, and the extent of their disappearance is an indication of the degree of weathering. In particular, the C_2 through C_4 naphthalenes are most useful for this purpose, since they can serve as reliable indicators of petrogenic hydrocarbons.

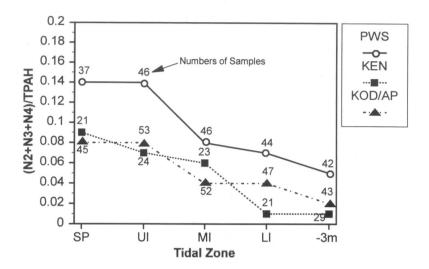

FIGURE 7A—Ratio of the C_2-C_4 naphthalenes/TPAH in 1989 sediment for PWS and the Gulf of Alaska region. (Tidal zonation definitions: SP-Splash Zone, UI-Upper Intertidal, MI-Middle Intertidal, LI-Lower Intertidal, -3m shallow subtidal three meters below zero tidal datum; Location: PWS-Prince William Sound, KEN-Kenai Peninsula, KOD/AP-Kodiak Island complex/Alaska Peninsula)

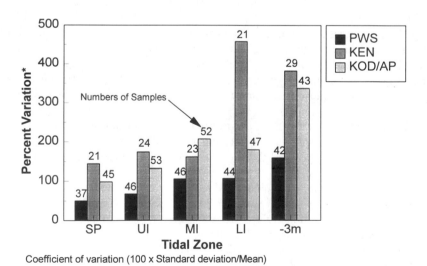

Coefficient of variation (100 x Standard deviation/Mean)

FIGURE 7B—The percent variation in the C_2-C_4 naphthalenes/TPAH ratio for sediment in the PWS and the Gulf of Alaska region in 1989

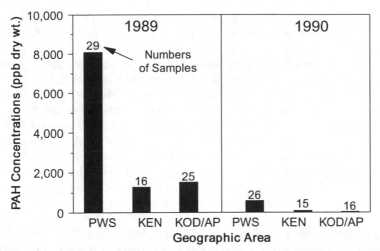

FIGURE 8A—TPAH concentrations in mussel tissue from oiled sites in PWS and the Gulf of Alaska region; 1989 vs. 1990. (Location: PWS-Prince William Sound, KEN-Kenai Peninsula, KOD/AP-Kodiak Island complex/Alaska Peninsula)

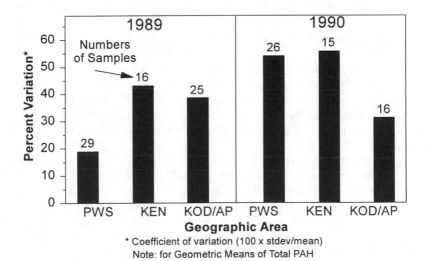

FIGURE 8B—The percent variation in TPAH concentrations in mussel tissue from oiled sites in PWS and the Gulf of Alaska region; 1989 vs. 1990.

The naphthalene content of shoreline sediment indicates that oil found along GOA shorelines was typically more weathered than that on PWS shorelines. Relative to other PAH compounds, lower levels of naphthalenes were present in GOA sediment than in PWS sediment. The relative weathering state of oil found at different tidal heights in PWS, the Kenai Peninsula, and the Kodiak/Alaskan Peninsula regions in the fall of 1989, as represented by the ratio of C_2-C_4 naphthalene/TPAH, is shown in Figure 7A. This figure shows that the PWS oil was less weathered than that in the other regions. Kodiak/Alaskan Peninsula sites and Kenai sites exhibited a similar weathering state of the oil on the shorelines. Mousse samples taken from PWS and GOA in April and May 1989 (Boehm, unpublished data) showed that the floating oil within PWS was less weathered than the oil in the GOA. Furthermore, the extent and variability of weathering, as shown in Figures 7A and 7B, increases at the lower tide zones, owing not only to lower initial oiling levels, but also to increased dissolution.

Bioavailability—Hydrocarbon analyses of mussel (*Mytilus sp.*) tissues are widely used to monitor "bioavailability" of oil residues to other biota. However, one must be careful when interpreting such data because hydrocarbons that are "bioavailable" to mussels are not necessarily "bioavailable" to all organisms. Mussels are filter feeders, processing large volumes of water hourly for food. By retaining free oil droplets or oiled sediment particles from the water or incorporating dissolved hydrocarbons into their tissue, mussels can concentrate analytes that occur at levels too low to measure in the water column.

In the late summer of 1989, TPAH levels in mussels in PWS were nearly 5 times higher than mussels in the Gulf of Alaska region (Figure 8A). The mean TPAH concentration in mussel tissue in all three areas parallels the trends measured for sediment TPAH concentrations. In both cases, lower concentrations of TPAH were reported at Kenai sites compared with the other locations (Figure 5A). Variability of mussel tissue TPAH measurements was higher in both the Kenai and Kodiak/Alaska Peninsula areas (Figure 8B), reflecting the patchy distribution of oil on the GOA shorelines in 1989 (Figure 5B).

A comparison of the TPAH levels observed in 1990 with those observed in 1989 (Figure 8A) indicate a marked decrease in the mussel TPAH values in all regions. These results indicate that even though the TPAH in intertidal sediment was still elevated compared with reference levels in 1990 (Table 3), the bioavailability (to epifaunal mussels) of the residual TPAH was much lower in 1990, suggesting that what remained in the sediment in 1990 was for the most part not generally available to filter-feeding bivalves and other epifauna immediately above those sediments.

Sediment toxicity—Sediment bioassays were conducted using the petroleum-sensitive infaunal marine amphipod *Rhepoxynius abronius* as the test species. Figure 9 shows the results of such bioassays on GOA and PWS sediments, both from 1989. Results are averaged over all sites by tide zone and region. GOA sediments are, on average, much less toxic than oiled PWS sediments. The differences between the means of percent mortality values for unoiled GOA sites and oiled GOA sites in each tide zone were tested for significance ($P = 0.05$) using Wilcoxon's/Kruskal-Wallace Rank Sums Test. None of the differences between oiled and unoiled means in the GOA sites were statistically significant.

BIOLOGY

1989 data (using shoreline survey team oiling designations)—The 1989 intertidal biological data presented here were analyzed for impacts using the oiling designations (none, light, moderate-high) referenced in Neff et al. (this volume) on a site-by-site basis. These results fall primarily into two categories: (1) biological percent cover data (for organisms covering more than 1% of the substratum) and (2) community data from scrape removals or cores (for organisms ≥ 1mm in size).

The results presented below are for the transect model. The site model was also run, but no significant differences were found for either percent cover or the community parameter variables.

Percent cover. In 1989 there were statistically significant decreases in biological cover with increasing oil. In the mid-intertidal zone, primary and tertiary biological cover were significantly reduced (compared with nonoiled reference sites) at rocky sites with moderate-heavy oiling, but not at sites with only light oiling (Figure 10A, B). No significant reductions were observed at boulder/cobble sites (Figure 10C, D).

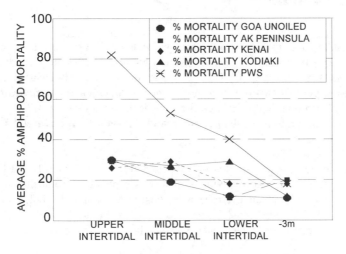

TIDE ZONE

FIGURE 9—Regional comparison of sediment toxicity values averaged over sites for intertidal and subtidal tide zones in 1989. The differences between the means for sediment from GOA unoiled sites and oiled values in each site were tested for significance ($P = 0.05$) using Wilcoxon's/Kruskal-Wallace Rank Sums Test. None of the GOA results were significantly different from controls.

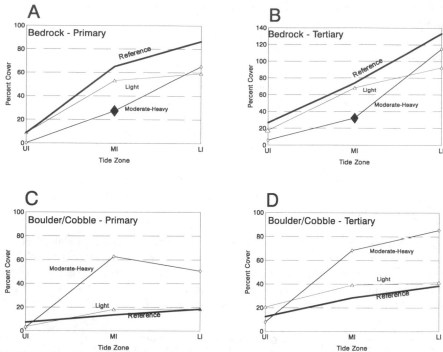

FIGURE 10—Percent cover (primary and tertiary) for bedrock and boulder/cobble habitats. (A) Primary cover on bedrock. (B) Tertiary cover on bedrock. (C) Primary cover on boulder/cobble substrata. (D) Tertiary cover on boulder/cobble substrata. Comparisons of each percent cover at different oiling levels which are statistically different ($P < 0.05$) from nonoiled reference sites are designated by large filled symbols. (Tidal zone definitions: UI-Upper Intertidal, MI-Middle Intertidal, LI-Lower Intertidal)

Community parameters. With respect to faunal abundance (Figures 11A, B and 12A, B top), significant differences (compared with unoiled sites) were observed at sites with moderate to heavy oiling. Significant decreases were observed in boulder/cobble cores (Figure 12A, MI and LI) and bedrock species removal samples (Figure 11A, MI). A significant increase in organism abundance was observed in pebble/gravel (Figure 12B, LI).

Species richness (Figures 11C, D and 12C, D middle) was variably affected by oiling. No significant differences from unoiled sites were observed in species removal samples from bedrock sites (Figure 11C). A significant increase in species richness was observed with light oiling in boulder/cobble species removal samples (Figure 11D, MI). In core samples there were significant decreases with moderate-heavy oiling at boulder/cobble sites (Figure 12C, LI) and with light oiling at pebble/gravel sites (Figure 12D, UI).

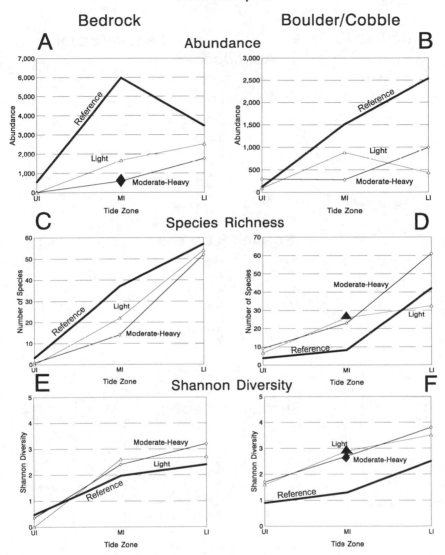

FIGURE 11—Community parameters (abundance, species richness, and Shannon diversity) shown as a function of oiling for scrape removal samples. Comparisons of each community parameter variable at different oiling levels which are statistically different (*P* < 0.05) from nonoiled reference sites are designated by large filled symbols. (Tidal Zone definitions: UI-Upper Intertidal, MI-Middle Intertidal, LI-Lower Intertidal.)

1989 Cores

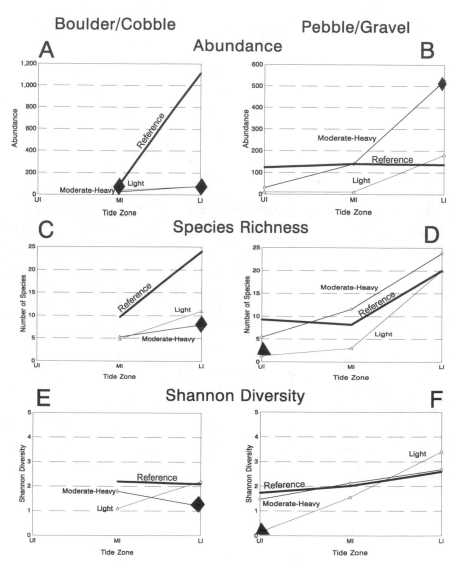

FIGURE 12—Community parameters (abundance, species richness, and Shannon diversity) shown as a function of oiling for core removal samples. Comparisons of each community parameter at different oiling levels which are statistically different (*P* < 0.05) from nonoiled reference sites are designated by filled symbols; nonsignificant differences are designated by open symbols. (Tidal Zone definitions: UI-Uppter Intertidal, MI-Middle Intertidal, LI-Lower Intertidal)

Shannon diversity (Figures 11E, F and 12E, F bottom) indicated that the responses to oiling were opposite in species removal and core samples. In boulder/cobble species, removal sample diversity was significantly increased with both light and moderate-heavy oiling (Figure 11F, MI). In core samples there were significant reductions in diversity in boulder/cobble with moderate-heavy oiling (Figure 12E, LI) and in pebble/gravel with light oiling (Figure 12F, UI).

1989 data (using "visible oil" designations)—The results presented above relate to qualitative oiling analyses, conducted on a site-by-site basis using the shoreline survey team oiling designations (Neff et al., this volume). Because of the patchiness of oil distribution on GOA shorelines, oiling estimates determined on a quadrat-by quatrat basis may reveal more of the within-site variability in the response of intertidal communities to oil. The "visible oil" determinations (see Methods) meet this criterion. However, relatively few samples had high values for "visible oil." Most had very low or zero values; there were very few with intermediate values. Many of the resulting regressions depended on samples from a small number of locations.

Linear regression of biological parameters (percent cover, abundance, species richness, and Shannon diversity) against percent cover of "visible oil" on a quadrat-by-quadrat basis were carried out. These results show trends in the data that were similar to analyses using site level oiling designations (as opposed to quadrat-by-quadrat oiling designations), with somewhat greater statistical significance. Primary and tertiary percentage biological cover on boulder/cobble substrata showed consistent decreasing trends with increasing percent cover of "visible oil" for the upper intertidal (i.e., tidal levels 1 and 2— see Figure 4), but none were statistically significant (at $P = 0.05$). Biological cover on solid rock substrata, however, showed a much stronger negative relationship to oiling than on boulder/cobble substrata; these negative trends extended down to intertidal level 4 for both primary and tertiary biological cover. On rock surfaces, there were statistically significant ($P < 0.05$) declines in biological cover at intertidal levels 1 and 2, nearly significant ($0.05 < P < 0.10$) declines at level 3, a clearly nonsignificant relationship at level 4, and no oiling seen at level 5.

For linear regression analyses of organism abundance, species richness, and Shannon diversity for scrape samples, there were more variable results. In general, there were negative trends for both organism abundance and species richness, with increasing visible oil on rock substrata but not for boulder/cobble substrata. The only statistically significant ($P < 0.05$) results, however, were those for both organism abundance and species richness at intertidal level 3. Shannon diversity showed no meaningful trends (some were negative, some positive).

Comparable linear regression analyses of core samples also showed decreasing trends in organism abundance and species richness (but not Shannon diversity) with increasing "visible oil" for pebble/gravel sites, but there were insufficient core samples to analyze boulder/cobble sites in this fashion. Despite these negative trends, none of the comparisons were statistically significant.

1990 core data—The site model was appropriate for all variables, as would be expected when the transects were much closer together than in the PWS SEP study (Page

et al., Shoreline Ecology Program: Part 1—Study Design and Methods, this volume).
The negative binomial distribution was appropriate for organism abundance from the
middle intertidal, lower intertidal, and -3m; normal-theory models were used for all other
analyses.

Figure 13 shows mean values for abundance, species richness, and Shannon diversity as
a function of tide zone for sites having heavy, moderate, light, and no oil. Examination
revealed that the sediments sampled in boulder/cobble and pebble/gravel habitats

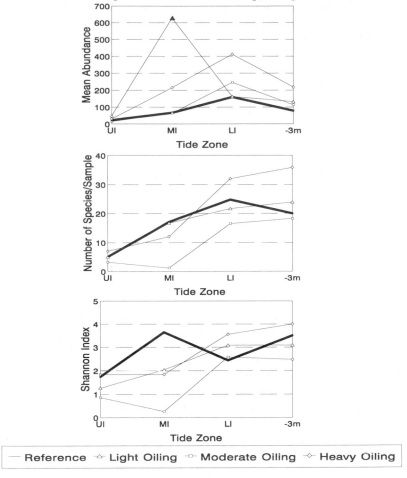

FIGURE 13—Summary of 1990 ecological community parameters for sediment
cores collected at boulder/cobble and pebble/gravel habitats (total abundance,
species richness, and Shannon diversity). Tidal zone definitions: UI-Upper
Intertidal, MI-Middle Intertidal, LI-Lower Intertidal, -3m- Shallow subtidal three
meters below zero tidal datum.

had similar grainsize distributions. As a result, data for these two habitats were combined. Significant differences are seen only for abundance where mean abundance in the middle intertidal zone of lightly oiled sites is greater than that found at reference sites. There is a tendency for abundance to be greater at oiled sites (11 of 12 means exceed reference means). There is no clear trend for species richness or Shannon diversity (5 of 12 means exceed reference; 7 of 12 means are less than reference).

DISCUSSION

The shoreline ecology program carried out in the GOA in both 1989 and 1990 was much smaller in scope than the work carried out in PWS at the same time. Study sites in the GOA were not chosen randomly, but were chosen to represent a complete range of both oiling conditions and habitat types. Hence, the GOA shoreline ecology program does not provide a basis for projecting results at the sampling locations to the GOA as a whole. However, the work was intended to assess the range of shoreline impacts in this region and to serve as a basis for comparison with PWS.

Chemistry

Sediments—The oil that exited PWS in early April 1989 was transported to the GOA and deposited along this very rugged and high-energy coastline from April through early May 1989. The oil that impacted most of the GOA shorelines was different in chemical composition and physical characteristics from the oil that impacted most of PWS. The weathering of the oil, which resulted in the loss of volatile constituents and significant portions of the two-ringed (more toxic) aromatic hydrocarbons, occurred while the oil was at sea during transport to the Kodiak/Alaskan Peninsula region.

When we compared *Exxon Valdez* cargo oil with "typical" samples collected from the waters of PWS and in the GOA area, we observed an extensive, but not complete, loss of the two-ringed aromatics (naphthalenes) in the GOA oil samples. After being deposited on the shoreline in April/May 1989, the oil was weathered extensively between May and August 1989 (Boehm, unpublished data). The extent of weathering was greatly accelerated after landfall, where the surface-area-to-volume ratio was increased by the spreading of the oil on the shoreline. The weathering of the oil deposited on the shoreline included biodegradation as well as the continued loss of the more volatile components.

The nature of the shoreline oiling in the GOA was also quite different from that in PWS, in that the oiling was much patchier in the GOA, as evidenced by the less-continuous shoreline oiling and localized distribution of oil within the study sites.

Mussels—Oil did remain in the GOA shoreline sediment in 1990; however, the oil was markedly less bioavailable as evidenced by the mussel body burdens. Due to the high energy of many of the oiled sites, the levels of shoreline oil residue are expected to have decreased even more rapidly than in Prince William Sound (Boehm et al., Shoreline Ecology Program: Part 2—Chemistry, this volume). The expectation is that the GOA intertidal sediments were almost completely cleaned by natural processes by 1991. Any small patches of oil residues remaining would be highly degraded and largely unavailable to marine organisms.

While *Exxon Valdez* crude oil residues were detected in the GOA subtidal sediments, there was no evidence of large-scale offshore transport and resulting deposition into the subtidal sediments. The oil that was removed from the shoreline as a result of the enormous physical energy experienced by the coastline was most probably dispersed in the water and degraded by natural processes. Overall, compared with the PWS sites, the hydrocarbon residues present in the GOA sediments and mussel tissues were significantly lower, more weathered, and much less uniform.

Sediment toxicology—Because it is possible to measure PAH at levels far below those associated with sublethal toxic effects, sediment bioassay measurements are needed to determine whether petroleum residues are acting as a toxicant or a carbon source. In fact, biological studies for PWS (Gilfillan et al., Shoreline Ecology Program: Part 3—Biology, this volume) indicate that petroleum residues that no longer exert a toxic effect, represent a carbon (food) source for marine biota, as is consistent with other studies (Spies et al. 1988). The fact that the overall means of the 1989 sediment bioassay results for GOA oiled sites were not significantly different from those of unoiled sites (Figures 2 and 3) indicates that, except for some heavily impacted isolated locations, the acute effects of the spill in the GOA were much less than those for PWS. The differences are a result of the progressive weathering and loss of toxic components of EVOS oil floating on the sea surface during the transit from PWS to the GOA sites. Results obtained for sediment toxicology in GOA are consistent with the biology results presented here for GOA and elsewhere for PWS (Gilfillan et al., Shoreline Ecology Program: Part 3—Biology, this volume).

In general measured PAH levels in the 1990 GOA sediment samples are well below those conservatively associated with adverse effects. Of the 248 individual sediment samples taken from GOA sites in 1990, only 16 exceeded the proposed sediment toxicity threshold value of 4 000 ppb for total PAH (Long and Morgan 1990). One of these 16 samples was a subtidal sample that consisted almost entirely of pyrogenic PAH not related to the spilled oil (Page et al., Shoreline Ecology Program: Part 1—Study Design and Methods, this volume).

Biology

1989 percent cover data—No matter which measures of oiling were used, i.e., shoreline survey team site oiling designations, "visible oil," or TPAH, the overall results were fairly consistent. The greatest oil impacts on both primary and tertiary biological cover were realized in the upper intertidal, typically from the mid (level 3) to upper (level 1) zones. Furthermore, these effects were more noticeable at rocky sites as compared with boulder/cobble sites. The most pronounced effects were documented for comparisons of percent cover as a function of "visible oil" with statistically significant decreasing trends of both primary and tertiary biological cover being documented down to intertidal level 2 (upper mid zone), trends that are close to significance at level 3 (mid zone), and nonsignificant but decreasing trends down to level 4 (lower mid zone).

1989 community structure parameters—Community structure parameters did not exhibit the level of demonstrable negative impacts found for biological cover (above). Of all the community structure parameters, organism abundance, species richness, and Shannon diversity, only the first two showed any significant response to oiling. Organism abundance, nearly without exception, exhibited consistent declines with increased oiling. Statistically significant declines in organism abundance were observed typically for sites exposed to moderate-heavy oiling (shoreline survey team oiling designations) or on more solid substrata such as rock or boulder/cobble as opposed to unconsolidated pebble/gravel substrata. On rocky shores this decline in organism abundance was statistically significant down to level 3 (only for analyses using "visible oil"), but for boulder/cobble sites (using shoreline survey team designations) it was significant down to level 5 (low intertidal zone).

Species richness was nearly, but not quite, as affected as organism abundance by increased oiling levels. Consistent trends of declining species richness with increasing oil were evident at rocky sites, but not at boulder/cobble or pebble/gravel sites. Only a few analyses of declining trends (e.g., scrape samples from level 3 at rock sites and core samples from level 5 at boulder/cobble sites) were statistically significant.

Shannon diversity showed variable responses to increasing levels of oil and in various cases exhibited increased or decreased diversity, and these trends were sometimes statistically significant.

1990 core data (community parameters only)—Results of ANOVA of samples taken in the summer of 1990 showed only one significant relationship between initial oiling and abundance, which was significantly higher in the middle intertidal zone of lightly oiled sites than at unoiled sites.

Similar increases in abundance were observed at some oiled sedimentary sites in PWS. It is likely that the same process, increased food availability as a result of bacterial metabolism of weathered oil, is responsible for the observed increase in abundance in the GOA region. There was much less oil in the GOA region; as a result the observed effect is less than in PWS.

CONCLUSIONS

- EVOS oil entering the GOA region was much more highly weathered than oil in PWS. It continued to weather extensively after being deposited on the shoreline.

- The distribution of oil deposited on the shoreline was very patchy; oil distribution on beaches was characterized by patches of oil separated by areas with very little oil. During the summer of 1989, mean PAH concentrations were 10- to 100-fold lower than in PWS.

- There was no evidence of large-scale offshore movement of oil deposited on the shoreline into nearshore subtidal sediment.

- Oil remaining on the shoreline in 1990 was not very bioavailable to epifauna; mussel tissue concentrations were near background levels.

- Sediment toxicology studies in 1989 showed that the sediment samples in the GOA region were essentially nontoxic to test organisms. None of the differences between oiled and unoiled sites in the GOA were statistically significant.

- In decreasing order of statistical significance, stranded oil had negative effects on biological cover, organism abundance, and species richness. The greatest negative impacts were realized at rocky sites and boulder/cobble sites and tended to be more concentrated in the mid to upper intertidal zone.

- In the summer of 1990 a significantly higher abundance was observed in the middle intertidal zone of lightly oiled sites (as compared with unoiled areas). This is similar to the situation observed in PWS in which oil-metabolizing bacteria became food for animals.

ACKNOWLEDGMENTS

This study was supported by Exxon Company, U.S.A. We acknowledge the participation of Cecile Krejsa and Nicole Maher of Bowdoin College; Bob Cimberg; Lane Cameron and others of Dames and Moore, Inc; Tony Parkin, Sandra Tate and others of Authur D. Little, Inc; Keith Parker of Data Analysis Group.

REFERENCES

Anderson J. W., S.L. Fiesser, D.L. McQuerry, R.G. Riley, and M.L. Fleischman. "Toxicity Testing With Constant Or Diluting Concentrations Of Chemically Dispersed Oil." *In: Oil Spill Chemical Dispersants.* T. E. Allen (ed.) ASTM Special Technical Publication 840. ASTM PNC 04-840000-24, Philadelphia, PA; 1984.

Anderson, J.W., R. S. Kiesser, and J. Gurtisen. "Toxicity Of Dispersed And Undispersed Prudhoe Bay Crude Oil Fractions To Shrimp And Fish." *In: Proceedings 1987 Oil Spill Conference, Washington, DC American Petroleum Institute.* pp 235-240; 1987.

Bonsdorf, E. and W. G. Nelson. "Fate and Effects of Ekofisk Crude Oil in the Littoral of a Norwegian Fjord." *Sarsia.* 66:231-240; 1981.

Chan, G. L. "A Study of the Effects of the San Francisco Oil Spill on Marine Life. Part II. Recruitment." *In: Proceedings 1975 Oil Spill Conference.* Environmental Protection Agency/American Petroleum Institute/United States Coast Guard; 457-461; 1975.

Chapman, P.M. and S. Becker. "Recommended Protocols for Conducting Laboratory Bioassays for Marine Sediment Toxicity." Puget Sound Estuary Program, US Environmental Protection Agency, Seattle: 55 pp; 1986.

Chasse, C. "The Ecological Impact on and Near Shores by the *AMOCO CADIZ* Oil Spill." *Marine Pollution Bulletin.* 9(11):298-301; 1978.

Clarke, R. C., B. G. Patten, and E. E. Denike. "Persistent Spill from the *GENERAL E.C. MEIGS.*" *Journal Fisheries Research Board Canada.* 35:754-765; 1978.

Commercial Fisherman's 1989 Guide. Volume 2; Central Alaska. Marine Trade Publications, 1989.

Connell, J.H. "Effects of Competition, Predation by *Thais lapillus,* and Other Factors on Natural Populations of the Barnacle *Balanus balanoides.*" *Ecological Monographs.* 31:61-104; 1961.

Dayton, P. K. "Competition, Disturbance and Community Organization: The Provision and Subsequent Utilization of Space in a Rocky Intertidal Community." *Ecological Monographs.* 41:351-389; 1971.

Druehl, L. D. "The Pattern of Laminariales Distribution in the Northeast Pacific." *Phycologia.* 9:237-247; 1970.

Gilfillan, E. S., D. S. Page, and J. C. Foster. "Tidal Area Dispersant Project: Fate and Effects of Chemically Dispersed Oil in the Nearshore Benthic Environment." Washington, DC: *American Petroleum Institute Publication No. 4440*; 215 pp; 1986 .

Glemarec, M. and E. Hussenot. " Reponses des Peuplements Subtidaux a la Perturbation Cree par l'*Amoco Cadiz* dans les Abers Benoit et Wrac'h." *In: Ecological Study of the* Amoco Cadiz *Oil Spill, Report of the NOAA-CNEXO Joint Sea Commission, Part II, Biological Studies of the* Amoco Cadiz *Oil Spill.* M. Marchand (ed.) National Oceanic and Atmospheric Administration; Washington, DC; pp 191-204; 1982.

Grant, W. S. "High Intertidal Community Organization on a Rocky Headland in Maine, USA." *Marine Biology.* 44(1):15-26; 1977.

Grassle, J. F. and J. R. Grassle. "Opportunistic Life Histories and Genetic Systems in Benthic Polychaetes." *Journal Marine Research.* 32:253-284; 1974.

Hanson, B. L. *Quality Control: Theory and Applications.* Englewood Cliffs: Prentice Hall; 1963.

Hurlbert, S. H. "Pseudoreplication and the Design of Ecological Field Experiments." *Ecological Monographs.* 54:187-211; 1984

Lindstrom, S. C. and N. I. Calvin. "New Records of Marine Red Algae from the Gulf of Alaska." *Syesis*. 8:405-406; 1975.

Long, E. R. and L. G. Morgan "The Potential for Biological Effects of Sediment-sorbed Contaminants Tested in the National Status and Trends Program." *NOAA Technical Memorandum NOS OMA 52*. National Oceanic and Atmospheric Administration, U.S. Department of Commerce, Rockville, MD; 175 pp + appendices; 1990.

McGuinness, K. A. "Disturbance and Organisms on Boulders I. Patterns in the Environment and the Community." *Oecologica*. 71(3):409-419; 1987a.

McGuinness, K. A. "Disturbance and Organisms on Boulders II. Causes of Patterns in Diversity and Abundance." *Oecologica*. 71(3):420-430; 1987b.

Mielke, J. E. "Oil in the Ocean: The Short- and Long-Term Impacts of a Spill." *90-356 SPR*. Congressional Research Service, The Library of Congress, Washington, DC; 34 pp; 1990.

Nakahara, H. and M. Ueno. "A Mechanism of Succession in Seaweed Communities." *Bulletin Japanese Society Fisheries*. 51(9):1437-1440; 1985.

National Research Council. *Oil in the Sea: Inputs, Fates, and Effects*. Washington, D. C.: National Academy Press; 601 pages; 1985.

Nelson, W. G. "Experimental Studies of Oil Pollution on the Rocky Intertidal Community of a Norwegian Fjord." *Ecology*. 65(2):121-138; 1982.

Osman, R. W. "The Establishment and Development of a Marine Epifaunal Community." *Ecological Monographs*. 47(1):37-63; 1977.

Paine, R. T. "Intertidal Community Structure: Experimental Studies on the Relationship Between a Dominant Competitor and its Principal Predator." *Oecologia*. 15:93-120; 1974.

Paine, R. T. and S. A. Levin. "Intertidal Landscapes: Disturbance and the Dynamics of Pattern." *Ecological Monographs*. 51(2):145-178; 1981.

Pearson, T. H. and R. Rosenberg. "Macrobenthic Succession in Relation to Organic Enrichment and Pollution of the Marine Environment." *Oceanography and Marine Biology Annual Review*. 16:229-311; 1978.

Sanders, H. L., J. F. Grassle, G. R. Hampson, L. S. Morse, S. Garner-Price, and C. C. Jones. "Anatomy of an Oil Spill Long Term Effects from the Grounding of the Barge *Florida* off West Falmouth, Massachussetts." *Journal Marine Research*. 38:265-380; 1980.

Shanks, A. L. and W. G. Wright. "Adding Teeth to Wave Action: The Destructive Effects of Wave Born Rocks on Intertidal Oorganisms." *Oecologica.* 69:420-428; 1986.

Shannon, C. E. "The Mathematical Theory of Communication". *Bell System Technology Journal.* 27:379-623; 1948.

Shannon, C. E. and W. Weaver. *The Mathematical Theory of Communication.* Urbana, IL: University of Illinois Press, 1949.

Sousa, W.P. "Disturbance in Marine Intertidal Boulder Fields: The Nonequilibrium Maintainance of Diversity." *Ecology.* 60(6): 1225-1239; 1979a.

Sousa, W. P. "Experimental Investigations of Disturbance and Ecological Succession in a Rocky Intertidal Algal Community." *Ecological Monographs.* 49(3):227-254; 1979b.

Sousa, W. P. "Disturbance and Patch Dynamics on Rocky Intertidal Shores." *In: The Ecology of Natural Disturbance and Patch Dynamics.* New York: Academic Press; 101-124; 1985.

Southward, A .J. and E. C. Southward. "Recolonization of Rocky Shores in Cornwall After Use of Toxic Dispersants to Clean Up the *TORREY CANYON* Spill." *Journal Fisheries Research Board of Canada.* 35:682-706; 1978.

Spies, R. B., D. D. Hardin, and J. P. Teal. "Organic Enrichment or Toxicity? A Comparison of the Effects of Kelp and Crude Oil in Sediments on the Colonization and Growth of Benthic Infauna." *Journal of Experimental Marine Biology and Ecology.* 124:261-282; 1988.

Suchanek, T.H. "The *Mytilus californianus* Community: Studies on the Composition, Structure, Organization and Dynamics of a Mussel Bed." Ph.D. Dissertation, University of Washington, Seattle; 1979.

Suchanek, T.H. "Mussels and Their Role in Structuring Rocky Shore Communities." *In: Ecology of Rocky Coasts,* S. P. G. Moore and R. Seed (eds.) Kent, United Kingdom: Hodder and Stoughton Educational Press; pp 70-96; 1985.

Suchanek, T. H. "Oil Impacts on Marine Invertebrate Populations and Communities." *American Zoologist.* 33:510-523; 1993.

Swartz, R. C., W. A. DeBen, J. K. Phillips, J. O. Lambertson, and F. A. Cole. "Phoxocephalid Amphipod Bioassay for Marine Sediment Toxicity." *Aquatic Toxicology and Hazard Assessment:* 7th Symposium. R. D. Cardwell, R. Purdy, and R. C. Banner (eds.) American Society for Testing and Materials STP 854:284-307; 1985.

Teal, A. R. "Shoreline Cleanup Following the *Exxon Valdez* Spill—The Decision Process for Cleanup Operations." *Proceedings of the 13th Arctic and Marine Oilspill Program (AMOP) Technical Seminar, June 6-8, Edmonton.* pp 422-429; 1990.

Impact Assessment for Fish and Fisheries

David A. Armstrong[1], Paul A. Dinnel[1], Jose M. Orensanz[1], Janet L. Armstrong[1], Trent L. McDonald[2], Robert F. Cusimano[3], Richard S. Nemeth[4], Marsha L. Landolt[1], John R. Skalski[5], Richard F. Lee[6], and Robert J. Huggett[7]

STATUS OF SELECTED BOTTOMFISH AND CRUSTACEAN SPECIES IN PRINCE WILLIAM SOUND FOLLOWING THE *EXXON VALDEZ* OIL SPILL[8]

REFERENCE: Armstrong, D. A., Dinnel, P. A., Orensanz, J. M., Armstrong, J. L., McDonald, T. L., Cusimano, R. F., Nemeth, R. S., Landolt, M. L., Skalski, J. R., Lee, R. F., and Huggett, R. J., "Status of Selected Bottomfish and Crustacean Species in Prince William Sound Following the *Exxon Valdez* Oil Spill," Exxon Valdez Oil Spill: Fate and Effects in Alaskan Waters, ASTM STP 1219, Peter G. Wells, James N. Butler, and Jane S. Hughes, Eds., American Society for Testing and Materials, Philadelphia, 1995.

ABSTRACT: Exposure and possible adverse effects of the *Exxon Valdez* oil spill (EVOS) at depth were studied between 1989 and 1991 on several species of crustaceans, molluscs, and finfish that are characterized by ontogenetic shifts in distribution from meroplanktonic larvae to benthic and demersal juveniles and adults. Our approach was to search for 1) evidence of exposure to *Exxon Valdez* crude oil (EVC) at depth (generally between 20 to 150 m) and 2) measurable perturbations at both the individual and population levels. Primary species targeted were Tanner crab (*Chionoecetes bairdi*), several pandalid shrimps (*Pandalus platyceros*, *P. hypsinotus*, *P. borealis*), flathead sole (*Hippoglossoides elassodon*), and several bivalves including scallops (*Chlamys rubida*) and infaunal clams (*Nuculana*, *Yoldia*, and *Macoma* spp.).
Our survey design provided a comparison between variables measured in

[1]Professor, Principal Research Scientist, Principal Research Scientist, Fisheries Biologist, and Professor/Director, respectively, School of Fisheries, University of Washington, Seattle, WA 98195.

[2]Pre-doctoral Research Assistant, Department of Statistics, Oregon State University, Corvallis, OR.

[3]Environmental Scientist, Environmental Investigations, Washington Department of Ecology, Olympia, WA.

[4]Pre-doctoral Research Associate, Department of Zoology, University of New Hampshire, Durham, NH.

[5]Professor, Center for Quantitative Science, University of Washington, Seattle, WA 98195.

[6]Professor, Skidaway Institute of Oceanography, University of Georgia, Savannah, GA 31406.

[7]Professor and Assistant Director, Division of Chemistry and Toxicology, Virginia Institute of Marine Science, College of William and Mary, Gloucester Point, VA 23062.

[8]Contribution No. 873, School of Fisheries, University of Washington, Seattle, WA 98195.

"oiled" bays around Knight Island and "non-oiled" bays at other locations within Prince William Sound. "Oiled" was defined in terms of degree of shoreline oiling, sediment and tissue hydrocarbon concentrations with the EVC signature, elevated concentrations of fluorescent aromatic compounds (FACs) in bile of flathead sole, and frequency of oil in benthic trawls. Statistical analyses of catch-per-unit-of-effort (CPUE; relative abundance determined by pots and trawls) were focused on detection of differences in trends through time (that is, "time-by-oil" interaction) rather than on magnitude of differences, thereby avoiding the problem of inherent differences in baseline CPUE levels between bays and the influence of non-random application of oil to bays.

Polycyclic aromatic hydrocarbons (PAHs) of petrogenic origin were measured in all bays sampled in this study and levels of PAHs derived from EVC were elevated in the "oiled" bays following the spill, yet attenuated to less than 200 ng/g sediment by 1991. Total PAHs in scallop tissues were higher in "oiled" bays in 1989 but decreased 15-fold to a mean of 16 ng/g by 1990. Clam tissues from "oiled" bays in 1991 had higher PAH concentrations, but only samples from Bay of Isles had alkylated PAHs (about 90 ng/g) indicative of EVC exposure. Mean concentrations of FACs in flathead sole bile were significantly higher in "oiled" than "non-oiled" bays (about 27 and 14 ng/g, respectively) in both 1990 and 1991, and corresponded to elevated tissue levels of PAHs in clams, which are the major prey of sole in these bays.

Virtually no evidence of significant adverse effects was detected at either the individual or population levels across all the life history stages sampled. Larval Tanner crabs were widely distributed in the plankton in early summer of 1989 and 1990; adult female fecundity and trends in CPUE of juveniles did not differ significantly between the two categories of bays. In spring of 1990, 16 dead juvenile Tanner crabs were caught in three "oiled" bays and mortality was significantly correlated with elevated FACs in bile of flathead sole. Such mortality was likely linked to inordinately low bottom-water salinity that spring, and dead crabs were not found on any other cruise prior to or after this event.

Pandalid shrimp were ubiquitous throughout the study area, and no significant differences were measured between "oiled" and "non-oiled" bays in trends of CPUE of *P. borealis* (the best quantified) and fecundity of *P. platyceros*. Fecundity in the case of *P. hypsinotus* was reduced in 1990 compared with 1989 irrespective of bay, but fecundity was also about 30% lower among females from the "oiled" compared with "non-oiled" bays. In the case of flathead sole, mean abundance of young-of-the-year fish declined significantly in "non-oiled" bays and mean abundance of older fish increased significantly in "oiled" bays.

In contrast to lack of evidence of adverse effects on target species caused by the EVOS, substantial declines in fishery landings of several crabs and shrimps had occurred in PWS, some to the point of closure, prior to the spill. Long-term trends in abundance of populations of these species due to natural environmental causes or fishing pressures are likely to be far more important than fluctuations attributable to EVOS.

KEYWORDS: *Exxon Valdez*, oil spill, Prince William Sound, Alaska, damage assessment, biological effects, subtidal, crustacean resources, Tanner crab, shrimp, bottomfish, flathead sole, polycyclic aromatic hydrocarbons, bile, sediments, bioaccumulation

Oil spills in marine environments quickly focus concern on biota most conspicuously associated with the surface distribution of hydrocarbons as they are spread by current and wind over an essentially two-dimensional surface. Marine birds and mammals, as well as sessile intertidal fauna, are obvious subjects of impact assessment because of their inextricable link to the surface and shorelines, where presence of and exposure to hydrocarbons is most dramatic. Invariably, extensive effort is put into documentation and quantification of these surface perturbations that tend to dominate the public and even scientific perspective of damage attributable to oil spills (Carr 1991; Bodin 1988). Yet the three-dimensional dispersion of oil is well documented *in situ* following spills (Cabioch et al. 1978, *Amoco Cadiz*) and is routinely considered an important component of risk analyses of offshore petroleum operations in Alaskan waters.

Proceedings of numerous conferences convened since the early 1980s by the Outer Continental Shelf Environmental Assessment Program (OCSEAP) highlight the transport and dispersion of oil at the surface, in the water column, and to the benthos via simulation models run under various scenarios for type and magnitude of spills, and physical processes operative after the spill (Liu and Leenderste 1981; Manen and Pelto 1984; Payne et al. 1984; Laevastu and Fukuhara 1985). Fisheries impact scenarios have been considered in detail for areas of Alaskan waters such as the SE Bering Sea for several commercial species (including flatfish), due to both well blowouts and tanker accidents at scales that approximate the *Exxon Valdez* spill (Fukuhara 1985; Laevastu et al. 1985). In general, these exercises are founded on fairly good information regarding species ecology and population dynamics because of long time-series of data collected annually by the National Marine Fisheries Service (Otto 1986) and physical oceanographic processes well described for the same systems (Kinder and Schumacher 1981a, b).

Such was not the case in Prince William Sound (PWS) at the time of the *Exxon Valdez* oil spill (EVOS) in March 1989. Apart from intertidal surveys at various locations and subtidal studies in the Valdez Arm and Port Valdez (O'Clair and Zimmerman 1986; Feder and Jewett 1986; Rogers and Rogers 1986), relatively few prespill data were available to guide in survey design and selection of target species for assessment of possible oil perturbations. In addition, the severity of bathymetry (changes of hundreds of meters in depth over comparable horizontal distances), convoluted coastline, variety of watersheds and freshwater input, intrinsic features such as sills and glaciers, all indicated high spatial heterogeneity within PWS in comparison with other Alaskan marine systems (for example, the eastern Bering Sea) better studied for the purpose of oil impact assessment.

As a consequence, it was assumed at the outset that data on mobile benthic and demersal animal species would be highly variable and so require a fairly comprehensive life-history orientation as a framework in which to measure and detect possible adverse effects of the EVOS. From this perspective, it was decided *a priori* that no single dataset would be regarded as definitive evidence for or against oil perturbation on any single target species. Rather, acquisition of data on two primary topics was viewed as essential: 1) evidence that species had been exposed to *Exxon Valdez* crude oil (EVC) at depth and 2) that such exposure had caused adverse changes in selected biota at the individual or population levels, measurable as change beyond the noise of natural variability so well documented in the populations of many marine finfish and invertebrates (Caddy and Gulland 1983; numerous articles in Caddy 1989).

We also faced a statistical challenge with respect to survey design and use of datasets to contrast conditions in areas eventually designated as "oiled" and "non-oiled." Standard statistical techniques rely on random allocation of treatments to experimental units, random samples from a population, and pre-event data as the bases for extrapolating conclusions and determining the validity of statistical tests. Damage assessment studies on subtidal populations in PWS possess none of these statistical qualities. It cannot be assumed that oil was deposited randomly nor can treatment conditions be replicated without another spill. Because of the sudden and unforeseen nature of the accident, there exist no usable prespill data for populations of the target species. Furthermore, because of highly variable bottom bathymetry in much of PWS, a limited number of sites exist where bottom trawls can be deployed.

This study defined a bay as the spatial unit of study and focused on differences in trends of catch-per-unit-of-effort (CPUE) in bays classified as "oiled" relative to bays classified as "non-oiled." By focusing on differences in trends through time rather than on differences in magnitude, equivalent to focusing on a time-by-oil effect interaction instead of the main effects of oil, this study avoids the problem of inherent differences in baseline CPUE levels between bays and is robust to nonrandom application of oil to bays (Skalski and Robson 1992). No attempt was made to obtain a random sample of bays in PWS and statistical inference is restricted to the bays sampled. However, the bays selected as "oiled" were among the most severely affected in the spill area, and in that respect they may represent a worst-case scenario for assessment of effects.

The question of interest in the analysis of CPUE data is inherently one-tailed, namely, "Did the oil spill adversely affect populations under study?" However, by focusing on the time-by-oil interaction and lacking a specific model for population decline and recovery in the aftermath of the spill, this study conducted two-tailed tests that allowed for testing for two types of oil effect. The first is an acute oil effect, which depresses population numbers immediately after the spill with a subsequent recovery to prespill conditions. The second is a delayed oil effect, which may depress population numbers from initially high levels immediately after the spill to lower levels one or two years later.

MATERIALS AND METHODS

Survey Design

Data were collected between May 1989 and September 1991 in the course of six cruises, referred to throughout the text as "Cruise 89/1, Cruise 89/2," etc. Baseline and survey data were sparse to nonexistent for many shellfish and bottomfish species in PWS (Hood and Zimmerman 1986), especially so in the many secluded embayments most affected by the EVOS. Cruise 89/1 (26 May to 21 June) was exploratory, designed for the selection of sampling locations, target species, and sampling equipment. Sampling gear included plankton nets (bongo and neuston), crab and shrimp pots (CP, SP), beam and otter trawls (BT, OT), and rock dredge. Sampling stations were spread throughout western PWS (Fig. 1a), from Port Wells in the north to the nearshore Gulf of Alaska in the south. Survey design was adjusted for Cruises 89/2 (24 July to 13 August) and 89/3 (20 September to 20 October) and maintained without change for

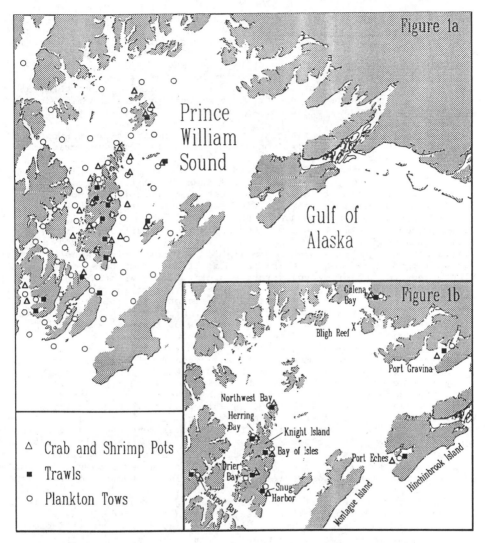

FIG. 1--(a)Broad-scale PWS sample sites and types of gear deployed during the exploratory Cruise 89/1.   (b).Repetitive sample sites, bay locations, and types of gear deployed for 1990 and 1991 cruises. "Non-oiled" bays (1 to 5): 1 = Galena Bay, 2 = Port Gravina, 3 = Port Etches, 4 = Jackpot Bay, 5 = Drier Bay. "Oiled" bays (6 to 9): 6 = Northwest Bay, 7 = Herring Bay, 8 = Bay of Isles, 9 = Snug Harbor.

Cruises 90/1 (26 May to 19 June), 90/2 (22 August to 14 September), and 91/1 (6 August to 5 September) (Fig. 1b). The definitive survey design was limited to a total of nine bays; the numbers of samples collected in each of them are summarized in Table 1. In the "oiled" group were Herring Bay, Snug Harbor, Northwest Bay, and Bay of Isles and in the "non-oiled" group were Jackpot Bay, Drier Bay, Port Etches, Galena Bay, and Port Gravina. Trawlable substrate was available in all of them, an important consideration because trawling was the primary sampling method for measuring abundance of juveniles and adults of several target species.

The experimental units of the study were the individual bays, which were classified as "oiled" or "non-oiled" using the following criteria (Table 2): 1) surveys of shoreline oiling during the months following the spill and 2) signs of oiling at depth based on trawl samples during Cruise 89/1 (for example, tar balls, oil sheen in sorting containers, heavy smell of hydrocarbons from the catch even when oil was not apparent at the water surface). Drier Bay, whose status was not clearly defined at the beginning of the study, was assigned *post-hoc* to the "non-oiled" group based on the absence of indication of subtidal oiling during this study.

A cluster analysis based on a compilation of observations made in 1991 was performed to validate the initial classification of bays. The clustering procedure was agglomerative hierarchical, with an average linkage criterion (Sokal and Michener 1958) for combining clusters containing the following four variables: percent length of shoreline oiling (heavy and moderate oiling combined), percent of trawls with oil, fluorescent aromatic compounds (FACs) in bile of flathead sole, and bivalve tissue hydrocarbon values (see *Laboratory methods*, below). Several of these variables were also measured in 1989 and 1990, and considerable improvement (50 to 100%) was evident between 1989 and 1991 in exposure indices for which comparable data exist. However, the analysis focused on 1991 data for the following reasons: 1) all four oiling indices were measured in all nine bays that year; 2) there were missing values in the 1989 and 1990 datasets; and 3) the clustering algorithm cannot proceed if there are missing values. Because the dependent variables represented a variety of measurement units (for example, μg/litre, percentages), all variables were standardized to a mean of zero and standard deviation of one with Z-scores. Euclidean distance (ED) was used to describe the distances betweeen bays in terms of the four oiling indices defined above. ED is the squared differences over all four oiling variables within each bay.

A second cluster analysis was performed using environmental variables to establish whether the initial classification of bays could be confounded with major environmental features (Table 2). The variables included were basin area (km^2), bay area (km^2), bay volume (km^3), compass azimuth of bay mouth (degrees), bottom temperature (°C), and bottom salinity (ppt). As above, all dependent variables were transformed into Z-scores.

Target Species

Species were selected for study based on several criteria: 1) ubiquitous distribution throughout PWS; 2) complex life history including meroplanktonic egg and/or larval stages and benthic juveniles and adults to maximize possibility of exposure to EVC; 3) commercial importance (or representative of a commercial group) to provide at least some history of abundance trends in PWS; and 4) fairly comprehensive

TABLE 1--Type and total number of samples collected in Prince William Sound in 1989 (three cruises), 1990 (two cruises) and 1991 (one cruise) in each of the primary study bays (exploratory Cruise 89/1 excluded; see footnote for cruise dates; abbreviation of bay names in parentheses). Bays PGR, PET and GB were not sampled in 1989.

Bay	Beam Trawl*			Otter Trawl			Crab Pots			Shrimp Pots			Plankton**			CTD***		
	'89	'90	'91	'89	'90	'91	'89	'90	'91	'89	'90	'91	'89	'90	'91	'89	'90	'91
Northwest (NWB)	4	10	5	5	6	8	4	15	8	4	37	12	7	20	0	1	7	6
Herring (HEB)	7	11	6	9	6	4	18	14	7	33	37	12	6	20	0	2	5	7
Bay of Isles (BOI)	10	17	6	7	8	3	12	10	5	10	37	12	6	20	0	2	7	6
Snug Harbor (SH)	11	12	5	7	8	7	12	2	2	22	37	12	6	20	0	2	5	5
Galena (GB)	0	14	8	0	7	6	0	16	7	0	37	12	0	20	0	0	4	5
Port Gravina (PGR)	0	15	7	0	14	7	0	16	8	0	37	12	0	20	0	0	4	4
Port Etches (PET)	0	14	7	0	11	11	0	13	8	0	37	12	0	20	0	0	3	8
Jackpot (JPB)	4	13	7	6	8	6	4	14	7	7	37	12	4	20	0	2	3	9
Drier (DB)	11	13	6	9	11	7	24	16	8	42	37	12	6	20	0	2	3	8
Total	47	119	57	43	79	59	74	116	60	118	333	108	35	180	0	11	41	58

* Cruise dates: 89/1 = 26 May-21 June; 89/2 = 24 July-13 Aug; 89/3 = 20 Sept-20 Oct;
90/1 26 May-19 June; 90/2 = 22 Aug-14 Sept; 91/1 = 6 Aug-5 Sept.

** Half of the tows indicated were bongo, the other half neuston.

*** A portion of the data collected in 1990 was with YSI meters due to a malfunctioning CTD unit.

TABLE 2--*Physical characteristics and degree of intertidal oiling of the PWS damage assessment sites sampled for crustacean and bottomfish resources, 1989 to 1991 (see Fig. 1b for locations). Bottom water values are averages for August/September (Cruises 89/2, 89/3, 90/2 and 91/1).*

Bay	Assigned Category	Percent Shoreline Oiled in 1989*	Maximum Depth (m)	Sill(s) Present ?	Bottom Temp., Range (°C)	Bottom Salinity, Range (ppt)	Bottom Diss. Oxygen, Range (mg/litre)	Bottom pH, Range
Northwest (NWB)	Oiled	59.6	210	Partial	5.1 - 5.4	32.5 - 32.6	4.4 - 5.1	8.0 - 8.2
Herring (HEB)	Oiled	47.8	230	Yes	5.2 - 5.4	32.4 - 32.6	4.2 - 4.7	7.7 - 8.3
Bay of Isles (BOI)	Oiled	30.7	130	Yes	4.6 - 5.4	31.5 - 31.7	3.5 - 4.7	7.7 - 8.2
Snug Harbor (SH)	Oiled	49.6	110	Partial	4.6 - 5.4	31.7 - 32.1	4.0 - 6.2	7.7 - 8.4
Galena (GB)	Nonoiled	0	220	Yes	3.9 - 4.0	31.7 - 31.9	5.2 - 5.6	8.1 - 8.3
Port Gravina (PGR)	Nonoiled	0	190	No	4.6 - 5.0	32.1 - 32.3	3.9 - 4.6	8.2 - 8.4
Port Etches (PET)	Nonoiled	0	160	No	5.8 - 5.9	32.4 - 32.4	5.4 - 5.7	7.8 - 8.2
Jackpot (JPB)	Nonoiled	0	150	Yes	4.0 - 4.6	31.6 - 31.6	3.7 - 4.6	7.8 - 8.2
Drier (DB)	Nonoiled	0.5	180	Yes	4.7 - 5.4	31.6 - 32.0	4.9 - 6.0	7.8 - 8.4

* Total of heavily + moderately oiled shoreline.

published literature on ecology and life history to facilitate interpretation of data. Consistent with these criteria, the target species selected were Tanner crab (*Chionoecetes bairdi*), several species of pandalid shrimp (*Pandalus platyceros, P. hypsinotus, P. borealis*), and the demersal flathead sole (*Hippoglossoides elassodon*). To the extent possible within certain limits of season deemed safe for field work and availability of vessels, all major life-history stages were sampled, and collections of attendant hydrocarbon data were made.

Tanner crab satisfies all of the criteria listed above and was the species most comprehensively investigated in this study. *Pandalus platyceros* (spot shrimp) is the major component of a shrimp pot fishery in PWS, with *P. hypsinotus* (coonstripe shrimp) contributing a small fraction of the commercial catch. PWS is divided into two management areas (Trowbridge 1992): "Traditional" (including all areas sampled by us around Knight Island, Jackpot Bay and Galena Bay), and "Eastern" (including Pt. Gravina and Pt. Etches), which contributes only a small fraction of the catch. Among study sites, only Jackpot Bay is a traditional shrimp pot fishing ground. *P. borealis* (pink shrimp), on the other hand, has been targeted primarily by a trawl fishery. The shrimp trawl fishery, however, has shifted (starting in 1985) from *P. borealis* in southwestern PWS to *Pandalopsis dispar* (sidestripe shrimp) in northwestern PWS. Two of the study sites (Pt. Etches and Pt. Gravina) are located within an area closed to trawling, a measure to protect crab recruitment.

Flathead sole has not been targeted by commercial harvesting in PWS, although it is an important component of the incidental catch in trawl fisheries. It was included in the study as an indicator of subtidal benthic environments and of *exposure* to oil, rather than because of specific interest in terms of the *effect* of the spill on its populations. It is a ubiquitous representative of a group of fishes that includes many commercially valuable species which may be exposed to pollutants because of their demersal life history and diet, which is composed of benthic invertebrate prey. Flatfish are studied extensively in other areas for evidence of contaminant-related injury as worst-case surrogates for other finfish (Varanasi et al. 1989).

Environmental Variables

Temperature, conductivity, density ("CTD"), salinity, pH and dissolved oxygen (DO) were measured on separate cruises parallel to Cruises 89/2 and 89/3 and on Cruises 90/2 and 91/1 using a "CTD" unit at one to nine stations in each bay. During Cruise 90/1, malfunction of the CTD unit led to the use of bench-type meters (various YSI® models) for measuring temperature, salinity, and DO of water collected with a Van Dorn bottle.

Population Structure and Abundance Sampling Methods

Plankton--Two collections were made at each station to obtain larval stages of target species. The upper 50 m of the water column was sampled by standardized oblique hauls of 60-cm-diameter bongo-rigged, 505-μm-mesh plankton nets. Surface plankton (neuston) was sampled with a winged frame (30 x 50 cm) rigged with a 505-μm-mesh plankton net, operated to a depth of 0.25 m. The bongo net was deployed and retrieved at standard rates (Incze et al. 1987) and towed at a target vessel speed of 2.5 to 3 km/h; the neuston net was towed 10 min at the same speed.

Both net types had calibrated flow meters mounted in the mouth to measure distance towed for conversion to volume filtered. During Cruise 89/1 (Fig. 1a), plankton was sampled in both open areas and bays (typically one station per bay). In 1990, collections were made at five stations in each bay, where depths were greater than 50 m. No plankton samples were collected on Cruise 91/1. Plankton collections were preserved onboard with 10% buffered formalin. Once in the laboratory, samples were rinsed, split if necessary with a Folsom splitter, and larvae of decapod crustaceans were sorted and identified in two steps: first, pandalid shrimp, other shrimp, anomuran and brachyuran crabs; second, the following species and stages: Tanner crab (zoea 1, 2, megalopae), spot shrimp (zoeal stages), and king crab (zoea 1-4, glaucothoe). Decapod larvae were preserved in an ethanol/glycerol solution, and remainders of the plankton samples were archived.

Trawls--Samples of benthic and demersal macrofauna were collected with BT and OT. The BT was effective in sampling benthic fishes and invertebrate fauna (particularly juvenile stages), while the OT was more efficient for sampling larger conspecific adults and more mobile epibenthic and demersal species (especially larger fishes). The BT was constructed with dual tickler chains in front of the lead line to move animals slightly off bottom and was towed approximately 230 m [1/8 nautical mile (NM)] at a target ground speed of 2.5 km/h; the net was made of 20-mm stretch mesh with a 10-mm stretch mesh cod end and had an effective fishing width of 2.3 m (Gunderson and Ellis 1986). The OT was a two-panel, semi-balloon design ("SCCWRP," 7.6 m; Mearns and Allen 1978), with an effective fishing width of 3.5 m, constructed with 32- to 38-mm stretch mesh and 6-mm stretch mesh cod end liner. It was towed approximately 370 m (1/5 NM) at a target ground speed of 4.2 km/h. The area swept in each haul, calculated from the width of the mouth and the distance trawled, was used to estimate catch-per-unit-effort (CPUE, expressed as catch per hectare swept). One to seven stations were sampled by BT in each bay; a subset of one to five of those was sampled by OT. The number of stations per bay was constrained by the extent of trawlable substrate. Target species caught in the trawls were identified, counted, and measured. Individuals of nontarget species were identified when possible and returned to the sea. Qualitative observations were made on any signs of oil in the catches (tar balls, oil sheens in the sorting pans, etc.).

Crab Pots (CPs)--Pyramid-style Tanner CPs (1.8-m^2 base x 1.2-m^2 top x 0.6-m height, 0.6-m-diameter top funnel entrance, weight approximately 125 kg) were deployed to sample Tanner and king crabs at as many as eight stations per bay. During Cruise 89/1, it was observed that adult female Tanner crabs escaped through the commercial size mesh (~10 cm), so mesh size was changed to 2.5 cm for all subsequent cruises. Each CP was baited with 0.5 kg of frozen herring. In 1989, data indicated that maximum catch was reached when pots were soaked for about 48 h, which became the target soak time in the 1990-91 cruises. Target species caught were identified, counted, and measured. Only data from CP hauls deeper than 50 m and soaked for 40 to 50 h were used in the analyses. CPUE was expressed as crabs caught per CP haul.

Shrimp pots (SPs)--Pots used to sample shrimp were of various designs, but always covered with a 2.5-cm stretch mesh, except for Cruise 90/1 when a wider mesh (3.1-cm) was used by mistake. SPs were used only as a qualitative sampling device, providing specimens for size-frequency, hydrocarbon, and fecundity analyses.

Data Analysis and Interpretation

Response variable in CPUE analyses--CPUE were computed on a per haul basis by dividing the number of individuals of a species caught by an amount of effort appropriate for the gear. The unit of CPUE for BT and OT is the number of animals caught per area swept (expressed in hectares), equivalent to density if efficiency of the gear is assumed to be 100%. CPUE for CPs is expressed as number of animals caught per CP fished for 40 to 50 h. CPUE for bongo and neuston nets (plankton) is expressed as number of animals per 1000 m^3 of water filtered. Sampling units in PWS were a hierarchy of stations within bays and hauls within stations. For trawl gear, multiple hauls could occur at a single station during a cruise. For CP gear, multiple pots ("hauls") could be deployed at a single station during a cruise. In 1989, some stations were visited during multiple cruises, while other stations were visited only once. An average log-CPUE for a bay during a year was computed by 1) averaging multiple hauls at a station (if any) during a cruise, 2) taking the mean of station averages across cruises in a given year (if multiple cruises were involved), 3) calculating arithmetic bay means per year, and 4) computing the ln(*mean CPUE+1*) of the latter; a value of one was added to each bay average to ensure that computation of ln(0) was not attempted. Transformation (natural logarithm) of the response variable forces the model of oiling effects to be multiplicative, and the units for two- or three-year comparisons to be reported as geometric means. For the data from a bay to be included in a test, at least one station had to be sampled in each time period (year).

Data subsetting in CPUE analyses--Tests were performed separately on subsets of the dataset defined by year, cruise, bay, species, sex (males, females, pools), size, gear type (BT, OT, CP), gear performance (hauls in which the gear did not perform adequately were not included in the analyses) and depth, as indicated in each case in the Results section. Size-frequency distributions (SFDs) indicated that size-related selectivity was different for each gear-species combination. Thus, results obtained with different types of gear emphasize different life history stages.

Statistical tests in CPUE analyses--The statistical procedure was a two-tailed test of the interaction between two factors: treatment (classification of bays as "oiled" or "non-oiled") and time (years); the null hypothesis (H_O) was "no treatment-by-time interaction." Data were partitioned in two ways for analyses. When the nine bays of the final survey design were considered, only the years 1990 and 1991 were included, because three of the bays were not sampled in 1989. When the three years (1989-1991) were included, the set of bays was smaller (generally six, four "oiled" and two "non-oiled") for the same reason. The two-degrees-of-freedom test across the three years was partitioned into two single-degree-of-freedom tests comparing trends over time in the linear and quadratic models. Significance levels for tests were adjusted to control the experimental error rate. Statistical significance was established at $\alpha = 0.1$ and a statistical power $(1-\beta)$ of 0.9 was defined as a goal, in an attempt to balance type I (α) and type II (β) error rates. *A posteriori* statistical power calculations were performed for each one-degree-of-freedom test. Statistical power was calculated given the observed variance and a 50% reduction in population numbers over what was expected if oil had no effect. However, because of the high natural variability in CPUE, the goal of achieving a statistical power of 0.9 was typically not achieved.

Occurrence of dead Tanner crabs--During Cruise 90/1 (late spring), a small number of dead juvenile Tanner crabs were collected with the BT in Galena Bay, Bay of Isles, and Snug Harbor. Because dead specimens were not collected in previous or later cruises, analyses similar in spirit to the interactive tests mentioned above for CPUE could not be performed. Instead, the relationship between catch of dead Tanner crabs during Cruise 90/1 and a measure of FACs in flathead sole bile during the same time was tested after adjusting for depth. This relationship was tested in a Generalized Linear Interactive Models (GLIM) framework assuming Poisson errors and log-link. Tests of significance were based on asymptotic F-tests using analysis of deviance (ANODEV, McCullagh and Nelder 1983).

Analysis of size frequency distributions--Size frequency distributions of the target species were decomposed into modal components (assumed to be normal) by an approach similar to that of MacDonald and Pitcher (1979), forcing the coefficient of variation to be constant. Components corresponded to the instars of the juvenile Tanner crab and to the year classes of the pandalid shrimp and flathead sole.

All of the results for Tanner crab are presented in terms of carapace length (CL). Alaska Department of Fish and Game (ADF&G) and National Marine Fisheries Service (NMFS), however, routinely use carapace width (CW) as the standard measurement. For juvenile crabs (CL <50 mm) a conversion factor was estimated on the basis of the data (n = 75, CL range: 5 to 47 mm): $CW = 1.282(CL)$. For larger crabs, the following relation has been estimated by Phinney (1977): $CW = -3.584 + 1.268(CL)$.

Reproductive Condition of Crab and Shrimp

Field methods--Tanner crabs larger than 20 mm CL were sexed in the field. Pandalid shrimp were sexed during Cruises 90/2 (second half only) and 91/1; spot shrimp and coonstripe shrimp were sexed on board and other pandalid species in the laboratory (samples were frozen on board). Gravid females of Tanner crab, spot shrimp, and coonstripe shrimp (mostly obtained with pots) were frozen whole in plastic bags and returned to the laboratory for fecundity analyses. No gravid coonstripe shrimp were sampled in 1991 because of the timing of Cruise 91/1.

Laboratory methods--Female Tanner crabs and shrimp were thawed and measured (CL). For Tanner crabs, shell condition and missing appendages were recorded. Eggs were stripped from pleopods. An aliquot of the eggs (200 eggs for shrimp, 400 for Tanner crabs), the remainder of the egg mass, and the body were dried to constant weight at 60 °C, cooled in a desiccator, and weighed.

Data analysis--Dry weights of the egg aliquot and the rest of the egg mass were used to estimate fecundity. Fecundity data were compared between years and between "oiled" and "non-oiled" areas by analysis of covariance (ANCOVA). *SIZE* (carapace length) was always the covariate, and *YEAR* and *OILING* were the factors. It is generally assumed that the relationship between fecundity and a linear measurement of size takes the form of a power function. For that reason, data were log-transformed for the analyses.

Petroleum Hydrocarbons in Sediments and Animal Tissues

Field sampling of animal tissues--Specimens were obtained from trawl and pot catches. Materials collected during 1989 and 1990 included whole body of pink scallops (*Chlamys rubida*), muscle and eggs of spot shrimp, and muscle and eggs of adult Tanner crabs. Whole bodies of surface deposit-feeding clams (*Nuculana, Macoma, Yoldia* spp.), which were often found in the gut of flathead sole, were collected during Cruise 91/1 only. Whole individuals were briefly rinsed in a 3% NaCl/distilled water solution, placed in precleaned glass jars, and immediately frozen to -10 to -20 °C. All species of clams were pooled for analysis of petroleum hydrocarbons. Adult Tanner crabs were cut into pieces with clean tools (NaCl solution/acetone/hexane rinses between use), and these pieces were frozen as above.

Field sampling of sediments--Grab samples of sediments were collected on separate cruises during 1989 (25 July to 17 August and 21 September to 20 October), 1990 (10 February to 10 March and 8 August to 10 September) and 1991 (9 July to 29 July) for analyses of petroleum and total hydrocarbon concentrations, total organic carbon, sediment grain size, benthic infauna and sediment toxicity bioassays. Sediment samples were collected with solvent-rinsed, Teflon-coated van Veen or Smith-McIntyre grabs, which were considered successful only if the surface of the sediment in the grab appeared undisturbed, water was overlying the sediment, and the grab contained a sufficient volume of unconsolidated (finer grain) sediment in subsamples. Water was siphoned from grab samples, and subsamples were removed from the top 2 cm with solvent-cleaned utensils. Subsamples of sediments from each grab were put into precleaned glass or plastic jars or bags and held at 4 to 20 °C.

Laboratory measurements--Sediments and tissues to be analyzed for hydrocarbons had moisture contents determined by weighing before and after drying. This allowed calculation of hydrocarbon concentrations on a dry-weight basis. Lipid contents of tissues were estimated by evaporating aliquots of solvent extracts of tissues and weighing the residues, which were assumed to be lipids. Total organic carbon contents of sediment samples were determined by combusting the samples in a LECO® carbon analyzer and determining the amount of carbon dioxide generated. Interferences due to calcium carbonate were eliminated by first treating the samples with hydrochloric acid. Particle size distributions were determined at 1-ϕ intervals utilizing sieving techniques for particles greater than 4.0 ϕ (63 μm) and gravimetric pipetting to determine the silt-clay fractions (Folk 1974).

Extraction procedures for hydrocarbons--Sediment hydrocarbons were extracted from desiccated samples. Sequential extractions with 1:1 dichloromethane and acetone, under sonication, removed the hydrocarbons from the bulk materials. Pooled tissue samples were macerated mechanically and saponified with $6N$ potassium hydroxide. The hydrocarbons were taken up in ethyl ether. Both sediment and tissue extracts were reduced in volume by Kuderna-Danish techniques and evaporation under flowing nitrogen.

Fractionation and cleanup--Column chromatography was used to fractionate and cleanup extracts. For sediment extracts, columns were packed with alumina. Activated copper and anhydrous sodium sulfate were added to remove sulfur and moisture, respectively. Saturated and aromatic hydrocarbons were eluted together with dichloromethane. Tissue extracts, after solvent exchange to *n*-hexane, were loaded onto columns packed with silica gel and deactivated alumina. Interferences due to extracted sulfur were removed by capping the columns with activated copper. Elution with *n*-hexane separated the saturated hydrocarbons. A 1:1 mixture of dichloromethane and *n*-hexane was used to elute aromatic hydrocarbons.

Quantification--Quantification of polycyclic aromatic hydrocarbons (PAHs) was achieved by high-performance gas chromatography-mass spectrometry (GC/MS) operating in the selected-ion mode. The GC columns were 25- or 30-m fused silica capillaries with DB-5 bonded phases. All samples were spiked with deuterated surrogate compounds before extraction to assess extraction efficiencies. Deuterated internal standards, added just before GC/MS analysis, were used to quantify the analytes. Table 3a lists the surrogate and internal standard compounds as well as the acceptance criteria for extraction efficiencies. Table 3b lists PAH and alkylated PAH analytes reported by the laboratories. In the following discussion, naphthalenes have been omitted from summations of PAH analytes (total PAHs) in tissues because of their occurrence, sometimes in high concentrations, as laboratory contaminants in reagent method blanks.

Data analysis--Data were always log-transformed to stabilize the variances. All tests were one-tailed, with $\alpha = 0.05$. The null hypothesis of equal mean sediment hydrocarbon concentrations among "oiled" and "non-oiled" bays was tested with an analysis of variance (ANOVA). Data for 1989 and 1990 were tested separately. Total PAHs and EVC PAHs were tested separately. Bays were used as replicates.

An ANOVA was used to test the null hypothesis of equal mean total tissue PAH concentrations among "oiled" and "non-oiled" bays for Tanner crabs, spot shrimp, scallops, and clams. Crabs, shrimp, and scallops were tested for 1989 and 1990. Data for clams were available for 1991 only. The null hypothesis of no time-by-treatment interaction (equal change in mean concentration between years for "oiled" and "non-oiled" bays) was also tested for crabs, shrimp, and scallops. Bays were used as replicates.

Flathead Sole Bile Metabolites and Gut Contents

Field methods--Bile was collected for metabolite analyses from up to 25 flathead sole individuals per bay per cruise. Specimens were kept alive until dissection and sacrificed within 2 h of capture. Bile was extracted with disposable syringes, transferred to specially cleaned amber glass vials, frozen immediately in liquid nitrogen, and kept in the dark. Contents of stomachs and intestines of fish sacrificed for bile extraction (see below) were identified during Cruise 91/1. Bivalve prey were identified to species, counted, and shell lengths measured.

Laboratory methods--FACs in fish bile are commonly used as indicators of exposure to aromatic hydrocarbons. The concentrations of FACs in fish bile were estimated using high-performance liquid chromatography (HPLC) with fluorescence detection (Krahn et al. 1986). Bile was injected directly into the instrument without extraction or cleanup. The excitation and emission wavelengths utilized for naphthalene equivalents were 292 and 335 nm; for phenanthrene equivalents, they were 257 and 380 nm. The areas for all peaks eluting between 5 and 22 min were integrated and summed to calculate naphthalene equivalents, and the areas for peaks eluting between 5 and 28 min were integrated and summed for phenanthrene equivalents. Sample FAC concentrations were determined by comparing peak areas with those obtained from calibration standards. A reference bile sample, provided by the National Oceanographic and Atmospheric Administration's (NOAA) NMFS Northwest Fisheries Center, was analyzed with each quality control (QC) sample batch in 1990 and 1991. Relative standard deviations of no more than ±15% of the mean were required in order to proceed with the bile sample analysis.

TABLE 3--(a): *Surrogate compounds and internal standards for PAH analyses.* (b): *PAH and alkyl PAH target compounds.*

a

Year	Surrogate Compounds	Internal Standards	Acceptance (%)
1989	Naphthalene-d8	Acenaphthene-d10	40-120
	Fluorene-d10	Phenanthrene-d10	40-120
	Chrysene-d12	Benzo[a]pyrene-d12	40-120
1990/91	Naphthalene-d8	Fluorene-d10	50-125
	Acenaphthalene-d10	Chrysene-d12	50-125

b

Compound	Compound	Compound
Naphthalene	Phenanthrene	Chrysene
C1-Naphthalenes	C1-Phenanthrenes	C1-Chrysenes
C2-Naphthalenes	C2-Phenanthrenes	C2-Chrysenes
C3-Naphthalenes	C3-Phenanthrenes	C3-Chrysenes
C4-Naphthalenes	C4-Phenanthrenes	C4-Chrysenes
Acenaphthylene	Anthracene	Benzo[b]fluoranthene
	C1-Anthracenes	
Acenaphthene	C2-Anthracenes	Benzo[k]fluoranthene
	C3-Anthracenes	
Biphenyl	C4-Anthracenes	Benzo[a]pyrene
Fluorene	Fluoranthene	Benzo[e]pyrene
C1-Fluorenes	C1-Fluoranthenes	
C2-Fluorenes		Indeno[1,2,3-c,d]pyrene
C3-Fluorenes	Pyrene	
	C1-Pyrenes	Dibenzo[a,h]anthracene
Dibenzothiophene		
C1-Dibenzothiophenes	Benzo[a]anthracene	Benzo[g,h,i]perylene
C2-Dibenzothiophenes		
C3-Dibenzothiophenes		

Data analyses--Two hypotheses were tested using ANCOVA on log-transformed bile FAC concentrations, with depth as the covariate. The null hypothesis of equal mean bile FAC concentration among "oiled" and "non-oiled" bays was tested (one-tailed test) separately for 1989, 1990, and 1991. The null hypothesis of no time-by-treatment interaction (equal change in mean concentration between years for "oiled" and "non-oiled" bays) was tested for 1989 to 1990 and 1990 to 1991.

The null hypothesis of no positive correlation between bile metabolites and PAH concentrations (total and EVC) in sediments was tested by linear regression for 1989 and 1990. Linear regression was also used to test the null hypothesis of no positive correlation between concentration of PAHs (total and pyrogenic) in clam tissues and FACs in flathead sole bile. Bay means were used in all of the analyses.

Flathead Sole Histopathology

Field methods--Tissue samples (liver, kidney, and gills in 1989; liver only in 1990 and 1991) from as many as 60 flathead sole per bay (including those sampled for bile) were collected during each cruise for histopathological study. Small pieces of tissue were fixed and preserved in 10% buffered formalin in seawater.

Laboratory methods--The preserved tissues were dehydrated through a graded ethanol series, cleared in xylene, embedded in paraffin, and sectioned (5 μm) using a rotary microtome. Tissue sections were stained with hematoxylin and eosin (Luna 1968) and examined by light microscopy. The pathologist examining the slides was not informed of the geographic sites from which the fish were collected ("blind reading"). Each tissue was first scanned at low magnification (40X) for general form and contour. Subsequently, the entire section was examined at high magnification (430X) for the presence of pathological alterations. A verbal description of each lesion was recorded, and the severity of the change was indicated by a numerical score equivalent to mild (severity score = 1), moderate (severity score = 2), or severe (severity score = 3). Numerical codes were assigned to each lesion according to the National Ocean Data Center's (NODC) histopathology coding system. Over the course of the entire study, tissues from 1062 flathead sole were examined.

Data analysis--Histopathology data were summarized to indicate the presence or absence of a particular lesion(s) in the fish tissues. These binary variables were analyzed using GLIM (NAG 1985) based on a binomial error structure and logit-link. Comparison of "oiled" and "non-oiled" bays was based on the proportion of fish possessing a histological anomaly after adjustment for depth. A second analysis determined the correlation between the binary histological responses and bile FAC concentration of individual fish collected. Tests of significance were based on asymptotic F-tests using analysis of deviance (ANODEV, McCullagh and Nelder 1983).

Assessment of Hydrocarbon Sources

Several chemical characteristics of PAH relative to their origin can assist in determining their sources. First, PAHs derived from the combustion of carbonaceous materials, such as wood, coal or petroleum fuels, have a preponderance of unsubstituted (no alkyl groups attached) compounds. Polycyclic aromatic hydrocarbons so created are referred to in this paper as pyrogenic PAHs. Crude oil and other petrogenic PAHs sources, on the other hand, contain a relatively high proportion of substituted PAHs, which have one or more alkyl groups in the chemical structure. Gulf of Alaska (GOA) seep oils and Alaska North Slope (ANS) crude and refined oils all contain high proportions of alkylated PAHs. Thus, differences in the abundance of unsubstituted or substituted hydrocarbons can assist in differentiating sources of PAHs in the sediments.

Second, the relative abundance of specific compounds within crude oils can be indicative of their sources. For instance, the ratio of C2-Phenanthrene or C3-Phenanthrene to C2-Dibenzothiophene or C3-Dibenzothiophene, respectively, in ANS oils are quite different from the ratios of the same compounds in crude oil derived from natural seeps in the Katalla and Yakataga-area of the Gulf of Alaska. Figure 2 illustrates the C3-Dibenzothiophene (C3-D) versus C3-Phenanthrene (C3-P) ratios for samples of ANS crude and diesel oils, as well as for GOA crude oils. While the ANS samples have a C3-D/C3-P ratio of about 1.2, the ratio for GOA oils is less than 0.2. The proportions of these compounds can be used to estimate the relative abundances of hydrocarbons from the two oil types, ANS and GOA, within the same sediment (Page et al., this volume). However, the variation in the GOA background ratio, compounded by the error in measurement as the concentrations of substituted dibenzothiophenes approach the detection limit, makes it impossible to accurately determine the ANS fraction at low PAH concentrations. Therefore, sediments with alkylated PAHs below 15 ng/g are called "indeterminate."

The *Exxon Valdez* crude oil (EVC) cargo was of ANS origin. Although numerous other sources of ANS oils may be locally important at sites of present and historical human activity throughout PWS (Page et al., this volume), in the following text PAH ratios typical of ANS crude oil will generally indicate the presence of EVC.

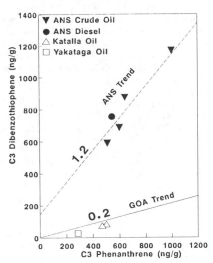

FIG. 2--*Relationship between C3-dibenzothiophene and C3-phenanthrene in crude oils and diesel from the Alaskan North Slope (ANS) and the Katalla and Yakataga seep areas of the Gulf of Alaska (GOA). All values are in ng/g of the whole oil.*

RESULTS

Characterization of Exposure

Bay physical features--Bays differed substantially in certain physical measurements and at times reflected different oceanographic features as well. Some had sills, and maximum depth differed by over 100 m (Table 2). Although the ranges of physical and chemical measurements were commensurate across bays, occasional values within bays were sometimes extreme seasonally, and the vertical structure of the water column was pronounced. Bottom water temperature and surface salinity were the two most noteworthy features. The former usually ranged between 3.8 to 6.0 °C (Table 2), and the latter often between 16 to 20 ppt at the surface in midsummer (Fig. 3). A thermocline was common at 40- to 50-m depths in most bays where surface and bottom temperatures often differed by 8 °C in July and August. Mean bottom water temperatures rarely exceeded 5 °C, and surface salinities were commonly 24 ppt to a depth of 10 to 20 m (Fig. 3).

Oiling indices--The cluster analysis based on the four oiling indices (percent shoreline oiling, bile metabolites in flathead sole, bivalve tissue hydrocarbons, percent of trawls with oil) identified several hierarchical subsets of bays, depending upon the ED selected. All "non-oiled" bays clustered tightly (ED <1.4, Fig. 4a). Only one of four "oiled" bays (Northwest Bay) clustered at some level with the "non-oiled" bays (ED = 3.3). The remaining "oiled" bays clustered together (at ED 4.0 and 13.1). Although Northwest Bay was one of the most heavily oiled in 1989 as indicated by shoreline oiling (60% of shoreline) and had a high proportion of trawls at depth with evidence of oil (30%), values of its "oiling indices" were reduced to levels comparable to some "non-oiled" bays by 1991. The mean of total bivalve tissue PAH in Northwest Bay was also comparable to "non-oiled" locations, but bile metabolites were somewhat elevated compared with the mean of "non-oiled" bays (see *Metabolites in flatfish bile* and Fig. 7, below). Thus, the cluster analysis based on oiling indices exhibiting subtle differences in exposure for 1991 generally supported the initial classification of bays as "oiled" versus "non-oiled" followed in survey design and statistical analyses.

Cluster analysis incorporating environmental indices (basin area, bay area, bay volume, compass orientation, bottom temperature, and bottom salinity) identified a hierarchy of similarity among bays. However, there was no dichotomy between "oiled" and "non-oiled" bays. Clusters were determined primarily by volume, surface area, and watershed (which tend to be correlated with each other). For example, three "oiled" bays (Herring Bay, Bay of Isles, and Snug Harbor) and two "non-oiled" bays (Galena Bay and Drier Bay) clustered into separate groups (ED about 1.5, Fig. 4b). However, together with Jackpot Bay, all six formed a major cluster (ED = 7.6). Moreover, one "non-oiled" (Port Etches) and one "oiled" (Northwest Bay) bay clustered together (ED = 5.8). Finally, Port Gravina ("non-oiled"), which is the largest of all the bays in both area and volume, did not cluster with any of the other eight bays. As far as we can ascertain, there is no confounding between oiling and a linear combination of the environmental indices. This is viewed as evidence that "oiled" and "non-oiled" bays were not coincidentally grouped by virtue of important physical features. Moreover, as far as we can ascertain, there is no confounding between oiling and environmental conditions that could flaw statistical comparisons of population abundance and hydrocarbon concentrations.

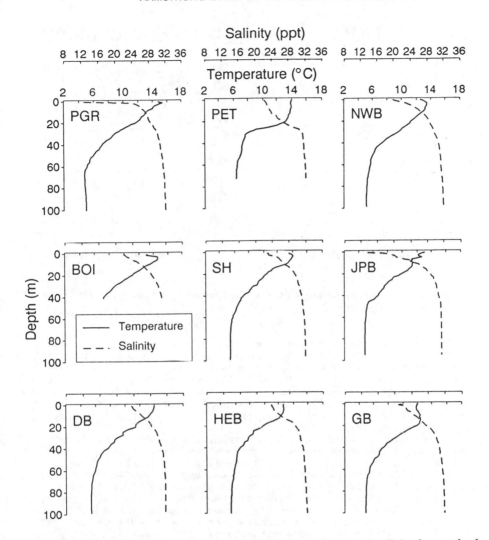

FIG. 3--*Representative water column profiles of temperature and salinity from each of the nine primary study embayments, recorded during Cruise 90/2 (22 August to 14 September). Note distinct thermocline and lowered surface salinity. See Table 1 for bay abbreviations.*

Sediment hydrocarbons--Polycyclic aromatic hydrocarbons (PAHs) of multiple origins, both natural and anthropogenic, are found in subtidal sediments throughout Prince William Sound. Petrogenic PAHs are generally the most abundant type of PAH, even in subsurface prespill sediments (Page et al., this volume). Figure 5a illustrates the overall average TPAH concentrations in sediments from "oiled" and "non-oiled" bays in this study as a function of time. While TPAH values in sediments varied

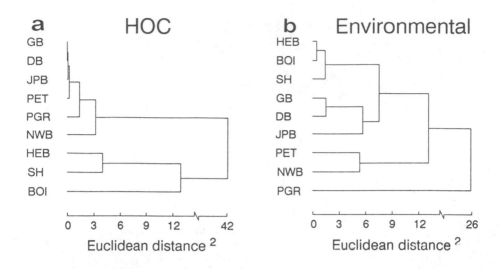

FIG. 4--*Results of cluster analysis of PWS bays based on (a) hydrocarbon (HOC) or (b) environmental characteristics.*

widely between sites, they were comparable, on average, between "oiled" and "non-oiled" bays. In 1989, the mean TPAH in subtidal sediments from "oiled" bays was 615 ng/g, and in "non-oiled" bays it was 469 ng/g. The mean TPAH concentrations in 1990 were 716 ng/g and 416 ng/g at "oiled" and "non-oiled" bays, respectively. In 1991, all but eight samples collected within study bays came from one "oiled" and one "non-oiled" site (Bay of Isles and Drier Bay); thus, they do not represent the broader range of sampling in earlier years.

Determination of the EVC component in sediments showed that such spill-related PAHs were present at many sites within heavily "oiled" bays, and that bays classified as "non-oiled" had little, if any, evidence of EVC PAHs relative to the total background PAH concentration (Fig. 5a). The data show a trend toward decreasing EVC PAH concentrations through time following the winter of 1989-90. Trends at individual sampling sites generally showed a similar pattern. Figure 5b illustrates trends at sites that were sampled repeatedly through 1991: the two "oiled" bay sites were situated off shorelines with heavy oiling in 1989. The EVC fraction was an increment above the natural background PAH concentrations and diminished with time. Visual sightings of oil in benthic trawls corroborate the identification of EVC PAHs in sediments by the fingerprinting techniques. Figure 5c illustrates the frequency of observations of oil in benthic trawls from "oiled" (Bay of Isles, Snug Harbor) and "non-oiled" (Drier Bay) bays through time.

The total organic carbon (TOC) content of the sediments collected for PAH analyses ranged from 0.1% to 10%. Highest TOC levels were generally found in the "oiled" bays. Highest TOC values in "non-oiled" bays were found in Drier Bay. PAHs in sediments tend to increase with increasing organic carbon: this relationship was best illustrated by sediments from Jackpot Bay ($r^2 = 0.55$) and Snug Harbor ($r^2 = 0.99$).

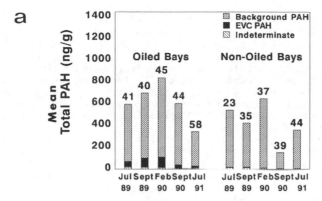

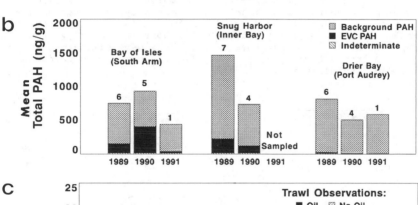

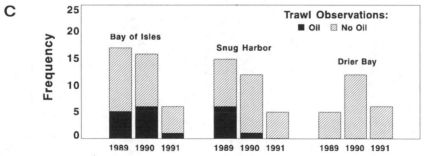

FIG. 5--*Evidence of background hydrocarbons and EVC in the study bays shown as average TPAHs, subdivided as* Exxon Valdez *crude (EVC) PAHs, background PAHs, and an indeterminate fraction. (a) Overall mean concentrations of PAHs in sediments of study embayments through time. (b) Temporal trends (averaged by year) in sediment PAHs at one subtidal station from each of three bays. The two "oiled" sites in Bay of Isles and Snug Harbor were near heavily oiled shorelines and represent a typical pattern of diminishing EVC PAH content with time, as well as a worst-case situation in terms of total EVC PAH content in the sediments. In both 5a and 5b, the number of samples analyzed is shown above each bar. (c) Frequency with which oil, as tar balls, small particles, sheen, or strong odor, was observed in the contents of bottom trawls from within three representative embayments.*

Hydrocarbons in tissues--Scallops are epibenthic filter feeders. Those collected in 1989 from the "oiled" bays had whole-body PAH concentrations averaging 292 *ng/g*, while in 1990 the concentrations had decreased substantially, averaging 16 *ng/g*. It should be noted that PAHs in scallops from the "non-oiled" bays also decreased by 1990 even though the initial 1989 levels were substantially less than those from "oiled" bays. This is addressed further in the discussion. Alkylated aromatics, indicative of petrogenic sources including oil, were prevalent in scallop tissues from "oiled" areas in 1989 but were rarely detected in 1990 tissue samples (Fig. 6a).

Analysis of infaunal bivalves collected in 1991 from "oiled" and "non-oiled" bays in PWS showed the presence of PAHs in tissue samples from all bays. *Macoma, Yoldia,* and *Nuculana* spp. collected in "non-oiled" bays had a mean PAH concentration of 30 *ng/g*. Bivalves collected from "oiled" bays had a mean of 70 *ng/g* and could be grouped into two classes on the basis of their PAH concentrations: samples from Bay of Isles showed two- to three-fold higher total PAH concentrations than samples from other "oiled," as well as "non-oiled" bays. In addition, four of five samples from Bay of Isles showed high proportions of alkylated PAHs (Fig. 6b). Bivalves from the other "oiled" bays were similar to bivalves from "non-oiled" sites in that they did not have detectable alkylated PAH concentrations.

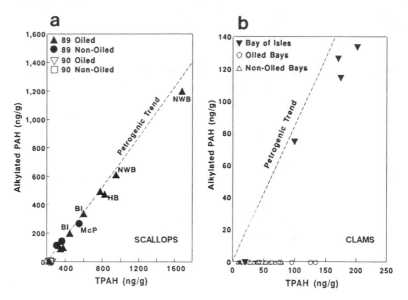

FIG. 6--*(a) Relationship between alkylated and total PAHs (TPAHs) in scallops collected in 1989 and 1990. Several samples collected in 1989, primarily from "oiled" bays, have abundant alkylated PAHs typical of a petrogenic source. All samples from 1990 plot near the origin, having low TPAH concentrations and nondetectable quantities of alkylated PAHs. (b) Relationship between alkylated and total PAHs in surface-deposit-feeding clams collected in 1991. Four of five samples collected in the Bay of Isles had abundant alkylated PAHs typical of a petrogenic source. All other samples from both "oiled" and "non-oiled" bays had nondetectable quantities of alkylated PAHs.*

Analyses of muscle tissues from adult Tanner crabs and spot shrimp from "oiled" and "non-oiled" sites generally showed low concentrations of total PAHs and substituted PAHs were nondetectable. Tanner crab muscle PAH concentrations ranged up to 32 ng/g with no difference in concentrations between 1989 and 1990. Spot shrimp muscle tissues generally contained <20 ng/g TPAHs, although a few samples ranged up to 117 ng/g TPAH. Alkylated PAHs were consistently low or nondetectable. The PAHs found were primarily non-alkylated 3-ring compounds with very low concentrations of 4- and 5-ringed PAHs. There was no difference in concentrations between "oiled" and "non-oiled" bays, or between 1989 and 1990. Analyses of PAHs in Tanner crab and spot shrimp egg masses showed that they were enriched in PAHs relative to muscle (up to 161 ng/g in Tanner crab eggs, 374 ng/g in spot shrimp eggs), but that there were no significant differences in TPAH concentrations between samples from "oiled" and "non-oiled" areas in either species, or between years in Tanner crab eggs. Little evidence of alkylated PAHs in muscle tissues of spot shrimp and Tanner crabs, and in Tanner crab eggs suggest a non-petrogenic source. Spot shrimp eggs, while not adequately sampled in 1989 for statistical comparison, show PAH compositions similar to the crustacean tissues.

Metabolites in flatfish bile--Both naphthalene and phenanthrene equivalent FACs showed similar spatial and temporal trends. Naphthalene and phenanthrene equivalent FAC values for the same bile samples were found to be highly correlated (r^2 = 0.91); therefore, only naphthalene equivalents will be reported and discussed. FACs occurred in the bile of all fish collected in PWS in 1989, 1990, and 1991, both within and outside of areas visually affected by the spill. Since the quantification procedure used in 1989 was different, i.e. only selected peaks were quantified rather than the total response, metabolite concentrations from 1989 are not compared with collections from 1990 and 1991. Flathead sole from "oiled" bays showed significantly higher FAC concentrations than fish from the "non-oiled" bays in 1990 and 1991 (P <0.001 both years; Fig. 7). However, FAC concentrations in fish from one of the "oiled" bays, Northwest Bay, were lower than in the other "oiled" bays and were not significantly different from those in fish from "non-oiled" sites. In 1990 and 1991, mean FAC values in fish from "oiled" and "non-oiled" bays were 27.1 and 14.5 $\mu g/g$, and 28.6 and 13.1 $\mu g/g$, respectively.

Characterization of Effect

Tanner crab planktonic larvae--Larval stages (primarily zoea 1 and 2; few megalopae) of Tanner crab were ubiquitous throughout all areas sampled in PWS during Cruises 89/1 and 90/1 (May to mid-June). Since Cruise 89/1 was exploratory, many bongo and neuston plankton samples were taken from "open" water as well as embayments, which averaged 354 and 201 larvae/1000 m^3, respectively (Fig. 8). As noted in Materials and Methods, many bays sampled during that first cruise were not retained in the long-term survey design; nonetheless, no evidence of lower larval density in "oiled" bays was detected. Larval densities in those bays initially classified as "non-oiled", lightly "oiled" (Lower Herring, Drier, and Mummy bays), and "oiled" averaged 153, 128, and 287 zoea/1000 m^3, respectively. When plankton samples collected from bays in 1989 were processed in the laboratory, an oil sheen was sometimes noticed in the sorting tray. Mean densities of Tanner crab zoea grouped in accord

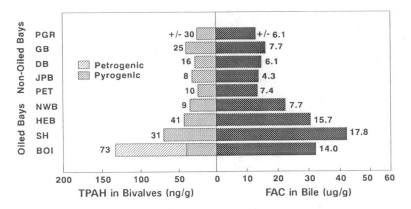

FIG. 7--*Comparison by bay of mean total PAHs (ng/g TPAHs) body burdens in deposit-feeding prey clams* (Macoma, Yoldia, *and* Nuculana *spp. combined) and mean FAC concentrations (as μg/g naphthalene equivalents) measured by bay in flathead sole bile in 1991. Total PAHs are subdivided as petrogenic (alkylated) and non-petrogenic (unalkylated) for Bay of Isles samples, the only samples containing detectable alkylated PAHs. Numbers beside each bar indicate the standard deviation about the mean value reported. TPAHs in clams and FACs in bile of flathead sole were both significantly elevated (P <0.05) in the "oiled" bays in 1991.*

with or without indication of oil in the preserved sample (irrespective of bay) were 290 and 145/1000 m^3, respectively. Of plankton samples from "open water" areas, nine contained an indication of oil and 53 did not, and respective larval Tanner crab densities were 434 and 337/1000 m^3.

Larval Tanner crab densities in 1990 bongo samples were substantially lower in the same month than the preceding year across all bays of the survey, irrespective of whether "oiled" or "non-oiled" (8.5 and 8.4 zoea/1000 m^3). Whereas substantial numbers of Tanner crab larvae were caught in neuston samples in 1989, no larvae at all were taken in the surface layer in 1990.

Tanner crab size and age structure, recruitment, and growth--Young-of-the-year (YOY) juvenile Tanner crabs (CL <12 mm) were not observed during cruises conducted between late spring and midsummer (May to mid-June, Cruises 89/1 and 90/1), when larvae were still found in the water column. Larval settlement takes place during midsummer, and YOY crabs were caught in BT samples collected between mid-July and October, producing a clear signal in the size frequency distributions (SFDs; Fig. 9a) for all three of the year classes that settled during this study. Largest catches were obtained during 1990 and 1991 in Port Etches.

Decomposition of juvenile/subadult Tanner crab (CL <50 mm) SFDs into modal instar components indicated that the number and spacing of instars were consistent with preliminary values estimated by Donaldson et al. (1981) for PWS (exact area not specified). At any given time, a typical year class of juvenile crabs was largely composed of two (sometimes three) instars. Approximate boundaries between year classes are indicated in Fig. 9a by vertical dashed lines. Most of the juvenile crabs in the 1989 samples corresponded to the 1987 and 1988 year classes, whose growth could be tracked through the duration of the study (Fig. 9a). Starting in the late summer of 1990, these year classes grew

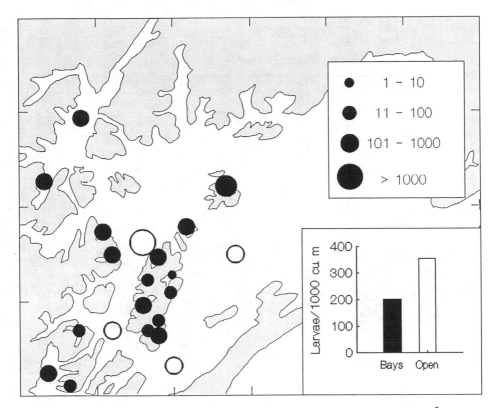

FIG. 8--*Tanner crab larvae (zoea 1 and 2) mean CPUE s (number of larvae/1000 m^3) from Prince William Sound, Cruise 89/1, shown as averages of stations from four areas of open water (open circles) and individual bays (closed circles). Lower right insert: mean density in bays and open areas.*

beyond the size threshold (50 mm CL) below which crabs are efficiently sampled by the BT, but started to appear in the CP catches (Fig. 9b, c). During 1989 and the late spring-early summer of 1990 (Cruise 90/1), few crabs smaller than 80 mm (males) or 65 mm (females) were caught in the CPs, but they were evident in late summer 1990 and fairly common by 1991 and were derived from the 87/88 year classes. There was no indication of recruitment to the legal size segment of the stock (CL >135 mm, CW ~110 mm; ADF&G 1991) during the study (Fig. 9b).

Tanner crab abundance (CPUE)--Density data were analyzed separately for YOY (CL <12 mm) and older (CL ≥12 mm) juvenile Tanner crabs caught with the BT. For YOY, Cruises 89/1 and 90/1 were not included because new year classes had not settled when sampling was conducted (late spring). CPUE of YOY was highest in Port Etches (2915 crabs/ha in 1990 and 4929 crabs/ha in 1991, Fig. 10); few YOY were caught in three other "non-oiled" bays (Jackpot, Drier, and Galena). Highest mean CPUE of YOY in an "oiled" bay was about 240 crabs/ha in Northwest Bay in 1989, but values more typically ranged from 20 to 150 crabs/ha (Fig. 10). Older

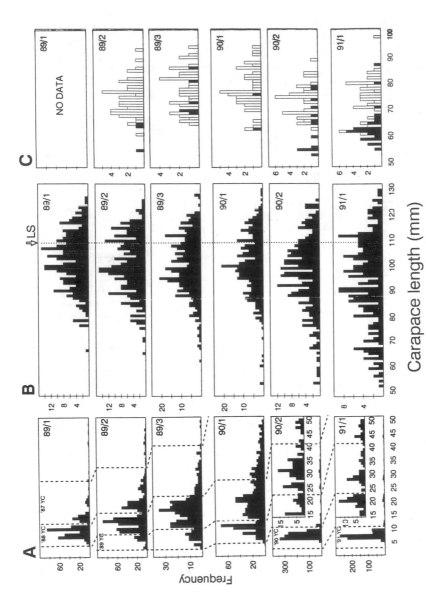

FIG. 9--(a) Juvenile Tanner crab size frequency distributions (SFDs) by cruise from beam trawl catches showing 1987 to 1991 year classes (YC). Vertical dashed lines correspond to the approximate mean boundaries between year classes. (b) Adult male Tanner crab SFD by cruise from the crab pots; LS = legal size. (c) Adult female Tanner crab SFD by cruise from the crab pots. Dark bars indicate nonovigerous females and open bars indicate ovigerous females.

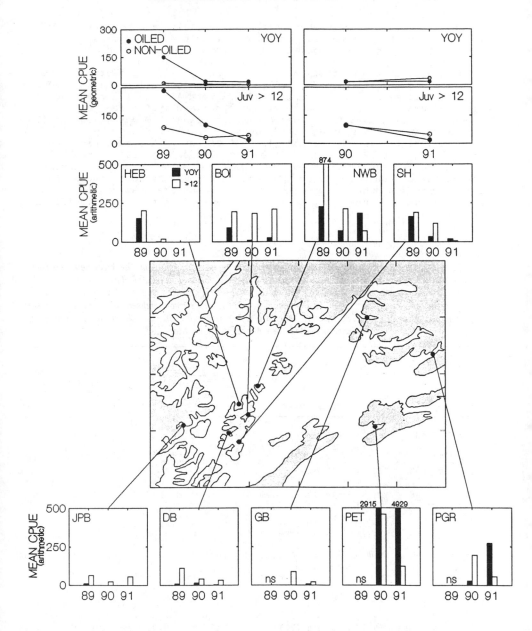

FIG. 10--*Juvenile Tanner crab mean CPUE (number/ha) shown separately for young-of-the-year (CL <12 mm, dark bars) and older (CL ≥12 mm, open bars) caught by beam trawl in the nine primary study bays. NS indicates not sampled. Upper panels show time trends in CPUE compared as means of values from the "oiled" and "non-oiled" bays based on two subsets (see Table 4 for test results).*

juveniles were relatively abundant in Bay of Isles and Northwest Bay (both "oiled" bays, about 240 crabs/ha across the three years), and generally less so in "non-oiled" bays (about 50 crabs/ha on average, Fig. 10).

During the three years of the study, mean CPUE of YOY declined after 1989, more drastically in the "oiled" than in "non-oiled" bays. Vectors of geometric means for the period 1989-91 were [151 18 17] crabs/ha and [10 4 2] crabs/ha for, respectively, "oiled" and "non-oiled" bays (vector notation used for annual geometric means). Older juveniles (CL ≥12 mm) displayed a similar trend; density in the first two years was generally higher in the "oiled" ([284 99 19] crabs/ha) compared with "non-oiled" ([86 32 43] crabs/ha) bays (Table 4, Fig. 10). Trends in CPUE in "oiled" and "non-oiled" bays were not significantly different for either of the two size groups considered, whether or not the two- or three-year data subsets were included, although the test result for the quadratic model (three-year data subset) was close to being significant ($P = 0.11$).

TABLE 4--*CPUE analyses and statistical comparisons. Results of the treatment-by-time interaction test. Treatments were "oiled" (O) and "non-oiled" (NO). Tests are two-tailed. Statistical power was calculated given the observed variances and a 50% reduction in population numbers over what was expected if oil had no effect. Subsets of data are analyzed for two time intervals, 1989 through 1991 and 1990 through 1991, and differ in the number of bays included (see Materials and Methods).*

Species	Gear	Data Subset	Restricted Set of Bays (1989-1991) Probability Linear Model	Quadratic Model	Full Set of Bays (1990-1991) Probability	Power
Tanner crab	BT	CL <12 mm (YOY) No Cr. 89/1, 90/1	0.77	0.28	0.44	0.18
Tanner crab	BT	CL ≥12 mm	0.12	0.11	0.26	0.20
Tanner crab	CP	Female, CW >60 mm No Cruise 89/1 Depth >50 m Soak time 40-50 h	0.24	0.49	0.21	0.50
Tanner crab	CP	Male, CW >60 mm Depth >50 m Soak time 40-50 h	0.07*	0.28	0.26	0.34
Pink shrimp	BT	CL <15 mm	0.65	0.36	0.58	0.13
Flathead sole	BT	TL <60 mm (YOY) No Cr. 89/1, 90/1	0.28	0.02*	0.90	0.19
Flathead sole	OT	TL ≥60 mm No Cruise 89/1	0.97	0.26	0.06*	0.30

*Significant at 0.10.

Adult male Tanner crabs were caught in all bays, while females were virtually never caught in several of them (for example, Herring Bay, Northwest Bay, Port Gravina, Port Etches). Mean CPUE of males was generally in the range of 4 to 8 crabs/CP in both "oiled" and "non-oiled" bays; mean female CPUE was typically a third to half of male CPUE. Linear trends of male CPUE over the three-year period (Fig. 11) were significantly different ($P = 0.07$, Table 4), largely due to a decrease in CPUE (8 to 2 crabs/CP) in the "non-oiled" bays from 1990 to 1991, concomitant with an increase in the "oiled" bays (Fig. 11). Trends in female CPUE did not differ significantly in any of the analyses.

Dead Tanner crabs--Sixteen dead juvenile Tanner crabs were caught in the BT in three bays (Galena Bay, Bay of Isles, and Snug Harbor) during Cruise 90/1, which equated to mean densities of 3, 5, and 44 crabs/ha, respectively. No dead Tanner crabs were collected from the other six bays, and none were collected throughout 1989 nor during subsequent Cruises 90/2 and 91/1. During Cruise 90/1, there was a significant relationship between the occurrence of dead Tanner crabs and an indicator of hydrocarbon exposure, the level of FACs in the bile of flathead sole ($P = 0.039$) sampled from the same bays, after adjustment for station depth ($P = 0.042$).

Tanner crab fecundity--Female Tanner crab fecundity was highly variable (Fig. 12a) and ranged from about 100,000 (68 mm CL) to a maximum of about 400,000 eggs/female (85 mm CL). Variability may in part be attributable to difference in fecundity between primiparous and multiparous females (Somerton and Meyers 1983), but it was not possible to separate these two groups with certainty. There were very few ovigerous females sampled from "oiled" bays in 1989 ($n_{oiled} = 3$) and 1990 ($n_{oiled} = 5$). For that reason fecundity was compared between "oiled" and "non-oiled" bays only in 1991 (Fig. 12b; $n_{oiled} = 26$, $n_{non-oiled} = 37$). The effects of the *OILING-by-SIZE* interaction and of *OILING* were not statistically significant. Data from "oiled" and "non-oiled" bays were pooled to compare fecundity across years (Fig. 12a). The effects of the *YEAR-by-SIZE* interaction and *YEAR* were not statistically significant.

Pandalid shrimp planktonic larvae--Larval hatching had already taken place in the three species by 26 May, when the sampling season started in 1989 and 1990. From the three 1989 cruises, pandalid larval density was higher within bays than in open areas; respective average densities for Cruise 89/1 (26 May to 21 June) were about 150 and 125 larvae/1000 m^3. Mean larval density declined rapidly through the 1989 sampling season to about 25 larvae/1000 m^3 during Cruise 89/2 (24 July to 13 August) and to fewer than 10 larvae/1000 m^3 during Cruise 89/3 (20 September to 20 October). Larvae of spot shrimp (the only larvae that could be identified to the species level) were present during Cruise 89/1 in five of the bays sampled, at densities of 10 to 40 larvae/1000 m^3. In both 1989 and 1990, pandalid shrimp larvae were present in the water column in greatest density during Cruises 89/1 and 90/1 only. Mean densities of pandalid shrimp larvae were consistently greater in 1989 than in 1990 for both "oiled" and "non-oiled" bays. As with Tanner crab larvae, there seemed to be a general decline in planktonic larval densities for shrimp in 1990 throughout all bays sampled. Whereas substantial numbers of shrimp larvae were observed in the neuston in 1989, no larvae at all were observed in the surface layer in 1990.

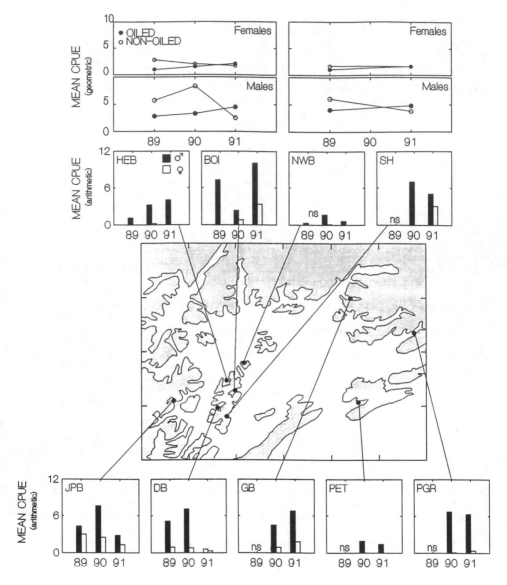

FIG. 11--*Adult Tanner crab (CL ≥60 mm) mean CPUE (crabs per pot fished 40 to 50 h) by bay (males, dark bars; females, open bars) and "oiled" versus "non-oiled" bay comparisons (see Table 4 for test results). NS indicates not sampled.*

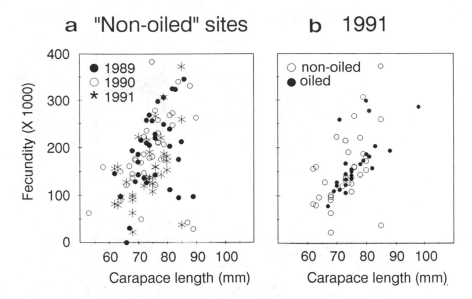

FIG. 12--(a)*Relationship between female Tanner crab fecundity (egg number) and carapace length for years 1989, 1990 and 1991 ("non-oiled" areas only) and (b) the same relationship from "oiled" versus "non-oiled" bays, 1991 only.*

*Pandalid shrimp size and age structure, recruitment, and growth--*Spot shrimp (*Pandalus platyceros*) from Alaska spawn in the deeper parts of bays, entering shallow, rocky, kelp-covered areas during or soon after settlement from the larval stage, and spend two growing seasons in these shallow areas (Barr 1971, 1973). All life history stages were sampled during the study (Fig. 13a): larvae with plankton nets (mostly during Cruises 89/1 and 90/1), juveniles (age classes 0+ and 1+) with the BT, and adults with the OT (age 1+ and older) and SPs (age 2+ and older). Post-larval YOY juveniles were not well sampled. SFD analyses indicate that maximum longevity in PWS is at least 10 years (Fig. 13a), consistent with preliminary conclusions from a tagging study conducted by ADF&G in Unakwik Inlet, PWS (Kimker and Donaldson 1987). During the first two years of life (ages 0+ and 1+) shrimp are immature; they start to mature as males during the third year (age 2+). Sex change takes place mostly during the fifth and sixth calendar years of life (ages 4+ and 5+). CL of the smallest ovigerous female caught was 31 mm, but most ovigerous females were larger than 37 mm (Fig. 13a, right). Most of the spawning stock is composed of females in age groups 5+ and older (a few are age 4+). Strongest new recruitment was observed in Galena Bay (BT and OT samples) during the late summer of 1990, corresponding to shrimp of age 1+ (1989 year class).

The coonstripe shrimp (*Pandalus hypsinotus*) measures 2.5 to 3.5 mm (CL) at the time of settlement (Baik et al. 1991). YOY (age 0+) in PWS reach a CL of 6 to 11 mm by the end of summer. Mean size-at-age was larger and longevity higher in Jackpot Bay (age 3+ well represented) than in bays around Knight Island (very few shrimp older than age 2+) (Fig. 13b).

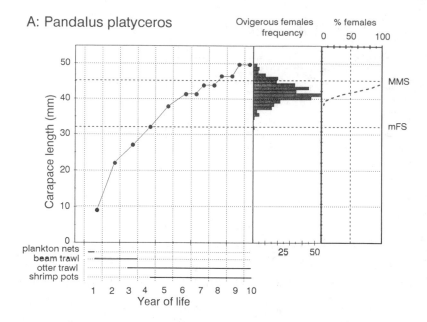

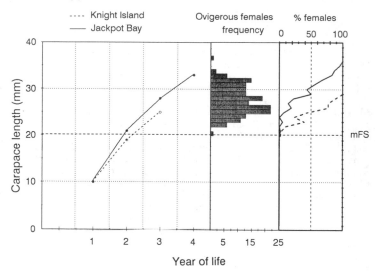

FIG. 13--*Schematic representation of the life history of spot shrimp (a) and pink shrimp (b) in Prince William Sound, based on our data. Left block: dots correspond to mean size-at-age in late summer (August-September). Middle block: size frequency distribution of ovigerous females. Right block: percent sex composition as a function of size. The size scale on the left applies to all three blocks. MMS = maximum male size, mFS = minimum female size.*

Most shrimp change sex during their third calendar year of life (age 2+), but given the differences in growth indicated above, size at which sex ratio is 1:1 is 25 mm around Knight Island and 31 mm in Jackpot Bay (Fig. 13b, right).

Pink shrimp (*Pandalus borealis*) larvae are generally assumed to hatch around April in the Gulf of Alaska (Anderson 1991). Juveniles of age 0+, 5- to 7-mm CL in size, were best represented in BT samples from Galena Bay obtained during Cruise 91/1. Average size of age classes 1+ to 3+ was larger in samples from the eastern sector (Galena Bay, Port Gravina, Port Etches) than from the western sector (Jackpot Bay). In late summer of 1991, for example, approximate mean size of age vector [1+ 2+ 3+] was [10 16 19] mm CL in the west sector, and [13 19 21] mm in the east sector. Largest male size (17 mm) and size range of the male-to-female transition (15 to 21 mm, modal size of transitional individuals = 18 mm) were the same in the two sectors. Given the differences in growth rate indicated above, age of transitional individuals was 2+ in east PWS, and 3+ in west PWS. Shrimp caught in the SPs (largely females) were mostly in age classes 3+ and older but could not be separated into year classes because of lack of distinct modes. The maximum size, 27 mm CL, was virtually the same in all of the areas sampled.

Pandalid shrimp abundance (CPUE)--The species with the most ubiquitous distribution and greatest abundance was pink shrimp (juveniles; <15 mm CL) captured by BT. Pink shrimp, however, were not common in most bays sampled, including all four of the "oiled" category and Galena and Port Gravina of the "non-oiled" group (Fig. 14). CPUEs were highest in Jackpot and Drier bays, where mean CPUE ranged from 100 to over 2000 shrimp/ha during the three survey years (Fig. 14). Mean density from 1989 through 1991 (restricted set of bays) was consistently higher in the "non-oiled" ([735 222 448] shrimp/ha) compared with "oiled" ([2 6 2] shrimp/ha) bays, but trends were parallel and time by treatment interactions were not statistically significant (for example, 1990-91, $P = 0.58$, power = 0.13; Table 4).

Pandalid shrimp fecundity--The three species of *Pandalus* selected as target species are protandric hermaphrodites. Spawning of spot shrimp and coonstripe shrimp occurred in late August and early September. No ovigerous females of *P. borealis* were found as late as October 20 (end of the 1989 sampling season); this species typically spawns later during the fall (Dungan et al. 1988). Fecundity of spot shrimp ranged between 450 and 4400 eggs/female (Fig. 15; size of females: 35 to 50 mm CL). Fecundity of coonstripe shrimp (size range: 19 to 35 mm CL) ranged from 450 to 4300 eggs/female (Fig. 15).

For spot shrimp, ANCOVA showed that neither the pooled *SIZE* by factors (*YEAR, OILING*) interaction nor the effects of *YEAR* or *OILING* (assuming homogeneity of slopes) were statistically significant. Data on coonstripe shrimp were available for 1989 and 1990 but not for 1991. In this case, ANCOVA indicated that interactions between covariate (*SIZE*) and factors (*YEAR, OILING*) were not significant, but that the effects of the two factors were highly significant (P <0.01). Fecundity was higher in 1989 than in 1990 (irrespective of oiling condition), and higher in "non-oiled" than in "oiled" bays (Fig. 15c, d). On average (and after adjusting for *SIZE*), fecundity in 1990 was about 63% that of 1989, and fecundity in specimens from "oiled" bays was about 70% of that observed in specimens from "non-oiled" bays.

Flathead sole size and age structure--Samples obtained with the BT and the OT (Fig. 16) complemented each other in providing a clear picture of recruitment and growth during the first four years of life. Recently

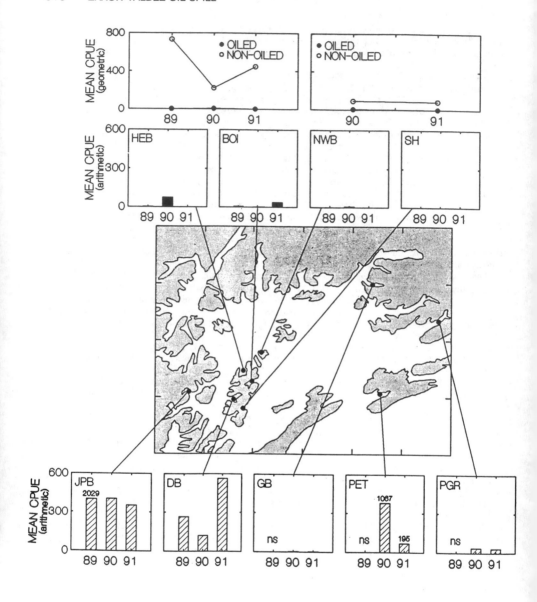

FIG. 14--*Juvenile pink shrimp (CL <15 mm) mean CPUE (number/ha) by bay from the beam trawl catches and "oiled" versus "non-oiled" bay comparisons, 1989 to 1991 (see Table 4 for result of tests). Dark bars indicate "oiled" bays; striped bars, "non-oiled" bays. NS indicates not sampled.*

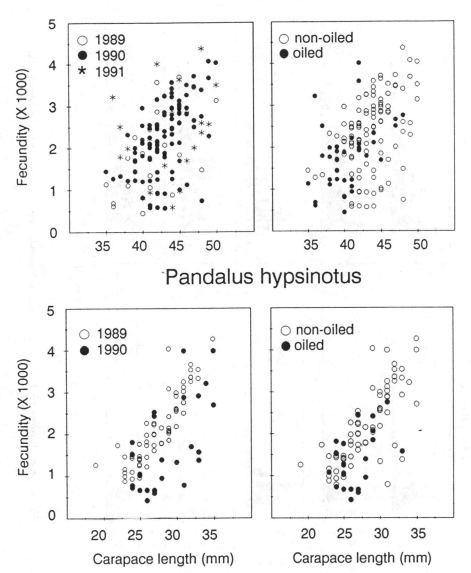

FIG. 15--*Relationship between fecundity (number of eggs) and carapace length for spot shrimp (a; 1989, 1990 and 1991), and coonstripe shrimp (c; 1989 and 1990); and the same relationship for shrimp from "oiled" versus. "non-oiled" bays (b and d; years pooled).*

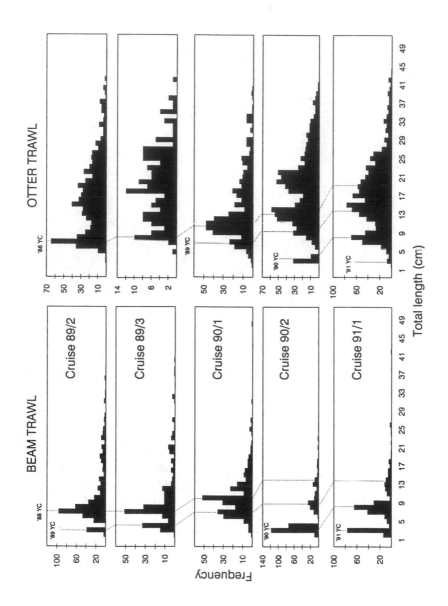

FIG. 16—Size-frequency distributions by cruise of flathead sole sampled with the beam and otter trawls. YC = year class.

metamorphosed juveniles started to appear in BT samples in late July to
early August and were 2 to 5 cm total length (TL) by September.
Juveniles of age 1+ (5 to 11 cm TL by late summer) were captured by the
two types of trawl gear. Fish of age 2+ (10 to 18 cm TL) and older were
poorly represented in BT samples. Beyond the fourth year of life, as
fish approach sexual maturity, males and females grow at different
rates, and separation of year classes is not possible in a pooled SFD.
Recruitment and growth of year classes 1988 to 1991 could be tracked
through the study period and were present throughout the area surveyed.

   Flathead sole abundance (CPUE)--Trends in density of juvenile flathead
sole (TL <6 cm) caught by BT were not parallel when compared between
"oiled" and "non-oiled" bays with the three-year data subset; the time-
by-treatment interaction was significant in the case of the quadratic
model (P = 0.02, Table 4; Fig. 17). This resulted from an increase in
mean CPUE between 1989 and 1990 in "oiled" bays ([11 69 29] fish/ha)
accompanied by a decrease in "non-oiled" bays ([28 10 8] fish/ha) (Fig.
17). The null hypothesis (parallelism) was not rejected for the two-
year (1990-1991) data subset (P = 0.90; power = 0.19; Table 4).
Juvenile fish were most abundant in Bay of Isles and Port Etches, but in
general fewer than 100 fish/ha (on average) were caught in most bays
during each of the three study years (Fig. 17).

   Trends in abundance of flathead sole caught with the OT (TL ≥6 cm)
were significantly nonparallel in the two-year (1990-1991) comparison
(P = 0.06, power = 0.30; Table 4) because of an increase in CPUE in
"oiled" ([83 238] fish/ha) and a slight decrease in "non-oiled" ([98 77]
fish/ha) bays (Fig. 18). A broad-scale pattern of geographic variation
in trends of abundance (independent of the "oiled" versus "non-oiled"
categories) is apparent in the data. Abundance declined or remained
constant from 1990 to 1991 in bays of eastern PWS (Galena Bay, Port
Etches, Port Gravina; Fig. 18) while at the same time increasing in *all*
of the bays sampled in western PWS (Jackpot Bay, Knight Island).

   Flathead sole diet analysis--Of 433 adult flathead sole caught in the OT
during Cruise 91/1 examined for stomach contents, 56% had empty
stomachs. Of the 191 with stomach contents, 60% were rated as 25% full
and 40% rated as 50-100% full. Analysis of the total number of prey
consumed grouped across all bays (evidence of consumption from both the
stomach and intestine) showed that the diet consisted primarily of
bivalve molluscs (88%), polychaete worms (7%), and crustaceans,
including crabs and shrimp (3%) (Fig. 19). Five clam species comprised
the majority of bivalves consumed: the trenched and smooth nut clams
(*Nuculana fossa*, 59%, and *N. tenuis*, 5%), heavy macoma (*Macoma brota*, 11%),
and yellow and axe yoldias (*Yoldia hyperborea*, 8%, and *Y. thraciaeformis*, 3%).
Since the bulk of flathead sole diet consisted of these infaunal
bivalves, which likely have low mixed function oxygenase systems and
would concentrate tissue hydrocarbons, flathead sole is a convenient
model to test for correlation between clam tissue hydrocarbon loads and
flathead sole bile metabolites. There is evidence of uptake of
hydrocarbons from the food via this predator-prey relationship (see
Fig. 7). The greater bivalve tissue PAH concentrations observed in the
"oiled" bays corresponded to the greater flathead sole bile FAC
concentrations when compared with the lower levels of both indices of
exposure in the "non-oiled" bays (r^2 = 0.46). The correlation was
somewhat stronger when comparing only the pyrogenic (unalkylated) PAH
concentrations in clam tissues with bile FAC concentrations (r^2 = 0.65).

   Flathead sole histopathology--Lesions in liver, kidney and gill tissue: Tissue samples
collected in 1989 were obtained on Cruises 89/2 and 89/3, within several
months of the spill. Liver, kidney, and gill tissues were examined for

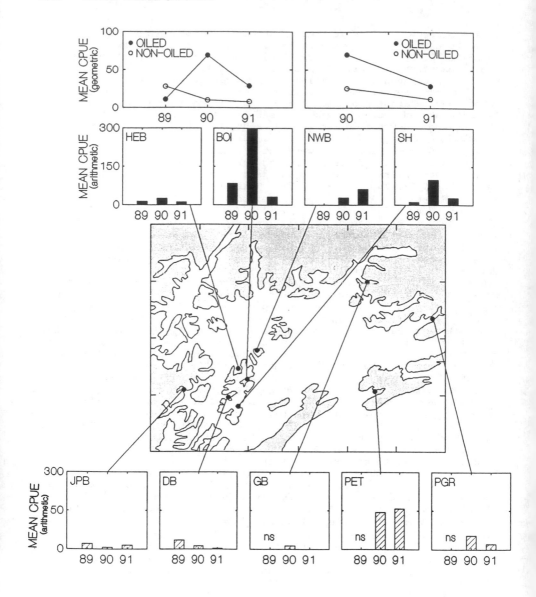

FIG. 17--*Juvenile flathead sole (TL <6 cm) mean CPUE (fish/ha) by bay from the beam trawl catches, and "oiled" versus "non-oiled" bay comparisons, 1989 to 1991 (see Table 4 for results of tests). Dark bars indicate "oiled" bays; striped bars, "non-oiled" bays. NS indicates not sampled.*

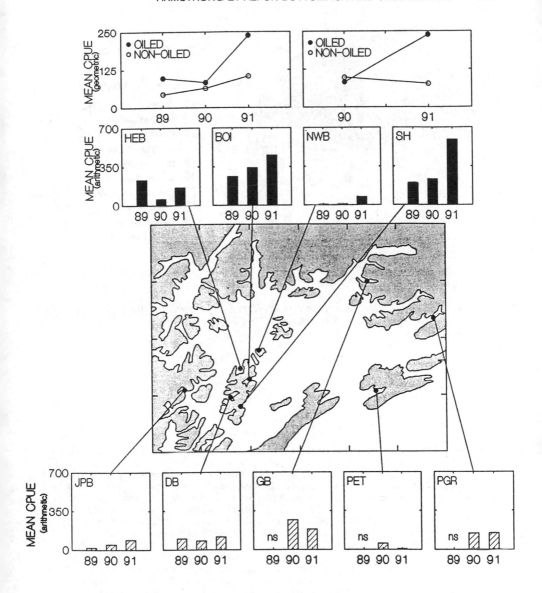

FIG. 18--*Mean CPUE (fish/ha) of flathead sole (TL ≥6 cm) by bay from the otter trawl catches, and "oiled" versus "non-oiled" bay comparisons, 1989 to 1991 (see Table 4 for results of tests). Dark bars indicate "oiled" bays; striped bars, "non-oiled" bays. NS indicates not sampled.*

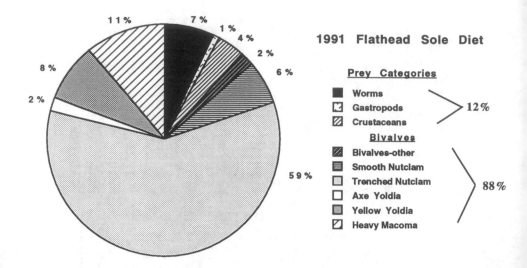

FIG. 19--*Flathead sole diet composition (expressed as percent of the total number of all prey items consumed) by taxonomic category. Data are from collections in 1991 only, all bays combined.*

evidence of acute or subacute effects. The results are summarized in Table 5.

In renal tissue, the most common lesions were changes associated with parasitism (free parasites, encapsulated parasites, parasitic granulomas). Frequency of parasitism was higher in "non-oiled" bays (39%) than in "oiled" bays (25%). A small percentage of fish in "oiled" (7%) and "non-oiled" (6%) bays possessed deeply pigmented melanin macrophage centers. A proliferative lesion that resembled a nephroblastoma was observed in one fish.

In gill tissue, focal epithelial hyperplasia and focal inflammation, probably resulting from parasite attachment, were observed in 20% of the fish collected. Microaneurysms were detected in 10% of fish from "oiled" bays and 9% of fish from "non-oiled" bays. Such lesions can result from a variety of infectious and noninfectious disease processes. Mild epithelial hypertrophy was observed in 20% of the fish collected from "oiled" bays, but was not observed in fish collected from "non-oiled" bays (P <0.01; Table 5).

The liver is the primary site of xenobiotic metabolism in fish (Lech and Vodicnik 1984). As such, it is the target organ most often affected by exposure to environmental contaminants (Myers et al. 1987). Liver

TABLE 5--*Summary of histological conditions in liver, kidney, and gills of flathead sole from Prince William Sound embayments, 1989 to 1991. Samples of kidney and gill tissues were collected only in 1989 and are indicated as "Na" in the table for 1990 and 1991.*

| Tissue | 1989 | | 1990 | | 1991 | |
Condition	Oiled	Nonoiled	Oiled	Nonoiled	Oiled	Nonoiled
Kidney						
Parasitism	0.25	0.39	Na	Na	Na	Na
Dark melanin macrophage pigment	0.07	0.06	Na	Na	Na	Na
Gills						
Parasitism	0.11	0.04	Na	Na	Na	Na
Focal epithelial hyperplasia	0.02	0.00	Na	Na	Na	Na
Microaneurysms	0.09	0.10	Na	Na	Na	Na
Epithelial hypertrophy	0.20	0.00	Na	Na	Na	Na
Liver						
Parasitism	0.35	0.50	0.40	0.60	0.41	0.62
Physiological conditions:						
Lipid vacuolation	0.21	0.32	0.29	0.10	0.20	0.09
Nonuniform vacuolation	0.00	0.02	0.04	0.04	0.06	0.04
Specific degenerative conditions:						
Nuclear pleomorphism	0.03	0.00	0.05	0.00	0.01	0.02
Intracytoplasmic storage disorders:						
Fatty infiltration	0.00	0.00	0.01	0.00	0.00	0.00
Foci of cellular alteration:						
Eosinophilic foci	0.00	0.00	0.00	0.01	0.01	0.00
Basophilic foci	0.00	0.01	0.00	0.00	0.00	0.00
Neoplasia	0.00	0.00	0.00	0.00	0.00	0.00

tissue was collected and examined in all three years of the study. Most of the lesions noted were conditions that could be attributed to parasitism (for example, free parasites, encapsulated parasites, parasitic granulomas, parasitic serositis). Parasitic lesions were observed in 35 to 61% of the fish during three years of study (Table 5). Although there was no statistically significant difference in prevalence of parasites between "oiled" and "non-oiled" bays in any year of the study, parasite infestation was consistently higher in the "non-oiled" bays. Conditions that represent nonspecific response to injury (for example, pyknosis, necrosis, mononuclear cell infiltrates) were also common. Some of these lesions probably arose due to parasite infestation.

Particular attention was paid to idiopathic hepatic lesions that have been shown by other investigators to correlate with chronic exposure to contaminants (Myers et al. 1987). Included in this category were specific degenerative conditions (for example, megalocytic hepatosis, nuclear pleomorphism), intracytoplasmic storage disorders (for example, fatty infiltration, hemosiderosis), foci of cellular alteration (for example, eosinophilic, basophilic, and clear cell foci), and neoplasms.

Table 5 shows the frequency of occurrence of idiopathic lesions in liver tissue. Such lesions were detected in relatively low incidence during the study. Hepatocellular lipid vacuolation is a physiological rather than a pathological condition. Vacuolation was recorded only when present at high levels (severity score = 3). No statistically significant differences in degree of vacuolation were noted in 1989, 1990 or 1991 ($P = 0.398$, Table 5). Hepatocellular lipid vacuolation is normally distributed uniformly throughout the tissue. The presence of nonuniform vacuolation is unusual and was recorded. Among the specific degenerative conditions, nuclear pleomorphism was significantly ($P < 0.05$) higher among fish from "oiled" compared to "non-oiled" bays in 1989 and 1990. In 1991, the prevalence was higher in "non-oiled" than in "oiled" bays, but the difference was not statistically significant. Foci of cellular alteration (putative preneoplasms) were observed in low frequency ($\leq 1\%$) and were present in fish from both "oiled" and "non-oiled" bays. Hepatocellular neoplasms were not detected.

DISCUSSION

Despite extensive research on impacts to biota following well-documented marine oil spills (for example, *Torrey Canyon, Amoco Cadiz, Ixtoc-1* well blowout, *Florida*, Santa Barbara spill), only slight evidence has been reported to suggest adverse, widespread effects on animal populations at depths >15 m (reviews by Laevastu et al. 1985; Clark 1992). Estuaries and shallow coastal waters (depth <15 m) are not within the scope of this study, because we focused on shelf areas generally deeper than 20 m, where extensive fishery resources are taken by trawl or pots worldwide. Where measurable adverse impacts of hydrocarbons in shallow nearshore waters have occurred, locations have usually been embayments and estuaries such as the abers of the Brittany coast (Glémarec and Hussenot 1982; Cross et al. 1978) and the West Falmouth area of Buzzards Bay (Sanders et al. 1980) and/or near sites of chronic discharge of petrochemicals such as the fjords of Sweden (Jacobsson and Neuman 1991).

Following the *Amoco Cadiz* spill, hydrocarbons were found associated with fine sediments at 18- to 70-m depths after periods of gale winds and extreme turbulence in the bays of Morlaix and Lannion (Cabioch et al. 1978). These authors also reported substantial declines in the number of amphipod species (24 to 10) and density (more than 8000 to fewer than 300 individuals/m^2) three weeks after the spill, and few signs of recovery until eight months after the spill (Laubier 1980). No evidence of decline in fishery landings of the edible crab (*Cancer pagurus*) was found, but some indication of reduced numbers of ovigerous female lobsters was reported; whether this affected the abundance of later year classes is unknown (Laubier 1980). In another case, Cross et al. (1978) found extensive mortality of heart urchins (*Echinocardium cordatum*), razor clams (*Ensis siliqua* and *Pharus legumen*), cockles (*Cerastoderma-Cardium edule*), and surf clams (*Mactra cinerea*) on the beach at Lieue de Grève, over 80 km from the *Amoco Cadiz* wreck site. The clam species were probably most affected at depths of <15m (the surf zone), although the authors speculated that oil may have been mixed into sediments at depths as great as 40 to 60 m. It also seems probable that

one year class of flatfish was negatively impacted (Conan 1982), but no
long-term adverse effects on fish stocks along the Brittany coast were
attributed to oil several years after the spill (McIntyre 1982).

Analyses of other oil spills reveal the same pattern of biological
impacts on shore and in estuaries, but no detectable long-term fisheries
effects for pelagic, demersal, or benthic species (see review by Clark
1992). The rich Gulf of Mexico penaeid shrimp fisheries were not
affected in the long term by the *Ixtoc-1* well blowout (Clark 1992), in
part due to the very short life span of the species and relatively rapid
degradation of the oil in subtropical waters. Although landings of
shrimp at U. S. ports in the Gulf of Mexico decreased 17% in 1979 (year
of the *Ixtoc-1* blowout) compared with 1978, landings increased 29% by 1981
over 1980 levels (NOAA 1980, 1982). Pelagic fisheries for anchovy,
bonito, and mackerel were little influenced by the Santa Barbara spill,
based on aerial surveys (Squire 1992). Short-term negative effects were
generally attributed to redistribution of fish that may have been able
to detect and avoid areas of greatest hydrocarbon coverage. Several
extenuating circumstances (for example, low abundance of some species
before the spill, long-term seepage of high levels of oil in the Santa
Barbara basin, pronounced effect of oceanographic phenomena like El Niño
years on fish stock abundance) make it difficult to identify any
relationship between post-spill fishery trends and the environmental
perturbation.

The extent of possible perturbations at the level of the individual is
dependent on the relative concentration of hydrocarbons per unit area,
the relative toxicity of specific compounds in the mixture, and their
bioavailability. It also depends on a broad suite of biochemical (for
example, mixed function oxygenase present or not) and physiological (for
example, molting, reproduction, feeding, environmental stresses)
processes and responses operative in the organism at different life
stages. On a population level, the extent of the negative effect is
often modeled and estimated at the spatial scale over which oil, in
excess of defined toxic thresholds, is dispersed relative to the
distribution of the population and the length of time such toxic levels
persist. Ecologically toxic concentrations of water-soluble fractions
(WSF) used in modeling impact scenarios for several Alaskan oil and gas
pre-lease sales are generally set at a lower limit of 0.01 ppm,
considered toxic to eggs and larvae of temperate water species, although
adult stages may be 10- to 30-fold less sensitive (Thorsteinson and
Thorsteinson 1984, their Table 4.6). The amount of oil estimated to
reach the benthos by various routes following a spill varies from 0.1%
(after 10 days, Manen and Pelto 1984) to 8% for the *Amoco Cadiz* (Gundlach
et al. 1983), to 10 to 30% for the *Tsesis* spill in the Baltic Sea (Linden
et al. 1979; Laevastu and Fukuhara 1985).

Extensive efforts to model trajectories and spatial scales of
hypothetical oil spills in the SE Bering Sea have incorporated much of
the data and experience gained from actual spills discussed above, in
order to anticipate the extent and severity of oil spills on several
fisheries resources along the Alaskan shelf (Laevastu et al. 1985;
Thorsteinson 1984). Recurrently, the results of these model scenarios
indicate no effect to very slight effect (less than the error in a
fishery resource estimate) on offshore species with broad distribution,
because the spatial scale of water column hydrocarbons at toxic levels
is very small relative to the distribution of the populations (Laevastu
and Fukuhara 1985). Under worst-case spill scenarios, less than 0.03%
of the yellowfin sole and crab populations of the Bering Sea would be
seriously affected. Since this value is nearly three orders of
magnitude less than the accuracy of the resource estimates, the authors

concluded that no quantifiable effect on offshore fishery resources could be measured following a major spill in that area.

Lack of findings that large marine oil spills *in situ* negatively affect coastal finfish and invertebrates at depth, and similar predictions derived from models of physical and biological events following spills, suggest that similar lack of effect on ubiquitous mobile demersal and benthic fauna would be expected for the EVOS in Prince William Sound. We designed our study to learn if exposure to EVC at depth had occurred and if measurable change could be detected in condition or abundance of target species across several life stages. While we found strong evidence of exposure to EVC that attenuated through the three years of this program, we did not find persuasive, recurring evidence of population impacts among the target species sampled.

Exposure and Uptake

Sediment PAH concentrations--Subtidal sediments in PWS contain a background of PAHs derived from both natural and anthropogenic sources. These background PAHs include pyrogenic materials that have entered PWS from runoff and atmospheric deposition and petrogenic materials whose likely sources include oil spills, natural seeps, and bilge water. Total PAH concentrations in fine-grained sediments from several sites in Alaska range from nondetectable to 1203 ng/g (NOAA 1988). Subsurface sediment samples from basin areas of PWS have average prespill TPAH concentrations of 1079 ng/g (Page et al., this volume).

In some locations within the spill area, an additional fraction derived from EVC is superimposed on these background sediment PAHs. It is important to differentiate the two fractions in order to assess the biological effects of EVC. The average TPAH concentrations in sediment from "oiled" and "non-oiled" bays through time are presented in Fig. 5a. The EVC PAH component, determined utilizing the C2-D/C2-P ratio method (see Materials and Methods: *Assessment of Hydrocarbon Sources*), indicates contamination attributed to the *Exxon Valdez* spill.

Total PAH concentrations in sediments and, where present, the EVC PAH fraction tended to reach peak concentrations in subtidal bay sediments during late 1989 (September sampling) or early 1990 (February sampling). Although background concentrations remain comparable from year to year during summer samplings, the EVC PAH fraction exhibits a steady decline following the winter of 1989-90 (Fig. 5a, b). As noted above, the correspondence between EVC PAHs in sediments and the observation of oil particles in benthic trawls (Fig. 5b, c) is good. Both indicators of the presence of EVC in subtidal habitats suggest substantial recovery with time.

A basic question relative to PAHs in subtidal bottom sediments of PWS centers on whether the sediments have been rendered toxic by the contamination. One approach is to compare the PAH concentrations found in the bottom sediments of a study site to those thought to be harmful to marine life. Long and Morgan (1991) reported TPAH concentrations in sediments above which adverse effects would be expected as estimated by field observations and bioassays. They estimated the lower concentration threshold for benthic effects at 4000 ng/g. The TPAH concentrations in subtidal sediments of "oiled" bays never exceeded this threshold and were generally an order of magnitude below that lower limit.

A second approach, utilizing the EPA's equilibrium partitioning (EqP) methodology, assumes that pore water concentrations of nonionic organic chemicals correlate best to biological effects and that pore water concentrations can be estimated using appropriate partitioning coefficients (Di Toro et al. 1991). The EPA has recently published proposed sediment quality criteria (SQC), based upon EqP, for three PAHs: fluoranthene, acenaphthene, and phenanthrene (Hansen et al. 1991a, b, c). Concentrations of these PAHs in study sediments, normalized to percent organic carbon per the method, were below the levels assumed to be protective of benthic marine life (Table 6). The one exception only slightly exceeded the lower 95% confidence value (75 ng/g versus 74 ng/g). This particular sample contained 0.2% organic carbon, which is at the lower threshold allowed by the EqP methodology.

These observations are supported by the results of 10-day amphipod (*Rhepoxynius abronius*) bioassays on sediments from "oiled" and "non-oiled" bays (Boehm et al., this volume). The data show that although some intertidal and shallow subtidal sediments had reduced amphipod survival in 1989, by 1990 there was no significant difference between "oiled" and "non-oiled" sites with respect to survival, emergence from the sediment during exposure, or the ability to rebury in clean sediment at the end of the bioassay.

The conclusion from all of these approaches is that after 1989 there was no indication of acute sediment toxicity in the subtidal settings studied.

Tissue PAH concentrations--Pink scallops, like other suspension-feeding bivalves, filter hundreds of litres of water per day. Thus, they may be used to indicate the presence of spill-related hydrocarbons in the water column. Scallops collected in 1989 showed the presence of petrogenic hydrocarbons (that is, substituted aromatics) at various sites, including low concentrations (up to 270 ng/g) in samples from "non-oiled" bays (Fig. 6a). The source of the petrogenic hydrocarbons in some scallop samples is ambiguous, but the PAH distribution in several samples from "oiled" bays, one sample collected just inside the mouth of Drier Bay, and from near "oiled" shorelines of Knight Island Passage resembled EVC PAH (Fig. 20a). In 1990, scallop tissues showed an absence of detectable petrogenic hydrocarbons from these same sites. Apparently, in 1989, low concentrations of EVC, either dissolved or

TABLE 6--*Sediment quality criteria (SQC) for phenanthrene, fluoranthene, and acenaphthene in marine sediments and organic carbon-normalized values for these PAH fractions in subtidal sediments from Prince William Sound embayments, 1989 through 1991. All values are reported in μg/g organic carbon.*

	Criteria			Observed		
	Lower 95% C.L.	SQC	Upper 95% C.L.	Maximum	Minimum	Median**
Phenathrene	74	160	340	75*	ND	0.82
Fluoranthene	620	1340	2880	65	ND	0.35
Acanaphthene	110	240	520	17	ND	ND

*Single sample exceeding the 74 μg/g lower 95% confidence limit had 0.2% organic carbon reported, which is at the margin of the acceptable range for determining SQC values.

**Determination of the median includes samples for which analytes were reported as nondetectable. Thus, for instance, acenaphthene was determined in <1/2 of the samples.

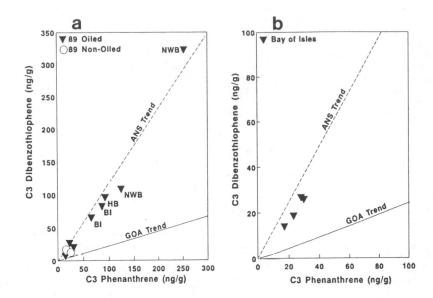

FIG. 20--(a)Relationship between C3-dibenzothiophene and C3-phenanthrene in scallops collected in 1989. Several samples from "oiled" bays and one sample from Drier Bay plot as being predominantly ANS-sourced. 1990 scallop samples do not plot on this figure because neither of these analytes was detected in those samples. (b): Relationship between C3-dibenzothiophene and C3-phenanthrene in four samples of prey clams collected in the Bay of Isles, 1991. These PAH fractions were not detected in any other clam samples from either "oiled" or "non-oiled" bays.

suspended, were present in the water at sites that lie along the spill path. By 1990, the concentrations of PAHs in the water column had returned to background (Neff 1991), and petrogenic hydrocarbons in scallop tissues were not detectable.

The decrease in PAH concentrations in scallops from 1989 to 1990 was also reportedly observed in mussels set out in cages in the Bay of Isles and Snug Harbor (Manen et al., in press). Mussels, which are also suspension feeders, are commonly used as sentinel organisms for monitoring marine pollution because of their ability to bioconcentrate contaminants from the water column. The mean PAH concentrations in mussels suspended at 25 m water depth in these bays was 635 ng/g in 1989, while in 1990 and 1991 the concentrations had decreased to 14 and 10 ng/g, respectively.

Whereas scallops, which are epibenthic, probably have PAH body burdens derived primarily from the water, infaunal deposit feeding bivalves live within the bottom sediment and feed on organic matter associated with the sediment. Consequently, their tissue PAH concentrations may be more reflective of sediment PAHs. In contrast to scallops, which were found to be free of petrogenic hydrocarbons by 1990, infaunal bivalves (*Macoma, Yoldia,* and *Nuculana*) showed the continued presence of petrogenic hydrocarbons at some localities in 1991. Substituted PAHs were found in infaunal bivalves from several stations within the Bay of Isles, but not in bivalves from the other "oiled" bays (Snug Harbor, Northwest Bay, and

Herring Bay), nor from the "non-oiled" bays (Fig. 6b). From the ratio of C3-Dibenzothiophene (C3-D) to C3-Phenanthrene (C3-P), the petrogenic hydrocarbons in the bivalve samples from Bay of Isles are interpreted to be of EVC origin (Fig. 20b).

Lack of petrogenic hydrocarbons in infaunal bivalves from "non-oiled" sites suggests that the background petrogenic hydrocarbons found in the sediment of those sites, discussed above, are less bioavailable than EVC. It may be that EVC in subtidal sediments is present mainly as droplets or micro-tar balls, as suggested by Figs. 5b and c. Hydrocarbons in such an oil phase could be concentrated at the sediment-water interface, to be fed upon by surface-deposit-feeding clams. The occurrence of EVC PAHs in undepurated whole clams may thus be explained by the presence of these whole oil particles in the gut. Weathered petrogenic hydrocarbons sorbed to sediment may not be readily removed by the biota, explaining the lack of detectable background petrogenic PAHs in organisms from "non-oiled" sites.

Crustaceans, including Tanner crabs and spot shrimp from all collection sites, showed the presence of PAHs in various tissues (muscle, hepatopancreas, gonads, egg mass). In 1989, 90% of the adult Tanner crab muscle samples did not show the presence of petrogenic hydrocarbons, and in 1990, 100% were free of petrogenic PAHs. Crustaceans showed much lower PAH concentrations than bivalves collected at the same sites. Whereas bivalves have a very limited ability to metabolize PAHs, and thus tend to bioaccumulate these compounds, crustaceans possess well-developed cytochrome P-450 systems, and most species can rapidly metabolize PAHs.

Bile metabolites--The concentration of bile metabolites in fish presumably reflects recent exposure to PAHs in the diet and ambient water. Concentration of bile FACs was significantly higher (approximately twofold) in flathead sole from "oiled" bays when compared with "non-oiled" bays in both 1990 and 1991 (Fig. 7). Infaunal bivalves (*Macoma, Yoldia, Nuculana*) were important food items in the diet of flathead sole in the study area. In the Bay of Isles, there was evidence of EVC PAHs in the infaunal bivalves sampled (Figs. 7, 20b). There was also evidence of EVC PAHs in subtidal sediments of all of the "oiled" bays sampled. Correlations of bile FACs with sediment and clam tissue PAHs indicate likely exposure routes. Mean bile FAC concentrations (by bay) showed a weak correlation (r^2 = 0.46) with TPAHs in bivalve tissues, but a somewhat stronger correlation (r^2 = 0.65) with the background pyrogenic PAH fraction. A weak correlation was also observed between mean bile FAC concentration and the EVC PAH fraction in sediments (r^2 = 0.43), but no correlation is evident with sediment TPAH concentration (r^2 = 0.05). Interestingly, although exposure of sole to EVC PAHs in subtidal sediments, possibly as weathered EVC particles, cannot be ruled out, bile FACs appear to exhibit the best correlation with nonalkylated (nonpetrogenic) PAHs in clams, suggesting uptake primarily through the diet.

Bile FACs were found in all fish from all stations. FACs derived from a petrogenic origin, particularly EVC, were not distinguishable from bile FACs from other sources by the method utilized. Krahn et al. (1992), using HPLC-MS techniques, have suggested that the presence of dibenzothiophenols found in bile indicates exposure of fish to crude oil. One confounding aspect of this approach is that some crude oils are very low in dibenzothiophenes (see discussion above on composition of GOA seep oil), while some refined petroleum products contain dibenzothiophenes. Thus, although use of bile FACs as an indication of environmental exposure to PAHs remains useful, it is problematic to presume a specific source for the substances.

Population Status of Target Species

Historical background--If stress caused by exposure to EVC is manifested across many individual animals, then harm at the population level might be detected in data (particularly CPUE) intended to contrast trends in abundance over time between "oiled" and "non-oiled" bays. This scale of effect is of greatest concern to the general health of the PWS ecosystem (Feder and Jewett 1986). From another perspective, the status of populations fished commercially and for subsistence is a vital concern for those whose incomes derive from these fisheries. Although specific prespill data on the ecology and population dynamics of many macroinvertebrates and finfish in PWS are notably lacking, commercial catch data for species targeted in our study are informative on status and trends before the EVOS.

Patterns in commercial landings may provide a relative measure of high or low abundance throughout the general population, including age and size classes that are not actually fished (see numerous reviews of crustacean fisheries in Jamieson and Bourne 1986; Caddy 1989). High or low landings in a given year are considered reflective of events and conditions (for example, predation, currents and transport, prey abundance, general physical and chemical stresses) that influence the relative success and survival of (for the most part) larval and early juvenile stages (Botsford et al. 1989; Staples 1985; McConnaughey et al. 1992). Conversely, abundance of early juvenile stages may be a predictor of the later magnitude of commercial adult stocks (Phillips and Brown 1989).

This sense of correspondence between abundance of early and late life stages is used as a rationale in interpreting trends in several Alaskan fisheries (see reviews by Otto 1985, 1986, 1990, for crab stocks), as an ancillary criterion to set harvest guidelines, and as warning of slow increase in abundance to levels that might support fisheries long closed in the Gulf of Alaska (for example, the Kodiak red king crab fishery has been closed since 1983; Otto 1990; Blau 1986). Catch data from PWS are especially informative about the historical onset of fisheries for a sequence of crustacean species that initially provided viable fisheries for several years, but eventually collapsed and were closed by ADF&G. The pattern shown in Fig. 21 is unique in our experience as an indication of a fishery where effort shifted sequentially from species to species, as each of them in turn was overfished in the relatively small area of PWS.

The data summarized in Fig. 21 suggest that fisheries for at least five commercial decapods had been substantially affected by the reduction of stocks (to the point of closure for red and brown king and Tanner crabs) before the EVOS. The long-term pattern for Dungeness crab is consistent with that for other stocks fished along the west coast of North America, from British Columbia to northern California, where cyclic landings are a pronounced feature of population abundance. But the trends for the other species are different. The decline in red king crab stocks in the mid-1970s to early 1980s (similar to a tenfold decline in abundance around Kodiak Island; Blau 1990) coincided with the onset of a fishery for Tanner crab, which lasted only about a decade before closure (Fig. 21). Trawl and pot fisheries for pandalid shrimp were reduced in landings by over 60 to 90%, from peaks in the mid-1980s to 1989, and the brown king crab fishery that was started around 1980 lasted about seven years (landings of 27,000 to 54,000 kg) before it closed the year before the EVOS.

The patterns of these fisheries suggest interesting biological features of decapod populations in PWS, but they also provide a

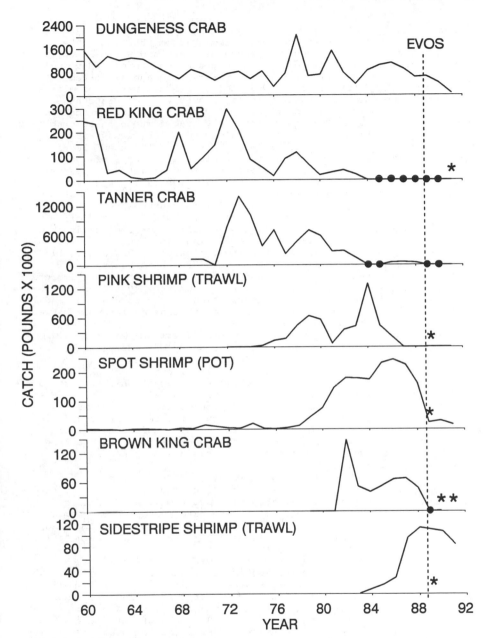

FIG. 21--Time trends in commercial landings of seven decapods fished in PWS since 1960. Indicated is the year of EVOS; solid circles are years closed by ADF&G; asterisks correspond to years in which few fishermen participated in the harvest and data were not released because of confidentiality (data extracted from ADF&G's "Prince William Sound Area Annual Shellfish Management Reports", 1987-1992).

cautionary note about interpreting trends in any set of CPUE data as reflecting hydrocarbon perturbations stemming from the EVOS. The relative speed with which several groups of crabs and shrimp were fished to unexploitable levels suggests both very slow growth of individuals to maturity and legal size (consistent with very cold annual bottom water temperatures throughout most of PWS; Fig. 3, see discussion of size-at-age below), and infrequent, strong year classes that generate huge fisheries (the latter was probably true for red king crab in the late 1970s in the SE Bering Sea and periodically true for Dungeness crab from California to Washington). At the time decapod fisheries started in PWS, high initial landings were likely based on an "accrued" legal population composed of survivors of multiple year classes of long-lived, slow-growing individuals that bottlenecked at an asymptotic upper size. Thus, abundance first encountered in the new fishery is in no sense reflective of stock productivity.

In light of these pronounced declines in adult abundance within PWS before the EVOS, it would be difficult to attribute further decline to oil perturbations since we have little capability to predict magnitude and rate of recovery of adult stocks following closures of fisheries (for example, the Kodiak king crab fishery closed in 1983 and little change in status of stocks has been measured to the present) under normal circumstances, without the added requirement to discern impacts of a major oil spill. Superimposed on this uncertainty is the high degree of spatial variability in distribution of the populations and low power of tests designed to show whether significant differences between groups over time can be detected.

Status of the populations during the study period--The effect of the *Exxon Valdez* oil spill on each of the populations under study was approached in two different, yet complementary ways. The first was a quantitative and comparative assessment of stock abundance in affected and unaffected areas over time (test of "year-by-treatment" interaction), the second a composite evaluation of life cycle continuity in PWS as a whole. Even if significant spill-related changes in population abundance were not statistically discernible, major disruptions of life cycles could become evident (albeit in a more qualitative sense) by considering jointly various pieces of information (qualitative and quantitative) pertaining to different life stages. The two approaches are combined in the following discussion.

Tanner crab--All life history stages of Tanner crab were sampled during the three-year study, including eggs, pelagic larvae, recently settled YOY, subadult juveniles, and reproductive adult males and females.

Observed fecundity was in agreement with data published by previous authors (Haynes et al. 1976; Hilsinger 1976; Paul 1982; Somerton and Meyers 1983), and no significant differences were found between "oiled" and "non-oiled" areas or among years.

No background data are available on the density of larvae in PWS. During Cruise 89/1 (two to three months after the spill), conducted when larvae are in the plankton, zoeal stages and megalopae were found in the neuston and upper 50 m of the water column of both "oiled" and "non-oiled" bays (mean density was virtually the same in the two groups), as well as in open waters within and outside the path of the spill. One year later (Cruise 90/1), the density of larvae in the water column was tenfold lower, and no larvae at all were found in the surface layer of bays in both categories, including some bays in eastern PWS far from the path of the spill. During the spring of that year there was exceptional freshwater runoff, resulting in low salinity over the entire water column measured during Cruise 90/1. Even by late summer (Cruise 90/2), very low salinities (fresh to brackish water) were observed at the surface of all bays (Fig. 3). No data are available for that year on larval abundance in open waters, but there must have been abundant larval supply to bays in eastern PWS traditionally known as settlement grounds. The densities of YOY crabs in Port Etches in 1990 and 1991 (Cruises 90/2 and 91/1) were more than 20 times higher than the mean for bays sampled in western PWS (Fig. 10). Eastern PWS has been closed to trawling by ADF&G as a protective measure for crab recruitment.

BT samples of juvenile Tanner crabs (CL <50 mm) revealed the ubiquitous presence of a relatively strong age/size group that had settled before the spill, corresponding to the 1987/88 year classes, which was followed through the three-year study and eventually grew to the size caught in CPs by 1991 (Fig. 9b, c). Assuming that the molting frequencies indicated by Donaldson et al. (1981) for crabs larger than 50 mm CL are at least approximately correct, recruitment of the 1987/88 year classes to the fishable population should be expected to start by 1993. This conclusion is consistent with results from ADF&G crab trawl survey (started in 1990), showing substantial numbers of "prerecruits 4" (CW <58 mm) and "prerecruits 3" (CW <74 mm), which are expected to support a fishing season in 1994 (Trowbridge 1992).

Trends in abundance in "oiled" and "non-oiled" bays were parallel (that is, no significant time-by-treatment interaction) for all the groups considered (YOY, juveniles in the size range 12 to 50 mm, adult females, adult males) in the two-year comparison (1990-91), but there was one significant difference in the three-year comparison (linear model), when abundance of adult males declined in the "non-oiled" bays in 1991, while it increased slightly in the "oiled" bays (Fig. 11).

Sixteen dead specimens of juvenile Tanner crabs were obtained in some BT and OT hauls, primarily from two of the four "oiled" bays (Bay of Isles and Snug Harbor) in the spring of 1990; in addition, a single dead Tanner female was found in a BT haul in Galena Bay. Similar mortality was not observed in these "oiled" bays in 1989, following the oil spill, nor later in 1990 or 1991 (although bile metabolites in flathead sole, an indicator of exposure to hydrocarbons, were comparable in 1989 and 1991 to levels measured during Cruise 90/1 when dead crabs were found). Occurrence of dead crabs appeared to be patchy and associated with the inner, shallower (generally, 20 to 40 m) depths and higher levels of FACs in flathead sole bile. However, the cause(s) of death is not presently known. Petroleum hydrocarbons reaching subtidal habitats should have been most toxic in the spring and summer of 1989, immediately following the spill, yet signs of acute toxicity to subtidal demersal organisms were not seen in trawl samples. Data from this study plus experiences from previous major oil spills suggest three possible causes: 1) salinity, which was anomalously low during the spring of 1990 due to runoff from a record snowpack; 2) chronic exposure to oil, especially if ingested; and 3) patchy areas of hypoxia or anoxia resulting from added organic material (including oil). All three factors may have acted additively or synergistically to affect benthic fauna, especially in some "oiled" embayments where circulation is restricted and high freshwater inflow occurred that spring.

Following initial detection of dead crabs in trawls during Cruise 90/1, salinity was measured in six of the nine bays with a YSI® meter (CTD unit malfunctioned). Bottom-water salinities were consistently low at about 20 ppt and ranged from 18 in Bay of Isles to 26 ppt in Herring Bay (Fig. 22). Given the stenohaline physiology of species like Tanner crab (and all other demersal target species of our study), we suspect that salinities approaching 20 ppt would be stressful. Since dead crabs occurred in "oiled" bays and bottom salinities were also low in "non-oiled" bays (only two of five sampled), we assume that oil and low

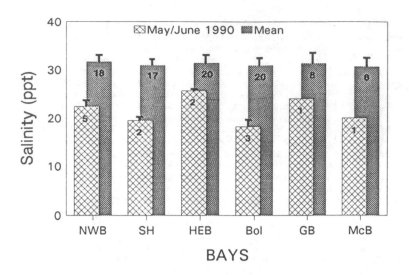

FIG. 22--*Bottom-water salinities during Cruise 90/1 (May/June 1990) compared with mean summer bottom-water salinities by bay over the three years of study. Data for Cruise 90/1 were collected with a YSI® meter after the first appearance of dead juvenile Tanner crabs. All other data were taken with a CTD unit. Number of samples included are shown on each bar. Positive standard deviation is indicated by error bar.*

salinity occurred as additive stresses that killed some animals. Yet, mortality did not seem pervasive throughout bays affected, since dead crabs were found at only 36% of stations sampled in Bay of Isles and Snug Harbor.

Pandalid shrimp--All stages in the life history of spot shrimp were sampled, but results for the other two target species were less comprehensive. In some cases, the sampling season was terminated before females of pink shrimp (all years) and coonstripe shrimp (1991 only) extruded eggs, so no data on fecundity were available, and larvae could not be identified to species level. Juveniles and adults were very patchily distributed in most cases. From the history of the fishery, it is clear that many bays were outside the area of distribution of the largest shrimp populations in PWS, a situation well exemplified by the absence of pink shrimp from bays around Knight Island. This, and the fact that SPs were not reliable for quantitative purposes, precluded CPUE analyses on most of the shrimp data subsets.

Estimated fecundity of spot shrimp in PWS (450 to 4400 eggs/female) matched values reported in previous studies: an average of 3900 eggs/female in Southeast Alaska (Hynes 1930), and ranges of 1393 to 3162 eggs/female from Vancouver Island (Butler 1964, 1970; size range: 33 to 41 mm; n = 21), and 1750 to 3750 eggs/female in Washington (Price 1969; size range: 39 to 44 mm; n = 28). No significant differences between "oiled" and "non-oiled" bays or between years could be detected. Measurable larval abundance was observed only during Cruise 89/1, when larvae occurred at low densities in both categories of bays. Surveys conducted by ADF&G in 1989 to 1991 (Trowbridge 1992, his Fig. 5) and data from this study indicate that the adult stock was dominated during that period by a strong 1987 year class, which could be tracked with SP samples during the three years of the study. Analysis of the spot shrimp SFD indicated that longevity (about 10 years) is much higher than previously reported for other areas (Butler 1970), suggesting that stocks of this species may be less productive and more sensitive to overharvesting compared with stocks of short-lived shrimp species.

Data on fecundity of coonstripe shrimp were consistent with previous studies. Fecundity in Southeast Alaska (based on five females) was 4000 eggs/female (Hynes 1930), and average fecundity in the Strait of Georgia was 2257 eggs/female (Butler 1980; size range: 25 to 31 mm; n = 15). Statistically significant differences in fecundity were detected between "oiled" and "non-oiled" areas and between years (1989 > 1990). Reduced fecundity in "oiled" bays (about 30% lower than in "non-oiled" bays) was probably inconsequential for the population dynamics of this species throughout PWS. Most decapods in this system have high fecundity and wide dispersal capability by virtue of planktonic larvae that may occur in the water column in excess of three months and be transported distances of hundreds to thousands of km (McConnaughey et al. 1992). Regional adult stocks are linked by such dispersal and not wholly dependent on long-term retention of local larval progeny for the supply of new juvenile recruits to a given area. Several decapod fisheries have interannual female abundance fluctuations (and, in turn, egg production) that may range from 50% to 80% (for example, Dungeness crab, Tanner crab, and pandalid shrimp; see reviews in Jamieson and Bourne 1986, PSMFC 1991) over a much wider geographic range than for our observations of reduced fecundity among coonstripe shrimp of PWS. Yet, from low levels of abundance, these populations build to higher abundance and such patterns, up or down, have not been linked to egg and larval production. Perhaps more significant to the future population dynamics of coonstripe shrimp in PWS than reduced fecundity in "oiled" bays will be the pattern of fisheries landings shown for other species in Fig. 21, in which fishing pressure is implicated as a major cause of reduced abundance.

The life history of natural populations of coonstripe shrimp has been best documented for British Columbia (Butler 1964), where maximum longevity is about three years. Size-at-age and longevity inferred for PWS are very similar to those indicated by Davis (1983) for Cook Inlet. Butler (1964) documented high variability in mean age and size of sex change in this area, between both populations and contiguous year classes in the same population. His results indicate that life history parameters of this species are extremely variable, both geographically and between years in a given area, which is consistent with the results of this study.

The estimated size-at-age vectors of pink shrimp from PWS are very similar to estimates for the well-documented population of Pavlof Bay, Alaska Peninsula (Anderson 1991). Trends in abundance of small shrimp (CL <15 mm) did not differ significantly between "oiled" and "non-oiled" bays.

Flathead sole--Having been selected as an indicator organism of exposure rather than of effect, less emphasis was placed on life history aspects of this species compared with target crustaceans. No data on fecundity or larval stages were collected, and individuals (except for those dissected for extraction of bile or histopathological study) were not sexed. Yet, the study yielded valuable information on recruitment and growth of age groups 0+ to 3+, which had been poorly documented in previous studies (Rose 1982). Four consecutive year classes were followed through the study period (Fig. 16) and were ubiquitous in their presence throughout bays sampled in PWS. Declines in mean abundance of

YOY in "non-oiled" bays (BT samples, three-year comparison, quadratic model) and increased abundance of older fish in "oiled" bays (OT samples, two-year comparison) resulted in two statistically significant outcomes.

Exposure of sole to oil through the diet via clams was reflected in relative concentrations of bile metabolites. Figure 7 indicates correlation between levels of total PAHs in tissues of clams consumed by sole and level of bile metabolites, particularly in Bay of Isles where there was a strong petrogenic signature in clam tissues. Since these bivalves have a low cytochrome P-450 system, long-term retention of tissue hydrocarbons (of pyrogenic origin in most bays, Fig. 6) is likely, and consumption of shallow infaunal clams by sole provides a route of exposure. This pattern is consistent with that reported by Elmgren et al. (1983; further discussion can be found in Laevastu and Fukuhara 1985, p. 131), who found that benthic effects of the *Tsesis* spill in the Baltic Sea included increased biomass of the clam, *Macoma balthica*. Tissue concentrations of hydrocarbons in flatfish feeding on *Macoma* were elevated one year after the spill (although the concentrations measured in the *Tsesis* instance were four orders of magnitude greater than found in clams in PWS, and tissue analyses of various fish from inside and outside of PWS have indicated no human health concerns related to hydrocarbon contamination; ADF&G 1991). While FACs in the bile are correlated with incidence of nonspecific necroses, foci of cellular alteration, and neoplasia in English sole in Puget Sound (Myers et al. 1987), there is no correlation with these parameters in flathead sole in Washington and Alaska based on data in Varanasi et al. (1989) and from this study.

CONCLUSIONS

The *Exxon Valdez* oil spill, like many other large marine spills, caused dramatic visual impacts at the surface and along intertidal shorelines and attendant species effects in some cases. But as in other instances of major oil spills (for example, *Torrey Canyon, Amoco Cadiz, Ixtoc 1*), we were not able to detect and document recurring and pervasive deleterious impacts at depth in PWS on the fauna of our study at either the individual or population levels, despite our best efforts to target species whose complete life cycle would cause persistent exposure in the water column or on benthos through ontogenetic changes in location from larvae to juvenile to reproductive adult. The species of decapod crustaceans and flatfish targeted in our study are in taxa inherently sensitive to chemical perturbations, have been well studied in laboratory bioassays, and have counterparts studied *in situ* following other major marine oil spills (NRC 1985)

We found evidence of EVC and other petrogenic hydrocarbons at depth following the EVOS in sediment, in animal tissue, and as elevated levels of bile metabolites consistent with time and space occurrence of exposure to EVC that attenuated during the three years of this study. In no instance was any route (for example, sediment concentrations) or evidence (for example, body burdens) of exposure gauged to be toxic or potentially lethal in the long term according to national standards or literature evaluations of toxic effects in response to dose (see Rice et al. 1979; numerous papers and reports listed in Johnson et al. 1992).

The two instances in which apparent negative changes were measured require special consideration. Observations of localized mortality events of juvenile Tanner crabs in some sites during the spring of 1990 were most likely negligible. Their cause remains unexplained but may be due, in part, to low bottom-water salinity. The observed difference in fecundity of coonstripe shrimp between "oiled" and "non-oiled" bays in 1989-1990, although statistically significant, may be biologically insignificant in terms of the dynamics of PWS populations when considered in the context of the documented variability of life history parameters of this species and of natural fluctuations in decapod crustacean populations (see reviews in Jamieson and Bourne 1986 and Caddy 1989).

Trends in abundance (CPUE) of the target species were not, for the most part, significantly different for populations in "oiled" compared with "non-oiled" bays, and in the cases of significant time-by-treatment interactions, the cause was usually a relative decrease of abundance in the "non-oiled" bays. From this perspective we found no evidence of biological damage to any of the populations in question, although the power of the tests was generally low (Table 4). In a broader context, most of the evidence accumulated on the life cycles of targeted species (larval distribution, fecundity, settlement during and after the spill, growth of juveniles and subadults, recruitment) indicated no deleterious impacts of the spill could be detected on populations at depth.

Few differences were noted in the prevalence of histopathological lesions in "oiled" versus "non-oiled" bays. In general, the prevalence of parasitism was higher in fish from "non-oiled" bays. Twenty percent (20%) of fish from "oiled" bays had mild epithelial hypertrophy in gill tissue; this condition was not observed in fish from "non-oiled" bays. In 1989 and 1990, fish from "oiled" bays had higher prevalence of mild hepatocellular nuclear pleomorphism; in 1991 the prevalence was higher in fish from "non-oiled" bays. Foci of hepatocellular alteration (putative preneoplasms) were observed in low frequency ($\leq$1%) in both "oiled" and "non-oiled" bays. Hepatocellular neoplasms were not observed.

Acknowledgments

This study was funded by Exxon Company, U. S. A., in conjunction with Dames & Moore, Seattle and Anchorage offices. Key personnel that provided excellent technical and logistical support were Perry Campbell, Greg Reub, Bill Mans, and Susan Payne (Dames & Moore) and Charles Eaton (Bio-Marine Enterprises, Seattle). We thank the captains and crews of the following support vessels: *Rapture, Dutch Omega, Discovery, Don Bollinger, Tradition,* and *St. George,* the last subsequently lost with all hands in the Bering Sea. Subcontractors responsible for physical and chemical support services were the Geochemical and Environmental Research Group, Texas A&M University; America North, Inc.; Kinetics Laboratories, Inc.; and Evans-Hamilton, Inc. (Curtis Ebbesmeyer and Jeff Cox). University of Washington personnel comprising the field and laboratory crews were: Helle Andersen, Julie Furstenberg, Oscar Iribarne, Gregory Jensen, Karen Larsen, Mary (Elger) Lonzarich, Jay Orr, Raul Palacios, Bill Patton, Andrew Shedlock, Anne Shaffer, Yunbing Shi, Pamela Wardrup, and Anthony Whiley.

REFERENCES

ADF&G (Alaska Department of Fish and Game), 1991, "Latest test results from two studies reconfirm that fish in the *Exxon Valdez* spill area are safe to eat," *September 1991 Report*, The Oil Spill Task Force, Division of Subsistence, ADF&G, Anchorage, AK, 4 pp.

Anderson, P. J., 1991, "Age, growth, and mortality of the northern shrimp *Pandalus borealis* Kroyer in Pavlof Bay, Alaska," *Fishery Bulletin*, Vol. 89, pp. 541-553.

Baik, K. K., Rho, Y. I., Hwang, Y. T., and Hong, G. E., 1991, "The larvae production of king shrimp, *Pandalus hypsinotus* Brandt," *Bulletin of the National Fisheries Research and Development Agency (Korea)*, Vol. 45, pp. 235-244.

Barr, L., 1971, "Methods of estimating the abundance of juvenile spot shrimp in a shallow nursery area," *Transactions of the American Fisheries Society*, Vol. 100, pp. 781-787.

Barr, L., 1973, "Studies of spot shrimp, *Pandalus platyceros*, at Little Port Walter, Alaska," *Marine Fisheries Review*, Vol. 35, pp. 65-66.

Blau, S. F., 1986, "Recent declines of red king crab (*Paralithodes camtschatica*) populations and reproductive conditions around the Kodiak Archipelago, Alaska," *Canadian Special Publication of Fisheries and Aquatic Sciences*, Vol. 92, pp. 360-369.

Blau, S. F., 1989, "Size at maturity of female red king crabs (*Paralithodes camtschatica*) in the Adak Management Area, Alaska," *Proceedings, International Symposium on King and Tanner Crabs*, University of Alaska, Fairbanks, Alaska, pp. 9-26.

Bodin, P., 1988, "Results of ecological monitoring of three beaches polluted by the *'Amoco Cadiz'* oil spill: development of meiofauna from 1978 to 1984," *Marine Ecology, Progress Series*, Vol. 42, pp. 105-123.

Boehm, P. D., Page, D. S., Gilfillan, E. S., Stubblefield, W. A., and Harner, E. J., 1993, "Shoreline Ecology Program for Prince William Sound, Alaska, following the *Exxon Valdez* oil spill: Part II-- Chemistry and toxicology," *This volume*.

Botsford, L. W., Armstrong, D. A., and Shenker, J. M., 1989, "Oceanographic influences on the dynamics of commercially fished populations," *In: Coastal Oceanography of Washington and Oregon,* Landry, M. R. and Hickey, B. M., Eds., Elsevier, Amsterdam, pp. 511-565.

Butler, T. J., 1964, "Growth, reproduction, and distribution of pandalid shrimp in British Columbia," *Journal of the Fisheries Research Board of Canada*, Vol. 21, pp. 1403-1452.

Butler, T. J., 1970, "Synopsis of biological data on the prawn *Pandalus platyceros* Brandt, 1851," *FAO Fisheries Report No. 57*, pp. 1289-1315.

Butler, T. J., 1980, "Shrimps of the Pacific Coast of Canada," *Canada Department of Fish and Oceans Bulletin No. 202*, 280 pp.

Cabioch, L., Dauvin, J. C., and Gentil, F., 1978, "Preliminary observations on pollution of the sea bed and disturbance of sub-littoral communities in northern Brittany by oil from the *Amoco Cadiz*," *Marine Pollution Bulletin*, Vol. 9, No. 11, pp. 303-307.

Caddy, J. F., 1989, "Marine Invertebrate Fisheries: Their Assessment and Management," John Wiley & Sons, New York, NY, 752 pp.

Caddy, J. F. and Gulland, J. A., 1983, "Historical patterns of fish stocks," *Marine Policy*, Oct. 1983, pp. 267-278.

Carr, T., 1991, "Spill!: The story of the *Exxon Valdez*," Franklin Watts, New York, NY, 64 pp.

Clark, B. R., 1992, "Marine Pollution", 3rd ed., Clarendon Press, Oxford, England, 172 pp.

Conan, G., 1982, "The long-term effects of the *Amoco Cadiz* oil spill," *Philosophical Transactions of the Royal Society of London*, Vol. B297, pp. 323-333.

Cross, F. A., Davis, W. P., Hoss, D. E., and Wolfe, D. A., 1978, "Biological observations," *In: The Amoco Cadiz Oil Spill - A Preliminary Scientific Report*, W. N. Ness, Ed., NOAA/EPA Special Report, pp. 197-215.

Davis, A. S., 1983, "The pandalid shrimp fishery of Cook Inlet, Alaska, from the initiation of the fishery through the spring of 1983," *Alaska Department of Fish and Game Informational Leaflet No. 220*, 37 pp.

Di Toro, D. M., Zarba, C. S., Hansen, D. J., Berry, W. J., Swartz, R. C., Cowan, C. E., Pavlou, S. P., Allen, H. E., Thomas, N. A., and Paquin, P. R., 1991, "Technical basis for establishing sediment quality criteria for nonionic organic chemicals using equilibrium partitioning," *Environmental Toxicology and Chemistry*, Vol. 10, pp. 1541-1583.

Donaldson, W. E., Cooney, R. T., and Hilsinger, J. R., 1981, "Growth, age and size at maturity of Tanner crab, *Chionoecetes bairdi* M. J. Rathbun, in the northern Gulf of Alaska (Decapod, Brachyura)," *Crustaceana*, Vol. 40, pp. 286-302.

Dungan, C., Armstrong, D., Sibley, T., and Armstrong, J., 1988, "Northern pink shrimp, *Pandalus borealis*, in the Gulf of Alaska and eastern Bering Sea," *In: Species Synopses. Life Histories of Selected Fish and Shellfish of the Northeast Pacific and Bering Sea*, Wilimovsky, N. J., Incze, L. S., and Westrheim, S. J., Eds., Washington Sea Grant Program and Fisheries Research Institute, Seattle, WA, 14 pp.

Elmgren, R., Hansson, S., Larsson, U., Sundelin, B., and Boehm, P., 1983, "The *Tsesis* oil spill: Acute and long-term impact on the benthos," *Marine Biology*, Vol. 73, pp. 51-65.

Feder, H. M. and Jewett, S. C., 1986, "The subtidal benthos," *In: The Gulf of Alaska: Physical Environment and Biological Resources*, Hood, D. W. and Zimmerman, S. T., Eds., U. S. Department of Commerce, NOAA/OCS Study No. MMS 86-0095.

Folk, R. L., 1974, "Petrology of Sedimentary Rocks," Hemphill Publishing Co., Austin, TX, 182 pp.

Fukuhara, F. M., 1985, "Estimated impacts of hypothetical oil spill accidents off Port Moller, Port Heiden and Cape Newenham on eastern Bering Sea yellowfin sole," *Final Report No. 36, Part 2, (1986),* U. S. Department of Commerce, NOAA/OCSEAP, pp. 1039-1128.

Glémarec, M. and Hussenot, E., 1982, "A three-year ecological survey in Benoit and Wrac'h Abers following the *Amoco Cadiz* oil spill," *Netherlands Journal of Sea Research,* Vol. 16, pp. 483-490.

Gunderson, D. R. and Ellis, I. E., 1986, "Development of a plumb staff beam trawl for sampling demersal fauna," *Fishery Research,* Vol. 4, pp. 35-41.

Gundlach, E. R., Boehm, P. D., Marchand, M., Atlas, R. M., Ward, D. W., and Wolfe, D. A., 1983, "The fate of *Amoco Cadiz* oil," *Science,* Vol. 221, pp. 122-129.

Hansen, D. J., Berry, W. J., Di Toro, D. M., Paquin, P., Davanzo, L., Stancil, F. E., Jr., and Kollig, H. P., 1991a, "Proposed sediment quality criteria for protection of benthic organisms: Acenaphthene," *U.S. EPA Office of Science and Technology Draft Report,* November, 1991.

Hansen, D. J., Berry, W. J., Di Toro, D. M., Paquin, P., Davanzo, L., Stancil, F. E., Jr., and Kollig, H. P., 1991b, "Proposed sediment quality criteria for protection of benthic organisms: Fluoranthene," *U.S. EPA Office of Science and Technology Draft Report,* November, 1991.

Hansen, D. J., Berry, W. J., Di Toro, D. M., Paquin, P., Davanzo, L., Stancil, F. E., Jr., and Kollig, H. P., 1991c, "Proposed sediment quality criteria for protection of benthic organisms: Phenanthrene," *U.S. EPA Office of Science and Technology Draft Report,* November, 1991.

Haynes, E., Karinen, J. F., and Hobson, D. J., 1976, "Relation of number of eggs and egg length to carapace width in the brachyuran crabs *Chionoecetes bairdi* and *C. opilio* in the southeastern Bering Sea, and *C. opilio* from the Gulf of St. Lawrence," *Journal of the Fisheries Research Board of Canada,* Vol. 33, pp. 2592-2595.

Hilsinger, J. R, 1976, "Aspects of the reproductive biology of female snow crab, *Chionoecetes bairdi,* from Prince William Sound and adjacent Gulf of Alaska," *Marine Science Commission,* Vol. 2, pp. 201-235.

Hood, D. W. and Zimmerman, S. T., Eds., 1986, "The Gulf of Alaska: Physical environment and biological resources," *Study No. MMS 86-0095,* U. S. Department of Commerce, NOAA/OCS.

Hynes, F. W., 1930, "Shrimp fishery of Southeast Alaska," *Appendix to the Report to the U.S. Commissioner of Fisheries for 1929, Bureau of Fisheries Document No. 1052, Appendix 1,* 18 pp.

Incze, L.S., Armstrong, D. A., and Smith, S. L., 1987, "Abundance of larval Tanner crabs (*Chionoecetes* spp.) in relation to adult females and regional oceanography of the southeastern Bering Sea," *Canadian Journal of Fisheries and Aquatic Sciences,* Vol. 44, pp. 1143-1156.

Jacobsson, A. and Newman, E., 1991, "Fish recruitment around a petrochemical centre in the North Sea," *Marine Pollution Bulletin,* Vol. 22, No. 6, pp. 269-272.

Jamieson, G. S. and Bourne, N., 1986, "North Pacific Workshop on Stock Assessment and Management of Invertebrates," *Canadian Special Publication of Fisheries and Aquatic Sciences,* No. 92, 427 pp.

Johnson, P. A., Rice, S. D., and Babcock, M. M., 1992, "Impacts of oil pollution and Prince William Sound studies: Bibliography of 1960-1991, 'Publications and Reports, Auke Bay Laboratory,'" *U. S. Department of Commerce, NOAA Technical Memorandum NMFS-AFSC-3.*

Kimker, A. and Donaldson, W., 1987, "Summary of 1986 streamer tag application and overview of the tagging project for spot shrimp in Prince William Sound," *Data Report No. 1987-07,* Alaska Department of Fish and Game, Division of Commercial Fisheries, Prince William Sound Management Area, 15 pp. + data appendix.

Kinder, T. H. and Schumacher, J. D., 1981a, "Hydrographic structure over the continental shelf of the southeastern Bering Sea," *In: The Eastern Bering Sea Shelf: Oceanography and Resources,"* Hood, D. W. and Calder, J. A., Eds., U. S. Department of Commerce, NOAA/OMPA, Juneau, AK, Vol. 1, pp. 31-52.

Kinder, T. H. and Schumacher, J. D., 1981b, "Circulation over the continental shelf of the southeastern Bering Sea," *In: The Eastern Bering Sea Shelf: Oceanography and Resources,"* Hood, D. W. and Calder, J. A., Eds., U. S. Department of Commerce, NOAA/OMPA, Juneau, AK, Vol. 1, pp. 53-76.

Krahn, M. M., Moore, L. K., and MacLeod, J. W. D., 1986, "Standard analytical procedures of the NOAA National Analytical Facility: Metabolites of aromatic compounds in fish bile," *NOAA Technical Memorandum NMFS F/NWC-102,* 25 pp.

Krahn, M. M., Burrows, D. G., Ylitalo, G. M., Brown, D. W., Wigren, C. A., Collier, T. K., Chan, S.-L., and Varanasi, U., 1992, "Mass spectometric analysis for aromatic compounds in bile of fish sampled after the *Exxon Valdez* oil spill," *Environmental Science and Technology,* Vol. 26, pp. 116-126.

Laevastu, T. and Fukuhara, F., 1985, "Oil on the bottom of the sea - a simulation study of oil sedimentation and its effects on the Bristol Bay ecosystem," *Final Report No. 36, Part 1 (1986),* U. S. Department of Commerce, NOAA/OCSEAP, pp. 395-454.

Laevastu, T., Marasco, R., Bax, N., Fredin, R., Fukuhara, F., Gallagher, A., Jr., Honkalehto, T., Ingraham, J., Livingston, P., Miyahara, R., and Pola, N., 1986, "Evaluation of the effects of oil development on the commercial fisheries in the Eastern Bering Sea," *Outer Continental Shelf Environmental Assessment Program,* Vol. 36, Part 1, pp. 1-47.

Laubier, L., 1980, "The *Amoco Cadiz* oil spill: An ecological impact study," *Ambio,* Vol. 9, No. 6, pp. 268-276.

Lech, J. L. and Vodicnik, M. J., 1984, "Biotransformation of chemicals by fish: An overview," *National Cancer Monograph*, Vol. 65, pp. 355-358.

Linden, O., Elmgren, R., and Boehm, P., 1979, "The *Tsesis* oil spill. Its impact on the coastal ecosystem of the Baltic Sea," *Ambio,* Vol. 8, No. 6, pp. 244-253.

Liu, S.-K. and Leendertse, J. J., 1981, "Oil spill analysis and simulation for the proposed oil-lease sale area in the St. George Basin, Alaska," *Report No. WD-1026-NOAA*, Rand Corporation, Santa Monica, CA, 75 pp.

Long, E. R. and Morgan, L. G., 1991, "The potential for biological effects of sediment-sorbed contaminants tested in the National Status and Trends Program," *NOAA Technical Memorandum No. NOS OMA 52*, Seattle, WA, 175 pp. + appendices.

Luna, L. G., 1968, "Manual of Histologic Staining Methods of the Armed Forces Institute of Pathology," McGraw-Hill, New York,NY, 258 pp.

MacDonald, P. D. M. and Pitcher, T. J., 1979, "Age-groups from size-frequency data: A versatile and efficient method of analyzing distribution mixtures," *Journal of the Fisheries Research Board of Canada*, Vol. 36, pp. 987-1001.

Manen, C. A. and Pelto, M. J., 1984, "Transport and fate of spilled oil," *Proceedings, The North Aleutian Shelf Environment and Possible Consequences of Offshore Oil and Gas Development*, Thorsteinson, L. K., Ed., OCSEAP/NOAA/MMS, Anchorage, AK, Chapter 2, pp. 11-34.

Manen, C. A., Price, J. R., Korn, S., and Carls, M. G., 1993 (in press), "Natural resource damage assessment database design and structure," *NOAA Technical Memorandum*, NOS/ORCA.

McConnaughey, R. A., Armstrong, D. A., Hickey, B. M., and Gunderson, D. R., 1992, "Juvenile Dungeness crab (*Cancer magister*) recruitment variability and oceanic transport during the pelagic larval phase," *Canadian Journal of Fisheries and Aquatic Sciences,* Vol. 49, No. 10, pp. 2028-2044.

McCullagh, P. and Nelder, J. A., 1983, "Generalized Linear Models," Chapman and Hall, New York, NY, 261 pp.

McIntyre, A. D., 1982, "Oil pollution and fisheries," *Philosophical Transactions of the Royal Society of London*, Vol. B297, pp. 401-411.

Mearns, A. J. and Allen, M. J., 1978, "Use of small otter trawls in coastal biological surveys," *Contribution No. 66,* Southern California Coastal Water Research Project (SCCWRP), EPA-600/3-78-083.

Myers, M. S., Rhodes, L. D., and McCain, B. B., 1987, "Pathologic anatomy and patterns of occurrence of hepatic neoplasms, putative preneoplastic lesions, and other idiopathic hepatic conditions in English sole (*Parophrys vetulus*) from Puget Sound, Washington," *Journal of the National Cancer Institute*, Vol. 78, pp. 333-363.

NAG (Numerical Algorithms Group), 1985, "The GLIM system release 3.77 Manual," Numerical Algorithms Group, Inc., Downers Grove, IL.

Neff, J. M., 1979, "Polycylic Aromatic Hydrocarbons in the Aquatic Environment," Applied Science Publishers, Ltd., London, 262 pp.

Neff, J. M, 1991, "Water Quality in Prince William Sound and the Gulf of Alaska," Arthur D. Little, Cambridge, MA, 37 pp.

Neff, J. M., Owens, E. H., Stoker, S. W., and McCormick, D. M., 1993, "Condition of shorelines in Prince William Sound following the *Exxon Valdez* oil spill: Part 1--Shoreline oiling," *This volume*.

NOAA (National Oceanic and Atmospheric Administration), 1980, "Fisheries of the United States, 1979," *Current Fishery Statistics, No. 8000, 2nd. Ed.*, Washington, D. C., 131 pp.

NOAA (National Oceanic and Atmospheric Administration), 1982, "Fisheries of the United States, 1981," *Current Fishery Statistics, No. 8200, 2nd. Ed.*, Washington, D. C., 131 pp.

NOAA (National Oceanic and Atmospheric Administration), 1988, "A summary of selected data on chemical contaminants in sediments collected during 1984, 1985, 1986, and 1987," *Technical Memorandum, NOS OMA 44*, National Status and Trends Program, Rockville, MD, 15 pp.

NRC (National Research Council, National Academy of Sciences), 1985, "Oil in the Sea, Inputs, Fates and Effects," National Academy Press, Washington D. C., 601 pp.

O'Clair, C. E. and Zimmerman, S. T., 1986, "Biogeography and ecology of intertidal and shallow subtidal communities," *In: The Gulf of Alaska: Physical Environment and Biological Resources*," Hood, D. W. and Zimmerman, S. T., Eds., U. S. Department of Commerce, NOAA/OCS Study MMS 86-0095, Chapter 11, pp. 305-344.

Otto, R. S., 1985, "Management of Alaska king crab stocks in relation to the possible effects of past policies," *Proceedings, International King Crab Symposium*, University of Alaska, Anchorage, AK, pp. 447-481.

Otto, R. S., 1986, "Management and assessment of eastern Bering Sea king crab stocks," *Canadian Special Publication of Fisheries and Aquatic Sciences*, Vol. 92, pp. 83-106.

Otto, R. S., 1989, "An overview of Eastern Bering Sea king and Tanner crab fisheries," *Proceedings, International Symposium on King and Tanner Crabs*, University of Alaska, Fairbanks, AK, pp. 9-26.

Page, D. S., Boehm, D., Douglas, G. S., and Bence, A. E., 1993, "Identification of hydrocarbon sources in the benthic sediments of Prince William Sound and the Gulf of Alaska following the *Exxon Valdez* oil spill," *This volume*.

Paul, A. J., 1982, "Mating frequency and sperm storage as factors affecting egg production in multiparous *Chionoecetes bairdi*," *Proceedings, International Symposium on the Genus Chionoecetes*, Alaska Sea Grant Report No. 82-10, pp. 273-281.

Payne, J. R., Kirstein, B. E., McNabb, G. D., Jr., Lambach, J. L., Redding, R., Jordan, R. E., Hom, W., de Oliveira, C., Smith, G. S., Baxter, D. M., and Gaegel, R., 1984, "Multivariate analysis of petroleum weathering in the marine environment-Sub Arctic," *Final Report No. 21, Vol. I-Technical Results*, U. S. Department of Commerce, NOAA, OCSEAP, Environmental Assessment of the Alaskan Continental Shelf.

Phillips, B. F. and Brown, R. S., 1989, "The West Australian rock lobster fishery: Research for management," *In: Marine Invertebrate Fisheries: Their Assessment and Management*, Caddy, J. F., Ed., John Wiley & Sons, New York, NY, pp. 159-181.

Phinney, D. E., 1977, "Length-width-weight relationships for mature male snow crab, *Chionoecetes bairdi*," *Transactions of the American Fisheries Society*, Vol. 75, pp. 870-871.

Price, V. A., 1969, "The post-embryonic development of laboratory reared 'spot' shrimp *Pandalus platyceros* Brandt," *MS Thesis*, University of Washington, Seattle, WA, 52 pp.

PSMFC (Pacific States Marine Fisheries Commission), 1990, "43rd Annual Report of the Pacific States Marine Fisheries Commission for the year 1990," Didier, A. J., Jr., Ed., Portland, OR, 26 pp.

Rice, S. D., Moles, A., Taylor, T. L., and Karinen, J. F., 1979, "Sensitivity of 39 Alaskan marine species to Cook Inlet crude oil and No. 2 fuel oil," *Proceedings, API, EPA and USCG, 1979 Oil Spill Conference (Prevention, Behavior, Control, Cleanup)*, pp. 549-554.

Rogers, D. E. and Rogers, B. J., 1986, "The nearshore fishes," *In: The Gulf of Alaska: Physical Environment and Biological Resources*, Hood, D. W. and Zimmerman, S. T., Eds., U. S. Department of Commerce, NOAA/OCS Study MMS 86-0095, Chapter 13, pp. 399-415.

Rose, C. S., 1982, "A study of the distribution and growth of flathead sole (*Hippoglossoides elassodon*)," *MS Thesis*, University of Washington, Seattle, WA, 59 pp.

Sanders, H. L., Grassle, J. F., Hampson, G. R., Morse, L. S., Garner-Price, S., and Jones, C. C., 1980, "Anatomy of an oil spill: Long term effects from the grounding of the barge *Florida* off West Falmouth, Massachusetts," *Journal of Marine Research*, Vol. 38, pp. 265-380.

Skalski, J. R. and Robson, D. S., 1992, "Techniques for Wildlife Investigations: Design and Analysis of Capture Data," Academic Press, San Diego, CA, 237 pp.

Sokal, R. R. and Michener, C. D., 1958, "A statistical method for evaluating systematic relationships," *University of Kansas Science Bulletin*, Vol. 38, pp. 1409-1438.

Somerton, D. A. and Meyers, W. S., 1983, "Fecundity differences between primiparous and multiparous female Alaskan Tanner crab (*Chionoecetes bairdi*)," *Journal of Crustacean Biology*, Vol. 3, pp. 183-186.

Squire, J. L., Jr., 1992, "Effects of the Santa Barbara, Calif., oil spill on the apparent abundance of pelagic fishery resources," *Marine Fisheries Review*, Vol. 54, No. 1, pp. 6-14.

Staples, D. J., 1985, "Modelling the recruitment processes of the banana prawn, *Penaeus merguiensis*, in the southeastern Gulf of Carpentaria, Australia," *In: Second Australian National Prawn Seminar, NPS2*, Rothlisberg, P. C., Hill, B. J., and Staples, B. S., Eds., Cleveland, Australia, pp. 175-184.

Thorsteinson, F. V. and Thorsteinson, L. K., 1984, "Fishery resources," *In: Proceedings, The North Aleutian Shelf Environment and Possible Consequences of Offshore Oil and Gas Development*, Outer Continental Shelf Environmental Assessment Program (OCSEAP), Juneau, AK, pp. 115-155.

Thorsteinson, L. K., Ed., 1984, "The North Aleutian Shelf Environment and Possible Consequences of Offshore Oil and Gas Development," Outer Continental Shelf Environmental Assessment Program (OCSEAP), Juneau, AK, 159 pp.

Trowbridge, C., 1992, "Prince William Sound management area, 1991 shellfish annual management report," *Regional Information Report No. 2A92-25*, Alaska Department of Fish and Game, 46 pp.

Varanasi, U., Chan, S.-L., McCain, B. B., Landahl, J. T., Schiewe, M. H., Clark, R. C., Brown, D. W., Myers, M. S., Krahn, M. M., Gronlund, W. D., and MacLeod, W. D., Jr., 1989, "National Benthic Surveillance Project: Pacific Coast, Part II. Technical presentation of the results for Cycles I to III (1984-86)," *NOAA Technical Memorandum NMFS F/NWC-170*, 158 pp. + appendices.

E. L. Brannon[1], L. L. Moulton[2], L. G. Gilbertson[3], A. W. Maki[4], J. R. Skalski[5]

AN ASSESSMENT OF OIL-SPILL EFFECTS ON PINK SALMON
POPULATIONS FOLLOWING THE *EXXON VALDEZ* OIL SPILL—PART 1:
EARLY LIFE HISTORY

REFERENCE: Brannon, E. L., Moulton, L. L., Gilbertson, L. G., Maki, A. W., and
Skalski, J. R., **"An Assessment of Oil-Spill Effects on Pink Salmon Populations
following the *Exxon Valdez* Oil Spill—Part 1: Early Life History,"** Exxon Valdez
Oil Spill: Fate and Effects in Alaskan Waters, ASTM STP 1219, Peter G. Wells,
James N. Butler, and Jane S. Hughes, Eds., American Society for Testing and Materials,
Philadelphia, 1995.

ABSTRACT: Pink salmon, *Oncorhynchus gorbuscha,* is the main salmon species of
commercial importance in Prince William Sound. Unlike other Pacific salmon, they have a
two-year life cycle and have adapted to spawn in the intertidal reaches of numerous small
streams throughout the oil-spill area. Thus, they represent the species at highest potential
risk for spill-related injury. This paper discusses results of field programs initiated within
a few days of the spill and designed to assess spill effects on critical early life stages of
pink salmon in postspill years.

Samples of water and stream sediments from throughout the spill area were used
to define the exposure of pink salmon to residual hydrocarbons from the spill. Mean
sediment concentrations of polycyclic aromatic hydrocarbons (PAH) up to 300 ppb were
measured in oiled streams in 1989 and generally followed a downward trend toward
background in 1990 and 1991. These PAH concentrations were then used in regression
analyses of potential effects on key early life stages of pink salmon. Water samples taken
from both nearshore feeding and rearing areas and offshore migratory areas show that
hydrocarbon concentrations were from one to four orders of magnitude lower than
concentrations reported in the literature to cause acute or chronic effects on fish species.

---

[1]University of Idaho, Moscow, ID 83843
[2]MJM Research, Bainbridge Island, WA 98110
[3]Genesis Technical Services, Pacific Beach, WA 98571
[4]Exxon Company, U.S.A., Houston, TX 77252-2180
[5]University of Washington, Seattle, WA 98195

The postspill field and laboratory studies of pink salmon early life stages included examination of potential effects on 1989, 1990, and 1991 eggs, fry, and juveniles. Generally high survival, ranging from 77% to 100%, was observed in both oiled and reference streams in 1989, and a weak correlation was indicated with stream sediment PAH at only one of the three tide levels sampled (12 feet). In 1990, egg viability was 90.6% from reference streams and 91.1% from oiled streams, as determined through incubation studies. Mean condition index, kD, was 1.76 for fry from reference streams and 1.79 from oiled streams, indicating normal developmental timing.

Study results show that no substantial effects on critical early life stages of pink salmon in Prince William Sound are attributable to the spill. Results of incubation experiments with eggs from the spill-affected area provide no indication of sterility or abnormal development. Our results are consistent with the pink salmon returns in 1990 and 1991 that yielded returns over three times the size of the parental year class.

KEYWORDS: pink salmon, toxicity, wildstock, oil pollution, Prince William Sound, *Exxon Valdez*

INTRODUCTION

During the two weeks following the March 24, 1989, *Exxon Valdez* grounding off Bligh Island, Prudhoe Bay crude oil was carried down the southwest side of Prince William Sound (PWS) and into the Gulf of Alaska by the southwesterly current characteristic of that coastal region (Reed and Schumacher 1986). Over the succeeding weeks crude oil at various degrees of weathering washed ashore along approximately 16% of PWS beaches (Neff et al. this volume) and entered the intertidal zones of many of the streams scattered along the spill pathway from Naked Island to the mainland and islands adjacent to Knight Island and Montague Strait, posing a risk to the pink salmon population (Figure 1). Streams that experienced oiling of their intertidal areas accounted for approximately 14% of the identified PWS pink salmon spawning streams in the spill-affected districts (Eshamy, Southwest, and Montague) according to the prespill inventory of pink salmon spawning areas (Alaska Department of Fish and Game [ADF&G] 1985).

This study was designed to assess the effects of the oil spill on the wildstock pink salmon population in PWS. This paper, Part 1, details results of field and laboratory investigations of critical early life stages of pink salmon. Part 2, the following paper, describes results of field studies designed to assess effects on pink salmon adult escapement and spawning behavior.

In the following sections, discussions of reasons for the selection of pink salmon as a sentinel species, a review of water-quality analyses, and a discussion of brood-year differences are presented to frame the study approach and objectives.

Sentinel Species

Major concerns about the effect of the spill on pink salmon were not based solely on the economic importance of the species in PWS, but also on life-history peculiarities of the species that make it the most susceptible among the PWS salmonids to a marine oil spill. Pink salmon follow a rigid two-year life cycle (Figure 2) that begins in the fall at spawning. After incubating all winter the fry emerge from the gravel in the spring and move directly into the marine environment, where they begin a year-long feeding circuit that runs counterclockwise around the Gulf of Alaska, as far south as the 40th latitude, and back up the eastern Pacific. They then home primarily to their natal streams and generally spawn within metres of where they incubated (Gharret and Smoker 1993).

Unlike most other salmonids, pinks use intertidal spawning areas, which leaves them potentially vulnerable to intertidal environmental perturbations. In PWS streams, intertidal areas account for a major portion of the wildstock pink salmon spawning habitat (Noerenberg, 1963). Thus, large numbers of incubating PWS wild pink salmon could be susceptible to deleterious environmental conditions affecting intertidal areas.

Developing salmonid embryos and alevins are life stages most vulnerable to environmental perturbation, and hatched alevins are the stage most sensitive to toxicity (Rice et al. 1975) because of their high ratio of body surface area per unit of mass. Salmonid incubation is a lengthy process, requiring several months before fry are ready to leave their redd (incubation site). This period provides ample opportunity for chronic exposure to potentially toxic conditions that exaggerate the effects of environmental alteration. Exposure to petroleum hydrocarbons during the period of intertidal incubation, therefore, was an issue of major concern. Any effect of oil exposure on pink salmon should be most readily detectable during incubation life stages. The incubation period is crucial to the assessment of potential oil-spill effects on PWS pink salmon specifically and, in general, is an indicator of effects on other salmonids.

The fact that pink salmon fry emerge and migrate immediately to salt water before feeding made the marine habitat conditions another issue of major concern. Emerging fry entering the marine environment carry minimal energy reserves and must begin feeding immediately to sustain their growth and survival. Altered feeding behavior or reduced food resources would have an immediate effect on fry growth and condition. Therefore, even subtle effects of oil on feeding behavior or on feeding opportunity would be readily detected during the first few weeks of pink salmon marine residence. The condition of pink salmon in the early marine environment is considered the next most critical stage to be examined. This is the earliest stage that most other salmonid species could be affected by the spill.

Water-Quality Analyses and Implications

Results of water-quality monitoring studies and pertinent literature on the toxicity of crude oil to salmon are reviewed in this section to provide background on risks to the pink salmon population. Measures of water quality with regard to polycyclic aromatic hydrocarbons (PAH), the most biologically active and major water-soluble-fraction (WSF) component of concern, were taken extensively following the oil spill. Levels at offshore sites averaged <0.1 ppb, and even the high range did not exceed 0.8 ppb. Levels of PAH

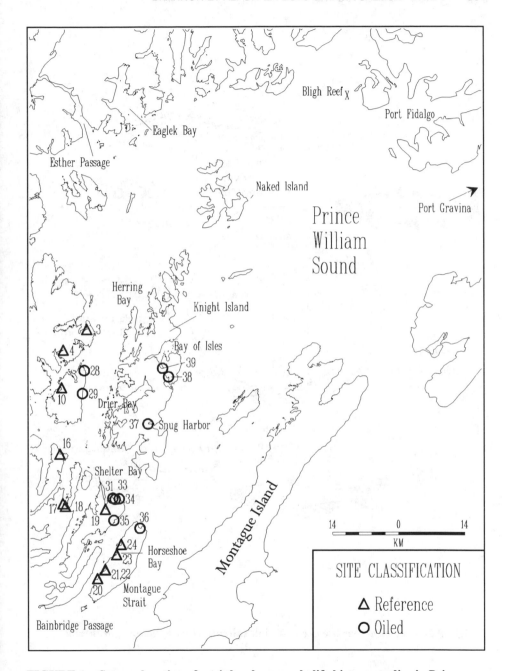

FIGURE 1—Stream locations for pink salmon early life history studies in Prince William Sound.

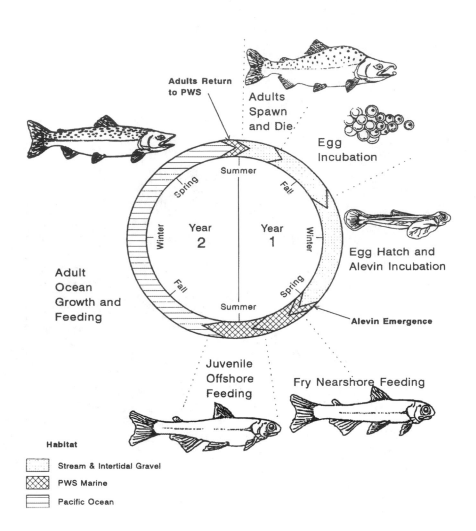

FIGURE 2—The two-year life cycle of pink salmon, *Oncorhynchus gorbuscha*.

from nearshore sites averaged <0.2 ppb, and in water adjacent to beaches where oil had stranded, surface levels ranged as high as 30 ppb (Neff 1991). The interval between the time of the spill and when oil reached the shorelines was sufficient for weathering action to remove most of the water-soluble toxic components, and those that remained in solution were at very low concentrations and continued to degrade. The rapid loss of acute toxicity of petroleum remaining in solution was demonstrated by toxicity tests on indicator organisms (Neff and Stubblefield this volume). In laboratory bioassays, exposure of sheepshead minnows, mysid shrimp, and algae to samples of PWS water taken in April 1989 showed no negative effects on any of the test organisms, indicating that concentrations of soluble oil remaining in the water column were low

Pink salmon have historically been one of the test organisms used in research on oil toxicity to fish. Data on the concentration of the WSF of crude oil at which 50% of the test organisms die (LC_{50}) in bioassay systems have demonstrated that the 96-hr LC_{50} for young pink salmon ranges from 1 500 ppb to 8 000 ppb (Korn and Rice 1981; Moles et al. 1979; Rice et al. 1975). Concentrations of the WSF of oil in water that evoke avoidance behavior in pink salmon fry have been shown to be as low as 1 600 ppb (Rice 1973), and avoidance reactions for salmonids in general occur around that concentration (Folmar 1976; Maynard and Weber 1981; Peters 1989; Weber et al. 1981). Concentrations of PAH components in the water column of PWS, therefore, were from 50 to 10 000 times less than those demonstrated to be deleterious to pink salmon.

Oil residues in the substrate of the oiled spawning streams were also low. Gravel samples taken from the intertidal areas of oiled streams showed mean PAH concentrations from 0.5 ppb to 267 ppb in 1989. Soluble components from oil residue in the gravel at those concentrations would be nearly undetectable in the water column. Because of these consistently low PAH concentrations both in the water column and throughout incubation substrates, direct mortality from oil exposure was considered unlikely.

Similarly, it was considered very unlikely that long-term effects from bioaccumulation would occur. Toxic substances from oil do not generally accumulate in salmonids because the fish metabolize and depurate petroleum hydrocarbons (Martinsen et al. 1992). Because available hydrocarbon monitoring data indicated that risks of direct pink salmon mortality were low, research emphasis was placed on sublethal effects of oil on early growth and development (Part 1) and on subsequent escapement and spawning behavior of adults (Part 2).

Brood-Year Differences

Brood year is used to identify adults and subsequent progeny of a particular spawning year. The 1988 and 1989 brood-year pink salmon had very different potentials for exposure to oil and could not be treated as replicate test groups (Figure 3). The 1988 brood-year adults were not exposed to oil, nor were the 1988 brood progeny during early incubation. They were not exposed to oil until late in incubation. The key life stages exposed to oiling included pink salmon alevins approaching yolk absorption and fry as they emerged and migrated to a recently oiled marine environment. Returns in 1990, therefore, were adults that had survived potentially acute exposure to oil as alevins and fry late in the 1989 incubation and emergence periods.

In contrast, the 1989 brood-year adults entered PWS along recently oiled nearshore migration routes, and their progeny were at risk of exposure to low residual concentrations of oil in the intertidal sediments during their entire incubation period. Fry emerging and migrating to the marine environment were exposed to conditions that prevailed a year after the oil spill. Consequently, some of the 1991 adult returns were fish that may have experienced chronic exposure to low levels of residual weathered oil throughout their entire incubation.

Research undertaken here on effects of oil on PWS pink salmon, therefore, had to consider the 1988 and 1989 broods as separate study projects. The brood years represented very different levels and times of exposure, and hence the questions that were asked addressed different exposure circumstances.

Study Approach

The study design focused on the relative survival and development of pink salmon early life stages from both oiled and control (reference) sites in the study area. Studies were designed to measure direct mortality and abnormal development from exposure to oil in the form of live/dead ratios and relative health of eggs and alevins just prior to their emergence from the incubation stream. Examination of factors that could reduce fitness, such as altered emergence timing or lower growth rates, were also included in the field studies. Although monitoring studies were necessary to define the situation in the field, such assessments could not identify the cause of any observed differences without specific controlled experiments to isolate the effect of the variable in question. Therefore, controlled field and laboratory experiments were also undertaken to isolate the potential effects of oil. These included controlled comparative studies of incubating eggs and alevins and studies of spawner fertility and gamete viability after exposure to oil as juveniles.

Objectives

The general goal of the study was to assess the response of salmonid species to the degree of oiling experienced in PWS from the *Exxon Valdez* oil spill by using pink salmon as the sentinel species. Specifically the study was designed to:

- Determine the effect of oil on incubation success by examining the survival, development, and emergence timing of PWS pink salmon in oiled and reference streams.

- Determine the condition of pink salmon fry and fingerlings during their early marine residence in PWS as a function of oiling.

- Determine the effect of the oil spill on reproductive performance and gamete viability using eggs from adult pink salmon returning to study streams in PWS.

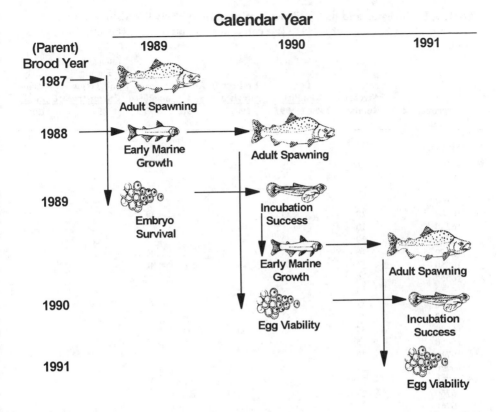

FIGURE 3—Field studies of oil effects were designed to examine key phases of the pink salmon life cycle.

METHODS AND MATERIALS

Stream Selection

Study streams were selected from pink salmon spawning streams identified by the ADF&G (1989) in the Southwestern and Eshamy harvest management districts of PWS (Table 1). Sampling was conducted in oiled and reference streams to examine effects of oil on the incubation success of pink salmon embryos and alevins. Streams were initially classified as "oiled" or "reference" on the basis of shoreline surveys in spring 1989 and according to measured PAH concentrations. These classifications were later reviewed, and adjusted if needed, according to the results of the final 1989 shoreline survey classification (Neff et al. this volume). The intertidal portions of the streams were divided into three tide strata shown to be the most utilized by pink salmon that spawn in the intertidal region. Boundaries of the strata were +1.8 m (6 ft), +2.4 m (8 ft), +3.0 m (10 ft), and +3.7 m (12 ft) above Mean Lower Low Water (MLLW). Observations and

TABLE 1—Streams and bays utilized in pink salmon early life history studies in Prince William Sound, 1989-1991 (R = reference stream or bay, O = oiled stream or bay).

Experimental Unit	Study Stream Number	Egg Viability 1990	Egg Viability 1991	Embryo Survival 1989	Alevin Survival and Anomalies 1990	Alevin Survival and Anomalies 1991	Emergence Timing and Tissue Chemistry 1990	Early Marine Condition 1990
STREAM[1]								
15163	3		R		R	R		
16010	4	R					R	
16030	5	R						
16100	8	R						
16180	28	O			O		O	
16210	10		R					
16280	29	O		O			O	
16370	16				R	R	R	
16550	17				R	R		
16557	18						R	
16610	19		R				R	
16620	31					O	O	
16630	33	O		O				
16640	34	O		O	O	O		
16650	35				O	O		
16710	20				R			
16720	21	R					R	
16730	22				R	R		
16760	23			R	R	R		
16768	24			R			R	
16780	36	O		O	O	O		
16820	37			O	O	O		
16850	38						O	
16860	39				O	O		
BAY								
Bainbridge Pass		R						
Shelter Bay		O						
Horseshoe Bay		R						
Bay of Isles		O						
Port Fidalgo								R
Port Gravina								R
Eaglek Bay								R
Esther Passage								R
Herring Bay								O
Drier Bay								O
Bay of Isles								O
Snug Harbor								O

[1]Salmon streams are identified by the five-digit number assigned by ADF&G.

measurements were recorded by tide stratum. Other information on the streams, including compass orientation upon entering the marine environment, general exposure to open water or wave action, and nature of stream bed (shale, cobble, or pebble) was also recorded.

Procedures

Embryo survival-1989—Controlled field studies were designed to assess the effect of oiling on pink salmon incubation success. Five oiled streams, selected to represent the greatest potential for substrate oiling, were compared with four unoiled reference streams. Whitlock-Viebert incubation chambers (Reiser and White 1981), modified by removing the interior partition to allow embryo contact with the gravel, were set in transects at four tide heights in each of nine streams during the 1989 spawning season. Tide heights were +1.8 m, +2.4 m, +3 m, and +3.7 m above MLLW. At each transect, three standpipes were buried across the stream and two incubation chambers were buried at each standpipe. The incubation chambers each contained 50 fertilized pink salmon eggs and gravel from the hole excavated at each standpipe. The gravel was sieved to provide incubation gravels of from 1.25 to 2.5 cm in diameter. The eggs were obtained by selecting three females and two males from the intertidal zone of each study stream. All eggs and milt were used within the stream of origin. The eggs from the three females were mixed and fertilized with milt from two males. After water hardening for 2 1/2 hr, the eggs were placed in the incubation chambers and planted in the stream bed at normal redd depths (20cm), in late August and early September. Fertilization success was checked by placing two test chambers in the upstream portion of the stream and, after about one week, by removing the eggs to check for signs of initial development. The incubation chambers were removed for assessment by mid-November 1989. The number of live and dead embryos were counted, and the embryos were classified as hatched or unhatched. If the number of live plus dead embryos was fewer than 50, the remainder were assumed to have hatched and escaped, which is consistent with the design of the box. After the incubation chambers were retrieved, the presence of egg capsules, indicating hatching, was recorded.

Sediment samples were taken from each tide level to analyze for sediment chemistry and grain size. The sediment samples for PAH analysis were collected from the surface of the stream, using a glass jar, and grain size was determined with a McNeil Gravel Sampler. Sediment samples were sieved according to particle sizes recommended by Platts et al. (1983) as those shown to be important for survival of incubating salmonid embryos. The sieving process consisted of flushing the core samples with water through a series of sieves. The contents of each particle-size class were then volumetrically measured on the basis of water displacement. The amount of water displaced determined the volume of the sediment plus the volume of any water retained in the pore space in the sediment. Because there is a differential retention of water at various particle sizes, wet volumes were corrected for each particle-size class by using the correction table provided by Platts et al. (1983). The grain-size data were used to generate a value termed the "fredle index," which is sensitive to both the permeability of the gravels and the pore size within the gravels (Lotspeich and Everest 1981). The fredle index is calculated by dividing the geometric mean grain size of each sample by a sorting coefficient. The fredle index at each tide level in each stream was used as a measure of sediment quality and as an environmental variable in the statistical analyses of oiling effects.

Dissolved oxygen, salinity, and temperature were also measured at each standpipe (20 cm depth). Measurements were taken at approximately one-week intervals during the first month of incubation and less frequently toward the end.

Alevin survival and development success-1990 and 1991—Monitoring studies were undertaken to assess differences in survival and development of eggs and alevins between oiled and reference streams. Pink salmon alevins were collected from 11 streams in April 1990 and from 12 streams in April 1991 by the standard technique of pumping water into the substrate and collecting individuals in a net that surrounded the 0.3-m^2 collection site (McNeil 1964). Samples were obtained from four tide strata within each stream. Tide strata were 1.8 to 2.4 m, 2.4 to 3.0 m, 3.0 to 3.7 m above MLLW, and upstream from + 3.7 m. Samples were examined for number of live and dead eggs and alevins, and for abnormal development. Because of the large variability in type of stream and subsubstrate, alevin density was not assessed.

Live and dead individuals in each sample were counted directly, and a sample of 140 alevins from each tide stratum was examined for developmental abnormalities with a binocular dissecting microscope in the laboratory. Individual alevins were examined with the use of a blind code, and any indication of an abnormality was assigned to one of nine categories: cranial, spinal column, eye, skin, muscle, yolk, pigmentation, and fin form. Within these categories abnormalities were ranked according to degree of severity from 1 to 4, with 4 the most severe.

As undertaken in analysis of embryo survival, sediment samples were obtained from each tide stratum to analyze for sediment PAH. The samples were taken from the surface of the stream bed with a stainless steel scoop, following the procedure previously discussed.

Emergent fry timing and condition-1990—Emerging fry were collected from oiled and reference streams to determine whether or not oiling affected emergence timing. In April and May 1990, emerging pink salmon fry were collected from nine streams by placing a 1-m^2 trap over the incubation gravels of spawning streams and removing fry daily as they emerged. The streams selected were different from those used in alevin survival studies to avoid interfering with survival and development investigations. Samples were obtained from three tide strata within each stream: 1.8 to 2.4 m, 2.4 to 3.0 m, and 3.0 to 3.7 m, above MLLW respectively.

The first 30 fry captured in each trap were retained for analysis of PAH in the tissues. The next 50 fry were preserved in 10% formalin or frozen to determine their condition. The samples were coded according to preservation methods. Enumeration of emerging fry was not attempted, and trapping was terminated at each site once sufficient samples were collected.

Both total length (tip of snout to tip of tail) and standard length (tip of snout to base of the notochord) were determined to the nearest millimetre for each fry retained. Damp-wet weight to the nearest 0.01 gram was also determined. The length and width of the yolk sac was measured if it was present.

The fry developmental index *(kD)* based on total length was used in the analysis and is derived from the formula developed by Bams (1970), expressed as follows:

$$kD = \frac{10 \times (\text{weight in mg})^{1/3}}{(\text{length in mm})}$$

Juvenile condition—Pink salmon fingerlings were sampled in PWS to determine if growth of juveniles was affected by the oil spill in 1989 or 1990. Analyses concentrated on the early marine growth period from May through June.

Juvenile pink salmon were collected with a surface trawl commonly referred to as a "tow net." The net is towed between two vessels and is designed to fish the top 1.8 to 3.0 m of the water column, where pink salmon juveniles typically feed. The tow net used in this study was 6 m across the head rope with 3-m vertical spreaders. The graded mesh bag tapered to a 3-mm mesh cod end. Samples were taken from areas offshore of major bays used by pink salmon as feeding areas.

In 1989, sample sites were two oiled bays on the east side of Knight Island, Bay of Isles and Snug Harbor. Tow net samples were collected from the bays, length measurements were taken from the pink juveniles, and temperatures were taken at each sample site. A total of 824 juveniles were measured in Snug Harbor and 373 juveniles from Bay of Isles. After measuring, most of the juveniles were released. The 1989 data were analyzed in growth increments/day based on the length measurements, and compared with expected growth (Brett, 1974) and with the ADF&G beach seine data from the same period.

In 1990 the number of sample sites was increased, and the experimental design expanded to overcome the difficulty in growth analysis caused from the size variability of juveniles. By adding Drier Bay and Herring Bay on the west side of Knight Island, four bays were included that had been heavily oiled in 1989. In addition , Esther Passage, Eaglek Bay, Port Fidalgo and Port Gravina, four bays that had not experienced oiling, were selected from the eastern and northern portions of PWS as reference areas (Figure 1). Net tows were made along four transects in each bay on every sampling day. Transect A was at the mouth of the bay. Transects B and C were north and south, or east and west of the mouth, while Transect D was offshore of the mouth. Juvenile pink salmon were collected from each transect and approximately 24 juveniles per sample site were preserved in 10% formalin for length/weight analysis. At the laboratory, fork length and damp-wet weight to the nearest 0.01 gram were measured to calculate a condition factor *(K)* for each juvenile by using the following formula:

$$K = (100 \times \text{weight in grams})/(\text{fork length in cm})^3$$

The *K* factor, therefore, allowed an examination of juvenile condition apart from absolute size as a measure of the general well being of the individual. If growing conditions were poor or the health of the fish was deteriorating, the *K* factor would demonstrate lower (< 0.75) or decreasing values throughout the sampling period.

Egg viability-1990 and 1991—Controlled laboratory incubation studies were designed to assess possible reduction in gamete viability of pink salmon juveniles exposed to oil. The 1990 and 1991 spawners were returns from the brood years potentially at greatest risk from oil exposure. Twenty ripe females were selected from the intertidal portion of each of four study streams (two oiled, two reference) during the spawning season in 1990 and from ten streams (five oiled, five reference) in 1991. The females were captured with a dip net, and an estimated 200 eggs were hand spawned from each of the twenty females into each of two glass jars. The eggs in each jar were fertilized by a different male; thus, 40 males were used from each stream. In the event of reduced survival, this design allowed us to determine whether the result was caused by a female effect or a male effect. The jars of fertilized and water-hardened eggs were placed in a padded, temperature-controlled cooler and transported to the Solomon Gulch hatchery in Valdez for incubation.

The eggs from each jar were incubated as separate lots in hatchery trays. The lots were coded so that the stream of origin was not known to the hatchery personnel. The eggs were examined daily during the development period, and dead eggs were removed. Well after the eggs hatched, the live alevins were counted, and the number of live alevins versus dead alevins and eggs represented the measure of viability.

Chemistry

Extensive sampling of stream sediments for petroleum hydrocarbons was done to assess the overall level of contamination of spawning/incubation gravel. Study streams were selected as worst-case examples since they were within the most heavily oiled areas of PWS. Thus the samples were not random samples, but were aimed at finding a problem related to hydrocarbons if one existed. Therefore the goal was not to get the exact hydrocarbon distribution within a specific stream, but instead to provide a synoptic sampling of sediment chemistry across impact-area streams as a basis for comparison with any biological effects observed in these streams.

Sediment samples were taken from the stream bed of study streams during the spawning season (mid-to late August) in 1989 through 1991, and during the late incubation season (April) in 1990. These samples were analyzed to determine the concentration and source (fingerprint) of the measured PAH components (Bence and Burns this volume). The PAH fraction includes some of the most biologically active components of crude oil.

Surface sediment samples for PAH determination were collected from intertidal spawning and incubation areas of both reference and oiled streams. During 1989, several individual samples were collected from the intertidal spawning areas, generally near the left and right banks of each stream at the 2.4- and 3.7- m tide levels. In 1990 and 1991, the sediment samples consisted of eight subsamples randomly collected and composited from spawning and incubation areas in the three tide strata for each stream: 1.8-2.4 m, 2.4-3.0 m, and 3.0-3.7 m above MLLW. Samples were collected in precleaned glass containers using methods developed to prevent contamination. In all years, the samples were frozen and transferred to the analytical laboratory. Samples were analyzed by gas chromatography/mass spectrometry (GC/MS) with quantification by selected ion monitoring (SIM) (Sauer and Boehm 1991).

The sediment PAH measurements from each stratum were used as an index of the degree of oiling in the intertidal spawning or incubation areas contained within that stratum. If more than one PAH value was available for a given stratum, the arithmatic mean was used. The use of surface PAH measurements was considered valid because female pink salmon turn over essentially the top 25-30 cm of stream bed during redd (nest) excavation. Contaminated sediments in the spawning areas are likely to be thoroughly mixed by spawning activity. Thus PAH values measured during the spawning season are more representative of PAH concentrations in the redd because of this mixing.

Statistical Analysis

Two approaches to analyzing salmon early life-history data were used to assess effects of oiling on survival, development, growth, and condition. One approach regressed the proportion live, proportion normal, and condition versus sediment and tissue PAH concentration. These dose response analyses were based on the premise that toxic effects on eggs and larvae would be caused by specific local concentrations and oil-derived PAH, i.e., concentrations measured at each sampling station. The experimental units used in regression were individual sampling stations at tidal heights within streams. The other approach compared proportion live, proportion normal, and mean condition between oiled and reference classifications. Here the premise was for an equal effect of oiling at all oiled streams. In these analyses, the sampling stations at tidal heights within streams, or bays in the case of juveniles, were used as experimental units. For analyses on stream data, tidal height was always used as a concomitant variable. Other environmental variables were used as concomitant variables, and these are indicated when appropriate.

Tests were made with two types of statistical distributions. Proportions of live and normal were modeled as binomial distributions and compared between oiled and reference classifications by analysis of deviance (ANODEV) with General Linear Interactive Modeling (GLIM) (Numerical Algorithms Group 1985). Conditions were log-transformed and analyzed using normal error comparing conditions between oiled and reference classifications by analysis of variance (ANOVA). We use the term regression for all dose response relationships, regardless of the type of statistical error.

Two-tailed and one-tailed tests were used. Tests on proportions were one-tailed because the effect of oil was known, i.e., oiling would have reduced proportions of live and of normal. The conventional Type I error (or α) of 0.05 was used for one-tailed tests. Two-tailed alternatives were used to test condition of emergent fry and juveniles. Condition was computed on a ratio of weight to length. Oiling could have resulted in either an increase or decrease in length or weight; therefore, a two-tailed test at $\alpha = 0.10$ was used for tests of effects of oil on either length or weight.

RESULTS

Stream Sediment Chemistry

To fully measure the potential for oil-spill effects on early life stages of pink salmon, regular sampling of the residual hydrocarbons present in the stream sediments was conducted in the falls of 1989, 1990, and 1991, and the spring of 1990. Analyses of these stream sediments for PAH concentrations, the biologically most active fraction of oil, permitted detailed statistical analyses and regressions of any observed effects attributable to the presence of oil. A summary of the PAH analyses for both reference and oiled streams throughout the study period of 1989 to 1991 is shown in Table 2.

A high degree of variability between years and among streams is evident from analyses of stream sediment PAH concentrations. Mean PAH concentrations up to 300 ppb were measured in three of the study streams in 1989 and low levels of 10 to 60 ppb were found in sediments of three reference area streams in 1989. In the spring of 1990 the highest concentration of PAH (7 680 ppb) in stream sediments was reported for stream number 36 in Sleepy Bay. This was approximately one order of magnitude higher than seen in any other stream sample and may have contained a small tar-ball, which would have caused the elevated concentration. Mean concentrations in this stream and the other streams showing measurable hydrocarbon concentrations dropped to levels below 110 ppb in summer of 1990 and between 0.7 and about 236 ppb in summer 1991 (Table 2). These measured concentrations of PAH from sediments were subsequently used in regression analyses for observed effects on key early life stages of pink salmon developing within the stream bed sediments.

Embryo Survival—1989 Spawners

This study, designed to evaluate the effect of oil exposure during the incubation period in five oiled streams and four unoiled reference streams, showed that survival was high in most chambers, averaging greater than 90% at all tidal elevations in seven of the nine study streams (Figure 4). Lowest survival was recorded in a reference stream (#10, 1.8-m tide level), followed by an oiled stream (#29, 3.7-m tide level). Overall, the oiled streams had a slightly higher proportion of live embryos (0.965), compared with the reference stream (0.951).

ANODEV with concomitant variables was used to test the null hypothesis that there were equal percentages of live eggs and alevins in both oiled and reference streams against the alternative hypothesis that the percentages live were less at oiled streams than at reference streams. Environmental variables included tide elevation, degree days, minimum dissolved oxygen, maximum salinity, and an index of gravel quality (fredle index). Analysis was also run on a truncated model with only tidal elevation fit before stream classification. Neither analysis indicated a significant difference in the proportion of live eggs and alevins because of stream oiling (ANODEV; with variables: $p = 0.870$; without variables: $p = 0.169$).

Regression was also used as a further test for a relationship between the proportion of live eggs and alevins and 1989 summer sediment PAH. The model was similar to the ANODEV model but used PAH instead of stream classification as a continuous variable . This statistically more powerful approach was used in analyses of effects, both with and without the environmental variables listed above. The relationship between PAH and the proportion of live eggs and alevins was significantly different for the three tide levels, 2.4-, 3.0- and 3.7-m (with variables: $p = 0.041$; without variables: $p = 0.018$). No stream PAH data were taken for the 1.8-m tide level. The high correlation for regressions with enviromental variables was due largely to temperature, minimum dissolved oxygen, and low degrees of freedom. A significant negative relationship was found only for the 3.7-m tide level with variables ($p = 0.080$) and without variables ($p =$

0.015); all others were not significant (Table 3). The significant relationship for the 3.7-m tide level was due to a single low survival in stream #29, which had a PAH value of 178 ppb. Figure 5a shows a plot of the proportion of live eggs and alevins versus 1989 sediment PAH. Several streams with higher PAH than stream #29 had higher proportions of live eggs, thus indicating that factors other than oil were responsible for the lower survival rates seen in stream #29.

Alevin Survival and Development Success

Alevins incubating in oiled streams in the spring of 1990 were assumed to have been exposed to oil in the incubation environment from late summer 1989 to spring 1990, as demonstrated by PAH analysis of incubation substrate (Table 2). The proportion of live alevins in streams was used as an index of alevin survival, and the proportion of normal alevins in streams was used as an index of alevin viability. ANODEV indicated there was no difference, either in the proportion of live alevins in oiled (0.845) and reference (0.851) streams ($p = 0.447$) or in the proportion of normal alevins in oiled (0.989) and reference (0.992) streams ($p = 0.285$) (Table 4).

As in the previous life-stage analyses, because measurements of sediment PAH were made in intertidal areas, regression was used as a further analysis of survival and development with regard to the presence of oil, independent of stream classification. Regressing proportion live against 1989 summer and 1990 spring sediment PAH showed no relationship in either case (1989 summer: $p = 0.958$, $R^2 = 0.22$; 1990 spring: $p = 0.767$, $R^2 = 0.15$). The regression of proportion abnormal against the same PAH values also indicated a nonsignificant relationship, although the relationships could be considered marginally significant (1989 summer: $p = 0.071$, $R^2 = 0.20$; 1990 spring: $p = 0.170$, $R^2 = 0.07$). The indication is that there may be an increase in the level of abnormality at the highest PAH levels (Table 3).

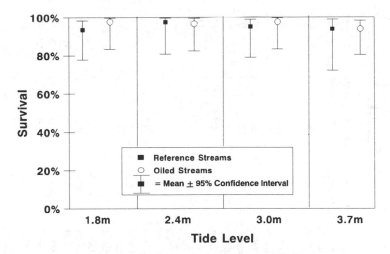

FIGURE 4—**Mean percentage of pink salmon embryos surviving in incubation chambers in intertidal areas.**

Table 2—Mean PAH (in μg/kg) measured in spawning substrates of Prince William Sound streams, 1989-1991.

Study Stream	Class	1989 Spawning			1990 Spring			1990 Spawning			1991 Spawning		
		Mean PAH (μg/kg)	Standard Deviation	Sample Size	Mean PAH (μg/kg)	Standard Deviation	Sample Size	Mean PAH (μg/kg)	Standard Deviation	Sample Size	Mean PAH (μg/kg)	Standard Deviation	Sample Size
3	Reference	0.9	1.4	5	0.6	0.1	3	1.3	0.8	3	1.3	0.0	3
4	Reference	1.2	0.3	4	0.9	0.4	3	1.5	0.3	3	1.7	0.5	3
5	Reference	9.3	17.2	4			0	1.2	0.4	3			0
8	Reference	12.6	16.6	4			0	1.8	0.6	3	0.8	0.1	3
10	Reference	64.0	39.3	7			0			0			0
16	Reference	16.3	19.5	4	1.6	0.6	4	0.7	0.3	3	1.0	0.4	3
17	Reference	28.7	32.6	4	1.2	0.3	3	0.8	0.3	3	2.4	0.7	3
18	Reference	0.9	0.5	4	1.0	0.2	3	1.0	0.2	3			0
19	Reference	1.8	1.0	6	1.8	0.5	3	1.3	0.4	3			0
20	Reference	0.2	0.1	3	1.8	1.2	3	3.2	1.1	3			0
21	Reference	0.4	0.2	4	0.7	0.3	3	1.7	0.3	3	1.5	0.6	3
22	Reference	0.9	1.0	4	1.8	0.6	4			0	1.5	0.1	3
23	Reference	3.2	5.8	7	1.0	0.1	3	2.9	0.4	3	1.5	0.3	3
24	Reference	0.7	0.2	5	35.1	30.3	3			0			0
28	Oiled	0.8	0.5	4	383.6	574.3	3	21.4	17.6	3	223.8	322.8	3
29	Oiled	194.3	83.9	6	181.5	175.7	3	2.2	0.7	3	4.7	4.7	3
31	Oiled			0	99.7	57.9	4			0	8.1	1.7	3
33	Oiled	232.8	262.5	4			0	30.8	25.3	3	96.4	94.2	3
34	Oiled	61.6	45.2	5	413.2	335.1	3	2.0	1.2	3	6.2	3.6	3
35	Oiled	5.4	6.2	4	12.4	17.8	3	2.0	0.7	3	2.1	0.4	3
36	Oiled	267.0	257.6	6	2817.9	3244.1	4	108.2	100.8	3	235.5	358.1	3
37	Oiled	0.5	0.3	6	0.8	0.3	4	1.8	0.5	3	1.1	0.4	3
38	Oiled	18.5	4.3	4	1.0	0.3	4			0			0
39	Oiled	17.4	5.0	4	0.9	0.1	3	3.0	1.7	3	0.7	0.2	3

TABLE 3—Result of regression analyses for pink salmon early life-stage measurements versus concentrations of PAH determined from stream sediments and tissue samples.

	P-Value	R^2	d.f.
1989 EMBRYO SURVIVAL ('89 brood)			
Proportion Live vs. '89 Sediment PAH			
With Environmental Variables			
2.4 m	0.939	0.812	3
3.0 m	0.828	0.921	2
3.7 m	0.080	0.880	2
Without Environmental Variables			
2.4 m	0.217	0.087	7
3.0 m	0.908	0.276	6
3.7 m	0.015*	0.567	6
1990 ALEVIN PUMPING ('89 brood)			
Proportion Live vs.			
'89 Sediment PAH	0.958	0.225	16
'90 Spring Sediment PAH	0.767	0.153	23
Tissue PAH	0.354	0.193	10
Proportion Normal vs.			
'89 Sediment PAH	0.071	0.201	15
'90 Spring Sediment PAH	0.170	0.069	22
Tissue PAH	0.130	0.156	10
1990 FRY TRAPPING ('89 brood)			
kD Index vs.			
'89 Sediment PAH	0.350	0.306	24
'90 Spring Sediment PAH	0.498	0.186	31
Tissue PAH	0.708	0.006	22
1990 EGG VIABILITY ('90 brood)			
Proportion Hatch vs.			
'89 Sediment PAH	0.825	0.421	3
1991 ALEVIN PUMPING ('90 brood)			
Proportion Live vs.			
'90 Summer Sediment PAH	0.500	0.262	17
'91 Sediment PAH	0.120	0.266	20
Tissue PAH	0.444	0.132	15
Proportion Normal vs.			
'90 Summer Sediment PAH	0.584	0.024	16
'91 Sediment PAH	0.871	0.082	19
Tissue PAH	0.528	0.127	15
1991 EGG VIABILITY ('91 brood)			
Proportion Hatch vs.			
'90 Spring Sediment PAH	0.933	0.391	5

* Significant at $p = 0.05$

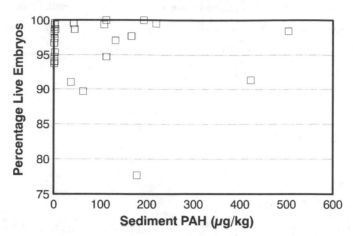

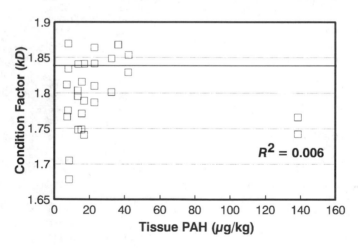

FIGURE 5—(a) Percentage live embryos in fall 1989 versus stream sediment PAH concentrations for 1989. (b) Condition of emergent fry in spring 1990 versus measured levels of PAH in tissues.

The 1991 alevins are the progeny of the juvenile pink salmon that had migrated seaward during the spring of 1989, when the potential for oil exposure was greatest. The 1991 alevins would also have been exposed to any residual oil present in the incubation environment in late 1990 and early 1991. Again, the proportion of live alevins was used as an index of alevin survival in oiled and reference streams, and the proportion of normal alevins was used as an index of alevin viability. In this instance, the proportion of live alevins in oiled versus reference streams showed mixed results. At the 1.8- to 2.4-m tide level, the proportion of live alevins was significantly lower in oiled (0.200) versus reference (0.950) streams ($p = 0.009$). For the combined 2.4- to 3.0-m and 3.0- to 3.7-m tide levels, the proportion of live alevins in oiled (0.991) versus reference (0.977) streams were not significantly different ($p = 0.920$). Because of these mixed results, a test on the proportion of live alevins for all three tide levels combined was not valid. The proportions of live alevins for all tide levels combined (Table 4, final column) are presented for visual comparison only. Regression of the proportion of live alevins against sediment PAH showed no relationship to 1990 summer sediment PAH ($p = 0.500$, $R^2 = 0.26$) or 1991 summer sediment PAH ($p = 0.120$, $R^2 = 0.26$), thus indicating that factors other than oil were responsible for the observed difference. Certainly, according to these statistics, if there was an effect, it was a very weak one.

TABLE 4—Proportion of live and normal pink salmon alevins by tide level for 1990 and 1991.

		Tide Zones		All Tide Zones Combined
	1.8-2.4 m	2.4-3.0 m	3.0-3.7 m	
		Proportion Live		
1990				
Reference	0.860	0.805	0.882	0.851
Oiled	0.842	0.735	0.979	0.845
1991				
Reference	0.950	0.971	0.988	0.966
Oiled	0.200	0.998	0.986	0.938
		Proportion Normal		
1990				
Reference	0.988	0.993	0.991	0.992
Oiled	0.986	0.989	0.990	0.989
1991				
Reference	0.993	0.998	0.991	0.994
Oiled	1.000	0.991	0.996	0.995

The absence of alevins in the 1.8 to 2.4- m tide zone combined with a weak indication of a correlation with oil warranted a further analysis of other factors possibly responsible for the differences in live alevins. In a classification of the stream substrate types this showed that shale was associated only with oiled streams and absent entirely from reference streams (Table 5a). Moreover, the presence of shale was related to the exposure of the stream, where wave action could erode the surface material, compared with the more protected reference streams with cobble and pebble substrates. The substrate types, therefore, as well as the general exposure of the oiled and reference streams (Table 5b), were very different. Also, yearly differences can exist in spawning behavior, especially when the even and odd brood years use different portions of the intertidal and upper sections of a stream.

The proportion of normal alevins in 1991 from oiled (0.995) versus reference (0.994) streams was not statistically different ($p = 0.521$). Similarly, there was no relationship with oil when proportion normal was regressed against 1990 summer sediment PAH ($p = 0.584$, $R^2 = 0.02$) and 1991 summer sediment PAH ($p = 0.871$, $R^2 = 0.8$) (Table 3).

Regressions of tissue PAH versus percentage of live and normal alevins were done to further examine potential relationships between residual PAH concentrations and any observed effects on development of alevins (Figure 6a, b). Tissue PAH were significantly higher in oiled streams for both 1990 ($p = 0.016$) and 1991 ($p = 0.029$). The geometric mean tissue PAH in 1990 and 1991 reference streams were 38.9 ppb and 38.5 ppb respectively, while oiled streams in 1990 and 1991 were 62.8 ppb and 94.6 ppb respectively. The proportion of live and normal alevins would have decreased if they had been affected by hydrocarbon residues present in their body tissues. This was not found to be the case. For 1990 alevins, no significant relationships with tissue PAH were found for either percentage live ($p = 0.354$, $R^2 = 0.19$) or percentage normal ($p = 0.130$, $R^2 = 0.16$). Similarly for 1991 alevins, there were no significant relationships between tissue PAH and either percentage live ($p = 0.444$, $R^2 = 0.13$) or percentage normal ($p = 0.528$, $R^2 = 0.13$) (Table 3).

Emergent Fry Timing and Condition—1990

The fry developmental index was taken as a measure of emergence readiness in five reference and five test streams. Mean condition index kD was 1.76 for fry from reference streams and 1.80 from oiled streams, indicating normal timing with regard to stage of advancement (Figure 7). The values were a little lower than the kD values reported for British Columbia pink salmon (Bams 1970). The kD index from reference stream fry proved significantly different than that from fry in oiled streams (ANCOVA: $p = 0.021$), but this was only because kD values of fry samples from two reference streams were very low, indicating that some fry in those sample areas delayed emergence nearly to the point of emaciation. However, because of such small differences in kD values between test and reference streams, no biological significance is implied.

When kD was regressed on tissue PAH (Figure 5b), there was no relationship between kD and tissue PAH ($p = 0.708$, $R^2 = 0.01$) (Table 3). Further analyses showed no relationship between kD and 1989 summer sediment PAH ($p = 0.350$, $R^2 = 0.31$) and no relationship with 1990 spring PAH ($p = 0.488$, $R^2 = 0.19$).

TABLE 5a—Presence or absence of alevins by substrate type in PWS oiled and reference streams.

	Substrate Type			Absence (A)* or
Stream #	Cobble	Pebble	Shale	Presence (P)
Reference				
3	X			P
16	X			P
22	X			P
17		X		P
20		X		A
23		X		P
Oiled				
37	X			P
39	X			A
28			X	P
31			X	A
34			X	A
35			X	A
36			X	A

* Absent in either 1990 or 1991 at any tide level.

TABLE 5b—Substrate type in PWS oiled and reference streams compared with exposure to wave action

	Substrate Type		
	Cobble	Pebble	Shale
Exposure			
Low	80%	100%	-
Moderate	20%	--	80%
High	--	--	20%

Juvenile Condition

In Snug Harbor and Bay of Isles, the two heavily oiled bays examined in the spring of 1989, growth analysis showed that mean growth rate of pink salmon from the 24th of May to the 8th of June was 3.0% and 2.4%/day at mean temperatures of 8.7° C and 9.2° C respectively, or an increase in length of 1.2 and 1.0 mm/day (Table 6). This rate was greater than that for pink juveniles demonstrated by Wertheimer et al. (1992) in either oiled or non-oiled areas for 1989. They reported growth rates no greater than 0.5 mm/day, and their early June samples averaged a little over 46 mm, or 9 mm less than samples in the Snug Harbor and Bay of Isles study on the same dates. Juvenile length increases of 1.2 and 1.0 mm/day in oiled bays were normal and, based on Brett (1975), comparable to those expected for pink salmon under the temperature regime experienced in 1989.

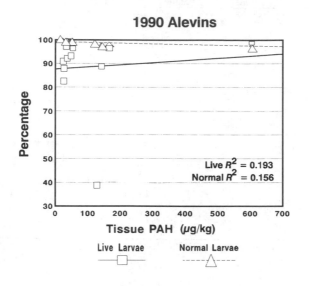

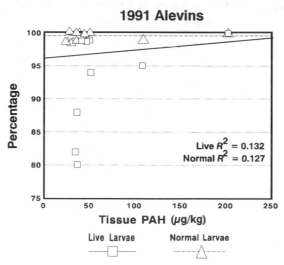

FIGURE 6—Percentage of live and normal alevins found in study streams in 1990 and 1991 versus measured PAH concentrations in tissues.

TABLE 6—Incremental growth in length of juvenile pink salmon in Snug Harbor and Bay of Isles, PWS, in spring of 1989.

	Snug Harbor 1989	Bay of Isles 1989
Study Period	5/25 to 6/8	5/24 to 6/7
Mean Temperature	8.7° C	9.2° C
5/24 length		41.6
5/25 length	39.6	
6/7 length		55.8
6/8 length	55.8	
Growth in mm/day	1.16	1.01

    In the expanded study of 1990, both mean size and condition of juvenile pink salmon that emerged and emigrated to the marine environment showed no differences between oiled and unoiled bays (Figure 8a and b). Temperature variation occurred among study sites in 1990, with mean temperatures as much as 4° C higher than 1989. Mean temperature in reference bays was 0.6° C warmer than in oiled bays (reference = 12.6° C, oiled = 12.0° C). Although an ANOVA showed that water temperatures were not significantly different ($p = 0.15$), to be conservative and increase the potential for detecting an oiling effect, temperature was included as a concomitant variable when testing for an effect of oiling on growth.

    The natural logarithm of weight was plotted against date (Figure 8a) since growth in weight was estimated to be exponential over the sampling period. Separate linear regressions were plotted for reference and oiled bays. Although oiled bays were cooler than reference bays, growth rates (slopes) were not significantly different ($p = 0.371$), and actually tended to be slightly greater in oiled bays.

    Mean condition of juvenile pinks measured during early marine residence in reference bays ($K = 0.889$) and oiled bays ($K = 0.891$) did not differ significantly ($p = 0.837$). Condition of the juveniles remained the same over the progress of the study (Figure 8b), indicating relatively constant feeding conditions.

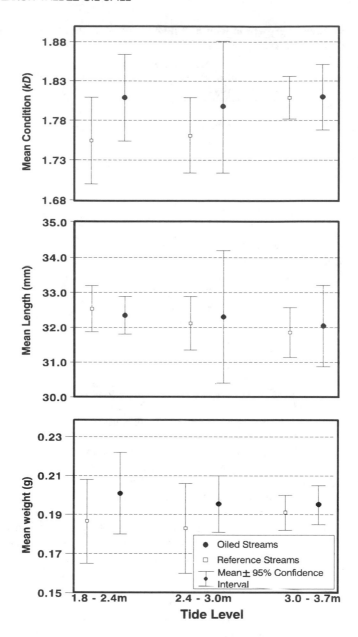

FIGURE 7—Mean length, weight, and condition (*kD*) of emergent fry by tide level in spring 1990.

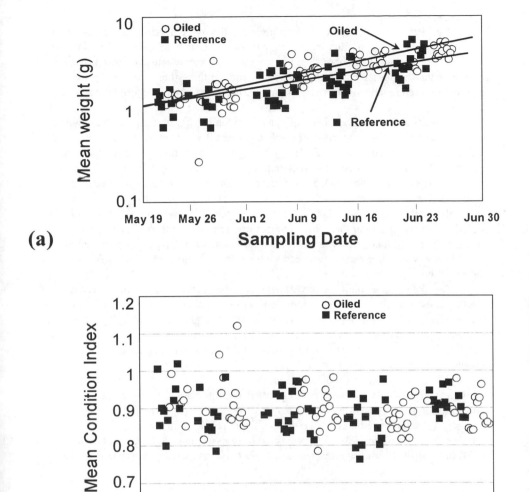

(a)

(b)

FIGURE 8a, b—Mean weight and condition of juvenile pink salmon captured in oiled and reference bays in 1990.

Egg Viability

The 1990 adult returns were from juveniles that were potentially exposed to oil late in incubation as alevins and fry in spring 1989. Forty females were selected from two streams representing sites where emerging fry could have contacted oil (test streams) upon entering the marine environment in 1989, and another 40 females were selected from the two reference streams representing marine environments where oil was not present.

Results showed high viability of eggs from females returning to both oiled and reference streams. The proportion of viable eggs was 0.897 from streams in reference bays and 0.910 in oiled streams (Table 7). No significant difference in egg viability between reference and test streams was demonstrated using ANODEV ($p = 0.574$). The effects of males on viability tended to be more variable than effects of females, but there were no differences between oiled and reference streams ($p = 0.424$).

In contrast, the 1991 adults were from juveniles that were potentially exposed to some level of oiling during their entire incubation period, from the fall of 1989 to the spring of 1990. In this case five streams were selected where spawning occurred in oiled intertidal areas, and five reference streams were selected where intertidal spawning areas were not oiled.

Results revealed high viability of eggs of females returning to both reference and oiled streams, with the proportion of viable eggs in reference streams at 0.962 (Table 7). Survival of eggs from oiled-stream females was 0.966, and no difference was shown between oiled and reference streams ($p = 0.656$). Again, male effects were more variable than female effects, but the variability of females did not differ between oiled and reference streams ($p = 0.903$).

Moreover, when intertidal sediment PAH was used as an indicator of the extent of oiling, and egg viability was regressed against PAH, no relationship between viability and concentration of oil present was demonstrated. When 1990 egg viability was regressed against 1989 summer sediment PAH, no significant relationship was found between the two ($p = 0.825$). When 1991 egg viability was regressed against 1990 spring sediment PAH, there again was no significant relationship between the two ($p = 0.933$) (Table 3).

DISCUSSION

After the *Exxon Valdez* oil spill, there was widespread concern that salmon resources in PWS would be seriously affected and that the economic effects from reduced survival would be long-term. The consensus was that pink salmon, because of their life history and behavior, were the most vulnerable to exposure and potential deleterious effects. Intertidal and nearshore areas received the most intense and prolonged exposure to the oil, and pink salmon utilize these habitats during sensitive and critical life-history stages. At the time of the spill, large numbers of pink salmon alevins were residing in the intertidal reaches of PWS streams, and they would soon emerge and move into nearshore marine waters to begin feeding.

Potential for Acute Effects

Although there was general concern about potential mortality of pink salmon early life stages, there was no prior body of evidence suggesting that exposure to oil concentrations as low as those in PWS would be deleterious to salmon survival. Evidence from other oil spills also indicated that direct mortality to stages in the water column would be unlikely. In California, no fish kills were observed when measurements of a chemically dispersed Prudhoe Bay oil slick near the point of spill showed that the concentrations of C_1-C_{10} hydrocarbons one hour after aerial spraying ranged up to 75 ppb (McAuliffe et al. 1981). These concentrations were several times higher than concentrations of undispersed oil measured in the water column in PWS following the oil spill, and still 20 to 100 times less than concentrations demonstrated lethal to pink salmon. Therefore, the WSF, which is the major harmful component of petroleum, dilutes and dissipates quickly enough to pose no acute hazard under environmental conditions associated with open water. Weathering effects on petroleum further reduce the WSF remaining in the water column that might be harmful to salmon.

Water chemistry determinations in PWS following the spill and toxicology studies exposing sensitive indicator organisms to PWS water samples from the spill trajectory (Neff and Stubblefield this volume) confirmed the view that oil levels encountered by emigrating salmon juveniles were far less concentrated than what would be necessary to cause direct mortality of fish or their food supply. Even at the most heavily oiled sites selected for monitoring, mean PAH levels at their highest concentration in April-May of 1989 were well below the Alaska State standard for petroleum aromatics, and those concentrations had returned to background levels by the end of May.

Our field program examined potential for acute effects of oil on each life stage of pink salmon. Emphasis was placed on development, behaviors, and survival of alevins during incubation, and no statistically significant effects of oil were found in those streams identified to have the heaviest level of oil contamination. Rice et al. (1975) showed that alevins were the most sensitive incubation stage to oil toxicity. The absence of any effect in the present study indicates that concentrations of oil in the incubation gravel were simply too low to negatively affect the developing pink salmon. There is little doubt that freshwater irrigating through the redd diluted the soluble components, but in the final analysis PAH concentrations present were below the acute toxicity threshold for pink salmon alevins.

Potential for Chronic Effects

Gametogenic effects from oil were considered remote because of the low WSF concentrations present; however, because toxicity tests with petroleum have not examined gametogenic effects from oil exposure of salmon, it was a possibility that needed consideration. Two different potential problems faced PWS pink salmon populations because of their exposure history. The first was reduced fertility or gamete inviability induced by exposure to oil during late incubation and early marine residence of the 1988 brood. The second was inviability from long-term exposure of the 1989 brood during the entire incubation period. However, gametes taken from returning spawners in test and reference streams, and incubated in isolation, revealed no gametogenic effects from the presence of oil.

TABLE 7—Proportion of hatched alevins from hatchery-incubated eggs taken from pink salmon females in oiled and reference streams, 1990 and 1991.

Sampling Year	Class	Stream or Bay	Proportion Live*
1990	Oiled		
		Shelter Bay	0.922
		Bay of Isles	0.898
		Oiled Bays:	**0.910**
	Reference		
		Bainbridge Pass	0.962
		Horseshoe Bay	0.839
		Reference Bays:	**0.897**
1991	Oiled		
		28	0.972
		29	0.954
		33	0.944
		34	0.974
		36	0.975
		Oiled Streams:	**0.966**
	Reference		
		3	0.961
		4	0.950
		5	0.973
		8	0.981
		21	0.944
		Reference Streams:	**0.962**

* Sample size was 20 females and 40 males for all bays and streams except #29, where 10 females were used.

This particular part of the study, conducted under controlled conditions, incorporated what might be considered the most sensitive tests for sublethal toxicity. Gametes taken from the returning spawners in test and reference streams, and incubated in isolation, however, revealed no differences in viability. Although viability was very high, the regression of PAH against viability should have detected even a subtle effect if one were present. These results indicated, therefore, that oiling to the extent experienced during incubation and rearing in the spring of 1989 and 1990 resulted in no gametogenic damage that would be demonstrated by higher egg mortality in returning spawners. We believe these studies address the question of long-term reduced gamete quality in fish exposed to oil from the *Exxon Valdez* spill.

Egg Incubation and Fry Survival in the Field

Egg incubation—Since direct mortality of incubating eggs and alevins in streams exposed to oil remained a potential effect, field studies of developing eggs and alevins were undertaken during the incubation period following the spill and executed at sites known to have heavy concentrations of oil reaching the intertidal incubation areas based on Shoreline Cleanup Assessment Team surveys. Results were a direct and immediate assessment of the effects oil may have on the incubation survival of eggs and alevins, including both direct toxic effects and indirect physical impairment of the incubation environment, such as material potentially coating the external surface of the eggs or physically reducing irrigating flow through redds.

Significant differences in incubation survival between streams were not demonstrated except in two instances. Reference stream # 10, at tide level 1.8 m, experienced the highest mortality, and other tide levels in the stream also experienced higher than average mortality. The second instance was an oiled stream (# 29) with intermediate PAH concentrations (194 ppb) at the 3.7-m tide level, where higher mortality in three of the six buried compartments reduced survival to 77% at that tide level (Figure 5a). This caused a statistically significant negative survival relationship with PAH. However, because high survival was recorded in the rest of that stream, and because survival was high in other streams at tide levels with equal or much higher PAH levels, it was concluded that reduced survival at the 3.7-m tide level in stream # 29 was not attributable to an oil effect. Therefore, insofar as these studies were concerned, where we investigated the worst cases, significant toxic effects of oil on the salmon population were not demonstrated, nor were there any effects on survival from poor gas exchange or reduced circulation in the incubation substrate, as might be hypothesized from the physical presence of oil.

Fry development—Examination of field samples for abnormalities of developing alevins was also given high priority as a potential cause of reduced pink salmon productivity. Deformed fry result from either poor incubation conditions or poor-quality gametes. A low percentage of deformed fry is normal in all salmonid populations, so the study looked for a marked increase in deformities among alevins incubating in oiled streams compared with those in reference streams.

A marked increase was not found, although there may have been a slight increase in abnormality at the highest PAH levels. However, at the level of analysis that was conducted in this study, the results indicated that neither a marked reduction in gamete quality nor a marked decrease in quality of incubation conditions were demonstrated in oiled streams. We would conclude that survival and development success in oiled streams were well within the range expected for normal pink salmon incubation success. These data, taken with the gamete viability and embryo survival data, are strong evidence that the oil spill had no significant effect on gamete quality or incubation success.

Statistical Significance

The summary of regression analyses presented in Table 3 indicates that, of the 20 separate regressions conducted, one embryo survival relationship is significant and four alevin development tests show weak but insignificant correlations with PAH. Although in some instances these probability values approach the level of statistical significance at $p = 0.05$, the uniformly low R^2 values indicate the lack of any meaningful relationship with measured PAH concentrations. Examination of residuals for all regressions in Table 3 showed that the linear model was appropriate. Overall the data indicate that viability of eggs was very good, embryo survival was very good in both oiled and reference streams, and differences in alevin survival and frequency of abnormalities significant to the pink salmon population were not detected.

Variables Influencing Salmon Production

One problem with a study design undertaken in response to a situation like the *Exxon Valdez* oil spill is that it is impossible to randomize or select paired streams that differ only in the variable of interest. The data to make such pairings are simply not available. The spill event dictates the circumstances around which the study design must proceed. The physical orientation of oiled streams places them in a category that is difficult to represent by control streams. We found that oiled streams differed from reference streams with regard to their orientation and exposure (Maki et al. this volume). A northeast-facing stream that was vulnerable to oil catchment was also vulnerable to the prevailing currents and storms sculpturing the intertidal area. Some streams had very little and poor- quality intertidal habitat that spawners tended to bypass. Others had unstable moraines where the channel would change between fall and spring, leaving the new stream mouth void of incubating fry.

This fact became apparent in the present study when several of the oiled streams showed no evidence of eggs or alevins, live or dead, at certain tide levels. The total absence of dead and live fish meant that these areas were most likely not used, because if something had been responsible for their mortality, ample evidence would have been available through the presence of dead eggs. Examination of stream exposure and the relationship with substrate types in streams selected in the present study revealed a high incidence of shale among oiled streams, whereas reference streams had cobble or pebble substrate, but no shale in the intertidal areas (Table 5a). The incidence of intertidal strata void of any eggs or alevins in the present study occurred primarily in streams with shale substrate. Because five of the seven oiled streams selected for fry-survival assessment in the present study had shale as intertidal substrate, and none of the reference streams, there was a bias in substrate type against oiled streams.

Void intertidal strata have been characteristic of some PWS streams. Recent historical spring stream fry-enumeration records (Table 8a) show that blank tidal zones are not rare. For example, in 1977 over 45% of the samples at the lowest tide stratum contained no eggs or alevins, whereas in 1980 void samples were found at all strata. It is clear there is substantial interannual variability in the occurrence of void zones. Most often, it was the 1.8- to 2.4-m tide zone that lacked alevins, and in some years the proportion was very high. In other cases no live alevins were found (Table 8b), which suggests the zone is poor incubation habitat or the live fry have emerged. Traditionally, the lower tidal zone is the poorer habitat because redds are left without irrigating flow when the tide floods. However, the lower tidal area is also the warmer incubation area of the stream, and emergence is usually earlier there. Olsen and McNeil (1967) showed that emergence timing in Sashin Creek, Alaska, can vary from year to year by as much as a month. When the mean incubation temperature for a year is higher, emergence is proportionally earlier. Another factor that would influence the occurrence of void zones is the frequency, intensity, and wind direction of winter storms. These storms have the potential to drastically rearrange the intertidal channel structure, particularly on the beaches with loose shale substrate, which would increase the chance that spring sampling occurs in areas that were not available to spawners the previous summer. These circumstances demonstrate the importance of controlled experiments to check against field observations. Without controlled experiments to isolate potential effects of oil, it is extremely difficult to attribute changes observed in fry survival to the presence of oil.

A very subtle effect of environmental perturbation on incubating salmon with important survival implications is altered emergence timing. Timing differences cannot be readily detected by just comparing emergence dates. Incubation temperature and slight differences in spawning time can result in marked changes in emergence timing under normal circumstances. Therefore, the weight/length relationship or developmental index (Bams 1970) can be used to assess the degree of advancement; thus, an assessment of appropriate timing is determined by the kD of emerging fry.

As the young fish converts yolk reserves into metabolizable energy for growth, the weight/length relationship decreases until no yolk remains, and an external energy source must be found. If emergence occurs too soon or too late, it will be demonstrated by the developmental index. In the present study, the index data as well as the general size of the fry indicated normal timing of progeny from oiled streams. This is a sensitive test for altered emergence behavior. According to unpublished studies of pink salmon early life history by the International North Pacific Fisheries Commission, incubating fry disturbed by the presence of poor-quality water or low dissolved oxygen would emerge prematurely and demonstrate a high index value (>2.0). Conversely, if fish could not orient to current or were hindered in leaving the gravel, they would delay emergence and show a very low index (<1.6). Neither result occurred in the PWS studies. The pink salmon fry emerged from both oiled and reference streams at the same developmental stage expected for the species.

Growth and Survival of Juveniles

Marine-entry timing is critical to pink salmon survival because it is linked with the immediate access to energy sources needed to sustain rapid growth. Consequently, this life stage in pink salmon is very sensitive to significant changes in water quality or food resources. If any altered behavior occurs, an immediate effect on their weight will be triggered because of the high metabolic demand of pink fry. If weight gain is slowed, the condition factor as a function of the weight/length relationship decreases even more rapidly because length continues to increase at the expense of weight even during starvation.

In 1989 and 1990 juveniles entering the marine environment were exposed to potentially very different consequences of oiling. In 1989 those fry emerging into recently oiled habitat would have encountered whatever the immediate effects of oil had been on the environment. By 1990, oil was off the waters of PWS and any oiling effect would have been limited to some remnant influence on productivity of feeding juveniles. Pink

TABLE 8—ADF&G historical fry-sampling data.

		A. Number of samples with no eggs or alevins (live or dead) by tide zone and year			B. Number of samples with dead eggs or alevins, but no live alevins	
Year	Tide Zone (m)	Total Zones Sampled	Zones with No Live or Dead Eggs/Alevins	Percentage Blanks	Zones with Dead but No Live Alevins	Percentage with No Live Alevins
1977	2.4	26	4	15.4	1	3.8
	3.0	31	3	9.7	0	0.0
	3.7	31	5	15.1	0	0.0
1978	2.4	31	14	45.2	4	12.9
	3.0	36	3	8.3	1	2.7
	3.7	36	5	13.9	2	5.5
1979	2.4	25	2	8.0	2	8.0
	3.0	30	1	3.3	1	3.3
	3.7	31	2	6.5	0	0.0
1980	2.4	26	9	34.6	0	0.0
	3.0	33	4	12.1	3	9.0
	3.7	33	5	15.2	1	3.0
1981	2.4	24	0	0.0	4	16.6
	3.0	31	1	3.2	0	0.0
	3.7	32	1	3.1	0	0.0
1982	2.4	18	4	22.2	2	11.1
	3.0	25	0	0.0	2	8.0
	3.7	24	1	4.2	0	0.0
1983	2.4	21	3	14.3	1	4.7
	3.0	24	2	8.3	1	4.1
	3.7	25	2	8.0	1	4.0
1984	2.4	18	5	27.8	1	5.5
	3.0	24	3	12.5	1	4.1
	3.7	23	2	8.7	0	0.0
1985		NA	NA	NA	NA	NA
1986	2.4	17	4	23.5	3	17.6
	3.0	21	2	9.5	0	0.0
	3.7	21	0	0.0	3	14.2
Composite 1977-1986						
	2.4	208	45	21.6	18	8.7
	3.0	255	19	7.5	9	3.5
	3.7	256	23	9.0	7	2.7

juveniles in the two oiled bays examined in 1989 showed very similar initial growth rates and were consistent with rates expected for pink salmon under the 1989 temperature regimes encountered in those bays.

In 1990 growth was similar among fry from oiled and non-oiled bays. No differences were found between the length, weight or condition of fingerlings from reference areas and test areas in 1990. This indicates that if there had been a latent effect on marine productivity from oiling, there was no apparent demonstration of such an effect manifested in the condition of juveniles in the marine environment one year after the spill. The size of fingerlings in this study was consistent with that reported by Hartt (1985) during the extensive studies undertaken and later reported by Hartt and Dell (1986).

The early life-history studies we conducted on the condition and survival of PWS pink salmon incubated in streams selected to represent the most severe effects of oiling demonstrated that the problems that might have been produced by the oil spill, in fact, did not occur. In each study case, sensitive measures were used to reveal changes in behavior, development, or survival both in controlled experiments and in field monitoring studies. In no instance was there a demonstrated effect that would be significant to the wildstock pink salmon population. Whether these data are interpreted to mean that pink salmon were not affected by oil, or alternatively, pink salmon must not have been exposed to biologically meaningful concentrations of oil, the result is the same. There was no detectable effect of the *Exxon Valdez* oil spill on the PWS wildstock pink salmon population.

CONCLUSIONS

This study was designed to discern oil-related effects using sensitive measures of the most vulnerable life stages of pink salmon. The study examined the survival and development of eggs and fry incubated in streams selected to represent the most severe effects of oiling. The intertidal incubation environment supported normal development and growth of pink salmon as determined by measures of fry survival, development abnormalities, and emergence timing. No differences were found in these parameters between oiled and oiled streams and bays. Condition of fingerlings during early marine residence in 1990 was the same between previously oiled and unoiled areas, indicating that both the stream and marine rearing habits were healthy and producing normally. Moreover, high gamete viability among the 1990 and 1991 adult returns suggested there was no effect of oil exposure on the long-term reproductive potential of the pink salmon populations. Comparisons of area-wide hydrocarbon contamination of stream sediments with sensitive biological endpoints of the pink salmon life cycle would have detected significant effects if present. However, there was no apparent effect from oil exposure that would have a significant effect on the wildstock pink salmon population in the sound.

Although negative indications of exposure to petroleum hydrocarbons have been reported in other studies related to the *Exxon Valdez* oil spill, neither results from the present early life-history studies nor the survival success of progeny of the 1988 and 1989 brood years would support such conclusions.

ACKNOWLEDGMENTS

The authors would like to thank Pentec Environmental, Inc., for their assistance in conducting the 1989 field program, and the staff and management of Dames and Moore for assistance with the 1989 and 1990 field program. K. R. Parker provided valuable support in the review of the experimental design and conduct of statistical analyses.

REFERENCES

Alaska Department of Fish and Game. *Catalog of Waters Important for Spawning, Rearing, or Migration of Anadromous Fishes: Southcentral Region, Resource Management Region II.* ADF&G Habitat Division, Juneau, Alaska; 109; 1985.

Bams, R A. "Evaluation of a Revised Hatchery Method Tested on Pink and Chum Salmon Fry." *Journal of the Fisheries Research Board of Canada.* 27: 1429-1452; 1970.

Brett, J.R. "Tank Experiments on the Culture of Pan-Size Sockeye (*Oncorhynchus nerka*) and Pink Salmon (*O. gorbuscha*) Using Environmental Control." *Aquaculture* 4: 341-352; 1974

Folmar, L.C. "Overt Avoidance Reactions of Rainbow Trout Fry to Mine Herbicides." *Bulletin of Environmental Contamination & Toxicology.* 15(5): 509-514; 1976.

Gharrett, A.J. and W.W. Smoker. "A Perspective on the Adaptive Importance of Genetic Infrastructure in Salmon Populations to Ocean Ranching in Alaska." *Fisheries Research.* 18 (1-2): 45-58; 1993.

Hartt, A.C., personal communication; 1985.

Hartt, A.C. and M.B. Dell. "Early Oceanic Migrations and Growth of Juvenile Pacific Salmon and Steelhead Trout." *International North Pacific Fisheries Commission Bulletin.* 46: 105; 1986.

Helle, J.H., R.S. Williamson, and J.E. Bailey. "Intertidal Ecology and Life History of Pink Salmon at Olsen Creek, Prince William Sound, Alaska." *U.S. Fish and Wildlife Services Special Scientific Report: Fish.* 483: 26; 1964.

Korn, S. and S. Rice. "Sensitivity to, and Accumulation and Depuration of, Aromatic Petroleum Components by Early Life Stages of Coho Salmon (*Oncorhynchus kisutch*)." *Report Conseil International Exploration de la Mer.* 178: 87-92; 1981.

Lotspeich, F.B. and F.H. Everest. "A New Method for Reporting and Interpreting Textural Components of Spawning Gravel." U.S. Forest Service Research Note PNW-369; 1981.

Martinsen, C., B. Lauby, A. Nevissi, and E. Brannon. "The Influence of Crude Oil and Dispersant on the Sensory Characteristics of Steelhead (*Oncorhynchus mykiss*) in Marine Waters." *Journal of Aquatic Food Product Technology.* 1(1): 37-51; 1992.

Maynard, D.J. and D.D. Weber. "Avoidance Reactions of Juvenile Coho Salmon to Monocyclic Aromatics." *Canadian Journal of Fisheries & Aquatic Sciences.* 38: 772-778; 1981.

McAuliffe, C.D., B.L. Steelman, W.R. Leek, D.E. Fitzgerald, J.P. Ray, and C.D. Barker. "The 1979 Southern California Dispersant Treated Research Oil Spills." *In: Proceedings of the 1981 Oil Spill Conference.* Washington D.C.: American Petroleum Institute; 269-282; 1981.

McNeil, W.J. "Redd Superimposition and Egg Capacity of Pink Salmon Spawning Beds." *Journal of the Fisheries Research Board of Canada.* 21: 6; 1964.

Moles, A., S.D. Rice, and S. Korn. "Sensitivity of Alaskan Freshwater and Anadromous Fishes to Prudhoe Bay Crude Oil and Benzene." *Transactions of the American Fisheries Society.* 108: 408-414; 1979.

Neff, J. M. "Water Quality in Prince William Sound and the Gulf of Alaska." Report 02140-2390 Cambridge, MA: Arthur D. Little; 37; 1991.

Noerenberg, W. H. "Salmon Forecast Studies on 1963 Runs in Prince William Sound." Information Leaflet 21. Alaska Department of Fish and Game. Juneau, Alaska; 27; 1985.

Numerical Algorithms Group. *The GLIM System Release 3.77 Manual.* Downers Grove, IL: Numerical Algorithms Group; 1985.

Olsen, J.M. and W.J. McNeil. "Research on Pink Salmon at Little Port Walter, Alaska, 1934-64." U.S. Fish and Wildlife Service Data Report 17. 301; 1967.

Platts, W.S., W.F. Megahan, and G.W. Minshall. "Methods for Evaluating Stream Riparian and Biotic Conditions." U.S. Department of Agriculture Forest Service General Technical Report NT-138; 1983.

Peters, R.J. *A Comparison of Two Methods for Determining Avoidance of Water-Soluble Petroleum Hydrocarbons by Salmonids.* MS Thesis. University of Washington; 1989.

Reed, R.K. and J.D. Schumacher. "Physical Oceanography." *In: The Gulf of Alaska.* D.W. Hood and S.T. Zimmerman, editors. U.S. Department of Interior, MMS Publish Number OCS Study MMS 86-0095:57-75;1986.

Reiser, D.W. and R.G. White. "Influence of Streamflow Reductions on Salmonid Embryo Development and Fry Quality." Idaho Water and Energy Resources Research Institute. University of Idaho. Research Technical Completion Report, Project A-058-IDA. Moscow, Idaho. 1981.

Rice, S.D. "Toxicity and Avoidance Tests with Prudhoe Bay Crude Oil and Pink Salmon Fry." *In: Proceedings of 1973 Joint Conference on Prevention and Control of Oil Spills.* Washington D.C.: American Petroleum Institute; 667-670; 1973.

Rice, S.D., A. Moles, and J.W. Short. "The Effect of Prudhoe Bay Crude Oil on Survival and Growth of Eggs, Alevins, and Fry of Pink Salmon." *In: Proceedings of the 1975 Conference on Prevention and Control of Oil Pollution. Washington D.C.: American Petroleum Institute.* 503-507; 1975.

Sauer, T. and P.D. Boehm. "The Use of Defensible Analytical Chemical Measurements for Oil Spill Natural Resource Damage Assessment." *In: Proceedings of the 1991 International Oil Spill Conference. March 4-7, 1991, San Diego, California.* 363-370; 1991.

Weber, D.D., D.J. Maynard, W.D. Gronland, and V. Konchin. "Avoidance Reactions of Migrating Adult Salmon to Petroleum Hydrocarbons." *Canadian Journal of Fishery and Aquatic Science.* 38: 367-372; 1981.

Wertheimer, A.C., A.G. Celewycz, M.G. Carls, and M.V. Sturdevant. "The Impact of the *Exxon Valdez* Oil Spill on Juvenile Pink and Chum Salmon and Their Prey in Nearshore Marine Habitats." Exxon Valdez *Oil Spill Symposium. February 3-5,* Anchorage, AK.1993. 115-117; 1993.

A.W. Maki,[1] E.J. Brannon,[2] L.G. Gilbertson,[3] L.L. Moulton,[4]
J.R. Skalski[5]

AN ASSESSMENT OF OIL-SPILL EFFECTS ON PINK SALMON
POPULATIONS FOLLOWING THE EXXON VALDEZ OIL SPILL--PART 2:
ADULTS AND ESCAPEMENT

REFERENCE: Maki, A. W., Brannon, E. J., Gilbertson, L. G., Moulton, L. L., and
Skalski, J. R., **"An Assessment of Oil-Spill Effects on Pink Salmon Populations
following the *Exxon Valdez* Oil Spill—Part 2: Adults and Escapement,"** Exxon Valdez
Oil Spill: Fate and Effects in Alaskan Waters, ASTM STP 1219, Peter G. Wells,
James N. Butler, and Jane S. Hughes, Eds., American Society for Testing and Materials,
Philadelphia, 1995.

This paper presents results of a field program designed to monitor the status of
wildstock pink salmon populations in Prince William Sound following the *Exxon Valdez*
oil spill. Field counts of spawning salmon were conducted each year from 1989 through
1992 to test for spill effects on the distribution and abundance of pink salmon adults
spawning in selected streams in the southwestern portion of Prince William Sound,
including streams from the most heavily oiled areas. Counts of whole-stream and intertidal
escapement density were statistically compared for 40 study streams in 1989 and for a
subset of those streams in successive years. Measurements of residual hydrocarbons were
made from stream-bed sediments to test for correlations with spawning behavior.

Adult pink salmon in the postspill years of 1990 and 1991, progeny of the year
classes considered most vulnerable to the oil spill, returned in high numbers, with the
wildstock spawners exceeding their parent year returns. In 1989, adult returns reflected
the relatively weak run for that year with a mean spawner density of 0.68 fish/m^2 in
reference streams and 0.69 fish/m^2 in oiled streams. In 1990, mean escapement density
for reference streams was 1.40 fish/m^2 and 1.55 fish/m^2 for oiled streams, indicating the
strongest run of the four study years. Trends in polycyclic aromatic hydrocarbon (PAH)
concentrations for the majority of oiled streams show a general decline from 1989 to

---

[1]Exxon Company, U.S.A., Houston, TX 77252-2180
[2]University of Idaho, Moscow, ID 83843
[3]Genesis Technical Services, Pacific Beach, WA 98571
[4]MJM Research, Bainbridge Island, WA 98110
[5]University of Washington, Seattle, WA 98195

background levels by 1990. The measured PAH concentrations indicate low-level exposure to residual hydrocarbons that have not produced detectable differences in spawning behavior or escapement between streams from oiled areas compared with unoiled streams.

In Part 1 of this paper, elements of the early lifestage survival of potentially affected year classes of pink salmon were examined by Brannon et al. (this volume). Conclusions indicate measures of early lifestages were largely indistinguishable between oiled and unoiled streams. The early lifestage data, in combination with observations of the strength of postspill returns and analyses of escapement reported herein, are the basis for the conclusion that changes in the wildstock pink salmon population in Prince William Sound could not be attributed to the oil spill.

KEYWORDS: pink salmon, escapement, wildstock, oil pollution, Prince William Sound, *Exxon Valdez*

INTRODUCTION

Pink salmon, *Oncorhynchus gorbuscha*, spawn throughout the coastal regions of Alaska and rank first in numbers of salmon harvested in commercial fisheries. Although all five species of Pacific salmon occur in Prince William Sound, pinks are by far the most abundant and economically important fishery resource. They have a rigid, two-year life cycle and can spawn in intertidal reaches of streams, a behavior that has served them well in the numerous short streams draining the mountainous coastlines of the sound.

This paper evaluates the status of wildstock salmon following the *Exxon Valdez* oil spill. Results from a field program that monitored adult escapement are presented with supporting data from the postspill commercial harvests. Published data from other spills are also included to test the hypothesis that a relationship exists between measured exposure to spill hydrocarbons and any adverse effects observed on pink salmon spawning behavior in Prince William Sound.

Stock Status and History

Adult pink salmon begin returning to Prince William Sound from the North Pacific in large numbers in July. Spawning generally occurs from mid-July through September, and intertidal reaches of streams are a major component of the total spawning habitat (Noerenberg, 1963; Helle, 1970; Thorsteinson et al., 1971). Embryos and larvae develop through the fall and winter within the stream-bed gravel. Juveniles emerge from the gravel in spring (April-June) and immediately move into estuarine habitats. The juveniles feed in the nearshore areas for a few weeks before moving into the Gulf of Alaska, where they begin their 12-month, open-water migratory circuit, counterclockwise around the north Pacific, before returning to their natal stream in Prince William Sound the following summer. The pink salmon's two-year life cycle is the shortest and least variable life cycle of all the Pacific salmon; as a consequence, there are two essentially independent populations, even- and odd-year spawners.

Commercial harvest of Prince William Sound pink salmon began in the late 1800's (Pirtle, 1976). The annual variability in run size has been considerable, with strong and weak runs correlated to some degree with long-term meteorological trends and resulting periods of warmer or cooler ocean temperatures (Cooney et al., 1992; Royer, 1990). In the early 1970's, returning runs were so weak that commercial fishing was restricted to allow adequate spawning escapement, prompting the development of hatcheries to augment natural runs and provide a more stable fishery. Hatcheries have been so successful they presently account for the majority of the population in Prince William Sound.

The return of natural spawners in the prespill year 1988 was the smallest since 1974 (Figure 1). However, return of natural spawners in the postspill years of 1990 and 1991, progeny of year classes most vulnerable to the oil spill, were in excess of their parent year classes.

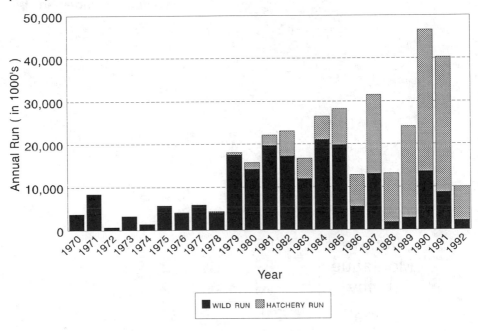

FIGURE 1--Annual run sizes of pink salmon in Prince William Sound for wildstock and hatchery runs (Donaldson et al., 1993)

Salmon Exposure to Oil

A perspective on the extent of oiled streams and their relative contribution to the Prince William Sound salmon population is shown in Figure 2. The total run size of pink salmon in Prince William Sound is shown as an average of the three years immediately preceding the spill, 1986 through 1988. During this period, hatchery production accountedfor approximately 64% of the total pink salmon run. The remaining 36% of

Percent of PWS Pink Salmon Total Run by Origin
1986-1988

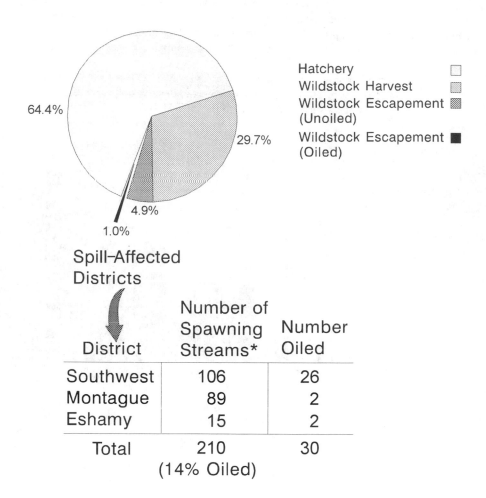

Hatchery ☐
Wildstock Harvest ▨
Wildstock Escapement ▦
(Unoiled)
Wildstock Escapement ■
(Oiled)

64.4%

29.7%

4.9%

1.0%

Spill-Affected
Districts

District	Number of Spawning Streams*	Number Oiled
Southwest	106	26
Montague	89	2
Eshamy	15	2
Total	210	30
	(14% Oiled)	

*1989 ADF&G Salmon Closed Water Map

FIGURE 2--An analysis of the origin of pink salmon constituting the total run for prespill years 1986-88 (ADF&G, 1985; Donaldson et al., 1993) the run was attributable to wildstock production within the eight Alaska Department of Fish and Game (ADF&G) fishery management districts. Based on present estimates, less than 20% of the wildstock escapement returns to streams in the three oil-affected management districts: Southwest, Montague, and Eshamy.

However, not all of the streams in the three districts were on oiled shorelines. Of the 210 spawning streams identified in these districts by the Alaska Department of Fish and Game (1985), 30 streams (14%) were actually on oiled shorelines. Thus, the total production of wildstock pink salmon attributable to streams in oil-affected areas was low, and potential spill impacts need to be assessed with a focus on that portion of the salmon population at risk.

Oil-Spill Effects on Adult Salmon

Laboratory toxicity data for crude oil or crude-oil fractions have not been appropriately examined for application to fish populations in actual field situations. Routinely, laboratory studies to assess oil effects utilize high levels of water-soluble fractions (WSF), which are the major toxic components of oil. Volatile aromatics can be toxic to aquatic life, particularly early life stages, in concentrations ranging from a few ppm to a few hundred ppb (Rice et al., 1984; National Academy of Sciences, 1985). However, WSF aromatics volatilize rapidly and high levels or even persistent low levels of WSF sufficient to be acutely toxic to aquatic life are atypical of oil spills (NAS 1985; Neff & Stubblefield, this volume).

Field studies have also generally failed to document widespread effects of oil spills on fish (Rice, 1985). Investigations following the spills of the *Argo Merchant* and *Amoco Cadiz*, and blowouts at Ekofisk Bravo and Santa Barbara recorded negligible effects of oil on resident fish populations (Longhurst, 1982; McIntyre, 1982; Sherman and Busch, 1978; Straughan, 1970). Although localized fish kills have been reported for oil spills in small estuaries and tidal flats such as the *Florida* spill near West Falmouth, Massachusetts, and the *R. C. Stoner* spill at Wake Island harbor (Hampson and Sanders, 1969; Gooding, 1971), there are no reports of major fish kills in open water.

Investigators have also examined the potential for oil spills to interfere with more subtle aspects of salmon life history, such as migratory behavior and homing. However, avoidance behavior or attraction of juveniles cannot be taken as evidence that homing of salmon will be disrupted by the presence of oil (Rice, 1973; Weber et al., 1981; Nakatani et al., 1986). When returning salmon were exposed to concentrations of Prudhoe Bay crude oil and various oil-spill dispersant concentrations exceeding the highest concentrations monitored under field conditions, subsequent homing success was not altered (Nakatani et al., 1985; Brannon et al., 1986).

In summary, neither existing toxicity literature nor prior field studies support the position that Pacific salmon were significantly affected by petroleum hydrocarbon concentrations from the *Exxon Valdez* oil spill. As will be discussed, our study of escapement and spawning distribution for the year classes at greatest risk to oil exposure was not able to demonstrate that changes in natural production of pink salmon within the spill-affected area were attributable to oil exposure.

STUDY FOCUS

Exposure Potential

The *Exxon Valdez* oil spill occurred on March 24, 1989. Oil spread on the water surface in a general southern trajectory so that the southwestern portion of Prince William Sound sustained the highest exposure. The oil washed ashore in many areas, coating beaches and exposing the intertidal reaches of some streams to oil. The exposure of the pink salmon population to spill hydrocarbons potentially involved both juveniles and adults of two year classes that migrated through spill-exposed waters in 1989 and specifically involved the streams that were directly oiled. Juveniles from the 1988 spawn could have been exposed as pre-emergent alevins in some streams and as free-swimming juveniles feeding in estuarine habitats or migrating out of Prince William Sound. Adults returning in 1989 could have been exposed to weathered oil as they migrated into Prince William Sound and during spawning activities in the intertidal reaches of exposed streams. However, the presence of oil on the shorelines and nearshore areas of Prince William Sound significantly decreased in 1990 and in subsequent years, thus diminishing potential for exposure and resulting risks to pink salmon populations (Neff et al , this volume).

Objectives

This study was part of an overall program designed to examine the oil-spill effects on critical life stages of pink salmon in Prince William Sound. Pink salmon were chosen for study because of their economic importance, abundance relative to other salmon species in southwest Prince William Sound, and their life-history characteristics. Additionally, they provide a surrogate for the other salmon species.

Part 1 (Brannon et al., this volume) reported the results of investigations into the survival, growth, and development of early life stages of pink salmon in oiled and unoiled areas. To build on those results, this study was designed to assess the effects of substrate oiling on distribution and density of spawning pink salmon in southwestern Prince William Sound following the oil spill. Specifically: (1) Did spawning pink salmon avoid oiled streams? and (2) Did pink salmon avoid oiled intertidal habitats by moving to upstream spawning areas in oiled streams?

Streams were selected in the most heavily affected areas of Prince William Sound to ensure an investigation of the worst-case effects of the spill. Additionally, monitoring of adult spawning abundance and distribution provided a test for overall, integrated effects of the spill since adult returns reflected survival during all life-history stages. The studies looked for evidence of both direct and delayed exposure effects on the abundance and behavior of spawning adults that would have migrated through spill-affected waters.

This part of the study was designed to provide analyses of effects at three levels of resolution: (1) through a qualitative comparison of the density of spawning salmon adults; (2) through statistical analyses comparing oiled and reference streams by ANOVA; and (3) by regression analyses wherein correlations between measurements of petroleum hydrocarbons (PAH) sampled from spawning stream sediments and several measures of spawning density were statistically analyzed for significant alterations in expected performance.

MATERIALS AND METHODS

The study design required accurate estimates of the numbers of pink salmon spawning in each of several streams (escapement), the distribution of spawning in each stream, and a measure of the amount of habitat available for spawning. Standard methods were used to quantify the abundance of pink salmon in each stream (Cousens et al., 1982), and total escapement was estimated by applying a modified integration method (Perrin and Irvine, 1980).

Study Area

Forty streams were studied in 1989 on the basis of location, potential for oil exposure, and the likelihood that large numbers of pink salmon commonly used the intertidal reaches for spawning. The selected streams were all in the southwestern part of Prince William Sound, and each stream was classified as either "reference" or "oiled" on the basis of levels of exposure recorded by shoreline survey teams during the summer of 1989 (Figure 3) (Neff et al., this volume). Streams with adjacent shorelines that received heavy, moderate, or light oiling were categorized as oiled. Streams with adjacent shorelines that received very light (<10% cover) or no oiling were categorized as reference streams. The stream beds did not contain visible oil because of hydraulic flushing from natural stream flow. Each stream was partitioned into sampling segments to provide information on the distribution of fish within streams. Boundaries between segments were located and marked by means of standard surveying methods. Each stream was divided into two major partitions identified as (1) intertidal, from 1.2 m to 3.7 m above mean lower low water (MLLW), and (2) as upstream, above +3.7 m to the farthest upstream location where pink salmon were observed (Pirtle, 1977).

Twenty streams, including those from the most heavily oiled areas, were selected from the 40 studied in 1989 for continued study in 1990 and 1991, and 22 streams were selected for study in 1992. Each stream was categorized and partitioned similarly to 1989 (Table 1).

Fish Counts

The study streams were periodically surveyed during the pink salmon spawning season, from early August through mid-September of each year. The procedure was to visit each stream approximately once per week and count and record the number of live pink salmon within each sampling segment. Observers walking along the stream tallied live fish and counted dead pink salmon during the first survey of each year in each stream. Dead fish accounted for any spawning before the first day of the survey.

To obtain consistent, accurate counts in the intertidal zone, the tide had to be below the lowest boundary (+1.2 m) of the sampling area. This was necessary to ensure that only the spawning salmon in the freshwater portion of the stream were counted, not those milling in the vicinity of the stream mouth.

The modified area-under-the-curve methodology used to estimate total escapement required an abundance curve for each stream that represented the total number of days that fish spent in the stream during the spawning period (Johnson and Barrett, 1986)--i.e., from the day before the first fish entered the stream to spawn (start date) to the day

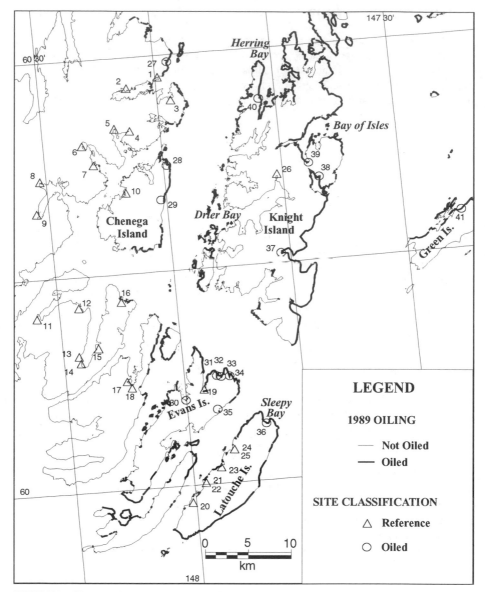

FIGURE 3 -- Map of pink salmon study streams, Prince William Sound

after the last fish died (end date). The periodic survey data for some of the streams included visits before and after the spawning season.

Resulting data were best described by curves plotted from the survey count data across time. The area under each curve was estimated by summing the areas of polygons formed between adjacent survey dates (Perrin and Irvine, 1980). The base of each polygon was measured in days, and the height was measured by counts of fish, so the area under each curve was an estimate of the number of fish-days accumulated in a stream for the entire spawning season. (A fish-day is the presence in the stream of one live fish for one day.)

Stream-Life Estimation

To estimate escapement, the total fish-days had to be divided by an estimate of the average number of days individual fish resided in the survey area. The estimate most commonly used is the mean residence time, or stream life (Bocking et al., 1988). The historical stream-life figures used to estimate pink salmon escapements in Prince William Sound are fixed values of either 17.5 days (2.5 weeks) or 28 days (4.0 weeks), depending on the particular stream (Pirtle, 1977). However, Helle et al. (1964) report that stream life in Olsen Creek averaged 11.1 days in 1961, ranging from 4.6 to 21.2 days, while Sharr et al. (1993) estimate that stream life for streams in western Prince William Sound range to values as low as 3.2 days. There are considerable differences in fixed stream-life estimates because of the high degree of variability among streams and areas and among years, as well as changes in stream life known to occur through a spawning season. For these reasons, we developed an approach to stream-life estimation that considered these sources of variability and used a series of stream-specific survival functions in lieu of a single fixed value for stream life.

Because stream life decreases through the spawning season (Helle et al., 1964; Thorsteinson, 1965; Neilson and Green, 1981; McCurdy, 1984), we estimated stream life for consecutive weeks through the spawning season. Four streams were selected for a detailed study in 1989 to estimate stream life. These were in the southwestern part of Prince William Sound but at locations not directly exposed to the spill. Once a week for six weeks, pink salmon were captured with seines near the mouth of each stream. Approximately 100 were marked with color-coded tags and released at the capture site. The four streams were surveyed daily and the number of live and dead, tagged and untagged pink salmon were recorded. Thus, for each tagged salmon, the number of days between tagging and recovery provided an estimate of individual stream life, and these data were used to calculate a survival function for each group tagged (Figure 4a). The application of stream life from four reference streams to represent stream life in oiled streams could lead to an underestimation of spawning density in oiled streams. This underestimate could occur because pink salmon populations in oiled streams tended to spawn later than populations in reference streams. Later spawning populations have, on average, shorter stream lives, thus applying a longer stream life than actual would lead to an underestimate of the spawning population.

For each tag group, the observed stream lives were modeled using an independent Weibull distribution (Lawless, 1982; Kalbfleisch and Prentice, 1980), a distribution

TABLE 1--Summary of study stream identifications and years that they were used for escapement counts of adult pink salmon in Prince William Sound

ADF&G Stream Identification Number	Districts	Study Stream Number	Escapement Counts			
			1989	1990	1991	1992
Reference Streams						
15070	Eshamy	1	x			
15080	"	2	x			
15163	"	3	x	x	x	x
16010	Southwest	4	x	x	x	x
16020	"	5	x	x	x	x
16030	"	6	x			
16040	"	7	x	x	x	x
16100	"	8	x	x	x	x
16130	"	9	x			
16210	"	10	x			
16300	"	11	x			x
16320	"	12	x			
16330	"	13	x			
16340	"	14	x			
16360	"	15	x			
16370	"	16	x	x	x	x
16550	"	17	x	x	x	x
16557	"	18	x	x	x	x
16610	"	19	x	x	x	
16710	"	20	x	x	x	
16720	"	21	x	x	x	x
16730	"	22	x			x
16760	"	23	x	x	x	x
16768	"	24	x			
16770	"	25	x			
16950	"	26	x			
Oiled Streams						
15060	Eshamy	27	x			x
16180	Southwest	28	x	x	x	x
16280	"	29	x	x	x	x
16590	"	30	x			
16620	"	31				x
16621*	"	32	x			
16630	"	33	x	x	x	x
16640	"	34	x	x	x	x
16650	"	35	x	x	x	x
16780	"	36	x	x	x	x
16820	"	37	x	x	x	x
16850	"	38	x			
16860	"	39	x	x	x	x
16920	"	40	x			
17880	"	41	x			

* The stream number 16621 was assigned to a stream not surveyed by ADFG.

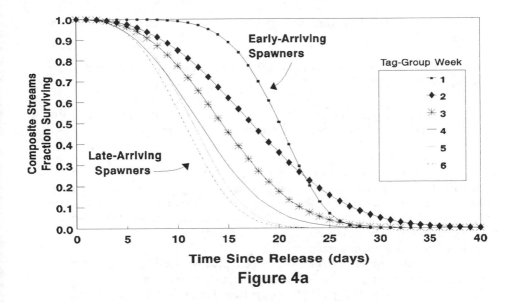

Figure 4a

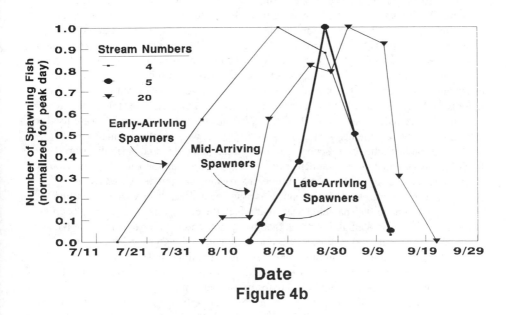

Date
Figure 4b

FIGURE 4a--Composite of Weibull survival functions used to calculate stream life.
4b--Examples of escapement data for early-, mid-, and late-arriving spawners at three
different streams in 1989

commonly used to model survival. The observed stream life, t, of a tagged salmon was defined as follows:

t = (Julian date of tag recovery – Julian date of tag release) – estimated milling time in intertidal zone

In turn, milling time for a tag group was measured as the time between release and entry of the first tagged fish of that release group into the stream.

Escapement Estimates

The survey counts showed that there was considerable variation among streams for patterns of relative abundance during the spawning season, i.e., in some streams, pink salmon were present throughout the spawning season, whereas in other streams salmon were present only in early or late season. Because the presence of pink salmon varied among streams, and stream life was related to arrival time, escapement could not be estimated by using a single, mean stream life.

To avoid errors caused by the variables listed above, survival functions for fish counted in study streams were assigned according to the observed arrival time and duration of escapement during the spawning season. Figure 4b shows actual count data for three streams in 1989. The length of the escapement time period decreased from early season to late season. Late-arriving salmon had less time to spawn, hence shorter stream life, than did salmon that arrived early in the season. Longer survival functions were assigned for streams with early-arriving adults than for streams where adults arrived later. Thus Stream 4 was assigned a longer survival function than was Stream 5.

Survival functions for shorter stream life were used for the 1990 and 1991 studies because there were relatively large escapements in these years compared with 1989, and there is evidence that stream life is shorter at higher spawning densities (Helle et al., 1964; van den Berghe and Gross, 1986). Survival functions for longer stream life were used to estimate the 1992 escapements since 1992 escapements were relatively small.

To calculate the total escapement for a stream, an individual Weibull survival function was assigned to the number of fish counted in a stream on each day that counts were made (Figure 4a). Since survival time of spawning salmon decreased as the spawning season progressed, each count was assigned a Weibull survival distribution relative to the time in the spawning season at which the count was made. Early counts were assigned earlier Weibull functions than were later counts. For example, the tag group Week 1 (Figure 4a) was assigned to early counts and tag group Week 6 was assigned to later counts. Using the Weibull survival functions, later counts were discounted for survivors from earlier entry to the stream. Escapement was then estimated by summing these daily discounted estimates of escapement.

Estimates of pink salmon that spawned in the intertidal zones of each stream were needed to test for some of the potential oiling effects. However, these estimates could not be made directly from the periodic counts of pink salmon in the intertidal zones because counts included both fish that were spawning in the intertidal zone and fish that were migrating through the intertidal to spawn in the upstream zone. Escapement to the upstream zone was estimated on the basis of periodic counts as described above. The total spawning escapement to each stream (whole-stream) and the escapement to only the upstream zones were estimated by using periodic counts and the survival functions previously described. The spawning escapements to the intertidal zones were then calculated as the differences between the whole-stream escapements and the upstream escapements.

Spawning Density

The escapement of pink salmon to streams is influenced by stream size. In general, since large streams have more spawning habitat than small streams, they have larger salmon runs. Because the influence of stream size on escapement numbers needed to be accounted for in the analyses, the extent of spawning habitat was measured in all 40 study streams in 1989. The width of each intertidal and whole-stream segment was estimated by the mean of several measurements of the width of wetted surface taken along the segment length. The segment area was then estimated as the product of the measured length and mean width. The stream areas were remeasured in 1990 to check for year-to-year differences. Since only small changes were seen between 1989 and 1990, the 1990 stream areas were used in density calculations in 1991 and 1992.

Spawning density for each entire stream, as well as for the intertidal area, was estimated by dividing the estimated annual escapement by the appropriate habitat area yielding the number of spawners per unit-area (m^2). These density estimates were used in the statistical tests for spill effects.

Sediment Chemistry

Sediment samples were taken from the stream bed during the spawning season (mid to late August) in all 40 study streams in 1989, in 20 study streams in 1990, and in 18 streams in 1991. These samples were analyzed to determine the concentration and source (fingerprint) of the measured PAH components (Bence and Burns, this volume). The PAH fraction includes some of the most biologically active components of crude oil.

Surface sediment samples for PAH determination were collected from intertidal spawning areas of both reference and oiled streams. During 1989, several individual samples were collected from the intertidal spawning areas, generally near the left and right banks of each stream at the 2.4 and 3.7 m tide levels. In 1990 and 1991, the sediment samples consisted of 8 subsamples randomly collected and composited from spawning areas in each of three tide strata for each stream: 1.8-2.4 m, 2.4-3.0 m and 3.0-3.7 m above MLLW. Samples were collected in precleaned glass containers using methods developed to prevent contamination. In all years, the samples were frozen and transferred to the analytical laboratory. Samples were analyzed by gas chromatography/mass spectrometry (GC/MS) with quantification by selected ion monitoring (SIM) analysis (Sauer and Boehm, 1991).

The mean of the sediment PAH measurements from the individual samples (1989) or tide strata (1990 and 1991) of each stream was used as an index of the degree of oiling in the intertidal spawning areas. The use of surface PAH measurements was considered valid because the female pink salmon turn over essentially the top 25-30 cm of stream bed during redd excavation. Contaminated sediments in the spawning areas are likely to be thoroughly mixed by spawning activity.

Escapement Ratios

Escapement ratios were used as an assessment of population trends in individual streams. A very significant influence affecting escapement is the fishery. Therefore, while equal fishery impacts can be assumed for purposes of comparing escapement trends, it is understood that the fishery is a major confounding factor that affects streams differently. The fishery may affect upstream, early spawning populations differently than later, intertidal spawning populations within a given stream. With this qualification, the escapement ratios were calculated as the number of spawners returning to a stream divided by the number of spawners from the parent year two years earlier. Two tests for oiling effects were run. First, the equality of escapement ratios for oiled and reference streams was tested statistically. For log-transformed whole-stream escapement, returns from the brood year were regressed against brood year escapement for both 1991 versus 1989 and 1992 versus 1990. The equality of regression slopes for oiled and reference streams was tested at $\alpha = 0.10$ because oiling could have affected either brood year escapement or progeny from the brood year. Second, a relationship between escapement ratios and PAH concentration was tested statistically. Whole-stream and intertidal escapement ratios (1991 to 1989 and 1992 to 1990) were regressed against PAH concentrations. Both sets of regressions were tested at a two-tailed $\alpha = 0.10$.

Data Analysis

Two approaches were used in analyzing escapement data. First, we tested the null hypothesis that there are no differences in mean escapement density between oiled and reference streams against the alternative hypothesis that escapement density was less at oiled streams. Densities were log-transformed to stabilize variances. Tests were made with a one-way ANOVA at $\alpha = 0.05$. Whole-stream and intertidal densities were tested separately.

The second, more sensitive, approach tested for a negative relationship between residual PAH concentration and escapement. Tests on spawning density were one-tailed at $\alpha = 0.05$. Tests on escapement ratios were two-tailed at $\alpha = 0.10$ since oiling could have affected either parent or progeny year. For regressions, data were log-transformed to normalize residuals.

RESULTS

Physical Characteristics of Study Streams

Figure 5 summarizes the size, orientation, and exposure to open water and wave action of each stream. Although attempts were made to ensure that reference and oiled streams were physically similar, significant differences did exist. The reference streams had an average whole-stream spawning area of 9 000 m^2 and generally exceeded the size of the spawning area in oiled streams, which averaged 4 600 m^2. Similarly, the intertidal spawning habitat available among the reference streams averaged 3 700 m^2, whereas the intertidal areas of oiled streams averaged 1 500 m^2.

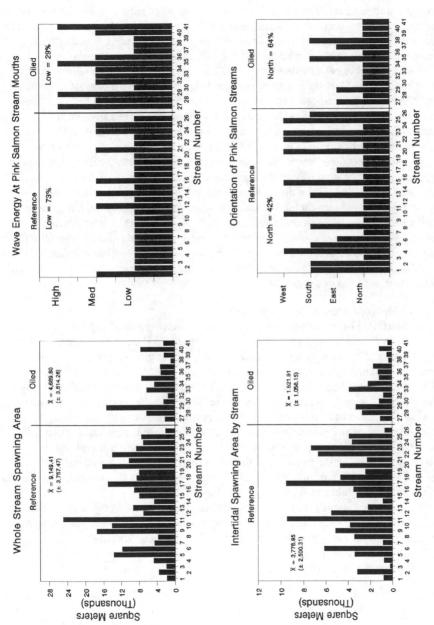

FIGURE 5--Physical characteristics of the Pink Salmon study streams comparing spawning area, wave energy, and orientation of oiled and reference streams, in Prince William Sound.

Analyses of total numbers of fish spawning show that more fish were in reference streams than oiled streams because of the larger amount of available habitat. For this reason, spawning numbers were normalized on the basis of density of spawners per unit-area of stream, and subsequent statistical tests for differences between oiled and reference streams were based on density comparisons. Although highly variable, whole-stream escapement data were used as an additional comparison of reference streams.

Two other physical variables that can affect stream production of salmon are intertidal exposure and stream-mouth orientation (Figure 5). The majority of reference streams (73%) have low exposure to offshore wave activity; however, only 29% of oiled streams have low exposure. Thus the intertidal segments of the oiled streams are subjected to higher wave activity and would be subject to more movement and storm-related displacement of substrate in the intertidal stream bed. Also more oiled streams than reference streams faced north (64% versus 42%). These north-facing streams in the spill-impacted area face directly into the southward water current in southwest Prince William Sound. Floating oil and mousse entrained in the southward flowing water affected many of these north-facing shorelines as it moved out of the sound, and these shorelines were shown to be among the most heavily oiled (Neff et al., this volume). Many of the same factors that caused shoreline oiling in the sound, such as orientation and exposure, would also be expected to cause differences in salmon spawning utilization even in unoiled areas; any postspill study of salmon spawning in the sound should consider such differences in order to assess spill effects.

Analyses of Stream Sediment for Hydrocarbons

Elevated PAH concentrations were present in numerous oiled and some reference streams in 1989 (Table 2). A high degree of variability in PAH concentrations is evident among streams and between years, reflecting the discontinuous and spotty nature of hydrocarbon presence in the stream sediment (Figure 6). Oiled stream mean PAH values varied from a low of 0.5 ppb to a high of 267 ppb. Fingerprint analyses confirmed that most of the PAHs were from *Exxon Valdez* crude oil (EVC). Several 1989 reference streams also showed mean PAH concentrations approaching 100 ppb; however, fingerprinting showed they were not crude oil but a refined product, such as diesel fuel. To avoid biasing the oil/reference comparison, 13 reference streams with refined product PAH levels greater than 10 ppb were omitted from the 1989 ANOVA analysis. Subsequent samples taken from 1990 and 1991 reference streams showed only trace levels of PAH from sources other than EVC.

PAH concentrations for the majority of oiled streams showed a general decline from 1989, declining to background levels by 1990. However, three north-facing streams with high exposure to wave energy continued to show a residual EVC signature through 1991. These streams were located at northern extremities of Chenega Island, Evans Island, and Latouche Island (Figure 3).

Table 2. *Mean PAH (in ug/kg) measured in spawning substrates of Prince William Sound streams, August 1989-1991.*

Study Stream	Class	1989			1990			1991		
		Mean PAH (ug/kg)	Standard Deviation	Sample Size	Mean PAH (ug/kg)	Standard Deviation	Sample Size	Mean PAH (ug/kg)	Standard Deviation	Sample Size
1	Reference	1.0	0.4	4			0			0
2	Reference	0.6	0.2	4			0			0
3	Reference	0.9	1.4	5	1.3	0.8	3	1.3	0.0	3
4	Reference	1.2	0.3	4	1.5	0.3	3	1.7	0.5	3
5	Reference	9.3	17.2	4	1.2	0.4	3			0
6	Reference	2.9	1.1	2	2.3	0.4	3	2.1	1.4	3
7	Reference	58.7	16.5	4	2.6	0.7	3			0
8	Reference	12.6	18.6	4	1.8	0.6	3	0.8	0.1	3
9	Reference	31.1	14.8	4	1.5	0.4	3			0
10	Reference	64.0	39.3	7			0			0
11	Reference	23.2	28.1	4			0			0
12	Reference	65.5	72.5	4	0.8	0.3	3			0
13	Reference	61.2	36.5	3	1.1	0.3	3			0
14	Reference	94.7	16.4	4	4.6	6.1	3			0
15	Reference	15.0	12.0	4			0			0
16	Reference	16.3	19.5	4	0.7	0.3	3	1.0	0.4	3
17	Reference	28.7	32.6	4	0.8	0.3	3	2.4	0.7	3
18	Reference	0.9	0.5	4	1.0	0.2	3			0
19	Reference	1.8	1.0	6	1.3	0.4	3			0
20	Reference	0.2	0.1	3	3.2	1.1	3			0
21	Reference	0.4	0.2	4	1.7	0.3	3	1.5	0.6	3
22	Reference	0.9	1.0	4			0	1.5	0.1	3
23	Reference	3.2	5.8	7	2.9	0.4	3	1.5	0.3	3
24	Reference	0.7	0.2	5			0			0
25	Reference	14.4	18.5	4			0			0

Table 2. Mean PAH (in ug/kg) measured in spawning substrates of Prince William Sound streams, August 1989-1991, cont.

Study Stream	Class	1989			1990			1991		
		Mean PAH (ug/kg)	Standard Deviation	Sample Size	Mean PAH (ug/kg)	Standard Deviation	Sample Size	Mean PAH (ug/kg)	Standard Deviation	Sample Size
26	Reference	18.6	16.4	4			0			0
27	Oiled	11.6	9.1	3			0			0
28	Oiled	0.8	0.5	4	21.4	17.6	3	223.8	322.8	3
29	Oiled	194.3	83.9	6	2.2	0.7	3	4.7	4.7	3
30	Oiled	2.1	1.2	3			0			0
31	Oiled			0			0	8.1	1.7	3
32	Oiled	120.0	157.1	4			0			0
33	Oiled	232.8	262.5	4	30.8	25.3	3	96.4	94.2	3
34	Oiled	81.6	45.2	5	2.0	1.2	3	6.2	3.6	3
35	Oiled	5.4	6.2	4	2.0	0.7	3	2.1	0.4	3
36	Oiled	267.0	257.6	6	108.2	100.8	3	235.5	358.1	3
37	Oiled	0.5	0.3	6	1.8	0.5	3	1.1	0.4	3
38	Oiled	18.5	4.3	4			0			0
39	Oiled	17.4	5.0	4	3.0	1.7	3	0.7	0.2	3
40	Oiled	15.3	3.3	4			0			0
41	Oiled	53.5	6.4	4			0			0

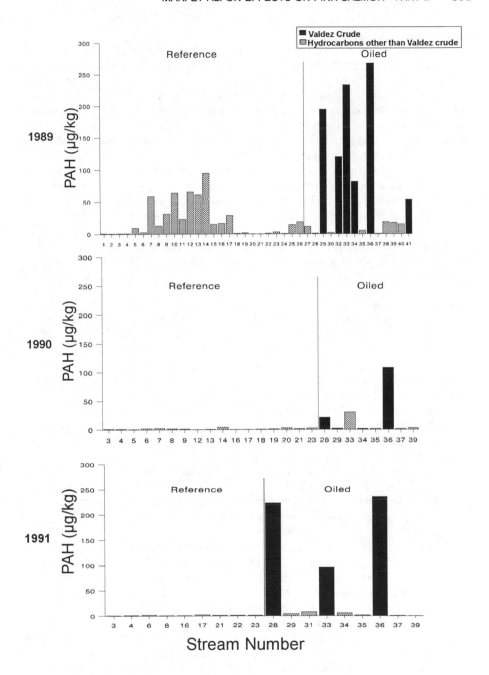

FIGURE 6--PAH concentrations measured from pink salmon intertidal spawning areas for 1989, 1990, and 1991, in Prince William Sound.

Calculation of Escapement

The sensitivity of escapement results to the choice of stream life value was tested by comparing them with historical data. The Weibull survival functions calculate mean stream life values equivalent to 12 to 13 days, approximately midway between the range of 3.2 to 19.6 days currently proposed by managers of the fishery (Pirtle, 1977; Sharr et al., 1993). Total stream escapements calculated using the ADF&G traditional fixed stream life of 17.5 days are consistently lower than those calculated using the Weibull survival functions (Figure 7), although there is strong correlation between escapements calculated by the Weibull and fixed stream life of 17.5 days.

The variable, stream-specific Weibull survival functions provide a more accurate estimate of escapement than does a single fixed stream-life value since the Weibull accounts for decreasing stream life values as the spawning season progresses. It also accounts for variations in timing of salmon spawning among individual streams.

Because of the high correlation ($R^2 = 0.99$) between the methods, statistical analyses would be similar regardless of the method used in estimating escapement. Hence, our conclusions are not dependent upon the specific method used in our escapement estimations.

Escapement Density

The escapement densities calculated for each stream are presented as fish/m^2 for odd years 1989 and 1991 (Figure 8) and even years 1990 and 1992 (Figure 9). In 1989, adult returns reflected the relatively weak run for that year, with a mean spawner density of 0.69 fish/m^2 in reference streams and 0.68 fish/m^2 in oiled streams. In 1990, mean escapement density for reference streams was 1.40 fish/m^2 and 1.55 fish/m^2 for oiled streams, indicating the strongest run of the four study years.

Adult returns for 1991 averaged 1.29 fish/m^2 for reference streams and 1.71 fish/m^2 for oiled streams. Further examination of the relative strength of postspill pink salmon returns indicates that the 1992 run had a mean density of 0.33 fish/m^2 in reference streams and a mean of 0.57 fish/m^2 in oiled streams (Figure 9).

The ratios of oiled to reference whole-stream densities increased from 1989 to 1991 (from 1.0 to 1.3) and from 1990 to 1992 (from 1.1 to 1.7) indicating a decrease in the effect of oiling on escapement over time. However, two-sample t-tests on ratios using streams as replicates showed that the progressions likely occurred by chance (for 1989 to 1991, $p=0.171$; for 1990 to 1992, $p=0.996$).

The intertidal density of spawning pink salmon was used to determine if fish avoided the intertidal spawning habitat in oiled areas by moving to unoiled streams or to upstream unoiled spawning habitat (Figure 10). A visual comparison of these data showed trends similar to the whole-stream density data with a high degree of variability in intertidal spawning density between streams and years. No visual trends existed between reference and oiled streams, and mean intertidal density was slightly higher for oiled streams versus reference streams for the postspill years 1991 and 1992. Results for 1989 and 1990 showed slightly lower mean densities for oiled streams versus reference streams.

The most striking differences result from a comparison of between-year adult returns. The return runs of 1990 and 1991 produced densities of intertidal spawners ranging up to almost three times the densities seen in the comparatively weaker

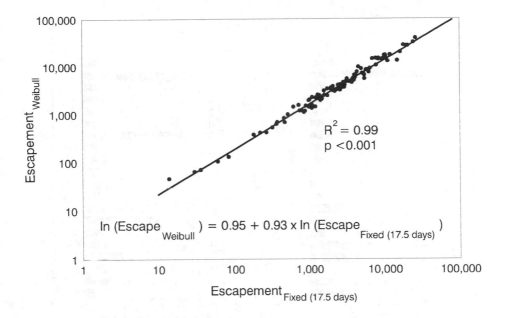

FIGURE 7--A comparison of whole-stream escapement numbers calculated by the Weibull estimate versus escapements calculated from fixed stream life of 17.5 days

parent run years of 1988 and 1989.

Comparison of Oiled and Reference Streams

An analysis of variance was conducted to test the null hypothesis that there was no difference between reference and oiled streams in either intertidal escapement density or whole-stream escapement density. The alternative hypothesis tested was that escapement densities were lower for oiled streams (Table 3). The results from the ANOVA for all four study years indicated no statistically significant differences between oiled and reference streams for either intertidal or whole-stream spawning density ($p > 0.05$). However, it must be noted that the high degree of between-year and among-stream variability seen in escapement data contributed to a low probability of detecting effects.

Response of Spawner Density to PAH

To further test whether there was a relationship between adult escapement and oiling, regression analyses were conducted by plotting measured in-stream PAH concentrations against whole-stream density, intertidal density, and whole-stream escapement numbers. All values were log-transformed before regression to normalize residuals. Results for 1989 and 1991 escapements are shown in Figure 11. The adults spawning in summer of 1989 were responsible for the progeny returning as adults in

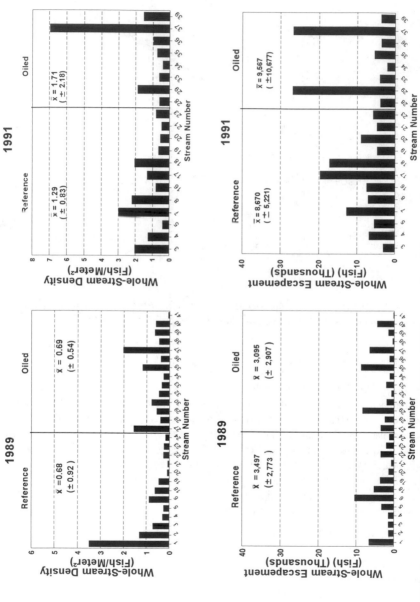

FIGURE 8—Annual escapement to study streams for 1989 and 1991 measured as whole-stream density and whole-stream escapement (± 1 standard deviation)

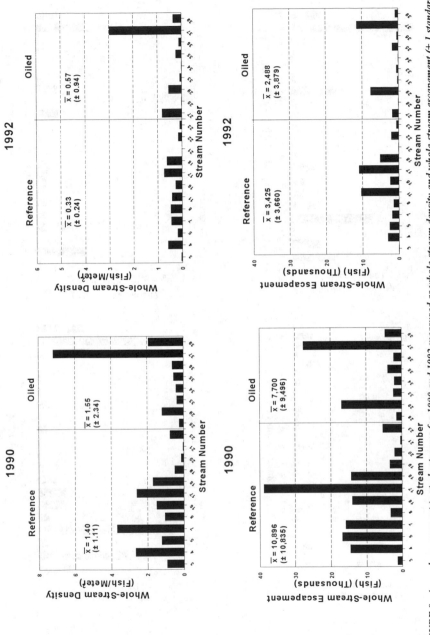

FIGURE 9—Annual escapement to study streams for 1990 and 1992 measured as whole-stream density and whole-stream escapement (± 1 standard deviation)

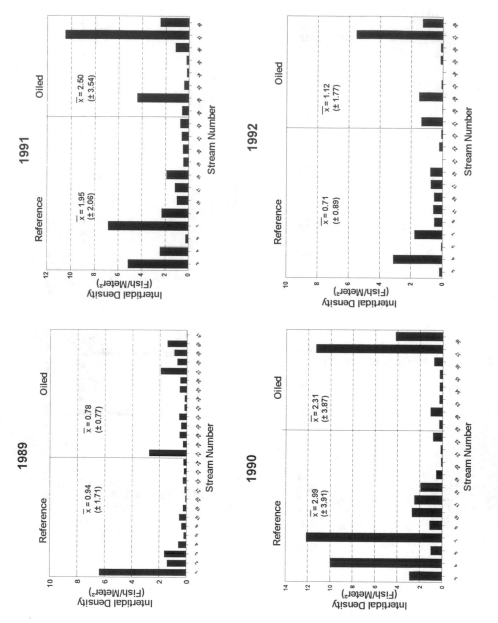

FIGURE 10—Intertidal density of pink salmon escapement for the four study years

1991. Data for 1989 were based on all 40 study streams and showed more frequent high PAH values than the 1991 data for 15 streams. Each data point represented the comparison of a stream's mean measured PAH and its escapement counts. Regressions for all three variables, whole-stream and intertidal densities, and whole-stream numbers of fish versus 1989 levels of PAH revealed no obvious relationships between escapement and sediment chemistry. Similarly, a regression of 1991 adult escapement data with measured PAH concentrations at the time of spawning indicated no obvious relationships between the two (Figure 11).

Statistical analyses of these regressions indicate that there were no relationships between 1989 or 1991 spawning densities and PAH concentrations (Table 4). The 1991 spawning density was tested against both 1989 and 1991 in-stream PAH values. A relationship with 1989 PAH values would test for potential significance of effects on incubation and hatch of eggs in 1989 and 1990. A regression against 1991 PAH values tests whether adults avoided oiled streams because of residual oiling. Calculated probability values confirm that there were no statistical relationships ($p \geq 0.05$) and coefficients of determination (R^2) are consistently low, reflecting the high degree of scatter and low correlation of any relationship between escapement and measured in-stream PAH values.

Statistical analyses of regression relationships for 1990 and 1992 spawning data indicate that there was no significant relationship between spawning adult numbers or densities and in-stream PAH values at $p = 0.05$ (Table 4). Regressions against 1990 chemistry were used to evaluate if residual PAH values caused adults to avoid oiled streams in the summer of 1990 (Figure 12). Regression analysis of returning adult statistics in 1992 against 1990 PAH values tested whether survival of those adults was affected by PAH concentrations during their in-stream incubation and hatching period in late 1990. No chemistry data were taken in 1992, so no further comparisons with PAH were possible. As with the even-year spawning data, coefficients of determination (R^2) are consistently low, again indicating the lack of a relationship between spawning adult numbers and in-stream PAH.

The probability of detecting R^2 of 0.50, where PAH concentration explained more than half of the variability in escapement, ranged from 0.85 to 1.0, with most probabilities above 0.90. These probabilities indicate relatively sensitive tests, with most having greater than 90% power of detection at $\propto\,= 0.05$ (Cohen, 1977). Therefore, the failure to detect a significant correlation between escapement densities and PAH is the result of little or no relationship between the two, rather than a lack of an adequate sample size.

Escapement Ratios

Each stream was compared with itself by measuring returns of progeny produced from spawning adults two years previously. It was recognized that the commercial fishery could substantially influence adult returns to an individual stream or area. The fishery was closed in the study area in 1989 but operated in the southwest district of Prince William Sound for the remaining postspill study years. This analysis assumed an equal distribution of fishing effort in postspill years and did not consider fishery effects. Since yearly changes in location and intensity of the commercial fishery would alter returns to

TABLE 3–ANOVA results of pink salmon escapement data for 1989 to 1992.

Response Variable	P-Values[1]	Means		Degrees of Freedom[2]
		Ref.	Oiled	
1989 Escapement				
Intertidal Density (#/m^2)	0.561	0.94	0.78	25
Whole-Stream Density (#/m^2)	0.749	0.68	0.69	25
1990 Escapement				
Intertidal Density (#/m^2)	0.332	2.99	2.31	18
Whole-Stream Density (#/m^2)	0.464	1.40	1.55	18
1991 Escapement				
Intertidal Density (#/m^2)	0.454	1.95	2.50	18
Whole-Stream Density (#/m^2)	0.551	1.29	1.71	18
1992 Escapement				
Intertidal Density (#/m^2)	0.465	0.71	1.12	19
Whole-Stream Density (#/m^2)	0.393	0.33	0.57	19

[1]P-value of 0.05 or lower (one-tailed) considered in rejecting null hypothesis of no difference between reference and oiled streams.

[2]Number of streams in the statistical comparison, minus two, the number of estimated parameters (means for oiled and reference streams).

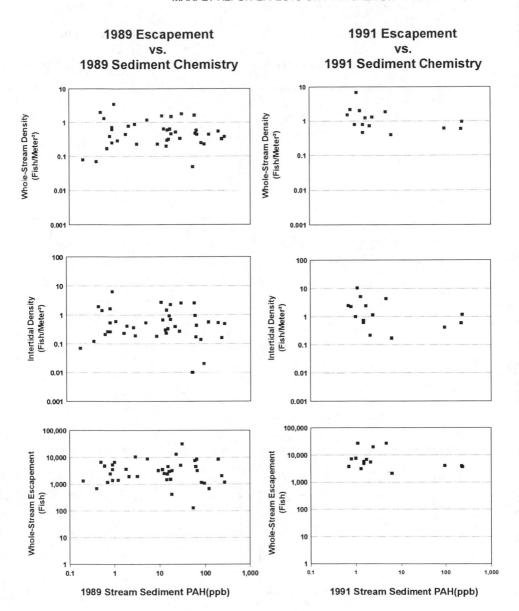

FIGURE 11--Comparison of pink salmon escapement for 1989 and 1991 versus sediment PAH concentrations

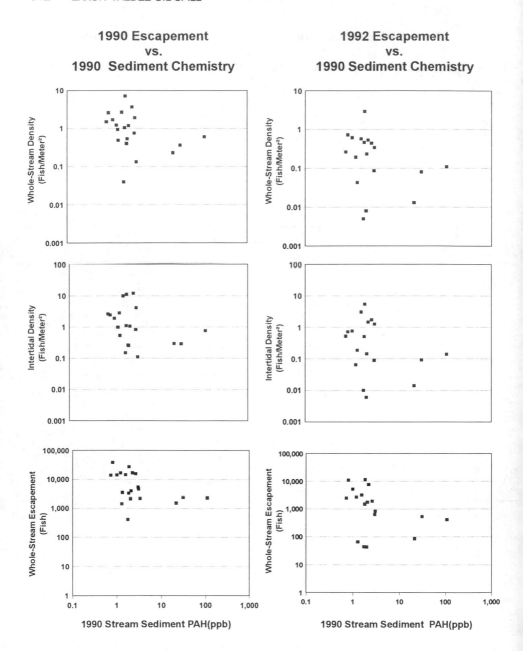

FIGURE 12--Comparison of pink salmon escapement for 1990 and 1992 versus sediment PAH concentrations

TABLE 4--Regression results of pink salmon escapement data for 1989 to 1992 vs. measured stream sediment PAH

Response Variable	P-Values[1]	Degrees of Freedom[+]	R^2	R
1989 Escapement vs. 1989 PAH				
Whole-Stream Density (#/m^2)	0.267	38	0.009	-0.095
Intertidal Density (#/m^2)	0.168	38	0.024	-0.155
Whole-Stream Escapement (fish)	0.239	38	0.013	-0.115
1990 Escapement vs. 1990 PAH				
Whole-Stream Density (#/m^2)	0.272	18	0.021	-0.144
Intertidal Density (#/m^2)	0.244	18	0.027	-0.165
Whole-Stream Escapement (fish)	0.137	18	0.066	-0.257
1991 Escapement vs. 1991 PAH				
Whole-Stream Density (#/m2)	0.155	13	0.079	-0.281
Intertidal Density (#/m2)	0.163	13	0.074	-0.273
Whole-Stream Escapement (fish)	0.122	13	0.103	-0.321
1991 Escapement vs. 1989 PAH				
Whole-Stream Density (#/m^2)	0.416	18	0.003	-0.050
Intertidal Density (#/m^2)	0.478	18	0.000	-0.008
Whole-Stream Escapement (fish)	0.395	18	0.000	-0.020
1992 Escapement vs. 1990 PAH				
Whole-Stream Density (#/m^2)	0.278	16	0.022	-0.149
Intertidal Density (#/m^2)	0.232	16	0.034	-0.185
Whole-Stream Escapement (fish)	0.213	16	0.040	-0.200

[1]P-values of 0.05 or lower required to confirm a significant regression relationship with PAH.

[+]Number of streams, minus two, the number of estimated parameters (slope and intercept).

specific spawning streams, results of this analysis provide a generalized basis for comparison of spawning behavior between oiled and reference streams.

The four-year study period allowed for the comparison of escapement data for two paired years, 1989 to 1991 and 1990 to 1992. Residual oiling could have reduced escapement in either brood year or progeny from the brood year. Thus, oiling could have either increased or decreased the escapement ratio and resulting regressions were tested at a two-tailed □=0.10.

For whole-stream escapement, the slope and intercept for progeny from the brood year versus brood-year escapement did not differ for oiled and reference streams for either sets of years (p=0.254 and 0.189 for 1991 versus 1989; p= 0.165 and 0.642 for 1992 versus 1990). Oiled and reference streams contributed similarly to the strong relationships for both sets of progeny from the brood year and brood-year escapements, and thus they are represented by single regression lines (Figure 13). Because of strong adult returns, escapement ratios were consistently above 2.0 for both oiled and reference streams, indicating more than a doubling of escapement over 1989. The weak 1992 escapement relative to 1990 escapement shifted the relationship away from parity in both oiled and reference streams. Resulting escapement ratios were all below 1.0, indicating that 1992 recruits did not fully replace the strong 1990 parent year.

There was no evidence for a relationship between PAH and escapement ratios (Table 5). The 1991 to 1989 escapement ratio was regressed against PAH concentrations and neither whole-stream nor intertidal escapement ratios were related to PAH concentration, $p > 0.10$ (Table 5). The 1992 to 1990 escapement ratio was regressed against sediment PAH concentration for 1990 and 1991. No PAH measurements were taken in 1992. Again, neither whole-stream nor intertidal escapement ratios were related to PAH concentration, $p > 0.10$ (Table 5). Therefore, although the 1992 returns were significantly lower than the 1990 parent year, the poor returns were experienced in both the oiled and the reference streams, and no correlation could be established between returns and residual hydrocarbons measured in stream sediments.

DISCUSSION

The intent of this investigation was to assess the effects of substrate oiling on distribution and density of spawning pink salmon in southwestern Prince William Sound following the oil spill. Data resulting from this field study provided three levels of resolution to assess potential spill effects on pink salmon: qualitative observations, ANOVA between reference and oiled streams, and quantitative regression tests for relationships between escapement and PAH concentration. Conclusions from each of these levels are discussed below.

Qualitative Observations

Comparisons at this level of resolution allowed an intuitive check of escapement data between oiled and reference streams. As expected, observations of escapement numbers for all four study years, 1989 to 1992, indicated a high degree of variability between years and among streams within each year. Escapement densities and whole-stream escapements varied consistently with the strength of the total run and commercial harvest. In addition, a visual comparison of results shows no obvious differences between oiled and reference streams. An examination of adult returns to oiled and reference streams for the two postspill year classes at greatest risk for spill effects, 1990 and 1991, shows strong wildstock returns relative to parent year class strength for both years.

Comparison of Oiled and Reference Streams

This second level of resolution tested for statistically significant differences in mean escapement measures between oiled and reference streams. Although the high

TABLE 5--Regression analyses of escapement ratios for oiled and reference streams

1989 to 1991

1989 to 1991 Escapement Ratio	P-Values	Degrees of Freedom[+]	R^2
1989 Summer Sediment PAH vs.			
Whole-Stream Ratio	0.905	18	0.001
Intertidal Ratio	0.635	18	0.013
1991 Summer Sediment PAH vs.			
Whole-Stream Ratio	0.550	13	0.028
Intertidal Ratio	0.872	13	0.002

1990 to 1992

1990 to 1992 Escapement Ratio	P-Values	Degrees of Freedom[+]	R^2
1990 Summer Sediment PAH vs.			
Whole-Stream Ratio	0.932	16	<0.001
Intertidal Ratio	0.888	16	0.001
1991 Summer Sediment PAH vs.			
Whole-Stream Ratio	0.497	13	0.036
Intertidal Ratio	0.395	13	0.056

[+] Number of streams in the statistical comparison, minus two, the number of estimated parameters (means for oiled and reference streams).

degree of variability between streams and among years tended to limit the power of these comparisons, each of the ANOVA tests indicated no statistical differences between oiled and reference streams. The oiled streams used in the comparison included the most heavily affected areas in Prince William Sound including Sleepy Bay, Snug Harbor, and Evans Island and Latouche Island (Figure 3). Using escapement data for streams from these heavily affected areas provided the basis for a worst-case comparison to detect effects on wildstock escapement. The fact that pink salmon runs in these worst-case streams did not appear to have been affected provided reassurance that there was minimal potential for impacts on overall wildstock returns.

Response of Spawner Density to PAH

The third level of resolution for examining spill effects was the regression analyses testing relationships between escapement data and measured PAH concentrations from spawning stream sediments. All regression analyses of escapement counts and spawner density indicated that there was no statistically significant relationship with measured PAH concentrations($p > 0.05$). Additional regression analyses of escapement ratios versus PAH concentrations provided a further test for potential escapement effects. These also indicated no relationship between the spill and adult returns.

Conclusion

Results of the study document some residual concentrations of hydrocarbons in three streams from the most heavily oiled area of Prince William Sound through 1991. These indices of exposure did not correlate with detectable differences in spawning behavior or escapement in streams from oiled areas compared with unoiled streams. Analyses of the data lead us to conclude that specific oil-related effects to the adult pink salmon population in Prince William Sound were not apparent.

ASSESSMENT OF OIL-SPILL RISKS TO THE PINK SALMON POPULATION

The two studies of potential impacts on pink salmon populations summarized as Part 1 and Part 2 in this volume, combined with supportive data from several other impact assessment studies as well as related literature, form a strong basis for determining potential risks to the pink salmon population. Specific issues addressed by the studies include:

- Quantifying and characterizing the degree of oil exposure to key life stages of pink salmon.

- Determining the effect of oil on the two brood years of wildstock pink salmon that were at greatest risk of exposure to oil.

- Assessing the potential risks of the oil spill to other salmonid species, using pink salmon as the sentinel species.

Quantification of Exposure Potential

The first objective addressed the fundamental need to assess the potential for spill-related effects on pink salmon by documenting the exposure to crude oil. This identified the probability that oil exposure could have posed significant risks to salmon populations. The need to adequately document exposure as a basis for establishing correlations with biological effects is fundamental to the injury assessment process. The establishment of this relationship is the basis for the Technical Information Documents (U.S. Department of the Interior, 1987 A&B) supporting the Type B natural resource damage assessment rule promulgated under Section 301(C) of the Comprehensive Environmental Response, Compensation and Liabilities Act (CERCLA). Furthermore, it is a requirement of sound science.

To document potential for exposure of pink salmon and other aquatic life to biologically significant concentrations of spill hydrocarbons, over 5 000 analyses of the concentrations of petroleum hydrocarbons in the water column of Prince William Sound and the northern Gulf of Alaska were made in 1989 and 1990 (Neff, 1991). As a complement to the water testing program, additional water samples were collected from more than 30 locations throughout the oiled area in 1989 to assess the toxicity of the water to representative species of marine organisms (Neff and Stubblefield, this volume). Over 500 sediment samples were also taken from salmon streams from 1989 through 1991 to monitor the potential for hydrocarbon exposure directly in the spawning stream substrate.

These studies showed that the average concentration of total PAH in the water samples was about 0.1 ppb and ranged from less than 0.005 ppb to about 1.0 ppb with maximum water column concentrations from even the most heavily oiled bays all less than 10 ppb. Acute and chronic toxicity tests with marine algae, mysid shrimp, and sheepshead minnows found no acute or chronic toxic responses related to water concentrations of total PAH. The nontoxic nature of the water column during spring 1989 is further underscored by the annual zooplankton biomass measurements taken by the commercial fish hatcheries in order to time the release of the yearly crop of pink salmon juveniles. Data taken in April and May of 1989, when exposure potential to hydrocarbons was greatest, showed that zooplankton density was among the highest on record, indicating a stable and strong food resource for growing juveniles (Olsen, 1992). The concentrations of petroleum hydrocarbons measured in the waters of Prince William Sound were also well below concentrations that have been shown to produce harmful effects on pink salmon growth, migration, or reproduction (Rice, 1985).

Similarly, the stream sediment chemistry data documented measurable PAH concentrations in several streams in 1989. Residual hydrocarbons remained in three of the most heavily oiled north-facing streams by 1991. These stream sediment concentrations were approximately one order of magnitude below hydrocarbon levels measured at adjacent oiled shorelines (Boehm et al., this volume).

In evaluating the NOAA National Status and Trends database for PAH effect concentrations, Long and Morgan (1990) concluded that a sediment concentration at the low end of the biological effects range (10th percentile) is 4 000 ppb total PAH. Except for one sample in spring 1990, all stream sediment values were well below this level, thus indicating minimal risks to aquatic species, including salmon eggs, juveniles, and adults found in close association with these stream sediments. Detailed chemical characterization of residual PAH concentrations on shorelines in 1990 and 1991 confirm that they are highly weathered and essentially devoid of the more biologically active components (Boehm et al., this volume).

A further analysis of these residual PAH concentrations found in the oiled streams in 1991 was done using equilibrium partitioning theory (Mackay et al., 1992). Calculated maximum PAH concentrations expected in pore water for fish stream sediment samples are on the order of 1 to 2 ppb, considerably below the PAH toxicity threshold.

An inventory of the Prince William Sound salmon streams indicates that streams in the spill-affected districts collectively account for approximately 20% of the wildstock

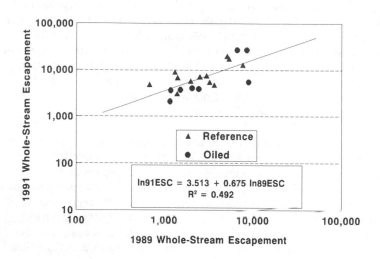

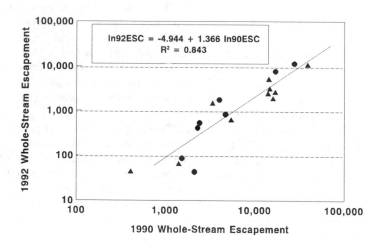

FIGURE 13--Comparison of escapement ratios for 1989 vs. 1991 and 1990 vs. 1992

escapement and approximately 1% of the total annual salmon harvest. In these districts, about 14% of the streams were directly exposed to oil. Thus, wildstock salmon streams potentially at risk of spill impacts account for a small percentage of annual pink salmon production.

In summary, these extensive monitoring programs demonstrate that risks to the pink salmon population from exposure to spill-related hydrocarbons were low.

Potential for Effects on the 1988 Brood Year

The second objective was to examine potential effects on the two brood years of wildstock pink salmon that were at greatest risk. Salmon embryos that were spawned in the fall of 1988 had hatched and were emerging from stream mouths and intertidal gravel in the spring of 1989, just after the oil spill. It can be argued that the 1988 brood year, with sensitive alevin and juveniles present throughout the spill-affected area immediately after the spill, had the highest potential for exposure to the oil spill, and thus represents the year class at greatest risk for spill impacts. These juvenile fish left Prince William Sound in the summer of 1989, at the height of the spill cleanup program, and matured in the Gulf of Alaska to return as adults in the summer and fall of 1990. Hatchery and wildstock components of this year class returned to constitute the 1990 all-time record pink salmon run for the sound. The return of wildstock adults from those fish that had migrated seaward in 1989 was estimated to be 8 times greater than the return during the parent year of 1988 (Donaldson et al., 1993).

Potential for Effects on the 1989 Brood Year

Pink salmon adults returning in summer 1989 spawned postspill and thus produced the first brood year with potential for oil-spill exposure and resulting effects throughout their entire life cycle. Eggs produced were incubated in gravels that, in some locations, contained residual hydrocarbons from the spill. Fry emerged from these gravels in spring 1990, and juveniles fed in nearshore waters off oiled shorelines to return as adults in 1991. It can be argued that this brood year thus represents the brood year at highest potential risk from the spill instead of the previously discussed 1988 brood. The return of these wildstock fish as adults was 1.4 times as great as the parent year return in 1989 (Donaldson et al., 1993). Hatchery and wildstock fish from this brood year contributed to the second largest pink salmon run in history, only slightly behind the all-time record 1990 run.

Postspill Run Size

Postspill studies of escapement and harvest statistics provided the data to further assess the extent and duration of spill effects. The Alaska Department of Fish and Game has monitored the productivity of pink salmon in Prince William Sound since well before the spill by sampling a subset of wildstock index streams. Observations from these index streams are used to guide management decisions for the entire wildstock population. Data for the period from 1982 to 1992 from the eleven index streams in the spill-affected area are shown in Figure 14. Data from these streams provided historical prespill escapement information for streams in the spill-impact area. The year classes at greatest risk for exposure to spill hydrocarbons (1990 and 1991) returned in large numbers, exceeding wildstock returns for immediate prespill years. Moreover, escapement trends for oiled and reference streams after the spill were similar to those observed prior to 1989.

Lower than expected returns of both hatchery fish and wildstocks combined to make 1992 the weakest run since 1978. Lower than average survival was predicted in the fall of 1991 by marine oceanographers documenting a high frequency of storms, overcast conditions, and resulting colder ocean temperatures (Cooney et al., 1992). These meteorological effects combined to produce poor ocean rearing conditions and a weaker zooplankton food base. These factors contributed to low ocean survival of juvenile salmon, which in turn contributed to the poor return of adults in 1992. Weak returns were observed for both oiled and reference streams, further suggesting regional conditions as a contributor to the weak runs.

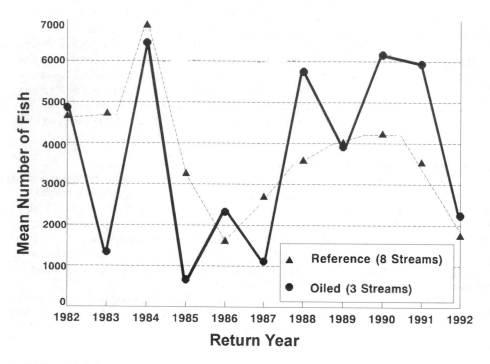

FIGURE 14--Mean escapement indices for eleven Alaska Dept. of Fish and Game index streams for 1982-1992

Risks to Pacific Salmon Populations
The final objective was to assess the risks of spill-related injury to other species of salmon. Our results are consistent with a fisheries risk assessment conducted by the U.S. Minerals Management Service (MMS) using oceanographic, fate and effects, resource assessment, and numeric-simulation studies (Meyer and Geiselman, 1990).

Results of that study of the effects of spilled oil on the homing of adult salmon suggested that adult salmon are able, even in the presence of spilled oil, to return to their natal rivers. This supports the conclusion of minimal risk to homing behavior of adult populations of the five species of Pacific salmon found in Alaska.

The four other species of Pacific salmon in Prince William Sound have longer life cycles, typically of three or four years duration, and thus were in the Gulf of Alaska, away from the spill area for longer time periods. Also, these species, except for some chum salmon populations, do not spawn in intertidal areas. Instead, spawning and early development occur in upstream freshwater areas, away from oil-affected shorelines. In addition, pink salmon have a much higher population density in the spill-affected areas and would consequently be expected to more readily show spill impacts. Thus, the empirical data developed in this study using pink salmon, the species with the greatest likelihood of exposure to oil and its subsequent effects, support the conclusion that the *Exxon Valdez* oil spill posed minimal risks to other salmon populations in the sound.

Conclusion

Each element of the early life-stage survival of wildstock pink salmon was examined in the study discussed in the preceding paper (Brannon et al., this volume). Conclusions from that study indicate that measures of early life stages were within the reported range of performance for pink salmon and that they were indistinguishable between oiled and unoiled streams. Field observations of adult spawning distribution and behavior reported herein for streams from the most heavily oiled areas were unable to measure differences attributable to spill hydrocarbons. In combination, these studies show that specific oil-related effects on wildstock pink salmon populations in Prince William Sound were not detectable.

ACKNOWLEDGMENTS

The authors would like to thank Pentec Environmental, Inc., for their assistance in conducting the 1989 field program. Also the staff and management of Dames and Moore provided support for the 1989 and 1990 field programs. K. R. Parker provided valuable assistance in reviewing the experimental design and conducting statistical analyses.

REFERENCES

Alaska Department of Fish and Game. 1985. *Catalog of waters important for spawning, rearing or migration of anadromous fishes: Southcentral Region.* Habitat Division. Alaska Department of Fish and Game. Juneau, Alaska. 109 p.

Bocking, R.C., J.R. Irvine, K.K. English, and M. Labelle. 1988. "Evaluation of random and indexing sampling designs for estimating coho salmon (*Oncorhynchus kisutch*) escapement to three Vancouver Island streams." *Canadian Technical Report of Fisheries and Aquatic Sciences Number 1639*, 95p.

Brannon, E., T. Quinn, R. Whitman, A. Nevissi, R. Nakatani, and C. McAuliffe. 1986. "Homing of adult chinook salmon after brief exposure to whole and dispersed crude oil." *Transactions of the American Fisheries Society* 115, 823-827.

Cohen, J. 1977. *Statistical Power Analysis for the Behavioral Sciences.* New York: Academic Press; 474pp.

Cooney, R.T., T.M. Willette, J. Sharr, D. Shaup, and J. Olsen. 1992. "The effect of climate on North Pacific pink salmon production: examining the details of a natural experiment." *International Symposium on Climate Change and Northern Fish Populations,* October 13-16, 1992, Victoria, Canada.

Cousens, N.B.F., G.A. Thomas, C.G. Swann, and M.C. Healey. 1982. "A review of salmon escapement estimation techniques." *Canadian Technical Report of Fisheries and Aquatic Sciences Number 1108,* 122p.

Donaldson, W., S. Morstad, E. Simpson, and E. Biggs. 1993. "Prince William Sound Management Area 1992 annual fin fish management report." Alaska Department of Fish and Game, Division of Commercial Fisheries, Anchorage Regional Information Report 2A93-12, 158 pp.

Gooding, R.M. 1971. "Oil pollution on Wake Island from the tanker *R.C. Stoner.*" National Oceanic and Atmospheric Administration, Special Scientific Report--Fisheries No. 636, Seattle, Washington.

Hampson, G.R. and H.L. Sanders 1969. "Local oil spill." *Oceanos* 15: 8-14.

Helle, J.H. 1970. "Biological characteristics of intertidal and fresh-water spawning pink salmon at Olsen Creek, Prince William Sound, Alaska, 1962-63." U.S. Fish and Wildlife Service, Special Scientific Report - Fisheries Number. 602. Washington, D.C. 19 p.

Helle, J.H., R.S. Williamson, and J.E. Bailey. 1964. "Intertidal ecology and life history of pink salmon at Olsen Creek, Prince William Sound, Alaska." U.S. Fish and Wildlife Service, Special Scientific Report Number 483, 26pp.

Johnson, B.A. and B.M. Barrett. 1986. "Estimation of salmon escapement based on stream survey data." Alaska Department of Fish. and Game, Division of Commercial Fisheries, Regional Information Report 4K88-35, 8p

Kalbfleisch, J.D. and R.L. Prentice. 1980. *The statistical analysis of failure time data.* New York: Wiley; 321pp.

Lawless, J.F. 1982. *Statistical models and methods for lifetime data.* New York: Wiley; 580pp.

Long, E.R. and L.G. Morgan. 1990. "The potential for biological effects of sediment-sorbed contaminants tested in the National Status and Trends Program." *National Oceanic and Atmospheric Administration Technical Memorandum National Ocean Service, Office of Oceanography and Marine Assessment 52*. U.S. Department of Commerce. 175pp.

Longhurst, A. 1982. "Consultation on the consequences of offshore oil production on offshore fish stocks and fishing operations." *Canadian Technical Report of Fisheries and Aquatic Sciences Number 1096*, Fisheries and Oceans, Ottawa. pp. 1-95.

Mackay, D., W.Y. Shiu, and K.C. Ma. 1992. *Illustrated Handbook of Physical Chemical Properties and Environmental Fate for Organic Chemicals Vol. II*. Ann Arbor: Lewis Publishers; 597 pp.

McCurdy, M.L. 1984. "Eshamy District pink salmon streamlife factor study." Alaska Department of Fish and Game, Division of Commercial Fisheries, Prince William Sound Area Data Report 84-18, 17p.

McIntyre, A.D. 1982. "Oil pollution and fisheries." *Philosophical Transactions of the Royal Society of London, Series B*, 279:217-25.

Meyer, R. and J. Geiselman. 1990. "Fisheries risk assessment in the Alaska OCS region." Minerals Management. Service, Alaska Outer Continental Shelf Region, Anchorage, Alaska, 9pp.

Nakatani, R., E. Salo, A. Nevissi, R. Whitman, B. Snyder, and S. Kaluzney. 1985. "Effects of Prudhoe Bay crude oil on the homing of coho salmon in marine waters." Report for the American Petroleum Institute by the University of Washington Fisheries Research Institute, Seattle, 55pp.

Nakatani, R., E. Salo, A. Nevissi, R. Whitman, B. Snyder, and S. Kaluzney. 1986. "Influence of crude oil and dispersant on the ability of coho salmon to differentiate home water from non-home water." Report for the American Petroleum Institute by the University of Washington Fisheries Research Institute, Seattle, 97pp.

National Academy of Science. 1985. "Oil in the sea--Inputs, fates, and effects." Washington, DC: National Academy Press, 601pp.

Neilson, J.D. and G.H. Green. 1981. "Enumeration of spawning salmon from spawner residence time and aerial counts." *Transactions of the American Fisheries Society* 110: 554-556.

Neff, J.M. 1991. "Long-term trends in the concentrations of polycyclic aromatic hydrocarbons in the water column of Prince William Sound and the western Gulf of Alaska following the *Exxon Valdez* oil spill." In: *Fourteenth Annual Arctic and Marine Oilspill Program Technical Seminar*. Environment Canada, Ottawa, Canada. pp. 27-38.

Noerenberg, W.H. 1963. "Salmon forecast studies on 1963 runs in Prince William Sound." Informational Leaflet No. 21. Alaska Department of Fish and Game, Division of Commercial Fisheries. Juneau, Alaska. 27 p.

Olsen, J. 1992. "Development and comparative performance of hatchery rearing strategies for pink salmon (*O. gorbuscha*) in Prince William Sound." Draft report for the Prince William Sound Aquaculture Corporation Board of Directors meeting Sept. 18-20, 1992. Cordova, Alaska.

Payne, J.F. 1989. "Oil pollution--A penny ante problem for fisheries (If it weren't for erroneous perceptions)." *Petro Pisces 89- International conference on fishing and offshore petroleum exploration., Bergen, Norway Oct. 23-25, 1989,* paper number E4

Perrin, C.J. and J.R. Irvine. 1980. "A review of survey life estimates as they apply to the area-under-the-curve method for estimating the spawning escapement of Pacific salmon." *Canadian Technical Report of Fisheries and Aquatic Sciences Number 1733,* 49p.

Pirtle, R.B. 1976. "Historical catch, escapement and related commercial fishery statistics of fish and shellfish, Prince William Sound Area, Alaska." Alaska Department of Fish and Game, Division of Commercial Fisheries, Juneau. *Technical Data Report Number 26,* 93pp.

Pirtle, R.B. 1977. "Historical pink and chum salmon estimated spawning escapements from Prince William Sound, Alaska streams, 1960-1975." Alaska Department of Fish and Game, Division of Commercial Fisheries, Juneau, *Technical Data Report Number 35.* 332pp.

Rice, S.D. 1973. "Toxicity and avoidance tests with Prudhoe Bay oil and pink salmon fry." In: *Proceedings of the 1973 Joint Conference on Prevention and Control of Oil Spills, March 13-15, 1973,* Washington, D.C. American Petroleum Institute; pp. 667 - 670.

Rice, S.D. 1985. "Effects of oil on fish." In: *Petroleum effects in the arctic environmental.* F.R. Englelhardt (ed.). New York. Elsevier Publishers. pp. 157-182.

Rice, S.D., A. Moles, J. Karinen, S. Korn, M. Carls, C. Brodersen, J.A. Gharrett, and M.A. Babcock. 1984. "Effects of petroleum hydrocarbons on Alaskan aquatic organisms: A comprehensive review of all oil-effects research on Alaskan fish and invertebrates conducted by the Auke Bay laboratory, 1970-81." National Marine Fisheries Service, Auke Bay, Alaska.

Royer, T.C. 1990. "High latitude oceanic variability associated with the 18.6 year nodal tide." *Proceedings of the International Conference on the Role of the Polar Regions in Global Change. June 11-15, 1990.* University of Alaska at Fairbanks. p. 150.

Sauer, T. and P.D. Boehm. 1991. "The use of defensible analytical chemical measurements for oil spill natural resource damage assessment." *Proceedings of the 1991 International Oil Spill Conference. March 4-7, 1991, San Diego, California*, pp.363-370.

Sharr, S., D. Sharp, and B. G. Bue. 1993. "Pink salmon spawning escapement estimation in Prince William Sound." *Program and Abstract Book, Exxon Valdez Oil Spill Symposium, February 3-5, 1993, Anchorage, Alaska*. Anchorage: Oil Spill Trustee Council; pp. 124-127.

Sherman, K. and D. Busch. 1978. "The *Argo Merchant* Oil Spill and the Fisheries." In: *In the Wake of the* Argo Merchant, *Proceedings of the Symposium Jan. 11-13, 1978 Center for Ocean Management Studies, University of Rhode Island Maragansett, RI*. August 1978. pp. 149-168.

Straughan, D. 1970. "Ecological effects of the Santa Barbara oil spill." In: *Santa Barbara Oil Symposium, Dec. 16-18, 1970*. University of California, Santa Barbara, CA. pp. 173-182.

Thorsteinson, F.V. 1965. "Some aspects of pink and chum salmon research at Olsen Bay Prince William Sound." Department of the Interior, U.S. Fish and Wildlife Service, Bureau of Fisheries Manuscript Report 65-3: 30p.

Thorsteinson, F.V., J.H. Helle, and D.G. Birkholz. 1971. "Salmon survival in intertidal zones of Prince William Sound streams in uplifted and subsided areas." In: *The Great Alaska Earthquake of 1964: Biology*, National Academy of Sciences, Washington, D.C. 1971.

U.S. Department of the Interior. 1987A. "Injury to fish and wildlife species." Type B Technical Information Document. CERCLA 301 Project; U.S. Department of Interior; Washington, DC, June 1987.

U.S. Department of the Interior. 1987B. "Guidance on the use of habitat evaluation procedures and suitability index models for CERCLA application." Type B Technical Information Document. CERCLA 301 Project; U.S. Department of the Interior; Washington, DC, June 1987.

van den Berghe, E.P. and M.R. Gross. 1986. "Length of breeding life of coho salmon (*Oncorhynchus kisutch*)." *Canadian Journal of Zoology* 64: 1482-1486.

Weber, D.D., D. Maynard, W. Grossland, and V. Konchin. 1981. "Avoidance reactions of migrating adult salmon to petroleum hydrocarbons." *Canadian Journal of Fisheries and Aquatic Sciences*. 38:779-781.

Walter H. Pearson,[1] Erlend Moksness,[2] and John R. Skalski[3]

A FIELD AND LABORATORY ASSESSMENT OF OIL-SPILL EFFECTS ON
SURVIVAL AND REPRODUCTION OF PACIFIC HERRING FOLLOWING
THE *EXXON VALDEZ* SPILL

REFERENCE: Pearson, W. H., Moksness, E., and Skalski, J. R., **"A Field and
Laboratory Assessment of Oil-Spill Effects on Survival and Reproduction of
Pacific Herring Following the *Exxon Valdez* Spill,"** Exxon Valdez Oil Spill: Fate and
Effects in Alaskan Waters, ASTM STP 1219, Peter G. Wells, James N. Butler, and
Jane S. Hughes, Eds., American Society for Testing and Materials, Philadelphia, 1995.

ABSTRACT: Pacific herring, *Clupea pallasi*, spawn along hundreds of kilometres of
shoreline in Prince William Sound. Herring eggs incubate in intertidal and shallow
subtidal areas attached to kelp and eelgrass. In April 1989, following the *Exxon Valdez*
oil spill, there was potential in Prince William Sound for localized effects on spawning
herring, their eggs, and the hatching larvae. Field and laboratory investigations in 1989
and 1990 were designed to assess potential injury to Prince William Sound herring by
testing for differences between oiled regions and unoiled reference areas and by relating
biological response variables to the concentrations of polycyclic aromatic hydrocarbons
(PAH) in eggs-on-kelp samples. Hydrocarbon analyses and laboratory incubation were
conducted on eggs-on-kelp samples from Prince William Sound and Sitka Sound. The
eggs and hatching larvae were examined to evaluate several response variables: egg
development, hatch, larval survival, abnormal development of larvae, larval length, and
larval yolk-sac volume.

Analysis of 1989 shoreline surveys indicate that about 96% of the total spawn
length (158 km) in Prince William Sound occurred along shorelines with no oiling, and
less than 1% of the 1989 total spawn length occurred along shorelines with moderate to
heavy oiling. Analysis of shoreline oiling in both 1989 and 1990 from all surveys
indicates that about 90 to 91% of the total 1989 spawn length occurred along unoiled

---

[1]Senior Research Scientist, Battelle/Marine Sciences Laboratory, Sequim, Washington
98382, USA.
[2]Senior Research Scientist, Institute of Marine Research, Flodevigen Marine Research
Station, N-4817 His, Norway.
[3]Associate Professor, Center for Quantitative Sciences, School of Fisheries, University
of Washington, Seattle, Washington 98195, USA.

shorelines. Effects on herring eggs were minor in 1989 even in oiled areas. No significant relationship was found between 1989 PAH burdens in eggs-on-kelp samples and 9 out of 10 biological response variables. In 1989, significantly lower proportions of developed eggs were observed for Cabin Bay samples visibly contaminated with tarry deposits. The location where these effects were seen represented less than 2% of total 1989 spawn length. No effects of the spill on herring were evident in 1990. No significant relationship was found between 1990 PAH burdens and the seven biological response variables studied. Biological response variables from Sitka Sound were either not significantly different from or significantly lower (more adverse) than those from Prince William Sound.

Our 1989 and 1990 results are consistent with the low exposure of herring to oil and do not indicate an extent of injury that would be significant to the Prince William Sound herring population. The biomass and harvests of Prince William Sound herring had reached record high levels in the three years immediately following the spill so that the minor effects observed in 1989 did not translate into decreases in the population level.

KEYWORDS: Pacific herring, *Clupea pallasi*, oil spill, *Exxon Valdez*, Prince William Sound, fish eggs, fish larvae

INTRODUCTION

Prince William Sound (PWS), Alaska, provides numerous spawning locations and important fisheries for Pacific herring (*Clupea pallasi*). In early April, large schools of spawning adult herring assemble in the nearshore waters of PWS. Herring deposit their eggs on eelgrass, seaweed, and kelp in the intertidal and shallow subtidal zones, where the attached eggs incubate for about 3 weeks before hatching (Hay 1985).

Following the *Exxon Valdez* oil spill in March 1989, concern about effects on Pacific herring arose for several reasons. First, the PWS herring fisheries have substantial economic value. The present commercial herring fisheries include (1) purse-seine fishery for sac roe, (2) gill-net fishery for sac roe, (3) natural or wild fishery for roe on kelp, (4) pound fishery for roe on kelp, and (5) bait and food fishery. Fisheries for sac roe and roe on kelp, which are sold primarily to the Orient, began in the early 1970s. In the 5 years prior to the spill, the PWS purse-seine and gill-net fisheries for sac roe had annual landings from 6 080 metric tons (mt) [5 515 short tons (st)] to 11 331 mt (10 277 st), with an average of 8 283 mt (7 513 st) (Brady et al. 1990; Figure 1). Over the same period, the estimated annual value of all five PWS herring fisheries ranged from $5.1 million to $12.2 million, with an average of $8.5 million (Brady et al. 1990; Figure 2). Historically, a strong year class emerges every 4 or 5 years and is the major support of the PWS sac-roe fishery (Figure 3). Concern for potential spill effects on the herring resource prompted the Alaska Department of Fish and Game (ADF&G) to close the 1989 sac-roe and roe-on-kelp fisheries.

Second, because herring deposit their eggs in the intertidal and shallow subtidal zones, shoreline stranding of oil in March and April of 1989 caused concerns about potential oil contamination of herring eggs on kelp. Over the 5 years prior to the spill, Pacific herring had spawned along 106 to 273 km (65.8 to 166.3 statute miles) of shoreline (Brady et al. 1990). The 1989 aerial survey by ADF&G observed herring spawning over 158 km (98.4 mi) of shoreline in PWS (Figure 4). There was little overlap between the distribution of herring spawning and oiling of the shorelines. The crude oil released into PWS was transported southwest by surface currents and moved past the Naked Island archipelago and the northern tip of Montague Island. Herring spawning locations in the northern, northeastern, and southeastern portions of PWS were not exposed to oil, and exposure in the other areas of PWS derived primarily from lightly oiled beaches (Figure 4). In 1990, herring spawned over 182 km (113.4 mi) of shoreline, including some shorelines that were oiled and cleaned in 1989 (Figure 5).

Third, previous laboratory studies suggested that oil can have harmful effects on fish eggs and larvae (NRC 1985). Eggs in static exposures to the water soluble fraction (WSF) of various oils and in static and flowing exposures to crude oils and specific monoaromatic hydrocarbons had shown increased mortality and increased frequency of gross morphological abnormalities in the hatched larvae of Pacific herring, *C. pallasi* (Struhsaker et al. 1974; Struhsaker 1977; Smith and Cameron 1979; Pearson et al. 1985) and Baltic herring, *C. h. membras* (Linden 1978; Vourinen and Axell 1980). For monoaromatic hydrocarbons, exposures to water concentrations from 700 to 35 000 ppb for several days produce larval abnormalities and other effects. For crude oils, effects are usually not evident until exposures reach 1 to 12 ppm for several days. Rice et al. (1986) found that Pacific herring eggs taken from unexposed adults and directly exposed to the WSF of Cook Inlet crude oil had normal hatching rates for 2-day exposures but decreased hatching rates for 12-day exposures above 1 ppm. Because Pearson et al. (1985) found that adherence of oil to eggs, not the hydrocarbon concentration in the water column, was the primary mechanism for increasing the frequency of abnormalities in larvae hatching from exposed Pacific herring eggs, direct oiling of the herring eggs was of the greatest concern.

This paper presents results from field and laboratory studies in 1989 and 1990 on naturally spawned herring eggs, the stage judged most likely to be exposed. In 1990, study of eggs on kelp was expanded to include more locations, and an aerial survey of herring spawning patterns was also conducted. This study considered the following questions:

- To what extent were eggs on kelp from the oiled and reference areas contaminated with oil?
- Were proportions of developed eggs and empty egg cases (hatching rate) for laboratory-incubated eggs on kelp from the oiled areas lower than those from the reference area?
- In larvae hatched from the incubated eggs on kelp, were mortalities or frequency of abnormalities greater for oiled than reference areas?
- Do the herring biomass and harvests in PWS following the spill provide any evidence of a spill effect?

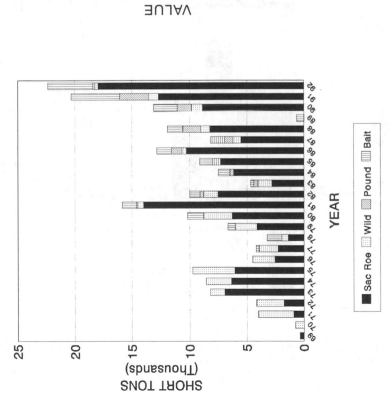

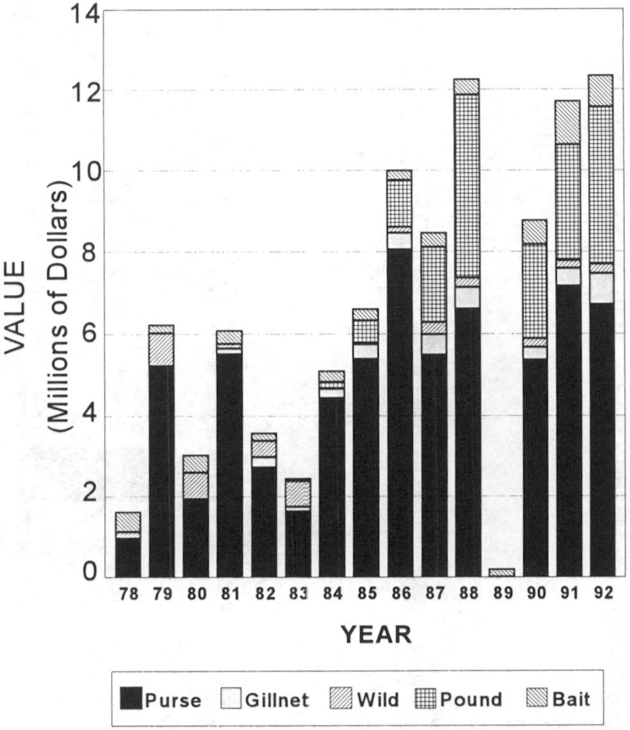

FIGURE 2—Estimated annual ex-vessel values for all herring fisheries in Prince William Sound from 1978 to 1992 (Brady et al. 1990, 1991; Donaldson et al. 1993).

FIGURE 1—Estimated annual harvest for all herring fisheries in Prince William Sound from 1969 to 1992 (Brady et al. 1990, 1991; Donaldson et al. 1993).

Purse-Seine Fishery for Herring Sac Roe in Prince William Sound

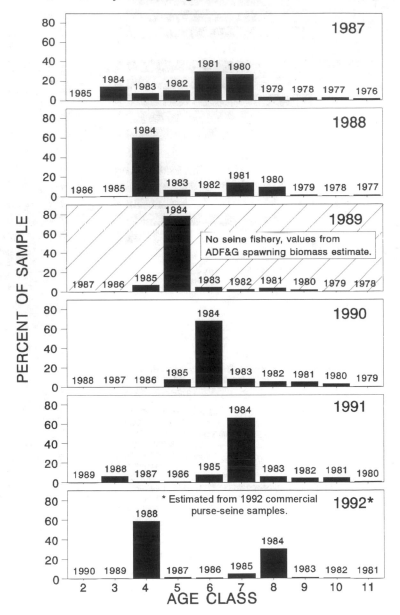

FIGURE 3—*Age-class distribution of herring in the sac-roe purse-seine fishery in Prince William Sound from 1987 to 1992 (Brady et al. 1990, 1991).*

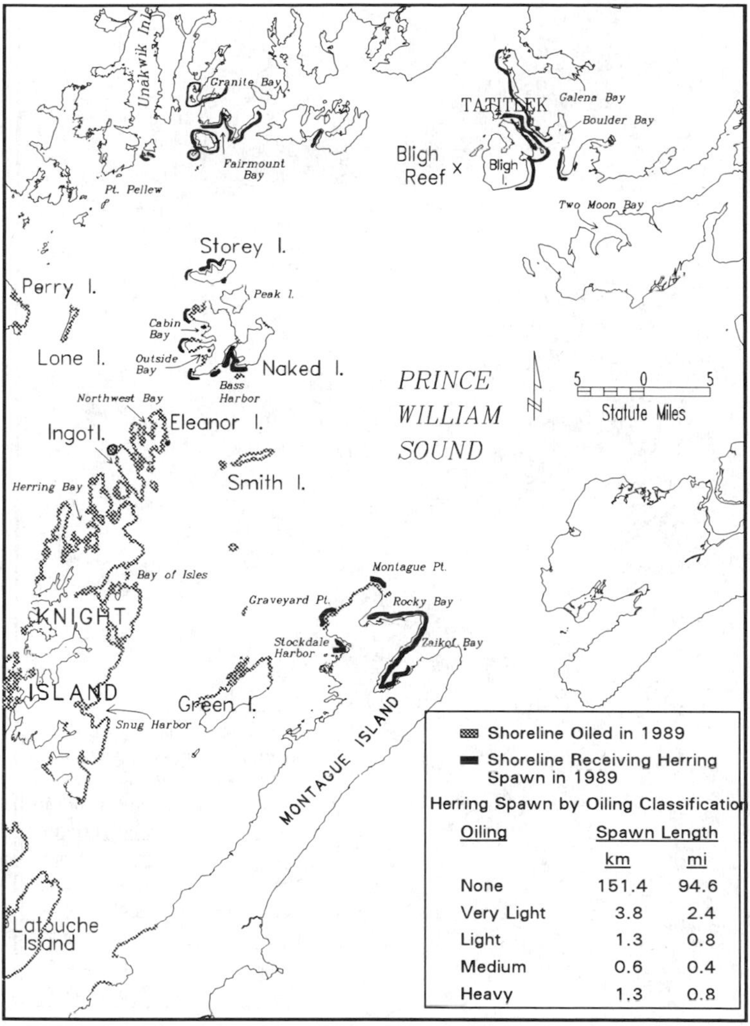

Unakwik Inlet
Granite Bay
Fairmount Bay
Pt. Pellew
TATITLEK
Galena Bay
Boulder Bay
Bligh Reef
Bligh I.
Two Moon Bay
Storey I.
Peak I.
Perry I.
Cabin Bay
Lone I.
Outside Bay
Naked I.
Bass Harbor
Northwest Bay
PRINCE WILLIAM SOUND
5 0 5
Statute Miles
Eleanor I.
Ingot I.
Herring Bay
Smith I.
Bay of Isles
Montague Pt.
Graveyard Pt.
Rocky Bay
KNIGHT ISLAND
Stockdale Harbor
Zaikof Bay
Green I.
Snug Harbor
MONTAGUE ISLAND
Latouche Island
Shoreline Oiled in 1989
Shoreline Receiving Herring Spawn in 1989
Herring Spawn by Oiling Classification
Oiling
Spawn Length
km
mi
None 151.4 94.6
Very Light 3.8 2.4
Light 1.3 0.8
Medium 0.6 0.4
Heavy 1.3 0.8

FIGURE 4—1989 locations of herring spawn (Brady et al. 1991) in Prince William Sound with 1989 locations of oiled shoreline (Koons and Jahns 1992).

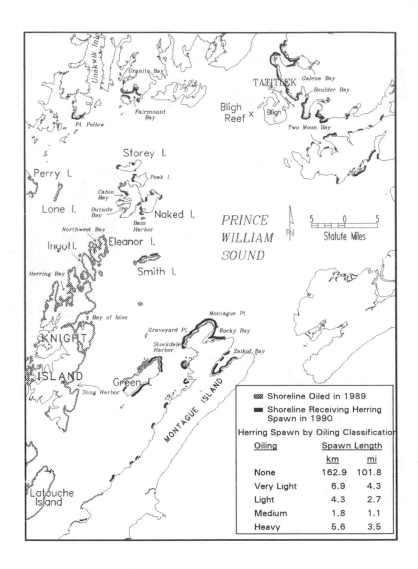

FIGURE 5—1990 Locations of herring spawn (Brady et al. 1990) in Prince William Sound with 1989 locations of oiled shoreline (Koons and Jahns 1992).

Our study design had the following attributes. First, the design compared potentially affected areas against reference areas and, for 1990, also compared PWS with Sitka Sound. The addition of Sitka Sound, which lies about 785 km southeast of PWS, enabled the measurement of the background frequencies of certain larval abnormalities in a geographical region free from any possibility of influence by the spill in PWS but still having similar herring spawning locations and a productive herring fishery. Sitka Sound provided a second reference area against which results from PWS could be compared. Second, measurements of hydrocarbon tissue burdens were directly coupled with biological response variables by subsampling from the same sample. Third, hydrocarbon analyses of water taken contemporaneously supplemented the hydrocarbon data for eggs on kelp. Fourth, the influence of natural factors on biological response variables was taken into account in the field and laboratory procedures and in the data analysis. For example, because the density of deposited eggs is known to affect egg survival and frequency of larval abnormalities (Galkina 1968, 1971), egg density was used as a concomitant variable in our study. Fourth, appropriate sample sizes were determined during planning. On the basis of published information on hatching rates and frequency of abnormal larvae (Pearson et al. 1985), the final sampling strategy selected in 1989 was designed to provide enough eggs to detect a 30% change in the frequency of abnormal larvae at a power of 0.80 and a significance level of 0.05. The 1989 data on the frequency of swollen pericardial regions were used to establish sample sizes in the 1990 sampling strategy. Fifth, field and laboratory processing included procedures to keep the origin of the samples unknown to the laboratory analysts (i.e., the analyses were performed "blind").

This paper reports our findings that there were minor effects of the spill on herring eggs in 1989 and no effects in 1990. In 1989, spill effects on herring eggs were observed in one location, Cabin Bay, in samples visibly contaminated with tarry deposits. The location where these effects were seen represented less than 2% of the total 1989 herring spawn length.

METHODS

Field and laboratory tasks were performed in 1989 and 1990 to (1) estimate the extent of herring spawn along the shoreline in the sampled locations, (2) observe oiling, herring spawn, and vegetation along transects, (3) collect samples of naturally spawned herring eggs deposited on seaweed and kelp, (4) collect supplemental samples of water and sediment, (5) evaluate egg density, proportion of developed eggs, proportion of empty egg cases, and proportions of normal and abnormal larvae hatching from laboratory-incubated eggs, (6) measure the level of hydrocarbon contamination in water, sediment, and herring eggs-on-kelp samples, and (7) measure length and yolk-sac volume in herring larvae without visible abnormalities (1989 only).

Sampling Schedules and Locations

The timing of the oil spill and herring spawning events established the sampling schedules. In 1989, eggs-on-kelp sampling occurred in PWS from April 22 to May 17th.

In 1990, sampling occurred in PWS from April 7 to May 7th and in Sitka Sound from April 12 to April 23th. We selected the sampling locations on the basis of spawn magnitude observed during aerial surveys, and on historical information about herring spawning locations (Brady et al. 1990, 1991).

We defined the reference area as a geographical area within which oil contamination from the spill had not occurred, that was otherwise similar to the oiled area, and that is comparable to a potentially affected area. For this study, locations south of the northern portion of the Naked Island archipelago and west of the most eastern portion of Montague Island were considered within the oiled area. Locations in the north, northeast, and southeast of PWS were considered within the reference area. Under this designation, the oiled area contained bays and shorelines past which the spill traveled.

In 1990, Sitka Sound was added as a reference area. The Sitka Sound herring sac-roe fishery had landings of 12 135 st during 1989 (Funk and Savikko 1990). In addition to its productive fishery, Sitka Sound has numerous herring spawning locations and was not exposed to oil from the *Exxon Valdez* spill.

In PWS during 1989, we made observations and collected eggs-on-kelp samples along 35 transects in 9 locations with observed spawn (Figure 6). In 1990, we collected herring eggs-on-kelp samples along a total of 53 transects from 12 PWS sampling locations and 14 transects from 6 locations in Sitka Sound (Figure 6). The 1989 and 1990 study locations were classified as oiled or reference, on the basis of the spill trajectory as follows:

1989 PWS Oiled	1990 PWS Oiled
Bass Harbor	Green Island
Cabin Bay	Montague Pt. to Graveyard Pt.
Montague Pt. to Graveyard Pt.	Peak Island
Outside Bay	Rocky Bay
Stockdale Harbor	Smith Island
Storey Island	Zaikof Bay

1989 PWS Reference	1990 PWS Reference	Sitka Reference
Granite Bay	Boulder Bay	Big Gavanski Island
Jack Bay	Fairmount Bay	Halibut Pt.
Rocky Pt.	Galena Bay	Lisianski Peninsula
	Point Pellew	Hot Springs Bay
	Rocky Pt.	Middle Island
	Two Moon Bay	Siginaka Islands

Because of hatching in the field or in transit, 1989 transects from Jack Bay, Rocky Point, and Storey Island did not yield measurements on all of the variables examined at the other 6 locations. In 1990, all of the samples shipped arrived before hatching and yielded the full set of measurements.

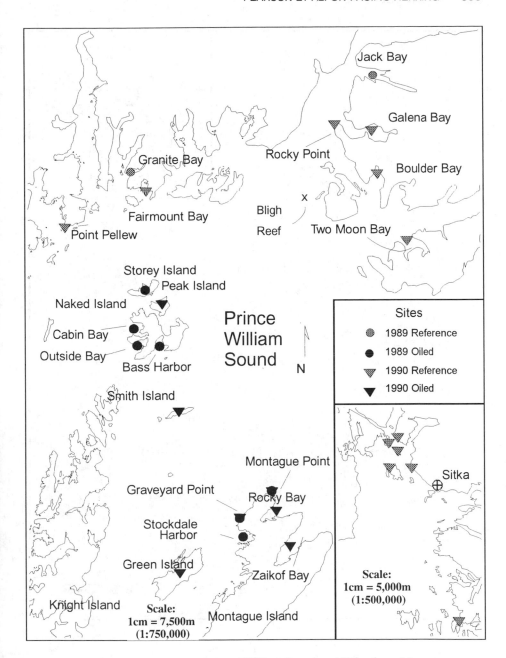

FIGURE 6—*General locations in Prince William Sound and Sitka Sound for transect observations and collection of eggs-on-kelp samples.*

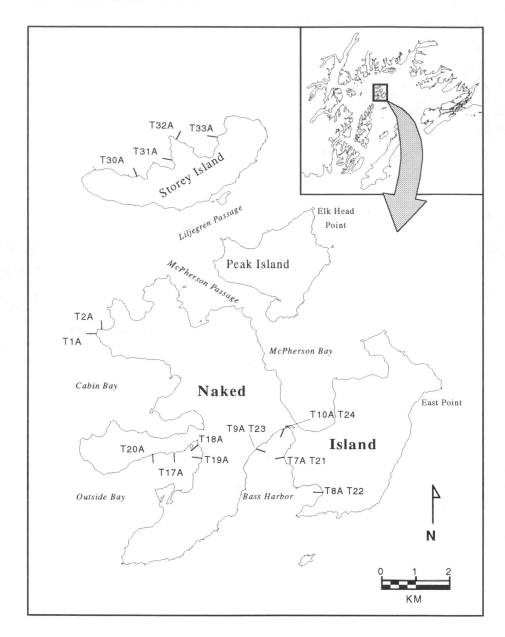

FIGURE 7—Positioning of transects for collection of eggs-on-kelp samples in the Naked Island Archipelago, 1989.

Spawn Reconnaissance

The extent of herring spawn along the shoreline at each location was estimated by observations from a launch. Stations marking the boundaries of spawn were located on a U. S. Geological Survey (USGS) topographical quadrangle, and the beach length containing spawn was digitized to provide the length in meters. A mean spawn width for each location was calculated from estimates of the distance along the transects over which spawn was observed.

Transect Observations and Sample Collection

The spawn reconnaissance information was used to position transects within the distribution of herring spawn. A systematic sampling protocol established transects that were evenly spaced with a random starting point for the first transect. In PWS, 2 or 4 transects per location were established during 1989 (Figure 7) and 4 per location during 1990. In Sitka Sound, 2 transects per location were established. The transects began at a tidal height of +1.23 m (+4 ft) referenced to Mean Lower Low Water (MLLW) and were oriented at right angles to the local shoreline (Figure 7).

Shore and diver teams made observations along each transect until the substrate became bare of vegetation, the water depth became greater than 11 m (36 ft), or herring eggs were no longer observed. When the diver or shore teams encountered the start or end of bands of spawn, they recorded the distance along the transect from its beginning and the depth or tidal height. At each of 7 tidal heights (nominally +1.23, +0.62, 0, -0.62, -1.85, -3.69, and -6.15 m MLLW [+4, +2, 0, -2, -6, -12, and -20 ft MLLW]), the shore and diver teams placed either a 1- or 0.25-m^2 quadrat. Only the smaller quadrat was used in 1989. The larger quadrat was used in 1990 where kelp density was too low or the kelp specimens too large for the smaller quadrat to have a plant count greater than one per quadrat. For each quadrat, the vegetation and substrate types were noted, and the number of plants or estimated percentage of plant cover recorded. At quadrats where herring eggs were present, an eggs-on-kelp sample was collected.

Water samples for hydrocarbon analysis were taken (5 to 10 cm below the surface) at the shoreward end of transects. One water sample was collected for each of the transects in each area in Sitka Sound. In PWS, one water sample was collected at each transect in 1989 and at two of the four transects in 1990. After each transect was completed, a YSI salinity-conductivity temperature meter was used to measure the water temperature and conductivity at the surface (0.1 m deep) and at depths of 1 m and either 2 m or 3 m. Salinity was calculated later from the temperature and conductivity.

Equipment was cleaned between locations to avoid cross-contamination. Any prelabeled sampling containers carried into the field at a location but returned unused were discarded.

Field Examination of Eggs-on-Kelp Samples

Eggs-on-kelp samples were examined on shipboard for oil, stage of embryonic development, and percentage of eggs that were dead (white opaque, or yellow opaque).

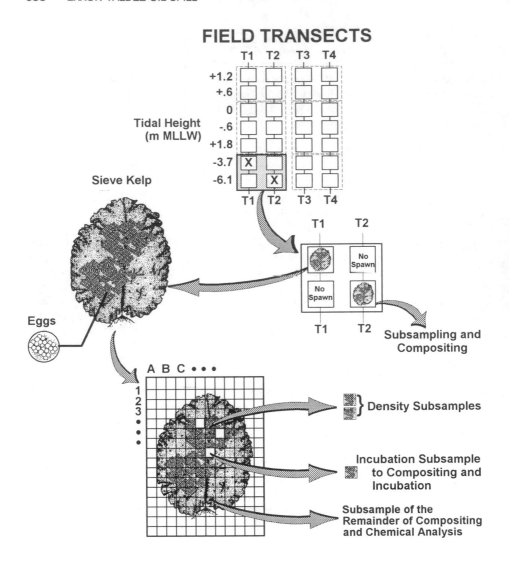

FIGURE 8—Compositing and subsampling of eggs-on-kelp samples collected in Prince William Sound and Sitka Sound in 1990.

The presence or absence of any visible oil, brown film, or tarry deposits was noted. General notes or scores were used to indicate the developmental stage of the eggs, following Outram (1955).

After examination, each kelp sample was placed into a precleaned glass jar. Each jar was rinsed three times with seawater drawn by teflon-sealed pump from 4 to 5 m depth in the middle of the bay being sampled. Enough seawater was added to cover one quarter of the kelp. Before sealing the jar lid, medical-grade oxygen was bubbled into each sample for 2 min. Oxygen was introduced into the sample again before shipping if there was more than a 12-hour delay between collection and shipping. The samples were placed into coolers with ice or Blue Ice. All samples were shipped by air along with chain-of-custody and sample log forms. Sample transport times were less than 48 h in 1989 and less than 24 h in 1990.

Laboratory Compositing and Subsampling of Eggs-on-Kelp Samples

Upon arrival of the samples at the Battelle/Marine Sciences Laboratory, Sequim Washington, temperature, dissolved oxygen, pH, and salinity were measured in each sample container. Field sample jars were then placed in a water bath for acclimation. Gentle aeration was provided during acclimation. Water-quality measurements (temperature, salinity, pH, and dissolved oxygen) were recorded each for day of acclimation.

Sample compositing was used to obtain large spatial coverage while reducing the time and costs associated with laboratory analyses (Strand et al. 1992). The eggs-on-kelp samples from each location were composited on the basis of transect position and tidal height of the sampling quadrats where herring spawn was found (Figure 8). Composites consisted of one or more kelp samples from a single sampling location. For compositing, three tidal zones were established as follows:

A   +1.23 m (+4 ft) to +0.031 m (+0.1 ft) MLLW
B   0 m (0 ft) to -2.43 m (-7.9 ft) MLLW
C   -2.46 m (-8 ft) to -6.15 m (-20 ft) MLLW.

The compositing strategy provided 6 samples (3 tidal zones × 2 pair of transects) from each sampling location. If any samples came from the field with low dissolved oxygen values, they were not composited with other samples but were processed as separate samples. In 1989, kelp samples were split into 2 portions (top and bottom of the kelp frond). Top portions of kelp fronds were composited with the top portions of other samples, and bottom portions with bottom portions. Because the results for top and bottom portions of kelp did not differ in 1989, such compositing was not performed in 1990.

Within 48 hours of beginning acclimation, each kelp sample to be composited was placed in a flowing water bath and subsampled for chemistry, egg incubation, and egg-density measurement. In 1989, the subsamples (25 cm^2 for density; minimum of 25 top-layer eggs for incubation, and minimum of 5 g for chemistry) were randomly drawn from the kelp area covered by herring eggs. In 1990, a sampling grid was used to measure the area of kelp and the area of kelp covered by eggs and to draw subsamples

(5 cm × 5 cm for density and incubation and minimum of 10 g for chemistry) at random (Figure 8). In compositing for incubation, pieces of kelp were randomly selected to provide at least 200 eggs per 1-L incubation jar. Subsamples were coded so that the observers and analysts did not know the sample origin.

Laboratory Incubation of Eggs-on-Kelp Samples

Kelp subsamples were placed into 1-L flow-through incubation jars that were then randomly positioned on flow-through water tables. Temperature, dissolved oxygen, pH, and salinity were monitored throughout incubation. Hatched larvae were removed daily for examination.

When daily inspections showed that no live eggs remained to hatch, the kelp and any loose eggs remaining in the incubation jar were removed and preserved for enumeration of unhatched eggs and empty egg cases. For 1990 incubation samples where fewer than 10 viable eggs remained to hatch and fungal infection was becoming evident, kelp and eggs were removed and preserved to prevent deterioration of the egg-density sample.

Examination of Hatched Larvae

Hatched larvae were examined daily for abnormalities under a dissecting microscope and sorted into primary and secondary categories. In 1989, the primary categories were Live and Dead. In 1990, the primary categories were Live, Moribund, and Dead. The secondary categories indicated normality or the type of abnormality.

In 1990, if a day's hatching produced too many larvae to process that day, the larvae were sorted into the primary categories and then fixed for subsequent detailed examination and sorting into the secondary categories. Fixation and preservation procedures included steps to ensure that all samples underwent the same preservation regimen.

Descriptions of larval abnormalities appearing in Galkina (1971), Linden (1978), Smith and Cameron (1979), and Pearson et al. (1985) were used to score individual larvae. Photographs and line drawings were used in the scoring process. The observers who scored larvae for scoliosis, swollen pericardial regions, and other abnormalities were trained with archived specimens using the following descriptions:

Normal—Normal larvae were fully developed with none of the conditions described below except that the yolk could have been depleted from the yolk sac.

Scoliosis—Larva had a lateral curvature of the spine. The diagnostic characteristic is irregularity of the notochord, including the notochord not being parallel with the body or the notochord having a bulge or constriction.

Swollen Pericardial Region—Larva had an enlargement of the area immediately anterior to the yolk sac and ventral and posterior to the heart.

Not Developed—Larva was not fully developed and was characterized by shortened body length, curled body sac, and a large yolk sac.

Yolk Depleted—Larva had a fully depleted yolk sac. The yolk sac was not detached from the body, but yolk was depleted from the yolk sac. Both normal and abnormal larvae may have this condition.

Damaged—A part of the larva was damaged or missing (e.g., yolk sac, tail section), impairing the observer's ability to distinguish normal from abnormal.

Abnormal Yolk Sac—Larva had deformities of the yolk sac, such as abnormally large or small and misshapen yolk sac, loss of compartmentalization, or discoloration (white or opaque yolk sacs).

Abnormal Pericardial Region—Larva had a pericardial region that was ruptured so that swollen and normal pericardial regions could not be distinguished.

Egg Density and Proportion of Developed Eggs and Empty Egg Cases

Eggs-on-kelp subsamples preserved both before and after incubation were examined under a dissecting microscope to measure egg density, proportion of developed eggs, and proportion of empty egg cases. Egg density was calculated as the number of eggs per cm^2.

Larval Length and Yolk-Sac Volume

The larval length and yolk-sac volume at hatching are general indicators of potential larval survival. A subsample of the preserved larvae without visible abnormalities was examined to measure these two characteristics. With an optical micrometer, the notochord length and two dimensions of the yolk sac were measured to the nearest 0.1 mm. Yolk-sac volume was calculated following Westernhagen and Rosenthal (1981).

Hydrocarbon Analyses

Procedures for determining concentrations of hydrocarbons in samples of water and eggs on kelp generally followed those developed for the *Exxon Valdez* Oil Spill Program (Page et al. this volume; Bence and Burns, this volume). Polycyclic aromatic hydrocarbons and heterocyclic hydrocarbons were determined by gas chromatography-mass spectrometry (GC-MS) with selected ion mode (SIM). The fingerprinting techniques of Page et al. (this volume) and Bence and Burns (this volume) were used to determine whether the hydrocarbon signatures in eggs-on-kelp samples were indicative of *Exxon Valdez* Crude (EVC).

Data Analysis

Results of the eggs-on-kelp study were analyzed to determine if there was a dose-response relationship between biological end points and concentrations of hydrocarbons in the eggs on kelp. For both years, end points with binomial response were as follows:

	1989	1990
Developed eggs as proportion of the eggs on the kelp	X	X
Hatched eggs as proportion of the eggs on the kelp		X
Empty egg cases as proportion of the eggs on the kelp	X	X
Dead larvae as proportion of those that hatched	X	X
Abnormal larvae as proportion of those that hatched alive	X	
Larvae with scoliosis as proportion of abnormal larvae	X	
Larvae with swollen pericardial regions as proportion of abnormal larvae	X	X
Larvae with abnormal yolk sacs as proportion of abnormal larvae	X	
Larvae with depleted yolk sacs as proportion of those hatched alive		X
Viable larvae, the live normal larvae as a proportion of the eggs on the kelp	X	X

Observed rates of success or failure at one stage of development were analyzed conditional to successful completion of a previous stage. For example, the proportion of abnormal larvae was based on the number of live larvae. Tests of significance on a later stage were therefore conditionally independent of results in previous stages. Empty egg cases as proportion of the eggs on the kelp was measured in both 1989 and 1990 and is one measure of hatching rate. In 1990, hatched eggs as the proportion of eggs on the kelp was determined by tracking all eggs and larvae in an incubation jar and is the better measure of hatch success. Analysis of the 1990 data indicated that the frequency of empty egg cases underestimates hatching rate by about 22.4% compared to the frequency of hatched eggs. The proportion of viable larvae is an overall indicator of the outcome of all the processes from embryonic development in the egg to being normal larvae on the first day after hatching. Because the proportion of viable larvae took into account all of the abnormalities observed and because the abnormalities tended to occur together, separate analyses for specific abnormalities were not performed in 1990.

The 2 continuous random variables analyzed were notochord length and yolk-sac volume measured for normal larvae in 1989. Because these variables proved to vary more with natural factors than with hydrocarbon burden, they were not measured in 1990.

The binomial response variables were analyzed using Generalized Linear Interactive Modelling [GLIM: Numerical Algorithms Group (1985)] based on a logit link function and binomial distribution for the error structure. Tests of dose response were based on analysis of deviance [ANODEV: McCullagh and Nelder (1983)] procedures and asymptotic F-tests. Continuous variables were log-transformed and analyzed assuming normally distributed error structure. For the 1989 data, the proportion of viable larvae was treated as a continuous variable and logit-transformed because the data were not in a form suitable for analysis by GLIM.

Hierarchical regression procedures were used to test the significance of hydrocarbon concentrations following inclusion of environmental and laboratory concomitant variables. Concomitant variables considered for inclusion in the analysis of both the 1989 and 1990 data included egg density and indicators for tidal zone. An indicator for top and bottom portions of kelp was included as a concomitant variable in 1989. Because there were generally no differences between top and bottom, kelp was not separated into two portions in 1990. Because the 1990 study included Sitka Sound, region was added as concomitant variable. Other concomitant variables in 1990 were indicators for thickness of egg deposition, minimum dissolved oxygen of sample upon arrival at the laboratory, maximum temperature of sample upon arrival at the laboratory, and difference in temperature between collection and arrival at the laboratory. The criterion for inclusion of concomitant variables was significance at $\propto = 0.05$, two-tailed. Interactions between region and hydrocarbon concentration and between tidal zone and hydrocarbon concentration were also included in the analysis.

Separate tests were conducted to assess the relationships between the biological end points and three chemical variables: total polycyclic aromatic hydrocarbons (PAH), total naphthalenes, and total phenanthrenes/anthracenes. This paper reports the results of the PAH analyses because the results for total naphthalenes and total phenanthrenes/anthracenes proved parallel to those for PAH. Tests of effects of hydrocarbon concentration were one-tailed at $\propto = 0.05$. In these analyses, eggs-on-kelp samples were considered independent experimental units assuming any observed effects of oiling would be directly related to the actual hydrocarbon concentrations measured in those tissues.

In another series of analyses with the 1990 data, the biological end points in three areas, PWS oiled, PWS reference, and Sitka Sound reference, were compared. Six spawning locations in each category served as replicates. Similar comparisons with the 1989 data were precluded by the unbalanced design (i.e., 6 oiled locations versus 1 or 2 reference locations). Analysis of deviance procedures were used to compare categories and construct contrasts between classifications. Separate analyses were conducted for each tidal zone because of unbalanced designs (i.e., not all tidal zones had spawn) and potential interactions between tidal zone and the oiled/reference category. Egg density was included as a concomitant variable. All tests were performed at $\propto = 0.05$.

RESULTS

Herring Spawning

The 1989 aerial survey by ADF&G observed herring spawn over 158 km (98.4 mi) of shoreline in PWS (Figure 4). In 1990, ADF&G used a fixed-wing aircraft to observe herring spawn over 151 km (94.1 mi) of shoreline in PWS. Our aerial survey, using a helicopter for 29 flying days in 1990, found herring spawn over 182 km (113.4

mi) of shoreline (Figure 5). The difference between ADF&G and our observations occurred in part because our survey included helicopter observations on several days during which fixed-wing aircraft were grounded due to weather conditions.

In addition to the aerial surveys, we examined spawn length by launch and spawn width along diver transects. In 1989, spawn length and mean width varied from 2.7 km by 31 m at Cabin Bay to 9.5 km by 56 m at Montague Point to Graveyard Point. Our 1990 launch reconnaissances found that spawn length in PWS varied from 225 m at Bass Harbor to 12 km at Fairmount Bay and Rocky Bay. Mean spawn width in 1990 varied from 33 m at Green Island to 105 m at Montague Point to Graveyard Point.

Spawning locations shifted somewhat between 1989 and 1990 (Figures 4 and 5). The Naked Island region received 22 km (13.7 mi) of spawn in 1989 (Brady et al. 1991) but only 8.4 km (5.2 mi) in 1990 (Brady et al. 1990). In 1989, spawn was not observed at Green and Smith islands, but our 1990 aerial survey found spawn along 12 km (7.4 mi) and 3.9 km (1.8 mi) at Green and Smith islands, respectively. Smith and Green islands had been oiled and then cleaned intensively in 1989. The Fairmount Bay region and the northern end of Montague Island were general regions of major spawning in both years.

Herring Spawn and Oiling

Analysis of 1989 shoreline surveys indicated that about 96% of the total spawn length in PWS occurred along shorelines with no oiling (Figure 4). Approximately 3% of the 1989 spawn length occurred along shorelines with oiling classifications of very light and light. Less than 1% of the 1989 spawn length occurred along shorelines with moderate to heavy oiling. In the moderately to heavily oiled Knight Island archipelago, ADF&G observed about 1 km (0.6 mi) of spawn in a shoal area northeast of Eleanor Island and around a small rocky island west of Ingot Island (Brady et al. 1991; Figure 4).

In 1990, approximately 90% of the total 1990 spawn length in PWS occurred along shorelines that received no oiling in 1989 (Figure 5). About 4% of the total 1990 spawn length occurred along shorelines in 4 locations that were moderately to heavily oiled in 1989. Naked Island, Montague Point, Green Island, and Smith Island had 0.19 (0.12), 0.60 (0.37), 3.9 (2.4), and 2.9 (1.8) km (mi) of spawn, respectively, along shorelines that were moderately or heavily oiled in 1989. About 32% of the 11.9 km (7.4 mi) of spawn miles at Green Island was along shoreline moderately or heavily oiled in 1989. All spawn length at Smith Island was along shoreline heavily oiled in 1989. The percentage of total PWS shoreline that was oiled decreased from 16.0% to 6.7% from 1989 to 1990 (Neff et al. this volume). Because of the combined effects of the cleanup program and winter storms in 1989 and 1990, the oil cover along the northeastern shoreline at Smith Island was substantially reduced in 1990. However, the upper intertidal and supratidal zones at Smith Island still had heavy oil cover in early 1990.

A worst case analysis of the overlap between 1989 spawn and oiled shorelines examined the extent of 1989 herring spawn along shorelines with any observation of oiling regardless of survey or year. This analysis accounts for slight interannual differences in survey coverage and for the observation of oiling in 1990 along beaches with no reported oiling in 1989. This worst case analysis found that 9% to 10% of the 1989 spawn length was along oiled shorelines.

Our diver and shore teams observed oil at 7 (3.8%) of the 182 quadrats examined in the oiled area in 1989. Oil was observed at transects in 4 locations: Cabin Bay (1 quadrat), Bass Harbor (2 quadrats), Outside Bay (1 quadrat), and Montague Point to Graveyard Point (3 quadrats). The only quadrats with both oil and spawn were those at Cabin Bay and Bass Harbor. All the quadrats where oil was observed were at or above -0.6 m (-2 ft) MLLW.

In 1989, shipboard examiners who were unaware of the diver observations found tarry deposits or brown film on eggs-on-kelp samples from the same 4 locations where divers had observed oil along transects:

	NUMBER OF SAMPLES			
LOCATION	Tarry Deposits	Brown Film	Confirmed EVC	Mean PAH in Eggs (ppb)
Bass Harbor	0	10	0	50.6
Cabin Bay	3	0	2	195.2
Montague/Graveyard Pt.	0	3	0	117.5
Outside Bay	0	3	1	127.5
Stockdale Harbor	0	0	0	27.9
Storey Island	0	0	0	71.7
Granite Bay	0	0	0	38.5
Jack Bay	0	0	0	61.6

Because diatoms and other epiphytic growth occur naturally on kelp, brown film on an egg-on-kelp sample may not always indicate the presence of oil. Most (62.5%) of the 16 samples with brown film came from quadrats at -0.6 and -1.8 m (-2 and -6 ft) MLLW.

In 1990, diver and shore teams observed no oil along the transects. At Smith Island, a supplemental beach survey in 1990 found oiling on and within the beach sediments in the high intertidal zone, well above the landward extent of herring spawn. In 1990, the shipboard examiners observed no oil or tarry deposits on any of the eggs-on-kelp samples.

Hydrocarbon Concentrations

Mean PAH concentrations in eggs on kelp from PWS in 1989 did not differ significantly between oiled and reference areas and (Figure 9a) were below 100 ppb within all tidal zones except at 3 locations: Montague Pt. to Graveyard Pt., Outside Bay, and Cabin Bay. Tidal Zone B of Cabin Bay had the highest mean PAH concentration in 1989. The eggs-on-kelp samples from Cabin Bay with high PAH concentrations (350 to 1000 ppb) were *Fucus* samples on which the field examiners had observed tarry deposits. Hydrocarbon fingerprinting techniques to identify the hydrocarbon source (Page et al. this volume; Bence and Burns, this volume) showed that 2 of the 1989 samples from

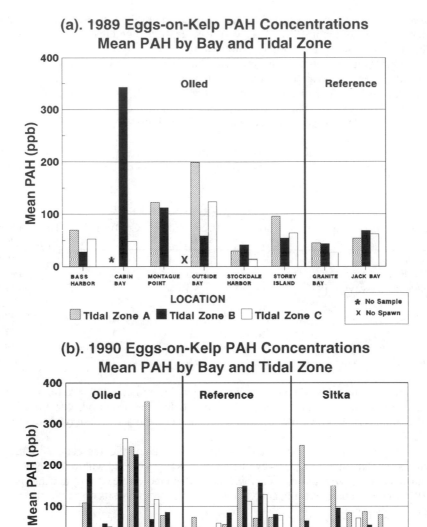

FIGURE 9—Concentrations of Polycyclic Aromatic Hydrocarbons (PAH) in 1989 (a) and 1990 (b) in eggs-on-kelp samples by tidal zone and location.

Cabin Bay with tarry deposits had signatures indicative of *Exxon Valdez* crude oil (EVC). The one other 1989 eggs-on-kelp sample with an EVC signature was from +2 ft MLLW in Outside Bay. No other samples were found with EVC signatures.

In 1990, PAH concentrations in egg-on-kelp samples did not differ among the three areas for Tidal Zones A and C but did for Tidal Zone B ($p = 0.027$). Concentrations above 100 ppb were found at Green Island, Peak Island, Point Pellew, Rocky Bay, Rocky Point, and Smith Island in PWS and Big Gavanski Island and Hot Springs Bay in Sitka Sound (Figure 9b). The 1990 PAH levels at Montague Point, the one location sampled in both years, were about half those observed in 1989. Fingerprinting analyses of a total of 157 samples from 1990 showed that only 2 samples indicative of weathered EVC, 12 samples indicated weathered Alaska North Slope crude oil and the remaining 142 were at background.had a signature

The water samples taken in 1989 at transect locations had low mean PAH concentrations ranging from 0.049 ppb at Outside Bay to 0.142 ppb at Montague Point to Graveyard Point.

Egg development, hatching, larval abnormalities, larval length, and yolk-sac volume

Mean proportions of developed eggs in 1989 ranged from 0.83 in Jack Bay to 0.98 in Bass Harbor. Multiple regression analysis revealed a significant relationship between the 1989 proportion of developed eggs and the PAH concentration in eggs-on-kelp samples (Table 1, Figure 10). The influential points in the relationship derive from Cabin Bay samples with tarry deposits (Figure 10). In 1990, the proportion of developed eggs ranged from 0.78 at Big Gavanski Island in Sitka Sound to 0.97 at Zaikof Bay in PWS. For 1990, multiple regression analysis revealed no significant relationship between the proportion of developed eggs and the PAH concentrations in eggs-on-kelp samples (Table 2).

For 1989 data, multiple regression analysis revealed no significant relationship between PAH concentrations in the eggs-on-kelp samples and the remaining response variables (Table 1). These 1989 variables include frequencies of empty egg cases, dead larvae, live larvae with scoliosis, larvae with abnormal yolk sacs, larvae with swollen pericardial regions, live abnormal larvae, and viable larvae as well as larval length and yolk-sac volume. Similarly, multiple regression analysis revealed no significant relationship between PAH concentrations in the eggs-on-kelp samples and all the 1990 biological response variables (Table 2).

Regional means of 1989 response variables averaged over tidal zones and locations are generally similar for PWS oiled and reference areas (Table 3). ANODEV analyses to compare oiled and reference areas were precluded by the unbalanced design and limited number of reference locations (1 or 2 depending on the variable).

The regional means of 1990 response variables averaged over all tidal zones and locations showed strikingly similar values for PWS and Sitka Sound (Table 4). The ANODEV to compare the response variables among the PWS Oiled, PWS Reference, and Sitka Sound Reference Areas (Table 5) revealed significant differences among the 3 areas for the frequency of hatched eggs in Tidal Zone A and the frequency of viable larvae in Tidal Zone A. In Tidal Zone A, Sitka Sound had both lower hatching rate and lower frequency of viable larvae than PWS Oiled. The ANODEV results for the pairwise comparisons (Table 5) showed no significant differences between PWS Oiled, PWS Reference, and Sitka Sound. In 1990, no effects related to hydrocarbon burden in eggs on kelp were seen. This lack of effect is observed for a dataset that includes locations such as Smith and Green islands that were heavily oiled in 1989.

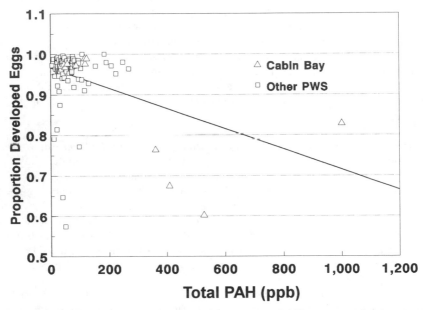

FIGURE 10—1989 proportion of developed eggs versus PAH concentration in eggs-on-kelp samples. Triangles indicate the Cabin Bay samples.

DISCUSSION

Concern about herring following the *Exxon Valdez* oil spill must ultimately center on potential injury to the PWS herring population. Elements in such concern include the actual degree of oil exposure, the potential injury to eggs in 1989 and 1990, and the fate of herring that were adults, juveniles, and eggs in 1989.

Potential Exposure of Herring Eggs to Oil

Although concern for potential exposure of herring eggs was initially great because of the uncertainties early in the spill about how much herring spawning occurred along oiled shorelines, the actual exposure of herring eggs proved quite low for several reasons. First, water-column concentrations of petroleum hydrocarbons did not approach toxic levels. Studies by Neff (1991) found that water-column concentrations of petroleum hydrocarbons in PWS peaked during April 1989, and then fell to background levels by August 1989. The peak in water-column concentrations

TABLE 1—*Results of multiple regression analyses between biological response variables and Polycyclic Aromatic Hydrocarbon (PAH) concentrations in eggs-on-kelp samples collected in 1989.*

| Biological Response Variable | Regression Results for PAH (a) | | | |
	P-Value	d.f.	Tails in Test	R^2 for Full Model
Developed Eggs	(e)	-	-	-
Tidal Zone A (b)	0.98	14	1	0.39
Tidal Zone B (c)	(e)			
Top	<0.0001	19	1	0.76
Bottom	0.0036	20	1	0.31
Tidal Zone C (d)	0.43	26	1	0.12
Empty Egg Cases	0.92	64	1	0.08
Dead Larvae	0.26	53	1	0.03
Larvae with Scoliosis	0.20	53	1	0.20
Larvae with Abnormal Yolk Sacs	0.58	48	1	0.21
Larvae with Swollen Pericardial Regions	0.95	48	1	0.25
Live Abnormal Larvae	0.39	52	1	0.22
Viable Larvae	0.58	47	1	0.01
Larval Length	0.45	10	2	0.16
Yolk-Sac Volume	0.98	10	2	0.10

(a) *P*-values are for PAH after adjustment for concomitant variables.
      P-Values of ≤0.05 are considered significant.
(b) Tidal Zone A +1.23 m (+4 ft) to +0.031 m (+0.1 ft) MLLW.
(c) Tidal Zone B 0 m (0 ft) to -2.43 m (-7.9 ft) MLLW.
(d) Tidal Zone C -2.46 m (-8 ft) to -6.15 m (-20 ft) MLLW.
(e) Significant interactions led to separate analyses for tidal zones and kelp portions (top and bottom).

TABLE 2—*Results of multiple regression analyses between biological response variables and Polycyclic Aromatic Hydrocarbon (PAH) concentrations in eggs-on-kelp samples collected in 1990.*

Biological Response Variable	Regression Results for PAH (a)		
	P-Value	d.f.	R^2 for Full Model
Developed Eggs	0.60	120	0.67
Hatched Eggs	0.48	122	0.25
Empty Egg Cases	0.35	122	0.42
Dead Larvae	0.83	120	0.34
Larvae with Depleted Yolk Sacs	0.84	121	0.39
Abnormal Larvae with Swollen Pericardial Regions	(b)	-	-
PWS	0.52	82	0.28
Sitka	0.99	31	0.30
Viable Larvae	0.63	122	0.18

(a)   *P*-Values are after adjustment for concomitant variables. All tests are one-tailed. *P*-Values of ≤0.05 are considered significant.

(b)   Significant interactions between geographic region and PAH concentration led to separate analyses for PWS and Sitka Sound.

TABLE 3—*Biological response variables for eggs-on-kelp samples from Prince William Sound, 1989.*

Mean Proportion

Biological Response Variable	PWS Oiled	PWS Reference	PWS All
Developed Eggs (a)	0.948	0.926	0.943
Empty Egg Cases (a)	0.462	0.658	0.501
Live (a)	0.551	0.358	0.458
Normal (b)	0.617	0.531	0.614

(a)   Proportion of total eggs.
(b)   Proportion of live larvae.

TABLE 4—*Biological response variables for eggs-on-kelp samples from Prince William Sound and Sitka Sound, 1990.*

Mean Proportion of Total Eggs

Biological Response Variable	PWS Oiled	PWS Reference	PWS All	Sitka Sound
Developed Eggs	0.938	0.891	0.899	0.893
Hatched Eggs	0.879	0.818	0.847	0.828
Larvae with Swollen Pericardial Regions	0.051	0.079	0.074	0.070
Viable Larvae	0.518	0.409	0.458	0.446

TABLE 5—*Results of ANODEV with concomitant variables for comparing biological response variables in herring eggs-on-kelp samples from Prince William Sound and Sitka Sound, 1990.*

Biological Response Variable	Tidal Zone	Proportion of Total Eggs			*P*-Value (a)
		PWS Oiled	PWS Reference	Sitka Sound	
Hatched	A (b)	0.93	0.82	0.82	0.01
Eggs	B	0.85	0.80	0.80	0.42
	C	0.89	0.86	0.93	0.25
Empty Egg	A	0.77	0.62	0.73	0.17
Cases	B	0.56	0.52	0.59	0.17
	C	0.72	0.68	0.75	0.94
Abnormal Larvae with	A	0.45	0.39	0.48	0.30
Swollen	B	0.42	0.38	0.47	0.51
Pericardial Regions	C	0.34	0.38	0.48	0.74
Viable	A (b)	0.60	0.39	0.45	0.002
Larvae	B	0.47	0.40	0.42	0.67
	C	0.53	0.48	0.52	0.85

(a)   Test assesses whether the means from all three areas are equal. All tests are two-tailed with d.f. = 2. *P*-Values ≤ 0.05 are considered significant.

(b)   Proportions of hatched eggs and viable larvae were not significantly different between PWS Oiled and PWS Reference and between PWS Oiled and Sitka Sound based on one-tailed tests. The one-tailed tests assume that an oiling effect would be evident as a decrease in proportion of hatched eggs or of viable larvae in PWS Oiled.

for 35 primary offshore stations within the spill trajectory averaged less than 2 ppb for volatile aromatic hydrocarbons (VOA) and about 0.2 ppb for PAH. For 51 shoreline monitoring stations, VOA water-column concentrations exceeded 5 ppb in less than 2% of the samples from March through October 1989. The highest VOA concentration (16 ppb) was observed in June 1989 for a surface water sample in Northwest Bay, a heavily oiled bay without herring spawn in the Knight Island archipelago.

The peak water-column concentrations found by Neff (1991) and Neff and Stubblefield (this volume) were about 100 to 1 000 times lower than levels known to be toxic to herring eggs. In a continuously flowing system, Pacific herring eggs taken from unexposed adults and directly exposed to the WSF of Cook Inlet crude oil had normal hatching rates after 2-day exposures to 5.3 ppm but decreased hatching rates after 12-day exposures above 1 ppm (Rice et al. 1986). Pacific herring eggs exposed for 24 hours to the WSF of Prudhoe Bay crude oil in a continuously flowing system did not show decreased hatching for exposures up to 4.7 ppm of monoaromatic hydrocarbons (Pearson et al. 1985). These studies indicate that the exposure of aromatic hydrocarbons in the water column that would affect hatching rate of herring eggs would be above 5 ppm for several days or above 1 ppm for about two weeks. Such levels were well above those observed in PWS even at the peak water column concentrations in 1989. McGurk (1992) also reports that, despite the initial concerns, herring eggs and larvae in PWS were not exposed to sufficiently high levels of hydrocarbons in the water column following the *Exxon Valdez* spill to affect their survival.

Second, claims of widespread exposure of herring spawn to oiling in 1989 (Biggs and Baker 1993) result from a focus on the gross features of the spill trajectory rather than on the distribution of oil in the 1989 spawning areas. In fact, there was little overlap between the 1989 oiled shorelines and locations of herring spawn. In 1989, about 3% of the herring spawn length occurred along very lightly oiled and lightly oiled shorelines (Figure 4), and less than 1% of the herring spawn length occurred in locations with moderately or heavily oiled shorelines (e.g., the northern end of the Knight Island archipelago; Figure 4). The 1989 occurrence of spawn in the Knight Island archipelago is a rare event historically. In 1988, 2.2 km (1.4 mi) or 0.8% of the total spawn length [268 km (166.3 mi)] was reported for Knight Island (Brady 1988). From 1978 to 1987, only 3.2 km (2.0 mi) of spawn in one year (1983) at Knight Island was observed (Brady 1987). Although Biggs and Baker (1993) reported that over 40% of the areas used by herring for staging, spawning, and depositing eggs, more recent estimates by Spies (1994) placed 5% to 10% of the PWS herring spawning habitat within the spill region. This more recent estimate is consistent with our worst case estimate of 9% to 10% of the 1989 spawn length occurring along oiled shorelines.

Third, direct, substantial oiling of herring eggs was not observed in 1989 or 1990. None of our field observations showed complete or even substantial coating of the eggs-on-kelp by oil. The samples with tarry deposits on *Fucus* derived from one transect at Cabin Bay and represented less than 4% of all the observations made during shipboard examination of eggs-on-kelp samples within the oiled area. The hydrocarbon concentrations in eggs-on-kelp samples parallel the field observations and do not indicate high levels of exposure.

Effects on Herring Eggs

The minor effects on herring eggs noted in 1989 were restricted to one location and a small percent of the samples. The four Cabin Bay eggs-on-kelp samples, which are influential in the relationship of decreased proportion of developed eggs with increasing PAH concentration, represent 4% of those analyzed for hydrocarbons in 1989. Spawn length in Cabin Bay represented less than 2% of total 1989 spawn length in PWS. The independent sets of observations, the diver observations, the field and laboratory examination of eggs-on-kelp samples, and the chemical analysis of the eggs-on-kelp samples, are all consistent in their results and indicate that the effects attributable to oil contamination are confined to a small percentage of eggs on kelp.

Currently available evidence does not indicate any failure of the 1989 year class, which was present as eggs during the *Exxon Valdez* spill. About 22% of the PWS herring recruit to the sac-roe fisheries at age 3, and 100% of the fish do not recruit until age 7 (Brannian 1989). From the historical trends (Figure 3), nondominant year classes comprise only a modest proportion of the fisheries, and only the dominant year classes that emerge every 4 years make up more than a small percentage of the sac-roe fishery when they are 3 years old. As expected, the strong 1988 year class has dominated the PWS fisheries since 1992. Therefore, the nondominant 1989 year class would be expected to constitute only a modest proportion of the 1992 fisheries, especially when at age 3 it is just beginning to enter the fisheries. The 1989 year class has constituted 1.3%, 2.6%, and 3.0% by number of the PWS age-class distribution in 1992, 1993, and 1994, respectively. The age-structured assessment (ASA) model of Funk (1994) for PWS herring indicates that initial year class strength of nondominant year classes ranged from 25 to 362 million fish from 1973 to 1993. Dominant year classes had initial year class strengths from 0.5 to over 1.5 billion fish. The initial cohort size of the 1989 year class was 83.8 million fish. The recruitment patterns of the 1989 year class are consistent with low exposure and minor effects from the 1989 oil spill.

Adult and Juvenile Herring

Early in the spill, concern focused on life stages other than adults because risk to adult herring was considered low. Potential for exposure of adult herring to oil is through the water column, and the levels at which water-column hydrocarbon concentrations become toxic to adult and larval herring are about 1 000 times higher than the peak concentrations in PWS during 1989. In continuously flowing exposure to the WSF of Cook Inlet crude oil, the 1.5 to 12 day median lethal concentrations (LC_{50}) are 2.2 ppm aromatic hydrocarbons for adult herring (Rice et al. 1987). Similarly, herring larvae with yolk sacs exposed to WSF of Cook Inlet crude oil have LC_{50} values of 2.8 and 2.3 ppm for exposures of 16 hours and 6 days, respectively (Rice et al. 1987). Also, the hatching rate of eggs taken from adult herring exposed to WSF of Cook Inlet crude oil is not affected for exposures at 1.6 ppm WSF for both 2 and 12 days (Rice et al. 1987). Because the peak water-column concentrations of hydrocarbons (Neff 1991; Neff and Stubblefield, this volume) did not approach toxic levels for adult and larval herring, effects on adult and larval herring would be low to nonexistent for this route of exposure.

Another potential route of exposure is through ingestion of oil droplets or oil-contaminated prey. Although we know of no studies on oil-contaminated prey and adult herring, laboratory studies by Carls (1987) found that highly contaminated prey (6 ppm of crude oil) affected survival but not swimming behavior, feeding, or growth of herring larvae. The water-column concentrations necessary to produce prey contaminated at 6 ppm are high enough to be directly lethal to herring larvae. The rapid depuration of hydrocarbons by zooplankton coupled with Carls (1987) findings indicate that ingestion of oil-contaminated prey would not be a major route by which spilled oil affects herring larvae. The low levels of hydrocarbons in the water column measured by Neff et al. (this volume) and by Short and Rounds (1993) included oil as droplets and bound to particulates so that direct ingestion of oil droplets by herring larvae would have been low and brief as a possible route of exposure.

Events following the spill confirm that the risk to the adult and juvenile herring during the spill was low. Year class strength is an important indicator of what happened to fish that were adults and juveniles in 1989. The PWS herring fisheries are dominated by one age class every 4 or 5 years (Figure 3). The 1984 year class dominated the fishery before, during, and after 1989 (Figure 3) and primarily supported record harvests in 1990 and 1991 (Figure 1). The 1988 year class, which is composed of fish that were 1 year old during the spill, now dominates the fishery and contributed to the 1992 record harvest in PWS (Figure 3). The continued strength of the 1984 year class, the expected emergence of a strong 1988 year class, and the record postspill harvests all provide evidence for no large-scale effects of the oil spill on the level of spawning biomass.

Other Studies

The minor extent of effects are consistent with those expected from the 1989 exposure levels and the results of other previous studies. Laboratory studies indicate that effects on herring eggs from oil exposure usually take the form of increased rates of larval abnormalities and premature hatch rather than decreased hatching rate or fertilization rate. Pearson et al. (1985) found no effect on fertilization rate or hatching rate for 24-hour continuously flowing exposures up to 28 ppm total hydrocarbons measured by infrared (IR) spectrophotometry and up to 4.7 ppm of monoaromatic hydrocarbons measured by helium equilibration gas chromatography. Rice et al. (1986) found that Pacific herring eggs exposed to the WSF of Cook Inlet crude oil had normal hatching rates for 2-day exposures but decreased hatching rates for 12-day exposures above 1 ppm.

Premature hatch in laboratory exposed eggs has been noted by Pearson et al. (1985) above 0.22 ppm measured by IR in continuously flowing exposure to fresh oil and by Kocan, Hose, and Biggs (1993) above 0.24 ppm in static renewal exposures with WSF. McGurk (1992) observed premature hatch by 1 to 2 days for herring eggs collected from potentially oiled areas in PWS, but interpretation of his finding is confounded by uncertainties about when his field collected eggs were fertilized and by temperature differences between his reference and oiled areas.

The previous study by Pearson et al. (1985) indicated that oil adhering to eggs is the major mechanism for inducing increased levels of larval abnormalities and other effects. In a series of experimental treatments, Pearson et al. (1985) found that water-column concentrations up to 4.7 ppm monoaromatic hydrocarbons and 28 ppm total hydrocarbons do not produce significantly higher frequencies of abnormal larvae unless oil visibly adheres to the eggs. For static renewal exposures of eggs to the WSF of Prudhoe Bay crude oil continuing over the incubation period, Kocan, Hose, and Biggs (1993) report that the 18-day median effective concentration (EC_{50}) for induction of larval abnormalities is 0.43 ppm. The water-column concentrations in PWS during April 1989 included both dissolved and particulate hydrocarbons and were about 200 times lower than the EC_{50} value determined by Kocan, Hose, and Biggs (1993).

Our results are consistent with other laboratory study results. In 1989, herring eggs generally received little or no exposure to oil, and effects were found only where oil had adhered to eggs on kelp and elevated hydrocarbon burdens were directly measured in the eggs-on-kelp samples. McGurk's (1992) independent study of PWS herring eggs and larvae in 1989 reached similar conclusions of no discernible effects because of insufficient level of exposure.

The 1989 Fishery Closure

Concern for herring resource effects from the spill caused ADF&G to close the 1989 sac-roe and roe-on-kelp fisheries. This closure had the effect of increasing the spawning biomass in subsequent years. In managing the PWS herring fisheries, ADF&G establishes an annual harvest allocation for the five fisheries that is not to exceed the maximum of 20% of the estimated total biomass. The PWS herring spawning biomass forecasted for 1989 was 54 899 st, of which a total of 10 980 st was allocated to the five fisheries (Brannian 1989). The 1989 sac-roe and roe-on-kelp fisheries had been allocated 9 580 st (10 562 mt) or about 17.5% of the spawning biomass. The 1989 bait fishery had an allocation of 1 400 st (1 543 mt), but only 646 st (712 mt) were harvested in November 1989 (Brady et al. 1990). With the 1989 spring fisheries closed and only a small harvest from the bait fishery, 10 334 st (11 394 mt) that normally would have been harvested were not harvested. One year after the spill (1990), annual total landings from all five PWS herring fisheries were above average with 13 098 st (14 441 mt) landed. The harvests in 1991 and 1992 [20 315 st (22 398 mt) and 25 140 st (27 718 mt), respectively] were the highest recorded in PWS since 1969, when the roe fisheries began. The previous post-1969 record for annual PWS herring landings was 15 878 st (17 506 mt) in 1981.

The 1989 fisheries closure allowed about 18% more spawning biomass to remain in the PWS herring population. The ADF&G has used a harvest model to forecast the herring biomass for the upcoming year (Brannian 1989). Comparison of harvest model runs assuming that the allocations for 1989 were taken and not taken (Figure 11) indicates that the effect of the 1989 closure was to pass about 8 773 st (9 672 mt) of herring to the 1990 spawning biomass. Because herring spawn over 8 to 10 years, the effects of the 1989 closure will extend until the strong 1984 year class fades from the spawning population, about 5 to 7 years after the 1989 closure. The combination of the increase in spawning population resulting from not removing about 18% of the herring biomass in 1989 and the long spawning life of herring would compensate for the loss of a few percentage of one year's egg deposition. The record high biomass in 1991 and 1992 resulted from the strong recruitment of the 1988 year class that was not subject to the fishery in 1989. It did not result from the 18% of the total biomass not harvested in 1989.

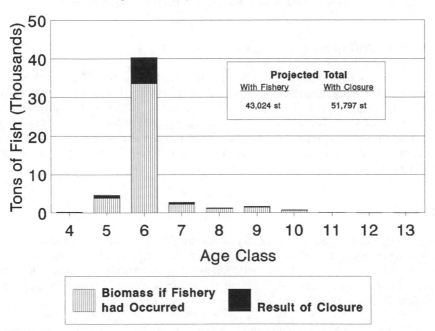

FIGURE 11—*Comparison of forecasts of 1990 herring biomass using ADF&G harvest model (Brannian 1989) assuming no sac-roe and no roe-on-kelp fisheries in 1989 vs. assuming the full 1989 allocations for the sac-roe and roe-on-kelp fisheries were harvested.*

CONCLUSIONS

Because less than 1% of 1989 herring spawning occurred along moderately and heavily oiled shorelines and because of the low (ppb) concentrations of hydrocarbons in the water column, the 1989 exposure of herring eggs on kelp to hydrocarbons was low. Minor effects were found in 1989 at one location where oil had adhered to eggs on kelp, and no effects were observed in 1990. Our 1989 and 1990 data indicate that the minor effects were restricted to less than 2% of the 1989 herring spawn length. The harvests and year class distributions in post spill years are consistent with our findings of little or no effects. The 1991 and 1992 sac-roe harvests in PWS established new records. The 1988 year class showed strong recruitment in 1991 and 1992. The minor effects observed in 1989 did not translate into decreases in the PWS herring population.

ACKNOWLEDGMENTS

We thank Dames & Moore for logistic and technical support. For their key scientific and technical contributions, we thank the following Battelle personnel. R. W. Bienert, B. J. Higgins, V. I. Cullinan, D. K. Nyogi, and M. R. Pinza. The scientific contributions of W. A. Laroche of Stonefish Environmental and Taxonomic Services is also gratefully acknowledged. To the more than 50 technical and other support personnel whose cooperative spirit and hard work were essential in completing this project, we give great thanks.

REFERENCES

Biggs, E. D. and T. T. Baker. "Summary of Known Effects of the *Exxon Valdez* Oil Spill on Herring in Prince William Sound and Recommendations for Future Inquiries." *Abstract Book for the* Exxon Valdez *Oil Spill Symposium.* Anchorage, Alaska: *Exxon Valdez* Oil Spill Trustee Council, University of Alaska Sea Grant College Program, and American Fisheries Society, Alaska Chapter; 264-268. 1993.

Brady, J. A. "Distribution, Timing and Relative Biomass Indices for Pacific Herring as Determined by Aerial Surveys in Prince William Sound 1978 to 1987." Prince William Sound Data Report No. 87-14, Alaska Department of Fish and Game, Juneau, Alaska. 38 p. 1987.

Brady, J. A. "Review of Prince William Sound Area Commercial Herring Fisheries, 1988." Regional Information Report No. 2C88-10, Alaska Department of Fish and Game, Anchorage, Alaska. 22 p. 1988.

Brady, J. A., E. D. Biggs, S. Morstad, and E. Simpson. "Review of the Prince William Sound Area Commercial Fisheries, 1990." Regional Information Report No. 2C90-09, Alaska Department of Fish and Game, Anchorage, Alaska. 31 p. 1990.

Brady, J. A., S. Morstad, E. Simpson, and E. D. Biggs. "Prince William Sound Area Annual Finfish Management Report, 1989" Regional Information Report No. 2C90-07, Alaska Department of Fish and Game, Cordova, Alaska. 186 p. 1991.

Brannian, L. K. "Forecast of the Pacific Herring Biomass in Prince William Sound, 1989." Regional Information Report No. 2A89-01, Alaska Department of Fish and Game, Anchorage, Alaska. 26 p. 1989.

Carls, M. "Effects of Dietary and Water-borne Oil Exposure on Larval Pacific Herring (*Clupea harengus pallasi*)." *Marine Environmental Research.* 22:253-270; 1987.

Donaldson, W., S. Morstad, E., Simpson, J. Wilcock, and S. Sharr. 1993. "Prince William Sound Management Area 1992 Annual Finfish Management Report." Alaska Department of Fish and Game, Regional Information Report No. 2A93-12.

Funk, F. "Forecast of the Pacific Herring Biomass in Prince William Sound, Alaska, 1993." Regional Information Report No. 5J94-04, Alaska Department of Fish and Game, Juneau, Alaska, 40 p. 1994.

Funk, F. and H. Savikko. "Preliminary Forecasts of Catch and Stock Abundance for 1990 Alaska Herring Fisheries." Regional Information Report No. 5J90-02, Alaska Department of Fish and Game, Juneau, Alaska. 92 p. 1990.

Galkina, L. A. "Survival of Herring Eggs and Larvae on the White Sea Spawning Grounds during a Period of Massive Spawning." *Voprosy Ikhtiologii.* 8:544-551; 1968.

Galkina, L. A. "Survival of Spawn of Pacific Herring (*Clupea harengus pallasi* Val.) Related to the Abundance of the Spawning Stock." *Rapports et Procès-Verbaux des Réunions, Conseil International pour l'Exploration de la Mer.* 160:30-33; 1971.

Hay, D. E. "Reproductive Biology of Pacific Herring *(Clupea harengus pallasi)*." *Canadian Journal of Fisheries and Aquatic Sciences.* 42 (suppl. 1): 111-126; 1985.

Kocan, R. M., J. E. Hose, and E. Biggs. "Herring Embyro Stage Sensitivity to Water Soluble Fraction of Prudhoe Bay Crude Oil." *Abstract Book for the* Exxon Valdez *Oil Spill Symposium.* Anchorage, Alaska: *Exxon Valdez* Oil Spill Trustee Council, University of Alaska Sea Grant College Program, and Amercian Fisheries Society, Alaska Chapter; 250-253. 1993.

Koons, C. B. and H. O. Jahns. "The Fate of Oil from the Exxon -- A Perspective." Marine Technology Society Journal. 26:61-69; 1992.

Linden, O. "Biological Effects of Oil on Early Development of the Baltic Herring *Clupea harengus membras.*" *Marine Biology.* 45:273-283; 1978.

McCullagh P. and J.A. Nelder. *Generalized Linear Models.* New York: Chapman and Hall; 261 pp. 1983.

McGurk, M. "Petroleum Effects on Herring Eggs and Larvae in Prince William Sound, Alaska, 1989." *Conference Proceedings of the Fourth Information Transfer Meeting, Alaska OCS Region.* Anchorage, Alaska: U.S. Department of the Interior, Minerals Management Service, Alaska OCS Region, OCS Study MMS 92-0046; 119-124 and 128-130. 1992.

NRC. *Oil in the Sea: Sources, Fates, and Effects.* National Academy Press, Washington, D. C.; 1985.

Neff, J. M. *Water Quality in Prince William Sound and the Gulf of Alaska.* Cambridge, Massachusetts: Arthur D. Little; 37 p. 1991.

Numerical Algorithms Group. *The GLIM System Manual, Release 3.77.* Downers Grove, Illinois: Numerical Algorithms Group Inc.; 1985.

Outram, D. N. "The Development of the Pacific Herring Egg and its Use in Estimating Age of Spawn." Circular No. 40. Pacific Biological Station, Nanaimo, British Columbia. 13 p. 1955.

Pearson, W. H., D. L. Woodruff, S. L. Kiesser, G. W. Fellingham, and R. A. Elston. "Oil Effects on Spawning Behavior and Reproduction in Pacific Herring (*Clupea harengus pallasi*)." API Publication No. 4412, American Petroleum Institute, Washington, D.C.; 105 p. 1985.

Rice, S. D., M. M. Babcock, C. C. Brodersen, M. G. Carls, J. A. Gharret, S. Korn, A. Moles, and J. W. Short. "Lethal and Sublethal Effects of the Water-Soluble Fraction of Cook Inlet Crude Oil on Pacific Herring (*Clupea harengus pallasi*) Reproduction." In: Outer Continental Shelf Environmental Assessment Program. Final Reports of Principal Investigators. U.S. Department of Commerce, National Oceanographic and Atmospheric Administration, and U.S. Department of the Interior, Minerals Management Service, Anchorage, Alaska; 423-490. 1986.

Rice, S. D., M. M. Babcock, C. C. Brodersen, J. A. Gharret, and S. Korn. "Uptake and Depuration of Aromatic Hydrocarbons by Reproductively Ripe Pacific Herring and the Subsequent Effect of Residues on Egg Hatching and Survival." In: *Pollution Physiology of Estuarine Organisms.* W. B. Vernberg, A. Calabrese, F. P. Thurberg, and J. F. Vernberg (eds.); Columbia, South Carolina: University of South Carolina Press; 139-154. 1987.

Short, J. W. and P. Rounds. "Determination of Petroleum-Derived Hydrocarbons in Seawater Following the *Exxon Valdez* Oil Spill I: Analysis of Seawater Extracts." *Abstract Book for the* Exxon Valdez *Oil Spill Symposium.* Anchorage, Alaska: *Exxon Valdez* Oil Spill Trustee Council, University of Alaska Sea Grant College Program, and American Fisheries Society, Alaska Chapter; 57-59. 1993.

Smith, R. L. and J. A. Cameron. "Effect of Water Soluble Fraction of Prudhoe Bay Crude Oil on Embryonic Development of Pacific Herring." *Transactions of the American Fisheries Society.* 108:70-75; 1979.

Spies, R. "Summary of Injuries," *Five Years Later: 1994 Status Report on the Exxon Valdez Oil Spill.* Exxon Valdez Trustee Council, Anchorage, Alaska, pp 7-17. 1994.

Strand, J. A., V. I. Cullinan, E. A. Crecelius, T. J. Fortman, R. J. Citterman, and M. L. Fleischmann. "Fate of Bunker C Fuel Oil in Washington Coastal Habitats Following the December 1988 *Nestucca* Oil Spill." *Northwest Science.* 66:1-14; 1992.

Struhsaker, J. W. "Effects of Benzene (a Toxic Component of Petroleum) on Spawning Pacific Herring, *Clupea harengus pallasi.*" *Fishery Bulletin. (U.S.)* 75:43-49; 1977.

Struhsaker, J. W., M. B. Eldridge, and T. Escheverria. "Effects of Benzene (a Water Soluble Component of Crude Oil) on Eggs and Larvae of Pacific Herring and Northern Anchovy." In: *Pollution and Physiology of Marine Organisms.* F. J. Vernberg and W. Vernberg (eds.); New York: Academic Press; 253-284. 1974.

Vourinen, P. and M. B. Axell. "Effects of the Water Soluble Fraction of Crude Oil on Herring Eggs and Pike Fry." *Conseil International pour l'Exploration de la Mer Meeting* E:30:1-10. 1980.

Westernhagen, H. v., and H. Rosenthal. "On Condition Factor Measurements in Pacific Herring Larvae." *Helgoländer Meeresuntersuchungen.* 34:257-262; 1981.

Impact Assessment for Wildlife

W.A. Stubblefield[1], G.A. Hancock[2], W.H. Ford[3], H.H. Prince[4] and R.K. Ringer[5]

EVALUATION OF THE TOXIC PROPERTIES OF NATURALLY
WEATHERED *EXXON VALDEZ* CRUDE OIL TO SURROGATE WILDLIFE
SPECIES

Reference: Stubblefield, W.A., Hancock, G.A., Ford, W.H., Prince, H. H., and
Ringer, R.K., "**Evaluation of the Toxic Properties of Naturally Weathered
EXXON VALDEZ Crude Oil to Surrogate Wildlife Species**," Exxon Valdez Oil
Spill: Fate and Effects in Alaskan Waters, ASTM STP 1219, Peter G. Wells,
James N. Butler, and Jane S. Hughes, Eds., American Society for Testing and
Materials, Philadelphia, 1995.

ABSTRACT: The toxic properties of naturally weathered *Exxon Valdez* crude oil
(WEVC) to avian and mammalian wildlife species were evaluated using the
surrogate species, mallard duck, *Anas platyrhynchos*, and European ferret,
Mustela putorius. This study was conducted to evaluate the potential for toxic
(rather than physical) injury to wildlife species that may have been exposed to
WEVC, either through external contact or through dietary uptake. Previous
studies have assessed the toxicity of unweathered crude oils, including Alaskan
North Slope Crude, but little information exists regarding the toxicity of a
naturally weathered crude oil, typical of that encountered following a spill.

A battery of laboratory toxicity tests was conducted, in compliance with
standard and published test procedures, to evaluate acute and subchronic toxicity
of WEVC. These included tests of food avoidance, reproductive effects, and
direct eggshell application toxicity. Naturally weathered EVC, recovered
postspill from Prince William Sound, was used as the test material. No
treatment-related mortalities or gross signs of toxicity were noted in ducks at oral
doses of 5 000 mg/kg body weight or at dietary concentrations up to 100 000 ppm
(mg WEVC/kg diet), or in ferrets at oral doses up to 5 000 mg/kg body weight.
Test animals did not avoid oil-contaminated food. No significant adverse effects
were noted in birds fed diets containing up to 2 000 mg WEVC/kg diet in the
reproductive toxicity test. However, significant reductions in mean eggshell
thickness and strength were observed in birds fed 20 000 mg WEVC/kg diets.
Applications of up to 92 mg/egg of WEVC to developing eggs produced no toxic

---

[1] ENSR Consulting and Engineering, 4413 West LaPorte Ave., Ft. Collins, CO 80521.
[2] Miles, Inc., 17745 South Metcalf Ave., Stilwell, KS, 66085
[3] Utah Biomedical Test Laboratory, 520 Wakara Way, Salt Lake City, UT 84108
[4] Michigan State University, Department of Fisheries and Wildlife, East Lansing, MI 48824
[5] Michigan State University, Department of Animal Science and Institute for Environmental
     Toxicology, East Lansing, MI 48824

effects.

Feeding weathered EVC to ducks and ferrets at oral doses or dietary concentrations exceeding those representing maximum likely field exposures from heavily affected spill areas did not significantly affect survival, growth, or reproduction. These results suggest that naturally weathered EVC posed little toxic risk to wildlife consuming oil or oiled food items following the *Exxon Valdez* spill, particularly considering the environmental exposure conditions that existed in the spill-affected area after 1989.

KEYWORDS: *Exxon Valdez*, Prince William Sound, avian, toxicity, mallard, ferret, weathered crude oil, reproduction

INTRODUCTION

The grounding of the *Exxon Valdez* on 24 March 1989, resulted in the discharge of approximately 10.8 million gal (41 million L) of Alaskan North Slope crude oil into the waters of Prince William Sound, Alaska. The spill occurred on Bligh Reef, located in the northeastern portion of the sound. Driven by winds and currents, the slick reached shorelines in western Prince William Sound (PWS), and in the following weeks, shorelines along the Kenai and Alaska Peninsulas, and Kodiak Island (Figure 1). Approximately 16% of the estimated 3 000 miles (4 800 km) of shorelines in PWS received some degree of oiling; about 5% of the shores were considered moderately to heavily oiled (Figure 2) (Neff et al., this volume). Outside of PWS in the Kenai-Kodiak region, oil reached approximately 14% of the 6 000 miles (9 600 km) of shorelines; about 2% (192 km) of these shores were considered moderately to heavily oiled.

Some of the largest populations of marine birds and mammals in North America reside in or migrate through Prince William Sound and the northern Gulf of Alaska. Avian species commonly found in the area include cormorants, kittiwakes, murres, puffins, loons, grebes, and a variety of sea ducks. At the time of the *Exxon Valdez* spill, an estimated 283 000 to 370 000 marine birds were at high risk in the spill-affected area (Piatt et al., 1990). In addition, substantial populations of marine mammals (e.g., sea otters) reside in this same general area. It is not surprising, therefore, that there was a great deal of concern regarding the potential effects of the oil on these wildlife species.

Physical oiling often results in the loss of the insulative properties of the feathers and fur of wildlife (Hartung, 1967; Davis et al., 1988); this can lead to hypothermia, stress, starvation, and can ultimately result in the death of an animal. Consequently, those animals that spend a majority of their time on the sea surface are at greatest risk in any oil spill. Approximately 35 000 bird and 1 000 sea otter carcasses were recovered following the *Exxon Valdez* spill (Piatt et al., 1990). The majority of the avian mortalities occurred among the alcids (e.g., common murres); however, populations of non-alcid species, such as the harlequin duck, bald eagle, and pelagic cormorant, also suffered substantial mortalities.

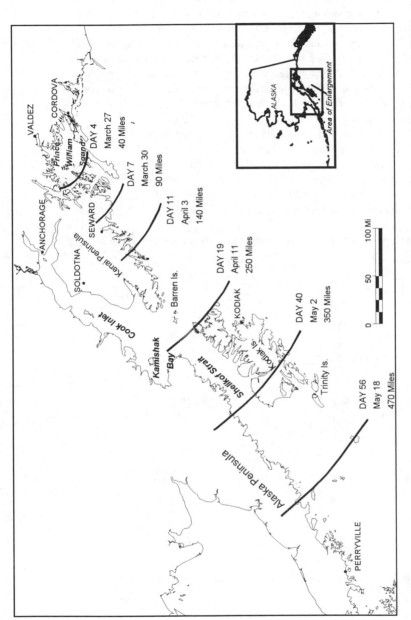

Figure 1. Map showing the entire Exxon Valdez spill-affected area, including western Prince William Sound (PWS), the outer Kenai Peninsula, Kodiak Island, and the Alaska Peninsula. Movement of the spill toward the southwest with time is illustrated by the dated contours emanating from the accident site at Bligh reef in north-central PWS. (Neff et al., this volume).

There is no doubt that the physical effects of oiling resulted in the deaths of many individuals of these species in the first months immediately following the spill. However, the potential for direct oiling decreased during the summer and fall of 1989, as evidenced by the number of oiled birds (Piatt et al., 1990) and number and degree of oiling observed on sea otter carcasses recovered (Osborn and Williams 1990). As a result of shoreline cleaning efforts and natural recovery processes in 1989, the potential for physical oiling was no longer a major concern by the winter of 1989 (Neff et al., this volume); future risks to wildlife were likely to occur through consumption of oil-contaminated food items.

A substantial body of literature exists regarding the effects of crude oils on wildlife, and a number of reviews have been published (Szaro, 1977; Leighton, 1982). Little information, however, is available regarding the toxicological properties of naturally-weathered crude oils. To address these concerns, a testing program was designed to assess the toxicological properties of weathered *Exxon Valdez* crude oil (WEVC) representative of the oil found on oiled shorelines after the spill.

Laboratory toxicity tests were conducted with surrogate wildlife species,

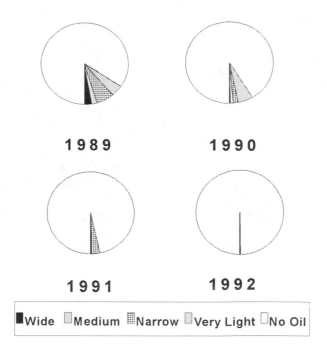

Figure 2. Surface oiling in the spill-affected area of Prince William Sound by year, 1989 through 1992. (Neff et al., this volume).

i.e., mallard (*Anas platyrhynchos*) and European ferret (*Mustela putorius*). Although not common to Prince William Sound, these organisms are considered appropriate surrogates for evaluating the toxicity of materials to other avian and mammalian species (USEPA 1982a). Ideally, in order to eliminate potential species sensitivity differences as a factor affecting conclusions about impacts to exposed populations, test data should be available for all "site species at risk" (i.e., Prince William Sound resident species). Practically, however, due to physical and legal limitations, it is not possible to conduct testing with these species. Therefore, potential differences in species sensitivity is an area of uncertainty that must be considered using best professional judgment in evaluating environmental impacts.

Study results provide information about potential effects resulting from short-term (acute) and long-term (chronic) exposures to WEVC when ingested directly, as would be expected in typical preening or grooming behavior, or as a dietary contaminant. Results from these studies were subsequently used to assess the toxic effects to wildlife in the context of environmental conditions prevailing in 1990 and beyond. The studies conducted followed standard or published methods in order to allow comparison to published data. Studies were not intended to directly model the acute exposure conditions existing in Prince William Sound during the few weeks immediately following the spill. However, the studies do serve as a basis for assessment of risks to wildlife from longer-term environmental exposures to WEVC.

MATERIALS AND METHODS

We focused on the potential effects of WEVC to exposed wildlife under the conditions prevailing at the time of the spill and during the ensuing postspill recovery period. Our laboratory test procedures and results are presented summarily in this paper; details of laboratory procedures and test results are in Stubblefield, et al., 1995a, b.

Weathered Exxon Valdez Crude Oil Sample

The test sample used in conducting the reported studies was a single sample taken from an oil-holding barge (Barge 251, Hold #3) in Seward, Alaska, on 1 July 1989, some 98 days following the *Exxon Valdez* spill. This barge had served as a reservoir vessel for oil skimming operations in the vicinity of Knight Island and lower Prince William Sound during the period immediately after the spill. The test material was a composite of recovered oils that had been skimmed from PWS and, therefore, had undergone a range of natural weathering processes. Physically the oil was a brown, viscous material having a consistency similar to that of chocolate pudding. Two 38-L, stainless steel drums were filled with the weathered oil, and any remaining headspace purged with nitrogen. Before and during testing, the weathered crude oil sample was maintained under a nitrogen atmosphere and refrigeration (<4°C). Analytical characterizations conducted prior to and at the completion of the testing program indicated that the test material remained chemically and physically stable throughout the testing period.

Subsamples of the test material were taken in July 1989 and analyzed for saturated and aromatic hydrocarbon content (Sauer and Boehm, 1991). Water content of the weathered oil sample was determined gravimetrically using solvent extraction and centrifugation. It was determined to be 7 to 8% by weight, suggesting that the oil had not undergone a great deal of mousse (water in oil emulsion) formation. Figure 3 presents the results of these analyses and contrasts them with the characterization of the unweathered cargo oil obtained directly from the *Exxon Valdez* and samples of oil obtained on shorelines in 1989 and 1990 (Bence and Burns, this volume). The test material had lost an appreciable amount of its $<C_{17}$ saturates and 2-ring aromatic content, indicating that it was slightly to moderately weathered (Boehm et al., 1987). However, it generally contained concentrations of the more biologically active polycyclic aromatic hydrocarbon (PAH) compounds similar to those found in the samples taken from shorelines in 1989. Thus, the tests were conducted with a sample representative of the oil found on shorelines at that time.

Test Procedures

A battery of seven acute and chronic toxicity tests were used to evaluate the toxicity of WEVC to surrogate wildlife species (mallard and ferret). The test battery was comprehensive and exceeded base testing requirements for USEPA pesticide registration (USEPA, 1982b). When available, standard test procedures, i.e., USEPA, OECD, or ASTM, were employed. When standard procedures were not available, test methods were patterned after those described in the peer-reviewed literature.

Specific test procedures and parameters evaluated in each of the toxicity tests are provided in Tables 1, 2 and 3. Doses/dietary exposure concentrations were selected either to bracket concentrations previously reported in the literature to elicit toxic effects with other crude oils, or were based on the maximum experimental doses recommended in the applicable standard test procedure. Each of the individual tests, the testing method used, and their utility in evaluating effects on spill-exposed animals are briefly described here.

Oral Toxicity Tests

Mallard acute oral toxicity--The selected procedures were designed to evaluate the acute oral toxicity of WEVC to birds when presented as a single large oral dose. This simulated the exposures encountered by birds ingesting oil as a result of preening behavior early in a spill episode. Study endpoints were survival and grossly observable signs of toxicity (e.g., lethargy, diarrhea). Test methods followed USEPA standard procedures (USEPA, 1985a).

Ferret acute oral toxicity--Procedures were designed to evaluate the toxicity of WEVC when presented as a large oral dose given daily over a 5-day period to simulate exposures from grooming of fur or eating oil-contaminated food. This test evaluated a number of secondary endpoints, e.g., blood parameters (Table 2 and 3), histopathological changes, as well as survival, and body weight change, among others. Test procedures were derived from standard ones used in conducting mammalian subacute toxicity tests (OECD, 1981).

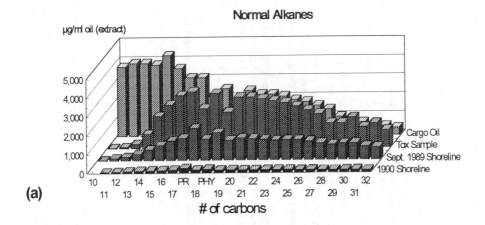

(a)

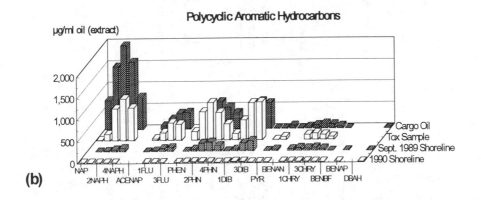

(b)

Figure 3. Plots of the normal alkane (PHC) (a) and polycyclic aromatic (PAH) (b) hydrocarbon distributions in samples of **Exxon Valdez** *cargo oil taken through time, illustrating characteristic compositional changes as the spilled oil weathered. "Cargo oil" is the unweathered cargo oil collected on board the* **Exxon Valdez** *immediately following spill in March 1989. "Tox Sample" illustrates the composition of test material collected in July 1989 and used in these studies. Samples of oil residues collected on shorelines in 1990 and 1991 illustrate the continuing effects of weathering and degradation on oil remaining in the environment.*

Table 1. Test procedures and parameters used for the mallard (*Anas platyrhynchos*) and ferret (*Mustela putorius*) toxicity tests with weathered *Exxon Valdez* crude oil (WEVC).

Test Type	Test Procedures	Test Parameters
Mallard Acute Oral Toxicity	16-wk old ducks were administered undiluted WEVC in gelatin capsules containing a dose of 5,000 mg WEVC/kg body weight; negative control group ducks received 5 empty gelatin capsules.	Signs of toxicity and mortality were recorded twice daily. Individual body weights were recorded for birds at test initiation, on day 7, and at test termination (day 14); food consumption was recorded daily (by cage) during the 14-day observation period.
Mallard Subacute Dietary Toxicity	Two groups of twelve, 5-d old ducklings were used. Diet concentrations of WEVC were 0, and 50,000 mg WEVC/kg diet. The ducklings were exposed to the appropriate dietary concentrations for 5 d and then maintained on a WEVC-free diet for an additional 3-d observation period.	Body weights were recorded for individual birds at test initiation, day 5, and at test termination (day 8). Food consumption was recorded daily by pen during the 5-day exposure period and also during the 3-day observation period. Signs of toxicity and mortality were recorded twice daily throughout the study.
Mallard Dietary Food Avoidance	Five treatment groups of ten, and one control group of twenty, 5-d old ducklings were used. Diet concentrations of WEVC were 0, 1,250, 2,500, 5,000, 10,000, and 20,000 mg WEVC/kg diet. Food, both contaminated and WEVC-free, was provided to the birds, *ad libitum*, over a 5-d period.	Food consumption was monitored daily. Other endpoints (body weight, gross observations, etc.) were measured as described for the subacute dietary toxicity test.
Mallard 14-Day Dietary Toxicity Test	Four groups of five pairs of 16-wk old ducks were used. Nominal dietary concentrations of 0, 10,000, 30,000, and 100,000 mg WEVC/kg diet were fed for a 14-day period. Clinical chemistry and hematological parameters were evaluated at study initiation and termination. At study termination, all birds were killed humanely and complete postmortem/histopathological examinations were performed.	Parameters analyzed included: body weights (by sex), growth (by sex), feed consumption, clinical chemistry (by sex), hematology parameters (by sex), organ weights (by sex), and organ pathology.
Mallard Reproductive Toxicity Test	Four groups of 15 breeding pairs of 16-week old ducks were fed dietary concentrations of 0, 200, 2 000, and 20,000 mg WEVC/kg diet. Adult birds were fed their respective diets throughout the 22 week study period. Clinical chemistry and hematological parameters were evaluated in 5 male and	Adult parameters included: body weights (by sex; weeks 0, 2, 4, 6, 8, final), growth (by sex; week 0 to week 8, week 8 to termination), feed consumption (bi-weekly, overall), feed wastage, clinical chemistry parameters (by sex), hematology parameters (by sex), and organ weights (by sex). Reproductive parameters

Table 1. (continued). Test procedures and parameters used for the mallard (*Anas platyrhynchos*) and ferret (*Mustela putorius*) toxicity tests with weathered *Exxon Valdez* crude oil (WEVC).

Test Type	Test Procedures	Test Parameters
	5 female mallards in each dose group on study weeks 0, 5, and 10 and at study termination. On study week 10, all birds were photostimulated into reproductive condition. All laid eggs were collected daily over a 10-week period; eggs were collected biweekly for measurement of eggshell strength and thickness. Eggs were artificially incubated and allowed to hatch; ducklings were monitored for 14 days post-hatch. At study termination, all surviving adult birds were killed humanely and complete postmortem/histopathological examinations were performed.	included egg production (per hen, weekly), number of eggs cracked, number of eggs set, number of eggs fertile (14 day), number of eggs viable (21 day), number of eggs hatched, percent of hens laying eggs, percent of eggs cracked, percent of fertile eggs of eggs set, percent of viable fertile eggs, percent hatch of eggs set, percent hatch of fertile eggs, eggshell thickness, and eggshell strength. Hatchling parameters evaluated were the number of 14-day survivors, percent of 14-day survivors of eggs hatched, hatchling body weights, and 14-day survivor body weights.
Direct Eggshell Application Toxicity Test	Nine groups of forty-five duck eggs were used. Each egg was divided into six equal application zones. Treatment groups included application to the top 1/3 and 1/6 of the shell, and the middle 1/3 and 1/6 of the shell area; the bottom portion of the shell was not tested. WEVC or white petroleum jelly, a control material, were applied as a single, direct application to the eggshells on incubation day 7. Eggs were incubated and allowed to hatch; ducklings were monitored for 14 days post-hatch.	Parameters included hatching success, 14-day hatchling survival and hatchling body weight at hatch, and 14 days post-hatch.
Ferret Subacute Oral Toxicity Test	Four groups of five male and five female ferrets were administered WEVC once daily by intubation at doses of 0, 500, 1,000, and 5,000 mg WEVC/kg body weight. Clinical chemistry and hematological parameters were evaluated at study initiation (day 0) and termination (day 5). At study termination, all surviving ferrets were killed humanely and complete post-mortem/histopathological examinations were performed.	Parameters included: body weights (by sex), growth (by sex), clinical chemistry parameters (by sex), hematology parameters (by sex), and organ weights (by sex).

Dietary Toxicity Tests

Mallard subacute dietary toxicity (LC$_{50}$)--Test procedures were designed to determine the toxicity of a test substance administered to 5-day old juvenile birds in their daily diet over a 5-day period. Test endpoints included survival, clinical signs of toxicity, feed consumption, and growth. This test is most appropriate for evaluating the potential acute effects associated with consumption of high doses of oil associated with contaminated food items. Test methods followed ASTM E857, "Standard Practice for Conducting Subacute Dietary Toxicity Tests with Avian Species" (ASTM 1990a).

Mallard dietary food avoidance--The procedures used in this test were designed to evaluate the tendency of birds to avoid food items contaminated with WEVC. Test endpoints were similar to those of the subacute dietary toxicity test, but include measurements of preferential feed consumption between WEVC-treated and control feed. Test methods followed those of Kononen et al. (1986).

Mallard 14-day dietary toxicity test--Procedures were designed to evaluate the toxicity of WEVC in the daily diet over a 14 day period. This test used adult rather than juvenile birds and was more complex than the subacute dietary toxicity test. Endpoints included survival, clinical signs of toxicity, feed consumption, body weight change, as well as a variety of secondary endpoints (e.g., hematological (Table 2) and clinical chemistry (Table 3), and organ weights). This test was conducted as a preliminary study to determine test concentrations for the longer-term reproductive toxicity test.

Reproductive Toxicity Tests

Mallard reproductive toxicity--Procedures were designed to determine the reproductive effects of WEVC consumed in the daily diet over a 20+ week period. All of the endpoints measured in the 14-day dietary toxicity test were monitored, in addition to a variety of endpoints associated with egg production, hatchability, and duckling survival. Test methods followed ASTM E1062, "Standard Practice for Conducting Reproductive Studies with Avian Species" (ASTM 1990b).

Direct eggshell application toxicity--This test was designed to evaluate the effects of WEVC when applied directly to the eggshell of developing bird embryos. The test endpoints relate to the hatching success of the eggs, and survival and growth of the ducklings. No standard test procedures have been developed for this test; however, the procedures used are similar to those of Couillard and Leighton (1989).

DATA ANALYSIS

Median lethal doses (LD$_{50}$), median lethal dietary concentrations (LC$_{50}$), and median food-avoidance concentrations (FAC$_{50}$) were calculated by probit analysis, using a computer program developed by Stephan (1977) that had been modified for use on a personal computer. Statistical analyses of all other endpoints were conducted using TOXSTAT Version 3.2 software (Gulley, Boelter, and Bergman, 1990). Feed consumption, body weights, organ weights, organ weights normalized for individual brain weights and body weights, clinical chemistry results, and hematology results were analyzed. Normality and homogeneity of variance assumptions were verified with the Shapiro-Wilks test and Bartlett's test, respectively. These tests were conducted at the more stringent significance level of $p \leq 0.01$ to assure that more powerful parametric procedures could be used in ensuing analyses. Two-tailed analyses, at a significance level of $p \leq 0.05$, were used in subsequent analyses of all experimental endpoints. If assumptions for normality and homogeneity were met, a one-way analysis of variance (ANOVA), followed by Dunnett's test (used for equal numbers of replicates) or the Bonferroni t-test (used for unequal numbers of replicates), was used to compare responses among WEVC treatment groups and the control group. If distributions were not normal or homogeneous, the data were normalized and/or homogenized via transformation (e.g., squareroot arcsin, log, $1/X$). Data transformation was followed by ANOVA and Bonferroni's or Dunnett's test as above; if the data could not be normalized and/or homogenized by transformation, the Kruskal-Wallis test was used, followed by Dunn's multiple comparison test.

Table 2. Hematological parameters evaluated in the mallard (*Anas platyrhynchos*) and ferret (*Mustela putorius*) toxicity tests with weathered *Exxon Valdez* crude oil (WEVC).

Parameters Evaluated	14-d Mallard Dietary Toxicity Test	Mallard Reproductive Toxicity Test	Ferret Subacute Oral Toxicity Test
Red blood cell count	X	X	X
White blood cell count	X	X	X
Differential count	X	X	X
Total hemoglobin	X	X	X
Mean cell hemoglobin (MCH)	X	X	
Mean cell hemoglobin concentration (MCHC)	X	X	
Mean cell volume (MCV)	X	X	
Packed cell volume (PCV)	X	X	X
Platelets			X
Reticulocyte count	X	X	

Table 3. Clinical chemistry parameters evaluated in the mallard (*Anas platyrhynchos*) and ferret (*Mustela putorius*) toxicity tests with weathered *Exxon Valdez* crude oil (WEVC).

Parameters Evaluated	14-d Mallard Dietary Toxicity Test	Mallard Reproductive Toxicity Test	Ferret Subacute Oral Toxicity Test
Albumin	X	X	X
Alanine aminotransferase (ALT/SGPT)	X	X	X
Alkaline phosphatase	X	X	X
Anion gap	X	X	
Aspartate aminotransferase (AST/SGOT)	X	X	X
Blood urea nitrogen			X
Calcium	X	X	X
Cholesterol			X
Chloride	X	X	X
Creatinine			X
Creatine phosphokinase (CPK)	X	X	
Gamma glutamyl transaminase (GGT)			X
Globulin	X	X	X
Glucose	X	X	X
Phosphorous	X	X	X
Potassium	X	X	X
Sodium	X	X	X
Total bilirubin	X	X	X
Total protein	X	X	X
Triglycerides			X
Uric acid	X	X	

RESULTS

Results for each part of the study are summarized in Table 4 and presented below:

Oral Toxicity Tests

Mallard acute oral toxicity--No deaths or signs of toxicity were noted in the mallards during this study. No significant effects on feed consumption, body weight, or treatment-related grossly observable pathological abnormalities were observed at test termination. The acute oral LD_{50} value and the No Observed Effect Level (NOEL) for WEVC exceeded 5 000 mg WEVC/kg body weight, the maximum dose tested.

Ferret acute oral toxicity--There were no deaths or gross signs of toxicity during the study, nor were there any observable effects on mean body weight in WEVC-dosed animals when compared with controls. No significant differences among clinical chemistry parameters were noted, except for lower mean serum albumin concentrations in females in the high dose group (5 000 mg WEVC/kg body weight). In this group serum albumin concentrations were slightly reduced (i.e., 3.44 mg/dL ± 0.19 for controls versus 2.66 mg/dL ± 0.78 for the high-dose group). No significant differences in any of the hematological parameters evaluated were observed among WEVC-treated ferrets. There were no organ weight differences among either sex, except for the significantly lower raw spleen weights observed in all female treatment groups. When spleen weights were normalized on the basis of body weight, ratios were significantly lower only in females in the three WEVC-treatment groups. However, when spleen weights were normalized on the basis of brain weight, ratios were significantly lower in only the 1 000 and 5 000 mg WEVC/kg body weight groups. Also noted were slightly decreased spleen weights in male ferrets in all WEVC treatment groups; however, spleen weights were not significantly different from controls. Microscopic examination of tissues failed to reveal any lesions considered related to WEVC treatment.

Dietary Toxicity Tests

Mallard subacute dietary toxicity (LC_{50})--There were no mortalities or signs of toxicity in the mallards during this study. Feed consumption was not significantly affected and no significant differences in body weight or growth were noted among treatment groups. Gross necropsies conducted on all ducklings at study termination revealed no evidence of systemic toxicity. The subacute dietary LC_{50} and NOEL of WEVC exceeded the highest test dose of 50 000 mg WEVC/kg diet.

Mallard dietary food avoidance--Calculation of a median food avoidance concentration (FAC_{50}) was not possible, because the ducklings did not avoid food treated with up to 20 000 mg WEVC/kg diet (i.e., the highest concentration tested). Other monitored endpoints indicated no WEVC-related mortalities or signs of toxicity among any of the dietary exposure groups. Food consumption

Table 4. Summary results for the mallard (*Anas platyrhynchos*) and ferret (*Mustela putorius*) toxicity tests conducted with weathered *Exxon Valdez* crude oil (WEVC).

Test	Results	Summary of Toxicity Tests[1]
ORAL TOXICITY TESTS		
Mallard Acute Oral Toxicity	No deaths or signs of toxicity were noted.	LD_{50} and NOEL > 5,000 mg/kg body weight
Ferret Acute Oral Toxicity	No mortalities or grossly observable signs of toxicity were observed.	NOEL = < 500 mg/kg body weight
	No significant differences in clinical or hematological parameters, except slightly reduced serum albumin concentrations (3.44 ± 0.19 vs. 2.66 ± 0.78) in high dose group (i.e., 5,000 mg/kg body weight) females.	
	Raw, and body weight normalized, spleen weights were reduced in all female treatment groups, relative to controls.	
DIETARY TOXICITY TESTS		
Mallard Subacute Dietary Toxicity (LC_{50})	No deaths or signs of toxicity were noted. No effects on feed consumption, body weight or growth endpoints were observed.	LC_{50} and NOEL > 50,000 mg WEVC/kg diet
Mallard Dietary Food Avoidance	No WEVC-related deaths or signs of toxicity were noted. Ducklings did not avoid food treated with up to 20,000 mg WEVC/kg diet.	FAC_{50} > 20,000 mg WEVC/kg diet

Table 4. (continued) Summary results for the mallard (*Anas platyrhynchos*) and ferret (*Mustela putorius*) toxicity tests conducted with weathered *Exxon Valdez* crude oil (WEVC).

Test	Results	Summary of Toxicity Tests
REPRODUCTIVE TOXICITY TESTS		
Mallard 14-Day Dietary Toxicity	No mortalities or grossly observable signs of toxicity were observed. No significant differences were noted in food consumption or body weights. No treatment related changes in clinical or hematological parameters were observed. No organ weight differences were noted, with the exception of increased liver weight (normalized by body weight) for high dose group males.	NOEL > 30,000 mg WEVC/kg diet
Mallard Reproduction	No significant effects on egg production, egg hatch or early development in hatchlings. Parental exposure to highest dietary exposure resulted in reductions in thickness and strength in eggshells. Females exhibited reductions in several clinical chemistry parameters (i.e., serum phosphorous, serum calcium, serum total protein, serum albumin) at the highest dose group; no such effects were observed among males.	NOEL = 2 000 mg WEVC/kg diet
Direct Eggshell Application Toxicity	No effects on embryo development or egg hatchability were observed at WEVC doses up to 92 mg/egg. Concurrent controls (petrolatum) showed significant effects on egg hatchability at dose levels as low as 24 mg/egg.	NOEL > 92 mg/egg < 125 mg/egg

[1] LD_{50} = Median Lethal Dose; NOEL = No Observed Effect Level; LC_{50} = Median Lethal Concentration
FAC_{50} = Median Food Avoidance Concentration

was not significantly affected by dietary concentrations of WEVC ($p \leq 0.05$). No significant differences in body weight or growth were found. No lesions consistent with WEVC exposure were noted in postmortem examination of test animals.

Mallard 14-day dietary toxicity--There were no mortalities and no gross signs of toxicity observed during 14-day exposures to concentrations of 100 000 mg WEVC/kg diet in food. No significant differences in mean food consumption or mean body weights between test and control groups were noted, nor were any significant treatment-related differences in clinical chemistry or hematological parameters observed between treatment and control group birds.

No organ weight differences were noted among male or female mallards except that statistically significant increases in the mean liver weights of male ducks, normalized on the basis of body weight, were found in birds in the high-dose (100 000 mg WEVC/kg diet) group. This difference was not significant on the basis of raw liver weight or brain-normalized liver weight. No consistent or substantive differences among the histologic appearance of the kidney, thymus, brain, or bone marrow of high-dose birds were noted when compared with those of control birds. Livers of high-dose birds were not affected in the appearance of the hepatocytes or the amount of vacuolation of hepatocytes.

Reproductive Toxicity Tests

Mallard reproductive toxicity--No statistically significant differences were observed between WEVC-treated and unexposed birds in terms of the numbers of eggs produced, egg hatchability, or offspring survival (Figure 4). Several other measures of growth and production in the test, including survival, food consumption, or body weight, were not affected by exposure to the highest concentrations of WEVC (20 000 mg WEVC/kg diet). Similarly, no effects among subtle indicators of toxicity such as hematological parameters, gross pathology, or clinical signs of toxicity of hatchlings were observed.

The highest dietary concentration produced several changes in clinical chemistry parameters; the most notable was reduced total serum calcium concentration. This is most likely related to the thinner and weaker shells of eggs laid by ducks exposed to the 20 000 mg WEVC/kg diet, when compared to unexposed controls (Figure 5). We noted an apparent trend among both male and female birds toward increased liver and decreased spleen weights; however, only in the case of male body weight-normalized spleen weights were these differences statistically significant relative to control mallards. Postmortem examinations of birds revealed no consistent, grossly or microsopically observable pathologies.

Direct eggshell application toxicity--Preliminary tests to define the general effects of oil on eggshells indicated that covering more than 1/3 of an egg shell with petrolatum resulted in significantly reduced egg hatching success relative to control (petrolatum-free) eggs. This presumably resulted from a reduction in gas exchange. While the authors do not exclude the fact that petrolatum exposure may have elicited the observed toxicity, it appears unlikely given the molecular size of its constituents (C_{16}-C_{50} paraffinic hydrocarbons) relative to eggshell pore size. Also, other researchers have reported little avian embryo toxicity associated with exposure to a mixture of aliphatic hydrocarbons (Hoffman and Albers 1984). Consequently, definitive testing applications with WEVC covered no more than 1/3 of total eggshell surface area.

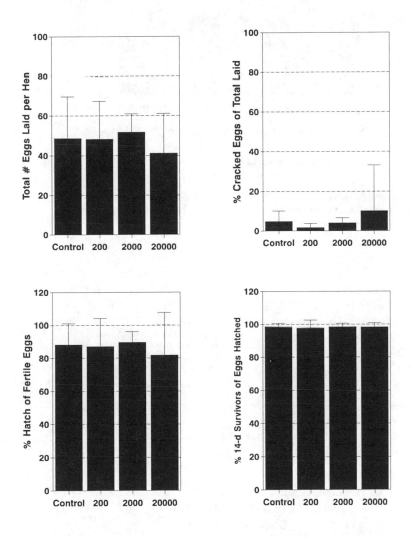

Figure 4. Reproductive parameters in mallards (Anas platyrhynchos) exposed to WEVC in their diet for 22 weeks.

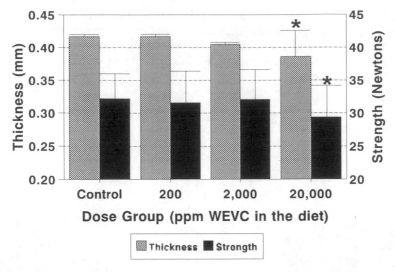

Figure 5. Mallard (Anas platyrhynchos) hen exposure to WEVC in their diet versus eggshell thickness and strength. Asterisks denotes significant difference from control ($p \leq 0.05$).

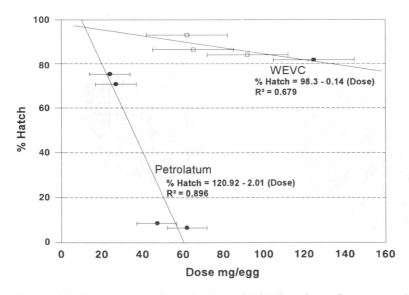

Figure 6. Effects of eggshell application of WEVC and petrolatum (petroleum jelly) on mallard (Anas platyrhynchos) egg hatching success. Solid symbols denotes significant difference from control value (95.6%) ($p \leq 0.05$).

WEVC application doses ranged from 62 mg (1/6 top) to 125 mg (1/3 middle), and petrolatum applications ranged from 24 mg (1/6 middle) to 62 mg (1/3 top). Hatching success was significantly reduced for all eggs treated with petrolatum (Figure 6). Among WEVC-treated eggs, hatching success was significantly reduced for only the group with 1/3 coverage of the middle of the eggshell; hatching success ranged from 82% to 93% for the WEVC groups. Neither petrolatum nor WEVC treatment significantly affected hatchling and 14-day survivor body weights. The NOEL for direct eggshell application toxicity with WEVC was > 92 mg/egg and < 125 mg/egg.

DISCUSSION

Wildlife, especially birds and shoreline mammals, are typically among the most visibly affected organisms in any oil spill. Early in most oil spills, the physical effects of oiling are the primary mechanism affecting exposed wildlife, sometimes leading to the deaths of large numbers of animals. The potential for exposure to free oil and the prevailing environmental conditions (e.g., water and air temperatures) in Prince William Sound at the time of the *Exxon Valdez* spill were such that aquatic birds and sea otters were at significant risk. This concern was borne out by the large numbers of birds and otters that died during 1989 (Piatt et al. 1990).

The effects of the loss of these animals to the spill-affected resident populations were probably short term in nature. With regard to the long-term health of birds and mammals, exposure conditions changed over the summer of 1989 as oil weathered and was removed from the water surface and shorelines (Neff et al., this volume).

Consequently, there remained concern for potential effects on wildlife species in two general areas. These included potential acute and chronic effects through ingestion of contaminated food, and the possibility of toxic effects on developing eggs due to oil exposure from contaminated feathers on the nesting adult. The potential for these effects and population implications are discussed below.

Field Exposure Conditions

Acute--In the case of the *Exxon Valdez* spill, field observations show that free oil was essentially gone from water surfaces after August 1989 (Taft et al., this volume). Also, the extent and degree of oiling on shorelines were substantially reduced after the 1989 cleanup (Neff et al., this volume). Therefore, the concerns over oiling from preening exposure were minimized post-1989, since oil coverage in the spill-impact areas diminished rapidly because of natural cleaning of shorelines during the 1989-1990 winter season. For this reason, the major exposure conditions being addressed here are based on consumption of food under worst-case oiling conditions observed in the field during 1990.

The exposure concentrations likely to be encountered by oiled wildlife after 1989 were within the range of doses used in conducting the present series of WEVC tests. Two factors were considered in estimating the amount of oil ingested by wildlife under spill conditions: (1) the amount of oil adhering to the feathers or hair of the organism, and (2) the amount of oil consumed from preening and from contaminated food. Hartung (1963) addressed the first factor, by quantifying the amount of oil on birds found dead at a spill site. These studies indicate that moderately oiled birds (described as being visibly oiled but with the details of their plumage readily visible) contained 1.3 to 5.6 g of oil on their feathers. Later studies by Hartung (1967) found that moderately oiled ducks acquired an average of 7 g of oil on their feathers and heavily oiled birds acquired loads of up to 124 g of oil.

To address the second issue, Hartung (1963, 1967) conducted studies to quantify the amount of oil that preening birds might ingest. His study results indicate that 50% of the applied oil was ingested over an eight-day period. Assuming the empirical observation of 7 g of oil on the feathers of moderately oiled birds, and the suggested 50% ingestion rate, oral exposures from preening of up to 3.5 g of oil could occur over an eight-day period (i.e., 0.437 g/day).

The contribution of oil via consumption of contaminated food items during this same period must also be considered. Using the highest monthly mean concentration of PAHs observed in the tissues of mussels in the spill affected areas, i.e., 27 884 μg PAH/kg mussel tissue (June 1989), assuming a PAH content in the oil of 8 050 mg PAH/kg oil, and feed consumption similar to that observed in our 14-d feeding study (approximately 100 g/bird/day), dietary uptake would be on the order of 0.35 g of total oil per bird per day, about 79% of the oil predicted to be consumed via preening. This analysis assumes that ducks are consuming only mussels from the most heavily oiled shoreline areas. In reality, their diet consists of numerous other prey species and virtually all mussels in the spill-affected areas have far lower hydrocarbon concentrations. Thus, the total worst-case daily oil consumption is estimated to be approximately 0.8 g oil day, well below the 5 g/kg body weight dose determined to cause no observable effects in the acute oral toxicity test. Therefore, risks to birds from consumption of weathered oil via preening are negligible.

Sea otters consume about 25% of their body weight daily in aquatic organisms. Thus a 30 kg sea otter would ingest about 7.5 kg of food per day (Cowan and Guiguet, 1978). Assuming again the maximum monthly mean of 27 884 μg PAH/kg of mussel tissue, the worst-case daily exposure to sea otters as a result of food consumption is estimated to be about 0.5 g WEVC/kg body weight, a factor of 10 below the dose determined to have minimal effects in the ferret 5-d gavage dosing study. This estimate does not address contribution of ingested oil resulting from grooming behavior; data similar to that reported by Hartung for mallards are unavailable for marine mammals.

Chronic--After chemical and physical dispersal and weathering processes have reduced the likelihood of heavy external exposure to oil, ingestion (i.e., from consumption of contaminated food) is the primary route for petroleum hydrocarbon exposure. To evaluate chronic wildlife exposures following the *Exxon Valdez* spill, we chose to use a worst-case approach and estimated dietary intake using the tissue hydrocarbon residue data from mussels collected from a number of shoreline sites throughout the spill-impacted areas in Prince William Sound, the Kenai Peninsula, and Kodiak Island (NOAA, 1992; Boehm et al., this volume). This approach is considered valid because mussels were shown to be among the highest accumulators of petroleum hydrocarbons following the spill and they make up a large portion of the diets of many wildlife species in Prince William Sound. Figure 7 presents the monthly mean ± SD of tissue residue concentrations of PAHs measured in mussels throughout the spill-affected areas. As expected, observed tissue residue concentrations were highest in the months immediately following the spill, but these rapidly declined by approximately an order of magnitude per year and many were at essentially background concentrations, i.e., approximately 0.01 to 0.1 μg PAH/g tissue (Bence and Burns, this volume), by 1991. These worst-case petroleum hydrocarbon concentrations in mussels were then used as discussed in the following section to evaluate the potential risks to bird and otter populations. Since neither birds nor otters feed solely on mussels, this worst-case scenario assumes an entire diet of oiled mussels from spill-affected areas.

Population Implications of WEVC Exposure

    Short-term--The results of acute oral and subacute dietary studies suggest that WEVC is not toxic to birds up to >5g/kg body weight or 50 000 mg WEVC/kg in the diet. USEPA has established standard evaluation criteria for

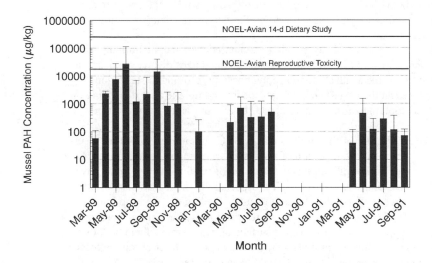

Figure 7. Mean polycyclic hydrocarbon (PAH) mussel tissue concentrations by month compared with no observed effects levels (NOEL), converted to dietary concentrations, for the 14-day dietary feeding and the reproductive toxicity studies. Data are from Exxon and NOAA NRDA databases (NOAA, 1992; Boehm et al., this volume).

agricultural-use chemicals defining as "practically nontoxic" those chemicals with LD_{50} values of >2g/kg body weight or 5 000 mg WEVC/kg in the diet. Thus WEVC would be considered practically nontoxic using the EPA criterion and this designation indicates that oral exposure to the material does not pose a substantial risk to biological species. Mammalian data for crude oils also support the prediction of no toxicity from such exposure amounts. In fact, studies by Smith, Haschek, and Witschi, (1980) indicate that LD_{50} doses for three crude oils (Mixed, Wilmington, and Recluse) in mice exceeded the highest doses tested, i.e., >10 to 16 g/kg.

For both birds and otters, predicted exposures via acute ingestion are well below the exposure levels (5 g/kg) used in our studies; therefore, no acute toxicity would be expected from oral ingestion of WEVC at doses predicted to occur with moderately oiled organisms under actual spill conditions. Obviously, oiled animals could succumb because of loss of insulative capabilities and associated environmental stresses; however, oiling conditions leading to such effects were not present after 1989.

No evidence of aversion to food contaminated with WEVC up to a concentration of 20 000 mg WEVC/kg diet was observed in the avian food avoidance test. Longer term feeding studies with adult mallards have not suggested food avoidance at substantially higher dietary concentrations. No differences in food consumption were observed between control and oil-exposure treatment groups fed either 5% unweathered South Louisiana crude (Szaro et al., 1978), or 10% WEVC in the case of the 14-d feeding study reported herein. These results indicate that birds show no preference or avoidance for oil-contaminated food.

Detection and avoidance of oil-contaminated food can be both beneficial and detrimental to wildlife. Although avoidance minimizes dietary exposure, it risks reduction of the available food supply, possibly resulting in starvation. Nonavoidance, on the other hand, risks exposure and uptake and, depending on the extent of contamination of the food and the amount eaten, can result in toxicity.

The implication of this study is that WEVC contamination of food items likely would not result in starvation of avian species owing to food avoidance. In the initial phases of the spill, localized disruption of feeding behavior may have occurred in areas that were severely oiled, especially in those instances where fledgling birds were physically oiled as a result of feeding on oiled food items (Sharp, 1990). However, by 1990 the degree of oiling observed on shorelines was reduced, i.e., approximately 75% of the surface oil was removed and bulk oil was essentially gone. At this point it is highly unlikely that acute or chronic effects on the feeding behavior of avian species would have occurred.

Long-term--Given that avian wildlife are not likely to avoid contaminated food, the results of our 14-day dietary toxicity test and the avian reproduction test offer a perspective on the risks associated with long-term consumption of such food.

Using the maximum measured PAH concentrations found in mussel tissues throughout the spill-impacted area post-1989, and assuming such mussels were the sole food source, avian diets would contain a maximum PAH concentration of 6 mg WEVC/kg. The NOEL from the reproductive toxicity test was determined to be 2 000 mg WEVC/kg, which equates to 16.1 mg WEVC/kg PAH. Thus, the worst-case dietary concentrations of PAH in 1990 (i.e., 6 mg WEVC/kg) were approximately 2.6 times lower than the concentrations shown to result in adverse effects on exposed birds.

This margin of safety is increased even more when one considers the transient nature of most wildlife, the extent of their home ranges, the sporadic nature of oil contamination of shorelincs and mussels, and the fact that, because of their opportunistic nature, their diets are generally composed of a variety of food items (both oil contaminated and not). For example, Harlequin ducks have been reported to feed on crustaceans, insects, echinoderms, and fish, with mussels contributing about 25% (Bellrose, 1976).

Reproductive--Clearly, the magnitude of cleanup efforts in 1989, and their associated disturbances to nesting birds, had the potential to affect the reproductive success of birds nesting in spill affected areas. The possible effects of consumption of hydrocarbon residues on avian reproduction in the post-1989 years are also of great concern.

These studies showed that chronic ingestion of diets containing up to 20 000 mg WEVC/kg diet had no adverse effects on the ability of parental birds to produce viable embryos, and no apparent effects were seen on the hatchability of their eggs, or on the survival or fitness of the hatchlings. Slight reductions in eggshell thickness and strength were observed in the 20 000 mg WEVC/kg diet dose group; this finding is consistent with the number of cracked eggs observed in the 20 000 mg WEVC/kg diet dose group.

Previous studies with unweathered crude oils tested at dietary concentrations up to 5% have reported a variety of adverse effects on reproductive parameters including reduced numbers of eggs, delays in onset of egg production, and reductions in eggshell thickness and weight (Coon and Dieter, 1981; Holmes, et al., 1978; Harvey et al., 1982; Ainley et al., 1981). Except for the previously discussed effects on eggshell thickness, none of these effects were observed in the WEVC test. This may be attributed to two factors: either (1) differences in the test exposure concentrations (i.e, 5% in the diet versus 2%) or (2) differences in the toxic properties of the oil materials used in the test.

Using the same assumptions previously described, doses comparable to maximum observed environmental exposures following the *Exxon Valdez* spill suggest no adverse effects after 1989 (Figure 7).

Eggshell contamination--Results of our studies indicate that WEVC was not toxic to developing mallard eggs, when applied at doses up to 92 mg/egg. This finding contrasts sharply with the extant literature regarding the toxicity of petroleum materials to developing bird eggs. Microlitre quantities of unweathered crude oils and a variety of petroleum products have been shown to be extremely toxic. For example, median lethal doses (LD_{50}) for unweathered Prudhoe Bay crude oil have been reported as 18.3 µL/egg and 4.2 µL/egg for mallards and leghorn chicken embryos, respectively (Hoffman and Albers, 1984; Couillard and Leighton, 1990). Comparison of these results to ours at 92 mg/egg suggest a 5- to 20-fold reduction in toxicity between fresh and weathered Prudhoe Bay crude oil. This difference is likely due to compositional differences resulting from weathering processes.

Previously, little data were available to address how much of the shell of a developing egg could be covered with a gas transport-inhibiting material before embryo asphyxiation occurred. The application of materials to the shell of a developing egg can have two possible effects, the material can penetrate the egg through the shell pores and exert direct toxic effects on the embryo, or it can block the shell pores resulting in inhibition of gas transport, ultimately suffocating the embryo. Our studies indicate that coverage of greater than about 17% of the surface area of an egg with an inert sealant, such as petrolatum, can adversely affect hatching success. Applications of WEVC covering areas of up to 33% of the shell area had no appreciable effect on embryo survival indicating that WEVC was not an effective sealant compared to petrolatum.

Field observations indicate that bird eggs were contaminated during the *Exxon Valdez* spill, especially the eggs of those species whose feeding characteristics predispose them to transport oil to developing eggs. However, the extent to which this occurred and its resulting effects are unknown. Studies conducted in 1989 to evaluate effects of oil on populations of pigeon guillemots and black oystercatchers in spill-impacted areas indicated that external oiling of eggs occurred but did not result in the deaths of all of the contaminated eggs (Oakley, 1990; Sharp, 1990).

Results of our studies indicate that WEVC is substantially less toxic to developing bird eggs when compared to previously reported data on unweathered EVC. These differences are probably attributable to the loss of the lighter aromatic components of the crude oil via weathering processes. Slight contamination of bird eggs with WEVC does not appear to be a major concern for developing eggs.

CONCLUSIONS

This study was designed to use standard or published toxicity test procedures and surrogate animals to test the effects of weathered EVC on avian and mammalian wildlife species. The battery of tests used in characterizing the toxic properties of WEVC was thorough, equaling or exceeding baseline testing requirements necessary for pesticide registration in the United States (USEPA 1982b). The test species used are commonly used laboratory test species that have been shown to be sensitive predictors of toxicity to free-ranging wildlife. Results of these tests show WEVC to be essentially nontoxic, except at the highest dosages tested. As in any well-designed toxicity study, subtle effects were observed at the highest exposure concentrations in a few of the studies discussed herein. The implications of even these subtle effects, however, must be considered in light of the actual environmental concentrations to which wildlife could be exposed. In the case of wildlife in the *Exxon Valdez* spill-affected areas, it appears that their potential exposures after 1989 were well below those shown in these tests to represent a substantial risk through diet or preening. This is especially true when one considers the transient residence time of most wildlife in Prince William Sound, the extent of their home range, and the sporadic nature of oil contamination of shorelines and food sources.

Substantial incongruity exists between the very low potential for effects to wildlife based on the results of our studies and the purported lingering toxic effects to wildlife (*Exxon Valdez* Oil Spill Trustee Council, 1994), especially avian species, in 1991 and 1992. Results from our studies indicate that WEVC is essentially nontoxic per EPA criteria (USEPA 1985a, b) and, at the exposure concentrations observed in PWS after 1989, would present negligible toxic risk to exposed wildlife.

ACKNOWLEDGEMENTS

The authors wish to thank the following persons for their valuable contributions in conducting these studies: Richard A. Leavitt, Ph.D., Michigan State University, analytical chemistry support; Julia E. Stickle, DVM, Ph.D., Michigan State University, clinical chemistry and hematology; and Alan Trapp, DVM, Ph.D., Dwight L. Schwartz, DVM, Michigan State University; and Svend W. Nielsen, DVM, Ph.D., University of Connecticut, for pathology support.

REFERENCES

Ainley, D.G., C.R. Grau, T.E. Roudybush, S.H. Morrel, and J.M. Utts. "Petroleum Ingestion Reduces Reproduction in Cassin's Auklets." *Marine Pollution Bulletin*. 12(9): 314-317; 1981.

ASTM. "Standard Practice for Conducting Subacute Dietary Toxicity Tests with Avian Species." ASTM E857, American Society of Testing and Materials. Philadelphia, PA. 1990a.

ASTM. "Standard Practice for Conducting Reproductive Studies with Avian Species." ASTM E1062, American Society of Testing and Materials. Philadelphia, PA. 1990b.

Bellrose, F. C. *Ducks, Geese, and Swans of North America*. Second ed. Harrisburg, PA.: Stackpole; 540pp 1976.

Boehm, P.D., M.S. Steinhauer, D.R. Green, B. Fowler, B. Humphrey, D.L.Fiest, and W.J. Cretney. "Comparative Fate of Chemically Dispersed and Beached Crude Oil in Subtidal Sediments of the Arctic Nearshore." *Arctic.* 40(1):133-148; 1987.

Coon, N.C. and M.P. Dieter. "Responses of Adult Mallard Ducks to Ingested South Louisiana Crude Oil." *Environmental Research.* 24: 309-314; 1981.

Couillard, C.M. and F.A. Leighton. "Comparative Pathology of Prudhoe Bay Crude Oil and Inert Shell Sealants in Chicken Embryos." *Fundamental and Applied Toxicology.* 13: 165-173; 1989.

Couillard, C.M. and F.A. Leighton. "The Toxicopathology of Prudhoe Bay Crude Oil in Chicken Embryos." *Fundamental and Applied Toxicology.* 14: 30-39; 1990.

Cowan, I. M. and C. J. Guiguet. The Mammals of British Columbia. British Columbia Provincial Museum. 1978.

Davis, R.W., T.M. Williams, J.A. Thomas, R.A. Kastelein, and L.H. Cornell. "The Effects of Oil Contamination and Cleaning on Sea Otters (*Enhydra lutris*). II. Metabolism, Thermoregulation, and Behavior." *Canadian Journal of Zoology.* 66(12): 2782-2790; 1988.

Exxon Valdez Oil Spill Trustee Council. Five Years Later. 1994 Status Report on the *Exxon Valdez* Oil Spill. Oil Spill Public Information Center, Anchorage, AK; 1994

Gulley, D.D., A.M. Boelter, and H.L. Bergman. "TOXSTAT version 3.2." Fish Physiology and Toxicology Laboratory. Department of Zoology and Physiology. University of Wyoming. Laramie, WY. 1990.

Hartung, R. "Wildlife Ingestion of Oil by Waterfowl." *Papers Michigan Academy Science Arts Letters.* 48:49-55; 1963.

Hartung, R. "Energy Metabolism in Oil-Covered Ducks. *Journal of Wildlife Management.* 31(4):798-804; 1967.

Harvey, S., P.J. Sharp, and J.G. Phillips. "Influence of Ingested Petroleum on the Reproductive Performance and Pituitary-Gonadal Axis of Domestic Ducks (*Anas platyrhynchos*)." *Comparative Biochemistry and Physiology.* 72C(1): 83-89; 1982.

Hoffman, D.J. and P.H. Albers. "Evaluation of potential Embryotoxicity and Teratogenicity of 42 Herbicides, Insecticides, and Petroleum Contaminants to Mallard Eggs." *Archives of Environmental Contamination and Toxicology.* 13: 15-27; 1984.

Holmes, W.N., K.P. Cavanaugh, and J. Cronshaw. "The Effects of Ingested Petroleum on Oviposition and Some Aspects of Reproduction in Experimental Colonies of Mallard Ducks (*Anas platyrhynchos*)." *Journal of Reproduction and Fertility.* 54: 335-347; 1978.

Kononen, D.W., J.R. Hochstein, and R.K. Ringer. "A Quantitative Method for Evaluating Avian Food Avoidance Behavior." *Environmental Toxicology and Chemistry.* 5(9): 823-830; 1986.

Leighton, F.A. "The Pathology of Petroleum Oil Toxicity in Birds: A Review." *in: The effects of oil on birds--Physiological research, clinical applications and rehabilitation.* 1982 Proceedings Tri-State Bird Rescue and Research, Inc. Wilmington, DE. 1982.

National Oceanic and Atmospheric Administration (NOAA). "Natural Resource Damage Assessment: PWSOIL Database." 1992.

Oakley, K.L. "Assessment of Injury to Waterbirds from the *Exxon Valdez* Oil Spill: Effects on the Population and Reproductive Success of Pigeon Guillemonts in Prince William Sound." *Exxon Valdez* Trustees Study-Bird Study Number 9 (Final Report). U.S. Fish and Wildlife Service, Anchorage, Alaska; 1990.

OECD. "Repeated Dose Oral Toxicity-Rodent: 28-Day or 14-Day Study" *in: OECD Guidelines for Testing of Chemicals.* Guideline number 407. Organization for Economic Co-operation and Development, Paris, France; 1981.

Osborn, K. and T.M. Williams. "Postmortem Examination of Sea Otters" *in: Sea Otter Rehabilitation Program 1989* Exxon Valdez *Spill.* T. M. Williams and R.W. Davis, eds. International Wildlife Research, pp. 134-146; 1990.

Piatt, J.F., C.J. Lensink, W. Butler, M. Kendziorek, and D.R. Nysewander. "Immediate Impact of the *Exxon Valdez* Oil Spill On Marine Birds." *The Auk.* 107:387-397; 1990.

Sauer, T. and P. Boehm. "The Use of Defensible Analytical Chemical Measurements for Oil Spill Natural Resource Damage Assessment." *Proceedings of the 1991 International Oil Spill Conference, March 4-7, 1991, San Diego, CA.* Washington, D. C.: American Petroleum Institute; Publication No. 4529; 1991.

Sharp, B. "Black Oystercatchers in Prince William Sound: Oil Spill Effects on Reproduction and Behavior in 1989." *Exxon Valdez* Trustees Study-Bird Study Number 12. U.S. Fish and Wildlife Services, Portland, Oregon; 1990.

Smith, L.H., W.M. Haschek, and H. Witschi. "Acute Toxicity of Selected Crude and Refined Shale Oil- and Petroleum-Derived Substances." *in: Health Effects Investigation of Oil Shale Development.* W.H. Griest, M.R. Guerin, and D.L. Coffin, eds. Ann Arbor Press, Ann Arbor, MI. pp. 141-160; 1980.

Stephan, C.E. Personal communication. USEPA. ERL - Duluth, Duluth, MN. 1977.

Stubblefield, W.A., G.A. Hancock, W.H. Ford, and R.K. Ringer. "An Evaluation of the Toxic Properties of Naturally Weathered *Exxon Valdez* Crude Oil to Wildlife Species--Part I: Acute and Subchronic Toxic Properties." *Environmental Toxicology and Chemistry.* (1995a). (In Review.)

Stubblefield, W.A., G.A. Hancock, H.H. Prince, and R.K. Ringer. "An Evaluation of the Toxic Properties of Naturally Weathered *Exxon Valdez* Crude Oil to Wildlife Species--Part II: Effects on Avian Reproductive Potential." *Environmental Toxicology and Chemistry.* (1995b). (In Review.)

Szaro, R.C. "Effects of Petroleum on Birds." *Transactions of the North American Wildlife Research Conference.* 42:374-381; 1977.

Szaro, R.C., M.P. Dieter, and G.H.Heinz. "Effects of South Louisiana Crude Oil on Mallard Ducks." *Environmental Research.* 17:426-436; 1978.

USEPA. "Surrogate Species Workshop: Workshop Report." Technical Report Number TR-507-36B. Available from Life Systems, Inc., Cleveland, OH, November, 1982a.

USEPA. Ecological Effects Branch. "Pesticide Assessment Guidelines Subdivision E, Hazard Evaluation: Wildlife and Aquatic Organisms." EPA-540/9-82-024, pp. 33-37; 1982b.

USEPA. "Standard Evaluation Procedure, Avian Single-Dose Oral LD_{50} Test." Office of Pesticide Programs--Hazard Evaluation Division. EPA-540/9-85-007. June, 1985a.

USEPA. "Standard Evaluation Procedure, Avian Dietary LC_{50} Test." Office of Pesticide Programs--Hazard Evaluation Division. EPA-540/9-85-008. June, 1985b.

R. Hartung[1]

ASSESSMENT OF THE POTENTIAL FOR LONG-TERM TOXICOLOGICAL EFFECTS OF THE EXXON VALDEZ OIL SPILL ON BIRDS AND MAMMALS.

REFERENCE: Hartung, R., "Assessment of the Potential for Long-Term Toxicological Effects of the Exxon Valdez Oil Spill on Birds and Mammals," Exxon Valdez Oil Spill: Fate and Effects in Alaskan Waters, ASTM STP 1219, Peter G. Wells, James N. Butler, and Jane S. Hughes, Eds., American Society for Testing and Materials, Philadelphia, 1995.

ABSTRACT: This paper assesses the potential for direct long-term toxicological effects of exposures to oils in birds and mammals by tracing exposures and effects from the initial acute phases through the sub-chronic to the eventual long-term exposures.

The immediate effects of oil spills are physical, the oil acting on the plumage of birds or the fur of mammals. This causes a loss of entrained air and a concomitant reduction in buoyancy and thermal insulation. Animals that escape the immediate impacts may be isolated from their food supply and often ingest large amounts of oil while attempting to clean themselves. At the comparatively high dose levels involved, these exposures can result in toxicologically significant responses in many organ systems.

In the course of an oil pollution incident, the amounts of biologically available oils decrease steadily, and simultaneously the composition of the oils shifts towards those components that have low volatility, and that resist photo- and bio-degradation. As this occurs, the primary pathways of exposure change from direct intakes to indirect routes involving the food supply. Although laboratory studies often report finding some adverse effects, the dose rates employed in many of these studies are extremely high when compared with those that are potentially available to animals in the wild, and very few actually use weathered oils.

An assessment of the toxicological literature and of the available empirical data on the Exxon Valdez oil spill leads to the conclusion that long-term sub-lethal toxic effects of crude oils on wildlife in such marine spills appear to be very unlikely.

---

[1]The University of Michigan, School of Public Health, Department of Environmental and Industrial Health, Ann Arbor, MI 48109-2029

KEYWORDS: Exxon Valdez, Prince William Sound, oil, toxicity, avian, mammalian, absorption, bioaccumulation, target organs, reproduction, dose-response.

INTRODUCTION

The waters and surrounding coastal habitat of Prince William Sound (PWS) and the adjacent Gulf of Alaska (GOA) are rich in marine and terrestrial wildlife, including many species of birds and mammals. The *Exxon Valdez* oil spill (EVOS) threatened individuals of many of these species. The magnitude of the threat and the resulting losses varied with the pattern of exposure to the oil, as well as with the abundance and life histories of each particular species. Carcasses of some 30 000 birds and about 1 000 sea otters were recovered in the months following the spill. Cleanup operations and the dynamic forces of nature have vastly reduced the amounts of biologically available oil residues in Prince William Sound since the early days of the spill. Yet concern lingers over what long-term effects the spill and its remnants may have had on the wildlife species inhabiting the spill-affected area.

The purpose of this paper is to explore the potential long-term toxicological impacts of the EVOS on birds and mammals. The acute, subchronic and chronic effects of the direct actions of oils are discussed in the context of the highly dynamic exposure conditions which existed in the field following EVOS.

The short term effects of oil spills on birds and mammals that have been heavily exposed are all too obvious. This paper addresses the matter of the survivors and how they can be expected to fare, subject to effects which may either be persistent or delayed in their expression. Long term toxicological effects may theoretically arise as a consequence of: (1) acute, but non-fatal, exposure leading to incomplete recovery and long term after-effects; (2) bioaccumulation of substances, under conditions of continued (chronic) exposure, to sufficiently high levels to produce adverse effects; and (3) the manifestation of delayed effects, involving a progression of pathological processes, after exposure has essentially ceased.

The paper describes the physical and biological processes that are responsible for acute effects as a consequence of high levels of exposure to oils, then explores the short-term effects on various organ systems and the types of exposure conditions that elicit them. Subsequently, the effects and dose-response relationships from longer term laboratory studies are assessed, making use of information on crude oils of various origins, on weathered oils, and specific petroleum fractions. Wherever possible, the exposure conditions and effects found under laboratory conditions are related to likely exposure conditions and effects found under field conditions, and long term effects on wildlife populations are considered.

OVERVIEW OF IMMEDIATE EFFECTS OF LARGE-SCALE OIL SPILLS.

Characteristically, toxicological assessments include information on dose-response relationships that range from acute to chronic durations of exposure and from lethal to subtle effects; furthermore the assessments seek to define target organs and mechanisms of toxicity (Klaassen and Eaton 1991; Mosberg and Hayes 1989; Stevens and Gallo 1989).

In any toxicological assessment the principal components to be considered are the identity and characteristics of the substance(s) to which the organisms are exposed, the dose rate, the duration of exposure, the number and characteristics of the exposed organisms, and the types and severity of effects that are elicited in the exposed organisms. Typically the experimental conditions (substance, dose rate, duration of exposure, choice of test organisms, and route of exposure) are carefully controlled and held constant. Usually, several dose rates are administered for fixed durations, and care is taken to eliminate other environmental stressors, so that the question of the causality of any observed effects can be more readily examined (Hartung 1987; Rand and Petrocelli 1985). Toxicological effects elicited under laboratory conditions cannot be extrapolated uncritically to field conditions. In contrast with exposure conditions in laboratory studies, oil spills, especially large-scale spills, represent dynamic and very changeable exposure scenarios for any organisms within their spheres of influence. Floating oils, and to a lesser extent beached oils, are the predominant stressors for aquatic birds and mammals during the acute exposure phase. Oiled foods, such as oiled mussels, can also contribute to the exposure. Although heavily oiled animals generally do not consume any food, the ingestion of oiled food becomes the most important exposure pathway among survivors after most of the floating oil has disappeared.

Environmental Fate and Transport Processes Influencing Exposure

There are very few fixed parameters during an oil pollution incident. The early stages of an oil spill are characterized by rapidly spreading, coherent layers of floating oil that are undergoing rapid changes. The more volatile fractions evaporate. Water-soluble and emulsifiable fractions enter the water column. The remaining floating oil is slowly oxidized through bacterial action and photo-oxidation, and water-borne and air-borne detritus is incorporated into the oil layer. Some of the oil residue is incorporated into sediments (Figure 1). Beached oil has often been of particular concern. It undergoes its own dynamics of dissipation and incorporation into beach material. During the "weathering" processes both the chemical and physical characteristics of the oil change markedly. The viscosity of the oil increases significantly, and the oil layer begins to break up into floating patches and "tar balls." Throughout this progression the total amount of floating oil continues to decrease (National Academy of Sciences (NAS) 1975; Neff 1990; Wolfe et al. 1993).

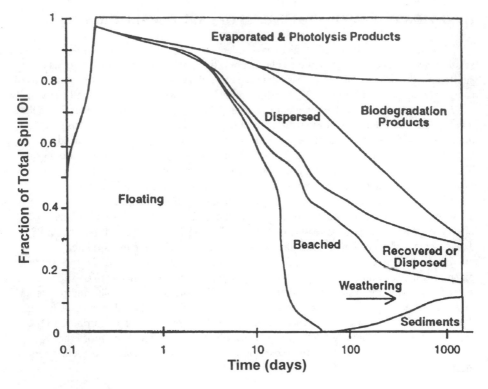

Figure 1--Overall fate of *Exxon Valdez* oil (from Wolfe et al. 1993).

The greatest number of deaths of aquatic birds have been observed following encounters with coherent floating oil layers (Giles and Livingston 1942; Hunt 1957; Hawkes 1961), rather than through contact with tar balls. The size of the oil spill is not the only determinant for wildlife losses. The potential for losses is also highly dependent upon the location and season of release of the oil in relation to the life-histories and habitat requirements of the species that might be exposed.

There are very few systematic observations of the behavior of animals during their initial encounter of oils, and the quality of the existing reports varies widely. Existing reports describe occasions when aquatic birds (Bourne 1976; Custer and Albers 1980; Flickinger 1981; King 1963), seals (St.Aubin 1990), sea otters (Davis, Williams and Awbrey 1988; Geraci and Williams 1990; Siniff et al. 1982), and cetaceans (Geraci 1990) were variously attracted to oils, were indifferent to oils, or avoided oils. Consequently, it appears that the risk of external oiling and the sensitivity to adverse effects from such oiling differs significantly among various species and is highly dependent upon local spill conditions and sites.

Physical Basis for Effects of Acute Oiling

Regardless of the attraction, avoidance, or initial indifference, the mechanisms of action by which the lower viscosity oil produces its adverse effects are remarkably similar among the exposed species. The most common scenario for acute toxicity begins either when a flying aquatic bird lands in an oil slick, or when a diving bird or mammal surfaces from underneath such an oil slick. The consequence of the contact with the oil is the matting of the plumage or pelage, which effectively destroys the buoyancy and the thermal insulation that is created by the entrained air, so that oil covered animals that are dependent upon it are likely to drown or suffer from hypothermia (Aldrich 1938; Wragg 1954). All of the aquatic birds, the sea otters and the river otters are dependent upon entrained air for buoyancy and insulation.

The mechanisms by which oils destroy the water-proofing and insulation provided by feathers or fur through entrained air is complex. The protective properties of feathers or fur are only partly due to the natural fats, oils and waxes on these structures. The orderly arrangement of individual hairs in fur, or of the barbules and barbicels of feathers (Fabricius 1958; Hartung 1967) is critical for normal functioning. The size of the openings provided by the arrangement of the fine structure of the feathers is so small that the high surface tension of the water prevents the penetration of water to the skin, and maintains entrained air for thermal insulation and buoyancy. In contrast, oils can readily wet hair or feathers; and, because many oils have a comparatively high viscosity, they tend to cause the barbules of the feather, and the feathers themselves, to stick together. This deranges the plumage so that air is no longer well entrained, and water can penetrate. The effects of oils on the fine structures have implications for the slowness of recovery of animals that have been cleaned of visible oils, but where the fine structures may still be deranged.

The immediate effects of oils on aquatic mammals depend upon the extent to which these mammals rely on the buoyancy and thermal insulation of their fur. Pinnipeds and cetaceans depend mainly upon cutaneous fat layers for this purpose, while species such as sea otters, river otters and muskrats depend upon their pelage. The pelage of aquatic mammals appears to be inherently less efficient as a provider of thermal insulation and buoyancy in a water environment than the plumage of aquatic birds. Fur simply lacks the orderly structure provided by interlocking barbules and barbicels provided in avian plumage. Even though individual hairs in a pelage are coated with lipids from sebaceous glands, this hydrophobic covering does not seem to include the long outer guard hairs, because the outermost layers of the fur of all aquatic mammals are readily wetted. Consequently, it is the density of the fur that governs the thermal insulation and buoyancy properties. For this very reason, aquatic mammals, such as muskrat, beaver, mink, river otter, and sea otter, have been the most desired fur bearers of commerce. Among these species, the sea otter is most closely linked to the aquatic environment, and it has the densest fur among all aquatic mammals (Costa and Kooyman 1982).

The most obvious initial impact of high dose external exposures to petroleum oils is the loss of buoyancy, which in turn leads to drowning or movement onto shore in aquatic mammals and birds, even when this is not part of their normal behavioral pattern. Animals which have sought refuge from drowning by moving ashore exhibit abnormal behavior patterns, such as excessive preening (Hunt 1957) and a loss of shyness, so that they can be readily approached by humans (Davis et al. 1988).

The loss of thermal insulation leads to extreme heat loss, which is counter-balanced by elevated metabolic rates in order to maintain normal core body temperatures (Hartung 1967; McEwan and Koelink 1973; Davis et al. 1988). The extent of heat loss is a function of the amount of oiling, the proportion of time spent in water, and the ambient temperature. It should be noted that most of the wildlife losses in any oil pollution incident occur during this initial phase, which tends to be characterized by massive exposures to biota through floating oils.

Furthermore, it should be noted that essentially all of the effects of oil on biota during the acute high dose exposures stage can be related to the physical properties of oils and their physical interactions with living systems. The external doses required to produce deaths in birds due to drowning and hypothermia are generally much higher than 1 gm per kg of body weight (Hartung 1964, 1967). Several authors have reported that only a "small spot" or a "few drops" of oil was sufficient to kill birds (Giles and Livingston 1960; Hawkes 1961; Hunt 1957). These are based upon isolated field observations on birds that were picked up dead, where no actual measurements of the amounts of oils on the feathers were made, and where no measurements of metabolic rates were made. The amounts of oil that are available during the early stages of catastrophic oil spills are very high, and the amounts of floating oils decline fairly quickly.

The decreases of floating oils over time were evaluated by Wolfe et al. (1993) as summarized in Figure 1. The number of heavily oiled sea otter carcasses found after EVOS peaked at three to four weeks and decreased significantly after that (see Figure 2 and DeGange and Lensink 1990). The relative recovery of oiled and non-oiled cormorant, duck, grebe and loon carcasses throughout the spill area between May and August of 1989 followed a similar decreasing pattern (Piatt et al. 1990), and most of the bird carcasses recovered after August 1, 1989 were unoiled. It should be noted that judging from the reportedly poor condition of many of the carcasses, there may have been considerable delays between the deaths of some of these animals and their collection.

THE TRANSITION FROM IMMEDIATE PHYSICAL EFFECTS TO SYSTEMIC TOXICITY

The information for this section is generally founded on observations of debilitated or moribund animals collected during oil pollution incidents, autopsies on such animals,

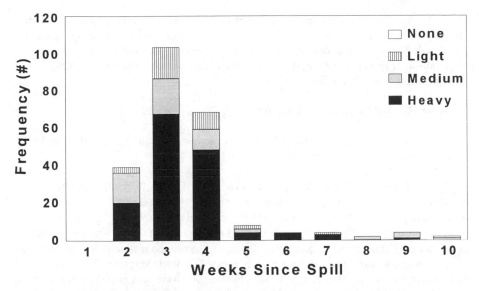

Figure 2--Degree of oiling of sea otter carcasses recovered in Prince William Sound, by week following the spill (Unpublished data C. J. Lensink, United States Fish and Wildlife Service, Anchorage).

and observations on laboratory animals that have received single large doses of oils. Although individual reports often contain glaring deficits, many of the reported phenomena have been replicated and form part of a coherent picture of the acute impacts of an oil pollution incident immediately after the initial mortalities by drowning and/or hypothermia.

This phase of the assessment of the impacts of oil spills covers the period from the end of the immediate mortalities due to drowning and/or hypothermia to disappearance of visible evidence of external oiling. During this phase, floating oil volumes are in continuous decline. The oil on the beaches changes from abundant free oil to weathered tarry residues. The floating oils assume a patchy distribution, and animals may move into or out of such areas. With the reduced concentrations of oils, the stresses imposed by external oiling are no longer immediately lethal, but are complicated by the effects of ingested oils.

Oiled animals that escape dying from drowning or hypothermia often seek refuge ashore. However, most of these animals are adapted to feed only in an aquatic environment; thus they do not consume any food while on land. This leads to a deterioration of their physical condition and to starvation.

Findings based on laboratory studies at steady exposure levels must be interpreted with great care, because of the continual qualitative and quantitative changes in the dosing spectrum during the progression of an oil pollution incident. The short-term effects at comparatively high dose levels must be interpreted with caution when extrapolating to longer term exposures in the field.

Uptake of Oils and Component Fractions

This section reviews the potential routes of exposure to and uptake of oil in the context of post spill environmental exposure levels.

Inhalation--Inhalation as an exposure route for the volatile fractions of freshly spilled crude oil has received limited study. Eley et al. (1989) measured benzene concentrations 2.5 cm above a 1 cm thick layer of mixed crude oils. The air velocity above the oil slick was 0.9 to 2.75 km/h, and the temperature of the oil was 43°C. The highest benzene concentration found was 80.5 ppm, the two-hour time-weighted average was 15.8 ppm, and the air concentration was reported to decline rapidly. The low environmental temperatures and high wind velocities that were common in Prince William Sound during and after the spill should have lead to much lower air concentrations, but also a slower rate of decline. The inhalation route of exposure is bound to fade to insignificance as the oils weather and the volatile fractions diminish greatly.

Ingestion--As the amount of floating oil diminishes and the characteristics of the remaining oil also change, the mortalities resulting from exposure to these oils decrease sharply, and the toxicological effects become more complex. While the initial mortalities were almost exclusively due to drowning and/or hypothermia, the ingestion of oils begins to contribute to the observed effects.

When birds seek to clean their feathers by preening, they ingest significant quantities of oil. Hartung (1963) showed that mallards (*Anas platyrhynchos*) were able to remove about 50% of 1 to 20 mL of radio-labeled oils from their plumage over a period of 10 days. The study did not determine the exact amounts of oil ingested, but significant levels of radio-activity were detected in the feces and on the cage walls. McEwan and Whitehead (1980) found evidence that ingested oils are only partially absorbed. They reported that Glaucous-Winged Gulls (*Larus glaucescens*) excreted 48% of a 500 mg oral dose of tritiated Boundary Lake crude oil, 47% of a similar dose of marine diesel oil, and 36% of a dose of Bunker C fuel oil. Mallard Ducks excreted about 43% of oral doses of marine diesel or Bunker C. There was evidence of absorption into plasma, gut, liver, kidney, muscle and fat. However, within 24 hours of dosing the residual concentrations of petroleum hydrocarbons declined to low or background levels. Gay et al. (1980) fed a synthetic aliphatic and aromatic hydrocarbon mixture to mallards at 1% in the diet for 7 months. The individual compounds from the synthetic mixture were found in liver, kidneys, fat and brain. The highest concentrations were found in the fat, but the total concentration of all hydrocarbons in the tissues was always considerably less than that in the diet.

Presumably, when oiled aquatic mammals clean their fur, they also ingest some of the oil. Engelhardt et al. (1977) immersed ringed seals (*Phoca hispida*) for 24 hours in sea water covered with a 1 cm layer of Norman Wells crude oil. They reported petroleum hydrocarbon residue estimates based on fluorimetric analyses in a number of body fluids and tissues. The highest concentrations found were 58 µg/g in bile two days after oiling. The daily administration of tritiated benzene in 5 mL Norman Wells crude oil for 5 days was followed by a rapid clearance of radio-label from blood, and no significant accumulation in other tissues. The oral administration of ^{14}C-naphthalene in Norman Wells crude oil resulted in the highest levels of ^{14}C activity in the water-soluble fraction from urine, moderate levels in fats, and very little activity in most other tissues (Engelhardt 1978), indicating that the naphthalene is readily metabolized to water soluble compounds which are then excreted.

Although there are no estimates of the amount of oil ingested by mammals as they clean their fur, Williams et al. (1990) report finding, on the day of capture, 20 to 800 ppm total petroleum hydrocarbons (TPH) in the blood of five heavily oiled sea otters, and 22 to 260 ppm TPH in the blood of nine heavily oiled harbor seals. A portion of these blood TPH levels may also have been due to the ingestion of food contaminated with oils.

Dermal absorption--The potential for the dermal absorption of petroleum oils and its component fractions is reasonably well understood for humans (Magee 1991), and the basic principles governing absorption seem to be universal. Thus, absorption rates through intact skin are much slower than those through the intestines or lungs. Substances with low molecular weight and high lipid solubility are generally absorbed most rapidly. High molecular weight non polar petroleum compounds are absorbed very slowly, usually to an insignificant degree, as illustrated through the wide-spread medicinal uses of mineral oils (baby oils) and petroleum jellies (Swinyard and Pathak 1985; Bogs 1967).

Effects on Target Organs

Lethality--The single oral doses of crude oils or simple fuel oils required to produce death among birds or mammals are very high, and the oral LD$_{50}$ values are commonly estimated as being greater than 10 mL/kg body weight (Hartung and Hunt 1966; Stubblefield et al. this volume).

Gastro-intestinal tract--The ingestion of high doses of oils leads to diarrhea, which has lead to the medicinal use of mineral oils as laxatives (Brunton 1985). Regardless of the detailed mechanisms, during the time that heavily oiled mammals and birds need to meet a greatly increased metabolic demand to maintain normal body temperatures, they can only rely upon their own internal reserves. Consequently, the elevated metabolic demands in the absence of dietary intake are likely to result in an accelerated starvation syndrome (Hartung 1967).

Pekin Ducks (*Anas platyrhynchos*) intubated with single large doses (2 - 24 mL/kg body weight) of diesel oils or lubricating oils exhibited irritated intestinal tracts, as demonstrated by the presence of hyperemia and traces of occult blood (Hartung and Hunt 1966). The intestinal tracts of moderately oiled ducks collected on the Lower Detroit River showed similar kinds of effects (Hartung, 1964). Baker et al. (1981) suggested that otter (*Lutra lutra*), which were autopsied after being found dead, exhibited hemorrhagic gastro-enteropathy after exposure to Bunker C fuel oil. Their observations need to be interpreted with caution, because of the presence of extensive post-mortem changes.

Crocker et al. (1974) demonstrated that a single oral dose of 0.2 mL ($\approx$ 1.3 to 2 g/kg body weight) of Santa Barbara Channel crude oil to Pekin Ducklings inhibited increased water and Na^+ ion absorption in salt water adapted ducklings. Subsequent studies showed that there were significant differences in the tendency of different crude oils to elicit this effect (Crocker et al. 1975). Daily doses of 2.5% Prudhoe Bay crude oil in the diet over a period of 7 days failed to produce any changes in the absorption of electrolytes (Eastin and Murray 1981).

The ingestion of mineral oils is also known to decrease the absorption of the oil soluble nutrients, such as vitamins A and D (Alexander et al. 1947). However, deficiencies of these vitamins have not been demonstrated in conjunction with oil pollution incidents.

Skin and eyes--The primary physical effects of oil on feathers and fur have been discussed in some detail in previous sections of this paper. The removal of the oil through the use of solvents or detergent solutions during wildlife rehabilitation efforts does not appear to return the water-proofing and insulating properties of pelage or fur to completely normal conditions. The major problems lie in reestablishing the orderly fine structure of fur and plumage, and the hydrophobicity of the surface of hair and feather elements, without matting them all over again. This process has required lengthy holding periods. Animals held in treatment facilities have experienced high mortality rates, and have also experienced reduced survival after release.

Oils are not inherently irritating to skin. Early observations by Phillips and Lincoln (1930), who reported that oiled birds preened so vigorously that they pulled out many feathers, have not been confirmed as a general occurrence. Autopsy reports of hyperemia of the skin in oiled birds (Hartung 1964) may also be related to freezing injuries.

Heavily oiled pinnipeds, and to a lesser extent sea otters, tend to exhibit eye irritation (probably conjunctival), which can be quite severe (St.Aubin 1990). The irritation tends to be transient and disappears when seals are placed in clean water (Engelhardt 1983).

Respiratory system--Materials may enter the lungs by inhalation of vapors or aerosols, and by inadvertent aspiration. Fresh crude oils contain a significant volatile fraction. However, the air concentrations near the oil-air interface the vicinity of a spill are going to be much less than a saturated vapor concentration in air, primarily because of the turbulent and diffusional mixing of the hydrocarbon vapors into the air column immediately above the water.

Studies on the inhalation of hydrocarbon vapors in humans (Ellenhorn and Barceloux 1988), even their intentional inhalation, have not demonstrated any adverse effects on the respiratory system. In a long series of studies on the toxicity of the vapors from various petroleum hydrocarbon solvents in laboratory animals and humans, Carpenter et al. (1975a; 1975b; 1975c; 1975d; 1975e; 1975f; 1976a; 1976b; 1976c; 1976d; 1977) did not report any adverse effects on the respiratory system. Only the inhalation of vapors of a rubber solvent was related to finding granulation nodules in the lung (Carpenter et al. 1975g). The authors regarded this response to be very unusual and questioned a possible causal relationship to the exposure.

Oil aspiration pneumonia (lipid pneumonia) has been reported when oils were administered by stomach tube or in gelatin capsules to waterfowl, as well as in oiled ducks collected in the field (Hartung and Hunt 1966). However, this type of pneumonia has not been reported in birds or mammals exposed to EVOS.

Many oiled sea otters that were collected early during the EVOS exhibited a high incidence of subcutaneous and pulmonary emphysema (Osborn and Williams 1990). There is no comparable response associated with exposures to oils in other species, either as part of any field observations or as part of any laboratory studies. The closest corollary appears to be the mediastinal and subcutaneous emphysema that is observed as a result of over-inflating the lungs as has been observed after excessively rapid ascents during diving (Berkow and Fletcher 1987).

Nervous system--The highly volatile components of crude oils are weak anesthetic agents by inhalation. High concentrations of several commercial petroleum solvent vapors produced incoordination and convulsions in rats, dogs, and cats at concentrations approaching saturation at room temperature (Carpenter et al. 1975a; 1975b; 1975c; 1975d; 1975e; 1975f; 1976a; 1976b; 1976c; 1976d; 1977). However, the findings of Eley et al. (1989), which were summarized in the Inhalation section, suggest that it is highly unlikely that the volatile components of EVOS could have reached levels sufficient to cause effects like those reported by Carpenter. The saturation levels in air at room temperature for neat petroleum distillates would obviously be much higher than the achievable air concentrations of the minor volatile components from a crude oil matrix at much lower environmental temperatures, evaporating into an unconfined and moving atmosphere.

Frost (1990) reported finding intramyelinic edema and axonal degeneration in the posterior ventral aspect of the thalamus (specifically in the ventral caudal lateral and ventral caudal medial nuclei of the thalamus, and to some degree in the lateral nuclear area and the reticular nucleus of the thalamus) of a heavily oiled harbor seal (*Phoca vitulina richardsi*) and similar but milder lesions in 5 other harbor seals collected three or more months after the spill. These findings are difficult to interpret, because histopathological lesions in isolated and specific regions of the brain have never been related directly to exposures to crude oil. Inhalation abuse of toluene associated with glue-sniffing has resulted in diffuse cerebral, cerebellar and brainstem atrophy in humans (Rosenberg et al. 1988). The exposures involved were much higher than the permissible worker exposure of 100 ppm (Cavender 1993). High doses of n-hexane and other substances that can be metabolized to γ-diketones, can produce axonal damage in the peripheral nervous system, leading to progressive sensory changes, weakness and paralysis of the extremeties (Cornish 1980; Anthony and Graham 1991), but no injuries are reported to occur in specific regions of the central nervous system. Toluene and n-hexane are minor constituents in crude oils.

Liver--The livers of birds show at most only slight elevations of the diagnostic enzymes (AST and ALT), even after large single doses (Hartung and Hunt 1966) or longer term feeding of high concentrations of 2.5 to 5% Louisiana crude oil in the diet (Szaro et al. 1978). Liver function as measured by BSP dye retention was only increased after single doses of 12 or 24 mL diesel oil/kg body weight (Hartung and Hunt 1966), and or ICG dye clearance was unaffected after feeding of 10 000 ppm paraffinic hydrocarbons in the diet for 7 months (Patton and Dieter 1980). However, the ICG dye clearance was stimulated when an aromatic hydrocarbon fraction was incorporated into the diet at 4 000 ppm for 7 months. Gorsline et al. (1981) reported increased metabolism of naphthalene by liver microsomal preparations derived from seawater adapted mallards (*Anas platyrhynchos*) that had been fed 1 to 5% of various crude oils in their diets for a period of 50 days. Prudhoe Bay crude oil was less effective than either South Louisiana or Kuwait crude oil, but more effective than Santa Barbara crude oil in stimulating hepatic microsomal metabolism of naphthalene.

Sea otters in EVOS rehabilitation centers demonstrated sizable elevations in ALT (SGPT) and AST (SGOT) diagnostic enzymes (Williams et al. 1990). On autopsy, the livers of 55% of the sea otters were found to be discolored and to exhibit an abnormal texture (Osborn and Williams 1990). Most of these animals were collected early during EVOS.

European ferrets (*Mustela putorius*) given daily oral doses of up to 5 g/kg body weight of weathered Exxon Valdez crude oil for a period of 5 days (Stubblefield et al. this volume) showed no effects on the liver as measured by clinical chemistry and histopathology.

Leighton (1990) reported increased liver weights in CD-1 mice that had received daily doses of 10 mL/kg body weight of Prudhoe Bay crude, Arabian Light crude, or Bunker C oils for a period of five days. Comparable doses of either mineral oil or corn oil did not produce the effect.

Kidneys--The kidney does not appear to be an important target organ after exposures to oils. Only slight increases in blood non-protein nitrogen (NPN) levels were reported in ducks after large oral doses of diesel fuel in mallards (Hartung and Hunt

1966). Sea otters in EVOS rehabilitation centers exhibited elevated blood urea nitrogen (BUN) levels (Williams et al. 1990) which may also have been due to decreased blood pressure during shock, which is known to decrease the glomerular filtration rate, which in turn increases the BUN.

Blood--Anemias have been frequently reported in birds after exposures to oils. The administration of single doses of 2 g/kg body weight of fuel oil by stomach tube resulted in decreased red cell counts, hemoglobin concentrations and packed cell volume (PCV) (Hartung and Hunt 1966). Feeding of South Louisiana crude oil at 2.5 and 5% in the diet of mallard ducklings for 8 weeks also resulted in a depression of the PCV. Herring gulls (*Larus argentatus*) and Atlantic Puffins (*Fratercula arctica*) given daily oral doses of 10 g/kg body weight or more of Prudhoe Bay crude oil for 5 to 7 days, developed profound anemias (Leighton 1985; Leighton et al. 1985; Leighton 1986). The anemias were associated with increased amounts of reduced glutathione, increased phagocytosis of degenerate red cells in liver and spleen, and increased numbers of red cell precursors in the bone marrow.

In contrast, Sandhill Cranes (*Grus americanus*) given daily oral doses of 2 or 10 mL/kg body weight of Prudhoe Bay crude oil for 25 days, did not develop any anemias (Fleming et al. 1982). Feeding a diet containing 1.5% Prudhoe Bay crude oil to mallards for seven days also failed to elicit anemias (Rattner 1981).

Wilson et al. (1990) report depressed PCVs in heavily oiled sea otters in captivity, but the values returned to normal PCV values within 3 months. Leighton (1990) reported slight reductions in PCVs in two out of four studies in CD-1 mice that received daily doses of 10 or 12 mL/kg body weight of Prudhoe Bay crude oil by gavage for a period of five days.

Endocrine system--The interactions that involve the endocrine system can be extremely complex. The adrenal gland has received the greatest amount of attention with respect to responses engendered by various types and amounts of oils. The major interests relate to induced responses to non-specific stresses and adaptation to salt-loading. The responses of the adrenal cortex differ significantly with respect to species, life-stage, characteristics of the oil, duration and dose rate, and environmental stresses.

A number of studies report adrenal hypertrophy after acute or short-term feeding of oils to mallards (Hartung and Hunt 1966), Black Guillemots (*Cepphus grylle*) (Peakall et al. 1980), Herring Gulls (Peakall et al. 1982), and in cold-stressed and seawater adapted mallards (Holmes et al. 1978a).

Plasma corticosteroid levels were not measured in all of these studies; they tended to be decreased in many of them, but were elevated in others.

Reproduction and development--Egg-laying can be readily inhibited in most species by the influence of sufficient environmental stress (Marshall 1961). A single oral dose of 2 g/kg body weight of a simple lubricating oil inhibited egg-laying in mallards for about 2 weeks (Hartung 1965). Japanese Quail (*Coturnix c. japonica*) fed 500 mg ($\approx$ 3.6 g/kg body weight) of No. 2 fuel oil stopped laying eggs for 6 to 8 days. The same dose of Bunker C fuel oil stopped egg-laying for at least 2 weeks, while the administration of the same dose of mineral oil had no effect on egg production. Lower doses of Bunker C (200 mg $\approx$ 1.4 g/kg body weight) reduced both egg laying and hatchability (Grau et al. 1977). When mallards were fed a diet containing approximately 3% South Louisiana crude oil for a period of 100 days, there was an 84% reduction in egg laying, and the same concentration of Kuwait crude oil in the diet stopped egg laying entirely (Holmes et al. 1978b). Coon and Dieter (1981) reported that mallards fed 2.5% South Louisiana crude oil in their diet laid approximately half the number of eggs as unexposed ducks.

Ainley et al. (1981) fed 1 000 mg of Prudhoe Bay crude oil or Bunker C fuel oil in gelatin capsules to Cassin's Auklets (*Ptychoramphus aleuticus*), which were free to leave and return to their nest boxes in a nesting colony on South Farallon Island, California. The authors did not report the weight of the auklets. Assuming a body weight of 200 g, the dose of 1 000 mg would correspond to a dose of approximately 5 g/kg body weight. The authors found slight, but statistically significant, reductions in egg laying. Furthermore, the hatchability of the eggs laid by Cassin's Auklets dosed with Bunker C fuel oil, but not with Prudhoe Bay crude oil, was reduced slightly.

Fry et al. (1986) dosed Wedge-Tailed Shearwaters (*Puffinus pacificus*) living in a colony on Manana Island in Hawaii with 2 mL of weathered Santa Barbara crude oil either orally by gelatin capsule, or by applying this amount on the breast feathers. The adult birds weighed approximately 400 g, so that this corresponded to doses of approximately 5 mL/kg body weight. Control birds were not sham treated. Birds were observed in their burrows; otherwise they were free to leave or return. The number of birds that returned to the colony to incubate eggs was reduced in both exposure groups, and the effects were greater among the externally oiled birds, which failed to hatch any eggs. Subsequently, Fry et al. (1986) applied 0.1, 0.5 or 1.0 mL ($\approx$ 0.25, 1.25 or 2.5 mL/kg body weight) to the breast feathers of both members of Wedge-Tailed Shearwater pairs. The authors observed decreases in the number of birds that returned to the colony to incubate eggs after exposures to 1.25 or 2.5 mL/kg body weight, and a decrease in the number of chicks raised at the 2.5 mL/kg body weight exposure level. Both of these studies (Ainley et al. 1981; Fry et al. 1986) combined laboratory and field conditions, which resulted in an expanded scope of study, but which also introduced other environmental factors that could not be controlled.

Butler et al. (1988) administered single doses of Prudhoe Bay crude oil to Leach's Storm Petrels (*Oceanodroma leucorhoa*) by stomach tube at 0.02, 0.1, or 0.3 mL (corresponding to approximately 0.4, 2.0, and 6 gm/kg bodyweight, respectively). The birds were captured in their burrows and released after dosing and banding. These authors also applied single doses of the same oil to the feathers at dose rates of 0.1, 0.5, or 1.5 mL (corresponding to approximately 2.0, 10, and 30 gm/kg bodyweight, respectively). Dose related effects were seen on hatching success and fledging. Reproductive success returned to normal in the following year.

Field observations by Rittinghaus (1956) first indicated that eggs which were oiled from the oil-covered plumage of Cabot's Terns (*Thalasseus sandvicensis*) did not hatch. The development of eggs is adversely affected in a dose-related manner when medicinal mineral oil is applied to mallard eggs (Hartung 1965), No. 2 fuel oil to mallard eggs (Albers 1977) or Common Eider (*Somateria mollissima*) eggs (Albers and Szaro 1978), Bunker C fuel oil to mallard eggs (Szaro 1979), and Prudhoe Bay crude oil to chicken eggs (Couillard and Leighton 1990). None of these oils had been weathered, and would therefore be expected to spread more or less readily over the surface of the eggs. Macko and King (1980) found that weathering of Lybian crude oil decreased the hatchability of Louisiana Heron (*Hydranassa tricolor*) eggs, but did not affect the hatchability of Laughing Gull (*Larus atricilla*) eggs, when compared to the effects of the unweathered oil. When petrolatum or weathered *Exxon Valdez* crude oil was applied to mallard eggs, with applications ranging from 1/6 to 1/3 coverage of the egg, the hatchability of the eggs covered with weathered Exxon Valdez crude oil was much higher than the hatchability of the petrolatum covered control eggs, even though the amount of weathered crude oil per zone was approximately twice as much as petrolatum (Stubblefield et al. this volume).

Immuno-toxicology--Rocke et al. (1982; 1984) gave daily doses of 1 to 12 mL/kg body weight of South Louisiana crude oil or Bunker C fuel oil by stomach tube to mallards for a period of 28 days. The authors reported no significant effects in the ducks exposed to South Louisiana crude oil, but reported increased liver weight/body weight ratios and decreased spleen weight/body weight ratios in ducks that had been given Bunker C fuel oil by stomach tube. Ducks which had been previously exposed to 2.5 or 4 mL/kg bodyweight per day experienced a higher degree of mortality than control ducks when an LD_{20} dose of *Pasturella multocida* (the causative agent of avian cholera) was administered. The authors were unable to detect any decrease in antibody mediated-immunity, even in the ducks that had a decreased spleen size. The daily doses used in these studies could have been attained during the early stages of direct contact with oil, but it is improbable that ducks would have survived for 28 days, the duration of experimental feeding, in an environment where the daily ingestion of 2.5 to 4 mL of oil per kg of body weight was likely.

Summary of Toxic Effects after Short-Term Exposures

Laboratory studies, and limited field studies, have shown that single or multiple doses ranging from 1 to 22 gm/kg body weight of various types of oils can produce toxic effects in many organ systems (Table 1). These doses appear to be possible during the early stages of an oil spill episode. However, as the oil weathers and becomes less available to biota, the likelihood of producing these effects on various organ systems diminishes. The most important route of exposure appears to be ingestion rather than inhalation or dermal exposure.

LONGER TERM CONSEQUENCES

There are no sharp demarcations between the short-term and long-term aspects of an oil pollution incident. In the usual classification of toxicological studies, all of the effects cited in this paper up to this point would have been classified as acute or subacute, and very rarely as subchronic. Furthermore the concepts of "acute," "subacute," "subchronic" and "chronic toxicity" are ambiguous because they focus primarily on the duration of an exposure, and secondarily on whether the effect is obvious or subtle. The term "chronic exposure" is usually reserved for exposures that last a full life-span, or, at a minimum, for a major portion of a life-span.

In the case of oil pollution incidents, the intensity of exposure decreases continually as the duration of exposure increases. From initial layers of oil that are centimeters thick, the abundance decreases until oil can be found only in thin layers, as consolidated solids, or in isolated pockets. In addition to the quantitative changes, the oil changes qualitatively as the lower molecular weight fractions are lost by evaporation and as weathering proceeds.

Initially it is easy to find effects in many biological systems, and laboratory studies are often able to mimic the effects found in the environment. It is tempting to believe that the effects found in the laboratory under relatively controlled conditions will persist in the environment. However, the available doses in the environment continue to decline until they are far below those which have elicited effects in the laboratory. Environmental factors may act as contributing causes. As available doses decline, effects tend to change from obvious to subtle (Hartung and Durkin 1986), until it becomes impossible to distinguish them from random events, or from events with other causes.

A few issues, potentially important for long-term assessments or having implications beyond the intermediate time scale discussed above, are addressed below.

Bio-Accumulation

In mammals or birds the extent of bio-accumulation can be expressed as a ratio of the concentration of a xenobiotic in the body of a consumer relative to the concentration of that xenobiotic in the food that is being consumed. If this ratio is determined when the concentration in the body of the consumer reaches equilibrium conditions, then this also presents the maximum bioaccumulation ratio, and it can be expressed as a bio-accumulation coefficient (BAF). As soon as a mammal or bird begins to absorb a xenobiotic, it also begins to clear it by a combination of metabolism and excretion. Equilibrium is reached when absorption equals clearance. Therefore, the major determinant of the time required to reach equilibrium is the clearance rate, simplistically expressed as the clearance half-life. If a bioaccumulation experiment has included feeding a substance for several half-lives, then equilibrium concentrations would have been substantially achieved.

The extent of bio-accumulation of the components of petroleum oils in vertebrates is remarkably limited, even though the compounds in the oil mixture tend to be characterized by high n-octanol/water partition coefficients, which are thought to be highly correlated with bioconcentration in aquatic organisms (Veith et al. 1979). The compounds with lower molecular weights tend to have sufficiently low vapor pressures, so that they are mostly exhaled unchanged in birds and mammals before they undergo significant metabolism. The polycyclic aromatic hydrocarbons (PAHs) are readily bio-accumulated in clams and mussels, but not in fish, birds or mammals, because vertebrate species are capable of metabolizing PAHs at rates that prevent significant bioaccumulation (Neff 1985).

For petroleum oils, McEwan and Whitehead (1980) reported that Glaucous-Winged Gulls (*Larus glaucescens*) and mallards absorbed tritiated Boundary Lake crude oil, a marine diesel oil, and a Bunker C fuel oil administered orally in gelatin capsules. However, within 24 hours of dosing the residual concentrations of petroleum hydrocarbons declined to low or background levels. This implies an excretion half-life of less than 24 hours. In addition this implies that these birds will achieve equilibrium concentrations with exposures derived from the environment within a few days, the time required to achieve equal intake and clearance rates.

Engelhardt et al. (1977) and Engelhardt (1978) immersed Ringed Seals (*Phoca hispida*) for 24 hours in sea water covered with a 1 cm layer of Norman Wells crude oil, and fed ^{14}C-benzene and ^{14}C-naphthalene in Norman Wells crude oil to seals for 5 days. These investigators reported a rapid clearance of radio-label from blood, and very little accumulation in other tissues. The oral administration of ^{14}C-naphthalene in Norman Wells crude oil resulted in the highest levels of ^{14}C activity in the water soluble fraction from urine, moderate levels in fats, and little activity in most other tissues, indicating that the naphthalene is readily metabolized to water soluble compounds which are then excreted. Thus, these data also indicate that the concentrations of at least the petroleum hydrocarbons that have been studied in seals will reach an equilibrium between the body burdens and the concentration in the food of seals within a relatively short time.

Based on the rapid clearance kinetics for both petroleum hydrocarbons and for PAHs, the concentrations of these substances found in vertebrates collected from the wild can be regarded as equilibrium concentrations. In other words, present body burdens in birds and mammals should fluctuate only in proportion to the concentrations of these substances in their food sources. Postulating continuing increases in body burdens in vertebrates in the absence of an increasing trend in environmental petroleum hydrocarbons and PAHs is inconsistent with known kinetic principles.

Sub-Chronic Toxicity Studies

Eastin and Rattner (1982) fed a diet containing 0.15% Prudhoe Bay crude oil to 4-day old Mallard ducklings. After 9 weeks of feeding, the authors found slight elevations in plasma triglycerides and sodium concentrations, and slight decreases in cholesterol and packed red cell volumes.

Coon and Dieter (1981) fed 0.25 or 2.5% South Louisiana crude oil in the total diet to adult mallards for a period of 26 weeks. They did not detect any changes in any blood chemistry values, including those reported by Eastin and Rattner (1982). However, they observed decreased egg production in ducks fed 2.5% oil in their diet. There were no effects on fertility, egg shell thickness, or hatchability.

Szaro et al. (1981) fed diets containing either 0.5 or 5% No. 2 fuel oil to Mallard ducklings from hatching until 18 weeks of age. No mortalities related to oil ingestion were observed. Subtle histopathological changes, thought to be treatment related, were observed in heart, liver, kidneys, intestines and gonads. Serum enzyme activities commensurate with mild effects on liver and perhaps kidneys were seen especially at 5% oil in the diet. Also, the ducklings consuming the higher oil concentration were more active and also showed less avoidance behavior. In an earlier study, Szaro et al. (1978) fed 0.025, 0.25, 2.5, or 5% South Louisiana crude oil to Mallard ducklings from hatching to 8 weeks of age. They reported more obvious histological changes in liver and kidneys than found in the 1981 study, while serum enzyme changes remained slight. They also reported decreased avoidance behavior, but no increased levels of spontaneous activity.

Stubblefield et al. (this volume) fed up to 20 000 ppm (2%) weathered *Exxon Valdez* crude oil to mallards for 20+ weeks. They found no effects on reproduction at any dose level. At the highest dose level they found reduced egg-shell thickness, increased liver weights, and decreased spleen weights.

When Fleming, Sileo and Franson (1982) dosed Sandhill Cranes (*Grus americanus*) with Prudhoe Bay crude oil at 2 or 10 mL/kg of body weight daily for 25 days by stomach tube, they found no significant treatment-related effects.

In mammals there are extensive 13 week inhalation studies of the volatile fractions from commercial petroleum distillate based solvents (Carpenter et al. 1975a; 1975b; 1975c; 1975d; 1975e; 1975f; 1976a; 1976b; 1976c; 1976d; 1977). At high exposure levels, often approaching saturated vapor concentrations, the major effects were signs of central nervous system depression and respiratory irritation. Some of the solvent vapors also produced kidney damage after 65 days of exposure.

Carcinogenicity

Crude oils have not been established to be carcinogenic in an extensive evaluation by the International Agency for Research on Cancer (IARC 1989), even though some highly processed oils and some of the individual components present in crude oils are known carcinogens. The compounds of greatest concern for this effect are benzene and benzo[a]pyrene (BaP), as a component of the PAHs. Nevertheless, for most crude oils there is no evidence that they are carcinogenic in humans, in spite of long histories of high levels of dermal and inhalation exposures.

Benzene is known to cause myelocytic leukemias in humans as a consequence of high occupational inhalation exposures (Aksoy et al. 1974). Exposures of laboratory rodents by inhalation or ingestion for their entire life spans produced tumors at various sites, mostly divergent from the human experience (National Toxicology Program 1986). Rinsky et al. (1981) observed 7 deaths from leukemia among 746 workers exposed to 10 to 100 ppm, as a time weighted average exposure for at least 24 years. Although high oral doses of benzene administered by stomach tube have produced excess tumors in laboratory animals at high levels of exposure, there is no evidence that oral exposures to benzene have resulted in the production of tumors in humans. Benzene has a moderately high vapor pressure, and therefore the highest inhalation exposures to benzene should have occurred early during the spill. Eley et al. (1989) found a maximum air concentration of 80.5 ppm of benzene 2.5 cm above the surface of a freshly spilled crude oil, and the benzene concentration in air was reported to decrease rapidly.

The PAHs and their fluorescent biliary metabolites have produced concerns about exposures to carcinogenic PAHs, especially BaP. The carcinogenicity of BaP has been demonstrated in skin painting, inhalation, and gavage studies in laboratory rodents (U.S. EPA 1980). In crude oils, BaP is a minor ingredient among the total PAHs, and the total PAHs in turn are minor ingredients ($\approx$ 8 g PAH/kg) in *Exxon Valdez* crude oil. PAHs are readily metabolized by vertebrate animals, but not by bivalve molluscs, which tend to bioaccumulate PAHs. Thus, total PAHs in various species of bivalves collected from uncontaminated remote areas ranged from $\approx$ 1 to 250 µg/kg wet weight (Eisler 1987). Following the *Exxon Valdez* oil spill, the highest monthly mean concentration of PAHs in mussel tissues from spill affected areas was $\approx$ 14 500 µg/kg wet weight (Stubblefield et al. this volume).

The potential significance of carcinogenicity to mammals and birds that may be exposed to crude oils is questionable. Cancers have been found fairly frequently in fish living on highly contaminated sediments (Mallins et al. 1987). Chemically induced cancers are characterized by long latency periods and a rising incidence towards the end of the lifespan regardless of the ultimate lifespan of the exposed species (Brown 1987). In general, wildlife population studies show that very few individuals reach old age or approach their ultimate lifespan, as a consequence of the normally occurring mortality factors, such as disease, predation, or accident. Tumors have been reported to occur in a California Sea Lion *Zalopus c. californianus* (Brown et al. 1980) and Beluga whales (Béland et al. 1991) without evidence of the causative agent. No evidence was found for chemical carcinogenesis among aquatic birds.

Consequently, given the relatively short durations of exposure of aquatic birds and marine mammals, as well as the probably low concentrations of benzene and/or BaP in air and/or diet, it is unlikely that the EVOS incident produced a significant impact on tumor incidence and/or population structure.

DOSE - DURATION - EFFECT RELATIONSHIPS WITH RESPECT TO POTENTIAL EXPOSURES

For long-term exposures the route of greatest potential concern is the ingestion of residual oils. Therefore, the literature was searched for studies where known amounts of various oils were administered either directly in capsules or by stomach tube, or where known concentrations of oils were administered in the diet (Table 1). When possible,

TABLE 1– Dose-Duration of Exposure-Effect Relationship for Ingested Oils

Dose(s)[1] (g/kg/d)	Duration (Days)	Species	Admin.	Oil Type	Organ or System Effects	Reference
					Survival	
22	1	Pekin Duck	Direct	Diesel	No mortality	Hartung & Hunt 1966
10	14	Mallard	Diet	Weathered EVC[2]	No mortality	Stubblefield et al. this symposium
5	126	Mallard	Diet	No. 2 Fuel	No mortality	Szaro et al. 1981
5	56	Mallard	Diet	S. Louisiana crude	No mortality	Szaro et al. 1978
2.5	182	Mallard	Diet	S. Louisiana crude	No mortality	Coon & Dieter 1981
5	5	Ferret	Direct	Weathered EVC	No mortality	Stubblefield et al. ibid.
					Gastro-Intestinal Tract	
1.3-2	1	Pekin Duck	Direct	Santa Barbara crude	Electrolyte absorption	Crocker et al. 1975
2.5	7	Mallard	Diet	Prudhoe Bay crude	No effect on electrolyte absorption	Eastin & Murray 1981
1	1	Mallard	Direct	Diesel or No. 2 Fuel	Intestinal irritation	Hartung & Hunt 1966
					Liver	
2.7-22	1	Pekin Duck	Direct	Diesel	Incr. enzyme activity	Hartung & Hunt 1966
10.8	28	Mallard	Direct	Bunker C	No change in liver wt. ratio	Rocke et al. 1984
10	14	Mallard	Diet	Weathered EVC	No effect on liver	Stubblefield et al. ibid.
2.5-5	56	Mallard	Diet	S. Louisiana crude	Incr. enzyme activity & wt.	Szaro et al. 1978
1	210	Mallard	Diet	Paraffinic Fraction	No effect on liver	Patton & Dieter 1980
0.4	210	Mallard	Diet	Aromatic Fraction	Incr. naphthalene metabolism	Patton & Dieter 1980
5	5	Ferret	Direct	Weathered EVC	No effect on liver	Stubblefield et al. ibid.
9-10.8	5	Mouse	Direct	Prudhoe Bay crude, Bunker C	Increased liver weight	Leighton 1990
					Blood, Immune System	
10	5-7	Gulls, Puffins	Direct	Prudhoe Bay crude	Anemias	Leighton 1985
10	14	Mallard	Diet	Weathered EVC	No anemias	Stubblefield et al. ibid.
2	1	Mallard	Direct	No. 2 Fuel	Slight anemias	Hartung & Hunt 1966
2	140	Mallard	Diet	Weathered EVC	No anemias	Stubblefield et al. ibid.
1.8-9	25	Sandh. Crane	Direct	Prudhoe Bay crude	No anemias	Fleming et al. 1982
1.5	7	Mallard	Diet	Prudhoe Bay crude	No anemias	Rattner 1981
5	126	Mallard	Diet	No. 2 Fuel	Decreased spleen weight	Szaro et al. 1981
2	140	Mallard	Diet	Weathered EVC	Decreased spleen weight	Stubblefield et al. ibid

TABLE 1 (continued)-- Dose-Duration of Exposure-Effect Relationship for Ingested Oils

Dose(s)[1] (g/kg/d)	Duration (Days)	Species	Admin.	Oil Type	Organ or System Effects	Reference
					Blood, Immune System, continued	
3.6-10.8	28	Mallard	Direct	Bunker C	Decreased spleen weight	Rocke et al. 1984
2.2	28	Mallard	Direct	S. Louisiana crude	No effect of avian cholera	Rocke et al. 1984
3.6	28	Mallard	Direct	S. Louisiana crude	Decreased resistance to avian cholera	Rocke et al. 1984
9-10.8	5	Mouse	Direct	Prudhoe Bay crude	Slight anemias	Leighton 1990
9-10.8	5	Mouse	Direct	Several crudes or Bunker C	Decreased spleen & thymus weight ratios	Leighton 1990
1-5	5	Ferret	Direct	Weathered EVC	Decreased spleen weight	Stubblefield et al. ibid.
					Kidney	
5	56	Mallard	Diet	S. Louisiana crude	Incr. enzyme activity	Szaro et al. 1978
10	14	Mallard	Diet	Weathered EVC	No effect on kidneys	Stubblefield et al. ibid.
1.8	1	Mallard	Direct	Diesel or No. 2 Fuel	Slight effect on kidneys	Hartung & Hunt 1966
2	140	Mallard	Diet	Weathered EVC	No effect on kidneys	Stubblefield et al. ibid.
1-5	5	Ferret	Direct	Weathered EVC	No effect on kidneys	Stubblefield et al. ibid.
					Reproductive System	
1.4	1	J. Quail	Direct	Bunker C	Reduced egg laying	Grau et al. 1977
3.6	1	J. Quail	Direct	Mineral oil	No effect on egg laying	Grau et al. 1977
4.5	1	Shearwaters	Direct	Santa Barbara crude	Decreased egg laying & hatchability	Fry et al. 1986
5	1	C. Auklets	Direct	Prudhoe Bay crude	Slightly reduced egg laying	Ainley et al. 1981
5	1	C. Auklets	Direct	Bunker C	Decreased egg laying & hatchability	Ainley et al. 1981
2.7	100	Mallard	Diet	Kuwait crude	No egg production	Holmes et al. 1978b
2.7	100	Mallard	Diet	S. Louisiana crude	Reduced egg production	Holmes et al. 1978b
2	140	Mallard	Diet	Weathered EVC	No effects on laying or hatchability	Stubblefield et al. ibid.
2	140	Mallard	Diet	Weathered EVC	Slight eggshell thinning	Stubblefield et al. ibid.
2.5	182	Mallard	Diet	S. Louisiana crude	Reduced egg production	Coon & Dieter 1981
0.25	182	Mallard	Diet	S. Louisiana crude	Slightly reduced egg production	Coon & Dieter 1981

1 When necessary, daily doses are converted from mL/kg to g/kg by assuming a specific gravity of 0.9. Daily doses are estimated from dietary concentrations by assuming that test organisms consume 10% of their bodyweight as food per day.

2 EVC = *Exxon Valdez* Crude Oil

these data were transformed to the approximate g/kg body weight per day dose-equivalents. When the dose of an oil was quoted in terms of mL/kg, the transformation was made assuming a specific gravity of the oil of 0.9. When doses were quoted only in absolute amounts, they were converted to g/kg body weight by using the best estimate of the adult body weights from published sources. When oils were administered in the diet, daily doses were calculated assuming that the exposed organisms consumed 10% of their body weight in the form of food per day.

The data in Table 1 show that the daily doses required to produce toxic effects decrease only slightly as the duration of exposure increases, indicating that oils do not have significant cumulative toxicity. There is also no indication of pronounced differences among the sensitivities of the various species that have been tested. Although there clearly are differences in the toxicities of various oils and oil fractions, these appear to fall within one order of magnitude for equivalent effects. And lastly, oils administered by intubation or through gelatin capsules appear to be more toxic compared with administration in the diet.

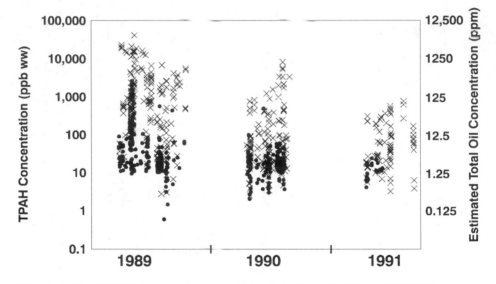

Figure 4--Total PAHs in mussels versus time; data from the NOAA PWSOIL database. Crosses indicate mussels in the spill path; dots indicate mussels outside the spill path. The total oil concentration in mussels is estimated by assuming that the oil contains 0.8% total PAHs.

The long-term potential exposures of oils in the environment are difficult to estimate. The bivalves, and particularly the mussels, seem to have the greatest potential to act as sources for the ingestion of PAHs and perhaps the associated oils. Figure 3 summarizes all analytical data for total PAHs in mussels that were analyzed by NOAA in conjunction with the *Exxon Valdez* oil spill. A hypothetical total oil concentration in these mussels was estimated by assuming that the oil contained 0.8% total PAHs. None of the estimated oil concentrations reach 12 500 ppm or 1.25%, and very few exceed 1 250 ppm. Only a few longer term toxicological studies have demonstrated effects at dietary levels of 12 500 ppm, and none have shown effects at 1 250 ppm. Furthermore, any assessment of potential effects needs to consider that the mussels with very high concentrations of PAHs were not very abundant, and that no aquatic animal has a diet that consists entirely of mussels for any extended period of time.

CONCLUSIONS

During the early phases of an oil spill the potential for significant exposures is very high, and can lead to extensive losses of aquatic birds and mammals, basically due to the physical actions of oils on plumage or fur. During the time course of an oil pollution incident, the local concentrations and chemical characteristics of oils change continuously as the oil weathers. Early during this transition from highly acute to sub-acute and sub-chronic exposures, many organ systems and biological processes can be affected. The exposures and effects characteristic of this transition phase have been studied most extensively in the laboratory, as well as the field. Most of the laboratory studies have been conducted on fresh crude oils or on refined products. The bio-accumulation of petroleum hydrocarbons or of PAHs in mammals or birds does not appear to be a significant phenomenon. Longer term studies conducted under laboratory conditions that have produced adverse effects have required exposures to higher concentrations than can be realistically sustained for an equal duration under environmental conditions.

An assessment of the toxicological literature and of the available empirical data on EVOS leads to the conclusion that direct, long-term sublethal toxic effects on wildlife appear to be very unlikely.

REFERENCES

Ainley, D.G., C.R. Grau, T.E. Roudybush, S.H. Morrell and J.M. Utts. "Petroleum Ingestion Reduces Reproduction in Cassin's Auklets." *Marine Pollution Bulletin.* 12(9): 314-317; 1981.

Aksoy, M., S. Erdem and G. Dincol. "Leukemia in Shoeworkers Exposed Chronically to Benzene." *Blood.* 44(6): 837-841; 1974.

Albers, P.H. "Effects of External Applications of Fuel Oil on Hatchability of Mallard Eggs." *in Fate and Effects of Petroleum Hydrocarbons in Marine Ecosystems and Organisms.* D.A. Wolfe (ed.); New York: Pergamon Press, Inc.; 158-163; 1977.

Albers, P.H. and R.C. Szaro. "Effects of No. 2 Fuel Oil on Common Eider Eggs." *Marine Pollution Bulletin.* 9: 138-139; 1978.

Aldrich, E.C. "A Recent Oil Pollution and its Effects on the Waterbirds in the San Francisco Bay Area." *Birdlore.* 40(2): 110-114; 1938.

Alexander, B., E. Lorenzen, R. Hoffman and A. Garfinkel. "The Effect of Ingested Oil on Plasma Carotene and Vitamin A." *Proceedings of the Society for Experimental Biology and Medicine.* 65: 275-278; 1947.

Anthony, D.C. and D.G. Graham. "Toxic Responses of the Nervous System." *Casarett and Doull's Toxicology - 4th Ed.* M.O. Amdur, J. Doull and C.D. Klaassen (eds.); New York: Pergamon Press; 407-429; 1991.

Baker, J.M., A.M. Jones, T.P. Jones and H.C. Watson. "Otter *Lutra lutra L.* Mortality and Marine Pollution." *Biological Conservation.* 20(4): 311-321; 1981.

Béland, P., S. DeGuise, and R. Plante. "Toxicology and Pathology of St Lawrence Marine Mammals." *Final Report Wildlife Toxicology Fund Research Grant.* St. Lawrence National Institute of Ecotoxicology. pp. 48-59; 1991.

Berkow, R. and A.J. Fletcher (eds.). *The Merck Manual - 15th Ed.* Rahway, New Jersey: Merck & Co.; 2377-2385; 1987.

Bogs, U. "Zur Kenntnis von pharmazeutischen Vaselinen." *Die Pharmazie.* 9: 502-506; 1967.

Bourne, W.R.P. "Sea Birds and Pollution." *Marine Pollution Bulletin.* 7: 403-502; 1976.

Brown, C.C. "Approches to Intraspecies Dose Extrapolation." in *Toxic Substances and Human Risk.* R.G. Tardiff and J. V. Rodricks (editors); New Yoek: Plenum Press; 237-268; 1987.

Brown, R.J., A.W. Smith, G.V. Morejohn and R.L. DeLong. "Metastatic Adenocarcinoma in Two California Sea Lions, *Zalophus c. californianus.*" *Journal of Wildlife Diseases.* 16: 261-266; 1980.

Brunton, L.L. "Laxatives." in *Goodman and Gilman's The Pharmacological Basis of Therapeutics - 7th Ed.* A.G. Gilman, L.S. Goodman, T.W. Rall and F. Murad (eds.); New York: Macmillan Publishing Company; 994-1003; 1985.

Butler, R.G., A. Harfenist, F.A. Leighton, and D.B. Peakall. "Impact of Sublethal Oil and Emulsion Exposure on the Reproductive Success of Leach's Storm Petrels: Short and Long-Term Effects." *Journal of Applied Ecology* 25: 125-143; 1988.

Carpenter, C.P., E.R. Kinkead, D.L. Geary, Jr., L.J. Sullivan and J.M. King. "Petroleum hydrocarbon toxicity studies. I. Methodology." *Toxicology and Applied Pharmacology*. 32: 246-262; 1975a.

Carpenter, C.P., E.R. Kinkead, D.L. Geary, Jr., L.J. Sullivan and J.M. King. "Petroleum hydrocarbon toxicity studies. II. Animal and human response to vapors of Varnish Makers' and Painters' Naphtha." *Toxicology and Applied Pharmacology*. 32: 263-281; 1975b.

Carpenter, C.P., E.R. Kinkead, D.L. Geary, Jr., L.J. Sullivan and J.M. King. "Petroleum hydrocarbon toxicity studies. III. Animal and human response to vapors of Stoddard Solvent." *Toxicology and Applied Pharmacology*. 32: 282-297; 1975c.

Carpenter, C.P., E.R. Kinkead, D.L. Geary, Jr., R.C. Myers, L.J. Sullivan and J.M. King. "Petroleum hydrocarbon toxicity studies. IV. Animal and human response to vapors of rubber solvent." *Toxicology and Applied Pharmacology*. 33: 526-542; 1975d.

Carpenter, C.P., E.R. Kinkead, D.L. Geary, Jr., L.J. Sullivan and J.M. King. "Petroleum hydrocarbon toxicity studies. VI. Animal and human response to vapors of "60" Solvent." *Toxicology and Applied Pharmacology*. 34: 374-394; 1975e.

Carpenter, C.P., E.R. Kinkead, D.L. Geary, Jr., L.J. Sullivan and J.M. King. "Petroleum hydrocarbon toxicity studies. VII. Animal and human response to vapors of "70" Solvent." *Toxicology and Applied Pharmacology*. 34: 395-412; 1975f.

Carpenter, C.P., E.R. Kinkead, D.L. Geary, Jr., L.J. Sullivan and J.M. King. "Petroleum hydrocarbon toxicity studies. VIII. Animal and human response to vapors of "140° Flash Aliphatic Solvent." *Toxicology and Applied Pharmacology*. 34: 413-429; 1975g.

Carpenter, C.P., E.R. Kinkead, D.L. Geary, Jr., R.C. Myers, D.J. Nachreiner, L.J. Sullivan and J.M. King. "Petroleum hydrocarbon toxicity studies. IX. Animal and human response to vapors of "80" Thinner." *Toxicology and Applied Pharmacology*. 36: 409-425; 1976a.

Carpenter, C.P., D.L. Geary, Jr., R.C. Myers, D.J. Nachreiner, L.J. Sullivan and J.M. King. "Petroleum hydrocarbon toxicity studies. X. Animal and human response to vapors of "50" Thinner." *Toxicology and Applied Pharmacology*. 36: 427-442; 1976b.

Carpenter, C.P., D.L. Geary, Jr., R.C. Myers, D.J. Nachreiner, L.J. Sullivan and J.M. King. "Petroleum hydrocarbon toxicity studies. XI. Animal and human response to vapors of deodorized kerosene." *Toxicology and Applied Pharmacology*. 36: 443-456; 1976c.

Carpenter, C.P., D.L. Geary, Jr., R.C. Myers, D.J. Nachreiner, L.J. Sullivan and J.M. King. "Petroleum hydrocarbon toxicity studies. XII. Animal and human response to vapors of "40" Thinner." *Toxicology and Applied Pharmacology.* 36: 457-472; 1976d.

Carpenter, C.P., D.L. Geary, Jr., R.C. Myers, D.J. Nachreiner, L.J. Sullivan and J.M. King. "Petroleum hydrocarbon toxicity studies. XIV. Animal and human response to vapors of "High Aromatic" Solvent." *Toxicology and Applied Pharmacology.* 41: 235-249; 1977.

Cavender, F. "Aromatic Hydrocarbons." *in Patty's Industrial Hygiene and Toxicology - 4th Ed. Vol. II Part B.* G.D. Clayton and F.E. Clayton (eds.); New York: John Wiley & Sons, Inc.; 1301-1442; 1993.

Coon, N.C. and M.P. Dieter. "Responses of Adult Mallard Ducks to Ingested South Louisiana Crude Oil." *Environmental Research.* 24: 309-314; 1981.

Cornish, H.H. "Solvents and Vapors." *in Casarett and Doull's Toxicology - 2nd Ed.* J. Doull, C.D. Klaassen and M.O. Amdur (eds.); New York: Macmillan Publishing Co., Inc.; 468-496; 1980.

Costa, D.P. and G.L. Kooyman. "Oxygen Consumption, Thermoregulation, and the Effect of Fur Oiling and Washing on the Sea Otter, *Enhydra lutris.*" *Canadian Journal of Zoology.* 60: 2761-2767; 1982.

Couillard, C.M. and F.A. Leighton. "The Toxicopathology of Prudhoe Bay Crude Oil in Chicken Embryos." *Fundamental and Applied Toxicology.* 14: 30-39; 1990.

Crocker, A.D., J. Cronshaw and W.N. Holmes. "The Effect of Crude Oil on Intestinal Absorption in Ducklings (*Anas platyrhynchos*)." *Environmental Pollution.* 7: 165-177; 1974.

Crocker, A.D., J. Cronshaw and W.N. Holmes. "The Effect of Several Crude Oils and Some Distillation Fractions on Intestinal Absorption in Ducklings (*Anas platyrhynchos*)." *Environmental and Physiological Biochemistry.* 5: 92-106; 1975.
Custer, T.A. and P.A. Albers. "Response of Captive, Breeding Mallards to Oiled Water." *Journal of Wildlife Management.* 44: 915-917; 1980.

Davis, R.W., T.M. Williams and F. Awbrey. "Sea Otter Oil Avoidance Study." Washington: OCS Study. Minerals Management Service, U.S. Department of the Interior. Report MMS-88-0051; 1-65; 1988.

Davis, R.W., T.M. Williams, J.A. Thomas, R.A. Kastelien and L.H. Cornell. "The Effect of Oil Contamination on Sea Otters (*Enhydra lutris*). II. Metabolism, Thermoregulation, and Behavior." *Canadian Journal of Zoology.* 66: 2782-2790; 1988.

DeGange, A.R. and C.J. Lensink. "Distribution, Age, and Sex Composition of Sea Otter Carcasses Recovered During the Response to the T/V Exxon Valdez Oil Spill." *Sea Otter Symposium: Proceedings of a Symposium to Evaluate the Response Effort on Behalf of Sea Otters After the T/V Exxon Valdez Oil Spill Into Prince William Sound, April 17-19, 1990, Anchorage Alaska.* K. Bayha and J. Kormendy (eds.). Washington: U.S. Fish & Wildlife Service; Biological Report 90(12): 124-129; 1990.

Eastin, Jr., W.C. and H.C. Murray. "Effects of Crude Oil Ingestion on Avian Intestinal Function." *Canadian Journal of Physiological Pharmacology.* 59: 1063-1068; 1981.

Eastin, Jr., W.C. and B.A. Rattner. "Effects of Dispersants and Crude Oil Ingestion on Mallard Ducklings (*Anas platyrhynchos*)." *Bulletin of Environmental Contamination and Toxicology.* 29: 273-278; 1982.

Eisler, R. "Polycyclic Aromatic Hydrocarbon Hazards to Fish, Wildlife, and Invertebrates: A Synoptic Review." *U.S. Fish and Wildlife Service Biological Report.* 85(1.11): 1-81; 1987.

Eley, W.D., R.J. Morris, L.L. Hereth and T.F. Lewis. "Is Overexposure to Benzene Likely During Crude Oil Spill Response?" *1989 Oil Spill Conference;* 127-129; 1989.

Ellenhorn, M.J. and D.G. Barceloux. *Medical Toxicology.* New York: Elsevier; 940-1006; 1988.

Engelhardt, F.R., J.R. Geraci and T.G. Smith. "Uptake and Clearance of Petroleum Hydrocarbons in the Ringed Seal, *Phoca hispida.*" *Journal of the Fisheries Research Board of Canada.* 34: 1143-1147; 1977.

Engelhardt, F.R. "Petroleum Hydrocarbons in Arctic Ringed Seals, *Phoca hispida,* Following Experimental Oil Exposure." *Proceedings of the Conference on Assessment of Ecological Impact of Oil Spills, 1978.* 614-628; 1978.

Engelhardt, F.R. "Petroleum Effects on Marine Mammals." *Aquatic Toxicology.* 4: 199-217; 1983.

Fabricius, E. "What Makes Plumage Waterproof?" *Severn Wildfowl Trust 10th Annual Report.* Slimbridge, England; 105-113; 1958.

Fleming, W.J., L. Sileo and J.C. Franson. "Toxicity of Prudhoe Bay Crude Oil to Sandhill Cranes." *Journal of Wildlife Management.* 46(2): 474-478; 1982.

Flickinger, E.L. "Wildlife Mortality at Petroleum Pits in Texas." *Journal of Wildlife Management.* 45(2): 560-564; 1981.

Frost, K.J. "Marine Mammals Study Number 5: Assessment of Injury to Harbor Seals in Prince William Sound, Alaska and Adjacent Areas." *State-Federal Natural Resource Damage Assessment for April 1989 - December 1990.* Fairbanks, Alaska: Alaska Department of Fish and Game; 1-22 + appendices; 28 November, 1990.

Fry, D.M., J. Swenson, L.A. Addiego, C.G. Grau and A. Kang. "Reduced Reproduction of Wedge-Tailed Shearwaters Exposed to Weathered Santa Barbara Crude Oil." *Archives of Environmental Contamination and Toxicology.* 15: 453-463;1986.

Gay, M.L., A.A. Belisle and J.F. Patton. "Quantification of Petroleum-Type Hydrocarbons in Avian Tissue." *Journal of Chromatography.* 187: 153-160; 1980.

Geraci, J.R. "Physiology and Toxic Effects on Cetaceans." *in Sea Mammals and Oil: Confronting the Risks.* J.R. Geraci and D.J. St.Aubin (eds.); San Diego: Academic Press; 167-197; 1990.

Geraci, J.R. and T.D. Williams. "Physiology and Toxic Effects on Sea Otters." *in Sea Mammals and Oil: Confronting the Risks.* J.R. Geraci and D.J. St.Aubin (eds.); San Diego: Academic Press; 211-221; 1990.

Giles, L.A. and J. Livingston. "Oil Pollution of the Seas." *Trans. 25th N. Am. Wildlife Conference.* 25: 297-303; 1960.

Gorsline, J., W.N. Holmes and J. Cronshaw. "The Effects of Ingested Petroleum on the Napthalene-Metabolizing Properties of Liver Tissue in Seawater-Adapted Mallard Ducks (*Anas platyrhynchos*)." *Environmental Research.* 24: 377-390; 1981.

Grau, C.R., T. Roudybush, J. Dobbs and J. Wathen. "Altered Yolk Structure and Reduced Hatchability of Eggs from Birds Fed Single Doses of Petroleum Oils." *Science.* 195: 779-781; 1977.

Hartung, R. "Ingestion of Oils by Waterfowl." *Papers of the Michigan Academy of Science, Arts, and Letters.* 43: 49-55; 1963.

Hartung, R. Some Effects of Oils on Waterfowl. Ann Arbor: University of Michigan Ph.D. Thesis; 141-161; 1964.

Hartung, R. "Some Effects of Oiling on Reproduction of Ducks." *Journal of Wildlife Management.* 29(4): 872-874; 1965.

Hartung, R. and P.R. Durkin. "Ranking the Severity of Toxic Effects: Potential Applications to Risk Assessment." *Comments on Toxicology.* 1(1): 49-64; 1986.

Hartung, R. and G.S. Hunt. "Toxicity of Some Oils to Waterfowl." *Journal of Wildlife Management*. 30: 564-570; 1966.

Hartung, R. "Energy Metabolism in Oil-Covered Ducks." *Journal of Wildlife Management*. 31: 798-804; 1967.

Hartung, R. "Dose-Response Relationships." *in Toxic Substances and Human Risk*. R.G. Tardiff and J.V. Rodricks (eds.); New York: Plenum Press; 29-46; 1987.

Hawkes, A.L. "A Review of the Nature and Extent of Damage Caused by Oil Pollution at Sea." *Trans 26th N. Am. Wildlife & Natural Resources Conference*. 26: 343-355; 1961.

Holmes, W.N., J. Cronshaw and J. Gorsline. "Some Effects of Ingested Petroleum on Sea-Water Adapted Ducks (*Anas platyrhynchos*)." *Environmental Research*. 17: 177-190; 1978a.

Holmes, W.N., K.P. Cavenaugh and J. Cronshaw. "The Effect of Ingested Petroleum on Oviposition and Some Aspects of Reproduction in Experimental Colonies of Mallard Ducks (*Anas platyrhynchos*)." *Journal of Reproductive Fertility*. 54: 335-347; 1978b.

Hunt, G.S. Causes of Mortality Among Ducks Wintering on the Lower Detroit River. Ph.D. Thesis, University of Michigan; 1-296; 1957.

IARC. "Occupational Exposures in Petroleum Refining; Crude Oil and Major Petroleum Fuels - Crude Oils." *IARC Monographs on the Evaluation of Carcinogenic Risks to Humans*. Lyons, France; International Agency for Research on Cancer; 119-158; 1989.

King, C.L. "Oil Sumps, Duck Nemesis." *Wyoming Wildlife*. 17(11): 32-33; 1963.

Klaassen, C.D. and D.L. Eaton. "Principles of Toxicology." *in Casarett and Doull's Toxicology - 4th Ed.* M.O. Amdur, J. Doull and C.D. Klaassen (eds.); New York: Pergamon Press; 12-49; 1991.

Leighton, F.A. "Morphological Lesions in Red Blood Cells from Herring Gulls and Atlantic Puffins Ingesting Prudhoe Bay Crude Oil." *Veterinary Pathology*. 22: 393-402; 1985.

Leighton, F.A., Y.Z. Lee, A.D. Rahimtula, P.J. O'Brian and D.B. Peakall. "Biochemical and Functional Disturbances in Red Blood Cells of Herring Gulls Ingesting Prudhoe Bay Crude Oil." *Toxicology and Applied Pharmacology*. 81: 25-31; 1985.

Leighton, F.A. "Clinical, Gross, and Histological Findings in Herring Gulls and Atlantic Puffins that Ingested Prudhoe Crude Oil." *Veterinary Pathology*. 23: 254-263; 1986.

Leighton, F.A. "The Systemic Toxicity of Prudoe Bay Crude and Other Petroleum Oils to CD-1 Mice." *Archives of Environmental Contamination and Toxicology.* 19: 257-262; 1990.

Macko, S.A. and S.M. King. "Weathered Oil: Effect on Hatchability of Heron and Gull Eggs." *Bulletin of Environmental Contamination and Toxicology.* 25: 316-320; 1980.

Magee, P.S. "Percutaneous Absorption: Critical Factors in Transdermal Transport." *Dermatotoxicology - 4th Ed.* F.N. Marzulli and H.I. Maibach (eds.); New York: Hemisphere Publishing Corporation; 1-35; 1991.

Mallins, D.C., B.B. McCain, D.W. Brown, U. Varanasi, M.M. Krahn, M.S. Myers and S.L. Chan. "Sediment-Associated Contaminants and Liver Diseases in Bottom-Dwelling Fish." *Hydrobiologica.* 149: 67-74; 1987.

Marshall, A.J. "Reproduction." *in Biology and Comparative Physiology of Birds. Vol. 2.* A.J. Marshall (ed.); New York: Academic Press; 169-213; 1961.

McEwan, E.H. and A.F.C. Koelink. "The Heat Production of Oiled Mallards and Scaup." *Canadian Journal of Zoology.* 51: 27-31; 1973.
McEwan, E.H. and P.M. Whitehead. "Uptake and Clearance of Petroleum Hydrocarbons by the Glaucous-Winged Gull (*Larus glaucescens*) and the Mallard Duck (*Anas platyrhynchos*)." *Canadian Journal of Zoology.* 58: 723-726; 1980.

Mosberg, A.T. and A.W. Hayes. "Subchronic Toxicity Testing." *in Principles and Methods of Toxicology - 2nd Ed.* A.W. Hayes (ed.); New York: Raven Press; 221-236; 1989.

National Academy of Sciences. Ocean Affairs Board. Petroleum in the Marine Environment. Washington: National Academy Press; 42-72; 1975.

National Toxicology Program. "Toxicology and Carcinogenesis Studies of Benzene (CAS No. 71-43-2) in F344/N Rats and B6C3F1 Mice (Gavage Studies)." *NTP Technical Report Series No. 289.* NIH Publication No. 86-2545; 1986.

Neff, J.M. "Polycyclic Aromatic Hydrocarbons." *in Fundamentals of Aquatic Toxicology.* G.M. Rand and S.R. Petrocelli (eds.); Washington: Hemisphere Publ. Corp.; 416-454; 1985.

Neff, J.M. "Composition and Fate of Petroleum and Spill-Treating Agents in the Marine Environment." *in Sea Mammals and Oil: Confronting the Risks.* J.R. Geraci and D.J. St.Aubin (eds.); San Diego: Academic Press; 1-33; 1990.

Osborn, K. and T.M. Williams. "Post-Mortem Examination of Sea Otters." *in Sea Otter Rehabilitation Program: 1989 Exxon Valdez Oil Spill.* T.M. Williams and R.W. Davis (eds.); Galveston, Texas: International Wildlife Research; 134-146; 1990.

Patton, J.F. and M.P. Dieter. "Effects of Petroleum Hydrocarbons on Hepatic Function in the Duck." *Comparative Biochemistry and Physiology.* 65C: 33-36; 1980.

Peakall, D.B., D. Hallett, D.S. Miller, R.G. Butler and W.B. Kinter. "Effects of Ingested Crude Oil on Black Guillemots: a Combined Field and Laboratory Study." *Ambio.* 9: 28-30; 1980.

Peakall, D.B., D.J. Hallett, J.R. Bend, G.L. Foureman and D.S. Miller. "Toxicity of Prudhoe Bay Crude Oil and its Aromatic Fractions to Nestling Herring Gulls." *Environmental Research.* 27: 206-215; 1982.

Phillips, J.C. and F.C. Lincoln. American Waterfowl. Boston: Houghton Mifflin Co.; 1-312; 1930.

Piatt, J.F., C.J. Lensing, W. Butler, M. Kendziorek and D.R. Nysewander. "Immediate Impact of the Exxon Valdez Oil Spill on Marine Birds." *The Auk.* 107: 387-397; 1990.

Rand, G.M. and S.R. Petrocelli. "Introduction." *in Fundamentals of Aquatic Toxicology.* G.M. Rand and S.R. Petrocelli (eds.); Washington: Hemisphere Publ. Corp.; 1-30; 1985.

Rattner, B.A. "Tolerance of 'Adult Mallards to Subacute Ingestion of Crude Petroleum Oil." *Toxicology Letters.* 8: 337-342; 1981.

Rinsky, R.A., R.J. Young and A.B. Smith. "Leukemia in Benzene Workers." *American Journal of Industrial Medicine.* 2: 217-245; 1981.

Rittinghaus, H. "Etwas über die "indirekte" Verbreitung der Ölpest in einem Seevogelschutzgebiete." *Ornithologische Mitteilungen.* 8(3): 43-46; 1956.

Rocke, T.E., T.M. Yuill and R.D. Hinsdill. "Oil and Related Contaminant Effects on Waterfowl Immune Defenses." *Toxicology of Petroleum Hydrocarbons, Proceedings of the First Symposium.* May 11-13, 1982, Washington, D.C.; 97-106; 1982.

Rocke, T.E., T.M. Yuill and R.D. Hinsdill. "Oil and Related Toxicant Effects on Mallard Immune Defenses." *Environmental Research.* 33: 343-352; 1984.

Rosenberg, N.L., M.C. Spitz, C.M. Filley, K.A. Davis, and H.H. Schaumburg. "Central Nervous System Effects of Chronic Toluene Abuse - Clinical, Brainstem Evoked Response and Magnetic Resonance Imaging Studies." *Neurotoxicol. Teratol.* 10: 489-495; 1988.

Siniff, D.B., T.D. Williams, A.M. Johnson and D.L. Garshelis. "Experiments on the Response of Sea Otters, *Enhydra lutris*, to Oil Contamination." *Biological Conservation.* 23: 261-272; 1982.

St.Aubin. "Physiologic and Toxic Effects on Pinnipeds." *in Sea Mammals and Oil: Confronting the Risks.* J.R. Geraci and D.J. St.Aubin (eds.); San Diego: Academic Press; 103-128; 1990.

Stevens, K.R. and M.A. Gallo. "Practical Considerations in the Conduct of Chronic Toxicity Studies." *in Principles and Methods of Toxicology - 2nd Ed.* A.W. Hayes (ed.); New York: Raven Press; 237-250; 1989.

Swinyard, E.A. and M.A. Pathak. "Surface-Acting Drugs." *in Goodman and Gilman's The Pharmacological Basis of Therapeutics - 7th Ed.* A.G. Gilman, L.S. Goodman, T.W. Rall and F. Murad (eds.); New York: Macmillan Publishing Company; 946-958; 1985.

Szaro, R.C., M.P. Dieter, G.H. Heinz and J.F. Ferrell. "Effects of Chronic Ingestion of South Louisiana Crude Oil on Mallard Ducklings." *Environmental Research.* 17: 426-436; 1978.

Szaro, R.C. "Bunker C Fuel Oil Reduces Mallard Egg Hatchability." *Bulletin of Environmental Contamination and Toxicology.* 22: 731-732; 1979.

Szaro, R.C., G. Hensler and G.H. Heinz. "Effects of Chronic Ingestion of No. 2 Fuel Oil on Mallard Ducklings." *Journal of Toxicology and Environmental Health.* 7: 789-799; 1981.

U.S. EPA. Ambient Water Quality Criteria for Polynuclear Aromatic Hydrocarbons. Washington, D.C.: Office of Water Regulations and Standards; EPA 440/5-80-069; 1980.

Veith, G.D., D.L. DeFoe and B.V. Bergstedt. "Measuring and Estimating the Bioconcentration Factor of Chemicals in Fish." *Journal of the Fisheries Research Board of Canada.* 36: 1040-1048; 1979.

Williams, T.M., R.K. Wilson, P. Tuomi and L. Hunter. "Critical Care and Toxicological Evaluation of Sea Otters Exposed to Crude Oil." *in Sea Otter Rehabilitation Program: 1989 Exxon Valdez Oil Spill.* T.M. Williams and R.W. Davis (eds.); Galveston, Texas: International Wildlife Research; 82-100; 1990.

Wilson, R.K., P. Tuomi, J.P. Schroeder and T. Williams. "Clinical Treatment and Rehabilitation of Oiled Sea Otters." *in Sea Otter Rehabilitation Program: 1989 Exxon Valdez Oil Spill.* T.M. Williams and R.W. Davis (eds.); Galveston, Texas: International Wildlife Research; 101-117; 1990.

Wolfe, D.A., M.J. Hameedi, J.A. Galt, G. Watabayashi, J. Short, C.O'Clair, S. Rice, J. Michel, J.R. Payne, J. Braddock, S. Hanna, and S. Sale. "Fate of the Oil Spilled from the *T/V Exxon Valdez* in Prince William Sound, Alaska." Draft Final Report Subtidal Study #4; 1993.

Wragg, L.E. "Effect of DDT and Oil on Muskrats." *Canadian Field Naturalist.* 68(1): 11-13; 1954.

Robert H. Day[1], Stephen M. Murphy[1], John A. Wiens[2], Gregory D. Hayward[2], E. James Harner[3], and Louise N. Smith[1]

USE OF OIL-AFFECTED HABITATS BY BIRDS AFTER THE *EXXON VALDEZ* OIL SPILL

REFERENCE: Day, R. H., Murphy, S. M., Wiens, J. A., Hayward, G. D., Harner, E. J., and Smith, L. N., **"Use of Oil-affected Habitats by Birds after the *Exxon Valdez* Oil Spill,"** Exxon Valdez *Oil Spill: Fate and Effects in Alaskan Waters, ASTM STP 1219*, Peter G. Wells, James N. Butler, and Jane S. Hughes, Eds., American Society for Testing and Materials, Philadelphia, 1995.

ABSTRACT: This study investigated the effects of the *Exxon Valdez* oil spill on the use of oil-affected habitats by birds during 1989-1991. We measured densities of birds in bays that had been subjected to various levels of oiling from the spill during survey cruises that were conducted throughout the year in Prince William Sound (PWS) and during summer along the Kenai Peninsula. Overall, 23 of 42 (55%) species in PWS and 22 of 34 (65%) species on the Kenai showed no evidence of oiling impacts on their use of habitats. Most species that did show initial negative impacts had recovered by late summer 1991 when our study concluded, although 6 of the 19 species initially impacted in PWS and 6 of the 12 species initially impacted along the Kenai did not exhibit clear signs of recovery by this time. A Principal Components Analysis of species examined from PWS revealed extensive overlap in ecological attributes among species that were and were not negatively impacted in their use of oil-affected habitats. Species that did not show clear evidence of recovery tended to be intertidal feeders and residents of PWS, but other ecologically similar species evidenced either no initial impacts or rapid recovery. These similarities suggest that the prognosis is good for the species for which we were unable to document recovery in habitat use. Our findings, together with the rapid rates of recovery in habitat features reported in other studies, suggest that impacts of the *Exxon Valdez* oil spill on avian use of oil-affected habitats generally were not persistent.

KEYWORDS: Alaska; *Exxon Valdez*; habitat; impact and recovery; oil spill; seabirds.

[1] ABR, Inc., P. O. Box 80410, Fairbanks, AK 99708 USA.

[2] Department of Biology, Colorado State University, Fort Collins, CO 80523 USA.

[3] Department of Statistics and Computer Sciences, Knapp Hall, West Virginia University, Morgantown, WV 26506 USA.

INTRODUCTION

Marine birds are among the most vulnerable and conspicuous organisms affected by accidents involving the production and transport of oil at sea. It is evident from the numbers of carcasses retrieved that major oil spills in productive areas (e.g., *Torrey Canyon* in 1967, *Amoco Cadiz* in 1978) often kill thousands of birds (National Research Council 1985; Burger 1993). Because oil spilled at sea initially floats on the sea's surface and often is deposited on shorelines, birds that use the water surface (e.g., loons, grebes, waterfowl, and seabirds) or intertidal habitats (e.g., shorebirds and wading birds) have a high probability of contacting spilled oil. This contact may cause direct mortality. Retrieving and enumerating oiled birds is the most common method of assessing impacts on birds following major oil spills (National Research Council 1985), although modeling estimates of actual mortality frequently are much higher than the dead bird counts (e.g., Page et al. 1990). Although few empirical data from field studies are available for evaluation of other impacts, there are a several pathways other than direct mortality through which oil spills can affect birds (Wiens, this volume). These include changes in population size or structure through decreased survival or emigration, changes in reproductive output, and reduced occupancy or use of spill-affected habitats.

When the tanker *Exxon Valdez* went aground on Bligh Reef on 24 March 1989, it spilled approximately 41 000 000 L (258 000 bbl) of crude oil into Prince William Sound (PWS). Oil spread through southwestern PWS, along the coast of the Kenai Peninsula (the Kenai), and into lower Cook Inlet and Shelikof Strait (see maps in Alaska Oil Spill Commission 1990; Galt et al. 1991). The leading edge of the oil slick moved from PWS into the Gulf of Alaska after about 1 week and reached the Kenai shortly thereafter (Galt et al. 1991). By that time, the slick had fragmented, most of the volatile fraction had evaporated, and the oil had mixed with seawater to form an emulsion, or "mousse" (Galt et al. 1991; Koons and Jahns 1992). Substantial amounts of oil were deposited on the shorelines of PWS and the Kenai, and these areas composed the majority of the estimated 2 000 km of shoreline that were oiled (Alaska Oil Spill Commission 1990).

Acute lethal effects of this spill on birds were well documented (Piatt et al. 1990; Maki 1991). About 30 000 carcasses were collected during the spring and summer of 1989, approximately 3 400 of them in PWS (12% of the total documented avian mortality) and 6 200 along the Kenai (21% of the total); the remainder (67% of the total) were retrieved primarily on the Barren Islands, around Kodiak Island, and along the Alaska Peninsula (Piatt et al. 1990). In decreasing order of abundance, murres, sea ducks, cormorants, tubenoses, murrelets, and guillemots constituted most of the mortality, with great regional variation in numbers and species killed (Piatt et al. 1990).

Considerable concern over the impact of this spill on birds has been voiced in the scientific literature, government documents, and the media. These concerns have focused on high mortality rates and long recovery periods (estimates of up to 70 years) for a variety of species (Piatt et al. 1990; Fry 1993; Heinemann 1993; Piatt 1993), uptake of hydrocarbons through contaminated food sources (Patten 1993a, 1993b; Sharp and Cody 1993), and long-term habitat degradation (Hodgson 1990). After 3 years of research, the *Exxon Valdez* Oil Spill Trustees (1992) issued a "Summary of Injury" that included claims of an estimated mortality of 375 000-435 000 birds in the months immediately following the spill, the complete reproductive failure of large murre colonies in 1989-1991 that led to an estimated lost production of 300 000 young, chronic uptake of hydrocarbons by sea ducks through contaminated food, reproductive failure of breeding species such as Black Oystercatchers and Harlequin Ducks, and population declines of a variety of species in oil-affected areas. (See Appendix Table for scientific names of bird species.)

The goal of this study was to evaluate impacts to and recovery of birds following the *Exxon Valdez* oil spill, focusing on their use of oil-affected habitats. To accomplish this goal, we pursued the following specific objectives: (1) to measure the abundance and distribution of birds in bays in PWS and along the Kenai that were exposed to various levels of oiling; (2) to assess impacts of this spill on birds and their habitats by comparing use among bays exposed to various levels of oiling, after accounting for the influence of habitat differences among bays; and (3) to evaluate and interpret the status of recovery of birds and their habitats by comparing use of oil-affected habitats through time. In the absence of adequate baseline data on affected populations, avian use of spill-affected habitats represents one of the few ways to assess the recovery of a species quantitatively. Although our study does not directly address demographic or reproductive recovery, the reoccupation of oil-affected habitats by birds is a clear sign that these other types of recovery can proceed (see Morrison 1986).

Because there are no universally accepted definitions of "impact" or "recovery" (Wiens, this volume), we will define these terms operationally and in the context of habitat use. A spill-induced impact is a statistical difference in the abundance of a species among bays exposed to various levels of oiling, after habitat differences among bays have been taken into account. A species has recovered from spill-induced impacts when a significant difference in a species' use of areas with respect to degree of oiling is no longer evident. In this study, we evaluated avian use of oil-affected habitats in PWS and along the Kenai and classified 47 species as "no apparent negative impact," "initial negative impact with recovery evident," or "impact persists or evidence of recovery unclear." We present detailed examples of species in each of these categories, then interpret these results in terms of ecological attributes of the species, vulnerability to oiling, and current thinking about the effects of oil on marine birds.

METHODS

Study Area

The PWS (Figure 1) and the Kenai (Figure 2) study areas are located in the northern Gulf of Alaska between 59° and 61°N and between 146° and 151°W. The physiography of the region is dominated by coastal mountain ranges (Kenai and Chugach) and numerous glaciers, both of which greatly influence climate, nearshore water masses, intertidal habitats, and numerous other factors that affect birds (Royer et al. 1990; Galt et al. 1991). Although the coasts of both areas differ in degree of exposure to the open ocean, both are dominated by complex rocky shorelines, numerous fjords, and active or recent glaciation. The climate of the region is cool maritime and is dominated in winter

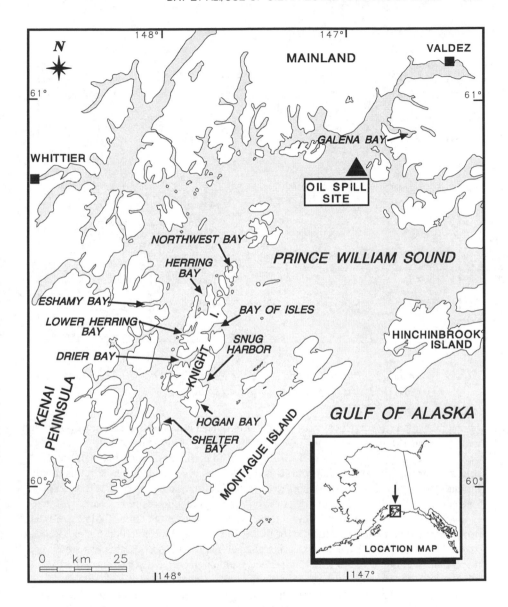

Figure 1—Locations of bays sampled in the Prince William Sound, Alaska, study area in 1989-1991, after the Exxon Valdez *oil spill.*

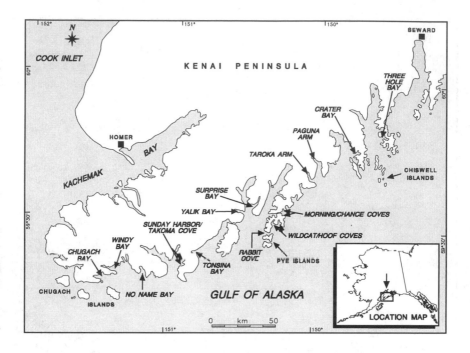

Figure 2—Locations of bays sampled along the Kenai Peninsula, Alaska, study area in 1989-1991, after the **Exxon Valdez** *oil spill.*

by the "Aleutian Low," which is the source of frequent, and often intense, storms (Wilson and Overland 1986).

Of the over 200 species of birds that occur in both areas, more than half are primarily marine-oriented (Isleib and Kessel 1973). Marine-oriented birds in this region include loons, grebes, tubenoses (e.g., shearwaters), cormorants, sea ducks, Bald Eagles, shorebirds, gulls, alcids (e.g., murres, puffins), and several corvids (e.g., Northwestern Crows). Because it is sheltered from intense winter storms in the Gulf of Alaska, PWS provides important wintering habitat for birds. In contrast, the Kenai coast is exposed to the Gulf of Alaska and lacks the estuarine characteristics of PWS. Both areas are important breeding areas for many bird species, although colonially nesting seabirds, which number in the millions along the Kenai, are less abundant in PWS (Sowls et al. 1978). The breeding bird community in PWS is dominated by noncolonial species such as Bald Eagles, Marbled Murrelets, Black Oystercatchers, and various species of ducks, although several small seabird colonies also are present (Sowls et al. 1978). The presence of large colonies of murres, Black-legged Kittiwakes, cormorants, and puffins along the Kenai is the most pronounced avifaunal difference between the two study areas; solitarily nesting species also breed in protected bays.

We used bays as our basic sampling unit because they are discrete areas that can be described quantitatively in terms of habitat and initial exposure to oil. Bays were not chosen randomly, but instead were selected to establish a gradient ranging from unoiled to heavily oiled. All bays were similar in that they were fjords with rocky shorelines, but they differed in size, shape, exposure to larger water masses, and other habitat features (see below).

We sampled 10 bays in PWS; 2 were on the mainland and 8 were on Knight, Eleanor, and Evans islands (Figure 1). These bays ranged in area from 1.5 to 24.3 km^2; four were unoiled or lightly oiled, and six were moderately to heavily oiled. Freshwater input and shelter from sunlight also varied among bays in PWS, as indicated by the formation of sea ice in some of the bays during winter.

We sampled 14 bays along the Kenai; 6 were sampled during all 3 years of study (1989-1991), 4 were sampled in 1989 and 1991, and 4 were sampled in 1990 and 1991. These differences in sampling occurred because weather and logistical constraints precluded sampling in 4 of the 10 bays scheduled for sampling in 1989. Four alternative bays were sampled that year but were not sampled in 1990, because we were able to visit all 10 bays originally selected for sampling that year. In 1991, we sampled all 14 bays. These bays ranged in size from 5.2 to 22.3 km^2; 10 were unoiled or lightly oiled, and 4 were moderately to heavily oiled.

Data Collection

Sampling schedule—Between 1989 and 1991, we sampled PWS up to six times per year and the Kenai up to two times per year (Figure 3) during research cruises that were timed to correspond with major phases of the birds' annual cycle (e.g., early breeding period, wintering). Each cruise (i.e., sampling period) was 14 to 20 days long, depending on the amount of inclement weather. During a cruise, we visited each bay one to five times, resulting in multiple samples (i.e., counts of each species of bird during each bay-visit) of avian abundance. We attempted to collect at least three samples in each bay during each cruise, although fewer were collected in PWS during early summer and fall 1989 and mid-winter 1990 and along the Kenai during late summer 1989.

Sampling methods—During each cruise, we collected data in each study bay with two sampling methods: nearshore surveys and offshore surveys. During nearshore surveys, we followed procedures previously used for counting nearshore and shoreline birds in PWS (Irons et al. 1988) and along the Kenai (Nishimoto and Rice 1987). In each bay, small boats were driven slowly along the shoreline at about 50 m from the beach, and all birds seen on the water within 200 m of the shoreline (nearshore zone), on the beach (intertidal zone), and on the shore within 100 m of the high-tide mark (supratidal zone; used primarily for sampling eagles and corvids) were identified and counted (Figure 4). Birds that occurred in the air over these three zones also were counted. Care was taken to avoid double-counting birds. We calculated linear densities of birds (i.e., an index of abundance) by dividing the total count for a species by the total length of shoreline sampled during each bay-visit.

Offshore surveys sampled birds that occurred in the centers of bays (>200 m from shore) and in waters off the mouths of bays. We modified the general strip-transect sampling technique used by the U.S. Fish and Wildlife Service (USFWS) (Gould et al. 1982; Gould and Forsell 1989) slightly, in that we sampled a transect trackline that was fixed in space rather than in duration (Figure 4); a similar technique has been used on

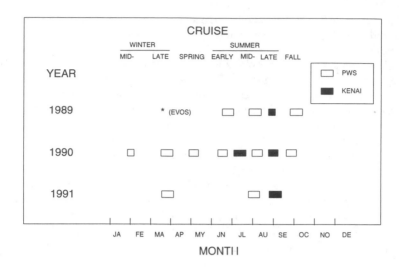

Figure 3—Dates of sampling cruises in Prince William Sound and along the Kenai Peninsula, Alaska, in 1989-1991, after the **Exxon Valdez** *oil spill (EVOS).*

Kodiak Island by the USFWS (Forsell and Gould 1981). In each bay, the ship followed a predetermined survey trackline, and we identified and counted all birds seen within 150 m of each side of the ship when it was within the bay and within 300 m of one side of the ship when it was off the mouth of the bay. The location and orientation of each survey trackline represented a compromise between avoiding shoal areas and maximizing the area sampled within the bay; hence, the size, shape, and bathymetry of a bay dictated the area sampled. We calculated densities of birds by dividing the total count for a species by the total area sampled (trackline length × width) during each bay-visit.

Before and during a cruise, we ensured quality control in data collection and handling. To minimize among-cruise effects of inter-observer variation in bird identification and distance estimation abilities, we conducted training sessions before each cruise, used a core of highly trained observers who participated in each cruise, constantly checked for agreement among observers, and had each team of observers sample all bays. We also checked the accuracy of the field data forms each night.

Oiling and habitat characteristics of bays—We developed an oiling index that reflected the initial oiling exposure for each bay. Data used in calculating this index were mapped in the field in 1989 by shoreline surveys and consisted of five possible categories for each uniformly oiled stretch of shoreline (Neff et al., this volume): no oil, very light oil (≤10% of the shoreline had spots of oil), light oil (band of oil <3 m wide), moderate oil (band 3 to 6 m wide), and heavy oil (band >6 m wide). For each bay, we calculated the percentage of the total shoreline length in each oiling category, then multiplied these percentages by a weighting factor for each category (from 0 for no oil to 4 for heavy oil) and summed them to obtain an oiling-index value. For example, a bay with light oil

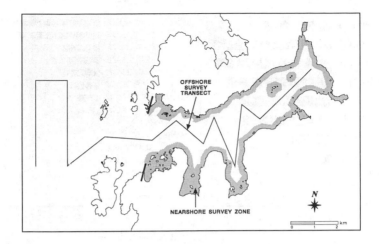

*Figure 4—Example of locations sampled by nearshore and offshore surveys in Drier
Bay, Prince William Sound, Alaska, in 1989-1991, after the* Exxon Valdez
oil spill.

along 44.5% of its shoreline and moderate oil along 55.5% would have an oiling index of
255.5 [(44.5 × weighting factor of 2 for light oil) + (55.5 × weighting factor of 3 for
moderate oil)]. Oiling-index values could range from 0 (100% no oil × weighting factor
of 0 for no oil) to 400 (100% heavy oil × weighting factor of 4 for heavy oil). Actual
index values ranged from 0 to 288.2 for bays sampled in PWS and from 0 to 222.5 for
bays sampled along the Kenai (Figure 5). Although most of the surface oil was gone
from bays and shorelines after 1989, we retained the oiling index to search for residual
impacts in 1990 and 1991.

    To describe other physical and biological characteristics of bays that may have
affected the distribution or abundance of birds, we mapped and measured habitat features
in each bay in 1990 and 1991. These measurements were treated as fixed values over all
cruises. Physical features that were measured from digital maps included bay area,
numbers of islands/km of shoreline, numbers of islets and intertidal rocks/km of
shoreline, shoreline complexity (fractal dimension--see Pennycuick and Kline 1986), and
overall shallowness (percentage of the bay area within 200 m of shore that was ≤18 m
deep). We also conducted surveys to determine the percentage of shoreline having each
of four substrates (bedrock, bedrock/rubble, boulder/cobble, and pebble/gravel), each of
three supratidal slope characteristics (0-30°, 31-60°, 61-90°), and special habitat features
(e.g., cliffs). Biological features measured and mapped during these surveys included the
percentage of shoreline having mussel (*Mytilus edulis* and *M. californianus*), fucus
(*Fucus distichus*), bullwhip kelp (*Nereocystis lutkeana*), and seagrass (*Zostera marina*
and *Phyllospadix scouleri*) beds and the percentage of shoreline bounded by each of nine
types of supratidal vegetation (e.g., coniferous forest). These vegetation types represent a
hybrid classification system derived from Kessel (1979) and Viereck et al. (1986).

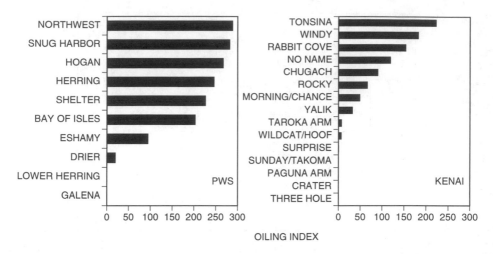

Figure 5—Initial oiling index values in 1989 for study bays in Prince William Sound and along the Kenai Peninsula, Alaska, after the **Exxon Valdez** *oil spill.*

In addition, we used historical data from the Alaska Department of Fish and Game (primarily from ADFG [1978]) and from our surveys to determine the number of salmon (*Oncorhynchus* spp.) runs/km of shoreline in each bay.

Data Analysis

Analytical strategy—Data from nearshore and offshore surveys were used to develop statistical models that related the abundance of a species (dependent variable) to initial oiling levels (i.e., oiling index, the primary independent variable) and habitat variables (secondary independent variables; see below). Three types of models were developed: "oiling analyses" and "oiling + habitat analyses" both tested for oiling effects within a particular year, whereas "among-year analyses" compared oiling effects during the same season over multiple years (Figure 6). Within-year analyses provided primary evidence of impact, and among-year analyses provided primary evidence of recovery. We also used data on the frequency of occurrence of species (i.e., the percentage of a cruise's bay-visits on which a species was recorded) in qualitative, among-year analyses that did not involve linear modeling and that provided secondary evidence of impacts (in a few cases) and of recovery.

Before constructing models, we calculated for each data set the percentage of bay-visits on which each species was observed. (A data set comprised density estimates or counts of a species for all of the bay-visits of a given survey type during a single cruise [e.g., Common Mergansers on nearshore surveys during spring 1990].) These frequency data were used to determine which analyses were to be conducted. If a species was recorded on <25% of the bay-visits on a cruise, we did not conduct within-year analyses; however, these data sets were used in among-year analyses if the frequency of occurrence of that species at that season in at least 1 year was ≥25%.

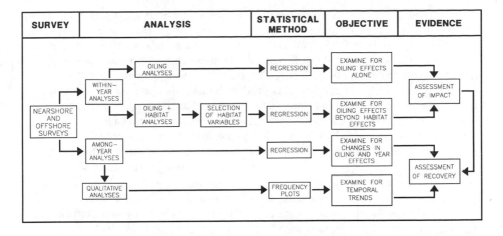

Figure 6—Strategy for analyzing and interpreting data collected on nearshore and offshore surveys in Prince William Sound and along the Kenai Peninsula, Alaska, in 1989-1991, after the **Exxon Valdez** *oil spill.*

If a species was recorded on ≥25% of the bay-visits, we used two main statistical procedures to analyze the data. For data sets in which the species was recorded on 25.0-74.9% of the bay-visits, we used Poisson regression with counts (not densities) of birds as the dependent variable (GLIM: Generalised Linear Interactive Models v.3.77; Royal Statistical Society, Oxford, United Kingdom). The count data were standardized by adding a constant term (log of shoreline length for nearshore surveys or of transect area for offshore surveys) to each model; such a constant functions much like an intercept value in normal regression. Poisson regression enabled us to analyze a large number of data sets that we would have been unable to analyze with normal regression. For data sets in which the species was observed on ≥75.0% of the bay-visits, we used normal regression with densities of birds as the dependent variable (Super ANOVA v.1.1; Abacus Concepts, Berkeley, CA). Densities were normalized with a common logarithmic transformation; before transformation, we added a small constant (0.167) to avoid computing the log of zero.

Our models and analytical strategy were designed to increase the likelihood that we would demonstrate both the existence of an oiling effect on a particular cruise and its persistence among cruises. We sought to minimize Type II errors (a failure to reject the null hypothesis that the oil spill had no effect on habitat use when in fact it did) by using error terms and α levels that maximized the likelihood of finding an impact and of not finding recovery. Determination of the most appropriate error term involved preliminary comparisons of the three sources of variation that were inherent in each data set: variation caused by multiple visits to a bay, variation caused by visits to different bays, and variation caused by oiling (a fourth source of variation, that caused by habitat variables, was considered only in an intermediate statistical step in the oiling + habitat analyses).

We used bays (i.e., a mean of multiple bay-visits for each bay during a cruise) or bay-visits as analytical sample units for regression analyses. Because we had only a limited sample of bays (10 in PWS and 10-14 along the Kenai), we preferred using bay-visits, because they considerably increased sample sizes and statistical power (i.e., the ability to detect oiling effects). The use of bay-visits, however, posed a problem if among-bay variability was significant, because their use made it difficult to determine whether a significant test statistic was caused by among-bay effects, oiling effects, or both. Consequently, we determined whether to use bays or bay-visits as the error term by testing each bay-visit data set to see whether the bay-to-bay variation explained a significant additional amount of the variation beyond that explained by the visit-to-visit variation ($\alpha = 0.05$ for oiling analyses; $\alpha = 0.20$ for among-year analyses). If the bay-to-bay variation explained a nonsignificant amount of additional variation, we used the bay-visit data set to determine the effects of oiling; otherwise, we used the bay data set. We used the same data set for both oiling analyses and oiling + habitat analyses.

The use of bay-visits posed another problem because the lack of statistical independence among replicate samples could lead to pseudoreplication (Hurlbert 1984). For example, repeated visits to a bay during the breeding season could result in repeated counts of the same pairs of nesting Bald Eagles; pseudoreplication also might affect data for some of the wintering species. If a bay-visit data set was used, however, pseudoreplication would increase rather than decrease the likelihood of demonstrating oiling effects. This potential problem did not arise when a bay data set was used. We used bay data sets in 41% of all models for PWS and in 53% of all models for the Kenai.

For both within-year and among-year analyses, we tested for oiling effects with a linear independent variable (*Oil*; the oiling index value for that bay) and a quadratic independent variable (Oil^2; the squared oiling index value for that bay) with three α levels (0.20, 0.10, and 0.05). All tests were two-tailed, because we were interested in both negative and positive relationships with oiling. For each analysis, we tested regression models that included *Oil* alone, *Oil* and Oil^2 together, and neither oiling term (i.e., just the intercept); we included the quadratic term to account for possible nonlinear relationships between bird densities or counts and oiling level. Quadratic models were interpreted by examining graphical plots of densities or counts versus oiling for evidence of a relationship. Because both oiling terms were tested at the three α levels to determine the strength of evidence of a relationship, different terms could be significant at different α levels. If the quadratic effect was significant at the same or a more significant α level (i.e., nearer 0.001) than the linear effect, the quadratic model was interpreted.

Within-year analyses—We examined the effects of oiling for each cruise separately within a particular year using (1) analyses of oiling effects among bays and (2) analyses of oiling effects among bays after the effects of habitat had been entered into the models. Oiling analyses measured the effects of oiling on abundance of birds through simple regressions of density or counts versus oiling. Oiling + habitat analyses were designed to evaluate the effects of oiling after the effects of habitat variation among bays had been accounted for by the model. To do these analyses, we first identified significant habitat variables for a data set. We then built habitat models from these variables, calculated the residuals from these models of densities or counts versus habitat variables, and regressed these residuals against oiling to determine the relationship between abundance and oiling after the effects of habitat had been removed. Significant habitat variables were selected by running an "all possible models" routine in SAS software (v.6.03; SAS Institute, Cary, NC) for each data set to find the habitat model that explained the greatest variation in density (i.e., had the highest R^2 value). During interpretation of oiling + habitat models, special attention was paid to the five habitat variables in PWS and the two habitat variables along the Kenai that were most collinear (i.e., were correlated most strongly) with oiling; this collinearity could mask the true effects of oiling on a species.

Among-year analyses—We examined changes in responses to oiling for the same season during different years (Figure 3) using statistical models and qualitative inspections of frequency of occurrence data (Figure 6). Among-year modeling extended the oiling models to allow for year effects and oil-by-year interactions. Such an approach was necessary because bird abundances at the same season could vary among years, either independently or as a function of oiling. A year effect would reflect a similar change in abundance across all bays among years, regardless of oiling level, but an oil-by-year interaction would reflect a change in effects of oiling among years.

We also compared the frequency of occurrence of each species on bay-visits for the same season among years to evaluate whether an impact or recovery was suggested. These comparisons provided an additional source of evidence of recovery if the regression results were ambiguous (see below).

Data Interpretation and Strength of Evidence

Oiling impacts and recovery were assessed by examining both within-year and among-year trends of oiling effects (Figure 6). We used the oiling + habitat analyses as the primary evidence of impacts, because these analyses revealed whether an oiling effect existed after habitat variation among bays had been taken into account. The oiling analyses were used to provide additional evidence of impacts. Recovery was assessed by examining both oiling + habitat analyses and among-year analyses. In the oiling + habitat analyses, recovery was indicated by the absence of an impact that had been detected earlier. In the among-year analyses, recovery was indicated by significant oil-by-year interactions that yielded increasingly positive regression slopes (i.e., increased use of heavily oiled bays). Increases in the frequency of occurrence on bay-visits through time also were used as evidence of recovery.

To increase the likelihood of detecting oiling effects in these statistical analyses, we departed from the customary practice of using an α level of 0.05 and instead used α levels up to 0.20, for two reasons. First, the combination of high variance in some data sets with small sample sizes when bays were used as analytical units reduced the power to detect an oiling effect. For example, quadratic regression models with bays as replicates had only 7 degrees of freedom; incorporating habitat variables reduced the number of degrees of freedom to <5 in some analyses. By using an α level of 0.20, we were able to detect possible spill-related impacts that we would not have found with a more stringent α level. Second, some analyses involved multiple tests for a species over time. The broader zone of "significance" provided by a less stringent α level enabled us to detect trends over successive cruises that probably would have been missed had we restricted our attention to the traditional α level of 0.05. If our sample sizes had been larger, estimates of densities less variable, and patterns of impact through time not so critical to our assessment of recovery, we could have used a more stringent α level.

Our conclusions about spill-induced impacts and recovery involved more than statistical tests for significant trends. We supplemented the statistical tests with other information, especially data on the frequency of occurrence of a species among bays over a series of cruises. We also categorized our conclusions for a given species as strong, moderate, or weak, based on the α levels at which statistical tests demonstrated significant effects and the number of tests available for interpretation. For example, we considered evidence of an oiling impact to a species to be strong if statistical tests indicated a negative relationship between abundance and oiling at $P \leq 0.05$ and if data were examined statistically for most or all of the cruises. On the other hand, if the analyses indicated an oiling relationship for a species at $0.10 \leq P \leq 0.20$ or if data could be analyzed for only a few cruises, we considered the evidence to be weak. Because the number of cruises varied seasonally and through time, determination of recovery was difficult for a few uncommon or seasonally restricted species.

To aid in the interpretation of our results, we categorized each of the 42 PWS species that we had analyzed according to features of its ecology and life history that might relate to impacts and recovery from oiling of habitats. These characteristics then were screened to delete variables that were highly correlated with other characteristics. We then iteratively conducted a series of principal components analyses (PCAs) based on a matrix of species-by-ecological trait that deleted additional variables until we selected the PCA with the greatest number of interpretable axes; our interpretation of all PCAs were similar, however. To conduct the PCA, we used JMP software (v.2.05; SAS Institute, Cary, NC). The variables retained in the analysis were residence status in PWS, the degree of breeding coloniality, primary food habits, and primary foraging location. We also tested for differences in PCA scores among the three oiling-impact groups (no apparent negative impact, initial negative impact with recovery, impact persists/evidence of recovery unclear) with a one-way Analysis of Variance (ANOVA); tests were performed separately for each axis.

RESULTS

We recorded 79 species of marine-oriented birds on nearshore and offshore surveys combined during 11 sampling periods in PWS and 70 species during 4 sampling periods along the Kenai (Table 1). Of these, 42 species in PWS and 34 species along the Kenai occurred frequently enough for quantitative analyses (i.e., in ≥25.0% of the bay-visits on at least one cruise). Of the 37 species in PWS and the 36 along the Kenai that were not examined quantitatively, some were at or near the edge of their ranges in this region (e.g., Ring-necked and Ruddy ducks, Thayer's Gull), some occurred in low numbers because of inadequate habitat in the study bays (e.g., Northern Fulmar, several

Table 1—Number of species of marine-oriented birds recorded on nearshore and offshore surveys combined during each cruise and year in Prince William Sound and along the Kenai Peninsula, Alaska, in 1989-1991, after the Exxon Valdez *oil spill.*

Location/cruise	Year		
	1989	1990	1991
PRINCE WILLIAM SOUND			
Mid-winter	nd[a]	40	nd
Late winter	nd	46	42
Spring	nd	63	nd
Early summer	32	46	nd
Mid-summer	48	47	43
Fall	40	45	nd
KENAI PENINSULA			
Mid-summer	nd	51	nd
Late summer	39	56	54

[a] nd = no data.

species of dabbling ducks, Least Sandpiper), and some simply were rare throughout this entire region (e.g., Yellow-billed Loon, Glaucous Gull).

Despite some seasonal differences, the number of species recorded was quite consistent among cruises. We recorded 40 to 48 species during most cruises in PWS and 51 to 56 species during most cruises along the Kenai (Table 1). The most species (63) were recorded in PWS during spring 1990, which coincided with spring migration in this region. The periods of low species richness in early summer 1989 (PWS) and late summer 1989 (the Kenai) were associated with the lower sampling effort on the initial cruises in each of the study areas. We expected to record fewer species on these cruises with lower sampling effort (Magurran 1988), but analyses of the effects of the spill on the entire bird community in PWS, which took sampling effort into account, indicated that species richness actually was negatively affected in oiled bays in summer 1989 (Wiens et al., in review).

The bird community also varied both seasonally and regionally. In PWS, gulls and alcids numerically dominated the summering community, whereas loons, waterfowl, raptors, and shorebirds were widespread but less numerous. In contrast, grebes, cormorants, and waterfowl dominated the wintering community, with loons, shorebirds, gulls, and alcids occurring in lower numbers. Along the Kenai, tubenoses, cormorants, and alcids dominated the summering community, with waterfowl, raptors, shorebirds and gulls occurring in lower numbers.

Oiling Effects in Prince William Sound

On the basis of our analyses, we classified each of the 42 species examined from PWS into categories according to initial impacts of oiling and subsequent recovery. Of these species, 23 (55%) exhibited no initial negative impacts of oiling and 19 (45%)

exhibited negative impacts (Table 2). Four species actually exhibited a positive relationship with oiling, even after habitat characteristics were taken into consideration. Species exhibiting no negative impacts included an assortment of loons, grebes, cormorants, waterfowl, shorebirds, jaegers, gulls, terns, alcids, and corvids.

Of the 19 species from PWS that exhibited an initial negative impact of oiling, 13 (68%) showed evidence of subsequent recovery (Table 2). Although only 1 of these 13 species had recovered by late 1989, an additional 7 had recovered by late 1990, and the other 5 had recovered by the end of our sampling in late 1991. Species exhibiting initial negative impacts were primarily waterfowl (37% of all negatively impacted species), grebes (11%), and gulls (11%). Six of the 19 species that exhibited an initial negative impact had exhibited no recovery or unclear recovery by late 1991 (Table 2). These six species included two grebe species, two sea duck species, a gull, and a corvid.

We classified 20 (48%) of the 42 species analyzed for PWS to specific oiling impact categories on the basis of strong evidence (Table 2). Another 13 (31%) species were classified from moderate-quality evidence, and the remaining 9 (21.4%) species were classified from weak evidence. Hence, we had moderate to high confidence in the accuracy of our classifications for nearly 80% of the species.

To clarify the analytical and interpretive steps that led us to assign species to these various categories, we will discuss in detail examples of two species that exhibited no initial negative impacts of oiling, two that exhibited initial negative impacts with subsequent recovery from those impacts, and two that exhibited initial negative impacts with no evidence of subsequent recovery or for which evidence of recovery was unclear.

Species exhibiting no initial negative impacts—The majority of the species examined statistically did not exhibit initial negative impacts of oiling (Table 2). The following examples are of one species that clearly exhibited no negative relationships with oiling and one that exhibited an apparent negative relationship that disappeared when habitat variables were included in the model.

Red-necked Phalaropes breed in freshwater marshes such as the nearby Copper River Delta (Isleib and Kessel 1973) and generally are open-water birds that feed at the sea's surface during migratory and nonbreeding periods. They were mid-summer migrants in our study bays (Figure 7) and occurred in sufficient frequencies for analysis only on offshore surveys. In the within-year analyses, phalarope densities exhibited no significant relationships with oiling in either the oiling or the oiling + habitat analyses (Table 3). There was a suggestion of increasing densities with increased oiling levels in mid-summer 1989, although that relationship disappeared when habitat variables were added to the model. In the among-year analyses, phalaropes also exhibited no negative relationships with oiling. Moreover, the mid-summer comparison revealed a significant year effect that did not consistently reflect time since the oil spill (i.e., numbers in 1990 > 1991 > 1989). This pattern occurred across all bays regardless of initial oiling levels, indicating no relationship to oiling. We conclude that, with respect to the use of oil-affected habitats, there was no evidence of negative impacts of oiling on Red-necked Phalaropes.

*Table 2—Classification of oiling impact and recovery based on use of oil-affected
habitats for bird species recorded in Prince William Sound, Alaska, in
1989-1991, after the* **Exxon Valdez** *oil spill.*

No apparent negative impact detected	Initial negative impact detected		
	Recovery evident	Year of recovery	Impact persists/ recovery unclear
EVIDENCE STRONG[a]			
Fork-tailed Storm-Petrel	Pelagic Cormorant	1990	Horned Grebe
Red-necked Phalarope	Harlequin Duck	1991	Red-necked Grebe
Black-legged Kittiwake (P)[b]	Common Merganser	1990	Barrow's Goldeneye
Pigeon Guillemot (P)	Red-breasted Merganser	1991	Bufflehead
Black-billed Magpie	* Bald Eagle	1990	Mew Gull
Common Raven	Black Oystercatcher	1991	Northwestern Crow
	Glaucous-winged Gull	1990	
	* Marbled Murrelet	1989	
EVIDENCE MODERATE			
* Common Loon	Mallard	1990	
Double-crested Cormorant	* Wandering Tattler	1990	
Surf Scoter	Common Murre	1990	
* White-winged Scoter (P)			
* Common Goldeneye			
Spotted Sandpiper			
Arctic Tern			
Tufted Puffin (P)			
Belted Kingfisher			
* Steller's Jay			
EVIDENCE WEAK			
Red-faced Cormorant	Great Blue Heron	1990	
Canada Goose	Black Scoter	1990	
Green-winged Teal			
American Wigeon			
Oldsquaw			
Pomarine Jaeger			
Herring Gull			

[a] The strength of evidence reflected both the statistical strength of the models and the number
  of cruises for which analyses were conducted; see Methods.
[b] (P) indicates that the species exhibited a positive response to oil.
* = our assessment of impact or recovery time changed as a result of the habitat analyses.

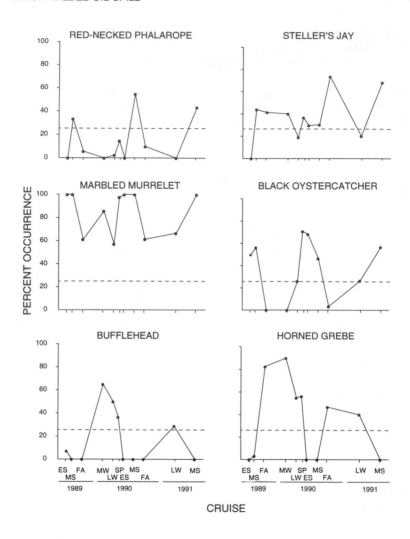

Figure 7—*Frequencies of occurrence (%) by cruise for six species of birds in Prince William Sound, Alaska, in 1989-1991, after the* **Exxon Valdez** *oil spill. The dashed line at 25% represents the minimal frequency of occurrence for which we could conduct quantitative analyses. Abbreviations for cruises are: ES = early summer; MS = mid-summer; FA = fall; MW = mid-winter; LW = late winter; SP = spring.*

Table 3—Results of regression analyses evaluating impacts of oil on use of oil-affected habitats by Red-necked Phalaropes and Steller's Jays in Prince William Sound, Alaska, in 1989-1991, after the **Exxon Valdez** *oil spill.*

Species/cruise	Analysis	Within-year analysis 1989	1990	1991	Oiling	Among-year analysis[a] Year	Oil-by-year interaction
RED-NECKED PHALAROPE[b]							
Mid-summer	Oil	*[c]	0	0	0	***	0
		+				90 > 91 > 89	
	Oil + Habitat	0	0	0	na[d]	na	na
STELLER'S JAY[e]							
Mid-winter	Oil	nd[f]	0	nd	na	na	na
	Oil + Habitat	nd	div[g]	nd	na	na	na
Spring	Oil	nd	*	nd	na	na	na
		−					
	Oil + Habitat	nd	0	nd	na	na	na
Early Summer	Oil	nd	*	nd	0	0	div
		−					
	Oil + Habitat	nd	0	nd	na	na	na
Mid-summer	Oil	0	***	0	0	***	0
		−				91 > 89 > 90	
	Oil + Habitat	0	0	0	na	na	na
Fall	Oil	*	*	nd	0	***	0
		−	−			90 > 89	
	Oil + Habitat	0	0	nd	na	na	na

[a] Comparisons are: late winter 1990 versus 1991; early summer 1989 versus 1990; mid-summer 1989 versus 1990 versus 1991; and fall 1989 versus 1990.

[b] Offshore data set.

[c] The number of asterisks indicates the statistical strength of the model, with $P \leq 0.20$, ≤ 0.10, and ≤ 0.05 represented by *, **, and ***, respectively. For all results except interactions, a "+" and a "−" indicate a positive and negative relationship with oiling, respectively; for interactions, a "+" indicates recovery, and a "−" indicates a lack of recovery. A "0" indicates no significant relationship with oiling.

[d] na = no analysis.

[e] Nearshore data set.

[f] nd = no data.

[g] div = divergence of GLIM model–no model could be calculated and no interpretation was possible.

Steller's Jays are forest birds that visit shoreline areas and therefore may have been exposed to oil. This species is resident in PWS (Isleib and Kessel 1973), was seen only on nearshore surveys, and occurred in highly fluctuating frequencies among cruises (Figure 7). In the within-year analyses, the oiling analyses suggested negative relationships with oiling on 5 of 7 cruises (Table 3). However, those relationships all disappeared in the oiling + habitat analyses, even though none of the habitat variables was strongly collinear with oil; hence, the significant oiling models were considered not to represent an actual oiling impact. The among-year analyses also indicated no negative effects. Significant year effects emerged in the mid-summer and fall comparisons. Only the fall comparison indicated a consistent increase in abundance with time since the oil spill; because this increase occurred across all bays, however, it did not indicate a relationship to oiling. We conclude that Steller's Jays were not impacted by the oil spill and that their apparent avoidance of oil-affected habitats actually was due to other habitat factors.

Species exhibiting initial negative impacts with subsequent recovery   Of the species exhibiting initial negative impacts of oiling (Table 2), most subsequently recovered. The following examples are of one species that exhibited an initial impact with rapid recovery and one that exhibited an impact with a more delayed recovery.

Marbled Murrelets are forest-nesting alcids that spend most of their time at sea. They are resident in PWS (Isleib and Kessel 1973) but are most abundant during the summer breeding season (Figure 7). Although murrelets occurred on both nearshore and offshore surveys, they exhibited a negative impact only on offshore surveys. In the within-year analyses, murrelets exhibited a moderate negative impact in the oiling analysis for early summer 1989; addition of habitat variables to the model resulted in weaker (but still convincing) evidence of a negative relationship with oiling (Table 4). In contrast, a strong negative relationship in the oiling analysis in mid-summer 1990 disappeared when habitat variables were added to the model. A weak negative relationship in the oiling + habitat analysis for mid-summer 1991 was not considered to be evidence of an oiling impact because no evidence of impacts was seen during the previous nine cruises. In the among-year analyses, significant year effects were found in 3 of 4 cruises. The population increases occurred across all bays, however, indicating a regional population increase that was not related to oiling. The one significant oil-by-year interaction (mid-summer) was positive, suggesting recovery, but the absence of negative relationships in previous surveys during this season suggested to us that it was not evidence of an oiling impact. We conclude that, with respect to the use of oil-affected habitats, Marbled Murrelets were weakly impacted early in the summer of 1989 but had recovered by mid-summer of that year.

Black Oystercatchers breed and feed in low numbers on beaches throughout the region. They are summer breeders that leave PWS by fall and return in late winter (Figure 7), although they occasionally overwinter in PWS in local, large flocks (Isleib and Kessel 1973). They occurred only on nearshore surveys. In the within-year analyses, consistent and strong negative relationships with oiling occurred in both oiling and oiling + habitat analyses for mid-summer 1989 and spring and mid-summer 1990 (Table 4). No negative relationships with oiling were recorded on surveys conducted

Table 4—Results of regression analyses evaluating impacts of oil on use of oil-affected habitats by Marbled Murrelets and Black Oystercatchers in Prince William Sound, Alaska, in 1989-1991, after the **Exxon Valdez** *oil spill. Explanations of footnote symbols are in Table 3.*

| Species/cruise | Analysis | Within-year analysis | | | Among-year analysis[a] | | |
		1989	1990	1991	Oiling	Year	Oil-by-year interaction
MARBLED MURRELET[b]							
Mid-winter	Oil	nd[f]	0[c]	nd	na[d]	na	na
	Oil + Habitat	nd	0	nd	na	na	na
Late Winter	Oil	nd	0	0	0	***	0
						91 > 90	
	Oil + Habitat	nd	0	0	na	na	na
Spring	Oil	nd	0	nd	na	na	na
	Oil + Habitat	nd	0	nd	na	na	na
Early Summer	Oil	**	0	nd	0	***	0
		−				90 > 89	
	Oil + Habitat	*	0	nd	na	na	na
		−					
Mid-summer	Oil	0	***	0	0	0	***
			−				+
	Oil + Habitat	0	0	*	na	na	na
				−			
Fall	Oil	0	0	nd	0	***	0
						90 > 89	
	Oil + Habitat	0	0	nd	na	na	na
BLACK OYSTERCATCHER[e]							
Late Winter	Oil	nd	***	0	***	0	0
			−		+		
	Oil + Habitat	nd	***	0	na	na	na
			−				
Spring	Oil	nd	0	nd	na	na	na
	Oil + Habitat	nd	0	nd	na	na	na
Early Summer	Oil	0	0	nd	0	**	0
						90 > 89	
	Oil + Habitat	0	0	nd	na	na	na
Mid-summer	Oil	***	***	0	0	0	***
		−	−				+
	Oil + Habitat	***	**	0	na	na	na
		−	−				

during the same seasons in 1991. In the among-year analyses, the mid-summer, oil-by-year interaction suggested recovery: the clear negative relationship with oiling level present in 1989 and (less strongly) in 1990 disappeared in 1991 (Figure 8). We conclude that impacts on habitat use by migrant Black Oystercatchers occurred in 1989 and 1990 in late winter and mid-summer. During the breeding season (in spring and early summer), however, birds occupied all bays without regard to oiling, and any evidence of negative impacts on use of oil-affected habitats disappeared by late winter 1991.

Species exhibiting negative impacts with no evidence of recovery—Of the species exhibiting initial negative impacts of oiling (Table 2), a few either did not recover during our study or exhibited unclear evidence of recovery. The following species exemplify these responses.

Buffleheads are mainland-nesting ducks that move to the sea during winter (Isleib and Kessel 1973). They were most abundant in PWS during winter and spring (Figure 7) and were seen only on nearshore surveys. In the within-year analyses, Buffleheads exhibited moderate to strong negative relationships with oiling in all four of the oiling analyses; all but one of these relationships remained significantly negative after habitat variables were added to the models (Table 5). The single among-year analysis also suggested an absence of recovery: the oil-by-year interaction term showed no clear evidence of recovery, the year term indicated lower abundance in 1991 than in 1990, and the oiling term indicated a highly significant, negative relationship with oiling.

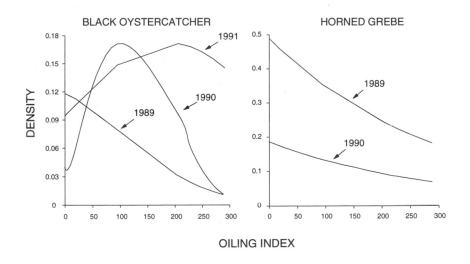

Figure 8—Between-year changes in the density (birds/km of shoreline) of Black Oystercatchers during mid-summer and Horned Grebes during fall in relation to the level of oiling for nearshore surveys in Prince William Sound, Alaska, in 1989-1991, after the **Exxon Valdez** *oil spill.*

Table 5—Results of regression analyses evaluating impacts of oil on use of oil-affected habitats by Buffleheads and Horned Grebes in Prince William Sound, Alaska, in 1989-1991, after the **Exxon Valdez** *oil spill. Explanations of footnote symbols are in Table 3.*

Species/cruise	Analysis	Within-year analysis			Among-year analysis[a]		
		1989	1990	1991	Oiling	Year	Oil-by-year interaction
BUFFLEHEAD[e]							
Mid-winter	Oil	nd[f]	***[c]	nd	na[d]	na	na
			−				
	Oil + Habitat	nd	***	nd	na	na	na
			−				
Late Winter	Oil	nd	**	***	***	***	0
			−	−	−	90 > 91	
	Oil + Habitat	nd	***	***	na	na	na
				−			
Spring	Oil	nd	***	nd	na	na	na
			−				
	Oil + Habitat	nd	0	nd	na	na	na
HORNED GREBE[e]							
Mid-winter	Oil	nd	***	nd	na	na	na
			−				
	Oil + Habitat	nd	0	nd	na	na	na
Late Winter	Oil	nd	***	***	***	0	0
			−	−	−		
	Oil + Habitat	nd	0	0	na	na	na
Spring	Oil	nd	***	nd	na	na	na
			−				
	Oil + Habitat	nd	**	nd	na	na	na
			−				
Fall	Oil	***	**	nd	**	***	*
		−	−		−	89 > 90	−
	Oil + Habitat	0	0	nd	na	na	na

We conclude that Buffleheads exhibited a clear and persistent negative impact with respect to their use of oil-affected habitats.

Horned Grebes also are mainland-nesting birds that move to the sea for overwintering (Isleib and Kessel 1973). They were most abundant in PWS from fall through spring (Figure 7) and concentrated in nearshore waters. In the within-year analyses, Horned Grebes exhibited moderate to strong negative relationships with oiling in all six of the oiling analyses, although only one model remained significantly negative after habitat variables were added (Table 5). Interpretation of these oiling + habitat analyses, however, was complicated by the presence of several habitat variables that varied collinearly with oiling, thereby possibly masking oiling effects. In the among-year analyses, the late winter and fall comparisons showed no oil-by-year interaction and, thus, no evidence of recovery. The fall comparison suggested that populations were lower overall in 1990 than in 1989 (Figure 8). Both analyses indicated moderate to strong and persistent negative impacts of oiling. We conclude that Horned Grebes were negatively impacted by the spill (although collinear habitat variables made that impact appear weaker than we believe it actually was), and there was no clear evidence of recovery.

Overall impacts through time—Perhaps the clearest indication of the overall patterns of impacts and recovery among marine-oriented birds in PWS emerges from examining the percentage of species on each cruise that exhibited negative impacts over the duration of our study (Figure 9). More than 50% of the species showed evidence of negative oiling effects on the first cruise in early summer 1989. The percentage of negatively impacted species decreased over time, especially after winter 1990, and by the time of the final cruise in mid-summer 1991, only 10% (3 of 30) of the species that were present still exhibited negative impacts. This percentage is lower than the 14% (6 of 42) of total species that had exhibited no recovery or unclear recovery by the final cruise, because the total species tabulation also included species that were present during winter.

Oiling Effects along the Kenai Peninsula

Because we conducted fewer surveys along the Kenai than in PWS (Figure 3), our ability to detect initial oiling impacts and to detect recovery for species exhibiting impacts was constrained. For this reason, a failure to detect recovery for a species along the Kenai should not be interpreted as strongly as a failure for a species in PWS.

Of the 34 species we analyzed quantitatively from the Kenai, 22 (65%) exhibited no initial negative impacts of oiling and 12 (35%) were negatively impacted; 36 species were not analyzed because of insufficient data (Table 6). Three species exhibited positive responses to oiling, even after habitat variables were added to the models. At least 2 of these 3 species (Pomarine Jaeger and Black-legged Kittiwake) probably were attracted to spill cleanup activities, but it is unclear why Northwestern Crows exhibited a positive response to oiling along the Kenai, particularly in view of the negative impact on their use of oil-affected habitats in PWS.

Of the 12 species that exhibited initial negative relationships with oiling along the Kenai, 6 (50%) had recovered by late 1991; the remaining 6 exhibited no recovery or unclear recovery by this time (Table 6). These latter species included a loon, a cormorant, a sea duck, a hawk, a gull, and an alcid. Recovery was suggested for Common Loons, Double-crested Cormorants, and Sharp-shinned Hawks, although the evidence was weak. A negative oiling effect was recorded for Ancient Murrelets during mid-summer 1990, but, because no subsequent samples were collected at that time of the year, we could not evaluate their recovery. Negative oiling effects were not seen initially in Common Mergansers and Glaucous-winged Gulls, but both exhibited negative relationships with oiling in 1990 and 1991. The gull probably was attracted to spill cleanup activities in 1989, masking a possible negative relationship, but it is unclear why the merganser exhibited no initial negative effects of oiling. Although we had moderate to high confidence in over 82% of the classifications, our ability to detect recovery was constrained by data limitations: 2 of the 6 species exhibiting no recovery or unclear

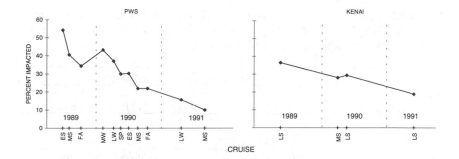

Figure 9—Percentage of species exhibiting negative impacts of oiling through time in Prince William Sound and along the Kenai Peninsula, Alaska, in 1989-1991, after the **Exxon Valdez** *oil spill. Abbreviations for cruises are: ES = early summer; MS = mid-summer; LS = late summer; FA = fall; MW = mid-winter; LW = late winter; SP = spring.*

recovery were classified from weak evidence, and 3 of the 6 species may have begun recovery but the evidence was not clear.

As in PWS, the overall percentage of Kenai species exhibiting negative impacts during a given sampling period declined through time (Figure 9). Negative impacts along the Kenai in 1989 were not as extensive as those found in PWS that year, but our ability to assess recovery on the Kenai was constrained by data limitations associated with the small number of cruises. During the final sampling period, about 19% (6 of 32) of the species that were present still exhibited negative impacts. This percentage is about the same as the 18% (6 of 34) of all species that had exhibited no recovery or equivocal recovery by the final cruise.

DISCUSSION

The goal of this study was to evaluate impacts to and recovery of birds following the *Exxon Valdez* oil spill, based on their use of oil-affected habitats. Overall, 23 of 42 (55%) species examined in PWS and 22 of 34 (65%) species on the Kenai showed no evidence of impacts: they were using habitats without regard to the level of oiling that the bays had experienced from the spill. Of those species that did exhibit initial negative impacts with respect to their use of oil-affected habitats, most had recovered by summer 1991.

There were many similarities between the effects of the *Exxon Valdez* oil spill on use of oil-affected habitats by birds in PWS and along the Kenai. Of 29 species examined in both locations, 16 (55%) were placed in identical impact categories, and another 8 (28%) exhibited stronger impacts in PWS. In contrast, only five (17%) species exhibited stronger impacts on the Kenai. A broader distribution of impacts among species in PWS was expected because the spill originated there: much more oil was present, the oil was

TABLE 6—Classification of oiling impact and recovery based on use of oil-affected habitats for bird species recorded along the Kenai Peninsula, Alaska, in 1989-1991, after the **Exxon Valdez** *oil spill.*

	Initial negative impact detected		
No apparent negative impact detected	Recovery evident	Year of recovery	Impact persists/ recovery unclear

		EVIDENCE STRONG[a]		
Sooty Shearwater	Wandering Tattler	1990	Double-crested Cormorant (R)[c]
Pelagic Cormorant	Red-necked Phalarope	1991	Common Merganser
Harlequin Duck	Mew Gull	1991	Glaucous-winged Gull
Bald Eagle (P)[b]	Rhinoceros Auklet	1991	
Black Oystercatcher	Tufted Puffin	1990	
* Spotted Sandpiper			
Black-legged Kittiwake			
Common Murre			
* Pigeon Guillemot			
* Marbled Murrelet			
* Horned Puffin			
Steller's Jay			
Black-billed Magpie			
Northwestern Crow (P)			

		EVIDENCE MODERATE		
Red-faced Cormorant	Green-winged Teal	1991	* Common Loon (R)
Pomarine Jaeger (P)			
Belted Kingfisher			
Common Raven			

		EVIDENCE WEAK		
Red-necked Grebe			Sharp-shinned Hawk (R)
Fork-tailed Storm-Petrel			Ancient Murrelet
Surf Scoter			
White-winged Scoter			

[a] The strength of evidence reflected both the statistical strength of the models and the number of cruises for which analyses were conducted; see Methods.

[b] (P) indicates that the species exhibited a positive response to oil.

[c] (R) indicates that recovery may have begun.

* = our assessment of impact or recovery time changed as a result of the habitat analyses.

more acutely toxic because it was less weathered, and the oil was present for a longer time than it was on the Kenai (Galt et al. 1991; also compare oiling index values in Figure 5).

There was a pronounced difference between PWS and the Kenai in the residence status of the impacted species. In PWS, more negative impacts occurred in the wintering bird community (35% of all impacted species) than in the summering community (15%), whereas along the Kenai, more negative impacts occurred in the summering bird community (41% of all impacted species) than in the wintering community (16%). Along the Kenai, however, we examined only those wintering species that were recorded on the late summer cruises as they were moving into the area to winter. The difference in impacts between study areas may have resulted from chronological differences in the movement of oil through the areas and from differences in the bird communities that occur there. The oil spill occurred on 24 March, and the main slick had left PWS before the arrival of the first spring migrants and summer visitants in mid-April (Isleib and Kessel 1973; Piatt et al. 1990). Although there still was a considerable amount of oil on the beaches in summer 1989, those species most likely to have suffered direct mortality and acute effects of the spill in PWS were birds that were present when the spill occurred. In contrast, the spill arrived on the Kenai 2 to 3 weeks later, when spring migrants and summer visitants had begun to move into the area. Thus, greater impacts (i.e., mortality, breeding, and habitat use) to spring migrants and summer visitants there were not unexpected.

Ecological Attributes, Oiling Impacts, and Recovery

Not all bird species occurring in the spill area were impacted, and rates of recovery varied among those species that were. For example, only one negatively impacted species in PWS (Marbled Murrelet) clearly had recovered in 1989, and it may have been affected more by disturbance associated with cleanup activities than by the oil spill itself (Kuletz 1993). Of the 13 species that recovered, 7 (54%) did so in 1990, within 1.5 years of the spill, and an additional 5 (38%) had recovered by late 1991, within 2.5 years of the spill. On the Kenai, we conducted only one cruise in 1989, so evaluation of recovery in that year was not possible. Of the 12 species there that were impacted by the spill, 2 (17%) had recovered by late summer 1990, and another 4 (33%) had recovered by late summer 1991. Differences among species in impacts and recovery rates were not unexpected, as differences in ecology and life history among these species are substantial. Do these differences provide any insights about why some species were impacted by the spill while others were not, and why impacted species apparently recovered at different rates?

To answer these questions, we used the results from PWS (where the data were more comprehensive than for the Kenai) in a PCA to examine relationships between ecological characteristics of the species and our assessment of their oiling-impact status. The PCA yielded two strong components (i.e., with eigenvalues >1.0) that collectively accounted for 73% of the variation in the original matrix of species-by-ecological trait. The first PCA axis (46% of the variance) represented a gradient in prey type and foraging location, ranging from species feeding on vegetation in intertidal areas to species feeding on fishes in subsurface waters (i.e., either mid-water or benthic fishes; Figure 10). The second axis (27%), which was strongly associated with residency, arrayed species along a gradient from migrants and summer visitants to winter visitants and residents (i.e., species present throughout the year).

There were no consistent differences in ecological attributes between species that exhibited spill-related impacts and those that did not: the distributions of species with and without impacts were broadly overlapping in the space formed by the first two PCA axes (Figure 10). Groups such as alcids and sea ducks, which generally are thought to be highly vulnerable to oil pollution (King and Sanger 1979), included both impacted and unimpacted species. Overall, there were no statistically significant differences ($P > 0.20$ for both axes) in PCA scores among the three impact groups (not impacted, impacted with recovery, and impacted without recovery or recovery unclear).

The six impacted species for which recovery did not occur or for which we lacked clear evidence of recovery (Table 2) occurred in two clusters along the first PCA axis. Bufflehead, Barrow's Goldeneye, Mew Gull, and Northwestern Crow were clustered toward the left side of the axis (species that feed primarily on invertebrates in either the exposed or submerged intertidal zone), whereas Red-necked and Horned grebes were clustered toward the right side of the axis (species that dive for fishes in the nearshore zone; Figure 10). In contrast, none of the primarily pelagic species (e.g., Fork-tailed Storm-Petrel) were impacted negatively by the spill, and all of the primarily offshore species that were initially impacted subsequently recovered. The habitats of intertidal and nearshore species seem to have been affected most heavily, probably because of the large amount of oil that washed ashore (Galt et al. 1991; Neff et al., this volume). Nonetheless, several species that shared ecological traits with the unrecovered species apparently suffered no spill-related impacts to habitat use or recovered rapidly.

The six unrecovered species tended to cluster toward the increasing residency (i.e., winter visitant/resident) end of the second PCA axis (Figure 10). As previously noted, a greater impact on wintering and resident species was not surprising. The spill spread through PWS in late March-early April, when the wintering community still was present, and resident species were exposed to the oil for the longest time. Again, however, other species that exhibited no impacts or that rapidly recovered also were residents of PWS (Figure 10). For example, Barrow's Goldeneyes and Buffleheads (species that showed no clear evidence of recovery during our study) occupied an intermediate position on the residency axis, whereas congeneric Common Goldeneyes (which were not impacted) had even greater residency.

Thus, despite the attractiveness of the notion that ecological characteristics of species determine their potential vulnerability to oil spills, such characteristics did not predict impacts of the *Exxon Valdez* oil spill on particular species of birds, at least as gauged by their use of oil-affected habitats. Instead, idiosyncrasies of the species and of when and where the oil was deposited during the spill seem to have played the dominant roles in determining which species were impacted and which recovered more rapidly than others. The lack of a distinctive and consistent set of characteristics distinguishing those species that did not show evidence of recovery by late 1991 suggests that the prognosis for recovery of these species is good: these species are not radically different ecologically from species that were not impacted or that already have recovered.

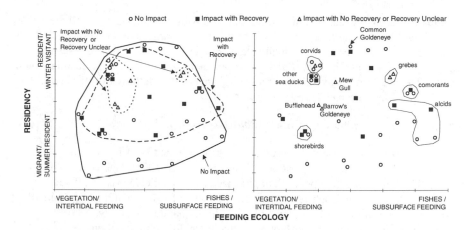

*Figure 10—Relationship between oiling impacts and recovery of marine-oriented bird
species (left) and particular species (right) in Prince William Sound,
Alaska, in 1989-1991, after the* **Exxon Valdez** *oil spill. Polygons enclose
species exhibiting no negative impacts of oiling (circles), species exhibiting
negative impacts with subsequent recovery (solid squares), and species
exhibiting negative impacts without recovery or with recovery unclear
(triangles). Axis 1 reflects prey type and foraging location; Axis 2 reflects
degree of residency in Prince William Sound.*

Comparisons with Other Findings

Our study was not the only investigation of changes in bird distribution and
abundance after the *Exxon Valdez* oil spill. In 1989-1991, Laing and Klosiewski (1993)
sampled a subset of transects in PWS that had been surveyed prior to the spill by Dwyer
et al. (1976) in 1972-1973 and by Irons et al. (1988) in 1984-1985. All of these
investigators used survey procedures similar to ours, including the use of a 200 m
nearshore zone. Laing and Klosiewski found nine species or taxa ("loons," "cormorants,"
Harlequin Duck, "scoters," Black Oystercatcher, Mew Gull, Arctic Tern, Pigeon
Guillemot, and Northwestern Crow) that declined significantly more in oiled than in
unoiled habitats relative to historical data.

We recorded impacts to more species than did the study of Laing and Klosiewski
(1993) for several possible reasons. First, our study sampled throughout the year,
whereas Laing and Klosiewski sampled only between the time of the spill (late March)
and late summer; many of the impacted species occurred in PWS primarily in fall and
winter. Second, our study used oiling as a continuous variable, whereas Laing and
Klosiewski used oiling as a categorical variable. Use of oiling as a continuous variable
allowed the use of regression statistics (including the use of covariates), which provided
more powerful analytical tools. Third, we used oiling maps to determine the initial level

of oiling that each bay received, whereas Laing and Klosiewski considered all areas that occurred within the general spill region to be oiled. This large area through which the oil passed included many areas that actually were not oiled (e.g., many bays on western Knight Island, most of Chenega Island). Such a generalized oiling categorization would result in the data from many unoiled areas being analyzed with those of oiled areas, thus increasing the variance and decreasing power.

Advantages and Limitations of the Habitat-Use Approach

Traditionally, impacts of oil spills on marine-oriented birds have been assessed by counting dead, oiled birds (e.g., National Research Council 1985; Page et al. 1990; Piatt et al. 1990) or by comparing postspill abundances with historical numbers, if such data exist (e.g., Harrison and Buck 1967; Richardson et al. 1981; Laing and Klosiewski 1993; Nysewander et al. 1993; Erikson, this volume). In our habitat-use study, we quantitatively analyzed use by birds of areas that were differentially oiled. A major advantage of this approach is that it does not require historical (prespill) baseline information. Quantitative, baseline studies of birds rarely have been conducted in locations where oil spills subsequently occur, and, if historical information is available, it usually is from many years before the spill occurred. Such data provide a reliable baseline only if the ecosystem has not varied or changed during the interim (Wiens, this volume). Comparisons with historical data also are limited by low statistical power (Laing and Klosiewski 1993). Collectively, these points suggest that the habitat-use approach is a better technique for evaluating the effects of an oil spill than are comparisons with historical surveys.

The habitat-use approach also has other advantages. First, this approach integrates the effects of oiling on both the birds and on critical components of their habitat, including secondary impacts of oil spills that affect either the birds or their habitat (e.g., chronic release of oil from sediments). Moreover, changes over time in the use of oil-affected areas by birds provide clear evidence of habitat recovery. By considering oiling level as a quantitative, continuous variable, one can conduct more powerful statistical analyses than would be possible if oiling were treated as a categorical variable (e.g., "oiled" versus "unoiled"). Analytical rigor also is enhanced by incorporating quantitative measurements of habitat features into the design, which permits one to separate the effects of habitat and oiling on the distribution and abundance of birds.

There are several limitations of the habitat-use approach, however. First, the approach does not provide direct evidence of the status of population-level recovery, because only inferential conclusions can be drawn regarding prespill populations. For example, a spill could have reduced overall abundance by 50%, but if the remaining birds were distributed among areas independently of oiling level, one would fail to document differences in the use of oil-affected habitats and would conclude that no impacts to habitat use had occurred. In the present situation, however, we compared our data with historical surveys, and found that the overall abundance of most species in these bays had not changed significantly since 1984-1985 (Murphy et al., in prep.). Hence, catastrophic population declines were not apparent. Second, the habitat-use approach requires an intensive, replicated sampling effort. Obtaining information for detailed population analyses usually requires an even greater effort, however (Wiens et al. 1984). A third limitation is that the habitat-use approach cannot be applied to rare species or those with extremely patchy distributions (i.e., those that occur in only a few bays). It is doubtful, however, that other approaches would be more successful in assessing impacts to these rare species. If determining impacts to such species is considered to be important, intensive, species-specific studies must be conducted. Finally, collinearity of some habitat variables with oiling occasionally makes unequivocal interpretation of oiling + habitat models difficult.

Conclusions about Impacts and Recovery

Evaluating the effects of a major oil spill on seabirds is complex because different species may be impacted in different ways. Some species may suffer immediate mortality, others may leave oil-affected habitats or areas, and still others may leave and return as soon as the major slick has passed through an area. Judging recovery is equally problematic, because adequate historical baseline data often are nonexistent or incomplete and because recovery can be measured in several ways (Wiens, this volume). It is difficult to design a research program that takes this complexity into account, and this study was no exception. We did not attempt to evaluate all aspects of impacts and recovery, but instead designed a study that provided quantitative information on impacts and recovery in the use of oil-affected habitats for a large number of species. Basic premises of this approach are that birds are effective biomonitors of their habitat conditions and that reoccupancy by birds of habitats that initially were contaminated by oil implies that habitat-based impediments to population recovery are dissipating or have disappeared (see Morrison 1986). Thus, our study provides perspective on the extent of long-term damage to the environment and on the potential for population recovery to occur for species that were displaced or that suffered high rates of mortality.

Our basic finding—that by 2.5 years after the spill, most marine-oriented bird species in PWS and along the Kenai were using habitats without regard to the initial oiling that the bays had experienced from the oil spill—suggests that the negative effects of the *Exxon Valdez* oil spill on bird habitats had largely dissipated by that time. This conclusion is consistent with the results of studies that have documented the recovery of other components of the habitat in PWS and along the Kenai. For example, the amount of oil in the water column in PWS had declined to background levels by June 1989 (Neff 1991), and the amount on and in beach sediments declined dramatically between 1989 and 1991 (Neff et al., this volume). In addition, although there was substantial mortality of intertidal life at Green Island in southern PWS in 1989 (Juday and Foster 1990), the more common species had begun recolonizing the area by 1990 (Juday and Foster 1991). Other studies indicated that most intertidal and nearshore subtidal communities of PWS recovered by 15-18 months after the spill (Gilfillan et al., this volume; but see Highsmith et al. 1993) and that epibenthic fishes and crustaceans occurred in similar densities in oiled and unoiled bays (Laur and Haldorson 1993; Armstrong et al., this volume).

Our findings also are consistent with those of other studies on the recovery of use of oil-affected habitats by birds (Harrison and Buck 1967; Chabreck 1973). In those studies, impacts were distributed across a range of species and were strongest in those areas that were oiled most heavily. Recovery in the use of oil-affected habitats was rapid and occurred in ≤ 2 years for all species. Our findings, together with these other reports of rapid rates of recovery of use of oil-affected habitats, suggest that impacts of the *Exxon Valdez* oil spill on avian habitat use generally were not persistent. Because the impacted species do not differ in general ecological characteristics from species that suffered no spill impacts or that were impacted and subsequently recovered, the prognosis for recovery of the species for which we were unable to document recovery in habitat use by the end of our study in 1991 appears to be good.

ACKNOWLEDGMENTS

This project was funded by Exxon Company, U.S.A. The opinions expressed here are those of the authors and do not necessarily reflect those of Exxon. Additional statistical advice and computations were provided by L.C. Byrne of ABR, Inc., J.N. Jonkman of Trilogy Consulting, G.R. Hobbs of West Virginia University, and K.R. Parker of Data Analysis Group. We thank all of the many people who helped collect data under often difficult conditions. We particularly thank ABR personnel who contributed to the success of this research program: D.A. Flint, B.E. Lawhead, L.C. Byrne, S.G. Speckman, J.R. Rose, B.K. Lance, C.B. Johnson, A.L. Zusi-Cobb, B.A. Cooper, R.M. Burgess, and T.D. Davis. This manuscript was critically reviewed by R.M. Burgess, B.E. Lawhead, and R.J. Ritchie of ABR, Inc., and T.O. Crist of Colorado State University.

REFERENCES

ADFG (Alaska Department of Fish and Game), 1978, *Alaska's Fisheries Atlas*, Vol. 1, State of Alaska, Juneau, AK.

Alaska Oil Spill Commission, 1990, *Spill: The Wreck of the* Exxon Valdez, Alaska Oil Spill Commission, State of Alaska, Juneau, AK.

American Ornithologists' Union, 1985, "Thirty-fifth Supplement to the American Ornithologists' Union *Check-list of North American Birds*," *Auk*, Vol. 102, pp. 680-686.

American Ornithologists' Union, 1983, *The A.O.U. Check-list of North American Birds*, 6th edition, American Ornithologists' Union, Washington, DC.

Burger, A. E., 1993, "Estimating the Mortality of Seabirds Following Oil Spills: Effects of Spill Volume," *Marine Pollution Bulletin*, Vol. 26, pp. 140-143.

Chabreck, R. H, 1973, "Bird Usage of Marsh Ponds Subjected to Oil Spills," *Proceedings of the Louisiana Academy of Science*, Vol. 36, pp. 101-110.

Dwyer, T. J., P. Isleib, D. A. Davenport, and J. L. Haddock, 1976, "Marine Bird Populations in Prince William Sound," Unpublished report prepared by the U. S. Fish and Wildlife Service, Anchorage, AK.

Exxon Valdez Oil Spill Trustees, 1992, "*Exxon Valdez* Oil Spill Restoration, Vol. I: Restoration Framework," Report prepared by the *Exxon Valdez* Oil Spill Trustees, Juneau, AK.

Forsell, D. J. and P. J. Gould, 1981, "Distribution and Abundance of Seabirds Wintering in the Kodiak Area of Alaska," U. S. Fish and Wildlife Service, Office of Biological Services, Report No. USFWS/OBS-81/13.

Fry, D. M., 1993, "How Do You Fix the Loss of Half a Million Birds?." Exxon Valdez *Oil Spill Symposium*, Abstract Book, *Exxon Valdez* Oil Spill Trustee Council, Anchorage, AK, pp. 30-33.

Galt, J. A., W. J. Lehr, and D. L. Payton, 1991, "Fate and Transport of the *Exxon Valdez* Oil Spill," *Environmental Science and Technology*, Vol. 25, pp. 202-209.

Gould, P. J., D. J. Forsell, and C. J. Lensink, 1982, "Pelagic Distribution and Abundance of Seabirds in the Gulf of Alaska and Eastern Bering Sea," U. S. Fish and Wildlife Service, Office of Biological Services, Report No. USFWS/OBS-82/48.

Gould, P. J. and D. J. Forsell, 1989, "Techniques for Shipboard Surveys of Marine Birds," U. S. Fish and Wildlife Service, *Fish and Wildlife Technical Report.*, No. 25.

Harrison, J. G. and W. F. A. Buck, 1967, "Peril in Perspective: An Account of the Medway Estuary Oil Pollution of September 1966," *Kent Bird Report* (Kent Ornithological Society), Vol. 16 (Special Supplement), pp. 1-24.

Heinemann, D., 1993, "How Long to Recovery for Murre Populations, and Will Some Colonies Fail to Make the Comeback?," Exxon Valdez *Oil Spill Symposium*, Abstract Book, *Exxon Valdez* Oil Spill Trustee Council, Anchorage, AK, pp. 139-141.

Highsmith, R. C., S. M. Saupe, K. O. Coyle, T. Rucker, and W. Erickson, 1993, "Impact of the *Exxon Valdez* Oil Spill on Intertidal Invertebrates Throughout the Oil Spill Region," Exxon Valdez *Oil Spill Symposium*, Abstract Book, *Exxon Valdez* Oil Spill Trustee Council, Anchorage, AK, pp. 166-168.

Hodgson, B., January 1990, "Alaska's Big Spill—Can the Wilderness Heal?," *National Geographic*, pp. 4-43.

Hurlbert, S. H., 1984, "Pseudoreplication and the Design of Ecological Field Experiments," *Ecological Monographs*, Vol. 54, pp. 187-211.

Irons, D. B., D. R. Nysewander, and J. L. Trapp, 1988, "Prince William Sound Waterbird Distribution in Relation to Habitat Type," Unpublished report, U.S. Fish and Wildlife Service, Anchorage, AK.

Isleib, M. E. and B. Kessel, 1973, "Birds of the North Gulf Coast-Prince William Sound Region, Alaska," *Biological Papers of the University of Alaska*, No. 14.

Juday, G. P. and N. R. Foster, 1990, "A Preliminary Look at Effects of the *Exxon Valdez* Oil Spill on Green Island Research Natural Area," *Agroborealis*, Vol. 22, pp. 10-17.

Juday, G. P. and N. R. Foster, 1991, "A Return to Green Island," *Agroborealis*, Vol. 23, pp. 26-28.

Kessel, B., 1979, "Avian Habitat Classification for Alaska," *Murrelet*, Vol. 60, pp. 86-94.

King, J. G. and G. A. Sanger, 1979, "Oil Vulnerability Index for Marine Oriented Birds," *Conservation of Marine Birds of Northern North America*, J. C. Bartonek and D. N. Nettleship, Eds., U. S. Fish and Wildlife Service, *Wildlife Research Report*, No. 11, pp. 227-239.

Koons, C. B. and H. O. Jahns, 1992, "The Fate of Oil from the *Exxon Valdez*—A Perspective," *Marine Technology Society Journal*, Vol. 26, pp. 61-69.

Kuletz, K. J., 1993, "Effects of the *Exxon Valdez* Oil Spill on Marbled Murrelets," Exxon Valdez *Oil Spill Symposium*, Abstract Book, *Exxon Valdez* Oil Spill Trustee Council, Anchorage, AK, pp. 148-150.

Laing, K. K. and S. P. Klosiewski, 1993, "Marine Bird Populations of Prince William Sound, Alaska, Before and After the *Exxon Valdez* Oil Spill," Exxon Valdez *Oil Spill Symposium*, Abstract Book, *Exxon Valdez* Oil Spill Trustee Council, Anchorage, AK, pp. 160-161.

Laur, D. and L. Haldorson, 1993, "Coastal Habitat Studies: The Effect of the *Exxon Valdez* Oil Spill on Shallow Subtidal Fishes in Prince William Sound," Exxon Valdez *Oil Spill Symposium*, Abstract Book, *Exxon Valdez* Oil Spill Trustee Council, Anchorage, AK, pp. 233-234.

Magurran, A. E., 1988, *Ecological Diversity and Its Measurement*, Princeton University Press, Princeton.

Maki, A. W., 1991, "The *Exxon Valdez* Oil Spill: Initial Environmental Impact Assessment," *Environmental Science and Technology*, Vol. 25, pp. 24-29.

Morrison, M. L., 1986, "Bird Populations as Indicators of Environmental Change," *Current Ornithology*, Vol. 3., Plenum Press, New York, pp. 429-451.

National Research Council, 1985, "Oil in the Sea: Inputs, Fates, and Effects," National Academy Press, Washington, DC.

Neff, J. M., 1991, "Water Quality in Prince William Sound and the Gulf of Alaska, March 1991," Unpublished report prepared by Arthur D. Little, Inc., Cambridge, MA.

Nishimoto, M. and B. Rice, 1987, "A Re-survey of Seabirds and Marine Mammals Along the South Coast of the Kenai Peninsula, Alaska, During the Summer of 1986," Unpublished report prepared by the U. S. Fish and Wildlife Service, Anchorage, AK, and the National Park Service, Anchorage, AK.

Nysewander, D. R., C. Dippel, G. V. Byrd, and E. P. Knudtson, 1993, "Effects of the T/V *Exxon Valdez* Oil Spill on Murres: A Perspective from Observations at Breeding Colonies," Exxon Valdez *Oil Spill Symposium*, Abstract Book, *Exxon Valdez* Oil Spill Trustee Council, Anchorage, AK, pp. 135-138.

Page, G. W., H. R. Carter, and R. G. Ford, 1990, "Numbers of Seabirds Killed or Debilitated in the 1986 *Apex Houston* Oil Spill in Central California," *Auks at Sea*, S. G. Sealy, Ed., Studies in Avian Biology, No. 14, pp. 164-174.

Patten, S. M., Jr., 1993a, "Acute and Sublethal Effects of the *Exxon Valdez* Oil Spill on Harlequins and Other Seaducks," Exxon Valdez *Oil Spill Symposium*, Abstract Book, *Exxon Valdez* Oil Spill Trustee Council, Anchorage, AK, pp. 151-154.

Patten, S., 1993b, "Reproductive Failure of Harlequin Ducks," *Alaska's Wildlife*, Vol. 25, pp. 14-15.

Pennycuick, C. J., and N. C. Kline, 1986, Units of measurement for fractal extent, applied to the coastal distribution of bald eagle nests in the Aluetian Islands, Alaska. Oecologia 68:254-258.

Piatt, J. F., C. J. Lensink, W. Butler, M. Kendziorek, and D. R. Nysewander, 1990, "Immediate Impact of the 'Exxon Valdez' Oil Spill on Marine Birds," *Auk*, Vol. 107, pp. 387-397.

Piatt, J., 1993, "The Oil Spill and Seabirds: Three Years Later," *Alaska's Wildlife*, Vol. 25, pp. 11-12.

Richardson, M. G., G. M. Dunnet, and P. K. Kinnear, 1981, "Monitoring Seabirds in Shetland," *Proceedings of the Royal Society of Edinburgh.*, Vol. 80 (B), pp. 157-179.

Royer, T. C., J. A. Vermersch, T. J. Weingartner, H. J. Niebauer, and R. D. Muench, 1990, "Ocean Circulation Influencing the *Exxon Valdez* Oil Spill," *Oceanography*, Vol. 3, pp. 3-10.

Sharp, B. E. and M. Cody, 1993, "Black Oystercatchers in Prince William Sound: Oil Spill Effects on Reproduction and Behavior," Exxon Valdez *Oil Spill Symposium*, Abstract Book, *Exxon Valdez* Oil Spill Trustee Council, Anchorage, AK, pp. 155-158.

Sowls, A. L., S. A. Hatch, and C. J. Lensink, 1978, "Catalog of Alaskan Seabird Colonies," U. S. Fish and Wildlife Service, Office of Biological Services, Report No. FWS/OBS-78/78.

Viereck, L. A., C. T. Dyrness, and A. R. Batten, 1986, *The 1986 Revision of the Alaskan Vegetation Classification*, U. S. Department of Agriculture, Forest Service, Institute of Northern Forestry, Fairbanks, AK.

Wiens, J. A., R. G. Ford, and D. Heinemann, 1984, "Information Needs and Priorities for Assessing the Sensitivity of Marine Birds to Oil Spills," *Biological Conservation*, Vol. 28, pp. 21-49.

Wilson, J. G. and J. E. Overland, 1986, "Meteorology," The Gulf of Alaska: Physical Environment and Biological Resources, D. W. Hood and S. T. Zimmerman, Eds., U.S. Department of Commerce, National Oceanic and Atmospheric Administration, Ocean Assessments Division, Anchorage, AK, pp. 31-54.

Appendix Table—Scientific names of bird species mentioned in text (following American Ornithologists' Union 1983, 1985).

Common name	Scientific name
Common Loon	*Gavia immer*
Yellow-billed Loon	*Gavia adamsii*
Horned Grebe	*Podiceps auritus*
Red-necked Grebe	*Podiceps grisegena*
Northern Fulmar	*Fulmarus glacialis*
Sooty Shearwater	*Puffinus griseus*
Fork-tailed Storm-Petrel	*Oceanodroma furcata*
Double-crested Cormorant	*Phalacrocorax auritus*
Pelagic Cormorant	*Phalacrocorax pelagicus*
Red-faced Cormorant	*Phalacrocorax urile*
Great Blue Heron	*Ardea herodias*
Canada Goose	*Branta canadensis*
Green-winged Teal	*Anas crecca*
Mallard	*Anas platyrhynchos*
American Wigeon	*Anas americana*
Ring-necked Duck	*Aythya collaris*
Harlequin Duck	*Histrionicus histrionicus*
Oldsquaw	*Clangula hyemalis*
Black Scoter	*Melanitta nigra*
Surf Scoter	*Melanitta perspicillata*
White-winged Scoter	*Melanitta fusca*
Common Goldeneye	*Bucephala clangula*
Barrow's Goldeneye	*Bucephala islandica*
Bufflehead	*Bucephala albeola*
Common Merganser	*Mergus merganser*
Red-breasted Merganser	*Mergus serrator*
Ruddy Duck	*Oxyura jamaicensis*
Bald Eagle	*Haliaeetus leucocephalus*
Sharp-shinned Hawk	*Accipiter striatus*
Black Oystercatcher	*Haematopus bachmani*
Wandering Tattler	*Heteroscelus incanus*
Spotted Sandpiper	*Actitis macularia*
Least Sandpiper	*Calidris minutilla*
Red-necked Phalarope	*Phalaropus lobatus*
Pomarine Jaeger	*Stercorarius pomarinus*
Mew Gull	*Larus canus*
Herring Gull	*Larus argentatus*
Thayer's Gull	*Larus glaucoides*
Glaucous-winged Gull	*Larus glaucescens*

Appendix Table—Scientific names of bird species mentioned in text (continued).

Common name	Scientific name
Glaucous Gull	*Larus hyperboreus*
Black-legged Kittiwake	*Rissa tridactyla*
Arctic Tern	*Sterna paradisaea*
Common Murre	*Uria aalge*
Pigeon Guillemot	*Cepphus columba*
Marbled Murrelet	*Brachyramphus marmoratus*
Ancient Murrelet	*Synthliboramphus antiquus*
Rhinoceros Auklet	*Cerorhinca monocerata*
Tufted Puffin	*Fratercula cirrhata*
Horned Puffin	*Fratercula corniculata*
Belted Kingfisher	*Ceryle alcyon*
Steller's Jay	*Cyanocitta stelleri*
Black-billed Magpie	*Pica pica*
Northwestern Crow	*Corvus caurinus*
Common Raven	*Corvus corax*

Clayton M. White[1], Robert J. Ritchie[2], and Brian A. Cooper[2]

DENSITY AND PRODUCTIVITY OF BALD EAGLES IN PRINCE WILLIAM SOUND, ALASKA, AFTER THE *EXXON VALDEZ* OIL SPILL

REFERENCE: White, C. M., Ritchie, R. J., and Cooper, B. A., **"Density and Productivity of Bald Eagles in Prince William Sound, Alaska, After the *Exxon Valdez* Oil Spill,"** Exxon Valdez Oil Spill: Fate and Effects in Alaskan Waters, ASTM STP 1219, Peter G. Wells, James N. Butler, and Jane S. Hughes, Eds., American Society for Testing and Materials, Philadelphia, 1995.

ABSTRACT: Helicopter surveys were conducted in Prince William Sound (PWS) to assess the effects of the 1989 *Exxon Valdez* oil spill on the reproductive success and densities of bald eagles *(Haliaeetus leucocephalus)* one and two years after the spill (1990 and 1991). Densities of bald eagles were compared between an oiled area in southwestern PWS and an unoiled area in northern PWS. In all surveys (four in 1990, one in 1991) densities of eagles in the oiled area generally were similar to or higher than those in the unoiled area. Reproductive success was compared between nesting territories that were oiled within 1 km of nests and nesting territories that were unoiled. In 1990, all measures of nest productivity, nest occupancy, and nesting success were similar between oiled and unoiled territories. In 1991, however, the number of young per successful nest was lower in oiled territories. The number of successful nests was slightly lower in 1991 than in 1990 in oiled territories but was significantly lower in 1991 in unoiled territories. Comparisons of nest occupancy and nesting success could not be made in 1991 because early surveys were not conducted. Differences between areas, territories, and years could not be attributed to oil, but rather appeared to be related to natural annual variability. Overall, no demonstrable effects of the oil spill on eagle density or reproduction could be detected in PWS one and two years after the spill.

KEY WORDS: Alaska, bald eagle, *Haliaeetus leucocephalus,* eagle densities, *Exxon Valdez* oil spill, nest densities, nesting success, nest occupancy, oiling, Prince William Sound, productivity.

1 Department of Zoology, Brigham Young University, 575 Widtsoe Building, Provo, UT 84602
2 Alaska Biological Research (ABR), Inc., P.O. Box 81934, Fairbanks, AK 99708

INTRODUCTION

On 24 March 1989, the oil tanker *Exxon Valdez* ran aground in northeastern Prince William Sound and spilled approximately 258 000 barrels of North Slope crude oil (Maki, 1991). Wind and currents moved oil from the spill site to the Gulf of Alaska and as far to the southwest as the Alaska Peninsula. The health of bald eagles was of concern because this extensive region supports approximately 8 000 bald eagles (Bowman and Schempf, 1993), roughly 25% of the Alaska population (Schempf, 1989). The coastal distribution of bald eagles and their reliance on marine prey make them vulnerable to a marine oil spill (King and Sanger, 1979).

Of particular concern was the effect of the spill on the bald eagle population in Prince William Sound. Surveys in late April and early May 1989 indicated that approximately 2 100 adult bald eagles were present in the Sound at that time (Bowman and Schempf, 1993). In the southwestern portion of the Sound, large amounts of floating oil persisted for 2 to 4 weeks following the spill, and some shorelines, including portions of the Knight Island group and Smith, Green, and Latouche islands, were heavily oiled (Galt et al., 1991). A total of 783 km (roughly 16%) of the shorelines in Prince William Sound was oiled to various degrees (Owens, 1991).

Following the spill, several impacts on bald eagles were documented, including direct mortality, displacement from nesting territories, and reduced reproductive success in 1989 (Bowman and Schempf, 1993; Bowman et al., 1993). Throughout the entire area affected, 153 bald eagle carcasses were found after the spill (Maki, 1991). Fewer than 50% of these were found in the Sound (U.S. Fish and Wildlife Service, 1989). Some authors (e.g., Piatt et al. 1990) projected substantially higher mortality figures, and Bowman and Schempf (1993) estimated that 900 eagles succumbed to oiling throughout the affected spill area. Estimates of the total mortality of bald eagles as a result of the spill are complicated by uncertainties related to the proportion of eagles killed but not found and uncertainties about the causes of death. There is little doubt, however, that more eagles died than were found.

The productivity of bald eagles in 1989 was reported to be lower in moderately and heavily oiled areas than in unoiled and lightly oiled areas (Bowman et al., 1993). A relationship was observed between reproductive failures and the extent and degree of shoreline oiling near nests, but this impact evidently was short-term and restricted to Prince William Sound (Bowman and Schempf, 1993). Two factors probably were responsible for this lower productivity in 1989: human disturbance and oiling.

During summer 1989, over 11 000 cleanup workers and hundreds of boats and aircraft were active in the spill cleanup, mostly along heavily oiled shorelines in the Sound (Maki, 1991). Although the reaction of eagles to humans can vary considerably depending on previous experience, type of disturbance, and season (Mathisen, 1968; Fraser, 1985; Fraser et al., 1985; Stalmaster, 1987; Grubb and King, 1991), the magnitude of human disturbance associated with the cleanup of oiled beaches probably increased the rate of abandonment of nests and subsequent mortality of eggs and nestlings.

Contamination of bald eagle eggs and prey remains in the Sound confirmed the direct exposure of nesting eagles to crude oil in 1989 (Bowman et al., 1993). Although studies have not examined the effects of oiling on the reproductive performance of raptors, research on other avian taxa has documented deleterious effects of crude oil on productivity. For example, oiling of plumage and ingestion of oil by adults reduce the hatchability of eggs of waterfowl and gulls (King and Lefever, 1979; Albers, 1980; Lewis and Malecki, 1984). Ingestion of oil may alter egg-laying and incubation behavior in waterfowl (Holmes et al., 1978; Cavanaugh et al., 1983). Ingestion of oil also retards the growth of nestling gulls and reduces their survival to fledging (Butler and Lukasiewicz, 1979). In addition, oil may reduce levels of nest occupancy after oiling: wedge-tailed shearwaters *(Puffinus pacificus)* that were oiled externally did not return to their breeding colony the year after oiling (Fry et al., 1986).

By the 1990 breeding season, conditions in the spill area had improved dramatically compared to the summer of 1989. The extent of shoreline oiling was greatly reduced by cleanup and natural processes. Surface oil remaining on shorelines was heavily weathered (Owens, 1991) and therefore less acutely toxic (Stubblefield et al., this volume). Floating oil, mainly in the form of thin sheens, occurred intermittently and was limited in extent. Significantly, blood samples from eagles in the spill area were essentially normal within 2 to 3 months following the spill (Gibson and White, 1990), and no oil-related eagle mortalities were reported after 1989. Further, human activity during the 1990 cleanup effort was much less intensive than in 1989 (1 000 versus 11 000 people; Harrison, 1991), and activities were scheduled to minimize disturbance of breeding eagles (Teal, 1991; Lockhart, 1993). Thus, by 1990, the risk of harmful exposure of eagles to oil and the effects of human disturbance probably had been reduced substantially.

It is not clear how the levels of exposure to oil that bald eagles experienced in Prince William Sound in 1990 and 1991 relate to those reported in the avian literature; further, previous research does not provide a good basis for predicting long-term effects of oil spills on raptors. Given these uncertainties and the importance of this species to the public, we undertook a field study to evaluate whether the effects observed in 1989 extended into two subsequent years. Specifically, we compared the densities and reproductive performance of bald eagles between oiled and unoiled portions of the Sound in 1990 and 1991. We investigated whether initial oiling of shorelines had an effect on densities and reproductive performance of eagles one and two years after the oil spill.

STUDY AREA

The coastal areas of Prince William Sound are dominated by spruce-hemlock forest (Viereck and Little, 1972). Bird habitats in this region were described by Isleib and Kessel (1973). Most of the bald eagle nests were located within 100 m of shore in western hemlock *(Tsuga heterophylla),* Sitka spruce

(Picea sitchensis), or dead trees of these two species; only one nest was located on the ground.

We did not have the option to select study areas in a totally random fashion. Instead, the size and dimensions of the study area were chosen to (1) provide adequate sample sizes, (2) avoid U.S. Fish and Wildlife Service (USFWS) monitoring programs associated with cleanup activities, (3) avoid overlap with USFWS eagle nesting surveys (e.g., the northern Knight Island group; Bowman et al., 1993), and (4) be within range of helicopter fuel sources. Although a portion of the area overlapped USFWS study areas (e.g., Green Island), our intent was to reduce duplication of effort and the potential disturbance-related impacts of repeated aerial surveys on bald eagles.

A total of 779 km of shoreline was surveyed, using the same survey boundaries in both 1990 and 1991. Those shorelines ranged from unoiled to heavily oiled in 1989 and were located primarily in the northern and southwestern portions of the Sound (Figure 1). Northern areas of the Sound were not oiled, whereas all shoreline impacts of oil occurred in the southwestern area. Our surveys in the southwestern portions of the Sound provided a relatively thorough and balanced sampling with regard to the inclusion of areas with various degrees of oiling impact. In this area, exclusive of Montague Island (a large but slightly oiled island that was not surveyed), surveys were conducted along 44% of the shoreline that had been heavily oiled in 1989, 25% of that with "medium" oiling, 30% of that with "light" oiling, 43% of that with "very light" oiling, and 30% of that with no oiling.

METHODS

Field Methods

In 1990, 4 helicopter surveys were scheduled to coincide with important life-history events and to minimize errors in estimates of reproductive performance (Fraser et al., 1983). Surveys I (27 April-3 May) and II (20-25 May) were conducted to establish the boundaries of the study area and to assess the status of each nest (e.g., occupied or unoccupied). Once established, however, the same area was surveyed on all subsequent surveys in 1990 and 1991. Survey III (28 June-4 July) measured productivity of pairs that had laid eggs in the early part of the season, and Survey IV (26 July-1 August) was used to estimate fledgling success.

This study was designed to be completed in one year. In 1991, however, the opportunity arose to conduct a single survey (comparable to Survey IV, 1990) during the late nestling period (24-28 July). Although definitive estimates of nesting success and productivity would have required at least 2 surveys (Postupalsky, 1974), the results of the 1991 survey provided data on numbers and productivity of successful nests and on densities of eagles late in the breeding season for comparison with 1990 data. This survey also helped us to evaluate whether many nests were constructed or lost between 1990 and 1991.

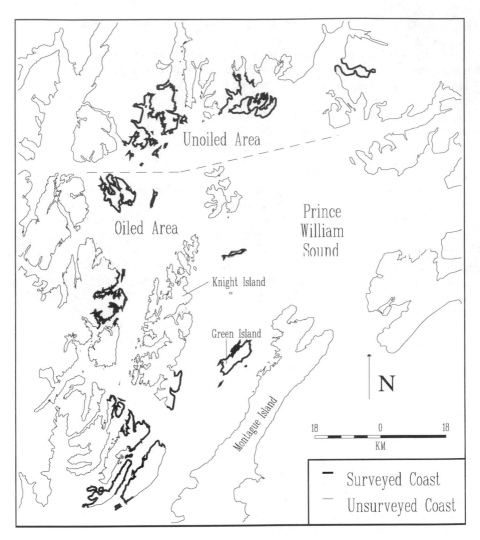

FIGURE 1--Study areas in Prince William Sound, Alaska, 1990 and 1991. Dark lines along
       coastlines indicate areas surveyed for eagles and nests. The area south of the
       dashed line is considered the oiled area, whereas the area to the north is
       considered the unoiled, or control, area.

       Standard protocol was followed in flying aerial surveys to locate and
determine the status of bald eagle nests (see Fuller and Mosher, 1987). An
Aerospatiale "Twin Aerostar" helicopter was flown at speeds of 65-80 km/h,

altitudes slightly above canopy height, and a distance of approximately 50 m from shore. Once a nest was located, a slower, closer pass by the nest (approximately 25 m away) was made if the numbers of adults and young could not be determined on the first pass. Flights directly over nests were avoided to lessen disturbance.

Two observers, seated on one side of the aircraft, conducted the surveys and recorded data. Each nest was assigned an individual number, and the following data were recorded for each nest: status (e.g., active, inactive), substrate (ground, tree), number of adults present, number of nestlings, and nestling age as indicated by plumage development (i.e., downy [white or gray], partially feathered, fully feathered). In addition, eagles not associated with nests were tallied and classified by plumage (i.e., adult, subadult) during each survey. Eagles without white heads were classified as subadults.

Terminology

Our terminology for nest status generally follows Postupalsky (1974). An *occupied nest* had an incubating or brooding adult, eggs, or nestlings present on any survey, or had a pair of adults within 250 m of a nest in good condition on Surveys I or II. An *active nest* had an incubating or brooding adult, eggs, or nestlings present. A *successful nest* had large, "nearly fledged young" present. We considered any nestlings that were well-feathered ($\geq$49 days; bodies mostly feathered with black, juvenal plumage) to be nearly fledged (see Bortolotti, 1984; Steenhof, 1987). Any reference to "young" in the text refers to young eagles that were nearly fledged.

Reproductive performance of raptors can be evaluated in several ways. In this study, we examined occupancy, nesting success, and productivity. Occupancy was calculated as the number of occupied nests/nesting areas. Nesting success was computed in four ways: the number of successful nests/active nests, the number of successful nests/occupied nests, the number of successful nests/total nesting area (which permitted a comparison of 1990 surveys with the single survey of 1991), and the Mayfield estimate of nesting success (Mayfield, 1961, 1975). The latter estimate is a technique used to reduce bias in estimates of avian reproductive rates that occurs as a result of survey timing. The Mayfield estimate was based on a 35-day incubation period (Stalmaster, 1987; Palmer, 1988) and a 49-day nestling period (for hatchlings to become large, feathered young). Four measures of productivity were calculated: young/occupied nest, young/active nest, young/successful nest, and total young.

Oiling Levels and Data Analysis

For statistical analyses, samples were partitioned in two ways. First, sightings of bald eagles were partitioned into two geographically separate areas, according to initial oiling levels, for all analyses of bald eagle and eagle nest densities (birds or nests/km of shoreline). Densities of eagles were compared in southwestern Prince William Sound, which was directly in the path of spreading oil (oiled area; 416.7 km of shoreline surveyed), with those in the northern Sound, an area that was not oiled (unoiled area; 362.0 km of shoreline surveyed; Figure 1).

For all other analyses, samples of nests were partitioned according to the occurrence of oil within 1 km of nest sites. Because of geographic variation in the amount of oil that washed up on shorelines, some unoiled territories occurred within the southwestern portion of the Sound. In our analyses, oiled territories included lightly, moderately, or heavily oiled shorelines within 1 km of nests, and unoiled territories included unoiled or very lightly oiled (<10% of shoreline had spots of oil) shoreline within 1 km of nests.

To determine whether a nesting territory was oiled or unoiled, oiling maps based on results of surveys performed following the spill in 1989 by Exxon Co., U.S.A., and approved by the U. S. Coast Guard (Neff et al., this volume) were used. Some portions of the study area were not surveyed for oil. Unsurveyed areas were considered unoiled if they were outside the path of oil (e.g., the northern shoreline of the Sound) as it spread southwest from the spill site. If <25% of the shoreline within 1 km of the nest was unsurveyed and the nest territory was in an area that may have been oiled, an oiling category was assigned based on the portion of shoreline that was surveyed. An oiling category was not assigned to a nesting territory in areas that may have received oil where >25% of the shoreline within 1 km of the nest was unsurveyed; such nests (n = 7)were discarded from analyses of nesting success and productivity.

The selection of a 1-km radius around nests as the sample unit in categorizing territory oiling status was based primarily on research in southeastern Alaska, where the mean distance between nests was 2 km (Hodges and Robards, 1982). The assumption was made that a 1-km radius encompassed the territory (defended area) and included portions of the home range (feeding area) of each pair of eagles. As a test of sensitivity, samples were also analyzed using 0.5- and 2.0-km territorial radii around nests. Because marked differences in results were not found using these different territory sizes, those results are not reported here.

All statistical tests followed methods in Conover (1980) and Zar (1984). The level of significance (α) was 0.05 for all tests. Nest occupancy, activity, and success were compared with Chi-square contingency table analyses (df = 1 for all tests). Productivity statistics were compared with Chi-square contingency table analyses by using nests with 0, 1, and 2 or more young as categories (df = 2 for all cases except Young/Successful Nest, where df = 1).

RESULTS

Densities of Eagles

In 1990, the density of adult eagles (birds/km of shoreline) in the oiled area was same as or higher than that in the unoiled area during each of the 4 sampling periods (Table 1). Densities of adult eagles in 1991 also were similar in both areas during the single survey conducted during the late nestling period. Densities ranged from 0.36 to 0.87 adults/km and were higher in late April 1990, the early part of the nesting season, than in any other sampling period.

In 1990, densities of total eagles (adults + subadults/km of shoreline) were greater in the oiled area than in the unoiled area on all but the July (final) survey (Table 1). Similarly, in 1991, densities of total eagles were lower in the oiled area than in the unoiled area during July. These differences were due to fewer subadults in the oiled areas in both years. Over the 2 years of the study, total densities ranged from 0.36 to 0.97 birds/km of shoreline.

Densities of Nests

Densities of total nests were slightly higher in the unoiled area than in the oiled area in both 1990 and 1991 (Table 2). In 1990, densities of occupied, active,

TABLE 1--Number and density (birds/km of shoreline surveyed) of bald eagles in oiled and unoiled areas of Prince William Sound, Alaska, 1990-1991.

| Year / | Oiled Area[a] | | | | Unoiled Area[a] | | | |
| | Adults | | Adults + Subadults | | Adults | | Adults + Subadults | |
Sampling Period	No.	No./km	No.	No./km	No.	No./km	No.	No./km
1990								
27 Apr - 3 May	363	0.87	406	0.97	285	0.79	326	0.90
20-25 May	177	0.42	205	0.49	153	0.42	170	0.47
28 Jun - 4 Jul	204	0.49	220	0.53	134	0.37	158	0.44
26 Jul - 1 Aug	150	0.36	150	0.36	132	0.36	158	0.44
1991								
24-28 Jul	228	0.55	253	0.61	203	0.56	258	0.71

[a] 417.6 km surveyed in the oiled area and 362.0 km surveyed in the unoiled area.

TABLE 2--Number and density (nests/km of shoreline surveyed) of nests of bald eagles in oiled and unoiled areas of Prince William Sound, Alaska, 1990-1991.

| Year/ | Oiled Area | | Unoiled Area | |
Nest Status	No.	No./km	No.	No./km
1990				
Occupied	91	0.22	89	0.25
Active	70	0.17	76	0.21
Successful	53	0.13	54	0.15
Total [a]	154	0.37	154	0.43
1991				
Successful	38	0.09	26	0.07
Total [a]	167	0.40	166	0.46

[a] These totals include supernumerary nests (i.e., unoccupied nests within 100 m of occupied nests). Different totals between years are attributed to a combination of some new nests being identified, and some old nests being lost.

and successful nests also were slightly higher in the unoiled area than in the oiled area, in proportions similar to those for total nests. In 1991, however, density of successful nests was slightly lower in the unoiled area than in the oiled area, but densities in both areas were lower than in 1990.

Nest Occupancy and Nesting Success

An oiling category could be assigned to 301 nests located in 1990 (Table 3A). Of these, 40% were in oiled territories and 60% were in unoiled territories. An oiling category also was assigned to 325 nests located in 1991 (Table 3A): 39% in oiled territories and 61% in unoiled territories.

In 1990, slightly higher proportions of nests (with respect to total nesting areas) were occupied in oiled territories than in unoiled territories; in contrast, a slightly lower proportion of nests was active in oiled territories than in unoiled territories (Table 3B). In addition, review of maps of occupied nests in oiled and unoiled areas revealed no gaps in the distribution of occupied nests in the most heavily oiled areas in 1990. No data on nest occupancy were available for comparison in 1991.

All measures of nesting success were slightly (but not significantly) higher in oiled areas relative to unoiled areas in 1990 (Table 3B). There were slightly (but not significantly) fewer successful nests in oiled territories in 1991 than in 1990, however ($\chi^2 = 1.33$, df = 1, P = 0.249). In unoiled territories there were significantly fewer successful nests in 1991 than in 1990 ($\chi^2 = 8.62$, df = 1, P = 0.003) (Table 3A). Comparisons of nesting success between oiled and unoiled areas could not be made in 1991 because early surveys were not conducted that year.

Productivity

Estimates of productivity (number of young/nest) did not differ significantly between oiled and unoiled territories in 1990 (Table 3C). In 1991, however, the number of young/successful nest was significantly lower in oiled territories than in unoiled territories (Table 3C). Consistent with the lower nesting success in 1991, fewer young were raised in both oiled (45% fewer young) and unoiled territories (47% fewer young) in 1991 than in 1990.

DISCUSSION

If the 1989 *Exxon Valdez* oil spill still had been affecting bald eagles in 1990 and 1991, one might have expected: (1) fewer eagles in oiled areas because of higher mortality there; (2) lower rates of nest occupancy and nesting success in oiled areas; and/or (3) fewer young produced per nest in oiled areas because of lower food availability or continuing effects of oil on reproductive physiology. In general, we found no consistent differences in densities of eagles, occupancy rates, nesting success (only measured in 1990), or productivity, and no gaps in the geographic distribution of

TABLE 3--Summary of bald eagle nest status, nest occupancy, nesting success, and productivity in oiled and unoiled territories in Prince William Sound, Alaska, 1990 and 1991.

	1990[b]				1991[b]			
	TOTAL	Oiled	Unoiled	P-value	TOTAL	Oiled	Unoiled	P-value
Part A - Nest Status								
Number of Nests								
Total[a]	301	120	181	-	325	127	198	-
Unoccupied[a]	127	48	79	-	-	-	-	-
Occupied	174	72	102		-	-	-	-
Active	141	55	86	-	-	-	-	-
Fate Unknown	3	2	1	-	-	-	-	-
Active/Fate Known	138	53	85	-	-	-	-	-
Successful	103	43	60	-	63	32	31	-
Part B- Nest Occupancy and Success								
Percentage of Nests								
Occupied/Total Nesting Area[c]	0.60	0.62	0.58	0.485	-	-	-	-
Active/Total Nesting Area[c]	0.48	0.47	0.49	0.811	-	-	-	-
Active/Occupied Nest	0.81	0.76	0.84	0.189	-	-	-	-
Successful/Occupied Nest	0.59	0.60	0.59	0.905	-	-	-	-
Successful/Active Nest[a]	0.75	0.81	0.71	0.166	-	-	-	-
Mayfield Estimate of Success	-	0.73	0.65	-	-	-	-	-
Part C - Productivity								
Mean Number of								
Young/Occupied Nest	0.96	1.01	0.92	0.538	-	-	-	-
Young/Active Nest[a]	1.21	1.38	1.11	0.204	-	-	-	-
Young/Successful Nest	1.62	1.70	1.57	0.269	1.43	1.25	1.61	0.004
Production of Young								
Nests with 1 young	40	14	26	-	36	24	12	-
Nests with 2 young	62	28	34	-	27	8	19	-
Nests with 3 young	1	1	0	-	0	0	0	-
Number of Young	167	73	94	-	90	40	50	-

[a] Excludes nests of unknown fate.
[b] Excludes nests where oiling level was unknown.
[c] These exclude supernumerary nests (i.e., unoccupied nests within 100 m of occupied nests).

occupied nests in the most heavily oiled areas that would indicate that eagles were doing poorly in oiled areas. Bowman et al. (1993) also examined the effects of the oil spill on reproductive performance of bald eagles in Prince William Sound. They found that the effects of the oil spill were short-term and were limited to direct mortality and impaired reproduction in 1989.

Besides a lack of consistent differences between oiled and unoiled areas, our estimates of productivity, nest occupancy, nesting success, and densities of eagles in oiled areas fall within the wide range of values measured for coastal eagle populations elsewhere in Alaska and British Columbia (Imler, 1941; Hancock, 1964; Hensel and Troyer, 1964; Troyer and Hensel, 1965; Robards and King, 1966; White et al., 1971; Sprunt et al., 1973; Bailey, 1976, 1977; Sherrod et al., 1977; Bailey and Faust, 1981, 1984; Hodges, 1982; Hodges and Robards, 1982; Hodges et al., 1984; Hansen and Hodges, 1985; Hansen et al., 1986; Hogan and Irons, 1988; Alaska Biological Research, Inc., 1990). Although some of the broad range of values reported for other populations may result from differences in survey techniques, productivity naturally can vary considerably among years and areas (Schempf, 1989).

Because the number of young per successful nest was significantly lower in oiled territories than in unoiled territories in 1991, however, we examined whether this difference could be attributed to oil. If an oil effect was evident in any year following the spill, a reasonable hypothesis might be that it should have been manifested most strongly in the first year after the spill (1990), not the second (1991). That is, any effect of oiling on productivity should have declined between 1990 and 1991 because the amount and toxicity of the remaining oil and disturbance due to cleanup activities had declined in that period. In addition, if there had been large-scale mortality or displacement of established territorial adults in the oiled areas in 1989, productivity might have been lower in oiled areas in 1990 than in 1991. The presence of fewer breeders or an influx of new breeding birds into oiled areas in 1990 could have been reflected in lower productivity, as has been associated with few or inexperienced breeders elsewhere (see Nelson, 1978:110, 456; Newton, 1979:145). Such was not the case, however; all measures of productivity were similar in the oiled territories and the unoiled territories in 1990. It is possible that mortality of adults was lower than projected by Piatt et al. (1990) and Bowman and Schempf (1993) and/or that losses of adults were compensated from a surplus of nonbreeding adults (see Hansen and Hodges, 1985), thereby limiting the impact of oil on productivity primarily to the year of the spill.

The fact that overall productivity (i.e., numbers of successful nests and numbers of young) was low in both oiled and unoiled territories in 1991 indicates that a regional factor (e.g., weather, food availability), and not a local factor (e.g., oiled shorelines), probably was most influential. Although a number of environmental factors could have contributed to lower productivity of eagles in 1991, at least two weather variables did differ substantially between the 1990 and 1991 breeding seasons in Prince William Sound: amount of rain and frequency of rainy days. On the basis of data from three NOAA weather stations in or close to our study area (Cannery Creek, Main Bay, and Port San Juan; National Oceanic and Atmospheric Administration, 1990a, 1990b, 1990c, 1991a, 1991b, 1991c), rainfall in 15 April—15 June 1991 (9.9 mm/d) was over three times higher than it was in the same period in 1990 (2.8 mm/d). In fact, mean precipitation at the Valdez weather station (where departure from normal data are available) was 87 mm above normal in April—June 1991 and only 19 mm above normal in 1990. Frequency of rainfall also was greater during the 15 April—15 June period in 1991, with 31 days with 0.5 inches (13 mm) or more of rain in 1991 compared with 15 days in 1990. In contrast, daily temperatures were similar between the two years. The April—June period considered above coincides with the incubation and early nestling stages of bald eagles, when the eggs and young would be most susceptible to exposure. Poor, wet weather conditions in spring (during incubation) have been found to depress the breeding performance of other raptors (Newton, 1979; Kostrzewa and Kostrzewa, 1990; Olsen and Olsen, 1989). It is possible that weather exerted such an effect in Prince William Sound in 1991.

Three lines of evidence indicate that environmental conditions for breeding by bald eagles improved after 1989; that improvement helps to explain the similarity in our results between oiled and unoiled areas in 1990. First, the amount of oil remaining on shorelines and on the water surface decreased greatly from 1989 to 1990 (Maki, 1990; Neff and Stubblefield, this volume), thus reducing the probability that eagles would come into direct contact with oil. In addition, concentrations of petroleum hydrocarbons in the water column, where they could affect eagle food resources, were negligible by mid-1990 (Neff and Stubblefield, this volume). Second, the number of humans involved in cleanup activities decreased greatly in 1990 and 1991 (Harrison, 1991), presumably decreasing the amount of disturbance to nesting eagles. Finally, cleanup operations in 1990 and 1991 were better coordinated with the USFWS to avoid eagle nests and reduce impacts by observing buffer zones around nests (Harrison, 1991; Lockhart, 1993).

With reduced oil in the Prince William Sound environment in 1990, the probability of uptake and accumulation of oil and, consequently, physiological impacts to surviving eagles should also have been reduced. Indeed, Gibson and White (1990) reported on eagles trapped in the spill zone within 2 to 3 months after the spill and found that most (101 birds, 89%) were in good or excellent physical shape. In addition, the hematocrit and blood protein levels of captured eagles (some with external oiling) generally were better than acceptable limits of the USFWS Protocol Guidelines. Bald eagles that had ingested large amounts of oil should have suffered some hemolytic anemia and kidney damage, but those were not indicated by these blood samples. Further, research by Pattee and Franson (1982) that examined the short-term, acute effects of ingesting unweathered crude oil on American kestrels (*Falco sparverius*) provides support for our contention that physiological impacts to eagles would be reduced once oil was limited in their environment. These authors reported that all of the birds that survived the feeding experiment (88% of the sample) recovered after oil was removed from the diet. They also provide an interesting behavioral observation: kestrels initially avoided oiled food during this experiment, suggesting to the authors that, in a free-choice situation, kestrels would probably avoid oiled food. Such avoidance of oiled areas by bald eagles was noted by Gibson and White (1990), providing additional explanations for reduced impacts of oil on surviving eagles in Prince William Sound.

CONCLUSIONS

The 1989 *Exxon Valdez* oil spill caused direct mortality and reduced reproductive success of bald eagles in Prince William Sound in the year of the spill. In general, one might have expected negative effects of the spill on reproductive performance of eagles still to be evident in years following the spill if: (1) nesting habitat had been severely damaged or nests were lost; (2) food resources had showed continuing population declines; or (3) eagle mortality, especially of breeding adults, had continued. There was no evidence that nesting habitat was damaged or lost, and the results of our study support the contention that the latter two events did not occur in 1990. There were no consistent differences in the density or reproductive performance of bald eagles between oiled and unoiled areas one to two years after the spill that would suggest that longer-term impacts occurred.

Our results reflect improved environmental conditions for bald eagles in the Sound in 1990 and 1991. We conclude that, despite the initial negative effects of oiling and related human disturbance in 1989, the oil spill did not have demonstrable effects on densities or reproduction of bald eagles in Prince William Sound one to two years after the spill.

ACKNOWLEDGMENTS

Support for this study was provided by Exxon Company, U.S.A. Several people were instrumental in this study. Paul W. Banyas and F. Lance Craighead of ABR participated in aerial surveys. Hilton Jones, David Pearson, and Ron Whipple, ERA Aviation, Inc., were excellent pilots. Gerry R. Hobbs of the Department of Statistics and Computer Sciences, West Virginia University, provided statistical advice. Robert H. Day and Stephen M. Murphy, and three anonymous reviewers provided critical review of the manuscript.

REFERENCES

Alaska Biological Research, Inc., unpublished data; 1990.

Albers, P. H. "Transfer of crude oil from contaminated water to bird eggs." *Environmental Research.* 22:307-314; 1980.

Bailey, E. P. "Breeding bird distribution and abundance in the Barren Islands, Alaska." *Murrelet.* 57:2-12; 1976.

____. "Distribution and abundance of marine birds and mammals along the south side of the Kenai Peninsula, Alaska." *Murrelet.* 58:58-72; 1977.

___, and N. H. Faust. "Summer distribution and abundance of marine birds and mammals between Mitrofania and Sutwik islands south of the Alaska Peninsula." *Murrelet.* 62:34-42; 1981.

___, and ___. "Distribution and abundance of marine birds breeding between Amber and Kamishak bays, Alaska, with notes on interactions with bears." *Western Birds.* 15:161-174; 1984.

Bortolotti, G. R. "Physical development of nestling bald eagles with emphasis on the timing of growth events." *Wilson Bulletin.* 96:524-542; 1984.

Bowman, T. D., and P. F. Schempf. "Effects of the *Exxon Valdez* oil spill on bald eagles." *in* Exxon Valdez *Oil Spill Symposium*, Abstract Book; Anchorage, Alaska: *Exxon Valdez* Oil Spill Trustee Council; 142-143; 1993.

Bowman, T. D., P. S. Schempf, and J. A. Bernatowicz. Effects of the *Exxon Valdez* oil spill on Bald Eagles: Bird Study #4. *Unpubl. final rep.* to USFWS, Anchorage, Alaska, 140 pp., 1993.

Butler, R. G., and P. Lukasiewicz. "A field study of the effect of crude oil on herring gull (*Larus argentatus*) chick growth." *Auk.* 96:809-812; 1979.

Cavanaugh, K. P., A. R. Goldsmith, W. N. Holmes, and B. K. Follett. "Effects of ingested petroleum on the plasma prolactin levels during incubation and on the breeding success of paired mallard ducks." *Archives of Environmental Contamination and Toxicology.* 12:335-341; 1983.

Conover, W. J. *Practical nonparametric statistics.* Second ed. John Wiley and Sons, New York; 493 pp; 1980.

Fraser, J. D. "The impact of human disturbance on bald eagle populations—a review." *in The bald eagle in Canada.* J. M. Gerrard and T. N. Ingram (eds.); Eagle Foundation; Apple River, Illinois; 1985.

___, L. D. Frenzel, J. E. Mathisen, F. Martin, and M. E. Shough. "Scheduling bald eagle reproduction surveys." *Wildlife Society Bulletin.* 11:13-16; 1983.

___, L. D. Frenzel, and J. E. Mathisen. "The impact of human activities on breeding bald eagles in north central Minnesota." *Journal of Wildlife Management.* 49:585-592; 1985.

Fry, D. M., J. Swenson, L. A. Addiego, C. R. Grau, and A. Kang. "Reduced reproduction of wedge-tailed shearwaters exposed to weathered Santa Barbara crude oil." *Archives of Environmental Contamination and Toxicology.* 15:453-463; 1986.

Fuller, M. R. and J. A. Mosher. "Raptor survey techniques." *in Raptor management techniques manual.* B. A. Pendleton, B. A. Millsap, K. W. Cline, and D. M. Bird (eds.); National Wildlife Federation; Scientific and Technical Series No. 10; 1987.

Galt, J. A., W. J. Lehr, and D. L. Payton. "Fate and transport of the *Exxon Valdez* oil spill." *Environmental Science and Technology.* 25:202-209; 1991.

Gibson, M. J., and J. White. "Results of the eagle capture, health assessment, and short-term rehabilitation program following the Valdez oil spill." *Paper presented at the 13th Annual Conference of the International Wildlife Rehabilitation Council;* Herndon, Virginia; 16 pp; 1990.

Grubb, T. G., and R. M. King. "Assessing human disturbance of breeding bald eagles with classification tree models." *Journal of Wildlife Management.* 55:500-511; 1991.

Hancock, D. "Bald eagles wintering in the southern Gulf Islands, British Columbia." *Wilson Bulletin.* 76:111-120; 1964.

Hansen, A. J., and J. I. Hodges, Jr. "High rates of nonbreeding adult bald eagles in southeastern Alaska." *Journal of Wildlife Management.* 49:454-458; 1985.

___, M. I. Dyer, H. H. Shugart, and E. L. Boeker. "Behavioral ecology of bald eagles along the northwest coast: A landscape perspective." Oak Ridge National Laboratory; Publication Number 2548; 166 pp; 1986.

Harrison, O. R. "An overview of the *Exxon Valdez* oil spill." *in Proceedings of the 1991 International Oil Spill Conference*; San Diego, California; 1991.

Hensel, R. J., and W. A. Troyer. "Nesting studies of the bald eagle in Alaska." *Condor.* 66:282-286; 1964.

Hodges, J. I., Jr. "Bald eagle nesting studies in Seymour Canal, southeast Alaska." *Condor.* 84:125-127; 1982.

___, J. G. King, and R. Davies. "Bald eagle breeding population survey of coastal British Columbia." *Journal of Wildlife Management.* 48:993-998; 1984.

___, and F. C. Robards. "Observations of 3850 bald eagle nests in southeast Alaska." *in Raptor management and biology in Alaska and western Canada.* W. N. Ladd and P. F. Schempf (eds.) U.S. Fish and Wildlife Service; Anchorage, Alaska; FWS/AK/PROC-82; 1982.

Hogan, M. E., and D. B. Irons. "Waterbirds and marine mammals." *in Environmental studies in Port Valdez, Alaska.* D. G. Shaw and M. J. Hameedi (eds.); Springer-Verlag; Berlin; 1988.

Holmes, W. N., K. P. Cavanaugh, and J. Cronshaw. "The effects of ingested petroleum on oviposition and some aspects of reproduction in experimental colonies of mallard ducks (*Anas platyrhynchos*)." *Journal of Reproductive Fertilization.* 54:335-347; 1978.

Imler, R. H. "Alaskan bald eagle studies." U. S. Fish and Wildlife Service; Denver, Colorado; 17 pp; 1941.

Isleib, M. E., and B. Kessel. "Birds of the North Gulf Coast-Prince William Sound region, Alaska." *Biological Papers of the University of Alaska.* 14:1-149; 1973.

King, J. G., and G. A. Sanger. "Oil vulnerability index for marine oriented birds." *in Conservation of marine birds of northern North America.* J. C. Bartonek and D. N. Nettleship (eds.); U.S. Fish and Wildlife Service; Wildlife Research Report No. 11; 1979.

King, K. A., and C. A. Lefever. "Effects of oil transferred from incubating gulls to their eggs." *Marine Pollution Bulletin.* 10:319-321; 1979.

Kostrzewa, A., and R. Kostrzewa. "The relationship of spring and summer weather with density and breeding performance of the buzzard *Buteo buteo,* goshawk *Accipiter gentilis,* and kestrel *Falco tinnunculus.*" *Ibis.* 132:550-559; 1990.

Lewis, S. J., and R. A. Malecki. "Effects of egg oiling on larid productivity and population dynamics." *Auk.* 101:584-592; 1984.

Lockhart, M., U.S. Fish and Wildlife Service, personal communication; 1993.

Maki, A. W. "The *Exxon Valdez* oil spill: Initial environmental impact assessment. *Environmental Science and Technology.* 25:24-29; 1991.

Mathisen, J. E. "Effects of human disturbance on nesting of bald eagles." *Journal of Wildlife Management.* 32:1-6; 1968.

Mayfield, H. "Nesting success calculated from exposure." *Wilson Bulletin.* 73:255-261; 1961.

___. "Suggestions for calculating nest success." *Wilson Bulletin.* 87:456-466; 1975.

National Oceanic and Atmospheric Administration. Climatological data, Alaska. 76 (4): 1—25; 1990a.

National Oceanic and Atmospheric Administration. Climatological data, Alaska. 76 (5): 1—25; 1990b.

National Oceanic and Atmospheric Administration. Climatological data, Alaska. 76 (6): 1—25; 1990c.

National Oceanic and Atmospheric Administration. Climatological data, Alaska. 76 (4): 1—25; 1991a.

National Oceanic and Atmospheric Administration. Climatological data, Alaska. 76 (5): 1— 25; 1991b.

National Oceanic and Atmospheric Administration. Climatological data, Alaska. 76 (6): 1—25; 1991c.

Neff, J. M., and W. A. Stubblefield. "Chemical and toxicological evaluation of water quality following the *Exxon* Valdez oil spill." *Exxon Valdez Oil Spill, Fate and Effects in Alaskan Waters. ASTM STP 1219*, R. G. Wells, J. N. Butler, and J. S. Hughes, eds., American Society for Testing and Materials, Philadelphia, 1994.

Neff, J. M., E. H. Owens, S. W. Stoker, and D. M. McCormick. "Condition of shorelines in Prince William Sound following the *Exxon* Valdez oil spill: Part I--shoreline oiling." *Exxon Valdez Oil Spill, Fate and Effects in Alaskan Waters. ASTM STP 1219*, R. G. Wells, J. N. Butler, and J. S. Hughes, eds., American Society for Testing and Materials, Philadelphia, 1994.

Nelson, J. B. *The Sulidae: Gannets and boobies.* Oxford University Press; Oxford; 1012 pp; 1978.

Newton, I. *Population ecology of raptors.* Buteo Books; Vermillion, South Dakota; 399 pp; 1979.

Olsen, P. D., and J. Olsen. "Breeding of the peregrine falcon *Falco peregrinus*: 2. Weather, nest quality and the timing of egg laying. *Emu.* 89:1-5; 1989.

Owens, E. H., "Shoreline conditions following the *Exxon Valdez* spill as of fall 1990." *Paper presented at the 14th Annual Arctic and Marine Oilspill Program*; Woodward-Clyde; Seattle, Washington; 1991.

Palmer, R. S. "Handbook of North American birds." Volume 4. Yale University Press; New Haven, Connecticut; 433 pp; 1988.

Pattee, O. H., and J. C. Franson. "Short-term effects of oil ingestion on American kestrels (*Falco sparverius*)." *Journal of Wildlife Diseases.* 18:235-241; 1982.

Piatt, J. F., C. J. Lensink, W. Butler, M. Kendziorek, and D. R. Nysewander. "Immediate impact of the *Exxon Valdez* oil spill on marine birds." *Auk.* 107:387-397; 1990.

Postupalsky, S. "Raptor reproductive success: some problems with methods, criteria, and terminology." *in Management of raptors.* F. N. Hamerstrom, Jr., B. E. Harrell, and R. R. Olendorff (eds.); *Raptor Research Report.* 2; 1974.

Robards, F. C., and J. G. King. "Nesting and productivity of bald eagles in southeast Alaska—1966." *Unpublished report to U.S. Bureau of Sport Fisheries and Wildlife*; Juneau, Alaska; 14 pp; 1966.

Schempf, P. F. "Raptors in Alaska." *in Proceedings of the Western Raptor Management Symposium and Workshop.* B. G. Pendleton (ed.); *National Wildlife Federation Scientific Technical Series.* 12:144-154. 1989.

Sherrod, S. K., C. M. White, and F. S. L. Williamson. "Biology of the bald eagle on Amchitka Island, Alaska." *Living Bird.* 15:143-182; 1977.

Sprunt, A., IV, W. B. Robertson, Jr., S. Postupalsky, R. J. Hensel, C. E. Knoder, and F. J. Ligas. "Comparative productivity of six bald eagle populations." *Transactions of the North American Wildlife and Natural Resources Conference.* 38:96-106; 1973.

Stalmaster, M. V. *The bald eagle.* Universe Books; New York; 227 pp; 1987.

Steenhof, K. "Assessing raptor reproductive success and productivity." *in Raptor management techniques manual*. B. A. G. Pendleton, B. A. Millsap, K. W. Cline, and D. M. Bird (eds.); *National Wildlife Federation Scientific Technical Series*. 10:157-170; 1987.

Stubblefield, W. A., G. A. Hancock, W. H. Ford, H. H. Prince, and R. K. Ringer. "Evaluation of the toxic properties of naturally weathered *Exxon Valdez* crude oil to wildlife species." *Exxon Valdez Oil Spill, Fate and Effects in Alaskan Waters. ASTM STP 1219*, R. G. Wells, J. N. Butler, and J. S. Hughes, eds., American Society for Testing and Materials, Philadelphia, 1994.

Teal, A. R., "Shoreline cleanup—reconnaissance, evaluation, and planning following the Valdez oil spill" *in Proceedings of the 1991 International Oil Spill Conference*; San Diego, California; 1991.

Troyer, W. A., and R. J. Hensel. "Nesting and productivity of bald eagles on the Kodiak National Wildlife Refuge, Alaska." *Auk*. 82:636-638; 1965.

U.S. Fish and Wildlife Service, unpublished data; 1989.

Viereck, L. A., and E. L. Little, Jr. "Alaska trees and shrubs." U. S. Department of Agriculture; *Agriculture Handbook*. 410:1-265; 1972.

White, C. M., W. B. Emison, and F. S. L. Williamson. "Dynamics of raptor populations on Amchitka Island, Alaska." *BioScience*. 21:623-627; 1971.

Zar, J. H. *Biostatistical analysis*. Second ed. Prentice-Hall, Englewood Cliffs, New Jersey; 718 pp; 1984.

David E. Erikson[1]

SURVEYS OF MURRE COLONY ATTENDANCE IN THE NORTHERN GULF
OF ALASKA FOLLOWING THE *EXXON VALDEZ* OIL SPILL

REFERENCE: Erikson, D. E., "Surveys of Murre Colony Attendance in the
Northern Gulf of Alaska Following the Exxon Valdez Oil Spill," *Exxon Valdez
Oil Spill: Fate and Effects in Alaskan Waters, ASTM STP 1219,* Peter G. Wells,
James N. Butler, and Jane S. Hughes, Eds., American Society for Testing and
Materials, Philadelphia, 1995.

ABSTRACT: Field surveys were conducted in July and August 1991 on 32 of the 36
murre (*Uria spp.*) colonies in the northern Gulf of Alaska to assess colony attendance
(number of birds present at a colony) two years after the *Exxon Valdez* oil spill. The
surveys focused on murre colonies because murres represented 74% of the recovered
seabird carcasses and because it had been claimed that there was large-scale mortality of
murres, leading to 60% to 70% decreases at some large colonies and population recovery
periods of 20 to 70 years.

Murres were present at all 32 colonies, and colony attendance estimates were generally
similar to those from historical (prespill) surveys, particularly for those colonies in the
direct path of the spill, i.e., the Barren Islands and Chiswell Islands. Colony attendance
levels in 1991 do not support the contention that murre colony attendance in the study
area was drastically lower than historical levels. When colonies were grouped according
to risk of oil exposure, the mean changes in attendance between 1991 and historical murre
surveys did not differ significantly among the groups. Factors that could account for the
observed similarity of 1991 and historical murre counts despite the high estimated
mortality are (1) overestimation of mortality or (2) replacement of lost breeders through
either recruitment of formerly nonbreeding individuals into the breeding population at
spill-affected colonies or immigration of murres from nonaffected colonies. The findings
of this study suggest that impacts of the *Exxon Valdez* oil spill on murre colony attendance
in the northern Gulf of Alaska were relatively short-term.

KEYWORDS: Common Murres, *Uria*, colony attendance, oil spill, environmental
effects, bird mortality, northern Gulf of Alaska

INTRODUCTION

On March 24, 1989 the oil tanker *Exxon Valdez* ran aground on Bligh Reef, in

[1]Environmental Scientist, Dames and Moore, P.O. Box 15204, Fritz Creek, AK 99603-6204

northeastern Prince William Sound, Alaska, and spilled approximately 41 million litres (11 million gallons) of North Slope crude oil into the waters of the sound (Galt and Payton 1990; Koons and Jahns 1992). The oil subsequently drifted through the western sound, into the Gulf of Alaska, then continued west along the Kenai Peninsula, into Lower Cook Inlet and to the northern end of the Kodiak Archipelago. Oil and mousse continued down Shelikof Strait and by May 18 had reached a distance of approximately 750 km from the spill site (Piatt et al. 1990; Galt and Payton 1990).

Seabirds are abundant in the northern Gulf of Alaska, with population estimates as high as one million in the spill area (Piatt et al. 1990). Because of these large populations and the vulnerability of seabirds to oil on the water, this spill caused considerable mortality to seabirds along its path. Approximately 36 000 seabird carcasses were collected from the affected areas. Two of the species most affected by the spill were Common and Thick-billed Murres (*Uria aalge* and *U. lomvia*), species that are vulnerable to spilled oil because they spend a high proportion of time on the water and dive repeatedly (King and Sanger 1979). Collectively, Common and Thick-billed Murres comprised 74% of the total bird carcasses collected following the spill and over 87% of the birds recovered from the Barren Islands, the Kodiak Island area, and the Alaska Peninsula (Piatt et al. 1990). Most of these mortalities resulted from physical effects associated with direct contact with the oil (Stubblefield et al. this volume). Relatively few birds were killed by oil after May 1989 (Piatt et al. 1990).

Murres are colonial-nesting seabirds whose life-history characteristics include delayed sexual maturation (generally mature at four to six years), low annual production capacity (typically one egg per year per breeding pair), high survival rate for adults, and high nest-site fidelity (Dunnet 1982; Harris and Birkhead 1985; Hudson 1985). In addition, a significant component of the murre population is nonbreeders and prebreeders (young birds). Although these birds do not occupy nesting sites at the colony, some may return to raft or roost in their breeding colony (Birkhead and Hudson 1977). Thus, this "reservoir" of birds may act as a buffer to replace lost breeders (Dunnet 1982; Stowe 1982b).

During the breeding season, birds present on the colonies are primarily breeding adults that are incubating eggs or brooding chicks. Such duties are shared by both parents. The off-duty member of the pair spends most of its time foraging at sea. The "at sea" component of the population, which includes the off-duty breeders along with nonbreeders and prebreeders, may represent as much as 140% of the number at the colony (Piatt and Ford 1993).

Common and Thick-billed Murres are among the most numerous seabirds in Alaska, with total population estimates up to 10 million. They are distributed throughout nearshore and offshore areas of the northern Gulf of Alaska (Sowls et al. 1978; Springer and Roseneau 1980). The populations for these species in the spill-affected area have historically represented approximately 5% of the statewide population. Murre abundance is significantly greater in the western Gulf of Alaska, at the Semidi Islands and Shumagin Islands, as well as in the eastern Aleutians, Bering Sea, and Bristol Bay areas (Sowls et al. 1978; Sowl 1979; Hatch and Hatch 1983; Nysewander et al. 1982; United States Fish and Wildlife Service [USFWS] 1991).

In Alaska, the Common Murre is the dominant species along the mainland coastline and nearshore islands; Thick-billed Murres are more common in the Aleutians and on offshore islands in the Bering Sea (Tuck 1961; Sowl 1979; Springer and Roseneau 1980). In this study area, over 90% are Common Murres (USFWS 1991). In colonies where both species are present, they occur together on nesting ledges. Because they are difficult to distinguish, most censuses report a single estimate for the combined total.

Some projections of murre mortality following the spill have approached total historical (prespill) numbers in the area affected by the spill. In the *Catalog of Alaskan Seabird Colonies* (Sowls et al. 1978; USFWS 1991), the number of murres in the region potentially affected by the spill, between Prince William Sound and the western end of Shelikof Strait, is estimated at approximately 330 000. Estimates of murre mortality have ranged from 74 000 to 220 000 (74% of the total seabird mortality estimate) (Piatt et al. 1990), and from 260 000 to 289 000 (Ford et al. 1990). Further, other claims include a 60% to 70% decrease in the number of breeding murres (i.e., at the Barren Islands) (*Exxon Valdez* Oil Spill Trustees' Restoration Plan 1992) and expected recovery times of 20 to 70 years (or sooner if birds immigrate) (Piatt et al. 1990, based on models from Ford et al. 1982 and Samuels and Lanfear 1982), with some colonies facing possible extinction (Fry 1993; Heinemann 1993). Thus, following the spill, the viability of murre populations in the northern Gulf of Alaska was in question.

To investigate the current state of murre colonies, a reconnaissance-level survey was conducted in 1991, approximately two years after the spill. The survey was designed to determine if murres were present at previously documented colonies and to compare colony attendance (number of birds observed at the colonies) with historical estimates. Statistical analyses were conducted to evaluate the relationship between changes in colony attendance and risk of oil exposure from the spill.

The results of this study are encouraging when they are contrasted with reported impacts (Department of Justice (DOJ) Summary 1991; *Exxon Valdez* Oil Spill Trustees' Restoration Plan 1992). Murres were documented at all colonies surveyed in the vicinity of the spill pathway. Although some murre attendance estimates were lower than historic estimates at some colonies, the observed changes were not correlated with the risk of exposure to the spill. Further, most colony attendance estimates, including estimates for colonies at higher risk of oil exposure, were within the range of historical estimates.

STUDY BASIS AND OBJECTIVES

Colony Attendance Estimates

Historical estimates of numbers of seabirds in the Gulf of Alaska generally were obtained with reconnaissance surveys. The purpose of many of the historical surveys was to document colony locations and the relative abundance of various seabird species. Results were usually reported as a single number for a given season and were obtained using a variety of methods under various field conditions (Bartonek et al. 1977; Sowls et al. 1978). Murre numbers at breeding colonies are generally difficult to assess (Sowls et al. 1978; Hudson 1985). Estimation error, including observer effects (number and skill of observers), visibility during the survey, weather conditions, and sea state (Slater 1980; Murphy et al. 1986; Hatch and Hatch 1989), can have a significant effect on survey results. Detectability of murres at the individual colonies also varies with height of nesting ledges on the cliffs, lighting conditions in caves or crevices, and density of breeding aggregations (Slater 1980). Techniques used to count or estimate (i.e., count by 10s or 100s, or general estimations) or survey methods (e.g., boat-based versus land-based surveys) can also have significant effects on the accuracy of a colony attendance estimate (Harris et al. 1983; Byrd 1989).

In addition, the ability to compare counts or estimates between years is complicated by the natural variability of murre colony attendance (Lloyd 1975; Slater, 1980; Murphy et al. 1980; Dunnet 1982; Harris et al. 1983; Piatt and McLagan 1987; Rothery et al. 1988; Hatch and Hatch 1989). Such variation can have significant effects on survey results and the interpretation of survey data. Sources of the variation include annual variation in populations, seasonal patterns of adult breeding activities, diurnal patterns of attendance, and disturbance.

Annual variations in attendance have been found to be significant at many colonies and make year-to-year changes difficult to interpret (Stowe 1982a; Wanless et al. 1982; Piatt and McLagan 1987; Hatch and Hatch 1989). For colonies within the study area, the protracted period of time since many of the historical surveys were conducted (up to 14 years for some colonies) opens the possibility of population decreases from natural "wrecks" (e.g., mortality events from starvation because of to prolonged storms, Bailey and Davenport 1972) or shifts in food availability (e.g., El Niño-Southern Oscillation or "ENSO" events from oceanographic disturbances that can affect forage fish distribution, Nysewander and Trapp 1983; Hatch 1987; Boekelheide et al. 1990).

Seasonal patterns include generally erratic attendance during the period before egg laying, with attendance gradually increasing and stabilizing from egg laying to the middle of the chick-rearing period (Gaston and Nettleship 1981; Hatch and Hatch 1989). Attendance variation during this latter period also reflects the number of nonbreeders (prospectors) visiting the colony and the length of time breeders (incubating or brooding birds and their off-duty mates) and failed breeders spend at the colony (Birkhead 1978; Lloyd 1975; Birkhead and Hudson 1977; Piatt and McLagen 1987). The amount of time breeders and nonbreeders are at the colony relative to the time they spend feeding at sea is probably a function of food availability near the colony (Gaston and Nettleship 1982) or other environmental conditions (Hatch and Hatch 1989).

Diurnal fluctuations in colony attendance also occur at many colonies; fewer birds are present early and late in the day because of the departure of nonbreeders, which spend the night at sea (Birkhead 1978; Slater 1980; Harris et al. 1983). The relative magnitude of daily fluctuations varies among colonies (Birkhead 1978; Gaston and Nettleship 1981; Piatt and McLagen 1987; Hatch and Hatch 1989).

Disturbance by humans or by predators such as gulls can cause temporary reductions in attendance. Once murres are flushed from the cliffs, attendance can be depressed for up to an hour (Slater 1980).

Because of natural variability, differences (increases or decreases) between historical survey estimates and those made after 1989 would be expected for some, if not all, of the colonies; changes may reflect estimation error in one (or more) of the counts or natural variation in population size unrelated to the spill.

Study Objectives

Even though they contain estimation errors, the historical data on murre colony attendance provide some indication of the range of attendance (natural variation) at these colonies. However, because of this variation, data from a single colony are of limited use in determining impact or recovery following an oil spill. Nonetheless, if colonies are considered collectively, the historical data can provide an adequate basis to assess the status and viability of murres in the spill-affected area. In addition, patterns in these data can be used to assess whether changes in the colony attendance are attributable to the spill.

This study was designed to achieve the following objectives: (1) determine whether murres were present at previously documented colonies; (2) compare murre attendance in the study area with historical levels of attendance; and (3) evaluate relationships between changes in colony attendance and exposure to oil from the spill.

STUDY AREA

The study area encompassed all murre colonies documented in the *Catalog of Alaskan Seabird Colonies* (USFWS 1991) from eastern Prince William Sound at Hinchinbrook Entrance (60°18'N, 155°44'W), along the southern shoreline of the Kenai Peninsula, within the lower Cook Inlet, around the Kodiak Archipelago, and along the southern coastline of the Alaska Peninsula to the southwest end of Shelikof Strait (57°34'N, 155°44'W, Figure 1). Middleton Island, located south of the spill pathway, was also surveyed.

Murres were usually found occupying nesting ledges in cliff-faced colonies, in small sea caves, or in dense aggregations in less-precipitous areas. Most of the colonies (31 of 36) were located on islands. The five mainland colonies were located on large, precipitous sea cliffs.

METHODS

Timing of Surveys

The numbers of murres attending colonies are highest and least variable between the end of egg laying and first-fledging of young when young jump from the cliffs and swim out to sea with one parent (Birkhead 1980; Slater 1980; Birkhead and Nettleship 1980; Gaston and Nettleship 1981). This period provides the best opportunity for censusing murre colonies. In the northern Gulf of Alaska, this period is from mid-July to mid-August (Petersen 1986). After this period, numbers decline sharply. This reconnaissance survey was conducted between July 18 and August 8, 1991, i.e., within the optimal censusing period on most of the colonies. Each colony was surveyed once, except for the largest colony, East Amatuli Island, which was surveyed three times because it was believed to have suffered the greatest reduction from the spill. In general, historical surveys were also conducted during optimal periods.

The time of day when a survey is conducted is also important; colony attendance is typically lower in the early morning and late evening than during midday (Birkhead 1978; Birkhead and Nettleship 1980; Slater 1980). For this reason, all but two surveys were conducted between midmorning and late afternoon. The exceptions were the Granite Island survey and the last of three surveys of East Amatuli Island.

Logistics and Survey Platform

The logistical support for conducting these surveys was provided by 80- to- 95-foot vessels (the *M/V Pacific Star* and *M/V Scorpius*), which provided quarters and transportation for the field crew and equipment. Colonies were generally surveyed either from inflatable boats or, when water depth adjacent to the colony permitted, from the support vessel. At Middleton Island, the colony was censused with spotting scopes from a vantage point on land.

Estimating Attendance

Murres were surveyed using techniques similar to those employed by Bailey (1976a, 1976b), Erikson (1977), Arneson (1978b), and Bailey and Faust (1984). Most historical data considered in this paper were collected using similar survey techniques.

To facilitate the estimation of murre attendance, nesting areas were divided into segments on the basis of landmarks and photographed. These photographs were marked with segment-boundary locations to document their location. The survey party (observer, recorder, and boat operator) would slowly cruise parallel to the shoreline of the colony and count or estimate numbers of murres, as well as other species of seabirds, both on the colony and near the colony (flying or rafting). Birds within each segment were either counted individually or estimated by 10s or 100s, and attendance totals from each segment were summed to estimate colony attendance. Common and Thick-billed Murres were not differentiated because of the difficulty in distinguishing these species at a distance.

Photo Documentation

Still-photo documentation of each colony included large-format, overlapping color panoramic photographs of the entire cliff-nesting areas and close-up 35-mm photos of seabird breeding behavior and general colony activity. Videotape footage using a Sony Betacam M-7 with a gyro-stabilized zoom lens was taken of each colony, including wide-angle panoramic shots of the entire cliff-nesting area and close-up footage. While useful for reference purposes, these formats were not as reliable as direct observation for colony-attendance estimation because of incomplete coverage.

Historical Estimates

The *Catalog of Alaskan Seabird Colonies* (Sowls et al. 1978) is currently available as a computer database (i.e., the "computer archives") maintained by USFWS (USFWS 1991). The catalog and computer archives contain counts and population estimates for all known seabird colonies in Alaska, but these numbers are not reported on a consistent basis (e.g., sometimes as pairs, sometimes as individual birds). In order to put historical count data on a common basis for comparison with postspill data, original references, field notes, maps of the original surveys, raw data on file with the USFWS, and discussions with field investigators were used to determine the actual number of birds observed at the colony. Documentation of field methods, when available, was also reviewed to assess the data quality of the historical surveys.

Categorization of Risk of Oil Exposure

In order to assess the relationship between changes in colony attendance and the risk level of oil exposure from the spill, the colonies were categorized into three groups: high, moderate, and low risk (Figure 1). Colonies were assigned to risk categories based on their proximity to the spill path, the estimated exposure to oil, and the residence time of oil in the area near the colony. The assumption was that, because murres were aggregating at their colonies when the spill occurred, risk of exposure to oil was considered greatest in the general vicinity of the colonies. There is also a risk of exposure while birds are dispersed at sea away from their colonies. This risk is assumed to be at least partly related to the geographic location of the colony. However, the pelagic distribution of murres for the individual colonies is not known.

Direct observations of the degree of oil exposure were not available for most colonies; therefore, hindcast projections, overflight data, and field observations from 1989 were used to categorize murre colonies according to their potential exposure to oil. During the first few months after the spill, considerable effort was directed at tracking and predicting the movement of oil in Prince William Sound and the Gulf of Alaska (Galt and Payton 1990). Hundreds of overflights conducted by the National Oceanic and Atmospheric Administration and the Alaska Department of Environmental Conservation (NOAA and ADEC 1989), remote sensing data, a weather observation network, satellite-tracked current drifters, and computer modeling techniques (Torgrimson 1981) were used to hindcast the movement of oil (Galt and Payton 1990).

High Risk of Exposure—Colonies at high risk were those closest to the path of the spill. Significant amounts of oil or mousse were in the vicinity of these colonies for up to several weeks. As oil left Prince William Sound, it was carried by the relatively strong nearshore Alaska Coastal Current along the Kenai Peninsula, with the highest concentrations within 24 km offshore (Galt and Payton 1990). Winds and freshwater runoff coming out of the fjords kept most oil away from much of the coastline, but offshore islands were moderately to heavily oiled (Galt and Payton 1990). Colonies classified in the high risk group include the Chiswell Islands and Barren Islands in the Gulf of Alaska and Point Elrington in southwestern Prince William Sound.

The Chiswell Island Group. These islands protrude into the Gulf of Alaska off the southern edge of the Kenai Peninsula and, therefore, were contacted by oil from the northern edge of the slick. Most of the oil passed just south of the Chiswells because of winds and currents, but portions of the slick tended to get caught in eddies west of the islands (Galt and Payton 1990). A large amount of mousse floated through the islands and left moderate deposits on some islands (Bailey and Rice 1989). Hence, all of the murre colonies in this group were placed in the high risk category.

The Barren Islands. By the third week in April 1989, scattered patches of oil were moving in the general vicinity of the Barren Islands, located between the Kodiak Island Archipelago and the western end of the Kenai Peninsula (Galt and Payton 1990). A significant amount of oil became trapped in current gyres near the islands, passed back and forth through the islands for up to one month, and left some heavy deposits on local beaches. Although only about 10% of the murre carcasses were recovered from beaches on the Barren Islands (Bailey 1989; Nysewander et al. 1992), some have speculated that the majority of murre mortalities resulting from the spill occurred in this area (Bailey 1989; Lensink 1990). The remainder of the carcasses were distributed along the Kenai Peninsula, Kodiak Island, and the Alaska Peninsula. Considering current and drift patterns, it is possible that many of the carcasses found at Kodiak and the Alaska

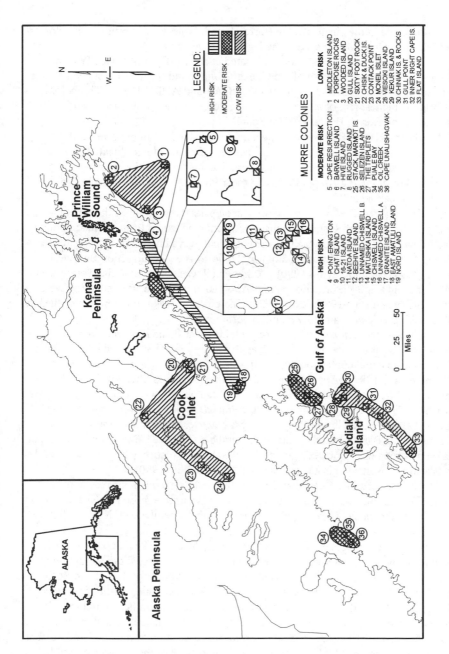

FIGURE 1—Locations of 36 murre colonies in the northern Gulf of Alaska. The degree of oiling risk (high, moderate, or low) for the colonies in different areas is indicated by the shaded patterns.

Peninsula originated in the vicinity of the Barren Islands. The two Barren Island colonies, Nord and East Amatuli, were placed in the high risk category.

Point Elrington. This colony is located at the west end of Prince William Sound and was directly in the path of the oil exiting the sound through Latouche Passage into the Gulf of Alaska (Galt and Payton 1990; NOAA and ADEC 1989). This colony was likely at the highest risk of any of the murre colonies in the study area because of its proximity to the oil exiting Prince William Sound.

Moderate Risk of Exposure—The amount and duration of exposure to oil or mousse were lower than for high risk colonies in a number of colonies located in areas peripheral to the spill path. Colonies in this group include those at the mouth of Resurrection Bay, along the Alaska Peninsula (near Puale Bay), and in Marmot Bay (northeast of Kodiak Island).

The Resurrection Bay Colonies. The oil passed just south of these colonies as it moved past the mouth of Resurrection Bay. After the oil exited Prince William Sound, it contacted many of the headlands along the coast, but prevailing winds and freshwater runoff kept most of the oil offshore and out of the fjords (i.e., Resurrection Bay) during early April 1989 (Galt and Payton 1990). Although oil was observed in the waters around Barwell Island and Cape Resurrection in mid-April, no appreciable amounts of oil were deposited (Bailey and Rice 1989; Rice 1992). Therefore, colonies at the mouth of the bay were all classified as having a moderate oil-exposure risk.

The Alaska Peninsula. The three colonies near Puale Bay were initially exposed to patches of mousse and sheen on approximately April 30 (based on overflight data), but after the initial contact, exposure appeared to decrease over the next week (NOAA and ADEC 1989). Approximately 2% of the oil entered Shelikof Strait and, by the time it exited (e.g., in the vicinity of Puale Bay), the oil was widely scattered (Galt and Payton 1990). Thus, although shorelines in the Puale Bay area received limited oiling (Dewhurst et al. 1990), the level of exposure was much less than that of the Chiswell Island group or the Barren Islands. Although a number of murre carcasses were found in the Puale Bay area, their advanced state of decay suggested that they had drifted from the Barren Islands and Kenai Peninsula (Lensink 1990; Piatt et al. 1990).

The Marmot Bay Colonies. The Triplets and Selezen Island were outside the primary path of the spill, but murres in this area may have been exposed to oil and mousse because limited oil deposits were found on beaches in the general area (NOAA and ADEC 1989; MacIntosh 1989).

Low Risk of Exposure—Colonies assigned to the low-risk category were located in areas outside the spill path but may have experienced a very limited degree of oiling from scattered mousse or tarballs. Such colonies included Middleton Island and Porpoise Rocks, all of the Cook Inlet colonies, and the Kodiak Island colonies south of Marmot Bay. Because the oil drifted west as it exited the sound, Middleton Island, in the Gulf of Alaska, and Porpoise Rocks, in the eastern sound, were well outside the spill path. Because only a part of the Alaska Coastal Current moves north into the inlet, and because of the prevailing strong northerly winds, only a small fraction of the oil moved into the inlet (Galt and Payton 1990). The colonies on the east side of Kodiak Island were potentially exposed to oil that was deflected south of the Chiswells (Galt and Payton 1990), but the extent and duration of exposure are unknown.

Statistical Analysis

Change in Colony Attendance—To evaluate relationships between changes in colony attendance and oil exposure risk, murre attendance data were examined on a regional basis. The model used to look for changes in murre attendance assumes that colonies within a geographic area fluctuate similarly in response to regional environmental conditions, such as decreases in forage fish populations or climactic changes such as ENSO events. The attendance at a given colony at a later time (N_2) can be represented as a multiple r of the attendance at an earlier time (N_1):

$$N_2 = r\,N_1$$

Under these regional influences, it can assumed that r would be similar for all colonies. Thus, if the regional population had doubled since the earlier time, $r = 2$ on average for the colonies in the area. If there were a significant effect of oiling by risk category, r would still reflect the overall population change but would differ by risk of oil exposure.

Test for a Change Caused by Oiling—Colony-attendance estimates were tested to determine whether the relative changes from historical levels were statistically different for the different risk categories. The null hypothesis was that the values of r were similar for the three levels of oiling risk (low, moderate, high). The alternative hypothesis was that r would be different for the three risk levels. It might be expected that if the colonies at greater risk were affected to a greater degree by the spill, r for those colonies would be lower. The effect of the degree of oil exposure was tested by using the most recent historical estimates of colony attendance (usually several years old) and estimates from this study in 1991. The rationale for using most recent historical estimates was to limit the effects of natural temporal variation on the analysis.

A one-way analysis of variance (ANOVA) with three treatment levels based on the risk of exposure (low, moderate, high) was used to test for an effect of oiling. Colonies within the same exposure-risk group were used as replicates. For each colony, the value of $\ln(r)$ was calculated as follows:

$$\ln r = \ln (N_{postspill}) - \ln (N_{prespill})$$

The use of logarithms changes the multiplicative population model above to an additive statistical model (tests of hypotheses are based on additive models) and stabilizes variances (Skalski 1992). This analysis is similar to a before-after control-impact (BACI) analysis (Stewart-Oaten et al. 1986; Skalski and McKenzie 1982).

In addition to comparisons among the three risk-category groups, a second ANOVA was performed in which the combined high and moderate risk groups were compared with the low risk group (equivalent to a t-test). This grouping also helped to determine whether the assignments of colonies to the different risk groups affected the results of the analyses.

ANOVA results are reported in terms of P, F and degrees of freedom $(d.f.)$. P is the probability of declaring a change in mean colony attendance when none actually occurred. F is a measure of variability of mean r values between risk groups divided by variation of r values of individual colonies within risk groups. Degrees of freedom are reported as two numbers *n*, *m*; where *n* = number of risk categories minus one, and *m* = number of colonies minus the number of risk categories minus one, respectively.

Other Tests

A paired *t*-test was also used to compare postspill estimates from this study with the 1991 USFWS postspill estimates of selected colonies in the area to assess possible differences caused by survey methods and timing of surveys.

RESULTS

Of the 36 colonies with nesting murre populations in the spill area that were listed in the *Catalog of Alaskan Seabird Colonies* computer archives (UFSWS 1991), 32 were surveyed during the course of this study (Figure 1). Four small colonies were not surveyed because of access restrictions or poor weather. Hence, these colonies were not included in the analyses. Stack-Marmot Island, a small colony (140 murres) in the Kodiak Archipelago, was not surveyed because of restricted access near a Steller's sea lion (*Eumetopias jubatus*) rookery. Wooded Island (80 murres), an unoiled site on the south side of Montague Island, on the Gulf of Alaska; Flat Island (less than 100 murres), on the south end of Kodiak Island; and Contact Point (290 murres), on the west side of Cook Inlet, were not surveyed because of adverse weather conditions. All four were categorized as low or moderate exposure risk.

Murre attendance at the colonies surveyed in this study ranged up to approximately 30 000 at East Amatuli Island in the Barren Islands. However, many of the colonies were small; murre attendance at 15 of the colonies was fewer than 100 birds. The two Barren Island colonies and the two large colonies in the Puale Bay area on the Alaska Peninsula made up 72% of the murres in the study area.

Historical data, as well as the estimates of colony attendance from this field survey in 1991 for the 32 colonies that were surveyed, are presented in Table 1, where colonies are grouped by risk category. Numbers of murres from the *Catalog of Alaskan Seabird Colonies* computer archives, and the latest (usually 1991) postspill counts by the USFWS are shown for comparison. Additional detail and references for all historical and postspill counts are provided in Tables 2-8. Total murre numbers are presented, but caution must be exercised in interpreting differences in totals, because these tend to be dominated bydifferences at large colonies.

One colony, Kekur Island, was surveyed but not included in the analysis. This colony, catalogued as a small colony of 40 murres based on a 1975 survey (USFWS 1991), is located in Chiniak Bay, Kodiak Island (low risk of exposure). However, the most recent historical survey of this colony (Nysewander and Trapp 1984) reported no murres usingmurres using the area. Similar to the 1984 survey, no murres were seen on the island, and only one murre was seen in the vicinity of the island on this survey.

Historical Information

The *Catalog of Alaskan Seabird Colonies* (USFWS 1991) values shown in Table 1 are generally higher than the latest historical estimates for most colonies. Although these

TABLE 1—Comparison of murre numbers listed in *Catalog of Alaskan Seabird Colonies—Computer Archives*, colony attendances from the latest prespill surveys, and colony attendance numbers from postspill surveys by this author and USFWS. Catalog values are as reported and were not corrected for known errors in counts.

| | | Prespill | | Postspill | |
| | | Colony Catalog Archives[1] | Latest Colony | This Study | Latest |
Colony	Year	Number[1]	Attendance	1991	USFWS[18]
HIGH OILING RISK					
Chiswell Island Group					
Beehive Island	1976	400	112[2]	32	95
Matushka Island	1976	3 040	1 135[2]	700	1 014
Notoa Island	1976	1 640	219[2]	315	521
16-21 Island	1976	120	10[2]	22	--
Chiswell Island	1976	520	239[2]	401	337
Unnamed Chiswell "A"	1976	280	279[2]	150	340
Unnamed Chiswell "B"	1976	150	385[2]	270	512
Granite Island	1976	200	18[2]	40	--
Chat Island	1976	160	14[2]	21	
Barren Island					
East Amatuli Island	1980	100 000	25 000[3]	30 294	--
Nord Island	1976	30 000	20 000[4]	16 592	13 333
Prince William Sound					
Point Elrington	1972	170	130[5]	30	--
MODERATE OILING RISK					
Resurrection Bay					
Barwell Island	1976	17 600	2 025[2]	7 420	--
Cape Resurrection	1976	4 300	1 079[2]	856	--
Rugged Island	1976	400	47[2]	87	--
Hive Island	1976	40	4[2]	21	--
Kodiak Island					
Selezen Island	1976	400	200[6]	63	--
Triplets	1984	1 400	1 300[7]	642	843
Alaska Peninsula					
Oil Creek	1976	80 000	30 000[8]	28 400	19 088
Cape Unalishagvak	1976	38 000	38 000[8]	30 700	14 374
Puale Bay	1976	8 000	6 500[8]	8 050	2 980
LOW OILING RISK					
Middleton Island	1978	10 100	7 899[9]	7 500	5 400
Prince William Sound					
Porpoise Rocks	1976	1 500	1 350[10]	1 241	--
Cook Inlet Group					
Sixty Foot Rock	1989	232	155[11]	100	--
Gull Island	1988	5 500	5 500[11]	1 732	5 075
McNeil Islet	1978	2 000	2 000[12]	15	--
Chisik & Duck Islands	1971	22 500	4 101[13]	7 536	--
Kodiak Island					
Viesoki Island	1975	200	168[14]	51	--
Inner Right Cape	1977	9	9[15]	81	--
Chiniak Island & Rocks	1975	18	136[7]	159	--
Gull Point	1976	500	500[16]	60	--
Kekur Island[4]	1975	40	0[17]	1	--
Totals		**329 419**	**148 514**	**143 582**	**112 010[19]**

See next page for footnotes.

TABLE 1—(continued).

Footnotes:
1 USFWS (1991).
2 Nishimoto and Rice (1987).
3 Manuwal (1978).
4 Bailey (1976a).
5 Irons et al. (1985).
6 Dick and Nelson (1976).
7 Berg et al. (1985).
8 Bailey and Faust (1984).
9 Hatch 1986-1991, unpublished data from Nysewander et al. (1992).
10 Lehnhausen and Quinlin (1977).
11 Nishimoto and Beringer (1989).
12 Arneson (1978b).
13 Nishimoto et al. (1987a).
14 Dick and McIntosh (1975).
15 Forsell and Sanger (1977).
16 Sanger and Handel (1976).
17 Nysewander and Trapp (1984), not used in the analysis.
18 USFWS surveys conducted in 1991, except for Triplets and Gull Island, which were conducted in 1989 and 1990, respectively.
19 Total is summation of counts for 14 colonies surveyed in 1989, 1990, and 1991 by USFWS and 1991 counts from this study for the additional 18 colonies in the study area.

numbers were included for completeness, they are not appropriate for direct comparison to the postspill data, for several reasons. First, the seabird catalog does not include the results of many surveys conducted since the mid-1980s. For example, surveys of 13 colonies along the Kenai Peninsula (Nishimoto and Rice 1987), Chisik and Duck Islands (Nishimoto et al. 1987a), and the three Alaska Peninsula colonies (Bailey and Faust 1984) were not included.

Second, the data on which the catalog values are based were not reported in a consistent fashion. In some cases, the number of murres seen at a colony was divided by two and the result was reported as the number of pairs, apparently assuming that both mates were present on the colony. In other cases, the number of murres seen was doubled in an attempt to correct for the fact that one mate of the pair is often foraging away from the colony.

Third, in some cases the cataloged values contain errors. For example, the attendance estimate for East Amatuli of 100 000 murres was obtained by inappropriately doubling the estimated number of birds present (25 000) twice (Manuwal 1992). In the case of Nord Island, an error was made in transcribing the field data (Bailey 1992).

The cataloged numbers appear in Table 1 as they did in the computer archives in 1991; errors have not been corrected, and the reported numbers do not always equate to colony attendance. Overall, the cataloged estimates were roughly 185 000 higher than the latest estimates reported before the spill. Most of the discrepancy was related to differences in the reported numbers for the colonies at Chisik and Duck, Barwell, Oil Creek, East Amatuli Island, Nord Island, and the Chiswell Islands.

Comparison with USFWS Postspill Data

In 1991, the USFWS conducted colony surveys using multiple observers at 11 of the 32 colonies examined in this study (Nysewander et al. 1992). Their survey results were reported as daily means obtained by averaging results from individual observers, and the reported number for each year for a colony was obtained by averaging these daily means. Most colonies had two to six surveys (Nord Island, Chiswells and Puale Bay), but two colonies (Cape Unalishagvak and Oil Creek) had only a single survey in 1991.

The means of the 1991 USFWS colony attendance estimates and the corresponding estimates derived from this study are very similar for most colonies (Figure 2). Paired t-tests performed on transformed data from the 11 colonies surveyed by the USFWS in 1991 show no significant difference ($P = 0.45$) between USFWS estimates and estimates from this study.

The field estimates from this study for three colonies in the Puale Bay area on the Alaska Peninsula were substantially higher than the counts by the USFWS. Two of these relatively large colonies had murres nesting on ledges over 100 m above the water and, therefore, presented particularly difficult survey conditions. After examining the photographs and videos of these colonies from this study, I concluded that the visual estimates in the field were probably too high. To test the effect of the discrepancies, duplicate ANOVA analyses were performed with two sets of data: (1) field data from this survey and (2) a dataset using 1991 survey results on all 11 colonies surveyed by USFWS personnel, supplemented with results from this study of the colonies they did not survey.

1991 MURRE COLONY ATTENDANCE USFWS ESTIMATES vs THIS STUDY

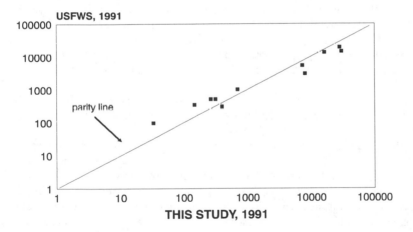

FIGURE 2—Comparison of the murre colony attendance estimates at 11 colonies surveyed in this study with counts at the same colonies made by USFWS during 1991. Counts were conducted during the nesting period in both cases, but counts at some of the colonies were separated by as much as three weeks. If estimates from this study and from USFWS for a given colony were equal, the point representing that colony would fall on the parity line. In general, our estimates were similar to those of USFWS (t-test, $P = 0.45$); however, our estimates tended to be higher than those of USFWS for larger colonies and lower for smaller colonies.

Comparison of Historical and 1991 Attendance Estimates

One would expect the greatest spill-related changes in murre attendance to occur at colonies at greatest risk from the spill. However, a comparison of estimates from this study with historical estimates shown in Figure 3 for each of the oiling risk categories is useful. In each plot, the historical data are shown as a range when multiple historical estimates were available and as a point when only a single historical estimate was available. If historical estimates were identical to estimates from this study, data points would fall on the parity line shown on each plot. When the line intersects a historical range, the values in this study are within the range of historical estimates. Points or historical ranges above the parity line indicate cases in which historical estimates were higher than those observed in this study. Overall, the postspill data are generally similar to historical data for all risk categories.

ANOVA analysis showed that changes in postspill colony attendance relative to historical estimates were not different among exposure-risk categories. The colony attendance data were first tested to see if the mean of the log-transformed difference (ln r) was the same for each of three risk categories (high, moderate, low) by comparing historical data with the postspill data from this study. The mean was negative in the high and low risk groups and slightly positive for the moderate risk group, but the differences between groups were not significant ($P = 0.33$, $F = 1.16$, $d.f.$ 2,28; Figure 4). Similar results were obtained when USFWS results were included in the analysis ($P = 0.36$, $F = 1.05$, $d.f.$ 2,28). Because of the broad range of the latest prespill estimates for East Amatuli, we also ran an analysis excluding East Amatuli and another using the high end of the 19 000 – 39 000 murre prespill range reported for the colony. Results of these analyses were similar to those above, showing no significant differences among risk groups.

An alternative grouping was tested to see whether moderate and high risk colonies taken together were different from low risk colonies. Again, the differences were not significant ($P = 0.15$, $F = 2.16$, $d.f.$ 1,29).

In all these analyses, murre attendance estimates in the low risk colonies decreased relatively more than in colonies at moderate and high risk to oil exposure from the spill. This indicates the absence of a trend related to the spill. Attendance counts from this survey were similar to the most recent historical counts for a majority of the colonies regardless of the oil-exposure risk. The following section integrates and summarizes the numerous sources of historical survey results as well as all available postspill estimates.

High Risk Category

Barren Islands—Of the seven islands in the Barren Islands group, only Nord Island and East Amatuli Island have significant nesting murre populations, and both of these colonies are relatively large for the region (Bailey 1976a). The Barren Islands were initially surveyed for seabird population levels in 1974 and 1975 (Bailey 1976a), over 10 years before the spill (Table 2, Figure 5a). Additional murre census work was conducted on East Amatuli Island from 1977 to 1979 in conjunction with other seabird research

HISTORICAL ATTENDANCE vs ATTENDANCE FROM THIS STUDY

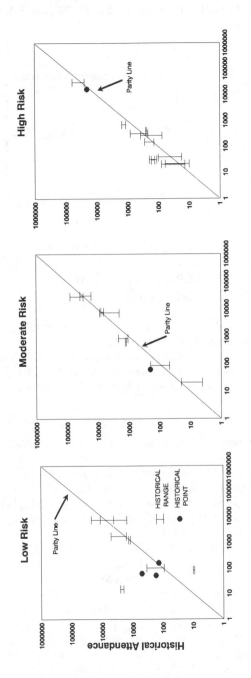

POSTSPILL MURRE COLONY ATTENDANCE ESTIMATES—THIS STUDY

FIGURE 3—Comparison of historical murre attendance estimates with data from this study for 31 colonies in the northern Gulf of Alaska. Data from each oiling risk group are presented separately. Single historical counts are represented by points (filled circles), and bars represent historical ranges where more than one count is available. When the points fall on the parity line or range bars intersect the line, postspill observations were equal to or within the range, respectively, of the historical estimate(s). Points falling above and to the left of the parity line represent cases in which historical numbers were higher, whereas points falling below the line represent cases for which our estimates are higher than historical estimates. In general, the 1991 numbers from this study are similar to the historical estimates.

CHANGE IN COLONY ATTENDANCE vs LEVEL OF OILING RISK

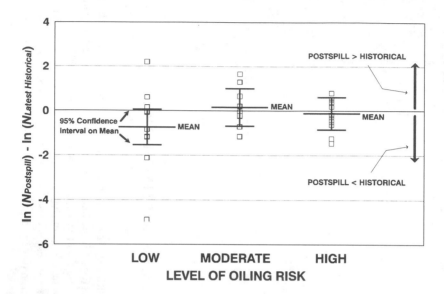

FIGURE 4—The difference between the natural logarithm of the postspill attendance from this study and the logarithm of the latest historical attendance estimate, as a function of oiling risk for 31 colonies surveyed in this study. The mean and 95% confidence intervals for each risk category are indicated by horizontal bars. The mean values for the different categories of risk are not statistically different ($P = 0.33$).

(Manuwal and Boersma 1978; Manuwal 1978; Manuwal 1980). The two colonies are discussed individually below.

East Amatuli Island supports one of the largest murre colonies in the northern Gulf of Alaska (USFWS 1991). The main nesting concentrations are located on the large, rocky headlands at the east end of the island and on a rock islet just offshore called Light Rock. Estimating colony attendance is difficult because of the very high density of nesting seabirds on the eastern headlands and on Light Rock.

The first survey for East Amatuli was conducted on July 10–11, 1975. Bailey reported 60 000 common murres present at the colony, flying and in the water at the east end of the island, with another 1 000 in two other small areas (Bailey 1975 field notes; Bailey 1976a). The colony attendance was estimated again in 1978, but few details were recorded as to methods, and the date of the survey was not recorded (Manuwal 1978). The colony status record submitted to the USFWS indicated that 9 000 murres were observed on the mainland and from 10 000 to 30 000 were recorded for Light Rock (Simons and Pierce 1978a), which results in a range of from 19 000 to 39 000 for the colony. This was reported as an estimate of 25 000 *pairs* for the colony (Manuwal 1978), with each observed bird representing one breeding pair (Simons 1992). The colony

TABLE 2—Comparison of murre colony attendance estimates from this survey July 27, August 2 and 8, 1991, with prespill data from surveys on the Barren Islands and postspill data collected by the USFWS, 1989 – 1991.

Barren Islands Colony Attendance[1]

	Prespill		Postspill			
				USFWS[4]		Present Study 1991
Colonies	Historic Estimates					
HIGH RISK	1975[2]	1978[3]	1989	1990	1991	
Barren Islands Group						
East Amatuli Island	61 000	25 000[5]	...	...	...	30 294[6]
(Range)		(19–39 000)				
Nord Island	20 000[7]	...	11 838[8]	12 277[8]	13 333[8]	16 592

[1]Colony attendance represents the estimated number of murres at the colony during the survey.
[2]Bailey (1976a).
[3]Manuwal (1978), Simons and Pierce (1978a,b).
[4]Nysewander et al. 1992.
[5]Originally recorded as pairs (one bird or occupied site = one pair).
[6]Mean of three counts (28 660, 25 213, 37 010) July 21, 27 and August 3.
[7]Bailey (1976a); Nord Island total is a correction from field notes (Bailey 1992 personal communication).
[8]Mean of two daily counts.

population estimate of 50 000 pairs (Manuwal 1980) was apparently obtained by inadvertently doubling the estimate developed in 1978 (Manuwal 1992). This estimate was doubled again to obtain the 100 000 murres reported in the *Catalog of Alaskan Seabird Colonies* (USFWS 1991).

This colony was surveyed three times in 1991 during this study. The mean attendance estimate of these surveys was approximately 30 000 individuals (Figure 5a). Surveys of this colony were also conducted by University of Washington personnel in August 1990 and late July–early August 1991. Estimated attendance was approximately 31 000 murres in 1990 and approximately 35 000 in 1991 (Boersma et al. this volume). Although the mean of the counts from this study were slightly lower than the results from the University of Washington study (which used more rigorous field protocols) results from both studies were significantly lower than Bailey's total estimate of 61 000 in 1975 (Bailey 1976a) but were within the range of 19 000 to 39 000 reported in 1978 (Simons and Pierce 1978a).

Nord Island is a relatively small island with a dense concentration of breeding seabirds. Murre attendance was originally estimated at 20 000 on July 12, 1975, or about 1/3 the number at East Amatuli (Bailey 1976a). However, Simons and Pierce (1978b) estimated only 1 500 murres (mostly rafting) on July 1, 1978, but their survey was probably conducted during the prelaying period when attendance is typically erratic. No other surveys during the breeding season were conducted until after the oil spill in 1989 (Nysewander and Dippel 1990).

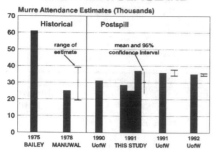

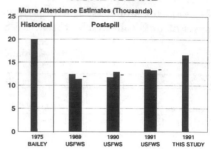

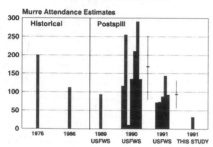

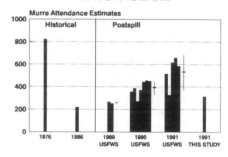

FIGURE 5a—Comparisons of the historical murre colony attendance estimates with postspill attendance estimates for four colonies in the high oiling risk group. Postspill estimates are from this study, the USFWS, and the University of Washington. The values shown represent either total estimates for single surveys or daily means when counts were conducted with multiple observers. USFWS surveys of the Chiswell Island Group (including Beehive and Natoa) in 1990 were probably conducted prior to the egg-laying period. The 1990 and 1991 USFWS results on Beehive and Natoa represent surveys conducted on separate days over 8-day and 6-day periods, respectively, and, therefore, show the range of daily variation in attendance for these colonies. Overall means with 95 percent confidence intervals are indicated where appropriate.

My reconnaissance survey estimate of approximately 16 600 murres on July 27, 1991, was lower than the 1975 estimate. However, considering that the historical estimate for this colony was also based on a reconnaissance-level survey, these differences may not be significant. During the present survey, the birds were very flighty, which suggested birds were not incubating at that time. The USFWS conducted two replicate counts about three weeks later and estimated a mean murre attendance of 13 333 (Nysewander and Dippel 1991).

MATUSHKA ISLAND

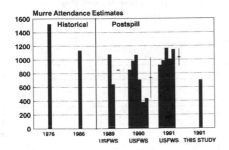

CHISWELL ISLAND

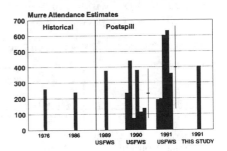

UNNAMED CHISWELL "A"

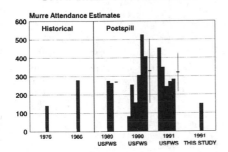

UNNAMED CHISWELL "B"

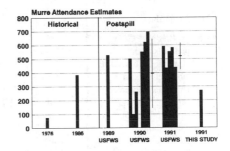

FIGURE 5b—Comparisons of the historical murre colony attendance estimates with postspill attendance estimates for four Chiswell Island Group colonies in the high oiling risk group. Postspill estimates are from this study and the USFWS. The values shown represent either total estimates for single surveys or daily means when counts were conducted with multiple observers. USFWS surveys at these islands in 1990 were probably conducted before the egg-laying period. The 1990 and 1991 USFWS data are from surveys done on separate days over 8-day and 6-day periods, respectively, and, therefore, show the range of daily variation in attendance for these colonies. Overall means with 95 percent confidence intervals are indicated where appropriate.

     Chiswell Island Group—For the purposes of this study, the Chiswell Island Group consisted of the seven Chiswell Islands, Granite Island (northwest of the Chiswells), and Chat Island (located northeast of the Chiswells off the Aialik Peninsula). This group of exposed offshore islands typically has steep sea cliffs with numerous ledges and some sea caves and supports diverse populations of breeding seabirds. These colonies were surveyed originally in 1976 and again in 1986 (Bailey 1976b; Nishimoto and Rice 1987).

TABLE 3—Comparison of murre colony attendance estimates from this survey (July 20–26, 1991) with prespill data from surveys on the outer Kenai Peninsula and postspill surveys data collected by the USFWS, 1989 – 1991.

Outer Kenai Peninsula Colony Attendance[1]

	Prespill		Postspill			
				USFWS		Present Study 1991
Colonies	Historic Estimates					
MODERATE RISK	1976[2]	1986[3]	1989[4]	1990[5]	1991[5]	
Resurrection Bay Group						
Cape Resurrection	2 150	1 079	267[6]	...	...	856(1 366)[7]
Barwell Island	8 800	2 025	1 830[8]	...	...	7 420[9]
Hive Island	20	4	...	...	...	21
Rugged Island	200	47	...	...	...	87
HIGH RISK						
Chiswell Island Group						
Natoa Island	820	219	260	424	521	315
Unnamed Chiswell B	75	385	528	624	512	270
Chiswell Island	260	239	375	251	337	401
Unnamed Chiswell A	140	279[10]	269	329	340	150
Matushka Island	1 520	1 135	858	507	1014	700
Beehive Island	200	112	93	212	95	32
Chat Island	80	14	...	...	...	21
16-21 Island	60	10	...	...	...	22
Granite Island	100	18	...	...	...	40

[1] Colony attendance represents the estimated number of murres at the colony during the survey.

[2] Bailey (1976b).

[3] Nishimoto and Rice (1987).

[4] Bailey and Rice (1989), single mean daily counts—Cape Resurrection, Chiswell A, Chiswell Island, and Beehive Island. Others are means of two counts (early July and early August).

[5] Nysewander et al. (1992) means of replicate daily counts, 1990 and 1991.

[6] Bailey and Rice (1989) July 7, single count, erratic attendance. More murres on cliffs in August, but no count was conducted.

[7] Higher number includes counts from additional areas at east end of the colony not surveyed on previous studies.

[8] Bailey and Rice (1989) August 4. Earlier count (July 6) found 550 on cliffs and 6 600 rafting off the island.

[9] Includes 4 000 in raft below the cliffs on the south side of the colony, many of which flew off colony before count.

[10] Number does not include large raft (1 000) offshore south of the island.

In my 1991 survey, murre colony attendance for seven of the nine islands in this group was within or above the range of historical surveys (Table 3, Figures 5a-b). Beehive and Matushka islands were the only Chiswell colonies for which counts were lower than both historical surveys. Beehive is a relatively small colony with limited murre nesting habitat.

Matushka Island supports the largest murre colony in the Chiswell Island group, as it has on previous surveys (Bailey 1976b; Nishimoto and Rice 1987), although numbers were lower in 1991.

Approximately three weeks before this survey, the USFWS conducted surveys on six of the Chiswell Islands on six consecutive days using multiple observers. Mean attendance estimates for each day of these surveys are presented in Figures 5a and 5b. Similar surveys were performed by the USFWS in 1989 and 1990 (Nysewander and Dippel 1991).

The timing (late June) and erratic attendance of the 1990 surveys suggest that these surveys may have been conducted before egg laying (Nysewander and Dippel 1991). The coefficients of variation (CV) for the 1990 surveys ranged from 17% to 70%. The 1991 counts were later in the season, when attendance is more stable (range of $CV = 10\%$ to 53%; CVs based on raw data from Nysewander and Dippel 1991). The high variability in daily attendance seen in Figures 5a and 5b in the USFWS data underscores the problem of using single census counts as a basis for determining population changes between years. Historical data for these colonies are limited to single census counts within a given year.

Point Elrington—Point Elrington is a small colony on the western end of Prince William Sound on the southwestern tip of Elrington Island. This colony had historical estimates of 130 to 170 murres and is located in the direct pathway of the spill (Table 4). Adverse weather hampered the survey of this colony. However, from an observation point on land, several small groups (30 murres) were observed rafting off the colony, and murres were observed flying to the colony. Survey results indicate that a few murres were using the site. Shoreline surveys by the USFWS on July 14, 1991, reported no murres on the colony (Laing and Klosiewski 1993).

Moderate Risk Category

Resurrection Bay—There are four murre breeding colonies at the mouth of Resurrection Bay, including two small colonies, on Hive and Rugged islands, and two large colonies, on Cape Resurrection and nearby Barwell Island. The Barwell Island and Cape Resurrection colonies support the largest murre populations (over 80%) on the outer coast of the Kenai Peninsula (Table 3). On Barwell Island, many murres nest on top of the island, in and on top of World War II bunkers, and on high ledges, and thus are difficult to see from water level. Scattered murre nesting areas are found along Cape Resurrection, a large headland at the mouth of Resurrection Bay that stretches for roughly 6 km.

The basis for comparison of murre colony attendance for these colonies was established by an initial survey in 1976 (Bailey 1976b) and another, ten years later, in 1986 (Nishimoto and Rice 1987). The 1976 survey at Cape Resurrection was abbreviated because of time constraints; and consequently, eastern portions of the colony were not surveyed. The 1986 survey covered the same area as the 1976 survey. This survey included murres nesting east of the former boundary, but for comparison purposes, the results are reported for both the original survey area and the additional area.

Postspill counts of murres on Barwell Island were conducted in early July and early August 1989 by USFWS and National Park Service (NPS) personnel, but erratic attendance on the colony made estimating attendance very difficult. At Barwell Island, approximately 7 400 murres were observed in early July, including roughly 6 600 murres

TABLE 4—Comparison of murre colony attendance estimates from this survey (July 22–23, 1991) with prespill data from colonies in Prince William Sound and south side of Montague Island.

Prince William Sound Colony Attendance[1]

Colonies	Prespill		Postspill	
	Historic Estimates		USFWS 1991	Present Study
HIGH RISK				
Point Elrington	1972[2]	170	0[3]	30
	1984[4]	130		
LOW RISK				
Porpoise Rocks	1976[5]	1 200	...	1 241
	1977[6]	1 350		
Wooded Island	1980[7]	80	...	(Not Surveyed)

[1]Colony attendance represents the estimated number of murres at the colony during the survey.
[2]Islieb and Sowl (1972).
[3]No murres observed at colony on shoreline survey, July 14, 1991 (Laing and Klosewski,1993), not used in analysis.
[4]Irons et al. (1985) database.
[5]Nysewander and Knudtson (1977).
[6]Sangster (1992) personal communication.
[7]Lehnhausen and Quinlin (1977).

(probably associated with both the Barwell Island and Cape Resurrection colonies) rafting off the island (Bailey and Rice 1989). Counts of murres on the cliffs were higher in August than in July but were slightly lower than the attendance found in 1986 (Nishimoto and Rice 1987).

At Cape Resurrection, murre attendance in July 1989 was lower than historical levels. Although the colony was not resurveyed in August, qualitative observations by USFWS and NPS personnel during that month indicated that murre numbers had increased (Bailey and Rice 1989). This increase in murres on the cliffs from July to August along with the rafting birds observed in the area in July indicates that the July survey may have been conducted during the prelaying period.

Murre attendance on this survey (July 1991) was within the range of historical estimates at three (Barwell, Hive, and Rugged) of the four Resurrection Bay colonies. The attendance estimate for Cape Resurrection was slightly below that of the last survey in 1986 (Nishimoto and Rice 1987).

Alaska Peninsula Group—The Oil Creek, Cape Unalishagvak, and Puale Bay colonies are located on the Alaska Peninsula mainland, all in the vicinity of Puale Bay. The Oil Creek (or Cape Aklek) colony is one of the largest in the study area (USFWS

TABLE 5—Comparison of murre colony attendance estimates from this survey (August 6, 1991) with prespill colony survey data from the Alaska Peninsula and postspill surveys data collected by the USFWS, 1989 – 1991.

Alaska Peninsula Colony Attendance[1]

	Prespill		Postspill			
Colonies	Historic Estimates		USFWS[2]			Present Study 1991
MODERATE RISK	1976	1981	1989	1990	1991	
Alaska Peninsula						
Puale Bay	8 000[3]	6 500[4]	1 790[6]	2 805[7]	2 980[6]	8 050
Oil Creek	80 000[5]	30 000[4]	20 400	16 970[8]	19 088	28 400
Cape Unalishagvak	16 500[9]	38 000[4]	14 246	14 496	14 374	30 700

[1]Colony attendance represents the estimated number of murres at the colony during the survey.
[2]Dewhurst and Moore (1992) cited in Nysewander et al. (1992).
[3]Bailey and Shad (1976).
[4]Bailey and Faust (1984).
[5]Powers and Gould (1976).
[6]Mean of 3 counts.
[7]Mean of 4 counts.
[8]Mean of 2 counts.
[9]Gould and Powers (1976).

1991), with nesting ledges extending approximately 100 m up sheer cliffs, thus making counting from the water extremely difficult. The Cape Unalishagvak (or Jute Peak) colony also supports a large murre population and is similar in topography to Oil Creek. Puale Bay is the smallest of the three colonies. These colonies were originally surveyed in 1976 (Gould and Powers 1976; Powers and Gould 1976; Bailey and Shad 1976) and were resurveyed in 1981 (Bailey and Faust 1984). There was wide variation between the 1976 and 1981 counts for the large colonies (Table 5); at least part of this variation may reflect the difficulty in counting murres at these colonies.

As discussed previously, my counts were generally similar to USFWS results in 1991 except for these three Alaska Peninsula colonies (Figure 2). Visual counts in this survey were similar to historical estimates. In contrast, USFWS counts of these colonies during the same time period were substantially lower than the historical estimates. After examining field photographs and video, it was concluded that the field counts from this study were probably too high, so analyses were also run using the lower USFWS counts for comparison.

Kodiak Island Group—Murres in the Kodiak Island area are typically associated with small seabird colonies on offshore rocks or islands, and numbers are usually relatively low (Dick et al. 1976). Of the nine colonies in the Kodiak region, the three northern-most colonies were categorized as having moderate risk of oil exposure (Table 6).

TABLE 6—Comparison of murre colony attendance estimates from this survey (July 29–August 2, 1991) with prespill survey data for colonies around Kodiak Island and with postspill data collected by the USFWS, 1989.

Kodiak Island Colony Attendance[1]

	Prespill		Postspill	
Colonies	Historic Estimates		USFWS	Present Study 1991
MODERATE RISK			1989	
Kodiak Island Group				
The Triplets	1975[2]	1 200	843[3]	642
	1977[4]	1 297		
	1984[5]	1 300		
Selezen Island	1976[6]	200	...	63
Stack, Marmot Island	1976[6]	70	...	(Not Surveyed)[7]
LOW RISK				
Kodiak Island Group				
Viesoki Island	1975[8]	168	...	51
Kekur Island	1975[8]	40	...	1
	1984[9]	0		
Chiniak Island & Rocks	1975[2]	136	...	159
Gull Point	1976[10]	500	...	60
Inner Right Cape Islets	1976[11]	10	...	81
	1977[12]	9		
Flat Island	1978[13]	<100	...	(Not surveyed)[14]

[1] Colony attendance represents the estimated number of murres at the colony during the survey.
[2] Dick and Warner (1975).
[3] MacIntosh (1989), mean of three counts.
[4] Nysewander et al (1977).
[5] Berg et al. (1985).
[6] Dick and Nelson (1976).
[7] Not able to survey because of proximity to Steller's sea lion rookery.
[8] Dick and McIntosh (1975).
[9] Nysewander and Trapp (1984).
[10] Sanger and Handel (1976).
[11] Handel and Sanger (1976).
[12] Forsell and Sanger (1977).
[13] Hatch (1978), estimate less than 100, only 4 eggs found.
[14] Three murres seen flying near colony; weather prevented survey.

The largest murre colony on Kodiak Island is located on The Triplets Islands in Marmot Bay on the northeast side of Kodiak Island. A second small colony, Selezen Island, is located on the north side of the bay. Stack-Marmot Island, just outside Marmot Bay, was not surveyed because of restricted access. Murre colony attendance at The Triplets on this survey was approximately half the numbers reported by Nysewander et al.

(1977) in 1977 and MacIntosh in 1984 (cited in Berg et al. 1985). Surveys conducted three months after the spill in 1989 found a mean colony attendance of 843, with a high count of 987; both were lower than historical levels (MacIntosh 1989). Attendance at Selezen Island was also lower than historical levels.

Low Risk Category

Kodiak Island Group—The six colonies located on the eastern and southeastern side of Kodiak Island have small murre populations. There was no clear pattern of attendance in 1991 compared with historical levels. Some colonies had slightly greater attendance (e.g., Inner Right Cape Islets) and others showed apparent reductions (e.g., Gull Point and Viesoki Island) (see Table 6) compared with historical levels.

Prince William Sound Group—Other than Point Elrington, the only murre colony in Prince William Sound is Porpoise Rocks, located in Port Etches off Hinchinbrook Entrance in eastern Prince William Sound. This colony was originally

TABLE 7—Comparison of murre colony attendance estimates from this survey (July 21, 1991) with prespill data and postspill from Middleton Island collected by the USFWS, 1975 – 1991.

Middleton Island Colony Attendance[1]

Colonies	Prespill		Postspill			
	Historic Estimates		USFWS[10]			Present Study 1991
			1989	1990	1991	
Middleton Island	1976[2]	5 851	5 846	4 431	5 400	7 500
	1978[3]	6 803				
	1981[4]	5 521				
	1982[5]	6 161				
	1983[6]	4 629				
	1984[7]	5 832				
	1985[8]	3 851				
	1986[9]	7 595				
	1987[9]	7 714				
	1988[9]	7 899				

[1] Colony attendance represents the estimated number of murres at the colony during the survey.
[2] Frazer and Howe (1977).
[3] Hatch et al. (1979).
[4] Gould and Zabloudil (1981).
[5] Gould and Nysewander (1982).
[6] Gould et al. (1983).
[7] Gould et al. (1984).
[8] Nysewander et al. (1986).
[9] Hatch 1986-91, unpublished data from Nysewander et al. (1992).
[10] Nysewander et al. (1992).

censused in 1976 (Nysewander and Knudtson 1977), with additional survey work conducted in 1977 (Sangster et al. 1978). This colony was not directly affected because the oil was carried toward the western side of the sound. Postspill murre attendance was found to be similar to historical levels (Table 4).

Middleton Island—Middleton Island is a large, relatively flat island located 80 km offshore in the northern Gulf of Alaska near the edge of the continental shelf. This colony has been the subject of long-term monitoring studies and is the most intensively studied of the colonies in the northern Gulf of Alaska. Island-wide counts were conducted once each year in 1976, 1978, and continuously from 1981 to the present (Table 7). In addition, repetitive counts on plots were conducted from 1987 to the present (Hatch 1991 in Nysewander et al. 1992).

Because of limitations of time and weather, only the nesting areas on the west side of the island were censused in this study. This side has supported almost all of the murre nesting on postspill surveys (Nysewander and Dippel 1991). Murre attendance since the spill suggests a reduction in numbers, but this was not significant (Nysewander et al. 1992). On this survey, I estimated a higher number for murres than did the USFWS survey conducted several weeks earlier.

Cook Inlet Group—Murre colonies in the Cook Inlet region consist of three moderately sized colonies, Chisik and Duck Island, Gull Island, McNeil Islet, and two small colonies at Sixty Foot Rock and Contact Point. At the Chisik and Duck Island colony, murre numbers appear to have declined in the 1970s (Snarski 1971; Jones and Peterson 1979) and have continued to decline in recent prespill years (Nishimoto et al. 1987a) (Table 8). Attendance in 1991 estimated from this study was higher than recent historical estimates. Murres were quite flighty, and many were rafting near the colony, suggesting that few were nesting.

Gull Island, in Kachemak Bay on the east side of Cook Inlet, is the second largest murre colony in this region and has been the subject of regular census efforts by the USFWS. No survey of Gull Island was conducted by the USFWS in 1991, but postspill attendance estimates in 1989 and 1990 were similar to the prespill count in 1988 (Nishimoto and Thomas 1991). I found colony attendance to be lower than previous counts, but this is likely related to erratic colony attendance on the day of the count, because other postspill counts indicate no significant reduction in attendance.

Sixty Foot Rock, a small, flat-topped offshore rock approximately 3 km from Gull Island, is the only other murre nesting area on the east side of Cook Inlet. Attendance on this survey was within the usual range for this colony.

McNeil Islet is a small, mushroom-shaped rock on the west side of Cook Inlet in Kamishak Bay. In July 1991 and before my survey on August 7, a "couple of hundred" murres were at the colony (Aumiller 1992). However, at the time of this survey, the colony was largely abandoned, there were no nesting murres on the colony, and only 15 were seen flying around the colony. However, murre numbers in 1992 were over 1 000 (Aumiller 1992).

Table 8—Comparison of murre colony attendance estimates from this survey (July 28–August 3 and 7, 1991) with data from prespill colony surveys in Cook Inlet and postspill data collected by the USFWS and Alaska Department of Fish and Game, 1989 – 1991.

Cook Inlet Colony Attendance[1]

Colonies	Prespill		Postspill			Present Study 1991
	Historic Estimates		USFWS			
LOW RISK			1989	1990	1991	
Cook Inlet						
Gull Island	1976[2]	1 146	5 176[5]	5 075[5]	...	1 732
	1984[3]	2 652				
	1985[3]	1 994				
	1988[4]	5 500				
Sixty Foot Rock	1976[2]	350	232[5]	190[5]	...	100
	1984[3]	234				
	1985[3]	91				
	1986[3]	99				
	1987[4]	221				
	1988[4]	155				
Chisik & Duck Islands	1971[6]	20–25 000	...	...	...	7 536
	1978[7]	10 000				
	1983[8]	5 000				
	1986[9]	4 101				
	1976[2]	2 500				
McNeil Islet	1978[10]	2 000	0[11]	+[11]	200[11]	15[12]
Contact Point	1978[13]	290	...	...	...	(Not Surveyed)

[1] Colony attendance represents the estimated number of murres at the colony during the survey.
[2] Erikson (1977).
[3] Nishimoto et al. (1987b).
[4] Nishimoto and Beringer (1989).
[5] Nishimoto and Thomas (1991).
[6] Snarski (1971).
[7] Jones and Peterson (1979).
[8] Muhlberg (1983).
[9] Nishimoto et al. (1987a).
[10] Arneson (1978a).
[11] Aumiller (1992), Alaska Dept. of Fish and Game; + = present; 200 not a count but listed as "a couple hundred" in text
[12] Seen flying; no murres on the colony.
[13] Arneson (1978b).

DISCUSSION

Because murres suffered greater losses than any other seabird from the *Exxon Valdez* oil spill, the overall impact on the breeding population and the potential for subsequent recovery have become significant issues. The primary focus of this study was to determine whether murres were attending previously occupied colonies and to compare postspill murre colony attendance with historical levels.

Murres were observed at all of the colonies in the spill path (high and moderate risk of exposure to oil), and numbers at colonies including those at highest risk generally were within the range of prespill estimates (Figure 3). Thus, claims of severely depressed numbers of breeding murres at colonies are not supported by the comparison of historical numbers with postspill counts (Figures 3, 5a, 5b). Although data from this study are limited to 1991, similar levels were reported by other investigators in 1989, 1990, and 1991 (Nysewander and Dippel 1991).

In this study, statistical analyses were used to test for the effects of oil by grouping colonies according to their risk of exposure to oil. If the spill had significantly reduced breeding populations, one would expect murre attendance at the colonies to have been greatly reduced, especially at colonies at high risk. Not only was there an absence of such a trend, but postspill estimates generally were within prespill ranges.

Although total attendance in the area appears to be lower than that recorded in the latest historical counts, these differences are much less dramatic than reported previously. According to the numbers from this survey, the total estimated murre attendance for the study area (143 582) is similar to but slightly lower than the total of the latest prespill estimates from the same colonies (148 514). For comparison, a second total attendance estimate was calculated by summing results for the 13 colonies surveyed by the USFWS in 1989–1991 with my attendance estimates for the colonies they did not survey. The total (approximately 112 000) is lower than the estimates generated using my numbers for all colonies (see Table 1), primarily because of differences in the 1991 counts at Cape Unalishagvak and Oil Creek, two large colonies on the Alaska Peninsula. The level of risk of oil exposure at these colonies was substantially lower than that at the colonies in the Barren and Chiswell islands, where postspill attendance was generally within historical ranges. This suggests that those apparent reductions may not be related to the spill.

For an individual colony, quantification of any spill-related mortality on the basis of comparisons between pre- and postspill colony attendance is often tenuous. Comparisons of numbers from historical and postspill surveys are complicated by two main factors: natural variability over time and observer effects. As an example of temporal variation, colonies in the eastern Aleutians, located well outside the spill-affected area, have shown declines of 60% to 90% in recent years that may be related to broad-scale environmental factors such as decreases in forage fish availability (J. Piatt, USFWS, personal communication). Decreases in murre numbers also have been observed from 1976 to 1986 at colonies in the Pribilof Islands in the Bering Sea (Byrd 1989). This natural variation confounds the ability to discern effects of a spill from prespill-postspill comparisons of attedance for an individual colony (Wiens and Parker, in press). Observer effects (e.g., different survey protocols and different observers) can cause similar difficulty in interpreting differences in numbers recorded at a single colony.

The approach used in this study helps to reduce the confounding effects of temporal variation and observer effects on an effect of oiling risk. Making comparisons among risk categories reduces the temporal variation as long as colonies across risk categories experience similar temporal variation—as might be expected with large-scale oceanographic changes. Similarly, this approach tends to eliminate observer effects when one observer counts all colonies prespill and one, either the same or different observer, counts all colonies postspill. Although more than one observer made prespill counts in this case, comparing among risk categories still works to reduce the observer effect. Using this approach, I found little evidence that changes in numbers at colonies in the spill-affected area were directly related to the risk of oil exposure.

As such, the findings of this study are inconsistent with conclusions reported by other investigators (Nysewander and Dippel 1991; Nysewander et al. 1993; Heinemann 1993; Fry 1993). I found no basis for reports of 40% to 60% decreases of breeding murres at the colonies in the spill path (60% to 70% in the Barren Islands). In fact, the results of this study showed that, as a group, colonies at high risk of oil exposure did not suffer larger reductions in attendance than those at low or moderate risk of exposure, but were generally within the range of estimates obtained before the spill. Published estimates of recovery times of 20 to 70 years or more assume substantial colony attendance reductions and no immigration from other colonies to replace lost breeding adults (Heinemann 1993; Piatt et al. 1990; based on models of Ford et al. 1982; Samuels and Lanfear 1982). The results of this study do not show substantial reductions in colony attendance in 1991. Therefore, one or both of these assumptions must be incorrect, and recovery times should be much shorter.

Although this study was not designed to estimate mortality, the data nonetheless shed light on the issue of murre mortality approaching estimated population levels. Specifically, the data from this study suggest that mortality of murres may have been considerably less than that predicted by computer simulation studies. The estimated total murre mortality estimate of 260 000 to 289 000 breeding murres was based on a computer model that includes several parameter estimates (e.g., the recovery rate of oiled birds), many of which are subject to significant uncertainty (Ford et al. 1990). If the local colonies had actually experienced the model-estimated magnitude of mortality, a large reduction in colony attendance would have been expected. No such reduction is evident from the field observations.

Whereas the model-predicted mortality estimates seem to be too high, there is no question that a large number of murres (i.e., tens of thousands) were killed following the spill. Given this mortality, the conclusion of this study of no major apparent effect on colony attendance may seem counterintuitive. However, breeding adult murres killed by the spill may have been replaced by birds from a reservoir of formerly nonbreeding birds. Murre populations are composed not only of breeding adults, which attend the colonies, but also of a substantial proportion of nonbreeding adults and prebreeding (sexually immature) individuals. This nonbreeding component may represent a significant portion of total murre populations (Dunnet 1982; Dunnet et al. 1990). Recruitment from this reservoir may compensate for breeders lost in one-time mortality events (Ford et al. 1982; Clark 1984; Stowe 1982b), as has been shown following natural wrecks (Birkhead and Hudson 1977). This surplus population also probably absorbed some of the mortality impact, thus diluting the impact on the breeding population. However, little is known about the size and distribution of this component of the population.

An alternative scenario that would allow the high rates of mortality to have occurred as estimated, while still allowing local colony attendance to be essentially unaffected, involves the mortality of nonlocal birds. More specifically, only a portion of the birds killed by the spill may have been breeding adults from local colonies. Substantial mortality of nonlocal murres may also have occurred. With regard to nonlocal birds, the winter-spring distribution of murres from the large colonies in the Semidi Islands, Shumagin Islands, and eastern Aleutian Islands (USFWS 1991), located to the south and west of the spill-affected area, is not well known. It is possible that murres from these areas were present in the spill-affected area as the oil moved through. If this were so, any population impact would have been distributed over a much larger geographic region. In this case, impacts to local colonies would have been less pronounced than would be expected by simply comparing the mortality estimates to the local population estimates.

Another scenario that could help to explain the findings of this study involves immigration of murres from other colonies in the area. Specifically, murres from the local colonies that died as a result of the spill could have been replaced by murres from other colonies in the region. Some studies suggest that seabirds that have bred successfully in one location display a high fidelity to that site (Birkhead 1977; Hedgren 1980). If this is so, it is unlikely that breeding murres from other colonies would have filled vacant sites at the affected colonies. Other authors cast doubt on this theory (e.g. Hudson 1985), and immigration is thought to be a factor in the recovery of colonies following major wrecks in the North Sea (Stowe 1982a). Although the site fidelity of nonbreeding murres in the Gulf of Alaska is not well understood, it is possible that recruitment of nonbreeders from other colonies in the general region could have filled some vacancies at the affected colonies. In the case of immigration, impacts on the available surplus population would be distributed over a large geographic region.

Considering these possibilities, it is likely that some combination of the first three factors discussed above (lower mortality than estimated, recruitment from the nonbreeding surplus pool, and the sharing of mortality impact by the nonbreeding pool) accounted for the observed similarities between the historical and postspill attendance estimates. The other scenarios (mortality of murres associated with colonies outside of the spill-impacted area, and large-scale immigration of breeding adults from other colonies) are largely suppositional. Regardless of the mechanism, the observation from this study that murres are occupying breeding colonies in numbers similar to historical levels underscores the continued viability of the murre populations in the area affected by the spill.

CONCLUSIONS

This study focused directly on the number of murres attending colonies following the spill, a key factor affecting the continued viability of the murre populations in the spill-affected area. The results of this study showed that murres were present at all colonies in the path of the spill, and attendance numbers were generally within historical ranges. Further, changes in murre attendance from historical levels were not related to the estimated levels of oil exposure. The colony-attendance levels documented on this survey in 1991 do not support the contention that murre colony attendance in the study area was drastically lower than historical levels. Thus, published estimates of long recovery times based on a premise of major reductions in breeding-colony attendance and no immigration, are not supportable.

ACKNOWLEDGMENTS

I thank the crew of the *M/V Pacific Star* and the *M/V Scorpius* for assistance in the field and logistical support, photographers Brad Anderson and Larry O'Donnel of Media Productions, Inc., Keith Parker of Data Analysis Group, and John Wiens, Colorado State University.

REFERENCES

Arneson, P.D. "Identification, documentation and delineation of coastal migratory bird habitat in Alaska." *in: Environmental Assessment of the Alaskan Continental Shelf. Quarterly Report.* National Oceanographic and Atmospheric Administration, Environmental Research Laboratory, Boulder, CO: 1:41-45; 1978a.

Arneson, P.D. "Colony of Alaskan seabird colonies, colony status record. Contact point (M051C002)." U. S. Fish and Wildlife Service. Anchorage, AK: Unpublished; 1978b.

Aumiller, L. "Notes on seabird colony survey of Kamishak Bay, 1989-1992." Alaska Department of Fish and Game. Unpublished report; 1992.

Bailey, E. and B. Rice. "Assessment of injury to seabird and marine mammal populations along the southeast coast of the Kenai Peninsula, Alaska, from the *Exxon Valdez* oil spill during summer of 1989." U.S. Fish and Wildlife Service and National Park Service. Anchorage, AK: Unpublished administrative report; 82 pages; 1989.

Bailey, E.P. "Barren Islands survey, 1975." U.S. Fish and Wildlife Service. Homer, AK: Unpublished field notes; 1975.

Bailey, E.P. "Breeding bird distribution and abundance in the Barren Islands, Alaska." *Murrelet.* 57:2-12; 1976a.

Bailey, E.P. "Distribution and abundance of marine birds and mammals on the south side of the Kenai Peninsula, Alaska." National Park Service and U.S. Fish and Wildlife Service. Anchorage, AK: Unpublished administrative report; 84 pages; 1976b.

Bailey, E.P. "Beached bird survey of Barren Island, April 6-June 16, 1989." U. S. Fish and Wildlife Service. Homer, AK: Unpublished administrative report; 21 pages; 1989.

Bailey, E.P. personal communication with David Erikson, Dames and Moore, Homer, AK; 1992.

Bailey, E.P. and N.H. Faust. "Distribution and abundance of marine birds breeding between Amber and Kamishak Bays, Alaska, with notes on interactions with bears." *Western Birds.* 15:161-174; 1984.

Bailey, E.P. and C. H. Davenport. "Dieoff of Common Murres on the Alaska Peninsula and Unimak Island." *Condor.* 74:213-219; 1972.

Bailey, E.P. and P. Shad. "Catalog of Alaskan seabird colonies. Puale Bay (M034013)." U.S. Fish and Wildlife Service. Anchorage, AK: Unpublished; 1976.

Bartonek, J., C. J. Lensink, P. Gould, R. Gill, and G. Sanger. "Population dynamics and trophic relationships of marine birds in the Gulf of Alaska and southern Bering Sea." *in: Environmental Assessment of the Alaskan Continental Shelf. Annual Report.* National Oceanographic and Atmospheric Administration, Environmental Research Laboratory, Boulder, CO: 4:1-13; 1977.

Berg, C.M., D.J. Forsell, and K.R. Emmel. "Census of seabirds nesting on the Triplets Islands, June 1985." U.S. Fish and Wildlife Service, Anchorage, AK: Unpublished administrative report; 16 pages; 1985.

Birkhead, T.R. "The effect of habitat and density on breeding success in the Common Guillemot (*Uria aalge*)." *Journal of Animal Ecology.* 46:751-764; 1977.

Birkhead, T.R. "Attendance patterns of guillemots (*Uria aalge*) at breeding colonies on Skomer Island." *Ibis.* 120:219-229; 1978.

Birkhead, T.R. "Timing of breeding of Common Guillemots *(Uria aalge)* at Skomer Island, Wales." *Ornis Scandinavica.* 11:142-145; 1980.

Birkhead, T.R. and P.J. Hudson. "Population parameters for the Common Guillimot (*Uria aalge*)." *Ornis Scandinavica.* 8:145-154; 1977.

Birkhead, T.R. and N.D. Nettleship. "Census methods for murres, *Uria* species: a unified approach." Canadian Wildlife Services. Occasional Papers; 43; 1980.

Boekelheide, R.J., D.G. Ainley, S.H. Morrell, H.R. Huber, and T.J. Lewis. "Common Murre" *in: Seabirds of the Farallon Islands.* D.G. Ainley and R.J. Boekelheide (eds.) Stanford, CA: Standford University Press; 245-275; 1990.

Byrd, G.V. "Seabirds in the Pribilof Islands, Alaska: Trends and monitoring methods." M.S. thesis; University of Idaho; Moscow, ID; 1989.

Clark, R.B. "Impact of oil pollution on seabirds." *Environmental Pollution (series A).* 33:1-22; 1984.

Dewhurst, D.A., K.K. Hankins, and P.W. Opay. "*Exxon Valdez* oil spill impact assessment on the Pacific Coast of the Alaska Peninsula and nearshore islands, Cape Kebugakli to American Bay, 26 April - 13 August, 1990." U.S. Fish and Wildlife Service. King Salmon, AK: Unpublished report; 1990.

Dewhurst, D. and M. Moore. "Population and productivity of seabirds on the Pacific coast of Becharof National Wildlife Refuge, Alaska in 1991." U.S. Fish and Wildlife Service. Homer, AK: Unpublished report; 1992.

Dick, M. and R. MacIntosh. "Catalog of Alaskan seabird colonies, colony status record. Kekur Island (M034C015)." U.S. Fish and Wildlife Service. Anchorage, AK: Unpublished; 1975.

Dick, M. and D. Nelson. "Catalog of Alaskan seabird colonies, colony status record. Selezen Island (M043C024) and Stack-Marmot Island (M043C041)." U.S. Fish and Wildlife Service. Anchorage, AK: Unpublished; 1976.

Dick, M. and I.M. Warner. "Catalog of Alaskan seabird colonies, colony status record. Chiniak Island and Rocks (M034C018) and The Triplets (M034C046)." U.S. Fish and Wildlife Service. Anchorage, AK: Unpublished; 1975.

Dick, M., I.M. Warner, and R. MacIntosh. "Distribution and abundance of breeding seabirds in Chiniak and southern Marmot Bays, Alaska, 1975." U.S. Fish and Wildlife Service. Anchorage, AK: Unpublished administrative report: 15 pages; 1976.

Department of Justice. "Summary of effects of the *Exxon Valdez* oil spill on natural resources and archaeological resources, U.S. Department of Justice." Washington, D.C. 1991.

Dunnet, G. M. "Oil pollution and seabird populations." *Philosophical Transactions of the Royal Society, London.* 297:413-427; 1982.

Dunnet, G.M., R.W. Furness, M.L. Tasker, and P.H. Becker. "Seabird ecology in the North Sea." *Netherlands Journal of Sea Research.* 26(2-4):387-425; 1990.

Erikson, D. "Distribution, abundance, migration and breeding locations of marine birds, lower Cook Inlet, Alaska, 1976." Vol.VIII. *in: Environmental studies of Kachemak Bay and Lower Cook Inlet.* Trask, L.L., L.B. Flagg, and D.C. Burbank (eds.) Unpublished Administrative Report, Alaska Department of Fish and Game Marine/Coastal Habitat Management. Anchorage, AK; 1977.

Exxon Valdez Oil Spill Trustees. "Draft Work Plan *Exxon Valdez* Oil Spill Restoration." Alaska Departments of Fish and Game, Law, and Environmental Conservation; U.S. Department of Agriculture, Department of the Interior; and the National Oceanographic and Atmospheric Administration. Anchorage, AK; 1992.

Ford, R.G., J.A. Wiens, D. Heinemann, and G.L. Hunt. "Modeling the sensitivity of colonially breeding marine birds to oil spills: Guillemot and kittiwake populations on the Pribilof Islands, Bering Sea." *Journal of Applied Ecology.* 19:1-31; 1982.

Ford, R.G., M.L. Bonnell, D.H.Varoujean, G.W. Page, B.E. Sharp, D. Heinemann, and J.L. Casey." Assessment of direct seabird mortality in Prince William Sound and the Western Gulf of Alaska resulting from the *Exxon Valdez* oil spill." Final report. Portland, OR: Ecological Consulting, Inc.; 1990.

Forsell, D. and G. Sanger. "Catalog of Alaskan seabird colonies, colony status record. Inner Right Cape Islets (M034C059)." U.S. Fish and Wildlife Service. Anchorage, AK: Unpublished; 1977.

Frazer, D.A. and M. Howe. "Seabird investigations on Middleton Island during the summer, 1976." U.S. Fish and Wildlife Service. Anchorage, AK: Unpublished administrative report; 1977.

Fry, D.M. "How do you fix the loss of half a million birds?" *in: Exxon Valdez Oil Spill Symposium, Program and Abstracts*; Anchorage, AK; 30-33; 1993.

Galt, G.A. and D.L. Payton. "Movement of oil spilled from the *T/V Exxon Valdez.*" *in: Proceedings of a Symposium to Evaluated the Response Effort on Behalf of Sea Otters after the* T/V Exxon Valdez *Oil Spill in Prince William Sound, Alaska.* Washington, D.C: U.S. Fish and Wildlife Service and National Fish and the Wildlife Foundation; 15 pages; 1990.

Gaston, A.J. and D.N. Nettleship. "The Thick-Billed Murres of Prince Leopold Island." *Canadian Wildlife Service Monograph No. 6.* 350 pages; 1981.

Gaston, A.J. and D.N. Nettleship. "Factors determining seasonal change in attendance at colonies of the Thick-Billed Murre *(Uria lomvia).*" *Auk.* 99:468-473; 1982.

Gould, P.J. and D.R. Nysewander. "Reproductive ecology of seabirds at Middleton Island, Alaska. Summer 1982." U.S. Fish and Wildlife Service. Anchorage, AK: Unpublished administrative report; 1982.

Gould, P.J. and K. Powers. "Catalog of Alaskan seabird colonies, colony status record. Cape Unalishagvak (M035005)." U.S. Fish and Wildlife Service. Anchorage, AK: Unpublished; 1976

Gould, P.J. and A.E. Zabloudil. "Reproductive ecology of seabirds at Middleton Island, Alaska. Summer 1981." U.S. Fish and Wildlife Service. Anchorage, AK: Unpublished administrative report; 1981.

Gould, P.J., D.R. Nysewander, J.L. Trapp, and M.L. Schaffer. "Reproductive ecology of seabirds at Middleton Island, Alaska. Summer 1983." U.S. Fish and Wildlife Service. Anchorage AK: Unpublished administrative report; 1983.

Gould, P.J., B. Roberts, D.R. Nysewander, and K. Omura. "Reproductive ecology of seabirds at Middleton Island, Alaska. Summer 1984." U.S. Fish and Wildlife Service. Anchorage, AK: Unpublished administrative report; 1984.

Handel, C. and G.A. Sanger. "Catalog of Alaskan seabird colonies colony status record. Inner Right Cape Islet (M034C059)." U.S. Fish and Wildlife Service. Anchorage, AK: Unpublished; 1976.

Harris, M.P., S. Wanless, and P. Rothery. "Assessing changes in the numbers of guillemots *Uria aalge* at breeding colonies." *Bird Study.* 30:57-66; 1983.

Harris, M.P. and T.R. Birkhead. "Breeding ecology of the Atlantic Alcidae." *in: The Atlantic Alcidae.* D.N. Nettleship and T.R. Birkhead (eds.) New York, NY: Academic Press; 155-204;1985.

Hatch, S.A. "Catalog of Alaskan seabird colonies, colony status record. Flat Island (M033C002)." U.S. Fish and Wildlife Service. Anchorage, AK: Unpublished; 1978.

Hatch, S.A. "Did the 1982-1983 El Niño-southern oscillation affect seabirds in Alaska?" *Wilsons Bulletin.* 99:468-474; 1987.

Hatch, S.A. and M. Hatch. "Population and habitat use of marine birds in the Semidi Islands, Alaska." *Murrelet.* 64:39-46; 1983.

Hatch, S.A. and M. Hatch. "Attendance patterns of murres at breeding sites: implications from monitoring." *Journal of Wildlife Management.* 53(2):483-493; 1989.

Hedgren, S. 1980. "Reproductive success of Guillemots (*Uria aalge*) on the Island of Stora Karlso." Ornis Fennica. 57:49-57; 1980.

Heinemann, D. "How long to recovery for murre populations, and will some colonies fail to make the comeback?" *in: Exxon Valdez Oil Spill Symposium, Program and Abstracts;* Anchorage, AK; 139-141; 1993.

Hudson, P.J. "Population parameters for the Atlantic alcidae." *in: The Atlantic Alcidae.* D. N. Nettleship and T.R. Birthed (eds.) New York: Academic Press; 235-261;1985.

Irons, D.B., D.R. Nysewander, and J.L. Trapp. "Distribution and abundance of water birds in relationship to habitat and season in Prince William Sound, Alaska, 1983-1984." U.S. Fish and Wildlife Service. Anchorage, AK: Unpublished administrative report; 1985.

Islieb, P. and L. Sowl. "Catalog of Alaskan seabird colonies. Colony status record, Point Elrington (M049C015)." U.S. Fish and Wildlife Service. Anchorage, AK: Unpublished; 1972.

Jones, R.D. and M.R. Peterson. "The pelagic birds of Tuxedni Wilderness." *in: Environmental Assessment of the Alaskan Continental Shelf, Annual Reports.* National Oceanographic and Atmospheric Administration, Environmental Research Laboratory, Boulder, CO: 2:187-232; 1979.

King, J. and G.A. Sanger. "Oil spill vulnerability index from marine oriented birds." *in: Conservation of Marine Birds of Northern North America.* J.C Bartonek and D.N. Nettleship (eds.) Washington, D.C.: U.S. Fish and Wildlife Service; 227-240; 1979.

Koons,C.B. and H.O. Jahns. "The fate of oil from the *Exxon Valdez*—a perspective." *Marine Technology Society Journal.* 26(3):61-69; 1992.

Laing, K.K. and S. Klosiewski. "Marine biological papers of Prince William Sound, AK, before and after the *Exxon Valdez* oil spill." U.S. Fish and Wildlife Service. Anchorage, AK: NRDA Bird Study 2; 1993.

Lehnhausen, W. A. and S. E. Quinlin. "Catalog of Alaskan seabird colonies, colony status record. Wooded Island (M049C008)." U.S. Fish and Wildlife Service. Anchorage, AK: Unpublished; 1977.

Lensink, C.J. "Birds and sea otters killed in the *Exxon Valdez* oil spill." *Endangered Species Update.* 7(7):1-2; 1990.

Lloyd, C. "Timing and frequency of census counts of cliff-nesting auks." *British Birds.* 68:507-513; 1975.

MacIntosh, R. "Census of seabirds on The Triplets Islands, Kodiak, Alaska. 23-25 July, 1989." Kodiak Audubon Society. Kodiak, AK: Unpublished report; 1989.

Manuwal, D.A. "Dynamics of marine bird populations on the Barren Islands, Alaska." *in: Environmental Assessment of the Alaskan Continental Shelf, Annual Report.* National Oceanic Atmospheric Administration Environmental Research Laboratory, Boulder, CO: 4:294-420; 1978.

Manuwal, D.A. "Breeding biology of seabirds on the Barren Islands, AK, 1976-1979." U.S. Fish and Wildlife Service. Anchorage, AK: Unpublished final report; 195 pages; 1980.

Manuwal, D.A. Personal Communication with David Erikson, Dames & Moore, Homer, AK. 1992.

Manuwal, D.A. and P. D. Boersma. "Dynamics of Marine Bird populations on the Barren Islands, Alaska annual report." National Oceanic Atmospheric Administration Environmental Research Laboratory, Boulder, CO: 4:294-420; 1978.

Muhlberg, G. "Status of seabirds at Chisik and Duck Islands during 1983." Kenai National Wildlife Refuge; U.S. Fish and Wildlife Service; Soldotna, AK: Unpublished administrative report; 1983.

Murphy, E.C., A.M. Springer, and D.C. Roseneau. "Population status of Common Guillemots (*Uria aalge*) at a colony in western Alaska: Results and simulations." *Ibis.* 128:348-363; 1986.

Murphy, E. C., M.I. Springer, D.C. Roseneau, and A.M. Springer. "Monitoring population numbers and productivity of colonial seabirds." *in: Environmental Assessment of the Alaskan Continental Shelf. Annual Report.* National Oceanic Atmospheric Administration Environmental Research Laboratory, Boulder, CO: 1:142-272; 1980.

National Oceanographic and Atmospheric Administration (NOAA) and Alaska Department of Environmental Conservation (ADEC). "Daily reports—*Exxon Valdez* oil spill. Overflight data and summaries." Unpublished. 1989.

Nishimoto, M. and B. Beringer. "Breeding seabirds at Gull Island and Sixty Foot Rock during 1987-88." U.S. Fish and Wildlife Service, Alaska Maritime National Wildlife Refuge. Homer, AK; 1989.

Nishimoto, M. and B. Rice. "A re-survey of seabirds and marine mammals along the south coast of the Kenai Peninsula, Alaska., during the summer of 1986." U.S. Fish and Wildlife Service. Homer, AK, and the U.S. Park Service, Seward, AK; 1987.

Nishimoto, M. and C. Thomas. "Breeding seabirds at Gull Island and Sixty Foot Rock during 1990." U.S. Fish and Wildlife Service, Alaska Maritime National Wildlife Refuge. Homer, AK; 1991.

Nishimoto, M., K. Thounhurst, and T. Early. "The status of seabirds at Chisik and Duck Islands during 1986." U.S. Fish and Wildlife Service. Homer, AK: Unpublished administrative report; 1987a.

Nishimoto, M., D. Debinski, K. Rose, and K. Thounhurst. "Breeding seabirds at Gull Island and Sixty Foot Rock, Kachemak Bay, during 1984-86." U.S. Fish and Wildlife Service, Alaska Maritime National Wildlife Refuge. Homer, AK; 1987b.

Nysewander, D.R. and C. Dippel. "Population survey of seabirds nesting in Prince William Sound, the outer coast of the Kenai Peninsula, Barren Islands, and other nearby colonies, with emphasis on changes in numbers and reproduction of murres." Bird Study No. 3. U.S. Fish and Wildlife Service. Homer, AK: Unpublished administrative report; 48 pages; 1990.

Nysewander, D.R. and C. Dippel. "Population survey of seabirds nesting in Prince William Sound, the outer coast of the Kenai Peninsula, Barren Islands, and other nearby colonies, with emphasis on changes in numbers and reproduction of murres. Bird Study No. 3." U.S. Fish and Wildlife Service. Homer, AK: Unpublished administrative report; 52 pages; 1991.

Nysewander, D.R. and P. Knudtson. "The population ecology and migration of seabirds, shorebirds and waterfowl associated with Constantine Harbor, Hinchinbrook Island, Prince William Sound, 1976." *in: Environmental Assessment of the Alaskan Continental Shelf, annual report*. National Oceanic Atmospheric Administration Environmental Research Laboratory. Boulder, CO: 4:500-575; 1977.

Nysewander, D.R. and J.L. Trapp. "Wide-spread mortality of adult Seabirds in Alaska, August and September 1983." U.S. Fish and Wildlife Service. Homer, AK: Unpublished administrative report; 1983.

Nysewander, D.R. and J.L. Trapp. "Catalog of Alaskan seabird colonies. Kekur Island (M034 C015)." U.S. Fish and Wildlife Service. Anchorage, AK: Unpublished; 1984.

Nysewander, D.R., B. Roberts, and S. Bonfield. "Reproductive ecology of seabirds at Middleton Island, Alaska. Summer 1985." U.S. Fish and Wildlife Service. Anchorage, AK: Unpublished administrative report; 1986.

Nysewander, D.R. C. Dippel, G.V. Byrd, and E. Knudtson. "Effects of the *T/V Exxon Valdez* oil spill on Murres: A perspective from observations at breeding colonies. Bird Study 3." U.S. Fish and Wildlife Service. Homer, AK: Final report; 1992.

Nysewander, D.R., D.L. Forsell, J.L. Trapp, E.P. Hoberg, and M.H. Dick. "Alaska seabird colony status record, The Triplets (M034C046)." U.S. Fish and Wildlife Service. Anchorage, AK: Unpublished; 1977.

Nysewander, D.R., C. Dippel, G.V. Byrd, and E.P. Knudtson. "Effects of the *T/V Exxon Valdez* oil spill on Murres: A perspective from observations at breeding colonies." *in: Exxon Valdez Oil Spill Symposium, Program and Abstracts*; Anchorage, AK; 135-138; 1993.

Nysewander, D.R., D.J. Forsell, P.A. Baird, D.J. Shields, G.J. Weiler, and J.H. Kogan. "Marine birds and mammal survey of the Eastern Aleutian Islands, summer of 1980-81." U.S. Fish and Wildlife Service. Anchorage, AK: Unpublished administrative report; 1982.

Petersen, M. "Murres (*Uria* spp). The Breeding Biology and Feeding Ecology of Marine Birds in the Gulf of Alaska." P. Baird and P. Gould (eds.) *in: Environmental Assessment of the Alaskan Continental Shelf, Final Reports*; National Oceanic Atmospheric Administration Environmental Research Laboratory. Boulder, CO: 45:381-399; 1986.

Piatt, J.F. and R.G. Ford. "Distribution and abundance of Marbled Murrelets in Alaska." *The Condor*. 95:662-669; 1993.

Piatt, J.F. and R.L. McLagan. "Common Murre *(Uria aalge)* attendance patterns at Cape St. Mary's, Newfoundland." *Canadian Journal of Zoology*. 65:1530-1534; 1987.

Piatt, J.F., C.J. Lensink, W. Buttler, M. Kendziorek, and D. Nysewander. "Immediate impact of the *Exxon Valdez* oil spill on marine birds." *The Auk*. 107:387-397; 1990.

Powers, K. and P.J. Gould. "Catalog of Alaskan seabird colonies, colony status record. Cape Unalishagvak (M035005)." U.S. Fish and Wildlife Service. Anchorage, AK: Unpublished; 1976.

Rice, B. Personal communication with David Erikson, Dames and Moore, Homer, AK; 1992.

Rothery, P., S. Wainless, and M.P Harris. "Analysis of counts from monitoring guillemots in Britain and Ireland." *Journal of Animal Ecology*. 57:1-19; 1988.

Samuels, W.B. and K.J. Lanfear. "Simulations of seabirds damage and recovery from oil spills in the northern Gulf of Alaska. *Journal of Environmental Management*. 15:169-182; 1982.

Sanger, G.A. and C. Handel. "Catalog of Alaskan seabird colonies, colony status record. Gull Point (M034C010)" U.S. Fish and Wildlife Service. Anchorage, AK: Unpublished; 1976.

Sangster, M.E. Personal communication with David Erikson, Dames and Moore, Homer, AK; 1992.

Sangster, M.E., C.T. Benz, and D.J. Kurhhajic. "Reproductive ecology of seabirds at Hinchinbrook Island and a census of seabirds at select sites in Prince William Sound." U.S. Fish and Wildlife Service. Anchorage, AK: Unpublished administrative report; 98 pages; 1978.

Simons, T. Personal Communication with David Erikson, Dames & Moore, Homer, AK; 1992.

Simons, T. and J. Pierce. "Alaska seabird colony status record. East Amatuli Island (M043C010)." U.S. Fish and Wildlife Service. Anchorage, AK: Unpublished; 1978a.

Simons, T. and J. Pierce. "Alaska seabird colony status record. Nord Island (M043C011)." U.S. Fish and Wildlife Service. Anchorage, AK: Unpublished; 1978b.

Skalski, J.R. "Techniques for wildlife investigations." San Diego, CA: Academic Press; 1992.

Skalski, J.R. and D.H. McKenzie. "A design for aquatic monitoring programs." Journal of Environmental Management. 14:237-251; 1982.

Slater, P.J.B. "Factors affecting the numbers of Guillemots (*Uria aalge*) present on cliffs." *Ornis Scandinavica.* 11:155-163; 1980.

Snarski, D.J. "Observations of birds on Tuxedni National Wildlife Refuge, Alaska." U.S. Fish and Wildlife Service. Soldotna, AK: Unpublished administrative report; 1971.

Sowl, L.W. "The historical status of nesting seabirds of the northern and western Gulf of Alaska." *in: Conservation of Marine Birds of North America.* J.C. Bartonek and D.N. Nettleship (eds.), Wildlife Research Report 11. Washington, D.C.: U.S. Fish and Wildlife Service; 47-71; 1979.

Sowls, A.L., S.A. Hatch, and C.J. Lensink. "Catalog of Alaskan seabird colonies." U.S. Fish and Wildlife Service. Office of Biological Services, FWS/OBS-78/78; Anchorage, AK; 1978.

Springer, A.M. and D.E. Roseneau. "Murres: distribution and abundance in Alaska." National Oceanic Atmospheric Administration Environmental Research Laboratory. Juneau, AK: Draft species account for Outer Continental Shelf Environmental Assessment Program; 1980.

Stewart-Oaten, A., W.W. Murdoch, and K.R. Parker. "Environmental impact assessment: pseudoreplication in time?" Ecology. 67:929-940; 1986.

Stowe, T.J. "Recent population trends in cliff-breeding seabirds in Britain and Ireland." *Ibis.* 124:502-510; 1982a.

Stowe, T.J. "An oil spill at a guillemot colony." *Marine Pollution Bulletin.* 13:237-239; 1982b.

Torgrimson, G.M. "A comprehensive model for oil spill simulation." *in: Proceedings of the 1981 Oil Spill Symposium.* Washington, D.C.: American Petroleum Institute; 1981.

Tuck, L.M. "The murres. Their distribution, populations and biology; a study of the genus *Uria.*" Ottawa, Canada: Canadian Wildlife Service Monographic Series No. 1; 1961.

U.S. Fish and Wildlife Service. "Catalog of Alaskan seabird colonies-computer archives." U.S. Fish and Wildlife Service. Anchorage, AK; 1991.

Wanless, S., D.D. French, M.P. Harris, and D.R. Langslow. "Detection of annual change in the numbers of cliff-nesting seabirds in Orkney 1976-1980." *Journal of Animal Ecology.* 51:785-795; 1982.

Wiens, J.A. and K.R. Parker. "Analyzing the effects of accidental environmental impacts: approaches and assumptions." *Ecological Applications.* In press.

P. Dee Boersma[1], Julia K. Parrish[2], and Arthur B. Kettle[2]

COMMON MURRE ABUNDANCE, PHENOLOGY, AND PRODUCTIVITY ON THE BARREN ISLANDS, ALASKA: THE *EXXON VALDEZ* OIL SPILL AND LONG-TERM ENVIRONMENTAL CHANGE

REFERENCE: Boersma, P. D., Parrish, J. K., and Kettle, A. B., "Common Murre Abundance, Phenology, and Productivity on the Barren Islands, Alaska: The Exxon Valdez Oil Spill and Long-Term Environmental Change," *Exxon Valdez Oil Spill: Fate and Effects in Alaskan Waters, ASTM STP 1219*, Peter G. Wells, James N. Butler, and Jane S. Hughes, Eds., American Society for Testing and Materials, Philadelphia, 1995.

ABSTRACT: The *Exxon Valdez* oil spill in 1989 caused substantial seabird mortality. By 1 August, more than 30 000 seabird carcasses (74% murres) were recovered, and it was initially estimated that between 100 000 and 300 000 seabirds were killed. The Barren Islands, in particular East Amatuli Island, support the largest seabird colonies within the path of the spill. With respect to murres nesting on the Barren Islands, claims were made that the population suffered at least a 50% loss and that the remaining population underwent a change in breeding phenology, a breakdown in breeding synchrony, and a widespread failure to fledge chicks in the years following the spill. As a result of these effects, it was projected that the population would take 20-70 years to recover.

Principally because of the paucity of prespill data on the Barren Islands murre population size and reproductive success, it is impossible to quantify any effect of the spill on these populations. Available prespill data (1976-1978) on the East Amatuli murre population size ranges from 19 000 to 61 000 birds. These data are not systematic, replicated counts but rather are estimates indicating a broad range within which the true attendance figure probably resided. Our postspill attendance counts range from 31 041 to 37 128 (1990-1992). Comparisons between matched historical and 1990s photographs showed nearly identical attendance patterns, although there were significantly more murres in the 1990s photographs. Postspill attendance data from multiply censused areas suggest a recovery may have been taking place because of greater than expected annual increases (+25% from 1990 to 1991).

Prespill data on reproductive activity of the murres nesting in the Barren Islands were collected from a single 5 × 5-m plot located in a dense, flat section of the East Amatuli Light Rock colony. Comparisons with similarly collected postspill data suggest that phenology, egg production, and chick production are extremely variable among

[1] Professor, Institute for Environmental Studies and Department of Zoology, University of Washington, Seattle, WA 98195

[2] Research Associate, and Technician, respectively, Institute for Environmental Studies, University of Washington, Seattle, WA 98195

years, athough chicks were fledged in all years. Egg and chick production were highest in 1977 and 1991 and lowest in 1992.

On the basis of these analyses, we conclude that, although murres rafting near the Barren Islands undoubtedly suffered substantial mortality as a result of the *Exxon Valdez* oil spill, there is no justification for claims of either a dramatic reduction in colony attendance or substantial failure of the remaining birds to settle and reproduce, in the years following the spill. In spite of continued perturbations to the system from both natural and human-induced sources, East Amatuli Island continues to support a large, reproductively active colony of murres.

KEYWORDS: Common Murre, Barren Islands, *Exxon Valdez*, attendance, reproductive success, environmental change

INTRODUCTION

Oil spills are highly visible and widely publicized. As a result, the public perceives that oil spills wreak lasting devastation on natural systems (Hunt 1987; Wiens, this volume). The *Exxon Valdez* oil spill (hereafter referred to as the spill) exemplifies these perceptions. On 24 March 1989, the supertanker *Exxon Valdez* ran aground on Bligh Reef just off the port of Valdez, Alaska. More than 41 million litres (11 million gallons) of Prudhoe Bay crude oil leaked into Prince William Sound and were carried by winds and the Alaska Coastal Current southwest along the Kenai Peninsula toward Kodiak Island (Figure 1) (Galt and Payton 1990; Royer et al. 1990). As the oil reached the southern tip of the Kenai Peninsula, a portion was pushed into Cook Inlet and some was held around the Barren Islands by wind and tidal currents (Figure 1) (Piatt et al. 1990). The first oil reached the Barren Islands around 14 April (Bailey 1989). By 22 May no oil was seen in the waters around the Barren Islands (Bailey 1989), the slick having moved southwest to Afognak Island and into Shelikof Strait (Figure 1) (Galt and Payton 1990).

Many organisms were affected by the spill, and seabird mortality was especially high. By 1 August, more than 30 000 seabird carcasses were recovered, and it was estimated that between 100 000 and 300 000 seabirds were killed (Piatt et al. 1990). Seabirds are vulnerable to oil spills because many species spend large amounts of time at sea. Diving seabirds are particularly susceptible to oiling because they spend most of their time at the surface, where oil is found (Sanger and King 1979; Hunt 1987), and these species often account for most of the bird mortality associated with oil spills (Wiens, this volume). In the northern hemisphere, the majority of these species are alcids, mainly murres (both Common Murres, *Uria aalge*, and Thick-Billed Murres, *Uria lomvia*; Sharp 1993). An extremely gregarious seabird, murres form large, tight aggregations ("rafts") on the water (Tuck 1960), making them especially vulnerable to oiling (Sanger and King 1979; Wiens, this volume). Piatt et al. (1990) reported that at least 20 000 murre carcasses were recovered following the spill and estimated that

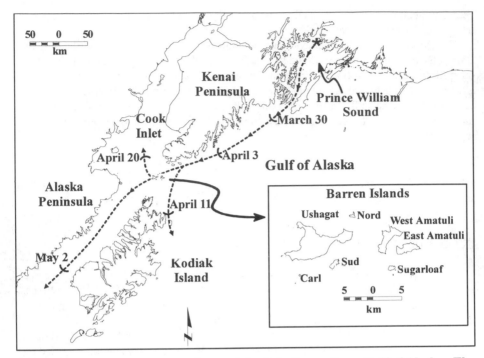

FIGURE 1—The location of the Barren Islands in the northern Gulf of Alaska. The generalized oil-spill trajectory (dashed line) and chronology (dates) following grounding of tanker in Prince William Sound on March 24, 1989, are shown (NOAA 1989). Oil was first sighted on the Barren Islands on April 14, 1989 (Bailey 1989). Inset: the Barren Islands including the study island, East Amatuli.

between 74 000 and 220 000 murres were killed by the spill. Other estimates ranged as high as 260 000 to 289 000 murre deaths (e.g., Heinemann 1993). This is compared with an estimated Alaskan population of 10 million murres (5 million Common Murres and 5 million Thick-Billed Murres; Sowls et al. 1978), and an estimated prespill Common Murre breeding population in the path of the spill of between 150 000 and 243 000 (Erikson, this volume; Piatt et al. 1990, respectively). Assuming murre mortality was principally confined to those colonies in the path of the spill, such losses should have noticeably depleted these colonies to roughly 50% of the former size of the entire population when the "at sea" proportion of the colony (i.e., 1.4 times as many as at the colony; Piatt et al. 1993) is included in the total.

   Determining the magnitude of the effect of this spill on the murre population in the spill path is difficult for several reasons. First, the potentially affected area is large, ranging from colonies along the Kenai Peninsula to colonies along the Shelikof Strait, several hundred kilometers away. Second, it is impossible to discern whether the spill had an even effect across its entire path, or if there were "hotspots" where mortality was higher.

Third, there is no precise information from the period immediately preceding the spill on population size, phenology, or reproductive success for most of the murre colonies within the path of the oil. Thus, current data must necessarily be compared with older, perhaps dated, information. Fourth, even though many carcasses were recovered, an unknown majority was lost (Ford et al. 1990). Even with careful calculation, murre mortality estimates are uncertain and range from 74 000 to 289 000. Piatt et al. (1990) suggested that 10% of the murre population in the Gulf of Alaska was killed by the spill. If estimated murre mortality was spread evenly over the entire population, rather than concentrated at a few colonies, each colony would have lost 5-15% of its attending birds, if no increases in recruitment or immigration took place. Without accurate, timely prespill data, these percentage changes would be impossible to detect (i.e., Hatch and Hatch 1989).

Finally, the observed "effect" of the spill is actually a combination of how many murres were killed and what the remaining murres, especially the "at sea component" (i.e., Piatt et al. 1993) did. For example, when examining the potential effects of the spill on a single population there are only three hypotheses: the population decreased, the population remained the same, or the population increased. If the population was reduced and no immigration took place, the observed attendance could have decreased markedly. On the other hand, if initial mortality was compensated for by immigration, observed attendance would remain the same or even increase, even though a large proportion of the original attending birds might have been killed. Unless the original breeders were banded, it would be impossible to detect such a turnover.

However, strong inferences can be made using only postspill data. Large annual increases in postspill attendance might indicate that a "recovery" was taking place. Steady declines in postspill attendance would suggest a continuing negative effect, either because young murres were not available to recruit, or because the existing population was emigrating. A stable postspill population could only be interpreted as no detectable effect. Of course, all of these scenarios must be set against natural variability, which can alter murre attendance by 5-10% in any given year (Birkhead 1978; Sydeman 1993).

The northern Gulf of Alaska supports several large seabird colonies (Sowls et al. 1978). One of the largest and most diverse of these colonies is found on East Amatuli Island at the eastern edge of the Barren Islands group (Figure 1) (Bailey 1976). East Amatuli Island supports the largest murre colony in the path of the spill (approximately 70% of the Barren Islands population and 5% of the western Gulf of Alaska population; Sowls et al. 1978; Piatt et al. 1990). Following the spill, initial claims were made that this population had been decimated, suffering losses of at least 50% (Piatt et al. 1990). There were also claims that the remaining Barren Islands population had undergone a change in breeding phenology, a breakdown in breeding synchrony, and a widespread failure to fledge chicks in the years following the spill (Fry 1993; Nysewander et al. 1993). Massive adult mortality, coupled with near-total breeding failure in the years following the spill, led several authors to suggest that the murre population might not recover for 20 to 70 years (e.g., Piatt et al. 1990; Ford and Piatt 1993; following model originally published in Ford et al. 1982). In principle, if the colony sustained massive mortality, differences in attendance should be detectable based on comparisons with historical information (assuming the system is relatively closed to immigration and the "at sea component" of the population did not immediately swamp the initial effect). However, we believe that the age and accuracy of the prespill population data on the Barren Islands precludes quantitative comparisons and is only useful for identifying a broad range within which the true population figure apparently resided.

In this paper, we present the results of a postspill study of the murres attending East Amatuli Island, with specific reference to interannual changes in adult attendance, phenology, and reproductive success. Contemporary data are compared to previous information on East Amatuli Island murre population dynamics, collected during 1977-1979. Our study did not extend to the murres nesting on Nord Island (the second largest island population within the Barren Islands system) because there was no prespill data on the breeding success of this colony.

Murre Biology

Like many other seabirds, murres are colonial nesters that often breed on offshore islands and stacks where there are few if any terrestrial predators (Harris and Birkhead 1985). Pairs lay one egg, usually within a body width of the nearest neighbor (Tuck 1960; Birkhead 1977; Hatchwell 1991). Although the female can relay if the first egg is lost early, many pairs abandon nesting for the year when they lose their egg or chick (Birkhead and Hudson 1977; Hedgren 1980). Chicks hatch within 30-35 days, and fledge 18-25 days later when they are about 25-30% of adult size (Boekelheide et al. 1990; Hatchwell 1991). Because of the large number of diurnal predators, chicks usually fledge at night. After leaving the breeding colony and often the area, fledglings are cared for by the male parent (Birkhead 1977; Hedgren and Linnman 1979; Harris and Birkhead 1985). After fledging, murres may spend 3-4 years at sea before attempting to breed, but many young murres may return to their natal area to raft or roost (Birkhead and Hudson 1977; Boekelheide et al. 1990). Murres live as long as 30 years (Campbell and Lack 1985) and have high adult survival (82-94% survival per annum in some colonies: Hudson 1985; Hatchwell and Birkhead 1991; Sydeman 1993). Breeding success is variable, and on occasion breeders may fail to return to the colony or abandon their egg in years when food is unavailable or breeding conditions are otherwise poor (e.g., Hodder and Graybill 1985; Boekelheide et al. 1990). High adult survival, coupled with a long life span, means that pairs can fail to rear a chick for several years without affecting the size of the breeding colony. These conservative life-history traits are probably the result of evolutionary adaptation to seasonal variation in the environment, which favors behaviors that increase adult survival rather than maximizing reproductive effort in any given year (Lack 1968; Furness and Monaghan 1987).

The Barren Islands System

The Barren Islands support the largest breeding colony of Common Murres in the path of the spill. In addition to murres, at least 14 other species of seabirds breed in the Barren Islands, including Horned and Tufted Puffins (*Fratercula corniculata* and *F. cirrhata*), a variety of smaller alcids (Alcidae), Fork-Tailed Storm Petrels (*Oceanodroma furcata*), Black-Legged Kittiwakes (*Rissa tridactyla*), and Glaucous-Winged Gulls (*Larus glaucescens*). The islands support this seabird community, in part, because the waters around the islands are highly productive. Large tidal fluctuations, coupled with steep topographical relief associated with the Amatuli Trench and strong local winds, combine to create turbulence and localized upwelling in the Barren Islands, providing a rich food supply for fish, seabirds, and marine mammals (Strauch et al. 1979). High secondary and tertiary productivity is evidenced by the rich fishing grounds in Kachemak and Kamishak bays (Blackburn et al. 1983) and the high density of seabirds around the Barren Islands (Erikson 1977; Gould et al. 1982).

Although the northern Gulf of Alaska is productive, it is also dynamically unstable. On both a regional (i.e., Gulf of Alaska) scale as well as a more global (i.e., the Pacific basin) scale, the environment is constantly changing. From the late 1970s to the present, the Pacific has experienced large-scale oceanographic events in the form of three El Niño-Southern Oscillation (ENSO) events (1982-1983, 1987, 1992). Although the power and magnitude of an ENSO may be muted in the northern hemisphere compared with southern systems, associated climatic change, including sea-surface warming, occurs globally (e.g., Monastersky 1992; Yan et al. 1992). This effect can have repercussions on both the offshore, nonbreeding season feeding regime of seabirds as well as the nearshore, breeding season food supply. This may ultimately affect the abundance of seabirds, such as murres, in the system (Hodder and Graybill 1985; Wilson 1991; Massey et al. 1992).

On a regional scale, the northern Gulf of Alaska (at and above 55°N) experiences 15-20 year reversals in sea-surface temperature (SST) spanning approximately 2°C (Royer 1989). Effects of ENSO are embedded within this signal, but they are apparently not responsible for it (Royer 1989). Changes in SST may also be coincidental with fluctuations in several oceanographic and atmospheric parameters that spread across the entire Pacific basin and fluctuate on a 6-12 year cycle (Hollowed and Wooster 1991). The initiation of the warm periods is correlated with strong recruitment of bottomfish stocks (Hollowed and Wooster 1991). Finally, a basinwide shift in some 40 climatological factors occurred in 1976 (Ebbesmeyer et al. 1991; Kerr 1992). It is likely that these long-term changes in the physical oceanography of the system are reflected by changes in productivity. Species composition and biomass of the plankton and baitfish communities may change, causing a change in food composition and availability to seabirds (Springer et al. 1986).

On a local scale, weather patterns can also alter seabird foraging and reproductive success. After severe storms thousands of murres have been found dead, apparently starved to death (Bailey and Davenport 1972). Hatch (1987) reported that kittiwakes have complete reproductive failures after storms in the north Gulf of Alaska, and Dunn (1973; 1975) found that tern foraging success was altered by windspeed and sea-surface conditions. Because periodic fluctuation in the environment acts as an important determinant of survival and reproductive success for seabirds, it is not surprising that most seabird species have evolved conservative life-history traits, particularly high adult survival, longevity, and small clutch size.

In the Barren Islands, the regional and basinwide patterns of environmental change in the Gulf of Alaska may be buffered by more stable localized productivity. Nevertheless, there is yearly variation in the attendance and breeding success of burrow-nesting seabirds on the Barren Islands that is loosely correlated with changes in oceanographic and atmospheric parameters (Boersma et al. 1980; Boersma unpublished data). Superimposed on this rich but unstable natural environment are the negative effects of human disturbance, exemplified most recently by the *Exxon Valdez* oil spill.

METHODS

Colony Attendance

We estimated colony attendance each year (1990-1992) by counting murres present on the island. Attendance was defined as all murres seen on the island, not those flying or rafting. In 1990, 36 census areas around East Amatuli Island, encompassing almost all of the murre breeding areas, were delineated by landscape features (Figure 2). In all years, two observers using binoculars conducted simultaneous, independent counts from a small inflatable boat. Before the official censuses were started, observers practiced counting selected areas by making independent counts and then comparing data. If these counts differed substantially, counts were repeated until the counters agreed which murres were missed or invented. One observer (Kettle) counted in all three years.

For most census areas, at least two independent counts per observer were made. Occasionally (three-year average = 20% of the time), only one count per observer was made and/or only one observer counted. The census dates were determined by the phenology of the murres and the weather (1990: 12 - 22 August; 1991: 19 July - 5 August; 1992: 8 August - 1 September). In all years we tried to census after the murres had laid eggs but before chicks had fledged (see Wanless et al. 1982; Hatch and Hatch 1989). Counts were made when the water around the island was relatively calm (seas less than 1 m) and visibility was good. Counts around Light Rock, where tidal currents are most pronounced, were made during periods of slack tide.

In most of the census areas, murres on the cliff were counted directly. In a few areas, murres were impossible to count individually because of high nesting density. Therefore, observers estimated attendance by counting by fives. On the top of Light Rock, counters estimated attendance by twenties. This latter portion of the census represented 22% of the Light Rock attendance, and 5% of the whole island census. In 1991 and 1992, all murre breeding locations on East Amatuli Island, including Light Rock, were censused. In 1990, the east and northeast sides of Light Rock and a small area on the main island were not counted. Therefore, interannual comparisons were made using only the original census areas set up in 1990 (i.e., the 36 census areas; Figure 2).

For each of the 36 census areas, the two counts for each observer were averaged and differences between the observers were compared with a sign test using a normal approximation (Zar 1974). In no year were the counts of one observer consistently higher or lower than the other (1990: $Z_c = 0.708$, $0.5 > P > 0.2$; 1991: $Z_c = 0.360$, $P > 0.5$; 1992: $Z_c = 1.195$, $0.5 > P > 0.2$). Therefore, counts were averaged among observers to produce a single count per area per year. Statistical tests were performed on this dataset, which excluded morning counts made in 1990 ($N = 3$) and 1991 ($N = 3$). Interannual comparisons were made with a sign test using a normal approximation (Zar 1974) because only one census was performed each year (i.e., $N = 1$). Results were graphed as the difference between years by area (1991-1990; 1992-1991).

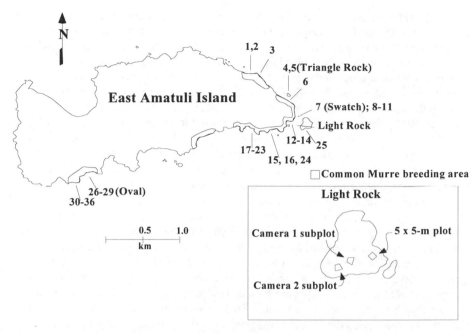

FIGURE 2—The location of all murre breeding areas, as well as the 36 census areas on East Amatuli Island, Barren Islands, Alaska. The shaded areas of the map show current (1990-1992) murre breeding and roosting areas. Inset: Light Rock, showing the placement of a 25m^2 plot used to assess annual phenology and productivity and the location of two time-lapse cameras installed during the 1991 murre breeding season.

In addition to the island census, four areas (Oval, Swatch, and Triangle Rock NW and S, respectively; Figure 2) were censused several times throughout the day on different dates throughout the breeding season to provide a more in-depth dataset for the determination of interannual trends. Censuses were performed either by direct counting (all years; see above) or by taking black-and-white photographs with a 300-mm lens (1992). Photographs were later censused repeatedly by two independent counters. Multiple counts for each counter were averaged to obtain a single value per counter per photograph. There was not a significant difference between counters (sign test on $N = 17$ photographs, $P = 0.629$). Therefore, counts were averaged for a single mean per photograph. Direct counts and counts made from concurrently taken photographs were not significantly different (Student t-tests on all photographic:direct-count pairs where the number of counts/sample > 2; $t = 1.67$, $P = 0.18$; $t = 0.25$, $P = 0.81$, respectively). Therefore, photographic and direct counts were used as equivalent sampling techniques. We used one-way ANOVA followed by a posteriori contrasts (1990 versus 1991; 1991 versus 1992) to assess yearly differences in attendance for each area, despite the fact that attendance values in the following year are somewhat dependent on the preceding year.

Oval, Swatch, and Triangle Rock S were also used to assess attendance differences as a function of time of day. Days were divided into three intervals: morning 0600 - 1059 h, afternoon 1100 - 1659 h, and evening 1700 - 2200 h. For each area, mean attendance was calculated for each of the 3 time intervals in 1990 and 1991, respectively. Percent differences between times of day (for example: [(*afternoon* – *morning*) ÷ *morning*] × 100%) were arcsine transformed to normalize the data. Afternoon and evening counts were significantly larger than morning counts (one-sample t-test on transformed percentages, H_0: the average difference is not different from zero; *afternoon* – *morning* $t = 4.23$, $N = 6$, $P < 0.005$; *evening* – *morning* $t = 2.30$, $N = 5$, $P < 0.05$). However, there was no difference between afternoon and evening counts (*evening* – *afternoon* $t = 0.49$, $N = 5$, $P > 0.05$). Therefore, afternoon and evening counts were pooled and morning counts were excluded from all attendance data analysis. All counts performed in 1992 were restricted to after 1100 h to facilitate interannual comparisons in the 1990s.

Changes in murre attendance were also assessed by comparing pre- and postspill photographs. We gathered photographs from field assistants (Mike Amaral, Curtis Bohlen, and Walt Reid) who had worked on the Barren Islands in the mid-1970s through the mid-1980s, and matched all photographs of reasonable clarity to pictures of these same areas taken in 1990 and 1991. Common areas in matched pairs of photographs were identified by topographical features. Two observers independently counted all the murres in these areas on the photograph pair at least twice. Student t-tests indicated that individuals did not differ in their counts for a given photograph ($P > 0.05$ for each comparison, $N = 14$ photographs). Therefore, counts were pooled and each counter value was used as a single sample (i.e., $N \geq 4$ for each photograph). Statistical comparisons between photographs were also made with a Student t-test.

Because some early photographs contained breeding ledges on which murres could not be accurately counted because of poor image quality, a second, more general, comparison was performed to assess changes in ledge-use by the birds. Thus, the ledge-use comparison included three photograph pairs that were not used in the direct count comparison. Without revealing the date of each photograph, all matched pairs were given to a "blind" observer who identified and numbered all ledges occupied by murres in each photograph. Ledge-use was assessed by matching and summing all occupied ledges in both years. Percent similarity in ledge-use was defined as all the ledges occupied in both photographs divided by all the ledges occupied in either photograph, multiplied by 100.

Phenology and Productivity

During boat trips we noted murre phenology by categorizing murre behavior as predominantly either occupation of the breeding ledges or rafting. If the murres were attending the island, we noted whether "flyoffs", defined as large numbers of murres (> 100) flying from the cliffs in unison, occurred. Because field seasons started after and ended before the onset/cessation of the murre breeding season (as defined by when the murres initially arrived and finally departed), it was impossible to determine when ledges were initially colonized or by what date the island was deserted. However, our field seasons usually started prior to the point at which the murres settled onto the cliffs throughout the day (i.e., no flyoffs were observed). Therefore, we operationally defined the beginning of reproductive activity as the time when most of the murres were present on the breeding ledges and remained there throughout the day (i.e., no flyoffs). We did not estimate the end of the breeding season, except by time-lapse photography in 1991 (see below).

Direct measurements of the number of breeding pairs, and the chicks they fledge, are difficult to make because most of the murres on East Amatuli Island nest on inaccessible ledges. Nonetheless, there are locations, such as Light Rock, where nest sites can be visited. A study plot, established on the top of Light Rock in a dense part of this colony (after Manuwal 1980), was used to determine interannual differences in productivity and, to a lesser extent, phenology. Counts of eggs and chicks were made in this area from 1977-1979 and again from 1990-1992. Every year, the plot was visited after the initiation of egg laying (usually two visits between late June and early August) and again after chicks started to hatch (one visit in late August). In 1977, the plot was only 17.6 m^2. In 1978, the plot was expanded to 25 m^2 and located in the same general area as in the previous year (P. D. Boersma personal observation). In 1990, the plot was re-established and permanently marked (Figure 2). Productivity could not be determined from data collected in 1977 and 1978 because the plot was visited only once (1977) or the last prechick visit was too early to determine total egg production (1978).

Reproductive success is usually measured as fledglings produced per pair. Because visiting the plot caused adults to temporarily abandon the area, we were unable to count the number of pairs directly. Therefore, we chose to assess reproductive success as a function of area, not pairs. During a good year, productivity could be high either because there were more pairs or because pairs were more successful. We assumed that although the actual number of pairs might vary between years, the number of potential breeders (i.e., the maximum number able to physically occupy the plot) was constant. Because the number of eggs produced in 1991 (263) was higher than in any other year, we assumed that this number represented maximum potential breeders. It was impossible to determine the number of fledglings by direct visits, so the number of eggs and chicks remaining on the plot during the last visit (late August) was substituted as an indirect measure of fledglings (even though this measure may inflate the number of actual fledglings). Therefore, our indirect measure of reproductive success equals the following:

eggs + chicks in late August ("fledglings")/eggs in late July in 1991 ("potential pairs")

In two of the years, 1979 and 1990, two visits were made to the plot to count eggs after eggs were laid but before chicks had hatched. Because plot visits disturbed nesting adults and allowed Glaucous-Winged Gulls, *Larus glaucescens*, to take unattended eggs, a weighting factor was added to estimate lost production during these years and to standardize our productivity estimate across all years. This factor was calculated by using known egg loss from the first to the second prechick visit in 1990 (39 eggs, as measured by marking). Because the number of eggs on the plot during the first prechick visit was identical in 1979 and 1990, the calculated loss is applicable to 1979, assuming that egg-predator pressure was not significantly different for the two years. Had all of these eggs survived to late August, the numerator of the production ratio would have increased by 39. When added to the equation, this extra factor estimates the highest possible production (i.e., additional eggs laid). In reality the number of chicks produced would probably have been somewhat less. Thus, the weighting factor represents a range within which actual productivity would have fallen.

To further quantify murre phenology and reproductive success, "natural" productivity was determined remotely in 1991 with two time-lapse 35-mm movie cameras located on Light Rock. Camera 1 was situated on a flat area similar to the 5×5-m plot, and Camera 2 was placed on a slope along the southern edge of the rock (Figure 2). The cameras were installed on 3 July and removed on 16 October, well after all the chicks had fledged and murres were no longer attending the cliffs. Each camera was programmed to record a single frame every six minutes, starting before dawn and ending after sunset. Overall, some 33 000 pictures were taken. The 35-mm movie prints were transferred to a Betacam SP video format for analysis. Each video frame indicated date and exact time.

For each camera view, clearly visible subplots were chosen for quantitative analysis (Figure 3). Reproduction of each pair was followed from laying to fledging. We recorded the presence, or absence, of an egg or a chick for each pair on each day. In the Camera 1 subplot, eggs were seen during the first few days that could not be ascribed to a pair. All of these eggs later disappeared, presumably because of egg predation. (In some frames we could see eggs outside of our subplot that were being eaten by gulls.) Although both the number of frames per day and the video resolution were high, it was nevertheless difficult, and sometimes impossible, to determine the nesting status of each pair on a given day. This was because the murres guarded their eggs and newly hatched chicks very closely, so they could not be seen. However, as the chicks aged they became more active and increasingly visible until fledging occurred. The night a chick fledged was operationally defined as the night after the last day it was seen. During the days leading up to fledging, the chick was active but closely attended to by its parents, whereas following fledging the remaining adult moved around its nest site, was not observed in brooding posture, and disappeared from the subplot within 2-3 days after the chick left.

Hatch dates were back-calculated from fledging dates by subtracting 21 days. Each hatch date was checked to determine whether it was a biologically reasonable estimate (i.e., that the chick had fledged instead of died). In cases in which the estimated hatch date conflicted with actual observations (i.e., an egg was seen after the calculated hatch date), the chick was scored as having died rather than fledged. In addition, if a chick was seen less than twice, it was also scored as having died rather than fledged.

To facilitate direct comparison with the 5×5-m plot data, we calculated Camera 1 reproductive success on the basis of plot area. For this analysis we used Camera 1 data because the topography was similar to that in the 5×5-m plot and because the camera angle was such that we could determine the nesting status of each pair. (Camera 2 was not used in this comparison because a sheer rock wall was present in part of the picture, and the camera angle made it more difficult to see eggs and chicks.) Values from the Camera 1 subplot were scaled to 25 m^2 by multiplying by 6.8 (the subplot area was 3.7 m^2 as measured in 1992). By direct observation and/or back-calculation of hatch dates, we could estimate the number of eggs and chicks on the Camera 1 subplot on any given day, allowing comparison of the phenology and productivity between the 5×5-m plot and the Camera 1 subplot on the same day. Because the Camera 1 subplot was followed throughout the breeding season, we also show fledging status on 10 September, because chicks had begun to fledge, and 18 September, because the last chick fledged on this date.

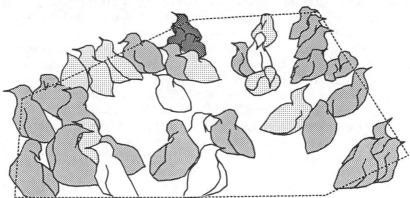

FIGURE 3—Top: A sample frame taken by camera 1, showing the density of breeding murres on the flat top of Light Rock (16 August at 0842 hours). The subplot used for assessments of reproductive success is outlined. Murres in view include breeding birds and some of their mates, as well as single attending murres. Bottom: A composite diagram showing the location of all pairs with eggs or chicks followed through the breeding season within the Camera 1 subplot, where each bird represents one pair. Note that there are postural differences between the sample frame and the diagram. The fate of each egg is indicated by the pattern for the corresponding adult: ☐ eggs that never hatched, ▦ chicks that died, ▨ chicks that fledged, ▧ chicks that presumably fledged, but were not specifically followed. This diagram does not include eggs lost early (N=12).

An independent dataset collected from the time-lapse cameras was used to calculate reproductive success as a function of the number of pairs attending each subplot. For this analysis, data from both cameras were used because we only needed to determine the number of pairs and the number of fledglings. Reproductive success was then calculated as the number of chicks fledged per pair followed.

RESULTS

Attendance

We counted more than 30 000 murres on the cliffs in 1990, 1991, and 1992 (Table 1). In all years, the majority (approximately 70%) of murres on East Amatuli nested on the southeast side of the main island (Figure 2); the second largest concentration (approximately 27%; Table 1) was on Light Rock. The distribution and density of murres in the 1990s appeared similar to those observed in the mid-1970s and early 1980s (P. D. Boersma; Davics personal observation, respectively). Although the number and placement of murre breeding areas was constant during 1990-1992, attendance differed significantly among years. From 1990 to 1991 the number of murres attending the 36 census areas (approximately 65% of the East Amatuli Island population) increased by an estimated 15%. Of the 36 census areas, only 8 had fewer murres in 1991, and there were significantly more areas with higher attendance in 1991 (sign test using normal approximation: $N=33$, $Z_c=3.27$, $P = 0.002$; Figure 4). However, there was no significant difference in attendance in the 36 census areas in 1992 compared with 1991 (sign test using normal approximation: $N = 36$, $Z_c =1.20$, $P>0.2$; Figure 4). Thus, attendance at breeding areas on the island appeared to increase from 1990 to 1991 but did not change from 1991 to 1992.

The 36-area census was made only once in each year. Observed change could therefore reflect a pattern of daily, rather than annual, variability. We made replicate counts of smaller areas (in total approximately 3% of the island's population) to substantiate the census results. Four areas (Oval, Swatch,and Triangle Rock NW and S, respectively; Figure 2) were counted 3 to 10 times within each season. However, counts made after the initiation of fledging were omitted from the analysis, as well as counts made before 1100 h, thereby lowering the final sample sizes. Annual attendance was significantly different among years in Swatch and Triangle Rock S ($F = 5.082$, $P = 0.025$; $F = 11.894$, $P = 0.001$), but not in Oval or Triangle Rock NW ($F = 1.873$, $P = 0.190$; $F = 3.436$, $P = 0.059$; Figure 5). In general, there was a consistent increasing trend from 1990 to 1991, mirroring the 36-area census data (Figure 3). If the yearly averages from each area are summed, cumulative average attendance rises, on average, 13% per year (principally because of the increases seen from 1990 to 1991).

Historical Counts

Historical accounts of the population of common murres nesting in the Barren Islands are available only from the mid- to late 1970s, more than 10 years before the spill. The methods used were only cursorily described (e.g., Bailey 1976; Manuwal 1980). In general, data were gathered during brief visits when observers made single counts or

TABLE 1—Contemporary murre (both common and thick-billed) attendance on East Amatuli Island, Barren Islands, Alaska.

Year	Light Rock	S. Colony	E. Amatuli Mainland	E. Amatuli Island Total	Source
1989	6 912				Nysewander et al. 1993
1990	5 865				Nysewander et al. 1993
		1 165-1 213**		31 041*	This study
1991	5 529				Nysewander et al. 1993
	8 918-9 594	1 988-2 113**	25 468-27 534	34 386-37 128	This study
1992	9 573-9 736	1 471**	24 814-25 444	34 387-35 180	This study

Blank spaces indicate that the census data was not specifically reported for a given location and year.

* Number estimated from a partial count of the island in 1990 (average count = 20 694, see 36 plot counts, Figure 3) and an additional 10 347 murres, estimated by subtracting the 36 plot count in 1992 from the 1992 whole island count (=11 626) and multiplying by the ratio of the 1990:1992 36 plot count (=0.89).

** These numbers represent totals from three separate murre colonies located on the southwest side of the island. While our counts encompass the earlier south colony counts, it is unclear whether our numbers include extra colonies or not.

TABLE 2—Historic estimates of murres (both common and thickbilled) on East Amatuli Island, Barren Islands, Alaska.

Year	Light Rock	S. Colony	E. Amatuli Mainland	E. Amatuli Island Total	Source
1975		600+		60 000	Bailey - Field Notes (a)
		1 000+		61 000	Bailey 1976
1977	10 000+				Manuwal and Boersma 1978
1978	20 000		5 000	25 000	Manuwal 1978
	10 000-30 000		9 000		Simons and Pierce, 1978
1979	20 000+	1 000+		100 000+	Manuwal 1980
				50 000+	Manuwal 1993 (b)

Blank spaces indicate that the census data was not specifically reported for a given location and year.

+ Originally reported as pairs (i.e., half the number presented in this table).

(a) Bailey's field notes (7/11/75), as cited by Nysewander et al., 1992.

(b) Manuwal, D. A. 1993 personal communication to P. D. Boersma: The original 1979 East Amatuli Island estimate was inadvertently doubled in the final report (i.e., Manuwal 1980).

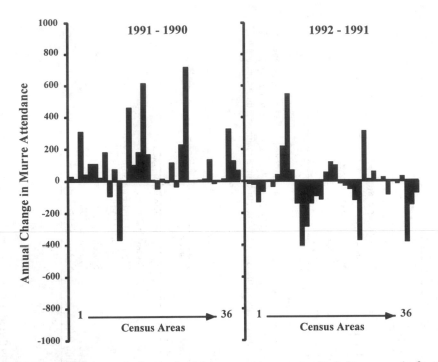

FIGURE 4—Differences between the 36 census area counts of adult murres (refer to Figure 2) during 1991-1990 and 1992-1991, respectively. Each bar represents a single census area from 1 to 36, left to right. Values above the horizontal axis indicate counts were higher in the following year. Values below the horizontal axis indicate counts were higher during the previous year.

crude estimates. For the most part it is unclear whether these counts were of murres flying, rafting, or attending the cliffs, or some combination of all three. Most of the historical data are presented as number of pairs without explicit reference to whether the number is the original estimate or is half of the original estimate (i.e., Harris 1989; but see Erikson, this volume). Murre numbers, sometimes reported in three subcategories—Light Rock, the south colony, and the East Amatuli headland (Figure 2; Table 2)—were estimated over an unknown span of days. Inspection of the historical data showed that the reported population ranged from 19 000 murres to 50 000 pairs. This latter figure was revised down to 25 000 pairs (D. A. Manuwal, personal communication), but not before the original figure (i.e., 100 000 birds) was included in the most recent *Alaska Seabird Catalog* (U.S. Fish and Wildlife Service 1991), the standard seabird population size reference (see also Erikson, this volume).

Because of the problems with the historical count data, we also used photographs of the colony taken in the late 1970s and early 1980s to assess whether the murre population had changed. We were able to match ten historical photographs to ones we took in the 1990s (e.g., Figure 6; Table 3), seven of which were sufficiently clear to allow

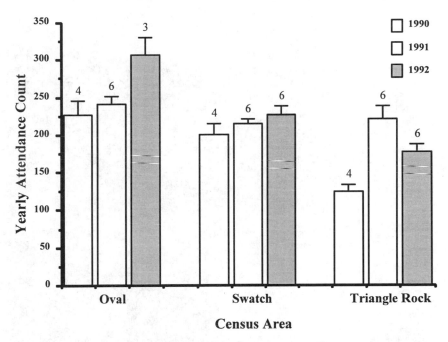

FIGURE 5—Mean and standard error of interannual variation in murre attendance at three sites (Oval, Swatch, and Triangle Rock) where multiple counts were made during each year (1990-1992). Numbers above the bars indicate the sample size. Average annual attendance increased significantly from 1990 to 1991 only at Triangle Rock. From 1991 to 1992 attendance increased significantly at Oval, and decreased significantly at Triangle Rock. Swatch showed only a positive trend in attendance over the three-year sampling interval.

for counting. The photographs represented approximately 5% of current murre attendance on Light Rock and East Amatuli Island. Direct counts of matched photograph pairs indicated that three were not significantly different and four contained significantly more murres in the 1990s photographs than in those from the 1970s and 1980s (Table 3). The circumstances under which the early photographs were taken (e.g., the exact date, time of day) are unknown. Because date and time could influence the number of attending murres, we also compared general ledge-use in all ten matched photograph pairs and assumed that large changes in murre population structure would be visible as abandonment of, or recruitment to, ledges, regardless of daily variation. The number of ledges in each photographic pair varied from 2 to 21. All matched pairs exhibited nearly identical ledge-use patterns (percent similarity ranged from 89-100%; Table 3).

Phenology and Productivity

The general pattern of murre phenology progressed from rafting below the colony early in the breeding period to unstable ledge colonization (during which time flyoffs were repeatedly observed), followed by stable colonization (when flyoffs were not observed).

FIGURE 6—An example of a pair of matched photographs (photographic pair 7) from Light Rock taken during 1976 (top) and 1991 (bottom), used to assess changes in murre attendance and ledge-use between years.

In general, the timing of egg laying, hatching, and fledging is only roughly known because observations began at different times each year (late June in 1990 and early July in 1991, 1992) and because we were limited to observations in our study plot for the time of egg laying and hatching. Therefore, our measures of phenology can only be used as a qualitative assessment of the timing of events. Murre phenology appears to be variable on East Amatuli, perhaps as a result of interannual differences in weather and/or food conditions. In 1990 and 1991 the majority of the murres on the Light Rock plots had settled and laid eggs by the middle of July (Figure 7). However, in 1992 murres continued flyoffs in large numbers throughout July and August, never settling as they normally do during egg laying. Relative to the 1990s, the timing of egg production in both 1977 and 1978 was early (Figure 7). In 1979, eggs were laid later, a pattern similar to that observed in the 1990s (Figure 7).

TABLE 3—Common Murre select subcolony attendance and ledge use.

Photograph Pair	Direct Counts of Individuals				Ledge-Use Patterns			
	Historic (x+SD)	Postspill (x+SD)	t	P	No. of ledges	Present: Absent	Percent Similarity	Comments
1	408+44	409+14	-0.031	0.978	21	21:0	100	
2	289+18	401+9	-7.740	**0.016**	16	16:0	100	
3*	59+3	91+1	-15.765	**0.040**				
4	542+13	539+14	0.223	0.844	19	18:1	95	absent in 1981
5	189+19	253+5	-4.661	**0.043**	17	16:1	94	absent in 1991
6	117+3	133+3	-4.808	**0.041**	2	2:0	100	
7	347+17	365+30	-0.774	0.534	2	2:0	100	
8**					15	14:1	93	absent in 1981
9**					19	17:2	89	absent in 1981
10**					21	21:0	100	

* No ledge data collected because of perspective problems between photographs.
** No direct count data collected because of poor photographic quality of prespill images.
Photograph credits:
1. Walter Reid, EALR, South side, 1981; Arthur Kettle, East Amatuli Light Rock (EALR), 1990.
2. Mike Amaral, EALR, South side, 1976-77; Arthur Kettle, EALR, South side, 1990.
3. Mike Amaral, EALR, South side, 1976-77; Arthur Kettle, EALR, South side, 1990.
4. Curtis Bohlen, EALR, South side, 1981; Arthur Kettle, EALR, South side, 1991.
5. Curtis Bohlen, EALR, South side, 1981; Arthur Kettle, EALR, South side, 1991.
6. Mike Amaral, EALR, upper East side, 1976-77; Arthur Kettle, EALR, upper East side, 1991.
7. Mike Amaral, EALR, upper East side, 1976-77; Arthur Kettle, EALR, upper East side, 1991.
8. Curtis Bohlen, EALR, Southwest side, 1981; Arthur Kettle, EALR, Southwest side, 1991.
9. Curtis Bohlen, EALR, Southwest side, 1981; Arthur Kettle, EALR, Southwest side, 1991.
10. Curtis Bohlen, EALR, Southwest side, 1981; Arthur Kettle, EALR, Southwest side, 1990.

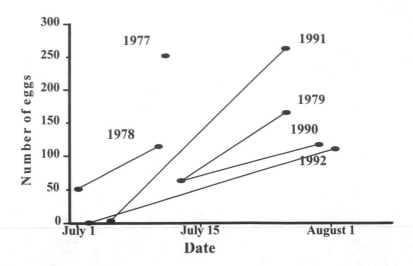

FIGURE 7—The number of Common Murre eggs counted on a 5 × 5-m plot on East Amatuli Light Rock during one (1977) or two visits (all other years). Sequential visits within a single year are connected by a line. During 1991 and 1992 the first egg check was made from outside the plot. Data presented are for visits in which only eggs were observed. These data were used to assess the relative timing of egg laying as well as differences in egg production, interannually.

During 1991, a more exact assessment of the onset of each reproductive stage was made possible by time-lapse photography. Although the camera plots were disturbed when cameras were placed in early July 1991, which may have retarded egg laying to some degree (five eggs were present on the entire area encompassing Camera 1 and Camera 2; Figure 2), they do provide a quantitative assessment of phenology under less-disturbed conditions than in the 5 × 5-m plot. Camera plots were placed within 20 m of each other. Nevertheless, there were striking differences in phenology. In the Camera 1 plot, located on the flat top of East Amatuli Light Rock, the first egg was seen on 5 July, flyoffs stopped on July 6, and the first chick was seen on 10 August. Phenology in the Camera 2 plot (located over the cliff's edge immediately northeast of Camera 1), was distinctly later as well as more difficult to assess: eggs were never seen, flyoffs did not stop until 18 July, and the first chick was seen on 18 August. Differences in laying and hatching translated into the fledging stage. Fledging took place in September over a 27-day period (mean date for Camera 1: 8 September, $SD = 5.5$ days; mean date for Camera 2: 19 September, $SD = 3.8$ days). In Camera 1, the first chick fledged on 30 August, and all chicks had fledged by 18 September. In Camera 2, the first chick did not fledge until 11 September, and all chicks were gone by 25 September. Adults usually left the plot within a day of fledging. In Camera 1, all adults had abandoned the plot by 18 September, and in Camera 2, adults were gone by 27 September.

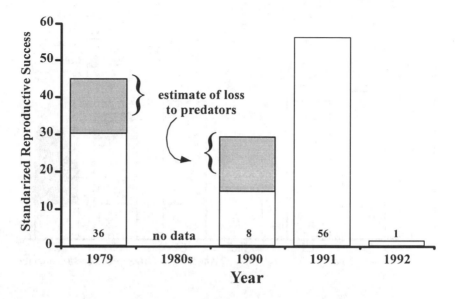

FIGURE 8—A standardized measure of the production of chicks from the 5 × 5-m plot on East Amatuli Light Rock, during the 1979 nesting season and the 1990-1992 nesting seasons. Standardized reproductive success = [(eggs + chicks in August) / (eggs in late July in 1991) × 100]. The number of eggs in 1991 was used as an indirect measure of potential pairs nesting within the 5 × 5-m plot. The combined total of (eggs + chicks) in August was used as an indirect measure of fledging. Numbers above each year indicate the actual count of chicks during the August plot check. Stacked bars above 1979 and 1990 indicate the theoretical maximum increase in production had only one visit (instead of two) been made during the egg laying period. Refer to the text for further explanation of the assumptions inherent in the ratio.

Although chicks were successfully reared in all years, there were marked differences in productivity. Differences in phenology can produce a difference in the number of eggs present on a given calendar date (e.g., Figure 7). However, this pattern may also be the result of absolute differences in egg production from year to year. For instance, phenology was similar among the 1990s; however, there were still differences in the number of eggs laid among years (111 in 1992 to 263 in 1991; Figure 7). This broad range of egg production is partially a result of human disturbance. The first visits to the 5 × 5 – m plot in 1991 and 1992 occurred before the murres had settled or laid eggs, so it was not necessary to enter the plot. In 1979 and 1990, however, both prechick visits to the plot occurred when eggs were present (Figure 7). Visits to the plot during egg laying and chick hatching invariably caused egg and chick loss. The numbers of eggs found on the second visit to the plot in 1979 and 1990 were therefore less than the number that might have been found had the plot not been previously visited during the egg stage. However, even after human disturbance is considered, 1992 was a very poor year.

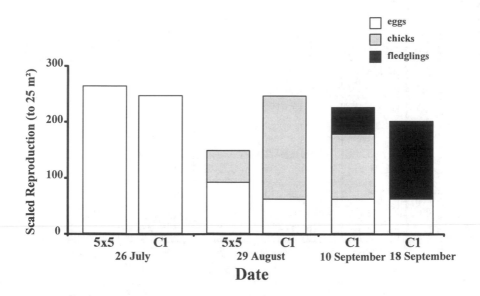

FIGURE 9—A comparison of reproduction from the 5 × 5-m plot and the Camera 1 (C1) subplot (scaled to 25 m²) in 1991. Data from the 5 × 5-m plot were collected by entering the plot. Data from the Camera 1 plot were collected by following chicks to fledging and then back-calculating hatch dates, as well as counting all lost and nonviable eggs. Although the plots appear initially comparable, the 5 × 5-m plot experienced delayed phenology and decreased reproductive output as a result of human-induced disturbance.

Productivity can also be assessed once chicks hatch. Our ratio (standardized reproductive success) suggests 1991 was the most productive year, followed by 1979 and 1990 (Figure 8). Although observations from 1978 are not directly comparable because of differences in the timing of visits, there were 60 eggs and 126 chicks in late August of that year, indicating that 1978 was also a very productive year. By contrast, 1992 was the worst year for which we have production data for the murres on Light Rock (Figure 8). In contrast to other years, in which August production (i.e., eggs + chicks) ranged from 38 to 147, during 1992 only two eggs and one chick were found in the plot. All of these data are compromised by the effects of human disturbance and by the fact that we concluded field observations before all eggs had hatched or chicks fledged. However, in 1991 we were able to use information from the time-lapse cameras to measure production (i.e., eggs, chicks, and fledglings) in the relative absence of human disturbance.

Data from Camera 1 were standardized to 25 m² to groundtruth the 5 × 5-m plot. Of 326 eggs estimated from Camera 1, 25% ($N = 82$) were lost to predators during the early part of the egg laying period. This left 244 eggs, a number similar to the measurement of egg production in the 5 × 5-m plot (263 eggs; Figure 9). By 29 August,

TABLE 4—Estimates of reproductive success from two time-lapse camera plots on Light Rock, East Amatuli Island, in 1991.

	Camera 1	Camera 2
Pairs followed	31	23
Eggs lost early	12	?
Chicks	24	20
Fledglings	20	16
Hatching success (chicks/eggs)	0.77* 0.56**	0.87
Fledging success (fledglings/chicks)	0.83	0.80
Reproductive success (fledglings/pair followed)	0.64* 0.46**	0.70

  * Calculations based on the assumptions that all eggs lost early were relaid.
** Calculations based on the assumption that pairs that lost eggs early abandoned and were replaced by new pairs.

the date of the last visit to the 5×5-m plot, all viable eggs in the Camera 1 subplot had hatched ($N = 183$, 56% of the total); the remaining eggs ($N = 61$, 19%) never hatched. This is in contrast to the 5×5-m plot, in which 44% of the eggs were lost from 26 July to 29 August. Therefore, the 2-3 visits to the 5×5-m plot decreased egg and chick survival and probably extended egg laying as a result of some relaying after early eggs were lost.

    The data from the time-lapse cameras were also used to estimate reproductive success per pair followed (Table 4). For this analysis, data were not standardized to 25 m^2; thus, numbers are lower than in the preceding analysis. It was impossible to tell whether early lost eggs were replaced, pairs abandoned the nest site, or new pairs recruited because all birds were relatively mobile during the early phase of laying as compared with later in the season when eggs had begun to hatch. Therefore, for Camera 1 we calculated reproductive success as a range between the two options (i.e., all relays versus all new pairs). As we were never able to see eggs directly in Camera 2, it is impossible to tell to what degree eggs were lost. Thus, assuming the relay estimate for Camera 1 is the most comparable value to Camera 2, fledglings produced per pair followed in two plots on East Amatuli Light Rock was somewhere between 64-70%.

DISCUSSION

Potential Effects of the Spill

Estimates of murre mortality during the spill, postspill estimates of murre demography and age structure, as well as ideas about natural factors limiting the prespill murre population, can lead to very different interpretations of the effects of the spill. Several studies have stated that the Barren Islands' murre population suffered a dramatic decline in numbers and a continuing depression of reproductive success as a result of the spill (Fry 1993; Nysewander et al. 1993). The explanation for these possible effects is based on the following assumptions. First, colony size, and thus attendance, would obviously decrease if murre mortality were high following the spill. Second, density within the colony might also decrease, increasing the spacing among birds. Alternatively, murres might rearrange themselves so that density would remain constant in some locations, opening up space on ledges formerly filled by murres. Either of these possibilities could have a negative effect on the productivity of the remaining murre population because egg and chick predators could gain access to a formerly better-defended colony (Birkhead 1977; Parrish unpublished data). Third, a major mortality event could change the age structure of the remaining population. Because the spill happened during the beginning of the breeding season, when prebreeders are by and large absent (e.g., Birkhead and Hudson 1977; Hudson 1979), breeders may have been differentially killed (Nysewander et al. 1993). If young murres recruited early, population-wide reproductive success might decline because young breeders and recent recruits are usually less successful than established breeders (Birkhead and Hudson 1977; Hedgren 1980). Thus, the spill could have reduced population size and lowered reproductive success of the remaining population, resulting in long-term damage to the colony.

An alternate scenario is that the spill could have killed large numbers of murres without significantly affecting the size of the breeding colonies within the spill area for several reasons. First, if murres breeding on East Amatuli were space-limited before the spill, a large reservoir of nonbreeders, both young and experienced, could have been present (the "at sea component" of Piatt et al. 1993). In this event, even a large loss of birds as a result of the spill might not have changed the number of murres occupying the breeding colonies, because nonbreeders would have filled the empty space. Second, because the spill happened early in the breeding season, at least three months before the initiation of egg laying, the murres killed may have belonged to a broad geographic distribution of breeding colonies. For example, murres killed in the *Nestucca* oil spill, off the coast of Washington during the winter of 1988, probably came from populations ranging from California to British Columbia (see Ford et al. 1991). Finally, some murres could have left the area as the spill arrived, returning only after the hazard diminished. Regardless of the mechanism, unless single colonies sustained massive losses as a result of this single event, it would be hard to discern any clear effect on subsequent attendance because the yearly variation in breeding colony attendance can be high (Hudson 1985; Hatch and Hatch 1989), and the annual mortality owing to natural factors (storms, starvation) can be high (e.g., North Sea colonies; Dunnet 1982). Piatt et al. (1990)

reported substantial end-of-season seabird mortality in 1989, which they attribute to a natural die-off rather than as a consequence of the spill.

Colony Attendance

Before interpreting changes in population size, any comparison must consider data quality. During the 1970s murre population size on the Barren Islands was estimated from the number of murres flying, rafting, attending nest areas, or some combination, over a wide range of the reproductive cycle, as well as over the day (see Bailey 1976; Manuwal and Boersma 1978; Manuwal 1980). Some estimates were reported as counts of individual murres (e.g., Bailey 1976), while other estimates were reported as pairs (i.e., the estimate was doubled to obtain an estimate of the breeding population, see Erikson, this volume). The early data were not intended as exhaustive innumerations, but rather as general indicators of population size in the late 1970s. Systematic, replicated, direct counts of the number of murres attending distinct colonies, where both diurnal and seasonal variability are controlled, are only available for East Amatuli Island during the 1990s. Nonetheless, several studies have based claims of significant mortality on a direct, even statistical, comparison of current census data with the historical figures (Piatt et al.1990; Fry 1993; Nysewander et al. 1993).

Previous studies on murre colony attendance have reported that census accuracy is affected by diurnal patterns in attendance, seasonal patterns in attendance, difference among counters, and the daily variation inherent in individual murre attendance (i.e., biological noise; Wanless et al. 1982; Hatch and Hatch 1989; Harris 1989). Our data address the first three sources of variance; however, we were only able to perform a single yearly census of the island. Although this may limit our ability to detect normal yearly variation, if large-magnitude changes in attendance occurred following the spill, we should have been able to detect them. If we compare our 1990 whole-island census total to the highest historical figure (i.e., 61 000 birds in 1975, Bailey 1976; Table 1), our data indicate that the population could have decreased by 51%. If we use the lowest presumed attendance count (19 000 birds in 1978; Simons and Pierce 1978; Table 2), the population may have increased by 39%. This is a range of change in attendance of 90% (-51% to +39%). The prespill information available is not good enough to detect either the amount or the direction of change in the murre population.

Even when making general comparisons about colony attendance with these data, several caveats should be observed. First, the only available historic estimates were made over a decade before the spill. Second, it is not clear which of these, if any, are based on attendance (as opposed to including flying and rafting birds). Without these pieces of information, one must assume that the murre population on East Amatuli was somewhere between 19 000 and 61 000 birds in the late 1970s (Table 2). Assignment of a discrete percentage decline in murre attendance in the Barren Islands pre- to postspill (e.g., "62% lower in 1989 than in 1979"; Piatt et al. 1990) was apparently made without reference to these issues. If the reported attendance decline from 1979 to 1989 was the result of oil-related mortality and the current East Amatuli population is really 50% lower than it was in the late 1970s (i.e., Piatt et al. 1990), we would expect to see evidence of this reduction tin the photographic comparison. However, the photograph analyses show no decline in the number of murres attending the ledges and little difference in ledge-use. Unfortunately extreme variation in dated prespill population estimates, and nonreplicated censuses in all years, preclude the use of the comparative approach in reaching any conclusion about the magnitude or significance of the spill effect on the East Amatuli murre population.

However, this does not mean that the spill did not have an effect on the population. There is postspill evidence that the East Amatuli murre population declined immediately following the spill. Taken cumulatively, murre attendance on the four multiple count areas (Oval, Swatch, Triangle Rock NW and S, respectively) rose over 25% from 1990 to 1991 (Table 5). Although not statistically comparable, our single yearly whole-island census follows the same increasing trend. Because our study began in 1990, it is unknown how large this increase might have been from 1989 to 1990. Murre populations in other parts of the world that have not experienced major perturbations show annual changes of -6% to +8%, on average (Table 5). Murre populations that have undergone dramatic declines in attendance those observed at East Amatuli. After the severe ENSO of 1983 on the Farallon Islands, (with a concomitant crash in murre attendance of 72%), recovery proceeded at 24% per year through 1985 (Sydeman 1993). Similarly, on the Semidi Islands the murre population declined for unstated reasons during 1977-1978 but then increased again, at a top rate of 25% from 1980 to 1981 (Hatch and Hatch 1989). We conclude that the large increase in murre attendance from 1990 to 1991 suggests that the murres were responding to a prior perturbation similar in scale to the 1983-1984 ENSO event.

The large annual increase in attendance from 1990 to 1991, could have come from three sources. Following the spill, the remaining East Amatuli prespill population may have been supplemented by immigration from outside populations. This increase may also have resulted from higher recruitment of first-time breeders, able to colonize vacant ledge space successfully. Finally, established breeders that left the area as a result of the spill may be returning after an absence of one or more years. Neither Sydeman (1993) nor Hatch and Hatch (1989) credit immigration or young recruits to account for the dramatic population increases they observed (Table 5), even though the populations took several years to recover, implying that established breeders can leave the colony for more than one sequential season and still return to breed.

Phenology and Reproduction

It has been suggested that the Barren Islands' murre population has undergone a change in phenology, a loss of egg-laying synchrony, and a widespread breeding failure as a result of the spill (Fry 1993; Nysewander et al. 1993). Fry (1993) stated that because older, mature birds were killed by the spill, younger, inexperienced birds are now breeding. Because the younger murres are poorly synchronized, they are breeding abnormally. This reasoning is based on evidence of earlier breeding at Middleton Island and the Semidi Islands, relative to breeding on the Barren Islands (Nysewander et al. 1993). There is no reason to expect that different sites should have the same phenology. Petersen (1986) shows that breeding in the 1970s at both Middleton and the Semidis occurred earlier than the Barren Islands. Moreover, we found differences in phenology for areas separated by 20 m (e.g., Camera 1 and 2 in 1991). We contend that the only reasonable comparison that can be used to elucidate spill effects is within site, among

TABLE 5—Annual change in Common Murre attendance at select colonies.

Location*	Year	Sample Size	Attendance	% change from previous year	Citation
East Amatuli	1990	2-5	648		This study
Barren Islands (4)	1991	5-6	811	25	
	1992	6-10	818	1	
Shubrick Point	1973-83	>>5**		8	Sydeman 1993
SE Farallon Island (1)	1983-85	>>5		24	
Semidi Islands (6)	1977	43	1 580		Hatch and Hatch 1989
	1978	9	1 380	-14	
	1979	43	1 250	-10	
	1980	43	1 300	4	
	1981	43	1 620	25	
Skomer Island (3)	1973	>120**	938		Birkhead 1978
	1974	>120	935	0	
	1975	>120	879	-6	

* Value in ( ) is the number of census areas, usually delineated by landscape features and counted remotely with the aid of binoculars and/or a spotting scope.

** Sample size was not explicitly stated in these references but was referred to indirectly as daily counts over the nesting season.

years. With the exception of 1992, our data from East Amatuli indicate that, at least on Light Rock, there were not dramatic changes in murre phenology and productivity between the 1970s and the 1990s. Although the 5 × 5-m plot is located in a dense, presumably optimal, breeding location, we assumed that massive mortality leading to changes in age structure and ensuing reproductive failures in the years following the spill (i.e., Fry 1993, Heineman 1993) would have been observable, even if muted in degree.

Reproductive success, however, is comparable among colonies. Murre reproductive success, measured as chicks fledged/pair, ranges from lower values in the north Pacific (e.g., 0.24-0.29 Ugaiushak Island: Wehle 1978; 0.34-0.46 Semidi Islands: Hatch and Hatch 1989) to high values in the North Atlantic (e.g., 0.72-0.79 Skomer: Hatchwell and Birkhead 1991; 0.77-0.82 Stora Karlso, Hedgren 1980). California colonies, exemplified by the Farallon Islands, have even higher annual reproductive success (average = 0.95 Farallons, Boekelheide et al. 1990) except in ENSO years, when massive breeding failures may occur (0.15 in 1983). Our time-lapse camera study in 1991 produced reproductive success values (0.64-0.70) comparable to the North Atlantic, well above other Alaskan colonies, and in sharp contrast to other estimates of Barren Islands murre reproductive success (i.e., 0.13 chicks per adult during early chick rearing for Nord Island, Nysewander et al., 1993). Although we were not able to follow every bird within the limits of our camera plots, it is unlikely that this differentially skewed our results, as pairs were followed based on their visibility to the cameras, a variable not likely to be correlated with eventual reproductive success. Our reproductive success calculations from Camera 2 may be somewhat inflated because we could not see eggs.

Both phenology and reproductive success appear to vary across small spatial scales (i.e., 0-20 m), thus our data may not represent average annual success of the murre population on East Amatuli, or the Barren Islands taken as a whole. However, they do contradict claims of continuing poor reproductive performance by murres on the Barren Islands (Fry 1993; Nysewander et al. 1993). We have no reason to believe that murres on East Amatuli Island would fail everywhere but in the 5 × 5-m plot, (and the time-lapse plots in 1991). Chicks fledged in this plot in spite of repeated disturbances that decreased reproductive success (Figure 9). Frequent disturbance is known to cause reproductive failure in Common Murres (Wehle 1978; J. K. Parrish in press). Moreover, because reproductive success is only available from the 5 × 5-m plot before the spill, this is the only location that can be used to make reasonable comparisons.

Postspill reproductive success data from other plots in the Barren Islands indicate that the murres experienced depressed reproduction and/or a total breeding failure in the years following the spill (Nysewander et al. 1993). Although it is entirely possible that reproductive success fluctuates within a single colony (e.g., Camera 1 versus Camera 2), the dramatic differences in reproductive success between this study and ours suggests that other factors may have been operating. The most obvious difference is methods. Nysewander et al. (1993) made single-visit estimates at Nord Island (reproductive success in 1991: 0.13). At Puale Bay, where murre reproductive activity was assessed every three-four days, fledging success in 1991 was listed as 0.38 fledglings per adult (Nysewander et al. 1993). Because of the difficulty of clearly identifying the presence of eggs and chicks in our time-lapse camera study (of which there were 33 000 frames), we believe the Nysewander et al. (1993) data may have been negatively biased as a consequence of site-visit limitation. Nysewander and Byrd (1993) state that the reproductive success of the murre colonies in the spill path began to return to normal in 1992. In contrast, our findings indicate that 1992 was a year of unusually low egg production followed by low chick production (Figures 7 and 8). Again, this discrepancy may be due to differences in methods, as well as the inherent differences in the breeding population between East Amatuli Light Rock (studied here) and other spill-path colonies. Murres are extremely sensitive to localized oceanographic fluctuations and the resulting changes in prey availability (Boekelheide et al. 1990). Because of this sensitivity, population size, growth rate, and reproductive success can differ among colonies on the same island (e.g., Sydeman 1993).

Environmental Variability

During the 1980s the Pacific experienced two ENSO events, one of which (1983) was the strongest recorded in the last 100 years (Barber and Chavez 1983). This particular event has been correlated with reductions in survival, attendance, and reproductive success in murre colonies in the Farallon Islands (Boekelheide et al. 1990; Sydeman 1993), in Oregon (Hodder and Graybill 1985), and along the coast of Washington (Wilson 1991).

Wilson (1991) found that the sudden drop in murre attendance at breeding colonies located along the Olympic peninsula has persisted at least through 1990. There is no reason to believe the Barren Islands were immune to such effects.

On a more local level, the Gulf of Alaska has experienced a warming trend in water temperature that started in the mid-1970s and lasted through the 1980s (Royer 1989). Increases in sea-surface temperature are generally associated with decreases in primary production, and therefore, in the food of seabirds. Although data are not available for the murres, information on Fork-Tailed Storm Petrels nesting on East Amatuli Island indicate that colony attendance and chick growth rates have decreased from the 1970s to the 1990s so that the earlier data are no longer representative of the current population size or reproductive activity (P. D. Boersma unpublished data). Furthermore, Steller's Sea Lion, *Eumetopias jubatus*, populations in the north Gulf of Alaska, including nearby Sugarloaf Island, have declined since the mid-1970s by nearly an order of magnitude (Hoover 1988; Merrick et al. 1987; Merrick et al. 1992).

Given that the marine environment is a dynamic system, and that the Gulf of Alaska experiences oceanographic and atmospheric fluctuations (particularly during the 1980s), we would expect the Barren Islands murre population to reflect these changes rather than remain stable. Thus, changes in attendance, phenology, and reproductive success should be the normal situation rather than the exception (see also Boekelheide et al. 1990; Furness and Barrett 1991). Claims that population size and breeding parameters, especially phenology and reproductive success, have changed must therefore be made with reference to a range of measurements, taken both before and after the event in question, rather than on the basis of single values, especially when those values are only coarse estimates. Unless a long-term dataset is available, it is extremely difficult to determine the true limits of the range of natural variability (Hunt 1987; see also Wiens, this volume).

CONCLUSIONS

The *Exxon Valdez* oil spill was responsible for the largest recorded seabird mortality resulting from an oil spill (31 000 carcasses collected) and, as such, should not be minimized. However, with reference to the Barren Islands, the lack of data from the 1980s, the ENSO events in the 1980s, and the fact that prespill surveys were crude at best, preclude our ability to detect a definitive effect, let alone assign a magnitude to it. Only our postspill attendance data suggests that a recovery may be taking place, and these data do not address whether these birds are returning breeders, young breeders, or immigrants from other Alaskan populations. Phenology and reproductive success is highly variable across all years for which we have data. There does not appear to be a clear pre- to postspill pattern. We can only conclude that claims of population decimation, disruptions in phenology, and a lowering of reproductive success in the Barren Islands murre population as a consequence of the spill are not scientifically supportable.

ACKNOWLEDGMENTS

Sonia deBary, Margie Blanding, Katie O'Reilly, Randy Mullen, David Socha, Carolyn Socha, Erica Acuña, Carin Chase, Emily Davies, and Mary Riley helped with field work. Jim Carroll of ICOM American provided us with side band communication equipment for the 1992 season. The research was funded under a contract with Exxon Company, U.S.A. (1990-1991) and by the Mineral Management Service contract 14-35-001-30670 (1992), and was allowed by United States Department of the Interior Fish and Wildlife Service Alaska Maritime National Wildlife Refuge Special Use Permit 50863 and 50890. The Maritime Refuge and Maritime Helicopter provided logistical support. We thank John Piatt, R.T. Paine, John Wiens, David Stokes, and Patti Char for improving the manuscript.

REFERENCES

Bailey, E. P. 1976. "Breeding Bird Distribution and Abundance in the Barren Islands, Alaska." *Murrelet*. 57: 2-12.

Bailey, E. P. 1989. "Beached Bird Survey of the Barren Islands, April 6 - June 6 1989." U.S. Fish and Wildlife Service; Homer, AK; administrative report (unpublished).

Bailey, E. P. and C. H. Davenport. 1972. "Dieoff of Common Murres on the Alaska Peninsula and Unimak Island." *Condor*. 74: 213-219.

Barber, R. T. and F. P. Chavez. 1983. "Biological Consequences of El Niño." *Science*. 222: 1203-1210.

Birkhead, T. R. 1977. "The Effect of Habitat and Density on Breeding Success in the Common Guillemot (*Uria aalge*)." *Journal of Animal Ecology*. 46:751-764.

Birkhead, T. R. 1978. "Attendance patterns of guillemots *Uria aalge* at breeding colonies on Skomer Island." *Ibis*. 120:219-229.

Birkhead, T. R. and P. J. Hudson. 1977. "Population Parameters for the Common Guillemot (*Uria aalge*)." *Ornis Scandinavica*. 11: 142-145.

Blackburn, J. E., K. Anderson, C. Hamilton, and S. Starr. 1983. "Pelagic and Demersal Fish Assessment in the Lower Cook Inlet Estuary System." *Outer Continental Shelf Environmental Assessment Program Final Report 17*. U.S. Department of Commerce, National Oceanic and Atmospheric Administration, 107-382.

Boekelheide, R. J., D. G. Ainley, S. H. Morrell, H. R. Huber, and T. J. Lewis. 1990. "Common Murre." *in: Seabirds of the Farallon Islands*. D. G. Ainley and R. J. Boekelheide (eds.); Stanford, CA: Stanford University Press; 245-275.

Boersma, P. D., N. T. Wheelwright, M. K. Nerini, and E. S. Wheelwright. 1980. "The Breeding Biology of the Fork-Tailed Storm-Petrel (*Oceanodroma furcata*)." *Auk*. 97: 268-282.

Campbell, B. and E. Lack. 1985. *A Dictionary of Birds.* Staffordshire, England: T. & A. D. Poyser, Ltd.

Dunn, E. K. 1973. "Changes in Fishing Ability of Terns Associated wtih Windspeed and Sea Surface Conditions." *Nature.* 244: 520-521.

Dunn, E. K. 1975. "The Role of Environmental Factors in the Growth of Tern Chicks." *Journal of Animal Ecology.* 44: 743-754.

Dunnett, G. M. 1982. "Oil Pollution and Seabird Populations." *Philosophical Transactions of the Royal Society of London.* 297: 413-427.

Ebbesmeyer, C. C., D. R. Cayan, D. R. McLaine, F. H. Nichols, D. II. Peterson, and K. T. Redmong. 1991. "1976 Step in the Pacific Climate: Forty Environmental Changes Between 1968-1975 and 1977-1984." *Proceedings: Seventh Annual Pacific Climate (PACLIM) Workshop, Asilomar, CA, 1990.* California Department of Water Resources, Sacramento, CA, Technical Report 26: 115-126.

Erikson, D. 1977. "Distribution, Abundance, Migration and Breeding Locations of Marine Birds, Lower Cook Inlet, Alaska." Alaska Department of Fish and Game; Anchorage, AK; administrative report (unpublished).

Ford, R. G., Wiens, J. A., Heineman, D. & Hunt, G. L. 1982. "Modelling the Sensitivity of Colonially Breeding Marine Birds to Oil Spills: Guillemot and Kittiwake Populations on the Pribilof Islands, Bering Sea." *Journal Applied Ecology.* 19: 1-31

Ford, R. G., M. L. Bonnell, D. H. Varoujean, G. W. Page, B. E. Sharp, D. Heinemann, and J. L. Casey. 1990. *Assessment of Direct Seabird Mortality in Prince William Sound and the Western Gulf of Alaska Resulting from the* Exxon Valdez *Oil Spill.* Final Report. Portland, OR: Ecological Consulting, Inc. (unpublished).

Ford, R. G., D. H. Varoujean, D. R. Warrick, W. A. Williams, D. B. Lewis, C. L. Hewitt, and J. L. Casey. 1991. "Seabird Mortality Resulting from the *Nestucca* Spill Incident, Winter 1988-89." Final Report to Washington Department of Wildlife (unpublished).

Ford, R. G. and J. F. Piatt. 1993. "Assessment of Seabird Mortality from the *Exxon Valdez* Oil Spill." Exxon Valdez *Symposium/Pacific Seabird Group Abstracts.* Seattle WA.; 25.

Fry, D. M. 1993. "How do You Fix the Loss of Half a Million Birds?" Exxon Valdez *Oil Spill Symposium Abstracts.* Anchorage, AK; 30-33.

Furness, R. W. and R. T. Barrett. 1991. "Seabirds and Fish Declines." *National Geographic Research and Exploration.* 7: 82-95.

Furness, R. W. and P. Monaghan. 1987. *Seabird Ecology.* New York: Blackie and Son, Ltd.

Galt, G. A. and D. L. Payton. 1990. "Movement of Oil Spilled from the *Exxon Valdez.*" *Proceedings Marine Mammal Conference, Anchorage, AK.* U.S. Fish and Wildlife Service, National Fish and Wildlife Foundation. 15 pp.

Gould, P. J., D. J. Forsell, and C. J. Lensink. 1982. "Pelagic Distribution and Abundance of Seabirds in the Gulf of Alaska and Eastern Bering Sea." U.S. Department of the Interior, Fish and Wildlife Service Biological Services Program, Fish and Wildlife Service, Office of Biological Services, 82/48: 1-294.

Harris, M. P. 1989. "Variation in the Correction Factor Used for Converting Counts of Individual Guillemots *Uria aalge* into Breeding Pairs." *Ibis.* 131: 85-93.

Harris, M. P. and T. R. Birkhead. 1985. "Breeding Ecology of the Atlantic Alcidae." *in: The Atlantic Alcidae.* D. N. Nettleship and T. R. Birkhead (eds.); New York: Academic Press; 164-171.

Hatch, S. A. 1987. "Did the 1982-1983 El Niño-Southern Oscillation Affect Seabirds in Alaska?" *Wilson Bulletin.* 99: 468-474.

Hatch, S. A. and M. Hatch. 1989. "Attendance Patterns of Murres at Breeding Sites: Implications for Monitoring." *Journal of Wildlife Management.* 53: 483-493.

Hatchwell, B. J. 1991. "An Experimental Study of the Effect of Timing of Breeding on the Reproductive Success of Common Guillemots (*Uria aalge*)." *Journal of Animal Ecology.* 60: 721-736.

Hatchwell, B. J. and T. R. Birkhead. 1991. "Population Dynamics of Common Guillemots (*Uria aalge*) on Skomer Island, Wales." *Ornis Scandinavica.* 22: 55-59.

Hedgren, S. 1980. "Reproductive Success of Guillemots *Uria aalge* on the Island of Stora Karlso." *Ornis Fennica.* 57: 49-57.

Hedgren, S. and A. Linnman. 1979. "Growth of Guillemot *Uria aalge* Chicks in Relation to Time of Hatching." *Ornis Scandinavica.* 10: 29-36.

Heinemann, D. 1993. "How Long to Recovery for Murre Populations and Will Some Colonies Fail to Make the Comeback?" Exxon Valdez *Oil Spill Symposium Abstracts,* Anchorage, AK; 139-141.

Hodder, J. and M. R. Graybill. 1985. "Reproduction and Survival of Seabirds in Oregon During the 1982-1983 El Niño." *Condor.* 87: 535-541.

Hollowed, A. B. and W. S. Wooster. 1991. "Variability of Winter Ocean Conditions and Strong Year Classes of Northeast Pacific Groundfish." *ICES 1991/Variability Symposium.* Paper No. 33, Session 3.

Hoover, A. A. 1988. "Steller Sea Lion." *in: Selected Marine Mammals of Alaska: Species Accounts with Research and Management Recommendations.* J. W. Lentfer (ed.); Washington, DC: Marine Mammal Commission; 159-193.

Hudson, P. J. 1979. *The Behaviour and Survival of Auks.* Ph.D. thesis, University of Oxford; 110 pp.

Hudson, P. J. 1985. "Population Parameters for the Atlantic Alcidae." *in: The Atlantic Alcidae.* D. N. Nettleship and T. R. Birkhead, (eds.); New York: Academic Press; 233-261.

Hunt, G. L. 1987. "Offshore Oil Development and Seabirds: The Present Status of Knowledge and Long-Term Research Needs." *in: Long-Term Environmental Effects of Offshore Oil and Gas Development.* New York: Elsevier; 539-586.

Kerr, R. A. 1992. "Unmasking a Shifty Climate System." *Science.* 255: 1508-1510.

Lack, D. 1968. *Ecological Adaptations for Breeding in Birds.* London: Methuen.

Manuwal, D. A. 1978. *Dynamics of Marine Bird Populations on the Barren Islands, Alaska.* U.S. Fish and Wildlife Service Coastal Marine Project Annual Report; (Unpublished); Anchorage, AK; 92 pp.

Manuwal, D. A. 1980. "Breeding Biology of Seabirds on the Barren Islands, AK. 1976-1979." Final report, U.S. Fish and Wildlife Service, Anchorage, AK; 195 pp.

Manuwal, D. A. and P. D. Boersma. 1978. "Dynamics of Marine Bird Populations on the Barren Islands, AK." *Environmental Assessment of the Alaskan Continental Shelf, Annual Report National Oceanic and Atmospheric Administration.* Environmental Research Laboratory. 4: 294-420.

Massey, B. W., D. W. Bradley, and J. L. Atwood. 1992. "Demography of a California Least Tern Colony Including Effects of the 1982-1983 El Niño." *Condor.* 94: 976-983.

Merrick, R. L., T. R. Loughlin, and D. G. Calkins. 1987. "Decline in Abundance of the Northern Sea Lion, *Eumetopias jubatus*, in Alaska 1956-86." *U.S. Fishery Bulletin.* 85: 351-365.

Merrick, R. L., Calkins, D. G., and McAllister, D. C. 1992. "Aerial and Ship Based Surveys of Steller Sea Lions (*Eumetopias jubatus*) in Southeast Alaska, the Gulf of Alaska and Aleutian Islands During June and July 1991." U.S. Department of Commerce *National Oceanic and Atmospheric Administration Technical Memo. NMFS* AFSC-1: 41 pp.

Monastersky, R. 1992. "Do Antarctic Seals Feel El Niño?" *Science News.* 142: 382.

National Oceanographic and Atmospheric Administration (NOAA) and Alaska Department of Environmental Conservation (ADEC). 1989. "Daily Reports—*Exxon Valdez* Oil Spill. Overflight Data and Summaries." Unpublished.

Nysewander, D. R., Dippel, C. H., Byrd, G. V., & Knudtson, E. P. 1992. "Effects of the T/V *Exxon Valdez* Oil Spill on Murres: A Perspective from Observations at Breeding Colonies." *Bird Study Number 3. Draft Final Report.* U. S. Fish and Wildlife Service, Alaska National Wildlife Maritime Refuge.

Nysewander, D. R. and G. V. Byrd. 1993. "Effects of the *Exxon Valdez* Oil Spill on Murres: A Perspective from Observations at Breeding Colonies." Exxon Valdez *Symposium, Pacific Seabird Group Abstracts.* Seattle, WA; 29.

Nysewander, D. R., C. Dippel, G. V. Byrd, and E. P. Knudtson. 1993. "Effects of the T/V *Exxon Valdez* Oil Spill on Murres: A Perspective from Observations at Breeding Colonies." Exxon Valdez *Oil Spill Symposium Abstracts*, Anchorage, AK; 135-138.

Petersen, M. R. 1986. "Murres (*Uria* spp.)." *in: The Breeding Biology and Feeding Ecology of Marine Birds in the Gulf of Alaska.* P. A. Baird and P. J. Gould (eds.). Final

Reports of Principal Investigators. Outer Continental Shelf Environmental Assessment Program 45: 388-399.

Piatt, J. F., W. Lensink, W. Butler, M. Kenzoirek, and D. Nysewander. 1990. "Immediate Impact of the *Exxon Valdez* Oil Spill on Marine Birds." *The Auk.* 107: 387-397.

Piatt, J. F., Gould, P., & Sowls, A. L. 1993. "Estimating Seabird Populations in Alaska from Colony and Pelagic Databases." *Pacific Seabird Group Bulletin.* 20(1): 59.

Royer, T. C. 1989. "Upper Ocean Temperature Variability in the Northeast Pacific Ocean: Is It an Indicator of Global Warming?" *Journal of Geophysical Research.* 94: 18,175-18,183.

Royer, T. C., J. A. Vermersch, H. J. Niebauer, and R. D. Muench. 1990. "Ocean Circulation Influencing the *Exxon Valdez* Oil Spill." *Oceanography.* 3: 3-10.

Sanger, G. A. and J. King. 1979. "Oil Spill Vulnerability Index for Marine Oriented Birds." *in: Conservation of Marine Birds of Northern North America.* J. C. Bartonek and D. N. Nettleship (eds.); Washington, DC: U.S. Fish and Wildlife Service.

Sharp. B. E. 1993. "Survival of Seabirds After Oiling, Cleaning and Release." Exxon Valdez *Symposium/Pacific Seabird Group Abstracts;* Seattle, WA; 26.

Simons, T. and J. Pierce. 1978. "Alaska Seabird Colony Status Record." U.S. Fish and Wildlife Service, unpublished report.

Sowls, A., S. A. Hatch, and C. J. Lensink. 1978. *Catalog of Alaskan Seabird Colonies.* U.S. Fish and Wildlife Service, Office of Biological Services.

Springer, A. M., D. S. L. Roseneau, C. P. McRoy, and E. C. Murphy. 1986. "Seabird Responses to Fluctuating Prey Availability in the Eastern Bering Sea." *Marine Ecology Progress Series.* 32: 1-12.

Strauch , J. G., Jr., E. G. Wolf, and K. W. Fucik. 1979. "Biological Populations and Ecological Systems." *Environmental Assessment of the Alaskan Continental Shelf: Lower Cook Inlet Interim Synthesis Report.* U.S. Government Printing Office, 1979-681-348, Region 8: 105-196.

Sydeman, W. J. 1993. "Survivorship of Common Murres on Southeast Farallon Island, California." *Ornis Scandinavica.* 24: 135-141.

Tuck, L. M. 1960. "The Murres: Their Distribution, Populations and Biology, A Study of the Genus Uria." *Canadian Wildlife Service Monograph Series.* 1-266.

U.S. Fish and Wildlife Service. 1991. *Catalog of Alaskan Seabird Colonies,* Computer Archives. Anchorage, AK.

Wanless, S., D. D. French, M. P. Harris, and D. R. Langslow. 1982. "Detection of Annual Change in the Numbers of Cliff-Nesting Seabirds in Orkney 1976-1980." *Journal of Animal Ecology.* 51: 785-795.

Wehle, D. H. S. 1978. "Studies of Marine Birds on Ugaiushak Island, Alaska." *Environmental Assessment of the Alaskan Continental Shelf, Annual Reports of Principal Investigators.* 3:208-312.

Wilson, U. W. 1991. "Responses of Three Seabird Species to El Niño Events and Other Warm Episodes on the Washington Coast 1979-1990." *Condor.* 93: 853-858.

Yan, X.-H., C.-R. Ho, Q. Zheng, and V. Klemas. 1992. "Temperature and Size Variabilities of the Western Pacific Warm Pool." *Science.* 258: 1643-1645.

Zar, J. H. 1974. *Biostatistical Analysis.* Englewood Cliffs, NJ: Prentice Hall.

John A. Wiens[1]

RECOVERY OF SEABIRDS FOLLOWING THE EXXON VALDEZ OIL SPILL:
AN OVERVIEW

REFERENCE: Wiens, J. A., "Recovery of Seabirds Following the Exxon
Valdez Oil Spill: An Overview," *Exxon Valdez Oil Spill: Fate and Effects in
Alaskan Waters, ASTM STP 1219,* Peter G. Wells, James N. Butler, and Jane
S. Hughes, Eds., American Society for Testing and Materials, Philadelphia,
1995.

ABSTRACT: Assessing oil-spill effects requires rigorous definitions of "impact" and
"recovery." Impact is defined as a statistically significant difference between samples
exposed to oil and reference samples. Recovery is then the disappearance through time of
such a statistical difference. Both impact and recovery must be assessed in relation to the
background of natural variation that characterizes marine environments. There are three
primary avenues of potential spill impacts on seabirds: on population size and structure,
on reproduction, and on habitat occupancy and use. Detecting oil-spill effects involves
comparisons of (1) observations taken following the spill with prespill data; (2) data
gathered following the spill from oiled areas ("treatments") and unoiled areas ("controls")
surveyed at the same time; or (3) measurements taken from sites along a gradient of oiling
magnitude. The strengths and weaknesses of these approaches are discussed. In many
situations, the third approach may be most useful.

Following the *Exxon Valdez* oil spill in March 1989, over 35 000 dead birds were
retrieved. Model analyses suggested that actual seabird mortality could have been in the
hundreds of thousands, prompting concerns about severe and persistent impacts on
populations of several species, especially murres (*Uria* spp.). Recovery for some
populations was projected to take decades. The findings of several studies conducted
following the oil spill, however, indicate that these concerns may not be justified. These
studies examined colony attendance and reproduction of murres as well as habitat
utilization for the prevalent species in Prince William Sound and along the Kenai
Peninsula. Surveys of attendance by birds at murre breeding colonies in 1991 indicated no
overall differences from prespill attendance levels when colonies were grouped by the
degree of oiling in the vicinity. At a large colony in the Barren Islands, where damage was
described as especially severe, counts of murres were generally similar to historical
estimates made in the late 1970s. In 1990 and 1991, murres breeding at the Barren

---

[1]Professor of Ecology, Department of Biology, Colorado State University, Fort Collins, Colorado 80523.

Islands colony also produced young at levels that were within the range of natural (prespill) variation for this site. Incidental observations indicated that several other species reproduced successfully in oiled areas in Prince William Sound and along the Kenai Peninsula following the spill.

Investigations of habitat occupancy indicated that the majority of species analyzed showed no initial oiling impacts on their use of habitats. Of the species that did exhibit initial oiling impacts, many had apparently recovered by late 1991, when the study ended. In Prince William Sound, there were no consistent differences in ecological or life-history attributes between the species that suffered impacts and those that did not. Although most of the species that did not show clear evidence of recovery in habitat use by the end of this study were wintering and resident forms, other ecologically similar species were not affected or recovered rapidly. Consequently, the prognosis for recovery of the species that continued to show evidence of oiling impacts on habitat use in late 1991 would seem to be good.

Overall, these studies indicate that recovery in use of habitats by many seabird species, and in colony attendance and reproduction by murres, appeared to be well advanced by late 1991.

KEYWORDS: Seabirds, oil spill, *Exxon Valdez*, impact, recovery, natural variation

---

INTRODUCTION

Birds are a major feature of marine environments. They are abundant, widespread, and conspicuous. Because of their numbers and their relatively high position in food chains, they can be an important component of energy flow in marine ecosystems (Wiens and Scott 1975; Furness 1978); at times they may compete with commercial fisheries for fish stocks (e.g., Furness 1982; Jones and DeGange 1988).

Seabirds live at the air-water or land-water interface, where floating oil accumulates. They are, therefore, extremely sensitive to oil pollution (Hartung 1967; Holmes and Cronshaw 1977; Dunnet 1982; Clark 1984; Leighton, Butler, and Peakall 1985; Hunt 1987). Certainly, oiled birds on beaches constitute one of the most visible and evocative signs of the release of oil into the environment. Counts of these beached birds form the basis of most estimates of avian mortality associated with spills. For example, nearly 8 000 dead birds were retrieved following the *Torrey Canyon* spill (Bourne 1967), and roughly 4500 were found after the *Amoco Cadiz* spill (Conan 1982). Only a fraction of the birds killed by a spill may be found on beaches, however (Tanis and Mörzer Bruyns 1968; Hunt 1987; Ford, Page, and Carter 1987; Page, Carter, and Ford 1990). Coarse estimates of the actual mortality for the *Torrey Canyon* spill ranged from 30,000 to 100,000 birds (Bourne 1967), while perhaps 15,000 to 20,000 birds died from the *Amoco Cadiz* spill (Conan 1982). Other spills or discharges of oil in the North Sea and Baltic Sea have resulted in estimated losses of 30 000 to 50 000 birds (Mead and Baillie 1981; Clausager 1983).

Seabirds were among the most conspicuous victims of the *Exxon Valdez* oil spill. Thousands of oiled birds were recovered from beaches and nearshore waters, and estimates of overall bird mortality from the spill ran into the hundreds of thousands (Piatt et al. 1990; Ford et al. 1991; Fry 1993; Piatt 1993). It has been claimed that the spill took an "unprecedented toll" on marine birds (Piatt and Lensink 1989) and that recovery of some populations might take several decades (Piatt et al. 1990; Temple 1990; Heinemann 1993; Piatt 1993). In fact, the studies described in this volume show that many bird species exhibited no detectable spill-related impacts, while many of the species initially affected appeared to recover relatively rapidly. This paper provides a context for evaluating the effects of the *Exxon Valdez* oil spill on marine-oriented birds.

INITIAL PROJECTIONS OF THE EFFECTS OF THE *EXXON VALDEZ* SPILL

The *Exxon Valdez* ran aground on Bligh Reef on 24 March 1989, spilling approximately 258 000 barrels (41 million L) of Prudhoe Bay crude oil into the waters of Prince William Sound (PWS), Alaska. Currents and winds moved the spill to the southwest, where large quantities were deposited on the western shores of PWS and adjacent islands (Galt et al. 1991). Over the next few weeks, the oil moved out of the sound, continuing southwest along the coast of the Kenai Peninsula to the Barren Islands, Kodiak Island, and Shelikof Strait. Eventually, oil from the *Valdez* spill extended more than 900 km from the spill site (Ciancaglini 1991).

As news of the spill reached the public, some of the first (and most lingering) images were of oil-coated seabirds and of beaches littered with oiled carcasses. These images fostered expectations among both the general public and scientists of a widespread and long-lasting ecological disaster for seabirds. The counts of dead birds retrieved during beach surveys reinforced these concerns. By 1 August 1989, over 29,000 bird carcasses had been recovered in Prince William Sound, along the Kenai Peninsula, and in the Kodiak Island region (Piatt et al. 1990). This mortality was unevenly distributed among species groups. In PWS, for example, sea ducks, grebes, and loons comprised 45% of the birds retrieved, while alcids (murres, murrelets, guillemots, and puffins) accounted for another 33%. In the Gulf of Alaska, murres constituted 58% to 89% of the bird carcasses recovered in various locations (Piatt et al. 1990). Extrapolations from the overall carcass counts produced initial estimates that 100,000 to 300,000 birds had been killed by the spill (Piatt et al. 1990); later revisions (Ford et al. 1991) increased this estimate to 300,000 to 645,000 birds.

These early estimates fueled an array of concerns and claims. Piatt et al. (1990), for example, asserted that "perhaps 10% of the existing Gulf of Alaska population" of Common Murres (*Uria aalge*) had been killed, and Fry (1993) concluded that 60% to 80% of the murres on the Barren Islands "were engulfed, carried away and killed by the oil." Local populations of Pigeon Guillemots (*Cepphus columba*) and Marbled Murrelets

(*Brachyramphus marmoratum*) were also thought to have been devastated by the spill. Recovery times of 20 to 70 years were projected for some species (Piatt et al. 1990; Piatt 1993). Temple (1990) noted that populations on several breeding islands seemed to have suffered very high losses, and his preliminary analyses suggested that the recovery of murre populations would "be slow without the help of immigration from other populations which is not likely to happen." These concerns were not based on careful, scientific studies, however, and the results of the investigations reviewed here indicated that they were not fully justified.

SEABIRD NATURAL HISTORY AND VULNERABILITY TO OIL

In general, high-latitude, coastal marine ecosystems support a diverse and abundant avifauna. Mickelson (1989) lists 125 bird species in PWS, of which 87 use shoreline or marine habitats extensively. Irons et al. (1988) tallied 75 marine-oriented species in their boat surveys in PWS, while Nishimoto and Rice (1987) recorded 40 species in their surveys along the Kenai Peninsula. Nearly 700 seabird breeding colonies have been documented in the northern Gulf of Alaska, supporting populations in excess of 6 million birds (U. S. Fish and Wildlife Service [USFWS] 1991). There are 485 cataloged colonies in the spill area, with a total of 1.4 million seabirds. The largest breeding concentrations are at the Barren Islands (510,000 birds) and the Kodiak archipelago (385,000 birds); few breeding colonies are located in PWS.

Several groups of species dominate these bird communities. Over 65% of the individuals recorded by Irons et al. (1988) in PWS were gulls, jaegers, and terns; another 15% were alcids. At seabird breeding colonies in the spill area, however, gulls accounted for only 29% of the individual counts, whereas alcids contributed 55% of the individuals (USFWS 1991). Murres comprised 22% of the colony survey counts.

Numerical dominance is not necessarily related to the mortality experienced by a group following an oil spill. In northern regions, alcids (especially murres) and sea ducks generally appear to be disproportionately affected, whereas cormorants, geese, and gulls often suffer lower mortality (Clark 1984; Vermeer and Vermeer 1975). In several spills, murres have made up over 90% of the recorded seabird mortality (e.g., Hope Jones et al. 1970; Diederich 1981).

These differences among species are related to features of their behavior, ecology and life history. For example, many seabirds form large aggregations at breeding colonies or in feeding flocks, often in response to limited nesting habitat (e.g., island cliff-ledges) or patchy distribution of their food (Ashmole 1971; Furness and Barrett 1991). This behavior places large numbers of birds at risk should a spill occur in breeding or feeding areas. Some seabirds, such as alcids and many sea ducks, escape disturbances by diving, whereas others, such as gulls and dabbling ducks, fly when disturbed (Bourne 1968a; Clark 1984; Eppley and Rubega 1990). Species that feed in the water may forage at the surface (e.g., phalaropes, storm-petrels) or dive (e.g., alcids, sea ducks), some to considerable depths (e.g., 180 m for Common Murres; Piatt and Nettleship 1985). If oil is present on the water, diving and resurfacing are likely to bring individuals into repeated contact with it (Peakall et al. 1987). Some species may be attracted to oil slicks, where wave action is less heavy (Curry-Lindahl 1960; Bourne 1968b), whereas others (e.g., gulls) may avoid oiled areas.

These features affect the probability that birds will encounter spilled oil. Other aspects of seabird life history and reproductive biology influence how spill-related mortality may affect population dynamics. Long-term studies of seabird populations (e.g., Dunnet and Ollason [Ollason and Dunnet 1988; Dunnet 1991] on Northern Fulmars [*Fulmarus glacialis*], Coulson [Coulson and Thomas 1985; Thomas and Coulson 1988] on Black-legged Kittiwakes [*Rissa tridactyla*], Birkhead and Hudson [1977] and Murphy, Springer, and Roseneau [1986] on Common Murres, Gaston and Nettleship [1981] on Thick-billed Murres [*Uria lomvia*], Potts [1969; Potts, Coulson and Deans 1980] on Shags [*Phalacrocorax aristotelius*], Harris [1984; Harris and Wanless 1991] on Puffins [*Fratercula arctica*]) have shown that adults of many species have high annual survival (often 80% to 95%; Hunt 1987; Harris and Wanless 1988; Hatchwell and Birkhead 1991) and may be long-lived (e.g., at least 45 years in Northern Fulmars; Dunnet 1991). Nonetheless, natural mortality associated with storms or crashes in the food supply may sometimes be great. In autumn 1969, for example, some 12 000 seabirds (mostly murres) died in the Irish Sea and West Scotland (Clark 1984), and tens of thousands of shearwaters, kittiwakes, and other seabirds died of starvation in the Gulf of Alaska and Bering Sea in August and September 1983 (Nysewander and Trapp 1984). Bailey and Davenport (1972) documented a "wreck" (as such large natural die-offs are called) in excess of 100 000 murres associated with sustained inclement weather and a severe storm in the Gulf of Alaska during April 1970 (see also Hudson 1985); similar losses have been recorded for Dovekies (*Alle alle*) (Murphy and Vogt 1933; Snyder 1953) and other seabirds (Harris and Wanless 1984). Because long-lived seabirds may experience several such events during their lifetime, and because young birds may be disproportionately affected, such die-offs may have profound effects on population structure (Nisbet 1989). However, Bailey and Davenport could find no obvious effects of the 1970 Alaska murre wreck on nearby breeding colonies (see also Harris and Wanless 1984).

In association with their long life-span, many seabirds exhibit delayed maturation (Ricklefs 1990; Wooller et al. 1992). Common Murres, for example, may not breed until they are 4 - 5 years old (Birkhead and Hudson 1977; Hatchwell and Birkhead 1991), Black-legged Kittiwakes until they are 3 - 5 years old (Coulson and Wooller 1976), and Northern Fulmars until they are 10 - 12 years old, on average (Dunnet and Ollason 1978; Dunnet 1991). Entry of individuals into the breeding population, however, may be determined more by social interactions with established breeders than by chronological age (Dunnet 1982). Among colonially breeding species, nonbreeding birds may join a "pool" of individuals that flock together during the breeding season (Tuck 1960; Birkhead and Hudson 1977; Klomp and Furness 1992). Because some adults may not attempt to breed every year (Wooller et al. 1992), this pool may also contain nonbreeding adults.

This pool of prebreeding and nonbreeding individuals may act as a "buffer," from which individuals may be recruited to replace losses from breeding populations (Dunnet 1982;

Stowe 1982; Klomp and Furness 1992). How the movement of individuals among different breeding colonies affects the recruitment of breeders into local populations is a critical, yet unresolved, issue. It is generally not known, for example, whether prebreeding individuals in a pool associated with a given breeding colony were hatched in that colony or whether adults that previously bred in one colony will move to another. The "conventional wisdom" is that breeding birds show strong fidelity to previous breeding colonies and nest sites (Birkhead 1977; Hudson 1985; Temple 1990; Harris and Wanless 1991). On the other hand, several recent studies document that prebreeding individuals may move among local populations (Harris and Wanless 1991; Coulson 1991), and it seems likely that emigration and immature survival may have been underestimated (Hudson 1985). Changes in population sizes within colonies suggest that some movement occurs among subpopulations (Hunt 1987; Hatchwell and Birkhead 1991). For example, on the Isle of May off the Scottish Coast, the Puffin population increased at an annual rate of 22% from 1951 to 1980, but local production of young birds could only account for an annual increase of 7% (Harris 1983). The degree to which individuals can be recruited to breeding colonies from nonbreeding pools or by immigration from other colonies is an important consideration in assessing the recovery of seabird populations from major mortality events, such as oil spills or natural wrecks.

Without external recruitment, the potential for recovery of a local seabird population is closely linked to reproduction. Many seabirds have low rates of reproduction (Lack 1968; Ricklefs 1990). Clutch sizes are low (all tubenoses and many alcids lay only a single egg per clutch), and development is often prolonged (e.g., storm-petrel chicks remain in the nest burrow for up to 61 days; Simons 1981). As a result, most species produce only one brood per year. Some species have precocial or semi-precocial young, which leave the nest shortly after hatching (e.g., shorebirds such as oystercatchers) or well before they have attained adult body mass (e.g., murres). Many of these chicks may be lost to predators or weather-related stress (Ydenberg 1989). Given these attributes, the inherent growth potential of seabird populations may be low. Leslie (1966), for example, calculated that the time required for a murre population to double in size, without immigration, would be on the order of 50 years.

Many seabird populations also experience episodic reproductive failures (Aebischer 1986; Springer et al. 1986; Boekelheide and Ainley 1989; Harris and Wanless 1991; Wooller et al. 1992). In 1983, for example, Black-legged Kittiwakes experienced almost complete breeding failure throughout their Alaska range (Hatch 1987), and several other widespread breeding failures of kittiwakes have occurred in the Gulf of Alaska or Bering Sea since then (including 1989, the year of the *Exxon Valdez* spill; Piatt et al. 1990). Large-scale oceanographic variations such as the El Niño Southern Oscillation (ENSO) may have spectacular and widespread effects on seabird populations (Schreiber and Schreiber 1984; Bayer 1986; Boekelheide et al. 1990; Croxall and Rothery 1991; see also Boersma et al., this volume). Because seabird reproduction is so closely tied to food abundance and distribution and is so sensitive to weather and predation, it may vary greatly from year to year under natural conditions (e.g., Murphy et al. 1986; Springer et al. 1986; Vader et al. 1990; Hatch and Hatch 1990).

The variations in annual mortality and reproduction, coupled with the uncertainties of recruitment from a nonbreeding pool or from other subpopulations, often produce substantial yearly variation in the sizes of breeding colonies (Richardson et al. 1982). Consequently, numbers of seabirds at particular colonies rarely remain unchanged for any length of time (Myres 1979; Hudson 1985; Cairns 1992).

EFFECTS OF OIL ON SEABIRDS

Birds may respond in several ways to an oil spill (Figure 1). Some birds may exhibit no apparent response to the oiling event. This may happen if they avoid direct contact with the oil, if they move from the area as the spill advances but return shortly after it has passed (and before researchers survey the area for spill effects), if there are no acute and sublethal effects on their behavior or physiology, or if their food supply or habitat is not affected by the oil.

Most attention has focused on mortality or diminished individual performance (Holmes and Cronshaw 1977; Dunnet 1982; Clark 1984; Leighton et al. 1985; Hunt 1987). When seabirds become oiled, they lose their buoyancy, which affects their ability to dive and feed. Thermoregulation becomes more difficult because insulation provided by the plumage is reduced, and because the feathers retain water, energetic costs of flight are increased. Energy demands therefore increase, requiring the birds to feed more when they are less able to do so. Oiled birds may also ingest oil while preening their plumage, producing physiological and endrocrinological changes that, combined with the other stresses, make it less likely they will survive. If the birds are breeding, oil may be transferred to eggs, affecting hatchability. Breeding and parenting behavior may also be altered, leading to a reduction in reproductive success (Fry et al. 1985; Eppley and Rubega 1990).

Many of these effects may be heightened in cold environments, where physiological stress may be extreme, harsh weather may preclude feeding, and the oil fractions may persist longer (Levy 1980; Brown 1982; Clark 1984). Seabird mortality associated with oil spills therefore tends to be greater in winter than in other seasons (O'Connor and Mead 1980; Clark 1984; Stowe and Underwood 1984) and greater in high-latitude than in tropical regions (Robertson 1982). Other factors, such as the type of oil, the dosage and duration of a spill, the proximity to breeding or feeding areas, prey abundance, and the composition of the bird community, may also influence spill-related mortality (Natural Research Council 1985; Mielke 1990). Because these factors vary among spills, the location and timing of a spill are generally more important in determining spill impacts than is spill size alone (Hunt 1987; Burger 1993).

The variety of direct and indirect effects of oil on seabirds culminate in three primary avenues of negative spill effects (Figure 1). First, there may be changes in population size or features of population structure, such as age distribution (the frequency of individuals of different ages in the population) or sex ratio. These changes may result directly from mortality and emigration, or indirectly, through alterations in food supplies or reduced reproductive success.

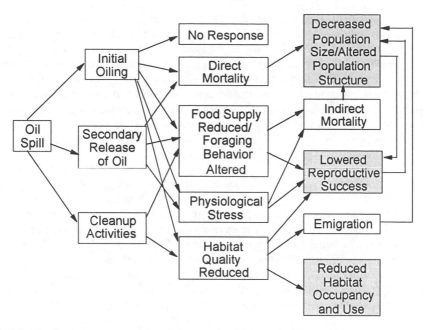

FIGURE 1—A schematic representation of the ways in which an oil spill can influence seabirds. The three primary avenues of effects, on population size and structure, reproduction, and habitat occupancy, are highlighted.

Second, reproduction may be affected by reductions in food availability, physiological stress on adults, loss of breeding or feeding habitat, or changes in the structure of the population. For example, if breeding densities are reduced or if young, inexperienced birds enter the breeding population to replace birds lost in a spill, they may be less effective at protecting their eggs or young against predators or in providing food for their young (Birkhead 1977). There has been speculation, but no firm evidence, that this happened in some murre breeding colonies following the *Exxon Valdez* oil spill (Nysewander et al. 1993; Fry 1993; Piatt 1993).

Third, the feeding or breeding habitat for a species may be altered by the spill or cleanup activities. For some species (e.g., some gulls), these changes may actually improve habitat conditions. Generally, however, oiling reduces habitat quality, which can diminish reproductive success, cause individuals to leave the area, or alter habitat-use patterns.

DEFINING IMPACT AND RECOVERY

Defining "impact" is not a simple matter. When birds die as a result of oil pollution, there is obviously an impact on those individuals. Whether these losses are biologically important, however, depends on whether there are effects on populations, not just individuals (Clark 1984; Hunt 1987). A loss of thousands of individuals from a large and widespread population may be biologically insignificant, whereas the same loss from a small or restricted population may be of much greater significance. Barrett (1979), for example, noted that the mortality of 10,000 to 20,000 seabirds (over 90% of them Thick-billed Murres) in a small spill off northern Norway probably had very little impact on the huge breeding colonies in the Barents Sea from which these birds most likely came. Clearly, some knowledge of the population at risk from a spill is needed to interpret mortality estimates. Such information is usually not available, in which case assessing the impact of mortality may be problematic and subjective.

Terms such as "impact" should be defined operationally and statistically. In this context, "impact" refers to a statistically significant difference between samples exposed to oil and control or reference samples (in this paper, I use "impact" to refer only to negative effects). Reference samples in such comparisons could be unoiled or lightly oiled sites in the same region or samples taken at the same site before the spill occurred (Wiens and Parker, in press). Biologically important impacts are those related to population size or structure, reproduction, or habitat use. If the impact of an oil spill is defined by a statistically recognizable departure of the state of a system in oiled samples from that in unoiled samples, then "recovery" from these spill effects can be defined as the disappearance through time of such a statistical difference. Because major oil spills occur at an identifiable point in time, impacts may occur over a short, definable time period. Recovery, on the other hand, is often played out over a longer, undefined period. As a consequence, environmental variation makes it much more complicated to assess recovery than impacts, and the context of natural variability of a system must therefore be part of the definition of "recovery." As with impact, there are several dimensions to recovery: population size and structure, reproductive rate and recruitment, and habitat occupancy or use. Obviously, if an impact is detected in one of these dimensions, recovery must be gauged using the same criteria. A variety of criteria may be used to assess impact and recovery, however, and differences in criteria may lead different workers to reach quite different conclusions. This may be one source of disagreement about the consequences of the *Exxon Valdez* oil spill.

EQUILIBRIUM AND NATURAL VARIATION

Recovery is often thought to have occurred when the system returns to its state before a disruption, such as an oil spill. Alternatively, one might consider a system to be recovered when a stable equilibrium is established in some feature of interest, such as population size or habitat occupancy. Commenting on the effects of the *Amoco Cadiz* oil spill on seabirds, for example, Conan (1982) observed that it was difficult "to give precise indications on how long it will take before the new or the former stable age distribution and equilibrium species assemblages will be attained," although he suggested that it might take up to 60 years for bird populations to regain a stable age distribution.

Computer models of murre and kittiwake population dynamics associated with oil spills (e.g., Ford et al. 1982; Samuels and Lanfear 1982; Samuels and Ladino 1984) have also used the attainment of a stable age distribution as a measure of population recovery. Such models generally predict long recovery times for populations impacted by oil spills (e.g., up to 70 years for murres; Ford et al. 1982; Samuels and Lanfear 1982). By applying such results to project possible recovery times for populations affected by the *Exxon Valdez* spill (e.g., Piatt et al. 1990; Heinemann 1993), one implicitly accepts a stable age distribution as a measure of recovery. Other demographic modeling exercises have projected that some seabird populations may require a long time to double in size (e.g., Leslie 1966; Temple 1990), reinforcing expectations of a long period of recovery following impacts.

Defining recovery in terms of such features as stable age distributions, equilibrium population sizes, or community composition reflects a narrow "balance of Nature" view, the notion that equilibrium is the natural state of Nature. By this view, recovery cannot occur until the equilibrium is reestablished. This view has long dominated Western thought (Worster 1977), and has been a prevailing paradigm in ecology as well. Most ecologists now recognize that equilibrium is a theoretical state that is probably infrequently attained in the real world (Wiens 1977, 1989; Chesson and Case 1986; Giller and Gee 1987). Natural systems are variable in time and space, and this variation produces a complex set of dynamics in which short-term variance may be superimposed on long-term trends.

Seabird populations are rarely stable at any location for any length of time (Myres 1979; Richardson et al. 1982; Cairns 1992). Moreover, some population parameters such as birth rate, death rate, and dispersal rate tend to vary more among years than do others, such as population size, distribution, habitat occupancy, age structure, sex ratios, and proportions of birds breeding (Ricklefs 1973; Temple and Wiens 1989). Long-term studies of seabirds generally demonstrate considerable yearly variation in reproductive success (Hunt 1987; Hatch and Hatch 1990). Superimposed on these natural variations are variations associated with survey procedures ("sampling error") (Gaston and Nettleship 1981; Richardson et al. 1982; Harris et al. 1983; Hudson 1985; Byrd 1989; Hatch and Hatch 1989). Richardson et al. (1982) found that murre counts varied among sites by -10% to +34% between consecutive years and concluded that changes of this magnitude could not be distinguished from "normal" variability over the longer term.

In high-latitude, coastal marine ecosystems such as the *Exxon Valdez* spill area, the natural environment is not only physically harsh, but tremendously variable as well (Cooney 1986; Sambrotto and Lorenzen 1986; Wilson and Overland 1986; Royer et al. 1990). The complex patterns of landforms and ocean circulation patterns may also produce considerable spatial variation in environmental conditions. These temporal and spatial variations in the physical environment affect the population dynamics and distributions of marine organisms, many of which are food for seabirds occupying the region. Seabirds are closely tied to their food resources (Springer et al. 1986; Furness and Barrett 1991; Hunt et al. 1991), and variation in food abundance or availability may cause major variations in seabird reproduction or population dynamics (Wooller et al. 1992; Cairns 1992).

Gauging the impact of an oil spill against the backdrop of such variation requires that the displacement be distinguished from natural variation in the system (Figure 2). Observing that the size of a breeding population after an oil spill is different from that recorded at some time before the spill, for example, does not in itself indicate a spill impact—the change could easily reflect natural variation in population size that is unrelated to the spill. In the same manner, recovery must be assessed in relation to the natural variability of the system. In a variable system, it is unrealistic to measure recovery in terms of the state of the system at some point before a spill unless one knows the temporal dynamics of the system. In a variable system, impact must be defined by a departure of the system from the "window" of natural variation, and recovery then occurs when the system returns to that "window" (Figure 2). In view of this variance, the need for statistical assays of impact and recovery is obvious.

There is an additional complication, because natural systems vary in space as well as in time (e.g., Springer et al. 1986; Mudge 1988). For example, the temporal dynamics of breeding colonies may differ in different areas, and the magnitude of decoupling may increase with distance between the areas. It may therefore be unrealistic to expect sites to display the same dynamics, or to behave in the same way at the same time. This lack of concordance has clear implications for the use of unoiled reference or "control" samples to establish the baseline conditions for gauging impact or recovery on oiled samples located some distance away (Wiens and Parker, in press).

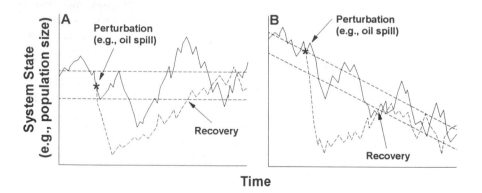

FIGURE 2—Hypothetical examples show how the impact of an oil spill and subsequent recovery can be assessed when the system under study undergoes natural variations (solid line). In A, the system varies in time, but the long-term mean remains unchanged. In B, there is a long-term decline in the state of the system (e.g., population size). Dashed lines indicate a "window" of normal variation about the mean (e.g., a 95% confidence interval). Operationally, "impact" occurs when the system is displaced outside this "window" of natural variation, and "recovery" occurs when the system returns to that "window." Note that it is unrealistic to define recovery as a return to exactly the state of the system before the perturbation. It is also unrealistic to require a "recovered" system to match exactly the state of an unperturbed system (e.g., a "control"). The "window" defines the zone within which the perturbed system cannot be distinguished statistically from an unperturbed system.

THE IMPORTANCE OF MEASUREMENT AND STUDY DESIGN

The studies conducted following the *Exxon Valdez* oil spill used a variety of measurements and followed different designs. Such differences in methodology can influence the conclusions one draws about oil-spill effects, and they may contribute to the continuing debate over the effects of the *Exxon Valdez* oil spill on seabirds. Any evaluation of the findings of the various studies must therefore include consideration of the measurements and study design.

One can investigate the effects of an oil spill on birds by studying one or a few focal species or by conducting a broader, multispecies assessment. In a single-species study, one can tailor the methods to the distinctive features of the species and examine particular aspects of its biology in some depth. Such investigations are particularly appropriate if, for some reason (e.g., high oiling vulnerability, threatened or endangered status), one wishes to target a particular species or group. Multispecies studies, on the other hand, enable one to assess how spill effects are spread over the entire assemblage occupying an area. This approach may permit a more balanced overview of spill impacts and recovery. Whichever approach one uses, the following comments apply.

Obtaining Measurements

Population size and structure—Each of the dimensions of assessing impacts and recovery carries with it some inherent limitations on obtaining measurements.The most frequently used measure of population impact and recovery is abundance, or perhaps an index of density or colony attendance. Estimates are generally obtained by survey counts, but seabirds are not easy to count (Lloyd 1975; Powers 1982; Tasker et al. 1984; Broni et al. 1985; Schneider and Duffy 1985), especially when they occur in large aggregations, and particularly at sea. Often it is not possible to distinguish sexes (or, in some cases, even species—e.g., Common versus Thick-billed murres). Seabird counts therefore have limited accuracy, and may contain systematic biases as well (Haney and Solow 1992).

The number of individuals in attendance at a breeding colony, however, can sometimes be estimated through direct counts (e.g., Lloyd 1975; Harris et al. 1983; Erikson, this volume) or from photographic records (e.g., Birkhead and Nettleship 1980; Boersma et al., this volume). The accuracy of such counts is usually greater from land-based vantage points than from boats at sea, but both are more accurate than counts of birds at sea. Because colony attendance varies with the time of day, the weather, sea state, and the stage of the nesting cycle (Birkhead 1976; Slater 1980; Byrd et al. 1983; Harris et al. 1983; Roby and Brink 1986; Rothery et al. 1988; Boersma et al., this volume), counts of the same colony made at different times may differ considerably. Moreover, to determine the size of the breeding population, one must know what proportion of the individuals present at a colony are actually nesting and whether one or both (or neither) members of a breeding pair are likely to be present at a given time. In murres, for example, one member of the pair usually attends the nest site while the other is at sea (Tuck 1960; Gaston and

Nettleship 1981). Some seabird biologists have multiplied colony-attendance counts by two to adjust for this behavior (see Harris 1989; Erikson, this volume).

Other measures of population structure—such as age distribution, sex ratio, proportion of birds breeding, and recruitment rates of nonbreeders into the breeding population—require detailed information on individual age, breeding experience, sex, etc. Such information is extremely difficult to obtain for seabirds without conducting long-term studies of marked individuals, and such studies must be confined to one or a few locations. These measures of population structure are therefore of limited value in assessing what actually happens following an oil spill.

Reproductive measures—Documenting breeding phenology and reproductive success requires careful, repeated on-site surveys throughout the breeding season (Gaston et al. 1983). Unless particular care is taken, repeated visits to a breeding colony by investigators may cause considerable disturbance, increasing the vulnerability of eggs and chicks to predation, neglect, or loss (Hunt 1987). Nesting surveys may be conducted more frequently after an oil spill in order to document reproductive performance more precisely. As a consequence, the effects of human disturbance on reproductive measurements may be especially great, and spill-related impacts may be overestimated. If automated camera systems are used to record breeding information (e.g., Boersma et al., this volume) the problem diminishes. However, this approach may be limited by the expense of monitoring many colonies, the formidability of quantifying results from the many photographic images produced, and the reduced effectiveness for noncolonial species.

Habitat use—Measuring habitat use requires that counts of birds present in various areas be coupled with measurements of relevant habitat variables. The bird counts are subject to the limitations noted above, although accuracy may be greater in nearshore or shoreline areas than in open seas. If appropriate historical survey data are available (see below), these counts may permit comparisons of abundance levels before and after the spill. One must generally use the published literature about the natural history of a species or one's intuition as a field biologist to determine which habitat variables should be measured and at what level of accuracy (Wiens 1989; Morrison et al. 1992), and there always exists the possibility that important habitat variables have not been measured. In this case, statistical analyses that use habitat measures to isolate the effects of oiling (e.g., Day et al., this volume) may not capture some of the important variation in habitat use. Relevant measurements are difficult to obtain for pelagic species, where the critical habitat variables may be oceanographic features that are expressed at multiple scales in both time and space (see Hunt and Schneider 1987; Wahl et al. 1989; Hunt 1990).

Sample sizes and natural variation—If impact and recovery are to be assessed statistically, sample sizes must be sufficient to permit valid statistical tests. Because the accuracy and precision of measurement of many attributes of seabird populations, reproduction, and habitat use are not great, there may be considerable sampling error. This weakens the power of statistical tests, requiring even larger samples to demonstrate a significant difference at a designated α-value. Unfortunately, the nature of marine environments and the remoteness of many coastal areas, especially at high latitudes, often place severe logistical constraints on sample sizes. In addition, because the effects of an oil spill are superimposed on natural variation, it is necessary to consider both sampling error and natural variation in assessing these effects (Richardson et al. 1982; Spies 1993). Unless measurements have been repeated over time, however, our knowledge of natural variation in variables of interest is likely to be limited.

Designing Comparisons

No matter which variables or criteria are emphasized, the basic design of a study of oil-spill impacts and recovery involves a comparison of oiled samples with reference samples. There are several ways to structure these comparisons (see also Wiens and Parker, in press).

Before-after comparisons—Comparisons of measures taken in an area before an oil spill with those made following the spill are often thought to provide a reasonable appraisal of spill effects (e.g., Kuletz 1993; Laing and Klosiewski 1993). Such "prespill" or historical comparisons are based on the premise that differences in the state of the system before and after the spill are due to spill effects alone. There are several problems with this approach.

First, oil spills rarely occur in well-studied areas. Available historical information may be limited, and this may lead one to use data that are of limited scope or are inappropriate. Many of the surveys of breeding colonies in the Gulf of Alaska (Sowls et al. 1978) were conducted to document the locations of colonies and to obtain a rough idea of their sizes—accuracy in the estimations of abundance was not a primary consideration. Using these early counts as a baseline for comparison with postspill counts, which have different objectives, therefore yields only general, qualitative results. Such information may be useful in indicating large-scale changes in abundance, but it does not allow one to specify the magnitude of those changes with much precision.

Second, the historical information was often gathered by different observers using different methods than those employed in postspill sampling. Some observers may consistently overestimate bird numbers, whereas others may habitually underestimate numbers. Weather conditions can dramatically affect counts, especially those made at sea. Interobserver variation may be a major source of "sampling error" in abundance estimates (Ralph and Scott 1981). If different survey procedures are used, the results cannot be quantitatively compared (Wiens 1989).

Third, if the historical information is based on a single survey, it will not capture the temporal variation of the system before the spill (Spies 1993). If variation is great, comparisons based on single-sample surveys can yield a wide array of results (Wiens 1981). Variation will also affect the sample sizes needed to document a statistically significant difference before and after the spill. For example, on the basis of information gathered before and after the *Arco Anchorage* oil spill, Speich et al. (1991) concluded that, for the species with the lowest variation in abundance in historical surveys, it would require more than 1 200 censuses both before and after the spill to detect a 5% change in abundance 80% of the time at the 0.05 significance level. To detect a 20% change in numbers would require roughly 80 censuses, while about 15 surveys before and after the spill would be needed to detect a 50% change. In most before-after comparisons, sample sizes are smaller and variation in species' abundances is greater.

If short-term variation in abundance is superimposed on long-term trends (e.g., Figure 2B), it becomes even more difficult to interpret the results of before-after comparisons. Populations of both Pigeon Guillemots and Marbled Murrelets, for example, were apparently declining in PWS before the *Exxon Valdez* oil spill, making it difficult to interpret low numbers following the spill (Oakley and Kuletz 1993; Kuletz 1993). Often, comparisons must be based on historical surveys conducted many years before a spill. In the absence of information documenting both short-term variations and long-term trends, old surveys may be useless as a baseline for comparison (Dunnet 1982).

Treatment-control comparisons—In the tradition of a scientific experiment, one may consider oiled areas as "treatments" and simultaneously unoiled areas as "controls." Given the general inadequacy of historical baseline data, this approach has the distinct advantage of requiring no prespill information. The premise of such a design is that the control sites differ from the oiled sites only in being unoiled. To some degree, the effects of other differences among treatment and control sites may be reduced by replicating samples within both groups (Spies 1993). Because of factors that affect the distribution of oil following a spill (e.g., prevailing currents, exposure), however, there may still exist systematic differences between oiled and unoiled areas that are not completely removed through replication (Wiens and Parker, in press). Logistical constraints often limit sampling, and investigators tend to sample far fewer control sites than treatment sites (being unoiled, they are considered to be uninteresting).

Moreover, it is often difficult to find suitable control areas. For example, in assessing the impacts of the *Exxon Valdez* spill on murre abundance and reproduction at breeding colonies, USFWS personnel used information from Middleton Island (near the mouth of PWS) and the Semidi Islands (off the Alaska Peninsula, west of Kodiak Island) to represent "control" conditions. Under normal conditions, breeding phenology at these colonies is earlier than that at many other colonies in the region (Petersen 1983). In addition, both of these colonies are at or near the continental shelf break and are much closer to oceanic waters than are most of the "treatment" colonies located in the path of the spill; consequently, the food base of the two groups of colonies is probably quite different (see Springer 1991).

Use of an oiling gradient—The problem of finding suitable control areas may be circumvented by using a number of sites that differ in the magnitude of the oiling effect. If these differences can be quantified, the sample sites can be arrayed on a gradient according to their relative oiling index value (e.g., Day et al., this volume). The null hypothesis is then that the variables of interest (e.g., population size, reproductive output, habitat occupancy) do not vary systematically along this gradient; this hypothesis can be tested statistically. Ideally, one should either sample a large number of sites along this gradient or select a set of sites that differ only in the level of oiling. In practice, however, it is often not feasible to sample many sites, and it is difficult to control for variation in environmental factors other than oiling. As a result, statistical tests may be complicated by differences in habitat features that parallel the oiling gradient to varying degrees. At the extreme, the oiling gradient may closely match a gradient in one or more environmental factors, so that it is difficult to separate the effects of oiling from those of the colinear environmental factors. However, by carefully measuring habitat features of the sites, it may be possible to factor out the effects of habitat differences from those of oiling (Spies 1993) and to identify situations in which colinearity of habitat variables and oiling intensity may pose problems in interpretation (Day et al., this volume).

Relative strength of these approaches—Spies (1993) has commented on the relative level of certainty that is associated with different sampling designs, in the context of determining impacts on seabird population sizes. He suggests that the evidence of an impact is strongest when direct counts of oiled carcasses are coupled with model estimates of mortality. Evidence is nearly as strong if a population decrease is recorded in oiled areas in relation to prespill levels but is not observed in unoiled locations, after natural fluctuations in population sizes have been taken into account. Inferences about impacts are weaker if the apparent population decrease in oiled areas is based on comparisons with historical data that are limited or old. Finally, if comparisons can only be made between oiled and unoiled sites sampled following the spill (i.e., a treatment-control comparison), Spies judges the evidence of impacts to be much less certain (although one's confidence is increased if many samples are available for comparison).

These approaches emphasize the determination of initial spill impacts. If samples are collected at repeated intervals over some time period following the spill, all except the first approach may permit some assessment of recovery as well. In my view, comparisons among sites studied following a spill are usually most feasible. Because the general inadequacy of the available historical data, comparisons among sites studied following a spill may often be more practical than comparisons that rely on prespill information. If one carefully selects well-replicated treatment and control sites and takes the measurements necessary to factor out variation in environmental factors among sites, such postspill comparisons may be quite powerful. By using sites along an oiling gradient one can deal with oiling as a continuous rather than a categorical variable, thereby enhancing certainty. This approach, however, may be better suited to determining impacts on habitat use than impacts on population sizes. By repeating such postspill comparisons over time following a spill, the effects of natural variability can be assessed and considered in the evaluation of recovery.

RESPONSE OF BIRDS TO THE *EXXON VALDEZ* SPILL

Initial Impacts

Although the effects of an oil spill on seabirds may be complex (Figure 1), it is likely that the extent of most direct impacts will be apparent within a few months of the spill (although some may last much longer). Accordingly, in evaluating initial impacts of the *Exxon Valdez* spill it is appropriate to focus on what happened during 1989. Several studies of oiling effects on seabirds were not initiated until 1990 and, therefore, do not document initial impacts (although impacts can be inferred if they persist); these studies are summarized under "recovery."

 Population size and structure—Overall, nearly 36,000 dead birds were retrieved following the *Exxon Valdez* spill (Table 1). Not all of these birds were killed by oil, however; many retrieved after 1 August were not oiled or probably became oiled after they died of other causes (Piatt et al. 1990). Perhaps 31 000 of the recovered carcasses could be directly attributed to oiling (*Exxon Valdez* Oil Spill Trustees 1992).

Overall, murres comprised 56% of the dead birds retrieved (Table 1), other alcids about 8%, shearwaters about 10%, and sea ducks 4%. Of the 29 175 carcasses retrieved before 1 August 1989, 74% were murres and 5% were sea ducks (Piatt et al. 1990); Ford et al. (1991) reanalyzed the dead-bird listing and calculated that 72% of the retrieved birds were murres. There were regional variations in mortality and in the species affected (Piatt et al. 1990). Most of the mortality occurred along the outer Kenai Peninsula and in the Kodiak area; roughly two-thirds of the carcasses were processed at the Kodiak receiving station (Piatt et al. 1990).

Counts of carcasses recovered on or close to beaches represent an unknown fraction of the actual mortality associated with a spill. Oiled birds may be lost at sea to scavengers, may move with currents away from land, or may sink before being beached. Once beached, carcasses may not be found because they are swept back out to sea, are scavenged, are buried by wave action, are not detected among masses of oiled detritus, or land in areas that are not searched. A series of probability functions therefore intercedes between the death of a bird at sea and its discovery on a beach. Most of these functions are not known, but all of them are sensitive to local shoreline, oceanographic, and weather conditions, making it "almost impossible to estimate from beached birds the population consequences of mortality due to oil pollution" (Hunt 1987).

For the *Exxon Valdez* spill, it has been suggested that only a small portion of the birds killed was recovered because of the large area affected, the long duration of the spill, and the high density of scavengers in coastal Alaska (Ford et al. 1991; Fry 1993). On the other hand, efforts to retrieve dead birds were substantially greater than is customary in beached bird surveys (Maki 1990). Model analyses (Ford et al. 1991) using "best estimates" of parameter values indicated that the probability of a carcass beaching before it sank was 42%, the probability that it would not be scavenged or otherwise removed from a beach was 31%, and the probability that searchers would find the carcass if it were present on the beach was 59%. The joint probability of these functions would be 8%, yielding an overall seabird mortality estimate of 375 000. The mean mortality estimated in Monte Carlo simulations was 435 000.

TABLE 1—Listing of dead birds retrieved from oiled areas following the *Exxon Valdez* oil spill from early April to 25 September 1989. The estimated population summering in the Gulf of Alaska and breeding at colonies in the region and in the spill area are shown for comparison.

Species Group	Dead Birds Retrieved[a]	Summer Regional Population[b]	Regional Colony Survey Counts[c]	
			Region[d]	Spill Area[e]
Loons	395			
Grebes	462			
Fulmars/storm-petrels	870	9 728 000	1 261 000	192 000
Shearwaters	3 399	34 493 000		
Cormorants	836	122 000	69 000	29 000
Herons	1			
Geese/swans	9			
Dabbling ducks/bay ducks/mergansers	121			
Sea ducks/eiders	1 440			
Cranes	2			
Shorebirds/phalaropes	49	>10 000 000[f]		
Gulls/jaegers	696	1 534 000		
Kittiwakes	1 225	3 526 000		
Terns	4	713 000		
[Gulls/jaegers + kittiwakes + terns]	[1 925]	[5 773 000]	[900 000]	[414 000]
Murres	19 948	4 865 000	1 827 000	306 000
Guillemots	614	140 000		
Murrelets	1 403	753 000		
Auklets	225	1 781 000		
Puffins	546	8 495 000		
[Total alcids other than murres]	[2 788]	[11 169 000]	[2 668 000]	[473 000]
Eagles	125			
Other raptors	13			
Corvids (jays, crows, magpies)	60			
Other birds	3 152			
TOTAL	35 595			

[a] Department of Justice (1991).
[b] From DeGange and Sanger (1986).
[c] From Seabird Colony Catalog files (USFWS 1991).
[d] For 691 cataloged colonies in area between Kayak Island, near the Copper River Delta, and Unimak Pass.
[e] For 485 cataloged colonies in the spill area.
[f] DeGange and Sanger (1986).

Overall, model-based estimates of total direct seabird mortality from the *Exxon Valdez* spill ranged from 300 000 to 645 000 (Ford et al. 1991; Heinemann 1993). It is important to remember that such values are derived from estimates of many parameters, and there is considerable uncertainty associated with the final estimates.

Mortality impacts are related to the size of the population at risk. The importance of the losses shown in Table 1 can be comprehended by comparing them with estimates of the at-sea population over the entire Gulf of Alaska (DeGange and Sanger 1986) or with surveys made at seabird breeding colonies in the spill region (USFWS 1991) (Table 1). Although these broad-scale estimates are necessarily coarse, it is apparent that the recorded mortality represents a small proportion of the regional species population estimated for the northern Gulf of Alaska. This proportion increases if one bases the comparison only on colony estimates from the spill area, although the values are still low. The magnitude of the factor one uses to adjust for the losses of carcasses before retrieval clearly has important effects on overall mortality estimates.

Other estimates of population losses have been based on comparisons of postspill counts with data gathered before the spill. In comparisons with counts of murres made at major breeding colonies (Sowls et al. 1978; USFWS 1991), it has been estimated that 120 000 to 140 000 breeding adult murres were killed (*Exxon Valdez* Oil Spill Trustees 1992; Heinemann 1993). Extrapolation to other unsurveyed colonies in the region yielded an estimate of 172 000 to 198 000 breeding adults, and the inclusion of wintering and nonbreeding birds brought the total area-wide murre mortality estimate to 300 000 birds (*Exxon Valdez* Oil Spill Trustees 1992). The assumptions underlying these estimations have not been clearly stated, and in some cases the historical colony-attendance values may be incorrect (see Erikson, this volume).

To estimate seabird populations at risk as a group, Piatt et al. (1990) conducted aerial surveys shortly before the oil reached certain locations. They concluded, however, that boat-based surveys conducted in PWS in the early 1970s (Dwyer et al. 1976) provided a better assay of the population at risk. In comparisons with these surveys, populations of 11 of 39 species or groups were reduced following the spill (Laing and Klosiewski 1993). Of the 11 species or groups, five (cormorants, Harlequin Ducks [*Histronicus histronicus*], Black Oystercatchers [*Haematopus bachmani*], Pigeon Guillemots, and Northwestern Crows [*Corvus caurinus*]) decreased more in oiled than in unoiled areas. In comparison with shoreline boat surveys conducted in the sound in 1984-85 (Irons et al. 1988), six taxa (loons, Harlequin Ducks, scoters, Black Oystercatchers, Arctic Terns [*Sterna paradisaea*], and Mew Gulls [*Larus canus*]) declined more in oiled than in unoiled areas (Laing and Klosiewski 1993). Overall, these assays suggest that populations of several taxa declined significantly in spill-affected areas in relation to historical (prespill) estimates, but they also indicate that populations of many other species apparently were not affected by the spill.

Mortality may alter the structure of a population as well as reduce its size. Following the *Exxon Valdez* spill, it was suggested that the composition of the breeding populations of several species (e.g., murres) was altered as younger, less-experienced birds replaced established breeders that were killed in the spill (Nysewander et al. 1993; Heinemann 1993; Piatt 1993). As a consequence, reproductive output was diminished. No data on the composition of breeding populations were gathered either before or after the spill, however, so such arguments are entirely speculative.

Overall, there is no question that many birds died as a consequence of the *Exxon Valdez* oil spill, although exactly how many will remain unresolved. Comparisons with historical data suggest that this mortality may have affected the populations of some species, but not others. There are problems in the design and interpretation of comparisons with prespill surveys, however (see Erikson, this volume, Boersma et al., this volume). As a result, it is difficult to determine the real impacts on population size or structure from such comparisons.

Reproduction—Although it is difficult to demonstrate changes in the breeding structure of a population, one can assess whether reproductive performance was affected by the spill. Few studies of reproduction were conducted during the summer following the spill. However, it has been claimed that murres suffered "nearly total reproductive failures" at many colonies within the spill area during 1989 and that breeding was later and less synchronous than normal (in relation to "control" colonies located outside of the spill area) (*Exxon Valdez* Oil Spill Trustees 1992; Nysewander et al. 1993; Heinemann 1993). Black Oystercatchers apparently laid smaller eggs, and chick survival was somewhat lower in oiled than in unoiled sites (Sharp and Cody 1993). There were reports of hydrocarbon residues on eggs of Pigeon Guillemots and in tissues of Harlequin Ducks following the spill (Oakley and Kuletz 1993; Patten 1993), although this evidence is equivocal (Bence and Burns, this volume).

Despite the oiling of feeding areas and the disturbance caused by cleanup activities, several species did breed successfully in the spill area in 1989. Incidental observations (Day et al. unpublished observations) indicated that in PWS Harlequin Ducks, Common Goldeneyes (*Bucephala clangula*), Common Mergansers (*Mergus merganser*), Mew Gulls, Glaucous-winged Gulls (*Larus glaucescens*), Black-legged Kittiwakes, Arctic Terns, Pigeon Guillemots, and Marbled Murrelets all nested and/or produced broods of young in bays that were heavily oiled. These surveys were not designed to document reproductive activity, so other species also may have nested successfully in the spill area.

Habitat use—One of the most powerful and persistent images of the *Exxon Valdez* oil spill was of a pristine wilderness awash in thick, black oil. Habitats were undoubtedly affected, first by the spill and then by the disturbances associated with cleanup efforts. One study (Day et al., this volume) was directed explicitly at evaluating patterns of habitat occupancy by birds as a function of oiling. Series of bays differing in oil exposure were selected in PWS and along the Kenai Peninsula, habitat features were quantified, and bird abundance was surveyed on a seasonal basis. By examining patterns of changing abundance along the gradient of oil exposure and including the effects of intrinsic habitat differences among bays, it was possible to determine whether a species demonstrated a clear, statistically significant impact in its use of bay habitats that was related to oiling. Of the 42 species in PWS that occurred frequently enough to permit statistical analyses, 23 (55%) exhibited no apparent negative impact in their use of habitats in 1989 (Table 2). The remaining 19 species showed some evidence of reduced occupancy of the more heavily oiled bays. On the Kenai, 22 of the 34 species analyzed (65%) showed no apparent negative oiling impacts (Table 2). In both areas, however, birds were present in bays that had been heavily oiled within a few months of the spill. Surveys conducted in heavily oiled bays in PWS recorded 22, 38, and 34 species in June, July-August, and September-October 1989, respectively. A survey on the Kenai in August 1989 recorded 38 species in heavily oiled bays.

Recovery

Population size and structure—Increases in population abundance following declines associated with an oil spill can occur through local reproductive recruitment or immigration of individuals from other areas. Measures of population recovery usually assume that the local population is closed (i.e., no emigration or immigration). If this is so, increases in population size can only occur by increased survivorship or reproduction. If there is much interchange of individuals among local populations, however, losses from local populations exposed to oil may be rapidly offset by immigration from populations in unoiled areas. Population dynamics are then played out on a regional rather than a local scale.

The magnitude of interchange among local populations depends on individual mobility and site fidelity. Although it is known that some seabirds exhibit remarkable fidelity to locations at which they have previously bred successfully (Birkhead and Hudson 1977; Coulson 1991; Harris and Wanless 1991), less is known about the fidelity of birds to their natal colonies or the extent of interchange of unsuccessful breeders among colonies (Wooller et al. 1992). Because site fidelity is usually documented from intensive studies of marked individuals at single colonies, little information is available on how widely individuals disperse.

Following the *Exxon Valdez* oil spill, population recovery (gauged by various measures of abundance) was monitored in several studies during 1990 and 1991. USFWS personnel conducted boat-based surveys of marine and shoreline birds in the spill area, made counts of individuals at murre breeding colonies, and undertook more focused investigations of several species thought to have suffered impacts as a result of the spill. Generally, these investigators concluded that many of the impacts they had recorded shortly after the spill continued over the next year or two. Decreases in murre numbers at several key breeding colonies were thought to persist in 1990 and 1991 (Nysewander et al. 1993), and counts of several other species remained low as well (Laing and Klosiewski 1993). Counts of Marbled Murrelets, on the other hand, generally returned to prespill levels by 1990 (Kuletz 1993). These studies were primarily directed toward documenting damages associated with the spill rather than describing population recovery, and it is difficult to determine whether the many species not mentioned in these conclusions had in fact recovered (or, indeed, whether they even suffered initial impacts).

Other studies give a somewhat different picture. In 1991, Erikson (this volume) surveyed murre attendance levels at 32 colonies in the spill area. He categorized these colonies according to their location relative to the spill trajectory, and he found that there were no statistically significant changes in colony counts from historical (prespill) estimates for any of the oiling-risk categories, nor were there significant differences in population changes among the oiling-risk categories. Murre attendance levels were lower at some colonies in

TABLE 2—Summary of oil-related impacts on habitat use by birds in bays in Prince William Sound and along the Kenai Peninsula. NI = no impact, IR = initial oiling impact with apparent recovery by 1991, IP = impact persists or recovery is equivocal in 1991, shading = sample size inadequate for statistical analysis. From Day et al. (this volume).

Species	Prince William Sound			Kenai		
	NI	IR	IP	NI	IR	IP
Common Loon	X					X
Horned Grebe			X	░	░	░
Red-necked Grebe			X	X		
Sooty Shearwater	░	░	░	X		
Fork-tailed Storm-Petrel	X			X		
Double-crested Cormorant	X					X
Pelagic Cormorant		X		X		
Red-faced Cormorant	X			X		
Great Blue Heron		X		░	░	░
Canada Goose	X			░	░	░
Green-Winged Teal	X				X	
Mallard		X		░	░	░
American Widgeon	X			░	░	░
Harlequin Duck		X		X		
Oldsquaw	X			░	░	░
Black Scoter		X		░	░	░
Surf Scoter	X			X		
White-winged Scoter	X			X		
Common Goldeneye	X			░	░	░
Barrow's Goldeneye			X	░	░	░
Bufflehead			X	░	░	░
Common Merganser		X				X
Red-breasted Merganser		X		░	░	░
Bald Eagle		X		X		
Sharp-shinned Hawk	░	░	░			X
Black Oystercatcher		X		X		
Wandering Tattler		X			X	
Spotted Sandpiper	X			X		
Red-necked Phalarope	X				X	
Mew Gull			X		X	
Herring Gull	X			░	░	░
Glaucous-winged Gull		X				X
Black-legged Kittiwake	X			X		
Arctic Tern	X			░	░	░
Pomarine Jaeger	X			X		
Common Murre		X		X		
Pigeon Guillemot	X			X		
Marbled Murrelet		X		X		
Ancient Murrelet	░	░	░			X
Rhinoceros Auklet	░	░	░		X	
Tufted Puffin	X				X	
Horned Puffin	░	░	░	X		
Belted Kingfisher	X			X		
Steller's Jay	X			X		
Black-billed Magpie	X			X		
Northwestern Crow			X	X		
Common Raven	X			X		

relation to historical estimates, but these changes were unrelated to the level of oiling in the area. Eleven of the colonies that Erikson visited were also surveyed by USFWS personnel in 1991: overall, there was no significant difference between the counts for the two studies. In a separate investigation, Boersma et al. (this volume) conducted colony counts on East Amatuli Island in the Barren Islands, where murre breeding populations were said to be devastated by the spill (Nysewander et al. 1993). Their counts were generally similar to historical estimates from the late 1970s. The studies of Erikson and of Boersma et al. indicate that breeding attendance at many murre colonies in the spill area had recovered from any initial spill impacts by 1991.

Although comparisons that are founded on old and relatively coarse historical data are not precise, the observations of Erikson and of Boersma et al. are clearly not consistent with fears of widespread devastation of murre breeding colonies. If the estimates of spill-related mortality of breeding adult murres in the region (about 172 000 to 198 000 birds, 60% to 80% of birds in the Barren Islands; *Exxon Valdez* Oil Spill Trustees 1992; Fry 1993) were correct, one would expect the numbers of birds in attendance at colonies to be severely reduced. This does not seem to be the case. Several factors might account for this apparent paradox (Erikson, this volume; Boersma et al., this volume). First, the mortality estimates, which were derived from model projections, might be wrong. Second, the mortality might have occurred primarily among nonbreeding individuals and therefore would have little immediate effect on breeding numbers. Third, a substantial number of breeding individuals may indeed have been killed by the spill, but they were rapidly replaced by new recruits drawn from nonbreeding "pools" (or perhaps other colonies) in the region (see also Bourne 1982). Finally, because the spill occurred in late winter, birds destined to breed at colonies covering a broad region may have died, and the mortality impacts were therefore diffused among a large number of colonies.

Reproduction—If reproductive activities or recruitment of young into the population is affected by an oil spill, the primary evidence of recovery will likely be an increase in rates of reproduction (eggs laid, chicks produced), enhanced reproductive success, or an increase in the number of birds breeding. To the extent that breeding phenology is influenced by a spill, recovery may also involve a return to "normal" phenology. Because breeding phenology is so sensitive to local or regional oceanographic conditions (e.g., location and availability of food concentrations) and to climatic events (e.g., late spring storms), however, it is difficult to determine what "normal" phenology really is without intensive, long-term studies.

Following the *Exxon Valdez* spill, the reproductive activity and output of several species were studied. There were reports that the reproductive success of murres in many colonies remained low in 1990 and 1991 and that nesting phenology was delayed (Nysewander et al. 1993; Heinemann 1993; Fry 1993). These reproductive failures were estimated to have resulted in "lost production of at least 300 000 chicks" (*Exxon Valdez* Oil Spill Trustees 1992). However, studies in the large murre colony on East Amatuli Island in the Barren Islands indicated that, on one carefully monitored plot, both phenology and reproductive output in 1990 and 1991 were within the range of counts for the same plot several years before the spill (Boersma et al., this volume). Over a larger area in one subcolony, reproduction in 1991 was within the range of normal variation for this site. As noted above, murre reproductive output is quite variable under natural conditions: during the period 1976 to 1979, reproduction in this subcolony varied considerably, and no birds bred successfully in 1976. Following the spill, reproduction also varied. Production of eggs and chicks was moderate in 1990, relatively high in 1991, and quite low in 1992. Data gathered from two automatic cameras in another part of this subcolony in 1991 indicated that reproductive success varied from 64% to 70%. The yearly variations in reproduction were most likely related to variations in food supplies brought on by oceanographic conditions, rather than delayed consequences of the oil spill (Boersma et al., this volume). During 1990 and 1991, breeding activity was late in relation to some prespill years (1977-78), but not to others (1979) (Boersma et al., this volume).

Other studies have suggested that Harlequin Ducks also experienced a "massive reproductive failure" in oiled areas of PWS from 1989 through 1992, which was attributed to continued oil contamination of the mussel beds on which the ducks feed (Patten 1993). Oakley and Kuletz (1993) reported that Pigeon Guillemot populations were still being exposed to oil in 1990, although they noted that the relationship of oiling to poor breeding success in that year was unknown. Black Oystercatchers nesting in heavily oiled areas apparently had lower reproductive success than birds nesting in moderately oiled areas in 1990, but not in 1991 (Sharp and Cody 1993).

All of these observations are consistent with the general expectation voiced by Holmes and Cronshaw (1977) that the effects of oil on birds may persist "long after the environment has returned to a relatively pristine state." They are inconsistent, however, with the empirical findings of several studies conducted following the *Valdez* spill. Although some shellfish did contain high levels of *Exxon Valdez* crude oil in 1989, spill hydrocarbon levels in mussels dropped by an order of magnitude in 1990 and again in 1991, when many samples had returned to background levels (Bence and Burns, this volume; Boehm et al., this volume). In studies in which Mallards (*Anas platyrhynchos*) were fed on food containing various concentrations of slightly weathered Prudhoe Bay crude oil (Stubblefield et al., this volume), effects on health and reproduction were noted only at concentrations significantly higher than those observed in mussels in the field after 1989. Moreover, much of the reported evidence of hydrocarbon exposure of Harlequin Ducks (Patten 1993) was apparently based on a misinterpretation of laboratory analyses of hydrocarbon residues in tissues (Bence and Burns, this volume). Harlequin ducks are sensitive to disturbance (Dzinbal 1982), and the reproductive failures noted following the spill may have been due to cleanup activities and, later, disturbance by researchers studying the birds.

Habitat use—A population may have the capacity to recover in terms of population and reproduction measures, but whether or not recovery can actually occur may be determined by the availability of suitable habitat. There is no question that large areas of shoreline and open-water habitats suffered impacts immediately following the *Exxon Valdez* spill. As a result of cleanup and natural weathering of the oil, many of these areas appeared visually to recover within 1 to 2 years of the spill. Studies of beach sediments, water quality, and intertidal organisms indicated that free oil was virtually gone and that intertidal biota had recovered by 1990 or 1991 (Koons and Jahns 1992; Bence and Burns, this volume; Boehm et al., this volume).

Such evaluations of habitat quality, of course, are based on human criteria and perceptions. What is more relevant is whether the birds consider habitats that have been oiled to be suitable at some point following the spill. We may use occupancy patterns (habitat use) of the birds as an assay of habitat suitability. Day et al. (this volume) used several tests to determine at what point habitat occupancy by species that had shown a significant negative impact following the spill could no longer be related to oiling level. In PWS, 19 of 42 species analyzed exhibited significant initial oiling impacts (Table 2); of these, 13 (68%) had apparently recovered (as measured by habitat occupancy) by late summer 1991 (Table 2). One (the Marbled Murrelet) had recovered by late 1989, another 8 by late 1990. On the Kenai, 6 of 12 species (50%) that initially showed negative oiling impacts had recovered by the end of the study in late 1991 (Table 2). In both areas, recovery of several of the remaining species could not be determined because the available data were limited.

CONCLUDING COMMENTS

When there is a large-scale environmental perturbation such as an oil spill, many people attribute all subsequent changes in variables to that event—a tight cause-effect linkage is implied. Yet there is considerable disagreement among scientists about the severity of oil-spill impacts on seabird populations and communities. Dunnet (1982), for example, suggested that mortality due to oil is relatively small compared with the annual mortality from natural causes. Several authors (e.g., Croxall 1975; Biderman and Drury 1980; O'Connor and Mead 1980; Clark 1984; Hunt 1987) have concluded that mortality associated with chronic oil pollution from vessel operations and small releases may be much greater than that associated with major (and well-publicized) spills. Modeling analyses (e.g., Ford et al. 1982) have reached similar conclusions. Seabird mortality associated with major spills may nonetheless be substantial, and it is unclear whether it occurs in addition to ongoing natural mortality or is compensated for by a reduction in density-dependent natural mortality (Dunnet 1982).

Similar disagreement has emerged about the *Exxon Valdez* spill. Claims that breeding colonies have been devastated, that reproductive performance is persistently depressed, that nearly half a million birds have been lost, and that potential recovery times may run into the decades (Piatt et al. 1990; Fry 1993; Piatt 1993; Heinemann 1993) seem to be contradicted by studies that show attendance at breeding colonies to be within the range of historical counts, successful reproduction occurring in many oiled areas, and relatively rapid recovery in the use of heavily oiled habitats by many species (Erikson, this volume; Boersma et al., this volume, Day et al., this volume).

Why do such disagreements persist, particularly in view of the large number of scientific studies that were conducted following the *Exxon Valdez* spill? One reason has to do with the nature of the investigations and the available data. Some studies have focused on documenting impacts, whereas others have targeted evaluating recovery as well. Moreover, recovery is sometimes thought to have occurred only when the system has returned to its state before the spill (e.g., Heinemann 1993). Such a view ignores the considerable natural variation that occurs in Alaskan coastal and marine ecosystems. Both impact and recovery must be defined, statistically, in the context of this variability. In a highly variable system, moderate or even large changes in population size, reproduction, or habitat use may not be statistically significant, especially when sample sizes are small or the historical baseline is weak. These circumstances produce considerable uncertainty in our conclusions about the ecological consequences of oil spills (Spies 1993). Following the *Exxon Valdez* spill, investigators have differed in the certainty they attach to conclusions based on historical or nonstatistical comparisons, and this has contributed to disagreements about the overall impact of the spill. Natural variation, and the multiplicity of factors influencing mortality, reproduction, and habitat use by seabirds, obscures the effects of a single event such as an oil spill.

A second reason may have to do with the birds themselves. The *Exxon Valdez* oil spill contributed to the deaths of tens of thousands of seabirds, perhaps even substantially more. Yet surveys conducted at breeding colonies or in heavily oiled bays a year or two after the spill documented significant oiling effects for only a few species or colonies. If hundreds of thousands of birds were killed by the spill, their absence from breeding colonies or bays should have been apparent. It seems likely that the vacancies in breeding populations created by the deaths that did occur (if, indeed, they were of adult, breeding individuals) were filled by recruitment from "pools" of nonbreeding individuals that may be regional in scope. If this is so, then impacts of the spill may have been diffused over a large area, facilitating local recovery, and making it difficult to detect any changes in local abundance or habitat occupancy. In any event, these findings agree with other observations of the remarkable resilience of seabirds following oil spills (Alexander 1983) and are consistent with Dunnet's (1982) suggestion that this resilience may depend, in large part, on the nonbreeding component of populations.

The *Exxon Valdez* spill clearly had effects on seabirds, but not all species were equally affected. As has been reported for other oil spills (Hunt 1987), some species showed no adverse effects, whereas others still exhibited impacts 2 years following the spill (see also Fry 1993). Some species that suffered apparent impacts on population sizes exhibited no oiling effects on habitat use, while others showed oil-related effects only on reproduction. Many of the species that suffered initial impacts had apparently recovered within a year or two of the spill. Overall, the initial concerns that the *Exxon Valdez* spill would create an environmental disaster that would last for decades seem not to have been realized.

These findings stand in sharp contrast to public perceptions of the *Exxon Valdez* oil spill. Scientists generally consider the consequences of an environmental accident in biological and statistical terms, whereas public perceptions are often based on other, more emotional criteria. Media coverage of a spill also tends to emphasize images with the greatest impact, and these images persist in the minds of the public much longer than they may in nature. The results of scientific studies emerge only some time after the spill has occurred, and they fail to have the same effect on the public that the more immediate press coverage does (Mielke 1990). By emphasizing the determination of damages resulting from a spill, the laws relating to oil spills in the United States (Clean Water Act, Oil Pollution Act) may also contribute to an unbalanced view of spill impacts. The focus is on those species that are apparently negatively affected, and the species that do not suffer impacts or that recover quickly are not given much attention.

Many people in Western cultures have a deeply ingrained feeling for the "balance of Nature," and they generally do not realize that natural systems may vary substantially in the absence of human-induced disruptions or that many biological systems may have considerable resilience. Understanding natural variability and its effects is the key to developing a proper perspective on the impacts of oil spills on seabirds and their potential for recovery. Variability complicates scientific analysis of spill effects, to be sure. But it is also an important part of the natural world in which these species have evolved. It has fostered the resilience that enables species to respond to environmental disruptions, whether they are natural or result from human activities.

ACKNOWLEDGMENTS

My thinking about seabirds and oil spills has benefited from my interactions with Dee Boersma, Tom Crist, Bob Day, Dave Erikson, Greg Hayward, and Steve Murphy. I thank all of these individuals for sharing their views and their findings with me. Financial support for this synthesis was provided by Exxon Company, U.S.A. Exxon personnel assisted in many ways; throughout this research, their interest has been only in establishing how the *Exxon Valdez* oil spill affected seabirds, with as much scientific rigor and responsibility as possible. The views expressed here are my own and not necessarily those of Exxon.

REFERENCES

Aebischer, N. J. "Retrospective Investigation of an Ecological Disaster in the Shag *Phalacrocorax aristotelis*. A General Method Based on Long-Term Marking." *Journal of Animal Ecology*. 55: 613-630; 1986.

Alexander, M. M. "Oil, Fish and Wildlife, and Wetlands." *Northeastern Environmental Science*. 2: 13-24; 1983.

Ashmole, N. P. "Sea Bird Ecology and the Marine Environment." *in: Avian Biology*. D. S. Farner, J. R. King and K. C. Parkes (eds.); New York: Academic Press; 1: 224-286; 1971.

Bailey, E.P. and C.H. Davenport, "Dieoff of Common Murres on the Alaska Peninsula and Unimak Island." *Condor*. 74: 213-219; 1972.

Barrett, R. T. "Small Oil Spill Kills 10-20,000 Seabirds in North Norway." *Marine Pollution Bulletin*. 10: 253-255; 1979.

Bayer, R. D. "Breeding Success of Seabirds along the Mid-Oregon Coast Concurrent with the 1983 El Niño." *The Murrelet*. 67: 23-26; 1986.

Biderman, J. O. and W. H. Drury. "The Effects of Low Levels of Oil on Aquatic Birds." FWS/OBS-80/16. Washington, DC: United States Fish and Wildlife Service, Biological Services Program; 1980.

Birkhead, T. R. "Effects of Sea Conditions on Rates at Which Guillemots Feed Chicks." *British Birds*. 69: 490-492; 1976.

Birkhead, T.R. "The Effect of Habitat and Density on Breeding Success in the Common Guillemot (*Uria aalge*)." *Journal of Animal Ecology*. 46: 751-764; 1977.

Birkhead, T.R. and P.J. Hudson. "Population Parameters for the Common Guillemot (*Uria aalge*)." *Ornis Scandinavica*. 8:145-154; 1977.

Birkhead, T.R. and N.D. Nettleship. "Census Methods for Murres, *Uria* species: A Unified Approach." *Canadian Wildlife Services. Occasional Papers*. 43; 1980.

Boekelheide, R. J. and D. G. Ainley. "Age, Resource Availability, and Breeding Effort in Brandt's Cormorant." *Auk*. 106: 389-401; 1989.

Boekelheide, R. J., D. G. Ainley, S. H. Morrell, H. R. Huber, and T. J. Lewis. "Common Murre." *in: Seabirds of the Farallon Islands*. D. G. Ainley and R. J. Boekelheide (eds.); Stanford, California: Stanford University Press; 245-275; 1990.

Bourne, W. R. P. "The Torrey Canyon Disaster." *Seabird Bulletin*. 3: 4-11; 1967.

Bourne, W. R. P. "Observations of an Encounter between Birds and Floating Oil." *Nature*. 291: 632; 1968a.

Bourne, W. R. P. "Oil Pollution and Bird Populations." *in: Symposium on the Biological Effects of Oil Pollution on Littoral Communities, Pembroke, Wales, 1968, February 17*. 99-121; 1968b.

Bourne, W. R. P. "Recovery of Guillemot Colonies." *Marine Pollution Bulletin*. 13: 435-436; 1982.

Broni, S. C., M. Kaicener, and D. C. Duffy. "The Effect of Wind Direction on Numbers of Seabirds Seen During Shipboard Transects." *Journal of Field Ornithology*. 56: 411-412; 1985.

Brown, R. G. B. "Birds, Oil and the Canadian Environment." *in: Oil and Dispersants in Canadian Seas— Research Appraisal and Recommendations.* J. B. Sprague, J. H. Vandermeulen, and P. G. Wells (eds.); Ottawa: Environmental Protection Service, Environment Canada; 105-112; 1982.

Burger, A.E. "Estimating the Mortality of Seabirds Following Oil Spills: Effects of Spill Volume." *Marine Pollution Bulletin.* 26: 140-143; 1993.

Byrd, G. V., R. H. Day, and E. P. Knudtson. "Patterns of Colony Attendance and Censusing of Auklets at Bulder Island, Alaska." *Condor.* 85: 274-280; 1983.

Byrd, G.V. "Seabirds in the Pribilof Islands, Alaska: Trends and Monitoring Methods." University of Idaho. M.S. thesis; Moscow, Idaho; 1989.

Cairns, D. K. "Population Regulation of Seabird Colonies." *in: Current Ornithology.* D. M. Power (ed.), New York: Plenum Press; 9: 37-61; 1992.

Chesson, P. L. and T. J. Case. "Overview: Nonequilibrium Community Theories: Chance, Variability, History, and Coexistence." *in: Community Ecology.* J. Diamond and T. J. Case (eds.); New York: Harper & Row; 229-239; 1986.

Ciancaglini, D. E. "The Federal On-scene Coordinator's Role in the *Exxon Valdez* Oil Spill." *in: Proceedings* of the *1991 International Oil Spill Conference (Prevention, Behavior, Control, Cleanup), March 4-7, 1991, San Diego, CA.* Washington, DC: American Petroleum Institute; 325; 1991.

Clausager, I. "Oil Pollution in Danish Waters." *Ornis Fennica Supplement.* 3: 110-111; 1983.

Clark, R.B. "Impact of Oil Pollution on Seabirds." *Environmental Pollution (series A).* 33:1-22; 1984.

Conan, G. "The Long-term Effects of the *Amoco Cadiz* Oil Spill." *Philosophical Transactions of the Royal Society of London, B. Biological Science.* 297: 323-334; 1982.

Cooney, R. T. "Zooplankton." *in: The Gulf of Alaska: Physical Environment and Biological Resources.* D. W. Hood and S. T. Zimmerman (eds.); Anchorage, Alaska: National Oceanic and Atmospheric Administration, Alaska Office, Ocean Assessments Division; 285-303; 1986.

Coulson, J. C. "The Population Dynamics of Culling Herring Gulls and Lesser Black-backed Gulls." *in: Bird Population Studies. Relevance to Conservation and Management.* C. M. Perrins, J.- D. Lebreton, and G. J. M. Hirons (eds.); Oxford: Oxford University Press; 479-497; 1991.

Coulson, J. C. and C. S. Thomas. "Changes in the Biology of the Kittiwake *Rissa tridactyla*: a 31-year Study of a Breeding Colony." *Journal of Animal Ecology*. 54: 9-26; 1985.

Coulson, J. C. and R. D. Wooller. "Differential Survival Rates Among Breeding Kittiwake Gulls *Rissa Tridactyla*." *Journal of Animal Ecology*. 45: 205-213; 1976.

Croxall, J. P. "The Effect of Oil on Nature Conservation, Especially Birds." *in: Environmental Protection*. H. A. Cole (ed.); Barking, Essex, UK: Applied Science Publishers; 93-101; 1975.

Croxall, J. P. and P. Rothery. "Population Regulation of Seabirds: Implications of their Demography for Conservation." *in: Bird Population Studies. Relevance to Conservation and Management*. C. M. Perrins, J.- D. Lebreton and G. J. M. Hirons (eds.); Oxford: Oxford University Press; 272-296; 1991.

Curry-Lindahl, K. "Serious Situation with Regard to Swedish Populations of the Long-tailed Duck (Clangula hyemalis)." *International Waterfowl Research Bureau Newsletter*. 10: 15-18; 1960.

DeGange, A. R. and G. A. Sanger. "Marine Birds." *in: The Gulf of Alaska: Physical Environment and Biological Resources*. D. W. Hood and S. L. Zimmerman (eds.); Anchorage, Alaska: National Oceanic and Atmospheric Administration, Alaska Office, Ocean Assessments Division; 479-524; 1986.

Department of Justice. "Summary of Effects of the *Exxon Valdez* Oil Spill on Natural Resources and Archaeological Resources." Washington, DC: U.S. Department of Justice; 1991.

Diederich, J. "Nur eine kleine Ölpest." *Regulus*. 15: 132; 1981.

Dunnet, G.M. "Oil Pollution and Seabird Populations." *Philosophical Transactions of the Royal Society of London (B)*. 297: 413-427; 1982.

Dunnet, G. M. "Population Studies of the Fulmar on Eynhallow, Orkney Islands." *Ibis*. 133 (supplement): 24-27; 1991.

Dunnet, G. M. and J. C. Ollason. "Survival and Longevity in the Fulmar." *Ibis*. 120: 124-125; 1978.

Dwyer, T.J., P. Isleib, D.A. Davenport, and J.L. Haddock. "Marine Bird Populations in Prince William Sound." Unpublished report; Anchorage, Alaska: U.S. Fish and Wildlife Service; 1-21; 1976.

Dzinbal, K. A. "Ecology of Harlequin Ducks in Prince William Sound, Alaska During Summer." Oregon State University. M.S. thesis; Corvallis, Oregon; 1982.

Eppley, Z. A. and M. A. Rubega. "Indirect Effects of an Oil Spill: Reproductive Failure in a Population of South Polar Skuas Following the *Bahia Paraiso* Oil Spill in Antarctica." *Marine Ecology Progress Series*. 67: 1-6; 1990.

Exxon Valdez Oil Spill Trustees. "*Exxon Valdez* Oil Spill Restoration 1993 Draft Work Plan." Alaska Departments of Fish and Game, Law, and Environmental Conservation; U.S. Department of Agriculture, Department of the Interior; and the National Oceanographic and Atmospheric Administration. Anchorage, Alaska; 1992.

Ford, R.G., M.L. Bonnell, D.H. Varoujean, G.W. Page, B.E. Sharp, D. Heinemann, and J.L. Casey. "Assessment of Direct Seabird Mortality in Prince William Sound and the Western Gulf of Alaska Resulting from the *Exxon Valdez* Oil Spill." Unpublished Final Report. Portland, Oregon: Ecological Consulting, Inc.; 221; 1991.

Ford, R. G., G. W. Page, and H. R. Carter. "Estimating Mortality of Seabirds from Oil Spills." *in: Proceedings 1987 Oil Spill Conference (Prevention, Behavior, Control, Cleanup), April 6-9, 1987, Baltimore, Maryland.* Washington, DC: American Petroleum Institute; 547-551; 1987.

Ford, R.G., J.A. Wiens, D. Heinemann, and G.L. Hunt. "Modeling the Sensitivity of Colonially Breeding Marine Birds to Oil Spills: Guillemot and Kittiwake Populations on the Pribilof Islands, Bering Sea." *Journal of Applied Ecology.* 19: 1-31; 1982.

Fry, D.M. "How Do You Fix the Loss of Half a Million Birds?" *Program and Abstracts Book* Exxon Valdez *Oil Spill Symposium, February 2-5, 1993, Anchorage, Alaska.* Anchorage: Oil Spill Trustee Council; 30-33; 1993.

Fry, D. M., R. Boekelheide, J. Swenson, A. Kang, J. Young, and C. R. Grau. "Long-term Responses of Breeding Seabirds to Oil Exposure." *Pacific Seabird Group Bulletin.* 12: 22; 1985.

Furness, R. W. "Energy Requirements of Seabird Communities: A Bioenergetics Model." *Journal of Animal Ecology.* 47: 39-53; 1978.

Furness, R. W. "Competition between Fisheries and Seabird Communities." *Advances in Marine Biology.* 20: 225-307; 1982.

Furness, R. W. and R. T. Barrett. "Ecological Responses of Seabirds to Reductions in Fish Stocks in North Norway and Shetland." *in: Proceedings 20th International Ornithological Congress.* 20: 2241-2245; 1991.

Galt, J.A., W.J. Lehr and D.L. Payton. "Fate and Transport of the *Exxon Valdez* Oil Spill." *Environmental Science and Technology.* 25: 202-209; 1991.

Gaston, A.J. and D.N. Nettleship. "The Thick-billed Murres of Prince Leopold Island." *Canadian Wildlife Service Monograph No. 6.* 350; 1981.

Gaston, A. J., D. G. Noble, and M. A. Purdy. "Monitoring Breeding Biology Parameters for Murres *Uria* spp.: Levels of Accuracy and Sources of Bias." *Journal of Field Ornithology.* 54: 275-282; 1983.

Giller, P. S. and J. H. R. Gee. "The Analysis of Community Organization: The Influence of Equilibrium, Scale and Terminology." *in: Organization of Communities: Past and Present.* J. H. R. Gee and P. S. Giller (eds.); Oxford: Blackwell Scientific Publications; 519-542; 1987.

Haney, J. C. and A. R. Solow. "Analyzing Quantitative Relationships between Seabirds and Marine Resource Patches." *in: Current Ornithology.* D. M. Power (ed.); New York: Plenum Press; 9: 105-161; 1992.

Harris, M. P. "Biology and Survival of the Immature Puffin, *Fratercula arctica.*" *Ibis.* 125: 56-73; 1983.

Harris, M. P. "*The Puffin.*" Calton, U.K.: T & AD Poyser; 1984.

Harris, M. P. "Variation in the Correction Factor Used for Converting Counts of Individual Guillemots *Uria aalge* into Breeding Pairs." *Ibis.* 131: 85-93; 1989.

Harris, M. P. and S. Wanless. "The Effect of the Wreck of Seabirds in February 1983 on Auk Populations on the Isle of May (Fife)." *Bird Study.* 31: 103-110; 1984.

Harris, M. P. and S. Wanless. "The Breeding Biology of Guillemots *Uria aalge* on the Isle of May over a Six-year Period." *Ibis.* 130: 172-192; 1988.

Harris, M. P. and S. Wanless. "Population Studies and Conservation of Puffins *Fratercula arctica.*" *in: Bird Population Studies. Relevance to Conservation and Management.* C. M. Perrins, J.- D. Lebreton, and G. J. M. Hirons (eds.); Oxford: Oxford University Press; 230-248; 1991.

Harris, M. P., S. Wanless, and P. Rothery. "Assessing Changes in the Number of Guillemots *Uria aalge* at Breeding Colonies." *Bird Study.* 30: 57-66; 1983.

Hartung, R. "Energy Metabolism in Oil-Covered Ducks." *Journal of Wildlife Management.* 31: 798-804; 1967.

Hatch, S.A. "Did the 1982-1983 El Niño-Southern Oscillation Affect Seabirds in Alaska?" *Wilson Bulletin.* 99: 468-474; 1987.

Hatch, S.A. and M. Hatch. "Attendance Patterns of Murres at Breeding Sites: Implications from Monitoring." *Journal of Wildlife Management.* 53: 483-493; 1989.

Hatch, S. A. and M. A. Hatch. "Breeding Seasons of Oceanic Birds in a Subarctic Colony." *Canadian Journal of Zoology.* 68: 1664-1679; 1990.

Hatchwell, B.J. and T.R. Birkhead. "Population Dynamics of Common Guillemots (*Uria aalge*) on Skomer Island, Wales. *Ornis Scandinavica.* 22: 55-59; 1991.

Heinemann, D. "How Long to Recovery for Murre Populations, and Will Some Colonies Fail to Make the Comeback?" *in: Program and Abstract Book, Exxon Valdez Oil Spill Symposium, February 2-5, 1993, Anchorage, Alaska.* Anchorage: Oil Spill Trustee Council. 139-141; 1993.

Holmes, W. N. and J. Cronshaw. "Biological Effects of Petroleum on Marine Birds" *in: Effects of Petroleum on Arctic and Subarctic Marine Environments.* D. Malins (ed.); New York: Academic Press; 359-398; 1977.

Hope Jones, P., G. Howells, E. I. S. Rees, and J. Wilson. "Effect of *Hamilton Trader* oil on Birds in the Irish Sea in May 1969." *British Birds.* 63: 97-110; 1970.

Hudson, P. J. "Population Parameters for the Atlantic Alcidae." *in: The Atlantic Alcidae.* D. N. Nettleship and T. R. Birkhead (eds.); New York: Academic Press; 233-261; 1985.

Hunt, G.L., "Offshore Oil Development and Seabirds: The Present Status of Knowledge and Long-Term Research Needs." *in: Long-Term Environmental Effects of Offshore Oil and Gas Development.* (D. F. Boesch and N. N. Rabalais (eds.); New York: Elsevier; 539-586; 1987.

Hunt, G. L. "The Pelagic Distribution of Marine Birds in a Heterogeneous Environment." *Polar Research.* 8: 43-54; 1990.

Hunt, G. L., J. F. Piatt, and K. E. Erikstad. "How do Foraging Seabirds Sample Their Environment?" *in: Proceedings of the 20th International Ornithological Congress.* 20: 2272-2279; 1991.

Hunt, G. L. and D. C. Schneider. "Scale-Dependent Processes in the Physical and Biological Environment of Marine Birds." *in: Seabirds. Feeding Ecology and Role in Marine Ecosystems.* J. P. Croxall (ed.); Cambridge: Cambridge University Press; 7-41; 1987.

Irons, D. B., D. E. Nysewander, and J. L. Trapp. "Prince William Sound Waterbird Distribution in Relation to Habitat Type." Unpublished Report. Anchorage, Alaska: United States Fish and Wildlife Service; 1988.

Jones, L. L. and A. DeGange. "Interactions between Seabirds and Fisheries in the Northern Pacific Ocean." *in: Seabirds & Other Marine Vertebrates: Competition, Predation and Other Interactions.* J. Burger (ed.); New York: Columbia University Press; 261-290: 1988.

King, J.G. and G.A. Sanger. "Oil Vulnerability Index for Marine Oriented Birds." *in: Conservation of Marine Birds of Northern North America.* J.C. Bartonek and D.N. Nettleship (eds.). U.S. Fish and Wildlife Service, Wildlife Research Report. 11: 227-239; 1979.

Klomp, N. I. and R. W. Furness. "Non-breeders as a Buffer Against Environmental Stress: Declines in Numbers of Great Skuas on Foula, Shetland, and Prediction of Future Recruitment." *Journal of Applied Ecology.* 29: 341-348; 1992.

Koons, C.B. and H. O. Jahns. "The Fate of Oil from the *Exxon Valdez*—A Perspective." *Marine Technology Society Journal.* 26: 61-69; 1992.

Kuletz, K.J. "Effects of the *Exxon Valdez* Oil Spill On Marbled Murrelets." *in: Program and Abstract Book* Exxon Valdez *Oil Spill Symposium, February 2-5, 1993, Anchorage, Alaska.* Anchorage: Oil Spill Trustee Council; 148-150; 1993.

Lack, D. *Ecological Adaptations for Breeding in Birds.* London: Methuen; 409; 1968.

Laing, K.K. and S.P. Klosiewski. "Marine Bird Populations of Prince William Sound, Alaska, Before and After the Exxon Valdez Oil Spill." *in: Program and Abstracts Book,* Exxon Valdez *Oil Spill Symposium, February 2-5, 1993, Anchorage, Alaska.* Anchorage: Oil Spill Trustee Council; 160-161; 1993.

Leighton, F.A., R.G. Butler, and D.B. Peakall. "Oil and Arctic Marine Birds: An Assessment of Risk." *in Petroleum Effects in the Arctic Environment.* F.R. Englehardt (ed.). New York: Elsevier; 183-215; 1985.

Leslie, P. M. "The Intrinsic Rate of Increase and the Overlap of Successive Generations in a Population of Guillemots (*Uria aalge* Pont.)." *Journal of Animal Ecology.* 35: 291-301; 1966.

Levy, E. M. "Oil Pollution and Seabirds: Atlantic Canada 1976-77 and Some Implications for Northern Environments." *Marine Pollution Bulletin.* 11: 51-56; 1980.

Lloyd, C. "Timing and Frequency of Census Counts of Cliff-Nesting Auks." *British Birds.* 68: 507-513; 1975.

Maki, A. W. "The *Exxon Valdez* Oil Spill: Initial Environment Impact Assessment." *Environmental Science & Technology.* 25: 24-29; 1990.

Mead, C. and S. Baillie. "Seabirds and Oil: The Worst Winter." *Nature.* 292: 10-11; 1981.

Mickelson, P. *Natural History of Alaska's Prince William Sound and How to Enjoy It.* Cordova, Alaska: Alaska Wild Wings; 1989.

Mielke, J. E. "Oil in the Ocean: The Short- and Long-term Impacts of a Spill." *CRS Report for Congress.* Washington, DC: Congressional Research Service; 1990.
Morrison, M. L., B. G. Marcot and R. W. Mannan. *Wildlife-habitat Relationships. Concepts and Applications.* Madison, Wisconsin: University of Wisconsin Press; 1992.

Mudge, G. P. "An Evaluation of Current Methodology for Monitoring Changes in the Breeding Populations of Guillemots *Uria aalge.*" *Bird Study.* 35: 1-9; 1988.

Murphy, R. C. and W. Vogt. "The Dovekie Influx of 1932." *Auk.* 50: 325-349; 1933.

Murphy, E.C., A.M. Springer, and D.C. Roseneau. "Population Status of Common Guillemots (*Uria aalge*) at a Colony in Western Alaska: Results and Simulations." *Ibis.* 128: 348-363; 1986.

Myres, M. T. "Long-term Climatic and Oceanographic Cycles Regulating Seabird Distributions and Numbers." *in: Conservation of Marine Birds of Northern North America.* J. C. Bartonek and D. N. Nettleship (eds.); Washington, DC: United States Fish and Wildlife Service, Wildlife Research Report 11; 3-7; 1979.

National Research Council. *Oil in the Sea: Inputs, Fates, and Effects,* Washington, D.C.: National Academy Press; 1985.

Nisbet, I. C. T. "Long-term Ecological Studies of Seabirds." *Colonial Waterbirds.* 12: 143-147; 1989.

Nishimoto, M. and B. Rice. "A Re-survey of Seabirds and Marine Mammals Along the South Coast of the Kenai Peninsula, Alaska During The Summer of 1986." Unpublished Report Prepared by the U.S. Fish and Wildlife Service and the National Park Service, Anchorage, Alaska; 1-63; 1987.

Nysewander, D.R. and J.L. Trapp. "Wide-spread Mortality of Adult Seabirds in Alaska, August and September 1983." Unpublished administrative report. U.S. Fish and Wildlife Service; Homer, Alaska: 1984.

Nysewander, D.R., C. Dippel, G.V. Byrd, and E.P. Knudtson. "Effects of the *T/V Exxon Valdez* Oil Spill on Murres: A Perspective From Observations at Breeding Colonies." *in: Program and Abstract Book,* Exxon Valdez *Oil Spill Symposium, February 2-5, 1993, Anchorage, Alaska.* Anchorage: Oil Spill Trustee Council; 135-138; 1993.

Oakley, K. L. and K. J. Kuletz. "Effects of the *Exxon Valdez* Oil Spill on Pigeon Guillemots (*Cepphus columba*) in Prince William Sound, Alaska." *in: Program and Abstract Book,* Exxon Valdez *Oil Spill Symposium, February 2-5, 1993, Anchorage, Alaska.* Anchorage: Oil Spill Trustee Council; 144-146; 1993.

O'Connor, R. J. and C. Mead. "Oiled seabirds." *British Trust for Ornithology News.* 110: 4; 1980.

Ollason, J. C. and G. M. Dunnet. "Variation in Breeding Success in Fulmars." *in: Reproductive Success: Studies of Individual Variation in Contrasting Breeding Systems.* T. H. Clutton-Brock (ed.); Chicago: University of Chicago Press; 263-278; 1988.

Page, G.W., H.R. Carter, and R.G. Ford. "Numbers of Seabirds Killed or Debilitated in the 1986 *Apex Houston* Oil Spill in Central California." *in: Auks at Sea.* S.G. Sealy (ed.). *Studies in Avian Biology.* 14: 164-174; 1990.

Patten, S.M., Jr. "Acute and Sublethal Effects of the *Exxon Valdez* Oil Spill on Harlequins and Other Seaducks." *in: Program and Abstract Book,* Exxon Valdez *Oil Spill Symposium, February 2-5, 1993, Anchorage, Alaska.* Anchorage: Oil Spill Trustee Council; 151-154; 1993.

Peakall, D. B., P. G. Wells, and D. Mackay. "A Hazard Assessment of Chemically Dispersed Oil Spills and Seabirds." *Marine Environmental Research.* 22: 91-106; 1987.

Petersen, M. R. "Murres (*Uria* spp.)." *in: The Breeding Biology and Feeding Ecology of Marine Birds in the Gulf of Alaska.* P. A. Baird and P. J. Gould (eds.); U. S. Department of Commerce, National Oceanic and Atmospheric Administration, OCSEAP Final Report; 45 (1986): 381-399; 1983.

Piatt, J. "The Oil Spill and Seabirds: Three Years Later." *Alaska's Wildlife.* 25: 11-12; 1993.

Piatt, J.F., C.J. Lensink, W. Butler, M. Kendziorek, and D.R. Nysewander. "Immediate Impact of the *Exxon Valdez* Oil Spill on Marine Birds." *Auk.* 107: 387-397; 1990.
Piatt, J. F. and C. J. Lensink. "*Exxon Valdez* Bird Toll." *Nature.* 342: 865-866; 1989.

Piatt, J. F. and D. N. Nettleship. "Diving Depths of Four Alcids." *Auk.* 102: 293-297; 1985.

Potts, G. R. "The Influence of Eruptive Movements, Age, Population Size and Other Factors on the Survival of the Shag (*Phalacrocorax aristotelis* L.)." *Journal of Animal Ecology.* 38: 53-102; 1969.

Potts, G. R., J. C. Coulson, and I. R. Deans. "Population Dynamics and Breeding Success of the Shag, *Phalacrocorax aristotelis*, on the Farne Islands, Northumberland." *Journal of Animal Ecology.* 49: 465-484; 1980.

Powers, K. D. "A Comparison of Two Methods of Counting Birds at Sea." *Journal of Field Ornithology.* 53: 209-222; 1982.

Ralph, C. J. and J. M. Scott. *Estimating Numbers of Terrestrial Birds. Studies in Avian Biology*; 6: 1981.

Richardson, M. G., M. Heubeck, D. Lea, and P. Reynolds. "Oil Pollution, Seabirds, and Operational Consequences, around the Northern Isles of Scotland." *Environmental Conservation.* 9: 315-321; 1982.

Ricklefs, R. E. "Fecundity, Mortality and Avian Demography." *in: Breeding Biology of Birds.* D. S. Farner (ed.); Washington, DC: National Academy of Sciences; 366-434; 1973.

Ricklefs, R. E "Seabird Life Histories and the Marine Environment: Some Speculations." *Colonial Waterbirds.* 13: 1-6; 1990.

Robertson, I. "Vulnerability of Seabirds to Oil In the Tropics: Modifying a North Pacific Index." *Pacific Seabird Group Bulletin.* 9: 78; 1982.

Roby, D. D. and K. L. Brink. "Breeding Biology of Least Auklets on the Pribilof Islands, Alaska." *Condor.* 88: 336-346; 1986.

Rothery, P., S. Wanless, and M.P. Harris. "Analysis of Counts from Monitoring Guillemots in Britain and Ireland." *Journal of Animal Ecology.* 57: 1-19; 1988.

Royer, T. C., J. A. Vermersch, T. J. Weingartner, H. J. Niebauer, and R. D. Muench. "Ocean Circulation Influencing the *Exxon Valdez* Oil Spill." *Oceanography.* 3: 3-10; 1990.

Sambrotto, R. N. and C. J. Lorenzen. "Phytoplankton and Primary Production." *in: The Gulf of Alaska: Physical Environment and Biological Resources.* D. W. Hood and S. T. Zimmerman (eds.); Anchorage, Alaska: National Oceanic and Atmospheric Administration, Alaska Office, Ocean Assessments Division; 249-282; 1986.

Samuels, W. B. and A. Ladino. "Calculations of Seabird Population Recovery from Potential Oil Spills in The Mid-Atlantic Region of The United States." *Ecological Modelling.* 21: 63-84; 1984.

Samuels, W.B. and K.J. Lanfear. "Simulations Of Seabird Damage and Recovery from Oilspills in the Northern Gulf of Alaska." *Journal of Environmental Management.* 15: 169-182; 1982.

Schneider, D. C. and D. C. Duffy. "Scale-Dependent Variability in Seabird Abundance. "*Marine Ecology Progress Series.* 25: 211-218; 1985.

Schreiber, R. W. and E. A. Schreiber. "Central Pacific Seabirds and the El Niño Southern Oscillation: 1982 to 1983 Perspectives." *Science.* 225: 713-716; 1984.

Seip, K. L., E. Sandersen, F. Mehlum, and J. Ryssdal. "Damages to Seabirds from Oil Spills: Comparing Simulation Results and Vulnerability Indexes." *Ecological Modelling.* 53: 39-59; 1991.

Sharp, B.E. and M. Cody. "Black Oystercatchers in Prince William Sound: Oil Spill Effects on Reproduction and Behavior." *in: Program and Abstract Book*, Exxon Valdez *Oil Spill Symposium, February 2-5, 1993, Anchorage, Alaska.* Anchorage: Oil Spill Trustee Council; 155-158; 1993.

Simons, T. R. "Behavior and Attendance Patterns of the Fork-tailed Storm-petrel." *Auk.* 98: 145-158; 1981.

Slater, P.J.B. "Factors Affecting the Numbers of Guillemots (*Uria aalge*) Present on Cliffs." *Ornis Scandinavica.* 11: 155-163; 1980.

Snyder, D. E. "A Great Flight of Dovekies (*Plautus alle*)." *Auk.* 70: 87-88; 1953.

Sowls, A.L., S.A. Hatch, and C.J. Lensink. "Catalog of Alaskan Seabird Colonies." U.S. Fish and Wildlife Service. Office of Biological Services, FWS/OBS-78/78; Anchorage, Alaska; 1-253; 1978.

Speich, S. M., D. A. Manuwal, and T. R. Wahl. "The Bird/Habitat Oil Index--A Habitat Vulnerability Index Based on Avian Utilization." *Wildlife Society Bulletin.* 19: 216-221; 1991.

Speich, S. M., T. R. Wahl, and R. U. Steelquist. "The *Arco Anchorage* Oil Spill—An Evaluation Of Avian Impact Assessment Methods." *Puget Sound Research '91 Proceedings.* 3: 383-392; 1991.

Spies, R. B. "So Why Can't Science Tell Us More about the Effects of the *Exxon Valdez* Oil Spill?" *in: Program and Abstract Book*, Exxon Valdez *Oil Spill Symposium, February 2-5, 1993, Anchorage, Alaska.* Anchorage: Oil Spill Trustee Council; 1-5; 1993.

Springer, A.W., D.S.L. Rosneau, C.P. McRoy and E.C. Murphy. "Seabird Responses to Fluctuating Prey Availability In The Eastern Bering Sea." *Marine Ecology Progress Series.* 32:1-12; 1986.

Springer, A. W. "Seabird Distribution as Related to Food Webs and the Environment: Examples from the North Pacific Ocean." *in: Studies of High-latitude Seabirds. 1. Behavioral, Energetic, and Oceanographic Aspects of Seabird Feeding Ecology.* W. A. Montevecchi and A. J. Gaston (eds.); Ottawa: *Canadian Wildlife Service Occasional Paper.* 68: 39-47; 1991.

Stowe, T. J. "An Oil Spillage at a Guillemot Colony." *Marine Pollution Bulletin.* 13: 237-239; 1982.

Stowe, T. J. and L. A. Underwood. "Oil Spillages Affecting Seabirds in the United Kingdom, 1966-1983." *Marine Pollution Bulletin.* 15: 147-152; 1984.

Tanis, J. J. C. and M. F. Mörzer Bruyns. "The Impact of Oil-pollution on Sea Birds in Europe." *in: Proceedings of the International Conference on Oil Pollution of the Sea.* 67-75; 1968.

Tasker, M. L., P. H. Jones, T. Dixon, and B. F. Blake. "Counting Seabirds at Sea From Ships: A Review of Methods Employed and a Suggestion for a Standardized Approach." *Auk.* 101: 567-577; 1984.

Temple, S. A. "Restoration Following the *Exxon Valdez* Oil Spill." Anchorage, Alaska: Restoration Planning Work Group; 43-45; 1990.

Temple, S. A. and J. A. Wiens. "Bird Populations and Environmental Changes: Can Birds Be Bio-indicators?" *American Birds.* 43: 260-270; 1989.

Thomas, C. S. and J. C. Coulson. "Reproductive Success of Kittiwake Gulls, *Rissa tridactyla.*" *in: Reproductive Success: Studies of Individual Variation in Contrasting Breeding Systems.* T. H. Clutton-Brock (ed.); Chicago: University of Chicago Press; 251-262; 1988.

Tuck, L.M. "The Murres: Their Distribution, Populations and Biology; A Study of The Genus *Uria.*"
Canadian Wildlife Service Monograph Series. 260; 1960.

U.S. Fish and Wildlife Service. "Catalog of Alaskan Seabird Colonies-Computer Archives." Anchorage, Alaska: U.S. Fish and Wildlife Service; 1991.

Vader, W., R. T. Barrett, K. E. Erikstad, and K. B. Strann. "Differential Responses of Common and Thick-billed Murres to a Crash in the Capelin Stock in the Southern Barents Sea." *in: Auks at Sea.* S. G. Sealy (ed.); *Studies in Avian Biology*; 14: 175-180; 1990.

Vermeer, K. and R. Vermeer. "Oil Threat to Birds on the Canadian West Coast." *Canadian Field-Naturalist.* 89: 278-298; 1975.

Wahl, T. R., D. G. Ainley, A. H. Benedict and A. R. DeGange. "Associations between Seabirds and Water-Masses in the Northern Pacific Ocean in Summer." *Marine Biology.* 103: 1-11; 1989.

Wiens, J. A. "On Competition and Variable Environments." *American Scientist.* 65: 590-597; 1977.

Wiens, J. A. "Single-Sample Surveys of Communities: Are the Revealed Patterns Real?" *The American Naturalist.* 117: 90-98; 1981.

Wiens, J. A. "The Ecology of Bird Communities." *in: Foundations and Patterns.* Volume 1. Cambridge: Cambridge University Press; 1989.

Wiens, J. A. and K. R. Parker. "Analyzing the Effects of Accidental Environmental Impacts: Approaches and Assumptions." *Ecological Applications;* in press.

Wiens, J. A. and J. M. Scott. "Model Estimation of Energy Flow in Oregon Coastal Seabird Populations." *Condor.* 77: 439-452; 1975.

Wilson, J. G. and J. E. Overland. "Meteorology." *in: The Gulf of Alaska: Physical Environment and Biological Resources.* D. W. Hood and S. T. Zimmerman (eds.); Anchorage, Alaska: National Oceanic and Atmospheric Administration, Alaska Office, Ocean Assessments Division; 31-54; 1986.

Wooller, R. D., J. S. Bradley, and J. P. Croxall. "Long-term Population Studies of Seabirds." *Trends in Ecology and Evolution.* 7: 111-114; 1992.

Worster, D. *Nature's Economy: The Roots of Ecology.* San Francisco: Sierra Club Books; 1977.

Ydenberg, R. C. "Growth-Mortality Trade-offs and the Evolution of Juvenile Life Histories in the Alcidae." *Ecology.* 70: 1494-1506; 1989.

Charles B. Johnson[1] and David L. Garshelis[2]

SEA OTTER ABUNDANCE, DISTRIBUTION, AND PUP PRODUCTION IN
PRINCE WILLIAM SOUND FOLLOWING THE *EXXON VALDEZ* OIL SPILL

REFERENCE: Johnson, C. B. and Garshelis, D. L., "**Sea Otter Abundance,
Distribution, and Pup Production in Prince William Sound Following the *Exxon
Valdez* Oil Spill**," Exxon Valdez *Oil Spill: Fate and Effects in Alaskan Waters*, ASTM
STP 1219, Peter G. Wells, James N. Butler, and Jane S. Hughes, Eds., American Society
for Testing and Materials, Philadelphia, 1995.

ABSTRACT: We investigated effects of the 1989 *Exxon Valdez* oil spill on the
abundance, distribution, and pup production of sea otters (*Enhydra lutris*) in Prince
William Sound (PWS) by comparing counts made during 1990 and 1991 with counts
made by researchers 5–12 years before the spill. We observed no evidence of avoidance
or attraction to spill-affected shorelines 1–2 years after the spill. Despite a substantial
loss of sea otters immediately following the spill, we counted fewer otters than prespill
investigators at only one of three heavily oiled islands, and from 1990 to 1991 our counts
at this one site increased to a level equivalent to the latest (1985) prespill count.

  We followed the methods of prespill investigators and found close agreement
between our counts of otters and those of two other concurrent investigations using the
same survey technique. This agreement among counts, and our involvement in counts
made prespill, suggested that inter-observer variability could not explain our
unexpectedly high counts at oiled sites. Some otters killed in the spill were likely
replaced by otters from other parts of PWS. However, we suggest that a modest
population increase prior to the spill, but after the last prespill counts, is the most
plausible explanation for the concurrence of our postspill counts and counts from the
early 1980s. At three heavily oiled sites, pup production 1–2 years after the spill was as
high or higher than witnessed before the spill. Although the increase in pupping observed
at one island was greater in lightly oiled than in heavily oiled areas, no such trend
occurred at another oil-affected island. Mortality, as indicated by the number of carcasses
found on beaches a year after the spill, was similar to what had been observed
historically. The diet also was unchanged. If the otter population indeed was growing
before the spill, these results indicate the potential for renewed population growth.

[1] ABR, Inc. P.O. Box 80410, Fairbanks, AK 99708.
[2] Minnesota Department of Natural Resources (MDNR), Grand Rapids, MN, 55744.
  Business address only; the MDNR was not affiliated with this work.

KEYWORDS: Alaska, counts, diet, *Exxon Valdez*, foraging, mortality, oil spill, population growth, Prince William Sound, pup production, sea otter, surveys

---

Since the completion of the Trans-Alaska pipeline in 1977, with its terminus in Valdez, the threat of an oil spill in Prince William Sound (PWS) has generated concern for the welfare of the sea otter population inhabiting PWS. Contamination of the marine ecosystem was foreseen as an inevitable result of petroleum-related development (Pitcher 1975) and prompted the first sound-wide survey of sea otters in 1973 to obtain baseline information on their abundance and distribution.

Sea otters are particularly vulnerable to floating oil because they spend most of their time on the water surface and rely on a dense, well-groomed pelage with an entrapped layer of air for both insulation and buoyancy (Kenyon 1969; Morrison et al. 1974; Tarasoff 1974). Oil contamination of a sea otter's pelage significantly increases thermal conductance, causing both elevated heat production (metabolism) and behavioral changes (especially increased grooming)(Siniff et al. 1982; Costa and Kooyman 1982; Davis et al. 1988; Williams et al. 1988). Sea otters have an unusually high metabolic rate (Morrison et al. 1974; Costa and Kooyman 1982), so they cannot readily compensate for the increased energy demands that result from lost insulation, decreased buoyancy, and increased grooming. Loss of insulation may be particularly demanding for sea otters in PWS, where they reach the northern limit of their range.

Toxic effects from oil inhalation or ingestion also pose serious risks to sea otters (Wilson et al. 1990a, 1990b). Otters may ingest oil while grooming, or may consume oil-contaminated prey. In combination, the effects of pelage contamination and ingestion often lead to death. Therefore, the diffusion of oil that leaked from the wreck of the *Exxon Valdez* in March 1989 prompted legitimate concerns for massive harm to the sea otter population in PWS.

Widespread adoration of the species, graphic depictions of oiled, moribund otters, and an indisputably high death toll focused much attention on the status of PWS sea otters after the *Exxon Valdez* spill. Initial efforts centered around capturing and rehabilitating oil-injured otters and recovering carcasses. Soon afterwards, various studies were undertaken to assess the effects of the spill on the population. Studies were necessary to determine both the immediate effect on the status of otters (how many survived?) and possible chronic injuries to survivors and/or their food supply, which could diminish the capacity of the population to recover.

In investigating the effects of this spill on sea otters, we must distinguish three issues: how many died?, how many remained?, and were there residual complications that could compromise recovery? Certainly the number killed directly affected the number remaining, but estimates of these numbers can be obtained independently, and, moreover, variation among estimates of the number killed does not affect the current status of sea otters. We know that the carcasses of 421 otters that were judged to have died after the spill were recovered from PWS, that another 84 died later at or en route to rehabilitation centers (Bayha and Kormendy 1990), and that some unknown fraction of the number killed were never recovered. An estimate of the spill-related mortality depends on the estimate of this unrecovered fraction. Such an estimate may be useful in assessing effects of the *Exxon Valdez* spill (cf. Estes 1991) and in projecting the effects of future spills in areas occupied by sea otters, but it is not needed to assess the current status of the PWS population and its probability of recovery.

We evaluated the status of the PWS sea otter population after the spill by comparing their numbers and distribution postspill with corresponding data from prespill investigations. The potential for population recovery also was assessed by comparing prespill and postspill data; we used pup production as a measure of growth potential, and food habits and over-winter mortality to evaluate possible oiling effects that might limit recovery.

STUDY AREAS

We selected eight sites in PWS (Figure 1) for which prespill data were available on sea otter numbers and pup production. Three of the sites had been affected by major amounts of oil (henceforth, "oiled"), one was close enough to oiled sites that otters likely moved between there and oiled areas, and the other four were distant, unoiled reference (henceforth, "control") sites. We used control sites to assess comparability of our data collection techniques with those of prespill investigators, and also to investigate possible population trends in areas unaffected by the oil spill. However, no true control sites were available, because all sites differed in physical characteristics and history of occupation by otters, and, consequently, population characteristics and dynamics probably varied among sites. We considered these factors in our choice of sites and in our study design.

History of Otter Occupation

The sea otter population in PWS was exploited to the point of near-elimination by the fur trade, first by the Russians (late 1700s–mid-1800s) and then by the Americans (mid-1800s–early 1900s) (Lensink 1960). After otters were protected from harvest by the 1911 International Fur Seal Treaty, the remnant population in PWS began to recover and recolonize vacant habitats. The size and location of remnant groups of otters during the early 1900s has never been established, but it seems certain that there were one or more groups in the southwestern portion of PWS. Sea otters were observed in the vicinity of Montague Island in 1936 (Williams 1938), at Latouche and Elrington Islands in 1949, and at Hinchinbrook Island in 1951 (Lensink 1960)(Figure 1). An aerial survey conducted in 1959 (Lensink 1962) located sizable numbers of otters at five of our study sites: Green Island (50–100), Applegate Rock (probably included in Green Island count), Stockdale Harbor-Port Chalmers (large proportion of the total 450–575 at Montague Island), and Port Etches and Constantine Harbor (both included in the Hinchinbrook Island estimate of 75–100). A large expansion of the otter population to the north, east, and west apparently occurred during the 1960s. Two of our other study sites, Knight Island and Port Gravina, were reoccupied by 1970 (Pitcher 1975). Expansion continued, particularly in the eastern part of PWS, during the 1970s, and otters moved into Sheep Bay in 1974 (A.M. Johnson, personal communication 1991). By 1980, otters had moved well past

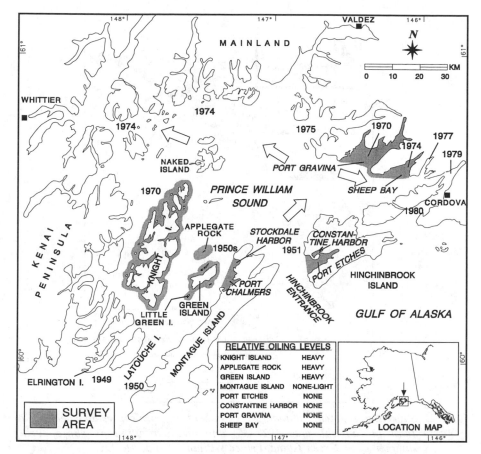

Figure 1. Map of survey areas in Prince William Sound, Alaska, 1990–91. Years indicate first recorded observation of groups of sea otters (Lensink 1960; Pitcher 1975; Garshelis et al. 1986; Johnson 1987). Arrows indicate general direction of population expansion.

Sheep Bay and had reinhabited virtually the entire eastern sound (Garshelis et al. 1986), and subsequently began recolonizing the Gulf of Alaska coast, south of Cordova (Simon-Jackson 1986; Monnett and Rotterman 1989).

Bays in eastern PWS were initially reoccupied by groups predominated by males; males were replaced by females and pups 7–9 years later (Garshelis et al. 1984; Johnson 1987). In the early stages of reoccupation, food was plentiful, but it dwindled with increased length of otter occupancy (Garshelis et al. 1986).

Description of Study Sites

Green Island, Applegate Rock, and Knight Island were all heavily oiled by the 1989 spill (Neff et al. this volume). The shoreline of Applegate Rock, comprising about 2 km, was almost entirely oiled (Figure 2). Oil was not distributed completely or uniformly

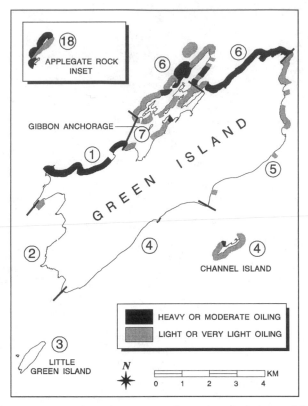

Figure 2. Shoreline segment boundaries (numbers in circles) established by A. Johnson (unpubl. data 1977–85) and oil distribution on shore during summer 1989, Green Island, Prince William Sound, Alaska.

around Green Island or its associated smaller islands (Little Green and Channel), which together constitute 66 km of shoreline, or at the Knight Island group (Knight, Eleanor, Ingot, Disk, Sphinx, Squirrel, Mummy, and Squire islands)(Figure 3), which constitutes 645 km of shoreline. Although northern Montague Island was oiled, our study sites in Stockdale Harbor and Port Chalmers (henceforth, Montague)(Figure 1), containing 66 km of shorelines, had only isolated patches of very light oil (mainly splashes and occasional tarballs). Green, Applegate, and Montague all have relatively large, shallow (<18 m deep) nearshore zones with abundant offshore rocks. Several kelp beds (*Nereocystis luetkeana*) were present at both Green and Montague. The nearshore zone at Knight Island drops off more steeply, except in some localized areas. Offshore rocks were abundant on the southwestern side of the island, but kelp beds were essentially absent.

The other four study areas were on the eastern side of PWS, and thus were not affected by oil from the *Exxon Valdez* (Figure 1). Port Etches on Hinchinbrook Island contains 38 km of shoreline, with shallow areas at the head of the bay and around a rock outcrop at its mouth. There were small patches of kelp and a few offshore rocks. Constantine Harbor, a distinct, enclosed shallow area (entirely <18 m deep) within Port

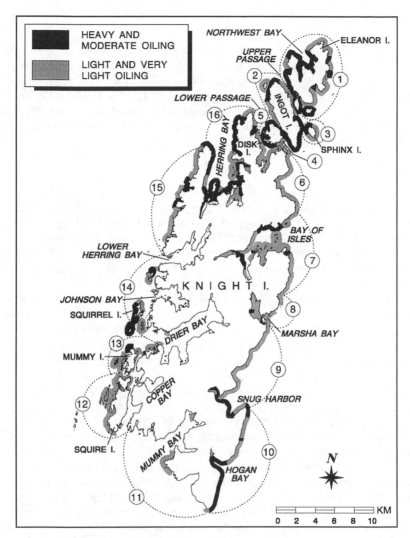

Figure 3. Shoreline segment boundaries (numbers in circles) established by Pitcher (1975) and oil distribution on shore during summer 1989, Knight Island, Prince William Sound, Alaska.

Etches contains 17 km of shoreline (at mean high tide) and extensive beds of eelgrass (*Zostera* spp.). Port Gravina and Sheep Bay, comprising 87 km and 59 km, respectively, of shoreline that we surveyed, are both on the mainland in eastern PWS. Nearshore habitats at these two sites are relatively deep, except at one headland and the heads of smaller bays and coves within these larger bays. There are few offshore rocks in these two areas, and no kelp beds.

METHODS

Survey and observational methods were designed to match those of the prespill studies that we used for comparisons. Protocols for data collection procedures were established on the basis of published accounts of procedures used previously, discussions with previous investigators, and personal experience (DLG) in collecting sea otter data before the spill. New observers read the protocols and practiced with an experienced observer before collecting data on their own. Three types of data were collected: counts of live otters, counts of carcasses, and foraging observations.

Counts of Live Otters

We counted live otters during boat surveys to assess changes in abundance, distribution, and pup production from prespill to postspill. We conducted surveys 2–4 times per month from May through August 1990 at Green Island, Applegate Rock, Montague Island, Port Gravina, and Sheep Bay. In 1991, we added three study sites—Knight Island, Port Etches, and Constantine Harbor—but surveyed all sites only during July and August; we surveyed each of the eight study sites 2–8 times during this period, allocating most effort to the oiled sites.

We started surveys generally at 0700–0800 hours, as was done by previous investigators, and completed them by mid- to late afternoon, when sea conditions tended to deteriorate. In a single day's survey we could count one of the following areas: Green Island and Applegate Rock, Stockdale Harbor and Port Chalmers (Montague), Port Gravina and Sheep Bay, or Port Etches and Constantine Harbor. Each area was surveyed at intervals of about 7 days, although we sometimes surveyed at shorter intervals (minimum = 3 days) when weather interfered. Knight Island required 8–13 days to complete, depending on the weather; each day we continued from where we finished the previous day. Surveys were postponed or prematurely terminated if weather or sea conditions were deemed unsatisfactory for viewing (heavy rain, fog, or seas > 0.6 m).

Prespill surveys were conducted with 5–10-m boats without a raised viewing platform (Table 1). The same types of boats were unavailable to us after the spill. Instead, we used a 13-m or 16-m boat with a 3-m high flying bridge for surveys that extended offshore; this gave us a somewhat better viewing range than that of the prespill investigators, but it did not alter the viewing area (i.e., we zigzagged less to cover the same area). In shallower areas that were difficult to navigate in a larger boat, like the shoal near Applegate Rock and in Constantine Harbor, we used a 4.5-m inflatable raft with an outboard motor. We used an inflatable raft also around Knight Island, where we followed the methods of a prespill survey that was conducted with 5–10-m boats close to shore.

At Green Island, Applegate Rock, and Montague Island, all open areas with undefined boundaries, the outer limits of the survey area were not specified by the prespill observer (Johnson 1987); however, on the basis of discussions with him and participation in some of his earlier surveys, we set an outer limit of 1500 m from shore. The survey areas for the enclosed sites—Port Gravina, Sheep Bay, Port Etches, and Constantine Harbor—were delineated by the boundaries of each bay with no distance limits from shore. At Knight Island, our survey area was restricted to 200 m offshore,

Table 1.   Sites surveyed and techniques used for sea otter counts in Prince William Sound, Alaska.

Sites	Prespill Surveys				Postspill Surveys		
	Survey Platform	Near-shore Zone[a]	Dates	Sources	Survey Platform	Near-shore Zone[a]	Dates
Green, Applegate, Montague, Sheep Bay, and Port Gravina	5–6-m open boat	no limit	1977–1985	Johnson 1987; and unpubl. data	13–16-m cabin cruisers with flying bridge[b]	no limit	May–August 1990, July–August 1991
Knight Island area	helicopter	200 m	June 1973	Pitcher 1975[c]	4.5-m inflatable raft with motor	200 m	July–August 1991
	5–10-m cabin cruiser	200 m	August 1984	Irons et al. 1988[c]			
Port Etches and Constantine Harbor	inflatable raft with motor	no limit	May–July 1976	Nyse-wander and Knudtson 1977	16-m cabin cruiser with flying bridge[b]	no limit	July–August 1991

[a]   Distance from shoreline that was searched for otters. The 200-m zone describes the primary search area; sea otters beyond 200 m were recorded with unknown accuracy. "No limit" indicates that researchers attempted to count all otters regardless of distance from shore, but within the general boundaries of the site.

[b]   During postspill surveys, a 4.5-m inflatable raft with motor was used in Constantine Harbor, in Gibbon Anchorage, and around Applegate Rock.

[c]   Pitcher (1975) and Irons et al. (1988) surveyed all of PWS during 1973 and 1984–85, respectively. Our comparisons with their data were made primarily for Knight Island.

although we also counted otters that were beyond 200 m, as set forth by Irons et al. (1988). Our survey route followed the contours of the shoreline 100 m offshore at Knight Island and about 500 m offshore at the other sites. At sites other than Knight Island, we deviated from the survey route to make more accurate counts of distant groups of otters and to survey the centers of large bays, as was done by Johnson (1987).

Survey boats traveled at 3–10 knots (6–19 km/hr), but we stopped to count large groups of otters. Two, or less commonly, three observers using 8–10x binoculars continually scanned the water surface to the sides and front of the boat. As we moved through an area, it was scanned more than once to improve our chances of observing an otter surfacing from a dive.

We differentiated two primary categories of otters: independent otters and dependent pups. We used the ratio of pups to independents (including mothers) as a measure of productivity. Pups were identified by a variety of criteria: being carried, groomed, or fed by a larger otter; swimming with a larger otter and exhibiting short, shallow dives, often with the tail breaking the water surface; or small physical size and proximity to a larger otter. Pups were subdivided into two categories. New pups had light, woolly pelage, rarely were unattended by their mother, and did not dive or swim without some assistance (Payne and Jameson 1984). Older pups had smooth dark pelage and were better able to swim and dive.

We mapped the location of each otter observed, recorded the time and group size, and, in 1991, noted which otters were within 200 m of shore. Otter numbers were tallied according to subunits of the shoreline, referred to herein as "shoreline segments." We used segment boundaries defined by previous investigators (A. Johnson [unpubl. data 1977–85] for Green Island [Figure 2]; Pitcher [1975] for Knight Island [Figure 3]), or created our own, on the basis of prominent shoreline features and areas where otters typically congregated. Shoreline data were measured from digitized versions of U.S. Geological Survey maps (1:63 360) and air photos (Aeromap, Anchorage, AK) using AutoCAD software (v.11, Autodesk, Inc., Sausalito, CA). Otter densities were calculated by dividing the number of otters by the area surveyed (calculated with AutoCAD).

Carcass Count

In late April 1990, prior to the spring growth of vegetation, we counted sea otter carcasses along the beaches at Green Island, Little Green Island, and Channel Island to assess mortality during the previous winter. One observer searched the upper third of the intertidal zone, and one searched the storm-tide line, where the terrestrial vegetation begins. We recorded the location of each carcass and indicated whether or not it was a pup (based on the presence of deciduous or partly erupted permanent teeth [Lensink, 1962]). We deleted from the count skeletal material that was bleached white and had no attached flesh or connective tissue, considering these remains to be from before the winter of 1989–90 (i.e., spill-related summer mortalities not previously recovered and mortalities from previous seasons). These were excluded from the count, because we compared winter mortality after the spill with counts of winter mortality made annually from 1976 to 1984 by Johnson (1987).

Foraging Observations

We observed foraging sea otters from onshore at various locations in and around Gibbon Anchorage, on the northwest side of Green Island (Figure 2), during May through August 1990 and July and August 1991. We followed the techniques used previously in this same area by Garshelis (1983) and Johnson (1987), and many of our observation locations were identical to the ones used in their prespill studies.

We collected foraging data opportunistically at different times of day, whenever we found an otter feeding close enough for us to identify food items through a 50–80x high-resolution telescope. Each time an otter surfaced from a foraging dive, we identified its prey to the lowest taxon possible. We attempted to watch a foraging otter for 30 min, but the observation period was cut short if the otter swam out of view or stopped feeding.

For analysis, each dive was treated as a sample unit and prey items were grouped into the following categories: clams, crabs, mussels, worm-like organisms (primarily *Echiurus echiurus*), urchins, sea stars, octopi, and kelp.

Quantification of Oiling Levels in Study Sites

To enable us to test for differences in otter population parameters related to degree of oiling, we quantified the amount of oil that stranded on each shoreline segment. Shoreline oiling levels were determined during the summer of 1989 by shoreline survey teams, which were reviewed by the Interagency Shoreline Cleanup Committee (Neff et al. this volume). We selected the shoreline oiling measurement from summer 1989 as most indicative of the original extent of oil in the shoreline environment and the extent of potential subtidal contamination. We converted oiling levels of very light, light, moderate, and heavy (Neff et al. this volume) to integer values 1 to 4, respectively. We then multiplied the percentage of each shoreline segment (or survey site) in each oiling category by the integer value of that category and summed these values to obtain an overall oil index for each segment. Oil indices could range from 0 (no oil) to 400 (heavy oil = 4 × 100% of shoreline length). An index of 100, for example, could represent light oil on 50% of the shoreline segment (2 × 50%), or heavy oil on one-quarter of the segment (4 × 25%), or some combination of oiling on different stretches of shoreline (Figures 2 and 3). Because we had no better information at the time for each shoreline segment on the actual quantity of oil, its mobility, its toxicity, or its potential to affect intertidal and subtidal habitats, we used these oiling indices as a means of quantifying the potential risk to sea otters.

Statistical Analysis

We primarily used analysis of variance (ANOVA) and regression to investigate possible effects of the oil spill on otter numbers and pup production. Dependent variables used in these analyses were transformed to approximate normal distributions and reduce patterns evident in plots of residuals. Counts and densities were log-transformed, whereas pup ratios were transformed by the arcsine of the square root. We constructed ANOVA models using all two-way and three-way interaction terms, after which we developed final models by eliminating two-way and three-way interactions that were not significant ($P > 0.05$). We made all possible pairwise comparisons of two-way factor means of each time period at each site (e.g., mean count in 1990 at Green with the mean count in 1991 at Green) using contrasts in the final model. The significance levels of the pairwise comparisons were not corrected for the number of comparisons made, but they reflected real differences because pairwise comparisons were made only when the overall comparison (two-way interaction) was significant ($P \leq 0.05$). Therefore, reported P-values for pairwise comparisons may be underestimated. All ANOVAs, regressions, and chi-square tests were conducted with JMP software (JMP, version 2.0.4, SAS Institute, Cary, NC).

Nonparametric tests were used to compare unreplicated counts of otters in various shoreline segments and at various sites during a single sound-wide survey in 1984–85 (Irons et al. 1988 and unpubl. data from their study) with the means of our multiple counts. We used nonparametric tests because they are not affected by departures of the data from normality or unequal variances (Conover 1980). We used Wilcoxon signed-ranks tests to compare paired counts (prespill and postspill), and we used Mann-Whitney U tests to compare counts between two samples (SPSS, v. 4.0, SPSS Inc., Chicago, IL).

RESULTS

Abundance and Distribution

Abundance of independent otters—Densities of independent otters surveyed at five sites (Green Island, Applegate Rock, Montague Island, Sheep Bay, and Port Gravina) before the spill (Johnson 1987 and unpubl. data 1985) and during 1990 and 1991 differed among sites, but this difference was not consistent among time periods (significant site by year interaction, Table 2). Because Green and Applegate were affected by the 1989 oil spill, Montague was adjacent to those two sites, and the two other sites were distant and clearly not affected by oil, we tested for prespill to postspill differences, which might relate to oiling, at specific sites.

At Green Island (excluding Gibbon Anchorage), prespill counts of independent otters from April to August varied from 73 to 196, with a coefficient of variation (CV [standard deviation/mean]) of 26%. This wide variation was probably attributable in part to year-to-year variation, although no consistent yearly trend was observed (Figure 4). Variation among postspill counts within a single year was nearly as large; for example, in 1990 the CV was 21% (range = 112–203). The mean numbers counted during prespill years (1977–85), 1990, and 1991 were 151, 150, and 176 otters, respectively; these means did not differ from one another (ANOVA, $P > 0.2$).

At Applegate Rock, the other spill-affected site with which we compared our data to Johnson's (1987) prespill data, counts of independent otters were highly variable during 1977–85 (Figure 5) (CV = 53%, range = 44–136). The first two counts were made by Johnson (1987) at this site consecutively on 9 and 10 May 1977 and, therefore, were not independent in time. These counts ($\bar{x}$ = 134) also were more than twice as high as Pitcher's (1975) count (42 including pups) in the summer of 1973 and Johnson's (1987) four later counts (1977–85, $\bar{x}$ = 54), suggesting that a temporary congregation of otters may have been present in May 1977. For these reasons, it seemed appropriate to exclude one or both of these May 1977 counts in making comparisons with our postspill surveys. With only one of these counts excluded, the mean counts in both 1990 and 1991 ($\bar{x}$ = 31 and $\bar{x}$ = 44, respectively) were significantly lower than the mean of 1977–85 ($\bar{x}$ = 70, ANOVA, $P < 0.01$), but with the two distinctively high counts from 1977 excluded, only the 1990 counts were significantly lower than prespill ($\bar{x}$ = 54, $P < 0.01$). The mean of the 1991 counts at Applegate was significantly higher than that in 1990 ($P = 0.02$), and equal to the tally obtained during the latest prespill survey available (44 independents, May 1985 [A. Johnson, unpubl. data 1985]).

Among the unoiled sites, differences between Johnson's (1987) prespill counts and our postspill counts were inconsistent (Figure 6). Postspill counts of otters at Montague Island during both 1990 and 1991 were higher than counts from prespill years ($P \leq 0.01$), suggesting that otters immigrated from nearby spill-affected areas and/or that the population increased. Counts at Montague in 1991 declined slightly, but insignificantly,

Table 2. Analysis of variance models comparing densities (log-transformed) of independent (non-pup) sea otters among prespill years (1976–85) (Nysewander and Knudtson 1977; Johnson 1987 and unpubl. data 1985), 1990, and 1991 at various sites in Prince William Sound, Alaska.

| Source | Green I., Applegate Rock, Montague I., Port Gravina and Sheep Bay 1977–85, 1990, and 1991 | | | Port Etches and Constantine Harbor 1976 and 1991 | | |
	Degrees of Freedom	Sum of Squares	F-ratio[a]	Degrees of Freedom	Sum of Squares	F-ratio
Site	4	1.48	25.63***	1	8.43	592.88***
Year[b]	2	0.01	0.41	1	0.05	3.72
Site by Year[b]	8	0.87	7.55***	1	0.05	3.32
Error	100	1.45		15	0.21	

[a] Regression mean square/error mean square
[b] Prespill years combined into one group: 1977–85
*** $P \leq 0.001$

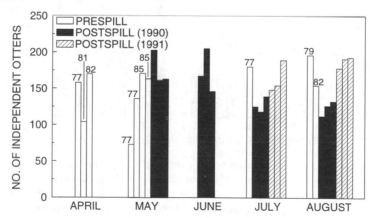

Figure 4. Counts of independent (non-pup) sea otters during prespill years (Johnson 1987 and unpubl. data 1985), 1990, and 1991, Green Island, Prince William Sound, Alaska. Numbers above prespill bars indicate year of count.

from counts in 1990 (P = 0.15). Across PWS in Sheep Bay a similar trend was observed: 1990 counts increased from prespill counts ($P < 0.01$), but numbers declined somewhat in 1991 ($P = 0.21$), and were closer to prespill levels (Figure 6). In contrast with Sheep Bay, neighboring Port Gravina's counts in both 1990 and 1991 suggested a slight but statistically insignificant decline from prespill counts ($P \geq 0.81$).

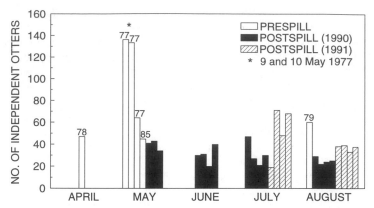

Figure 5. *Counts of independent (non-pup) sea otters during prespill years (Johnson 1987 and unpubl. data 1985), 1990, and 1991, Applegate Rock, Prince William Sound, Alaska. Numbers above prespill bars indicate year of count.*

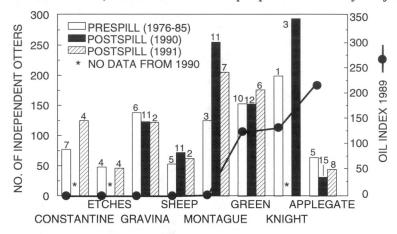

Figure 6. *Mean counts of independent (non-pup) sea otters at sites surveyed during prespill years (Nysewander and Knudtson 1976; Johnson 1987 and unpubl. data 1985; Irons, unpublished data 1984), 1990, and 1991, Prince William Sound, Alaska. Numbers above bars represent sample sizes.*

Counts at two other unoiled sites, Port Etches and adjacent Constantine Harbor, were compared with prespill counts made by Nysewander and Knudtson (1977) (Figure 6). Constantine Harbor had significantly higher densities of otters than Port Etches during both pre- and postspill periods (site effect, Table 2), and the density in Constantine increased from 1976 to 1991 ($P = 0.01$), whereas the density in Port Etches remained constant ($P = 0.94$).

At Knight Island, a heavily oiled area, we used a different observational protocol so that we could compare our data with prespill data collected in 1984 (Irons et al. 1988) (Table 1). A survey conducted during 1973 from a helicopter by Pitcher (1975) did not provide valid baseline data for our comparisons; pups were not discriminated from independent otters, and the count likely was biased low because otters were less detectable from the air than from a boat (Pitcher [1975] counted three times as many otters from a boat as from a helicopter along portions of Knight Island). Nevertheless, Pitcher's (1975) count, including pups, was not much different from Irons et al.'s (1988) boat-based count, also with pups, and both were much lower than our counts in 1991 (Figure 7). The difference between the 1984 and 1991 counts, excluding pups, was statistically significant (1-tailed Wilcoxon signed-rank test for 16 paired transects, $Z =$ 1.96, $P = 0.02$).

Considering all eight study sites, we found no consistent trend in population change with time or among sites that coincided with degree of oiling (Figure 6). Among the five control sites, three increased significantly from prespill levels (although one later returned to the prespill level) and two showed no significant change. Among the three oil-affected sites, one declined significantly the year following the spill, one did not change, and one increased significantly.

Irons et al. (1988) conducted a prespill count in each of our survey areas, but Knight Island was the only site where we specifically duplicated their methodology, using a small boat 100 m from shore (Table 1). At most of the other sites, we counted from a higher platform farther from shore, and thus saw more otters >200 m offshore than they did (although this was true also at Knight Island, Applegate Rock, and Constantine Harbor, where we did not have the advantage of a high observational platform)(Table 3). To compare our counts at all sites with those of Irons (unpubl. data 1984–85), we limited the data set to otters seen within 200 m of shore, where, if anything, his route close to shore should have yielded an observational advantage. Nevertheless, at six of eight sites we saw more otters close to shore than did Irons (unpubl. data 1984–85, Table 3); overall

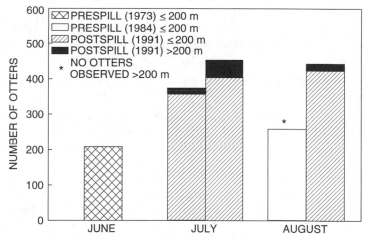

Figure 7. Counts of sea otters (independents and pups) within 200 m and beyond 200 m of the shoreline during prespill years (Pitcher 1975; Irons et al. 1988) and 1991 at the Knight Island area, Prince William Sound, Alaska. Prespill counts in 1973 were conducted from a helicopter.

Table 3. Counts of independent (non-pup) sea otters during the summers of 1984 and 1985 (Irons et al. 1988 and unpubl. data from their study) and 1991 along shorelines in Prince William Sound, Alaska. One count in 1984 and 1985 was made in western and eastern Prince William Sound, respectively, from 5–10-m boats. Counts at Knight Island, Constantine Harbor, and Applegate Rock in 1991 were made from a 4.5-m inflatable raft with outboard. Counts at the remaining sites in 1991 were made from a 3-m high flying bridge aboard a 16-m boat.

| | ≤200 m | | | | >200 m | | | |
| | | 1991 | | | | 1991 | | |
Site	1984–85	$\bar{x}$	SD	n	1984–85	$\bar{x}$	SD	n
Green Island[a]	58	99.0	17.75	6	4	85.2	15.16	6
Applegate Rock	22	21.0	14.34	8	0	23.1	18.84	8
Knight Island[b]	199	273.3	16.56	3	0	17.3	11.02	3
Stockdale Harbor and Port Chalmers	104	120.3	9.62	7	40	85.0	12.99	7
Port Etches	51	18.0	6.68	4	12	28.2	14.86	4
Constantine Harbor	50	92.0	52.78	4	0	32.8	30.63	4
Port Gravina	49	65.5	19.09	2	19	61.0	21.21	2
Sheep Bay	21	25.0	14.14	2	2	42.5	4.95	2

[a] Includes Green Island, Little Green Island, Channel Island, and Gibbon Anchorage
[b] Includes Knight, Eleanor, Ingot, Disk, Sphinx, Squirrel, Mummy, and Squire islands

this represented a significant increase (1-tailed Wilcoxon signed-ranks test, $Z = 1.68$, $P = 0.046$).

Distribution of independent otters—Oil-affected sites were not oiled along the entire length of shoreline (Figures 2 and 3), so we examined changes in distribution at these sites relative to oiling levels among shoreline segments. Among the shoreline segments at Green Island, differences in densities of independent otters from prespill to postspill appeared unrelated to the degree of oiling (Figure 8). Two of the three most heavily oiled segments had higher densities postspill than prespill. Applegate Rock, which above was considered a separate site and here, because of its proximity, is considered a segment within the Green Island complex, was the only heavily oiled area to show a decline (with or without the anomalous May 1977 counts included). We found no relationship between 1989 oiling levels and otter density in each of eight Green Island shoreline segments in 1990 ($r^2 < 0.01$, $P = 0.45$), but, in 1991, density decreased significantly with increasing oil levels ($r^2 = 0.21$, $P < 0.01$); however, a similar inverse relationship (i.e., negative slope) was observed in the 1977–85 data ($r^2 = 0.16$, $P < 0.01$),

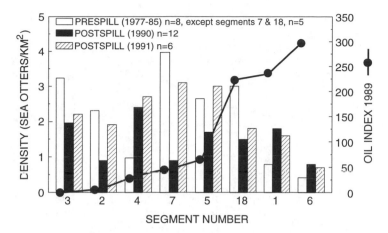

Figure 8. Mean density of independent (non-pup) sea otters within boundaries of shoreline segments (Figure 2) and up to 1500 m from shore at Green Island and Applegate Rock during the summers of 1977–85 (Johnson, unpubl. data), 1990, and 1991. The count on 10 May 1977 at Applegate Rock was not included (see text and Figure 5).

indicating that the shoreline segments at Green Island that were affected by oil had historically supported relatively low densities of otters.

An analogous situation occurred at Knight Island. Comparing the 1973 helicopter count (Pitcher 1975) to the 1984 boat count (Irons, unpubl. data 1984), we found evidence of a prespill shift in otter distribution from the northern to the southwestern part of this area (Figures 3 and 9), and it happened that the northern end of the island was more heavily oiled by the 1989 spill. During 1991, otter densities among shoreline segments decreased with increasing oiling levels measured in 1989 ($r^2 = 0.45$, $P < 0.01$), but this relationship also was apparent during 1984 ($r^2 = 0.47$, $P < 0.01$). Furthermore, the relative distribution of otters between heavily oiled (oil index ≥ 100) and lightly oiled (oil index <100) segments at Knight Island did not change between 1984 and 1991 (Mann-Whitney U-test comparing 12 heavily oiled with 4 lightly oiled segments for the difference from 1984 to 1991 in the proportion of the total count on each segment, $Z = 0.85$, $P = 0.4$).

Pup Production

Level of pup production—Timing of pup production during 1990 and 1991 was similar at oiled and unoiled sites (Figure 10). A high percentage of the pups observed during May at all sites were recent births, as indicated by their small size and buffy pelage. Birthing slowed but continued into July, so the cumulative number of pups in the population increased. Consequently, pup:adult ratios (pup ratios) in July and August generally were higher than in May and June (Figures 11 and 12). That seasonal change confounded some of our analyses because prespill data were not available for all months, and 1991 data were collected only in July and August.

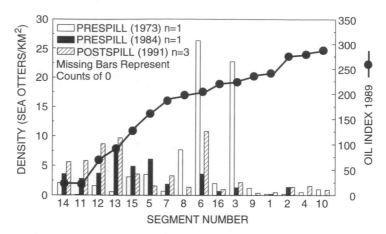

Figure 9. *Mean density of sea otters (independents and pups) within boundaries of shoreline segments (Figure 3) and up to 200 m from shore, Knight Island area, Prince William Sound, Alaska, during the summers of 1973 (Pitcher 1975), 1984 (Irons, unpubl. data), and 1991. Count in 1973 was made from a helicopter, whereas counts in 1984 and 1991 were made from boats.*

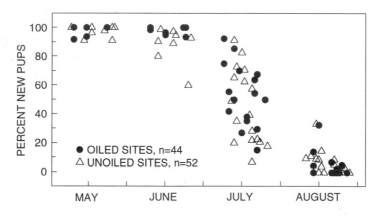

Figure 10. *Percentage of new pups ([new pups/total pups] × 100) by date counted at oiled (Green I., Knight I., and Applegate Rock) and unoiled sites (Montague I., Port Gravina, Sheep Bay, Port Etches, and Constantine Harbor), Prince William Sound, Alaska, May–August 1990 and July–August 1991.*

A preliminary ANOVA model of our 1990 pup ratios with prespill ratios reported by Johnson (1987 and unpubl. data 1985) at Green Island, Applegate Rock, Montague Island, Sheep Bay, and Port Gravina indicated significant variation by month (May–June versus July–August) and by site, but differences among sites were inconsistent from prespill to postspill (i.e., significant site by year effect). The monthly variation in pup ratios was consistent among sites and consistent between pre- and postspill periods

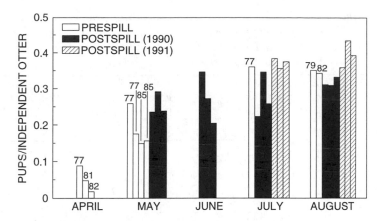

Figure 11. *Ratios of pups/independent sea otter during prespill years (Johnson 1987 and unpubl. data 1985), 1990, and 1991, Green Island, Prince William Sound, Alaska. Numbers above bars indicate year of count.*

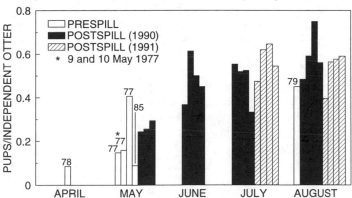

Figure 12. *Ratios of pups/independent sea otter during prespill years (Johnson 1987 and unpubl. data 1985), 1990, and 1991, Applegate Rock, Prince William Sound, Alaska. Numbers above bars indicate year of count.*

(i.e., insignificant month by site and month by year effects). The significant relationships remained in the model when insignificant interaction effects were removed (Final Model 1, Table 4).

Pup ratios from the same five sites, including 1991 data and excluding the months of May and June, differed significantly among sites and among years, but changes in pup ratios among sites were, as above, inconsistent from prespill to 1990 to 1991 (significant site by year effect, Final Model 2, Table 4). No difference was found between pup ratios in the months of July and August.

At oiled sites, pup ratios either increased or remained the same from prespill to postspill years. Pup ratios at Green Island did not differ between prespill and either 1990 or 1991 ($P > 0.54$), but pup ratios increased from 1990 to 1991 ($P = 0.04$)(Figure 11). At

Table 4. *Analysis of variance models comparing ratios (arcsine-square-root transformed) of pups/independent sea otter among prespill years(1977–85) (Johnson 1987 and unpubl. data 1985), 1990, and 1991 at various sites in Prince William Sound, Alaska.*

Source	Preliminary Model Prespill and 1990, May–August			Final Model 1 Prespill and 1990, May–August			Final Model 2 Prespill, 1990, and 1991, July–August		
	df[a]	SS[b]	F-ratio[c]	df	SS	F-ratio	df	SS	F-ratio
Corrected total	82	1.72		82	1.72		62	1.27	
Site	4	0.20	4.65**	4	0.16	3.40*	4	0.25	11.41***
Year[d]	1	0.02	1.44	1	0.00	0.37	2	0.16	14.64***
Month[e]	1	0.14	12.72***	1	0.12	10.56**	1[f]	0.01	1.84
Site by Year	4	0.18	4.11**	4	0.23	4.86***	8	0.11	2.62*
Site by Month	4	0.10	2.27	-	-	-	-	-	-
Year by Month	1	0.03	2.76	-	-	-	-	-	-
Error	67	0.74		72	0.86		47	0.26	

[a] Degrees of freedom
[b] Sum of squares
[c] Regression mean square/error mean square
[d] Prespill years combined into one group: 1977–1985
[e] Months combined into two groups: May–June and July–August
[f] July and August treated separately
* $0.01 < P \le 0.05$
** $0.001 < P \le 0.01$
*** $P \le 0.001$

Applegate Rock, pup ratios increased from prespill years to 1990 when one or both of the seemingly anomalous May 1977 counts were included ($P = 0.04$ and $P < 0.01$, respectively), but not when both were excluded ($P = 0.60$) (Figure 12). Pup ratios at Applegate in 1991 did not differ from those of prespill years or those of 1990 ($P = 0.20$ and $P = 0.75$, respectively), but the mean (0.55) was the highest of our eight study sites for both prespill and postspill observations (Figure 13). At Knight Island (not included in the above ANOVAs), pup ratios observed during all three surveys in 1991 were higher (range = 0.40–0.52) than observed during a single survey in 1984 (0.30)(Irons et al. 1988); however, the increase was not statistically significant when comparisons were made for each shoreline segment (1-tailed Wilcoxon signed-rank test, $Z = 0.45$, $P = 0.33$). The validity of this statistical test was compromised by the exclusion of four segments where we saw pups but Irons (unpubl. data 1984) observed no otters. However, the number of pups (rather than pup ratio) in 1991 was significantly higher than in 1984, when compared segment by segment (1-tailed Wilcoxon signed-ranks test, $Z = 2.30$, $P = 0.01$).

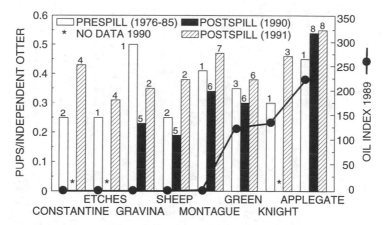

Figure 13. *Mean ratios of pups/independent sea otter counted during July and August of prespill years (Johnson 1987 and unpubl. data 1985; Irons, unpubl. data 1984), 1990, and 1991, at sites in Prince William Sound, Alaska. Numbers above bars indicate number of replicate counts.*

Of the three control sites—Montague, Sheep Bay, and Port Gravina—only Port Gravina had a significant ($P = 0.01$) decline in pup ratio from prespill to 1990 (Figure 13). Pup ratios at all three sites increased significantly between 1990 and 1991 ($P \leq 0.03$), although the 1991 ratios did not differ significantly from prespill ratios in any of these areas. A separate ANOVA model was run for the other two control sites—Port Etches and Constantine Harbor—because 1990 data were not available. The 1991 pup ratios appeared higher than prespill records (Figure 13), but these differences were not statistically significant.

Overall, changes in pup ratios from prespill to postspill were apparently unrelated to the degree of oiling at these eight study sites (Figure 13). The only consistent trend was markedly high pup production in 1991, compared with both 1990 and prespill data.

Distribution of pupping—Among eight shoreline segments in the Green Island-Applegate Rock area, we observed no relationship between pup production and degree of oiling. In 1990, there was a weak positive relationship between pup ratios and the 1989 oiling level (more pups in segments where there was more oil) ($r^2 = 0.06$, $P = 0.02$), principally because pup production at Applegate Rock was so high (segment #18, Figure 14), but this relationship disappeared in 1991. Changes in pup production from prespill to postspill years also were unrelated to oiling. Compared to historical records, pup production increased at one heavily oiled segment (#18) and one lightly oiled segment (#5), whereas it declined at one heavily oiled segment (#6) and two segments with very little oil (#2, #4)(Figures 2 and 14).

At Knight Island, pup ratios in 1991 were significantly inversely related to the degree of oiling along shoreline segments ($r^2 = 0.38$, $P < 0.01$), but pup ratios in 1984 were not ($r^2 = 0.03$, $P = 0.59$). However, pup ratios in 1984 could not be calculated for four segments that were later oiled, because Irons (unpubl. data 1984) saw no otters there. When regressing pup density rather than pup ratios against oiling level, we found a

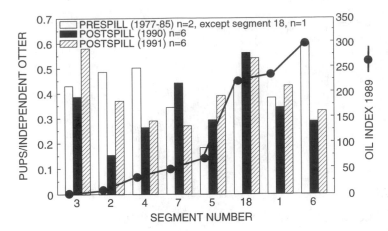

Figure 14. **Mean ratios of pups/independent sea otter counted during July and August of prespill years (Johnson, unpubl. data 1977–85), 1990, and 1991, within shoreline segments (Figure 2) at Green Island and Applegate Rock, Prince William Sound, Alaska.**

significant inverse relationship for both prespill ($r^2 = 0.29$, $P < 0.01$) and postspill data ($r^2 = 0.53$, $P = 0.01$). We observed higher densities of pups in 1991 than were observed in 1984 on 12 of 14 segments, including eight heavily oiled segments (oil index ≥ 100) and four lightly oiled segments (oil index < 100) (Figure 15). Nonetheless, pup densities increased significantly more on lightly oiled segments than on heavily oiled segments from 1984 to 1991 (Mann-Whitney U test, comparing four lightly oiled and twelve heavily oiled segments, $Z = 2.43$, two-tailed $P = 0.02$). Likewise, although the pup ratios for 1984 (0.34) and 1991 ($\bar{x} = 0.30$, $n = 3$) were similar for heavily oiled parts of the island, pup ratios in lightly oiled areas increased noticeably from 1984 (0.28) to 1991 ($\bar{x} = 0.53$, $n = 3$). The changes in pup ratios from 1984 to 1991 differed significantly between heavily and lightly oiled segments (Mann-Whitney U test, comparing eight heavily oiled and four lightly oiled segments, $Z = 2.04$, two-tailed $P = 0.02$), but we had to pool the data from some geographically adjacent segments to calculate pup ratios for segments where no otters were seen in 1984 (Figure 16).

Winter Mortality

During the spring of 1990, we counted 19 sea otter carcasses on the beaches of Green Island, Little Green Island, and Channel Island (Figure 2). This count, representing the observed mortality during the winter of 1989–90, was slightly above the mean (15.9) observed during 1976–84 (Johnson 1987), but well within the prespill annual variation (range = 2–37). The number of adult (non-pup) carcasses found in 1990 was above the prespill mean, whereas the number of pup carcasses was slightly below the prespill mean, yet both were within their respective 95% confidence intervals (Figure 17). Together, though, the above-average number of adults and below-average number of pups resulted in a pup ratio that was lower than the 95% confidence limits around the historic mean.

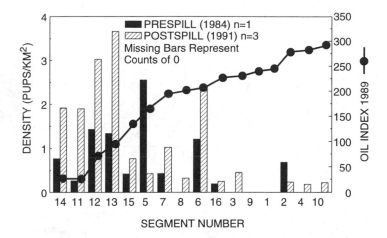

Figure 15. **Mean densities of sea otter pups counted during August 1984 (Irons, unpubl. data 1984) and July and August 1991 within boundaries of shoreline segments (Figure 3) and up to 200 m from shore, Knight Island area, Prince William Sound, Alaska.**

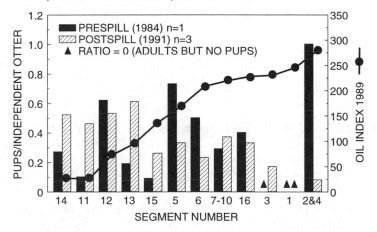

Figure 16. **Mean ratios of pups/independent sea otter counted during August 1984 (Irons, unpubl. data 1984) and July and August 1991 within boundaries of shoreline segments (Figure 3) and up to 200 m from shore, Knight Island area, Prince William Sound, Alaska.**

Food Habits

Prior to the spill, otters observed foraging on the northwestern side of Green Island, in or near Gibbon Anchorage, consumed primarily clams (several species), with lesser quantities of crabs (mainly *Telmessus cheiragonus* and *Cancer* spp.), mussels, and worm-like organisms (mainly *Echiurus echiurus*). Two prespill data sets were available, one

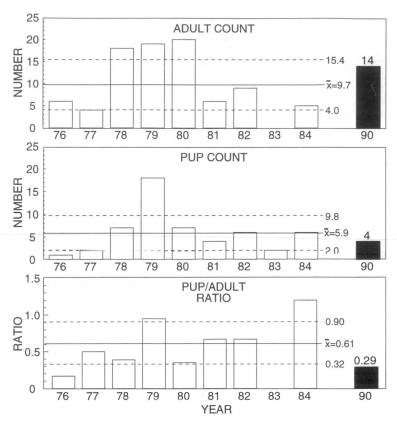

Figure 17.   Counts of sea otter carcasses during April and May of 1976–84 (Johnson 1987) and 1990 at Green, Channel, and Little Green islands, Prince William Sound, Alaska. Dashed lines represent 95% confidence intervals. One carcass from 1977, two carcasses from 1978, and one carcass from 1990 do not appear on the figure because their ages were unknown.

collected by Johnson (1987) and one by Garshelis (1983), and the years of data collection overlapped (1977–84 and 1980–81, respectively). The results of each study were similar, with minor differences probably due to variation in the sex, age, and location of otters observed feeding. Our observations of the percentage of the diet made up of each of the major prey types during 1990 and 1991 fell within the range of values established by the two prespill data sets (Figure 18). We observed otters more frequently eating kelp, a food of low nutritional value, although we could not see whether otters sought the kelp or small animals that were attached. We also observed more frequent captures of preferred but rarely obtained food items, like octopuses (*Octopus* spp.) and urchins (*Strongylocentrotus* spp.). Therefore, 1–2 years after the spill, we detected no substantial change in the composition of the diet resulting from the heavy oiling in the Gibbon Anchorage vicinity (Figure 2).

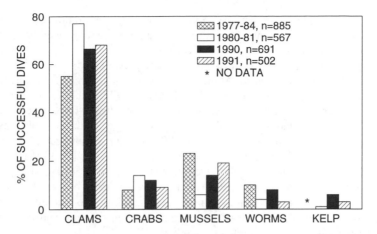

Figure 18. *Frequency of occurrence of major foods obtained by sea otters during 1977–84 (Johnson 1987), 1980–81 (Garshelis 1983), 1990, and 1991, Gibbon Anchorage, Prince William Sound, Alaska. Sample size (n) is the number of dives on which food was retrieved.*

DISCUSSION

Abundance and Distribution

Estes et al. (1981) and Johnson (1987) believed that by the late 1970s sea otters had reached carrying capacity at Green Island and other sites of prolonged occupation in western PWS. Assuming a population at carrying capacity and given the substantial number of otters killed or removed from western PWS after the spill in 1989, our counts there should have been conspicuously lower than prespill counts. Johnson (unpubl. data 1985) tallied 217 independent otters in his last complete count at Green Island and Applegate Rock in 1985; 40 carcasses of independent otters were collected in this area in 1989 (about 34 of which were judged to be spill-related) and another 41 independent otters were captured and brought to a rehabilitation center (and not returned to this site)(USFWS, unpubl. data 1989), yet our counts just a year after the spill averaged considerably higher ($\bar{x} = 181$) than expected after subtraction of just the known removals from the last prespill count (217 – 75 = 142). At Knight Island, our counts were even higher than the last prespill count, made by Irons et al. (1988) in 1984. Below we discuss four hypotheses to account for the unexpectedly high numbers of otters observed at oiled sites.

Inter-observer variation—One potential explanation for our high counts is that despite our attempt to replicate the methodology of prespill observers, we may have seen a higher proportion of otters. Otters can be missed during boat surveys because they are underwater or obscured (Schneider 1971). The proportion of otters sighted varies with weather and sea conditions, the speed and stability of the boat, observer height above water, the skill of the observers, and the behavior of the otters. We established minimum weather and sea state criteria for conducting our surveys, although our counts often were made under less than ideal circumstances; Johnson's (1987, pers. commun.) weather criteria for surveys were apparently more stringent than ours, so if weather was a factor in comparability of counts, ours may have been biased low.

Survey platforms differed between our study and prespill studies, possibly resulting in differences in sighting efficiency. At most sites we used a higher, more stable platform than did Johnson (1987) and Nysewander and Knudtson (1977)(Table 1), but we zigzagged less to cover the same area and thus tended to be further from the otters, so it is unclear which, if either, platform offered a viewing advantage. In the control areas, our counts ranged from higher than prespill in both 1990 and 1991 (Montague), higher in only one year (Sheep Bay and Constantine Harbor), about the same (Port Etches), to slightly lower (Port Gravina)(Figure 6). Overall, these results do not suggest any consistent observer-related variation between our counts and those of these two prespill investigators. We are especially confident in the comparability of our counts to those of Johnson (1987), as one of us participated in some of Johnson's counts, and we designed our postspill methodology accordingly.

We used a poorer viewing platform (inflatable raft in which we could not stand) than Irons et al. (1988) at the single site (Knight Island) where we followed their survey route, 100 m offshore; nevertheless, at Knight Island, our counts were considerably higher than theirs (Table 3, Figure 7). A potential explanation is that we counted only otters, whereas Irons et al. counted both otters and birds. However, counts of both sea otters and birds conducted during the summer of 1991 in two other independent investigations, also using Irons et al.'s survey route and methods, compared favorably to ours. Day et al. (this volume) surveyed selected bays at Knight Island, and although they counted birds and marine mammals, their otter tallies were similar to ours (Table 5). Burn (1994) made counts of otters and birds along 38 randomly-selected shoreline segments around Knight

Table 5. *Counts of independent (non-pup) sea otters during July and August 1991 by researchers counting only sea otters (this study) and researchers counting marine mammals and marine-oriented birds (Day et al., unpubl. data 1991) within 200 m of shore in selected bays in the Knight Island area, Prince William Sound, Alaska.*

Bay	Day et al. unpubl. data			This Study		
	$\bar{x}$	SD	n	$\bar{x}$	SD	n
Northwest Bay	0.8	0.84	5	0.7	0.58	3
Herring Bay	4.8	3.27	5	7.7	0.58	3
Lower Herring Bay	8.8	2.77	5	8.3	0.58	3
Drier Bay	20.2	9.36	5	17.0	9.54	3
Hogan Bay	0.4	0.55	5	1.0.	1.00	3
Snug Harbor	0.6	0.55	5	1.0	1.00	3
Bay of Isles	4.6	2.61	5	11.7	7.02	3

Island; his otter count (133 including pups [Burn, unpubl. data 1991]) was nearly identical to the mean (136.4) of our three counts along these same segments the same summer. The match between our results and those from studies that counted both birds and otters indicates that, despite our singular attention to otters, our counting efficiency at Knight Island was likely very similar to that of Irons et al. (1988).

We also compared our counts at other sites to those of Irons et al. (1988), but at most of these sites we used a larger boat and followed a survey route further from shore (about 500 m); consequently, the counts were not directly comparable. In the control areas (Montague, Sheep Bay, Port Gravina, Port Etches, and Constantine Harbor) we counted 64% more otters, 17% more in the zone within 200 m of shore (Table 3). Assuming that our higher counts in these control areas were due to methodological differences, we increased Irons et al.'s (1988) counts by these same percentages at the two oiled areas where we did not use their methodology (Green Island and Applegate Rock). Even making this adjustment, our counts at these oiled sites were higher than Irons et al.'s (1988) counts (our mean total count of 228 at Green and Applegate was greater than their adjusted count of $84 \times 1.64 = 138$, and our mean count of 120 in the nearshore zone exceeded their adjusted count of $80 \times 1.17 = 94$).

These comparisons, either adjusted for differences in methodology or where no adjustments were necessary, provide compelling evidence that there were indeed as many or more otters in the oiled sites in 1990–91 as there were 5–12 years before the spill. That is, our high counts were not simply an artifact of inter-observer variation.

Immigration of otters from unoiled to oiled areas—If sea otters in western PWS were at carrying capacity before the oil spill, then vacancies created by the spill might have been filled by otters from less-desirable areas. Our data indicated little change in the distribution of otters around Green Island and Knight Island from prespill to postspill, and what change did occur was unrelated to shoreline oiling. Considering that many otters along oiled shorelines in 1989 either moved away or were killed, reoccupation of these shorelines in 1990 and 1991, in numbers comparable to those before the spill, suggests immigration from somewhere else.

If otters repopulated oil-affected sites from nearby unoiled areas, then their distribution throughout the area could be similar (assuming uniform emigration) but their overall abundance would be less than during prespill years. However, because our analyses of pre- and postspill otter numbers indicated no decline in abundance for Green, Knight, or Montague islands, a simple reshuffling of otters around or among these islands could not explain our results. If immigration accounted for the high numbers we observed in southwestern PWS, the otters must have come from farther away.

One possible source of repopulating otters was the eastern part of PWS. However, studies of radio-tagged female sea otters in PWS have shown that few venture across Hinchinbrook Entrance and the open expanse of water to the north of the entrance that separates western and eastern PWS (Figure 1)(Garshelis and Garshelis 1984; Monnett 1988). Whereas females routinely move among the various bays in eastern PWS (Monnett 1988), it is unlikely that many would have been aware of possible habitat vacancies in western PWS after the spill. Moreover, if some of these eastern females happened to journey west, it is unlikely that large numbers would have settled there, because prolonged occupation by otters in western PWS has reduced food supplies compared to more recently populated areas in the east (Garshelis et al. 1986; VanBlaricom 1987; 1988)(Figure 1). Other favorable features like exposed mudbars for resting, shallow water for feeding, and protection from storms attract extraordinarily high densities of otters (particularly pup-rearing females in recent years) in some parts of eastern PWS (Garshelis and Garshelis 1984; Simon-Jackson 1986; Monnett and Rotterman 1989). Furthermore, the number of otters at areas we surveyed in eastern PWS remained the same (Port Gravina, Port Etches) or increased (Sheep Bay, Constantine Harbor) compared with prespill numbers, suggesting that there was no mass exodus of otters from these areas to fill vacancies created by mortality in the spill area.

In contrast, adult males regularly do travel between eastern and western PWS (Garshelis and Garshelis 1984). Upon reaching breeding age, males may wander over large areas in search of vacant breeding territories or territories they might usurp. Males that establish territories in western PWS generally remain there through the late summer and fall, but most return after breeding to male-dominated areas at the fringe of the expanding population, where food is more plentiful (Garshelis et al. 1984). Some males stay in the west through the winter or at least travel back periodically during the winter, and many return to their territory or seek out a new territory during early spring (Garshelis et al. 1984). Consequently, about 33% of the sea otters that died as the oil spread through western PWS in the spring of 1989 were males (Doroff et al. 1993). It is likely that these animals were rapidly replaced by other males from eastern PWS, making up for some of the losses to the male segment of the population in the west. However, because pup ratios remained high in western PWS in both 1990 and 1991 (Figure 13), it is clear that males did not replace females.

Movement of otters from offshore to better habitats nearshore—Offshore habitats might have been an alternative source of otters that replaced those killed in the spill. Nearshore habitats are preferred by otters because foraging is easier in shallower water, water conditions tend to be calmer, and, in severe weather, kelp beds or haul-out areas are more available (Kenyon 1969). Consequently, at places like Knight Island, where water depths increase rapidly away from shore, most otters tend to remain close to shore (Table 3). Conversely, at places with extensive shallows and more offshore rocks and small islands, otters were found farther from shore. Nearly half the otters we observed around Green, Applegate, and Montague were >200 m from shore (Table 3), and several were >1 km from shore. Similarly, in large enclosed bays like Port Gravina, Sheep Bay, and Port Etches, roughly half or more of the otters were >200 m from shore.

If otters that had formerly spent much of their time offshore moved toward shore to fill vacancies after the spill, we should have seen fewer otters offshore than did prespill investigators. Only Irons et al. (1988) recorded the position of otters with respect to shore (≤200 m or >200 m), so we compared our results only with theirs. At every site, we saw proportionately more otters offshore than did Irons (unpubl. data 1984–85)(Table 3); however, this comparison is not appropriate at most sites because we used a higher viewing platform and traveled farther offshore (Table 1). At Knight Island, we followed the same course (100 m from shore) as Irons et al. (1988) and used a viewing platform that was not as good as theirs. Nonetheless, on average, 6% (17/291) of the otters we counted in this area were >200 m from shore, where Irons et al. (1988) counted none.

Comparisons of our counts with those of Irons (unpubl. data 1984) at Applegate Rock also suggest that more otters were using offshore areas 1–2 years after the spill than during the 1984 survey. We used the same viewing platform as at Knight Island, but did not restrict our course to 100 m from shore; yet, on average, 52% (23/44) of the otters we observed at Applegate Rock were >200 m from shore, whereas Irons (unpubl. data 1984) again recorded no otters beyond 200 m (Table 3).

Even at Green Island, where we surveyed an area much farther from shore than 200 m, there was no evidence that the number of otters offshore had declined, as our counts extending 1500 m from shore were similar to prespill counts.

Population increase prior to the spill—If sea otter numbers were increasing before the spill, then the population would have been higher at the time of the spill than it was when the last prespill counts were made in the mid-1980s. If the spill then removed this increment of growth, this could explain why our postspill counts at Green Island, for example, were similar to prespill counts there.

Johnson (1987) made repeated surveys around Green Island from 1977 to 1985 and found no consistent trend in population size, leading him to conclude that otters in this area were at carrying capacity. However, variability in the timing of the surveys and large fluctuations in counts just a few days apart (e.g., 46% decline in 11 days followed by an 86% increase in 7 days) may have obscured an annual trend. At neighboring Montague Island, Johnson (1987) completed only three prespill counts, but these suggested an increasing trend (from 96 independent otters in 1977 to 125 in 1983 and 155 in 1984). This area was not greatly affected by the spill, although some otters may have crossed over to Montague from nearby spill-affected sites. Thus, our extraordinarily high counts ($\bar{x}$ = 254 independents) at Montague in 1990 may have been due to both a continued population increase, as well as temporary immigration from oiled areas. In 1991, our Montague counts declined (and Green Island and Applegate Rock counts increased) by about 50 otters, leaving what may have been a better representation of the average population size unaffected by the spill. Fitting these 1991 data in a regression with Johnson's (1987) three previous counts yields a 5.5% annual rate of population growth for Montague (r^2 = 0.96, P = 0.02), which is comparable to annual growth rates in other established sea otter populations (Kenyon 1969; Estes 1990). If the number of otters in western PWS did increase about 5–6% annually since the mid-1980s when the last counts at Green and Knight islands were conducted, the total population there would have climbed about 25–30% by the time of the spill, and thus could have sustained a substantial loss that would not have been detected by comparing postspill abundance with the latest prespill counts.

Although this explanation for our high counts seems contrary to what was previously supposed about the population trend in this area, it is not implausible. It is possible, for example, that otter numbers were indeed fairly stable at Green Island during the late 1970s and early 1980s, when Johnson (1987) conducted his investigation, but then increased during the late 1980s. We witnessed exceptional pup production in 1991, compared with Johnson's (1987) prespill records. In fact, the pup ratios that we observed were even higher than those recorded for populations with annual growth rates of 17–20% (Estes 1990). If relatively high pup production characterized the late 1980s, it seems logical that the population might have grown.

Pup Production

Historical data indicate that the birthing period for sea otters in PWS begins in April, rises to a sharp peak in May and June, and then tapers off through the late summer, with rare sporadic births during the fall (Garshelis et al. 1984; Johnson 1987; Monnett et al. 1991). Pups usually remain with their mothers for 5–6 months, with the family generally breaking up during the September–November breeding season (Garshelis et al. 1984; Monnett et al. 1991). Females are capable of producing a single pup annually (Loughlin et al. 1981; Wendell et al. 1984; Siniff and Ralls 1991; Jameson and Johnson 1993; Riedman et al. 1994), although females in poor condition may be forced to skip years, and early pup mortality may cause females to produce a second pup at an unusual time of year. Therefore, we would expect food-stressed females to exhibit more variable reproductive cycles with less-synchronized pup production (although pupping synchrony may be constrained by other environmental variables).

The oil spill could have affected reproduction in a number of ways. Because the spill occurred during the spring, it caused mortalities of newborn pups. If some mothers of these pups survived, they might have produced another pup later that year, thereby perturbing the pupping chronology. This perturbation then could have persisted into the next year (1990), manifested either by an extended pupping period, or alternatively, reduced pup production if these females were compelled to skip a year. Pup production in 1990 also could have been reduced if females that survived or escaped the spill were stressed by chronic effects on their health, contamination of their food, or forced emigration to an unfamiliar area. Conversely, pup production could have been enhanced in 1990 if losing a pup in the 1989 spill left females in better condition than if they had cared for a pup for 5–6 months (what might be called a "rebound effect").

Contrary to these scenarios, at oiled survey sites we observed both normal pupping chronology (based on a peak occurrence of small, woolly pups in May and June, with subsequently increasing pup ratios as some new pups were added through July)(Figures 10–12) and levels of pupping equal to or higher than the historical records. Furthermore, we found no consistent relationship with oil when comparing pre- and postspill pup production at the finer level of shoreline segment within these oiled sites. On Knight Island, pup production increased dramatically from 1984 to 1991 on some lightly oiled segments without a concomitant increase among the heavily oiled Knight Island segments (Fig 16); however, at Green Island, increases and decreases in pup ratios from prespill to postspill occurred irrespective of oiling level (Figure 14). Applegate Rock was heavily oiled, yet mean pup ratios there increased after the spill to an extraordinarily high level. Taken together, these data do not demonstrate any clear effect of shoreline oiling on pup production 1–2 years after the spill.

Mortality

Pup production after the spill could have been normal and, at the same time, pup mortality could have been high, resulting in decreased recruitment and consequent population stagnation or decline. However, because pup ratios remained high through August in spill-affected areas, despite a decline in new births in July and August (Figures 10–12), pup mortality during the period of dependency must have been rather low.

We have no direct information concerning the effects of the spill on pup survival after weaning, although two lines of evidence may suggest that weanling mortality was not abnormally high: (1) otter numbers at two spill-affected sites, Green Island and Applegate Rock, increased from 1990 to 1991, and (2) the number of pup carcasses found during our beach search at Green Island, during spring 1990, was equivalent to the average number found during prespill years (Figure 17). Both of these findings, however, may have been related to or confounded by other factors. Increased otter numbers at Green and Applegate could have been due to immigration (e.g., from Montague, but see immigration discussion above) rather than high recruitment of weanlings. Secondly, the spring 1990 tally of pup carcasses at Green Island may have been normal, and the pup ratio among carcasses below normal, not because of low over-winter pup mortality, but because of low pup production during the summer of 1989. Our data indicated that pup production was high the next summer, but we did not conduct another mortality survey; however, Monson (1992) did, and again found few pup carcasses (4), as well as a low total number of carcasses (9) in the spring of 1991. Monson's (1992) carcass count in 1990 (18) was nearly identical to ours (19), leading us to conclude that our and Monson's count efficiencies were similar, that the otter mortality around Green Island during the winter following the spill was not abnormally high (Figure 17), and that pup and adult mortality in this area over the winter of 1990/91 was low.

Monson (1992) correctly noted that if the otter population at Green Island had been reduced by the spill, then the mortality rate would be higher, even though the number of mortalities was similar to prespill values. However, as discussed earlier, we suspect that the spill reduced the population at Green Island to a number equivalent to what existed there during the late 1970s and early 1980s; consequently, the mortality rate in 1990 would be equivalent as well. The actual mortality rate is a reflection of the winter rather than the summer population, and indications were that the Green Island population during the winter of 1989 was low compared with normal summer numbers (Rotterman et al. 1990); however, consistently low winter counts in this area were observed before the spill (Pitcher 1975; Garshelis and Garshelis 1984; Johnson 1987).

Foraging

We detected no change in diet 1–2 years after the spill in an area that had been heavily oiled. We used methodology identical to that used by one of us to collect the prespill foraging data (Garshelis 1983) and conducted observations in the same small area on the northwest side of Green Island. However, even in this small area, there was some variation in the specific locations where otters were observed feeding; because of patchy food distribution, small differences in feeding locations can radically affect the types of prey obtained during an observational period (Garshelis 1983). Thus, just as we observed some slight differences in dietary composition between the 2 years of our study and between our data and prespill information, as much or more variation exists within the prespill data (Figure 18). In a similar study, Doroff et al. (1994) found no detectable shifts in prey from prespill to postspill or among sites that had different levels of oiling.

The reliance on opportunistic observations of unmarked foraging otters to obtain information on dietary composition may preclude detection of small changes in selection for, or availability of, different food types. However, it is clear that there were no major differences in otter diets between prespill and postspill.

In theory, the dietary composition could have remained unchanged after the spill even while the overall abundance of prey declined. Success rates of foraging otters and the number of prey items captured per dive should be indicative of prey abundance; that is, if the availability of prey declined, because of either oil-related mortality or rejection by otters of oil-contaminated items, otters should surface less often with food and obtain less food per dive. Doroff et al. (1994) found, however, that foraging success was high (87%–92%) and did not differ among three sites ranging from heavily oiled to unoiled, and that otters caught nearly the same number of items per dive at each site.

Mussels appear to be a critical food source for pups, especially after pups leave their mother, because large quantities can be easily obtained in shallow water (Garshelis 1983; Johnson 1987). Highsmith et al. (1993) reported a reduction in mussel abundance at some oiled sites in 1990, but by 1991 this was no longer evident. Various studies reported retention and/or continued uptake of oil by mussels from sources contained in the sediment (Babcock et al. 1993; Rounds et al. 1993; Shigenaka and Henry 1993), which raises the possibility that isolated mussel beds still contaminated with oil could have chronic effects on newly weaned pups that feed there intensively; however other evidence indicates that such effects would not be widespread enough to affect the population. By 1991, mussels with elevated polycyclic aromatic hydrocarbon levels were rare in oil-affected areas of PWS (Boehm et al. this volume). Furthermore, the weathered oil present at that time under some mussel beds had appreciably lower toxicity than fresh oil; reduced survival and growth, at least, were not apparent in a laboratory experiment of short term effects on another mustelid (European ferret [*Mustela putorius*]) that was fed weathered oil in concentrations far exceeding worst-case daily exposures expected for sea otters (Stubblefield et al. this volume). Notably, blood and tissues collected from PWS sea otters showed little evidence of hydrocarbon contamination in 1990 and no evidence in 1991, indicating infrequent exposure of the population as a whole, low assimilation, and/or effective metabolism (Bence and Burns this volume). Thus, 1–2 years after the spill, oil from the *Exxon Valdez* was having little apparent effect on the sea otter population through the food chain.

CONCLUSIONS

A slightly increasing population of sea otters in western PWS prior to the spill may explain our finding that at least as many otters occupied some of the most heavily oiled areas 1–2 years after the spill as were counted there 5–12 years before the spill. We could not determine whether the high number of otters observed in two oil-affected areas during 1990 and 1991 was due to reproductive recruitment or to immigration, but in either case, otters clearly were not avoiding oiled sites.

We found that pupping rates equaled or exceeded prespill levels, and we deduced that pup mortality during the summer was low, thus providing a source for population growth. Our study design did not enable us to assess mortality of weaned pups, although we saw no indication of increased mortality in counts of carcasses found on beaches the first winter after the spill. Furthermore, our observations of foraging and observations made at other oiled and unoiled locations (Doroff et al. 1994) did not indicate that the food supply would deter population growth any more than in the recent past.

Taken collectively, our findings bode well for the recovery of the sea otter population. Although we cannot discount the possibility that the spill may have had chronic effects at the local or individual level, we find it improbable that these effects would hinder population growth. However, we feel it is unjustified and unwise to make predictions of future population change, because the population in PWS may be affected by both natural and spill-related factors that were beyond the scope of this study. Nevertheless, our results indicate that 1–2 years after the spill, otters remained abundant in the oil-affected area of PWS and showed no apparent spill-related effects on their distribution or pup production.

ACKNOWLEDGMENTS

We appreciate the contributions made by B. Cooper, T. Davis, T. DeLong, D. Flint, J. Garshelis, B. Lance, T. Mabee, M. MacDonald, J. Schauer, K. Selhay, L. Smith, S. Speckman, T. Stone, and A. Zusi-Cobb. J. Harner and J. Jonkman helped with statistical analyses. We appreciate the reviews by B. Anderson, S. Murphy, R. Ritchie, and four anonymous reviewers. We are especially grateful to D. Burn, D. Irons, and A. Johnson for allowing use of their unpublished data. Exxon Company, U.S.A. supported this study. The results reflect the opinions of the authors and not necessarily those of Exxon.

REFERENCES

Babcock, M., Irvine, G., Rice, S., Rounds, P., Cusick, J., and Brodersen, C., 1993, "Oiled Mussel Beds Two and Three Years After the *Exxon Valdez* Oil Spill," Exxon Valdez *Oil Spill Symposium*, Abstract Book, Anchorage, AK, *Exxon Valdez* Oil Spill Trustee Council, pp. 184–185.

Bayha, K. and Kormendy, J., 1990, *Sea Otter Symposium: Proceedings of a Symposium to Evaluate the Response Effort on Behalf of Sea Otters After the T/V* Exxon Valdez *Oil Spill into Prince William Sound, Anchorage, Alaska, 17–19 April 1990*, U.S. Fish and Wildlife Service Biological Report, Vol. 90, No. 12, pp. vi–x.

Bence, A.E. and Burns, W.A., 1995, "Fingerprinting Hydrocarbons in the Biological Resources of the *Exxon Valdez* Spill Area," Exxon Valdez *Oil Spill: Fate and Effects in Alaskan Waters*, ASTM STP 1219, Peter G. Wells, James N. Butler, and Jane S. Hughes, Eds., American Society for Testing and Materials, Philadelphia.

Boehm, P.D., Page, D.S., Gilfillan, E.S., Stubblefield, W.A., and Harner, E.J., 1995, "Shoreline Ecology Program for Prince William Sound, Alaska, Following the *Exxon Valdez* Oil Spill: Part 2—Chemistry and Toxicology," Exxon Valdez *Oil Spill: Fate and Effects in Alaskan Waters*, ASTM STP 1219, Peter G. Wells, James N. Butler, and Jane S. Hughes, Eds., American Society for Testing and Materials, Philadelphia.

Burn, D.M., 1994, "Boat-Based Population Surveys of Sea Otters in Prince William Sound," *Marine Mammals and the* Exxon Valdez, T.R. Loughlin, Ed., Academic Press, New York, pp. 61–80.

Conover, W.J., 1980, *Practical Nonparametric Statistics,* 2nd Edition, John Wiley and Sons, New York.

Costa, D.P. and Kooyman, G.L., 1982, "Oxygen Consumption, Thermoregulation, and the Effect of Fur Oiling and Washing on the Sea Otter, *Enhydra lutris*," *Canadian Journal of Zoology*, Vol. 60, pp. 2761–2767.

Davis, R.W., Williams, T.M., Thomas, J.A., Kastelein, R.A., and Cornell, L.H., 1988, "The Effects of Oil Contamination and Cleaning on Sea Otters (*Enhydra lutris*). II. Metabolism, Thermoregulation, and Behavior," *Canadian Journal of Zoology,* Vol. 66, pp. 2782–2790.

Day, R.H., Murphy, S.M., Wiens, J.A., Hayward, G.D., Harner, E.J., and Smith, L.N., 1995, "Use of Oil-affected Habitats by Birds after the *Exxon Valdez* Oil Spill," Exxon Valdez *Oil Spill: Fate and Effects in Alaskan Waters*, ASTM STP 1219, Peter G. Wells, James N. Butler, and Jane S. Hughes, Eds., American Society for Testing and Materials, Philadelphia.

Doroff, A.M. and Bodkin, J.L., 1994, "Sea Otter Foraging Behavior and Hydrocarbon Levels in Prey," *Marine Mammals and the* Exxon Valdez, T.R. Loughlin, Ed., Academic Press, New York, pp. 193–208.

Doroff, A.M., DeGange, A.R., Lensink, C., Ballachey, B.E., Bodkin, J.L., and Bruden, D., 1993, "Recovery of Sea Otter Carcasses Following the *Exxon Valdez* Oil Spill," Exxon Valdez *Oil Spill Symposium*, Abstract Book, Anchorage, AK, *Exxon Valdez* Oil Spill Trustee Council, pp. 285–288.

Estes, J.A., 1990, "Growth and Equilibrium in Sea Otter Populations," *Journal of Animal Ecology*, Vol. 59, pp. 385–401.

Estes, J.A., 1991, "Catastrophes and Conservation: Lessons from Sea Otters and the *Exxon Valdez*," *Science*, Vol. 254, p. 1596.

Estes, J.A., Jameson, R.J., and Johnson, A.M., 1981, "Food Selection and Some Foraging Tactics of Sea Otters," *Worldwide Furbearer Conference Proceedings, Frostburg, MD,* A. Chapman and D. Parsley, Eds., pp. 606–641.

Garshelis, D.L., 1983, "Ecology of Sea Otters in Prince William Sound, Alaska," Ph.D. thesis, University of Minnesota, Minneapolis.

Garshelis, D.L. and Garshelis, J.A., 1984, "Movements and Management of Sea Otters in Alaska," *Journal of Wildlife Management*, Vol. 48, pp. 665–678.

Garshelis, D.L., Garshelis, J.A., and Kimker, A.T., 1986, "Sea Otter Time Budgets and Prey Relationships in Alaska," *Journal of Wildlife Management*, Vol. 50, pp. 637–647.

Garshelis, D.L., Johnson, A.M., and Garshelis, J.A., 1984, "Social Organization of Sea Otters in Prince William Sound, Alaska," *Canadian Journal of Zoology*, Vol. 62, pp. 2648–2658.

Highsmith, R.C., Saupe, S.M., Coyle, K.O., Rucker, T., and Erickson, W., 1993, "Impact of the *Exxon Valdez* Oil Spill on Intertidal Invertebrates Throughout the Oil Spill Region," Exxon Valdez *Oil Spill Symposium*, Abstract Book, Anchorage, AK, *Exxon Valdez* Oil Spill Trustee Council, pp. 166–168.

Irons, D.B., Nysewander, D.R., and Trapp, J.L., 1988, "Prince William Sound Sea Otter Distribution in Relation to Population Growth and Habitat Type," Unpublished report, U.S. Fish and Wildlife Service, Anchorage, AK.

Jameson, R.J. and Johnson A.M., 1993, "Reproductive Characteristics of Female Sea Otters," *Marine Mammal Science*, Vol. 9, pp. 156–167.

Johnson, A.M., 1987, "Sea Otters of Prince William Sound, Alaska," Unpublished report, U.S. Fish and Wildlife Service, Anchorage, AK.

Kenyon, K.W., 1969, "The Sea Otter in the Eastern Pacific Ocean," *North American Fauna*, Vol. 68, U.S. Government Printing Office, Washington, D.C.

Lensink, C.J., 1960, "Status and Distribution of Sea Otters in Alaska," *Journal of Mammalogy*, Vol. 41, pp. 172–182.

Lensink, C.J., 1962, "The History and Status of Sea Otters in Alaska," Ph.D. thesis, Purdue University, Lafayette, Indiana.

Loughlin, T.R., Ames, J.A., and Vandevere, J.E., 1981, "Annual Reproduction, Dependency Period, and Apparent Gestation Period in Two Californian Sea Otters, *Enhydra lutris*," *Fisheries Bulletin*, Vol. 79, pp. 347–349.

Monnett, C.W., 1988, "Patterns of Movement, Postnatal Development, and Mortality of Sea Otters in Alaska," Ph.D. thesis, University of Minnesota, Minneapolis.

Monnett, C.W. and Rotterman, L.M., 1989, "Distribution and Abundance of Sea Otters in Southeastern Prince William Sound," Unpublished report to U.S. Fish and Wildlife Service, Alaska Pacific University, Anchorage, AK.[3]

Monnett, C.W., Rotterman, L.M., and Siniff, D.B., 1991, "Sex-Related Patterns of Postnatal Development of Sea Otters in Prince William Sound, Alaska," *Journal of Mammalogy*, Vol. 72, pp. 37–41.

Monson, D.H., 1992, "Post-spill Sea Otter Mortality in Prince William Sound," *Natural Resources Damage Assessment Draft Preliminary Status Report*, B.E. Ballachey, J.L. Bodkin, and D. Burn (project leaders), U.S. Fish and Wildlife Service, Anchorage, AK.[3]

---

[3] Available from the Oil Spill Information Center, 645 G Street, Anchorage, AK, 99501.

Morrison, P., Rosenmann, M., and Estes, J.A., 1974, "Metabolism and Thermoregulation in the Sea Otter," *Physiological Zoology*, Vol. 47, pp. 218–229.

Neff, J.M., Owens, E.H., Stoker, S.W., and McCormick, D.M., 1995, "Condition of Shorelines in Prince William Sound Following the *Exxon Valdez* Oil Spill: Part 1—Shoreline Oiling," Exxon Valdez *Oil Spill: Fate and Effects in Alaskan Waters*, ASTM STP 1219, Peter G. Wells, James N. Butler, and Jane S. Hughes, Eds., American Society for Testing and Materials, Philadelphia.

Nysewander, D. and Knudtson, P., 1977, "The Population Ecology and Migration of Seabirds, Shorebirds, and Waterfowl Associated with Constantine Harbor, Hinchinbrook Island, Prince William Sound, 1976: Appendix 3—Summary of Non-Cetacean Marine Mammal Observations, Hinchinbrook Island Field Camp, 1976," *Environmental Assessment of the Alaskan Continental Shelf, Vol IV, Receptors—Birds*, J.C. Bartonek, C.J. Lensink, R.G. Gould, R.E. Gill, and G.A. Sanger (principal investigators), Annual Report, U.S. Dept. of Commerce, NOAA, pp. 565–568.

Payne, S.F. and Jameson, R.J., 1984, "Early Behavioral Development of the Sea Otter, *Enhydra lutris* ," *Journal of Mammalogy*, Vol. 65, pp. 527–531.

Pitcher, K.W., 1975, "Distribution and Abundance of Sea Otters, Steller Sea Lions, and Harbor Seals in Prince William Sound, Alaska," *Distribution and Abundance of Marine Mammals in the Gulf of Alaska*, Appendix A, D.G. Calkins, K.W. Pitcher, and K.B. Schneider (authors), Alaska Department of Fish and Game, Anchorage, AK.

Riedman, M.L., Estes, J.A., Staedler, M.M., Giles, A.A., and Carlson, D.R., 1994, "Breeding Patterns and Reproductive Success of California Sea Otters," *Journal of Wildlife Management,* Vol. 58, pp. 391–399.

Rounds, P., Rice, S., Babcock, M.M., and Brodersen, C.C., 1993, "Variability of *Exxon Valdez* Hydrocarbon Concentrations in Mussel Bed Sediments," Exxon Valdez *Oil Spill Symposium*, Abstract Book, Anchorage, AK, *Exxon Valdez* Oil Spill Trustee Council, pp. 182–183.

Rotterman, L.M., Monnett, C.W., Doroff, A., Garrott, R., Bowlbey, E., Stack, C., Ranney, G., and Ranney, S., 1990, "Fixed-Wing Surveys," *Assessment of the Magnitude, Extent, and Duration of Oil Spill Impacts on Sea Otter Populations in Alaska: Marine Mammals Study Number 6*, A.R. DeGange and D.M. Burn (project leaders), U.S. Fish and Wildlife Service, Anchorage, AK. [3]

Schneider, K., 1971, "An evaluation of sea otter survey techniques," Unpublished report, Alaska Department Fish and Game, Anchorage, AK.

Shigenaka, G. and Henry, C.B., Jr., 1993, "Bioavailability of Residual PAHs from the *Exxon Valdez* Oil Spill," Exxon Valdez *Oil Spill Symposium*, Abstract Book, Anchorage, AK, *Exxon Valdez* Oil Spill Trustee Council, pp. 163–165.

---

[3] Available from the Oil Spill Information Center, 645 G Street, Anchorage, AK, 99501.

Simon-Jackson, T., 1986, "Sea Otter Survey, Cordova, Alaska—1986 (Orca Inlet to Cape Suckling)," Unpublished report, U.S. Fish and Wildlife Service, Anchorage, AK.

Siniff, D.B. and K. Ralls, 1991, "Reproduction, Survival and Tag Loss in California Sea Otters," *Marine Mammal Science,* Vol. 7, pp. 211–229.

Siniff, D.B., Williams, T.D., Johnson, A.M., and Garshelis, D.L., 1982, "Experiments on the Response of Sea Otters *Enhydra lutris* to Oil Contamination," *Biological Conservation,* Vol. 23, pp. 261–272.

Stubblefield, W.A., Hancock, G.A., Ford, W.H., Prince, H.H., and Ringer, R.K., 1995, "Evaluation of the Toxic Properties of Naturally Weathered *Exxon Valdez* Crude Oil to Wildlife Species," Exxon Valdez *Oil Spill: Fate and Effects in Alaskan Waters,* ASTM STP 1219, Peter G. Wells, James N. Butler, and Jane S. Hughes, Eds., American Society for Testing and Materials, Philadelphia.

Tarasoff, F.J., 1974, "Anatomical Adaptations in the River Otter, Sea Otter, and Harp Seal," *Functional Anatomy of Marine Mammals,* Vol. II, R.J. Harrison, Ed., Academic Press, New York, pp. 111–142.

VanBlaricom, G.R., 1987, "Regulation of Mussel Population Structure in Prince William Sound, Alaska," *National Geographic Research,* Vol. 3, pp. 501–510.

VanBlaricom, G.R., 1988, "Effects of Foraging by Sea Otters on Mussel-Dominated Intertidal Communities," *The Community Ecology of Sea Otters,* G.R. VanBlaricom and J.A. Estes, Eds., Springer-Verlag, Berlin, pp. 48–91.

Wendell, F.E., Ames, J.A., and Hardy, R.A., 1984, "Pup Dependency Period and Length of Reproductive Cycle: Estimates from Observations of Tagged Sea Otters, *Enhydra Lutris,* in California," *California Fish and Game,* Vol. 70, pp. 89–100.

Williams, C.S., 1938, "Notes on Food of the Sea Otter," *Journal of Mammalogy,* Vol. 19, pp. 105–107.

Williams, T.M., Kastelein, R.A., Davis, R.W., and Thomas, J.A., 1988, "The Effects of Oil Contamination and Cleaning on Sea Otters (*Enhydra lutris*). I. Thermoregulatory Implications Based on Pelt Studies," *Canadian Journal of Zoology,* Vol. 66, pp. 2776–2781.

Wilson, R.K., McCormick, C.R., Williams, T.D., and Tuomi P.A., 1990a, "Clinical Treatment and Rehabilitation of Sea Otters," *Sea Otter Symposium: Proceedings of a Symposium to Evaluate the Response Effort on Behalf of Sea Otters After the* T/V Exxon Valdez *Oil Spill into Prince William Sound, Anchorage, Alaska, 17–19 April 1990,* U.S. Fish and Wildlife Service Biological Report, Vol. 90, No. 12, pp. 326–337.

Wilson, R.K., Tuomi, P.A., Schroeder, J.P., and Williams, T.D., 1990b, "Clinical Treatment and Rehabilitation of Oiled Sea Otters," *Sea Otter Rehabilitation Program: 1989* Exxon Valdez *Oil Spill,* T.M. Williams and R.W. Davis, Eds., International Wildlife Research, pp. 101–117.[3]

---

[3] Available from the Oil Spill Information Center, 645 G Street, Anchorage, AK, 99501.

Impacts on Archaeological Sites

Christopher B. Wooley[1] and James C. Haggarty[2]

ARCHAEOLOGICAL SITE PROTECTION: AN INTEGRAL COMPONENT OF THE *EXXON VALDEZ* SHORELINE CLEANUP

REFERENCE: Wooley, C. B. and Haggarty, J. C., "Archaeological Site Protection: An Integral Component of the Exxon Valdez Shoreline Cleanup," Exxon Valdez Oil Spill: Fate and Effects in Alaskan Waters, ASTM STP 1219, Peter G. Wells, James N. Butler, and Jane S. Hughes, Eds., American Society for Testing and Materials, Philadelphia, 1995.

ABSTRACT: A major cultural site identification and protection program in Prince William Sound and the Gulf of Alaska was conducted as part of the *Exxon Valdez* spill response. In cooperation with state and federal agencies and Native corporations with historic preservation mandates, the four-year program was designed to identify archaeological sites in the area of the spill, determine the effect of planned cleanup on them, and mitigate impacts to sites during cleanup.

Archaeological site protection constraints, augmented by an extensive cultural resource training program, were an integral part of each shoreline-specific cleanup plan. As a result, impacts attributable to the cleanup were limited to minor disturbances and two vandalism incidents. Impacts from oiling were minimal largely because most intertidal cultural sites had lost their fragile constituents and contextual integrity as a result of prespill erosion. State and federal studies confirmed the efficacy of the site identification and protection program, finding negligible impacts attributable to either direct oiling or the cleanup at intact sites.

The Cultural Resource Program also developed innovative management strategies with implications for future emergency responses involving complex land management and site protection issues. The program greatly enhanced the knowledge of the area's history by collecting and synthesizing considerable new archaeological information.

KEYWORDS: *Exxon Valdez*, cultural resources, archaeology, historic preservation, archaeological sites, Alutiiq, natives

---

INTRODUCTION

Programs aimed at minimizing effects of the oil or the cleanup on sensitive environmental and cultural resources were integral components of the response to the *Exxon Valdez* oil spill. This paper describes the development, evolution, and implementation of the Cultural Resource Program (CRP), including the procedures employed to identify and protect archaeological sites. This paper also addresses

---

[1]Chumis Cultural Resource Services, Anchorage, AK
[2]Shoreline Archaeological Services, Inc., Victoria, British Columbia, CANADA

the results and scientific contributions of the four-year program reported in program publications (Mobley et at. 1990, Haggarty et al. 1991, and Haggarty and Wooley 1993). The program was designed and implemented by professional archaeologists to protect cultural resource sites during cleanup and to address cultural resource issues by working with state, federal, and Native organization cultural resource managers in the spill area. The CRP was compatible with existing state and federal historic preservation laws since it aimed to preserve the information integrity of sites potentially affected by cleanup. The Coast Guard's involvement in the *Exxon Valdez* Oil spill cleanup made the cleanup a federal undertaking. By law, such undertakings require assessment of potential impacts to cultural resources. Potential site impacts included direct oiling of archaeological sites, and human impacts such as unmonitored cleanup on or near sites and unauthorized digging into archaeological sites (coloquially termed site vandalism).

Implementing a program to identify and protect archaeological sites widely scattered over 5 000 km of remote coastline presented unique challenges for the project managers. Successful implementation required daily communication between staff and agency and Native organization cultural resource managers, remote field personnel, and cleanup supervisors. The extensive transportation and communications network developed by Exxon to conduct response activities allowed field surveys and site protection tasks to be implemented in a systematic and timely fashion.

The size of the CRP effort each year was linked directly to the extent of shoreline cleanup. In 1989, 24 program archaeologists conducted reconnaissance surveys over 5 400 km (3 400 mi) of shoreline, developed site protection plans, and monitored culturally sensitive shoreline segments during cleanup. Consistent with the reduced need for cleanup in 1990, 15 archaeologists intensively surveyed 265 km (164 mi) of shoreline, developed site protection plans, and inspected or monitored over 100 beach segments. The 1991 and 1992 cleanup programs and CRP efforts, although more limited because of the diminishing scope of the cleanup, also involved site protection, inspection, and monitoring in the spill area.

The coastal area affected by the spill had never been the focus of systematic archeological survey, and only 283 archeological sites were known before 1989. In the process of identifying and protecting sites, the CRP found and recorded 326 new sites of cultural importance, more than doubling the sites known in the spill area, and collected new information on 200 previously known sites.

The CRP was successful in achieving its cultural site protection goals. Only two cases of vandalism were directly linked to the cleanup activity that involved thousands of people working on more than 1 000 miles of shoreline during four cleanup seasons. State of Alaska (Reger et al. 1992) and U.S. government (Dekin 1993) damage assessment studies confirmed that the cleanup activities did not significantly affect archaeological or historical resources. In fact, considerable new information on the history and prehistory of the area was gained through the unprecedented level of shoreline surveys and site studies.

BACKGROUND

Environmental And Cultural Setting

The area associated with the spill extends roughly 750 km (466 mi) east to west by 500 km (310 mi) north to south, encompassing Prince William Sound, the outer coast of the Kenai Peninsula and the Barren Islands, the Kodiak Archipelago, and the Pacific coast of the Alaska Peninsula from Cape Douglas to Stepovak Bay (Figure 1). Less than 15% of the 14 500 km (9 000 mi) of shoreline in the area were actually touched by oil (Owens 1991).

The tectonic history of the area is complex, with profound implications for the study of the history of the region's maritime people. The area is a tectonically active "collision coast" where two of the earth's major crustal plates converge, causing earthquakes and continual modification of the region's shorelines. Buried peat deposits in the adjacent Cook Inlet region indicate six to eight major subsidence events occurred over the past 4 700 years (Combellick 1991:22). Much of Prince William Sound and small portions of the Kenai Peninsula and Kodiak Archipelago were uplifted by the 1964 earthquake (Plafker 1965, 1967). Most of the Kodiak Archipelago and the Kenai Peninsula subsided during the quake, while the Alaska Peninsula remained largely unaffected by the event. Numerous drowned trees and intertidal peat deposits marking former landforms inundated by saltwater as a result of subsidence were noted during CRP surveys (Mobley et al. 1990: Figure 9). Birket-Smith (1953:179) and de Laguna (1956:3) attributed a lack of early village sites in Prince William Sound to destruction caused by shoreline submergence and erosion.

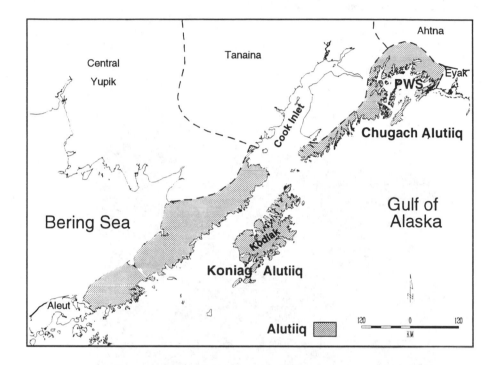

FIGURE 1—Ethnic boundaries in the Alutiiq region (19th century)

Prince William Sound and the Kenai Peninsula are the ancestral homeland of the Chugach Alutiiq people, while the Kodiak Archipelago and the Alaska Peninsula are home to the Koniag Alutiiq people. The term "Alutiiq" refers to the language, culture, and historic territory of these people (Pullar and Knecht 1990:9). The Alutiiq region roughly coincides with the area affected by the *Exxon Valdez* spill. The archaeological record of the Alutiiq region spans 10 000 years, encompassing a wide range of prehistoric and historic sites that record occupation and use by people of Native, Russian, and American ancestry.

Range Of Cultural Resource Sites

Most sites in the project area are located near the coast because of past human reliance on ocean resources. Some sites (or portions thereof) have eroded or subsided and now are located in the intertidal zone, whereas others are still located in the adjacent upland areas. Many sites are difficult to recognize, even by the trained eye. Some sites in this region consist of a single stone tool lying on the beach. Other sites such as villages occupied by hundreds of people a few generations ago may now be noticeable only as a cluster of depressions in the earth where semi-subterranean houses once stood.

Various site types are present in the project area. *Middens* are sites where human refuse has been deposited. Thickness may range from a few centimeters to several meters, with the remains of marine shellfish often forming the dominant cultural material, though bone or fire-cracked rock middens occur. These sites are not always visible on the surface, but can be detected in cut banks, steep erosional slopes (Figure 2), caves, rockshelters, and rocky promontories. Middens generally are located in the uplands (above the intertidal zone) although some are being eroded by wave action, resulting in disturbed archaeological material accumulating in the intertidal zone. At a few places, past subsidence preserved intact midden material beneath beach cobbles.

FIGURE 2—Eroding coastal midden, Kodiak Island (1989)

Wet midden sites (sites that have remained water-saturated) are extremely rare. These sites are usually found when wave or stream action erodes a portion of the site, exposing well-preserved materials. Such sites have the potential to clarify aspects of prehistory not possible under normal preservation conditions (Jordan and Knecht 1988; Haggarty et al. 1991:182-183; *Anchorage Daily News* 1992) because they can include preserved wood and plant fiber artifacts including masks, basketry, and other organic items. They also may be located entirely in the subtidal zone as a result of tectonic subsidence.

Caves and *rockshelters* (rock overhangs, the walls and ceilings of which provide natural shelter) may contain artifacts, faunal debris, burials, rock art, or other evidence of human occupation or use. Although generally located in the uplands, some examples are close to sea level. *Rock art* sites, including *pictographs* (rock paintings) and *petroglyphs* (rock carvings), are relatively rare in the Alutiiq region. *Petroglyphs,* when found, are usually in or near the intertidal zone, while *pictographs* are generally in the uplands. Most petroglyphs known in the project area are in the Kodiak region, whereas most pictographs are located in Prince William Sound.

Fish traps are a type of prehistoric structure used by Alutiiq people to capture salmon and other fish. These structures generally consist of rock walls or wood stake fences located in streams, tidal channels, or intertidal flats adjacent to streams.

Post contact (1741-present) Native, Russian, and Euroamerican sites occur sometimes as isolates (individual objects), but more often in association with other features. These include cabins, fox farms and fox traps, docks, roads, shipwrecks, World War II bunkers, and mining and logging camps. Historic structures and artifact scatters (multiple objects) are most common in the uplands, although some are present in the intertidal zone.

At eroded prehistoric and historic sites, fragile organic midden elements (shell, bone, charcoal, etc.) are destroyed by wave or stream action, leaving only scattered deposits of more resilient artifacts in the intertidal zone or in stream channels. Eroded sites were classified as *artifact scatters* or *isolates.* Most intertidal artifacts, such as prehistoric adzes, projectile points, and stone lamps (Figure 3) or historic mining equipment, are erosional remnants of upland villages, camps, or industrial sites.

Figure 3—Stone lamp, (17 cm long) used to burn sea mammal oil for light, found during shoreline survey

Along the coast, many environmental forces affect site integrity, which is a critical factor in determining the scientific value of an archaeological site. Site integrity is better preserved in upland or subtidal sites because they usually are less exposed to the wind and wave action that rapidly alters sites. When upland sites are exposed to wave and tidal action, either through subsidence or erosion, the remaining intertidal portion of these sites loses the contextual integrity of an intact upland site.

Potential Site Impacts

The scientific value of an archaeological site is measured by its contextual integrity-- preservation of the spatial relationships between site constituents (artifacts, features, and other cultural remains). Disturbance due to erosion, vandalism, or other forces may decrease the scientific value of a site if it alters or destroys the spatial relationships between site constituents. Alteration of these relationships at a site adversely impacts the site's potential contribution to the reconstruction of a region's history.

Archaeological sites in the spill area were potentially at risk from direct oiling and cleanup activities. The degree of risk depended on site location, site composition, the degree of oiling, and the intensity of cleanup activity. The risk to upland sites from direct oiling was negligible. However, cleanup crews working near sensitive upland sites introduced the possibility of site disturbance from pedestrian traffic and vandalism. Conversely, intertidal sites, including intact subsurface middens, fish traps, rock art sites, and artifact scatters, were potentially at risk from direct oiling and from cleanup activities. Sites and artifacts could potentially be coated with oil, disturbed, or removed.

Legal Requirements For Cultural Resource Protection

At the time of the spill there were state and federal laws that protected cultural resource sites on public land. These included the National Historic Preservation Act (NHPA), the Archaeological Resources Protection Act (ARPA), and the Alaska Historic Preservation Act (AHPA). The aim of historic preservation legislation is to preserve the information integrity of cultural resources that may be adversely affected by construction projects or other land altering actions.

Under Section 106 of NHPA, a consultation process among all interested parties is triggered when the federal government becomes involved in an undertaking with the potential to affect cultural resources. Under normal conditions, this process involves identification of the cultural properties that could be affected, determination of the potential impacts to these properties, and mitigation to minimize or avoid any adverse effect. This process is routinely handled by the State Historic Preservation Officer (SHPO), with oversight by the Advisory Council on Historic Preservation (ACHP), often through a Memorandum of Agreement (MOA) that identifies steps and considerations specific to the undertaking.

Archaeological permits are commonly required when activities are proposed that might affect sites on public land. These permits stipulate how archaeological investigations should be conducted and reported. The permits normally require participants to have at least an M.A. in archaeology or anthropology plus appropriate regional field experience.

CULTURAL RESOURCE PROGRAM

Objectives

The primary objective of the CRP was to protect cultural resources from impacts during cleanup without slowing or unduly hindering cleanup operations. Specific goals of the CRP were to 1) locate and assess archaeological sites; 2) determine the potential effects of treatment on them; 3) mitigate potential impacts through avoidance, site inspection, site monitoring, and education; and 4) maintain site location confidentiality. The objectives of the CRP were consistent with the intent of the laws and regulations-the preservation of cultural resource site information integrity.

Design

No model existed for conducting a site protection program under an emergency situation for a large and virtually unsurveyed area with undocumented coastal sites. With input from the ACHP, the SHPO, the Forest Service, other agency and Native organizations, and Exxon, a MOA was developed that spelled out responsibilities specific to the undertaking and provided a framework for the CRP.

The general design of the CRP included the following elements: 1) extensive shoreline surveys were conducted by CRP archaeologists to identify and document cultural sites; 2) survey data were synthesized with existing site data to document sensitivities to consider in developing cleanup plans; 3) archaeological protection strategies (constraints) were developed on the basis of specific site sensitivities to ensure sites would not be impacted by cleanup operations (these constraints were an integral part of the cleanup plan for each shoreline unit); 4) education programs were conducted to ensure all response workers were aware of laws and procedures related to cultural resources; 5) special responses to issues such as reported artifact finds were investigated to ensure that sites were protected.

Consistent with provisions of the MOA and the permits, procedures were set up to document findings in interim and final reports and to provide for curation of all artifacts and samples collected during the program, as well as the project's administrative documents, field notebooks, photographs, and videotapes.

Methods

Standard archaeological field methods were employed throughout the program, including systematic shoreline archaeological surveys, site testing with soil probes and test pits, site documentation, and collection of diagnostic surface artifacts, ^{14}C samples, and tephra (volcanic ash) samples.

In the field, archaeologists used notebooks, recording forms, sketch maps, 35-mm film, and videotape to document cultural resource sites. Standardized forms for recording specific confidential site data, program tasks (survey, inspection, monitoring, incidents, etc.), and general shoreline sensitivity evaluations were developed in 1989 and enhanced in 1990.

Tests for subsurface cultural deposits were only conducted where deposits were suspected. Tests consisted of either probing with one-inch diameter soil samplers or 20-cm^2 shovel tests to the depth necessary to determine the presence of cultural material. There was no mechanical screening of sediments, but shell, tephra, and ^{14}C samples and artifacts were collected when encountered in test pits. No further subsurface testing was conducted once a site was identified as cultural in origin.

CRP archaeologists designed and implemented cultural resource education and training programs. They also assisted with constraint implementation by meeting regularly with cleanup supervisors before sensitive segments or subdivisions were cleaned, providing guidance for site protection, and monitoring treatment when appropriate. Archaeologists also recorded site conditions before and after cleanup. In some cases, they personally cleaned areas near intertidal artifact scatters so that artifacts were not inadvertently damaged or removed. This minimized impacts to cultural resources and conveyed the importance of site protection to treatment crews and agency representatives.

Implementation

Throughout the four-year treatment program, the CRP worked closely with representatives from the State Historic Preservation Office, Alaska Department of Natural Resources Office of History and Archaeology, USDA Forest Service, National Park Service (NPS), Fish and Wildlife Service, Bureau of Indian Affairs, Chugach Alaska Corporation (CAC), and Kodiak Area Native Association. When extensive field work was in progress in 1989 and 1990, interactions with agency colleagues were frequent. Copies of all project data were made available to the four permitting agencies and, through the SHPO's office, to authorized parties, including Native organizations.

Site identification—In 1989, archaeologists conducted reconnaissance surveys as members of the teams that assessed oiling conditions, geological characteristics, and biological and cultural sensitivities of area shorelines (Neff et al., this symposium). This type of survey initially appraised the location and general nature of cultural resource sites and was conducted both to identify sites and document sensitivities. These surveys, covering over 5 400 km (3 400 mi), were conducted by aircraft, boat, and on foot. The extent of the survey was determined by the distribution of stranded oil, with nonoiled shorelines receiving cursory review and more heavily oiled shorelines receiving more detailed surveys.

Since most areas had never been systematically surveyed by professional archaeologists, existing documentation was often incomplete,thus requiring the archaeologist to describe the visible site features and components of each site whether new or known. On the basis of information gathered, archaeologists assessed the potential for site impact should cleanup occur.

In 1990, additional reconnaissance survey data were not necessary, however, there was a need for separate intensive archaeological survey information in selected cleanup areas. Approximately 262 km (164 mi) of shoreline were surveyed intensively by teams composed of two archaeologists. The objective of the 1990 survey was to collect archaeological data from the intertidal and near upland zones of all locations scheduled for cleanup in 1990 should the SHPO require additional documentation before approving a site protection constraint for a cleanup plan. The 1990 intensive survey located 62 new sites, 29 of which were in upland locations with low visibility from shorelines where cleanup was conducted. The relatively few and generally small new sites found in 1990 confirmed that the 1989 reconnaissance surveys had been effective for developing emergency site protection constraints.

Determining potential cleanup effects—Through a review process, CRP managers and agency cultural resource representatives examined the updated archaeological information from each shoreline segment or subdivision and determined the potential effect cleanup might have on sites. A segment (1989) or subdivision (1990 onward) was defined for cleanup operations as a contiguous length of shoreline with similar characteristics that could be addressed by a single cleanup plan. A segment might contain a single cultural site, multiple cultural sites, or no sites at all.

In 1989, the CRP managers and the SHPO (representing the permitting and land managing agencies) reviewed each shoreline segment's survey report. These reports contained cleanup plans, biological, and nonconfidential archaeological data, proposed cultural resource constraints (to mitigate any adverse effects), and other guidelines to be followed in the segment during cleanup (Teal 1991). Each shoreline-specific cleanup plan and cultural resource constraint had to be approved by the SHPO before it could be submitted to the Interagency Shoreline Cleanup Committee (ISCC) for review and to the Federal On-Scene Coordinator (FOSC) for approval. This committee was composed of up to 24 agencies and interested parties, including Native groups, and provided the primary forum for their input into the review process.

In 1990, in an effort to streamline and improve the multi-agency review process, a Technical Advisory Group (TAG) replaced the ISCC groups for cleanup plan reviews, and the Cultural Technical Advisory Group (CTAG) was formed to address archaeological issues. This group was composed of cultural resource representatives from the Coast Guard, state and federal agencies, relevant Native organizations, and Exxon. The group reviewed cleanup plans and archaeological constraints recommended by the CRP (Haggarty et al. 1991:33-34). The SHPO endorsed a work plan for review and approval by the FOSC only after the CTAG members met in person and reached consensus on the level of cultural resource protection. CTAG continued to operate on a much-reduced scale during 1991 and 1992, consistent with the smaller cleanup programs and increased knowledge of the area.

Impact mitigation through constraints—A cultural resource constraint (protection strategy) was integral to each of the more than 1500 segment-or subdivision-specific cleanup plans developed during the four seasons of cleanup. The cultural resource constraints were determined after the cleanup plans were developed to account for the specific sensitivities of the site and type of work. Constraints included avoidance, access restrictions, and requirements that treatment take place in the presence of a monitor. The most restrictive constraint, having an archaeologist on site during cleanup activities, was included in only about 6% of the cleanup plans during the four-year program.

In 1989, specific archaeological constraints were written for each cleanup segment. In conjunction with a blanket prohibition on unauthorized access to the upland areas (which remained in effect throughout the project), the primary constraint to mitigate potential adverse impacts during cleanup was site avoidance. Cleanup supervisors were directed to contact an archaeologist when working in a segment requiring a monitor, to avoid sensitive areas for segments containing sites near a cleanup area, or to contact an archaeologist if any cultural material was encountered.

Before the 1990 cleanup program, archaeological constraints were standardized to simplify the review process and implementation of the constraints in the field. One of three working constraints was applied to each subdivision in which cleanup was planned: (1) a standard constraint for subdivisions with no known sites or where known sites were not in conflict with planned cleanup; (2) consultation and inspection constraint for subdivisions with sensitive sites that could be avoided with archaeological input; and (3) a monitoring constraint for subdivisions in which sensitive sites were known to be near cleanup locations.

The standard constraint allowed cleanup to be conducted without further archaeological input unless previously undiscovered cultural materials were encountered. Under the consultation and inspection constraint, the sensitive area had to be inspected by a CRP archaeologist and a determination made as to whether cleanup could proceed with or without a monitor. Many of these subdivisions were worked on several times, and the process was repeated each time to ensure that no impacts to sites occurred. Site monitoring constraints required that an archaeologist be present during subdivision cleanup. Field archaeologists normally documented the condition of sites in subdivisions with inspection and monitoring constraints before and after cleanup. These procedures also were employed during 1991 and 1992.

Impact mitigation through education—The CRP implemented a training and education program to familiarize cleanup personnel with the policies that applied to cultural resources during cleanup. Written information and a 20-minute video were developed to instruct cleanup personnel on the confidential and sensitive nature of cultural resources, their protection under state and federal laws, and the strict procedures to follow should cultural material be encountered during cleanup. The education program operated throughout the four-year treatment program and was an important step in mitigating potential human impacts to cultural resources.

Maintaining site confidentiality—In accordance with the MOA, all parties agreed that sensitive data would be treated in such a way as not to reveal the specific location of sites. General shoreline segment sensitivities were identified on shoreline survey forms and other public paperwork, but the descriptions of the nature and specific location of archaeological sites were limited to CTAG discussions, inspection and monitoring discussions with cleanup supervisors, and restricted access-files. Site location data were intentionally left out of nonconfidential publications, and separate confidential reports containing the sensitive data were compiled and transmitted to the SHPO for distribution only to authorized parties.

RESULTS

Program Implementation

Design and implementation of a program to protect cultural resources in the spill area was a monumental challenge, given the size and remoteness of the area and the paucity of information on the resources to be protected. Although laws and regulations to protect cultural resources were in place well before the spill, there were no precedents for implementing a program of the size and nature of the CRP.

The normal Section 106 sequence in which potential site impacts are identified, assessed, and mitigated was compressed into a short period of time because of the emergency cleanup and the short summer season. The CRP conducted what amounted to many years' worth of archaeological shoreline surveys in the space of a few months in order to assess the potential impact of the cleanup on sites.

Site Identification

All shorelines that had the potential to be affected by oil were surveyed at least at a reconnaissance level. Previously documented cultural resource sites near oiled shorelines were located and descriptions updated. In addition, 326 new sites were located, documented, and reported by the CRP (Figure 4). Surveys conducted by the CRP more than doubled the total number of known sites in the area from 283 to 609. Archaeologists visited and gathered data at 526 cultural resource sites during the four-year program. Only 83 (14%) of the 609 known sites in the area affected by the spill were not inspected by CRP archaeologists, and none of these were near shorelines that involved cleanup.

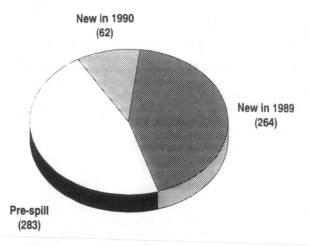

New in 1990
(62)

New in 1989
(264)

Pre-spill
(283)

FIGURE 4—Number of culture sites in Valdez spill area - 609 sites on 1/91

The distribution of different types of cultural sites recorded by the CRP is summarized in Figure 5. Of the total 609 sites, about 70% were categorized as primarily prehistoric, with the remaining 30% classified as primarily historic, although many sites include both prehistoric and historic material. The distribution of new sites documented by the CRP is roughly the same as the distribution of pre-1989 sites, which illustrates the success of the CRP surveys in identifying sites of all types.

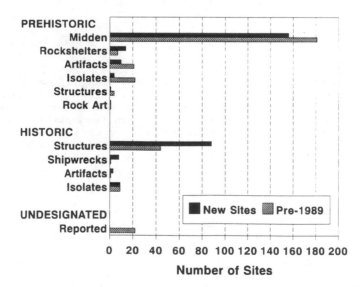

FIGURE 5 —Types of cultural sites in spill area - 609 sites on 1/91

Table 1 summarizes the oiling conditions near upland and intertidal sites on shorelines in areas initially affected by the spill. It was constructed using a Geographic Information System (GIS) by overlaying the 609 Alaska Heritage Resource Survey (AHRS) sites on a map of initially oiled shorelines and computing the worst oiling condition within 200 m of each site. As can be discerned from the table, the oiling conditions of shorelines near sites varied greatly. Although site-specific protection constraints were developed on the basis of a site's location, sensitivity, and proposed cleanup methods, the intensity of cleanup and the level of constraint generally were proportional to the degree of initial oiling. Not all intertidal sites shown in the table to be near an oiled shoreline were directly touched by oil because the amount of oil ranged from tarballs or sporadic patches (very light) to a continuous band with a width greater than 6 m (heavy) (Owens 1991). It was possible that a site might be mapped on an oiled shoreline but actually located between widely spaced tarballs or above or below a band of heavy oil and not physically touched by oil at all.

TABLE 1—1989 Shoreline oiling conditions near cultural resource sites on shorelines potentially affected by Valdez spill

1989 Shoreline Oiling Category [2]	Number and location of sites on potentially affected shorelines [1]								
	Upland only [3]		Upland/Intertidal [4]		Intertidal [5]		All sites		
	PWS	GOA	PWS	GOA	PWS	GOA	PWS	GOA	Total
No oil	20	107	6	93	10	13	36	213	**249**
Very light	6	76	7	94	0	9	13	179	192
Light	9	10	5	8	2	1	16	19	35
Moderate	11	5	3	7	1	0	15	12	27
Heavy	51	18	10	14	10	3	71	35	106
Total near oil	77	109	25	123	13	13	115	245	**360**
Total near oil	186		148		26		360		
Total no oil	127		99		23		249		
Total Sites	313		247		49		609		**609**

1) Highest level of initial oiling within 200 m of site location.

2) Based on 1989 SCAT initial oiling maps (Owens 1991).

3) Sites entirely in upland areas.

4) Sites with both intertidal and upland portions.

5) Sites entirely in intertidal areas.

Of the 609 sites, 249 (41%) were located more than 200 m from an oiled shoreline and thus not directly exposed to oil. Of the 360 sites within 200 m of an oiled shoreline, 245 were in the Gulf of Alaska, where the oil continuity and degree of shoreline oiling were lower and the oil more weathered than in Prince William Sound. Although there were more than three times the number of sites in the Gulf of Alaska, the intensity of cleanup, and the effect of direct oiling or cleanup activities on cultural sites was generally less than in Prince William Sound.

Of the 360 sites (59%) that were within 200 m of an oiled shoreline, over half (186) were located entirely in the uplands, with no direct exposure to oil. These sites were protected from the indirect effects of cleanup activities by individual site protection constraints, the level of which generally increased as the degree of shoreline oiling and the need for cleanup increased.

Of the other 174 sites near oiled shorelines that had intertidal components, 126 were near lightly or very lightly oiled shorelines where the level of cleanup was generally low compared with moderately or heavily oiled shorelines. Forty-eight intertidal sites were located near moderately and heavily oiled shorelines, and 34 of these had upland components that were not exposed to direct oiling. Intertidal sites were inspected and monitored by CRP staff consistent with the degree of oiling and the intensity of cleanup conducted.

Special Responses

In addition to implementing constraints, the CRP investigated and documented suspected artifact finds, site vandalism reports, and related site issues. A number of reported artifact finds were found to be authentic. The fact that archaeological finds were reported by cleanup supervisors indicated that the training program had increased awareness of the crews, thus mitigating further impact. In 1989, 16 site vandalism reports were investigated, and only 2 were found to be directly related to the spill cleanup. One report resulted in the apprehension and prosecution of a vandal by the Forest Service. The other incident in 1989 involving the collection of artifacts from a beach by members of a local crew resulted in several artifacts being turned over to the SHPO and the CRP. There were no known incidents of vandalism related to Exxon treatment activities in 1990, 1991, or 1992. Copies of all special response documentation were sent to the SHPO.

Cleanup near a newly discovered site in Kenai Fjords National Park illustrated the CRP's responsiveness to agency and Native concerns (Betts et al. 1991). At the request of the National Park Service (NPS) and Chugach Alaska Corporation (CAC), the CRP implemented a cautious site protection strategy involving careful monitoring of four beach cleanup events at the site. Archaeologists established a grid over the cleanup area, enabling them to map and collect artifacts found as oil residue was manually removed from the intertidal zone. Under CRP direction, crews cleaned the oiled shoreline while protecting the redeposited lithic scatter. Thirty-nine lithic artifacts were collected from the intertidal area. Joint NPS/CAC investigations of the intact upland portion of the site resulted in two dates that place site occupation at approximately 1400 years ago.

Documentation

Updating the documentation of known sites was an important result of the CRP because it substantially increased the amount of site information for the area. Many of the 283 sites known before the spill were inadequately documented. CRP staff visited and documented 200 of them with maps, photographs, and videotapes. Many of the sites that were documented superficially during 1989 reconnaissance surveys were documented in greater detail in 1990 and 1991. Inspection and site monitoring took precedence over improving site documentation; nevertheless, records of known sites were updated whenever archaeologists were in the vicinity. Archaeologists recorded important new data at many of these sites, including observations on the effects of tectonic processes on sites in the region.

Thousands of pages of site descriptions, maps, field notes, Alaska Heritage Resource Survey (AHRS) site forms, over 15 000 photographs, and 50 hours of videotape of sites and artifacts amassed by the CRP provided detailed information for determining impacts of oiling and for developing plans and constraints to protect the sites during cleanup. Three hundred thirty-three artifacts that either were at risk during treatment or provided evidence of a site's age were collected and subsequently archived at the University of Alaska Museum, Fairbanks.

DISCUSSION

The CRP was a massive undertaking that was developed and implemented under emergency conditions. Procedures to identify and protect cultural resources without impeding the effectiveness of the cleanup were rapidly and successfully implemented. Extensive shoreline surveys provided information on previously known and unknown sites, which was synthesized and used to develop site protection constraints for all cleanup activities. Cultural sites experienced minimal disturbance during cleanup because of specific constraints such as avoidance, access restrictions, and working only with an archaeological monitor at sensitive locations. These constraints were integral to each cleanup plan and were taken into consideration during the approval and implementation of those plans.

All personnel involved in the cleanup were made aware through cultural resource education and training programs of the cultural sensitivities, the regulations protecting them, and strict procedures to follow if cultural materials were encountered during cleanup. Documentation describing the precise location and nature of cultural sites were made available only to authorized personnel to ensure that site confidentiality was maintained. The CRP was successful largely because of the cooperation and support of the federal and state agencies, Native organizations, and others involved in the cleanup.

Assessment Of Archaeological Impacts

No significant injuries to cultural resources were documented by the CRP during the extensive four-year program. Although some injuries were documented, they were largely minor and far less significant than the observed injuries from chronic erosion and prespill vandalism. The primary goals of the program--to protect sites that had direct oiling from cleanup activities and to protect all sites near cleanup operations from vandalism--were achieved with a high degree of success through site protection constraints and education.

Government-sponsored damage assessment studies confirmed the effectiveness of the CRP site identification and protection approach--an approach conducted with input from and the approval of SHPO, agency, and Native organization representatives. Dekin (1993:6) surveyed 60 shoreline segments previously surveyed by the CRP and relocated all 17 sites that the CRP had identified. While his survey identified new sites in 4 of the 45 segments in which the CRP had reported no sites, the sites were "small and low in visibility." Dekin (1993:6) stated that his damage assessment survey "confirmed the efficacy of their [CRP survey] efforts," and that "the most widely observable injury was from coastal erosion in areas of tectonic subsidence" (1993:1).

Direct oiling—Most surface intertidal archaeological deposits in the spill area lacked integrity, and, therefore, were relatively less important archaeologically than intact upland sites (see McMahan and Holmes 1987:22). Some oiled intertidal sites or artifacts suffered minor, short-term cosmetic injuries. Some artifacts were collected and cleaned, while others were left to be cleaned by tidal action. Careful inspection and monitoring of sites helped protect intertidal artifacts from damage or removal. The CRP documented two intertidal sites that contained intact subsurface cultural material, but neither site was oiled. Since it was recognized that there could be additional, nonvisible, subsurface sites, careful inspection and monitoring of cleanup areas where such deposits were possible ensured that they were protected from physical disturbance during cleanup.

An issue considered, but not directly addressed by CRP, studies involved the potential interference of *Exxon Valdez* oil on ^{14}C dating. CRP staff expected the impact of direct oiling on the overall archaeological framework of the area to be negligible because only sites in the intertidal could be directly touched by oil, and very few intertidal sites were expected to have either the integrity or the organic artifacts that would allow effective dating. It also became apparent through the CRP that relatively few sites were initially touched by oil and that the combination of the extensive cleanup effort and natural cleaning rapidly removed the oil that was initially stranded on the shorelines.

Government-sponsored damage assessment studies have confirmed that significant impairment to ^{14}C dating did not occur. Reger et al. (1992) investigated the presence of oil at 13 intertidal sites in the spill area. Four of these sites yielded collections and radiocarbon samples suitable for assessing the impacts of oiling. Although two of the sites contained sediments that tested positive for traces of oil, the study concluded that ^{14}C dates from artifact-bearing levels at these sites were well within the range of dates established for artifact assemblages in the region.

A federal damage assessment study of the effect of oil on ^{14}C dating of wood, peat, and charcoal samples (Mifflin & Associates 1991) concluded that "^{14}C ages are severely affected (appear older) by the introduction of ^{14}C-deficient crude oils." The study was performed in a laboratory and used high-speed centrifuge to saturate the samples before analysis. The study indicated that weathered crude oil penetrates organic material poorly--even in a high-speed centrifuge. This suggests that the potential for oil contamination of organic archaeological materials decreased with time as the crude weathered and emulsified, and was slight outside Prince William Sound. The study also concluded that oiled samples could be successfully decontaminated and radiocarbon dated, though the time and cost of dating would be substantially increased.

Dekin (1993:1) found no evidence that the *Exxon Valdez* spill had oiled any upland deposits, but he did find widespread low-level hydrocarbon contamination from other sources at these sites. He also identified intact intertidal deposits at seven sites (Dekin 1993:5), but found no evidence of damage to the sites by *Exxon Valdez* oil. From these investigations, Dekin (1993:4) concluded,

> . . . small, but detectible, amounts of petroleum hydrocarbons may occur in most archaeological sites within the project area. However, we do not find evidence of extensive soil contamination from a single definable source (the crude oil spilled from the *Exxon Valdez*).

Both Reger et al. (1992) and Dekin (1993) conducted actual field investigations at more than 20 of the sites most likely to have sustained damage by direct oiling. Their studies indicate that direct oiling did not injure archaeological sites in the spill area.

Vandalism—During CRP surveys, archaeologists found many sites that had never been recorded by an archaeologist but that had been vandalized, indicating that prespill vandalism was a serious problem lacking baseline data.

The CRP instituted an extensive education program to instruct cleanup personnel about site protection procedures and to combat potential site vandalism associated with the cleanup. During the four-year period, only two incidents of vandalism were found to be directly related to the spill cleanup and one was prosecuted by federal authorities.

Dekin's study was the only damage assessment study that dealt with vandalism. He concluded, "Vandalism was limited and could not be associated with the oil spill and cleanup activities" (Dekin 1993:1).

Other studies—Jesperson and Griffin (1992) and McAllister (1993) conducted other damage assessment studies that did not involve fieldwork. Jesperson and Griffin evaluated CRP and agency archaeological documentation for evidence of site injury and concluded that 19 (3%) of the 609 sites in the spill area showed "substantive" injury due to direct oiling or cleanup, and an additional 16 (2.5%) demonstrated "circumstantial" evidence of injury. Their classification of "substantive" injuries is not supported by field surveys and documentation by the CRP. Their damage assessment was essentially a library exercise based on review of CRP documentation. CRP data were not collected for damage assessment purposes. The Dekin and Reger studies superseded the Jesperson and Griffin study. Dekin (1993) and Reger et al. (1992) actually conducted field investigations and found no site impacts from either direct oiling or the oil spill response at four sites they inspected that had been identified by Jesperson and Griffin as having sustained "substantive" injury.

Dekin (1993:6) and McAllister (1993) report that 1 287 cultural resource sites exist in the spill area, and McAllister bases a gross estimate for damage restoration costs on this figure; "spill area" is not defined. Dekin (1993:2) reports that the spill area includes "1 287 known sites from the Alaska Heritage Resource Survey files," even though the AHRS (as of January 1991) files included 609 sites in the actual spill area--that is, on or adjacent to shorelines where oil was either present or possible. (These 609 sites include 249 sites [Table 1] located more than 200 m from oiled shorelines.) The undefined "1 287 known sites " referred to by Dekin and McAllister, therefore, apparently include sites remote from the actual area of the spill and subsequent cleanup, raising questions concerning the basis McAllister used for estimating restoration costs.

The data from the CRP and damage assessment studies by the State of Alaska (Reger et al. 1992) and the US Government (Dekin 1993; Mifflin & Associates 1991) indicate that damage to cultural resource sites resulting from the *Exxon Valdez* oil spill and the cleanup was negligible.

Program Contributions
The CRP greatly increased the knowledge of the Alutiiq region archaeology by identifying and documenting a wide range of significant sites, by identifying new intertidal sites with organic artifacts and subtidal deposits, by conducting the first systematic archaeological surveys of the outer Kenai Peninsula, and by dating several important new sites in Prince William Sound and the Gulf of Alaska. ^{14}C dates for two sites extended the known age of human habitation in Prince William Sound to earlier than 4 000 years ago (Haggarty et al. 1991:175). Tephra samples identified from sites on the outer Kenai Peninsula coast provide initial chronological data for this little-known area (Haggarty et al. 1991:176). The CRP also gathered important new data on large village sites and fort sites, and at significant wet sites in the area. Numerous postcontact sites throughout the Alutiiq region containing valuable information on the Russian fur trade, fox-farming, mineral prospecting, mining, and World War II-era military defense were also recorded and analyzed (Haggarty and Wooley 1993).

Reports describing the goals, methods, implementation, and results of the program were written each year as required by the MOA and permits and were reviewed by the permitting agencies and Native organizations before publication. They document the nonconfidential findings of the program and have been widely distributed to universities, museums, and agencies (Mobley and Haggarty 1989a; Haggarty and Wooley 1990; Mobley et al. 1990; Betts et al. 1991; Haggarty et al. 1991; Haggarty and Wooley 1993). These and other project reports (Haggarty 1989; Mobley and Haggarty 1989b; Erlandson et al. 1992; Wooley et al. 1992) provide a better understanding of the culture and history of the Alutiiq area.

The preservation of program artifacts, samples, and documentation was covered by separate agreements with the University of Alaska Museum and with the University of Alaska Fairbanks Rasmuson Library for curation of all project collections and data. These will provide bases for continuing studies of the Alutiiq area.

The process of coastal site identification and protection developed by the CRP during the *Exxon Valdez* response is serving as a model for oil spill response plans in other regions. Canada has produced shoreline assessment manuals that include procedures developed by the CRP for British Columbia, the Great Lakes, and the Atlantic Coast. Also, the British Columbia government has published oil spill response atlases incorporating key aspects of the CRP's approach.

CONCLUSIONS

Implementing a program to identify and protect cultural resource sites in the area of the oil spill was a massive and unprecedented task. The Cultural Resource Program was rapidly developed and implemented with input from the SHPO, government agency, and Native organization representatives and achieved its fundamental goals of site identification and protection.

Although vandalism attributable to cleanup activities was documented at two sites, serious damage to archaeological sites in the spill area did not occur from either direct oiling or cleanup activities. Field damage assessment studies conducted by government agencies support these conclusions.

During the four-year program, the CRP collected, analyzed, and synthesized a considerable amount of high-quality archaeological data from sites located along large stretches of previously unsurveyed remote coastline. This new information represents a major contribution to the study of the human history of the Alutiiq region. The CRP effectively protected cultural resource sites in the spill area and, in the process, provided important baseline data on the nature and location of cultural resource sites in the Alutiiq region.

REFERENCES

Anchorage Daily News. 1992. "Archaeologists Claim Village 2,000 Years Old." *Anchorage Daily News*, June 20, 1992.

Betts, R.C., C.B. Wooley, C.M. Mobley, J.C. Haggarty, and A. Crowell. 1991. *Site Protection and Oil Spill Treatment at SEL-188, an Archaeological Site in Kenai Fjords National Park, Alaska*. Exxon Company, U. S. A., Anchorage, Alaska.

Birket-Smith, Kaj. 1953. *The Chugach Eskimo*. National museets Skrifter, Etnografisk Raekke 6. Copenhagen.

Combellick, R.A. 1991. *Paleoseismicity of the Cook Inlet Region, Alaska: Evidence From Peat Stratigraphy in Turnagain and Knik Arms*. Alaska Department of Natural Resources, Division of Geological and Geophysical Surveys Professional Report No. 112. Fairbanks.

Dekin, A. A., Jr. 1993. "The Impact of the *Exxon Valdez* Oil Spill on Cultural Resources." Draft preprint of paper presented at: Exxon Valdez *Oil Spill Symposium, February 3-9, 1993, Anchorage, AK*. Anchorage: Oil Spill Trustees Council.

de Laguna, F. 1956. *Chugach Prehistory: The Archaeology of Prince William Sound*. University of Washington Press, Seattle.

Erlandson, J.M., A. Crowell, C.B. Wooley, and J.C. Haggarty. 1992. "Spatial and Temporal Patterns in Alutiiq Paleodemography." *Arctic Anthropology*. Vol. 29, No. 2.

Haggarty, J.C. 1989. "Overview of the *Exxon Valdez* Shoreline Cleanup Assessment Team Activities." Paper presented at the British Columbia Oil Spill Prevention Workshop, University of British Columbia, Vancouver, B.C.

Haggarty, J.C. and C.B. Wooley. 1990. *Interim Report of the 1990 Exxon Cultural Resource Program*. Exxon Company, U. S. A., Anchorage.

Haggarty, J.C. and C.B. Wooley. 1993. *Final Report of the Exxon Cultural Resource Program*. Exxon Company U.S.A., Anchorage.

Haggarty, J.C., C.B. Wooley, J.M. Erlandson, and A. Crowell. 1991. *The 1990 Exxon Cultural Resource Program: Site Protection and Maritime Cultural Ecology in Prince William Sound and the Gulf of Alaska*. Exxon Company, U. S. A., Anchorage.

Jesperson, M. and K. Griffin. 1992. "An Evaluation of Archaeological Injury Documentation "*Exxon Valdez* Oil Spill." Prepared at the direction of the Comprehensive Environmental Response, Compensation, and Liability Act, and the Archaeological Steering Committee. Paper on file, Exxon Cultural Resource Program Files.

Jordan, R. H. and R. A. Knecht. 1988. "Archaeological Research on Western Kodiak Island, Alaska: The Development of Koniag Culture." In: *The Late Prehistoric Development of Alaska's Native People*, edited by R. D. Shaw, R. K. Harritt, and D. E. Dumond. Aurora: *Alaska Anthropological Association Monograph*. 4:225-306.

McAllister, M.E. 1993. "Generating Damage Restoration Costs for Archaeological Injuries of the *Exxon Valdez* Oil Spill." In: *Program and Abstracts Book, Exxon Valdez Oil Spill Symposium, February 2-5, 1993, Anchorage, AK*. Anchorage: Oil Spill Trustee Council; 219-222.

McMahan, J.D. and C.E. Holmes. 1987. *Report of Archaeological Findings at Nuke Island and the Adjacent Kenai Peninsula, Gulf of Alaska.* Alaska Department of Natural Resources; Office of History and Archaeology Report 5; Anchorage.

Mifflin & Associates, Inc. 1991. Exxon Valdez *Oil Spill Damage Assessment Contamination of Archaeological Materials, Chugach National Forest: Radiocarbon Experiments and Related Analyses.* Final Report on Contract No. 53-0109-1-00305. Report on File, Oil Spill Public Information Center. Anchorage.

Mobley, C.M. and J.C. Haggarty. 1989a. *Interim Report for the* Exxon Valdez *Cultural Resource Program.* Exxon Company, U. S. A., Anchorage.

Mobley, C.M. and J.C. Haggarty. 1989b "The *Exxon Valdez* Cultural Resource Program." In: *Proceedings of the British Columbia Oil Spill Prevention Workshop,* edited by Paul H. LeBlond, Manuscript Report No. 52, Department of Oceanography, University of British Columbia, Vancouver, B.C.

Mobley, C.M., J.C. Haggarty, C.J. Utermohle, M. Eldridge, R.E. Reanier, A. Crowell, B.A. Ream, D.R. Yesner, J.M. Erlandson, and P.E. Buck. 1990. *The 1989* Exxon Valdez *Cultural Resource Program.* Exxon Company, U. S. A., Anchorage.

Neff, J.M., E. H. Owens, S. W. Stoker, and D. M. McCormick. 1993. *"Conditions of Shorelines in Prince William Sound Following the Exxon Valdez Oil Spill: Part 1 -- Shoreline Oiling."* Third Symposium on Environmental Toxicology and Risk Assessment: Aquatic, Plant, and Terrestrial. ASTM STP###, American Society for Testing and Materials, Philadelphia. 1993.

Owens, E.H. 1991. *Changes in Shoreline Oiling Conditions 1-½ Years after the 1989 Prince William Sound Spill.* Unpublished report; Seattle, WA: Woodward-Clyde.

Plafker, G. 1965. "Tectonic Deformation Associated with the 1964 Alaska Earthquake." *Science* 148:1675-1687.

Plafker, G. 1967. "Surface Faults on Montague Island Associated with the 1964 Alaska Earthquake." *United States Geological Survey Professional Paper 543-G.*

Pullar, G. L. and P. Knecht. 1990. "Continuous Occupation of Larsen Bay/Uyak Bay by *Qikertarmiut.*" Paper prepared for the Native American Rights Fund, January 29, 1990. Paper on file at Exxon Cultural Resource Program Office, Anchorage.

Reger, D., J.D. McMahan, and C.E. Holmes. 1992. *Effect of Crude Oil Contamination on Some Archaeological Sites in the Gulf of Alaska, 1991 Investigations.* Alaska Department of Natural Resources, Division of Parks and Outdoor Recreation, Office of History and Archaeology Report Number 30.

Teal, A. 1991. "Shoreline Cleanup--Reconnaissance, Evaluation, and Planning Following the *Valdez* Oil Spill." In: *Proceedings of the International 1991 Oil Spill Conference (Prevention, Behavior, Control, Cleanup), March 4-7, 1991, San Diego, CA.* Washington, D.C.: American Petroleum Institute; Technical Publication 4529.

Wooley, C.B., J.C. Haggarty, and J.M. Erlandson. 1992. "Exxon's Cultural Resource Program: Process and Results of Site Protection in Prince William Sound and the Gulf of Alaska." Paper presented April 12, 1992, Society for American Archaeology Meeting. Pittsburgh.

Author Index

A

Armstrong, D. A., 485
Armstrong, J. L., 485

B

Bence, A. E., 41, 84
Boehm, P. D., 41, 263, 347, 398, 444
Boersma, P. D., 820
Bragg, J. R., 178
Brannon, E. L., 548, 585
Burns, W. A., 84
Butler, J. N., 3

C

Cooper, B. A., 762
Cusimano, R. F., 485

D

Day, R. H., 726
Dinnel, P. A., 485
Douglas, G. S., 51

E

Egging, D. E., 215
Erickson, W. P., 296
Erikson, D. E., 780

F

Ford, W. H., 665

G

Garshelis, D. L., 894
Gilbertson, L. G., 548, 585
Gilfillan, E. S., 263, 347, 398, 444

H

Haggarty, J. C., 933
Hancock, G. A., 665
Harner, E. J., 263, 347, 398, 444, 726
Hartung, R., 693
Hayward, G. D., 726
Henry, C. B., Jr., 239
Huggett, R. J., 485
Hughes, J. S., 3

J

Johnson, C. B., 894

K

Kettle, A. B., 820
Kuhn, H. A., 215

L

Landolt, M. L., 485
Lee, R. F., 485

M

Maki, A. W., 548, 585
McCormick, D. M., 312
McDonald, L. L., 296
McDonald, T. L., 485
Moksness, E., 626
Moulton, L. L., 548, 585
Murphy, S. M., 726

N

Neff, J. M., 141, 312
Nemeth, R. S., 485

O

Orensanz, J. M., 485
Owens, E. H., 312

951

Subject Index

A

Abundance
 birds, 820–847
 Common murres, 820–847
 flathead sole, 521, 537–538
 fucus, 413
 limpets, 413–415
 littoral snails, 413–415
 mussels, 413–415
 of species, 289, 306–308, 402,
  417, 424, 430, 432, 451,
  458, 470–473, 477
 seabirds, 820–847
 sea otters, 904–908, 917–922
 shrimp, 517, 537
 Tanner crabs, 509–513, 534–535
Alaska Coastal Current, 44–45,
  315
Alaska North Slope crude oil
  (ANS). *See also Exxon Valdez*
  crude oil (EVC).
Alaska North Slope crude oil
  (ANS), 56, 500–501
Alaska Peninsula
 ecology, 444–481
 murres, 791, 802–803
 recovery, 444–481
Alutiiq, 935
Amoco Cadiz oil spill, 349,
  526–527, 589, 727,
  855–856
Analysis of deviance, 561–562,
  642–643
ANCOVA/ANOVA, 284–285, 356,
  461, 498, 561, 571, 590,
  598, 610, 615, 675, 735,
  738, 789–790, 794, 827,
  903–904, 910, 913
ANODEV, 561–562, 642–643,
  648, 652
Archaeology, 933–947
Auklets, 871–875

B

Background polycyclic aromatic
  hydrocarbons, 62–64,
  69–72, 165–166, 380,
  500–501
Bald eagles. *See* Eagles.
Barren Islands
 murres, 786, 791–792,
  794–799, 820–847
Bears
 fingerprinting hydrocarbons in,
  121–122
 hydrocarbon exposure, 131
Bioaccumulation
 of petroleum hydrocarbons,
  708–709
 of polycyclic aromatic
  hydrocarbons, 239–260,
  375, 708–709
Bioavailablity
 of polycyclic aromatic
  hydrocarbons, 239–260,
  468, 475
Biodegradation, 380–381
Biogenic polycyclic aromatic
  hydrocarbons, 55–56, 67,
  74, 90
Birds. *See also* Ducks, Eagles,
  Guillimots, Kittiwakes,
  Murres, Murrelets,
  Oystercatchers, Seabirds, etc.
Birds
 abundance, 820–847
 fingerprinting hydrocarbons in,
  107–115
 Gulf of Alaska, 780–807
 hydrocarbon exposure,
  125–128, 694–725
 Kenai Peninsula, 726–756
 mortality, 727–728, 781–782,
  808–811, 820–824,
  842–847

953